s

AFRICAN-AMERICAN BUSINESS LEADERS

AFRICAN-AMERICAN BUSINESS LEADERS
A Biographical Dictionary

JOHN N. INGHAM
AND
LYNNE B. FELDMAN

GREENWOOD PRESS
WESTPORT, CONNECTICUT • LONDON

Library of Congress Cataloging-in-Publication Data

Ingham, John N.
    African-American business leaders : a biographical dictionary /
John N. Ingham and Lynne B. Feldman.
        p. cm.
    Includes bibliographical references and index.
    ISBN 0–313–27253–0 (alk. paper)
        1. Afro-Americans in business—Biography—Dictionaries.
I. Feldman, Lynne B.   II. Title.
HC102.5.A2I52   1994
338.6′42′08996073—dc20   93–20430

British Library Cataloguing in Publication Data is available.

Library of Congress Catalog Card Number: 93–20430
ISBN: 0–313–27253–0

First published in 1994

Greenwood Press, 88 Post Road West, Westport, CT 06881
An imprint of Greenwood Publishing Group, Inc.

Printed in the United States of America

The paper used in this book complies with the
Permanent Paper Standard issued by the National
Information Standards Organization (Z39.48–1984).

10 9 8 7 6 5 4 3 2 1

CONTENTS

PREFACE

This collection contains the biographies of 123 individual African-American business leaders in seventy-seven separate biographical entries. Since several individuals were members of the same family, or were involved in the founding or development of the same companies, they were included in multiple biographies. What we have endeavored to do is include within this volume the historically most significant black business leaders from the early days in America until the present time. We tried to make the entries as comprehensive as possible, both in terms of the biographies themselves and the accompanying bibliographies. We concluded that it was more valuable to have a complete treatment of these one hundred or so individuals, with full information on collections of manuscript materials and published biographical data, than to have short biographies with rudimentary bibliographic information, on twice the number of individuals.

We have endeavored to provide extensive and analytic biographical information on those included here. Obviously, there was more information available on some individuals than with others, but we have tried to make each as complete as humanly possible. Further, we have included the most complete and extensive bibliographical information for each of the entrants as we were able. We have noted if or where personal or corporate materials may be found for more in-depth studies, we have indicated the published biographical sources for each entrant, and we have also included background bibliographical information for the city and industry in which the person was involved.

The resultant collection, therefore, is designed to provide students of African-American history, individuals interested in business history, and the casual reader with biographies that place the individual fully within the context of his or her times, dealing with the relevant economic, social, and cultural issues that impinged upon that person's life and upon the lives of other African-Americans in that city and at that time. To assist the reader in understanding that historical context, we have also provided a bibliographic essay at the end of the volume that provides information on general works in African-American history, general writings on blacks in the principal cities covered in this volume, and also background information on industries in which the present biographical entries were most involved. In this manner we hope to provide students and other scholars with a useful and convenient starting place from which to pursue their own investigations.

In order to fulfill our goal of providing the most detailed and comprehensive biographical and bibliographical information on about 100 individuals, we found it necessary to restrict our focus somewhat to certain cities and time periods. Our own research interests have tended to concentrate on the period after 1880, so the bulk of the biographical entries tend to be clustered in the period from 1880 to World War II. We did, however, try to include most of the important business leaders from the periods before and after that time. We should also emphasize that our most complete listings are for a broad range of southern cities—especially Atlanta, Birmingham, Charleston, Durham, Memphis, Nashville, New Orleans, Richmond, Savannah, and Washington, D.C., along with such major northern centers as Chicago, Detroit, Indianapolis, St. Louis, New York, Philadelphia, and Pittsburgh, and Los Angeles and San Francisco in the Far West. As indicated, most of the business leaders considered were located in urban areas of the North and South, although we did have a few eminent individuals from rural areas in Mississippi and Alabama, and one individual from Iowa. As a result of these decisions, some deserving individuals were inevitably left out of this collection. Our coverage of New England, and of Cleveland, Detroit, and Buffalo, among some other areas, was not complete, and due to contraints of time and money, we were not able to include individuals from these areas.

Whenever reference is made to a person in a biography who is also included as a biographical entrant in this volume, that name is followed by an asterisk[*]. Several abbreviations are used in biographical entries: Ingham, BDABL refers to John N. Ingham, *Biographical Dictionary of American Business Leaders*, 4 volumes (Greenwood Press, 1983) and Ingham and Feldman, CABL refers to John N. Ingham and Lynne B. Feldman, *Contemporary American Business Leaders* (Greenwood Press, 1990). At the end of the volume are four appendices that allow the reader to access the biographies according to place of birth, principal place of business, type of business, and women business leaders.

AKNOWLEDGMENTS

Alabama

Birmingham

Birmingham and Jefferson County Public Library, Linn Healey Research Library

Marvin Whiting, archivist

Yvonne Crumpler, Tutweiler Room on Southern History

Booker T. Washington Insurance Company

Mattie M. Frierson

Viki Harrison

University of Alabama at Birmingham

Mrs. Bonnie Ledbetter, reference librarian, Mervyn H. Sterne Library

Montgomery

Alabama Department of Archives and History

Keeta Kendall

State of Alabama

Frances Smiley, black heritage coordinator

Roanoke

Terry Manufacturing Company

Jesse Terry

Tuscaloosa

University of Alabama, University Libraries

Clark Center, reference librarian

California

Los Angeles

Huntington Library, San Marino

Peter Blodgett, curator, Western Manuscripts

University of California, Los Angeles

Staff of Special Collections, University Research Library

Jerry Wright, Afro-American Studies Library

Alva Stevenson, Oral History Program, Powell Library

Michael Woodard, visiting scholar, Afro-American Studies Program

San Diego

San Diego Historical Society

Sallie West, Research Archives

San Diego State University

Robert Fikes, Jr., and Carole Wilson, reference librarians

Connecticut

New Haven

Yale University

The staff of the Beinecke Rare Book and Manuscript Library

Georgia

Atlanta

Atlanta Daily World

Portia Scott

Atlanta University, Robert W. Woodruff Library

Wilson Flemister, head, Special Collections

Elaine Williams, Special Collections

Jacqueline E. J. Daniels, periodical librarian

Emory University

Linda Matthews, head, Special Collections

Herndon Home

Carole Merritt, archivist

Martin Luther King Center for Non-Violent Social Change, Inc., Library

Diane Ware, archivist

Danny Bellinger, assistant archivist

Paschall's Motor Lodge

James Paschall

Columbus

Covered Bridges of Georgia

Thomas L. French, Jr.

Savannah

Chatham-Effingham Public Library, Main Branch

Nick Bazemore, reference department, Georgia Collection

Georgia Historical Society

Debbi Willis

Guaranty Life Insurance Company

Bowles Ford

King-Tisdale Foundation

W. W. Law

Savannah State University

Sheldon Rice, A. H. Gordon Library

Illinois

Chicago

Burrell Communications Group

Leslie Cole

Chicago *Defender*

Michael Brown and Dr. Marjorie Stewart Joyner

Chicago Historical Society

Emily Clark, assistant librarian

Chicago Municipal Research Library

Staff

Chicago Public Library, Carter G. Woodson Branch

Edward Manney and Beverley Cook

Chicago Public Library, Main Branch

James Stewart

DuSable Museum

Ramon Price, curator

Johnson Products, Inc.

Adrienne Hamilton and Carrie Duncan

Johnson Publishing Company

Pamela J. Cash

Procter and Gardner Advertising

George Miller

Mrs. E. Brown

Seaway National Bank

Constant W. Watson III and Cornelia Ryan

Soft Sheen, Inc.

Andrea Smith

Supreme Life Insurance

Betty Dickson

Travis Realty

Dempsey Travis

Louisiana

Baton Rouge

Louisiana State Library

Virginia R. Smith, head, Louisiana Section

Louisiana State University, Hill Memorial Library

Claudia Holland, Special Collections

Judy Bolton, Public Services, Louisiana and Lower Mississippi Valley Collections

New Orleans

New Orleans Public Library

Collin B. Hammer, Jr., and staff of the Louisiana Division

Tulane University

Ulysses Ricard, archivist, Amistad Research Center

Wilbur Minard, Archives and Special Collections, Howard-Tilton Memorial Library

Joan Caldwell and Ann Smith, Louisiana Room, Howard-Tilton Memorial Library

University of New Orleans

D. Clive Hardy, head, Archives and Special Collections, Earl K. Long Library

Xavier University

Lester Sullivan, archivist, Archives and Special Collections

Mississippi

Jackson

Staff of the Mississippi Department of Archives and History

Missouri

Jefferson City

Lincoln University Library

Perry Douglas, librarian, Ethnic Collection

Oi-Chi Hui (Ivy), reference librarian

Missouri State Archives

Mary Rick

St. Louis

Harris-Stowe State College Library

Martin Knorr, library director

Missouri Historical Society

Emily Miller, Public Services Librarian

Missouri Historical Society, Education Department

Ernestine Hodge

St. Louis Mercantile Library

John N. Hoover and Charles E. Brown

St. Louis Public Library, Julia Davis Branch

Lou Emma Robinson

St. Louis Public Library, Main Branch

Matthew Nojohen, Information Division

University of Missouri at St. Louis

Natalie Drew, Archives and Special Collections

Washington University, Olin Library, Special Collections

Carole Prietto, university archivist

New York

New York City

Brooklyn Public Library

Judy Walsh, History Division, Local History

CNN

Tony Chappelle, associate producer, "Pinnacle"

Columbia University

Bernard Crystal, assistant curator for manuscripts, Butler Library

Jane Rogers

Earl G. Graves, Ltd.

Charles Smith

Essence Magazine

Carol Patterson

Long Island University, Brooklyn Campus

M. B. Wenger, reference librarian

New York City, Central Reference Library

David Beasley, Economics Department

New York City Department of Records and Information Services— Municipal Reference and Research Center

Devra Zetlan, department supervising librarian

New York City Historical Society

Staff

New York Public Library, Schomburg Center

Staff

Philadelphia Coca-Cola Bottling Company, New York

Linda Harris

North Carolina

Chapel Hill

University of North Carolina, North Carolina Collection

Jeffery Hicks

Alice Cotton

University of North Carolina, Southern Historical Collection of the Manuscript Department

Richard A. Schrader, research archivist

Concord

Charles A. Conner Memorial Library

Kathryn Bridges, Local History Room

Durham

Duke University, William R. Perkins Library, Manuscript Department

Linda McCurdy

William Erwin

Durham Public Library, Main Branch

Anne Berkeley, North Carolina Room

Stanford-Warren Branch of the Durham Public Library

Darlene Brannon

St. Augustine's College

Linda Simmons-Henry

Raleigh

John W. Winters, Inc.

John W. Winters

Donna LaRoche

Shaw University, Archives

Benjamin Williams, archivist

Wake County Library, Richard B. Harrison Branch

Sandra Chambers

Pennsylvania

Philadelphia

Balch Institute Library

Pat Proscino

Free Library of Philadelphia

Staff

Library Company of Philadelphia

Staff

Pennsylvania Historical Society

Staff

Temple University

Urban Archives, Margaret Jerricho, head, and George D. Brightbill, assistant curator

Charles L. Blockson Collection, staff

Pittsburgh

  Carnegie Mellon University

    Joe W. Trotter, Jr.

South Carolina

Charleston

  Charleston Library Society

    Staff

  Charleston Museum

    Kathryn Gaillard

  Charleston Public Library

    Victoria West, Main Branch

    Rebecca M. Stepney, J. L. Dart Branch

  College of Charleston, Avery Research Center for African-American History and Research

    Myrtle G. Glascoe, director

    Donald West, archivist

    Millicent E. Brown, Education and Public Programs Specialist

  College of Charleston, Libraries

    Oliver Smalls, archivist, special collections

  South Carolina Historical Society

    Stephen Hoffius

Columbia

  State of South Carolina

    Staff of the Department of Archives and History

    Staff of the South Carolina State Library

  University of South Carolina

    Thomas L. Johnson, South Carolina Library

Tennessee

Memphis

  Lemoyne-Owen College, Hollis F. Price Library

    Marcia Morrison, Afro-American History Collection

  Memphis Room, Memphis-Shelby County Public Library

    James Johnson, head, Afro-American Collection

    Patricia LaPointe, reference librarian, History and Travel

  Mississippi Valley Collection, Memphis State University

    Ed Frank, assistant curator

    Ms. Sara Roberta Church

  Universal Life Insurance Company

    Frances Hassell

Nashville

  National Baptist Publishing Board

    Pamela Yates

  Public Library of Nashville and Davison County, Main Branch

    Laura Rehinert, Nashville Room

  Research Library of the Sunday School Board

    Ray Minardi, archivist

  Southern Baptist Historical Archives

    Bill Summers, archivist

  Staff of the special collections at Fisk and Vanderbilt Universities

  Tennessee State Library and Archives

    Mary Dessypris

  Tennessee State University

    Sharon Hull, Special Collections, Library

    Bobbi Lovett, History Department

Texas

Dallas

  Southern Methodist University

    Kenneth M. Hamilton, History Department

Virginia

Charlottesville

  University of Virginia Library

    Laura A. Endicott, Special Collections and Manuscripts

Hampton

  Hampton University

    Cora Mae Reid, Peabody Collection

    Fritz J. Malval, university archivist

    Donzella Willford, Archives

Petersburg

  Virginia State University

    Lucius Edwards, Jr., university archivist

Richmond

  Maggie Lena Walker Home

    Cecelia Suggs

  Richmond Public Library, Literature and History Department

    Bill Simpson

  Valentine Museum

    Greg Kimball

    Theresa Roane, assistant supervisor of reference services

  Virginia Historical Society

    Linda H. Jons

  Virginia State Library

    Roseann N. Meagher, reference librarian

Washington, D. C.

  Library of Congress, Manuscript Division

    Staff

  Martin Luther King Public Library, Washingtonia Collection

    Roxana Dean and Kathryn Ray

  Moorland Spingarn Research Center, Howard University

    Manuscript Division, Esme E. Bahn, manuscript research associate

    Reading Room, staff

  Washington Historical Society

    Bonnie Hedges, curator, and Jim Brewer

We would like to extend special thanks to Abbie and Barry Segall of Atlanta, Georgia, Robert and Karen Gourlay of Tampa, Florida, Hugh and Margaret Reat of Napa, California, Steve Keller of Nashville, Tennessee, and Dwayne Hillard of Columbia, South Carolina, for friendship and encouragement extended to us during our long travels throughout the United States. And we would also like to thank Professor Neil Betten and the History Department at Florida State University for providing office space and library privileges during the critical writing stage of the project.

Finally, most important, we would like to thank the Humanities and Social Sciences Committee of the Research Board of the Office of Research Administration at the University of Toronto, which provided two research grants to help defray travel and other research expenses connected with this project.

AFRICAN-AMERICAN BUSINESS LEADERS

A

Abbott, Robert Sengstacke (November 28, 1868/70–February 29, 1940) and
John Herman Henry Sengstacke (November 25, 1912–   ). Newspaper publishers: Robert Abbott Publishing, Sengstacke Newspapers, Chicago *Defender,
Abbott's Monthly,* and *New Pittsburgh Courier.* Abbott's editorials have been
described with such vivid adjectives as flaming, caustic, and uncompromising,
while the man himself has paradoxically been referred to as humble, inarticulate,
and gentlemanly. How could one man exhibit such a calm, controlled exterior
when his internal being was plagued with the highly explosive realities of the
injustices of segregation and discrimination? Robert Abbott was certainly the
embodiment of a complex, sometimes contradictory, set of values that have
caused confusion among his admirers and dissenters alike. Nonetheless, this man
created a national newspaper that penetrated the soul of the black community in
such a way that his legend persists until this day—more than fifty years after
his death.

Robert Sengstacke Abbott was born on November 28, 1868 or 1870, on St.
Simons Island, Georgia. Several reputable sources list 1870, but his biographer
insists on 1868. He was the son of former slaves. His father, Thomas Abbott,
was a house servant of Captain Charles Stevens. Their close relationship ensured
Thomas a relatively comfortable existence in the confines of slavery, but Robert's
mother Flora (Butler) suffered the demands of hard labor as a field slave. Although their experiences in slavery were extremely diverse, the two joined in
wedlock in 1867 after a brief courtship, much to the horror of the Abbott family,
who felt themselves superior to any field hand. With the close of the Civil War,
both Thomas and Flora were granted their freedom and proceeded to make a
life for themselves. Thomas first worked as a surveyor for a streetcar line in
Savannah, but with insufficient work to support his wife he began a grocery
business on St. Simons Island that catered to former slaves. Shortly thereafter,
Robert was born, followed by the birth of a sister who died in infancy. Upon
the death in 1869 of Thomas Abbott, Flora married John H. H. Sengstacke, with
whom she had a total of seven children. John Sengstacke, the stepfather of

Robert Abbott, became the most influential figure in his stepson's life. Throughout the formative years of his life, Abbott used his stepfather's surname and was known as Robert Sengstacke. Yet, years later when Robert had achieved a modest degree of wealth, he erected a monument on St. Simons Island in memory of his natural father, Thomas Abbott. Sengstacke, a very light-skinned mulatto of German descent, had received a formal education. He was ordained a minister by the Congregational Council in 1876 and installed as a missionary in Woodville's Pilgrim Congregation Church. Savannah, just three miles from Woodville where the Sengstacke family had relocated, was hardly an environment that encouraged positive race relations, even within the African-American race itself. Fair-complexioned blacks, who could boast white blood and its derived social distinction, perceived their lot in life as superior to their brethren who were darker skinned. Yet, at the same time, a new black elite was emerging in the city, many of whom were darker complected ex-slaves, opening lunch counters, saloons, groceries, and a funeral home, all designed to service the black community. Members of the older black business elite made their living as barbers or caterers, trades that relied heavily on white customers. Such distinction made for a divisive class structure within the black community, noticeable in church and educational institutions. Robert Perdue reports that skin color differences split the prestigious St. Stephen's Episcopal Church in the city: "The lighter-skinned Negroes in Savannah were clannish and constituted a colored aristocracy that had little in common with blacks."

Although Sengstacke was very light skinned, his wife and her young son Robert were ebony colored and thus were poorly treated by the elites of Savannah. Abbott years later recalled bitterly the scars he bore from poor treatment by lighter skinned teachers and students at Beach Institute, the city's elite private school for blacks. Abbott internalized the resulting feelings of inferiority and inadequacy from a very young age—feelings that were to haunt him throughout his life. At the same time, his stepfather actively challenged the deeply entrenched system and forged ahead with a relentless vitality, with Abbott benefiting by the example of this role model. Abbott would remain a crusader for the rights of the masses of blacks throughout his life.

Abbott's early education was provided by his father who was the teacher in Woodville's only school in the parsonage. Despite the great disadvantages that were operating against the success of a school for black children, Sengstacke's ambition and determination achieved a modicum of success. Over and above his teaching responsibilities, Sengstacke assumed the role of Woodville's leader, owing to his position in the church. Sengstacke, who had gained the confidence of the blacks in Woodville, proceeded to educate, inform, and lift his people. His struggle to attain these goals were later adopted by his stepson. Abbott's education continued at Beach Institute, a small Congregationalist institution that opened in 1868 as the first school for Savannah's black children. Unfortunately Abbott, as noted above, experienced the same color discrimination here he had found in Woodville. The students were primarily descendants of Savannah's fair-skinned first families. Without completing his studies there, Abbott moved on to Claflin University in Orangeburg, South Carolina. After six brief months, during which time he worked on the school's farm and received some elementary schooling, Abbott returned home to apprentice with the Savannah *Echo*, a local militant black newspaper that competed with the more conservative Savannah *Tribune*, another black publication.

At that point, Abbott's stepfather became involved in the newspaper trade. In November 1889, Sengstacke introduced the first issue of the Woodville *Times*, on which young Abbott performed a variety of duties. Robert soon left the city to resume his education, but the *Times* continued to be published by his stepbrother Alexander, who renamed the paper the West End *Post*. The paper's editorial policy was rather curious, given the racial climate at that time: Not one item was printed that covered the social or political situation of blacks. Nonetheless, one can fairly draw the conclusion that Abbott's interest in newspaper work resulted from his father's entrepreneurial pursuit in the same field.

In November 1889, Abbott left again to pursue an education, this time at the highly regarded Hampton Institute. Hampton provided Abbott with an environment in which he could develop a stronger sense of self than he had yet experienced. This industrial school was the alma mater of Booker Taliaferro Washington,* who spoke at several functions attended by Abbott. The young man was mesmerized by the eloquence with which Washington spoke, but, more important, he was enthralled with the strength and commitment of Washington's words, words that were to remain with him for years to come. At Hampton, Abbott received training in the printing trade that provided him with skills and advantages which, in the future, probably exceeded even his own dreams. While enrolled at Hampton, Abbott participated in the school's choir and eventually made his way into the illustrious Hampton Quartet. This involvement allowed him to travel the country, visiting numerous cities that he otherwise would never have seen. In 1893, while performing at the World's Columbian Exposition in Chicago, Abbott attended Colored American Day. There he heard the resounding speeches of Frederick Douglass and Ida B. Wells, who had recently suffered the indignity of being driven out of Memphis, Tennessee, where she published the newspaper *Free Speech*.

As at Hampton, Abbott was given the opportunity to hear leaders of his race speak emotionally and critically of the cruelties endured by African-Americans. Abbott undoubtedly was inspired by these dynamic speakers and was now prepared to press forward and take control of his life. After briefly returning to Woodville to work part-time on the *Times* and teach school on a plantation, Abbott relocated to Chicago, a city which then included 40,000 blacks. After facing numerous rejections for printing jobs for which he was qualified, his frustration began to mount. Abbott was horrified that he was denied work, while non–English speaking white immigrants who could belong to unions that did not enroll blacks were hired. Consequently, Abbott's focus changed to law, and he enrolled at the Kent College of Law in the fall of 1897 as Robert Sengstacke

Abbott, the first time he had assumed the surname Abbott as his own. After completing law school, Abbott was again frustrated by the discrimination operating against him because of his dark complexion.

Upon graduation, Abbott sought counsel from Edward H. Morris, a fair-skinned, prominent, black attorney who primarily serviced white clients. Morris had only disappointing advice for Abbott: He was told he was "a little too dark to make any impression on the courts in Chicago." Despite this disheartening news, Abbott tried his luck first in Gary, Indiana, and then in Topeka, Kansas. Although neither venue proved to be any different from Chicago, all was not lost. While in Topeka, Abbott made arrangements to handle local distribution of the *Plaindealer*, a Topeka paper, in Chicago. To enhance his meager income from the paper, Abbott took on short-term stints doing piecework for job printers, and he even managed to work on the National Negro Business League's program when it held its meeting in Chicago. He also practiced setting type in the print shop of Ferdinand L. Barnett (husband of Ida B. Wells), the editor and publisher of the Chicago *Conservator*. Despite this, Abbott was not faring well at all in Chicago, the vaunted northern city of opportunity. Nonetheless, although Abbott was struggling financially as well as socially, he was still determined to educate his people and change the all-consuming racism of the city and nation.

After considerable cajoling from some skeptical friends and acquaintances and an unsuccessful attempt at publishing a daily that lasted only two or three issues, Abbott introduced the first issue of the Chicago *Defender* (a name suggested by James A. Scott, a lawyer and confidant of Abbott's) on May 5, 1905. The initial printing of 300 copies cost $13.75 to produce. A six-column, four-page sheet of handbill size, the *Defender* closely resembled John Sengstacke's Woodville *Times* publication. (It has been suggested by Abbott's sister Rebecca that the *Times* was actually the precursor to the *Defender*.)

The content of the first issue did not reflect the confrontational, angry tone that later issues would exhibit, but rather, in the style of Booker T. Washington, it focused on the achievements of notable blacks. Although considerable errors are evident in the first issues, Abbott's accomplishments in overcoming the obstacles is particularly noteworthy inasmuch as he alone was responsible for all the work involved. Through a generous arrangement with the Western Newspaper Union, which printed primarily small country weeklies, the *Defender* was extended a $25.00 line of credit. Since Abbott was financially unprepared to prepay for the service, it was agreed that he would pay the printer's fee upon sale of the papers. With an introduction to a foreman who worked at the Chicago *Tribune* engraving plant, Abbott was able to secure one month's credit for engraving. Others also supported his dream: He rented limited space from George W. Faulkner, in whose real estate and insurance offices Abbott set up a card table and single chair. With a total capital of twenty-five cents, Abbott purchased notebooks and pencils. His only means of distributing the paper was by personally peddling it to locales in which blacks frequently congregated: churches, barbershops, poolrooms, night clubs, and the like. While visiting these various venues, Abbott also collected news and advertising that appeared in subsequent issues of the paper.

Despite Abbott's undying commitment, his paper was not prospering and was on the verge of collapse. When the printer threatened to interrupt his service unless he received payment, Abbott had no other option than to decrease his overhead by moving his "office" to Henrietta Lee's home, in which he also lived. Her interest in helping Abbott stemmed from her equally deep commitment to her race. Without Lee's support and generosity, it is doubtful that the *Defender* would have survived. At this new address of 3159 State Street, the *Defender* finally began to take a turn for the better.

Abbott proceeded to recruit volunteers to write articles on sports, health, and social events that added flavor to the paper. Accomplished individuals like lawyer Louis B. Anderson, Henry D. Middleton, and Julius Nelthrop Avendorph, along with others, agreed to offer their services free of charge. Gradually, additional people who shared Abbott's ideals but had no place in which to vent their sentiments joined the effort with no monies exchanged. Abbott appealed to people in all walks of life to collect newsy items for him and to deposit papers wherever they felt they would sell. The black community supported his venture. A distribution network began to take shape, and circulation started to climb. When the paper outgrew the capacity of the Western Union Printing Company facilities, Abbott made an alternative arrangement with Chicago's *Daily Drovers Journal*. This new business alliance brought with it an added bonus: A foreman of the *Journal* offered suggestions on the *Defender*'s layout. He recommended a more sensational approach that would feature eye-catching headlines. Given the design of the *Defender* and its remarkable similarity to the *Evening American,* a Hearst paper, newsstand buyers often bought the *Defender* in error. Rumors circulated that the *Defender* was owned by William Randolph Hearst—rumors that were laid to rest when the Hearst paper filed suit against the *Defender* for infringement of copyright (given the likeness of the two papers' mastheads). Abbott responded quickly by changing his masthead, since he hardly had the resources to tangle with Hearst.

The *Defender* was successfully reaching a local audience but had yet to assume a national reputation. As Roi Ottley asserts, "Not until the *Defender* assumed its inherited role as an organ of racial propaganda, did it leap into prominence." Although in later years the *Defender* became the "voice of the People," and despite its aggressive slogan, "American race prejudice must be destroyed," it remained rather mild in its approach. J. Hockley Smiley, who was hired as managing editor (without the title) in 1910, took the "bull by the horns." Having had considerable experience in the newspaper field, Smiley helped Abbott transform the *Defender* from a " 'boiler plate' sheet to a standard weekly." It also was transformed, in the words of August Meier, "into the first modern Negro newspaper." From that point forward, the *Defender* unabashedly proclaimed itself "The World's Greatest Weekly," which was incorporated into the masthead. Not by coincidence this also began the transformation of the *Defender* into a "race" paper. Abbott had long been uncomfortable with the labels ascribed to his people: Negro, colored, Afro-American, and so forth. Jointly Smiley and Abbott decided upon the word "race," and as such it was the only word used for African-Americans in the paper.

Smiley also addressed the issue of distribution and identified Pullman porters and the like as crucial people in his proposed strategy. Chicago was a principal railroad terminal and thus had hundreds of railway employees entering and exiting the city daily. They, along with theater people who also traveled extensively, provided the *Defender* with a vast distribution network. In time, a collection of highly competent individuals, who created a cooperative spirit, were hired. With such a coterie of workers, all of whom shared Abbott's ideals, it was only a matter of time before the *Defender* reached blacks throughout the United States.

During the first two decades of the twentieth century, when the *Defender* was coming into its own and establishing Abbott as a local race leader, two major figures came to the forefront nationally as leaders of African-Americans. Both dynamic individuals had strong camps of support that were radically divergent in their dogmas. Booker T. Washington emphasized the importance of industrial education and economic stability within the race as foundations on which to gain ground socially. Succinctly, he was labeled an accommodationist. Conversely, W.E.B. Du Bois, an intellectual, unequivocably stated that the only means of advancement of the race was through confrontation by the "talented tenth," who were intellectually superior and thus better equipped to challenge the status quo. Although Washington had greater mass appeal among blacks, as well as the support of wealthy whites, Du Bois was gaining ground in the early twentieth century. These great leaders both understood the political and influential might of newspapers, and each attempted to recruit editors and publishers who would openly challenge and thus weaken the strength of the other camp. Although other race newspapers did comply and thus advocated the beliefs and strategies of one of the two leaders, Abbott was not willing to be used as a pawn. In Chicago, Claude Barnett, the *Conservator*'s founder, and corporate lawyer and activist E. H. Morris were relentless and consistent opponents of Washington. In other cities, opposition to the Tuskegean was spearheaded by William Monroe Trotter, publisher of the Boston *Guardian*, and J. Max Barber of the *Voice of the Negro* in Atlanta. (In later years, the *Conservator* was seduced into Washington's arena.) In support of Washington were such newspapers as W. Calvin Chase's Washington *Bee* (sometimes) and T. Thomas Fortune's *New York Age*, which was sold to Frederick Randolph Moore* and Booker T. Washington in 1907. Du Bois and Washington wielded considerable power and reached significant numbers of people using "their" newspapers as vehicles in which to assert their doctrines. Chicago proved an elusive city for Washington. Abbott never openly sided with either camp, and thus was never forced to compromise his principles. He adhered to his own beliefs and stood somewhere in the middle of the doctrines of these two very powerful men.

Unquestionably, Abbott's stepfather's belief that a newspaper was one of the strongest weapons a black could have in the defense of his race penetrated the young man's soul. He fought loudly and hard to eradicate discrimination and prejudice, and he strove to educate his race on the importance of protest. Abbott created a platform which became the *Defender*'s "bible." It included the eradication of all race prejudice and any form of segregation, the extension of equal opportunity in employment and education, the abolition of lynching, and the institutionalization of enfranchisement for all American citizens. Clearly Abbott demanded equality in all areas of life—political, social, and economic—and in so doing expressed the sentiments of his race at large. He was the champion of "the masses" and often relentlessly fought a specific injustice that caught his attention. Abbott renounced his support of the Republican party when he witnessed the irresponsible machinations of the two-party political system. He declared himself an Independent politically and urged other members of his race to follow suit. By doing so, he reasoned, they could play one party against the other and perhaps gain more ground. Abbott's distrust of the political system is aptly illustrated in the following quote: "If we are depending on them [politicians] to solve our problems, we shall wait for a long, long time."

As early as 1905, when the Pullman Company threatened to replace blacks with Oriental labor, the *Defender* featured the controversy on page one of several issues of the paper. Abbott's commitment to his race was complete, and although he relied on porters, dining car waiters, and other employees of the railroads to distribute his paper and collect competitors' newspapers that had been left on the trains, he undoubtedly was more concerned with the injustice of the Pullman Company's policies than with the loss of revenue. He had aggressively crusaded against the "red light" district in Chicago's black ghetto. Although Abbott's campaign proved effective and organized the black community sufficiently to have a decision instituted in their favor, he expressed some misgivings over the results of the campaign. When the red-light district officially closed, the *Defender* no longer had a "first-rate issue to exploit." Subsequently he ordered, "Never choose a campaign you can win!"

Outside of Chicago, the *Defender*'s appeal was growing as a result of the effort of Phil Jones, who headed the circulation department. Jones successfully established a distribution network that recruited representatives to act as agent-correspondents. By 1916, seventy-one localities had been adequately organized to make the *Defender* the first black newspaper in history with a mass circulation. It was widely read in the South, and actually its largest readership outside of Chicago was in Kentucky, Tennessee, and the Gulf states. Abbott had long recognized that the opportunities afforded blacks were far greater in the North than in the South. He had been able to succeed despite some major setbacks, and he felt others should avail themselves of similar opportunities. He therefore put special efforts in attempting to convince Southern blacks to pull up stakes and migrate to the North, especially Chicago, where greater opportunities awaited them.

By 1915, the *Defender* had achieved the status of the most successful black paper in Chicago, and it was well on its way to becoming one of the largest black-owned businesses in the United States. Abbott's influence was far-reaching, and through the *Defender* he played a major role in instigating the mass migration that ensued during World War I. Although blacks in the South prior to the war had more than ample reason to migrate to the North, relatively few did. As Allan H. Spear explains, "The ties of home and family exercised a natural restraining influence. But, more important, Negroes had few opportunities outside the South before 1915." Traditionally, industry vacancies in the North had been filled by European immigrants rather than by African-Americans. However, with the outbreak of the war, a variety of circumstances encouraged blacks to head to the North. Employment opportunities had opened up with increased war production combined with the absence of the able-bodied men who were actively engaged in the war effort. Immigration fell considerably between 1914 and 1918, and companies had no readily available source of manpower other than black workers. Without sufficient numbers to support the demand for workers in the North, labor recruiters (who often enticed southern blacks with free transportation and the allure of high wages) headed South to raid the rural and urban centers of their black employees. Offers were particularly attractive for several economically related reasons: the ravages on cotton caused by the Mexican boll weevil, irreversible soil erosion, unrelenting floods, and general economic depression. To add fuel to the fire, Abbott's cries of "Come North, where there is more humanity, some justice and fairness!" reached desperate ears. He instigated a campaign, called "The Great Northern Drive," that helped to set in motion the mass migration. Many relatives of southern blacks who had fled the South earlier appealed to their southern counterparts with letters describing Chicago and the opportunities with which it had provided them. The *Defender* further raised their consciousness. Abbott's ideology of racial solidarity and self-help no doubt motivated his involvement in the mass migration. His appeal to black southerners is exemplified in the following passage from the October 7, 1916, issue of the *Defender* cited in Spear's *Black Chicago*:

Every black man for the sake of his wife and daughter should leave even at a financial sacrifice every spot in the south where his worth is not appreciated enough to give him the standing of a man and a citizen in the community. We know full well that this would almost mean a depopulation of that section and if it were possible we would glory in its accomplishment.

The *Defender*'s influence becomes starkly apparent with the overwhelming response from readers inquiring about the details of the drive: who to contact? where to go? what time? The paper attempted to answer most of these queries to ensure an organized campaign. The potential impact was anticipated by the white population in the South who attempted to confiscate copies of the *Defender* or to punish those found with an issue. Their attempts at confounding the migration were based on the realization that they were faced with an impending crisis without black labor. They were unsuccessful in their efforts to stop it.

Chicago had absorbed a gradual influx of blacks between 1900 and 1914 with little fanfare or problem. Such was not the scenario when masses of people arrived between 1916 and 1920. By 1920, according to the census of that year, Chicago's black inhabitants had reached 109,458, which was an increase of 65,355 since 1910. The city's white population reacted with a threatened and ugly response. Several white newspapers repeatedly printed headlines that further exacerbated the hostile sentiments, and the Baptist church made no attempt to hide its repulsion at the black invasion. Abbott and the *Defender* offered the migrants encouragement with success stories of individuals who had preceded them. Unabatedly, the South was depicted as a place unfit for blacks, and the North was depicted as a place of promise and opportunity. The threat of this mass migration was too great for the whites of Chicago to bear, and time and time again they resorted to unlawful activities such as bombings (Jesse Binga,* a prominent black banker, was a target five times), which the police repeatedly ignored, further aggravating the situation. Confrontations escalated between the races until it was only a matter of time for a full-scale "war" to erupt.

In 1919, with the tragic drowning of a young black boy at the hands of whites, a riot ensued that had national repercussions. The *Defender* covered the daily events of violence and destruction, and it was not until the hostilities persisted that Abbott courageously spoke out against the situation and urged blacks to exercise restraint. Despite risking being labeled an Uncle Tom, Abbott issued a five-point plea to discourage further destruction and disobedience. Not until the state militia intervened did the hostilities cease. To determine the causes of the violence, a Commission on Race Relations was organized that had six appointed representative members from both races. Abbott participated in this forum, which published its results in a book entitled *The Negro in Chicago* (1922). During the proceedings, Abbott was politely criticized for the *Defender*'s irresponsible reporting of race issues. The publisher respected this recommendation and ultimately altered the *Defender*'s tone and appeal.

Shortly thereafter, Abbott reflected on the paper's format, perhaps in response to the commission's criticisms. The stinging label of "yellow journalist" troubled him as did his paper's sensationalistic approach to the news. After consulting an old friend, Abbott adopted a "policy of gradualism." He continued to feature stories of protest, but he encouraged patience (which was also put forward in his five-point plea during the 1919 riots); no longer were immediate action and gratification demanded. Additional items appeared featuring blacks' achievements in all fields, including art, education, literature, and the theater. It has been suggested by Ottley that Abbott assumed this less aggressive tone in response to Marcus Garvey, a West Indian black whose racial philosophy encouraged blacks to take pride in their race and to return to their homeland. His "Back to Africa" rhetoric appealed primarily to recently migrated lower class blacks who were unable to identify with the philosophy of the leadership class. Garvey had become a national figure by the time he made his first personal appearance before black Chicagoans in 1919. His United Negro Improvement

Association (UNIA), by this time, had a large membership, although it is unlikely that it had successfully recruited two million people, as Garvey claimed, and his newspaper *Negro World* had an impressive circulation. Garvey's visit to Chicago was an attempt to attract additional members for the recently organized Chicago branch of the UNIA. Some Chicago blacks enthusiastically supported Garvey, but generally speaking the city was somewhat hostile to his "flamboyant nationalism." Abbott was particularly determined to undermine Garvey's movement, and he mounted vigorous opposition to him. Abbott twice went to great lengths to tarnish Garvey's reputation: once in 1919 and once in 1920. Garvey, in due time, lost his prestige and was ultimately deported from the United States. However, his presence in the United States aroused the level of race pride and certainly threatened Abbott enough to cause the publisher to expend considerable energy, time, and money to undermine Garvey.

By 1920, the circulation of the *Defender* was approximately 230,000. Two-thirds of the issues were sold outside of Chicago; 23,000 of those were sold weekly in New York City. Such numbers were achieved through great toil and trouble. Abbott had taken an aggressive step when he was faced with a near disaster. During the race riot of 1919, the *Drovers Journal*, which had previously provided Abbott with good service, had to desist, since its white printers refused to print the *Defender* out of fear for their lives. Some of the worst violence had occurred near the *Journal*'s facilities, and the white employees expressed understandable nervousness at having to print the black paper. After considerable deliberations, they agreed to do all of the production work, with the exception of the printing. Then, when rioting occurred directly in front of the plant, all production ceased. Abbott's near disaster was saved by the Gary (Indiana) *Tribune* and its presses. After this close call, Abbott decided to avoid the possibility of this ever happening again. He purchased a high-speed cylinder press from Goss Printing Press Company (one of two he later purchased) and bought a building on Indiana Avenue in the primarily black South Side of Chicago, as defensive measures. The equipment and the building were both acquired through cash transactions in the name of the Robert S. Abbott Publishing Company, which was established in 1918.

Two revolutionary steps followed: First, Abbott hired a white foreman, Clarence Brown, and, second, he agreed to unionize the shop. By signing with the Chicago Typographical Union No. 16 (which, incidentally, was the same union that had denied Abbott membership early in his career), the *Defender* became the first unionized black newspaper. From there another first was achieved: Brown was allowed to hire his own staff and recruited skilled white workers, making the *Defender* the first newspaper, white or black, in the United States to employ an integrated staff. It must be recognized, however, that Abbott had little choice in hiring white linotypists, stereotypists, and pressmen, since, after a search had been conducted, it was discovered that all such skilled blacks were already employed and had no interest in leaving their jobs.

With a new home equipped with production facilities and a highly skilled staff, an unveiling took place, in May 1921, to present Abbott's pride and joy to the public. The modernization of his operations provided a role model for other black newspapermen. The financial benefits were soon apparent: Printing costs were cut by more than $1,000 weekly and other overhead costs were modest, which allowed for a greater profit to be realized. With sixty-eight employees paid substandard wages and branch offices in several American cities and London and Paris (although some of these were merely mailing addresses), the business was in fine shape. The *Defender* proved to be a money-maker for Abbott. Generally, white publications make money by selling advertising; traditionally, black publications have relied on circulation for the bulk of their revenues. Such was the case with the *Defender*. As a former business manager of the *Defender* reported to Ottley, "Out of every ten cents the *Defender* netted one cent. With the circulation roughly 200,000, the paper earned nearly $1,500 weekly, on circulation alone. The costs of production were broken down in this way: five cents a copy to produce the paper (including printing, processing, mailing, paper and salaries); four cents for the agent's share, with a profit of one cent for the *Defender*." Of course, Abbott also earned money from advertising. To boost circulation further, he implemented a variety of promotional campaigns, including the sponsorship of the first all-star black football team.

Abbott garnered the attention and status of a national leader and successful businessman, and he aspired to all the accoutrements of upper class elitism, including a weekly salary of $2,000 and monthly bonuses in 1929. He included among his acquaintances some of the most prominent black businessmen of the time: Anthony Overton* and Charles Clinton Spaulding.* He was generous with his time, and he offered family members (including his German relatives) gifts of money to provide for their education. However, despite his financial success, Abbott could hardly be considered a financial wizard. The paper seemed to take on a life of its own given its enormous popularity, and Abbott, from early on, had rarely been aware of the actual monetary transactions. When he was informed that longtime employees of his, including Phil Jones, the managing editor, had been dishonest and had helped themselves to company money to finance a magazine called *Reflexus* (which only published two issues), Abbott perceived a conspiracy at work and fired these highly capable employees. It is important to note that, although Abbott had expressed the intention of publishing *Reflexus*, he had later abandoned the idea. His employees had stepped in at this point. Abbott was continually out of touch with the business side of the *Defender*; his primary concern was the paper's editorial orientation. During the latter part of the 1920s, Abbott retained a commitment to the paper, but his involvement had somewhat diminished given his trips abroad and his responsibilities as a race leader.

During this time, the *Defender* took on a new format with one entire page devoted to the arts. An offshoot of the *Defender* was *Abbott's Monthly*, which made its first appearance during the Chicago renaissance. According to Johnson and Johnson, the magazine's first printing consisted of 50,000 issues, which then was increased to 100,000 soon thereafter. Despite the implications of such a sizable print run, the monthly never enjoyed the success of the *Defender*. No other magazine matched its popularity until John Harold Johnson's* *Ebony* appeared in 1945. *Abbott's Monthly* had a broader range of features than the *Defender* and appealed to a more specialized audience. According to George H. Hill, *Abbott's Monthly* was published from October 1929 to September 1933, at which time it became a monthly and then a weekly newspaper, *Abbott's Weekly and Illustrated News* from October 1933 to March 1934, when it ceased publication. Despite the success reflected in the volume of sales, the magazine could not withstand the effects of the Great Depression.

The Depression of the 1930s was ruthless in the number of businesses and individuals it felled. Some of the most reputable and seemingly solid companies were unable to survive its onslaught. Although Abbott and the *Defender* managed to remain above water, the newspaper's appeal declined significantly during the 1930s because it failed to grow with its readers who were becoming "better educated and more urbanized," according to George Hill. Additionally, during this time, Abbott was suffering from tuberculosis and Bright's disease, and his subsequent absenteeism from the paper negatively affected its content and circulation. When Abbott died on February 29, 1940, the *Defender*'s future slipped smoothly into the capable hands of young John Sengstacke.

John Herman Henry Sengstacke was born in Savannah, one of six children of Herman Alexander and Rosa Mae (Davis), a missionary worker. Herman Sengstacke, a stepbrother of Robert Abbott, was a clergyman who was the founder and principal of Sengstacke Academy and the publisher of the Woodville *Times* and West End *Post*. As a young man in Savannah, John Sengstacke was involved in his father's newspaper business, beginning at the bottom as a printer's devil and eventually working his way up to assume the position of assistant to his father. Robert Abbott took a keen interest in his young nephew and actually took charge of his education and future. Sengstacke was educated at the grade schools in Savannah and then attended Knox Institute in Athens, Georgia, and Brick Junior College in North Carolina, from which he graduated in 1929. Sengstacke next enrolled in Hampton Institute, the institution that had offered Abbott a valuable education and a strong sense of self-worth. There he studied business administration and involved himself in such extracurricular activities as track and football, as well as writing for and editing the school newspaper, the Hampton *Script*. Like his uncle, he also participated in the Hampton Quartet and spent his summer vacations working in Chicago on the *Defender*. In 1933, after graduation from Hampton with a Bachelor of Science degree, Sengstacke accepted permanent employment as Abbott's assistant. Sengstacke continued to learn all aspects of the newspaper industry by working in every department of the *Defender* and taking courses intermittently at the Mergenthaler Linotype School, the Chicago School of Printing, and Northwestern University, where he attended night classes in journalism. In 1933 Sengstacke did postgraduate work at Ohio State University. As Abbott's assistant and as vice president and general manager of the Robert S. Abbott Publishing Company, Sengstacke contributed articles to the company's two affiliated weekly publications—the *Louisville Defender*, founded in 1933, and the *Michigan Chronicle*, established in 1936. He also wrote for the flagship paper in Chicago, which had achieved a national status and was valued at $300,000 in 1940. In that same year, when Abbott succumbed to a lengthy illness, Sengstacke assumed leadership.

The 1940s was a decade of prestige and expansion for many of the large black papers, and Sengstacke's *Defender* followed suit by building the largest black newspaper chain of all. Sengstacke aggressively enlarged the scope of the *Defender* beyond what it had already achieved. He organized the *Columbus News*, *St. Louis News*, *Toledo Press*, and *Cincinnati News*, and in 1951 he founded the *Tri-State Defender*, a weekly published in Memphis, Tennessee. In 1952 he purchased the venerable *New York Age*. Sengstacke's next significant step came in 1956 when he founded the *Chicago Daily Defender*, which focused on covering local news. In that same year, he moved the company's operations to a grander building on Michigan Avenue to accommodate the growing need for additional space. In no time, the daily became a true Chicago paper with in-depth reporting on the activities of the city's enormous black population. Circulation subsequently increased as did advertising revenues from local department stores and supermarkets. Classified and real estate advertising enhanced revenue for the Chicago paper, as it did for the *Michigan Chronicle*.

Sengstacke was the acting editor and publisher of the daily while he continued to serve as the publisher of the weekly and national editions of the *Chicago Defender* in addition to his responsibilities as president of the parent company. Under his direction, in 1966 the *Daily Defender's* circulation reached approximately 50,000 copies daily with approximately 40 percent of that circulation in the form of home deliveries. At this same time, the company had a staff of 150 and annual sales of more than $2 million. Sengstacke maintained a hands-on approach that proved highly effective. As publisher of the *Michigan Chronicle* and chairman of the board of its parent publishing company, the paper achieved a weekly circulation of about 50,000 copies with fifty employees and annual sales in excess of $1 million. Sengstacke was also the publisher of the *Tri-State Defender* and president of its parent publishing company and a stockholder in and a director of the *Louisville Defender*. In 1980 the *Chicago Tribune* reported that Sengstacke Publications owned a total of ten papers, which also included papers in the *Courier* chain that he bought in the late 1960s from S. B. Fuller.* The *Courier* had become the largest black newspaper chain, with a national circulation of 300,000 weekly, compared to 275,000 for the weekly *Defender*. But the *Courier* had run into financial trouble, and an urgent call from Fuller, then chairman of the board, appealed to Sengstacke's sensibilities and a deal was made. According to the staff at the *New Pittsburgh Courier*, the new paper was "a creature of John Sengstacke of Chicago. It's not like the old *Courier* at all. The old *Courier* died."

Sengstacke's syndicate by 1982 included the following publications: the Chicago *Defender*, the Memphis *Tri-State Defender*, the *Michigan Chronicle*, and the *Courier* newspapers published in Pittsburgh, Philadelphia, Ohio, Detroit, Georgia, and Florida. In 1980 Sengstacke Publishing was the seventy-third largest black business in the United States, with sales of $7 million. That was the last year it appeared on the *Black Enterprise* list. The *Louisville Defender* was sold in 1979. In addition to his newspaper activities, Sengstacke published a monthly magazine in New York City, entitled *Headlines and Pictures*, and a trade publication for the black press, known as *PEP*, an acronym for publisher, editor, and printer. He participated in the organization of Amalgamated Publishers, Inc., an advertising agency for the black press and has been acting president since 1961.

Although the editorial policy of the *Defender* continued to urge integration, equal opportunity, and civil rights, when a study was conducted, as early as 1942, that examined readers' attitudes, surprising results emerged. Consuelo Young found that 75 percent of the readers found the paper too radical. They expressed discomfort about the paper's attempt to inflame the passions of blacks against prejudice and discrimination. The readers preferred a more cooperative effort with a more peaceful approach to solving race problems. Although in retrospect the *Defender*'s approach hardly seems radical, at the time it represented a militant approach to the majority of its readers. However, the *Defender* by the 1990s was no longer perceived as the guiding light on race issues and perhaps could even be considered somewhat conservative in its policy, which undoubtedly prompted Chuck Stone, a former *Defender* editor, to label Sengstacke a "journalistic coward." To defend the charge, Sengstacke says, "I'm responsible for the editorial policy. We can't publish our paper on personal whims. Our stories affect a lot of underprivileged people. If it's not in their interest, I don't print it."

The prestige and appeal that the *Defender* enjoyed and the power that it once wielded have diminished considerably in more recent years. Sengstacke, according to one former national correspondent for the *Defender*, over the years placed more emphasis on finances than on editorial quality. In doing so, the paper became riddled with typographical errors, and its circulation has decreased continually since the 1950s. In 1982 the *Chicago Reporter* estimated the *Defender*'s circulation at 18,000 a day; this is hardly an impressive figure when compared to its 1947 claim of 275,000 copies sold weekly: 200,000 of its national edition and 75,000 of its local edition. By 1990 the *Chicago Defender*, still published daily, had 22,044 readers; the weekend edition had 27,044. It also continued to publish three other weeklies—the *Tri-State Defender*, the *Michigan Chronicle* (with 23,669 readers), and the *New Pittsburgh Courier*, which had the largest circulation: 80,000 readers.

The *Defender* and other black newspapers that had so actively fought for civil rights ironically felt the effect of the movement when it came to national attention and the white media provided extensive coverage. The readers that the race papers traditionally appealed to and relied upon were lured away by the mainstream media accounts of the events. Sengstacke also suffered a loss of credibility when he supported Chicago's Mayor Richard Daley, who was not particularly sympathetic to blacks. Such an alliance between the two men undoubtedly caused black organizations to question Sengstacke's politics. He was also strongly antiunionist and created problems with the *Defender*'s staff when in 1972 he broke several unions at his shop. As August Sallas, secretary of the Typographers Union Local 16 noted, "Twice we tried to organize workers at the *Defender* and both times we were stymied by the publisher's anti-trust tactics." The profile of the readership has dramatically changed from the early years when younger blacks particularly responded to Abbott's plea to come North. In more recent decades, the younger black population has turned to the metropolitan dailies or television for news, and the majority of readers of the *Defender* are older black Chicagoans. Financially, the paper has struggled because of the absence of such large department store advertisers as Marshall Field and Company and Carson Pirie Scott. They no longer felt that the *Defender* wielded the influence it once had.

One of Sengstacke's greatest accomplishments was the trade organization he developed that was designed to improve the black newspapers themselves and to offer assistance to black business in general. Abbott, when presented with the idea, was pessimistic about the possibility of creating such an organization because competition among black newspapers had been so fierce that he thought it impossible for them to meet in one room, let alone form an association. Sengstacke proved him wrong. The conference of National Negro Publishers was the beginning of a new era in black publishing, and, as noted in the Birmingham *Times*, "Ironically, the transition and meeting were marked by the death of the preeminent figure in black journalism of that day—the *Defender*'s Abbott." Representatives from thirty-one papers from across the United States organized the Negro Newspaper Publishers Association, which later became the National Newspaper Publishers Association (NNPA). Sengstacke, the organizer, became the association's first president. In 1986 he was serving his fifth term in that capacity. The organization initially met with cool responses from such notable black papers as the *New Pittsburgh Courier* (which had the highest circulation of any black newspaper); however, it did receive support and participation from the *Norfolk Journal and Guide*, the *Baltimore Afro-American*, and the *Kansas City Call*. Others outside of the publishing industry in government and active in civil rights also attended the founding session of the NNPA.

The strength and viability of the NNPA first came to light during World War II when the black press received relentless criticism for its disloyalty. Its loyalty was questioned because the black press was conducting its famous "Double V" campaign, fighting a battle on American soil for equal rights while at the same time supporting the war abroad. The black press was perceived as unpatriotic. Undeterred, the black press pushed war bonds and civil defense, but also continued to protest conditions at home. Since its early years, the association has grown and has become increasingly influential in the United States and beyond, fighting "for the dignity and benefit of those, particularly blacks and the poor, who are in need and entitled to a square deal."

Sengstacke, at the peak of his career, controlled three major communications enterprises: Robert S. Abbott Publishing Company, which published the *Daily Defender* and which was the holding company for four publishing firms; Sengstacke Enterprises, which owned stock in all the publishing companies; and Amalgamated Publishers, which handled national advertising accounts for several black-owned newspapers. When Sengstacke reached his eightieth birthday in 1992, a successor was yet to be named. At that time, Sengstacke was editor and chairman of the *Defender* organization and continued to report daily to work. His commitment to the *Defender* would have made Abbott proud. Shortly before his death, Abbott had expressed his concern about John Sengstacke's abilities when he spoke the following words to Mary McLeod Bethune: "John is my nephew. I am depending upon him, Mamie. I am committing my unfinished task to him. Mamie, do you think he can do it?" Sengstacke proved that he could.

Sources

The personal papers of Robert Abbott and John Sengstacke are both held in the archives of the Chicago *Defender*, under the personal supervision of Sengstacke. They are not at the present time generally open to researchers. There are clipping files on both men in the Schomburg Collection of the New York Public Library. There are a few letters from Robert Abbott in the Booker T. Washington Collection in the Library of Congress. There is also a letter in the archives of Hampton University concerning Abbott's name change. There is a solid, full-length biography of Abbott by Roi Ottley, *The Lonely Warrior: The Life and Times of Robert Abbott* (1955), which was written with Sengstacke's cooperation; Ottley had access to at least some of Abbott's papers. There are also solid shorter biographies by Armistead Price in the *Dictionary of American Biography* and Doris E. Saunders in the *Dictionary of American Negro Biography*. See also treatments in Madeline Stratton, *Negroes Who Helped to Build America* (1965), 122–33; Mary White Ovington, *Portraits in Color*, (1927), 118–26; Ingham, BDABL; Edgar A. Toppin, *Biographical History of Blacks in America* (1971), 244–45; Saunders Redding, *The Lonesome Road* (1958); William M. Tuttle, Jr., *Race Riot: Chicago in the Red Summer of 1919* (1970); Arna Bontemps, *Anyplace But Here* (1966); St. Clair Drake and Horace Cayton, "The Power of Press and Pulpit," chap. 15, vol. II of *Black Metropolis* (1945); Frederick H. Robb, *The Negro in Chicago* (1929); *Ebony*, June 1955, 69–75; Nicholas P. Georgrady and Louis N. Romano, *Robert S. Abbott: Negro Businessman* (1969); *Southern Workman*, February 1919; *Afro-American*, February 6, 1937; *Opportunity*, March 1929 and April 1940; Metz T. P. Lochard, "R. S. Abbott: Race Leader," *Phylon*, 2d quarter, 1947, 124–32; *New York Amsterdam News*, October 8, 1930. There is an extensive obituary of Abbott in the March 9, 1940, issue of the *Defender*. For other obituaries, see *New York Times* and *New York Herald Tribune*, March 1, 1940; the *Norfolk Journal and Guide*, March 9, 1940; *Journal of Negro History*, April 1940. The basic facts of Abbott's life are given in *Who's Who in America*, 1938–39, and *Who's Who in Colored America*, 1938. The single best source of information on Abbott and Sengstacke and the *Defender* are the back issues of the newspaper itself, which are available on microfilm. George N. Hill, ed., "Robert Abbott: Defender of the Black Press," *Bulletin of Bibliography* 42, 2 (1985), 53–55, is an excellent bibliographic source on Abbott and the *Defender*.

Some scholarly articles and books deal with specific aspects of Abbott and the *Defender*: Carolyn A. Strohman, "The Chicago *Defender* and the Mass Migration of Blacks, 1916–1918," *Journal of Popular Culture* 15, 2 (1981), 62–67; James S. Finney and Justice J. Rector, *Issues and Trends in Afro-American Journalism* (1980), 20, 38–39 + ; George N. Hill, *Black Media in America: A Resource Guide* (1984), 18–19, 22, 54, 204, 207; Abby Johnson and Ronald M. Johnson, *Propaganda and Aesthetics: The Literary Politics of Afro-American Magazines in the 20th Century*; M. L. Stein, *Blacks in Communications* (1972); T. Ella Strother, "The Black Image in the 'Defender,' 1905–1975" and Albert Krieling, "The Rise of the Black Press in Chicago," both in *Journalism History* 4, 4 (Winter 1977–78); Joseph B. LaCour, "The Negro Press as a Business," *The Crisis* 48 (April 1941); Charles Allen, "A Readership Survey of the Chicago Defender" (1951). Four issues of the *Defender* are particularly helpful for understanding the operation of the paper: May 3, 1930, which is a recapitulation of the first twenty-five years of the paper; May 4, 1935, an anniversary issue which shows how the paper is put together; March 23, 1940, where Abbott talks about his accomplishments shortly before his death; May 10, 1947, another anniversary issue.

On John Sengstacke, see Gerri Major, *Black Society* (1976), 188–89 (photos); and *Current Biography* (1949), 557–58; *Ebony Success Library* II, 232–35; Doris F. Innis, *Profiles in Black* (1976), 224–25; *National Cyclopedia of American Biography*, K: 257–59; *Chicago Reporter*, June 1982; *Chicago Tribune*, June 18, 1955, May 2, 1980, and June 25, 1982; *Who's Who in Black Corporate America* (1982); Frank J. Johnson, *Who's Who of Black Millionaires* (1984), 126; *Argus*, July 3, 1980; *Pittsburgh Courier*, June 19, 1974.

Alexander, Archie Alphonso (May 14, 1888–January 4, 1958). Contracting engineer: Alexander and Higbee, A. A. Alexander, Inc., and Alexander & Repass; governor of the Virgin Islands of the United States. "Alexander the Great" was a sobriquet given to Archie Alexander when he proved his mettle as a tackle on his college football team. But his accomplishments in business were also sufficient to earn him the title. He accomplished feats that few other African-Americans had managed at the time, and he overcame obstacles, specifically race barriers, as if they did not exist. Alexander seemed to have the ability to bridge the gap between the races in the same way that he bridged the gap between two landmasses. How did a black man from the Midwest achieve this during the first half of the twentieth century when racism ran rampant across the nation? His life history reveals a man of strong will whose determination afforded him opportunities, in both his private and public life.

Archie Alphonso Alexander was born to Price and Mary Alexander in the Iowa town of Ottumwa. The family resided in South Ottumwa, which contained the town's industrial area and the neighborhoods reserved for poor whites and for blacks. The small minority of blacks in Ottumwa numbered only 467, just 3 percent out of a total population of 14,000, according to the census of 1890. Price Alexander worked as a coachman and janitor there until the family relocated to Des Moines, the state capital, in 1901. There the elder Alexander was again employed as a janitor, and the family lived on a small farm on the outskirts of town. African-Americans composed an even smaller percentage of the population in Des Moines, so Archie Alexander early learned how to function in a largely white environment. Since the school system was not segregated in Des Moines, Alexander was allowed to attend Oak Park grammar school and Oak Park High School, graduating from the latter in 1905. From there he attended Highland Park College and the Cummins Art School before he entered the State University of Iowa, in Iowa City, in 1908. Growing up in the Midwest certainly provided him with advantages denied his brethren in the South. Alexander was the first, and only, black enrolled in the College of Engineering at the State University, where he was quickly warned that "a Negro could not hope to succeed as an engineer." He accepted this warning as a challenge and proceeded to prove himself one of the most capable among his peers. Working part-time to support his education and playing on the school football team failed to hamper his success. He was the first African-American to be recruited by the team, and he became a three-letter football tackle. It was during this time that the other students began to refer to him as "Alexander the Great." In 1912 Alexander graduated with a Bachelor of Science degree in civil engineering.

When he was unable to find a job during the summers while going to school, Alexander simply took matters into his own hands. He found himself painting houses, building screens, and repairing porches. He was his own foreman, skilled workman, laborer, and superintendent until he engaged sufficient business to hire help. He learned a valuable lesson at this time: "[He] found that if you delivered a good job when and as your clients wanted it—no particular attention was paid to racial identity." When he founded his own firm, he applied this knowledge when bidding for contracts.

The next several months were difficult ones for Alexander. Convinced of his abilities, he applied to every construction firm in Des Moines, only to be rejected by each one. Thus, he was forced to take a job for twenty-five cents an hour as a laborer in the steel shop at the Marsh Engineering Company of Des Moines. When he resigned his position in 1914 to form his own engineering company, he was earning $70 a week as an engineer responsible for bridge construction for the company in Iowa and Minnesota. Impatient to strike out on his own, Alexander established the general contracting firm of A. A. Alexander, Inc. In 1917 he and George F. Higbee, a white colleague from Marsh Engineering, formed a partnership and renamed the company Alexander and Higbee. The firm specialized in building bridges, viaducts, and sewage systems throughout Iowa. The biracial organization thrived and endured until the accidental death of Higbee in 1925. Alexander proceeded on his own for the following four years and was granted contracts with Iowa State. In 1926 he built for his alma mater a $1 million heating plant, and in 1928 he constructed a new power plant and a tunnel system that ran below the Iowa River. Alexander's expertise overcame whatever color barriers there might have been.

Although Alexander had landed substantial contracts on his own, in 1929 he entered into a new partnership with Maurice A. Repass, another white engineer and former classmate. They renamed the firm Alexander & Repass, and Alexander became the senior partner and assumed responsibility for making contacts, landing contracts, and engaging in public relations activities—a prototypical "Mr. Outside." Alexander nurtured good relations with his business associates, including bankers, material dealers, bondsmen, insurers, and even salesmen. He cherished the value of what he termed "friendliness." During economic hard times, his firm was saved the embarrassment of bankruptcy by the assistance of those Alexander had "been friendly with over a period of years." Repass, on the other hand, became "Mr. Inside," a role which entailed verifying contracts and handling the internal affairs of the business. The firm did remarkably well, so well, in fact, that *Ebony* in 1949 called Alexander & Repass the "nation's most successful interracial business." Their individual skills complemented one another, and the firm prospered handsomely in its early years. Their reputation was far-reaching; they were involved in projects in nearly all forty-eight states (Alaska and Hawaii had not yet been annexed), and they had offices in Des Moines and Washington, D.C. In 1929 Alexander and Repass pooled their resources to construct a $1 million, fifty-two-acre sewage treatment plant at Grand Rapids, Michigan, and in 1933 they built a large power house at Columbus, Nebraska, which was a major unit of the Loup River Power Project. Their most noted accomplishments, though not necessarily their most brilliant, were those projects constructed in the nation's capital: the $1.5 million Tidal Basin bridge and seawall, which they completed in 1943; the K Street elevated highway and underpass from Key Bridge to 27th Street, N.W., constructed from 1947 to 1949; and the $3.35 million Whitehurst Freeway along the Potomac River, which required the labor of 200 workers for two years. The firm also constructed various bridges for the Chicago, Rock Island and Pacific Railroad in western Iowa and Missouri; and the civilian Moton Airfield at Tuskegee, his only black contract at the time. The firm also constructed a $1 million apartment building on six acres of the Frederick Douglass Memorial Estate at Anacostia, Maryland, for the National Association for Colored Women, a project completed in 1954.

All these contracts required strategic bidding because the competition was stiff, particularly from white organizations. But Alexander's careful calculations enabled the firm to make reasonable bids, bids that considerably undercut the competition. In 1946 he declared, "In thirty years of building both public and private work I have never been refused a contract when my proposal was the lower. Some contracts have been awarded our firm when the proposal was much higher than the low one." Alexander asserted that all his contracts were won fairly and that his political affiliations did not win him any business. In 1949 *Ebony* quoted him, "Some of [his competition] act as though they want to bar me. I walk in, throw my cards down and I'm in. My money talks just as loudly as theirs." By 1950 the total number of projects the firm had completed since its original founding in 1914 exceeded 300.

Alexander & Repass landed a broad array of contracts that required both skilled and unskilled labor. The owners employed an integrated work force, although the vast majority of skilled workers were white. Alexander was skilled at public relations both outside of and within the company. He maintained respectable relationships with his employees which enhanced their productivity. Before visiting any of the project sites, he would learn the names of those employees on the payroll of that particular job and, upon arrival, Alexander would greet each individual with a friendly "hello." As he recalled, "I have found that this small courtesy not only pleases each individual workman but also builds up an esprit de corps and an unwavering loyalty that pervades the whole organization." When he encountered Washington union rules that required separate restrooms and separate drinking fountains for blacks, Alexander resourcefully implemented the use of paper drinking cups and labeled the two restrooms "skilled" and "unskilled." This tactic allowed him to maintain his principles without directly challenging the unions. But labor policies were not always so easily resolved. In 1935 a labor dispute interrupted the progress of a construction project in Chicago. Alexander & Repass lost most of its capital, and the founders were forced to rebuild their firm with just $4,000. This controversy was only a minor setback for the firm. The founders' optimism and diligence pushed the company forward onto the national scene.

How does one account for Alexander's success during a time when blacks were facing considerable discrimination? Clearly, his Iowa rearing contributed significantly to how he perceived matters of business and the issue of race relations. Unhampered by bitterness or hostility, Alexander pursued his business goals with the same determination as any other entrepreneurial-minded individual. He focused on what he could do, rather than on what he could not do. After having succeeded as an engineer, Alexander wanted to share the possibility of success in the profession with other aspiring African-Americans. He wrote an article that appeared in a 1946 issue of *Opportunity*, in which he urges young people to become engineers because of the possibilities the profession offered. In it he accounts for his own personal success and encourages African-Americans to take hold of the opportunities available in engineering. He further discredits claims that his color had in any way impeded his progress and articulates several personality traits that are essential for success as an entrepreneur. In addition, he cites other black architects and contractors across the nation who have achieved a modicum of success.

Alexander particularly urged blacks to enter into the construction business because it was lucrative and offered more opportunities than any other branch of the profession. "There is not a city in the United States with a Negro population of three thousand or more that does not offer a splendid opportunity to a Negro engineer to lay a foundation for a successful career in the construction field. Houses need repair, most of them need paint, screens and porches. In every community new homes, too, are needed." He worked his way up in the profession in this manner and he encouraged others to start at the bottom and work their way up. This self-help philosophy can be likened to that of Booker T. Washington's,* for it was he who urged members of his race to lift themselves up from their bootstraps. Alexander identified several essential traits needed for one to succeed in the profession—the willingness to be venturesome, friendly, diligent, and honest. Alexander had learned the importance of these virtues while still in school, and his adherence to them had earned him respect and success in the profession.

African-Americans had long been staunch supporters of the Republican party, the party of Abraham Lincoln. And Archie Alexander was as devoted to the party as other members of his race. When Franklin Roosevelt, a Democrat, assumed the presidency after 1932, blacks shifted their alliance. Roosevelt's New Deal was designed to create greater economic and social equality for all American citizens, and blacks across the nation rallied to his side. But Alexander deviated from this trend. He remained a vocal supporter of the Republican party. His privileged upbringing and subsequent comfort in engaging in business with whites caused him to perceive matters from a different vantage point from that of his brethren. He was active in Iowa's state Republican party, serving as assistant to the chairman of the Republican State Committee in 1932 and 1940, and was active in the presidential campaign of Dwight D. Eisenhower in 1952. When Eisenhower won the presidency, he not surprisingly nominated Alexander for the post of governor of the Virgin Islands. Alexander received the endorsement of both the Democratic and the Republican senators from Iowa, and his nomination was confirmed by the U.S. Senate in January 1954.

The Virgin Islands became a U.S. possession in 1917, when the United States purchased them for $25 million for strategic reasons. In 1927 the islanders were granted American citizenship, and in 1936 Roosevelt granted the islands greater self-government. The population of the islands was largely black descendants of slaves, along with a minority of whites of Danish, Dutch, French, and English ancestry. When Alexander was granted the governorship, a $15,000 a year post, he became the second black to assume that position. (William H. Hastie, a black lawyer and educator had been the first.) The islands' dependence on the United States caused considerable dissonance between the islands' representatives and Congress. When the original Organic Act of 1936 was replaced by a revised Organic Act of 1954, it ensured that the United States would retain "absolute veto power . . . over any bills passed by the legislature over the Governor's veto." It also left the governorship an appointive position, much to the chagrin of the islanders who were denied the right to choose their own representative.

Alexander took the oath of office on April 9, 1954, in Charlotte Amalie's Emancipation Garden, where the Danes had freed their slaves in 1848. The new governor pledged to be "Governor of all and every segment of the population. . . . Prejudice is born in ignorance and dispelled by knowledge. . . . We have room on these islands for but one flag, the American flag." He committed himself to work for a larger tourist trade, while reminding them that "an economy based on tourist trade alone is not a stable one," to aid schools, and to help end the islands' water shortage. Alexander possessed little knowledge of the Virgin Islands. He had vactioned there and had unsuccessfully sought contracts for sewage disposal plants there. His lack of experience in political affairs and his narrow-mindedness resulted in what Charles Wynes has termed "the Virgin Islands fiasco."

Alexander had little understanding of the ethos of Virgin Islanders and of their aspirations. He dispensed with the services of experienced natives in top government positions and replaced them with officials from the United States. Consequently, relations between Alexander and the legislature started poorly and deteriorated over time. What further exacerbated the situation was Alexander's manner: "dogmatic, paternalistic, undemocratic, and with an openly stated contempt for the easy-going Virgin Islanders," as defined succinctly by Wynes. Or as Paiewonsky perceived the problem, Alexander had tried to push his way around without understanding the local personality. Despite Alexander's race, he appeared incapable of comprehending the people or their plight. The island was on the verge of changing character with the introduction of the revised Organic Act, and Alexander did little to ease the transition. He lacked support from the black population and fared little better with the whites, who were uncomfortable with a black governor. Alexander was highly critical of the slower paced islanders who failed to adopt the Protestant work ethic that he had internalized as a driven entrepreneur. He even had the gall, as governor of the Virgin Islands, to identify them as "wards of the nation." One scholarly critic perceived Alexander to be a "midwestern Babbit who brought all the values of small-town America to the Caribbean." He also brought with him "an openly contemptuous attitude toward the local people, a brash manner more befitting a gang foreman than a diplomat, and a complete inability to comprehend the subtleties of West Indian intercourse." No wonder Alexander's governorship was short lived, lasting only sixteen months.

Although several works attribute Alexander's truncated political career to poor health, more in-depth analyses suggest that his stubbornness lay at the root. Alexander claimed that most of his troubles stemmed from the revised Organic Act, which did not provide for an elected governor. As an appointed governor he encountered a hostile legislature. Island critics cited his hardheadedness and his appointment of nonislanders to administrative posts. Wynes, who has conducted the bulk of the research on the situation, concluded that Alexander had controlled his own business for years without having to account to a board of directors, and he mistakenly thought he could run a country in the same fashion. When legislative investigation of his regime brought a vast array of charges, including illegal expenditures of public funds, Alexander's tenure was cut short. The final blow came when Alexander was accused of creating a new corporation with some of his business associates and providing it with advantages that would have ensured a successful low bid and the winning of a contract. Alexander failed to emerge from this controversy unscathed; on April 9, 1955, his resignation was requested. After covering his tracks by claiming ill health, Alexander offered his resignation to Eisenhower, who anxiously accepted it. Alexander's term as governor of the Virgin Islands proved an embarrassment to Eisenhower and a nightmare to the Virgin Islanders.

Alexander's business affiliations extended beyond Alexander & Repass. He founded the American Caribbean Contracting Company in Des Moines in 1950 and served as its president thereafter. It did contracting work in Venezuela and Puerto Rico. He also was president of the Cedar Hill Construction Corporation and secretary treasurer of the Douglas Glen Garden Corporation, both of Washington, D.C., from 1932. He served as a director of the Supreme Liberty Life Insurance Company of Chicago from 1927, maintaining all these positions until his death. Earlier in his career he served as a member of a government commission that investigated economic and social conditions in Haiti, with a view for improvement. A trustee of Tuskegee Institute from 1941 and of Howard University from 1951, Alexander donated $10,000 to cover the cost of books for the library and Tuskegee Institute's engineering school, and he lectured at Howard University. Alexander also engaged in activities for the betterment of his race: He was president of the Des Moines branch of the National Association for the Advancement of Colored People and president, in 1940–1941, of the Des Moines Interracial Commission, and he was a member of a committee that in 1947 met with the Des Moines Board of Education and arranged for the employment of African-American teachers in mixed schools. Several awards were conferred on him during his lengthy career. He was awarded the Spingarn Medal in 1926 for outstanding contributions to industry by a black businessman and a certificate of merit in 1947 from the State University of Iowa, as one of the institution's 100 most outstanding graduates. He, too, held a membership in the Boule, an elitist organization that was organized to bring together blacks who had "demonstrated outstanding ability to compete successfully with whites." Alexander's business accomplishments opened this door.

Alexander's abilities as a businessman are well proven, and in retrospect, he likely would have admitted that he should have remained an engineer and avoided politics altogether. Upon returning to civilian life, Alexander was sixty-seven years old and ailing. Three years later, he died of a heart attack at his home in Des Moines. He left an estate worth $140,505 to his wife, upon whose death the remaining monies were equally divided among the University of Iowa, Tuskegee Institute, and Howard University for engineering scholarships. In 1975, each of the three institutions received $105,000.

Publications that celebrate blacks' contributions to society have overlooked Archie Alexander's success, and his omission is a travesty. He achieved success in a profession where few blacks had before or after. Like Horace King* of Georgia, Sam Plato of Louisville, the Aiken brothers of Atlanta, and the McKissack brothers of Nashville, black engineers have failed to draw the accolades they deserve. Alexander saw the possibilities afforded blacks in the profession and shared his knowledge and enthusiasm with them. He wrote, "The profession of engineering is such a splendid one. . . . It is creative. Truly the engineer is a partner of the gods and the master of gravitation." And Alexander enjoyed the splendor of it all.

Sources

Archie Alexander's personal papers are held in the Special Collections Department of the University of Iowa Libraries, Iowa City. However, the holdings are limited to mostly trustees' records from Howard University and articles and clippings about Alexander, with a minimal amount of personal correspondence. Alexander authored an article, "Engineering as a Profession," which appeared in the April–June 1946 issue of *Opportunity*. His own personal account of his success also appears in Vishnu V. Oak's *The Negro's Adventure in General Business*, vol. II of the series *The Negro Entrepreneur* (1949).

The most comprehensive account of Alexander's career is found in Charles E. Wynes, " 'Alexander the Great,' Bridge Builder," *The Palimpset* LXVI (May–June 1985), 78–86. See also Wynes's treatment in *American National Biography* (forthcoming). Alexander prepared an autobiography for his nomination hearing: U.S. Congress, Senate Committee on Interior and Insular Affairs, *The Nomination of Archie A. Alexander to Be Governor of the Virgin Islands*, 83rd Congress, 2d session, 1954. Briefer sketches appear in the *National Cyclopaedia of American Biography* XLIX; *Current Biography* (1955); and Ralph Bullock's *In Spite of Handicaps* (1968). E. A. Toppin's *Biographical History of Blacks* (1971), Ingham BDABL, and W. S. Robinson's *Historical Negro Biography*, offer concise biographical profiles. He appears in the *Negro Year Book* (1952) and in *Who's Who in Colored America* (1950). National coverage of Alexander's business activities appears in *Ebony*, April and September 1949 and November 1952; the *New York Times*, April 11, 1954, April 12, 13, and 18, and August 18 and 19, 1953; the *Des Moines Tribune*, November 25, 1947; and the *Grand Rapids Herald*, October 4, 1954. Also, a brief press release from the Office of War Information is held in the Schomburg Collection. Alexander's college football career is offered in Raymond A. Smith, Jr., "He Opened Holes Like Mountain Tunnels," *The Palimpset* LXVI (May–June, 1985), 87–100. Obituaries appear in the *Des Moines Sunday Register* and the *New York Times*, January 5, 1958.

Alexander's public position as governor of the Virgin Islands is chronicled in *Time*, April 19, 1954, and July 25, 1955; as well as in *Current Biography* (1955). A very brief treatment of Alexander's role in the Caribbean appears in former governor's Ralph M. Paiewonsky's autobiography *Memoirs of a Governor: A Man for the People* (1990). More complete accounts of the nature of his governorship is offered in William W. Boyer's *America's Virgin Islands: A History of Human Rights and Wrongs* (1983) and Gordon K. Lewis's *The Virgin Islands: A Caribbean Lilliput* (1972).

Amos, Wallace, Jr. (Wally) (July 1, 1936–   ). Cookie company founder: Famous Amos Chocolate Chip Cookie Company. In 1944 the sociologist Leo Lowenthal wrote a famous article, in which he talked about the rise of what he called "idols of consumption" in America after the 1920s. In this new framework, people were encouraged to believe, not so much that they could become successful in a Horatio Alger–like manner, but that by eating the same cereal, drinking the same tomato juice, or smoking the same cigarette, they could share the celebrity status and success of a number of popular entertainers. Wally Amos, creator of Famous Amos Chocolate Chip Cookies, created the first "celebrity cookie," that is, the first cookie that was merchandised and purchased because Carol Burnett, Ann-Margret, John Denver, Elton John, Marvin Gaye, or any one of a number of other stars loved it. However good and unique the taste of the cookie, it achieved popularity primarily because it had "celebrity chic"; consumers wanted to share in the lives of the stars by sharing their cookie.

Wally Amos was born in the black ghetto of Tallahassee, Florida, the son of Ruby and Wallace Amos, neither of whom could read or write. Suffering miserably, as did most blacks, from the Great Depression, the Amos family relied on prayer and hope to get them through the hard times. But Wally Amos has happy memories of growing up; he does not even remember much poverty. When he was asked by Tom Cassidy on the CNN program "Pinnacle" if he was poor, he said: "Yes, I guess by today's standards, even by standards then . . . but even though I was a poor kid, I always had nice clothes, always ate enough, so there were people who were poorer than I was." Mostly he just remembers being happy, as he says in his autobiography, *The Famous Amos Story*: "My childhood in Tallahassee was like kids everywhere; living my life to the fullest every day, going to bed every night tired and happy." Of course, even the eternally optimistic Amos knew he grew up in the Deep South in the 1940s and 1950s. He told Cassidy about Tallahassee's segregation: "I had to walk all the way to the other side of town to go to the one movie that was in town for blacks, there were no swimming pools, no recreational areas and whatnot, you know; you had to ride in the back of the bus; you had to ride in the front of the train, because it was the car that was right next to the engine, and the dirtiest car on the train, but, you know, you lived through all that. You knew that was the way of life and you accepted that."

Then, when he was twelve years old, Amos received devastating news—his parents were divorcing, and his mother was moving in with her mother in Orlando, Florida. Young Wally was to be sent to live with his Aunt Della in the Washington Heights section of New York City without his mother. It was Aunt Della who introduced young Wally Amos to chocolate chip cookies. It was her cookies that, years later, inspired Amos to found his own company. While living with Aunt Della, Amos attended the Edwin W. Stitt Junior High School. This was a difficult transition for him, since it was the first integrated school he had ever attended. He also had to adjust to the tough street gangs in Harlem, who often shook him down for money. During this period, Wally Amos also began working part-time, first delivering newspapers, then groceries for local supermarkets, and then ice. After junior high school, Amos decided to attend Food Trades Vocational High School, with the idea of becoming a chef, since the school's recruiter told him that "cooks make a lot of money."

Amos recalled later that he loved his time at Food Trades, and he especially looked forward to his second year, when he would alternate a week of school with a week of on-the-job training, for which he got paid. For his training, Amos was assigned to the pantry of the Essex House Hotel, one of the prestige hotels in the city. But, as Amos recalls, "I wasn't happy about the assignment," since he found he spent most of his time preparing salads, desserts, pancakes, and waffles, rather than cooking main courses. When he complained to his counselor, Amos was told the assignment was temporary, but after a year he knew this was not the case. As he reported, "I was discouraged, to say the least, and I felt that racism was the reason I didn't get what I deserved. Therefore, I started thinking again about whether I really wanted to be a cook." Amos then went through a difficult period, where he dropped out of school, gambled away his Aunt Della's utilities payments, and ran away to live on the streets. When he finally returned home, Amos told his aunt that he did not want to return to school but wanted to join the U.S. Air Force instead. She agreed to sign the required papers for the seventeen-year-old to enlist in 1953. Amos was assigned to Sampson Air Force Base in Geneva, New York, where he spent two months of basic training.

After basic training, however, Amos was sent to Keesler Air Force Base in Biloxi, Mississippi, a rigidly segregated city and state in the early 1950s. Tallahassee may have been the South, but Mississippi was something else again. It was, as historian James W. Silver called it, a "Closed Society." Amos was to learn to repair airplane radar and radio equipment. After nine months there, Amos was assigned to Hickham Air Force Base in Honolulu, Hawaii, which introduced him to a city and a society that he grew to love, and where he would return to live later in his life. It was during this time that he also got his high school equivalency. After four years in the Air Force, Amos came back to New York, where he looked for a job. He decided to get his diploma at the Collegiate Secretarial Institute, and at the same time he got a job working in the supply department of Saks Fifth Avenue department store. Amos started there as a stock clerk, unloading cartons from trucks, and receiving and storing cartons and office supplies. He worked there mornings and evenings and went to school during the afternoons.

While working at Saks, Amos impressed his supervisor, Ernie Riccio, and when Riccio was promoted, he recommended that Amos be his replacement. The store agreed, and Wally became an executive with an increase in salary. Amos then was sent to New York University's retail and merchandising course, but he had such trouble with the math involved that he decided he no longer wanted to be a buyer. So, in 1961, Amos decided to leave Saks to look for other employment. Jobs were not easy to come by, but an employment counselor at Collegiate Secretarial got him an interview with the William Morris Talent Agency in New York City. After several interviews, Amos was hired and was informed that he would be given no special treatment because he was black— he would be judged solely on the quality of his work and attitude. Starting in the mailroom, in two months Amos became a substitute secretary by continuing school and practicing typing during his lunch hours. His next step on the ladder was in the music department of the firm, where Amos became one of two secretaries to Howard Hausman, one of the firm's top executives.

Even though Amos was not an agent, he wanted to be one, and he kept his eye out for new talent. One night he caught the act of two young, white singers in a local club. Impressed with their talent, Amos invited Hausman down to hear the duo, who turned out to be Simon and Garfunkel. Hausman was tremendously impressed, signed the young singers to a contract, and made Amos an assistant agent at William Morris, the first black agent ever at the company. Amos later said that he was the firm's "token black trainee." "I was," he added, "the Jackie Robinson of the theatrical-agency business." Hausman remembers Amos rather fondly: "My first impression of Wally was that he was a likeable long drink of water because he's tall, skinny and ingratiating. When he became my secretary, I quickly found him to be a hardworking young man. On the average I turn in a ten-hour workday, with a lot of overtime, but Wally would be in the office before me, with anything I had given him to do ready first thing in the morning." What ultimately impressed Hausman most about Amos, however, was his "tremendous eye and ear for talent."

While at William Morris, Amos experienced a good deal of success, booking the Supremes, the Temptations, and Marvin Gaye, along with Simon and Garfunkel. By all accounts, Amos did a fine job. "Wally was trusted as a manager and knew what would catch on," Hausman recalled. But, by 1967, Amos felt he was "burned out" with the agency. He had been booking rock and roll acts for the firm for over six years, but by then he felt the music scene was changing too radically. He had trouble relating to the hard rock and acid rock emerging at that time. Also, there were a number of personnel changes in the music department at William Morris, which made Amos feel less comfortable. Worst of all, was the fact that he found he would not be able to advance any further in the firm, since the executives thought the other agents would not take direction from a black.

So, in 1967, Amos left to manage talent on his own. He moved to Hollywood, and there he took over management of the careers of singers Abby Lincoln and Oscar Brown, Jr., actress Pat Finley, and comedian Franklin Ajaye. He had some success with these acts, but then he decided to devote himself solely to managing the career of trumpeter Hugh Masakela. But, after several months, that relationship ended. As Amos tells it, "Masakela came off the most successful tour ever and told me he didn't like the way I was managing his career. . . . It was the low point of my life."

The next months and years were difficult for Wally Amos. He went from job to job in the entertainment industry—working for a time for John Levy, a personal management firm, as a manager of acts for Venture Records; and then trying to go out on his own again as a personal manager. After that, he formed his own production company and a number of other short-lived ventures. During this same troubled period (when two of his marriages also dissolved), Amos turned to baking his Aunt Della's chocolate chip cookies for therapy. He also often brought a bag of cookies with him to parties and other engagements. Putting his card in the bag of cookies, they became his own unique calling card, his "gimmick." Unfortunately they did not do much to get his career going.

One day, while munching on his cookies with Quincy Jones' secretary at A&M Records, Amos was bemoaning his hopeless future. The secretary said, "Why don't we go into business together selling your chocolate chip cookies?"

Amos smiled and said, "That's a great idea. But I don't have any money."
Nonetheless, an idea had been planted in Amos's mind, and soon he became
committed to it—the problem was finding some financing. For that, Amos turned
to his friends in the music and entertainment industry. He first approached his
longtime friend, singer Helen Reddy. She and her husband agreed to put up
$10,000 if he also found some other investors. Then Artie Mogull, a recording
executive, put up $5,000, as did Herb Alpert, band leader and founder of A&M
Records. The final $10,000 came from singer Marvin Gaye.

With his financing lined up, Amos next had to establish a business. Again,
Quincy Jones's secretary suggested a name—"Famous Amos"—and he began
to call his product "the superstar of cookies." Amos rented a storefront on the
corner of Sunset Boulevard and Formusa Avenue. It was not a prime location—
next door was the Exotica School of Massage ("Sindy's Nude, Nude, Nude
Girls, Girls, Girls"), and across the street was the American School of Hypnosis
and the Seventh Veil Restaurant, which billed itself as "The Home of Camel
Juice." But Wally Amos was determined to make his opening a celebrity event—
a "happening." He sent out 2,500 invitations to his opening. It turned out to
be a magnificent event: Some 1,500 people showed up on March 10, 1975; many
of them were celebrities, and some even arrived in chauffeured limousines. Amos
provided all with free champagne and had a strolling Dixieland band on hand.

Wally Amos was a genius for promotion. Truly the showman, Amos applied
all the techniques he learned flogging musical acts to promoting his celebrity
cookies. He made himself the star of the "cookie extravaganza" he was developing, and he played the role to the hilt. He appeared in various locations
where there were crowds of people and began singing "Fa-mous Amos!" to the
tune of "Hallelujah Chorus." With a tin of cookies in hand, he began to chant:
"Here, have a Famous Amos cookie. I am *the* Famous Amos. Whoop! Cookie
time here, cookie time! I am *the* Famous Amos and there's my store right there.
Oh, please take my cookies! How can I sell 'em if I can't give 'em away? Oh
me, let's talk about it! Hey, we got two left. One for you." But what really
gave his cookies cachet was the fact that various stars were reported to love his
cookies. These stories first ran in the Los Angeles papers, and then were picked
up and syndicated across the United States. As a result, the demand for his
cookies became nationwide.

In 1976 a dress designer friend took some of Amos's cookies to Bloomingdale's
in New York. The buyers there, having already heard something about the
cookies, were excited and contacted Amos about carrying the cookies in their
twelve New York stores. He agreed, but to do so he had to set up a factory and
wholesaling operation on the East Coast. To service his rapidly expanding East
Coast business, Amos soon decided he would set up a factory in Nutley, New
Jersey. At the same time, he began opening other Famous Amos cookie stores
in the Los Angeles area. But all of this was really just preparation for what
happened in the spring of 1977, when Famous Amos Cookies skyrocketed in
popularity.

Media hype had made Famous Amos Cookies reknowned as the "cookie of the jet set," and when they began to be handled by the famous Neiman-Marcus department stores, they really hit the big time in prestige. At the same time, Amos abandoned selling cookies at Bloomingdale's to sell them in the basement boutique at Macy's. The big clincher in making this move was that Macy's promised Amos that he and his cookies could be part of the great Macy's Thanksgiving Parade. Famous Amos would be visible to at least 20 million television viewers. For four years, Wally Amos was in the parade, and he became a true media celebrity himself.

By 1979 Wally Amos was in charge of a mammoth operation. His factories turned out 7,000 pounds of handmade cookies every day; the company had $4 million in revenue annually; and his first store in Los Angeles was included on the Grayline Sightseeing Bus Tour of Hollywood. Over the next three to four years, his cookies also began appearing on supermarket shelves, and Amos expanded his production facilities extensively. But, at the same time, a number of problems began to surface. First, Amos faced increasing competition. New cookie companies, like Mrs. Field's and David's, were taking a good deal of the upscale cookie business away from Famous Amos. Also, he made the mistake of not franchising his operation when it was the leading cookie business. By 1983 he had just eight franchises, with most of his business focused on wholesaling, and the newcomers were gaining momentum via specialized prestige cookie kiosks, rather than in department stores or supermarkets.

Although Amos was able to ride a tremendous media hype to the top of the cookie world in the 1970s and 1980s, some of that also turned against him. Perhaps because he was black, or because he had been in show business and could attract the testimonials of stars for his cookies, he enjoyed nearly unprecedented media coverage during his early years. Geraldo Rivera featured his cookies on "Good Morning America," they were also on the "Mike Douglas Show," and Amos and his cookies were extolled in the pages of *Time*, *People*, and *Vogue* magazines, in the *New York Times*, *New York Daily News*, the *Chicago Tribune*, *Black Enterprise*, *Family Circle*, and many others. Almost universally, it was claimed that his cookies were the best tasting and that Amos himself was a genius. On December 19, 1983, *People* magazine rated the Famous Amos Chocolate Chip Cookies as "the winner, by a crumb," over other contenders. Whenever someone is on top, however, the criticism becomes intense, and Amos soon experienced some of that. This was particularly true over what some people believed was deceptive advertising. Some people complained that the cookie in the bag was not like the cookie pictured on the bag. The latter was large, with enormous chocolate chips and chunky nuts protruding from it. The cookies in the bag were much smaller, about the size of a half-dollar, and the nuts and chocolate chips were submerged in the cookie. When challenged about this, Amos admitted the cookies were different from the picture. "That's why we carry a disclaimer on each bag which says the cookies inside may be different in appearance from the cookie in the photograph on the bag."

Of greatest significance, however, was the fact that, although Wally Amos was perhaps the greatest cookie salesman and promoter who ever lived, he was not an effective businessman. He was uninterested in the mundane chores of managing the company, and he was unable to assess others who were hired to do the job for him. Further, although the company's headquarters remained in Los Angeles, in 1977 Amos moved to Hawaii, where he was able to neglect his obligations even more easily. Amos himself recognized this years later when he said, "You can't run a business unless you're there. In 1977 I moved from Los Angeles to Hawaii. Other people tried to run the company but they really weren't qualified to do so." As a result, the firm was soon in a chaotic state and suffering from a severe cash flow problem.

In 1985, on sales of more than $10 million, Amos's company was losing $300,000. Facing bankruptcy, Wally Amos had to look for additional financing. In February of that year he sold a majority of the stock to the Bass brothers of Texas. "With the infusion of capital, I thought, 'This is what I've been waiting for,' " Amos said, "but the chemistry wasn't there." Thus he struck a deal with a group of private investors that included former Senator John Tunney to buy out the Bass brothers. Amos explained, "All the money went into the company. None of it went into my pocket. We were in such bad shape it was either that or try to reorganize under Chapter 11." Amos kept just 8 percent of the firm's stock, and the new investors instituted stiff financial controls on the lax company. This was a difficult situation for Amos, but he adjusted to it after a time. With new management, the firm was revitalized and expected to reach $12 million in sales in 1987.

Wally Amos himself went back to doing what he did best—promoting the company. Like Orville Redenbacher and Colonel Saunders, company founders who sold their concerns to others, Amos spent little time at company headquarters after the sale. He no longer ran the business; he was solely a spokesman. But, as he said, "I'll always be part of the business because I *am* the business." He also commented once, "I started the cookie business just to make a living, and that's still all I'm concerned with." Yet there is no question that he made a profound cultural impact on America, even if it was for just a brief time. As Libby Clark wrote in the *Los Angeles Sentinel*, "Wally (Famous) Amos has done for the chocolate cookie what Barnum, Bailey and Ringling Brothers did for the circus—glamorized it, made it an integral part of our lifestyle . . . and an American institution."

Some of his most visible work in the 1980s was as a spokesman for the Literacy Volunteers of America. He told audiences about his illiterate parents, about how he never could have even followed a cookie recipe if he couldn't read, and he stressed the message: "If you can't read, you can't succeed." On November 18, 1980, however, Wally Amos achieved true immortality. On that date he was selected by the Smithsonian Institution of the National Museum of History to donate his trademark embroidered shirt and Panama hat to become part of the exhibits in the Business Americana Collection. Famous Amos was the first food company to have anything accepted at the Smithsonian, and he was the first black businessman to be represented in the collection. Wallace and Ruby Amos and Aunt Della would be very proud of him indeed.

Sources

No business or family papers of Wally Amos are currently available. He has written his autobiography: Wally Amos with Leroy Robinson, *The Famous Amos Story: The Face That Launched a Thousand Chips* (New York, 1983). Wally Amos and his cookies were covered in a number of press accounts. See *Time*, June 13, 1977; *Ebony*, September 1, 1979, and May 1983; *Essence*, May 1977 and December 1981; *Nation's Business*, December 1981; *Newsweek*, November 14, 1983; *Black Enterprise*, January 1981 and June 1987; *People*, September 20, 1986; *Minorities and Women in Business*, November/ December 1986; *Sepia*, December 1976 and June 1978; *Forbes*, March 10, 1986; *The Argonaut*, February 10, 1983; *Los Angeles Sentinel*, April 12, 1979, June 25, 1981, June 3, 1982, February 10, 1983, and June 5, 1986; *LA Magazine*, March 1980 and May 1984; *Los Angeles Herald Examiner*, October 12, 1978, and April 18, 1979; *Los Angeles Times*, October 7, 1986; *About Time*, January 1982; *Pittsburgh Courier*, October 7, 1976. See Joseph J. Fucini and Suzy Fucini, *Entrepreneurs* (1985); Frank J. Johnson, *Who's Who of Black Millionaires* (1984). See also the transcript for the "Pinnacle" television show on CNN, January 10, 1987. Lowenthal's article "Biographies in Popular Magazines," in Paul F. Lazarsfeld and Frank Stanton, eds., *Radio Research, 1942–43* (1944).

Antoine, Cesar Carpentier (1836–September 1921). Politician, businessman, and editor: *Black Republican, New Orleans Louisianian*, Cosmopolitan Life Insurance Company. C. C. Antoine, like his fellow business leader, Thomy Lafon,[*] was a member of the prestigious Creole community in New Orleans, but he was not part of its older aristocracy. Unlike Lafon, however, Antoine made his money and status largely through his political connections. Most of what we know of Antoine's early life, unfortunately, comes from his own recollections, which appear to be colored with a good deal of inflated rhetoric. Antoine was born in New Orleans, according to him, to a mother who was descended from an African chief and whose grandmother had been brought to America as a slave. His father served as a soldier in the battles around New Orleans in 1812.

C. C. Antoine spent his childhood in New Orleans, and he was educated in private schools in his native city, indicating a fair affluence for his free black parents. Antoine as a member of the Creole class in the city, became fluent in both French and English, and after completing his education he entered the barbering trade—one of the few professional occupations open to blacks at the time. According to the 1850 census, there were forty-one free black barbers in the city. None of them, however, attained the kind of wealth and influence accorded to the Creole aristocrats who worked as tailors or real estate brokers or in a few other elite occupations. Antoine, like the great majority of free black businessmen before the Civil War, in New Orleans and elsewhere, was a small businessman, and in the 1860 census his wealth was not sufficient enough to warrant mentioning. Also, C. C. Antoine, unlike the other Antoines listed in that census, was recorded as "black" rather than mulatto.

Antoine's great opportunity came when Union troops marched into New Orleans, and he allied himself with a group of free blacks in the city, often in opposition to the older Creole mulatto aristocracy. After Union troops had occupied the city, Antoine began recruiting African-Americans to serve in the "Native Guards," which later evolved into Company I, Seventh Louisiana Colored Regiment, with Antoine as its captain. He served, evidently with distinction, during the balance of the war, and at the end of the Civil War, Antoine moved to Shreveport, where he opened a grocery. This business prospered, and Antoine garnered a good deal of respect from both blacks and whites. As a result, he decided to try his hand at politics.

While still in New Orleans, Antoine had already begun staking out his political territory. In 1864, members of the Creole mulatto aristocracy, including Thomy Lafon, had formed the *Tribune*, ostensibly to fight for the rights of all blacks. Many recent slaves and other dark-skinned blacks, including Antoine, were convinced that the Creoles were more interested in their own respectability to be concerned with the rights and needs of the freedmen. When the *Tribune* took issue with the policies of General Nathaniel P. Banks, the military governor of Louisiana, Antoine and others organized the *Black Republican* to represent those blacks who felt they were ignored by the *Tribune*. This brought Antoine into the company of a number of the most powerful rising Republicans in Louisiana, black and white. Of greatest consequence was his budding relationship with P.B.S. Pinchback.*

On the political side, Antoine was elected a delegate to the Louisiana Constitutional Convention in 1867–1868. There, he advocated an extensive Bill of Rights, tax reforms, and a petition to Congress requesting the extension of the Freedmen's Bureau. Upon completion of the new constitution, Antoine was elected as state senator from Caddo Parish and served until 1872. During this time, a power struggle developed between the followers of the governor, Henry Clay Warmoth, and an opposition group, termed the Custom House Ring. Antoine increasingly threw his allegiance behind the latter group, which was allied to Oscar Dunn, the black lieutenant governor. Antoine's associate, Pinchback, since he held appointive office, remained loyal to the "carpetbagger" Warmoth. Thus began a split between the two former allies that revealed itself in a number of ways.

During this same period of time, Antoine and Pinchback engaged in joint business enterprises. In 1869 the two men formed a cotton factorage concern. Called Pinchback and Antoine, it was based at 114 Carondelet Street, New Orleans. The concern proved to be a success, and it was carried on by the two men for a number of years. In December of that year, Pinchback and Antoine became the owners of the *New Orleans Louisianian*, a semiweekly. Antoine was with the paper from December 25, 1869, to April 27, 1872, when Pinchback became the sole owner and continued to run the paper for over a decade. Antoine also invested in a number of other business enterprises in New Orleans on his own account during these years. One other venture the two men engaged in together was of questionable legality and reflects on their political involvement. Pinchback, as park commissioner in New Orleans in 1871, was involved in buying a parcel of land that was to be sold to the city as parkland. He and the other commissioners paid $60,000 down for a $600,000 parcel. They sold one-half of this land to the city at a much higher sum and pocketed the balance. Antoine was rumored afterward to have gone around complaining that Pinchback had cheated him out of about $40,000 he had expected to make on the deal. It is not clear just why he thought he was owed the money, but it helped drive a wedge between the two men, and it demonstrates some of Antoine's and Pinch-back's attitudes toward the use of politics for personal advancement.

By 1872 Antoine was ready for what became his biggest triumph in politics. In that year he received the Republican nomination for lieutenant governor, with William Pitt Kellogg as the gubernatorial candidate. At first, there were two Republican tickets: the Custom House Republicans, who had nominated Kellogg and Antoine, and the Pinchback Republicans, who ran an alternate ticket. Pinchback soon realized that the split could result in a Democratic victory, and he threw his support to Kellogg and Antoine, with Pinchback as a candidate for congressman-at-large. Kellogg and Antoine were ultimately put into office in a highly disputed election in which there was a great deal of fraud on both sides. It was resolved only when President Ulysses Grant upheld the election of Kellogg and Antoine.

Antoine himself had become quite a lightning rod of white opposition during the election. Kellogg was a northerner who was reputed to hate living in Louisiana. Many opponents, then, suggested that, if his ticket were elected, Antoine would be the real chief executive of the state, since Kellogg would always be absent. This sentiment was expressed most bluntly in the *Times* in an editorial entitled ''The Triumph of Africa'' on June 25, 1872:

[Antoine's] choice with Mr. Kellogg for the Governorship, is a distinct announcement to the people of Louisiana that General Grant desires this state to be delivered over to rule of the recently emancipated Africans. . . . [Kellogg] has never passed eight consecutive months in this city . . . [and that] give[s] pretty satisfactory assurance that our Caesar Anthony would wield the sceptre of Louisiana for at least half the year.

Soon after the disorder and violence of the 1872 election had passed, a number of black and white businessmen in New Orleans organized the Unification Movement. In this, the white unionists were willing to recognize the validity of the Fourteenth and Fifteenth amendments to the United States Constitution and that all public places be open to all people, regardless of race or color. It also called for equal employment opportunities for both races and for the equal division of public offices between the two. C. C. Antoine was one of the principal black signatories to the agreement, along with members of the old Creole aristocracy, Aristede Mary, P. Bonsegneur, Dr. Roudanez, and William Randolph. The movement, however, did not catch on with the masses of either whites or blacks, and it was dismissed by many as a Quixotic scheme.

While Antoine was serving as lieutenant governor, he, for reasons not fully clear, came under withering attack from the Creole aristocracy. Antoine and Pinchback were often viewed as symbols of new black usurpers, who had ascended to roles in the black community that they felt should rightfully be held by them. Thus, both endured great criticism, but Antoine, perhaps because he was also Creole, was most rudely treated. They attacked him as a "dandy" and particularly used the black pidgin French, a blend of French and African grammar, to attack him. The *Carillon*, a Creole weekly, began an uninterrupted barrage on Antoine after he was elected. They accused him of deserting one woman for a huge "cala woman," who sold hot rice cakes and weighed "214 pounds net." This was couched in verses that went on for pages:

> Ah, then its you Caesar Alligator,
> You who dresses like a peacock,
> Who makes love to a young Negress,
> and never looks at old age.

Another rhyme described his rise from poor barber to acting governor in uncomplimentary terms:

> That monkey, he was little,
> That monkey, he grew large,
> He who was but a mouse,
> He's bigger than an elephant.
> That monkey was once a dirty nigger.
> He's better than all white men now.
> Because tis he who makes our laws,
> Tis he who's our governor.

Seldom has a public official been subjected to such abuse, and what made it all the more difficult was that it came from members of his own race.

In 1876 Antoine was renominated for the lieutenant governor spot, along with Stephen B. Packard as governor, and the result was again a disputed election, with two slates claiming victory. This time, however, federal troops were withdrawn from Louisiana shortly after the election, and the government set up by Packard was soon toppled, and Antoine was pushed permanently out of state politics. He did, however, serve as a member of the school board for Caddo Parish for a time after 1875, and he was long an advocate of better public education for blacks in the state. Antoine himself, quite naturally, saw his political career as exceptionally honest and free of corruption. Whites in the state hardly agreed. A master's thesis, written at Louisiana State University in 1945, calmly referred to Antoine as "a symbol for the corruption of the Republican party in Louisiana." No doubt this was greatly overstated, but the fact that Antoine never again held public office, even when some blacks like Pinchback did, lends some credence to the charge.

During the 1870s, Antoine continued to be involved in a number of business activities, including extensive investment in railroad and lottery stocks. He also raised a number of race horses. In 1880 Antoine became president of the Cosmopolitan Life Insurance Company, but it is not clear how long his affiliation with that concern lasted. After 1887 he largely disappeared from public view, though in later years he did purchase a plantation in Caddo Parish and also owned several lots in New Orleans, along with a $1,300 residence there.

Antoine's last political involvement came in the 1890s, ironically in concert with the old Creole aristocrats who had so greatly vilified him some twenty years earlier. In 1890 the state of Louisiana passed new Jim Crow legislation which mandated separate seating for blacks on streetcars and trains. Prominent members of New Orleans' Creole community organized the Comité des Citoyens in 1891 to protest the new law. Their complaint, rather significantly, was not so much that blacks were forced to sit in separate cars, but that, under the new law, mulattos, who had enjoyed an elevated status in the city and state since the early nineteenth century, were now being classified with blacks and forced to sit in the separate black cars. C. C. Antoine was chosen vice president of this committee, which also included such eminent members of the Creole aristocracy as Aristede Mary, Paul Bonseigneur, R. L. Desdunes, and Firmin Christophe. On February 5, 1892, the committee reported that it had collected $2,767.25 with which to pursue court action to test the constitutionality of the law.

To attack the ruling, the committee chose Homère Plessy as its representative. They fought the case up to the United States Supreme Court, where, in the fateful case of *Plessy vs. Ferguson* in 1896, the Court upheld the concept of separate but equal facilities, not just in transportation, but also in education and in virtually every other aspect of southern life. The committee also fought against a number of other segregation ordinances in Louisiana and New Orleans. In 1895, when St. Katherine Church was opened as the first Jim Crow Catholic church in the city, the committee protested mightily. Prior to this time, the city's Creoles had worshipped (although in separate pews) in the city's white Catholic churches. They lost this protest, and separate parishes became the rule in the city. The committee also lost their fight against the passage of a law forbidding interracial marriage. By the turn of the century, the rigid Jim Crow system was in place; Creoles had been placed on the same level as the rest of the city's blacks; and Antoine and all the Creoles had largely retreated from public view.

When C. C. Antoine died in 1921, he was a forgotten man. Louisiana's whites wished to wipe out all memory of the days of Reconstruction, of that "angry scar" that had frightened them with the specter of "African domination." But Antoine was also a symbol of a new breed of African-American who was rising at this time, and he was himself a transitional individual. The old elite of New Orleans were the refined, light-skinned Creoles. A new business elite emerged in the segregated black communities of New Orleans and the nation around the turn of the century. Followers of Booker T. Washington,* they turned their backs on politics and protest and put their energies into building strong, independent black communities. Antoine represented that generation of Civil War blacks who viewed politics as the avenue to wealth and prosperity and as the way to provide equal rights and privileges for all African-Americans. Whatever mistakes Antoine might have made along the way, he was a fighter for these rights, and as long as there was some hope of success he gave great service to blacks in New Orleans, Louisiana, and the nation. He deserved better than he got.

Sources

There are no personal or business papers on C. C. Antoine, nor is there much other information, but the most helpful single source is a scrapbook held at Southern University. There is a short biography of Antoine in the *Dictionary of American Negro Biography* (1982), as well as a sketch (probably written by Antoine himself) in William J. Simmons, *Men of Mark* (1887), 1132–34. There is a biography of Antoine in the *Times-Picayune*, September 15, 1921. Some additional information can be found in Rudolphe Desdunes, *Our People and Our History*, trans., Dorothea O. McCants (1973), 141–48. Information on Antoine's role in Reconstruction politics can be derived from Agnes Smith Grosz, "The Political Career of Pinckney Benton Stewart Pinchback," *Louisiana Historical Quarterly* 27 (1944), 538–39, 544–45, 560; Sidney James Romero, Jr., "The Political Career of Murphy James Foster, Governor of Louisiana, 1892–1900," *Louisiana Historical Quarterly* 28 (1945), 1134–35, 1138; John Edmond Gonzalez, "William Pitt Kellogg, Reconstruction Governor of Louisiana, 1873–1877," *Louisiana Historical Quarterly* 29 (1946), 403–6; Hilda Mulvey McDaniel, "Francis Tillou Nicholls and the End of Reconstruction," *Louisiana Historical Quarterly* 32 (1949), 399–400; Ted Tunnell, *Crucible of Reconstruction: War, Race and Radicalism in Louisiana, 1862–1877* (Baton Rouge, 1984); Joe Gray Taylor, *Louisiana Reconstructed, 1863–1877* (Baton Rouge, 1974); and James Haskins, *Pinckney Benton Stewart Pinchback* (New York, 1973).

B

Banks, Charles (March 25, 1873–1923), **Benjamin Thornton Montgomery** (1819–May 12, 1877), and **Isaiah T. Montgomery** (May 21, 1847–March 6, 1924). Businessmen, town developers, and banker: Mound Bayou, Mississippi; W. T. Montgomery & Co.; Montgomery & Sons; Mound Bayou Oil Mill and Manufacturing Company; Bank of Mound Bayou. Benjamin and Isaiah Montgomery, along with Charles Banks, had a magnificent dream—a vision of vast plantations owned and managed by African-Americans, of massive manufacturing enterprises, of banks that would finance an ever-expanding network of black homes and businesses. They dreamed of a colony of African-Americans, separated from whites, yet acting as a "City on a Hill," a beacon for both blacks and whites to prove that the recently freed slaves could accomplish great things. It all seemed to have so much potential, so much promise in the years of Reconstruction and the late nineteenth century—and it all ended in failure or near failure. Mound Bayou—the glittering jewel of that great dream in 1900—was described by J. Saunders Redding when he visited it in 1940:

[Mound Bayou] does not look like a town with such a legend. It is a gray town, flung like rubble into a dull-red field just off the highway that runs north to Memphis and south to the Gulf. . . . We passed no one on the roads. Many of the scattered houses looked deserted. There were many fire-blackened heaps of rubble. With no tree in the landscape to soften it, the naked ugliness took on the concrete hardness and reality of a brick wall . . . . "It's mostly a town of old folks an' folks getting old," Mrs. Tilman said. "It's nothing here for young people."

Benjamin Montgomery started it all. He was born a slave in Loudoun County, Virginia, spending his boyhood as the companion for his young master. Ben learned to read and write from the young white boy. In 1836, however, the seventeen-year-old Ben was sold to a trader who carried him south to Natchez, Mississippi. This was the period of time when slave sales in the Deep South states were at their peak, and from 1834 to 1837 the slave population more than doubled, with average prices per slave of $1,000. Benjamin was purchased by

Joseph Davis. Joseph Davis's family had followed the frontier as they moved from Georgia to Kentucky to Mississippi Territory, prospering as they went along. Joseph became a country lawyer, making a handsome fortune and becoming one of the most prestigious members of the young state. Like most everyone, he wanted to become a planter, and he began acquiring land and slaves. By the 1820s, Joseph Davis owned some 11,000 acres of fertile land in the area around Vicksburg, in an area that came to be known as Davis Bend. He sold off parts of this land but retained 5,000 of the best acres for himself. This vast plantation he called Hurricane, and he retired there in 1827 to establish a model plantation based upon Robert Owen's humanitarian principles. Joseph Davis's vision was that he believed it was possible to make profits while at the same time practicing a humane, utopian form of paternalism on his plantations. This is the environment Benjamin Montgomery was brought to in 1836.

It was a large, modern plantation, with over 200 slaves, a steam gin for cotton, and neat, two-room, whitewashed cabins to house the slave population. In addition, Davis shunned the authoritarian methods used on most plantations, instead practicing a form of self-government among the slaves themselves. No slave was punished except after conviction by a jury of his or her peers. At about the same time Benjamin came to Davis Bend, Joseph Davis's younger brother, Jefferson Davis, resigned his army commission to take up a tract of land adjacent to Hurricane. This new plantation, called Brierfield, was run in a somewhat less enlightened manner, but Joseph encouraged Jefferson to adopt his methods.

One of Joseph Davis's ideas was that slaves should be allowed to engage in individual enterprise and to keep what they earned beyond the value of their labor as field hands. This encouragement of individual talent was a godsend to the ambitious young Benjamin Montgomery, and by 1850 he was, by far, the most influential slave on the plantation. It was not, however, an automatic fit. Ben, who had been used to town life in Virginia, did not immediately take to the isolated, rural plantation. As soon as he arrived, Ben ran away, only to be recaptured. Joseph Davis then "inquired closely into the cause of [Ben's] dissatisfaction," and the two men "reached a mutual understanding and established a mutual confidence which time only served to strengthen throughout their long and eventful connection."

Benjamin Montgomery was given complete and free access to the Davis library and even accumulated his own small library. He also became a proficient surveyor of land and was particularly skilled at building and maintaining the ditches and levees that were essential to flood control in the area. Also an excellent mechanic and an adept inventor, he developed a boat propeller that Joseph Davis tried to get patented for him but failed since the U.S. Patent Office would not patent the invention of a slave. Ben Montgomery, however, achieved his greatest success during his slave days as a retail merchant. In 1842 he established a store on the plantation, in which he sold drygoods and staple items to the other slaves in exchange for the wood, chickens, eggs, and vegetables they were allowed to produce in their own gardens. Joseph Davis guaranteed Ben's first consignment of goods, but after that he maintained his own line of credit with wholesalers in New Orleans.

After a time, Benjamin became the business manager for the Hurricane plantation, and sometimes for Brierfield also. With the profits he made from these ventures, Ben built a combined store building and living quarters near the steamboat landing and also was able to pay his master the equivalent of the labor of his wife, Mary Lewis Montgomery, so that she could stay home and tend the home and their four children. They had been married on December 24, 1840. There is some wonder that a person of Benjamin Montgomery's talent and ambition could be content to remain a slave, but there is no evidence that he was discontent. The first Union officer Ben encountered in 1863 said of him, "I don't see how so inteligent [sic] a man could have consented to remain so long a slave." Yet, he did, and as Janet Hermann commented, "It seems unlikely that so sophisticated a man could have been held against his will." The Montgomerys were always the white man's favorite blacks because they "proved" the white philosophy that slavery and, later, segregation and racism were kind and benevolent systems under which blacks could flourish.

The two parents were concerned that their children, especially the two boys, get a good education. So, they arranged for George Stewart, an educated slave belonging to Jefferson Davis, to give them lessons from the Webster's speller. The youngest son, Isaiah, showed particular promise. Isaiah was born at Davis Bend, and by the time he was seven years old, Ben found an educated white man, George Metcalf, to tutor him. Joseph Davis, on hearing of this, had Metcalf move his family nearby and sent the Davis children to be schooled with him also, thereby creating a unique situation of integrated education on the plantation. This system, however, was a bit too daring for the area, and, as Isaiah later commented, "The school was finally discontinued because of its existence being too publically known of." When Isaiah was ten, Joseph Davis decided he should come to live in the plantation mansion, to be trained as Joseph's personal valet and private secretary. Ben objected, but Joseph promised that Isaiah would be allowed to continue his education and put him to work copying and filing letters. Isaiah also had full access to the Hurricane library, which resulted in the young boy's extraordinary literary competence. According to Redding, by age twelve, young Isaiah was doing all the plantation accounts. By reading newspapers and periodicals, Isaiah also acquired knowlege of national and international affairs, and he was reportedly so well-informed that white visitors to the Davis plantation often asked him about current events rather than read the newspapers themselves.

This somewhat idyllic, if circumscribed, world for Ben and Isaiah came to an end when the Civil War broke out in 1861. Jefferson Davis was elected president of the Confederacy, and he and his family left to live in the new nation's capital. Joseph Davis and his family also left for the capital for the summer months. Life at Davis Bend, though, went on much as before until April 1862, when the Union Army marched into northern Mississippi. Later that month, New Orleans fell to the northern troops. At that point, Joseph Davis took his family and escaped from Mississippi, leaving Benjamin Montgomery in charge of the plantations. Later, Davis returned and took one hundred slaves with him to another plantation in the interior of the state. Ben remained behind, with a few slaves, while the Union armies pillaged and ransacked the plantation, and even more slaves ran off or were driven off. Isaiah remained on the plantation as his father's assistant.

In February 1863, Admiral David D. Porter, commander of the Union fleet on the Mississippi, came to Davis Bend. There, captivated with the intelligence and charm of the fifteen-year-old Isaiah Montgomery, he virtually adopted him, making Isaiah his cabin boy and personal attendant. Later, Porter sent Ben Montgomery and his wife to Cincinnati, where Ben found a job as a carpenter in a canal boat yard. A few months later, when Isaiah's health became imperiled, Admiral Porter also sent him north to Cincinnati. With Ben Montgomery gone, Porter, who took responsibility for the entire black community at Davis Bend, decided to try a grand experiment at the plantation. He decided, in Hermann's words, to "foster an independent colony of contrabands, as the government called freed slaves, under the supervision of the commander of the gunboats that patrolled the adjacent river."

For a variety of reasons this plan did not work well, but a year later, General Ulysses Grant decided that the irony of turning Jefferson Davis's old plantation into a refuge for freed slaves was too good a propaganda ploy to pass up. He told John Eaton, Jr., superintendent of freemen, that he would like to see it become "a negro paradise." Plans had progressed far enough by the end of 1863 that a New York newspaper could proclaim: "Jeff's Plantation Turned into a Contraband Camp." The army began dividing the land among the black lessees, with the government providing supplies and equipment on credit. There were some 3,000 freedmen on the lands at Davis Bend by 1864. It was hardly a paradise, however, and Henry Rountree, a northern visitor, said, "I never saw such degradation." Although the wartime experiment with establishing a black utopia at Davis Bend did not work well, it did set the stage for a larger experiment during Reconstruction.

During these last years of the war, the Montgomery family remained in Cincinnati but had not been happy there. According to Saunders Redding, a rigid class structure had developed among African-Americans, with the large number of mulattoes there forming the cream of the black aristocracy. Most were offspring of white southern planters, who had been established in the city with some education and money and, by the 1860s, were doing very well. The Montgomerys, who were of pure African extraction and very dark skinned, according to Redding, were not accepted in the older free black community. Their cousin, Ben Green, had remained in Mississippi, working as a mechanic in Vicksburg, and he was doing quite well. His letters after the war enticed the Montgomerys to return home in 1865.

They arrived at Hurricane and determined to reopen their store, now called Montgomery and Sons, but found they were directly opposed by the northern officials of the Freedman's Bureau. Samuel Thomas, who ran the program in Mississippi, did not like Ben Montgomery. Thomas had envisioned a plantation with 5,000 acres of land turned over to a community of 1,750 former slaves. It was to be done in a system in which whites monitored closely the actions of the blacks. Thomas was, in Hermann's words, "paternalistically protective." Ben Montgomery challenged that. He organized a group of black lessees who proposed to increase their profits by ginning and baling their own cotton. They also decided to form a partnership to reopen the Hurricane sawmill. Thomas's negative reaction was fueled by his dislike of speculators, especially black ones like the Montgomerys, who he believed had relocated to the Bend to make money "off the ignorance of their former fellow servants." Ben Montgomery then enlisted the support of Joseph Davis to help him in the fight to set up the gin.

  They were not successful in this quest, but by 1866 Joseph Davis had been informed of his impending pardon from the government, which would allow him to reacquire the plantations at Davis Bend. When the plantations were finally restored to him in 1866, Davis promptly sold them to Benjamin Montgomery and his sons, who promised to set up a cooperative community of freedmen and freedwomen. The price for the 4,000 acres at Davis Bend was negotiated at $300,000 on November 19, 1866, with interest to be paid at 5 percent in gold or 7 percent in paper currency. Because the 1866 Mississippi Black Code forbade the selling of real property to freedmen, Davis and Montgomery had to keep their deal secret, proclaiming publicly that he was leasing the land from his former masters. Nonetheless, with a single stroke of the pen, Ben Montgomery had the distinction of owing more money that any other ex-slave in the state, perhaps more than any other in the nation.

  But he also had plans for a magnificent enterprise at Davis Bend, one that harked back to Joseph Davis's old dreams of combining profit with humanitarian ideals. Ben Green joined them in the venture, restoring the forge for making and repairing tools, and a number of other former slave families also became part of the experiment. The first cotton crop was planted in the spring of 1867, and although they had to battle the army worm and although the levee and docks had to be rebuilt, they picked nearly 600 bales of cotton in the fall. The big problems most planters had in the immediate postwar period was the shortage of labor, but Montgomery avoided this by publicizing the details of his planned utopian community. Advertising in the *Vicksburg Daily Times*, Montgomery invited people "such as are recommended by honesty, industry, sobriety and intelligence" to participate, informing them that the community would "adopt such rules and regulations as experience shall show to be necessary to its welfare." Kenneth Hamilton has recently expressed some reservations about the true utopian nature of this enterprise.

  Ben Montgomery's plan attracted a good deal of attention in both the North and the South. In the North, stressing the utopian aspects, the reaction was positive, but in the South, there was concern. These tensions became greater when William T. Montgomery, Isaiah's older brother, was selected as postmaster for a new postal station at the Bend plantations, and they reached a boiling point when Ben accepted an appointment in 1868 by General E.O.C. Ord as justice of the peace. This was the first political office held by a black in Mississippi, and it stirred a wave of negative reaction by local whites, which Isaiah Montgomery was able to defuse only by promising that his father would not hear cases involving whites. He also assured them that Ben had not sought the appointment in the first place.

These problems, however, were relatively minor compared to the blows nature was dealing the infant enterprise. First came the disastrous floods of 1867, which caused a number of the tenants to leave to go elsewhere, followed by a massive invasion of insects in the same year. The result was a severely reduced crop yield for 1867: just 620 bales of cotton. In response, Joseph Davis forgave the interest payment for that year. 1868 was not much better, although they were able to gin 790 bales. Ben Montgomery thought the year was "generally disastrous," and Joseph again told him to forget the interest payment for the year. Jefferson Davis, however, grumbled loudly from England that the yield from the plantations was very disappointing. The growing antipathy of the younger Davis brother did not bode well for the future.

In March 1869, the increasingly infirm Joseph Davis revised his will: "It is my will and desire that my executors should extend a liberal indulgence to B. T. Montgomery or their survivors . . . by extending time for the payment, as long as they pay the interest thereon." He also stipulated that $200 per year was to be provided to Ben Montgomery "for the benefit of the aged and infirm on the plantation." Eighteen months later, on September 18, 1870, the elderly planter died and was buried at Hurricane. On one hand, this had a liberating effect on the Montgomerys, since Davis had remained the ultimate authority as long as he lived. On the other hand, it now opened them to a series of attempts made by Jefferson Davis and other relatives to recover the plantations from them.

During the years Ben Montgomery and his family ran the plantations, they did very well. The quantity of cotton they produced went up steadily, with 1,900 bales in 1869 and 2,500 the following year. Even though cotton prices were down, they still should have been able to net some $50,000 on the latter crop, although heavy interest payments absorbed much of that. In any event, by the early 1870s, it was estimated that the Montgomerys were the third largest planters in the state. Not only was the quantity high, but so was the quality. They won a series of awards for their short staple cotton, the most important at the Philadelphia Centenary Exposition in 1876, where they won a medal for "about the best bale of cotton on exhibition." Ben Montgomery also began diversifying the crops and greatly expanded the operations of his store, Montgomery and Sons, turning it into a large regional market center, with a store, a steam-driven gin and a press, and warehousing facilities. The expanded firm was given an excellent credit rating from R. G. Dun Mercantile Agency, which considered them "very reliable and safe." Significantly, they were rated among the wealthiest merchant planters in the entire South by 1872.

By this time also, Isaiah Montgomery had emerged as a forceful entity on the plantation. Since 1866, Isaiah had been given full responsibility for keeping the records of the family's business ventures. By 1872 he was manager of an office staff that included a professional bookkeeper and a clerk, and he was also in full charge of Hurricane, the largest plantation. Isaiah was also beginning to expand his activities and influence outside the plantations, establishing fruitful connections with white agents and suppliers in New Orleans, Vicksburg, Cincinnati, and St. Louis. His father, however, continued active management of the plantations and other business activities. As Janet Hermann has commented, "Ben and his family were prototypes of the New Southerner, displaying a 'time is money' industriousness, no prejudice against work, no habits of extravagance, and great pride in their ability to overcome obstacles."

Nonetheless, by the late 1870s, decline had set in at the Davis Bend colony. It was a victim of declining cotton prices, of repeated floods and invasions of insects, and also of worsening political conditions, as Reconstruction came to an end with a vengeance in the state. The crumbling of the family fortunes took its toll on Ben Montgomery, and his health began failing in the mid–1870s. He died in 1877, at the age of fifty-eight. A year later, the courts reversed an earlier ruling and awarded the Brierfield plantation to Jefferson Davis, and in 1879 Montgomery and Sons mercantile firm failed. At the same time, their planting activities were also curtailed, so that during the 1879 season they tilled only 1,000 of the 3,700 acres they controlled. From this, they got just 800 bales of cotton, with more attention now on livestock and other crops. Finally, in 1881, Isaiah was informed that unless he immediately remitted $392,000, the Hurricane and Brierfield plantations would be sold at public auction. Of course, he could not pay that amount, and the plantations were auctioned to Jefferson Davis's family and Joseph Davis's grandchildren for just over $75,000. The Montgomerys were left to run Ursino, a plantation they had purchased later, which Isaiah ran until the late 1880s. By 1886 all the Montgomerys had left Davis Bend, and their grand experiment in a communal dream was at an end. But Isaiah had visions of reviving it elsewhere.

According to Kenneth Hamilton, the Montgomerys also lived a life-style that would have been the envy of all but the wealthiest white planters in the state. They entertained lavishly in a twenty-one-room mansion, had subscriptions to scores of magazines, and hired servants to tend an extravagant floral garden. Also, instead of using their profits during several of these years to retire their enormous debt, the Montgomerys used their profits to purchase more land in a speculative manner and to open another merchandising business. Also, the great "Kansas fever" of the late 1870s and early 1880s had a negative impact on their operations. In 1879 a number of their tenants migrated to Kansas, creating a severe labor shortage. Isaiah's response was to engage in yet another, utopian/speculative venture.

Early on, Isaiah had begun looking for a new site to establish an all-black community. In 1879 he went to Kansas in an attempt to persuade his workers to return to Davis Bend. He provided transportation back for those who agreed to return. But a number wished to remain in Kansas, so after consulting with the governor and securing the support of the Kansas Freedmen's Relief Association, Isaiah bought a section of land in Kansas for his own use and employed nine black families from his Mississippi plantations to work it. It was not, as Hamilton points out, a utopian venture, since his employees would never be allowed to own the land, and Montgomery planned to exploit them as sharecroppers. Isaiah ultimately decided that it was not a viable plan and sold his holdings there if, indeed, he ever actually bought the land. He did not stop looking for another site, though—one more isolated from white interference where he might play out his father's dream of a black community that could be utopian and profitable at the same time.

In 1885 Isaiah moved to the outskirts of Vicksburg, where he set up a small mercantile operation and became active in civic affairs in the city's black community. But he was contacted by James Hill, a leading black Republican political figure in Mississippi, who had become a land agent for the Louisville, New Orleans and Texas Railroad (LNO and T). Hill told him that the railroad was offering bargains in rich alluvial, delta land along its route, and Isaiah determined to investigate. After several trips to the area, he chose a site about halfway between Memphis and Vicksburg. He then persuaded his cousin, Ben Green, to sell his small store and join him in the venture, and they bought 840 acres there. They then persuaded blacks in the Vicksburg area, especially those who had been at Davis Bend, to join them in this great new experiment. In 1886, Isaiah returned with Ben Green and seven other blacks to begin clearing the land, land that was so wild and untamed as to be daunting to nearly anyone. Montgomery supposedly gave an inspiring speech to the men, telling them "that they might as well buy land and own it and do for themselves what they had been doing for other folks for two hundred fifty years." In any event, they set off into the wilderness with axes and shovels and, by the fall of 1886, despite swarms of mosquitos and other pests, had managed to clear ninety acres. Erecting a crude sawmill, they cut and stacked enough lumber to build several rude cottages.

During the next several months, they continued to clear the land, selling the timber to the railroad, and despite floods in the first winter that wrecked the sawmill and swept away much of the lumber, the land was ready for permanent settlement in February 1888. Naming the place Mound Bayou, Isaiah by that time had sold more than 700 acres for $7 per acre, with one dollar down, and the balance in five equal installments. The settlers continued to cut timber, selling it as ties for the railroad, which kept the settlement afloat during the first few difficult years. They also began producing cotton and other crops, and soon they had a post office on the site. The settlement was beginning to take shape, and, as Booker T. Washington[*] commented, "The wilderness had become the frontier. The colonists came in faster now. The ragged outline of the forest steadily receded in all directions." Isaiah Montgomery and Ben Green, meanwhile, purchased an additional 700 acres, and the early pioneers from the old Davis Bend experiment were later joined by large numbers of blacks who were fleeing from the violence of the "whitecappers" in the southern part of the state. Green and Montgomery spent most of their time traveling the state, advertising the advantages of their new, all-black community.

Isaiah established a very paternalistic form of government and social mores at Mound Bayou. By the 1890s the community had over 1,000 persons on 20,000 rich alluvial acres. In 1898 the town of Mound Bayou was incorporated, and two years later it had 287 persons in the town itself, and about 1,500 in the surrounding area. Isaiah Montgomery was elected mayor, and he also chose the town constable, hired the first schoolteacher, and guaranteed the salary of the first preacher. Although the sheriff of Bolivar County was white, he allowed Montgomery to appoint a black deputy for the town. At other times, he also served as justice of the peace and postmaster. In addition, Isaiah owned, either in whole or in part, the cotton gin and warehouse, the feed and fertilizer store, the lumberyard, the large retail emporium, and the burial business. He and Ben Green also engaged in land speculation and large-scale cotton production. Montgomery also held uncounted first mortgages on land in the colony and grossed a profit of $8,000 per year on lumber sales alone. His reputation was that he was the only black person in the United States who could put his hands on $50,000 "cash money" with an hour's notice. He was, as Saunders Redding commented, "The Boss of Mound Bayou."

Ben Green and Isaiah, however, became increasingly estranged from one another. Green, who was more suspicious of whites and was less idealistic, disagreed with Isaiah on the way profits were distributed and with the future of the settlement. The two men dissolved their partnership in 1895, and a year later Green was murdered by a customer in his store, who argued over "five cents worth of rivets." Green's net worth when he died was $35,000, and his widow soon married John W. Francis, her former store manager. Capitalizing on Green's investments, Francis went on to become Mound Bayou's most successful merchant.

The rift between Green and Montgomery may have been made greater by Isaiah's sensational speech to the Mississippi Constitutional Convention in 1890. Few speeches by blacks in the nineteenth century had a greater impact, or caused more controversy, and perhaps none did more ultimate damage to black political rights than Montgomery's utterances. Isaiah was always, as Redding has said, skilled at the "ceremonial submissiveness" required of blacks who wanted to stay on good terms with southern whites. He was, in fact, better at this than his father, who was often too proud or militant to show this submissiveness. This is why Isaiah was increasingly made the "outside" contact man at Davis Bend in the 1870s.

Isaiah Montgomery, if anything, became increasingly conservative on race issues as Mississippi turned more overtly racist. He continually criticized black political leaders in the Republican party, such as Blanche K. Bruce and Hiram Revels as "outsiders" and John Roy Lynch as a "Douglass man." Isaiah also withdrew from the Colored Farmers' Alliance when it became aligned with the white Southern Farmers' Alliance and began becoming "too political." An "accommodationist" well before Booker T. Washington made it a household word in 1895, Isaiah acquiesced in the white rule of the South, saying, "This is a white man's country, let them run it." What he wanted was to be left alone in Mound Bayou, to have him and his tenants given full protection of the law, and to be allowed to pursue their dream of economic independence and capitalist utopia. To do that, he was prepared to make, as he said, a "sacrifice on the altar of liberty," in which he would sanction the disfranchisement of 124,334 blacks and just 11,889 whites, so that whites would have a permanent majority of more than 40,000 votes in the state.

Isaiah Montgomery made this "generous offer," he said, as an attempt to "bridge a chasm that has been widening and deepening for a generation," making a "generous offer of peace [that] affords the white men of Mississippi an opportunity to settle the race question once and forever." The reaction, from both blacks and whites, from North and South, was immediate and electric. Most African-Americans, including many in Montgomery's own settlement, were horrified. He was called a "traitor" and a "turncoat" by prominent black leaders in Mississippi for decades. Fifty years after his speech, Sidney D. Raymond, one of the state's most prominent black politicians, thought Montgomery always would be remembered as "the Judas of his people." Another said that he was "thoroughly hated" by a younger generation of black Mississippians, who remembered him as the "dictator . . . who had sold them out." Even the official historian of Mound Bayou conceded that the speech "was received with varying emotions throughout the country, many of his own people dissenting from the compromising tenor assumed by him."

Whites, especially in the South, and most particularly in Mississippi, were elated. After all, just as whites were trying to find some way to justify disfranchising millions of blacks throughout the South, Isaiah Montgomery provided them with just the excuse they needed. As his white eulogist said, "He was the first to draw the color line in the South." The white delegates at the convention received the speech with a "deep sense of relief and surprised wonder," and the *New York World* reprinted the entire speech and gave it headline treatment, calling it "A Noble Speech," and saying that Isaiah was "an orator of whom any race might be proud."

What would prompt Isaiah Montgomery to make such a concession? Historians have been confused about it, calling his speech "strange," "unfathomable," and a "jangle of contradictions." Yet, as Neil McMillen has pointed out, Isaiah's own instincts were intensely conservative and he had little faith in political solutions. Further, his experience with whites like Joseph Davis had taught him the positive value of trusting his fate to white paternalism. And, finally, disfranchisement was an accomplished fact anyway; all he gave was his consent. Whites could make much political capital out of that, but little else, and it is certainly difficult to imagine that blacks might have been in better circumstances if he had not made the speech. It was deeply embarrassing to many blacks, and it provided whites with a patina of black acceptance of their actions, but it really changed little or nothing. Even Isaiah Montgomery, though, came to regret the speech. In 1904 he wrote to Booker T. Washington that he felt a growing sense of betrayal over the actions of Mississippi's whites, and that only federal intervention could restore democracy to the state. By then, of course, it was too late.

What Isaiah Montgomery still had, though, was his vision: his dream of an independent black community that would shine as a beacon for blacks and whites alike. And one that would make money, not only money for the black families who settled there, but most of all money for Isaiah Montgomery and the small corps of families who had early on made speculative investments in the community. In the early years of the twentieth century, blacks owned four cotton gins that processed nearly 2,500 bales of cotton and three sawmills that cut more than one million board feet of lumber.

In 1900 the railroad built a new depot in Mound Bayou, and two years later eighteen black-owned businesses shipped and received goods worth nearly $150,000 through the station. By 1907, twenty years after its founding, Mound Bayou was a thriving colony of some 800 families who owned 30,000 acres, 5,000 to 6,000 of which were under cultivation. These industrious blacks produced 3,000 bales of cotton annually, along with more than half the corn and fodder consumed in the community. In the town itself, there were by then thirteen stores and a number of small shops, doing a combined business of $600,000 a year. There was a train station in the center of town that was a hub of activity, handling $40,000 in freight and $60,000 in passenger traffic. There was a thriving sawmill, three cotton gins, a telephone exchange, a weekly newspaper (*The Demonstrator*), six churches, and two private schools. The heart of the business community, however, was the Bank of Mound Bayou, which had been organized in 1904 with capital stock of $10,000. The bank also brought a powerful new business influence into the town: Charles Banks.

Charles Banks had been born in a log cabin in Clarksdale, Mississippi, the son of Daniel and Sallie Ann Banks. Banks, a "tall, big-bodied man of pure African blood," lived in extreme poverty, but he was educated in the public schools of his hometown and at Rust University in nearby Holly Springs. He then returned to Clarksdale, where he engaged in business as a speculator in land and cotton. Ultimately, Banks became the senior member in the general mercantile firm of Banks & Co. Banks was called "the most influential Negro business man in the United States" and "the leading Negro banker in Mississippi" by Booker T. Washington, and he served as the third vice president of the National Negro Business League from 1901 to 1905 and as first vice president from 1907 until his death in the mid–1920s. Another black admirer said that Banks found the music of the cash register "as pleasing . . . as the rhapsody of a Beethoven sonata."

In 1893 Banks married Trenma O. Booze, of Natchez, Mississippi. He took her brother, Eugene Parker Booze, in as his apprentice in the general store and cotton trading operations. Booze later went with Banks to Mound Bayou, where he married Isaiah Montgomery's daughter. In 1903 Banks visited Mound Bayou and a short time later wrote to Emmett J. Scott, "I am going out of the merchandise business . . . to engage in the banking business." A year later Banks moved to Mound Bayou where he opened the Bank of Mound Bayou. The president of the bank was John W. Francis, but Charles Banks, who owned about two-thirds of the bank's stock, as cashier was the dominant influence in the enterprise.

Banks, at the 1906 meeting of the National Negro Business League, gave his appraisal of how the Bank of Mound Bayou might fare in the future:

Located in a town and surrounded by a community whose citizenry is composed almost exclusively of our people, our bank has had a splendid opportunity to indicate the Negro's capacity to operate a financial institution among themselves.

Explaining that they had started without "any experience, no correspondents or financial connections," the bank by 1906 had $40,000 in resources, was doing an attractive business, and paid a dividend of 6 percent. By 1910 the bank was in a two-story brick and plate-glass building and had resources of over $100,000.

The Bank of Mound Bayou played an extremely important economic role in the community. As Kenneth Hamilton has pointed out, "It enabled area blacks to keep a great deal of their money circulating in their own town and hinterland, while providing capital for new investments at a reasonable rate." It was also a source of tremendous pride in the local black community and also attracted attention nationally. It perfectly symbolized Booker T. Washington's concept of self-help and also demonstrated how blacks could use a bank to establish further economic independence from the white community. Charles Banks also established, with E. P. Booze, the Farmer's Cooperative Mercantile Company in 1909 which they capitalized at $10,000. Targeting the area's farmers, the firm was organized to provide the necessities of life at reasonable prices.

Charles Banks, however, was apparently not as good a bank manager as Washington and Montgomery believed. As early as September 1913, Washington urged Banks to get his bank "in a strong and active condition," but, in spite of a loan from Julius Rosenwald, president of Sears, Roebuck, the Bank of Mound Bayou went under in the recession of 1914. This apparently caused some rift between Banks and Isaiah, but both men cooperated to set up a new bank in less than eighteen months. The second bank, called Mound Bayou State Bank, lasted a decade, but it was not much stronger than the first, and it was never able to meet the community's demand for credit in ensuing months and years.

Charles Banks was also involved with William Thornton Montgomery in organizing and running the Mound Bayou Loan and Investment Company. This was intended to prevent the intrusion of white ownership into the colony by accumulating local capital which would then be used to cover defaulted mortgages for farmers who were in financial trouble. His most ambitious venture, however, and the one that had the most traumatic impact on his own fortunes and on those of the black colony was the Mound Bayou Oil Mill and Manufacturing Company.

Banks had begun writing to Booker T. Washington in 1902, a year before he ever moved to Mound Bayou, about the opportunity for organizing a cotton manufacturing concern. Then Banks convinced the Mississippi Chapter of the National Negro Business League that it should sponsor a manufacturing venture "that would broaden the racial activities, and afford legitimate channels for the encouragement of the mechanical and business development of our people." The group chose a cottonseed-oil mill as their project, and this seemed eminently logical. Since, as they stated, "our people are cotton-growers; whatever money they make is from handling cotton," it made sense to integrate vertically into the production of cotton by-products. Further, cottonseed-oil mills were extremely profitable, often earning from 15 to 40 percent on their investments. They quite naturally decided to locate the new venture in Mound Bayou and to offer stock at just one dollar a share, "in order that every negro in Mississippi might have the chance of investing his savings in the venture."

In 1908 Banks and Isaiah Montgomery began selling shares of stock in the firm, and in 1910 construction of the plant had begun. But the whole enterprise was fraught with difficulties—one of those situations where everything that could go wrong, did go wrong. Banks and Montgomery held massive revival-style meetings at Mound Bayou where they stimulated the enthusiasm of the gathered crowds of blacks for the venture. These meetings did much to enhance race pride but did little to generate the capital with which to start the business. Montgomery and Banks then had to turn to Booker T. Washington, who put them in touch with a number of white philanthropists in the North. By 1912 they had raised enough money to finish the plant, which was valued at $100,000, and on November 25, 1912, it was dedicated by Washington in a grand ceremony.

Banks and Montgomery, however, did not have sufficient funds to begin operations. They enticed Rosenwald to buy $25,000 of the remaining $40,000 in stock and sold the balance to B. B. Harvey, a Memphis mill owner. The mill was then leased to Harvey and commenced operations on October 9, 1913. Harvey, however, proved to be a real problem, as he refused to make financial statements to Banks and Montgomery and probably diverted funds from the black enterprise to his own mill. There were a number of other problems during this early period, and they had to turn to Rosenwald again for money to force Harvey out so that they could run the plant themselves. They had a chance to sell the plant at that point to a subsidiary of Procter and Gamble, but Banks refused, fearing it would mean "the loss of our identity as a race with the Oil Mill." By 1915, however, all was lost, and the plant suspended operations entirely. The building stood for later generations as a "tragic reminder of a more prosperous past . . . [and] a loss to stockholders and promoters of $100,000."

Mound Bayou enjoyed a brief splurge of prosperity, along with other cotton farmers, during the period of high prices caused by World War I. After the war, however, prices plummeted, and the situation in the town became increasingly dismal. A number of the families after the war joined the exodus to Chicago and other northern cities, until the community's population stabilized at about 800. Many of these, however, had been wiped out financially, and they were now forced back into tenancy, with their wives going into domestic service in increasing numbers. After 1917, also, Banks and Isaiah Montgomery parted ways when a group of Banks's supporters defeated Montgomery in the municipal elections. Montgomery was angry and alleged fraud and persuaded racist governor Theodore G. Bilbo to oust the winners. This split between the two wealthiest and most powerful figures in the town also stunted Mound Bayou's growth. After the split, Montgomery increasingly focused on simply enhancing his own wealth, with little concern for the town's welfare.

Banks remained more concerned with racial solidarity and advancement than Montgomery, but his own resources began tumbling during these years. In 1922 the town's largest retail establishment, the Farmers' Cooperative Mercantile Company, which E. P. Booze managed for Banks, failed. A year later, Charles Banks, a broken man who had been driven into virtual poverty by his losses, died. Then, in 1924, Isaiah Montgomery, the "black Moses" who had helped run Davis Bend and then had led "his people" to the new promised land, the new Canaan, died.

Isaiah Montgomery and Charles Banks, who had both become close associates of Booker T. Washington, were primary spokesmen for the Tuskegean's policies and were instrumental in the organization and running of the National Negro Business League for many years. Isaiah and Washington had become quite close after the latter's Atlanta Exposition speech in 1895, and together they worked out the ideas of accommodation and self-help. If Washington was the "drum major" for these ideas in the national consciousness, it was Montgomery who put them into action at Mound Bayou. In 1911 Washington labeled Mound Bayou a "place where a Negro may get inspiration by seeing what other members of his race have accomplished . . . [and] where he has an opportunity to learn some of the fundamental duties and responsibilities of social and civic life." For his part, Montgomery wrote in *The Outlook* in 1901, "I think the education and training that Mr. Washington is endeavoring to give will help the progress of the colored people anywhere, whether North or South."

When Washington founded the National Negro Business League in 1900, Isaiah Montgomery was at his side in Boston, giving empassioned speeches endorsing the Tuskegean's philosophy and describing Mound Bayou and its glowing prospects. Montgomery served for many years on the executive board of the league. Soon after, Charles Banks was also involved, becoming vice president of the national group and organizer and president of the Mississippi branch. Both Banks and Montgomery, despite the fact they denigrated the role of politics for blacks in the South, were very politically active with the "Black and Tan Republicans" in Mississippi until their deaths in the 1920s.

Succeeding years were not terribly kind to the Mound Bayou community. The depression years were hard. When Saunders Redding visited it in 1940, he found it "more dead than alive," a place of "naked ugliness." By then another visionary had taken leadership. Benjamin A. Green, son of one of the founders and a graduate of Harvard Law School, had become mayor, and he had hopes for the future. With a population of 1,700 and 30,000 acres of rich farmland to build on, Green set about on a project of rehabilitation. By the early 1950s, some of this seemed to have been realized. In 1951 reporters for *Coronet* magazine marveled at the town's prosperity and ambiance. Calling it "Mississippi's Miracle Town," they exclaimed in wonder, "The town is unique. It is all-Negro—and it is all happy." They talked of the fact that there was no jail and no major crime in the town, and that most of the Mound Bayou families were landowners. It was, withall, seemingly a happy place in the days of segregationist Mississippi.

Twenty years later, though, Mound Bayou was struggling again. *Black Enterprise* reported that the town was trying to recapture some of its past glory but that progress was painfully slow. Its one source of strength was the Delta Community Hospital and Health Center, Inc., a black-run medical complex which had been set up by the Delta Ministry and the Tufts Medical School. It brought about 450 jobs and $5.5 million in revenue to the beleaguered town. When the Nixon administration dismantled the Office of Economic Opportunity, which had been providing funds for the center, and transferred the health services program to the Department of Health, Education and Welfare, town leaders knew the future of the town was uncertain. They realized that diversification was the key to long-term survival. Earl Lucas, the mayor in 1972, said, "Right now we're almost totally dependent upon the health center for jobs and commerce here, and that's a shaky foundation." They tried to attract industry, perhaps trying to relieve Charles Banks's old dream, but had little success.

Mound Bayou struggled on for another several years more until 1982, when the town was on the verge of bankruptcy. A victim of massive cuts in spending by the Reagan administration, it lost the funding for more than half of the town's employees who had been paid with CETA and VISTA funds. The town thus had a debt of $209,000 and faced bankruptcy. African-Americans across the nation sent in funds to save the town, raising more than $120,000 in individual contributions. Mayor Lewis was overwhelmed and exclaimed, "Black Folks did to Mound Bayou what the Jews did in Israel. They gave us rebirth." Without industry, though, Mound Bayou's future is still uncertain. In 1990 the town looked much as Saunders Redding saw it in 1940—grey, tired, and mired in poverty. Ben and Isaiah Montgomery and Charles Banks were dreamers. Perhaps their dream has turned to dust, perhaps the accommodation and conservatism they displayed in pursuing their dream was foolhardy, but it did fire the imagination. As Isaiah Montgomery himself said in a brief autobiography in 1887, he "sought to begin anew, at the age of forty, the dream of life's young manhood."

Sources

There is, relatively speaking, a massive amount of material, both primary and secondary, available on the Montgomerys and Mound Bayou. These is less on Charles Banks. At the Library of Congress, there are the Benjamin Montgomery Family Papers and a large number of letters from both Isaiah Montgomery and Charles Banks to Booker T. Washington and Emmett J. Scott in the Booker T. Washington Papers. At the Mississippi Department of Archives and History in Jackson, Mississippi, there are many letters from Benjamin Montgomery to Joseph Davis in the latter's papers, and there are also papers on Mound Bayou. There are letters between Benjamin and Jefferson Davis at the Alabama State Department of Archives and History in Montgomery, Alabama, and the Confederate Museum at Richmond, Virginia, and other letters in the Jefferson Davis Papers at the University of Alabama and Transylvania University in Lexington, Kentucky. There are important materials on the Davis plantations after they were taken over by the Montgomerys in the Records of the Bureau of Refugees, Freedmen and Abandoned Lands, Record Group 105, in the National Archives in Washington, D.C. The mortgage on the Davis Bend plantation is recorded at Warren County, Mississippi, Land Records, Office of Chancery Clerk, Deed Book VV, 14. The estate of Benjamin Montgomery is contained in Probate no. 3029, Warren County, Mississippi. There are other materials of use scattered in various collections. The best source for these is an excellent scholarly account of the experiments conducted at Davis Bend, with some information on Mound Bayou: Janet Sharp Hermann, *The Pursuit of a Dream* (New York, 1981). Hermann's account, however, should be supplemented by the material on Mound Bayou contained in Kenneth M. Hamilton's *Black Towns and Profit: Promotion and Development in the Trans-Appalachian West, 1877–1915* (Urbana, Ill., 1991). Hamilton has some additional factual material not used by other authors, but mostly he views Mound Bayou within the context of a black promotional and capitalist undertaking, with less acceptance of the utopian overtones insisted upon by most other authors.

Besides Hermann, the best published material on Benjamin Montgomery is James T. Currie, "Benjamin Montgomery and the Davis Bend Colony," *Prologue*, Spring 1978, 5–21; Janet S. Hermann, "Reconstruction in Microcosm: Three Men and a Gin," *Journal of Negro History* LXV, 4 (Fall 1980), 312–35; George Alexander Sewell, *Mississippi Black History Makers* (Jackson, Miss., 1977), 154–63. Isaiah Montgomery also wrote a biography of his father, which is included in Lewis O. Swingler, ed., *Jewel of the Delta, A Souvenir Bulletin* (1962).

On Isaiah Montgomery, the Southern Historical Collection at the University of North Carolina has his "papers," which consists primarily of his speech at the 1890 Mississippi Constitutional Convention, as reported in the *New York World*, September 27, 1890. The full text of that speech is also included in the Benjamin Montgomery Papers in the Library of Congress. There is a letter from Isaiah to Governor John P. St. John in the Department of Archives, Kansas State Historical Society, Topeka, Kansas, and from Isaiah to Jefferson Davis in Dunbar Rowland, ed., *Jefferson Davis, Constitutionalist: His Letters, Papers and Speeches* 10 vols. (Jackson, Miss., 1923). There are some materials on Isaiah in the Hemingway Papers at the MDHA. Some of Isaiah's letters to Booker T. Washington are reprinted in Louis R. Harlan, ed., *The Booker T. Washington Papers* (Urbana, Ill., 1972–1979); see especially vol. 8, 61–63. Janet S. Hermann has written a short biography of him in Leon Litwack and August Meier, eds., *Black Leaders of the Nineteenth Century* (Urbana, Ill., 1988), 290–304; and Rayford Logan wrote one for the *Dictionary of American Negro Biography* (1982). There is a useful account of Isaiah and Mound Bayou in Janie Stennis, "Mound Bayou—An Example of Negro Community Building," Master's thesis, University of Mississippi, 1930; and Maurice Elizabeth Jackson, "Mound Bayou—A Study in Social Development," Master's thesis, University of Alabama, 1937. J. Saunders Redding discusses the Montgomerys and Mound Bayou somewhat impressionistically in *Lonesome Road* (New York, 1958), 93–121. He also visited Mound Bayou in 1940, calling it "River City," in *No Day of Triumph* (New York, 1942), 289–307. A clipping file at the Mississippi State Department of Archives has sketches of Isaiah in Florence Warfield Sellers, *History of Bolivar County* (Jackson, Miss., 1948); *Evening Post* (Vicksburg, Miss.), February 17 and March 24, 1885; *Bolivar Commercial* (Cleveland, Miss.), November 8, 1876; *Weekly Mississippi Pilot*, November 19, 1870; *Daily Clarion-Ledger* (Meredian, Miss.) Centennial Edition, December 13, 1937, June 23 and 30, 1974. See also *National Cyclopedia of the Colored Race* (Montgomery, Ala. 1919); Hiram Fong, "The Pioneers of Mound Bayou," *Century Magazine* LXXIX, 3 (January 1910); *The Crisis*, March 1942; Booker T. Washington, "A Town Called Mound Bayou," *World's Work* XIV, 3 (July 1907). There is an obituary from an unidentified newspaper from 1924 in the MDAH clipping file as is "The Negro in Business," by Isaiah in *Outlook*, November 16, 1901, which is a representative sample of his philosophy, which is also dealt with in August Meier, *Negro Thought in America* (Ann Arbor, Mich., 1963); Louis R. Harlan, *Booker T. Washington, The Wizard of Tuskegee* (1983); and John Hope Franklin, ed., *The Autobiography of John Roy Lynch* (1970). There are many speeches by Isaiah Montgomery and Charles Banks in the *Annual Reports* of the National Negro Business League. See especially the reports for 1900, 1904, 1905, 1908, 1913, and 1916. These are available in the Archives at Hampton University and in the National Negro Business League Records in the Library at Tuskegee University. See also John Howard Burrows, "The Necessity of Myth: A History of the National Negro Business League, 1900–1945," Ph.D. diss., Auburn University, 1977. There is some information concerning Isaiah Montgomery's role as a member of the auditing committee of the African Methodist Episcopal Church in Benjamin W. Arnett, *The Budget Containing the Annual Reports of the Officers of the African Methodist Episcopal Church of the U.S.A., 1881–1884*. There is a brief mention of Isaiah's investment in lands for development in Kansas in Robert G. Athearn, *In Search of Canaan: Black Migration to Kansas, 1879–80* (Lawrence, Kans., 1978), 79. His political role is briefly dealt with in Buford Satcher, *Blacks in Mississippi Politics, 1865–1900* (Washington, D.C., 1978).

Other useful items on Mound Bayou include Norman L. Crockett, *The Black Towns* (Lawrence, Kans., 1979); G. F. Richings, *Evidences of Progress among Colored People* (1897); Booker T. Washington, *The Negro in Business* (1907); Vernon Lane Wharton, *The Negro in Mississippi, 1865–1890* (Chapel Hill, N.C., 1947); A. R. Taylor, "A Brief History of the Town and Colony of Mound Bayou," *Semi-Centennial Program*, July 1937; G. A. Lee, "Mound Bayou, the Negro City of Mississippi," *Voice of the Negro* III, 1 (December 1905); "Mound Bayou—Past and Present," *Negro History Bulletin*, April 1940; *Pittsburgh Courier*, December 6, 1952; *Baltimore Daily Herald*, November 3, 1919; B. F. Ousley, "A Town of Colored People in Mississippi," *American Missionary Association Bulletin*, 1904; *Black Enterprise*, December 1972, 37–40, and July 1982, 20; Robert Fulton Holtzclaw, *Black Magnolias: A Brief History of Afro-Mississippians—1865–1980* (Shaker Heights, Ohio, 1984); Aurelius P. Hood, *The Negro at Mound Bayou* (1909); August Meier, "Booker T. Washington and the Town of Mound Bayou," *Phylon* 15 (Winter 1954); Neil R. McMillen, *Dark Journey: Black Mississippians in the Age of Jim Crow* (Urbana, Ill., 1989); Dickson Hartwell and Carol Weld, "Mississippi's Miracle

Town,'' *Coronet* 30 (September 1951), 125–28; Day Allen Willey, ''Mound Bayou— A Negro Municipality,'' *Alexander's Magazine* 4 (July 15, 1907), 159–66; *Newsweek*, July 24, 1939, 14; *Time*, July 26, 1937, 14, November 25, 1974, 107; Webb Waldron, ''All Black: A Unique Negro Community,'' *Survey Graphic* 27 (January 1928), 34–36.

Charles Banks is primarily dealt with in many of the above works, but also see *Who's Who of the Colored Race* (1915); and J.W. Gibson and W.H. Crogman, *Progress of a Race* (1902, 1969) for a bit more biographical material. There is a clipping file in his name at Tuskegee University, and Booker T. Washington wrote a brief biography of him: ''Charles Banks,'' *American Magazine* 81 (March 1911). For some general information on black banking in Mississippi, and on Banks's role in that, see Tommy Lee Johnson, ''The Development of Black Banking in Mississippi,'' Master's thesis, Jackson State University, 1977; W. E. Mollison, ''What Banks Managed by Colored Men Are Doing for Their Communities,'' *Colored America* 12 (August 1907), 191–92; and Abram L. Harris, *The Negro as Capitalist: A Study of Banking and Business among Negroes* (Philadelphia, 1936). Charles Banks himself wrote of the situation in Mississippi in ''Negro Banks of Mississippi'' in D.W. Woodard, ed., *Negro Progress in a Mississippi Town* (Cheyney, Penn., 1909), 9–11.

Information on the Davis plantations and family can be found in Frank E. Everett, Jr., *Brierfield: Plantation Home of Jefferson Davis* (Hattiesburg, Miss., 1971); Hudson Strode, *Jefferson Davis, American Patriot 1808–61* (New York, 1955); *Jefferson Davis Confederate President* (New York, 1959) and his *Jefferson Davis, Tragic Hero: The Last Twenty-Five Years, 1864–1889* (New York, 1964). Varina Howell Davis, *Jefferson Davis, Ex-President of the Confederate States of America: A Memoir*, 2 vols. (New York, 1890).

Bartholomew, Joseph Manuel (August 1, 1890–October 12, 1971). Contractor, real estate developer, golf course designer, businessman, and insurance company executive: Bartholomew Construction, Douglas Life Insurance. For most businessmen, the game of golf is something they dream of retiring to when they are either old enough or have made enough money. For Joseph Bartholomew, however, golf was the means to a successful business career and a substantial fortune. The fact that he was an African-American, and that he made most of his money designing and running golf courses for whites, is even more fascinating. But Joe Bartholomew was a real hero in the golf world, so much so that he was honored for his achievements by *Sports Illustrated* and became the first black man to be inducted into the Greater New Orleans Sports Hall of Fame in 1972.

Bartholomew was born in New Orleans, the son of Manuel and Alice Bartholomew. It is not known what his parents did, but they were not part of the city's black elite, and they must have been rather poor, since young Joseph was able to get only an elementary school education. At age seven he supposedly began working after classes at McDonough public school as a caddie at nearby Audubon Park Club. He held a number of other jobs, including one where he got up at four in the morning to clean a white man's pantry, but the golf course kept pulling him back. Continuing his caddying in the afternoon, Bartholomew determined to become the best caddy on the course. As he remembered later, ''It distracts a golf player to lose his ball. . . . I never lost one golf ball a year.'' After a time, he became so popular with the most prestigious members of the club that they put him in charge of the greens. Soon, according to *Fortune* magazine, "Joe Bartholomew had all but cornered the golf industry in New Orleans. He worked in the locker room, waited on tables, acted as a steward."

During this same period, Bartholomew found time to teach himself to play golf, and soon he was good enough to be appointed assistant pro at the course, which allowed him to give lessons—often twelve per day at two dollars each. One businessman later recalled, "Hell, Joe Bartholomew taught about every good player in town how to play this game." A man of infinite energy and ambition, Bartholomew was not satisfied with these accomplishments but kept pressing for new frontiers and new challenges. One year, when fire destroyed the Audubon clubhouse, he made nearly $10,000 replacing the members' lost golf clubs, balancing and assembling his own models.

When the new eighteen-hole Metaire golf course was being planned, a member's committee came to Bartholomew, who had become widely respected for his expert handling of the Audubon greens, and asked him to design and build their new course. "Whooo, but I was surprised," Bartholomew recalled. "They gave me a bunch of money and told me to go and find the best golf course in the world and bring it back." So, in 1922, Bartholomew headed north, where first he attended the Golf Architectural School in New York, and then traveled around to various golf courses until he found what he was looking for. He then brought a scale model of it back to New Orleans, along with his first piece of dirt-handling equipment. The club's executive board approved the plan, and he built the Metaire Country Club course.

At the end of the job, Bartholomew had a lot of fine new equipment and no other work, so he decided to rent the equipment out to white contractors, giving him a chance to observe firsthand a variety of construction techniques, enabling him to expand his own construction business. In the meantime, he made money by running a cartage concern. With a wagon and a pair of mules, he would haul anything people wanted, and he gave them a guarantee of delivery when he took the job. It was to be satisfactorily done or they did not have to pay him. In this way, he built a strong reputation throughout the community for his dependability and his honesty.

Having made some money, built an excellent reputation, and learned various aspects of the construction trade, Bartholomew decided that, in addition to golf courses, he would expand into drainage, foundation, and landscape work. His next big job, however, was for construction of another golf course, the famous City Park, a public golf course paid for by the state of Louisiana, with the city of New Orleans supplying the manpower. The end result was another superb job, and the two courses, Metaire and City Park, stood as monumental masterpieces of his design genius and expert landscape techniques, and years later they still stand as showplaces among southern golf courses.

With these successes, the business began pouring in to Bartholomew Construction. He did the landscaping, excavating, grading, and so forth at both Dillard and Xavier universities, and, under subcontracts, he did the excavating, hauling, demolishing, and other such jobs on Louisiana's massive Charity Hospital and also on each of New Orleans' public housing projects built during the 1930s and 1940s. During World War II, he was a subcontractor at Higgins Industries, excavating, hauling, and laying the framework for the largest shipyard building program in the state's history. He also provided the foundations for several factories and office buildings, including the Johns-Manville plant in the city.

One of Joseph Bartholomew's biggest jobs involved the grading and excavation for the Parkview Gardens housing project, built in the late 1940s. This was a $300,000 job. His most difficult project, however, was the repaving of Tulane Avenue, a wide commercial artery, for which he received $250,000. The job involved digging and blasting out tons of old, steel-meshed concrete and dirt before he was able to lay a new foundation and repave the highway. By that point, he was running a massive construction operation. He had over twenty three- and four-ton trucks for hauling, several caterpillar tractors for excavating, three huge cranes and one smaller crane for lifting, and numerous other pieces of equipment. He often had as many as 300 men working on a job.

He talked about both his equipment and his work force: "A man must have good machinery to do efficient work," he stated. "And next to good machinery, he must have capable men. I've made heavy investments in both." His regularly employed 50 to 100 men, with far larger numbers brought on for large jobs. He used both white and black workers; the only requirement was that they must all be members of the American Federation of Labor. In later years, Bartholomew also built the New Orleans Country Club and Pontchartrain Park, a relatively successful, privately financed housing project for blacks. Located about six miles from mid-city, it provided fifteen different house styles, of two or three bedrooms each, on lots of varying sizes. Intended for the black middle class, homes ranged in price from $9,800 to $27,000. The streets were all well paved, there were concrete sidewalks and driveways, and all the homes had adequate plumbing, good water and sewage facilities, and good drainage, the latter due to Bartholomew's excellent construction techniques. The project was completed in 1956.

Bartholomew also began to get into the real estate business in the late 1930s. He and a white partner began buying up several acres of low-quality land throughout the city for from $40 to $50 per acre. Then Bartholomew, using his massive equipment and construction expertise, drained and leveled the property, while his partner took charge of reselling the land. They often got as much as $600 per acre. The biggest venture of those two men was the Plum Orchards development, on which in 1942–1943 they spent $640,000 building eighty-two houses on reclaimed land. These houses were then rented to white families for $43 per month. Bartholomew and his partner brought in $6,500 monthly in rents on these properties. In another real estate deal, Bartholomew and an associate bought 400 swamp lots for $60,000. He then drained, leveled, and improved the lots, and sold all but forty of them for black homes, making a total of $250,000.

In 1940, Bartholomew took some of his profits from construction and real estate and used them to purchase the Douglas Life Insurance Company, an ailing black-owned firm. The company had a deficit when he took it over, but he turned it around over the next several years until it was showing a profit. By 1946 it had assets of $147,253, showed a profit of $11,453, and had 14,441 policy-holders, most of whom took out sickness and disability insurance by paying premiums of five or ten cents a week. Bartholomew, who owned 51 percent of the stock in the firm, also owned the building where it was housed. The neat white building was assessed at $60,000, and he rented it to the company for $1,000 per month, a rather nifty return, considering he had bought the building earlier for $16,000.

Bartholomew also went into the ice cream business. With a partner, John Creech, he put up $75,000 to build a modern ice-cream plant where they manufactured a rich, 12.5 percent butterfat ice cream. Bartholomew's initial investment was soon paid off, and the ice-cream firm became very profitable. "That's the difference between me and most of the rest of the colored people," Bartholomew declared. "They won't take a chance because they been skinned before. I take 'em all the time."

The brusqueness was characteristic of Joseph Bartholomew. He was regarded as pretty much of a lone wolf in New Orleans' largely Creole business community. Also, the fact that whites gave Bartholomew his start, and acted as his partners in many of his business ventures, set him apart. Nor did he join many clubs or other social organizations that were central to the black community, explaining that he had no time to "socialize." On the other hand, he was always willing to give advice to young blacks who wanted to succeed in business: "There's no such thing as get rich quick. Take your time. Don't try to outsmart the white folks—they're smart. Be honest, listen and learn."

Despite the fact that Bartholomew was never an intimate element in the city's largely Creole upper class, he did play a major role in the civic life of blacks in the city. He was a member of the NAACP and the Urban League, and he did a good deal of unpaid work at such black universities as Xavier and Dillard. Bartholomew was also a member of the Mayor's Advisory Board. In addition, he donated the land and built Crescent City Golf Club, a private nine-hole golf course for blacks. A modest man, he lived simply with his wife, Ruth Segue, two daughters, and one son, and attended St. Joan of Arc Roman Catholic Church.

Golf, like tennis, is one of those sports where few African-Americans have been influential. The playing surfaces for both sports are generally located in largely white suburban areas, many of the clubs are private, and even the public ones are fairly expensive for poor, inner-city youth. On top of that, most of the private clubs, and many of the public ones, were restricted to whites only. Yet, Joseph Bartholomew was able to break through these barriers, achieving success not just as a fine athlete, that is, a golfer, but also as a designer and builder of golf courses, as well as a large number of other impressive projects. He was one of those very few blacks who were somehow able to transcend massive racial barriers, and oftentimes to get whites to become their biggest boosters. A couple of comments from whites should demonstrate this: deLesseps S. Morrison, one-time mayor of New Orleans, said of him, "Joe's got fine equipment—build with him, you save money." Abe Goldberg, a fellow contractor, commented, "Every time I get to feeling a little discouraged about a job, I just look up and say 'If Joe Bartholomew, with two strikes against him can do it, then I ought to be ashamed of myself.' Why, the fellow's an inspiration." In 1979, in recognition of all he had accomplished, the city named the Joseph M. Bartholomew Memorial golf course in his honor.

Sources

There are no personal or business papers of Joseph Bartholomew available. There are biographical sketches of him in *Forget-me-knots* (New Orleans, n.d.); *Fortune*, November 1947; *Sepia Socialite*, April 1942; and there are some clippings in the Marcus Christian Collection in Special Collections, Earl K. Long Library, University of New Orleans. There is a short obituary in the *Times-Picayune*, October 14, 1971. There is a photograph of him in *Etches of Ebony Louisiana* (1981). See also *Times Picayune*, January 28, 1972.

Beavers, George Allen, Jr. (October 30 or 31, 1891–October 13, 1989), **Ivan James Houston** (June 15, 1925–   ), **Norman Oliver Houston** (October 16, 1893–October 20, 1981), and **William Nickerson, Jr.** (January 20, 1879–November 14, 1945). Insurance company founders and executives: Golden State Insurance. William Nickerson, Jr., was born, somewhat like Abraham Lincoln, in a log cabin. His father, William Nickerson, and his mother, Emma Poole, were natives of Louisiana who had married in 1877. Neither of the parents ever knew their white fathers, and both were raised by their mothers, who subsisted in desperate poverty. The elder Nickerson and his wife went to San Jacinto County, Texas, where he got a small plot of land and built a log cabin made of timber sawed by hand, with two doors, a chimney, and no stove. The Nickerson family homestead was five miles from the county seat of Cold Springs and three miles from the nearest public road. The elder Nickerson slowly began to carve out an independent existence for himself. Engaging in farming during the day, he did blacksmithing at night, and soon he had accumulated a small nest egg. In time, he had saved enough money to buy 50 acres of land, for which he paid cash, which was followed by 50 more acres a short time later and, subsequently, another 165. In the beginning, this property was all woodland, but the older Nickerson cleared 35 acres in short order, and soon he was engaged in diversified agriculture and hog raising.

Young William's early years were not luxurious, but neither was he deprived of educational opportunities. When he was eight years old, he began attending school, and his father was so concerned that the son get a good education that he once drove thirty miles to Huntsville to get a book for him. William's mother also gave him all the help and encouragement he needed to progress during this time; she even secured a needed book from white children for William to use. The school William attended was at Wolf's Creek, about three miles from his home, and it was in session just five months a year. Later, when it became clear he could get a better education in Cold Springs, William and his sisters walked the five miles to attend elementary school there. At this time, William became enamored of history, which became his favorite subject, and he decided he would teach history when he was older.

After completing elementary school, Nickerson went to Huntsville to attend high school and boarded with Professor Peter Abner, the principal. He did very well in all his subjects there, so his parents decided to send him to Bishop College in Marshall, Texas, where he took a normal course to prepare him to teach history. Eight years later, he completed the requirements for the four-year course, and he graduated in 1904, at the age of twenty-five. During these eight years, however, he had not been able to attend school full-time. In 1898, in order to help out with expenses at home, Nickerson spent a year and a half teaching at Prairie View Normal and Industrial College, and he also taught for two months at Holland's Quarter in Panola County, Texas. There he met and married his wife, Bertha B. Benton.

In April 1905, after having spent a number of years teaching history in Texas, Nickerson went to Houston, where a chance encounter changed his career and his life. Shortly after arriving there, Nickerson had breakfast with an old friend, J. J. Hardaway, who was working as an agent with Southern Mutual Benefit Association, a white-owned insurance firm with head offices in Dallas, which had a division to solicit business among African-Americans. Hardaway, who sold industrial insurance to blacks, convinced Nickerson of the value of the product for his race and also of the great career opportunities in the field. Nickerson was so impressed that he left Sapenter's Restaurant, went straight to Southern Mutual, and joined the agency staff. This was the beginning of what was to be a long and distinguished career in the insurance business.

Nickerson began slowly and steadily to increase the amount of premium business he brought to Southern Mutual each month and soon became one of the top agents with the firm. Southern Mutual, however, went through a reorganization, and it was taken over by American National Insurance of Galveston. This disrupted the firm and caused Nickerson to begin looking for another line of work. He took and passed the civil service exam for a postal carrier, and his wife encouraged him to take the security of that position instead of the uncertainty of insurance. Nickerson, though, was "hooked" by his new career and decided to stay with insurance. This did not necessarily mean, though, that he was going to remain with Southern Mutual.

In March 1908, as Nickerson himself later explained, there were " 'labor troubles' between our superintendent and the agents." As a result, Nickerson and several other agents at the firm decided to go out on their own. He left Southern Mutual on July 1, 1908, and, with J. B. Grigsby, Forrest T. Perkins, London Franks, W. H. Parker, and C. H. Green, got a charter from the state of Texas to form the American Mutual Benefit Association. Offices established at 409½ Milam Street in Houston, the new insurance firm began to sell aggressively "fraternal insurance" to blacks in Texas. Nickerson served as secretary of the company, W. B. Cogle as president, Perkins as vice president, and Franks as treasurer.

When the American Mutual Benefit Association proved successful, American National Insurance filed charges against the new firm because of the similarity of their names and also because they said it was not operating under the fraternal system as their charter stipulated. Nickerson and the other officers were called before the state insurance commissioner, and things looked, in Nickerson's words, "mighty dark" for a time. But the night before the meeting, Nickerson had drafted a formal ritual for policyholders in the organization, thereby formally satisfying the requirement that they be a "lodge" or fraternal order, and the Department of Insurance ruled that the two names were not similar enough to disturb the business of the white company. This whole incident, however, caused Nickerson to make a detailed and intensive study of insurance law and the entire insurance field. As a result of this, he became convinced that industrial and fraternal insurance schemes were not good for either the black insurance firms or the African-American consumer. Instead, he advocated the establishment of "old-line" legal reserve insurance firms that sold regular, whole life insurance. He suggested this to his associates at American Mutual Benefit, but they did not share his enthusiasm.

As a result, while still shouldering the extensive duties of secretary of American Mutual Benefit, Nickerson set up an agency for south Texas for the Standard Life Insurance Company of Atlanta, Georgia, an ordinary life insurance company recently established by Heman Edward Perry.* This provided Nickerson with important experience in whole life insurance and also showed him the advantages of operating in more than one state. Therefore, he next suggested to his associates at American Mutual Benefit that they set up a tristate operation, with offices in Oklahoma and California, in addition to Texas, but, again, they were not responsive to the idea. Nickerson later recalled that period:

For a long time this was debated without a decision. In the meantime other things (politically) were happening in the state, one of which was the riot [Longview, Texas, in 1919 and perhaps Tulsa in 1921] and its consequences. So becoming disgusted, I decided to take my wife and eight children and move to California, regardless of whether a conversion plan was effected . . . believing in another state I could effect my plan as Heman Perry had done in Georgia.

Nickerson had also been politically active in Texas, pushing for voting rights for blacks. The riots undoubtedly made him feel less secure there. Thus, Nickerson decided to leave Texas for California on June 11, 1921, and arrived in Los Angeles with his family by train two days later. They rented a house at 1543 East 22nd Street, but after just a month they bought a home at 1214 E. 20th Street.

Los Angeles in 1920 was just beginning to explode as an attractive place for migrants, and the importance of its African-American community was growing apace. Although blacks were among the first settlers of the area and received a certain amount of recognition for that, by the turn of the century the black community was still very small and its leadership structure was weak and fragmented. Blacks in 1870 made up just 1.6 percent of the city's population, with just 93 souls. The next thirty years brought the first significant migration of African-Americans to Los Angeles, so that by 1900 there were 2,131 living there, constituting 2.1 percent of the total. Although blacks were still a negligible portion of the total population, the number living there by 1900 was sufficient to create an important social and economic structure, and for a small black elite to emerge.

This fact was recognized just after the turn of the century, when Booker T. Washington* visited the city. Among those African-American business and social leaders to greet Washington were B. W. Brown, a graduate chemist who ran a hardware store and manufactured grocery specialties; a Mr. Strickland, who was a successful butcher; M. R. Dunston, who had established a large and successful van and storage business; a Mr. Jamison, who was known as the "scrap iron king"; G. W. Holden, the "hog king"; and, perhaps most important, J. L. Edmonds, editor of *The Liberator*, the first African-American newspaper in the city. Blacks had also established a rich institutional structure in Los Angeles, with five African Methodist churches and one each black Presbyterian, Christian, and Episcopal churches. Angeleno blacks had also set up some twenty-nine lodges of the major fraternal orders in the city, such as the Odd Fellows, Masons, Knights of Pythias, United Brothers of Friendship, and the True Reformers, and it may have been this fact that attracted Nickerson to the city to push his fraternal insurance program.

The population of Los Angeles exploded between 1900 and 1920, growing fivefold from 102,479 to 576,673. The number of African-Americans there increased from just over 2,000 to 15,579, but their percentage of the total population grew only from 2.0 percent to 2.7 percent. During the next decade, the general population of Los Angeles exploded again, to 1,238,584 by 1930, and the black population increased to nearly 39,000, 3.1 percent of the total. Thus, Nickerson was pursuing his business interests in one of the most rapidly growing cities in America. The black community there had, by the early twentieth century, begun to be concentrated in a large colony on Central Avenue, with the business section at Twenty-Second Street and Central.

J. Max Bond, in his study of blacks in the city, described the Central Avenue area at that time:

Here many newcomers from Texas, Louisiana, Arkansas, Georgia, and Alabama—have settled; most of the business and professional men of the race have their offices in and are residents of this large community; here are found the business concerns of Negroes living in other communities; and here resides still a large number of the first families of Los Angeles. In the Central Avenue community, poverty and prosperity exist side by side. On every hand conservative old families are surrounded by people of a lower level of culture.

The lure of Los Angeles for African-Americans was perhaps no different than it was for other Americans. As Frank Fenton wrote in *A Place in the Sun* (1949): "This was a lovely makeshift city. Even the trees and plants did not belong here. They came, like the people, from far places, some familiar, some exotic, all wanderers of one sort or another seeking peace or fortune or the last frontier, or a thousand dreams of escape."

Nickerson secured a license to sell insurance in California and, at the same time, also got a real estate license. He rented an office for five dollars a month at 1804 South Central Avenue, in the heart of the black business district. A great need, however, was to get someone, in Nickerson's words, who was a " 'live wire' to assist me in getting the American Mutual properly established in the state of California." This was Norman O. Houston, of whom Nickerson said, "At first I didn't think so much of this young man, but he was very insistent, so much so that I concluded to give him a decent hearing. I reasoned I needed someone with experience who could help me and was known here." Houston became the first employee of American Mutual in California, and he would be one of the founders of Golden State Insurance.

Nickerson and Houston set out to drum up business in Los Angeles. They concluded that the various African-American churches would be a good starting point. Houston was made superintendent of agents, and three young men were hired as the first agents. Nickerson then accompanied Houston and his wife to the African Methodist Church at Eighth and Towne, and upon ascertaining that it was a fertile ground for selling insurance policies, Nickerson requested that Houston become a member of the church, which he did. Although Houston had some experience with insurance, he had little in managing people, but he proved an "apt pupil" and soon had established a smoothly functioning sales force. One of the agents hired by Nickerson and Houston during these early months was George Beavers. Nickerson later recalled his first impressions of Beavers: "He was a short, stocky young fellow and wore glasses. He was quiet and unassuming. One thing I soon found out about him was as represented, he was not only a 'beaver' but of the bull dog type as well—he was a hard worker and a fighter as well." These three men would dominate the African-American insurance business in California for decades to come.

Norman Houston was a rarity—a native Californian—who had been born in San Jose. His mother was also a native of the state, having been born in San Francisco. The first member of his family in the "Golden State" was his grandmother, who had come from Virginia, sailing around Cape Horn to settle in San Francisco, as one of the earliest black settlers in the city. Houston's father was a native of Georgia. His parents were divorced when Norman Houston was twelve, and he was subsequently raised by his mother and stepfather in Fruitland, just outside Oakland. Upon graduating from high school, he went to the University of California at Berkeley, where he took classes in business administration for two years. Then, he worked for about a year as a clerk with the board of insurance underwriters in California, before returning to UC Berkeley to continue his education. He had been there only a short time, however, before the United States entered World War I and Houston was drafted into the U.S. Army, where he served as the regimental personnel adjutant with the 32nd Division—the only black person to hold such a position in the entire army. After being discharged from the service, Houston attended summer school at UC Berkeley but left the following fall to become an agent with the National Life Insurance Company in Los Angeles, where he sold insurance to black waiters and cooks at the railroad commissary. Although his family had spent several generations in California, Houston, like so many northern Californians at that time, had never before visited Los Angeles. That city, however, would be his home and source of business success for the rest of his life. In his adopted city, Houston soon acquired a reputation as an affable, friendly, and aggressive businessman.

George Beavers was born into a poor family in Atlanta, Georgia. He received his early education in that city, but when he was twelve years old, his father, a laborer in a wholesale grocery store, and his mother, who took in laundry, decided to move to California. There they hoped both to find better economic opportunities and to escape the increasingly brutal and violent race relations of the South. George Beavers's first job in California was as a water boy for the Pacific Electric Railway during his summer vacation from Los Angeles High School and he became very active in the African Methodist Church. His father, who was employed as a laborer at the railway, had gotten George the job. Later, the elder Beavers moved on to a permanent position with the Sante Fe Railway Company in the building maintenance department, where he remained until he retired.

Young George Beavers graduated from high school, got married in 1911, and got a job at the German-American Bank as an elevator operator. This bank later developed into the Security Pacific National Bank, and Beavers rose to stock clerk and then messenger at the firm. During World War I, he went to work in the Los Angeles Foundry as a molder's helper since he had a deferred classification in the draft because of the loss of an eye as a teenager. Because of Beavers's longtime interest in the church, he got involved after World War I in organizing the People's Independent Church, which was designed to serve the needs of the large influx of African-Americans from the South that had flooded into Los Angeles during and immediately after the war.

A major activity of Beavers during this early period was to help establish the People's Independent Church of Christ. The principal driving force in its establishment was J. H. Shackelford, who had a prosperous business on Central Avenue selling furniture and household goods and who became a leading real estate broker in the community. Through these connections, George Beavers also became involved in selling real estate at G. W. Wheatley Real Estate, with which he was affiliated for the next several years. The People's Church was established at 1025 E. 18th Street in 1915 and remained at that location for the next sixty-five years. Shackelford was chairman of the board of trustees; Beavers was acting secretary. When Nickerson first came to Los Angeles, he asked to speak to the congregation there and finally was able, after much discussion, to persuade many in the congregation to purchase insurance. Presumably, Beavers first encountered Nickerson and his insurance programs there. The church was closely tied to the Masons.

In any event, it was not until the spring of 1922 that George Beavers had official contact with American Mutual. Caldwell Jones, a leading agent for the firm, called on Beavers at his place of business, trying to sell him an insurance policy. On his next visit, he brought Norman Houston with him, and shortly after Beavers met Nickerson in the meeting described above. After meeting Nickerson, Beavers paid the premium on his insurance policy and became an agent for the firm on a part-time basis. At the same time, he began to study the insurance business under Houston and Nickerson and began taking courses at the University of California, Los Angeles' extension division. The three men worked closely together over the next year or so, and by that time they had a staff of eight agents. Then, in 1923, Houston came to Nickerson and told him he had signed a contract with Liberty Building and Loan Association. Feeling he could make more money with this other company, he resigned from American Mutual, and Beavers took his place as superintendent of agents.

Houston was named field manager of Liberty Building and Loan, which had the unlikely goal of trying to sell bonds to blacks with barely adequate incomes. Houston's principal reason for this was that he disliked being an employee of anyone, even someone he respected as much as Nickerson. He had wanted to run his own business ever since he was a child, and Liberty Building and Loan seemed like a surer road to that than his association with an insurance firm based in Houston, Texas. The prime mover behind Liberty Savings and Loan was Louis M. Blodgett, who also started the Angelus Funeral Home in 1925. Although Liberty Building did well enough in the 1920s, both it and the Angelus Funeral Home had serious problems during the Great Depression of the 1930s. It was ultimately bought by Beverley Hills Savings and Loan, and then by Coast Federal. Houston, however, did not remain long with Liberty—some significant changes brought Houston back into association with Nickerson and Beavers.

In November 1924, the executives at the Houston office of American Mutual decided that they no longer wanted to pursue a tristate operation, and they decided not to renew their license for the next year. Nickerson was thrown off stride by this decision for a short time, but soon he decided he wanted to establish his own insurance firm in California. Contacting Norman Houston, who had worked in the state insurance office earlier in his career, Nickerson sent him to see the insurance commissioner about the requirements for doing so. They decided to establish the firm under Chapter 6 of the Insurance Code which required that 500 life insurance applications be secured and paid for in advance, and that a fund of $15,000 be deposited with the Department of Insurance. The three men decided to go ahead with their project, and Nickerson later recalled coming up with the name: ''One morning while in the office of the American Mutual, I called in Mr. George A. Beavers, Jr. and told him I had found a law upon which our organization could be founded and I was about to select a name for it. I suggested several names . . . among which was 'Golden State Guarantee Fund Insurance Company.' Golden State meant 'California.' We needed as part of the name something that would serve as a confidence builder among the public.'' It would be the first insurance firm to be owned, operated, and controlled by African-Americans in the state of California.

The three men split the organizational duties. Beavers, who was head of the agency staff, was assigned the job of signing up 500 applicants for policies; Houston, the man with financial contacts, was supposed to sell $50 certificates to raise the $15,000; and Nickerson, who had studied insurance law, acted as the firm's counsel and also, as a man of boundless energy and enthusiasm, was the front man, convincing everyone of the new company's worth. When the company opened for business in a one-room office at 1435 Central Avenue, its total capital was $17,800 and its physical assets were a desk, a table, an adding machine, a file cabinet, and a few chairs. It was granted its license to operate on July 23, 1925.

In less than three months, the new firm had outgrown its cramped office and moved to a large storeroom at 3512 Central Avenue. By the end of the first year, it had a surplus of over $16,000, nearly $12,000 was placed in real estate loans, $16,700 was paid to policyholders, and over $6,000 had been placed in reserve. Income for that year was over $60,000, and new life insurance amounted to in excess of $260,000. Expansion outside the Los Angeles area came that same year, with the establishment of a district office in Oakland. The company continued its rapid growth over the next several years, opening branch offices in Pasadena, Bakersfield, San Diego, and Fresno. By 1928 Golden State had 100 employees, including sixty agents, ten medical examiners, a claims adjuster, an actuary, twelve committeemen, and fourteen home office clerical help. As a result of this expansion, it was necessary to move to a new and larger home office in 1928. A new building was erected at 4261 Central Avenue. The building was entirely planned and constructed, including the architect and contractor, by African-Americans. The insurance firm occupied the second floor of this large, new building; the first floor was rented out to various black merchants.

In the same year, Nickerson decided to join the National Negro Insurance Association. This organization was an outgrowth of the National Negro Business League. In 1920 the heads of several African-American insurance firms felt their needs were not getting the attention they deserved at the NNBL, so they advocated the organization of an association of the largest and most stable black insurance firms. Thirteen of the largest firms did join, and Charles C. Spaulding* of North Carolina Mutual was named the first president of the group. Nickerson decided to join because, in his words, ''We reason that these companies, at least some of them, should have very valuable experience that we should have by contact. That's why we joined the organization.'' It also helped to enhance the young firm's status as a viable, reputable organization.

Although Golden State was operating as an assessment company, which allowed them to organize on a more liberal basis, they actually ran it as a legal reserve firm, setting aside reserves for each policy sold, and steadily building its reserve fund. To reflect this, in 1931 the name was changed to Golden State Mutual Life Insurance Company. But the Depression years for Golden State, as for most African-American firms, were difficult ones. To economize, in 1930 the number of directors was reduced from fifteen to nine, and other efficiencies were exacted. As a result, the firm was not only able to continue to grow during the Depression years, but it also remained profitable. In July 1930, dividends were paid to Golden State policyholders for the first time. They were paid each year afterward without interruption. Assets, which stood at $73,000 in 1929, had grown to $437,000 by the end of the 1930s. Surplus funds had grown from about $28,000 to $108,000 during this same period, and insurance in force rose from just under $1 million to nearly $6 million.

One key to this expansion by Golden State was the judicious use of advertising. In 1939 Nickerson and Harry H. Pace* of Supreme Liberty Life in Chicago had exchanged letters concerning the importance of advertising. Pace wrote to Nickerson:

Our experience in advertising in church bulletins is not a satisfactory one. We regard any advertising in a church bulletin as a contribution to a church and do not expect any results from the advertising. . . . We regard the most effective form of advertising as premiums and prizes for the agents.

Golden State did both. The three officers were very closely tied to African-American churches and secured many of their policyholders from their ranks, but they also provided a good deal of incentive and encouragement for their agents with various premiums and prizes.

Golden State was so successful during these years that they began plans to expand operations outside of California. Viewing Chicago as the ''center'' of black business and culture in the North, they set up operations in Illinois in 1938, and in 1944 they expanded into Nickerson's home state of Texas. In the meantime, the three officers had decided it was time to convert the firm officially from assessment to old-line legal reserve status. A capital reserve of $250,000 was needed for this conversion, and, in 1938, the officers asked the insurance department for permission to sell additional certificates of advancement. The permission was granted, and a total of $241,840 was secured from this source. In 1941 the sale of certificates was completed, the $250,000 fund was set up, and in December 1941 the firm was converted to an old-line legal reserve company, depositing the $250,000 with the state of California. By the end of World War II, Golden State had over $1 million in policy reserves, $2 million in assets, $750,000 in surplus funds, and nearly $24 million of insurance in force. Within the firm, Norman Houston was usually the strongest voice calling for expansion, while Beavers was far less expansion minded.

During the war years, massive numbers of African-Americans had moved to California, particularly to Los Angeles, to work in the war industries. This not only was a source of much potentially lucrative business for Golden State, but also encouraged the firm to lobby for the best interests of these newcomers. Golden State organized the Allied Organization against Discrimination in National Defense, which spearheaded the fight to help open doors of the area war industries for blacks.

In 1945, however, William Nickerson, the driving force behind Golden State from its very beginning, died. His death was greatly mourned in the black community; he was valued not just as a businessman, but as a man who, in the words of the *Chicago Defender*, "Made Good." By that they meant that he was a "top businessman—yet, human to the 'core.' " They went on to say: "William Nickerson, say those who knew him well, was made of solid stuff. He had pioneering courage and steadfastly refused to bow to defeat. Those who knew him well . . . still talk of his smile, his work, his contributions to his country and to his fellows."

George Beavers echoed that sentiment,

During my association with Mr. Nickerson, which covered almost a quarter of a century, I always admired his magnetic personality and enthusiasm. These characteristics, together with his remarkable vision and dogged determinism, contributed greatly to the birth and noteworthy progress of Golden State Mutual. . . . He demonstrated the wisdom of mixing religion with business. . . . Among the many qualities possessed by Founder Nickerson that fit into the pattern of by the life of Christ was his *friendliness, love of children and young people, enthusiasm, courage,* and *his unselfishness and deep concern for others.*

In 1925, when Nickerson was first setting up Golden State, Reverend N. P. Griggs of the People's Independent Church, said of him: "My friends, we may not and possibly cannot fully appreciate the sterling worth of a man like this to our race and age. This is more than likely to be true with us, because he is contemporaneous with us. Unfortunately, people are so constructed as to be almost unable to see or appreciate the noble characters that live among them. That has been true of every generation."

William Nickerson left two monuments to his life. The first, of course, was Golden State Mutual, which continues as one of the most successful black insurance companies in the nation. The other is Nickerson Gardens, an infamous public housing project in Los Angeles. The California State Association of Colored Women and the Los Angeles Urban League campaigned for the creation of this project and to have it named after Nickerson. It opened with much fanfare and optimism in March 1954 at Imperial Boulevard and Compton Avenue. Thirty-five years later, however, the projects were among the most crime filled and violent in the city. Celes King III, owner of King Bail Bonds Agency, whose family owned the Dunbar Hotel and were close friends of the Nickersons, commented in 1988 that "William Nickerson would crawl out of his grave if he knew that Nickerson Gardens would have gotten to the point where it is now."

With Nickerson's death, the official mantle of leadership of the firm shifted to Norman Houston, who became the second president of the company. Even

Houston's son, Ivan Houston, however, recognized that "Beavers and my father were essentially co-equal" in running the company over the next several decades. Norman Houston remained president and chief executive officer of Golden State until January 1967, after which he was chairman of the board and chief executive officer until 1970. He was then chairman of the board and chairman of the board emeritus until his death in 1981. These were years of great consolidation and growth for the company, and Houston himself emerged as one of the most important and respected African-American business leaders in Los Angeles. By 1954 Houston had increased the policy reserves of Golden State from just over $1 million to $7.5 million. Assets increased from $2 million to nearly $10 million; surplus funds went up from $750,000 to $1.6 million; and insurance in force increased from $23 million to nearly $84 million.

In expanding the firm, Houston brought Golden State into new areas. In 1946, for example, the company set up its Funeral Service Division, under the supervision of John M. Nelson. Then, in 1948, new emphasis was placed upon the enlargement of policyholder service in California, and new districts were set up on the west side of Los Angeles, in San Bernadino, and in Vallejo, and the Sacramento office was enlarged to include Stockton. Services outside of California were also enlarged and enhanced. In 1948 Houston brought in a team of management consultants to survey the company and its personnel. His son later commented, "He always wanted us to be the best-run and best-managed company in the industry."

Most significant, Houston began preparations to move into a new home office. Ground was broken at the corner of Western Avenue and Adams Boulevard, and on July 15, 1949, the historic move was made from the Central Avenue building, which had been the firm's headquarters for twenty-one years. The new, modern, six-story building was designed as the central clearinghouse and headquarters of executive and administrative management and business operations. During the grand opening week, more than 10,000 persons from all over the United States came to visit. It was one of the most important events in the history of the African-American community of Los Angeles to that time.

Golden State's vigorous expansion continued throughout the 1950s, as Oregon, Washington, and Arizona were added to the earlier three states where the company did business, and in 1959 electronic data processing systems were set up. The company ended that decade with $133 million of insurance in force and over $16 million in assets. They also broadened their services to include mortgage insurance and group insurance. In 1962 George Beavers, who had served as chairman of the board since 1945, retired from active management. Beavers had been vice president and director of agencies from 1925 to 1945, chairman of the board and of the executive and agency committees from 1945 to 1951, chairman of the board until 1965, and then chairman emeritus and director from 1965 to 1980. From 1980 until his death at ninety-seven in 1989, he was chairman emeritus and director emeritus. Beavers, in addition, had been vice president of the National Negro Insurance Association in 1931–1932 and president of that group in 1962–1963. He was also very involved in the Los Angeles Urban League, which he served as president for a number of years, and he received a number of awards during his lifetime, including honors from presidents Franklin Roosevelt and Harry S. Truman, along with awards from Los Angeles mayors ranging from Fletcher Bowron to Tom Bradley. He was also a member of the NAACP, the Los Angeles County Conference on Community Relations, and the National Conference of Christians and Jews.

Tom Bradley, a particularly close friend of Beavers, called Beavers, on his death, "A dynamic leader [and] a source of inspiration to others who wished to get into business and improve the quality of life in the community." Los Angeles supervisor Kenneth Hahn remembered Beavers as a "long-time friend and community leader." Beavers combined the practical and the emotional, the business and community side of African-American life in Los Angeles as well as anyone. Revealing, perhaps, is a letter he wrote to William Nickerson in 1938. Nickerson had turned down a plan for reorganization of the company that Beavers had proposed. Purely an unemotional, business decision perhaps, but not in Beavers's mind:

It is 4 a.m. as I pen these lines. My heart has been wounded by my best friend. I can't sleep. . . . I am wondering if our years of friendship mean anything to you. If you care about our cordial business relations or if you are only concerned about the employment of a stranger. Do you want efficient office help? Do you want a private secretary to do your work? Do you want harmonious cooperation in the office? Don't you think the plan *I* suggested would accomplish these purposes. *I am convinced* that this plan *is the best solution* to the problem. . . . Mr. Nickerson, my friend, you will make a serious mistake if you disregard friendship, cordial business relations and harmonious cooperation in the one institution that means so much to us all, for the sake of the association and employment of a stranger.

George Beavers, for over sixty years, was the conscience of Golden State Mutual.

Norman Houston, like Beavers, was involved in a number of other business and community ventures. He became one of the organizers in 1947 and served for many years as chairman of the board of Broadway Federal Savings and Loan Association. By the mid–1970s, Broadway was credited with having made more loans to black churches than any other firm. It was also by far the largest black-owned savings and loan in California, with $62 million in assets in 1980. Ten years later, however, Broadway had lost momentum to Family Savings and Loan Association, whose assets were about 40 percent greater than Broadway's. Robert Bowdoin of Family Savings had by that time become the chief voice of black savings and loans in California. Both firms survived the disastrous savings and loan crisis of the late 1980s and early 1990s, but Broadway had slipped all the way to the thirteenth spot among black-owned financial institutions in the United States, and had experienced little or no growth during those years. Norman Houston was also involved in the organization of the National Bank of Los Angeles in 1949, which was the brainchild of H. A. Howard, manager of Broadway Federal Savings. A short time later, however, Houston resigned his association with the bank and with Broadway Savings, and the effort failed to go very far.

Norman Houston was elected to the California State Athletic Commission, the first black to be appointed, and later also served as chairman of the commission. He was chairman of the committee of management of the 28th Street YMCA. In 1976 he was a member of the 1976 Olympic Games Committee appointed by Mayor Sam Yorty. He served as president of the Los Angeles branch of the NAACP and presiding cochairman of the Southern California regional board of the National Conference of Christians and Jews, and as a member of Los Angeles' first Human Rights Commission. Houston received the Brotherhood Award of the National Conference of Christians and Jews and the U.S. Department of Commerce National Award for Achievement, and he was named to the Golden Book of Distinguished Service, the highest award from the YMCA. His proudest achievement came in 1975, when he, along with Beavers and Nickerson, received awards from the Brotherhood Crusade, a black charity organization. At the time, that organization said, ''These men represent the top money in black business. They are also regarded as pioneer institution-builders in the black community. That is why we want to honor them now and hold them up as examples of what blacks can do.''

Upon Houston's death, the *Los Angeles Sentinel* commented, ''Mr. Houston, a true pioneer in the business field, helped provide jobs and a better life for Black Americans and others from coast to coast.... During his career, Mr. Houston was just as well-known and respected for his business acumen and community involvement in board rooms of the business world as he was in Watts and other Black communities.'' In 1975 both Governor Edmund G. Brown and Mayor Tom Bradley honored Houston as a ''pioneer of black industry.'' In truth, though, Houston was from an older school, one rather out of touch with the militance and activism of the 1970s and 1980s. In an interview he once admitted that he had always escaped the personal consequences of being black and said that ''good fortune, good friends, intelligence, education, and courage have all conspired to help [me] sidestep the personal frustrations and humiliations of humble status.'' He even went on to say that he felt it was ''an advantage to be a Negro,'' since in his success and in the success of other blacks around him, he learned a deeper joy than nonblacks could ever experience. Perhaps so, but few other blacks in America would be inclined to share his joy in their deprived status.

Norman Houston was succeeded as chief executive officer of the company by his son, Ivan J. Houston. Ivan was born in Los Angeles and educated in the city's schools, graduating from Polytechnic High School. During this time, Ivan's father and mother were divorced, and both parents remarried, with his mother moving for a time to Seattle, Washington. Ivan had a good deal of contact with both parents during this time, however.

With World War II on, Ivan went into the U.S. Army, where he served with the all-black 370th Regimental Combat Team of the 92nd Infantry. He saw a good deal of action in Italy in 1944 and 1945, for which he received medals of commendation, but he also experienced a lot of discrimination and racism, really for the first time in his life. Houston later reflected that, after his army experience, "nothing worse in my life could happen." Ivan then went on to his father's alma mater, UC Berkeley, where he graduated in 1948. His father then persuaded him to go to the University of Manitoba, where he received his degree in actuarial science.

Upon returning to Golden State, Ivan Houston worked as an accountant until 1950, when he was promoted to supervisor for two years. He continued to work his way slowly up the ladder of the company during the 1950s, serving as administrative assistant, assistant secretary, actuary, and head of personnel. In that last position, Ivan Houston had a baptism of fire. In 1957 there was a strike by the California agents of Golden State which lasted for some two months. Ivan was ultimately named the negotiator in this dispute. It was a tough and bitter fight, especially since the agents had become affiliated with the AFL-CIO, but it was ultimately resolved to the satisfaction of all concerned. Ivan Houston was named vice president in 1962 and senior vice president in 1966.

In 1970 his father decided to step down as chief executive officer of the firm. Upon his resignation, the elder Houston asked that his eldest son, Norman B. Houston, who was also a senior vice president and investment officer of the company, be named chief executive officer and Ivan Houston be named chief operating officer. Ivan Houston was terribly upset by this decision, since he believed he had played a more important role in the development of Golden State than his brother. Norman B. Houston was two years older and had joined Golden State after graduating from UCLA. Norman B. Houston's major interests, however, had always been in politics and various African-American organizations. At UCLA he had gone to school with H. R. Haldeman and John Erhlichman, and they had brought him into the inner sanctum of the California Republican party. He was also active as an officer in the NAACP and other organizations. The two sons were, in a word, "Mr. Inside and Mr. Outside," and the father had opted for the flashier, more gregarious "Mr. Outside" to run the firm.

Ivan Houston, however, did not meekly accept the decision. He went to George Beavers, who was chairman emeritus, and to Edgar J. Johnson, who was president and chief administrative officer of the company, and he presented his case. They overruled Norman O. Houston's decision, and Ivan became president and chief executive officer of Golden State. Norman B. Houston was equally upset by this turn of events, and six months later he resigned from Golden State to become deputy secretary of the Department of Health, Education and Welfare in the Nixon administration. He remained there until the Carter administration took over in 1977, when he became a consultant in Washington and Rhode Island.

Ivan Houston faced a number of difficult challenges during his tenure as head of Golden State, and he made a reputation as an innovative and aggressive leader. Throughout most of the 1970s, Houston and Golden State still depended strongly on its "bread and butter" trade—selling small "funeral insurance" policies to poor blacks—policies in which they had to employ an army of agents to make monthly calls to collect the premiums on policies that had a face value of only from $500 to $1,000. Golden State was one of the last of the large black companies to continue this practice. Houston, however, by using his actuarial skills, had managed to make the insuring of poorer blacks a more profitable operation. He determined that the lower life expectancy of blacks compared to whites was not genetic but environmental and that, further, blacks who had been born in California, regardless of their economic situation, had a greater life expectancy than migrant blacks. They had, in fact, a life expectancy slightly higher than whites. Houston focused upon these facts in selling policies, and the bulk of its 300,000 customers in the early 1970s were in this category. "Other companies won't let their agents even drive into the areas we sell in," said Houston, "much less let them walk around collecting money. Yet most of our customers don't have checking accounts. And they can't afford to pay quarterly or semi-annual premiums."

Even then, however, Houston realized that in order to survive Golden State had to expand into servicing a newer, and wealthier, clientele. There was an attempt to expand into the Mexican barrios (which duplicated an effort made in the 1920s), but it was not very successful. The company also began to target upper-middle-class blacks by using celebrity advertising with sports stars such as Hershel Walker. One of his most important decisions was to bring Golden State into the group insurance field. As pressures developed for large corporations to spread their group insurance policies out to include smaller, minority-owned firms, Golden State, along with North Carolina Mutual, was among the most active and successful of the black firms that pursued this business. By the late 1980s, Golden State carried more than $4 billion worth of group insurance for large, white-owned companies such as Ford Motor, Chrysler, General Motors, American Airlines, Rockwell International, AT&T, and Pacific Bell. The first white firm Houston was able to convince to place some of its group insurance with Golden State was Crown Zellerbach, which was followed shortly afterward by Pacific Bell. There was, however, a certain irony in this. As a mutual company, Golden State is owned by its policyholders, so as both Golden State and North Carolina Mutual successfully pursued the group insurance business of white firms, it became a real question as to whether these insurance companies could be considered black-owned any longer. They continued to be managed and staffed by blacks, but the ultimate ownership now lay outside the black community.

Golden State also did a good deal during the 1970s and 1980s in providing mortgage money to blacks who were moving into new areas of the city. Often, white-owned financial institutions would not provide these mortgages. As Ivan Houston commented, "I think our company was sort of in the vanguard of helping to open up housing in Los Angeles by providing mortgage loan money for blacks who wanted to move into certain areas, especially the west side.''

The mid–1980s were a critical period for Golden State and Ivan Houston. The amount of new insurance the company issued in 1982—$98.2 million—was the lowest in two years, and its premium income also dropped slightly. This was at a time when premium income for the industry generally was rising. The problem, according to Houston and other industry analysts, was that the recession had hit Golden State's low-income policyholders very hard. ''We got clobbered last year,'' said Houston, but felt that ''we are stronger now'' for having survived the recession. It was clear to him, however, that the firm would have to pursue some new approaches. It planned to expand into the real estate and service industries and purchased Winston Mutual Life in Winston-Salem, North Carolina, which brought it into a lucrative new market area. By the end of the 1980s it was selling insurance in twenty-two states, with offices in Hawaii, Florida, Arizona, and Minnesota, as well as California. The company also completely computerized all of its sales and bookkeeping operations by 1988 and continued its push for greater sales to middle and upper income blacks. Golden State also began selling insurance in Liberia, its first venture outside the United States.

Houston put Golden State on an austerity campaign, designed to reduce operating expenses. In 1988 the number of employees (not agents) was drastically reduced from 925 to 410, partially as a result of Houston's computerization program. They were still trying to focus on upper income blacks as their major market, since those policies required less servicing than those for poorer blacks. That goal, however, remained somewhat elusive: ''We haven't completely worked it all out, yet,'' Houston said, ''but we're trying our best to make middle-income blacks our major market.'' The firm launched an aggressive fourfold marketing campaign in the late 1980s to accomplish this. The effort included offering a greater array of insurance policies, upgrading the company's sales force, opening two additional California offices, and increasing visibility through advertising.

In addition to these ventures, Houston continued and further institutionalized Golden State's longtime commitment to the black community. Houston's most innovative move in that direction was to set up the Golden State Minority Foundation, which was designed to enable disadvantaged minority students to pursue careers in business administration and life insurance. Ivan Abbott Houston, his oldest son, served as executive director of the foundation, which gave out some 1,200 scholarships and grants worth $1.25 million during its first fifteen years. This community involvement by Golden State reflected Ivan J. Houston's own dedication.

He served on the board of directors of the Los Angeles Area Chamber of Commerce and the Los Angeles Urban League. He was also a founding member of Black Agenda, Inc., and a life member of the NAACP. Houston served as board chairman of the local chapter of the National Conference of Christians and Jews and on the board of trustees of the National Urban League from 1980 to 1986. He was also on the boards of the United Way and the YMCA. In 1984 Ivan Houston won the Brotherhood Award from the National Conference of Christians and Jews.

Like his father, Ivan Houston was relatively oblivious to racial discrimination. Although both he and his wife, the former Philippa Jones, remembered segregation and discrimination when they were growing up in Los Angeles and although Houston had experienced even more of it when he served in the army, it never had much impact on him. Although, "I could see how unfair it was," it was as if he were above it all. Like his father, he led a rather charmed life in this regard. "I always felt I could do anything," he said. "I never had any sort of inferiority complex, and I was always for integration." Despite this somewhat Pollyannaish attitude, Houston was able to respond relatively well to the increasingly militant demands of blacks in the 1970s and 1980s. Discussing the protests and riots of the period, he said, "[Y]ou knew some historic things were going on and that life was never going to be the same." And so, in a series of low-keyed decisions, he continued to push for civil rights and to use the offices of Golden State as a place where Dr. Martin Luther King, Jr., and other black leaders could meet to plan their strategy.

Houston saw a continuity in all of this: "The people who started the company were always active in civic affairs and I'm always out nowadays telling people to get involved—not only because the community needs volunteers, but also because it's another way of making the company known. It's the same as in the beginning; one thing feeds on the other." By 1992 Golden State remained the third-largest black insurance company, behind only North Carolina Mutual and Atlanta Life. With assets of over $100 million, and nearly $6 billion of insurance in force, it remained a powerful force in the black community of Los Angeles, one that would have to respond to yet another crisis, the devastation of the South Central community in the riots following the Rodney King decision in May 1992. It is not clear how well Houston and other traditional black leaders will be able to deal with this crisis. They may be, as Manning Marable has said, "several steps behind the times." Only time will tell.

Sources

The most important sources for information on these four men and on their company are the records of Golden State Insurance held at the University of California, Los Angeles. There is a wealth of material there, ranging from company histories, clipping files, correspondence between executives of the firm, cash books, and some other company materials. There is also a diary of Norman Houston and memoirs of William Nickerson. Beyond that, items on the four men and their company are a bit scarce. For William Nickerson, see *Los Angeles Sentinel*, April 14, 1983; *Chicago Defender*, August 27, 1949; *Negro Who's Who in California* (1948); and *Oakland Herald*, November 16, 1945, for a short obituary. There are obituaries of Norman O. Houston in the *Los Angeles Sentinel*, October 22, 1981, and *Los Angeles Times*, October 16, 1981. Information can also be obtained from the *Los Angeles Sentinel*, January 29, 1948, and April 10, 1975; *Negro Who's Who in California* (1948); *Oakland Tribune*, August 19, 1949; *Chilton's*

Spectator, February 1970; *News Guardian*, December 23, 1937; *Los Angeles Herald-Examiner*, May 10, 1975; and *Who's Who in Colored America* (1950). The best source for Ivan Houston is in the Oral History Collection at UCLA in an item entitled "Black Leadership in Los Angeles," in which Houston is interviewed by Ranford B. Hopkins in 1989. See also *Los Angeles Sentinel*, May 29, 1975, January 27, 1977, September 28, 1978, July 21, 1983, June 12, 1986, and June 14–20, 1990; and *Los Angeles Times*, December 5, 1976, and September 10, 1984. The information on George Beavers is least extensive, but see "In Quest of Full Citizenship," an interview in 1985 held in the Oral History Collection at UCLA. See also an obituary in the *Los Angeles Times*, October 14, 1989; see also *Los Angeles Sentinel*, September 18, 1980; *Christian Science Monitor*, November 9, 1954; and *Negro Who's Who in California* (1948).

Some additional information on Golden State Mutual can be obtained from *Black Enterprise*, June 1989, June 1990, and June 1992; *Los Angeles Sentinel*, July 25, 1985; *Los Angeles Times*, September 24, 1984; David Lavender, *Los Angeles 200* (Tulsa, Okla., 1980); "Ownership Vested in the People It Serves," *The Messenger* (a company publication), July/August, 1950; and *Pittsburgh Courier*, May 15, 1948.

Binga, Jesse (April 10, 1865–June 13, 1950). African-American banker and realtor: Binga State Bank. Jesse Binga, tall, handsome, and distinguished, represented for many African-Americans in Chicago during the 1920s the great hopes and dreams they had for the future of black business and for the "black metropolis" on the South Side of Chicago itself. The failure of Binga's bank in the early months of the Great Depression; his conviction and imprisonment for embezzlement; and his later years spent as an elderly, stooped, white-haired janitor recalled for many the great failure of those grandiose dreams and the cruel toll that racism and discrimination took of even the most promising blacks.

Born in Detroit, Michigan, the son of Robert Binga, Jr., and Adelphia Powers, Binga's father was a native of Ontario, Canada, who owned a barbershop in Detroit. His mother, a native of Rochester, New York, who reportedly had the business acumen in the family, developed an active interest in real estate and conducted a trade in the interstate shipment of whitefish and sweet potatoes. Both of Binga's parents came to Detroit in the 1840s. Young Jesse assisted his mother in collecting rents and doing repairs on tenement properties, in what was known as "Binga row" in Detroit. The tenants were mostly black migrants on the way to and from Canada during these years.

Jesse Binga dropped out of high school after two years to learn barbering from his father, and he also worked in the office of Thomas Crispus, a young black attorney. Despite a seemingly promising business career in Detroit, in 1885 Jesse Binga embarked upon a seven-year itinerant journey as a barber and entrepreneur. He worked as a barber in Kansas City, Missouri; St. Paul, Minnesota; and Missoula, Montana. In Tacoma and Seattle, Washington, he opened his own shop, but each venture lasted only a short time. Binga then went to Oakland, California, where he worked as a barber and as a porter for the Southern Pacific Railroad. Then, while in Ogden and Pocatella, Utah, he made a prudent investment in land on a former Indian reservation. Thus, by the time Binga arrived in Chicago in 1893, he had already tasted some of the fruits of his business endeavors.

Despite the success of his Utah investments (which might have just helped him get out of debt), Binga started in Chicago with only about $10. It is not clear just what he did during his first few years there; some reports had him running a fruit stand and others had him working as a wagon driver peddling coal, but all agree that between 1896 and 1898 he entered the real estate business there. Binga opened his first real estate office in a former apartment at 3331 South State Street, with his office equipment consisting of a desk, three chairs, and a "worn-out stove resting on two legs and a brick."

Binga's rise to prominence as a businessman for over twenty years before the collapse of his empire in the Depression illustrates a common pattern for black businesses. He began by buying run-down properties in Chicago's existing black ghetto, and he improved them by doing the necessary repairs and maintenance himself. As he noted, "Many a night I worked all night on boilers and plumbing, and wiping joints, and mending stairs, and hanging paper. I knew materials and I knew when work was right." When the properties were renovated, Binga then leased them at increased rents to African-American migrants from the South who were beginning to pour into the city. By 1905 Binga's former shoestring enterprise had become one of the major businesses in the black community.

Binga's success, however, did not come from just improving properties in the existing black ghetto. The great need of African-Americans in Chicago at this time was for more housing, and this could come only from what were then all-white areas. Binga prospered by seeking rental properties throughout the South Side, regardless of racial restrictions. Binga's first venture of this kind came in 1905, when he took a long-term lease on the seven-story Bates apartment building located at 3637 South State Street as headquarters for his real estate office. At the time, the tenants were all white, but they left as soon as Binga took control. This opened that building and the surrounding area to blacks, who were generally willing to pay higher rents for the same accommodations as the former white tenants. Despite hostile reactions against this practice of "block busting" to bring black tenants into formerly white areas, it is clear that Binga and others were fulfilling a need not being met by existing shelter patterns. The African-American population of Chicago was growing rapidly after 1900, and it simply could not be contained within the traditional black ghetto.

During the next fifteen years, Binga purchased the homes of more affluent whites who were fleeing the encroaching black population and divided those homes into smaller units for single black men and families, which allowed him to serve an important social need while at the same time turn a nice profit. The high rents he charged, though, and the profits he made did generate some antagonism to Binga in the African-American community. Nonetheless, by 1907 Binga was one of the most prosperous African-American realtors in the city.

A year later, he opened the Binga Bank in a newly constructed office building next door, at 3633 South State. A private bank, it was the first one owned, managed, directed, or controlled by blacks in the North. As Binga's bank and fortune grew, the area became the center of black business development in South Side Chicago, and Anthony Overton* located his Hygienic Manufacturing Company on one side and his *Chicago Bee* offices on the other side of Binga's bank. The two men became closely allied in business, politics, and social matters. According to Carl Osthaus, the corner of State Street where Binga's bank was located in the 1920s was rivaled only by Harlem's 135th and Lenox as a commercial center for black Americans.

Binga's small bank and his own fortune grew impressively during the years of massive black migration around World War I, but white resentment in Chicago grew apace. Although Binga had never posed as a ''race leader'' and had never taken a stand on controversial public issues of the time, he was nonetheless recognized by many whites as a causal factor in the expansion of blacks into formerly white neighborhoods. At several points during the years from 1917 to 1921, his properties were vandalized, and during the so-called Red Summer of 1919, Binga's real estate office and home were bombed several times. Binga stood up to the white bombers, hired guards, and carried a gun himself, thereby attaining the status of a martyr and militant for the black cause among other African-Americans—a status he had not previously enjoyed. Despite the opposition of whites, however, Binga's holdings grew so much that at one point in the mid–1920s he owned 1,200 leaseholds on flats and residences; by 1926 the Chicago *Broad Ax* reported that he owned more frontage on State Street south of 12th Street than any other person.

All of this made possible Binga's next step, the opening of Binga State Bank in January 1921. Viewed as a ''History-Making Event among Colored People Residing in Chicago'' by the *Broad Ax*, the bank's board of directors was composed of the leading African-American businessmen in the community. Binga State Bank itself set out its goals in an advertisement in the *Chicago Defender* (April 20, 1920):

People are spending money, people are saving money, people are investing money as never before in the history of the Race. We see them standing in line supporting banks, real estate brokers, doctors, dentists . . . helping those who are attempting to blast their future as well as those who are giving them a square deal. The Binga State Bank arrives at a time when it can be of unlimited assistance to such a public in such times.

By 1924 Binga was able to increase the capital and surplus of Binga State Bank to $235,000, and he also opened the Binga Safe Deposit Company and organized a black insurance firm. At the same time, Binga in many ways became a hero and model for young people in the community. He responded to that new status by publishing a small pamphlet entitled ''Certain Sayings of Jesse Binga,'' filled with Benjamin Franklinesque homilies of hard work, seriousness, and success.

Despite the fact that Binga had gotten a state charter for his bank, he continued as the largest shareholder, and he ran it as if it were a private, solely owned fiefdom. This would engender much criticism later on. So, too, did his marriage in 1912 to Eudora Johnson, the daughter of John "Mushmouth" Johnson, the gambling kingpin of Chicago's South Side. According to Gerri Major, Miss Johnson, neither young nor attractive, looked "like a caricature of a 'big, fat, black, mammy,' " and many were convinced that the handsome Binga married her for her money. Whatever the truth of that accusation, it is true that, when the senior Johnson died in 1907, his daughter inherited an estate worth $200,000. This made her quite a "catch," and it did much to enhance Binga's economic prospects during these years.

Although Binga's marriage caused some critical comment over the years, it is also true that it brought the ambitious young migrant into one of the oldest and wealthiest first families of the city's African-American community. Their marriage was the most fashionable of the year in 1912, and the couple became particularly noted for their annual Christmas parties and their philanthropic endeavors, especially to the Old Folks Home and the YMCA. Binga himself was also involved in a number of important civic organizations, the most significant of which was the Associated Business Club, which was affiliated with the National Negro Business League. Preaching Booker T. Washington's* gospel of self-help and independence, the ABC actively worked to provide business opportunities for other South Side blacks.

Binga's accomplishments brought him both praise and censure from the city's black and white communities. He was lauded for his business acumen and for his philanthropy, but he was also criticized for rent gouging and for his hard-driving personality. Many years after his death, the prominent African-American leader Earl Dickerson* still remembered Binga as "a mean son-of-a-bitch." He was also often perceived as an arrogant man, for example, in a statement he made to the *Chicago Daily News* in 1916: "I'm an Irishman. You won't find any other colored people like me. . . . Few of them, aside from professional men, have got beyond the stage of 'small business.' " Nonetheless, it is clear that Binga played a major role in developing Chicago's black community during the 1920s. That community, along with Binga's own empire, came crashing down with the economic collapse of 1929.

The pinnacle of Binga's success came in 1929, when he constructed the Binga Arcade, a five-story building and ballroom on the corner of 35th and State streets. This area had once been the center of black business in Chicago, but by 1929 it had deteriorated badly. Binga who hoped his building would revitalize the area, expressed his feelings in an interview on July 21, 1928 with the *Chicago Defender*:

Most people don't realize it, but practically all our business institutions and our substantial investments are located on or near 35th Street. . . . That new investments and new enterprises are being opened by our people in this neighborhood means that 35th Street will always be Colored Chicago's most important commercial center.

Alas, this was not to be. Instead, Binga's whole empire soon came unraveled, and the black commercial center of Chicago suffered along with it. In 1930 Binga State Bank collapsed, destroying Jesse Binga's fortune of $400,000 and taking with it the savings of thousands of black Chicagoans. Although the Depression was partly to blame for this, Binga himself had also made a number of unwise or illegal financial decisions. The state banking examiner concluded that the institution had been conducted in an illegal and unsafe manner; Binga himself was convicted of embezzlement in 1933 and sentenced to ten years in prison.

The failure of Binga Bank and the subsequent imprisonment of Binga occasioned some bitter resentment in the African-American community. W.E.B. Du Bois, writing in *Crisis* in December 1930 laid the blame squarely on the white banking community: "[I]t was not necessary for the Binga Bank to fail. . . . It was necessary that the banking world, which means the white banks of Chicago, should stand behind Mr. Binga." Other analysts have not been prone to accept Du Bois's judgment without qualification. F. Cyril James, in his broad study of the growth of Chicago banks, saw the failure of the Binga Bank as just one of many in a process by which weaker banks were either merged with stronger ones, or winnowed out of the system. Abram Harris, in his study of the bank, also countered Du Bois's claim, pointing out that by 1930 the bank's securities had already been pledged with white banks for money previously borrowed and that Binga had indeed engaged in a number of fraudulent practices. Carl Osthaus echoes this argument. Yet, a couple of points should be remembered. The Binga Bank was the largest and most important black bank in Chicago—it was not just another small bank that failed. True, the failure of whites in private institutions or government to come to its aid did not single it out negatively from many other small and weak white banks. But the Binga Bank was different, and the failure to recognize this, as Du Bois intimates, may indeed constitute a form of semiconscious racism on the part of whites.

Despite Binga's mixed reputation, and despite the fact that many lost their savings when his bank collapsed, leading citizens in the African-American community organized a petition drive to secure his release. After several attempts, it was finally successful, and Binga was freed from prison after three years. Spending the rest of his life as a custodian at St. Anselm's Catholic Church (Binga had converted to Catholicism earlier in his life), he died after a fall at his nephew's home in Chicago in 1950. By 1992 there were few tangible references to Jesse Binga's achievements in Chicago. His first office, his bank building, and the Binga Arcade have all been demolished. The corner of 35th and State is now occupied by the campus of the Illinois Institute of Technology. Other parts of the once thriving business area are simply crumbling relics of a bygone age in a horribly depressed black ghetto. Binga was a tragic meteor in Chicago's black community, one whose fortunes so nearly reflected the complex web of hope and despair that characterized the city's black business community during these years.

Sources
None of Binga's personal papers, nor those of his various enterprises, are extant. Nor does one find his letters or other information in the files of other prominent black Chicagoans. The Peabody Collection at Hampton University (available on microfilm) has clippings on Binga from a number of published sources. Nearly all sources state that Jesse Binga was the son of William W. Binga. These are all based on an article published in *Crisis* in December 1927 (329, 350–52) by Inez V. Cantley, which may not be reliable. A family member, Anthony J. Binga, Sr., after conducting research in the census records from the Courts of Records of the Dominion of Canada, claims that Jesse Binga's father was Robert Binga, Jr. *Who's Who in Colored America* (1928–1929), also names Robert Binga as his father. Consulting United States census records, Anthony Binga asserts that Binga was married twice, not once, and that he had two children by his first marriage. See Anthony J. Binga, Sr., "Jesse Binga: Founder and President, Binga State Bank, Chicago, Illinois," *Journal of the Afro-American History and Geneology Society* 2, 4 (1981), 146–52. David Katzman, in *Dictionary of American Biography* (1946–1950), supplement 4, 72–74, has a biography of Binga, as do Carl Osthaus, in the *Dictionary of Negro Biography* (1982), 43, and John N. Ingham, in *Biographical Dictionary of American Business Leaders* (1983), I, 73–74. There is a short obituary of Binga in the Chicago *Herald American*, June 14, 1950, and a longer one in the *Chicago Defender*, June 24, 1950.

See also Carl Osthaus, "The Rise and Fall of Jesse Binga, Black Banker," *Journal of Negro History*, January 1973, 39–60; Abram L. Harris, *The Negro As Capitalist* (1936), 153–64; Gerri Major, *Black Society* (1976), 304–6; F. Cyril James, *The Growth of Chicago Banks* (1938), vol. 2, 959, 994. Many articles on Binga were published in the Chicago *Defender* and the *Broad Ax* during the period of his influence. See especially the *Defender*, February 24, 1912, December 16, 1916, April 20, 1920, July 21, 1928, October 11, 1930, February 14 and 24, March 7 and 14, April 18, May 16, and November 7, 1931, and March 5, 1938; and the *Broad Ax*, September 21, 1907, and October 23, 1926. See also *The Freeman* (Indianapolis), April 17, 1909; the *Chicago Daily News*, December 14, 1916; *Commercial and Financial Chronicle*, CXXXI (August 2, 1930), 735; *The Crisis*, March and May 1925, December 1, 1927, and September 1932, 289; and *Opportunity*, September 1930, 264. Later brief treatments include *Ebony* 29 (February 1974), 66–70+; and *Sepia*, October 1972, 18.

Blayton, Jesse B. (December 6, 1897–   ), **Lorimer D. Milton** (September 8, 1898–February 8, 1986), and **Clayton R. Yates** (?). Bankers and businessmen, certified public accountant: Citizens Trust Bank, Mutual Federal Savings and Loan, Yates and Milton Drugstores, Top Hat Club, radio station WERD, Brown Boy Bottling Company, J. B. Blayton and Company, and Blamiya, Inc. Jesse Blayton, L. D. Milton, and Clayton Yates were all outsiders to the Atlanta establishment when they arrived there in the 1920s. They nonetheless moved quickly into the corridors of power of the African-American community and came to control the largest constellation of black businesses in the city from the 1930s to the 1970s. And, by that time, they were widely regarded as the oldest of the "old guard" among the African-American elite in the city. That was one of the defining characteristics of Atlanta in the twentieth century. Unlike most other older southern cities, it has remained remarkably open to black men and women of talent and ambition. Another aspect of these three men also illustrates an important element of Atlanta's appeal to outsiders—the importance of education and specialized skills. Blayton and Milton particularly fueled their rise in Atlanta's black community with their specialized education and skills and their continuing connections to the Atlanta University complex—the training ground for future generations of the black elite.

Lorimer Milton was born in Prince William County, Virginia, the son of an ex-slave. He grew up in Washington, D.C., and was the second black to graduate from the prestigious Ivy League school, Brown University in Providence, Rhode Island, where he earned both his bachelor's and master's degrees. Milton was lured to Atlanta by John Hope in 1920 to teach at Morehouse College. Hope was the first black graduate of Brown, and while president of Morehouse, from 1906 to 1929, and then as head of the Atlanta University system, he kept his eye out for promising Brown graduates. Milton was the first of those. B. R. Brazeal, who became dean at Morehouse, took courses from Milton during his early years there. He recalled the experience many years later, "I took 'Introduction to Economics and Banking' under him. And when I got to Columbia I found out that what I had been taught held up well. And I didn't have any unusual difficulties at Columbia working for a masters degree and subsequently a Ph.D."

Not long after Milton arrived in Atlanta, though, he also became associated with Citizens Trust, part of the vast black business empire then being constructed by the dynamic but erratic Heman E. Perry.* Milton recounts being lured into the bank's fold:

The bank was opening, Citizens Trust, and I had acquired three shares of that stock, and I went down to talk with the officers about getting me a job. At first they said, "No, you don't know anything about banking." I said, "Well, you don't know anything about me." They evidently got in touch with Brown University and then they got in touch with me and told me to come down, they wanted to give me a job.

This offer, of course, created a problem for Morehouse College and John Hope, who was in the process of trying to create a premier black educational institution. "Dr. John Hope begged me to change my mind and come back to Morehouse," Milton recalled. "I subsequently did, [and I] accepted the job in the bank. They set the time of my classes at 7:30 in the morning. But I did that, [then] went to work in the bank in the accounting department. And I learned how to run the accounting department."

This dual role for Milton, from 1921 to 1923, was a taxing but exhilarating experience for him. "I was at Morehouse and I was at Citizen's Trust Company, and I was head over heels in both places. There were no [black] majors in economics except for majors that we began to turn out at Morehouse College after my third year on the faculty. They kept me on that faculty for eighteen or twenty years." But the situation at Citizens Trust was more shaky. Perry's business empire began crumbling in 1923, and in that year Milton left the bank. He did not, however, completely sever his connection with the Perry enterprises.

In that year, he and Clifton Yates bought an interest in the Gate City Drug Store, which had been part of Perry's Service Pharmacy chain. Milton and Yates had little capital of their own, but they "agreed to get together and buy the drugstore from [Perry], with the assistance of the wholesale druggists to whom the drugstore owed money." It was a difficult situation for the two young men, as Milton later recounted:

We had to go through the wholesale druggists who had loans on that property, and make arrangements with them to take charge of those loans. And they gave us a tight package, requiring us [to] pay them everything we owed them in about a year and three months. But instead of that, I paid them out in nine months. Now, when a white man finds out a Negro jumps up and pays him a debt far in advance of that debt, they say, "Umm-hmmm. I've got myself a good nigger here." And they went on then to even loan us money to pay out the other creditors that we had.

Yates and Milton Drugstore became a smashing success. The two partners made the store on Auburn Avenue a clean and attractive place, and they made sure that blacks in the area could get every product and service available in white-owned drugstores. "People knew that they could get what they wanted at Yates and Milton," L. D. Milton said, "when it could not be found anywhere else." Phoebe Hart, who lived in the Auburn Avenue neighborhood, later remembered the critical role the drugstore played in the daily life of the community. "There are plenty of people," she related, "who have never been to pay a light bill or a water bill anywhere other than Yates and Milton drugstore. The bills were paid there. The post office and your Christmas shopping and all—you see, they brought as much business down there that kept you out of having to take the slurs and all of downtown."

Milton and Yates built on that success: "And we developed crowds of people coming to that drugstore," said Milton. "On Sunday, my Lord, you couldn't get in the drugstore for the people piled in there. After one year, we were opening our second drugstore, on the west side. In subsequent years we opened three more stores until we had five drugstores in the city of Atlanta. No white chain in this town had as many drugstores as we had."

As important as Milton was to the success of the drugstore, he had his fingers in too many other pies then and later to play the dominant role in its success. This part was taken by Clayton Yates. Yates, who graduated from Morehouse College, was a trustee there and at Atlanta University. In 1964 he was named to the Fulton-Dekalb County Hospital Authority, the first black to be appointed to that board, was vice president of Southeastern Fire Insurance and Mutual Federal Savings and Loan, and president of South View Cemetery Association. Unfortunately, there was no information readily available on Yates, who tended to keep a much lower profile than his two associates. The most significant aspect to remember about him, though, is that it was he more than anyone else who made such a smashing success of the Yates and Milton drugstore chain.

Milton was able to devote even less time to the drugstores after 1927, since in that year he rejoined Citizens Trust as a cashier. According to his own account, he had been "thrown out" in 1923 for "interfering with the policies of the board," most likely the dangerous expansionist tendencies of Heman Perry. In any event, by 1927 the Perry empire was in ruins, and Citizens Trust was still struggling to survive. It had led a rather charmed life in the four years Milton had been gone. As one observer commented at the time, "This institution must have a soul, for it could not have withstood the steady withdrawals of deposits and common street conversation to the effect that 'the Bank is going to close.' " Yet, it did not, as every demand was met. In September 1927, however, Citizens Trust was reorganized when a 100 percent stock assessment was levied and collected. This action eliminated a number of old stockholders who had not paid the assessments and also brought the National Benefit Life Insurance Company of Washington, D.C., to the forefront. National Benefit was the owner of Citizens Union Investment Company, which was the principal stockholder of Citizens Trust, owning 911 of the 1,000 outstanding shares. When Citizens Union could not make the levy, National Benefit emerged as the principal stockholder.

It was obvious to the new owners that wholesale changes in the management of Citizens Trust were in order. As a result, they called for the resignations of the chairman of the board, the vice president, and the cashier. They then consulted with John Hope as to the best person to entrust with resurrecting the bank. Hope asked Milton to take the job of cashier, which would in effect be the chief executive officer of the bank, since the president was merely a figurehead. Milton had a daunting task ahead of him. Citizens Trust, which had been founded with $250,000 in capital, and in 1921 had $230,000 in cash reserves out of total bank assets of $657,000, had slipped badly during the 1920s. Capital stock had dropped to $120,000, while cash reserves were just $40,000, and total bank assets stood at $323,000. It was merely a shell of its former self.

Milton set to work reorganizing, systematizing, and streamlining the bank. He had luckily made great improvements in the overall financial condition of the bank when the Great Crash of 1929 and subsequent severe depression set in. During the four years between the crash and the banking crisis of 1933, Milton somehow kept the bank afloat. The lowest point came in 1933, when total bank assets dropped to $191,000, the lowest in the bank's seventy-year history, but Milton amazingly kept losses to just $3,000. While the banking system in America almost totally collapsed, Milton kept Citizens Trust afloat. There were about 26,000 state and national banks in the United States in June 1929, and just over half that number (15,600) in June 1933. Milton kept the confidence of his depositors during this period, and there was no run on Citizens Trust.

After the crisis of 1933, Milton undertook a thorough and patient rebuilding job during the subsequent four years. In 1935, Citizens Trust became a member of the Federal Deposit Insurance Corporation, providing greater protection for the bank's depositors. By June of that year, Citizens Trust was finally showing a profit on its operations. A new opportunity presented itself. National Benefit Life Insurance, the bank's majority stockholder, had gone into receivership. Milton, in concert with his partners Clayton R. Yates and Jesse A. Blayton, formed a coalition to take a controlling interest in Citizens Trust. Since the three relatively young men did not have sufficient capital to undertake this venture, they were financed in the effort by Rybun Clay, president of the white-owned Fulton National Bank.

Jesse Blayton, Milton's and Yates's partner in the Citizens Trust venture, was born in Garden, Oklahoma, the son of Lester B. Blayton and Mattie E. Carter. He was educated at Langston University in Oklahoma from 1915 to 1918. After serving in the 92nd Division of the U.S. Army during World War I, Blayton came to Atlanta, where he became an auditor with Heman Perry's Standard Life Insurance Company from 1922 to 1929. Blayton also became, like Milton, a teacher at Morehouse College, serving as professor of accounting there, from 1925 to 1930, and as Carnegie Professor of business administration from 1930 until his retirement. Blayton became the first black certified public accountant in Georgia in 1928, and in that year he formed his own accounting firm, J. B. Blayton and Company, which he ran throughout his life. Also, in October 1925, he helped organize the Mutual Federal Savings and Loan Association. Blayton and fourteen other black investors (not including Yates or Milton) put in $100 each to found the savings and loan.

Mutual Federal became, like Citizens Trust, a bulwark on the city's black financial scene. Starting with just $1,500 in assets in 1925, it had grown to over $10 million by 1959. Mutual Federal never missed paying a dividend, even during the difficult days of the 1930s. Always closely associated with Citizens Trust, especially after 1935, its office was located directly across the street. Like Citizens Trust, Mutual Federal was an important element in the financing of black homes during the next sixty-five years. By 1990 Mutual Federal was the ninth largest black savings and loan in the United States, with assets of nearly $37 million, 3,000 depositors, and a staff of seventeen. About two-thirds of its loans continued to be residential. Perhaps most significant, it had managed to weather the horrific savings and loan debacle of the late 1980s, when countless black and white savings and loan institutions went under. From 1972 to 1991, according to *Black Enterprise* magazine, the number of black thrifts declined from forty-four to eighteen. The carnage among white savings and loans was even higher.

Meanwhile, the three men took the reins of Citizens Trust. Milton remained cashier until 1938, when he moved up to president of the concern, serving in that capacity until his retirement in 1971. Blayton became vice president, and when Milton moved up to the presidency, Blayton also took on the duties of cashier. Yates, who spent most of his time as chief operating officer of the rapidly expanding Yates and Milton drugstore chain, served as chairman of the board. Their first significant move after taking over in 1936 was to join the Federal Reserve, becoming the first black bank in the country to do so.

The key to Citizens Trust's growth during the 1930s and after, according to Reverend William Holmes Borders, pastor of Wheat Street Baptist Church, lay in the ties of the three men to various churches in the black community. Milton was a member and trustee of the elite First Congregational Church; Yates was chairman of the board of that same church; and Blayton was a Baptist. According to Borders, "The preachers made Citizens Trust Bank. They put in deposits that Monday morning. Around 11:00 o'clock the lobby would be full of nothing but preachers. And the people, seeing their preacher deposit God's money from the churches in Citizens Trust, put their money into it and helped put it over, in a great way."

This support helped Citizens Trust become one of the leading black banks in the country by the 1940s. By 1947, for example, it had total assets of over $4 million, trailing only the Industrial Bank of Washington and Mechanics and Farmers Bank of Durham, North Carolina, among the black banks. By 1969 Citizens Trust's assets had reached $20 million. In this position, according to Milton, the role of Citizens Trust had been to set up "pilot institutions." As he related, "We have been economic interpreters of Negro life addressing a white financial community. We have simply given the needed proofs. The institution can say 'It is a lie to say that a Negro is a bad mortgage risk.' "

Although as a state bank Citizens Trust faced stringent rules on mortgage lending, it nonetheless was able to participate increasingly in financing homes for blacks in Atlanta after 1940. The three largest black financial institutions in Atlanta by the mid–1950s were Citizens Trust, Mutual Federal Savings and Loan, and Atlanta Life Insurance Company, with combined assets in 1955 of $57.3 million, of which nearly $14 million or 24.4 percent were invested in first mortgage loans. Of this amount, Citizens Trust and Mutual Federal had $10.75 million, the bulk of that amount ($9.2) from Mutual Federal, since Citizens Trust did not set up a mortgage department until 1952. Citizens Trust played a particularly crucial role in the conversion of the desirable Hunter Hills section.

This was an area out Hunter Road (now Martin Luther King, Jr., Drive), which in the 1930s was "in the country," and generally peopled by whites. In 1940, the Federal Housing Administration agreed to work with Citizens Trust to develop this area for middle-income blacks. Eighty or ninety homes were to be developed there, with the Works Progress Administration cutting roads through the area. This became a particularly prestigious locale, with many homes of the black elite there. One of the first to move out there was Clayton R. Yates and his family, followed closely by Jesse Blayton. One early resident recalled, "The C. R. Yates moved out here years before anyone else, and at one time the people in the little house across the street worked for the Yates." Another longtime resident commented, "That's the Blayton home. Oh honey, this was considered it." The development of this area, however, was not accomplished without friction, as many whites felt blacks were coming too close to desirable white areas. One early resident recalled Ku Klux Klan crosses being burned on the lawns.

After World War II came the development of the Collier Heights section, which passed from white to black occupancy. Next came Crestwood Forest, developed by a number of executives of Citizens Trust and other prominent blacks, which was followed by home construction in the Bankhead area and a whole series of other all-black developments financed by the bank through the early 1960s. Milton had also gotten involved in public housing developments during the 1930s. As a trustee of the University Homes Board, he shared responsibility for building the nation's first public housing project for blacks. "It was," as a landscape architect for the project said, "a totally different concept. It was a different concept of the way people could live. It was clearly an introduction of all that was to come. It was really a very exciting thing for the city to have the first and watch it grow."

The University Homes project enlisted the support of John Hope, who, as Clarence Bacote observed, "had been interested in improving the area around [Atlanta University]. He could see this would be an asset to the university . . . and it would eliminate that terrible residential area which was known as Beaver Slide." But Milton got involved in a controversy over the fact that white land owners were paid more for their slum property than were their black counterparts. "That land [owned by blacks] was not as valuable as the land that was purchased for the white project," explained Milton. "University Homes was built in an area that was considered to be mainly Negro. And white land cost more than Negro land." The controversy blew over, but it was indicative of the conservative, fiscally rigid leadership that Milton often brought to the black community over the years. It was one of the reasons he encountered increasing resistance to his influence.

Besides mortgage financing, Citizens Trust played a critical role in financing the development of black businesses. As Milton said, "The bank was a powerful negotiator for Negro businesses in the city of Atlanta, and helped these businesses to grow and to get started and expand. Oh, there were gracious plenty of businesses started." Citizens Trust helped the first black in Atlanta get a service station franchise, the first black liquor store owner to get his bond, the first black general insurance agent to get connected with a major insurance company. Plus, they assisted a myriad of small black businesses to get under way—barber and beauty shops, sandwich shops, grocery stores, and dry cleaning establishments.

This aid to black businesses began very early and involved a number of the most important entities in Atlanta. The *Atlanta Daily World*, for example, had its genesis with L. D. Milton and Citizens Trust. "I started that paper," Milton recalled. "W. A. [Scott]* went to Morehouse College while I was teaching at Morehouse, and that's how he got to know me. I had a printing company which I took from Perry and his crowd when they failed in running a printing company successfully. And when Scott knew that I owned that printing shop, that is, my bank owned that printing shop, then he came to me to let him use it. And so I let him use the damn equipment. I didn't charge him a damn thing for it."

Another major black business enterprise financed by Milton and Citizens Trust was the large construction firm of Herman Russell.*

The classic example of a business loan made by Citizens Trust to a black was one given to the Paschal brothers. Robert and James Paschal were born in the rural area around Thomson, Georgia, the sons of a man who was a waiter and bellboy at the Knox Hotel there. When they were still quite young, the two boys began filling in for their father, and in the late 1930s James opened a small sandwich and short-order shop that became quite popular. Robert, meanwhile, had gone to Atlanta when he was fifteen, where he got a job as a busboy in a restaurant, and never left. Three years later, he went to work for Yates and Milton Drugstores, setting up soda fountain operations in each of its stores. After serving in the U.S. Army during World War II, James also came to Atlanta, and in 1947 they borrowed $3,000 from Citizens Trust and scraped together $2,000 of their own money to open a restaurant on Hunter Street, near Atlanta University. Specializing in fried chicken, with Robert doing the cooking and James serving as the business partner, the venture over time became very popular with both blacks and whites in Atlanta.

In 1959, with $85,000 borrowed from Citizens Trust and $30,000 from Atlanta Life, the Paschals moved into expanded quarters a short distance from their old store. Customers began to ask for drinks to be served with their meals, so the brothers in the next year borrowed more money from Citizens Trust to open La Carousel Lounge. This became an extremely popular meeting place for the emerging black middle class and college students in the area, and it began to book top-name jazz talent into its room. Movie stars and other celebrities began dropping in at Paschal's. Finally, in 1966, they decided to take a major step forward and build a 120-unit first-class motel with dining facilities and other public space. Getting a loan for $1 million from Citizens Trust made this possible; it was at the time the largest black-to-black financial transaction in Atlanta's history. The motel was opened in January 1967. The record for the largest transaction was surpassed seven years later, in July 1974, when the Paschals borrowed, to expand their motor hotel, a total of $3.5 million from a consortium of black lenders (Atlanta Life, $1.3 million; Mutual Federal, $1 million; North Carolina Mutual, $500,000; and Pilgrim Health and Life, $100,000). Citizens Trust was responsible for putting together the package, and added $250,000 to consortium funds. The Paschals in 1978 put in a successful bid of $116.9 million, in conjunction with Dobbs House, Inc., to form a joint venture to run the concessions at Hartsfield Atlanta International Airport.

The Paschal's dining room and motel gained fame over the next several years as the "war room for a nonviolent revolution," when the Southern Christian Leadership Conference used the motel and dining room to conduct its strategy sessions during the civil rights crusade. It was there that the first Freedom Riders in the early 1960s came for nourishment and moral and legal support. The strategy for integrating lunch counters was also developed there, as was the decision to carry the war for civil rights into Selma, Alabama. It was also at Paschal's that black leaders from around the nation met to mourn the death of Dr. Martin Luther King, Jr., in 1968, and where they decided to carry on his work in the future. It remained in the 1980s and 1990s, as Atlanta became a more integrated city, the place where the major officeholders in city government met for lunch and other matters. As John Turner, a longtime Fulton County assistant district attorney commented, "When you mention the name Paschal's, two things come to mind, chicken and politics."

During these same years, Citizens Trust continued to grow and expand. In 1964, under the direction of L. D. Milton, it opened a modern new office building on Piedmont, just off Auburn Avenue. In 1971 Milton stepped down as president and was succeeded by Charles McKinley Reynolds, Jr., a Morehouse College economics student of Milton's who had become the nation's first black bank examiner.

During those forty-odd years that Milton had headed the bank, it was run pretty much as a one-man show. It was claimed that Milton ran the bank with a small group of secretaries, and maintained what many felt was an excessively conservative loan policy. Reynolds, eager to take part in the expansive mood of the early 1970s, liberalized Milton's credit policies and moved into such services as mortgage banking, credit cards, and auto leasing, none of which worked out well. To be fair to Reynolds, many of Milton's later decisions had not been inspired either, and that made Reynolds's task more difficult. Despite Milton's conservatism, he had made a number of bad loans, and the magnificent office structure he had built, which was larger and more expensive than they needed, saddled the firm with debt. Then, the oil embargo–induced recession of 1973 hit Citizens Trust harder than most banks, and it paid a steep price for the poor loans it had made in the previous two years. Reynolds finally stepped down amidst chaos in 1974. The bank had lost money for two years, writing off $900,000 in 1974 alone. The board chairman of Citizens Trust, Herman Russell,* brought in I. Owen Funderberg to rescue the bank. Funderberg was also a graduate of Morehouse, had gone to the graduate school of business at the University of Michigan with Jesse Hill, Jr.,* and had begun his career as a cashier at Mechanics and Farmers Bank in Durham, North Carolina. In 1966 he joined the biracially owned Gateway National Bank in St. Louis as executive vice president and chief executive officer. During his time there, assets grew from $2.5 million to $21 million.

Funderberg brought about an immediate transformation in the fortunes of Citizens Trust. By 1977 it had jumped two places on the *Black Enterprise* list of black banks to fifth place in the nation. By 1982, eight years after assuming the helm of Citizens, Funderberg had raised its assets from $29 million to more than $50 million. He became known as "the man who saved Citizens Trust Bank." Part of his plan of salvation was to develop deposit and loan relationships with large, white-owned companies like Coca-Cola, Delta Air Lines, Bell South, and Atlanta Gas and Light. It also gets about one-fourth of its deposits from various government units. In 1990 Citizens Trust had assets of $127 million, with 157 employees. Despite its success, and its growing relationship to white institutions, Funderberg remained aware of its origins and mission: "Historically we have been oriented toward Atlanta's black community. But the underlying economic situation we have is not similar to what other banks have. We probably have to work a little harder."

Besides the above-mentioned enterprises, the Blayton-Milton-Yates combination was involved in a number of other significant ventures. In 1938 the three men opened the city's first black night club, the Top Hat, on Auburn Avenue. "Mr. Milton and Mr. Yates redecorated an old building on Auburn and made it look like something," an old resident commented. "When the Top Hat opened, it became the place where everybody migrated to have a dance—if you were a member, let's say, of the Masons or some fraternity and your group wanted to give a dance. . . . They had dances, they had floor shows. . . . Basically what it was, it was the same thing as what you'd have in a place like one of your better night clubs in New York. Cotton Club format, that's what it boiled down to."

The Top Hat was open from Monday through Friday for blacks, but "Saturday night was reserved for whites," another Auburn resident recalled. "The same band, the same waiters, the same bartenders. The only difference was that Saturday night was reserved for white patrons. They would be packed in there Saturday night at the Top Hat." It was later sold to Carrie Cunningham and became known as the Royal Peacock Club, which provided an elegant setting to showcase the likes of Duke Ellington, Harry Belafonte, and the Supremes.

Blayton, Milton, and Yates also owned Brown Boy Bottling Company, which produced various kinds of soft drinks that were distributed locally; Southeastern Fidelity Fire Insurance Company, organized in 1950; and Blamiya, Inc., a holding company, named for the three men, which made loans considered too large for the bank to make. In addition, Blayton had his accounting firm, which had branches in Dayton, Ohio, and in Charlotte and Durham, North Carolina. That firm had mostly black clients, particularly religious, fraternal, and business organizations. In 1949 Blayton got a license from the Federal Communications Commission to operate radio station WERD, reportedly the first long-wave radio station operated by a black in the United States. By the 1970s, WERD was one of three black stations in Atlanta and was beaming a gospel-only format during the daytime only. By then, its connection to the black community was rather tangential. As the station manager affirmed, "[W]e get some spots from black-owned businesses, but most come from white-owned businesses that realize they have to work through the black media to get black business."

Blayton also opened Midway Television Institute, which provided training in television and radio mechanics, and he operated the Blayton Business School, which operated for many years on Auburn Avenue. He was the first president of the Atlanta Negro Chamber of Commerce and an officer of the National Negro Business League, and he contributed many articles to *Bankers Magazine* and the *National Accountant*. Blayton, it has been claimed, "through his researches and teaching, has been largely responsible for training many young men for successful business careers and in helping Negro businessmen to conduct their operations in a more efficient manner.''

Blayton, Milton, and Yates were all behind-the-scenes operators and negotiators in the civil rights crusades. They donated a good deal of money to various efforts, and they were often invaluable in providing assistance at critical times. In the mid–1950s, when the city of Montgomery, Alabama, indicted Dr. Martin Luther King, Jr., along with eighty-eight other leaders of the bus boycott there, Milton and Yates, along with several other old-line members of the black community, met with King to plan strategy. Ultimately, King decided to move his Southern Christian Leadership Conference offices to Atlanta to relieve some of the pressure on him and the organization. When he did, Milton and Yates, along with T. M. Alexander, provided him with free office space until he was able to get his organization back on its feet.

Yet the three men remained lifelong conservative Republicans, even after the mass of blacks had converted to the Democratic party. Although they were affiliated with the Urban League and the NAACP, along with other black organizations, there was always a certain distaste—not for the goals, but for the tactics of the new civil rights movement. As Lucy Rucker Aiken, one of the ''old colored aristocracy'' of Atlanta commented, ''We wish to give [Dr. King] all the credit that can be given a person, but as lawful people we should obey the law even if it doesn't suit us. There are a lot of things that don't suit us in this life.'' That would tend to concur with the observation of Hoyt Fuller, editor of *First World*, who said, ''Martin Luther King did not march in Atlanta because he was opposed not only by the white power structure, but also by the black power structure.''

Sources

Biographical information on Jesse Blayton is found in *Who's Who in Colored America*, (1950). Lorimer D. Milton can be found in Mildred Daniel, ''L.D. Milton—Banker,'' *Opportunity* 25, 2 (April-June 1947), 71, 111; *Atlanta Daily World*, February 9 and 13, 1986; *Jet*, March 3, 1986. General information on the three men and their various enterprises can be gathered from Robert J. Alexander, ''Negro Business in Atlanta,'' *Southern Economic Journal* 17, 4 (April 1951), 456–58; *Atlanta Journal and Constitution*, August 12, 1984; *Atlanta Daily World*, June 18, 1976, and May 12, 1988; *Pittsburgh Courier*, July 15, 1961, and February 1988. Bobby J. Lamar, ''Citizens Trust Company and Its Role in the Development of the Atlanta Black Community with Emphasis on the Loan Function,'' Master's thesis, Atlanta University, 1969, is a good study of those aspects of the bank. Robert C. Vowels, ''Atlanta Negro Business and the New Black Bourgeoisie,'' *Atlanta Historical Society* Spring 1977, 48–63, has some useful information on the later years of Citizens Trust. See also, Sheila M. Poole, ''Mutual Federal Chugs Along,'' *Atlanta Journal/Constitution*, November 8, 1992.

Information on Owen Funderberg and Citizens Trust in later years is contained in *Atlanta Journal and Constitution*, August 18, 1971, June 2 and August 8, 1972, October 26 and November 11, 1974, August 10, 1975, April 22, 1979, January 21 and October 15, 1982, March 30, 1986, and November 19, 1988; and *Atlanta Constitution, Intown*

Extra, February 16, 1984. Some general information on black banking and Citizens Trust can be found in Robert H. Kinzer and Edward Sagarin, *The Negro in American Business* (1950), 104–7; *Black Enterprise*, October 1971, June 1977, and June 1990; Arnett G. Lindsay, "The Negro in Banking," *Journal of Negro History* XIV, 2 (April 1929), 189–90.

Biographical, business, and other data on the Paschal brothers come from promotional materials and press releases supplied by James Paschal; *Black Enterprise*, March 1971 and June 1979; *Ebony*, November 1979; *Pittsburgh Courier*, July 15, 1961; *Atlanta Journal and Constitution*, July 25, 1974, October 28, 1978, September 4, 1983, November 16, 1985, and August 5, 1987; *Atlanta Daily World*, February 5, 1967, and February 12, 1984; *Atlanta Tribune*, 1987; *Saturday Review*, August 23, 1969; and *Pride*, November 1972.

Boutte, Alvin Joseph (October 10, 1929–). Banker, drugstore chain owner, and race leader: Independence Bank of Chicago, Lakeside Pharmacies; Chicago Urban League and Chicago School Board. Alvin Boutte was part of a new generation of black business leaders in Chicago in the 1960s and 1970s. Born into a prestigious, though evidently not very prosperous, family in Louisiana, Boutte came to Chicago in 1954, merely one of hundreds of thousands of black southern migrants who were streaming into the city during those years. But unlike most of those, Boutte had a number of advantages: He was educated, he had served as an officer in the U.S. Army, he was alert to business opportunity and success, and he was tremendously ambitious. Thus, contrary to the experience of many of his fellow African-Americans who came to Chicago during this time, Alvin Boutte experienced a steady diet of success, wealth, and recognition.

Boutte was born in Lake Charles, Louisiana. Little is known about his parents, but in a later interview he said his father was a "working man," who was self-educated although he finished grammar school. The Louisiana where Boutte grew up in the 1930s was rigidly segregated. He lived in segregated neighborhoods and went to segregated schools, and he faced an intense system of racism and discrimination. Yet, neither he nor his family seemed to have been discouraged by that. Alvin Boutte tells a story of his father that is very revealing:

You know, my father lived his entire life in America, and he never once voted. I can remember how he'd dress me up and we'd walk down to the voting place and they'd tell him, "You know you can't vote." He'd just walk back and try again the next time. I guess I should be bitter, but I'm not.

The Bouttes, however, were an old and prominent family in Louisiana, with many members of the extended family having reached positions of importance in the community. A number had also, like Alvin Boutte, chosen pharmacy as a career. Matthew V. Boutte, for example, was a native of Oliver, Louisiana, who got a degree in pharmacology at the University of Illinois and ultimately owned a successful drugstore in New York City during the 1920s.

After graduating from local schools, Alvin Boutte went to Xavier University in New Orleans, the center of higher education for affluent and privileged blacks in the state, on an athletic scholarship. He received his bachelor's degree in pharmacology in 1951. At that point, Boutte joined the U.S. Army where he took the examinations for Officer's Candidate School. This was, he later recalled, the first time he had competed against people other than blacks. He did extremely well, finishing second in a class of 220 people. He then spent three years in the service.

When he left the army in 1954, the first thing Boutte had to decide was where he wanted to live. One thing was certain—he had no desire to live in Lake Charles: "I knew I wanted to live in a large city with a large group of Blacks." First, Boutte tried California, but soon after arriving, he found that California did not reciprocate with Louisiana on the pharmacy exams, so that he would have to take them again after a one-year waiting period. Boutte decided he would go to New York City. On the way there, he stopped off in Chicago to stay for a few days, but he never left. Boutte had saved some money while in the service, and he decided to find a job that would allow him to save enough money to buy a business. Looking through the classified ads in the newspaper, he found one from a man who wanted to sell his drugstore. "I took a look at the store," remembers Boutte, "and I liked it, but I had never run a drugstore or even worked in one. I made a deal with him that he would give me a job for one year, and I would give him a deposit to buy the store."

During that first year, Boutte worked in the store and studied the way in which the owner, Tom McCauley, ran it. But he did more than that. Boutte also visited other stores in his spare time to find out what they were doing. In addition, he took business courses at the University of Chicago. At the end of the first year, Boutte bought the store, called Lakeside Pharmacy, with the help of a loan from Sealtest Dairy. He got the loan from them because he was unable to get a loan from a bank:

The banks just didn't have any money to lend to a small businessman, if he were black. The assumption was that we didn't know what we were doing. . . . In any event, I was able to get a loan from the Sealtest ice cream people. They would back you in hopes of getting another outlet for their products.

Two years later he bought another store, deciding he wanted to become the black version of a chain like Walgreen's. He called his chain Independent Drug Stores, Inc. Over the next several years, Boutte expanded his chain to four stores. They were very successful, and Boutte became one of the leaders of the black business community on the South Side of Chicago. By the mid–1960s, Boutte's chain was doing business in excess of $3.5 million.

During these years, Boutte became a close friend and business associate of George Johnson,* the head of Johnson Products, the large black cosmetics and hair care firm. In 1964 Boutte and Johnson became involved in the organization of Independence Bank. The evolution of this institution, however, was twisted and complex. The genesis of the bank came in 1963 when Chatham Bank failed, leaving the black, middle-class Chatham neighborhood around Cottage Grove Avenue on Chicago's South Side without a nearby banking institution. George Johnson, whose Johnson Products had been one of the largest depositors at Chatham Bank, led the movement to start a new bank, and he enlisted his friend Alvin Boutte and others in the effort. A split soon emerged among the group, however. Johnson's group wanted to get a state charter for the bank, while the other group preferred to obtain a federal charter, a far more difficult endeavor.

As a result, instead of one bank being organized in the Chatham area, there were two, and they were destined to be lifelong, albeit friendly, rivals. The group that wanted the federal charter was led by Ernie "Stu" Collins, who owned a small chain of grocery stores, and Dr. Jasper Williams. They got the endorsement and support of a number of black business leaders on the South Side, including Dempsey J. Travis,* and they organized Seaway National Bank. This had a serious impact on Johnson and Boutte's plans for a bank, since Seaway drained off a good deal of the potential capital in the black community.

Joining Johnson and Boutte in organizing Independence Bank were Henry P. Hervey, then manager of a savings and loan association, H. Ernest Lafontant, vice president and general counsel of Johnson Products, and Robert H. Bacon, Jr., president of Bacon's Clipping Bureau. The five organizers put up $60,000 each, then went about raising the balance of the $1 million required for minimum capital through the sale of stock. They fell short of their goal by some $200,000, but the state banking agency allowed them to proceed with just $800,000. Seaway, on the other hand, easily raised the $1 million needed for its federal charter, and it went through its first few years with little apparent difficulty. Bringing in an experienced white banking executive as president and chief executive officer, Seaway had few serious management problems during its early years. That was definitely not the case with Independence Bank.

Since none of the organizers of Independence Bank had any banking experience, they too hired a white as president. Unlike the situation at Seaway, however, the man Boutte and Johnson hired had little experience in senior management. At the end of the first year, Independence wrote off $175,000 in losses. "Every deadbeat in town came knocking on our door for a loan," recalls Johnson. The problem was the president they had hired. Johnson explained, "He was a cashier. Academically he had some depth, but he was not a senior banking official. He stayed about a year and a half. It took us that long to find out what he didn't know." By 1967 the prospects for Independence Bank were grim, indeed. To stave off what looked like certain failure, Johnson and Boutte approached the board of directors of Seaway Bank and proposed a merger. Seaway, understandably, declined. "I can't say I blame them," said Boutte. "We really didn't have that much to offer. Our loan portfolio was dotted with bad loans, we weren't growing, we weren't making money, we had had four presidents the first four years."

To solve their critical problems, and to save the significant sums of money they had already invested in the bank, Johnson, chairman of Independence's board, asked Alvin Boutte to assume the presidency. Although Boutte had no banking experience, he had superb managerial skills, and he was asked to apply those skills to the task. Boutte had just passed his fortieth birthday. He agreed to sell his prosperous drugstore chain, invested $400,000 in Independence Bank, buying out a number of other stockholders, and increased his holdings to 25 percent. Johnson also invested another $400,000, raising his share in the bank to 28 percent. The two men, however, were just about the only ones who had any faith in the future of Independence Bank. "Everybody else was afraid of it," said Boutte. "It was a speculative investment to say the least."

Boutte's first day on the job as president was hardly one to inspire confidence in the future—Independence Bank was robbed. Armed robbers drove up to the drive-in window and demanded and got some $5,000. Boutte, however, was not to be deterred, as he steered Independence on a conservative course. "I cut out all the foolishness," he said. His first task was to develop a competent management team. To do so, he developed a three-year development program. "There was not a single MBA in the place in those days," he said. "Today we have five." Having strengthened that end of the operations, Boutte then launched an aggressive marketing program, designed to attract mainstream white corporate accounts. This campaign coincided with the federal government's promise to make deposits in black-owned banks, and it also pressured big business to do likewise. Over the next few years, Boutte was successful in his quest. By the 1970s, Independence held deposits for a large number of corporations, including CBS, Chrysler, and General Motors. It also handled the payroll account for a division of Johnson & Johnson baby products, an operating account for Delta Airlines, and one for a CBS-owned radio station in Chicago.

In addition, Boutte was able to attract accounts from a number of the larger black businesses. In addition to Johnson Products, it also handled accounts for Golden State Insurance, Johnson Publishing, Parker House Sausage, Supreme Life Insurance, and Tuesday Publications. All of this business brought significant growth to Independence. When Boutte took over it had assets of just $16 million. Three years later, he had increased assets to $55 million. Of this $39 million increase, $16 million came from black businesses, $15 million from white corporations, and $8 million from the retail banking sector.

Having greatly increased the operating base of the bank, Boutte, in 1973, embarked upon a second three-year phase, concentrating totally on developing a high-quality staff. This was a costly procedure, as the bank spared little expense to bring in top-flight personnel. At the end of the period, though, Boutte had brought in an experienced investment officer, two lending officers, and a comptroller. He also had several staff members undergoing training with large downtown Chicago banks. At that point, Boutte pushed Independence into its third phase—called the Retail Program—another three-year plan to enhance the bank's image in the community.

Since its founding, Independence Bank had its headquarters in the old Chatham Bank building, an architectural curiosity that had been built at the turn of the century. They had chosen it when they opened because it "looked like a bank," and therefore would give the fledgling institution credibility in the community. In 1977, however, they began construction on a new, five-story, $4 million headquarters. The new building also marked the beginning of an important new alliance for Independence—with Chicago Metropolitan Mutual Assurance Company. The two rapidly growing black firms agreed to share the new headquarters, both in construction costs and space, which signaled a broader, mutually beneficial, alliance between the two firms.

Founded in 1927, Chicago Metropolitan Mutual was an outgrowth of a consortium of black funeral companies that had banded together in 1925 to provide death benefits for poor black Chicagoans. The man who was responsible for the development of the firm during its early years was Robert A. Cole, once manager of a gambling den in the city. Cole died in 1956, and the following year there was an agent strike at the firm, which stymied its growth and development for a time. After George S. Harris took control of the firm in 1961, Chicago Metropolitan began to expand. In 1965 Harris explored the possibility of merging his firm with Supreme Life, but the plans were stillborn, largely because of resistance among personnel of both companies. From that point onward, Chicago Metropolitan allied itself with the causes of black power, black pride, and race consciousness, which resulted in a higher profile for the firm and increased profitability.

Another turning point for Chicago Metropolitan came in 1971, when Anderson M. Schweich replaced Harris. Schweich and Boutte became close associates, and Schweich became a member of the board of directors of Independence Bank. In 1977 Boutte also became a member of the board of directors of Chicago Metropolitan, the first nonemployee to be so designated. Schweich took Chicago Metropolitan, like North Carolina Mutual, into the group insurance market, getting some of the group insurance business of General Foods, Jewel Companies, and Commonwealth Edison. By 1992 Chicago Mutual had over $2.8 billion of insurance in force, making it by far the largest black insurance firm in Chicago. It was, by 1992, the fifth-largest black insurance firm in the United States. Throughout much of the 1970s and 1980s, Chicago Metropolitan and Independence Bank were among the most dynamic black institutions in Chicago. By 1973, in fact, Independence had become the largest black bank in America.

The 1980s signaled yet another important stage in the development of Independence under Alvin Boutte. In 1980, when two black-owned banks—Gateway National Bank and Guaranty Bank & Trust—became insolvent and were closed, Boutte moved in and made an offer for them to the Federal Deposit Insurance Corporation. "I knew that we had to make a bid for those banks," he said. "[R]umors were going back and forth and it was bad for black banks in general." Neither Gateway nor Guaranty had any major commercial accounts, but both had a strong base in the retail community (Guaranty was owned by the Nation of Islam). Both banks had a large number of black workers among their customers. "What you had [as bank customers]" Boutte said, "were the community people, basically the consumers.'' It was a chance for Independence to do good and do well at the same time. By taking over the two banks they would be helping their community, and Independence could expand its retail consumer base, which was part of Boutte's master plan. Seaway, always a competitor, also bid for the two banks, but Independence emerged victorious.

Boutte's next major thrust came in the late 1980s. In July 1988, Independence, by then having slipped to become the fourth-largest black bank in the nation with assets of $106 million, announced an agreement to purchase Drexel National Bank, a white-owned, Chicago-based institution with considerable presence in the South Side black community. It would be the first time a healthy, white-owned banking institution had been acquired by a black-owned bank. The acquisition would more than double Independence's assets to $230 million, thereby again making it the nation's largest African-American bank, toppling Seaway from the position it had wrested from Independence a few years before. Independence proposed to pay $10 million for Drexel, financed with a $4 million loan from First National Bank of Chicago. The purchase would have pushed Independence's capital from $9 million to around $17 million and would have given it a large number of new black customers on the South Side. "What we are doing by acquiring Drexel," said George Johnson, "is just fulfilling our mission to provide good banking services to the community." The merger, however, was never consummated, and the result was a relative decline for Independence Bank.

By 1992 Independence had slipped to become the sixth-largest black-owned bank in the United States, continuing to trail its main rival Seaway, which itself had fallen to third place. Independence's assets had climbed to only $138 million in four years, its capital remained at just under $9 million, and deposits were $126 million, well behind Seaway's $151 million. Alvin Boutte continued as chairman and chief executive officer, with a staff of 106 at his command.

Boutte was also involved in a number of other aspects of the African-American community in Chicago. In the late 1960s, he joined the board of the Small Business Administration, in an effort to promote black ownership of business. "You know the first thing we have to do?" Boutte asked at the time. "We have to encourage industry to come back into depressed areas so that people can get jobs. Once a man has a job he can be a better father, he can gain the respect of his children. It has to start somewhere." In the heady days of racial protest in the 1960s, however, this kind of approach did not always elicit a favorable response from black militants. Thus, Boutte was greatly pleased when Dr. Martin Luther King, Jr., upon visiting Johnson Products' new wing, stood on the stairs, looked around and announced, "Now *this* is black power." Boutte also served as president of the Freedom Development Corporation, founded by King to help African-Americans become property owners.

In 1969 Boutte was nominated by Mayor Richard Daley to serve a five-year term on the Chicago School Board. The nomination was opposed by a number of whites, who complained that Boutte was not a good example for school children since he had once been arrested, even though those charges were ultimately dropped. The Chicago Urban League, whose president was George Johnson (Boutte was vice president), announced that it was supporting the nomination of Boutte "150%." Boutte was elected and he served on the school board until 1974. In 1982 Boutte was asked to serve as chairman of the Chicago Housing Authority, but he declined, citing ill health (he had been in an accident that had injured his spinal cord) and overwork with Independence Bank and his other interests. Boutte suggested Dempsey Travis, who also declined. Both were no doubt aware that the CHA was the graveyard of reputations and careers and did not want to be tarred by any connection with it. In 1971 Boutte was selected as the Man of the Year by the Chicago Urban League, and he received a similar designation by the Chicago Economic Development Council. Married, he and his wife had four children.

Boutte in 1992 remained in many ways the eternal optimist: a man who is never down or depressed. Of course, the man in 1969 proclaimed, "You know, it's fun to be black. It's a challenge. Sure, it can be tough, but that's what makes it worthwhile." As the years went on, and as the fortunes of the mass of blacks remained depressed, a new realism crept into Boutte's tone:

As a black man in this country, even today with all the things that have changed, some attitudes are not changed. The black man finds himself isolated, no matter who is he. There is a relationship with the white businessman downtown, but it's a limited relationship.

Sources

There are no personal papers of Alvin Boutte available, nor are the records of Independence Bank or Lakeside Pharmacies available to researchers. There are brief biographies of Boutte available in a number of places: John Seder and Berkeley G. Burrell, *Getting It Together* (1971), 192–96; and Frank J. Johnson, *Who's Who of Black Millionaires* (1984), 119. A number of articles deal with various aspects of Boutte's life: *Chicago Defender*, July 20, 1969, September 25, 1972, November 15, 1979, and April 26, 1980; *Chicago Sun Times*, July 16, 1969, and August 4, 1982; *South Side Scene*, July 7, 1984; *Chicago Metro*, August 15, 1981; *Chicago Daily News*, July 29, 1969; *Chicago Tribune*, May 14, July 16, 20, and 29, 1969, and June 14, 1970. There is also a press release from the Chicago Urban League, dated August 7, 1969, held at the Chicago Historical Society, dealing with Boutte's nomination to the Chicago School Board. There are many articles dealing with Independence Bank and Boutte's role in it: *Chicago Sun Times*, April 6, 1971; *Chicago Tribune*, July 22, 1979; *Black Enterprise*, June 1977, June 1980, October 1988, June and October 1989, April and June 1990, and June 1992; *Richmond Times Dispatch*, July 29, 1979; and *Chicago Defender*, September 22, 1973. There are also a number of brochures and company reports from Independence Bank, available at the Chicago Historical Society.

Boyd, Richard Henry (March 15, 1843–August 23, 1922) and **Henry Allen Boyd** (April 15, 1876–May 28, 1959). Publishers; bankers; business, civic, and religious leaders: National Baptist Publishing Board, *Nashville Globe*, National Negro Doll Company, National Baptist Church Supply Company, One Cent Savings Bank and Trust, Citizens Savings Bank and Trust, and National Negro

Press Association. Richard Boyd lived one of America's most extraordinary lives. Born a slave, he was unable to read, write, or even spell his own name until after emancipation. He was almost thirty before he taught himself the rudiments of the alphabet and English grammar, using *Webster's Old Blue Black Speller* and *McGuffey's First Reader*. Armed with this elementary education, Boyd then enrolled in college and became an ordained minister; he later owned the largest black publishing house in America, owned and edited a militant and literate black newspaper, wrote several books and articles, and was president of the first black-owned bank in the twentieth century. A present-day researcher, reading Boyd's long, eloquent, moving letters to J. M. Frost and Booker T. Washington* must continually remind himself or herself that this man was almost wholly self-educated. Richard Boyd was a brilliant, charismatic, controversial man; one who was filled with pride of his own accomplishments and those of his race—the first generation of freed blacks. And he was a militant advocate of black rights at a time when segregation and racism were growing rapidly in the South.

When Richard Boyd was born on the Gray family plantation in Nexube County, Mississippi, he was given the name of Dick Gray. His mother, Indiana Dixon, was born in Richmond, Virginia, but she was sold to slave traders in 1840 and carried to Mississippi where she was acquired by the Gray family. In 1849 the Grays moved to Washington County, Texas, and during these years, Indiana Dixon gave birth to ten children. There is no information on Boyd's life as a slave, but when the Civil War broke out, he accompanied his master as a servant to the fighting. After the plantation owner and two of his sons were killed in battle, Boyd returned to manage the family plantation until the end of the war. As manager, he did an excellent job, not only raising cotton, but selling it successfully at several points across the border in Mexico.

After emancipation in 1867, Boyd's true feelings about slavery perhaps emerged, and he discarded his slave name of Dick Gray and took the new name of Richard Henry Boyd. During the first few years after the war, Boyd worked as a cowboy, a cotton trader, and a sawmill laborer, all the time educating himself to fulfill his deep-seated ambitions. In 1869 came two significant events in Boyd's life: He married Hattie Moore, who would be his lifelong mate and with whom he would produce nine children, and he enrolled in Bishop College in Marshall, Texas. Although he did not graduate, Boyd became a Baptist preacher, which began his long career as an influential religious leader.

Boyd soon displayed his remarkable talents for leadership and organization. In 1870 he organized the first Negro Baptist Association in Texas, with just six churches. He also served as a pastor and organized Baptist churches in a number of Texas towns, including San Antonio, during the twenty-six years he spent as a minister in the state. In 1876 Boyd was selected to represent Texas Baptists at the Centennial Exposition. He was also superintendent of home missions in the state, and Boyd's relationship to the Baptist Home Missionary Society of New York (which had founded Bishop College) was to prove fruitful for him throughout his life. Boyd was also what one source called a "vehement prohibitionist'' and was the most "prominent and conspicuous Negro personality'' in the great Prohibition campaign in the state in 1880. While serving in these various positions in Texas, Boyd developed the idea of publishing literature for the Black Baptist Sunday Schools, and he brought out his first religious pamphlets in 1894 and 1895. By this time, he had become convinced of the necessity for black Baptists to publish their own religious materials. This concept was to create great debate and schism within the Baptist community, but it also opened enormous opportunities to Richard Boyd.

At the end of the Civil War, African-American Baptists had come together in the Consolidated American Baptist Missionary Convention, which united the efforts of black Baptists in most sections of the country. This lasted until 1880, when disagreement between white and black missionaries over the treatment of natives in Africa brought into being the Foreign Mission Baptist Convention of the U.S.A. and the dissolution of the earlier organization. The Foreign Mission Convention gave black Baptists a new sense of power and responsibility, but they were left without a broader organization. In the same year, the American National Baptist Convention was also organized, with the objective of working for the unification of all black Baptists in America. Finally, in 1893, another organization, called the Baptist National Educational Convention, was formed to create an educated ministry in the leadership of the churches. Thus, African-American Baptists were operating in a dispersed fashion, and there was much pressure to create a united organization.

This came to fruition in 1895, when the three were united into the National Baptist Convention of the U.S.A. in Atlanta, Georgia. E. C. Morris of Arkansas was elected its first president, and three boards—the Foreign Missions Board, under Lewis G. Jordan; the Home Mission Board, headed by Richard Boyd; and the Educational Board, under A. Wilbanks—were formed. Although Boyd's formal mission was to expand the missionary activity among black Baptists at home, he quickly redirected its emphasis toward the establishment of a publishing house. At the 1895 convention, Boyd had argued strenuously for black Baptists to begin publishing their own materials, but the larger group had decided against it. Some were concerned with the expense of starting this operation, others were content to continue buying materials from northern white Baptists.

Boyd, however, was keenly sensitive to the elements of white racism that existed, and he made stirring pleas for blacks to stand on their own two feet and continually criticized blacks "who would try to sell" the "race to a white man's soulless corporation." Thus, Boyd, along with E. C. Morris and Reverend Walter H. Brooks of Washington, began a relentless campaign to establish a black Baptist publishing house. All three believed that the very dignity of the African-American race was at stake in this venture. This came to fruition in 1896 when the National Baptist Publishing Board was established under the aegis of the Home Mission Board and Richard Boyd. Boyd decided to establish the new publishing concern in Nashville, and in the latter part of that year he moved to the city to commence operations. Thus Richard Boyd, at fifty-three years of age, started his life work in a city in which he was a complete stranger. Over the next few years, he would profoundly transform both the black Baptist church and the city of Nashville.

Little is known of the size or nature of the plant that Boyd set up in Nashville, but it was no easy venture. Doors were repeatedly slammed in his face in the city, as he attempted to purchase printing equipment. Failing that, Boyd then appealed to Dr. J. M. Frost, secretary of the Baptist Sunday School Board of the Southern (white) Baptist Convention, to assist him in getting items published. Frost arranged to have some of this done through the board's publisher. Then, through the University Printing Company, he was able to get access to electroplates and other materials to publish his materials. Boyd finally succeeded in buying his own printing equipment by hiring a white man to act as a front to bid on the equipment at auction. This allowed Boyd to obtain the equipment he needed to publish materials in his own plant, and within three years he had published nine titles and distributed over six million copies of *The National Baptist Magazine*. In 1912 the physical plant was valued at over $350,000, and during these same years it had issued over 128 million periodicals. The operation had become an enormous success—it was one of the largest and most prosperous black businesses in Nashville; it was the most successful black publishing venture in the country; and it was the only arm of the Baptist church that was not losing money. In fact, it was making money, lots of it, and that was at the root of many of the problems Richard Boyd encountered during the next two decades.

There was a group within the black Baptist church who had never been in favor of either the amalgamation in 1895 or the establishment of the Publishing Board in 1896. In large measure, they had opposed separatism, hoping black and white Baptists would continue to work together, and they viewed the Publication Board as further evidence of schism. Thus, when Boyd made his first report for the Publication Board in 1897, this group, called the Lott Cary supporters, criticized it and decided to withdraw from the larger group to form the Lott Cary Baptist Foreign Mission Convention. Boyd, fearing for the independence and continuation of the Publication Board, decided to incorporate it as a separate body in 1898, thus giving it a status unique within the Baptist Convention. Independently chartered, it was wholly under Boyd's management and provided the larger board with only cursory accounts of its affairs in succeeding years. Boyd invested a good deal of his own money in the venture, and by the second decade of the twentieth century it was a highly successful black enterprise, profiting from its connection to the Baptist Convention, which placed mammoth orders for religious materials for its Sunday School operations with it, but had little or no control or influence over its operations. In that context arose an increasing crescendo of protest with the black Baptist church to bring the Publishing Board to accountability.

This all came to a head at the national convention held in 1915. There, President E. C. Morris laid down the gauntlet: "There is but one issue before the Baptists of the country, and that is, shall the Baptists of this country own

and control that which they, through their principal organization, have found
and built up, or shall its control be left to a few to be used for personal gain?''

Lewis G. Jordan, head of the Foreign Mission Board, recalled in his subsequent
history of the black Baptists that the Publication Board "rapidly became the
most efficient, influential department of the National Baptist Convention. In the
language of many of its critics, it was 'the most arrogant department of the
whole Convention.' '' At the convention, it was reported that the income of the
Publication Board had reached an aggregate total of $2.4 million during the
previous nine years. Little wonder the Baptists wanted control of Boyd's enterprise.

They decided the best way to accomplish their ends was to incorporate the
parent body, which would then give it legal authority and control over all its
subsidiaries, including Boyd's renegade Publication Board. On Boyd's part, it
was clear that this move would not only destroy his control over the board, but
would, in effect, take his own private property away from him, since he had
invested so much of his own time, money, and energy into the enterprise. He
therefore resisted the convention's attempt to take control by incorporation, and
the convention filed a lawsuit to take over. In the ensuing trial, however, the
court case revealed that Boyd had bought property and enlarged buildings and
printing facilities with his own money and had kept the title, deeds, and copy-
rights in his own name. The court therefore allowed Boyd to retain ownership
and control of the Publication Board.

Boyd himself was devastated by what happened, and he appealed to powerful
friends to intercede on his behalf. He complained to Booker T. Washington in
September 1915:

Yes, they have sought to ruin my reputation. They have sought to ruin my credit. They
have sought to break up my business. They have sought to destroy my family. . . . The
Convention has never given me $1,000. I have built up this institution on manufacturing
and trade and in this effort I have turned from time to time for denominational purposes
as benefits out of the two million dollars handled, more than Six Hundred Thousand
Dollars free or separate from actual running expenses.

Boyd also wrote a whole series of letters to Dr. Frost at the Sunday School
Board, pleading for his support. At one point, Boyd stated that "each member
of our Board is firm and determined that this property belongs to the Negro
Baptists of the United States of America. We are determined that it shall be
administered according to the charter carrying out the purpose for which it was
incorporated." Frost replied with a somewhat noncommital, but supportive,
letter, and this perhaps gave Boyd the courage to go ahead with his next move.

As John Lewis Hill wrote in the 1920s of Richard Boyd, "He had the friendship
and cooperation of the late Dr. J. M. Frost, and the friendship and cooperation
of practically all the outstanding leaders of the Southern Baptist Convention."
Possibly because of this support and cooperation, Boyd was confident enough
to pull the Publication Board out of the convention and form his own—the

National Baptist Convention, USA—which was often just called the "Boyd Convention." The National Baptist Publication Board continued to prosper over the years, and by the time of Boyd's death in 1922, it was one of the largest black business enterprises in the United States.

In the meantime, Richard Boyd was busy creating a large black business empire in Nashville, and he also became one of the most militant and dynamic leaders of black protest and black pride in the city. Increasingly participating with him in these ventures was his eldest son, Henry Allen Boyd. The younger Boyd was born in Grimes County, Texas, and grew up in San Antonio. Educated in the schools of that city, Henry Boyd became the first black to hold a clerk's position in the San Antonio post office. He also worked alongside his father in many of the family's business holdings and religious ventures in that city. When his father moved to Nashville in 1896, Henry, along with his wife and daughter, moved there also. Henry became his father's "Man Friday" in the publishing venture, and he also became an ordained Baptist minister in 1904. As Richard Boyd's business empire expanded during the first decade of the twentieth century, Henry Boyd was a close associate and partner in every endeavor. They worked out a rough division of interest—Richard Boyd was the idea man, the charismatic leader, the one with the entrepreneurial initiative; Henry was the administrator and organizer, the one who nurtured the infant enterprises and carried out the essential day-to-day functions of the business that his father did not have the time or patience to pursue. Between the two of them they made a remarkably successful business team.

In 1903 James C. Napier,* a prominent black Nashville politician, a business and civic leader, and a close associate of Booker T. Washington, convinced Washington to hold the annual convention of the National Negro Business League in the city. Washington agreed, Richard Boyd was elected vice president of the organization, and he and Napier were responsible for the highly successful meeting held there in August of that year. John L. Barbour, a local black merchant, welcomed the delegates to Nashville, declaring, "If the colored merchant of [this city] is not a success, it is not at all due to race prejudice but is due entirely to his own incapacity." Boyd, in his own speech, was not quite so certain of that, but he conceded that blacks, no longer distracted by political and social concerns, could now "concentrate on raising [themselves] economically." This fervor for the creation of a vibrant black business community in Nashville caused Boyd, Napier, and several other leading African-American leaders in the city to meet several months later to make plans for the creation of a black-owned bank.

On the night of November 5, 1903, these men met in an upstairs room in Napier Court to make plans. Each of the nine men present pledged to contribute no less than $100 to the capital stock of the bank, which was to be a total of $25,000. The theme heard over and over from them was that of "race confidence," the idea that African-Americans could not continue to be scarred by the failure of the Freedman's Bank a generation earlier. This was a new day;

there was a new, confident, and successful black community in Nashville; and they could make a go of any enterprise to which they turned their hands. Boyd, after all, had created a massive religious publishing business from virtually nothing in less than a decade. These were not timid, kerchiefed, forelock-tugging blacks; these were strong, confident, capable black men who were determined to create an independent economic entity.

Thus, on January 16, 1904, when One Cent Savings Bank and Trust Company opened its doors in donated quarters in Napier Court, its announced purpose was "to encourage frugality and systematic saving among our people, to secure the safe keeping and proper investment of such savings and set in motion business enterprises." This was to be the linchpin to the creation of a strong, dynamic black community. But Boyd, Napier, Preston Taylor, and the other black founders were in a quandary. On one hand, they wanted to invest in the black community and create a phalanx of business enterprises. On the other, they were concerned that the black community have complete trust in the safety of their funds. In the end, as one officer later commented, the policy was "first confidence, and second, financiering."

Thus, over the years, One Cent Bank would follow an excessively conservative lending policy which resulted in stability but very slow growth. When some stockholders complained about this slow growth, Richard Boyd, the bank's first president, reminded them that the idea of "getting rich quick" was never in the minds of the founders of the institution. He asserted that the bank wished to deal only in "gilt-edged securities," which, of course, were a scarce commodity in the black community. Thus, the bank, which opened with healthy deposits of $6,500, had less than $36,000 six years later. Nor did many pay in their capital stock, so that by 1910, only $4,290 of the $25,000 was actually paid in. Although Boyd stoutly defended this conservative policy, and probably did agree with it, most analysts have concluded that James Napier was most responsible for it. Napier, to ensure against default of the bank in the early months, had pledged his personal fortune as security. He had been in Nashville when the Freedman's Bank failed, and he had invested in a scandal-scarred black bank in Chattanooga in the 1890s. Thus, he was determined that One Cent Bank would not fail. Time and again, when members of the black community complained about this policy, Boyd and Napier would reply, "Remember the Freedmen's Bank."

In response, a number of previous directors of One Cent Bank resigned and formed a new bank on July 31, 1909: People's Savings Bank and Trust Company. Headed by Dr. Richard F. Boyd (no relation), even Richard H. Boyd recognized the concerns of these men, saying that they "thought the officers of the One Cent Savings Bank were too exacting in their . . . securities and made money a little too hard for borrowers to obtain." His newspaper, the *Nashville Globe*, called the appearance of the new bank, run by younger members of the black business community, a "healthy sign." Its stated purpose was not stability, but a more active and direct promotion of black economic growth.

Both banks grew during the next decade and experienced particularly pronounced growth during World War I, when each had its demand deposits and time savings accounts double during a period of eighteen months. In 1920 One Cent Bank reorganized itself as Citizens Savings Bank and Trust, but it continued its conservative investment and lending policies. In February 1922, shortly before Richard Boyd's death, Citizens Savings moved to new quarters in the old Duncan Hotel building, at the corner of Cedar and Fourth Avenue, near Napier Court. Then, in August of that year, upon the founder's death, Henry A. Boyd ascended to the presidency. The younger Boyd had joined the bank as assistant secretary and worked his way up the ranks over the years. As president until his own death in 1959, Henry Boyd continued to run Citizens Trust in the same manner as his father, despite the fact that he had supported aggressive banking as editor of the *Globe*.

Throughout the boom times of the 1920s, Citizens Savings invested its funds in blue-chip railroad stocks, rather than more risky black businesses or home mortgages. People's Bank, on the other hand, made hundreds of short-term loans, mostly on real estate in the black community. This made the latter bank more of a viable community institution, but proved its undoing when the Great Depression hit in the 1930s. On November 21, 1930, People's Savings Bank and Trust closed its doors, a victim of its own liberal lending policies. The crisis at People's also almost brought down Citizens Bank, when rumors spread through the black community that it also was on the verge of collapse. It survived a two-day run on the bank in October 1931 by placing stacks of currency in its windows and drawing on the financial and public support of the white-owned American National Bank. In 1934 it received a large Reconstruction Finance Corporation loan, and bank examiners throughout the decade allowed Citizens to continue running with some questionable loan conditions.

In 1954 Henry Boyd as president celebrated Citizens Bank's fiftieth anniversary. By that time, its capital stock stood at $200,000, it had deposits of nearly $1.7 million, and it declared that it was ''as safe as any bank in the United States, because it has the same government insurance of Ten Thousand Dollars on every deposit.'' After Henry Boyd's death, Meredith G. Ferguson. a longtime employee of the firm, became president for the next fifteen years. But the Boyd family continued to have a powerful say in the bank's operation. Serving as chairman of the board from 1959 to 1978 was Richard Boyd's grandson, T. B. Boyd, Jr. Born and educated in Nashville, T. B. Boyd, Jr., attended Fisk University and graduated from Tennessee State in 1940. After serving in the U.S. Army during World War II, he became a Baptist minister and served as pastor of Greater Salem Baptist Church in Louisville, Kentucky, and as assistant superintendent of Mount Olive Baptist Church in Nashville.

In 1958 T. B. Boyd, Jr., became secretary treasurer of the National Baptist Publishing Board, which by then printed material for more than 68,000 Baptist churches, and a year later he became chairman of the board of Citizens Bank. He was also president of Citizens Realty and Development Corporation until his death in 1979. Active in civic affairs, T. B. Boyd, Jr., was appointed to a seat on the Metro Human Relations Committee in 1978. In that year, the elder T. B. Boyd stepped down, and he was succeeded as chairman of the board of Citizens Bank by his son, T. B. Boyd III, who was still serving in that capacity in the early 1990s. Upon the death of his father, T. B. Boyd III was elected executive secretary of the National Baptist Publishing Board, the fourth generation of the Boyd family to run the firm. The younger Boyd, a native of Nashville, graduated from Tennessee State University in 1969 and did graduate work in economics at the University of Tennessee at Nashville. In 1974 he became personnel director of the National Baptist Publishing Board.

When T. B. Boyd III took command of National Baptist Publishing, the firm was in a precarious position, and young Boyd was just thirty-two years old. Nor had he shown much leadership potential to that point. But, as he later said, ''My father's death woke me up. . . . It made me recognize my inadequacies.'' He gave a speech to 32,000 members of the National Baptist Congress that year, in which he pledged to continue the firm's growth and excellence. He performed as he promised. Whereas the publishing house produced 3.5 million publications in 1979, ten years later it produced more than 12 million books and periodicals worldwide. Boyd also supervised the building of a new 55,000-square-foot headquarters in West Nashville, with plans for even greater expansion.

T. B. Boyd III also took an active role in the development of the bank. During his first ten years as chairman, assets grew from $30 million to $35 million, but he was frustrated in his attempts to attract more white patrons. He insisted that ''Citizens Bank serves the entire community . . . and while the bank continues to be an avenue for small businesses and minorities to conduct business, it will always be a bank for all of the community.'' He projected a goal of $50 million in assets by 1994. In 1985 he watched proudly as Citizens Bank moved into a gleaming new office tower at Citizens Plaza. Boyd was also a pioneer in community race relations. In 1989 he was elected the first black member of the sixty-nine-year-old Richland Club, and he commented, ''I hope that Nashville can realize and appreciate what Richland has done by including an Afro-American in its social base.''

Although Richard Boyd was a follower of Booker T. Washington, an officer in the NNBL, and a firm believer in the gospel of economic self-improvement, he could hardly be termed an accommodationist. On the contrary, the black pride aspect of economic development, which was somewhat muted in Washington's espousal, was given full and complete development by Boyd. At the turn of the century, despite his affiliation with Washington, Boyd protested the political disfranchisement of blacks, saying that if African-Americans did not ''carefully guard [their] . . . interests,'' white politicians would ''turn the hand backward on the political dial by a quarter of a century.'' Boyd was also extremely sensitive to individual or collective slights to his race. For this reason, during these years he and other black business leaders often took the lead in racial protest against elements of the emerging Jim Crow system in the South. The streetcar boycotts in Nashville in 1905 and 1906 are perfect examples of this phenomenon.

Whites in Tennessee had for some time been pushing for the complete segregation of blacks and whites in all public facilities, and streetcar lines were a particular bone of contention. Whites in letter-writing campaigns in Nashville and Memphis complained of ''the odor of sweaty negroes'' and the disrespectful conduct of black males toward white women. They therefore asked for the creation of separate ''Jim Crow'' streetcars for blacks, and the Tennessee legislature tried to pass a number of acts between 1900 and 1905.

The controversy built further in 1903 when the West Nashville trolley line added an extra car for black workers traveling to the fertilizer plants in that area. This fed into growing demands by whites to segregate the trolley lines completely, and by January 1905, the state legislature enacted a Jim Crow streetcar law for all Tennessee cities, to go into effect on July 5. In the spring, well before the law went into effect, black leaders in Nashville began preparing the African-American populace for a boycott. Reverend Edward W. D. Isaac, editor of the *Nashville Clarion*, advised readers ''to trim their corns, darn their socks, wear solid shoes . . . and get ready to walk.'' When the law went into effect, it was clear that few blacks were riding the cars.

After three weeks of the boycott, the leaders of the local chapter of the NNBL, then headed by Richard H. Boyd, and including James Napier, Preston Taylor, and several others, met on July 31 and declared that blacks should use the trolleys only in ''absolute necessity'' and that owners of express wagons in the city should use them to transport people to their destination. Shortly afterward, they quietly went about organizing their own traction company. Taylor, Richard Boyd, and Napier emerged as the leaders of this new race-conscious enterprise, called the Union Transportation Company. The firm purchased five steam-driven ''auto buses,'' which were in operation in black neighborhoods by October 1905, but they soon proved to be underpowered to handle Nashville's hilly terrain. In response, Taylor, Boyd, and Napier brought in fourteen electric buses, each capable of carrying twenty passengers, to replace the steamers. Rather than purchase power from the white-owned Nashville Railway and Light Company, the main culprit in the Jim Crow dispute, the company installed its own dynamo in the basement of Boyd's National Baptist Publishing Company.

The whole enterprise, however, was undercapitalized, and the city fought back by levying special taxes on the buses. The operation was also strained by the great dispersion of Nashville's blacks, who lived and worked in all parts of the city. The company was able to continue operations until July 1906 but a short time thereafter went out of business. By this point, the boycott had been abandoned by most of the city's blacks. Nevertheless, it was one of the longest boycotts in the history of American cities, and it provided a beacon for blacks in the 1950s when they prepared their successful protests against segregated transit systems in Montgomery, Alabama, and elsewhere. Boyd, Napier, and Taylor were joined in leadership of the protest by one of the city's ministers,

Reverend Sutton E. Griggs. Like Boyd, he was a Texas-born Baptist who became pastor of Nashville's First Baptist Church. During the first decade of the twentieth century, he was a vehement foe of discrimination and the caste system, and he supported W.E.B. Du Bois, the Niagara Movement, and the formation of the National Association for the Advancement of Colored People (NAACP), and he was a militant leader of the Nashville boycott. Later, however, he moved to Memphis, where he became the supreme accommodationist, encouraging co-operation with whites and blaming the blacks' problems not on racism but on their own "adverse mental attitudes." By this time, also, Griggs was one of the leaders in the movement of the National Baptist Convention to take control of Boyd's National Baptist Publishing Board in 1915.

Boyd, however, continued his race militance, and this was reflected most graphically in his founding and sponsorship of the *Nashville Globe*, which Henry A. Boyd ran for many years. The *Globe* was a direct outgrowth of the ill-fated streetcar boycott. Believing the city's African-American community needed an independent newspaper, Richard Boyd put his entrepreneurial talents, his fortune, and his good name behind the enterprise. In December 1905 he founded the Globe Publishing Company, and in January 1906 it began publishing the news-paper. Its editorial policy was a combination of Washington's economic self-help and an uncompromising sense of black pride and racial protest. In this respect, it was very much like John Mitchell, Jr.'s* *Richmond Planet*. Boyd was convinced of the importance of developing black business in Nashville, and this was a constant theme in the paper. But the Union Transportation Company, despite its failure, had taught him something also—that business development was intimately connected with black social and economic independence and that this, in turn, was the key to true freedom for his race. Boyd may have been an ally of Booker T. Washington, and he was conservative in many respects, but one could hardly call him an accommodationist.

However important Richard Boyd was to the founding of the paper, and however much it drew its strength from his pride and resolve and from his financial resources, it was Henry Boyd, along with Joseph Oliver Battle and Dock A. Hart, who actually ran the paper and set its editorial policy. They continually stressed the potential strength of the black community and were staunch opponents of discrimination, but they seldom opposed segregation laws per se. This was particularly shown in its crusade for the development of black business, editorializing in 1907 that "slowly but surely, the Negroes of this city and of the country at large [would reach] the conclusion that a black man [would] come nearer giving a square deal to a black man than [would] those of another race." Thus, they continually urged the black community to "buy black," which, of course, would help the One Cent Bank. Henry Boyd attacked black fraternal organizations that did not patronize black banks and other businesses, and they continually ran articles praising the stability of black banks. They also reported extensively on the activities of the Nashville Negro Board of Trade, the National Negro Business League, and other black business associations.

It was not long, however, before the *Globe* began attacking the NNBL and Washington's philosophy. The *Globe*'s editors were upset because the NNBL showed little concrete or tangible local results. Instead, they wanted to follow W.E.B. Du Bois's plan of organizing local organizations first. As a result, when A. N. Johnson, a young newcomer and black undertaker, decided to organize a new Business and Professional League in Nashville, the *Globe* gave it full support. James Napier, however, did not join the new association and did everything he could to heal the breech that had developed. To this end, he convinced Washington to visit Nashville in late 1909, and he and Richard Boyd and Preston Taylor organized a statewide tour for him. The new local organization also "agreed to cooperate" with the NNBL, while remaining separate. Nonetheless, the *Globe* remained unimpressed with the work of the NNBL, and in 1911 said that it "never seriously grappled with the real problems of Negro Business." Richard Boyd, however, continued to hold national office in the NNBL, and he remained an associate of both Napier and Washington throughout his life.

One black enterprise that the Boyds and the *Globe* supported fully was the creation of the National Negro Doll Company, which was organized as early as 1909. This was a "race enterprise" of the highest sort—it was intended to instill race pride, yet also was designed to make money. In November 1909, Henry Boyd wrote to Emmett J. Scott, Washington's secretary, telling him that he was sending three "Negro dolls." Boyd asked Scott to accept and keep them as Christmas presents for the children, saying, "These we consider the very best playthings that could be offered for children of our own race. We are very desirous of having the endorsement of our leader [Washington]."

The Boyds began advertising the new dolls, not just in the pages of the *Globe*, but also in national publications like *The Crisis*. They urged all black Baptists to purchase them, saying that "your child would be happy if it had a Negro doll. . . . The Negro doll is calculated to help in the Christian development of the race." In the pages of the *Globe*, August 28, 1908, the Boyds went even further:

These toys are not made of that disgraceful and humiliating type that we have been accustomed to seeing black dolls made of. They represent the intelligent and refined Negro of today, rather than that type of toy that is usually given to the children, and as a rule used as a scarecrow.

Collier's Weekly, in commenting on the dolls, said; "There is more involved than appears on the surface in encouraging little Negro girls to clasp in their arms pretty copies of themselves. The white race doesn't monopolize all the beauty and lovableness, and it will be a happy day when this is realized."

The dolls were produced for some twenty years, and although they never made a great deal of money on the enterprise, it was a self-sustaining operation that invoked much pride in the black community. Nearly a century after the Boyds brought out their doll, the New York Toy Fair was all agog over the fact that Tyco Industries had produced an African-American doll—Kenya—which had no white counterpart. The marketing director for the company commented in 1992, "Traditionally black dolls were an afterthought to white dolls. Kenya is not a 'Roots' doll. She is for contemporary African-American girls." The Kenya doll was produced in response to a study undertaken in Connecticut in the late 1980s that showed that 75 percent of African-American children preferred white dolls to black dolls. There was a need, the study concluded, to produce a doll that did not reinforce stereotypes, for example, Mammy dolls, or that looked like white dolls with a coat of brown dye. The Boyds were obviously light-years ahead of their time in the early twentieth century.

Henry and Richard Boyd and the *Globe* also took the lead in fighting for better schools for African-Americans in the city. They were less concerned with the fact that the schools were segregated than that the black schools were inferior to the white ones. In 1907 the *Globe* demanded that money be appropriated for the erection of two new black schools: "In most of the affairs of the South 'for the colored race' is synonymous with inferior accommodations. We hope that such will not be the case with the Nashville schools." The *Globe* played an even more dramatic role in investigating the disparities in educational opportunities between blacks and whites in higher education. It particularly raised questions about the manner in which federal land grant monies under the Morrill Acts were being distributed. With James Napier in Washington to champion their cause, the Boyds hammered away on the subject between 1907 and 1912.

Henry Boyd, to speed things along, founded and served as chairman of the Tennessee Normal, Agricultural and Mechanical Association, formed in 1909. This became a particularly effective lobby group for the school. Finally, largely as a result of their own efforts and those of Napier, the Boyds were able to secure the establishment of Tennessee Agricultural and Industrial School in the city in 1912. This school ultimately became Tennessee State University, which the Boyds supported with their money, their interest, and their children's education. They were also instrumental in getting the establishment of a black YMCA in the city in 1913, running front page editorials on the issue on a daily basis for nearly two weeks in June.

Another educational issue in which Henry Boyd and the *Globe* became intimately involved was the whole question of white control of Fisk University. Almost from its beginning, the *Globe*, under Boyd's direction, expressed irritation at the paternalism and aloofness of the white administrators who controlled the school. One confrontation emerged in 1911 when a friend of Henry Boyd was visiting the school and was treated in an excessively rude manner by George A. Gates, the university president. The *Globe* attacked Gates, warning him, "The Negroes always looked upon Fisk University as theirs." Few of Nashville's blacks, however, were willing to support the Boyds in their militant stand against white paternalism at that time. The issue reemerged in the 1920s when a more activist student movement began to take issue with the administration's restrictive measures. W.E.B. Du Bois, a Fisk alumnus, took up the cause in speeches and letters, much to the irritation of James Napier. The students ultimately called a strike to protest conditions there, and Henry Boyd and the "young Negroes" at the *Globe* were among those in Nashville's black community who supported the strike. The Negro Board of Trade of Nashville also supported the students' action.

Throughout all these years, the *Globe* continued to grow and prosper and to have a profound impact upon the development of the African-American community in Nashville. By 1929, 20.5 percent of the black families in the city subscribed to the paper, and it also reached nearly every black community in Tennessee. This was a considerable achievement when one takes into account the poverty of the audience they were addressing. Between 1900 and 1940, five additional black newspapers came to life in the city, but none represented a significant challenge to the *Globe*'s leadership. By 1940 not one of the competitors was still in operation. The *Globe* managed to sustain its impact on black Nashvillians for fifty-five years. Through most of these years, the paper reflected the race pride, militance, and desire for economic betterment of Henry Boyd. As a comtemporary commented; "[H]e had various titles, but H. A. Boyd was the *Globe*." After his death, the *Globe* ceased publication. He also served as an organizer and longtime corresponding secretary of the National Negro Press Association. At his funeral, he was called by many who came to speak in his behalf a "first class citizen" of the city.

When Richard Henry Boyd died in 1922, 6,000 people crowded Nashville for his funeral. Twenty-five years later, a life-sized bronze statue of him was erected in his honor by the National Baptist Publishing Board. About 1,000 persons were present to witness the ceremony, which also announced the opening of a new publishing plant for the firm. Dr. G. L. Prince, president of the National Baptist Convention of America, made the dedication speech:

This publishing plant will always speak for the greatness of Dr. Boyd, one of the greatest Negroes his race has ever produced. He was great in intellect, and great in the power to execute those things his intellect discovered. He was great in sensibility and a fearless pioneer who paved the way for the kind of institutions which would bring a better life for people.

Sources

Most of the Boyd family papers are still in private hands and not available to researchers. This is true also of company records for the various Boyd business enterprises. Valuable sources are, however, scattered in a number of collections. The richest source of letters, particularly those relating to the heated controversy over the Publishing Board in 1915, is located in the Frost-Bell Papers at the E.C. Dargan Research Library at the Sunday School Board Library in Nashville. A number of helpful letters from Richard and Henry Boyd to Booker T. Washington and Emmett J. Scott can be found in the B. T. Washington Papers at the Library of Congress. Richard Boyd also wrote a number of books and pamphlets which are generally available at the Special Collections at Tennessee State University, which also has the *Nashville Globe* on microfilm from 1907 to 1960, with some gaps. Copies of some of Boyd's writings are also available at the Southern Baptist Historical Library Archives in Nashville. Richard and Henry Boyd also gave numerous speeches at the National Negro Business League, which are recorded in the annual reports of that organization, available at the Archives of Hampton University.

There is no full-length biography of the Boyd family or any of its members. Nor are there extensive studies of any of their business organizations, save for several partisan writings on one side or the other of the National Publishing Board dispute in 1915. The best short biographies of Richard and Henry Boyd are in the *Dictionary of Negro Biography* (1982), by Richard F. Hildebrand and Lester C. Lamon, respectively. There is also a short biography of Richard Boyd in the *Dictionary of American Biography Supplement 1* (1944). There are obituaries of Richard Boyd in the *Nashville Banner*, August 24, 1922, and the *Chicago Defender*, September 2, 1922. Additionally, there is biographical information in Samuel W. Bacote, *Who's Who among Colored Baptists of the United States*, 1912, 73–76; *Who's Who of the Colored Race* (1915); *Who's Who in Colored America* (1927, 1928–1929); *Black Enterprise*, June 1980; and *Negro History Bulletin* V, 5 (February 1942), 114–15. There are also some short notices in the *Nashville Banner*, March 17, 1947; *Leaders of Afro-American Nashville* (1983, 1987); *Leadership in Nashville* (n.d.); and *Los Angeles Sentinel*, February 17, 1981. Obituaries of Henry Boyd appeared in the *Nashville Banner*, May 28, 1959; *Nashville Globe*, June 12, 1959; and the *Pittsburgh Courier* (national edition), June 6, 1959. There is additional information in the *Louisiana Weekly*, December 3, 1932. There is an article by Henry Boyd on banking in the *Christian Recorder*, June 1910.

There is biographical information about Theophilus B. Boyd, Jr., in the *Nashville Banner*, April 13, 1947, April 19, 1972, January 29, 1974, July 25, 1975, April 2 (obituary), April 3, and April 18, 1979. There is also an obituary in *The Tennessean*, April 2, 1979. Information on T. B. Boyd III appears in the *Nashville Banner*, March 24, 1978, October 21, 1979, February 2, 1984, October 23, 1985, and February 5, 1988; and in *The Tennessean*, May 13, 1979, October 13, 1980, December 11, 1981, June 16, 1988, February 19, 1989, and December 8 and 17, 1989.

Information on the National Baptist Publishing Board is voluminous, but much of it is partisan either pro- or anti-Richard Boyd and the controversy surrounding the board, so it must be used with care. Older accounts include Richard Boyd's *A Story of the National Baptist Publishing Board* (Nashville, 1915) and W. H. Moses, *The Colored Baptists' Family Tree* (Nashville, 1925) by one of Boyd's enemies. *Negro Baptist History, U.S.A.*, by Reverend Lewis G. Jordan (Nashville, n.d.) is also an antagonistic account by a partisan. Booker T. Washington gives a favorable story of the Publishing Board in Chapter XVIII of *The Negro in Business (1907)*. There is another account of the organization of the board in typescript at the Southern Baptist Historical Library and Archives, entitled "The National Baptist Publishing Board" (n.d.). Even recent scholarly studies display a marked bias. J. H. Jackson, *A Story of Christian Activism: The History of the National Baptist Convention, U.S.A. Inc.* (Nashville, 1980), is strongly anti-Boyd; H. Leon McBeth, *The Baptist Heritage* (Nashville, 1987) gives a more favorable account. Similarly, accounts published by the Publishing Board continue to give Boyd's side: *National Baptist Union-Review*, April 2, 1983; George Rollie Adams and Ralph Jerry Christian, *Nashville: A Pictorial History* (Virginia Beach, 1981), 228–29; and a video produced by the Publishing Board. More balanced accounts appear in *The Crisis*, April 1914, 314–16; W. A. Low and Virgil A. Clift, eds., *Encyclopedia of Black America*, 164–65; James Melvin Washington, *Frustrated Fellowship: The Black Baptist Quest for Social Power* (Mercer, Georgia, 1986); Donald Franklin Joyce, *Gatekeepers of Black*

Culture (1983), 75–77, 200–01; August Meier, *Negro Thought in America* (1963), 132. See also John Louis Hill, *When Black Meets White* (Cleveland, 1924), 77–78.

Information on Citizens Bank and Trust can be obtained from articles in the *Nashville Globe* and *New York Age* in the Peabody Collection at Hampton University, as well as from the bank's own publications available from the bank. Information on the *Nashville Globe* comes from Samuel Shannon, "Tennessee," in Lewis Suggs, *The Black Press* (1983), 328–35. August Meier, *Negro Thought in America*, discusses the Boyd's "colored" doll company on p. 270; and there is a series of articles in the Peabody Collection at Hampton on the doll company: *Christian Index*, October 1, 1908; *Afro-American Ledger*, December 4, 1909; and *New York Age*, September 21, 1910. Bill Bell, "Introducing Kenya," *New York Daily News*, February 1992, discusses the history of African-American dolls in America. Regarding the Boyd's involvement with educational institutions in Nashville, particularly Tennessee State University, see a series of articles in the *Nashville Globe* from 1909 to 1912. These have been collected in the clipping file in Special Collections at Tennessee State University.

Browne, William Washington (October 20, 1849–December 21, 1897). Insurance company founder, banker, religious leader, and fraternal order organizer: United Order of True Reformers; True Reformers Bank. Contemporaries in the late nineteenth century recognized W. W. Browne as one of the most powerful and important leaders of the African-American community. This appraisal was also shared by many influential members of the white community. The measure of Browne's regard can be gauged by the fact that he was one of just eight blacks nationwide chosen to be in the audience when Booker T. Washington* delivered his famous "Atlanta Exposition" speech in 1895. Yet, until very recently, Browne has been almost completely ignored by historians of the black experience. Only in the last fifteen years has Browne begun to be restored to his rightful place in history. A temperance agitator, fraternal society founder, pioneer black banker and businessman, community leader, minister, and national spokesman, William Washington Browne, despite his short life, was a giant in the African-American community at the turn of the century.

W. W. Brown's early years are somewhat clouded in mist. All we know is what was written shortly after his death by admirers who may have embroidered the truth. The following "facts" must therefore be taken with some caution. It seems quite clear that Browne was born a slave on the plantation of Benjamin Pryor in Habershaw County, Georgia. His parents were Joseph and Maria Browne, natives of Virginia, and the baby was given the name of Ben. While still quite young, "Ben", who early showed flashes of intelligence and initiative, was made a servant in the Pryor household. At about the same time, his master died and his mistress married A. G. Pitman of Rome, Georgia. At that time she sold the old plantation, Ben's parents along with it, and brought him with her to Rome.

Within a few years, young Ben was being hired out to local businessmen and professionals. He worked for a time for a storekeeper, during which time Ben learned the rudiments of that trade. Then he worked as an office boy for a local lawyer. At about this time Ben asked that his name be changed to Washington and prefixed William to that, becoming William Washington Browne. Next, Browne was sold to a horse trader who trained the compact young man to be a jockey. Given the opportunity to travel throughout the South in this capacity, Browne soon acquired an enormous thirst for freedom and became an avowed abolitionist. When tensions developed between Browne and his young master, Browne supposedly gave him a thrashing for insults. His master decided to send Browne to a plantation in Mississippi, where his "uppity" behavior would be curtailed. By this time, though, the Civil War was raging, and Browne heard that Union armies were advancing on Memphis, so he fled the plantation and began walking toward Union lines, ultimately meeting up with companies of the Sixth Missouri regiment. As owners were coming to the camp to claim runaway slaves, however, Browne decided he should push further north.

Arriving at Cairo, Illinois, Browne worked for a time as a saloon servant, giving him a lifelong aversion to alcohol, and then joined the navy as a bootblack. Aboard the gunboat *National*, Browne saw several battles, but he left the ship at Vicksburg and went to Wisconsin where he joined the Eighteenth U.S. Infantry. With that unit, Browne evidently distinguished himself; he was mustered out as a sergeant major at the end of the war. Browne then returned to Wisconsin, where he attended school in Prairie-du-Chien for a short time before going back to Georgia. In his native state, Browne began teaching in the new freedmen's schools and became a leader of blacks in the local area. His movement onto a broader stage came when he began speaking out against the Ku Klux Klan in the early 1870s, at some very real peril to his own life. Allying himself at times with Reverend Henry M. Turner, who later became a powerful force in the African Methodist Episcopal (AME) Church and one of the most radical voices in the late nineteenth-century black community, Browne was equally controversial. Recognizing the fear the Ku Klux Klan was instilling in his people, Browne encouraged blacks to arm themselves for their own protection. Browne argued that a bullet from a Winchester would do much to convince lawless whites not to trifle with blacks. This militant stance made Browne a man to be reckoned with in both the black and white communities.

Using that newly acquired prestige, Browne became a prominent temperance lecturer in Georgia and Alabama. He viewed "King Alcohol" as one of the major scourges in the postbellum black community. Not only, he stated, did newly freed African-Americans have high rates of alcoholism, with its attendent psychological and social problems, even moderate drinking among blacks could have dire consequences. Being convicted for public drunkenness, he argued, often meant the chain gang for blacks, resulting in loss of income and disfranchisement. Thus, for Browne, alcoholism was a key social and political issue, a symbol for the rapidly diminishing role of blacks in the economic, social, and political life of late Reconstruction South. Browne's speeches were effective, but he was still just a single individual. He decided he needed an organization to fight "demon rum" more effectively.

To that end, Browne, with a few other leaders of the local African-American community, approached the Grand Lodge of Good Templars. The Good Templars, a white organization in Alabama devoted to temperance, was intrigued with Browne's ideas for promoting abstinence among blacks but reluctant to associate formally with him. Striving to find a compromise, the Good Templars proposed to Browne that he receive a charter and sponsorship from them, but under a separate name—the United Order of True Reformers. At around this same time, Browne married Mary A. (Molly) Graham. Childless, they adopted two children.

William W. Browne was thus launched into the beginnings of one of the most significant and, until recently, largely ignored, social developments among blacks in the late nineteenth and early twentieth centuries. The newly freed blacks at the end of the war were without the most basic institutions and organizations that went into the making of communities. For a time this vacuum was filled by the Freedman's Bureau, but as the North withdrew its support for Reconstruction, it was necessary for African-Americans to develop their own institutional framework. A key element in this was black fraternal organizations, and the benefit societies, insurance companies, banks, and businesses that soon came in their wake. Browne, with the United Order of True Reformers, created one of the first, and certainly one of the most influential, of these organizations.

In 1874 Browne quit his teaching job in Georgia and moved to Alabama to work full-time for the True Reformers. Canvassing the state, the dynamic and charismatic Browne had soon set up enough "sub-fountains" to establish a "Grand Fountain." This was an enormous accomplishment on the part of Browne, but his ambition pushed him to yet greater lengths. To further enhance his appeal as a temperance speaker, Browne was ordained a minister of the AME Church in 1876. The AME Church had high social status among nineteenth-century blacks, so his ordination had the additional significance of increasing Browne's popularity among the middle classes of African-American society.

Over the next few years Browne worked as a minister, temperance agitator, and fraternal organizer in Selma and Montgomery, Alabama. Although he had achieved no small measure of success in his endeavors, Browne was becoming increasingly frustrated with his situation in Alabama. He, first of all, disliked being under white control with his sponsorship by the Good Templars. He also bemoaned the fact that the Good Templars and True Reformers had no membership dues, making it difficult either to build a stable organizational base or to put the group on a sound financial footing. Finally, he had begun to visualize the possibilities of a broader financial empire among blacks that could not be accomplished within the confines of Alabama.

Searching for a new base of operations, Browne recalled the cordial treatment he had received when he organized a branch of the True Reformers in Richmond, Virginia, in 1875. Richmond's blacks had experienced traumatic times during the Civil War and Reconstruction period. Conditions during the war were very trying for African-Americans, slave or free. As Union armies put pressure on the Confederate capital, slaves were impressed into service of the Confederate army, and the property of free blacks was often seized.

These actions did much to undercut the independence and stability of the prewar free black group. Loren Schweninger has found that only one in seven of the antebellum black businesses survived the war. At the same time, the war also created some opportunities for new black entrepreneurs. Property was much cheaper because of the trauma of the times, and a large number of whites who might have provided business services after the war had been killed or crippled in the conflict. Thus, as the war came to an end, a small group of black entrepreneurs emerged with new strategies and attitudes. Although it would take time for it to bear fruit, this new group of blacks laid the basis for the future expansion of the black business community in postwar Richmond.

With the end of the war, massive numbers of newly freed black slaves poured into Richmond. The city, with 12,296 African-Americans in 1850, watched that total nearly double to 23,110 by 1870. Since the 1870 census drastically undercounted blacks in the South, the latter total was undoubtedly much higher. To many Richmond natives, black and white, it seemed as if their world had been turned upside down. This situation also created social chaos for the black community. What few independent social institutions they had had before the war were destroyed, and they sorely needed a whole network of social organizations to create a sense of community among the group of desperate newcomers. To that end, the black churches particularly played a leading role in creating a dense network of self-help organizations.

Temperance groups like the True Reformers were key elements in this new self-conscious effort on the part of blacks to create a sense of community in Richmond. Along with these organizations arose also a number of new businesses designed to cater to this black community, and a new middle class who, having experienced much hostility and repression by whites during Reconstruction, began developing a philosophy of militant race pride to go along with their ideals of self-help. Like Browne himself, this new black middle class in Richmond joined more conservative beliefs in individual mobility and the gospel of wealth with radical race pride and separatism. The confluence of this set of ideals helped create a whole new panoply of black businesses in Richmond in the 1870s, several of which developed directly from fraternal and social organizations.

Thus, when W. W. Browne arrived in Richmond in 1880, he came to a city that was tailor-made for his abilities and ambitions. Upon his arrival, Browne was named a minister of the Leigh Street African Methodist Episcopal Church, a position he maintained until the church demanded that he spend less time with the True Reformers. In response, Browne resigned from the pulpit, leaving no doubt where his primary sympathies lay. He was concerned with building a large and vibrant social and temperance society and, even more important, to convert that into the largest, most important black financial institution in the state.

When Browne helped organize the True Reformers in Richmond in 1875, the leadership of the organization was composed primarily of members of the city's newly emergent black elite—storekeepers, undertakers, ministers, and the like. During the next five years, the True Reformers experienced modest growth, but when Browne took over in 1880, he determined to change the entire nature of the organization. Browne's first step came in his acceptance speech. There, he unveiled plans to convert the True Reformers into a benefit and relief society. That is, each member would be required to purchase a death benefit certificate for $1.50 as a condition of membership, in return for which his or her heirs would receive a death benefit of $100 upon death. This modest start laid the basis for what one historian has called "a black-owned, black-operated financial empire, the size of which had not been seen before in America."

To achieve this end, Browne also had to change the social composition of the organization's leadership in order to make it more attractive to the city's rank-and-file black community. Of the fourteen delegates and officers who attended the first assembly in 1881, just two, Browne and Peter H. Woolfolk, were members of the city's black elite. The rest were all day laborers and other members of the city's lower ranks of the working classes. Upon this new basis, the True Reformers began to grow in the 1880s, but not without tensions and difficulties. The first of these came when many original members of the True Reformers objected to the deemphasis on temperance reform. What ensued was a terrible struggle between the temperance advocates and Browne, as they felt he was perverting the mission of the True Reformers beyond any recognition, and, in fact, many felt he was concerned only with his own personal gain. Therefore, they resolved to strip him of his powers and "send him back to the state of Alabama." To do so, they filed suit against him, but the judgment was ultimately in Browne's favor. As a result, the dissidents broke away and formed their own branch of the True Reformers, allowing Browne to pursue his business interests with his rump group. With just fourteen fountains, 150 members, and a total capital stock of just $150 for the entire state, Browne had his work cut out for him.

William W. Browne was, by all accounts, a profoundly charismatic leader, known far and wide as "True Reformer Browne," as he traveled the land in his long clerical-cut coat. His organizational and inspirational abilities gave fruit in the growth of the new organization. A year later he had 600 members in the True Reformers, and in 1883 it was officially and formally incorporated. Browne's grand vision was finally on its way. By 1885 there were fifty-one fountains in the state, and at the same time a system of levying fees on the members according to age was instituted, thus making the True Reformers the first black benefit society to be based on the sound actuarial principles of the insurance industry.

With these changes, money began to accumulate in the organization's treasury, and Browne conceived the idea of establishing a bank to handle them. This was a revolutionary step. The African-Americans' only previous experience with banking had been a disaster. The federal government had set up the Freedman's Bank at the end of the Civil War, but corruption and mismanagement by politicians, together with the impact of the depression of the 1870s and the federal government's new callous attitude toward the needs of blacks, caused the bank to fail, taking with it the savings of some 70,000 black depositors. To start a black-owned bank to handle the savings of blacks, therefore, was a risky venture, but Browne's charisma was again sufficient to overcome negative reactions. Browne got a charter for the True Reformers Bank from the Virginia legislature on March 2, 1888, making it the first black-owned and black-operated bank in America. Browne had problems getting it actually operating, however, and by the time he commenced operations in his home on April 3, 1889, the Capitol Savings Bank of Washington, D.C., also organized by blacks, had been operating for several months.

On its first day of business, the True Reformers Bank received $1,200 in deposits. The bank was authorized not only to act as a depository for the order's funds, but also was able to do a general banking business. The bank, contrary to the predictions of most whites, and even many blacks, was an instant success, and it continued to be so for more than twenty years. At the same time, Browne began to network the bank, the order, and himself more tightly into the newly emerging black middle class in Richmond. Giles B. Jackson, the bank's attorney, became one of Browne's closest associates and one of the most important leaders of the city's African-American community for many years. Involved in management of the bank were R. T. Hill, a successful small businessman in the city, and W. P. Burrell and Joseph Jones, both teachers at Navy Hill School, P. S. Lindsay, a shoemaker, and W. L. Taylor, a minister. Most important, on the board of directors, was John Mitchell, Jr.,* editor of the *Richmond Planet*, next to Browne the single most important member of the city's black elite.

The bank was really just the cornerstone of a whole business empire Browne was creating in Richmond. The order began acquiring an impressive amount of real estate, much of it funded through loans from the bank. Its first property was the Centralia Mills in Chesterfield County, and the second became the site of the True Reformer's new hall in Richmond. On the site they erected in 1890 an impressive three-story building to house their general offices and a large auditorium. The bank itself was also moved there. Throughout the early 1890s, Browne continued to expand the economic interests of the True Reformers. He organized its own real estate agency in 1892 and started a newspaper, *The Reformer*, in 1895. The Reformer's Mercantile and Industrial Association was established in the late 1890s to conduct a chain of stores, and to erect a 150-room hotel for blacks. It also took over management of the newspaper and printing establishment and the real estate operations. In 1900 the Mercantile and Industrial Association was incorporated. In addition, an Old Folks Home was set up in 1898, and, at about the same time, the Westham Farm was founded. The latter was, next to the bank, the order's most ambitious undertaking. Some of the 634 acres were set aside for agricultural production; the rest were subdivided into lots and sold to individual blacks to create a new, all-black town called Browneville in honor of its founder.

Browne and the Order of True Reformers had achieved wondrous things in Richmond, given the extent of white racism and the severity of the depression of the 1890s. In recognition, Browne, along with Booker T. Washington and seven other African-Americans, was invited to attend the Atlanta Exposition in 1895. Prior to going to Atlanta, Browne addressed Richmond's blacks. He advocated, like Washington, a continued separation of the races in both business and social affairs. He also argued against pressing for social and political equality with whites, asserting that these demands simply brought lynchings and other forms of white retribution without gaining any benefits for blacks. Browne went so far in 1895 as to criticize Mitchell and a black Massachusetts legislator for provoking white racism by visiting the governor's mansion along with white members of the Massachusetts delegation. As a result, Mitchell and other critics of Browne often accused him of subservience toward the state's white supremacists. Browne took great umbrage at this criticism, and often asserted that his critics were light-skinned African-Americans who desired acceptance by white society. Browne himself was a dark-skinned man of pure African heritage.

Browne's great plans and visions, however, had to be achieved without his participation. Soon after the Atlanta Exposition, he discovered he had cancer on his arm, and because he refused to have the limb amputated, the cancer rapidly spread to the rest of his body. Upon his death in December 1897, eulogies were delivered by prominent blacks in Richmond, and Browne's associates vowed to carry on his work. To some extent they did, but serious problems ultimately emerged. Reverend W. L. Taylor took over leadership of the order, and W. P. Burrell assumed control of the bank, but neither of them had the sort of leadership and charisma that Browne possessed. Although the order's financial empire grew, it was loosely and not terribly effectively managed, and the whole organization collapsed in 1910 due to a scandal within the bank.

The crisis was caused by the news that R. T. Hill, the bank's cashier, had embezzled $50,000, but this just hastened the end of what had been a very shaky financial organization for a number of years. As Abram L. Harris reported, the bank had long subordinated its own interests, and those of its depositors, to the financial and social needs of the order. They had given the order extensive loans to engage in its grandiose projects, usually without sufficient equity to back them up. Thus, when the loans began to default, the bank was not able to pay the claims brought against insurance policies held by the order. The state's banking examiner ordered the bank closed on October 20, 1910, and the rest of the order's financial empire came tumbling down in short order.

The magnitude of the failure probably explains why William W. Browne slipped from the view of historians. The world loves a winner, and Browne's empire, like so many other ambitious black enterprises during these years, was undercapitalized, pursued plans that were far too grandiose, and was poorly managed. But this should not obscure Browne's enormous accomplishment. He combined a number of real needs in the African-American community in the traumatic years of the late nineteenth century into a dynamic and successful business enterprise, one that was copied by other blacks for example, John Merrick* and the North Carolina Mutual Insurance Company. Even W.E.B. Du Bois, who was geneally quite critical of economic self-help ventures, characterized the True Reformers as "probably the most remarkable Negro organization in the country" in 1907.

Starting with temperance reform, Browne understood the need blacks had for the symbols of belonging, community, and togetherness. He thus formed a fraternal organization that provided just that sense of belonging, and a sense of being somebody important in a world that otherwise severely undervalued their existence. The parades, the regalia, the rituals, and secret handshakes and passwords were important touchstones of community in a hostile and rapidly changing world. But Browne soon went beyond that, recognizing that even poor blacks, in sufficient numbers, possessed sufficient capital to engage in independent economic activity. Browne's empire in Richmond failed, but his grand vision was picked up by others. In Richmond, John Mitchell, Jr., and Maggie Lena Walker* picked up Browne's banner as it was falling; in other cities, his success inspired other African-Americans to do likewise. Only Booker T. Washington may have had more importance in developing independent black business and black communities in the later years of the nineteenth century. William W. Browne was not only an "organizer extraordinary" as one historian has called him; he was a powerful pioneer in the development of a whole range of important African-American institutions. He was a giant among men.

Sources

No personal records of W. W. Browne or the True Reformers appear to exist, although the Virginia Historical Society in Richmond has a photocopy of the order's 1904 charter and a broadside from 1911 announcing the need to raise $37,000 to relieve financial difficulties. The most detailed, though not wholly reliable, sources for Browne and the order are Daniel W. Davis, *The Life and Public Service of Rev. William Washington Browne: Founder of the Grand Fountain* (Richmond, 1910), written at the behest of Browne's widow. A new edition of the book, with an introductory essay by David M. Fahey, was published in 1992. See also Walter P. Burrell, *Twenty-Five Years History of the Grand Fountain of the United Order of True Reformers* (Richmond, 1909). Abram L. Harris, *The Negro As Capitalist: A Study of Banking and Business among American Negroes* (College Park, Md., 1936), chapter IV, has an extended analysis of the True Reformers Bank, based at least partly on an examination of the bank's annual statements after 1900. See also Arnett G. Lindsay, "The Negro in Banking," *Journal of Negro History* XIV (1929).

The most important studies by recent historians are by James D. Watkinson, "William Washington Browne and the True Reformers of Richmond," *Virginia Magazine of History and Biography* 97, 3 (July 1989); and "W. W. Browne: Organizer Extraordinary," *Richmond Literature and Historical Quarterly* 2, 3 (Winter 1979). There are short biographies of Browne by David Fahey in *American National Biography* (forthcoming) and Ingham, BDABL. There is also some information on the order or Browne in G. F. Riching's *Evidences of Progress among Colored People* (1897); *The Afro-American*, October 29, 1910; *The Ninth Annual Report of the Hampton Negro Conference* in 1905;

The World's Work, June 1908; and W. H. Quick, *Negro Stars in All Ages of the World* (1898).

The broader influence of fraternal organizations and the economic significance of Browne and the True Reformers can be ascertained from Walter B. Weare, *Black Business in the New South: A Social History of the North Carolina Mutual Insurance Company* (Urbana, Ill., 1973); Howard Rabinowitz, *Race Relations in the Urban South* (Urbana, Ill., 1978); and August Meier, *Negro Thought in America* (1963). Oral history tapes of Anthony Binga (a descendent of Jesse Binga* of Chicago), held at the Maggie Lena Walker Historical Site in Richmond, give testimony to the great importance of fraternal organizations for blacks in the late nineteenth century.

Burrell, Thomas J. (March 18, 1939–   ). Advertising agency founder: Burrell Advertising Inc. It was a television ad for Crest toothpaste. The ad showed a black father lovingly teaching his son how to knot a tie. A simple message, one most whites would find familiar and unremarkable. But this kind of sensitivity to the emotional needs of the black market has made the Burrell Advertising Agency the largest black-owned agency in the United States. Thomas Burrell, the agency's founder, continually makes the point that white agencies do not know how to reach the black market. Since 40 percent of blacks grow up in fatherless households, it is necessary to present an image to them, not of what is, but of what could and should be. "There's a tremendous difference in the way we came here," says Burrell, "and this affects our buying behavior. Targeting for the black consumer is an anthropological consideration more than a marketing consideration. We simply look at things differently. Lots of customs and habits came with us, only vestiges of which are left today, but we're still very different from Europeans." Most white advertisers, he claims, have missed this important emotional point when dealing with blacks. Thus, emotional appeal became the hallmark of Burrell's advertising approach. As he often noted, "[T]o reach the purse strings, you must first touch the heartstrings."

Thomas Burrell was born in Chicago and grew up in Englewood, a tough neighborhood in the South Side black ghetto. Englewood was one of the formerly white areas in the South and Southwest side of Chicago that was rapidly converted to a majority black population during the massive migration of southern blacks in the 1940s. The transition was not peaceful. During the 1940s, when Tom Burrell was a small child, there was a series of mob attacks on blacks in the area. It had the second-highest number of mob attacks of any area in Chicago during this time. The worst of the disturbances was the Englewood Riot, which occurred at 56th and Peoria in November 1949, when Tom Burrell was just ten years old. Thereafter, the area rapidly became an all-black ghetto, inhabited by the poor and characterized by gang violence and other crime. Not much is known about his parents, but his father was a tavern owner and his mother worked as a beautician. She was the one who tended to give Burrell the greatest encouragement to succeed in life. "My mother always treated me as if I was a person," he later reflected, "not just a kid. She knew I'd be something." His father, however, was less optimistic, and what drove Burrell to become successful was the contrast in the way he was treated by his parents. "What drove me [to be successful]?," he asked. "It was probably to prove my mother right and my father wrong."

But none of this was a foregone conclusion in the tough Englewood area. "I have a hard time describing myself as anything when I was growing up," Burrell admits. "I wasn't a good athlete, I wasn't a good gang fighter, I wasn't a good bike rider—I was outside every group and that's probably what saved me. Otherwise, I'd probably be in Englewood, still hanging out." Burrell was educated in the city's public schools, but he did not distinguish himself as a student; his grades were mostly average or below average. The problem, Burrell admits, was that he just was not interested in anything—certainly not in school, but not even in "gang fighting or sports or girls or marbles. I can't recall being interested in anything." At Englewood High School, Burrell managed to stay out of trouble, because he was an outsider, but that is about all. Then he transferred to Parker High School and, as part of the assessment process, was forced to take an aptitude test. On the test he scored well in the areas of artistic and persuasive abilities. But not having a clue as to what that meant, Burrell went to his teacher. The teacher told him that it meant that Burrell had a bent for writing advertising copy. That struck a spark in Burrell. "I glommed on to it," Burrell later recalled. "It was an exotic, unknown occupation in my neighborhood. I was able to say I was going to be something."

After graduating from Parker High, Burrell enrolled in Roosevelt University on a probationary status—and promptly flunked out. He then took a job working on the assembly line at a local paint factory. That experience told him he had better go back to college and to apply himself to his studies this time. "I knew I didn't fit in at the factory," he said. "I tried to change the way things were done, things that had been going on for years. The older employees didn't like it." He reentered Roosevelt majoring in English and advertising. "It was hard," admitted Burrell. It meant giving up a lot of other things, but he stuck with it and graduated in 1961. About a year before graduating, Burrell joined the now-defunct Wade Advertising Agency of Chicago as a mailroom clerk.

Burrell spent six months working in the mail room, always "comport[ing] myself in a way that I should be doing something more," said Burrell. As he pushed his cart around the office, he picked up information on problems the agency was having. Learning of a problem in the creative area, Burrell went into the creative director's office, telling him that he could help him with some of his problems. The director was persuaded to take a chance. "Two weeks later I was a copy trainee," remembers Burrell. He asserts that, at the time, he was almost certainly the only black working on the creative side of advertising in Chicago.

After graduation from college, Burrell was promoted to copywriter. Before long, he was working on television and print ads for Alka-Seltzer, One-a-Day Vitamins, and Falstaff. At the time, Wade, as was true of all other white-owned agencies, paid virtually no attention to the black market. It was, therefore, a big breakthrough for Burrell, and for the black community overall, when he landed the Toni account, which was attempting to market a hair product to black women. "There wasn't much of that going around then," he said.

In 1964 Burrell moved on to the giant Leo Burnett Company of Chicago as a copywriter. There he found that "there wasn't much acknowledgment that there was a black consumer market. The only thing they ever heard was television reaches everybody." This was characteristic of highly successful large agencies in the 1960s. They were so imbued with the magic of communications technology, so caught up in the concept of a homogeneous American marketplace, that they simply gave no thought to a segmented market approach. It was not just that the black market was ignored; there was no recognition that one needed to develop alternative approaches to market goods effectively. America, to their mind, was a melting pot, and television was the crucible in which everybody was reduced to a common denominator. But blacks and advertising had been a particularly nettlesome area for some time.

During the 1940s, a few pioneer black admen started their own agencies in New York, Detroit, and Chicago. They serviced a profoundly limited market— selling black products through the black media to black customers. However, none of these agencies ever achieved any significant size. The major white agencies had little interest in the black market either and hired very few blacks. The first white agency to recognize that there might be a special market niche for blacks was Batten, Barton, Durstin and Osborn in the 1950s. They started a "special markets" unit staffed by blacks to sell to blacks. The few blacks hired at other agencies during the 1950s were simply so good that their credentials outweighed their color and they were assigned to work on general accounts. By the early 1960s, when Thomas Burrell broke into advertising, a survey conducted by the Urban League showed there were fewer than twenty-five blacks at creative or executive jobs in the top ten agencies. Whites simply dismissed the problem by claiming they never hired blacks because there were so few qualified black applicants.

The impact of all of this on the black community, and on America generally, was profoundly disturbing. A study of ads featuring blacks in 1946 showed that 78 percent were depicted in laborer or service jobs: maid, waiter, slave, field hand, personal service—the typical Aunt Jemima or Uncle Tom. Only 3 percent of the blacks were depicted in even remotely higher status occupations. Ten years later, blacks who were depicted as sports heroes or entertainers increased from 15 percent to 36 percent, while those in the service or laborer categories dropped to 52 percent. There was just one ad in each year that depicted blacks in a white-collar occupation. Even by 1965, during Burrell's early years in Chicago advertising, the number of blacks depicted in professional, managerial, and clerical occupations had risen just 1 percent from the previous decade, although only 13 percent were shown in menial jobs. Virtually no ads throughout this entire twenty-year period showed blacks and whites as equals.

By the mid–1960s, civil rights pressures for the hiring of blacks had intensified, resulting in a slight increase in blacks at white-owned agencies. The push by civil rights organizations in the later 1960s, though, went beyond merely hiring more blacks. They also began demanding that more blacks be shown in the agencies' ads and a greater sensitivity in the advertising copy directed toward blacks. They demanded that the old white stereotypes of blacks—Aunt Jemima, the Gold Dust twins, Cream of Wheat's smiling black chef, and Hiram Walker's butler—be eliminated. All these characterizations depicted blacks either in demeaning service roles, or tended to perpetuate the image of blacks as smiling, happy "pickaninnies" in a way that was extremely offensive to the black community. The black organizations had some success in their campaign, with Doyle Dane Bernbach, headed by William Bernbach leading the way. DDB's ad for Levy's Jewish rye bread, showing a picture of a smiling black child with the caption "You don't have to be Jewish to love Levy's," won praise from the black community. Malcolm X, the black militant, was so impressed he told a photographer, "Take my picture by this sign, I like it."

Heavy pressure was mounted by the Congress of Racial Equality on Procter & Gamble, Coca-Cola, Colgate-Palmolive, and other major advertisers to develop more sensitive advertising campaigns aimed at blacks. The subtext of these demands was the necessity to hire more blacks to handle these campaigns, since only they understood the unique cultural role of blacks in America. Progress came, but it came very slowly during the 1960s. A survey of ads run in New York, monitored by the New York City Commission on Human Rights, showed that just 314 of the 7,340 commercials in the city during 1966 and 1967 had blacks represented in them—just 4 percent of the total. There was also minimal progress at best in securing the employment of blacks in white-owned agencies. An EEOC study conducted in 1966 showed that just 2.5 percent of the white-collar jobs at sixty-four New York agencies were held by blacks, even though blacks made up over 18 percent of the city's population. At the largest ad agencies, blacks fared even more poorly, accounting for just 1.9 percent of the total.

Consequently, Thomas Burrell during these years was in a lonely and often neglected situation. In 1967 he left Leo Burnett to become a copywriter in the London office of Foote, Cone & Belding. "I went there," said Burrell, "and almost starved to death, *with* a job. Until then, I'd been thoroughly nonentrepreneurial. I came back really hot to make money." A year later he returned to the United States as copy supervisor at Needham, Harper & Steers. Although Burrell was advancing within a largely lily-white advertising community, he was not happy with the kind of work he was doing, nor was he impressed with the ads Needham, Harper and other white agencies were producing. Even though the murder of Martin Luther King, Jr., in 1968 had brought about a characteristic surge of concern for blacks, with a flood of ads and pious statements, blacks already employed in advertising decided to organize themselves, starting the

Group for Advertising Progress. The message was clear: "You white advertising folks are a lot happier about the progress of integration than us black advertising folks."

No matter what small gains were made, by then it seemed far too little and too late for many blacks in advertising. Edgar Hopper, a former account executive at Foote, Cone & Belding said, "We have to become black Anglo Saxons to make it. If you let your hair grow out, you're Rap Brown. Speak out and you're coming on too strong." Hopper, Burrell, and others insisted, "When you hire a black creative person, hire him for his lifestyle, not because you want him to imitate the white." As this sense of nationalist pride grew in the late 1960s and early 1970s, several blacks, Thomas Burrell among them, decided to open their own agencies. Burrell remembers that he was particularly tired of having to "think in reverse." This was no big deal, he insisted, since "that's one of the unique gifts we have had by necessity, of being able to think in reverse and in our terms. We have to live in a White world and have to deal with the world. Selling things to White people was no big thing because my whole life revolved around trying to figure out what White people were thinking."

In 1971 Burrell left Needham, Harper and, along with two associates, rented a small, one-room office in Chicago to house his Burrell McBain Advertising Agency. "We had no secretary, one telephone, and three old desks," he recalled, "which we painted red, green, and orange." He then waited six agonizing months before he got his first piece of business, which paid the agency a piddling $3,000 a month. But they were finally on their way. Burrell Advertising was one of about a dozen black-owned agencies spawned during the early 1970s to operate on a nationwide basis. Some failed, and some survived, but Burrell's became the largest, by far.

The key to Burrell's success was the pitch he used with white advertisers. He argued that blacks were "not just dark-skinned white people," but a group with a unique heritage, with distinctly different tastes and formidable buying power. Further, the best way to reach this black market, he argued, was not with a sales pitch oriented to the product, which was characteristic of most white advertising, but to pursue a form of "lifestyle advertising," to create and celebrate an image of black people that is positive and uplifting, which at the same time reflected positively upon the product. He warned advertisers who were beginning to use increasing numbers of blacks in their ads that this was a path fraught with dangers. "As soon as a black face appears on the screen," he said, "it's 'Okay. How you gonna be usin' us now?' White people don't have to go through that."

From the start, Burrell determined to go after only big clients, and his big breakthrough came in 1972 when he garnered the Coca-Cola soft drink account for the black market. Burrell was invaluable in the early years in providing Coca-Cola with insights into the black market. In 1974 Coke decided to run a campaign entitled "Look up America and see what you've got." Burrell did not think it would work in the black community. He argued that the time had not yet come when blacks could take pride in the American experience. So he persuaded them to run ads that said, "For the real times, it's the real thing." Similarly, Burrell picked up McDonald's black advertising account in the 1970s. At that time, McDonald's slogan in the white community was "You deserve a break today." This, argued Burrell, implied that going to McDonald's was a special dining treat. But in the black neighborhoods, "kids were running into [McDonald's] four and five times a day." As a result, Burrell substituted the theme "McDonald's is good to have around" for the black market. Burrell also lined up a number of other blue-chip firms, including Ford Motor Company and Stroh's Brewery. The only black-owned businesses among his client mix were Johnson Publishing, Chicago-based publisher of *Ebony* and *Jet*, and Johnson Products, a Chicago hair products manufacturer. Burrell pointed out that, although he never went after black businesses, he did not turn them away either.

By the early 1980s, Burrell had used this strategy to build Burrell Advertising into an agency with $30 million in bookings. It was still a midget compared to such huge international agencies as J. Walter Thompson, which had U.S. billings of about $1.5 billion. Compared to most other black agencies, however, Burrell was huge. Only Uniworld, started by Byron Lewis, and Mingo-Jones, set up by Frank Mingo, both in New York, even approached Burrell's size. The problem that Burrell and many of the other black agencies encountered was that the black advertising business had arisen in the 1960s and early 1970s for the most part as a result of a response by white advertisers to the riots of the late 1960s when the government and many white firms began putting money into black-owned businesses. Blacks usually referred to this as "conscience money," but by the mid–1970s it began withering away. As a result many of the black agencies went out of business, but Burrell continued to grow, with almost twice as many billings as the next largest black agency. Burrell's explanation for that is that from the very first, "we [were] interested in clients who think we can help them, not who are trying to help us."

Despite Burrell's impressive earlier growth, 1983 was a major turning point for the agency. In that year, they began to escape the "ghetto" in which all black agencies had been confined, and acquired accounts to service the broad general market. The first step in this important watershed came with Burrell's acquisition of Procter & Gamble's Crest account for the black market. Heretofore, the account had been handled by Benton & Bowles, which had argued that its ads reached the white and black markets equally well. Burrell convinced P&G's management that African-Americans' "behavior is different and interests are different, [and] that can certainly translate into different buying habits, different brand preference, different ways of looking at a particular product category or a particular brand." This persuasive argument was enough to win the Crest account, and Burrell was well aware of its significance: "The acquisition of [a P&G account] was the major package-goods consumer company in the U.S. saying that the black consumer market was big enough, important enough and unique enough to require a special effort. That was the first step out of the quick-service restaurant, soft-drink, and distilled-spirits categories,'' which along with cigarettes made up the bulk of products advertised to blacks.

More important, however, was a smaller account Burrell picked up that year: Brown-Forman's Jos. Garneau Co.'s Martell Cognac. For some time, the advertising for Martell's cognac had been split between Benton & Bowles, which produced advertising for the white market, and Burrell, which handled the black market. In late 1983, Burrell made a bid to consolidate the entire $2.5 million ad budget in his shop. He developed an integrated advertising program that changed the cognac advertising from what was called the "big bottle" approach, which were print ads dominated by a large photo of the bottle, to the use of Burrell's familiar "life-style" advertising. Burrell came up with an "I assume you drink Martell" campaign, which was originally used for the black market with great success. When Brown-Forman found that Burrell's ad tested better than B&B's in the general market, he just switched the black models for white models and the ad ran very successfully.

With the success of the Martell ads, Brown-Forman gave Burrell an assignment in 1984 to develop ads for its Jack Daniel Distillery. Jack Daniel, an old, white, southern company in Lynchburg, Tennessee, was given a new image by Burrell. Whereas earlier ads had stressed models dressed in upwardly mobile attire, Burrell instead stressed Jack Daniel's lineage, its heritage, and its quality in a highly successful series of long-copy, product-oriented ads. Burrell's success in landing these general market accounts stemmed from his conviction and argument that not only are white agencies unable to understand the nuances of black culture and the black market, but that black agencies are uniquely qualified to deal with the white market. Black consumers, explained Burrell, are "a much more complex and more sensitive audience" than white consumers. "If I can sell to black consumers," he argued, "I can sell to anybody." Therefore, contrary to what had been conventional wisdom in the advertising community, Burrell felt that the special sensitivity needed to reach black consumers made it more likely that a campaign developed for a black audience could be used successfully for whites, rather than the reverse. "Blacks, in order to be successful," Burrell said, "have to know the white world and culture. I had to when I worked at Leo Burnett and had to sell Robin Hood flour to whites in West Virginia. But whites can live their white lives and never know anything about the black world. And that's why we wouldn't have any problems with general-market advertising."

In addition to the Crest and Brown-Forman accounts, Burrell also regained the Coca-Cola account in a big way in 1983. Coca-Cola had been one of his earliest accounts, but it had been lost to another agency. Burrell, however, became the beneficiary of the confluence of a number of forces in the early 1980s. Jesse Jackson's black activist PUSH organization lobbied Coca-Cola to increase its ad spending in the black community and to use black agencies more extensively. The soft drink company responded by naming Burrell as its worldwide agency of record for black consumer advertising for its food and soft drink brands. The contract was worth about $7.5 million annually, which was by far the largest account Burrell had landed to that point. Part of the goal of Coca-Cola was to reach new markets—in this case, the vast black population on the Africa continent, especially in Nigeria.

Burrell first led a fact-finding tour through several African markets and then began designing a comprehensive worldwide program to meet these needs. Ira C. Herbert, Coca-Cola's executive vice president noted, "This is believed to be the first time a black-owned agency has received international agency of record status for all brands of a major consumer products company." Burrell, for his part, said he was pleased to be a pioneer in the concept of reaching blacks on a worldwide basis. "We see potential for other American marketers as well who do business in parts of the world populated by blacks." The Coca-Cola account, plus the other new business, pushed Burrell's billings to $40 million in 1984, one-third higher than the year before. In 1985 they went past $50 million. The plans for Coca-Cola in Nigeria, however, hit a snag when a military coup in 1984 dashed all hopes of developing a campaign for that country.

Burrell compensated for that loss by increasingly effective advertising for the black market in the United States. A particularly effective series of ads for Coke in 1985 featured five black kids on a Manhattan stoop singing the "Coke adds life" jingle. This spot won a Clio, the advertising industry's equivalent of an Oscar, for Burrell. He also won a Clio for his ads for McDonald's. In 1985 Burrell picked up yet another new client—Beatrice Co., the giant, Chicago-based food conglomerate, and one of America's biggest advertisers, with total billings of some $680 million. Burrell argued that America's 30 million blacks spent about $23 billion a year on food, and no one was doing a good job of reaching that market. Beatrice was convinced by his argument and gave Burrell a large account. As a result of all these accomplishments, Burrell was named the Advertising Person of the Year by the Chicago Advertising Club in 1985.

By the late 1980s, Burrell Advertising was not only the largest black-owned agency in America, but Thomas Burrell had done much to change the nature of advertising and marketing in the United States. His effective campaigns had shown companies how better to reach the black market and, in the process, greatly enhanced their market share there. A good example was McDonald's, a longtime Burrell client. His decade-long campaign to win the black community over to McDonald's was an outstanding success. While blacks composed just 12 percent of the nation's population, they accounted for 20 percent of the McDonald's business by 1986. "All of a sudden," said Chuck Wimbley, Burrell's director of account services, "blacks are being talked to," and advertisers were finding an untapped gold mine there. The country's 30 million blacks had an estimated annual income of $203 billion and, if they were a separate nation, would rank twelfth in buying power in the free world. For decades they were taken for granted by the white corporate world. Thomas Burrell and his black advertising cohorts were crucial in creating an awareness of this vast and important market.

Burrell at times has thought of moving to New York City, the center of the advertising world, and a place of brighter lights and enhanced prestige. In the end, however, he always decides to remain in Chicago: "I love Chicago as a city. There's a good, strong black entrepreneurial tradition here, and that makes it a healthy environment in which to do business." The late 1980s brought a slowing of the Burrell agency's growth. Billings were flat during the latter years of that decade, growing by a small percentage each year, from $53.8 million in 1986 to just over $60 million in 1989. In 1988 Burrell was forced to lay off thirteen people. Thomas Burrell continued to own 80 percent of the stock of the privately held company. In 1990 Burrell received the Missouri Honor Medal for Distinguished Service to Journalism from the University of Missouri's School of Journalism. By 1992 Burrell Communications, the parent firm for Burrell's various advertising and public relations companies, was the 100th largest black firm in America, down from number 84 the year before. It had revenues of just over $10 million.

Burrell also tried a new kind of ad for McDonald's that year that drew a good deal of commentary. Entitled "Second Chance," it showed a young black teenager named Calvin walking through his neighborhood. Neighbors wonder where he is going and he says he has to go to work. A woman says, "I wonder where he's working?" The next thing you see is Calvin in uniform behind the McDonald's counter, saying "Welcome to McDonald's." The ad stands out, according to Anna Morris of Burrell Advertising, because it suggests that "maybe [Calvin] was on the wrong path for a while," and because it attacks stereotypes about "street-looking kids. The impression people may get from kids, because they may wear their hair funny or dress funny, is that they're not good kids. That may not be the case." She added, "Since unemployment is a problem in the African-American community, a lot of it is based on the Anglo employer's lack of familiarity with black kids. If it [the ad] dispels some stereotypical myths in the general market, that'll be wonderful."

Even with his success, however, Burrell has often experienced frustration. Frequently, when he calls upon a potential general-market client with six members of his staff to make a presentation they will remark, "You must have brought your whole staff." That was a common perception: Since it was a black agency serving a niche market, it must be tiny. Burrell would respond, "No, these are seven of our 115 employees." Burrell had great hope for the continuing expansion of his agency and saw his own role in that expansion very clearly: "My duty is very narrow and very simple. My job, no matter what size this agency gets to be, is to be in charge of quality control for the product that we manufacture, which is advertising. I have always been inclined that way and I think it is key to the success of the agency."

Sources

No personal or corporate papers on Thomas Burrell or his advertising agency are currently available. The best short biography of Burrell is in Ingham and Feldman, CABL. See also *Who's Who among Black Americans* (1986) and Frank Johnson, *Who's Who of Black Millionaires* (1984), 116–17. The most useful biographical information on Burrell and his agency is available in a number of magazine and newspaper articles: *Advertising Age*, April 11, 1966, October 30, 1967, January 22, March 25, May 27, 1968, May 5, 1969, March 1, 1982, January 24, 1983, September 17, 1984, December 19, 1985, and August 28, 1989; *Fortune*, September 2, 1985; *Black Enterprise*, September 1979, January and December, 1985; *Jet*, December 16, 1985; *Newsweek*, February 10, 1986; *Chicago Tribune*, April 8, 1981, October 5, 1990; *Chicago Sun-Times*, August 26, 1984, October 27, 1985, November 11 and 23, 1986; *Encore*, September 7, 1976; *Crain's Chicago Business*, May 30, 1988; *Chicago's Reader*, October 20, 1989; *Norfolk Journal & Guide*, May 12, 1982; *Chicago Advertising & Media*, November 15–30, 1990; *Chicago Defender*, November 19, 1990; *CAC Voice*, November/December 1990; *Adweek*, July 24, October 29, and September 27, 1990; *USA Today*, August 13, 1990, 5B. Some informational materials were supplied by Burrell Communications Group.

General material on black business in Chicago includes ''Business in Bronzeville: The Center of U.S. Negro Business,'' *Time*, April 18, 1938, 70–71; ''Chicago: Money Capital of Negro America,'' *Our World* 6, September 1951, 15–19; ''How Chicago Strikes It Rich,'' *Color* 11 (March 1956), 22–33; Barbara Reynolds, ''Business without the Crystal Stair,'' *Chicago Tribune Magazine*, Janary 22, 1978; *Chicago Tribune*, June 12 and 13, 1972, May 4, 9, and 24, and July 31, 1976, March 20, 1988; *Ebony*, September 1978; *Chicago Daily News*, June 23–24, 1973, and August 4, 1975; *Chicago Sun-Times*, June 16, 1976, and February 18, 1979; *Chicago Defender*, August 2, 1978, July 3, 1979, and February 15, 1986; *Crain's Chicago Business*, August 14, 1989; *Daily Press* (Newport News, Va.), July 29, 1979; and *Richmond Times-Dispatch*, July 29, 1979.

C

Chase, W[illiam] Calvin, Sr. (February 2, 1854–January 3, 1921). Newspaper publisher and editor: *Washington Bee*. Calvin Chase was one of the most dynamic and caustic African-American newspaper publishers and editors during a critical period for blacks in America, and he was located in the epicenter of national black and white consciousness—Washington, D.C. Chase was born into relatively privileged circumstances six years before the Civil War. His father, William H. Chase, a native of Maryland, moved to Washington as early as 1835, where he worked as a blacksmith, wheelwright, and mechanic. He married Lucinda Seaton, a dressmaker from one of the most prestigious black families in Alexandria, Virginia. Her father had one of the largest black-owned grocery stores in the city, served in the Virginia legislature, and was worth $50,000. Both parents were free people of color, were literate, and owned their own home at 1109 I Street, NW when Calvin was born. They were members of the socially prominent Fifteenth Street Presbyterian Church. Although the status of the Chase family was well above that of the mass of African-Americans in Washington, and Chase was always cognizant of this, it is equally true that his family was no where near as wealthy or as socially eminent as the Wormleys (see James Wormley) or several other black families. The Chases were comfortably middle class, but not upper class. The elder Chases had five daughters and one son, and William Chase was accidentally killed when Calvin was just nine years old.

Although William Chase left real property worth $4,000 and personal property of at least $200, and although Mrs. Chase was able to ensure that all her children were to receive a good education, times were harder than before, and for a time she operated an Ice Cream Saloon and Confectionary Resort out of her home. Calvin Chase also did his part. While attending John F. Cook's private school for blacks in the basement of the Fifteenth Street Presbyterian Church, Calvin Chase began selling newspapers to help support his family. One of his white customers was so impressed with Chase that she arranged for him to go to Massachusetts to work for a hat manufacturer. He soon found that he had no interest in that business and that he terribly missed his native Washington. When he returned, Chase attended public school and also worked in the printing trade. He then enrolled in the Howard University Model School "B" class, and within two years he had passed the exam to enter the preparatory department. He did not attend college, but later, in about 1883 or 1884, he took courses at the Howard Law School and in 1889 was admitted to the bar in both Virginia and the District of Columbia. Since the newspaper business was never very lucrative for blacks, Chase also actively practiced law until his death.

During these early years, Chase became involved in the mutual supportive careers of politics and journalism. In 1875 he began working as a temporary clerk in the office of his former teacher, John F. Cook, Jr., who then headed the tax collector's office in Washington. At about the same time, Chase became the Washington correspondent for the *Boston Observer*. While in this position, he launched a withering attack on Frederick Douglass. This attack grew out of Chase's ambition for a political patronage position. When Douglass refused to support him, Chase used the columns of the newspaper to vilify his opponent. The *Observer* soon ceased publication and Chase went to work for the *Boston Co-operator* in 1879 in its Washington office. This lasted only a short time before he became a reporter and society editor for the *Washington Plain Dealer*. There his irascible personality and outspoken stances had him in continual hot water until he was forced to resign. Chase then assumed editorship of the *Argus*, owned by Charles Otey, and changed the name of the paper to the *Free Lance*.

Again, Chase's strident and outspoken opinions got him and his newspaper into trouble. He fearlessly attacked the press, government officials, police brutality, and the National Republican party for its failure to protect the rights of blacks. This stance incurred the enmity of Chase's coworkers, and the owners of the paper ultimately had to sell the concern because of the controversy caused by Chase's editorial policies. In 1880 Chase went to work for the *Washington Bee*, which had been started a year earlier by William V. Turner. Before long, Chase became the chief editor and proprietor of the paper. There he adopted a motto for the masthead that was to clearly identify the goal of the paper and its bombastic editor: "Honey for our friends and stings for our enemies." I. Garland Penn, in his hisory of the black press, thought the name fit the paper well: "Nothing stings Washington City, and in fact, the Bourbons of the South, as [does] the *Bee*."

Chase was the supporter of black rights in a number of important areas. One of the most critical of these was lynching. Although no African-Americans were ever lynched in Washington while Chase ran the *Bee*, his concern for the issue indicated the degree to which he viewed himself as a spokesman for national causes. Through editorials and cartoons he dramatized and publicized the issue of lynching and violence against blacks in a strikingly forceful manner. Also, like his counterpart in Richmond, John Mitchell Jr.,* Chase advocated that African-Americans use any means to defend themselves against this violence:

Our condition demands . . . that when our homes are invaded the shotgun shall be the direct resort in their protection . . . when our property is destroyed . . . the torch of retaliation shall be lighted and applied until devastation, destruction, blood, tears, misery and starvation shall teach our white oppressors that the colored man . . . can and will fight and die to assert his rights by the dreadful instruments of revenge.

Chase also waged an unending battle against discrimination in the federal civil service. Time and again he publicized the unfair employment practices of the government, pointing out instances where blacks had been denied employment, placed in segregated situations, or in other ways treated unfairly. He also attacked local officials for their attitudes. In one particularly irate editorial, Chase criticized district court commissioners for singling out black criminals and insinuating that the black crime rate was disproportionately high. He pointed out that the mayor and police department had recently issued a report showing that the number of offenses committed by whites far exceeded those by blacks.

Governmental racism also caused Chase to take a militant stand regarding the Brownsville affair in Texas in 1906. After a so-called riot by black troops there, President Theodore Roosevelt summarily discharged three companies of black infantrymen for their alleged involvement. Chase badgered Roosevelt in the pages of the *Bee* for over a year concerning this incident. This attack was just part of a long-standing crusade on Chase's part against racism in the American military. It was the treatment of African-American soldiers during the Spanish American War that had first angered Chase, and this concern continued into America's involvement in World War I. He refused to support America's war aims in that conflict until blacks were given more equal treatment. After 1918, however, he came to feel that the hopes and future of blacks were "indissolubly bound" to those of whites in the conflict. When vicious antiblack riots occurred after the war in 1919, including a particularly violent one in Washington, Chase felt betrayed, but he continued to press his belief that equal rights and justice for all were possible under the American system.

If Chase crusaded for the integration of blacks into the mainstream of white America in a number of areas, in some he accepted, or even advocated, a separation of the races. He did not, for example, see anything wrong with discriminatory policies of white social clubs in Washington. When the Harvard Club rejected membership applications of Richard T. Greener and Robert H. Terrell, both eminent African-Americans, Chase did not protest. Nor did he feel private universities or churches had an obligation to integrate their facilities, since, in his mind, they were essentially private social organizations. Chase did not even support the idea of integrated public schools; in this instance, he argued that calling for such schools "debase[d] the memory of our ancestors," who had founded their own.

These attitudes were part, however, of a fierce race pride and consciousness on the part of Chase. In a talk at the Berean Baptist Church, he spoke on "The Blunders of Negro Leadership," in which he militantly stressed the need for economic solidarity and cooperation among blacks. He believed blacks should become involved in their own businesses and that these should be supported by the broader African-American community. All of this, in his formulation, was designed to build a stronger, more self-reliant black community in Washington and the nation.

Although some of Chase's ideas smacked of the accommodationism and self-help philosophy of Booker T. Washington,* his relationship with the Tuskegee leader was anything but tranquil or cordial. He had bitterly criticized Washington's Atlanta Exposition Address in 1895 as a "bait of Southern fancy," and in 1900 he called Washington a "Negro Apologist." By 1906, however, Chase's financial problems caused him to accept Washington's monetary help, and he began printing his speeches and writing favorable editorials concerning Washington's proposals. The two men never coexisted comfortably though, and in 1912 Chase wrote Washington a bitter letter stating that he had not received the financial support he had been promised. When the organizer for the National Negro Business League, Ralph W. Tyler, offered Chase $20 out of his own pocket and informed him that there would be no further payments, Chase retorted that he could not "allow the *Bee* to be used any longer for their personal use without giving money." Nonetheless, Chase remained in Washington's camp until the latter's death in 1915.

If Chase had earlier opposed Washington as an accommodationist, he called W.E.B. Du Bois a "water-brained theorist." Although Chase had served as a delegate to the second annual meeting of the Niagara Movement in 1905 and strongly supported its work in the early years, he became alienated when Du Bois took control, particularly when Du Bois's paper *The Crisis* became a competitor for the *Bee*'s readers. After 1915, Chase took a more active role again in the work of the National Association for the Advancement of Colored People, possibly because that organization began placing articles in the *Bee* (presumably for payment).

Chase's apparent inconsistency or confusion on the issues of support of Washington and Du Bois was partially the result of shifting and uncertain alliances among the city's black elite, as many tried to satisfy the demands of both camps. Then, too, it had to do with competition among black newspapers. *The Crisis* was not the only newspaper Chase feared; he was also concerned with an upstart local African-American paper, *The Colored American*. That paper had been started in Indiana as the *Indianapolis Freeman* by Edward Elder Cooper. In 1893 Cooper started the *Colored American* in Washington. Cooper's major competition was the already established *Bee*, and he tried to attract readers by taking a strong stand on various political and social issues. This, of course, aped what Chase was already doing, but what made Cooper's threat very real was the fact that he was the first black publisher to make extensive use of pictures and illustrations.

Cooper during these early years was a strong advocate of Booker T. Washington's policies, and in 1904 he had a special four-page pictorial insert honoring the "Wizard of Tuskegee." For this, Washington sent Cooper regular amounts of money. This type of journalism was very expensive, however, and Washington evidently viewed Cooper as a bit of a loose cannon, so that when Cooper and the *Colored American* got into severe financial trouble in 1904, Washington sent him just $20 and the paper folded. Chase was most bitter in his attacks on Washington between 1904 and 1906, when the Tuskegean was financing the *Colored American*, and it was after 1906 that Chase and Washington were able to reach their agreement. So perhaps these editorial affiliations had less to do with ideology than they did with finances. David Howard-Pitney, observing these vacillations by Chase, is more charitable, saying that Chase ''is one more example of an important intellectual figure whose thought was neither exclusively accommodationist nor protest-oriented, but a pragmatic blend of the two.''

Chase married Arabella Virginia McCabe in 1886. She was a graduate of the Preparatory Department of Howard, and a writer and musician. They had a son and a daughter, both of whom worked for the *Bee* when they were old enough. Despite Chase's pugnacious personality, he was a highly esteemed man by the time of his death in 1921. Some 3,000 persons, both black and white, attended his funeral, and seventy-four cars took part in the funeral cortege. One of the speakers at the service summed up Chase's life well: ''We shall listen no more to his timely admonitions and advice, we shall read no more the informating editorials of his trenchant pen, but he leaves a blessed heritage, not only to his family, but to his race.''

Sources

Calvin Chase's correspondence is located in a number of collections, as well as in the National Archives. There is a microfilm copy available at the Moorland-Spingarn Research Center at Howard University. They also have microfilm copies of the *Washington Bee*. There are some letters between Chase and Booker T. Washington in the latter's papers at the Library of Congress. Information on relations between Edward E. Cooper and Washington is contained in the BTW Papers.

There is no published full-length biography of Chase, but the most comprehensive study of his life is Hal S. Chase, ''Honey for Friends, Stings for Enemies: William Calvin Chase and the *Washington Bee*, 1882–1921,'' Ph.D. diss., University of Pennsylvania, 1973. He has published a more specialized study entitled '' 'Shelling the Citadel of Race Prejudice': William Calvin Chase and the Washington 'Bee,' 1882–1921,'' *Records of the Columbia Historical Society* 49 (c. 1976), 371–91, and a short biography in the *Dictionary of Negro Biography* (1982), 99–101. There are also biographies of Chase in Afro-American Bicentennial Corp., *A Study of Historic Sites in the District of Columbia* (Washington, D.C., May 1976), 54–63; William J. Simmons, *Men of Mark* (1887), 118–32, and I. Garland Penn, *The Afro-American Press and Its Editors* (1891), 287–90. See also David Howard-Pitney, ''Calvin Chase's Washington *Bee* and Black Middle-Class Ideology, 1882–1900,'' *Journalism Quarterly*, Spring 1986, 89–97.

Church, Robert Reed (June 18, 1839–August 2, 1912). Real estate developer, banker, businessman, and philanthropist: Solvent State Savings Bank; Church Park and Auditorium. The Church family is probably about as close to aristocracy as you get in the African-American society of the United States. As Stephen Birmingham commented in *A Certain People*, his book about the black upper classes, "[T]he Churches of Memphis are often considered—and certainly consider themselves—the grandest black family in America. For nearly three-quarters of a century the early remains of various illustrious Churches have reposed in the vast marble Church mausoleum in Memphis' Elmwood Cemetery, which is now regarded as something of a family shrine." It was Robert Church, Sr., who accumulated the fortune to make this possible, and Robert, Jr., who gave the name its panache of political power. Robert, Sr.'s, daughter, Mary Church Terrell, brought exquisite dignity and literary prestige to the name.

Robert Church, Sr., was born a slave in Holly Springs, Mississippi, the son of a wealthy white owner of two palatial steamboats that plied the river and his house slave. Church was proud of the fact that he had little African blood, telling a congressional committee: "My father is a white man; my mother is as white as I am." Church's mother, Emmaline, was described by contemporaries as "a born aristocrat" with "exquisite manners." She worked as a seamstress on the Church plantation and, according to a later descendent of Charles Church, was "never treated as a slave." She also claimed to be the daughter of Lucy, a beautiful Malay princess who had been enslaved after her family fell from power. The family's evidence for this came from the grandson of the planter who purchased Lucy during the first decade of the nineteenth century. He wrote to Robert Church:

My grandfather, who was a wealthy planter at Lynchburg, Virginia attended a sale of African slaves at Norfork, Virginia between 1805 and 1810. Among them was a bright red young girl with very long straight hair. She was not of African descent but Malay. She attracted a great deal of attention by her beauty and the jewelery she wore. . . . Her name was Lucy and she could speak the French language. . . . She was the daughter of a royal family of one of the Malay Islands and in the civil strife had been taken prisoner and sold.

Robert Church's father, Charles B. Church, reared his son to be a gentleman, and young Robert never considered himself a slave. He maintained a close relationship with his natural father, who seemed to return the affection, although he withheld formal acknowledgment. As Robert Church commented: "Captain Church is my father; he used to have a packet line. My father owned my mother. . . . My father always gave me everything I wanted, although he does not openly recognize me." Although Robert Church never claimed that these arrangements troubled him, one cannot help but wonder what impact they had on his psyche. In later years, the family, including Church himself, challenged the idea that he and his mother had been slaves. Col. James Lewis,* a close friend who had worked with Church on the steamboats, wrote him in 1891 saying:

I do not think it a proper thing on the part of our southern press to refer to you as a slave. I have known you for many years; we were together on the steamboat *Ingomar* long before the war, and I never heard of you being classed as a slave.

Despite these protestations, it appears that Robert Church was officially a slave until he was emancipated on January 1, 1863.

Robert Church received little in the way of formal education, but Captain Church did see to it that he was trained in the management of the passenger steamboat business. At an early age, the elder Church brought Robert on board as a dishwasher, and the young man began progressing up the ladder to cook, and finally to steward, the highest post a black could achieve on these boats. In this position Robert Church learned how to purchase provisions wholesale, keep accounts, and manage the eating, drinking, and gambling operations on his father's boats. Captain Church also instilled a sense of pride and combativeness in his son. "He taught me to defend myself," Robert later recalled, "and urged me never to be a coward. 'If anyone strikes you, hit him back, and I'll stand by you.' " The result was a man who, although he was never involved to any extent in organized struggles for black rights throughout the late nineteenth and early twentieth centuries, was personally ready to stand up to any hint of personal slight or discrimination. He often carried a pistol and would pull it at the slightest provocation on policemen, sheriffs, a snowball-throwing crowd, or anyone else who got in his way. His pugnaciousness resulted in serious injury and near death on at least one occasion.

After working the river trade throughout the 1850s, Church's career on steamboats came to a dramatic end in 1862. At that time he was working as a steward on the steamer, *Victoria*, when it was captured by the federal fleet during the Battle of Memphis. Robert, by then a young man of twenty-three, was unhurt and was released by the Union forces to make his own way in Memphis. Robert Church had a small amount of savings from his years on the river boats, he was familiar with Memphis, his father had extensive connections there, and Robert himself was intensely ambitious and trained in the ways of dealing with whites in matters of business and service. He therefore decided to strike out on his own there and got involved in the saloon business.

During the twenty years prior to the Civil War, Memphis had grown to become the sixth-largest city in the South, largely profiting by the cotton trade on the Mississippi River. There were relatively few blacks in the city in the antebellum years, and by 1860 there were just 3,882 African-Americans. They constituted 17 percent of the population, of whom just 198 were free. One of Church's problems was that pre–Civil War Memphis had tried to place severe restrictions on the drinking of alcohol by slaves and other blacks. Although many of these laws were later lifted or ignored, the police often used them as a pretext for harassing Church and his patrons at his various saloons.

At the end of the war, Church purchased his own saloon at 29 Monroe Street, but during the Memphis riots of 1866, he nearly lost his own life. The riots there were some of the worst that took place in the postwar South. On May 1, 1866, a street brawl erupted between several Irish policemen and a group of blacks who were recently discharged from the Union army. It soon escalated into a full-scale battle between the police and virtually all the African-American soldiers. Before long, a large mob of whites descended into the city's black community and went on a rampage for an entire night. By the time martial law was declared, forty-six blacks and two whites lay dead, and Robert Church was among seventy-five others who received gunshot wounds. Church learned that rioters, including Irish members of the police force, were determined to put him out of business. Undaunted, Church opened his establishment and was purposely shot in the back of the head while defending his saloon from police who were looting his liquor and cash box. Church's revenge came in being one of the few blacks to testify before the federal officials sent to investigate the riot. At that tribunal he boldly identified a number of city policemen who were among the rioters.

Church continued to have trouble with the police at his establishments over the years, however, and George W. Lee,* who would later be an associate of Church's son, recalled, "Whenever officers arrested men loitering around his place he always paid their fines . . . whenever officers approached Church's place he made everybody there stand up, had the officer count heads, and then paid their fines [for vagrancy] on the spot." He also had problems with white hoodlums. Operating businesses that featured drink, gambling, and probably prostitution, Church's operations were often targets for underworld figures. Lee tells of a "group of white hoodlums from the underworld" who had been "regarding [Beale Street] with envious eyes. They wanted to gain control over the great spending power of the Negroes, and in order to accomplish this they found it necessary to put Church 'on the spot.' " Church, however, refused to be intimidated and retained full control of his operations.

The shady side of Robert Church's operations continued throughout his life, although they have been largely sanitized in recent accounts. On August 7, 1876, he complained to the *Memphis Evening Ledger* when they reported that "this mulatto runs a lively trap [Church's Billiard Hall, which they described as a "bar, gambling hall, pawnshop, etc."], and many a good Negro has been run through and robbed there by the sharpest gamblers in the city." Church responded, "I am too well known in this community to ask for endorsement of my conduct during my long residence in Memphis." Two years later, on January 11, 1878, the *Commercial Appeal* reported that

Six shots reverberated through the air at Second and Gayoso last night, where Bob Church's saloon stands on the southeast corner. The neighborhood was electrified by the news that Church had been shot by Sheriff Furbush of Lee County. The row was about a colored woman, not about politics as first thought. Furbush was arrested and taken to the stationhouse. Mr. Church was shot in the head and neck but may recover. He is an influential and prosperous member of his race in this city.

Twenty-five years later, when Church was sixty-four years old, he got into another brawl. The *Commercial Appeal*, in September 20, 1903, reported that

Two brothers, John H. and R. H. West, white, had a street fight with Robert Church, wealthy Negro, on Beale yesterday, and are now incarcerated with their heads broken. Church is at his home on Lauderdale recuperating from a wound on the head and cuts. . . . Officer Matthews told the *Commercial Appeal* that the West brothers started the fight by insulting and provoking Church.

The Reconstruction years were heady ones for the black community in Memphis, and Church aggressively pursued his fortune during this time. He traded up to a saloon and billiard parlor at 81 DeSota and then to 360 Main Street. At the same time, he also began buying real estate in black residential areas. His policy was to continually buy, and never sell, these properties while always exercising close supervision over them. George W. Lee recounts the elder Church's activities during these years:

R. R. Church on Beale Street had much to do with making it the center of commercial life for the Negroes of Memphis . . . [he was] the acknowledged and accepted Boss of Beale Street, who held the old thoroughfare completely in his grip and directed its course for many years.

Another elderly black resident of Memphis recalled Church's technique:

Old Bob Church made piles of money on saloons and rent houses. Went round ev'y night and poured up that liquor to see ef'n his barkeeps git the right number of drinks out'n a quart. Made 'em put all the money in a glass bowl, too. Yet Old Man Bob was friendly.

By the middle of the 1870s, Bob Church had already made a sizable fortune and had a tidy amount of money that was not tied up in his various properties. His great challenge and opportunity came with the repeated yellow fever epidemics that struck Memphis in the late 1870s. The city's population had declined by nearly 7,000 (out of 40,000) during this decade, and Memphis fell behind in its quest to become one of the leading metropolitan centers of the South. Most of those who left were white, often either Irish- or German-born immigrants. The percentage of blacks in the city, on the other hand, which stood at 39 percent in 1870, increased to 44 percent in 1880. Bob Church moved his family out of the city during the great epidemics in 1878 and 1879 but returned himself to begin purchasing land and houses at distress prices. White Memphians were willing to sell him property previously worth thousands for just a few hundered dollars. By the time the 1880s began, Church had accumulated a massive real estate empire in the center city. This enabled him to become a rentier on a large scale, and it is said that by the time of his death he was regularly collecting $6,000 a month in rents. His properties included undeveloped land, residential housing, and commercial buildings, and a good portion of this was located in the city's red-light district.

Much has been made of Church's risk-taking at this time, and to a certain extent this must be acknowledged. But it must also be remembered that the black population was not declining during this time, and therefore it was perhaps easier for Robert Church to see opportunity where others saw only disaster. Nonetheless, he made an enormous fortune during this time, most of it in real estate, and was reputed to be the first African-American millionaire. This has been disputed by more recent historians, however, who place his actual fortune at closer to $700,000 in 1912 dollars. Whatever the truth in this matter, it is certainly clear that he was a very wealthy man by the time of his death. Another myth disputed by recent historians is the tale that when Memphis, which was totally insolvent by the end of the 1870s, wanted to resurrect itself with a new bond issue, Church became a true founding father of the new Memphis by purchasing Municipal Bond no. 1 for $1,000. Professor David Tucker, however, reports that city records do not report his name among the first bond buyers. More well known, and probably true, is the fact that Church in 1901 did donate $1,000 to help finance the official Confederate reunion held in Memphis. The *Evening Scimitar* boasted about Church's contribution in headlines the next day, and white southerners generally were enthralled by this. A. R. Pickett, chairman of the finance committee for the fund, wrote to the paper, saying, "It is by no means a surprise to find "Bob" Church in a generous mood, but to find in an unobtrusive colored man the ability as well as the disposition to voluntarily donate so large a sum for the entertainment of veterans of the Southern armies furnish beyond a doubt the greatest surprise." John Overton wrote, "I am exceedingly gratified and well pleased at your contribution to the Confederate reunion. I have never seen a more striking act, to show what should be the real genuine feeling between the races here. . . . It should be a shining example to the people of your race." Church replied to the paper, "I have been a citizen of Memphis all my life and believe this is a great opportunity which I am sure the people of Memphis will approve." It was a good bit of street theater on Robert Church's part, if nothing else.

Although a man who was primarily concerned with making money from the city's black community, Church also exhibited at times a paternalistic attitude toward it. In 1899, since Memphis did not provide parks for blacks, Church developed a park on his own Beale Street property and equipped it with a large auditorium. Known as Church Park, it also had a playground and concert hall. Admission was charged for most affairs there, but there were free times and free Thanksgiving dinners for the poor. Most significant, the auditorium and concert hall became the cultural center of the black community. The event that gained nationwide recognition at the time occurred in 1902, when President Theodore Roosevelt spoke to 10,000 people in the auditorium. In 1909, Booker T. Washington[*] was feted at a breakfast banquet at the auditorium, and later a public ceremony was held in the same building to commemorate the Tuskegean's tour of the city.

Most significant in the long run, however, were the black entertainment acts that played the venue. Among the popular black acts that played the Church Park Auditorium were the Black Patti Troubadours, along with a number of early jazz and blues musicians. The most important of these was W. C. Handy, who later wrote to Annette Church,

I appreciate so much your memories of the days when I played for dances at Church's Auditorium and elsewhere in Memphis, and for me these are unforgettable memories. . . . I got a start as an orchestra leader there, and in declining years it is a pleasure to think of those humble beginnings. . . . In those days it was the name of Bob Church that drew people to Memphis, from all over the South.

The auditorum was also used for annual conventions of black church groups, such as the Church of God in Christ, which had been founded in Memphis.

In 1906 Church took the lead in founding the Solvent Savings Bank and Trust Company. Organized with capital stock of $25,000, Robert Church was its president; prominent black undertaker Thomas H. Hayes was the vice president, and Harry H. Pace* was the cashier. Its board of directors was composed of most of the leading members of the city's African-American business community. Located at 392 Beale Street, it was designed to receive the savings of and provide credit to the city's black community. A year after its founding, the panic of 1907 hit, and banks across the nation were faced with a run by their depositors. Black-owned banks, particularly after the demise of the Freedmen's Bank, had little credibility, so it was a dire time for Solvent Savings. In response, Church placed sacks of money in the windows with a large sign that said, "This Bank Is Paying off All Depositors." It worked. The bank survived the crisis and continued to grow. By the time of his death in 1912, it had deposits in excess of $100,000 and passed the $1 million mark in 1920. Speculations in the 1920s, however, doomed the institution to ultimate failure.

Robert Church, whose own career depended in some measure upon maintaining open contacts with the dominant white system, remained largely aloof from politics and the dominant social issues that divided the black and white communities. In a few instances, however, he did take a stand in these areas. Church, for example, always rode in the white section of streetcars, and few appeared willing to challenge him on this. His daughter, Mary Church Terrell, later recalled when she was four years old riding with her father on the train. They were sitting in the white section, and the elder Church went to the smoker for a time. While he was gone, the conductor tried to force young Mary to move to the colored section. When she refused to move voluntarily, he took her arm to remove her forcibly. Just then her father returned, saying, "What's the trouble?" The conductor replied, "This little girl, you too, don't belong in here. You . . . " At that, Church exploded: "My daughter is riding here, with me! We have first-class tickets." The conductor, thoroughly cowed by Church's presence and demeanor, backed down and left them where they were.

When Memphis passed a Jim Crow ordinance in 1906, Church allowed a rally to be held in Church Park, in which $5,000 was raised to test the constitutionality of the law, but this effort failed. Robert Church, Jr., later recalled that he carried lasting and "bitter memories" of the passage of the Jim Crow law and the failure of his father's efforts to overturn it. Church also allowed his name to be put forward for city government positions in 1882 and 1886, but he was soundly trounced by more popular black candidates each time. From then on he eschewed politics except in 1900, when he was a delegate to the Republican National Convention.

Church was reputed, however, to wield considerable political influence behind the scenes. He reportedly played a role in securing the appointments in the Department of State's foreign service for two black Memphians, I. N. Ruttin and W. J. Yerby. Also, in 1901, the *Colored American* in Washington, D.C., reported, "In the early days when the Negro was first enfranchised, [Church] was a fearless leader of the black voters and many time took his life in his hands while insisting upon the full and free exercise of their rights at the polls."

Robert Church was married three times, and several of his children distinguished themselves in later years. In 1857 he had a slave marriage in New Orleans to Margaret Pico which produced one child—Laura Napier—whose education he financed. Then, in Bluff City, Tennessee, a few years later, he married Louise Ayers, a maid in that city. That union produced two children, Mary Church Terrell and Thomas Ayers Church. Thomas Church went to law school at Columbia University and later became a police clerk and lawyer in New York City. Mary Church became one of the most accomplished black women in America. She graduated from Oberlin College and moved to Washington, D.C., where she married Robert H. Terrell, the first black judge in that city. She became the first president of the National Association of Colored Women, the first woman elected president of the Bethel Literary and Historical Association, and the first black woman to serve on a board of education in the United States. She also served as a national officer of the NAACP, and in 1919 she was invited by the International League for Peace and Freedom to represent the United States in Zurich. She fought for woman's suffrage and against segregation and mistreatment of women and blacks throughout her life. Her autobiography, *A Colored Woman in a White World*, published in 1940, is an eloquent plea for racial justice with its recital of the indignities suffered continually even by someone as talented, cultured, and distinguished as she.

Robert Church divorced Louise Ayers in 1870. She got custody of their two children, and evidently she secured a goodly sum of money from Church, which enabled her to establish a highly prosperous hairdressing business, first in Memphis, and then in New York City. In 1885 Robert married Anna Wright, a college-educated principal of Winchester Colored School, who bore him two more children, Robert, Jr., and Annette Church. Descended from a long line of aristocratic southern whites, with just a trace of African blood, Anna Wright was "so fair as to be hardly recognizable as a Negro." Nonetheless, according to Stephen Birmingham, "she became the unquestioned leading *grande dame* in Memphis's black society."

Robert Church, Jr., was born in 1885. He was educated by private tutors, private schools in the city, Oberlin College, and the Packard School of Business in New York. After young Church served a three-year apprenticeship on Wall Street, from 1904 to 1907, he returned to Memphis as cashier at his father's Solvent Savings Bank. In 1909 his father stepped aside as president, and the younger Church guided the affairs of the family-controlled banking business until the death of his father in 1912. After that, however, his carefully prearranged career began to come unraveled. He resigned his position at the bank in that year and restricted his economic activity to his father's sprawling real estate empire. Even this, however, failed to capture his interest. Young Robert's consuming fascination was with politics. In 1916 he founded the Lincoln League, with the goal of increasing the number of blacks who could vote and wield political influence in western Tennessee.

The Lincoln League organized voter registration drives, established voting schools, and paid poll taxes for black voters. Within a few months, the league had registered over 10,000 voters. A Lincoln ticket was entered in the 1916 election which included an African-American candidate for Congress. The ticket lost, but Robert, Jr.'s, influence in the Republican party was solidified for decades to come. Over the years, Church, who became the most influential black political leader in the South, was often referred to as the "dictator of the Lincoln Belt." As a political boss of the old order, Church shunned the public eye and operated as a dispenser of patronage and a political strategist. He and E. H. Crump, the white boss of Memphis, "coexisted" with one another, and the presence of Church and his powerful black political machine did much to blunt the potential racism and race-baiting of politics in the city. His principal lieutenant in much of this was George W. Lee, also a prominent African-American businessman and politician.

Robert Church, Jr.'s, political and economic power began to wane in the 1930s. The depression lowered the value of his real property, undercut the ability of his tenants to pay their rents, and saddled Church with real estate taxes he had difficulty paying. Ultimately, the city claimed Church's property in lieu of a sizable back-tax debt. The Democratic victory in the 1930s also undercut Church's influence, and "lily-white" Republicans were able to blunt his political power. In 1940 Church left Memphis for Chicago, where he continued to have a voice in Republican circles, albeit with diminished impact. He died in 1952. As historian Roger Biles said of him: "Church's obstinacy, stubborn loyalty, and lack of political acumen led him to an inglorious end."

The elder Churches lived in a rambling mansion situated on South Lauderdale Street, surrounded by upper class white neighbors. Many years later, his daughter, Annette, was asked by an interviewer about her home:

[I]t was of Queen Anne style of architecture and was three stories high. On the first floor it contained five rooms, one was a double parlor, and there were halls that ran through the center of the house. On the second floor were five bedrooms; one servant's room and four family rooms. On the third floor situated like the first floor was a long double room and two rooms. It had a basement and a servant's house and a laundry in the back, and some horse stables and a large lot . . . in those days Memphis wasn't as segregated as it became later. The corner of [Lauderdale and] Vance was very exclusive.

The once-grand home came to an inglorious end a generation later. In 1940, in the midst of Bob Church, Jr.'s, financial problems, the family home on Lauderdale was sold. As the *Press Scimitar* reported,

Time was when this two-story brown frame house with 13 rooms was a show-piece of Memphis, ranking with the best mansions of the white folks. . . . But things didn't go so well with Church during this past decade. Much of his estate was tied up. . . . Much of this property was in the red light or twilight sections of Memphis. . . . The passing of the red light district is reported to have ruined the value of the last of Church's property.

The house, which had cost in excess of $15,000 when it was built in the 1880s (a princely sum at the time), was sold for just $4,250. The purchasers planned to convert it to a boarding house.

When Robert Church, Sr., died in 1912, a large funeral was held, and he was honored by citizens of the city, both black and white. The white newspapers of the city, contrary to normal practice, ran long obituaries on his passing. One year and four months after his death, the *Commercial Appeal*, in its Southern Prosperity Edition, extolled his virtues:

A substantial story of the triumph of Memphis as a great city could not be written without an account of the marvelous career of the late R. R. Church, who built a fame on character and left two fortunes, one consisting of a great estate as men appraise wealth, and the other a heritage for his children and all the people . . .

Through forty years or more of business activity he saw this town grow from a boasting village to a city of renown, and he was part of the bravery of those who grappled with such problems as few builders have been compelled to overcome . . .

A quarter of a century ago his discerning eye saw the present Memphis.

In his last will and testament, he listed hundreds of properties to be inherited by his two wives and four of his children. And his economic power on Beale Street was unquestioned. As Shields McIlwaine commented, "Everyone knew Old Man Bob Church had been Kingpin of Beale Street business for over thirty years. No one opened a liquor or gambling place without his consent. Much of the property in the white and black red-light districts on and around Gayoso Street was his, and it brought skyhigh rent." David Tucker said it more succinctly, "Robert Church never attended school, wrote a letter, or made a public speech, but he gained the respect and admiration of his community, black and white."

The power of the Church family has been pretty well destroyed in Memphis, but old Bob Church's ambition and aggressiveness were not in vain. The Churches remained part of the "old money" set of wealthy African-Americans, and two generations of Churches lived in splendor at the black resort at Highland Beach, Maryland. This resort drew the black crème de la crème of the South and Middle Atlantic states, and the *Commercial Appeal* said that its residents could be considered a "who's who of Black America." Sara Roberta Church, granddaughter of Bob Church, Sr., after living in Chicago and Washington, D.C., returned to Memphis. She told Stephen Birmingham: "I will always consider Memphis my home." In Memphis, they put it more bluntly: "The Churches *are* Memphis."

Sources

The Robert R. Church Family Papers are deposited at Memphis State University. They are, however, still restricted, and family permission must be obtained for access. Professor David Tucker, who has used them, indicates they are not of great value. The papers are described in *The Robert R. Church Family Papers of Memphis: Guide to the Papers with Selected Facsimiles of Documents and Photographs*, by Pamela Palmer, Mississippi Valley Conference, Bulletin no. 10 (Memphis, 1979). Mary Church Terrell's papers are located at the Library of Congress, as are those of her husband, Robert Terrell. The Shelby County Public Library in Memphis has acquired the papers of Mrs. Sarah Roberta Church, which were still uncatalogued at the time of this writing and will likely be restricted when completed. Robert Church, Sr.'s, will can be found in "Document— Last Will and Testament of R. R. Church, Sr. (1839–1912)'', by M. Sammye Miller, *Journal of Negro History* LXV, 2 (Spring 1980). Interviews of Roberta Church and Annette E. Church by Charles W. Crawford are held in the Oral History Office at Memphis State University. A few letters involving Robert Church, Jr., are found in the Booker T. Washington Papers in the Library of Congress.

The only full-scale biography of the Churches is by the elder Church's daughter and granddaughter: Annette E. Church and Roberta Church, *The Robert Churches of Memphis* (Ann Arbor, Mich., 1974). It is, unfortunately, rather too laudatory to be fully reliable. A more insightful memoir that also has reference to the two Churches is Mary Church Terrell's magnificent *A Colored Woman in a White World* (1940). See also "M. C. Terrell's Letters from Europe to Her Father," *Negro History Bulletin* 39, 6 (September/ October 1976). There is a rather brief biography of Robert Church, Sr., by Lester C. Lamon in the *Dictionary of American Negro Biography* (1982), and another by David M. Tucker in the forthcoming *American National Biography*. There is also biographical information in G. P. Hamilton, *The Bright Side of Memphis* (1908), 91–92, 98–100. See also U.S. Congress, *Memphis Riots and Massacre* (1866), microfiche no. 1274, card 4, 226–27. There is an obituary in the Memphis *Commercial Appeal*, August 30, 1912, and the estate controversy is covered in the *Commercial Appeal*, November 16, 1928. See also Paul R. Coppock, *Memphis Sketches* (Memphis, 1976), 243–46; Stephen Birmingham, *A Certain People* (1977), 138–42; George W. Lee, *Beale Street: Where the Blues Began* (New York, 1934), 24–29, 168, 250–57, 282–85; M. Sammye Miller, "Portrait of a Black Urban Family," *Negro History Bulletin* 42, 1 (April/May/June 1979), 50–51; *History of Memphians of Color* 16–18; *Commercial Appeal*, January 1, 1940, June 15, 1969, July 1, 1973, October 30, 1984, September 15, 1986; *Colored American*, February 16, 1901; Charles R. Crawford, *Yesterday's Memphis* (Miami, 1976), 43, 54, 118; Memphis *Evening Scimitar*, Souvenir Edition, October 1891, Art Supplement, April 1899, January 30, 1901; Memphis *Press-Scimitar*, November 26, 1941, January 1, 1970; *The Vision* (house publication of Atlanta Life Insurance Company), March 1971, 29–30; *Tri-State Defender*, October 2, 1972, October 25, 1975, May 14, 1988; *Congressional Record*, September 7, 1972; *Dawn Magazine*, October 11, 1975.

There are obituaries of Robert, Jr., in the *Press Scimitar* and *Commercial Appeal*, April 18, 1952, and *Journal of Negro History* XXXVIII, 2 (April 1953). The best short biography of Church is by Lester C. Lamon in *Dictionary of American Negro Biography* (1982). A good summary of his political activities is by Roger Biles, "Robert R. Church, Jr. of Memphis: Black Republican Leader in the Age of Democratic Ascendency, 1928– 1940," *Tennessee Historical Quarterly* 42, 4 (1983), 362–82; and Clarence L. Kelly, "Robert R. Church, A Negro Tennessean, in Republican State and National Politics from

1912–1932,'' Master's thesis, Tennessee State University, 1954. See also Estes Kefauver, "How Boss Crump Was Licked," *Collier's Magazine*, October 16, 1948, 24; "G.O.P. South," *Time* XIII, 7 (February 18, 1929). See also *National Cyclopedia of American Biography*, C. Stone, *Black Political Power in America*; *Crisis* XII (June 1916), 67; *Tri-State Defender*, May 21, 1988, 7-A; *Commercial Appeal*, April 18, 1936, March 8, 1948, February 27, 1953, April 18 and August 9, 1977, July 24, September 20, and December 5, 1978; *Press Scimitar*, January 1, 1976; *Pittsburgh Courier*, May 3, 1952; *Who's Who in Colored America*, 1928–29; George A. Sewell and Margaret L. Dwight *Historic Black Memphians* (n.p., n.d.) 20–25.

There is additional information on the Churches and the black community of Memphis in Shields McIlwaine, *Memphis Down in Dixie* (1948); Lester C. Lamon, *Black Tennesseans, 1900–1930* (Knoxville, 1977). Biographical information on Mary Church Terrell is found in *Journal of Negro History* XXXIX, 4 (October, 1954), 334–37; and "Tribute—Mary Church Terrell," *Negro History Bulletin* XVIII, 2 (October 1960), 6; Elizabeth F. Chittenden, "As We Climb: Mary Church Terrell," *Negro History Bulletin* XXXVII, 1 (February/March 1975), 351–54; Beverley Washington Jones, "Quest for Equality: The Life and Writings of Mary Eliza Church Terrell, 1863–1954," *Black Women in United States History*, vol. XIII; Dorothy Sterling and Benjamin Quarles, *Lift Every Voice: The Lives of Booker T. Washington, W.E.B. Du Bois, Mary Church Terrell, James Weldon Johnson* (Garden City, 1965). The Churches are also discussed rather extensively in Willard Gatewood, *Aristocrats of Color: The Black Elite, 1880–1920* (Bloomington, Ind., 1990).

Cohen, Walter I. (January 22, 1860–December 29, 1930), **James Lewis** (1832–1914), and **James Lewis, Jr.** (1867–   ?). Businessmen, politicians, civic leaders: People's Industrial Life Insurance, People's Drug Stores; Register of the Land Office in New Orleans, Controller of Port of New Orleans, National Negro Business League; Harry L. Haws and Company.

Walter Cohen once remarked partially in jest when the Ku Klux Klan surged back into prominence in the 1920s that in him—a black, a Jew, and a Catholic—was embodied the three groups the Klan was most bitterly attacking. Cohen, an exceptionally light-skinned African-American, was also, as his name attests, partially of Jewish extraction, and he was also, as was true of many of New Orleans' blacks, raised a devout Catholic. Thus embedded in Walter Cohen were many of the contradictions and inconsistencies of life in New Orleans in the late nineteenth and early twentieth centuries.

Cohen was born in New Orleans, the son of Bernard Cohen and Amelia Bingaman. Walter Cohen's mother had received her freedom in 1857, so Walter was born free on the eve of the Civil War. When young Walter was in fourth grade his parents died, forcing him to drop out of St. Louis Catholic School. There is not a great deal of information on his life during this period, but as a young boy Cohen took up the cigar-making trade, at which he worked for a time, and he was also employed in a saloon for four years. Sometime during this period, Cohen attended Straight University for several years. During the 1870s, when the Reconstruction legislature sessions were held in New Orleans, Walter Cohen worked as a page. While in that position, he met a number of

Republican politicians who influenced his career. Most important were Oscar J. Dunn, C. C. Antoine,* and especially P.B.S. Pinchback.* Cohen became Pinchback's protégé and remained closely tied to him throughout the older man's life.

Cohen became a member of the Fourth Ward Republican organization in the city, which had been founded and dominated by Pinchback. There Cohen also enjoyed the influence of James Madison Vance, another noted political figure. Cohen's first political appointment obtained through these men was as a night inspector on the riverfront in the city. As Reconstruction came to an end, and the older men, all of whom had been scarred by the bitter battles of the period, were forced to retreat from the political stage, Cohen came forward. He soon was appointed to the powerful position of secretary of the Republican State Central Committee, and he was by far its most influential member until he was removed from that post by Herbert Hoover in the late 1920s.

In 1889, Cohen was appointed as United States Inspector in New Orleans and promoted to lieutenant of inspectors sometime later. He resigned when the Democrats took charge of the White House in 1893. His first major federal appointment, however, came in 1898, when President William McKinley appointed Cohen Register of the United States Land Office in New Orleans. He was reappointed to the office by President Theodore Roosevelt, but not without some difficulty. Both Cohen and Colonel James Lewis, another prominent black politician and businessman in New Orleans, were up for reappointment at the same time in 1904, and when Lewis was given his appointment, and Cohen was not, Cohen appealed to Booker T. Washington* to intercede on his behalf. The problem was that F. B. Williams, chairman of the state Republican Committee, and Henry McCall, collector of customs, as heads of the so-called "lily-white" Republican faction, wanted to destroy the career of Cohen, who headed up the "black and tan Republicans." Washington wrote to Cohen that he had talked to President Roosevelt about the matter but had not been able to make much progress. In another letter to Cohen sometime later, Washington declared exasperation over the opposition of lily-white Republicans to Cohen's appointment: "I confess I am thoroughly disgusted with conditions in Louisiana as far as the treatment of Negroes is concerned by the Republican party." Washington ultimately made a direct appeal to the president and, with the additional backing of Pinchback, was able to secure the appointment for Cohen. In 1910, however, the office was abolished by President William H. Taft. Taft offered Cohen the same position in Baton Rouge or Natchitoches, but Cohen replied that he had lived in New Orleans his entire life; it was his home, and he was not about to move.

For the first time in a quarter of a century, Cohen was without a political position and had to find a new line of work. In that same year, along with a few of his close friends, Cohen organized the People's Benevolent Life Insurance Company and became president of the firm. On May 10, 1910, Cohen wrote to Booker T. Washington, informing him that he was getting ready to publish a brochure announcing the formation of his company. He assured Washington,

"We will make an excellent showing," but, said, "What I would like from you is a letter congratulating our company on its organization and giving your opinion on some of the members of the board." Cohen then planned to include Washington's letter in the bulletin. The Tuskegean wrote, "I congratulate you upon the success of the work of this company, and I congratulate you also upon the high character of the men associated with you on the board of directors." The company was successfully launched and was a profitable business for decades thereafter. Cohen served as head of the firm until his death. In 1942, the company, then called People's Industrial Life Insurance, had assets of over $300,000 and total insurance in force of $5,874,946. By 1961, its assets stood at $2,847,269.

Walter Cohen also established a drugstore in New Orleans, which later grew into a second store. Called People's Drug Store, the first was located at 624 S. Rampart Street. Cohen wrote to Washington on May 2, 1914, informing him that "I have an opportunity of purchasing a drug store and I believe it a very safe investment. . . . I am sure in the course of time it will be very profitable." But Cohen had some problems, as he explained to Washington: "To complete the purchase and stock the place as it should be with some improvements I will need about $250." Cohen was short of cash and was not able to get a loan on his own account, so he asked Washington "if [he] would accept my note for the above amount. I assure you I would appreciate same." Cohen also again asked Washington to provide him with a letter endorsing his new drug business and "wishing me all the success as all Negroes ought to get into business." Washington again provided him with a letter and also backed Cohen for a loan through the Macon County Bank but had to badger Cohen later in the year to repay the note.

Nonetheless, Cohen was excited about the prospects of his store, which he endeavored to make the finest in the city for blacks. As he pointed out, "It is situated on a street where more colored population pass on than any other in the city." Cohen installed a soda fountain and ice cream parlor, which he saw as a "great revenue getter," and sent letters to the various benevolent and fraternal organizations in the city, requesting that they add his firm to their list of druggists. Another important feature that he added was to have a physician on duty during the period between 9 A.M. and 7 P.M. As he explained, "This will be a good thing as it will guarantee to [the customers] the services of a physician in the event of an emergency."

Besides these business activities, Cohen was one of Booker T. Washington's point men in Louisiana, especially in regard to the activities of the National Negro Business League. In 1910 Cohen reported to Washington that they had a "very successful Business League Convention." He further predicted that the "League will be a success and it is my intention to lend my earnest efforts in making it a success." Shortly thereafter, Cohen also became involved in the roof garden business at the Pythian Temple with his old political sponsor James M. Vance, along with Lewis Joubert and Edward Barnes, who were both officers of his insurance company. In 1912 Cohen decided to pull out of the roof garden business since he could not get along with one of his partners, presumably Vance, since the other two men remained allied with his insurance firm. Cohen sold out his interest and complained to Washington that it had not been a profitable season and he had had to spend $600 of his own money to "fix the place up."

Walter Cohen's life underwent substantial changes during the 1920s. His first wife, Wilhelmina Selden, whom he had married in 1882, died in 1920. A short time later, he married Antonia Manade from Lutcher, Louisiana. The other major change at this time came with Cohen's appointment to high political office by President Warren G. Harding. Harding created the post of controller of the Port of New Orleans. The appointment brought forth a storm of protest from white southerners, and Cohen was rejected by the Senate three times before President Calvin Coolidge finally pushed it through in 1924. When Herbert Hoover assumed the presidency in 1929, however, he abolished the office but permitted Cohen to remain in office until his death in 1930. Hoover had offered him the post of minister to Liberia, but Cohen, as was always the case if he would have to move from his beloved New Orleans, refused the position.

Cohen suffered from unremitting attacks on his character throughout his career. Because this was typical of the sort of vilification white southerners heaped upon any blacks who had the temerity to try to remain involved in politics, it is difficult to know if there was much substance to the various charges. In 1908 his son Walter Cohen, Jr., was convicted of a crime dealing with his work as a letter carrier with the U.S. Postal Service and was sentenced to two years at the federal prison in Atlanta. His father, along with several of New Orleans' most prominent black leaders—Aristede Dejoie (see DeJoie, Geddes, and Misshore Families), James Lewis, and George D. Geddes—petitioned for his release. In 1925 the elder Cohen was indicted, along with fifty-two white officials, for accepting bribes to permit the smuggling of liquor through the port of New Orleans in violation of the prohibition law. Cohen was later fully exonerated by the jury in a directed verdict.

While Cohen was involved in running the customs office at the port of New Orleans, the insurance business was largely run by his daughter, Camille. After graduating from Straight University, she went to work in her father's office and was later to become his private secretary. As such, she virtually ran People's Benevolent Insurance Company until she married Oscar D. Jones and moved to Chicago.

Walter Cohen attended every national Republican Convention from 1896 through 1928, and he became a close confidant of many of the party's top leaders, including Marcus A. Hanna, Boies Penrose, and Will Hays. He was also a member, and for many years president, of the Iroquois Literary and Social Club, founded in 1899, an essentially Republican organization that included many of the city's black elite: James Lewis, Aristede DeJoie, and J. R. Joubert. He was also elected president of the prestigious Société d'Economique from the late 1890s onward. The club, which had been organized in 1836, was as Cohen himself said, "composed of the oldest and best French families who are very careful and scrupulous as to the reputation and character of the officers to serve them.'' David Rankin, in his study of black leadership, described it as the most exclusive black organization in America. Cohen was also a leader for the social and economic betterment of blacks in Louisiana and a member of the NAACP, the Knights of Pythias, Odd Fellows, and Elks.

Funeral services for Cohen, held in the Corpus Christi Roman Catholic Church, were attended by a large number of people from the city and around the nation. S. W. Green, who succeeded Cohen as president of the San Jacinto Club said, ''The race has lost one of its ablest men. He was one of the leaders of the race in civic and political matters.'' J. D. Brown, of Liberty Insurance, commented, ''I had known Mr. Cohen for the past twenty years. He was possessed of sterling character and a strong will power. The colored people have lost in him a leader, and the party owes more to him than any man ever connected with it. He kept the fires burning.'' The *Louisiana Weekly* said it most simply, mourning the death of the ''Last of the Old Guards.''

Succeeding Cohen as head of People's Insurance was James Lewis, Jr., the son of Col. James Lewis, an ally and sometime adversary of Walter Cohen. The elder Lewis was a native of Woodville, Mississippi, and, like P.B.S. Pinchback, started his career working as a cabinboy on river boats. Working his way up to steward, the highest position a black could achieve on the river, Lewis made his way to New Orleans after the Union troops took it over. There he raised a company of black troops, of which he was appointed captain. After General Nathanial P. Banks took command of the Department of the Gulf, he began a concerted campaign to get rid of black officers. After receiving discriminatory treatment from Banks's white officer, Lewis resigned on March 8, 1864.

After 1864 Lewis joined with the Freedmen's Bureau helping to establish schools for blacks all around the state. At the end of the war, Lewis was appointed collector of the port at New Orleans, the first black man to be given a federal civil position in Louisiana. Later, Lewis became a sergeant of the metropolitan police, and in 1870 he was appointed colonel of the second regiment state militia by Governor Warmoth. Lewis became a major force in the state's Republican party during Reconstruction, serving in a number of offices and as a member of the state senate. As such, he played a crucial role in getting Pinchback elected president pro tem of that body. In 1877 Lewis was appointed naval officer of the port of New Orleans, a post he held for three years. Later in the 1880s Lewis was appointed superintendent of the United States bonded warehouse in New Orleans. In 1884 and 1885, when the World's Industrial and Cotton Exposition was held in New Orleans, Lewis opened the Experimental Restaurant on the grounds to ensure that blacks would be served on the same basis as whites.

James Lewis had early become an advocate of the idea of self-help and economic betterment for blacks, insisting as early as 1875 that the question of civil rights would be resolved by industry and acquisition of wealth on the part of blacks themselves. At the same time, he had said, ''Our labor and our crops bring us money; we need banks wherein we have an interest in which to deposit.

We like to insure our houses and our furniture, we then need insurance companies. The fact is we need to enter all branches of trade.'' It was natural, therefore, that, when Booker T. Washington rose to prominence with the same message in the 1890s, James Lewis would become closely associated with the Tuskegean.

In the controversy in 1904, mentioned above, when both Lewis and Cohen were up for appointment, Cohen became rather critical of Lewis's integrity and courage and asked Washington to talk to "Col. Lewis in such a way as to put some stiffener in his backbone—he has done nothing in the fight.'' Aristede DeJoie shared that feeling, writing to Washington in 1905 that "Lewis is a negative character,'' while he viewed Cohen as "a fearless leader.'' In the end, however, Lewis and Cohen remained friends, and after the elder Lewis died in 1914 his son became closely associated with Cohen. The elder Lewis left a large fortune when he died, most of which he had made by investing in real estate.

A tall, dignified man, with an imperial beard, James Lewis was widely respected by both whites and blacks in New Orleans, although there were those like Aristede DeJoie and Walter Cohen who were critical of him at times. Unlike most of the New Orleans African-American elite, James Lewis and his son were Methodists, and the elder Lewis had done much to help establish a number of benevolent institutions connected with that faith, including the Louisiana Educational Relief Association, which helped support the St. James AME Church School among others.

James Lewis, Jr., was educated in New Orleans public schools and Straight University. Early in his life he joined the sugar brokerage firm of Harry L. Haws and Company as a stenographer. Later, he became cashier of the enterprise and directed the lending of as much as $3 million a year to sugar planters. "And,'' Lewis proclaimed proudly, "I wasn't bonded.'' Ultimately Lewis spent over fifty-five years with the company until he retired in 1941. In 1931 Lewis joined People's Insurance, as a director, and in 1935 he became head of the company. At that time, it was not in particularly good shape, since it had a $14,000 deficit. "You can't make money,'' Lewis declared, "by spending more than you are taking in.'' By economizing, he was able to cure that imbalance. Then, he started investing People's funds with the same care he used with his own fortune of some $500,000, putting it into blue-chip stocks like General Motors, General Electric, United Fruit, and Standard Brands. Lewis, unlike most black insurance executives, refused to make loans on farms or real estate.

As his chief aide, and the man who handled the day-to-day operations of People's, Lewis promoted Haydel Christophe, who started at People's as a sweeper. "I have surrounded myself with good men,'' Lewis said proudly. "You take Mr. Christophe. His life is clean, and that's all that counts with me. We don't have 'em around here gambling, Not with our money. God's blessed us.'' Lewis ran People's in a highly paternalistic fashion, declaring, "It's just like a big family here. It's cool and everybody's happy. We all work together. The Almighty's watching over us. And we're making money.''

Lewis was involved with Cohen in running the Fourth Ward Civic Organization and with the development of the Republican party in the state. He was also a major benefactor of black charities throughout his life. He sent a number of black young men through Southern University, and he planned on donating his fortune after he died to Charity Hospital's "Negro Ward." "I've been fixed all my life," he admitted, but "I want to show white people we appreciate what they've done for us." He firmly believed that New Orleans was the best city for blacks in America, saying, "I don't think business opportunities are as good in Chicago. Northerners are cold—cold and sharp. Let me tell you about Southern people. You can get your program over with them. They'll help you if you help yourself."

Sources

Neither Walter Cohen's private papers nor those of People's Industrial Life are currently available. There is, however, extensive correspondence between Cohen and Booker T. Washington and Emmett J. Scott in the Booker T. Washington Papers at the Library of Congress. There also are some important references to Cohen in letters between P.B.S. Pinchback and Blanche Kelso Bruce, located in the Pinchback Papers and the B. K. Bruce papers, both held in Special Collections at the Moorland-Spingarn Research Center, Howard University. Biographical information on Cohen, however, is rather limited. The best printed sources are *The National Cyclopedia of the Colored Race* (Montgomery, Alabama, 1919); Charles B. Rousseve, *The Negro in Louisiana: Aspects of His History and His Literature* (New Orleans, 1937), 130–31; *Who's Who in Colored Louisiana* (1930), 112–13; and *Sepia Socialite*, April 1942. There are obituaries in the *Times-Picayune*, December 30, 1930, and *Louisiana Weekly*, January 3, 1931. There is information on his daughter, Camille Cohen, in *Crisis* XXXVI (December 1929), 410, and on his son, Walter L. Cohen, Jr., in the *Times-Picayune*, September 10, 1959. Information on the Lewises is also very limited. James Lewis, Sr.'s, biography is in William J. Simmons, *Men of Mark*, 954–58, and he has a very few letters in the Booker T. Washington Papers in the Library of Congress. The best information on James Lewis, Jr., is found in *Fortune*, November 1947, 186–88.

Coleman, Warren Clay (March 28, 1849–March 31, 1904); **Richard Burton Fitzgerald** (c. 1843–March 24, 1918); and **Edward Austin Johnson** (November 23, 1860–July 24, 1944). Textile manufacturers, banker, merchants, brickworks owner, politician, educator, and insurance company founder: Coleman Manufacturing Company, Mechanics and Farmers Bank, North Carolina Mutual Insurance Company. It was an ambitious dream—not just for the men involved—but for the African-American people of the South as a whole. The symbol of the rapidly industrializing New South at the turn of the century was the cotton mill. It was cotton mill production that fueled the growth of cities in rural North Carolina and provided the fastest growing area of employment for persons being pushed off the land. Yet it was precisely this new avenue of opportunity that had been cut off to poor blacks. It was common wisdom in the South that blacks could not and should not work in these new mills. Most whites believed, as one mill manager stated, "I do not believe a genuine negro can ever be profitably used in a cotton mill." And if they could, by some stroke of luck, be taught these skills, they still should not be used because, according to the manager, "they would be twice as hard to manage and control as white people." Moreover, whites, he reasoned, would not work with blacks, and it was especially taboo for white women to work alongside blacks. It was this impression that Warren Coleman, Richard Fitzgerald, Edward Johnson, and other black leaders wanted to alter in 1896 when they began plans for their black-owned and black-run cotton mill. It was not just a plan to make money. It was far more than that— it was a magnificent dream of race uplift—a classic working out of Booker T. Washington's* ideas of self-help and example. It was a grand dream, and for Warren Coleman it became a magnificent obsession.

Warren Clay Coleman, as Allen Burgess has commented, was "exceptional: exceptionally active, exceptionally successful, exceptionally ambitious, and exceptionally wealthy." He was born a slave on the William M. Coleman plantation in Cabarrus County, North Carolina. His mother was a slave woman named Roxie, and his father was white, but there is some conjecture about who he was. Warren Krieger states that his father was Rufus Clay Barringer, who became a general in the Confederate Army during the Civil War, and then became a lawyer and farmer. Others have simply noted that he was a white man "distinguished by military and financial ability." Whatever the case, it is clear that Barringer guided Warren Coleman in his early development and was his financial backer in a number of his ventures. Warren's mother later married John F. Young, a household slave and blacksmith, and had a total of three sons: Thomas Clay Coleman, Joseph Smith, and Warren.

Warren Coleman's master, William M. Coleman, owned a good deal of property in Cabarrus County, but during the Civil War he liquidated much of his holdings. After the war he became involved in Republican politics, but he so embarrassed the party that he was appointed consul to a city in Germany to get him out of North Carolina. Warren Coleman spent his youth on the Coleman plantation, learning the shoemaking trade which he practiced until the end of the Civil War. He was then, according to Krieger, apprenticed to William Coleman, who "educated and trained" him until 1867. Warren Coleman himself, however, recalls this period as a time when he was "required to perform drudgery work," which he disliked intensely.

At eighteen, Coleman's apprenticeship ended, and he began to engage in trading and peddling, which allowed him to develop a number of valuable business skills. In 1869, at just twenty years of age, the young ex-slave bought his first piece of property—a half-acre business site in the town of Concord for $600—paying for it in cash. Nonetheless, Coleman soon grew restless in Concord. Like so many blacks in this period right after the war, he lusted for economic opportunity, so he left for Alabama, where he spent a year. When he got back to Concord in 1871, Coleman began to be tutored by his old master, who by then had come back from Germany. During this same period, Warren Coleman continued his business activities, peddling groceries and a number of other items. He also began farming.

In 1872 William M. Coleman persuaded Warren that he should pursue his education and recommended he go to the Model School at Howard University. To finance his education, Warren Coleman had to sell his business, which he did in the late fall for $671. While in Washington, D.C., Coleman continued his business interests, trading and peddling a number of items. He entered Howard in the fall of 1873, but he found that the formal pursuit of knowledge was not for him. He began returning to Concord to purchase land while he was still in school. In September 1873, Coleman bought ninety acres of land for $600, paying cash for the entire amount. He returned again in December, this time to marry Jane E. Jones, whom he had evidently met while he was in Alabama. She was eight years his senior.

By early 1874, Coleman was back in Concord permanently, and he began to act as a moneylender. He also purchased additional property during this time. Finding success in these ventures, by 1876 Coleman was also selling land as a real estate agent and was also acting as a broker for the sale of a number of other kinds of goods. By the late 1870s, Coleman was regularly purchasing lots in and around Concord, building up a rather tidy real estate empire, but little else is known about his business activities during this time. It was also during this time that Coleman became a leader in the African Methodist Episcopal (AME) Zion Church in Concord. Next to his business ventures, the church was the most important element in Warren Coleman's life, and the AME Zion Church was the most aggressive and expansionist in North Carolina during these years. Coleman was instrumental in getting the national leaders of the AME Zion Church to locate a denominational school in Concord.

For a number of years, Coleman had wanted to own a business in downtown Concord, and in 1881 he purchased from William M. Coleman a half-interest in a lot on Main Street for $850. This was an exceedingly valuable piece of land that William Coleman and his brother Daniel had inherited. Daniel retained his half-interest. On this lot Warren Coleman erected a simple wood frame building. Coleman's mercantile operations appear to have flourished from the beginning, and he also became, as did most general merchants in the South, an important credit source for local farmers. A man who traded with Coleman in the late nineteenth century commented, "Coleman was a shrewd business man that could go up a tree naked and come down with a suit of clothes on."

Some sense of Coleman's business acumen, and his flair for advertising, can be gained from several ads he ran in the *Concord Register*. The first one, in June 1880, proclaimed: "Coleman is selling at very small profits teas, coffee, sugar, syrups, home and imported molasses. Received this day is another lot of fresh cakes and candies." Eleven years later, in January 1891, he ran the following ad: "I am offering some choice bargains in canned goods for the next few days. I wish to unload a heavy stock of molasses. I will make close figures that will startle you. Houses for rent in different parts of town.'' As the final line indicates, Coleman continued to buy real estate property during this time and was also involved as a landlord, renting these properties to tenant farmers and others.

In 1885, however, Coleman suffered a terrible setback when his mercantile store burned to the ground. His losses totaled $7,000, and he had no fire insurance—a failure that would cause him trouble again later. But Coleman was determined to rebuild his business, and he accomplished his purpose with surprising speed, although he may have incurred large debts in doing so. By 1886, however, he seemed to be back on his feet, because he purchased twenty-eight lots in the Concord suburb of Coleburg from William M. Coleman, bringing to forty the number of lots he owned there. In December 1887, he purchased another thirty-eight lots in Coleburg from Daniel Coleman. All of this land was part of the former plantation on which Warren Coleman had been born a slave. During this same period, Coleman continued to make extensive real estate purchases in other parts of Concord. In addition, he made some advantageous sales of these properties. One of his best transactions was a half-acre plot he sold in 1889 to Odell Manufacturing Company, the town's largest and oldest cotton manufacturer. He sold the property for $600, realizing a profit of between 500 and 900 percent from when he had bought it in 1883. In the early 1890s, Coleman also began to purchase properties outside of Concord, adding to his already large holdings.

But Coleman was not just speculating in land, he was also developing it. On many of these lots, especially in Coleburg, he was building houses, dozens of them. These were generally not much more than cabins, which he rented out to black tenants for anywhere from fifty cents to $1.25 per week. These rentals, by the end of the 1880s, were grossing Coleman about $200 a week; R. G. Dun & Co. estimated the worth of his general store at $5,000. Edward A. Johnson, later to be Coleman's partner, estimated in his *A School History of the Negro Race in America*, published in 1890, that Coleman was worth $100,000 in that year. By 1895 Coleman was one of the largest merchants and landowners in Concord, white or black, and he was considered one of the South's wealthiest blacks.

Besides these business activities, Coleman was involved in a number of other important areas during the years prior to 1896. In 1881, for example, he became a stockholder and member of the North Carolina Industrial Association. This organization was formed to hold an annual fair in Raleigh, at which North Carolina blacks could display all sorts of items they had grown or made. The association had a dual purpose: first, to encourage blacks to develop their own business interests and, second, to persuade whites of the industry and ability of African-Americans. Coleman brought his indefatigable energy and enthusiasm to this enterprise, was elected treasurer of the group, and became quite active in planning the 1886 fair. Two years later, in October 1888, he was elected president and served in this capacity until 1891. In 1895 he was made responsible for North Carolina's exhibit at the Cotton States Exposition held in Atlanta, where Booker T. Washington made his famous speech. Being appointed to this position was both an honor and an opportunity for Coleman, since it allowed him to come into contact with prominent blacks and whites from throughout the South.

Coleman, as mentioned above, was active in his church, but in 1895 he had a falling out with the AME Zion Church, withdrew with nineteen other members, and organized the Price Memorial AME Zion Church in Coleburg. He was also an active temperance advocate and played a prominent role in the election to make Concord a dry town. His campaign in this regard stirred up some animosity toward him from antiprohibitionists in the town. Besides his activity in prohibition matters, Coleman was fairly active in politics as a Republican. In 1895 he was appointed justice of the peace, but there was a great outcry over this because he was black. He nonetheless fulfilled the office, and in 1896 he was nominated as a Republican to run for county commissioner. A week after the Republican Convention, however, Coleman withdrew from the race, probably because of pressure put upon him because of his race.

At about that time, in 1895 or 1896, Coleman decided to build a cotton mill. It was the most momentous decision of his life, and one with vast potential importance for other African-Americans in the state and nation. What impelled him to take this plunge? He, after all, for all his wealth and business success, knew nothing of manufacturing, let alone cotton production. Holland Thompson, who wrote an early history of North Carolina's cotton mills and lived in Concord at the time Coleman built his mill, probably understood his motivation:

[Coleman's] motivation was complex. The other mills in the town were almost phenomenally successful; his own past success as a financier had made him ambitious to be recognized in a broader field. Further, his race consciousness was strong and he desired to be considered the negro Moses, and to receive the applause gained by opening a new field of activity to his people.

So, according to Thompson, Coleman Manufacturing was a combination of personal and racial betterment. What could be a more apt embodiment of Booker T. Washington's ideas of self-help and economic enterprise that Coleman had recently heard him espouse at the Atlanta Exposition?

This dual ambition was further fueled by the fact that once sleepy Concord had become a major center of cotton manufacture in North Carolina. The transformation of Concord, a sleepy agrarian village of 700 in the 1880s, began with the arrival of Captain J. M. Odell. He bought a floundering mill in the Forest Hill section of the city, which had been organized as Concord Manufacturing Company in 1839, and he transformed it using poor hill farmers and widows as a labor force. By the 1890s Odell, a "master mill man," employed 800 hands, and the mill produced 15 percent of the cotton produced in the state. It was generally recognized as the best mill in North Carolina. A little later, Odell helped James W. Cannon, who had worked for him for a time, to start Cannon

Mills, and the two men then started a number of other mills in various parts of the town. By 1900 Concord's population had exploded to 8,000, and it had surpassed Durham and Salisbury in size. This prosperity and growth for Concord was not to last, but no one, certainly not Warren Coleman or J. M. Odell, knew it at the time. Then, too, both Odell and Cannon had operated general merchandise stores in Concord. Now they were both wealthy men and accorded enormous respect by everyone in the community. If they could do it, why not Coleman?

Having decided that he wanted to start a cotton mill using black labor, Coleman next had to face the difficult task of securing financing. Although he had a good deal of capital himself, little of it was liquid, and he did not want to have to liquidate all of his holdings to engage in this enterprise. He decided to incorporate and gather investors in the project. One of the first things Coleman did was to approach Odell and Cannon for their support. They heartily gave their endorsement (though, of course, not their money) and even appeared at the first stockholder's meeting to speak in its favor. Daniel Augustus Tomkins, the great mill owner of Charlotte, also pledged support of the concept. Coleman then went ahead and got an option on land near the Cabarrus Mill, owned by the Cannon family, which a representative from the *Manufacturer's Record* called the best site possible for the experiment. Things looked rosy indeed for Coleman's grand vision.

In June 1896, Coleman wrote to Booker T. Washington about his plans:

Knowing you as we do to be a man of worth, talent and influence and one who is interested in the industrial development of the race, we hope that you will help by influencing those around you and by sending us your subscription, not as a donation but as a stockholder.

Washington evidently did not heed Coleman's pleas for, in February 1897, Coleman complained that the Tuskegean had still not given his support to the mill. On the same day he first wrote to Washington, Coleman also sent a letter to Washington Duke, scion of the North Carolina tobacco family, asking him to "kindly aid in the undertaking by taking stock." Several months later, in March 1897, Duke wrote to Richard B. Fitzgerald, "It is my pleasure to subscribe one thousand dollars to the capital stock of the Coleman Manufacturing Company." He stated further, "I commend the enterprise of the colored people in establishing a cotton mill for the employment of their people. I wish for the institution that success its worthiness merits." Coleman could also announce by 1897 that two wealthy blacks from Durham, Richard B. Fitzgerald and Dr. James E. Shepard, had pledged support for the enterprise. Fitzgerald would soon be appointed president of the company.

Getting the Duke family to support his enterprise with actual cash was an enormous coup for Coleman, and he used it to persuade other wealthy whites of the worth of his venture. Nevertheless, he ran into a great deal of trouble raising capital. First of all, there was a serious downturn in the textile trade in 1897 and 1898, which made investors very wary; second, the rise of virulent white supremacy, coupled with the Wilmington Riot, after 1898, made whites leery of becoming involved. In that year, two tenements built to house workers near the Coleman Mill were burned down. Additionally, many of the blacks who had promised their support failed to pay their pledges. Coleman found his plans for opening the plant on the scale he intended to be continually frustrated.

Coleman was therefore forced to make a public appeal to blacks of North Carolina. In it, he used the full flourish of his rhetorical talents:

Please allow me to call attention of the public to the fact that a movement is on foot to erect a cotton mill at Concord to be operated by colored labor . . . the enterprise will prove to the world our ability as operatives in the mills, thereby solving the great problem "can the Negroes be employed in cotton mills to any advantage?" . . . But don't think for a moment that this desirable and enviable position can be obtained by merely a few of our people, . . . it will require a united effort of the race.

The appeal was evidently a success; by the time Coleman incorporated the company in 1897, he had secured twenty individuals to serve as incorporators. Many of them were there for the prestige they lent the project, rather than any money they invested. This included seven black ministers. The most prominent among them was Bishop James Walker Hood of the AME Zion Church, possibly the most widely known African-American in the state. Another prestigious group were the presidents of denominationally affiliated black colleges, such as Dr. D. J. Sanders of nearby Biddle University and Charles Francis Merserve of Shaw University in Raleigh. Merserve was one of three whites among the incorporators. Other important individuals were Dr. Lawson Andrew Scruggs of Raleigh, one of the best-known black physicians in the state. The two most important black incorporators for the future of the company, though, were Edward A. Johnson, an attorney from Raleigh, and Richard B. Fitzgerald, a wealthy brickyard owner from Durham. Fitzgerald assumed the largely honorific position of president of the concern, and Johnson was named vice president. Warren Coleman was to be secretary and treasurer and chief operating officer of the concern.

Johnson, like Coleman, was an ex-slave with enormous ambition and great abilities. He was born in Wake County, North Carolina, one of eleven children of the slaves Columbus and Eliza Johnson. While still very young, Edward Johnson was educated by a free black, Nancy Walton, and after emancipation attended a school in Raleigh conducted by two Yankee teachers from New England. These teachers introduced Johnson to the Congregational religion, and he remained active in the church for the rest of his life. Edward Johnson graduated from Washington High School in Raleigh and decided to attend Atlanta University in 1879.

Upon his graduation four years later, Johnson decided to remain in Atlanta, where he opened a wood and coal yard in the city. The business was apparently successful, but Johnson evidently did not feel that it suited his needs or ambitions. He enjoyed far more his association in publishing the *Atlanta Pilot*, which he ran with Dr. Henry A. Rucker and others. By 1883, however, Johnson had decided on education as his profession, and he became principal of Mitchell School, the largest black school in Atlanta. After two years there, however, he eagerly accepted a chance to return to Raleigh as principal of his old high school. Johnson remained principal until 1891, during this time writing and publishing *A School History of the Negro Race in America*, which was designed to provide black children with role models and information about "the many brave deeds and noble characters of their own race." It was the first textbook by a black author to be approved by the North Carolina Board of Education for use in the public schools.

During this same period, Johnson attended law school at Shaw University, getting his law degree in 1891, the first graduate of their program. He practiced law for two years but complained about the fact that neither whites nor blacks would use black attorneys. Business was so bad that in 1893 the *Raleigh Gazette* told its readers that Johnson and the other black attorney in town were considering leaving Raleigh because of lack of business. Johnson was kept in Raleigh by giving him an appointment to the law faculty at Shaw, where he served until 1907 as professor and then dean. This gave him more financial security than the law practice, which he also continued during these years.

Johnson was also strongly involved in politics in Raleigh during the 1890s. He was a prominent factor in local and state Republican circles and served as assistant district attorney and an alderman in the city of Raleigh. He was also a delegate to the Republican National Convention in 1892 and 1896. Johnson was therefore a man of some importance in North Carolina by the late 1890s, yet his political career was also under great jeopardy because of the movement to exclude blacks from political positions in the state. If Warren Coleman needed Edward Johnson, Johnson needed the success of the Coleman mill just as much.

Richard Fitzgerald, along with his brother, Robert G. Fitzgerald, were probably the wealthiest and most respected blacks in Durham. Richard was born in New Castle County, Delaware, the son of Charles Thomas Fitzgerald, a mulatto who had been manumitted when he was twenty-four, and Sarah Ann Burton, a white woman. The elder Fitzgeralds were small-scale farmers in Delaware, but a few years before the outbreak of the Civil War they moved to Chester County, Pennsylvania. Not much is known of Richard Fitzgerald's early life, but he and Robert were probably educated at Ashmun Academy in Chester. Both of them served in the Quartermaster Corps of the Union Army from 1861, working as civilian contract laborers driving mule teams. Richard served in Virginia, near Fortress Monroe and Harrison's Landing, but after a time he enlisted in the navy and went to sea. Robert joined the Union Army, serving with the Fifth Massachusetts Cavalry. After the war, both the Fitzgeralds returned to the family farm in Pennsylvania, and two years later they moved to a larger farm in Nottingham Township. During this time Robert went to school to prepare himself to begin teaching in the Freedman Bureau's schools in the South. Richard, on the other hand, opened a brickyard in Nottingham Township. After his first year of operation, Richard had lost $500 on the enterprise, and Robert began to encourage his brother to join him in moving South. In 1868 Robert left for North Carolina. Richard remained behind to continue trying to make a go of his brick-yard.

In the spring of 1869, Fitzgerald's parents also moved to North Carolina, and Richard began to give the matter serious consideration. Thomas Fitzgerald sold the family farm for $1,500 and bought Woodside Farm in Orange County, North Carolina. In July of that year, Richard moved to North Carolina, and, upon his arrival, the family began to operate a small brickyard at Woodside to supplement the family's income. At this same time, Richard met Sallie Williams, daughter of Reverend Samuel Williams, an AME Church missionary from Philadelphia, who was living in Woodside, and in 1870 they were married.

In the meantime, Robert Fitzgerald, in desperate need of money to support his family and his school, began selling larger and larger orders of bricks, traveling to Raleigh to get orders for construction of a new state prison there. He was ultimately successful in getting an order for 4 million bricks, and immediately he sent word of the order to Richard. To fill the order, the brothers set up a new, much larger brickyard in Raleigh and began making bricks there. They had nothing but problems, however, trying to fulfill the order, as rain and floods damaged some of their equipment and bricks. Finally, they were forced to renegotiate the contract, supplying the state with 525,000 bricks, and making less than $85 for four months' work. They were, however, able to show people in Wake and Orange counties that they were reliable brick makers.

At this point the two brothers at least partially went their separate ways. In September 1870, Robert Fitzgerald qualified as a teacher in the public school system, but Richard, according to Pauli Murray, a granddaughter of Robert, had few of his brother's idealistic impulses and was more interested in making money. Richard continued to expand his brick-making business, and Robert ran a smaller brickyard while teaching school. In 1879 their father died, and the two brothers decided it was time to pull up stakes again and head for a new frontier—the raw "new South" town of Durham. Murray describes Durham at that time:

Durham was a village without pre–Civil War history or strong ante-bellum traditions. In some ways it was like a frontier town. There was considerable prejudice, of course, but there was a recognition of individual worth and bridges of mutual respect between the older white and colored families of the town which persisted into the twentieth century. Robert and Richard Fitzgerald were respected as builders of this tobacco center and their families were held in high esteem.

Both men started brickyards, but Richard's was by far the larger of the two enterprises.

Richard, a blue-eyed, blond-haired, fair-skinned man, in business "was quick to drive a hard bargain . . . [and] had a genius for making a dollar." His personality was characterized by those who knew him by a "pugnacious stubborn-ness." These traits allowed him to overcome virtually any hardship put in his way, and by 1884 he was running the largest brickyard among the eight located in Durham. By this time he had expanded his business beyond that of making simple brick to the manufacture of ornamental brick for more elaborate buildings and residences. By the 1890s, Fitzgerald was doing a good deal of business with the Duke family, and the bricks he manufactured were used not only by American Tobacco Company, but also by Trinity College, the Oxford Orphan Asylum, and a number of local churches funded by Duke philanthropy. Fitzgerald in the 1890s was estimated by the *Raleigh Blade* to regularly employ between "fifty and one hundred ten hands," making him by far the largest black employer of African-American labor in the state.

Richard Fitzgerald also began purchasing a good deal of real estate in Durham. He not only owned an impressive amount of property in Hayti, the black section of town, but by the 1890s was also buying substantial acreage in or near downtown Durham. In 1894, for example, he acquired a business property on Main Street that he bought from the trustees of the bankrupt tobacco tycoon, William T. Blackwell. He bought several other parcels in the next few years also. As a result of his business and real estate interests, Richard Fitzgerald was considered the wealthiest black in the area. A natural leader in the city's black community, he lived in a beautiful eighteen-room, slate-roofed mansion with many turrets and gables and a wide piazza that he purchased from T. J. Walker, an executive of American Tobacco Company who was transferred to Richmond.

Thus Richard Fitzgerald was a prize catch for Coleman. Not as significant a one as the Duke family, perhaps, but having Fitzgerald's financial support, and having him listed as president of the concern, gave Coleman Manufacturing a good deal of prestige, particularly among blacks in eastern North Carolina. Coleman tried to persuade Washington Duke to allow his name to be used as one of the officers, but Duke declined. He did, however, allow Coleman to continue making use of his name, saying, "You can use my name in connection with your enterprise to the extent I told you in my office." In another letter, Duke indicated his pleasure at the selection of Fitzgerald as president. He noted that he had "known the bearer, R. B. Fitzgerald, of our town for twenty years." Further, he said, "He is reliable in business matters and worthy of the attention and consideration of any one from whom he may solicit subscriptions to the capital stock of his mill."

By the end of 1897, the mill building had been substantially completed, but Coleman was still having difficulty securing sufficient capital. He planned an impressive cornerstone-laying ceremony in February 1898 and asked Booker T. Washington to attend. The Tuskegean was unable to do so, but Coleman was nonetheless able to convince an impressive array of white and black dignitaries to be there. By April of that year the main building and tower were complete, and it was time to begin purchasing mill machinery. But Coleman was woefully short of capital to do so, and the rising racial tensions of the summer of 1898, culminating in the tragic Wilmington Riot, only made his task more difficult. By early summer, the total number of subscribers to stock in Coleman Manufacturing was 800, but only about 100 had paid even a portion of the money they owed. Nonetheless, Washington Duke paid in his $1,000, which enabled

Coleman to buy the Corliss engine and boilers to power the works. The next step, however, was to purchase the actual manufacturing machinery.

Coleman decided that his original plans for a 3,000-spindle mill were too small and therefore determined that he would purchase used machinery so that he could engage in a larger operation. The mill machinery he wanted was purchased from a factory in Nashua, New Hampshire, and had 150 looms and 5,104 spindles. To make even this purchase, though, it was necessary for Coleman to ask Benjamin N. Duke on March 8, 1899, for a "loan of $10,000 or $15,000" for which he promised to "give the property as security." Buying the machinery through Lafayette Godfrey of Providence, Rhode Island, the latter also helped finance the sale by taking stock in Coleman Manufacturing. The loan agreement also required Coleman to have insurance on the building, but he procrastinated on this matter, to the point that Duke's private secretary was forced to secure the insurance himself and bill Coleman Manufacturing for it.

By February 1900, the spinning, weaving, and belting machinery was in place, and the mill had been tested but was still not in operation. The problem now was to purchase some cotton to be spun and woven and sold. This, however, would take a good deal of cash, money they did not have. Coleman therefore proposed to the board that they approach Benjamin Duke for another loan. He reported that the mill building and machinery had cost $51,000, although he felt they were valued at $75,000. The firm carried an indebtedness of over $15,000, mostly to Benjamin Duke. Thus, on February 21, 1900, Coleman wrote to B. N. Duke: "We are in need of money to get Cotton. The machinery is all ready to go to work. We need the cotton and a few other things and wanted to see if you would increase yours—that is your loan—make us another [loan]." Duke gave no immediate response, and the mill continued to sit idle for months on end for want of raw material.

In August 1900, however, Coleman had an opportunity to present the prospects for his firm at the first annual meeting of Booker T. Washington's recently organized National Negro Business League. He had Roscoe Murray Simmons, who was identified as his "private secretary," make the presentation. Simmons painted a grandiose, and totally false, picture. He said the plant was valued at $100,000; it was not. He claimed, "We employ between two hundred and two hundred and thirty colored boys and girls," when they had recently scaled down even their plans, let alone their actual employment, to one hundred hands. He claimed, "We manufactured there cotton goods and yarn." At this point no yarn or cloth was being produced.

Finally, in March 1901, Benjamin Duke agreed to loan the firm another $10,000, but this time he deducted $1,200 unpaid interest on the first loan from this total, so that Coleman received only $8,800. Coleman's response was hardly what one would expect, given the generally servile relationship between blacks and wealthy whites. He wrote to Duke's private secretary:

Now listen! . . . it was decided that . . . [with] a loan of $10,000 we could start up at once and these were very close figures. We are aware that we owe Mr. Duke $1,200 . . . [but] when we made our application for the second loan . . . our calculations did not include the $1,200.

Coleman asked that the $1,200 be sent immediately, but Duke refused.

Finally, in early June of 1901, the Coleman Mill began operating. In the fall, Coleman wrote Washington Duke that "the mill is in excellent running order with a full force [of operatives] on duty." It was, however, a terrible time to start making cotton yarn, since the market was in its most depressed state since the Civil War. In the spring of 1901 all mills in the Concord area cut wages by 10 percent, and J. W. Cannon posted notices that his heavily capitalized and highly efficient mills might be forced to close at any time. During the next few years, a number of mills in the area were forced to close, including Coleman Manufacturing. Another casualty a few years later came when the huge Odell mill went bankrupt.

Thus, business conditions were terrible for Coleman's fledgling, undercapitalized enterprise. This was compounded by the fact that Coleman, a wonderful promoter, a good trader, and a keen judge of real estate and business opportunity, was not a good manager or administrator. He was a continual procrastinator, and he was poor at attending to details. The situation reached such a stage that, in the fall of 1903, Richard Fitzgerald met with Morrison H. Caldwell, the firm's white attorney, and decided to ask for Coleman's resignation as secretary treasurer. Coleman resigned in December 1903 and was replaced by E. F. White, a white Concord merchant and cotton buyer. White did manage to get the mill operating a bit more efficiently, but by then it was too late. Finally, in June 1904, Benjamin Duke was forced to foreclose on the property to have a chance at recovering any part of the $20,000 he had loaned the firm. There was little interest in the property, and Duke was forced to buy it himself for $10,000. He held on to it for two years, for a time leasing it out to Edward A. Johnson and a few other blacks, who again tried to make a go of it as a black-owned and black-managed mill. In 1906 the property passed into the hands of J. W. Cannon, and it became part of his massive cotton textile mill empire in North Carolina, continuing to function as plant number nine of the Cannon Mills.

Warren Coleman was not around to watch the denouement of his once glorious dream. Perhaps it was just as well. At the end of March he died, exhausted and disillusioned in his home in Concord. Even by then, his faltering mill was just barely a black enterprise. It had a white chief operating officer, and it was financially controlled by whites. Allen Burgess has said of Coleman that "[he] epitomized the nineteenth century entrepreneur: he was aggressive, self-possessed, relatively well educated, highly motivated, individualistic, and materialistic. He was, in short, a black capitalist." In February 1988, the North Carolina Department of Cultural Resources placed a historical marker on Highway 601, about 300 yards from the site of Coleman's mill: "Warren Coleman—1849–1904—Founder of the nation's first textile factory owned and operated by blacks, 1897–1904. Mill building is 350 yds N." William Morrison, president of the Cabarrus County NAACP, who led the fight to get official recognition of the site, commented, "This is a part of Cabarrus County history that will always be recognized. . . . I think it was indeed remarkable that Coleman was able to get the plant up and going. We should all be proud."

The years after 1904 were unsettled ones for Edward Johnson also. He deeply resented the disfranchisement of blacks in North Carolina, partly for philosophical reasons, and partly because it ended his political influence in the area. He had been serving as assistant District Attorney in the Eastern District of North Carolina since 1900, but in 1907 he asked Booker T. Washington to help him keep that job. Washington wrote a letter for him, but it did not do any good, and Johnson was dismissed. Then, too, his involvement in North Carolina Mutual Insurance had been cut short when that firm was reorganized by John Merrick,* and his tenure as dean at Shaw was coming to an end. Thus, in 1907, he decided to move to New York City and settled in Harlem.

There he opened a law office and began investing in real estate. He also became prominent in the political, social, and cultural life of that community, becoming an active member of the Harlem Board of Trade and Commerce and the Upper Harlem Taxpayers Association. Johnson also began acquiring political influence in New York, and for many years he served as Republican committeeman for Harlem's Nineteenth Assembly District. In 1917 he was elected to the state legislature in Albany, the first black member of that body. He was defeated for reelection when his seat was redistricted, but Johnson remained active in Republican circles. In 1928 he waged a vigorous, but unsuccessful, effort to gain election to Congress as a Republican. During the final decade of his life, Johnson was nearly blind, and he developed a concern for sightless blacks. Upon his death in 1944, he left a bequest that half of his $76,000 estate be placed in a trust fund for the benefit of sightless blacks in Wake County, and he also gave $2,000 to Shaw University to be used for music scholarships. In 1951 the Raleigh Ministerial Alliance named a junior high school in the city in Johnson's honor.

Richard Fitzgerald continued his illustrious business career in Durham. In 1899 Fitzgerald, Dr. A. M. Moore, James E. Shepard, and others established the Durham Drug Company which had a drugstore in the white area and later one in Hayti. He was also involved in the Durham Real Estate, Mercantile and Manufacturing Company, and in 1910 he got involved with John Merrick and A. M. Moore in trying to make a success of another black-owned textile mill, the Durham Textile Company. Unlike Coleman's enterprise, which lacked capital, this venture had plenty of funds but could not find enough competent skilled black mill laborers to make a go of it. It did, however, struggle along for six years before it was shut down. Of greater importance for the future, however, was his involvement in the founding of the Mechanics and Farmers Savings Bank in 1907. There is some debate over just how the bank got started.

Moore said that Johnson and Dr. M. T. Pope of Raleigh had come to Durham and talked about the idea of starting a building and loan association in 1907. "Soon after," according to Moore, "R. B. Fitzgerald, John Merrick and others began to show activity toward starting a bank." William Gaston Pearson, the bank's first cashier, however, has a different version. He said, "The idea of a Negro bank originated in the minds of R. B. Fitzgerald and myself. I talked with John Merrick about it but at first he did not think the time was quite ripe to launch it.'' Later, Merrick subscribed $10,000 to the venture. Another account by J. A. Dodson claimed that Fitzgerald had been ''agitating the matter'' for several years and that ''[he] and Dr. J[ames] E. Shepard got together and the latter wrote out a form of charter for the institution.'' No matter which version of the founding of the bank is accepted, it is clear that Fitzgerald was the key individual in its origin and founding, and his name, along with several others (not Johnson's) are on the state incorporation papers in 1907. Richard Fitzgerald was elected first president of the bank, serving until 1910, when he was succeeded by John Merrick.

The original capital stock of the bank was just $10,000, which was increased to $15,000 in 1909, when the bank declared its first dividend. The bank was in large measure an adjunct of North Carolina Mutual over its entire history. The presidents of the insurance company were often also the presidents of the bank, and the single most dominant influence on Mechanics Bank during much of its history was Charles Clinton Spaulding.[*] After Spaulding died in 1952, John H. Wheeler, son of the Mutual's John L. Wheeler, became the bank president. Young John Wheeler was a magna cum laude alumnus of Morehouse who came from Atlanta in 1929 to work at Mechanics Bank as a teller at $60 a month.

Wheeler became vice president of the bank in 1944 and president upon Spaulding's death in 1952. Wheeler remained president of the bank until his retirement in 1978. Mechanics Bank, which had assets of about $6 million in 1952, grew slowly and steadily over the years. In 1983 Julia Wheeler Taylor, John Wheeler's daughter, was elected president and chief executive officer of the bank, the first woman to hold the position. She was born in Durham in 1936, attended North Carolina Central, and started as a trainee at the bank in 1955. After living in Los Angeles for a time, she came back to Mechanics Bank in 1965 as a teller. Julia Taylor progressed through the ranks, going from vice president and manager of one of the bank's two Raleigh branches to senior vice president and city executive for Raleigh.

John Wheeler became a prominent figure in the fight for integration and black rights in Durham. He was a leader of the Durham Committee on Negro Affairs, which became the most important political force in the black community in Durham. Organized in 1935, it openly asserted that its goal was to put political power in the hands of black people. Wheeler, unlike his mentor C. C. Spaulding, was an aggressive campaigner for integration, and he filed suits to integrate the public schools of the city and the law school of the University of North Carolina. A critical turning point for Wheeler came in the early 1960s, when a series of more violent sit-ins and other protests erupted. Many of the state's more conservative black leaders drew back from these protests, but Wheeler joined right in with several of them. Dr. Martin Luther King, Jr., praised Wheeler for ''unswerving commitment to the cause of freedom and justice.''

Wheeler was appointed a member of President John Kennedy's Equal Opportunity Committee; he also received a multitude of other honors. Despite these accolades and successes, Wheeler felt that the most important economic legacy of the bank, and of North Carolina Mutual and Mutual Savings and Loan, was the granting of long-term loans to blacks, which ultimately persuaded white banks to do likewise. Wheeler's daughter continued his sense of social commitment when she took over the bank. In 1986 venerable Shaw University was in severe financial difficulty. It was viewed by most banks as a risky client that should be allowed to die a quiet death, but Julia Taylor stepped in with bank loans and financial strategies that enabled the school to survive. A year later Shaw had repaid the bulk of its loan and was back on the road to financial health. John H. Lucas, the interim president of the university, commented, "It made everyone here realize how vital it is to have black financial institutions to which to turn." Mechanics and Farmers, which by 1992 had assets of over $100 million, was the eleventh-largest bank on the *Black Enterprise* list and was rated among the nation's safest by a credit rating bureau. It stood as a proud heritage of the dreams and vision of Richard Fitzgerald.

It is clear that Richard Fitzgerald was a man of great accomplishment at a critical period in the history of African-Americans. He, as much as John Merrick or Dr. Aaron M. Moore, must be given credit for creating the "capital for Black Business" that Durham became in the twentieth century. Yet, there are no plaques to Fitzgerald or his brickyard. His magnificent home was destroyed long ago, and although Coleman Manufacturing and Mechanics and Farmers Bank both were most fully the creations of other men, Fitzgerald's role in all of these endeavors cries out for recognition. His exact date of birth is not known; what little we do know of him comes from the fact that his brother's granddaughter wrote a history of that branch of the family. Coleman, Fitzgerald, and Johnson—three giants of the emerging black business, political, and cultural world of the twentieth century—deserve to be remembered.

Sources

There is a rather impressive amount of material on the Coleman Manufacturing Company scattered in a number of archives and collections. In the William R. Perkins Library at Duke University are letters and other materials pertaining to the enterprise and to Warren Coleman himself in the Benjamin Newton Duke Papers, the Washington Duke Papers, and the Daniel Augustus Tomkins Papers. In the Southern Historical Collection at the University of North Carolina at Chapel Hill there are items in the Julian Shakespere Carr Papers and the Charles N. Hunter Papers. In addition, there are a number of letters to and from Warren Coleman or Edward A. Johnson to either Booker T. Washington or Emmett J. Scott in the Booker T. Washington Papers in the Library of Congress. There are some additional legal materials pertaining to the enterprise in the North Carolina Department of Archives and History in Raleigh.

Some other basic information on the business can be culled from a number of sources: *Directory of Concord, North Carolina*, vol. 1 (Charlotte, N.C., 1902); *Branson's North Carolina Business Directory, 1896* (Raleigh, N.C., 1896); *Davison's Blue Book Textile Directory, 1896–97* (New York, 1896); *1904–05* (New York, 1904); *Textile World's Official Directory of the Textile Mills in the United States* (Boston, 1899, 1901).

The best overall account of Coleman Manufacturing is found in "Tar Heel Blacks and the New South Dream: The Coleman Manufacturing Company, 1896–1904," by Allen

Edward Burgess, Ph.D. diss. Duke University, 1977. There is another interesting and useful presentation in *The Noble Experiment of Warren C. Coleman*, by J. K. Rouse (Charlotte, N.C., 1972). There is a biography of Coleman by Warren A. Krieger in *Dictionary of North Carolina Biography*, edited by William S. Powell, vol. 1 (Chapel Hill, N.C., 1979), and his Master's thesis, "Warren Clay Coleman," Wake Forest University, 1969. Other biographies appear in William Harvey Quick, *Negro Stars in All Ages of the World* (Richmond, 1898); James Walker Hood, *One Hundred Years of the African Methodist Episcopal Church* (New York, 1895); *Dawn Magazine*, May 1977; and *Evidence of Progress among Colored People* (1897), 301–4. Some information on Coleman's white ancestors can be found in the *Charlotte Observer*, February 2, 1930; the "Family Tree of the Barringer Family" held at the Concord Public Library; and the *Dictionary of North Carolina Biography*, vol. 1. Robert F. Durden, in his *Dukes of Durham, 1865–1929* (Durham, N.C., 1975), has a good account of the Duke family's participation in Coleman's venture.

Additional contemporary information on the Coleman enterprise can be obtained from National Negro Business League, *Proceedings*, Annual Convention, August 23, 24, 1900; *Voice of the Negro*, August 1905; *Daily Standard*, February 23, 1897; Jerome Dowd, "Colored Men as Cotton Manufacturers," *Gunton's Magazine* 23 (September 1902), 254–56; and Holland Thompson, *From Cotton Field to the Cotton Mill: A Study of Industrial Transformation in North Carolina* (New York, 1906). Recent articles dealing with Coleman and mill ventures are found in "Historic Mill," *Cabarrus Neighbors*, June 5, 1986; *Concord Tribune*, February 28, 1988; *Cabarrus Voice and News*, February 24, 1988; *Charlotte Observer*, February 25, 1988; *Daily Times* (Wilson, N. C.), March 14, 1973; and *Raleigh News and Observer*, March 23, 1975.

Some sources dealing with Concord generally or with other textile mills in the area that are useful for understanding the Coleman attempt are "Life in a Southern Mill Town," *Political Science Quarterly* XV, 1 (March 1900); James L. Moore and Thomas H. Wingate, *Cabarrus Reborn: A Historical Sketch of the Founding and Development of Cannon Mills Co. and Kannapolis* (Kannapolis, N.C., 1940); Gary Richard Freeze, "Master Mill Man," Master's thesis, University of North Carolina at Chapel Hill, 1980; and Peter R. Kaplan, *The Historic Architecture of Cabarrus County, N. C.* (1981).

Some information on the Fitzgerald family is available in the Fitzgerald Family Diary and other items in the Fitzgerald Family Papers at the Southern Historical Collection, University of North Carolina at Chapel Hill. Almost all of this, however, deals with Robert rather than Richard. There are a few letters from Richard Fitzgerald in the Benjamin N. Duke Papers at Duke University. See also Pauli Murray, *Proud Shoes* (1956) for an account of the family. There is a biography of Robert G. Fitzgerald in the *Dictionary of North Carolina Biography* by Marvin Krieger. A biography of Richard B. Fitzgerald is found in the *Durham Recorder*, April 16, 1900. There is a short item on Richard in the *Urbana Illinois Informer*, March 1910, dealing with his involvement in the Durham Textile Mill.

Edward A. Johnson's papers are not available, but there are a number of letters between Johnson and Booker T. Washington or Emmett J. Scott in the Booker T. Washington Papers in the Library of Congress. Willard Gatewood has done a biography of Johnson in the *Dictionary of North Carolina Biography*, and another appears in *Black Americans in North Carolina and the South*, edited by Jefferey J. Crow and Flora J. Hatley (Chapel Hill, N.C., 1984). There are older biographies in the *Journal of Negro History*, October 24, 1944; *New York Times*, July 24, 1944; and *Who's Who in Colored America, 1938–*

40 (1940). Some earlier summaries of his life were "The Life and Work of Edward Austin Johnson," *The Crisis* 40 (April 1933); *Indianapolis Freeman*, July 6, 1907; and *Evidences of Progress among Colored People* (1897). See also *The Raleigh Times*, December 18, 1951. There is some information about Johnson's political career in New York City in Gilbert Osofsky, *Harlem: The Making of a Ghetto* (1966), 170ff; and his career there can be followed in the *Amsterdam News, Negro World*, and other black newspapers which are in the clipping files at the Schomburg Collection, New York Public Library. His real estate dealings in New York can be ascertained from Wilfred R. Bain, "Negro Real Estate Broker," WPA Paper in the Schomburg Collection.

An appraisal of Johnson as a writer and historian may be found in Willard Thorpe, *The Black Historian: The Layman as a Writer of History* 149–50; and "School and Society," July 29, 1944, *Negro Almanac*, 73. His writings are not readily available but include *A School History of the Negro Race in America* (1891); *History of the Negro Soldiers in the Spanish-American War* (1899); *Light ahead for the Negro* (1904); *Negro Almanac and Statistics* (n.d.); and *Adam vs. Ape-Man and Ethiopia* (1931).

D

Davis, Willie D. (July 24, 1934–   ). Entrepreneur and professional football player: All-Pro Broadcasting, Willie Davis Distributing Company, WANA, Inc., Valley School and Office Supplies; Green Bay Packers. Willie Davis was one of the first of a new breed of black entrepreneur—the ex–professional athlete who parlays his or her sports fame, along with an astronomical income, into the creation of a significant business empire. In recent years, such ex–ball players as Dave Bing in Detroit, Julius Erving in Philadelphia, Mel Farr in Royal Oak, Michigan, Oscar Robertson in Cincinnati, and Gale Sayers in Chicago have followed a similar pattern. More recently, active sports stars, such as Bo Jackson, "Magic" Johnson, and Michael Jordan, have used their visibility in sports to create a huge financial empire based on testimonials. Willie Davis differed from most of these stars in one significant way; he never had a large salary. The most he ever made from sports was $47,000 a year. He combined sports fame with education, hard work, dedication, and a keen business sense to create a highly successful and diversified business empire.

Willie Davis was born in Lisbon, Louisiana, but moved to Texarkana, Arkansas, as a boy. His family was very poor, and his mother was forced to raise her three children as a single parent. Despite these difficulties, she instilled in her children a great will to succeed and carefully monitored their progress. She did not allow young Willie to play football, out of fear he would be injured, but he joined the team anyway. She found out only when his team played a game in another city and Willie had to stay away overnight. She was not pleased but agreed to allow him to continue playing. Willie Davis was educated in the segregated public schools, shining as a three-sport athletic star at tiny, all-black Booker T. Washington High School. Despite his achievements, Davis apparently did little to impress his classmates, who voted him "Least Likely to Succeed" when he graduated in 1952. Davis's athletic prowess, however, won him a scholarship to Grambling College in Louisiana, where he became the captain and a star player on the school's well-regarded football team under legendary coach Eddie Robinson. No slouch as a student, he made the Dean's List several times and graduated with a Bachelor of Science degree in industrial arts with minors in mathematics and physical education. After graduation, Davis spent two years in the U.S. Army, where he won Army and All-Service honors as a football player.

Davis, who stood six feet, three inches tall and weighed 260 pounds when he graduated, was drafted in the seventeenth round by the Cleveland Browns football team, where he played with no particular distinction for two years. He was traded to the Green Bay Packers in 1960, which was then the worst team in the National Football League, with a 1–10 won-lost record. Being traded to Green Bay was regarded as the equivalent of being sent to Siberia. An admonition of NFL coaches to their players was, "If you don't like it here, we'll send you to Green Bay." In the year Davis arrived, however, the team had been taken over by coach Vince Lombardi, who molded Davis and a number of other players into one of the greatest football dynasties of all time—one that won six division championships and five world championships during the time Davis was there. Davis himself became defensive team captain during the ten years he played there; he was selected to the All-Pro team for six years; and, after he retired, he was selected to the National Football League Hall of Fame in 1981. He also established a record for durability; he never missed a game in ten seasons of play. It was this sense of tenacity and reliability that was a tip-off to Davis's later success as a business executive.

Unlike many other professional athletes, Davis realized that fame and fortune in sports was fleeting, and he began to prepare himself early for a business career. Also, unlike so many of his colleagues, he really never tried to capitalize much on his name, setting up franchised restaurants or the like, reasoning that if he was traded or retired, the name recognition would fade and the businesses would probably fail. "I realized how frustrating it would be when the day finally arrived that I couldn't play football," Davis said, "and would have to face the world with a reduced salary and no talents. So I planned for a career. I liked football, but it offers limited opportunities for a lifetime career. On the other hand, the world of business is boundless."

Therefore, for five years while still playing football, Davis pursued his MBA at the University of Chicago. It was a difficult task, especially since he played in the world championship and Pro Bowl in most of these years. Thus, Davis usually started his semester two or three weeks late, even though he had registered and tried to keep up with his reading while still playing football. Once, in the winter of 1968, Davis found he was flunking his course at Chicago. He went to coach Lombardi, and told him how he seemed to be unable to do well. Lombardi responded, "It isn't easy to suck it up and go harder late in the game—when you'd rather quit. You've never been a quitter, have you?" "I guess not coach," Davis replied, and he returned to the university and in the next two quarters missed the Dean's List by only a fraction of a point before making it in his final quarter. He got his MBA in 1970, and in 1982 he was named MBA of the Year by the National Association of Black MBAs because of his outstanding contributions to business. George P. Schultz, former U.S. secretary of state, and later dean of the business school at Chicago, commented, "This doesn't surprise anyone who knows him. Willie was well-respected on campus as a student. I'm not an expert on pro football, but I'm sure nobody captains a successful football team except a guy who is looked up to by his teammates. In whatever setting you place Willie Davis, he'll be a leader. People pay attention to him."

Not at first, though. In 1964 Davis went to Jos. Schlitz Brewing Company in Milwaukee for a job in the off season and was turned down. Rather than discourage him, however, it intensified his determination to succeed and started him on his quest of the MBA so that he would have the qualifications Schlitz felt he lacked. In 1967 he won the Byron "Whizzer" White award as the NFL player who best served his team, community, and the nation. When he retired at the end of the following year, Davis was inundated with fifty-one job offers from various firms. He decided, however, to take an executive training position with Schlitz Brewing—one that promised to lead one day to a vice presidency of the company. While still playing football, he also had pursued a series of astute investments: a $200,000, twenty-four-unit apartment building he owned in Green Bay with former teammate, Herb Adderley, and a part ownership (with ex-teammates Bob Skronski and Ron Kostelnick) in Valley School and Office Supplies, based in Appleton, Wisconsin.

In 1970 Schlitz made Davis an offer he could not refuse: ownership of a Schlitz distributorship in Los Angeles. This would not be easy. The distributorship cost him $500,000, and Davis was not a wealthy man. Nor would he apply for any of the kinds of minority, set-aside financing the government had made available. "My initial inquiries [to the government]," Davis recalled later, "really convinced me that there is so much paperwork and red tape associated with compliance that you almost need extra staffing to handle compliance. I felt that if I was able to put it together without going to the government I would be better off." Davis had $150,000 in savings, and he was able to get the rest on a bank loan secured with his home and other properties he owned.

Davis then proceeded to set up Willie Davis Distributing in the Watts section of South Central Los Angeles. A dozen years later he recalled, "Willie Davis Distributing has a special significance for me, since it was my first business venture." During his first decade and a half as a beer distributor, Davis experienced phenomenal success. He doubled its business in the first three years. By 1973 it had sales of $4.5 million, with thirty employees. Growth continued during the next decade, so that by 1982 Davis Distributing had 180 employees and sales of $17.5 million. At that point, however, the beer industry began to experience problems, and this affected Davis's operation. Schlitz Brewing had been ailing for years, and in 1982 it was taken over by Stroh's Brewing. Davis continued to handle the product, but beer sales of the major brewers dropped 5 percent overall during that year. "The beer industry is in all-out war," said Davis. "Busch, Miller and Schlitz/Stroh have tremendous brewing capacities, but sales have fallen. Companies are now fighting harder over market shares.

The critical point in the future will be who is cost efficient enough to cut price and still make a profit.'' Davis Distributing remained the largest beer distributorship on the West Coast.

To enhance his position in the industry, Davis made a number of bold moves. In 1981 he decided to add wines to his distributorship, carrying Inglenook and Colony wines, Jacques Bonet Champagne, and a number of smaller wine labels for Heublein. It made up about 10 percent of his distributorship business in the early years, but sales of that product grew faster than beer. Davis made another daring move in 1986, when he teamed with actors Tom Selleck and Larry Monetti in securing a distributorship for Coors beer in West Los Angeles. Davis was the principal operating partner in the arrangement, with Selleck and Monetti as secondary partners. Called West Coast Beverage Co., a year later the firm was grossing $23 million. By that time, Davis Distributing was ringing up more than $25 million in sales. Davis, however, had developed other business interests by the late 1980s and was increasingly convinced that he had neither the capital nor the desire to continue fighting the ''beer wars'' in a dwindling market. Therefore, in 1988, he sold out his beer interests to an undisclosed white-owned firm and concentrated on his other holdings.

Davis continued to own 20 percent of Valley School and Office Supplies and 28 percent of Shelter Media, Inc., a bus shelter manufacturing company, and he was a founder and major stockholder in Alliance Bank in Culver City, California. His major interest, however, was increasingly All-Pro Broadcasting. The genesis for this operation came in 1976, when he purchased radio station KAGB-FM at a bankruptcy auction for $225,000. When he reopened the station a few months later, it had the call letters KACE. He had become interested in the radio industry at the urging of Curt Gowdy, a noted sportscaster with whom Davis had worked as a color man doing commentary for football games for six years. It was an astute investment: ''If you can steal something for $225,000,'' Davis said, ''I guess you could say I did that with KACE.''

That investment did not look quite so great when he first bought the station. ''At the time it seemed like I was putting all the things I had worked for in jeopardy,'' said Davis. ''I ended up with a lot of beat-up equipment and a piece of paper representing a license. In retrospect, it was the greatest business opportunity in my life.'' In six months, KACE was turning a profit, and seven years later it was worth $4 million. Los Angeles is a tough radio market, with eighty-two stations competing, of which forty-eight are on the FM band. There were, however, some 7 million listeners in the 1980s, with some $56 billion in purchasing power. This brought advertisers to Davis's station, and it remained a highly profitable venture. The attraction for Davis, however, was less its profitability than its manageability: ''As an industry, radio is not necessarily more profitable than beer,'' said Davis. ''A radio station is far more manageable, however, than the beer business. In beer you get hooked into a numbers game of whether you can generate enough volume.''

Davis positioned KACE to appeal to upscale, middle-class blacks, playing a wide variety of music from rhythm and blues, to jazz, to pop. The station's promotional materials referred to this as "Soulful Bouillabaisse." Some critics found this mix confusing, but it paid off for Davis and KACE. There were then five black-oriented radio stations, of which four were black owned; KACE was the number two–rated station among them. Davis said, "People love music and people enjoy a variety of music. We've listed ourselves as a contemporary station because, frankly, I couldn't think of anything else to call it. We don't want to be typed." The station, which had just 3,000 watts of power when Davis bought it, had 40,000 watts just five years later.

With the success of that investment, Davis began buying other stations. Along with Northwestern Mutual in Milwaukee, he bought WLUM-FM and WAWA-AM in Milwaukee in 1979 for $1.25 million, and in 1981 he bought KQIN-AM in Seattle for $750,000. A year later he purchased KYOK-AM in Houston for $1.5 million. Later he also purchased KDHT-FM in Denver. For the most part, Davis allows his stations to operate autonomously, since, as he said, "I think radio in its best operating form is really a localized medium." He therefore sets up operating guidelines but tries to leave to those in the programming areas the discretion of being sensitive to what each local market demands. Each station therefore presents a different mix of information and music in its format.

This approach reflects Davis's general management style. Borrowing from his days in football, he sees himself as the quarterback who calls the plays but then allows his "players" to find the best way they can to perform. The general manager of KACE said of him, "Willie makes the people who work here feel they are part of a process instead of just working for a company. I think it is one of the reasons we have such a low employee turnover rate." Bob Skoronski, ex-teammate at the Packers and longtime business partner, says of him: "Davis is a good administrator and assigns responsibility well. He's cool. He doesn't fly off the handle and make rash decisions."

Davis's most recent economic venture was his attempt to secure a National Football League expansion franchise for Memphis. Becoming a partner in Memphis Pro Football, Inc., Davis and his partners made the first "cut" in March 1992, when they were not among those eliminated for further consideration. Davis was confident they would be awarded a franchise for the team, tentatively called the Memphis Showboats, but they had not been successful by the fall of that year.

Willie Davis has remained very community oriented also, never forgetting his roots in the African-American community. Early on, he joined with former NFL star Jim Brown in the Negro Industrial Economic Union, which was instrumental in securing loans for newly organized small black businesses. "We're not looking for fabulous success stories," he said in 1968, "just guys who can succeed in small businesses like dry cleaning, small stores, restaurants, anything. This is probably more important to the average Negro than seeing a Negro senator or supreme court justice. It's not something out of reach." This reflected Davis's essentially conservative and nonconfrontational approach to race relations and the betterment of his race.

Davis was often asked to speak to groups of black youth, particularly African-American male teenagers. His approach was consistently upbeat. When he was asked in 1981 by the Black Business Association of Los Angeles to address 500 local high school students, he encouraged them to consistently pursue excellence and reminded them that it was his attitude, not the money he made or the fame he earned as a football player, that made him a successful businessman. He has also been very involved in a number of other community activities, especially in the Watts area. He personally was involved in helping to provide scholarship opportunities for minority and disadvantaged students, and for years the Willie Davis Distributing Company sponsored three adult softball teams, a Pop Warner League football team, a basketball team at the Challengers Boys Club, the annual Inter-Frat Basketball Series, and a woman's volleyball team. He also served as president of the Los Angeles Urban League.

Davis explained that one reason for his company's charitable giving was that it was just "good business." But Davis also explained that "another is giving-back consideration based on what was an outgrowth of my own personal achievements. . . . I'm particularly proud of our scholarship programs. I'm a great believer in education. After football, I equate that more with my success than anything else." Bill Barkin, one-time part owner of the Milwaukee Brewers, said that "Willie Davis is a very special person, a very in-depth person. One of the most significant things about him is that he has never forgotten his community."

His involvement in community affairs was always very much the up-beat, self-improvement type, promoted years earlier by Booker T. Washington.[*] In 1968 he said,

I don't think bitterness helps. I've seen a good deal of progress in the last 15 years or so. Texarkana is a good example. I went to a segregated school there, and none of us got the opportunity white kids got. It was tough for a Negro growing up in the South to keep a sense of direction. Why bother to study when your ability and knowledge won't help you get a job? Now the schools are integrating, even in Texarkana, and opportunities are gradually opening up. But, oh, so slowly. We're in a transitional period. I'm not bitter now. But if I look around in 15 years and see the same conditions, maybe I will be bitter.

Fifteen years later, much of Watts and South Central Los Angeles lay in ruins after perhaps the most destructive urban riot in American history. William Justus Wilson, University of Chicago sociologist, commented after the Los Angeles riots:

I think there is an association between declining neighborhoods and increasing social problems. A lot of people important for maintaining stability in innercity neighborhoods have left. That leaves behind what I call the truly disadvantaged population. . . . In time, you have the potential for a violent uprising if you get the right spark. It didn't shock me that Los Angeles blew up.

Did it shock and surprise Willie Davis and other conservative black leaders? Did this finally cause him to be less optimistic about the outlook for blacks in America? We have yet to hear from him on that score. Is Willie Davis bitter?

Sources

There are no personal or business papers of Willie Davis currently available. There are short biographies of Davis in Doris Innis, ed., *Profiles in Black* (1976); and Frank J. Johnson, *Who's Who of Black Millionaires* (1984). The best sources on his career, however, are various magazine and newspaper articles: *Ebony*, October 1968, May 1983; *Black Enterprise*, November 1979, June 1983, June 1992; *Sepia*, July 1975, March 1978; *Atlanta Daily World*, February 3, 1981; *Los Angeles Times*, May 15, 1977, June 7, 1986, March 14 and June 6, 1990; *Los Angeles Sentinel*, May 5, 1977, September 21, 1978, April 16 and May 21, 1981, November 18, 1982, June 12, 1986; *Chicago Tribune*, September 5, 1971; and *Black Sports*, August 1974. See also "How Athletes Handle Their Money," *Ebony*, June 1987.

DeJoie, Geddes, and Misshore Families: Aristede DeJoie (d. 1917), **Paul H. V. DeJoie** (July 2, 1872–October 1921), **Ella Brown DeJoie** (d. October 15, 1929), **Constant C. DeJoie** (November 11, 1881–March 23, 1970), **Constant C. DeJoie, Jr.** (b. October 25, 1914), **Prudomme John Earl DeJoie** (d. October 10, 1955), **Clem J. Geddes** (d. August 22, 1913), **Gertrude Geddes Willis** (d. February 20, 1970), **George D. Geddes** (d. 1915), **Joseph P. Geddes** (d. January 16, 1948), **Joseph Osceola Misshore, Jr.** (b. 1932), and **Willis Joseph Misshore** (d. September 20, 1967). Insurance executives and funeral parlor owners, editors and publishers: Unity Industrial Life Insurance Company, Unity Mutual Life Insurance of Chicago, Louisiana Industrial Life Insurance, Gertrude Geddes Willis Funeral Parlor, Gertrude Geddes Willis Life Insurance, *Louisiana Weekly*, Louisiana Undertaking, George D. Geddes Undertaking. The DeJoie, Geddes, and Misshore families were all Creole families, but they were not among the antebellum or even early post–Civil War leaders of that aristocratic group. They were relative newcomers, but by the late twentieth century the families were pretty close to the cream of that city's African-American aristocracy. Aristede DeJoie was of Creole heritage, but he was not from one of the older aristocratic families. Like so many other blacks in New Orleans and Louisiana, DeJoie rose to prominence on the back of the Republican party during Reconstruction. No information is available on DeJoie's early life, but he was not one of the black leaders who emerged during the Civil War period itself. By the 1870s, however, he was representing the 12th, 13th, and 14th Wards of New Orleans in the state legislature. He later became a city commissioner, an official gauger, and an internal revenue officer. DeJoie began to develop his business interests during this period, opening a bakery, restaurant, and confectionary on Canal Street. By the 1890s, DeJoie had become convinced of the futility of politics for blacks, and he began to develop an alliance with Booker T. Washington.* In the early twentieth century, Aristede DeJoie served as president of the local National Negro Business League affiliate.

Married to Ellen Chambers, DeJoie had two sons, Paul H. V. and Constant

C. DeJoie, whom he instructed to eschew politics in favor of business careers. Both sons complied. Paul DeJoie was educated at Southern University and then at New Orleans University, where he got his medical degree in 1895. He became the first black man to pass the Louisiana State Board of Medical Examiners. He worked for a number of years in New Orleans as a physician and also opened up a drugstore for blacks called DeJoie Cut Rate Pharmacy. The drugstore, which was later joined by a second, was managed by a relative, Joseph DeJoie, after Paul DeJoie became occupied with other business matters. In 1907 Paul DeJoie became president of Unity Industrial Life Insurance Company, which his father had organized.

The genesis of Unity Life came when Aristede DeJoie united four small burial relief societies into a single larger insurance firm. The tradition in New Orleans had been for doctors and medical societies to offer insurance to their own patients and others on a small scale. Several black firms operated in this manner. By 1906, however, the larger white insurance companies were beginning to suffer from competition from these black firms and also from a number of small white organizations. In response, they lobbied the Louisiana state legislature to pass a law requiring a $5,000 cash deposit by each and every doctor and medical society and insurance company operating in the state. This was a devastating blow to the black firms, which did not have sufficient resources. The officers of four of these organizations, including three of the top black firms—the Philadelphia, the George D. Geddes, and the International—were brought together by Aristede DeJoie to form Unity Insurance.

The name Unity was chosen because it signified a union of the black firms, and it took as its motto: "In Union There Is Strength." George D. Geddes was made president of the new concern, with Paul DeJoie as secretary and actual operating head and W. E. Robinson as treasurer. The company was founded with capital stock of $10,000, nearly all of which was owned by the DeJoie family. Aristede DeJoie did not take an active role in the management of the firm but spent his time with the Negro Business League and other matters until his death in 1917.

Although Unity Industrial had been organized according to the new laws, and had more than the proper minimum balance for operation, the secretary of state of New Orleans arbitrarily refused to grant an operating permit to the firm. The officers of the new firm, especially Paul H. V. DeJoie, carried the legal fight to the state supreme court, where they were finally vindicated, and the secretary of state was compelled to issue them a permit to do business. On July 7, 1907, Unity Life issued its first policy, making it the oldest black insurance company in the state and the one that paved the way for a number of other African-American firms. When George Geddes died in 1915, he was succeeded as president by Paul DeJoie, and C. C. DeJoie became the new secretary.

Constant C. DeJoie had been educated in the public schools of New Orleans and graduated from Southern University in 1898. He then worked in Burbridge & DeJoie's Drug Store on Canal and Liberty Streets, after which he worked for the United States Railway Mail Service, running on the Texas Pacific Railroad from New Orleans to Ferreday, Louisiana. After Unity Life was organized in 1907, C. C. DeJoie became business manager of the concern, accepting a 40 percent cut in salary from his previous position. At that time, the new combined firm had just three people working in the office and another fifty in the field. Income was less than $35,000 per year and was paying just $2 per week in benefits. This was about to change.

After 1910 Unity Life began expanding outside of New Orleans to other parts of the state, and soon it became the largest industrial life insurer in Louisiana, black or white. This position was maintained at least up until World War II. During World War I, the firm purchased over $10,000 worth of Liberty Bonds, paying cash for them. The first great expansion of the company, however, came during the 1920s. Much of the expansion took place in Louisiana, and by 1927 the company's annual income amounted to $637,635.61. It paid out claims amounting to $2,729,255.55 in that year and had over 80,000 policyholders with $8 million of insurance in force. Three hundred men and women worked for the firm. Unity Life owned the building from which it conducted business at 535–37 South Rampart Street, and by that time it had become the sixth largest black-owned, black-operated insurance company in the nation. In 1921 Paul H. V. DeJoie died and was succeeded as president of Unity Life by his brother, C. C. DeJoie.

It was in the decade after C. C. DeJoie took over Unity Life that the firm experienced some of its most significant expansion. A year earlier, the two brothers had decided to expand the operations of Unity Life outside of Louisiana. To meet the needs of migrants, especially the large number of black Louisiana natives who were moving to Chicago, they organized the Unity Agency and Loan Company of Illinois, with offices in Chicago. For the first eight years of its existence, the Chicago firm was only able to write sickness and accident insurance, but in 1928 it was reorganized and licensed by the state of Illinois to also write life insurance. Although C. C. DeJoie was chairman of this new concern, the actual operating manager was A. W. Williams, a native of Philadelphia who had been with National Benefit Life Insurance Company there for many years.

Also, in 1926, Unity began supporting, through the Child's Welfare Association at its home office building, a clinic for expectant mothers and babies, when the service had been discontinued by that organization. Unity Life continued to house the clinic as a permanent feature of its health extension bureau, and it annually contributed through its officers and employees more than $10,000 to the Community Chest. It also donated $5,000 to the new Flint-Goodridge Hospital, which was headed by Dr. Rivers Frederick, who also owned the Louisiana Industrial Life Insurance Company, in which the DeJoies had an interest. Unity contributed $19,000 to the YMCA building fund, as well as to a number of other charities. In 1925 the DeJoie family, especially C. C. DeJoie, founded the *Louisiana Weekly*, which soon became the largest and most important black-owned newspaper in the state. It continued to be published by the family for a number of years, with circulation rising from 12,149 in 1950 to 19,319 in 1965. C. C. DeJoie married Vivian Baxter in 1914, and they had three children, including C. C. DeJoie, Jr.

Louisiana Industrial Life had been organized by Dr. Frederick in 1920 and, ten years later, had become the second-largest black-owned insurance company in Louisiana. It had assets of $500,000 in 1930, capital stock of $50,000, and paid out over $150,000 in benefits to policyholders that year. The company also owned a large building in downtown New Orleans and had a Life Extension Department which was an important factor in improving the health of blacks in the state. Prudomme J. E. DeJoie was first vice president of the firm, and Pearl DeJoie, daughter of Dr. Frederick and wife of Prudomme, known as P.J.E., was assistant secretary.

When Paul H. V. DeJoie died, his widow, Ella Brown DeJoie, also assumed a prominent position in Unity Life, becoming treasurer of the firm. She had been born in St. John the Baptist Parish in Louisiana, and over the years she became involved in a variety of business, social, and civic responsibilities. By the time of her death in 1929, the *Times-Picayune* was able to call her "One of the County's Best Known Negro Women." In addition to Unity Life, she also organized Broadmoor Laundry, Cleaning and Dyeing Company, which was forced into receivership after she became ill in 1929. Ella DeJoie had two sons, Paul H. V., Jr., and P.J.E. DeJoie, the latter of whom was to play an important and dramatic role in the company's future.

Unity Life had grown rapidly and was very profitable during the 1920s, but the depression decade of the 1930s was a difficult time. Income, which stood at over $600,000 in 1929, declined steadily throughout the 1930s, until it reached just $273,261 in 1937. C. C. DeJoie decided at that point to discontinue the health and accident insurance business and substitute industrial whole life policies. This decision probably caused much of the firm's later decline. In 1939 deep family jealousies that had simmered under the surface for years exploded into the public domain in a sensational manner. In the late 1930s, when C. C. DeJoie attempted to place his son, C. C. DeJoie, Jr., on the board of directors, the move was adamantly opposed by P.J.E. DeJoie, then vice president and treasurer of the company. In response, Henry L. Wilcox, general manager of the company, and an intimate friend of C. C. DeJoie, Sr., shot and severely wounded P.J.E. DeJoie. C. C. DeJoie, Sr., despairing of ever developing harmonious relations among his warring relatives, decided to sell controlling interest in the company to a group of whites.

Few matters upset the elite black population of New Orleans as much as this whole "DeJoie Affair." C. C. DeJoie, Sr., was viciously attacked for his actions. The *Sepia Socialite* (April 1942) commented in pained fashion:

This "leader," this "has been" patriot of his own race sold out or has caused to be sold out to nine members of the white race his control of this pioneer company. The worst tragedy of this act lies in the fact that Mr. DeJoie dealt this black-eye to all that racial cooperation could ever mean, deliberately, and with cold calculated interest. . . . It is a serious indictment to brand C. C. DeJoie a traitor to the race; but unless he speaks for himself and offers some explanation, the 46,000 policy holders and 170,000 Negroes of New Orleans . . . should henceforth despise him and consider him the TRAITOR THAT HE IS!

On September 16, 1939, in the family's *Louisiana Weekly*, C. C. DeJoie, Jr., gave the family's explanation for the sale:

Climaxing irreconcilable differences between members of the DeJoie family . . . results in a split within the family. The C. C. DeJoie faction sold the stock (the majority) to an unnamed insurance company Saturday afternoon. The minority faction was represented by P.J.E. DeJoie, nephew to C. C. DeJoie.

C. C. DeJoie, Sr., left Unity Life at that time, but he continued to act as publisher of the *Louisiana Weekly* until 1969. He died in 1970.

After that time, P.J.E. DeJoie concentrated his activities on Louisiana Undertaking Company, of which he was president, and Louisiana Life Insurance, of which he became chairman of the board until his death in 1955. A graduate of Xavier University, he had married Pearl Frederick, daughter of Dr. Rivers Frederick, founder of Louisiana Life. P.J.E. DeJoie was also involved with Broadmoor Laundry, which his mother had founded and of which his brother, Paul H. V., Jr., was president. He had one son, Prudomme J. E. DeJoie, Jr., who succeeded him as president of Louisiana Life Insurance. C. C. DeJoie, Jr., was educated at Talladega College, from which he graduated in 1937. He then took over the *Louisiana Weekly*, serving as business manager from 1938 until 1969, and president and publisher after that time. He was also on the board of Liberty Bank and Trust, and he had been one of the owners of the New Orleans Saints football team in the National Football League. Members of the family also owned the DeJoie Taxicab Company.

Although George D. Geddes had just a limited impact on the development of Unity Life, his family was one of the most prominent in African-American business circles in New Orleans. As noted above, he ran one of the largest and most prosperous undertaking firms, George D. Geddes Company, which continued as one of the most important in the city long after his death in 1915. Joseph P. Geddes, his son, who was a graduate of Tuskegee Institute and a prominent funeral director in New Orleans, ran his father's old firm as Joseph P. Geddes Undertaking. He also served as vice president of Unity Life Insurance in the 1920s and 1930s and was a member of the National Negro Business League in the city. He died in 1948.

Other members of the Geddes family also owned important funeral parlor and insurance ventures. Clem Geddes, a Creole like the members of the DeJoie family, was born in rural Louisiana, and came to New Orleans shortly after the Civil War. Upon arrival, he worked for a number of years for a white funeral home. Later, in 1873, he set up his own mortuary business. He was succeeded by his son, Clem J. Geddes, who ran the mortuary until his own death in 1913. At that time he was succeeded by his wife, Gertrude Geddes. In 1919 she married

Dr. W. A. Willis, a dentist, who became head of the Gertrude Geddes Willis Burial Association and was also vice president of the funeral home. Mrs. Geddes Willis, however, remained the dominant force in the latter business, as it grew to become the largest and most successful black-owned mortuary business in the city.

The Burial Association had first been established by Clem J. Geddes in 1909 and was reestablished by Mrs. Willis and her husband in 1940. The funeral home employed nineteen persons in the 1940s and had two hearses and four ambulances. Mrs. Willis also became a leader in the social and civic circles of the black community in New Orleans, and she and her husband were prominent members of the NAACP in the city as well as leading proponents of black business. Mrs. Willis, a Roman Catholic like the members of the DeJoie and Misshore families, died on February 20, 1970.

Another officer at Gertrude Geddes Willis Funeral Parlor in the 1940s was Joseph O. Misshore, who served as secretary and later as vice president. Another Louisiana Creole, Misshore was related to the Geddes family and was succeeded by his own son, Willis J. Misshore. Willis Misshore was born in New Orleans, graduated from Xavier University Preparatory School, and attended Clark College in Atlanta. He joined the family funeral parlor, and when he died in 1967 he was executive vice president and chairman of the board and held the same positions with the Gertrude Geddes Willis Insurance Company and Gom's Delivery Service. He was a prominent member of a number of city and state trade associations, along with a large number of civic enterprises in his native city. By 1961 the insurance firm was the twenty-first largest black insurance company in terms of asset strength, with assets of $2,847,269. By 1990, with Joseph Misshore still its head, it was the seventeenth largest, with assets of over $4 million, insurance in force of $33 million, and premium income of $1.14 million.

Willis's brother, Joseph Osceola Misshore, Jr., became head of the various Geddes-Willis enterprises upon the death of Gertrude Geddes Willis in 1970. By that time, the various firms employed over 150 people and were among the most substantial black-owned enterprises in the city and the funeral parlor was the largest for blacks there. Joseph attended Catholic grammar schools in the city and Booker T. Washington High School. By the 1970s, Joseph Misshore enjoyed a position at the very apex of the city's Creole aristocracy, with money, education, and family heritage. He was also a director of Liberty Bank; a member of Zulu, of which his father was King Zulu in 1932; a member of the Original Illinois Club, of which his daughter was Queen Illinois in 1972; and a member of the exclusive Top of the Line Club.

Speaking about his social position as a leading member of the city's esteemed Creole community, Joseph Misshore said:

There might be blacks who hate me because of my success, but I think that the majority do not. There is no longer much importance placed on so-called "Creole" backgrounds, or on the lightness of a black man's skin—although we have always had a certain number of what we call "passant blancs"—so there is really not that divisive an element around affluence in New Orleans. . . . I don't care how integrated you get, when you're black, you're just black. (*Figaro*, December 26, 1973)

Yet, in the late 1950s, when two social scientists, John H. Rohrer and Munro S. Edmonson, did a study of New Orleans' Creole community, they found a very different mindset in at least one man Joseph Misshore's age. A colored Creole who had been born in 1923, like Misshore, he was a light-skinned, dapper man with a good education, who confined all of his social contacts to other Creoles who lived in the same neighborhood. He rarely identified with the aspirations of blacks in general and usually displayed hostility toward lower class blacks in the city. Rohrer and Edmonson reported that he was always ambivalent about his social classification and that he lived ''in a kind of chronic identity crisis.'' Joseph Misshore did not appear to share that anxiety. According to an article appearing in *New Orleans* magazine in 1976, much of the color exclusiveness of Creoles by that time was a function of the generation gap. Whereas most Creoles of Misshore's age would probably be like the young man described above, younger members tended to celebrate their blackness and their oneness with other, dark-skinned, non-Creole blacks. The DeJoies, Geddeses, and Misshores had been transported to the upper reaches of New Orleans' African-American society, but through their ownership of the *Louisiana Weekly* and other endeavors, they evidently remained closely linked with the larger number of blacks in the city.

Sources

There are no papers of the DeJoie, Geddes, or Misshore families currently available, nor are there any records of their various business enterprises in the public domain, although there are twenty boxes of correspondence from the *Louisiana Weekly* and other black newspapers in the Marcus Bruce Christian Collection in the Holdings of Special Collections at the Earl K. Long Library of the University of New Orleans. Biographical information on the families is also somewhat scattered and limited. There are no full-length biographies of any of the family members, and their companies have not received any scholarly treatment. There are a few letters from Aristede DeJoie to Booker T. Washington in the Washington Papers in the Library of Congress. The biographical information that is available is in *Who's Who in Colored Louisiana* (Baton Rouge, 1930, 1990–91); Clement Richardson, *National Cyclopedia of the Colored Race* (New York, 1919); *Who's Who in Colored America* (1927); and *Figaro* (New Orleans), December 26, 1973. Obituaries and death notices are found in the *Times-Picayune*, November 14, 1913, August 22, 1917, October 16, 1929, January 16, 1948, October 11, 1955, September 23, 1967, and March 23, 1970; and *Louisiana Weekly*, October 19, 1929, and October 15, 1955. Information on the companies was retrieved from *Louisiana Weekly*, May 24, July 19, and October 11, 1930; *Sepia Socialite*, April 1942. Henry and C. C. DeJoie, Jr., wrote an article on black politics entitled ''Politics: From Slave to Freeman?'' in *New Orleans*, June 1972, 38–39. The best coverage of the family split over control of Unity Life, and of the resulting shooting, is found in M. S. Stuart, *Economic Detour* (New York, 1940), 92–93, 165–68.

de Passe, Suzanne Celeste (1947–   ) and **Berry Gordy, Jr.** (November 26, 1929–   ). Entertainment company founder and executives: Motown Industries, Inc. Berry Gordy, flush with success in 1965, told *Newsweek* magazine: "This organization is built on love. We're dealing with feeling and truth." There were many artists at Gordy's Motown Records over the years who would have disputed that statement, since Gordy was infamous for his cavalier treatment of some stars. Yet, it reflected a form of reality. David Szatmary, in his history of rock and roll, calls the "Motown sound" the "music of integration." He explains: "Gordy, sounding much like Martin Luther King, Jr., created a music empire that exemplified the peaceful integration advocated by King and reflected in the progress of the civil rights movement. . . . It was the first label that successfully groomed, packaged, marketed, and sold the music of black artists to the white American masses." Yet, there was a supreme (no pun intended) irony here: America's black ghettoes, especially those in Detroit in the 1960s and Los Angeles in the 1990s, sequentially homes to Motown Records, were ripped apart by riots and violence. Full integration of the masses of blacks in those cities, and in America generally, was more remote than ever by the end of the twentieth century. But this has never been reflected in the music of Motown. It is, as Gordy once claimed, "ghetto music," but ghetto music of a peculiar kind. Motown music might have its roots remotely in the ghetto, but it was hardly "of" the ghetto. Yet Gordy knew what he was doing. Motown became one of the largest, most successful black-owned firms in America; it was the first African-American firm to challenge the domination of the white giants—Columbia, R.C.A. Victor, and Decca—and it represented a success story with great social meaning.

Berry Gordy, Jr., was born in Detroit, the son of Berry (Pops) and Bertha Gordy. The elder Gordy was a native of rural Georgia who had come north to Detroit during the great migration of the early 1920s. Although the mythmaking machine of Motown liked to portray the family as poor and deprived, this was not quite the case. Berry, Sr.'s, father had been a very successful landowner and businessman in Georgia who had been killed in a storm. Pops continued in his father's footsteps: "I always had money," he later revealed in his autobiography. "I had money all the time." Gordy's success in farming and with a produce and meat business led to his being forced to leave Georgia by jealous whites. He came to Detroit, where he worked as a plasterer and later owned a successful printing shop in which he employed all of his eight children. Bertha Gordy was also in business, working as an insurance agent. At one point Gordy, Sr., ran a grocery store, which he revealingly named the Booker T. Washington Grocery Store. In this way, Pops Gordy was paying tribute to a man and set ideals of self-improvement and racial pride. Those Washingtonian virtues were also instilled in his children, although he must have wondered for a time whether they had been adopted by his eldest son, Berry, Jr.

Berry, Jr., grew up in the Detroit ghetto of the 1930s. At that time there was a powerful competitor for the homage of young black males—the heavyweight boxer, Joe Louis. Louis, like the Gordy family, had moved from the South to Detroit, and he became the personification of black triumph over whites. Because of the model of Louis, and also because there were few economic opportunities for young black males during the Depression, Gordy, like so many of his racial counterparts, was determined to become a professional boxer, hoping to match Louis's fame and wealth. Gordy began boxing in Golden Gloves and then turned professional. At that point he dropped out of Northeastern High School in his junior year. A fairly good boxer, he won twelve of his fifteen fights, but he decided that, as a welterweight, he could never make the kind of money Louis was making, so he abandoned that dream.

According to Gerald Early, Berry Gordy combined these two youthful influences to later make a successful career:

[Gordy] came to epitomize both the "realistic" virtues of industry and tenacity espoused by Booker T. Washington and the "idealistic" possibility of an extravagant impact on the American popular culture held out by the example of Louis. After all . . . both Louis, who was cheered by whites for beating white opponents and was an idol of World War II, and Washington, who ate dinner in the White House with Theodore Roosevelt, and extolled white examples for blacks, were essentially crossover heroes.

This was the ideological background and preparation for Berry Gordy to create one of the greatest crossover phenomenons in African-American business.

Gordy had a ways to go, however, before he could achieve that distinction. In 1951 Gordy was drafted into the U.S. Army, where he served for two years and received his high school equivalency diploma. Upon his release, Gordy returned to Detroit, where he used his savings from military service along with a $700 loan from his father to open a record store. Gordy and his partner, Marvin Johnson, had set it up to sell jazz recordings.

I loved jazz. Stan Kenton, Thelonius Monk, Charlie Parker—and so I decided to concentrate on jazz. I wanted to let people know I was modern, so I called the place Three-D Record Mart. But people started coming in and asking for people like Fats Domino. Pretty soon I was asking "Who is this Fats Domino? What is this rhythm-and-blues stuff?" I listened and ordered a few records by these people and sold them. But my capital was all tied up in jazz, and jazz didn't have the facts, man, the beat.

A short time later the 3-D Record Mart went bankrupt.

After the store's failure, Gordy became something of a "street hustler." He worked for his father as a plasterer but continued to hang around the city's rhythm and blues (R&B) clubs, passing himself off as a songwriter. In 1953 Gordy married Thelma Coleman, with whom he had three children. To achieve a more secure income to support his growing family, Gordy got a job on the line at Ford Motor Company's Wayne Assembly plant. The pay was good for the time ($85 a week), but the work was horribly monotonous. While doing the boring task of tacking upholstery into Lincoln automobiles, Gordy kept himself sane by composing songs in his head while he worked. On weekends he took his songs around to the R&B bars he had been frequenting, trying to get the artists working there to perform them.

With the help of his sisters Anna and Gwen, who had gotten the photography and cigarette concessions at the Flame Show Bar, Gordy met a number of the city's top musicians, including Maurice King and Thomas "Beans" Bowles, both of whom would eventually work for Motown. He also met managers, hustlers, nightclub owners, and others who populated the underworld of African-American popular music during that time of strict segregation. Gordy was able to convince a few of the R&B groups to record some of his songs, but the results were undistinguished. Then, in 1957, Gordy began writing songs for Jackie Wilson, another ex-prizefighter in Detroit, who was known on the club circuit as "Mr. Excitement" and who had one of the truly great voices of rhythm and blues. Gordy rented a small recording studio, hired some musicians, and put some of his songs on tape with either Wilson or himself as the vocalist. Gordy took his demonstration tapes to New York City, hoping to convince one of the major record producers to distribute them.

Gordy's first sale, to Decca, was a song called "Reet Peteet," which he wrote with his sister Gwen. Wilson was the vocalist on the song, and Decca bought it for $1,000. Over the next several years, Gordy and Wilson produced a number of successful hits for Decca, including "Lonely Teardrops," "To Be Loved," and "That's Why I Love You So." But he realized little profit from these songs. Royalties for songwriters took a long time to appear, and often they were not paid completely by the white-owned record firms to black songwriters. Moreover, Gordy did not publish his own songs, which meant he was essentially at the mercy of the music publisher and the record company that Wilson recorded for. A turning point for Gordy came in 1958, when he met Raynoma Liles, a trained musician who became his second wife in 1959. She convinced him that he should begin producing his own records—in other words, to assume full responsibility for a song's arrangement, harmonies, mix, and the overall structure and presentation of a record.

Following this advice, in 1959 Gordy borrowed $700 from his family and founded Motown (short for "Motor Town") Records in an eight-room bungalow at 2648 Grand Boulevard. Gordy's aspirations at this time, however, were still relatively modest: "If I ever get this house and get it paid for, I'll have it made. I'll live upstairs, I'll have offices down in the front part, and I'll have a studio out back where I can make demonstration records or masters to sell to record companies." Gordy began to record a number of the city's rhythm and blues artists. He scored a minor hit with Marv Johnson's "Come to Me," and later in his first year of operation he cowrote and released "Money," recorded by Barrett Strong.

The real turning point for Motown came in September 1959, when it released "Bad Girl," recorded by William "Smokey" Robinson and the Miracles. Robinson, a 1957 graduate of Detroit's Northern High School, would always hold a special place at Motown, and he was the only performer in the company's history to become a corporate executive, although Diana Ross later was placed on the board of directors. Robinson was not only a riveting performer with a distinctive, high-pitched singing voice, he was also a magnificent songwriter, and it was his latter talent that was particularly important for the early success of Motown. "Bad Girl" was issued locally in Detroit on the company's Tamla label and was distributed nationally by Chess Records. A mild success, the song reached ninety-three on the charts for two weeks before sinking into oblivion.

Robinson had another important influence on the early development of Motown. He convinced Gordy himself to begin to distribute the records nationally. "When I started," Gordy told *Black Enterprise* in 1974, "we licensed our singles to other companies such as United Artists. Smokey Robinson gave me the idea to go national with my own product; my attorneys and other people said it was madness, that I shouldn't do it because a hit would throw me into bankruptcy since [we were] undercapitalized." In spite of this advice, in 1960 Gordy cowrote with Robinson and distributed nationally on the Motown label "Shop Around," which became Motown's first gold record in 1960, selling 1 million copies. This firmly established Motown as an important independent record company.

Although Motown was certainly the most successful black-owned record label, it was not the first. There had been a number of small, transient black labels over the years, including Harry Pace's[*] pioneering Black Swan Records, but the most important forerunner to Motown was Vee Jay Records in Chicago. Founded in 1953 by Vivian Carter and James C. Bracken, along with Clarence Carter, it was one of the most successful independent record firms, bringing out a stable of R&B hits, along with a number of jazz and gospel recordings. By the early 1960s, however, Vee Jay was on the verge of bankruptcy, and it would be Motown and Berry Gordy who would reap the rewards of a society suddenly interested in racial integration and the crossing over of black culture into the white mainstream.

It turned out to be a propitious time for this. The civil rights movement in the South was gathering a full head of steam; Martin Luther King, Jr., was becoming a national icon, and the Kennedy administration was instilling the country with a new sense of hope. "It was an awe-inspiring time," wrote Raynoma Gordy in her autobiography. "JFK was new and fresh, young and exciting. So was his wife. And we [Berry and I] were all those things. I'd look at their picture in the paper and think how romantic they were. Like us." According to Gerald Early, "At no time in their history did blacks feel more optimistic about the future than in 1960, when a young president's rhetoric promised so much so richly, when a young black Southern preacher spoke so eloquently for a brave new humankind, when it was quite possible, at last, to think of entering the world of whites without going through the back door of culture."

This optimism about the possibilities of American society in 1960 built upon a tradition of black cultural crossover into the white mainstream. African-American poet Gwendolyn Brooks in 1950 won the Pulitzer Prize, and Ralph

Ellison in 1952 won the National Book Award for *Invisible Man*. Also, during the 1950s, James Baldwin became one of the most popular black American writers; Sidney Poitier became a major film star; Lorraine Hansbury's *Raisin in the Sun* became a hit film; and Jackie Robinson, named the National League's Most Valuable Player in 1949, not only integrated baseball, but also brought blacks to the pinnacle of success in "America's pastime." This was also true in music. Although ragtime, jazz, and blues, all forms of music with African-American roots, had early passed into the mainstream, black R&B music in the late 1940s was confined to a cultural ghetto called "race music." Appealing to recent southern black migrants to the city, it was an electrified blues sound that became popular in black clubs in cities all over the United States. But these blacks also wanted to have this entertainment in their homes, and this meant that the music was recorded by a number of independent record companies. For some time, these "race records" remained segregated from white America.

But several white disc jockeys, including Alan Freed, became attracted to this music and began to play it for dedicated legions of white teenagers. White artists began to "cover" some of these black R&B hits, with "Sh-Boom" by the Crewcuts in 1954, the first commercial success for what came increasingly to be called "rock and roll" music when played by whites. This African-American music was then integrated with country and western by Bill Haley and Elvis Presley to create a new homogenized art form that had enormous appeal in the late 1950s. By 1960, however, the formerly "authentic" black sound of early R&B had been diluted by Dick Clark, "American Bandstand," and the so-called Philadelphia sound. Just as in the early 1950s, there was an interest among white teenagers by the early 1960s for a more authentically "black" music. And it was this demand that Berry Gordy and Motown were to provide throughout the 1960s and part of the 1970s.

Just what kind of music Motown produced is open to debate. To Gordy, as mentioned above, it was ghetto music: "It's rats and roaches, love, guts, and talent. . . . We haven't forgotten where we came from. We were like a thousand other kids on the streets of the Brewster and Douglas Projects. . . . Don't misunderstand rats and roaches. It's not just climbing out of poverty, escaping from it—it's being young, creating, doing things with dignity. It's pride." Many music critics and black artists were not so sure. To them, the Motown or "Detroit" sound is just pop music, so homogenized and attenuated as to lose all connection with its African-American roots. Yet, to the teenagers who bought and listened to its records by the millions, and perhaps more to whites, it was clearly "black" music. Even if they recognized that the rough edges of the ghetto had been smoothed out, that it was not the blues, or even the more raucous rhythm and blues, it nonetheless retained an unmistakable element of its origins. None of the Motown acts, not even the Jackson Five, could ever be confused, for example, with the Osmonds. The distinctiveness of Motown stemmed perhaps more from church and gospel singing than from more secular black music. Its not that their young performers were originally part of church groups—most were not—but they did bring with them some elements of that form. As Charlie Gillette noted, ''From 1963 onwards, the emphasis was placed more definitely on the gospel qualities of [Gordy's] singers' voices, and the musical arrangements, accordingly, were closer to the accompaniments that commonly backed up gospel singing.''

Throughout the next four years after the success of Robinson's ''Shop Around,'' Berry Gordy continued to produce hits, largely by capitalizing on the girl-group craze that was developing at that time. This seemed a perfect vehicle for crossover music to Berry. Black women, he reasoned, would be less threatening to a white audience than black men. He first began to groom a young black teenager, Mary Wells, for stardom, and she teamed with Smokey Robinson on a number of hits in the early 1960s. In 1964 she topped the charts with her hit ''My Guy.'' During this same period, Motown also topped the charts with a number of hits from the Marvellettes. The most significant was ''Please Mr. Postman'' in 1961, which was the first time Motown hit the top of the pop, as opposed to the R&B, charts. Gordy signed Martha and the Vandellas, and in 1963 they had a monster hit with ''Heat Wave.'' Through this period, however, Gordy continued to record a number of rawer, less processed records, especially those by Marvin Gaye, which became very popular.

In October 1962, Gordy decided to send out the first Motown Revue, which left Detroit on a ten-week tour with the Marvellettes, Marvin Gaye, the Supremes, the Contours, and a number of other performers. They toured through the Midwest and the South at about the same time as the Freedom Riders were challenging segregation statutes throughout the region. To some white southerners, the Motown Revue must have seemed almost as threatening: Their bus was shot at, and segregated facilities and rude treatment greeted them at nearly every stop. Nonetheless, Katherine Anderson of the Marvellettes said, ''[We] did what we could to play for integrated audiences.''

Despite the string of successes Motown racked up, the early years were nonetheless difficult and exciting. Gordy, who was reputed to have ''the best ear in the business'' for a talented performer or a hit song, was a neophyte businessman. Motown ran into a problem that plagued many independent companies—slow payments and even bankruptcy among its distributors. As a newcomer, Motown had to rely on smaller, marginal distributors to get its records to retailers, some of which overextended themselves when Motown records became hits and ran out of money. When Motown tried to collect, the distributors were frequently out of money, and this put Motown into a severe financial crisis. Finally, one of Gordy's sisters, Lucy Wakefield, took over the job of collecting the money and was aggressive enough at her job to recoup enough receivables to keep the firm on its feet.

But the excitement in these early years also came from the fact that Berry truly did create a sense of family at Motown. Gordy astutely realized that he was taking raw, unformed, unsophisticated youngsters from the city streets and trying to turn them into pop stars. They were not professionals. Therefore, he hired Mazine Powell, who had formerly operated a finishing and modeling school, to teach them dress and manners: "The singers were raw," she remembers. "They were from the streets, and like most of us who came out of the [housing] projects, they were a little crude: Some were backward, some were arrogant. They had potential, but they were not unlike their friends in the ghetto. I always thought of our artists as diamonds in the rough who needed polishing." Another Motown staffer said, "We really wanted young blacks to understand that you do not have to look like you came out of the ghetto in order to be somebody other blacks and even whites would respect when you made it big. They'll believe you had a rough childhood; you don't have to prove it to them by looking like hell."

They not only had to teach these youngsters how to dress, talk, and act; they also had to provide many of them with a sense of family, a feeling of belonging. "Loyalty, honesty, and obedience were demanded and often given," wrote Mary Wilson of the Supremes in her autobiography. "Joining Motown was more like being adopted by a big loving family than being hired by a company," said Otis Williams of the Temptations. Gordy said the same thing: "Our loyalty to one another and to our goals was so strong that the only reasonable description of that energy was something beyond business and beyond contracts—it was the sticking together that only happens in families. . . . Though we did not coin the term ourselves, the 'Motown Family' was not a description that any of us took lightly." This strong sense of family was given its ultimate expression in the large number of members of the Gordy family who themselves held executive positions with Motown. It was family nepotism at the extreme, and it reflected the nearly fetishistic attraction that the concepts of "family" and "unity" were gaining in the black communities of the North. "My own family was close," wrote Smokey Robinson, "but I'd never seen anything like the Gordys. . . . The Gordys took care of business, but mainly they took care of each other."

This paternalism of the early years was also part of a broader message and mission. There was a sense of the need to fulfill racial uplift and create a feeling of community for a black company trying to succeed in a racist society. Gordy, therefore, liked to foster the image that Motown was not merely a privately owned company, but was also some kind of communal "race enterprise." "For a time," Gerald Early has written, "Gordy was able to manipulate his black and white audiences brilliantly with a 'race company' that satisfied the nationalistic yearnings of blacks and an 'assimilationist success story' that edified whites." For that was another important element of Motown in those early years; Gordy had long supported the peaceful integrationist program of Martin Luther King, Jr., who had once paid a brief visit to the Motown offices. Gordy also recorded King's "I Have a Dream" speech at the end of the March on Washington in 1963. "Motown was a very strong supporter of Martin Luther King's total program," said Mickey Stevenson of Motown. "Berry felt that our job in Detroit

was to make blacks aware of their culture, of the problems and some of the
ways out of the problems. . . . Motown was a tremendous avenue of escape and
hope.''

This sense of family and of social mission was then melded, somewhat in-
congruously, with the rather ruthless plant-floor logic of factory production.
Berry Gordy did not bring to Motown just an ear for music and a heart of youth
and families; he also had been made aware while working at Ford of how
production could be efficiently organized and automated for the highest quality.
He provided a series of attractive rewards and incentives for hard work, and he
instilled at the firm an almost unbearable atmosphere of competition. When the
young performers wilted and were on the point of cracking from the strain of
this pressure, the ''family'' side of Gordy would then emerge and he would, in
his famous phrase, say, ''I'll take care of you.'' This system produced an
unprecedented ratio of hit records in relation to the number of records released.
And that was another part of Gordy's genius and system—he saw himself and
Motown not as a producer of records, but a producer of only hit records.

''Gordy was musically illiterate,'' wrote Gerald Early. ''He could neither play
an instrument nor read music. Still, he possessed a remarkable sense of what
constitutes a good pop-cum-R and B song.'' It was this keen musical sense that
caused Gordy to turn away from the blues and R&B to find a new sound, one
that would be pleasing to the American, largely white, mainstream. What he
settled upon was a formula, one characterized by an insistent, pounding rhythm
section, punctuated by horns and tambourines, and featuring often shrill, echo-
laden vocals that carried with them some sense of the call-and-response tradition
of gospel music. Gordy called this music ''The Sound of Young America'' and
called his recording studio on Grand Boulevard ''Hitsville, U.S.A.'' The key
for Gordy, however, was to find a group or a singer who fully reflected this pop
sound he was trying to create. He found it in the Supremes.

The original Supremes were four teenage girls out of the low-income Brewster
housing project: Diana Ross, Mary Wilson, Florence Ballard, and Mary Travis.
In 1960 they were signed to a contract at Motown but performed the next several
years with no particular success. Around 1964, however, when Gordy's attempts
to make Mary Wells his great crossover success failed, Motown began to polish
the Supremes. They were taught proper etiquette and attire, and their resultant
popularity was in many respects a consequence of that visual image they created,
rather than their music. Gordy would later boast that he ''made'' the Supremes,
and he probably was not too far off the mark.

In the early years, Flo Ballard was the lead singer of the Supremes, and her
rich, powerful voice made them a solid R&B act. As Gordy began priming them
for stardom, he had Ross sing more and more lead, and this was an important
transition for the group, as Diana Ross ''had a truly 'pop' voice, that is, a
completely synthetic voice.'' Thus, as the Supremes became less rooted in the
black R&B tradition, they became more popular in the mainstream, and Motown
rode their popularity to big time status. That they did become so popular is in

retrospect a bit confounding. As *Sepia* commented, "Diana [Ross] lacked feeling and conviction, sang in a narrow range, a whining tone that would have been difficult for a less attractive woman to succeed with. Her sighs and pauses for breath were often more expressive than her words. She sang like her delivery was coming right through her nose. Still, they made Motown's best records."

The key for the Supremes was that they looked professional: They sang the right notes, smiled the right smiles, and moved like "synchronized robots." They were "sexy and a bit naughty, but in a polite sisterly way. With droll feline moves, they flashed their white teeth, rolled their eyes, fluttering them with large false eyelashes, and lapped their pink tongues." United with the songwriting team of Holland-Dozier-Holland, the Supremes had a string of incredible hits: "Where Did Our Love Go?," "Baby Love," "Back in My Arms Again," "Stop! In the Name of Love," "I Hear a Symphony," and many others. During the 1960s, the Supremes sold 12 million records, second only to the Beatles. In 1969, however, the Supremes (by then called Diana Ross and the Supremes) lost Diana Ross as a member of their group because she wanted to begin her solo singing career. Replaced by Cindy Birdsong, the new Supremes had a number of hits during the early 1970s.

By that time, the biggest Motown recording group was the Jackson Five. Headed by the preteen Michael Jackson, they had an enviable series of hits during these years, such as "I'll Be There" and "We're Almost There," and an unprecedented series of four straight number-one hits. This was the advent of what some critics called "bubble gum soul," a counterpart to "bubblegum rock" designed to appeal to a preteen audience. At the same time, however, Motown continued to produce music closer to its roots in the 1960s. Gladys Knight and the Pips won a string of Grammy Awards for Motown, even if their commercial success did not quite match that of some of the other artists. Marvin Gaye and Smokey Robinson also continued to have hit records, and they were joined by another monstrously talented performer who was closer to soul and R&B origins, young Stevie Wonder, whose first big hit was "For Once in My Life."

During the 1960s, Berry Gordy had established a music empire that included eight record labels, a management service, and a publishing company (Jobete), and was grossing millions of dollars a year. From 1964 to 1967, Motown placed 114 number-one pop singles, 20 number-one singles on the R&B charts, 46 more top twenty fifteen singles, and 75 other top fifteen R&B singles. In 1966 alone, 75 percent of the Motown releases hit the charts. "It is no coincidence," wrote a British newspaper, "that while 10,000 Negroes are marching for their civil rights in Alabama, the Tamla-Motown star is on the ascendent." But after 1967 the Motown empire began to decline, and in the early years of the 1970s Gordy pointed the company in radically different directions.

In 1967 the black ghetto in Detroit exploded in rage and frustration, and this was followed over the next several years by a rolling fireball of violence in America's inner cities and on college campuses. At the same time, both blacks and whites began turning increasingly to the more gutsy, inner-city sound of artists like James Brown, Aretha Franklin, and Otis Redding. The white market was also turning toward the San Francisco sounds of the Grateful Dead and others. Motown fought back musically by making its music more complex than in earlier years, and by adding African rhythms. These changes brought Motown back into the vanguard of pop music by the end of 1969. But Gordy realized that his formerly unerring "feel" for the popular music pulse was slipping and that, if Motown was to survive, it was going to have to diversify into other aspects of the entertainment business.

The first step in this transformation came in 1970, when a number of offices of Motown were moved from Grand Boulevard to several stories of a modern building on Sunset Boulevard in Los Angeles. Although Gordy and others denied they were leaving the "Motor City," in 1972 the move became official, and Motown became based in Hollywood. This was in many respects a devastating blow for Detroit, one that profoundly changed the nature of Motown itself, once the quintessentially inner-city, urban company. For Detroit, it seemed like the last straw. Lawrence M. Carino, chairman of the Greater Detroit Chamber of Commerce said in 1972, when Motown moved to Hollywood, "Detroit is the city of problems. If they exist, we've probably got them. We may not have them exclusively, that's for sure. But we probably had them first. . . . The city has become a living laboratory for the most comprehensive study possible of the American urban condition." There was in Detroit's black community a great deal of bitterness over Motown's move. It was made particularly poignant by the fact that Gordy had for so long, and so clearly, identified Motown as a community institution, as a machine for racial uplift, and, of course, as a family. Even twenty years later, there was still a strong sense of abandonment among blacks in the city.

But the move to Hollywood was an accurate signal of a new Motown. The company was no longer "the ghetto" or "roaches and rats." It was not "family" or "community" or "racial uplift." It was a business, and it was going to make movies and television shows and other entertainment ventures. Motown was not only located in Hollywood, it *was* Hollywood. Gordy in 1974 explained his reasons for moving to Hollywood to *Black Enterprise*:

Motown moved west to get into the action, to be closer to the scene, because we feel that the West is certainly the entertainment capital of the future, if it's not the entertainment capital now. And I think that in a growing operation such as ours, we just had to either come to New York or to California. And because I personally like the movie industry and the charisma of California, I chose California. I like the weather.

Gordy did leave his recording studios on Grand Boulevard in Detroit ("Hitsville"), and the building became a museum in 1987 and the state of Michigan made it a historic landmark in 1988. It thus became, in the words of Gerald Early, "a combination tourist trap and institution of memory, a little like Graceland; and it operates upon the nostalgia that the merchants of popular culture strive to stimulate to reach everyone about his or her (or somebody else's) youth.''

The first fruits of Gordy and Motown's new direction came in 1972 when its first motion picture, *Lady Sings the Blues*, a biography of singer Billie Holiday starring Diana Ross, was released. Distributed by Paramount, it was a stunning commercial and artistic success. It garnered five Academy Award nominations and grossed more than $8.5 million. That was the first of several films, none of which matched the success of *Lady*. Motown's second feature-length film was *The Bingo Long Traveling All Stars and Motor Kings* about a Negro League baseball team. It was a moderate financial and artistic success. The next two films, *Mahogany* and *The Wiz*, however, were absolute disasters with the critics. *Mahogany* was especially hurtful to Gordy because he not only financed and produced the film, he also directed it. Gordy bristled at the critics, characterizing their complaints as ''attacks on an uppity black.''

Increasingly in the 1970s Gordy began delegating more and more of the daily authority of Motown Industries and of Motown Records to others. For a time in the 1970s, two white men, Michael Roshkind, a former television executive who acted as Gordy's spokesman on many issues, and Berle Adams, chief operating officer, appeared to be in line to succeed him. Gordy, however, continued as at least the titular head of the entire massive Motown complex. In 1983 he and the company were feted in the press and elsewhere on their twenty-fifth anniversary. Motown was at that point the largest black-owned business in America (it would soon be surpassed by Johnson Publications, and then both would be dwarfed by TLC Beatrice International). *Newsweek* commented, ''Berry Gordy doesn't sleep over the store anymore. Now he lives in a hilltop estate, and Motown's offices fill three floors of a Hollywood highrise, where 200 employees supervise an entertainment empire that includes a music-publishing house and a TV movie production arm. But the heart of it all is still Motown Records.'' By this time, too, a new star had emerged on the horizon at Motown—a black woman named Suzanne de Passe.

Suzanne de Passe, like Berry Gordy, is secretive about some elements of her past, especially her exact age, but most reports indicate she was probably born in 1947. A native of New York City, de Passe was born into that city's African-American elite. Her grandfather, Lucian Brown, was a physician in Harlem, and her father was in the liquor business and worked for Seagrams, and her mother was a schoolteacher. Suzanne grew up in the middle-class Riverton Apartments on Harlem's Seventh Avenue and attended the prestigious and integrated Jack and Jill School. She spent her summers on Martha's Vineyard. She grew up enjoying the pampered life of an upper-middle-class New Yorker, taking ballet, going to the theater and the circus. ''I was at home on 135th Street just as I was on Sutton Place,'' she commented. ''It was much later that I realized it wasn't that way for everybody.''

The idyllic nature of de Passe's childhood was marred only slightly by the divorce of her parents when she was three. To ease the trauma of the separation, however, her grandfather sent her and her mother on a long trip to Europe. "The only other black people on the boat sailing first class were the John Johnsons"* (publisher of *Ebony*), she later recalled. She was fortunate, however, in that her mother and father appeared to remain on good terms. She spent the week with her mother and weekends with her father, and when her father remarried when she was nine, it only made her situation better, since she "had the benefit of an extremely harmonious relationship between three people." This gave her an extraordinary support system as she was growing up.

De Passe then went on to New Lincoln, a progressive, integrated school: "New Lincoln made a tremendous contribution to my development," she said. "The environment there was very conducive to expressing oneself. It was a little melting pot and you were rubbing shoulders with some of the most dramatic opposites." Fellow students at New Lincoln remembered de Passe fondly: "She was a very popular girl," said writer Jill Nelson. "If they had a homecoming queen she would have been it. She was the kind of black woman you aspired to be—worldly and very sophisticated. All the women in her family were like that. Tall, strong, and independent. They were feminists before it was fashionable."

When de Passe graduated in 1964, she decided to enroll in Syracuse University, but this turned out to be one of the down points in her life. She found Syracuse too cold, and too lonely, with only 80 blacks out of 20,000 students, and too far away from the world she knew. The following year she transferred to Manhattan Community College. This was closer to home, but de Passe still found she was getting nothing out of her education. When she told her father she wanted to quit school, in her words, he "went flako, beserko." What she wanted to do was work at Cheetah, a New York disco. De Passe had been spending more time at Cheetah than she had at her books during that year. "I've always had this urge to tell people what I think," she said. "I would go up to the manager or the owner and say, 'This band really stinks' or perhaps 'This band is great.' " Eventually, they asked her if she wanted to come to the weekly auditions to give her opinions. She agreed, and after a time they fired their booking agent and hired de Passe as talent coordinator.

At that point, de Passe moved into a fourth-floor walk-up on East 57th Street and began handing out business cards with a pink cheetah on them. She also became, in her words, "the last living authority on live music in New York. I guess I was pretty obnoxious." It was while doing this job that de Passe met Berry Gordy. Motown artists had appeared often at Cheetah, and the bigger stars often liked to come there to party when they were in New York. Because of that, they often sought out de Passe: "I was queen of the hop," she said. "I was the New York correspondent for entertainment." One night after a show, Supreme Cindy Birdsong introduced her to Gordy. She used a limousine to ferry important people around New York, and when de Passe offered Gordy a lift in it, he was a bit taken aback, asking her if she was "a go-go dancer." That was the extent of their first meeting.

Later, however, de Passe was working for a booking agent and was having considerable difficulty getting through to the proper people in the Motown offices. When she met Gordy a second time, she let him have it: "You know," she said. "Mr. Gordy, your company is the pits. I can't get answers and I have to do my job. I want to book Smokey and Martha and the Vandellas and your man won't return my calls." Gordy challenged her to join the company and "help us straighten it out." That was in 1968, and three weeks later de Passe moved to Detroit to become an assistant to Gordy. After working for several months out of New York, de Passe was one of the first Motown officials to set up an office in Hollywood. She soon proved her worth to the company and to Berry Gordy. "She's one of the brightest people I've ever met—black or white, male or female," he said. "She has worked hard to attain the status she has in the entertainment industry and it is extremely pleasing to me that she should happen to be a black woman."

Within a short time, de Passe was named vice president in charge of creative operations. She offered her input on all aspects of Motown's operations, and during these years she "did everything but type" for the company. De Passe traveled on the road with the Jacksons, critiqued performances of Motown stars, held artists' hands to help them through emotional crises, assisted producers in the studio, and performed in every aspect of the business. De Passe's greatest asset in her rapid ascent at Motown was her close ties to Gordy. "She certainly knows what Mr. Gordy expects," said Fay Hale, another Motown vice president. "She's prepared herself well and she's had the benefit of working with Mr. Gordy." De Passe's relationship with Gordy fueled rumors and suspicions in the corridors and in the press. "Some people want to say that the only reason I'm in my position is because I slept with somebody," she said. "I never did, and nobody wants to believe that either. That's their problem. I would never have had to work so hard if I were Berry Gordy's old lady." De Passe married Hollywood actor Paul LeMat.

In 1981 de Passe was named president of the production division of Motown. "She has complete authority to run that operation," Gordy said. "She has more leeway than any previous director. I'm looking forward to great things from her. . . . She understands my philosophy completely." Her job was primarily to beef up the nonrecording side of Motown industries, particularly to develop better movie, theater, and television projects. She was given a $10 million budget by Gordy to develop these ventures. "We have a backlog of concepts and properties that will now be developed," she announced. "We will place strong emphasis on creative talent existing in our organization." It was a difficult transformation, however, and was not achieved overnight. Several movie ventures were not successful, and the theater projects met only mixed success. De Passe's great contribution to Motown was to turn the company increasingly toward television production.

De Passe put on a few television specials, such as "Motown Review" and "Motown 25—Yesterday, Today, and Forever," which were successes, and also had some failed television movies. She also participated in backing some terrible feature films, such as the 1985 film "The Last Dragon." The big breakthrough for de Passe and Motown, however, was the hugely successful television miniseries, "The Lonesome Dove" in February 1989, which became the highest-rated miniseries of the past five years. It was an enormous gamble, and one that demonstrated clearly that Motown was no longer a firm purveying African-American culture to a white audience. "Lonesome Dove" was from a Pulitzer Prize–winning novel by Larry McMurtry, but because the conventional wisdom said that westerns were passé, all three networks turned down a chance to bid on it. When de Passe first approached McMurtry about it, however, he told her that she would not like it because it was a Western. "I told him I like Westerns, and I do," she commented to the *Los Angeles Times*. She optioned the book for $50,000 in the spring of 1985 and became coproducer of the television film, for which she won an Emmy. With the success of that venture, de Passe has had a number of others in the works: "Bridesmaids," a television movie, an ABC-TV miniseries called "Sacrifices," "Heatwave," a movie about growing up in Harlem, and several others. A decade earlier, de Passe had waxed about what Motown meant to her:

I'm proud of the fact that we are a black-owned company, but that doesn't mean we are a black company. We are a corporation. We want to be big. We want to grow and Motown has always made music for the masses of people. You don't get millions of dollars just from blacks. The American economic system is such that you can succeed and grow and make money. I want my 40 acres and a mule. (*Black Enterprise*, July 1981)

She got that, but by then Motown was not only not a black company; it was no longer black owned. Gordy and de Passe's "40 acres and a mule" seemed to come at the expense of the broader black community.

The success of "Lonesome Dove" delivered $10 million in profits to Motown Industries, which desperately needed it, since Gordy had earlier sold off the Motown Records arm of the business. The 1980s generally had not been terribly kind to Motown. In 1987, for example, Motown Records had just one album on *Billboard*'s Top Forty, and that was "One Heartbeat" by Smokey Robinson, the old warhorse of the studio. Black music, with its emphasis on rap, and the music industry generally, was passing Motown by, and Gordy, de Passe, and the other executives seemed to have little clue as to how to fix the problem. In 1987 Gordy announced that Motown would spend $38 million to develop new artists. Although all agreed it was necessary, not many analysts were confident that Motown would be able to turn itself around. An executive from a rival record firm commented, "Stevie Wonder and Lionel Ritchie have been able to keep the lights on at Motown, but it has not been a cutting-edge label in over fifteen years."

Nothing Gordy and the others tried seemed to work. By 1988 it was apparent that the $38 million push of the year before was not working, and Motown slipped to eighth place among black record producers on *Billboard*'s annual recap of the industry. By that time most of the top stars from the company's heyday, including Michael Jackson and the Jackson Five and Diana Ross, had left the firm, although Robinson and the Temptations remained. People wondered what Gordy would do, and as early as 1986 rumors were rampant that he was planning to sell Motown Records (but not the entertainment end of Motown Industries) to MCA, which acted as the label's distributor. Finally, after protracted negotiations, Gordy sold Motown Records to MCA and Boston Ventures for $61 million. Gordy and Motown Industries still retained control over Jobete, which owned the vast library of Motown hits, and was worth between $100 and $150 million, and Hitsville, the recording studios in Detroit. Mostly what MCA was getting in the deal were a few big-name artists and a name. But it was a name that, in the words of record producer Dick Griffey,* "is the most important name in American music. There is no Warner Brothers sound, no CBS sound, no MCA sound. But the Motown sound was so successful that they now call Detroit 'Motown'—they named the city after the company! That's worth something!"

Others were not so certain that MCA had gotten much of a deal. "Right now, the company has nothing on the charts, it's internally shot, people are looking to get out," said a rival producer. "It's a sad ending to a good piece of American history. Berry Gordy is a great creative guy, but is not a strong manager." Gordy also came under withering criticism from many black organizations for having sold one of the largest and most important black-owned businesses in America to whites. Undeterred, Gordy formed the Gordy Company to contain Motown Production, Jobete Music, and Hitsville. In 1990 the new firm's revenues were about $100 million, and it continued to seek out new television, cable and film projects. Even the Gordy Group, however, was not considered by *Black Enterprise* to be 51 percent black-owned in 1992.

Berry Gordy and Motown for many years were intimately involved in the black community. In 1968 Gordy set up the Gordy Foundation, which was established to help "a unique kind of inner-city youth who has great promise and potential but has not been properly motivated towards higher education." The foundation six years later had granted sixty-eight scholarships to Wayne State University. It also granted twelve scholarships to minority law school students at the same school. Motown also set up the Sterling Ball to fund scholarships for blacks. A black-tie affair for the African-American elite of Detroit, it raised some $50,000 in 1971. Increasingly, though, Gordy lost his contact and interest with Detroit and with the black community, especially after he moved to Hollywood.

There he lived in a massive mansion in Beverly Hills that once belonged to comedian Tommy Smothers. Stephen Birmingham described the house as "the scene of Mr. Gordy's most opulent parties, and its most arresting feature is perhaps the life-size portrait of the diminutive president of Motown that hangs in the dining room. It depicts a bearded Berry Gordy dressed in full imperial regalia, posing as Napoleon.'' A friend said of Gordy, ''He flashes money like an old-time street person. He's basically still a street hustler from Detroit.'' Gordy spent much of his time at the Hugh Hefner mansion, and the two became close friends. Although Gordy made some attempts to connect with the black community in South Central Los Angeles, the scene was rather strange. Gordy would pull up outside a drug rehabilitation clinic in Watts in his stretch limo, wearing designer clothes and diamond rings. He would then address the poor and downtrodden: ''Anybody can do anything. It's just a matter of believing in yourself.'' Pure Washingtonian ideology, but one wonders what effect it had on the denizens of the clinics.

As for Motown itself, it stands in 1992 as an odd monument to a man, a people, and a time. It's a mixed legacy. *Newsweek* commented,

Motown goes on and on . . . even if, sad to say, the Motown Sound is just a beautiful memory now for a generation of teenagers grown old. It really *was* The Sound of Young America throughout much of the 1960s, instantly recognizable on a car radio or hi-fi; it was sweet but soulful, polished but nakedly emotional. And always, without fail, there was the beat. Gordy's true genius was to recognize that, above all, young America—black and white—wanted to *dance*.

By the 1990s, Motown signified, to Gerald Early, ''finally, a modern black urban community of hierarchically arranged talents, a community built on technology but not controlled by it, on the American bourgeoisie values of consumption and production, and on the Washingtonian principles of casting down one's bucket where one is. Motown was for a time the fulfillment of a philosophical and communal ideal.'' As he says elsewhere, however, ''In the dangerous business of judging American popular art, certainly, it is difficult to tell what was Armageddon and what was just passing fancy.''

Sources

Berry Gordy, Jr., has deposited some materials in the Gordy Archives at the University of Michigan in Ann Arbor, but the papers of Suzanne de Passe are not available, nor are the corporate records of Motown, or of any of its divisions, currently available to researchers. There are, however, a number of books and articles that deal in some detail with the Motown empire and especially with Berry Gordy's role within it: J. Randy Tarabelli, *Motown: Hot Wax, City Cool, and Solid Gold* (Garden City, N.Y., 1986); Don Waller, *The Motown Story* (New York, 1985); Nelson George, *Where Did Our Love Go?: The Rise and Fall of the Motown Sound* (New York, 1985); David Bronco, *Heat Wave: The Motown Fact Book* (Ann Arbor, Mich., 1988); Sharon Dairs, *Motown: The History* (New York, 1988). See also Berry Gordy, Sr., *Movin' Up: Pops Gordy Tells His Story* (New York, 1979), written for juveniles. There is biographical information on Berry Gordy in *Current Biography*, July 1975; *Ebony Success Library*, vol. II (1973), 88–91; Stephen Birmingham, *Certain People* (1977), 259–66; Louis Robinson, Jr., *Black Millionaires* (1973); *Who's Who among Black Americans* (1988); *Detroit Free Press*, October 29, 1972, and September 2, 1973; and Ingham BDABL. See also *Los Angeles Herald Examiner*, March 9, 1980, on Gordy's winning the Whitney Young Award.

Biographical information on Suzanne de Passe can be found in *Los Angeles Times*, February 13, 1973, September 26 and October 14, 1983; Diane Haithman, ''How Motown

Corraled 'Lonesome Dove,' " February 19, 1989; *Ebony*, August 1977; *Los Angeles Sentinel*, February 5, 1981, October 13, 1983, and September 26, 1985; Joel Dreyfuss, "Motown's $10 Million Gamble," *Black Enterprise*, July 1981, 26–29; Solomon Herbert, "Motown Soars with 'Dove,' " *Black Enterprise*, May 1989, 40; June 1989, 300–1; Bonnie Allen, "Suzanne De Passe: Motown's $10 Million Boss Lady," *Essence*, September 1981, 90ff.; *LA Magazine*, September 1984; *Time*, January 30, 1989; *People Weekly*, Spring 1991, 64–65; *Esquire*, August 1989, 86ff.; Moris Gelman, "Motown's 'Lonesome Dove' Gamble Pays Off: de Passe Declares Herself Vindicated," *Variety*, February 15, 1989, 85–86; Graham Button, "The Golden Dove," *Forbes*, January 23, 1989, 58–59.

Much information about Motown and its influence has been published over the years: "No Town Like Motown," *Newsweek*, March 22, 1965, "Motown's 25 Years of Soul," May 23, 1983; *Ebony*, February 1966, July 1971, and November 1985; Stanley H. Brown, "The Motown Sound of Money," *Fortune*, September 1, 1967, 103ff.; *Michigan Chronicle*, October 23, 1970; Nadra Woods, "How Motown Made Millions in Music," *Sepia*, July 1971, 34–37; Patrick Salvo and Barbara Salvo, "The Motown Empire," *Sepia*, September 1974; *Sepia*, October 1974; Herschel Johnson, "Motown: The Sound of Success," *Black Enterprise*, June 1974, 71–80; 85–88, 151; "Motown Sings a New Tune," *Black Enterprise*, November 1987, 22; "The Motown Lament: Where Did Our Company Go?," *Black Enterprise*, August 1988; *Black Enterprise*, June 1992, 219–20; Robert A. Wright, "The Dominant Color Is Green," *New York Times*, July 7, 1974; *Time*, October 27, 1974; Robert Hilburn, "Motown's Berry Gordy Looks Back on 25 Years," *Los Angeles Times*, March 22, 1983; William K. Knoedelseder, Jr., *Los Angeles Times*, "Motown Tries to Get Back in the Groove," August 21, 1987; Paul Grein, "Motown Retunes Its Sputtering Hit-Making Machine," *Los Angeles Times*, February 10, 1988; Paul Grein, "Busby Writing Next Chapter of Motown," *Los Angeles Times*, August 8, 1988; John Spano, "Man Who Built Motown Spins Words of Hope," *Los Angeles Times*, December 7, 1988, Paul Grein, "Motown on the Road to a Comeback," *Los Angeles Times*, July 30, 1989; "That Ol' Black Vinyl," *The Economist*, September 7, 1986, 74–75; *Rolling Stone*, February 11, 1988; Michael Goldberg, "Berry Gordy: Motown's Founder Tells the Story of Hitsville, U.S.A.," *Rolling Stone*, August 23, 1990, 66ff.; Richard L. Hudson, "Bidding Contest Shapes Up for Rights to Motown Hits," *Wall Street Journal*, August 30, 1989; Gary Graff, "The Rise and Fall—and Rise—of Motown Records," *Tampa Tribune*, April 13, 1990; Michelle Green, "After Decades of Silence, Raynoma Singleton Is Singing the Blues about Her Ex-husband Berry Gordy," *People Weekly*, November 5, 1990, 107ff.; Gerald Early, "One Nation under a Groove: The Brief, Shining Moment of Motown—and America," *New Republic*, July 15, 1991, 30ff.; Elvis Mitchell, Jr., et al., *Motown Album: The Sound of Young America* (New York, 1990). There is also a wealth of shorter articles in the *Los Angeles Times*; see the index to that publication for details. The operations of Motown were also covered regularly in *Variety* and *Billboard*; consult back issues of those publications. There are, in addition, numerous "kiss and tell" autobiographies by a number of the artists who made their careers at Motown: Mary Wilson, *Dreamgirl: My Life as a Supreme* (New York, 1986); Mary Wilson and Patricia Romanowski, *Supreme Faith: Someday We'll Be Together* (New York, 1991); Smokey Robinson and David Ritz, *Smokey: Inside My Life* (New York, 1991); Raynoma Gordy Singleton with Bryan Brown and Mim Eichler, *Berry, Me, & Motown: The Untold Story* (New York, 1991); J. Randy Taraborrelli, *Call*

Her Miss Ross: An Unauthorized Biography of Diana Ross (New York, 1991); Otis Williams and Patricia Romanowski, *Temptations* (New York, 1991).

Dickerson, Earl Burrus (June 23, 1891–October 2, 1986), **Truman Kella Gibson, Sr.** (August 5, 1882–August 27, 1972), **Truman Kella Gibson, Jr.** (January 22, 1912–   ), and **Frank L. Gillespie** (November 8, 1876–May 8, 1925). Insurance company executives, entrepreneurs, community leaders, boxing promoter, lawyers, and politicians: Liberty Life Insurance, Supreme Life Insurance, Supreme Liberty Life Insurance, Joe Louis Enterprises, Inc., and International Boxing Club. Supreme Life Insurance was once the largest black-owned business in the North, and it is still the oldest African-American insurance company in Chicago. But it is no longer the largest black insurance firm in that city. Chicago Metropolitan Assurance has nearly five times the assets, and three thousand times the insurance in force. Yet Supreme Life is still the tenth-largest black insurance firm in the country and remains a profitable entity. By the 1990s it was merely a cog in John H. Johnson's* massive black Chicago business empire, but from its origins seventy years earlier, Supreme has played an important and dynamic role in the development of Chicago's black community.

Supreme Life got its start as the Liberty Life Insurance Company, receiving a charter from the state of Illinois in 1919. It was founded by an assertive and dynamic young black migrant to Chicago from the South, by way of Boston: Frank L. Gillespie. Gillespie was born in Osceola, Arkansas, a small village in Mississippi County consisting of a post office, a few houses, and a couple of stores situated in the flat, muddy bottom of the Mississippi River Valley. While he was still very young, Gillespie's parents relocated to Memphis, Tennessee, where the boy was educated in the public schools. Later, they moved on to St. Louis, Missouri, where Frank Gillespie attended Sumner High School for three years. At that point he was sent to the Boston Conservatory to study music, and while there he also completed his high school studies. Gillespie then went to Washington, D.C., where he enrolled in the law school at Howard University. Family financial difficulties, however, forced him to forsake his pursuit of a law degree. Gillespie relocated to Chicago just after the turn of the century, where he became the private secretary to J. C. Yeager, an important white capitalist in the city.

After Yeager's death Gillespie had to find a means to support himself, and he was able to secure a position as the first black employee of the Automatic Telephone Company, where he remained for just a short time because he left to join Oscar DePriest, the powerful Chicago black politician and U.S. congressman, in the real estate business. Gillespie remained there for two years, when in 1916 he joined the agency force of the Royal Insurance Company of Chicago, a white firm that was beginning to pursue the growing black market in the city. Gillespie was placed in charge of the "department for colored people" but, by August of that year, was so successful that he was promoted to superintendent of the company, becoming the first black superintendent of a northern, white, old-line legal reserve insurance firm in America. This was an exceptional position for the time, since Gillespie was the superior of a number of young, bright, and ambitious white men, as well as a number of blacks. This was a time of growing racial tensions in the city, so Gillespie's success in this endeavor is that much more remarkable, but it is also true that Royal Insurance made impressive efforts to hire and promote a number of African-Americans during this time.

Gillespie's success at Royal ultimately brought him frustration, however, as he found his opportunities for further advancement thwarted. Thus, in the fall of 1917, he became an organizer and officer of the Public Life Insurance Company of Illinois. This firm was organized by a group of black former employees of Royal Insurance, and Gillespie remained an officer of that firm for two years, making a moderate success of it. This turned out to be short lived, though, and as early as 1918 Gillespie met with a group of prominent black businessmen in the city to discuss founding a new, black-owned insurance company. When they received their state charter and opened for business, the company's advertisement was effusive:

At last! At last! The Negroes are going to get together. . . . If we ever expect to get anywhere as a race of people we must first learn to stick together. . . . The day of Negro enterprises of every kind has arrived. . . . The Liberty Life Insurance Company [is] the first old line reserve company ever incorporated north of the Mason-Dixon Line that will be owned and controlled by Negroes.

Gillespie had arrived in Chicago at a propitious time for blacks and had founded his insurance company in the wake of a massive migration of African-Americans from the South to the city. Chicago's black community had gotten its start in the 1840s, when a group of fugitive slaves came to the city. By 1860 nearly a thousand blacks lived there, and a small leadership group headed by a prosperous tailor, John Jones, was participating in antislavery activities and protesting discrimination and segregation. From 1870 to 1890, the black community grew to nearly 15,000 people, and a well-delineated class structure had begun to emerge. The center of this community was on the South Side of Chicago, but a number of blacks were interspersed throughout the city.

Between 1890 and 1915, the black population of Chicago grew to over 50,000, and a massive, segregated black ghetto had taken shape on the South Side, with a smaller offshoot on the West Side. Nearly all this population increase came from the migration of southern blacks to the North. Most of the city's blacks, male or female, worked as domestic and personal servants; only 8 percent of the men and 11 percent of the women engaged in manufacturing. A significant professional class, however, had also emerged, accounting for about 3 percent of the group. An African-American elite had also begun to emerge, made up of ministers, physicians, lawyers, and business leaders. Of the businessmen, the wealthiest in the early twentieth century was a caterer, Charles J. Smiley, who served exclusively the wealthy white community.

Increasingly, however, a black business elite began to emerge which, as in other cities, primarily serviced the increasingly large and segregated black community. Among the most important of these new business leaders was Theodore W. Jones, a Canadian-born black who owned a large South Side express company and who was a strong supporter of Booker T. Washington* and the National Negro Business League. Others who were prominent in Chicago's Negro Business League in these years was S. Laing Williams, an attorney, and Sandy W. Trice, an owner of a clothing store. By 1910, however, the black community's leading businessman was Jesse Binga,* a wealthy real estate broker and banker who had married the daughter of John "Mushmouth" Johnson, the city's king of the black gambling establishment. Other prominent blacks owned saloons and other businesses of marginal repute, such as Pony Moore and Robert T. Motts, who also became members of the business establishment during this time. Motts, a gambling figure, opened the Pekin Theater, billed as "the only Negro-owned theater in the world."

Other members of the black elite emerging at this time were politicians, who were perhaps more numerous here than in any other city. Edward H. Wright, the city's first black ward committeeman, was a leading force, but the most prominent was Oscar DePriest, Gillespie's one-time employer. DePriest was a native of Alabama who started his career as a painter in Chicago, attained a minor civil appointment, and built up the Second Ward Republican organization. He later became an alderman and then a congressman, in addition to his lucrative real estate business and activities as one of the founders of the National Negro Business League in Chicago. Finally, and perhaps most important, there was Robert Abbott,* who founded the *Chicago Defender* in 1905. The paper soon grew to have a national circulation, was a major factor in inducing blacks to migrate from the South to Chicago, and became the leading black newspaper in the country.

After 1910 Chicago increasingly became the magnet for black business in the North. Anthony Overton* moved his highly successful Overton Hygienic Manufacturing Company to Chicago in 1911, and in 1913 Robert Abbott and others organized the short-lived Progressive National Life Insurance Company. Black baseball teams were also organized, as were development companies and other organizations. The greatest explosion in the city's black population came during World War I and continued into the afterwar years, as Chicago became the focal point of the massive migration from the South.

Whereas the prewar migration to Chicago had been relatively gradual, during the war years it was large scale and sudden. The city, which had 63,355 blacks in 1910, counted 109,458 ten years later, an increase of 72 percent in just one decade. Ninety-four percent of this increase was the result of migration. As Allan Spear has commented, "[A]n unprecedented influx of Negro migrants from the Deep South swelled Chicago's black belt and converted it into a solidly Negro community that cut through the heart of the South Side." It also intensified the racism and racial violence that had been growing during the prewar years, resulting in one of the bloodiest, most violent racial confrontations in the nation's urban history in the summer of 1919, at the very same time that Frank Gillespie was launching his new insurance firm. It was a time fraught with promise and uncertainty.

Blacks by 1919 had a greater presence in manufacturing employment in Chicago than ever before, as 45 percent were so employed by 1920. This resulted in generally higher wages in the black community, and, therefore, a greater propensity to afford premiums on whole life, as opposed to industrial insurance, which formerly had been the mainstay of the black insurance business. Gillespie and his colleagues, however, overestimated the capacity of the city's black community. They offered 10,000 shares of Liberty Life's stock at $30 a share. Although all shares were sold by November 13, 1920, the required $100,000 deposit to begin business could not be made until June 1921. Gillespie's chief appeal, as demonstrated above from a company brochure, was racial pride. Stock sales were carried out by salesmen traveling throughout the South and Midwest, but there was not much success in this operation. Most of the stock was finally purchased by company officers and employees.

Even as late as June 1921, only $65,000 of the required $100,000 had actually been raised, so Gillespie was forced to resort to a subterfuge. He announced a director's meeting to celebrate the sale of all the company's stock. Then, when the directors arrived, he informed them that the deposit could not be made, and that they must come up with the $35,000. Pledges were made at that time to make up the difference. Liberty was thus able to begin operations that summer, and Frank Gillespie served as the company's first president. Two other early officers were W. Ellis Stewart, secretary, and Earl B. Dickerson, legal counsel.

The ordinary life market appeared lucrative at this time. No other black firms sold that type of insurance; instead, they concentrated on industrial insurance, which collected premiums of just a nickle or a dime a week to supply what was essentially burial insurance. Gillespie's company collected premiums just once or twice a year, and the amount was higher, but the insurance provided was of greater substance. It was a type of insurance designed to be sold to the expanding African-American middle class. And there was no real competition, since white companies refused to sell this kind of insurance to blacks, on the pretext that African-American mortality rates were higher than white.

But these positive factors were negated by the growing racism of the white community and the deleterious effects of the 1919 race riot. Blacks were highly disillusioned by what had happened in a city trumpeted in the *Chicago Defender* as a relative haven of economic opportunity and racial justice. By the early 1920s blacks in Chicago had faced the ugly reality of racism in the North and had also been hit with a short but sharp economic recession and massive layoffs as the soldiers returned home. So, Gillespie and his staff had to convince these people that they had a future in Chicago and that they should invest their hard-earned and scarce earnings in relatively expensive life insurance.

To achieve this goal, Gillespie hired and trained a corps of well-educated, young African-Americans. He tried to obtain as many experienced salesmen as possible, and when he found a man he wanted, he went to any lengths to obtain his services. One potential agent had received a letter from Gillespie instructing him, "Name your own salary and get the next train." When a man arrived, however, he found a company with little cash to pay the salary. Instead, the man would be given a one-way ticket to his market and told to deduct the cost of the return ticket from his policy sales. The salary was even less secure. Thus, Gillespie was not successful in hiring as many full-time agents as he desired, being forced, like most black insurance firms, to rely on part-time ministers and postal workers instead. Although sales rose each year through 1925, sales expenses and lapsed policies were very high. Gillespie himself was forced to spend a great deal of his time selling insurance himself and training new agents.

First-year premiums were used up in payment of the agents' commissions and the establishment of policy reserves. To survive, Liberty Life in 1922 had to sell an additional 10,000 shares at $40 per share. This stock sale was not completed until 1928. By 1923 sales income was adequate to cover operating expenses, but policy reserves still had to be covered from surplus funds. The situation slowly improved, however, and by the end of 1925 Liberty Life had over $8 million of insurance in force and $495,000 in admitted assets. Investments throughout the 1920s were primarily in real estate, and in 1924 a home office building was erected at the cost of $250,000. The firm also purchased a large number of mortgages on black residential property in the city, providing an economic benefit to themselves and a social service to the city's blacks, who were unable to get financing from white institutions.

In May 1925, though, the firm suffered an enormous setback when Gillespie, the company's founder and driving force, died. During this same time, Gillespie had also been one of the founders of the National Insurance Association, a trade association of black insurance firms. He had married Edreaner Poree of New Orleans, Louisiana, in 1903, and they had two children. Upon the death of Gillespie, the presidency was turned over to Dr. M. O. Bousfield, a native of Missouri and a graduate of the University of Kansas and Northwestern Medical School. After serving internships and traveling in various countries, Bousfield came to Chicago. Here, while working for the Railway Man's International Benevolent Association (later the Brotherhood of Sleeping Car Porters), he met Frank Gillespie who invited him to join in organizing Liberty Life. Bousfield became vice president and medical director of that firm until 1925 when he assumed the presidency. Bousfield ran the company in a competent, but somewhat dilatory, fashion for the next four years. Nonetheless, in 1928 Liberty Life earned a profit of $12,000, the first in its history. It was clear, however, that something radical had to be done to reenergize the firm. As a result, Bousfield began to discuss the possibilities of merging with a number of other black-owned insurance firms.

In 1929 Liberty Life merged with the Supreme Life and Casualty Company of Columbus, Ohio, and the Northeastern Life Insurance Company of Newark. This merger brought a number of inestimable advantages to Liberty Life. Supreme Life had large holdings of industrial insurance, with salesmen trained in those operations. Northeastern had an excellent investment portfolio and highly experienced management. Neither firm, unlike Liberty Life, had been profitable in 1928. The merger also brought two tremendously talented and energetic chief executives to the new firm. Harry H. Pace,* who had been president of Northeastern, became the president of the new Supreme Liberty Life, and Truman K. Gibson, formerly president of Supreme Life, became the chairman of the board of the new concern. Together they formed a powerful tandem that allowed Supreme Liberty Life to weather the Great Depression. Bousfield returned to his position of medical director and vice president, while also serving as director of medical services for the Julius Rosenwald Fund.

Harry Pace, one of the most dynamic and multifaceted African-American businessmen of the first half of the twentieth century, is covered in his own biography. But some points should be made about him here, particularly in relationship to his running of Supreme Liberty Life. Both Pace and Gibson were natives of Georgia; Pace was born in Covington and Gibson in Macon, within two years of each other. Both were also drawn to Atlanta University where they received their educations; Pace graduated in 1903 and Gibson in 1905. Both men ultimately also became officers of important black insurance firms in Atlanta—Pace as secretary treasurer of Heman Perry's* Standard Life Insurance and Gibson as vice president and secretary of Alonzo Herndon's* Atlanta Mutual Life Insurance. Gibson also managed the health and accident insurance department at Standard Life in the 1920s. So the two men shared some similar backgrounds and associations. It was Gibson who reputedly worked out the complicated merger of the three black insurance companies in 1929 to form Supreme Liberty Life.

Pace had various disagreements with Heman Perry and left Standard Life in 1920, becoming involved in the music publishing and record business with the famous W. C. Handy. In 1925 he left as president of Black Swan Records and formed Northeastern Life Insurance in Newark, New Jersey, with the aid of a number of wealthy blacks. After becoming president of Supreme Liberty, Pace also attended law school in the evenings, gaining his law degree from Chicago Law School in 1933. He practiced law as a member of the firm of Bibb, Tyree and Pace during the later 1930s while continuing as president of Supreme Liberty until his death in 1943.

Truman K. Gibson grew up in Macon, Georgia, the son of John Arthur and Annie C. Gibson. Although raised in a family of moderate means, Gibson was able to acquire a good education. He attended the Ballard Normal School in Macon, working after school at a number of jobs—messenger, clerk in a drugstore, and so forth. At age eighteen, he went to Atlanta University, where he graduated four years later, in 1905. The following year he decided to go to Harvard University, where he received another bachelor's degree, this one in business administration, in 1908. Well armed with an exceptional education for the time, Gibson taught at St. Paul School in Lawrenceville, Virginia, for the next two years. At that point a teacher and friend of his appealed to Gibson to enter the insurance field. Like so many other bright young African-Americans of the time, particularly graduates of Atlanta University, he obtained employment with Atlanta Mutual Life, starting in the agency end. Many of his acquaintances thought he was crazy. As he later recalled, "I recall most vividly the concern and incredulity which met my decision, because there were only three companies operated by Negroes then and they looked none too promising." During the nine years he was with the firm, he advanced from agent to manager, and his annual earnings increased from $600 to over $2,000.

Gibson, however, wanted to be more than just a well-paid member of management—he wanted to be an entrepreneur—the owner and chief executive of his own firm. He had also tired of the increasing white racism of the South. "It was natural that in 1917," he later said, "partly from a desire to educate our children in a freer climate and partly in order to carry out my own predictions, that I left a steadily growing Atlanta company I had joined and journeyed North." With a number of others in 1919 he organized the Supreme Life and Casualty Company of Ohio. At about the time of its founding, Gibson wrote a letter to the *New York Age*, explaining his hopes and plans for the new insurance firm:

It is a matter of common knowledge that most large companies of the country persistently refuse to insure our people upon any terms or conditions. . . . It is intended to fill just that need along with others. . . . This company feels that it is blazing the trail for similar companies in the future.

Gibson was named the company's first president and served in that capacity for ten years. Despite his optimism, however, the young firm struggled until it was merged with Liberty Life and Northeastern Life. After that time, and until Harry Pace's death, Gibson served as chairman of the board of Supreme Liberty. He then became president and ran the firm until 1955, when he again became chairman of the board and then chairman emeritus until his death in 1972. For his part in bringing about the merger, Gibson was awarded the Harmon Medal for distinguished achievement.

The years of the joint management of Supreme Liberty Life by Pace and Gibson were ones of survival. Just after the merger in 1929, the devastating Great Depression struck. The young firm had not even fully coordinated its procedures at that point, but the great problem was simply to survive in an economic crisis of unprecedented proportions. The Depression hit urban blacks in the North harder than any other group, as African-American unemployment hit astounding levels. Even as late as 1940, fully 36 percent of the black males in Chicago were still unemployed or only had relief work. As they lost their jobs, and as income levels fell, blacks could not afford to keep up their insurance premiums. The effect on black insurance companies nationwide was traumatic, and two of the larger black-owned firms went out of business during the decade.

The situation for Supreme Liberty Life was more desperate than for many others for two reasons. First, it relied more heavily on the ordinary life market, which was more expensive, and therefore blacks were more likely to allow those policies to lapse. Also, Pace and Gibson's company had invested very heavily in the real estate market, and with the rapid devaluation of real estate, especially in black areas, the value of these assets held by the firm shrank accordingly. Then, too, as hard-pressed blacks, unemployed and underemployed, could not meet their mortgage payments, Supreme Liberty Life was faced with a difficult situation. Foreclosures would only saddle the firm with property that either could not be sold, or could be liquidated only at a fraction of its former value.

To deal with the crushing problems, Pace and Gibson reduced operating expenses and cut the par value of the stock from $10 to $2.50 a share. They also focused the firm more on the industrial insurance market, which, with its low weekly premiums, was the only area of even moderate growth among the black population. The key element was to maintain the policyholders' confidence. To do so, the executives made sure they paid off all death claims, and they were even ready and willing to continue loaning money at up to 50 percent of the cash surrender value of the policy. It was, withall, a difficult time, as Supreme Liberty Life's assets fell from $1,830,000 in 1930 to $1,575,000 in 1934, and investment income virtually disappeared.

Then, Gibson and Pace were faced with an even more desperate situation. In 1933 the Illinois Department of Insurance began an examination of all insurance firms. In the course of their examination, they drastically reduced the book value of most of the real estate items in Supreme Liberty's investment portfolio. As a result, its real estate holdings were revalued from $743,000 to just over $380,000. Since the company had only a small surplus of just over $76,000, and were making no profits on current operations, bankruptcy seemed inevitable. At that point, Earl Dickerson, the corporate counsel, came up with a brilliant and unorthodox scheme. He persuaded the company's policyholders to sign a lien by which they acknowledged an indebtedness to the firm of either 50 percent or the entire amount of their policies' reserves. It was a maneuver of somewhat questionable legality, that was later made illegal by statute, but after a court battle, the Illinois Supreme Court allowed the use of the liens as admitted assets. Dickerson, who was also assistant attorney general of Illinois at this time, was a key factor in the firm's legal victory. However dubious were the assets, the action saved Supreme Liberty Life, allowing it to add some $300,000 in policyholders' liens to the asset list.

That was the turning point. Supreme Liberty Life became increasingly profitable in the late 1930s. The liens were retired in 1937; the surplus funds grew from $100,000 in 1935 to $280,000 in 1941; and in 1941 a dividend of 30 cents a share was declared. This recovery, as suggested above, was based largely on the sales of industrial life insurance. The key figure in this drive was James G. Ish, the agency director, who developed a concept he called "mass production." Under this system, largely untrained agents were sent out to write as many policies as they could without even requiring any financial settlement at the time of signing. After the policy had been processed and issued, the agent would then try to get the client to sign it, stressing the very small weekly premiums to be paid. This technique allowed a rapid expansion of Supreme Liberty's industrial insurance holdings, as $460,000 of these policies were sold from 1935 to 1942. This brought the company's total industrial insurance in force by 1942 to over $53 million.

This expansion was, however, very expensive. Supreme Liberty's lapse rate was the highest among black insurance firms; thirteen policies were issued for every one that remained in force. Then, too, the expense of collecting the premiums on those policies in force was also high, and there was a very high turnover among the inexperienced and untrained agents. Nor did it do much for the reputation of Supreme Liberty Life. As Robert Puth has commented, "Agents learned almost nothing about the sales approaches necessary to sell life insurance as a long-term contract, or in selling large policies—both sources of reduced operating expenses. Supreme Liberty Life agents were not well paid, and the company lost many of its better sales personnel to other firms."

After America's entrance into World War II, black employment and wages began rising rapidly. Black mortality rates also began dropping sharply, becoming closer to the national average. On one hand, this increased the opportunity for Supreme Liberty to sell more profitable ordinary life insurance; on the other hand, it made the black market more attractive to large white firms. With Pace's death in 1943, these new challenges were met by Truman Gibson alone. The first seven years of his solo management of Supreme Liberty were tremendously successful. The firm experienced phenomenal growth and financial success from 1943 to 1950. One of its sources of strength was the fact that the firm invested a higher proportion of its funds in mortgages than other firms. Operating expenses, however, due to continuation of the "mass production" policy, remained high.

By the end of World War II, Supreme Liberty Life seemed to be sitting on top of the world. The young *Ebony* magazine, whose publisher, John H. Johnson, had gotten his start with the firm, extolled its virtues in 1946, calling it the "[b]iggest business owned and operated by Negroes above the Mason and Dixon Line," when it celebrated its twenty-fifth anniversary that year. Johnson attributed its success to the fact that it was "deliberately conservative." Despite this innate conservatism, Gibson pushed foward some aggressive plans. In 1949 he absorbed the Carver Mutual Insurance Company of Detroit and, in 1952, took over the business of Twentieth Century Life Insurance Company of the same city.

Yet the conservative policies were also to cause some problems in later years. They began to have a negative impact on Supreme Liberty Life after 1950. Profits never rose above $180,000 after 1951, below the average of the preceding eight years, despite a greater volume of business. Supreme Liberty Life was also growing more slowly than other black insurance firms during this period, whereas it had exceeded their growth rate before 1950. Its failure, according to Robert Puth, was due to "the shortcomings of its sales force and increased competition from white firms for the Negro market.'' Industrial insurance in force fell by nearly $10 million between 1950 and 1955. Even though its holdings of ordinary life rose by 33 percent, this was well behind the 50 percent increase in this category enjoyed by the rest of the black insurance firms.

Not only that, it became increasingly clear that Supreme Liberty Life, under the guidance of Truman K. Gibson, was not particularly well managed. The firm's administrative structure had been designed for a much smaller firm, run by men who supervised their departments directly. By the 1950s, with a greater number of employees, more complex problems, and more business, it was clear that changes would have to be made. The most critical area was the Agency Department, which was run at very high cost, and was no longer producing as it had in the 1930s and 1940s. After 1953 a number of changes were made to improve the administrative structure and the flow of communications at the firm, and in 1955 a modern profit and expense control system was established. The most important change in that year was the replacement of Gibson as president with Earl B. Dickerson.

Despite Supreme Liberty Life's decline in later years, Gibson's achievement with Supreme Liberty Life was impressive, and by the time he stepped out of the presidency the company had insurance in force of $124 million, had more than 1,000 employees with offices in twelve states, and had assets of more than $15 million invested in buildings and equipment. Gibson by that time was seventy-three years old, but he remained hale, hearty, and deeply involved in the firm's operations and future for several years to come. At the time, he told the *Chicago Tribune,* ''I have found complete satisfaction in my work, because I have touched the lives of people in a positive and constructive way.'' Gibson was chairman until 1971 and honorary chairman emeritus until his death in 1972. A member of the Congregational Church, Gibson had married Alberta Dickerson of Jersey City, New Jersey, in 1910. It is not known whether she was related to Earl Dickerson. They had three children, two of whom, Truman K., Jr., and Harry H. became important factors in the business world.

Earl Dickerson was born in Canton, Mississippi, the son of Edward Dickerson and Emma Garrett. The family had a difficult life, similar to that of many blacks in Mississippi at that time. Dickerson's mother worked as a laundress, and he later remembered, ''My mother was a washerwoman, and I would take my little wagon to the white section of town to pick up the clothes and deliver them at the end of the week.'' He also experienced the violence of white racism of the time: ''I was about 5 then, I think—[passing a group of white boys] one yelled, 'There's nigger; let's get him,' and they let fly. One boy put a rock in his snowball and it struck me on the temple. I was knocked unconscious. They carried me to a store and I came around.'' He also saw a relative shot in the knee by a policeman for simply brushing against the policeman in a street crowded with Christmas shoppers. ''It was seeing that sort of thing, seeing my mother wash all those clothes for $1.50 or $2 a week, that made me want to get away.''

Earl Dickerson was educated in his hometown and in 1907, at the age of sixteen, went to Chicago to attend school. Over sixty years later, he recollected that time: "I was filled with those youthful visions of a new-found freedom that looked for a personal and tangible solution to the problems and injustices of life that had stricken my life as a child in Mississippi." Upon arrival in Chicago, Dickerson enrolled in Evanston Academy, then the preparatory division of Northwestern University, graduating from there in 1909. He then went to Urbana to attend the University of Illinois, from which he graduated in 1914. It was one of the proudest days of his life, as his mother was there to attend the graduation ceremonies. "Somehow I felt that she was living through me," he said.

After two years of teaching at Booker T. Washington's Tuskegee Institute in Alabama and at a high school in Vincennes, Indiana, Dickerson entered law school at the University of Chicago. Before he could finish, however, the United States entered World War I, and Dickerson became a first lieutenant in the 365th Infantry and served in France. After completing his service, Dickerson returned to Chicago, where he completed his law degree in 1920. A year earlier he was asked to attend a convention in St. Louis, Missouri, where he gave a speech and became one of the founders of the American Legion. In later years he became highly critical of that group (and they of him), but he said, "I don't like the American Legion, and I haven't for many years, but that doesn't take away the fact that I am one of the founders."

In 1921 Dickerson was admitted to the bar, and in the same year he was asked by Frank L. Gillespie to draw up the articles of incorporation for Liberty Life Insurance, and he also became general counsel of the firm. Over the next three decades, Dickerson continued in that capacity, while also building an important career as a lawyer, politician, and civil rights leader in the city. His role in those other endeavors are handled in more detail below. As Truman Gibson's hand faltered at the helm of Supreme Liberty Life in the early 1950s, Dickerson began to take a more active role in the management of the company. Dickerson became the major voice calling for dramatic changes during this time, and in 1954 he became executive vice president and a year later became general manager before being named president and chief executive officer the following year. Dickerson remained in those positions until 1971, when he stepped up to chairman of the board for two years. After that, he was honorary chairman emeritus until his death in 1986.

When he took over in April 1956, Dickerson's main objective was to increase the company's rate of growth. His principal step was to change the emphasis of the firm from industrial to ordinary life. To do so, he replaced James G. Ish as agency director with J. F. Morning. Morning made great improvements in the selection, training, and compensation of agents and made great strides in reducing agency expenses. Dickerson reflected on the problem, saying, "Manpower is the problem, we must have competent people. Before we can branch out any further along those lines, we have to undertake the consolidation and rebuilding of home office personnel to handle efficiently the business we already have." Emphasis gradually shifted to quality production and larger policies. Five years after he assumed command of the firm, Dickerson's policies were bearing fruit. By 1961 Supreme Liberty Life remained the largest Negro-owned business in the North, and the third largest in the nation. It had over $200 million of insurance in force, with $31.5 million in assets and thirty-eight branch offices in twelve states with 600 employees and more than 350,000 policyholders.

In that year, *Ebony* magazine gave most of the credit for this transformation to Dickerson's influence:

For much of the entrenched security and rock-hard respectability identified with their company, Supreme Life officers and stockholders must thank their president, a man whose debonair presence and business acumen might qualify him as a model executive. In the six years since he moved into the top spot in the company, Dickerson has effected both a literal and a figurative face-lifting of the corporate image.

In 1956 he renovated the corporate headquarters building at a cost of $400,000, and over the next five years he absorbed Friendship Mutual Life Insurance Company, the Beneficial Life Insurance Company of Detroit, the Dunbar Life Insurance Company of Cleveland, and the Federal Life Insurance Company of Washington, D.C. Then, in 1961, in his most dramatic move to that time, Dickerson bought the Domestic Life Insurance Company of Louisville, Kentucky, for $1.8 million, adding one-third as many policyholders as before and bringing the firm into the new areas of Kentucky, Ohio, Indiana, and Tennessee. These acquisitions by 1962 added nearly $59 million to Supreme Life's insurance holdings. They were made possible by the increased administrative capacity Dickerson had brought into the firm after 1956. By 1962 Supreme Life was able to report a profit of $500,000, by far the largest in the company's history. Its growth rate from 1957 to 1962 was much higher than the average of black insurance firms, and it was far better equipped to compete in a changing market by that time than it had been in the mid–1950s.

Dickerson, who had been deeply involved in politics and civil rights for decades, understood the mission of Supreme Life in the more socially complex ways than Gillespie, Pace, or Gibson:

We seek to become a powerful factor in all the communities where we operate. We work toward bringing the people together to achieve their objectives. A company with a program in all these communities can fight to bring about equality by by-passing city and state lines. We cooperate with churches and civic and social groups to rally the spirit of the people in a common effort to attain their common mission. The idea, of course, is to get Negroes to invest in their own future and security. Supreme Life emphasizes that economic strength is the key to real equality.

Dickerson continued to run Supreme Life until 1971, when he retired as chief executive at the age of eighty. At that time, John Johnson, the majority stockholder in the company, took over active management. By then, Dickerson's decade and a half transformation of Supreme Life had gone stale. In 1970 the firm lost more than $500,000, had assets of $37 million, and insurance in force of $222 million. Its annual premium income amounted to $7.3 million. It stood at number 517 among all insurance companies in the United States and was slipping badly among black insurance firms as well.

Johnson, who is handled in detail in a separate biography, was born in Arkansas City, Arkansas, in 1918, the son of a sawmill worker and a domestic servant. His father died when he was young, and his mother remarried another sawmill worker. When Johnson was fifteen, his mother took him to Chicago to visit the World's Fair. They decided to stay, and Johnson soon became a part-time worker in a National Youth Administration work relief program. He became an honor student at DuSable High School, the premier school for blacks on the South Side of Chicago, and in 1936 he was asked to speak at a meeting of the Chicago Urban League. There he caught the eye of Harry Pace, then president of Supreme Life. Pace gave him a job with the insurance firm as a teenaged office boy, as Johnson himself said, a "go-fer," since executives would tell him to "Go for" this and "Go for" that. He attended the University of Chicago part-time during this period and began to edit Supreme Life's company publication. This gave Johnson the idea to start the *Negro Digest*, from which grew his massive publishing empire.

He began to publish the *Negro Digest* in 1942 and brought out *Ebony* in 1945. By the 1960s, *Ebony* had passed the 1 million mark in circulation, putting it among the nation's fifty largest magazines, and it had yearly advertising revenues of $7 million. He also brought out a number of other magazines and expanded into cosmetics and other fields. In 1955 Johnson began buying Supreme Life stock; by 1964, he was the firm's largest stockholder. Becoming increasingly concerned with Supreme Life's performance in the late 1960s, Johnson became more and more involved in company affairs. In 1971 Johnson's black Fleetwood Cadillac began appearing outside the doors of Supreme Life at 8 A.M., and it was clear that changes were going to be made. He then "kicked" Earl Dickerson "upstairs" to board chairman and took control of the firm himself.

During his first two years as head of Supreme Life, Johnson, applying the genius and energy that made him such a success in other endeavors, brought about a transformation of the insurance firm. By 1973 insurance in force had climbed to over $1 billion, assets stood at $41 million, and premium income had increased over 40 percent to $10.2 million. It was by then the 346th largest insurance company in the land, an upward climb of 171 positions. Then, in the fall of 1973, Johnson moved up to chairman, while retaining the role of chief executive, and installed Ray Irby as president. Irby had been vice president and agency director of the firm and a key right-hand man in Johnson's shake-up of the company over the previous two years. Supreme Life continued to grow over the next several years. In 1975 it had a record year, when it reached over $1.5 billion of insurance in force and ranked 244th among all insurance firms in America.

As America entered the 1980s, though, pressure on black insurance companies became more intense, and many were forced to adopt new marketing tactics in order to survive ferocious competition from giant white firms, both for policyholders and for agents. The Chicago firm that was to perform best in this new environment was Chicago Metropolitan Mutual Assurance Company. Founded in 1927, it was an outgrowth of a consortium of black funeral companies, which had banded together in 1925 to provide death benefits for poor black Chicagoans. The man who was responsible for the development of the firm over its early years was Robert A. Cole, once a manager of a gambling den in the city. Cole died in 1956, and the following year there was an agent strike at the firm, and its growth and development were stymied for a time. But, after George S. Harris took control of the firm in 1961, Chicago Metropolitan began to expand.

In 1965 Harris and Dickerson explored the possibility of merging their two firms, but the plans were stillborn, largely because of resistance among the personnel of both companies. From that point onward, Chicago Metropolitan allied itself with the causes of black power, black pride, and race consciousness, which resulted in a higher profile for Chicago Metropolitan and increased profitability. Then, in 1971, Anderson M. Schweich replaced Harris, and he guided the firm into the 1990s. He took Chicago Metropolitan, like North Carolina Mutual, into the group insurance market, getting some of the group insurance business of General Foods Corporation, Jewel Companies, Inc., and Commonwealth Edison. By 1992 Chicago Mutual had over $2.8 billion of insurance in force, compared to just $1 billion for Supreme Life. Its premium income was nearly $19 million; Supreme's was $10.5 million. Supreme's assets, however, were almost the equal of Chicago Metropolitan's, and it remained relatively profitable.

Supreme Life's performance between 1989 and 1992 was curious. In the former year, it had $2.3 billion of insurance in force, a premium income of $21 million, and assets of over $55 million. In 1991, however, Supreme Life appeared to hold a virtual fire sale of its assets. During that year, Johnson sold off $39 million of assets to the United Insurance Company of America, cutting its total from $53 million to just $12 million. Johnson also claimed he wrote off nearly $4 million in real estate loans between 1985 and 1990. In 1987 he had stated, ''The real reason Supreme Life hasn't run into serious financial problems is because I put more money into it. It's that simple. We've written off just about all our bad properties; now we have a strong, viable real estate portfolio.'' He said that he wanted to sell the assets to black insurance companies, but they declined after reviewing the asset portfolios.

In 1992 Johnson claimed he had Supreme Life in ''fighting trim.'' ''All claims have been paid,'' he said, ''the staff has been trimmed; and Supreme Life still handles group and real estate insurance.'' Yet, Supreme Life was hardly the giant, dynamic firm it had been for decades. It had settled into an apparently profitable niche in the market, but was hardly the ''largest Negro business in the North'' any longer, nor was it even close to being the third-largest black insurance company, and it continued slowly sliding down *Black Enterprise*'s listings of top firms, resting at tenth place in 1992.

Yet Supreme Life had a grand past, and it was a past that included more than simply business influence. Harry Pace, as noted above, was a protean capitalist who was involved in a large number of highly creative enterprises. Truman K. Gibson was also a man of many parts. He was chairman of the Joint Negro Appeal Drive, a sponsor of the United Negro College Fund, and a member of the National Negro Insurance Association, the Urban League, and the NAACP. Vernon Jarrett, a writer for the *Chicago Tribune*, caught the significance of Gibson nicely. At the time of Gibson's death he was visiting Fisk University. Jarrett, who had known Gibson for many years, was badly shaken by the news, but when he asked the students if they had heard of him, they gave him only blank stares. Jarrett related that

all 15 [students] looked in amazement that I should ask such a question about this 90-year-old black man who grew up poor in Macon, Ga. and died last week in Chicago. Many of today's younger generation will tell you that the T. K. Gibsons of the world were merely a group of black people who failed because they attempted to be "just like whites." At the same time these young people will praise Marcus Garvey as being a "true black man." What they don't realize is that the Gibsons of America collectively contributed just as much, if not more, to black nationalism and black awareness as Garvey and his followers.

Gibson's two sons also had significant careers. Harry H. C. Gibson was for many years executive vice president of Supreme Life. Truman K. Gibson, Jr., was born in Atlanta, educated in Chicago, and graduated from the University of Chicago in 1932. While there, Gibson came under the tutelege of Professor Harold Gosnell, earning money as a 60-cents-an-hour "political observer" on assignment in the black political world. Much of the material he uncovered went into Gosnell's classic book, *The Negro Politician of Chicago*. This research gave Gibson access to William L. Dawson, then a leading Republican and later a Democratic congressman. Dawson was also closely allied with Earl Dickerson of Supreme Life. At Dawson's urging, Gibson attended law school at the University of Chicago, getting his degree in 1935. He then started practicing in Dawson's law firm and worked as an attorney in the city from 1935 to 1940. In that year he became assistant to Dr. William H. Hastie, a civilian aide to the secretary of war in Washington, D.C.

Hastie, dean of the Howard University Law School, was appointed by Secretary of War Stimson as a sop to blacks who were demanding integration of the armed forces. After three years of frustration in dealing with racism and segregation in the military, Hastie quit in disgust. Gibson was chosen as his replacement, but he also found himself powerless to effect any changes. He created a major controversy in early 1945 when he visited the all-black 92nd Division which had served in North Africa and Italy. In the latter theater, after a number of successes, it had suffered several defeats for which it was severely criticized. Gibson visited the division and was reported to have said that the 92nd "melted away" when faced with opposition. This seemed to reflect the sort of racist attitudes held by most whites at that time, and Gibson received a fire storm of criticism from the black press and black leaders. He responded by claiming he had been misquoted, that, in fact, he had been expressing the thoughts of a white general, Joseph T. McNarney. At another time, he claimed the statement was that of a reporter and he was just answering a question. Still later, he said that whatever defects the black troops had were due to the low educational equipment of the rank-and-file soldiers, which was, of course, no fault of the blacks. Soon after Gibson's statement, however, the army stopped recruiting blacks to serve as combat troops in the European theater. Gibson was under fire from all sides after that, and he resigned his post in 1945.

There were two events of significance for his later career during this period, however. First of all, Gibson intensified his relationship with Joe Louis, the heavyweight boxing champion of the world, for whom he had done some legal work before the war. Louis during the 1940s was serving in the army, and Gibson had frequent contact with him as the most famous African-American in the service. This would lead to Gibson's prominent career in boxing. Second, Gibson appeared before the Committee on the Armed Services of the U.S. Senate in 1948, which was discussing the question of universal military training. In his speech, he supported the idea of universal military training, basing that conclusion on the "aggression of the Soviet Union." He further made the point that "Universal Military Training, if adopted, should be truly universal in application . . . all physically qualified youth must be trained. This means that Negroes, comprising as they do 10 percent of the available manpower potential must be trained and must be used." This was an important factor in getting President Harry Truman's concept of the integration of the armed services accepted. In 1947 Truman awarded the Medal of Merit Award for Civilians to Gibson, who was the first African-American to receive the award. During this same period (1948–1951), Gibson was also a member of the President's Committee on Religion and Welfare in the Armed Forces.

Gibson's connections with Joe Louis served him well in the postwar years. Although he had done some legal and tax work for the champion prior to the war, Gibson had never had much interest in boxing itself. During the war, however, he caught the "bug." In 1943 Gibson suggested that Joe Louis head up a traveling troupe of black boxers to tour Army bases in an attempt to build morale. The War Department approved, and another future great boxer, Sugar Ray Robinson, became part of the troupe. Louis and Gibson soon developed a fast friendship, and Gibson continued to help Louis with his tax, financial, and legal problems. Gibson at the same time became addicted to the prize ring and to the tough, black "street kids" in the troupe.

After the war, Gibson helped Louis establish Joe Louis Enterprises as a means to handle the many promotional deals that were coming to the popular champion. Gibson also continued to fight the myriad of tax and financial problems Louis had. At the same time, the empire of Mike Jacobs, the boxing promoter who had managed Louis's career from the early days, was crumbling. Louis, in consultation with Gibson, decided to announce his retirement from boxing in

1948, and they negotiated a retirement package with the 20th Century Sporting Club. Then, Gibson and Louis went about setting up their own rival boxing promotion company, to be called the International Boxing Club (IBC). The idea was that, with Louis giving up his heavyweight title, they would sign the leading contenders, Ezzard Charles and Jersey Joe Walcott, to exclusive contracts and thus fully control the most lucrative end of professional boxing. Gibson then approached James Norris of Chicago for financial backing.

Norris was a millionaire grain speculator who had built a massive sports empire. He owned the 20,000-seat Chicago Stadium, where many of the matches promoted by the new organization would be held. Norris also owned the Chicago Black Hawks and the Detroit Red Wings hockey teams in the National Hockey League and had a large interest in Madison Square Garden in New York City. Having set up the IBC with Norris, Gibson went out and signed Charles and Walcott to contracts; Louis was paid $350,000 for the contracts along with a salary of $20,000 a year in the future. In doing so, Gibson hoped he had guaranteed Louis's financial security. This was not to be, but through no fault of Gibson's. Louis, who did not understand money well, continually withdrew funds from Joe Louis Enterprises and from IBC to continue living the good life. He was therefore forced to go back into the ring to pay his back taxes and other debts.

Gibson became secretary of the IBC, and, although Norris was the ultimate boss, Gibson was the man who ran the company on a day-to-day basis. His status with the organization was so important by 1951 that *Ebony* called him a "one-man brain trust of the pugilistic profession—the man to whom both champions and challengers must eventually come if they are to amount to much in boxing." The IBC was often referred to at that time as "Octopus, Inc.," because its tentacles seemed to reach everywhere. Gibson and Norris were also credited with changing the principal locale of professional boxing in the late 1940s and early 1950s from New York's Madison Square Garden to Chicago Stadium. Gene Ward, boxing reporter for the *New York Daily News*, acknowledged that change: "Chicago is the new boxing capital of the world. Madison Square Garden is just another Friday night stop on the television dial. Truman Gibson is a major factor in Chicago's new role." Gibson handled all aspects of the boxing game, from studying the contracts for fine-print clauses and setting ticket prices, to fending off summons servers and paying off the boxers.

Ebony reported that Gibson's "upper-crust Negro social friends" were skeptical as to just how long he could stand the "daily rubbing of elbows with the riff-raff and nondescripts who speckle the 'fight mob.' " But he displayed a remarkable comfortability in his new surroundings, perhaps conditioned by his political involvements of earlier days. Although Gibson and Norris had started out with a stable of mostly black boxers, and one in which Louis, Charles, and Walcott (all black) were the main drawing cards, it soon became clear that other talent had to be found. By 1951 the IBC's "great white hope" was Rocky Marciano, a tough but unschooled fighter from Boston. In October of that year,

Marciano was matched against the aging Joe Louis. Marciano beat Louis in a technical knockout and emerged as the new, hugely popular, heavyweight champion. Gibson, when criticized for the fact that the IBC was now pushing a white champion, replied, "We are out to make money, and I'll match an Eskimo with a Pampas bull if it'll bring people through those turnstiles out front. We try to present fighters who have the ability, the prestige and the correct ratings whether they are Negro or white."

Gibson's later career in boxing and other endeavors was fraught with problems. Until 1953 Gibson and Norris in the IBC promoted fights generating $2.3 million in revenues. In 1957, however, a New York federal judge ordered the IBC dissolved as a monopoly that violated federal antitrust laws. Two years later, on September 22, 1959, Gibson was arrested by the Federal Bureau of Investigation. He had been indicted in Los Angeles, along with four other men, on charges of extortion involving an attempt to take a share of the earnings on welterweight champion Don Jordan. On May 30, 1961, Gibson and the others were convicted, and Gibson received a suspended five-year sentence and a $5,000 fine. During his testimony, Gibson gave graphic testimony of the extent to which organized crime and gangsters dominated the fight game, claiming that it was just one of the facts of life of the business.

Gibson then returned to his law business, running his own firm of Gibson and Gibson, and served as a longtime director and member of the executive committee of Supreme Life. Then, in 1977, he again got in trouble with the law. He was indicted in a stock-swindle suit in federal court in New York City. In this, Gibson was involved with several other men in a venture to transform a rundown resort in the Bahamas into a vacation spa. Five years later, he pleaded no contest to that suit, and he was placed on six months' probation on the condition he make monthly payments of $1,000 on the principal sum and penalties. By the late 1980s, the total amount with interest, amounted to more than $200,000. By 1988 Gibson was in deep default on his payments, and he owed the government an immediate $13,000 payment in order to avoid jail. Gibson pleaded poverty, claiming to be broke. The government contended that the seventy-six-year-old man had deposited $80,000 into his bank account during the previous year. Judge Frank McGarr said, "Mr. Gibson has deliberately avoided the payment of this judgement over many years. He has frequently and admittedly commingled his clients' funds and his own funds, in violation of the canons of ethics binding upon him as an attorney."

Gibson, for his part, feigned surprise and hurt, claiming he could not afford to pay the money: "I get $1,000 a month from Social Security. . . . I don't know what is going to happen to me. I don't know what is going to happen next month. . . . I have no knowledge about any money coming in." He had other problems, too. In September 1987, Gibson was indicted by a federal court jury in Montana on charges involving an $80,000 bank fraud. He was placed on probation for five years on that charge and ordered to make restitution of $20,000. A separate state court ruling ordered him to pay $138,000 to two men who claimed they had lost their investment in a Gibson deal to take over an Italian winery.

In 1988 he emerged as one of the key figures in a nationwide dental health-care firm, Dental Health Care Alternatives. In 1986 he had become the chief salesman for the company, which was seeking government contracts in Chicago. Gibson was able to obtain contracts with the Chicago Transit Authority, the Chicago Board of Education, the Chicago Teachers Union, and Cook County. For his work, Gibson was promised a 7 percent commission and an unlimited expense account.

The contracts that Gibson negotiated were to generate more than $7 million a year in gross revenue, if all the contracts were signed. Gibson's commission thus would amount to more than $500,000 a year. In early 1988, however, the federal government launched an investigation into whether the firm had paid bribes to get contracts for health benefits programs. Gibson was unable to meet his January 1 deadline to cement the contracts. By February of that year, Gibson said that the contracts "never will come to anything because of the publicity" of the government investigation. It was all an ignominious denouement of what once seemed a spectacular career. As of 1992, he was still alive in Chicago, and had apparently avoided the clutches of the law on all the indictments against him.

Earl Dickerson, as noted above, had a spectacular career as a leader in Chicago politics and civil rights. He had cultivated his interest in politics as a student at the University of Illinois, and he made his first formal entrance into Chicago politics in 1923, when he was named head of the Negro Division of Democratic Mayor William Dever's campaign. As a result, he was named assistant corporation counsel for the city, a plum political appointment. It was a significant move for Dickerson, since at that time virtually all of the city's blacks were supporters of the Republican party. Dickerson continued to work for Democratic national, state, and citywide candidates throughout the 1920s, but he never ran for office himself during that time. Dickerson's first attempt to run for public office came in 1929, when he ran as an independent for the position of alderman of the Second Ward. He fared poorly, and two years later he returned to the Democratic fold.

During this same period, Dickerson became a leader in both the NAACP and the Urban League, as well as an outspoken protest leader in behalf of public housing. In 1931 he protested police brutality both in person to Mayor Cermak and through leading public protests, and in 1939 he began to represent Carl Hansberry, father of Lorraine Hansberry, author of *Raisin in the Sun*, in a case involving restrictive covenants in housing. In the meantime, his own career in elective politics took off. As one of the first black Democrats in Chicago, Dickerson was in an enviable position in the late 1930s, when Franklin Roosevelt's New Deal policies converted the mass of African-Americans in the city to the Democratic column. As a result, Dickerson again ran for the aldermanic position in the Second Ward in 1939, this time winning handily. At the same time, he had reached an agreement with William Dawson, the longtime black Republican alderman of the Second Ward, to join forces after the election, when Dawson crossed over to the Democratic party. Dickerson thus became a cog in the black subgroup of the powerful, new, Democratic machine that was emerging in the city.

Dickerson entered office as a fervent New Dealer but soon became a burr under the saddle of that machine, and much of the disagreement centered around the issue of housing and over Dickerson's role as a "reformer." Dickerson joined a series of organizations, such as the Midwest Committee for Protection of the Foreign Born, National Lawyers Guild, Free Earl Browder Conference, Abraham Lincoln School, International Labor Organization, and the Progressive party. All of these were advance guards of the great civil rights struggle of the 1950s and 1960s. Soon, Dickerson and Dawson were "at each other's throats."

Dickerson's most sensational public stance during this time, however, involved the Hansberry case. Carl A. Hansberry and Harry Pace had both purchased homes on Rhodes Avenue in 1937. This was an area where the property was covered by a restrictive covenant, and when the neighbors complained, they were instructed to move by court order. The state supreme court sustained the lower court. Dickerson pursued the case through the state courts to the U.S. Supreme Court. There, he won an impressive victory in 1940, when the Court ruled the restrictive covenants as nonexistent. The *Chicago Defender* was ecstatic, declaring, "Hansberry Decision Opens 500 New Homes to Negroes." It did, in fact, open up the Washington Park Subdivision for black residence and brought much fame and notoriety to Earl Dickerson. One of Dickerson's cocounsels in the case was Truman Gibson, Jr.

Dickerson also became involved in the "Double V" campaign during World War II, which urged, "You who are ready to enlist in the fight against Hitler abroad must seek to enlist in the fight against Hitler at home." As Charles Branham had commented, "[b]oth Dickerson's tactics and ideology were alien to the modus operandi of urban machine politics. He eschewed backroom politics, the trading of votes for patronage and enforced party discipline of the machine." When he disagreed with the city council's decision on an issue, he did not acquiesce; instead he organized a mailing campaign among blacks that flooded the council with thousands of letters and postcards on behalf of improved educational facilities for blacks. He outspokenly attacked the Chicago Housing Authority for being "over-cautious" in building low-income housing and rehabilitating old buildings. He demanded more "recognition" for blacks on all levels and on every issue, and he threatened mass demonstrations against proposed cuts in federal and state relief programs and in social security benefits.

Dickerson's pursuit of these social goals, and the abrasive tactics he used to try to attain them, did not endear him to his political colleagues. To get him out of their hair, the Democratic machine persuaded Roosevelt to appoint Dickerson to the Committee of Fair Employment Practices in 1941. This group was to investigate complaints of discrimination and make recommendations to the government, although it had no enforcement powers. Dickerson used his position to expose discrimination against blacks in an aircraft plant in Melrose Park, Illinois, and charged there was a "conspiracy" to keep blacks out of the various skilled craft unions in the city.

When Dickerson ran for U.S. Congress in 1942, he was opposed for the seat by Dawson, who had the full backing of the party. Dickerson ran as an independent, announcing that he "felt duty bound to fight against . . . the domination of ward politics by downtown political big-wigs who tell the people of the ward who their candidate shall be even though the downtown selections are against the will of the people." Dickerson received the endorsement of several black organizations and the *Chicago Defender*, as well as the Chicago AFL and CIO, but he had few allies within the Democratic party itself, and he suffered a devastating defeat, finishing third.

In 1943, when Dickerson ran for reelection to his aldermanic seat, he was opposed by a virtually unknown former city fireman, William Harvey, one of Dawson's henchmen. Dickerson ran largely against Dawson, launching bitter attacks on his one-time ally, whom he called "a big noise, gilt-edged uncle." Dickerson was soundly defeated in the election, and his political career was over. As he later reflected, he probably was not cut out for party politics: "I never was a fellow to hang around bars, fool around, kid and cajole people. I'd come in, sit down and talk, and speak . . . I'd go on my way." Many blacks in his ward thought of Dickerson as a "silk stocking," or elitist. Dickerson said, "I did everything wrong from the standpoint of promotion of myself." Charles Branham said, "He was too intellectual, too politically and philosophically radical, too litigious, too tied to community groups and public protest to fit him into the generations of old patterns of ethnic politics in Chicago. . . . He preferred the public protest style of pressure politics to the backstage negotiations which had always been the staple of party politics."

Throughout the late 1940s, and on through the 1950s, 1960s, and 1970s, Dickerson remained an important figure in the civil rights struggle in Chicago. He served as president of the Chicago Urban League and was a director of the National Urban League and the NAACP. He spent most of his life fighting discrimination and pushing for integration. By the mid–1970s, when much of what he had fought for had been accomplished, he expressed disappointment. At eighty-two years of age, he mused, "For over 50 years . . . I have been dedicated to the ultimate attainment of an integrated society as the means to solving this country's racial dilemma. But for the past few years now, I have seriously questioned whether integration, per se, is the appropriate answer." When he died in 1986, he was praised as one of the most important leaders of Chicago's black community. Dickerson himself, a few months before his death, said it best: "I left the desperate life of a black person in feudal Mississippi. I fled, clothed with little else than a burning sense of outrage and a driving resolve, cradled in the Declaration of Independence, not to be bullied, browbeaten, or held hostage, in fact or in spirit, ever again."

Certainly he was not. Dickerson was, as he himself said, "always something of a rebel," and each in their own way, Frank Gillespie and both Truman Gibsons were also. They were born into a world of prejudice and discrimination; one in which blacks were denied economic, political, and social opportunity, and they bent every effort in an attempt to create a better world for their race.

Sources

The company records of Supreme Liberty Life are not generally open to researchers, but some were used by Robert C. Puth in his dissertation on the company: "Supreme Life: The History of a Negro Life Insurance Company," Ph.D. diss., Northwestern University, 1967. Portions of his research have also been published as "Supreme Life: The History of a Negro Life Insurance Company," *Business History Review* XLIII, 1 (Spring 1969), 1–21; and "From Enforced Segregation to Integration: Market Factors in the Development of a Negro Life Insurance Company," in *Business Enterprise and Economic Change: Essays in Honor of Harold F. Williamson*, edited by Louis F. Cain and Paul J. Uselding (Kent, Ohio, 1973), 280–301. There is some other useful information on the company in *Ebony*, August 1946, November 1956, and October 1973; and *Chicago Defender*, November 18, 1969, and January 18, 1975. There is also a great deal of information on Supreme Liberty Life and its workings during the times when Harry H. Pace and John H. Johnson were running the firm. Those references can be found in the biographical sections in this volume on those men.

Personal papers and letters of Frank Gillespie and Truman Gibson are not currently available, but there is a clipping file on Gibson and his son at the Chicago Historical Society. That organization also has a scrapbook and clippings of Earl Dickerson in the Earl Dickerson Papers. There is little biographical information on Gillespie. The best is found in M. S. Stuart, *An Economic Detour* (New York, 1940). See also a very short obituary in *The Crisis* XXX (July 1925), 142; and some brief biographies in *Jet*, May 7, 1964; and *Ebony*, November 1956. An announcement of Gillespie's promotion at Royal Life is found in *The Crisis*, January 1916, 115.

On Gibson, the company had a brief biographical sketch giving the main events and affiliations of his life, but the best published biography is in Ingham, BDABL. *Harvard Class of 1908: Fiftieth Anniversary Report* (Cambridge, Mass., 1958), has a brief account of Gibson's life, as does *Atlanta University Bulletin* (July 1960 and December 1972), *Who's Who in Colored America, 1928–29*; and Cornelius V. Troup, *Distinguished Negro Georgians* (n.p., 1962), 64–65. There is also information in *Ebony*, August 1946; *Chicago Tribune*, July 23, 1955, September 1 and 2, 1972 (obituaries); *Sepia*, August 1962; and a very brief obituary in *Jet* 42 (September 14, 1972), 42. Gibson wrote an article for *New York Age*, March 27, 1920, on the founding of Supreme Life. There is information on his son, Truman K., Jr., in Chris Mead, *Champion—Joe Louis* (New York, 1985); and Roi Ottley, *Black Odyssey* (New York, 1948), 293–94; *Ebony*, June 1949, November 1951, November 1956, and June 1969; *Time*, December 19, 1960; *Norfolk Journal & Guide*, October 5, 1946; *Afro-American*, February 13, 1943; and *Chicago Tribune*, February 21, 1988. Gibson's speech to Congress on the draft is found in U.S. Congress, Senate, Committee on the Armed Services, "Universal Military Training" (Washington, D.C., 1948).

There is an abundance of material on Dickerson, but most of it deals with his political and civil rights activities; there is less coverage of his business life. Portions of a more extensive oral interview with Dickerson is published in Dempsey Travis, *An Autobiog-*

raphy of Black Chicago (Chicago, 1981). See also *Ebony*, December 1961, December 1984, and November 1985; and Frederick H. Robb, *The Negro's Progress in Chicago: A Who's Who of a Thousand in 1929* (Chicago, 1929). There are obituaries and memorials to Dickerson in several Chicago newspapers; see especially *Chicago Sun Times*, June 27, 1976, September 3, 4, and 5, and October 21, 1986; *Chicago Tribune*, September 4, 1986; and *Chicago Daily News*, January 19, 1974. See also Robert McClory, "A Supreme Life: Earl Dickerson at 92," *Reader* 13 (January 1984); *Illinois Democracy*, vol. II (1935); Ed Wilson, "The Chicago Negro in Politics," *The Voice*, March 1907, 102. There is important contextual information on Dickerson's career in politics in Charles Russell Branham, "The Transformation of Black Political Leadership in Chicago, 1864–1942," Ph.D. diss., University of Chicago, 1981. See also Harold Gosnell, *Negro Politicians: The Rise of Negro Politics in Chicago* (Chicago, 1935); Dianne M. Pinderhughes, *Race and Ethnicity in Chicago Politics: A Reexamination of the Pluralist Theory* (Urbana, Ill., 1987); Paul Kleppner, *Chicago Divided: The Making of a Black Mayor* (DeKalb, Ill., 1985); and Dempsey Travis, *An Autobiography of Black Politics* (Chicago, 1987). A general understanding of Chicago politics when Dickerson was emerging is found in John M. Allswang, *A House for All Peoples, Ethnic Politics in Chicago, 1908–1936* (Lexington, Ky., 1971).

Durnford, Andrew (1800–July 12, 1859). Sugar planter, Louisiana. Andrew Durnford was a sugar planter and land speculator. Like William Ellison[*] and William Johnson,[*] he was an African-American who used slaves to increase the size of his business operation and make more money. Although historian John Hope Franklin said, "There is no doubt that most of the free blacks who owned slaves did so for humanitarian reasons," Andrew Durnford certainly was not one of those. He was a stern master; one whose only revealed concern about his slaves was the financial gain or loss that they might bring him. He made little or no profit over the years in his sugar production, but he did grow wealthy over his purchases and exploitation of land and slaves. Durnford, the son of a white father and an African-American mother, by all accounts felt more comfortable with, and kinship toward, whites than blacks. But as Joel Williamson pointed out in *The New People*, he was of a race apart, a third caste in the South, that of the mulatto who existed on the margins of both societies, never quite fitting into either one.

Andrew Durnford was born in New Orleans, Louisiana, in 1809, the son of Thomas Durnford, a wealthy white merchant, moneylender, and slave owner, and Rosaline Mercier, a free woman of color. Thomas Durnford was a native of England who came to America as a boy of fourteen in 1776. He settled with his cousin in Pensacola, Florida, where he worked as a clerk for the British army and then began to engage in trade between British Florida and New Orleans. While in Pensacola, Thomas Durnford evidently had a relationship with a free woman of color there, producing a mulatto son, Joseph Durnford, a free black who would be Andrew Durnford's half brother, and who later visited Andrew on several occasions. When Thomas Durnford moved to New Orleans, he established a housekeeping relationship with Rosaline Mercier. Although they were not married, there was evidently a legal agreement between them, and she was referred to as the *placée*. As such, she was guaranteed that she would be supported in a particular manner and that any children produced by the union would be secure, in financial terms and as to their status as free persons of color. After Thomas Durnford died in 1826, his will stipulated that Rosaline Mercier receive $1,716 for services rendered. John McDonough was appointed curator of the estate and, in this way, became the guardian of Andrew Durnford and later also his close friend and protector.

John McDonough was a wealthy, successful, New Orleans businessman who was also a staunch foe of slavery and a major benefactor of the American Colonization Society. McDonough was also an important philanthropist in other areas, and he left a good deal of money in his will for the public schools of New Orleans. When Andrew Durnford came of age, McDonough acted as financier and business advisor to the young man and remained a lifelong friend, even maintaining a room in his home for Durnford when the young man visited New Orleans. The nature of McDonough's affection for Durnford can be gleaned by a comment he made when young Andrew did not stay with him during a trip to New Orleans: "You profess great friendship," McDonough lectured, "[but] you come to the city and stay several days and away you go without giving me sight of you."

Andrew Durnford's life prior to 1828 is obscure. He was relatively well educated in both French and English and knew enough mathematics to be able to practice medicine. He also probably received business training from his father and from McDonough. In addition, McDonough, who owned sugar plantations, undoubtedly schooled the young black man in the intricacies of sugar cultivation and manufacture. By 1828 Durnford had accumulated enough capital to be able to purchase ten arpents (about eight and one-half acres) of frontage on the Mississippi River in Plaquemines Parish, along with fourteen slaves. Much of this capital was inherited in the form of cash from his mother and tracts of land in New Orleans and McDonoughville, some of which he sold. By this time he had also married Charlotte Remy, a free woman of color, who may have brought a dowry with her. Durnford purchased the land which would become St. Rosalie Plantation from John McDonough, who accepted a 6 percent mortgage, less than the 10 percent McDonough had charged Andrew's father. The price was $25,000. In addition, Durnford paid about $500 a piece for his slaves, a total investment of about $32,000.

Andrew Durnford's plantation was located about thirty-three miles south of New Orleans, on a bend in the Mississippi River. Over the next four years, Durnford acquired other contiguous acres from McDonough, for another $47,500. Then, in partnership with McDonough, Durnford began to cultivate and produce sugar. Durnford ran his plantation for some thirty years with indifferent results. David Whitten, who has done an in-depth analysis of his operation, concluded, "Andrew Durnford cannot be considered a successful sugar planter." The cause of this situation was the deterioration of the general condition of the plantation, along with possible soil exhaustion, which reduced output. This had a negative impact on the profitability of the sugar production aspect of his operations. He was, however, far more successful as a landowner and speculator and particularly, as a slave owner. Durnford's sugar plantation, like most others, was vertically integrated forward to include manufacturing. Because sugarcane was too bulky to transport economically, it was the practice to process it at or near the point of cultivation. He therefore transported heavy machinery by river to his plantation. His farm machinery was ultimately worth some $10,000. Durnford produced both sugar and molasses.

In the early years of his operation, Durnford particularly had problems securing sufficient labor to run his operations profitably. Although he had fourteen slaves, this was not enough. Over the next three years, he purchased additional slaves, so that by 1831 he had twenty-two slaves, of whom just three were under ten years of age. In 1832 Durnford bought an additional male slave for $620, the highest sum Durnford had expended to that date for a slave. He complained bitterly to McDonough about the high prices of slaves: "I fear that Negroes will sell high in six months or a year, therefore I hope ere this you have met with a bargain for me." These slaves were not enough to provide all of his labor needs, so during these first few years Durnford was also forced to hire white and black free labor and to rent slaves from other owners. Hired labor, however, was scarce and expensive, so Durnford determined to go to Virginia in 1835, where he hoped to secure better bargains in his slave purchases. Durnford revealed his plans to McDonough in a letter on February 8, 1834: "I came down with P[ackwood]. He advised me very much to gett people and says that I cannot do as my neighbors to make 3 and 400 hogsheads without augmenting my force."

In May 1835, Andrew Durnford landed in Philadelphia, where he sold his sugar for $8,312 and departed for Richmond. There he found the prices for slaves to be higher than he expected: "Slaves are high. The Alabamian[s] are paying high prices, they have spoiled the market. . . . I have fears that people could nott be gott easy and at our premeditated prices, butt I will and must do for the best." Despite the high prices, Durnford did manage to make a number of purchases: "I have bought a woman with two children for the sum of 625$ one of about 4 years old the other a couple of month's, both boys." Because of the high prices in Richmond, Durnford decided to ride out to the countryside, attempting to buy slaves from the farmers themselves. He found this was not as fruitful as he had hoped, and complained: "I could have bought some cheaper but, they are what I call rotton people. My thighs is all blistered riding round of within twenty miles of Richmond. . . . I can't stay no longer. Blacks are getting higher every day, even the Negro traders are surprised at the prices demanded." Ultimately, Durnford bought twenty-five slaves in Virginia for a total of $6,876. Durnford made no further purchases of slaves until 1842, when he bought five adult slaves from McDonough for $5,500. By the end of Durnford's life in 1859, he owned seventy-seven slaves with a market value of $71,550.

Durnford also worried about the difficulty and expense of transporting the slaves back to Louisiana: "If a few getts sick on the way I will have to stay and expend what few dollars I may have left." Later he complained, "My lot is children. They can't walk, and if half a dozen get sick on the way, it would fill up my waggon, prevent my traveling." Later, when he had an accident on the trip home, Durnford showed more concern for his financial loss than for the life of the young African-American boy that was lost: "I had the misfortune to have lost the biggest of those boys that I brought from Virginia by a cart running away with him last monday. He died in the night, the Lord's will be with us all!" Later that year he commented, "Lost another child. All is well." The latter phrase seems particularly heartless but may simply mean that no epidemic or mass death was expected. Nonetheless, it was clear that Durnford had little personal involvement with his slaves.

Durnford was, in David Rankin's terms, a "tough and tight-fisted master." He apparently did not clothe his slaves well, since he wrote in 1834 that he needed "a piece of linsey [because] some of my people is naked." He also fed them the cheapest food available, which may account for their sickliness, and may be one reason that productivity on St. Rosalie Plantation declined over the years. Although there is, according to Whitten, "little evidence" of corporal punishment at St. Rosalie, Durnford's treatment of slaves who disobeyed or ran away was stern. His slave Jackson was a troublesome presence, and in 1836 Durnford ordered him whipped for stealing corn. The next day Jackson ran away, and Durnford wrote, "I wish to lay eyes on him once more. I will fix him so the dogs will not bark at him." When he recovered the slave seven months later, Durnford noted that Jackson "had the audacity to go away [again] with all the iron I had putt on him." By 1847 Durnford had dismissed Jackson as crazy, saying, "I believe him to be a little out of his head."

Unlike McDonough, Durnford never had much interest in emancipating his own slaves, nor was he all that impressed with the work McDonough was doing. McDonough had emancipated some eighty-five slaves and had sent them to the colony in Liberia that had been started by the American Colonization Society. McDonough would allow his slaves to work for their freedom, earning enough money to buy a slave to replace their labor in the fields. The plan required years of labor, but then they would be transported to Liberia to begin life anew. In 1843 McDonough asked Durnford's opinion of his plan for emancipation. Durnford did not think much of it, believing it was ultimately impractical because masters would not part with their slaves, if they had any business sense at all, and the slaves would never be able to save enough money to free themselves and finance a new start in Africa. Durnford addressed the latter issue, saying, "Of all your slaves sent to Africa how many of them went away with any pecuneary [sic] means called their own. Nely probably and her mother are the only ones, depend on it." The problem, Durnford believed, was that neither masters nor slaves "have the moral courage to deprive themselves of luxuries." But, of course, neither did Durnford. He needed labor on his plantation, and labor was scarce and expensive. The most efficient form of labor available to him was slaves, and he was determined to use them. If he was troubled by this, the evidence in his letters is scant indeed. In fact, one might surmise that McDonough's great wealth allowed him the luxury to follow his expensive plan of emancipation. Most other planters, black or white, could not afford to do this. Then, too, for a black like Durnford, owning slaves was a form of insurance as white southern society became more alarmist about free blacks and the influence of abolitionists. They could hardly worry about Durnford becoming an advocate of abolition if he owned slaves himself. That certainly must have been in the back of his mind when he gave his exceedingly lukewarm support to McDonough's emancipation schemes.

Although Durnford and his family did not live in luxury on their plantation, they did experience the life of a comfortable farm family. Durnford kept up with the news of the world and was quite well read, with his own impressive library. In addition, Durnford purchased and transported to St. Rosalie a fancy carriage and leather to make its harness equipment, which was his one real luxury item. He also bought an armoire, cigars, a coop of chickens, soap, sweet oil, bologna, chocolate, chewing tobacco, roach poison, and other sundries. He sent his son away to a good school in New Orleans. In most respects, Durnford lived the life of a solid, respectable planter in rural Louisiana. There is little or nothing in his actions to distinguish him from fellow white planters of the same socioeconomic level. To be sure, he must have suffered discrimination, but that seldom, if ever, was alluded to in his letters.

Andrew's oldest son, Thomas McDonough Durnford, was educated at a private school in New Orleans and then sent to Lafayette College in Easton, Pennsylvania. Following his graduation there, he went to medical school and became a physician in New Orleans, dividing his time between that city and Paris. Another son, Andrew Jr., along with his sister, Rosema, continued to run the family plantation after the Civil War but were not successful. In 1874, beseiged by creditors, they were forced to sell St. Rosalie for a few thousand dollars. Sarah Mary Durnford, daughter of Andrew, Jr., and granddaughter of the original Andrew, taught for many years in the schools in New Orleans, retiring in 1952.

David Whitten wrote that "Andrew Durnford was a rare American." That certainly seems to be the case. Part of a privileged elite, he was able to move with ease in the refined circles of white aristocratic planters and merchants. Yet, he also knew the pain of discrimination and racism and must, of necessity, have learned the subtle nuances of racial etiquette in order to survive. Mostly, he probably saw himself as existing in a raw jungle, one in which he had to be smarter and tougher than the next person. This is reflected in a quote from Durnford:

I think society is made up of two distinctive parts. On one hand wolves and foxes, and on the other lambs and chickens providing food for the former. In the forest a lion recognizes another lion, tiger does not make another tiger his prey, only man is man's enemy.

Sources

A large number of Andrew Durnford's letters are contained in the John McDonough Collection in the Manuscripts, Rare Books and University Archives, Tulane University Library. That library also has Andrew Durnford's St. Rosalie Plantation Journal. In the same library, there are also some letters and other materials on Durnford in the Rosamund E. and Emile Kuntz Collection. See also Plaquemines Parish Notarial Books (Pointe-a-la-Hache, Plaquemines Parish Court House).

David Whitten has written a biography and a number of important articles about Andrew Durnford. The biography is *Andrew Durnford: A Black Sugar Planter in Antebellum Louisiana* (Natchitoches, La., 1981). See also his "Slave Buying in 1835 Virginia as Revealed by Letters of a Louisiana Negro Sugar Planter," *Louisiana History* 11, 3 (1970), 231–44; "A Black Entrepreneur in Antebellum Louisiana," *Business History Review* 45, 2 (1971), 201–19; and "Rural Life along the Mississippi: Plaquemines Parish, Louisiana, 1830–50," *Agricultural History* 58, 3 (1984), 477–87. Durnford's slave owning is put into a broader perspective by David Rankin's "Black Slaveholders: The Case of Andrew Durnford," *Southern Studies* 21, 3 (1982), 343–48. Durnford is also mentioned in Herbert E. Sterkx, *The Free Negro in Antebellum Louisiana* (Rutherford, N.J., 1972), 203; and his descendents after the Civil War are briefly treated in Loren Schweninger, "Antebellum Free Persons of Color in Postbellum Louisiana," *Louisiana History* 30, 4 (Fall 1989), 355.

Dutrieuille, Peter Albert (1838–1916) and **Albert E. Dutrieuille** (July 26, 1877–April 25, 1974). Caterers: P. Albert Dutrieuille Caterer and Albert E. Dutrieuille Catering. From a family of French West African descent, Albert Dutrieuille was the last of the great African-American caterers in Philadelphia. As such, he proudly represented a magnificent family and a racial heritage that lasted over 150 years. Henry M. Minton in 1913 sang the praises of this group: "No other city in America has been so famed for its efficient and successful caterers as this." Minton would know. His grandfather, also Henry Minton, had migrated from Virginia to Philadelphia in 1830. After apprenticing as a shoemaker, he became a waiter and then opened his own very successful dining room and catering service. His son, Theophilus, became a lawyer, and his grandson, Henry M., opened the first black-owned licensed pharmacy in Pennsylvania and went on to become a doctor. Catering built some of Philadelphia's largest and most important black fortunes.

The most famous of Philadelphia's early caterers, and the man who was said to have "set in motion catering as we know it today," was Robert Bogle. He was a waiter who recognized that, although wealthy individuals liked to entertain, they did not wish to expand the retinue of their own kitchens to throw a formal dinner party. Bogle thus contracted to furnish the entire meal with his own personnel. His charm and polished manners so impressed the banker Nicholas Biddle that in 1829 he immortalized Bogle's accomplishments in an "Ode to Bogle." Bogle was also an astute businessman who ran a popular funeral service and was active in the civic life of the city's black community.

Bogle's contemporary as a caterer was Peter Augustine, who began his concern in the city in 1816 where it was still operating over a century later. Augustine, a native of the West Indies, set up his business on Third Street above Spruce. He served the best white families of the city and included a number of famous foreign visitors among his clientele. Perhaps the most famous was Charles Dickens, who praised the terrapin prepared by Major Teagle, one of Augustine's chefs. Dickens's acclaim made Augustine's fame worldwide, and he was often asked to send his terrapin as far away as Paris. Three sons and their mother carried on the business after Peter's death. When one of these sons married Clara Baptiste, the family became allied with another great catering family, and they created the firm of Augustine and Baptiste.

Eugene Baptiste, the progenitor of that family, came to Philadelphia in 1811 and settled in the French Colony, an area now known as Society Hill. There he first worked as a cabinetmaker, but, because of his wife's skill in the culinary arts, they decided to go into the catering business together in about 1818. They soon were running a large and successful business on Walnut Street. When Clara Baptiste married Theodore Augustine, the two great catering dynasties were united under the name Augustine and Baptiste, which flourished at 255 South 15th Street for years. Its successor, John J. Baptiste, located his business in West Philadelphia, where it continued as the oldest catering firm in the city. It was into this dynamic family and bustling business that Peter Albert Dutrieuille married and began to serve an apprenticeship. It was, however, a time of painful transition for the great black catering families of the city.

During the period from 1845 to 1875, Philadelphia catering had been ruled by what W.E.B. Du Bois called the "triumvirate" of Dorsey, Minton, and Jones. We have already met Minton, and Jones was another Virginia native who developed a reputation for care and faithfulness, building an excellent business catering to families in Philadelphia, New Jersey, and New York until he died in 1875. The most important of the triumvirate, however, was Thomas J. Dorsey. Dorsey was born a slave in Maryland in 1810, and in 1856 he and his family left for Philadelphia by way of William Still's* Underground Railroad. His master made an attempt to have Dorsey returned to slavery, but he was rescued by his friends through a payment of $1,000. Although he had been born a slave and had little formal education, Dorsey developed a refined instinct for dining and entertaining, so that some of the greatest luminaries of nineteenth-century Philadelphia dined at his table on Locust Street. Like Jones, Dorsey also died in 1875. His progeny were among the most eminent of African-Americans in the city.

In the late 1870s the place of African-Americans in the catering and restaurant profession in Philadelphia began to decline. There were a number of reasons for this change. New styles of European cooking were introduced by immigrants coming into the city during these years. Many of these individuals were able to put far greater amounts of capital into their enterprises than the average black caterer could afford. At the same time, elegant hotel dining rooms and other upscale dining rooms began to replace home dining to a certain extent. Black caterers thus had to refocus their business on the middle class rather than the upper class and also had to combat increasing prejudice and racism against blacks in industries serving a white clientele. Thus began a long, slow decline of the black catering profession in Philadelphia. The Dutrieuille family, however, was able to continue this tradition successfully for a longer period than anyone else.

The first of the Dutrieuilles in America, Pierre Albert, had come to Philadelphia from Bordeaux, France, by way of the French West Indies. He married Mary Lambert and had two sons. One of them was Peter Albert Dutrieuille, who was born in the city in 1838. Peter was educated in the public schools and then worked as a shoemaker for seven years. After he married Amelia Baptiste, daughter of Mr. and Mrs. Eugene Baptiste, in November 1864, Dutrieuille decided to enter the catering field and worked as an apprentice in the Augustine and Baptiste firm. Having gotten a good foundation in both the culinary and business aspects of the industry, Peter Dutrieuille decided to open his own operation in 1873. He set up business in his own home at 108 S. Eighteenth Street, just below Chestnut. Dutrieuille soon attracted the business of a number of Philadelphia's financial tycoons, including T. DeWitt Cuyler, who even offered to finance him in establishing a branch operation in New York City. Mrs. Dutrieuille reportedly summarily dismissed that idea.

In company with others, Peter Dutrieuille also organized the Caterer's Manufacturing and Supply Company for furnishing caterers with tables, chairs, linens, glasses, silver, and chinaware. He served several terms as president of this concern and was also intimately involved with the Philadelphia Caterers Association, which was essentially a trade union for the city's black caterers. The elder Dutrieuille also was the promoter of the Pioneer Building and Loan Association, called "one of the best of its kind in Philadelphia" by the attorney Charles Fred White. Dutrieuille served as treasurer of that organization for twenty-five years, and was also connected with the Quaker City Beneficial Association, in which he held a number of offices, the Negro Historical Society, and St. Mary's Catholic Beneficial Society. Dutrieuille also belonged to a number of literary clubs in the city. Toward the end of his life, the *Commercial Journal* of Philadelphia in 1910 said of Dutrieuille: "We have in this city a number of the best caterers in the East . . . men, who from broad experience, have truly made catering a fine art. Prominent among them is Mr. P. Albert Dutrieuille, who for many years has had charge of the gastronomic features and feasts of the very generous properties of the elite and exclusive functions that have been given in this city." He was a staunch Roman Catholic and a member of St. Joseph's Catholic Church throughout his life.

Albert E. Dutrieuille was educated in the city's schools, but at an early age he began to assist his father in the catering business in the fashionable Rittenhouse Square area. After his marriage to Florence May Waters in 1900, Albert was given increasing authority in running the operation, although the elder Dutrieuille refused to cede ultimate control to him. Albert's most important independent venture during these years was when he headed the concession at several army camps during World War I. After his father's death, Albert took full control of the business and changed the name to Albert E. Dutrieuille Catering in 1917.

A typical meal catered by Albert Dutrieuille was one prepared for the Mutual Assurance Company in 1937. He served caviar on toast, a horseradish chili sauce, bisque of mushroom soup, currant jelly, spinach and eggplant, Virginia ham, celery salad, ice cream cakes, coffee, and various hors d'oeuvres. Although Albert retained many of his father's fashionable clients, increasingly his business came from the Roman Catholic clergy and church-related events and celebrations. Some of the most important of his clients were Dennis Cardinal Dougherty, of Philadelphia, and Gerald P. O'Hara, apostolic delegate to London for the pope. Dutrieuille himself was deeply religious and much involved in Catholic lay activities.

Albert Dutrieuille and his family were very much part of which became the "Old Philadelphia" black elite, especially after the great migration of southern blacks during and after World War I. He took particular pride in his participation in the founding of the Olde Philadelphia Club, and he was the last surviving founder when he died. The other founders, including Henry M. Minton, were from among Philadelphia's oldest and most revered black elite families. Albert continued to operate the catering business until 1967, when he retired at the age of eighty-nine. When Albert Dutrieuille died in 1974, at the age of ninety-seven, it marked the end of a truly important era in the history of Philadelphia and America.

Sources

The Albert E. Dutrieuille Catering Records are available at the Balch Institute for Ethnic Studies. Two daybooks and a financial ledger make up the largest part of the collection, but also included are correspondence, receipts, invoices, and other materials. The collection also contains a biography of the Dutrieuille family and a few newspaper clippings. The Historical Society of Pennsylvania has a history of the family, written by Bernice Dutrieuille Shelton. Other sources of information include Charles Frederick White, *Who's Who in Philadelphia* (Philadelphia, 1912); G. James Fleming and Bernice D. Shelton, "Fine Food for Philadelphia," *The Crisis*, April 1938, 107, 114; R. R. Wright, Jr., *The Philadelphia 1908 Colored Directory* (Philadelphia, 1908); *Nixon's Classified Directory of Negro Business Interests and Professions in Pennsylvania* (Philadelphia, 1928); and WPA Project, "The Negro in Philadelphia" (Philadelphia, 1938). Information on the black elite of Philadelphia, and the Dutrieuilles' place within that comes from Linn Washington, "In the Shadows of History: Philadelphia's Black Achievers," *Philadelphia Daily News*, Educational Supplement, February 11, 1988; Emma Jones Lapsansky, "Before the Model City: An Historical Exploration of North Philadelphia" (1969); Willard Gatewood, *Aristocrats of Color* (Bloomington, Ind., 1990); and Charles Ashley Hardy III, "Race and Opportunity: Black Philadelphia during the Era of the Great Migration, 1916–1930," Ph.D. diss., Temple University, 1989.

E

Ellison, William (1790–December 5, 1861). Planter, Stateburg, South Carolina.
Michael P. Johnson and James L. Roark recount a poignant incident in Ellison's
life in their book *Black Masters*. On June 20, 1820, a free black man by the
name of April Ellison appeared before a magistrate in Sumterville, South Carolina, to change his name to William. "April" was recognizable as a slave
name, and the name change, his lawyer argued, "altho' apparently unimpor-
tant[,] would yet greatly advance his interest as a tradesman." It would also
"save him and his children from degradation and contempt which the minds of
some do and will attach to the name 'April.' " The judge granted the request,
and Ellison was able, in effect, to nearly start his life anew as a free man with
a new name. He went on to become the largest cotton gin maker in the state,
the wealthiest free black in South Carolina, and a "black master," a free black
who owned a large number of African-American slaves in his own right.

William Ellison's early life, like that of so many other black slaves, is shrouded
in mist. From his tombstone, we learn that he was born in 1790, but not the
day or the month. He was a slave on the Ellison plantation near Winnsboro, in
the Fairfield district of South Carolina. His master was either William Ellison,
or Ellison's father, Robert. His mother was a slave, probably on that plantation.
Since April Ellison was of mixed racial origins, we know his father was white,
and, given his treatment in later years, was probably either William or Robert
Ellison, but that is conjecture. The area in South Carolina, as Johnson and Roark
note, was "barely a generation removed from the frontier" at that time. The
white Ellison family was not among the elite of that upcountry area of the state,
owning about fifteen slaves, but Robert Ellison was in a comfortable, even
prosperous situation.

The young slave April received exceptional treatment from his master, even
while still a slave, providing strong evidence for one of the white Ellisons being
his father. Rather than sending the young man into the fields to work as was
customary, in 1802 April's master apprenticed him to William McCreight, a
young white gin maker in Winnsboro. He worked there for four years, receiving

training in every phase of that vitally important, growing business. April not only learned the mechanical rudiments of the design, construction, and repair of the newly developed cotton gin, but also learned to read and write and acquired basic skills in bookkeeping. Working in McCreight's shop also taught April a number of important social skills, which would later allow him to conduct business with white planters in the efficient, yet delicately nuanced, way so important for blacks.

Evidence indicates that April's master, William Ellison, was preparing him for freedom by providing him with the gin making apprenticeship. The skills would be of only limited use on the master's plantation, and April was given an education similar to the one Robert Ellison gave to his own sons. In January 1811, the twenty-year-old April had a daughter with a slave woman named Matilda on his home plantation. His daughter, Eliza Ann, automatically inherited the slave status of her mother. Five years later, on June 8, 1816, William Ellison, with April, appeared before a magistrate and five freeholders from the district to seek permission to emancipate his slave. A key to granting this request was proof presented by them that April had the "ability to gain a livelihood in an honest way." Later testimony indicated that April purchased his freedom from his master; that it was not given solely out of benevolence.

Upon his emancipation, the twenty-six-year-old ex-slave set himself up in business as a maker and repairer of cotton gins in Stateburg, South Carolina, about forty miles from Winnsboro. Stateburg in 1816 was a sleepy little settlement with a tavern, an academy, a store, and a church. But it was surrounded by vast estates capable of supporting a "small aristocracy in splendid style." Thus, there was a ready market there for young April's expertise, and the area also had a reputation for relative tolerance toward free blacks. In 1820 there were more free African-Americans in the Sumter district, of which Stateburg was a part, than in any other rural district in South Carolina. Within a year, Ellison had purchased the freedom of his wife and daughter, and they joined him in Stateburg. During the next five years, three sons—Henry, William, Jr., and Reuben—were born as free men in Stateburg. As they grew older, the three sons joined their father's gin business, becoming important cogs in its operation.

Even more important for the growth and prosperity of Ellison's business, however, was his use of slave labor. By 1820 Ellison had already managed to purchase two adult male slaves to work in his shop, and over the years he continued to add to the number of slaves he employed. This decision seems ironic in many respects. Here is a man, who had recently won his own freedom and that of his wife and children, turning around and owning slaves himself. Nor was there much sense of racial solidarity here, of identifying with the plight of those he enslaved, because they shared a common skin color and heritage. As Johnson and Roark note, there was never a hint in the Ellison letters that he ever had the slightest guilt or compunction about the ownership of slaves. There were several reasons for this. First of all, slave ownership was the key to enhanced prosperity in the South, for blacks or whites. If Ellison wished to become something more than a simple tradesman, and the evidence is abundant that he did, he would need to use the labor of slaves, since the acquisition of each slave allowed him to build and repair more gins and thereby make more money.

Also, the ownership of slaves protected Ellison and his family, as free African-Americans, from insinuations that they might be antislavery. How could they be against slavery if they shared a stake in the South's "peculiar institution?" Nor, as Johnson and Roark argue, was skin color and cultural heritage a link between Ellison and his slaves. He and his family were light-skinned mulattoes, whereas all of his slaves were classified in the federal census as "black." The evidence for this insistence on a racial difference by light-skinned African-Americans to differentiate them from their darkhued brethren is legion, both in contemporary accounts and historical analyses. Perhaps one observation may suffice. An agent of the American Colonization Society (not, to be sure, a totally disinterested observer) attended a large Methodist Church in Charleston in 1847 and reported "that the blacks and mulattoes did not sit together," and he was informed that mulattoes "utterly refused to sit promiscuously with blacks; and that, in all relations in life, they maintain the same dignified reserve; that the two classes are as totally distinct as it is possible for them to be." Thus, there appeared to be little racial affinity between William Ellison and his black slaves.

Nor is there any evidence that Ellison owned slaves in order to free them, or because they were members of his own family, or in some way to protect them from greater abuse by white slaveholders. Every shred of evidence Johnson and Roark were able to uncover indicates that Ellison was a stern taskmaster. Local gossip claimed he was an unusually harsh owner. This claim cannot be substantiated with any confidence, but neither is there any evidence that Ellison showed any exceptional kindness toward his slaves. In fact, the evidence that does exist portrays a rather cold and heartless attitude. Calculating from the federal census rosters in 1850 and 1860, Johnson and Roark determined that Ellison must have sold a goodly number, perhaps as many as twenty, female slave children. Furthermore, in his will he directs the sale of a female child slave, so there is little question that he had few guilty feelings about this practice. That which was considered the most reprehensible practice of slaveowners, that is, the breaking up of families and the selling of small children to owners of other plantations, was evidently freely practiced by William Ellison. The sale of these female children allowed Ellison to buy more adult slaves and thereby expand his highly profitable operations still further. It was an economic calculation, but one unfettered by even the slightest blush of racial solidarity or compassion with persons who shared a status endured by Ellison himself not too many years before. Also, when Ellison's slaves ran away, which they did on occasion, he was not loath to use the services of slave catchers to bring them back. So the specter of runaway slaves being pursued through the swamps by baying dogs and cruel white mercenaries also tainted Ellison's career as a slaveholder.

As the cotton economy of the South and of South Carolina boomed, the number of slaves owned by Ellison increased, and as his slave population increased, Ellison's gin making business grew along with it, Furthermore, as Ellison made more and more money from the manufacture and repair of cotton gins, he began to invest part of the profits in land, and, by buying still more slaves, both male and female, began to grow cotton himself. Finally, to these profitable lines he added a general blacksmithing and carpentry business that also brought in a good deal of money.

Ellison's gin making operations, although he was not without competition, became the largest in the area, and he also shipped his gins as far away as Mississippi. By 1850 his annual income from his shop was $3,000, of which one-half came from his general blacksmithing and carpentry work. Although this does not sound like a great deal of income, Ellison's expenses were low, and he was able on this steady, dependable income rapidly to achieve a comfortable economic status in Stateburg. A visible manifestation of this came in 1835, when he purchased the home and fifty-four acres that belonged to Stephen D. Miller, former governor of the state, for $1,200. The home, a large and comfortable two-story frame structure, was hardly ostentatious, which might offend some of Ellison's white neighbors.

The growth of Ellison's fortune in slaves and land was impressive. In 1820, as mentioned above, he had two adult male slaves. By 1830 he had doubled the number of his slaves to four, and during that decade he also put his sons to work in the gin shop. The result was a great increase in Ellison's prosperity, which was reflected in his ability to manufacture and repair more gins, buy more slaves, and purchase additional lands. By 1840 Ellison owned thirty adult slaves, a 750 percent increase from the previous decade, and his profits skyrocketed. Because nine of these thirty slaves were women, it meant two things—he also now had some slave children on his property, and he could buy lands on which to plant foodstuffs and cotton, which could be at least partially worked by the female slaves. Therefore, during the 1830s, Ellison began to buy more and more land, most of it in fields in which he could use the labor of his slave women. By 1840 he owned more than 330 acres of prime acreage in the Sumter District.

Ellison's pattern of success continued during the 1840s and 1850s. In the prior decade, he also watched his sons make highly successful marriages to members of the prestigious mulatto aristocracy of Charleston. William, Jr., married Mary Thompson Mishaw, whose father, John, was a prosperous bootmaker and member of the select Brown Fellowship Society. Henry and Reuben married sisters from the Bonneau family, whose father, Thomas S. Bonneau, was a highly respected mulatto schoolmaster and also a member of the Brown Fellowship Society. In this manner, the Ellison family, just thirty years out of slavery, gained entrance into the select African-American aristocracy of Charleston. At about the same time, William's daughter, Eliza Ann, married James M. Johnson, son of James D. Johnson, a respected tailor in Charleston. The Johnson family, who ranked just a notch below the Bonneaus and Mishaws, were not members of the Brown Fellowship. Ellison's three sons and their wives, along with his daughter and son-in-law, all lived in a family compound in Stateburg. They lived in houses provided by their father, and the three sons worked in their father's shop. James Johnson, a tailor, took in sewing in Drayton Hall, the home built as a wedding present by his father and father-in-law.

By 1860 William Ellison was in his seventieth year, and he had long since become a wealthy man. He now owned sixty-three slaves and nearly 900 acres of land. For the federal census he estimated that his slaves were worth $53,000, while his land was valued at $8,250. As Johnson and Roark note, this was a severe undervaluation on both counts. They estimate his slaves were worth somewhere between $100,000 and $150,000, and the value of his land was at least twice what Ellison claimed. "Although Ellison's wealth did not rival the white aristocracy's, he was among the top 10 percent of all Sumter slaveholders and landowners. In the entire state, only 5 percent of the population owned as much real estate as Ellison."

Ellison, because of his wealth and success as a businessman, came to be held in high regard by the white planters of the Stateburg area. One clear demonstration of Ellison's elevated, but still circumscribed status, was his membership in Holy Cross Episcopal Church. The Stateburg white gentry worshiped at this church, and the Ellisons, along with a few other free African-American families, were allowed to participate. What set the Ellisons apart was that they, unlike the other black families, were allowed to become full-fledged members, and in 1844, after twenty years of sitting in the gallery with other blacks, they were allowed to purchase a pew at the back of the "white" section downstairs.

The unique respect and status that William Ellison and his family achieved in the Sumter area can also be attested by a number of other things. First of all, William H. Bowen, a longtime white resident of the area, in 1856 wrote a letter to the *Saturday Evening Post* about Ellison. In it, he said, "William Ellison is respected by all classes of citizens, and is honorable in all his dealings." At about the same time, Ellison "proved his mettle" to his white planter associates by becoming one of the founders of the Kansas Association of Sumter, which was organized to raise money in support of guerillas fighting the Free Soil forces in Kansas.

Shortly after the Civil War erupted in Charleston Harbor, William Ellison slipped quietly into a coma and died at his home in Stateburg. At his funeral, according to one account, both blacks and whites served as pallbearers, and condolences came in from a number of people in Charleston and elsewhere. Ellison's sons continued to run the family businesses after his death, but the situation was altered markedly by the war and postwar conditions. As with most planters, the war put a virtual end to cotton production. The sons, therefore, converted the entire land holdings to food production and became a veritable storehouse of grains and other food items for the state. They also hired out their horses and mules when the supply of those animals became scarce during the war. Most of their profits during this time, however, were in Confederate notes, which had little or no utility at war's end. At the end of the war they also had to face the emancipation of their large force of slaves, which involved a loss of capital of some $100,000.

Although cotton production resumed after the war, the Ellisons did not engage in it. For a variety of reasons, they would not participate in the sharecropping system that emerged after the war, trying instead to hire freed blacks as wage labor on their plantations. Although sharecropping today has an odious reputation, to the newly emancipated blacks it was greatly preferable to wage labor, which they associated with a lack of independence. So, they refused to work for the Ellisons. Thus, the Ellison family virtually ceased its farming activities after the war.

Nor was the gin shop continued on its old level, and again the lack of slave labor appears to be the key to its demise. Unable to hire their former slave artisans, the Ellisons were dependent on their own family for labor. By 1870 just one member of the family still listed himself as a gin maker, William Ellison's grandson, John Buckner. He was hardly able to maintain a thriving business, and by 1870 his $300 in personal property speaks volumes for the extent to which the Ellison gin business had withered and was near death.

What the Ellison sons decided to do was to become merchants. In the late 1860s they built and began operating a general store that catered primarily to the white trade in the area. Most country store owners would have catered to the freed blacks of the area, but the Ellisons refused to do this. This, again, was an astute business decision. All of their business lives as gin makers and repairmen, the Ellisons had dealt with the white families of the area. To focus their general store on the black trade would have made little sense; with whites, on the other hand, they had a good rapport and track record reaching back decades that could be exploited for profit in postwar South Carolina. The new business was a success, and the credit rating firm of R. G. Dun & Co. always gave them solid reviews. In 1877, for example, it said: ''Doing well. Honest and industrious. Temperate Reliable & in good credit for business wants.'' Their worth was estimated at between $7,000 and $8,000, a tidy enough sum to be sure, but just a fraction of what their father's estate had been worth at its peak. The store was run, with declining profits, until the 1890s, when it was closed. In 1920 the last of the Ellison clan died, alone and nearly forgotten in William Ellison's beloved Wisdom Hall. Just one member of the far-flung Ellison family returned for the funeral.

Johnson and Roark eloquently summarized William Ellison's status and challenge in antebellum South Carolina:

Ellison built his refuge in Stateburg at a very high price. He enslaved other Afro-Americans, ignored most free people of color, dominated members of his own family, and spent his life trying to please whites. The cost, however, did not include the sacrifice of his own personality or the elimination of his will. . . . He stood as far from the river of heroic, militant black protest as any man of his era. He did not challenge Southern society, but he did seek to defend himself from the degradation it reserved for people of color.

Sources
The Ellison Family Papers are held at the South Caroliniana Library, University of South Carolina. Michael P. Johnson and James L. Roark have masterfully edited a collection of these letters and published them as *No Chariot Let Down: Charleston's Free People of Color on the Eve of the Civil War* (Chapel Hill, N.C., 1984). They have also written an excellent history of the family entitled *Black Masters: A Free Family of Color in the Old South* (New York, 1984). The first book has a good bibliography. See also H. J. Quin, "William Ellison: Black Slave Owner," *Sandlapper*, November 1974, 47–49, which was written without benefit of the information in the Ellison Papers; see also James L. Roark, "Address to the South Carolina Historical Society" (n.d.).

Other manuscript collections of interest are the Holloway Scrapbook, 1811–1964, held at the Robert Scott Smalls Library, College of Charleston. They also have the *Minutes of the Brown Fellowship Society*, 1869–1911, and the minutes of the *Friendly Moralist Society*, 1841–1856. At the South Carolina Department of Archives and History there is the Charleston *Free Negro Tax Books*, 1816–1857. Several directories are of assistance also, including, T. C. Fay, *Charleston Directory and Stranger's Guide for 1840 and 1841* (Charleston, S.C., 1840); W. Eugene Ferslew, *Directory of the City of Charleston, 1860* (Charleston, S.C., 1860); and Frederick A. Ford, *Census of the City of Charleston, South Carolina, for the Year 1861* (Charleston, S.C., 1861). See also *Rules and Regulations of the Brown Fellowship Society* (Charleston, S.C., 1844).

F

Fitzgerald, Richard Burton (see Coleman, Warren Clay, Richard Burton Fitzgerald, and Edward Austin Johnson).

Forten, James (September 2, 1766–February 1842). Sailmaker and abolitionist. James Forten was one of the wealthiest and most honored of the early African-American business leaders. He was also perhaps the earliest ''true'' abolitionist. That is, unlike nearly all of the white abolitionists of the early nineteenth century, Forten did not subscribe to the idea of black inferiority to whites. Nor did he support the concomitant idea of colonization of blacks back to Africa. His idea was that the slaves should be freed, educated, and then fitted to take their rightful place in society. This idea, which became the credo of the American Anti-Slavery Society, was taken up a few years later by William Lloyd Garrison and Theodore Dwight Weld, with whom Forten developed an intimate association.

Forten was born in Philadelphia, the son of free black parents. His family had lived as freemen in Pennsylvania for at least two generations, since, according to Forten's own account, his great-grandfather had been brought from Africa as a slave, but his grandfather had obtained his freedom. James was educated for a time at the Quaker school of Anthony Benezet, but the death of his father in 1775, when the boy was just nine years old, forced him to help support the family. He worked for a few years in a grocery store, but as the Revolutionary War proceeded, James wanted to participate. Thus, in 1781, at age fifteen, he enlisted as a powder boy aboard the *Royal Louis*, a Pennsylvania privateer commanded by Stephen Decatur, Sr. It was not long, however, before the ship was captured by the British. This created a dangerous situation for the young boy. Although he was free born, it was not the custom of the British to exchange black prisoners with the Americans. Instead, they were usually sold into slavery in the West Indies. Forten was able to escape this fate by striking up a friendship with the young son of the captain of the British ship, teaching him to play marbles. As a result, Forten was transferred to another prison ship with white captives and was not sent to the West Indies. He commented later, "Thus did a game of marbles save me from a life of West Indian servitude."

After a year on board the prison ship, Forten was released in a general exchange of prisoners, and he arrived home just as the Revolutionary War came to a close. At that point, Forten decided he could no longer tolerate second-class citizenship in the newly formed independent country, and he decided to move to England. While there, Forten came under the influence of prominent British abolitionists, such as Granville Sharpe, who did much to shape his later ideas on the subject. Returning to Philadelphia after a year, Forten was apprenticed to Robert Bridges, a sailmaker whose loft dominated the south wharves of the city. Thus commenced Forten's spectacular business career.

Bridges, unlike most white Americans at that time, seemed remarkably free of prejudice, since in 1786 he promoted Forten to foreman of the loft. Forten at that time was just twenty years of age, about half the workmen in the shop were white, and many had been there years before Forten's arrival. But Bridges reportedly recognized Forten's "skill, energy, diligence and good conduct" in promoting him to foreman. Nor did this appointment cause problems with the rest of the work force, since Forten was also their unanimous choice. In 1798, when Bridges died, Forten became owner of the firm. During the next forty years, Forten conducted the large shop very successfully, employing as many as forty men at times and amassing over $100,000, a very large fortune for the time. Part of his wealth also came from royalties on a device Forten invented to handle sails. This became very popular with other sailmakers, and, although it was never actually patented, it brought him a comfortable income that allowed him to purchase homes for his widowed mother and his sister, along with his own large and comfortable home at 92 Lombard Street for his wife and eight children.

Although James Forten became perhaps the most prominent African-American businessman of his time, he was hardly the only one, as Philadelphia became a major center of black business in the early nineteenth century. As early as 1789, many blacks were doing well keeping small shops, a beneficial insurance society among blacks was organized in 1796, and an African-American insurance company was founded in 1810. By 1820 the black population of the city had grown to 11,891, and they owned about $250,000 worth of property. An Englishman in 1823 reported that a number of blacks by that time had "amassed fortunes," presumably Forten was one of those he had in mind. In the late 1830s, the Pennsylvania Society for Promoting the Abolition of Slavery reported that blacks were engaged in virtually every occupation pursued by whites.

Yet, during this same period of time, the situation for free blacks, always far from perfect, began to worsen. The arrival of large numbers of immigrants in the 1820s brought about increasingly violent confrontations, culminating in a series of riots of whites against blacks throughout the 1830s and beyond. Further, legislation was introduced into the state legislature, but never passed, to halt the further migration of southern free blacks into Pennsylvania. W.E.B. Du Bois summarized the situation with his customary eloquence:

The new industries attracted the Irish, Germans, and other immigrants; Americans too, were fleeing to the city and soon to natural race antipathies was added a determined effort to displace Negro labor. . . . To all of this was added a problem of crime and poverty. . . . The tide had set against the Negro strongly, and the whole period from 1820 to 1840 became a time of retrogression for the mass of the race . . . and of repression from whites.

It was in this context that Forten turned increasingly to abolitionism and racial protest.

Forten had for some time been a civic leader among Philadelphia's black population. He had on four occasions saved persons from drowning near his loft, and in 1821 he was given an award from the Humane Society for his efforts. During the War of 1812, when the city of Philadelphia was threatened by British troops, Forten enlisted 2,500 blacks to fight for the city's defense. In addition, in 1796, he had helped organize St. Thomas Episcopal Church, and he was later instrumental in purchasing the freedom of the wife and children of Reverend Gloucester, the founder of the First African Presbyterian Church. Forten was also a leader in movements for temperance and moral reform in the city. These activities, as Ray Allan Billington has noted, ''prepared James Forten for a role in the cause that interested him most—abolitionism.''

Forten's interest in the problem was first awakened in 1800 when Reverend Richard Allen, pastor of the African Methodist Church, and Absalom Jones, another of the founders of the St. Thomas Church, circulated a petition among the city's blacks, urging Congress to modify the Fugitive Slave Act of 1793. Forten signed the petition and then watched its overwhelming defeat in Congress by a vote of eighty-five to one. This convinced Forten that he had to become a more active abolitionist and champion of black rights. In 1813 he was the author of a pamphlet that protested against the bill to bar free blacks from migrating to Pennsylvania. He was successful in that endeavor. During these early years Forten also began to turn against the idea of recolonizing slaves back to Africa. Until Paul Cuffe died in 1819, however, Forten did not speak out publicly against colonization. Thereafter, he became a militant opponent of the idea and did much to convince other abolitionists to oppose the idea.

By the 1830s, Forten had become so well known as an abolitionist, and as an opponent of colonization, that he is given credit for convincing William Lloyd Garrison to oppose it also. Forten's sizable fortune allowed him to be a generous contributor to Garrison's *The Liberator*, and it is said that only Arthur and Lewis Tappan gave more to the cause. It was in Forten's home in 1833 that the American Anti-Slavery Society was organized in 1833, and he served on its board of managers and acted as a principal fund-raiser for the organization. At the same time, he also became an advocate of woman's rights and universal peace, and he served as president of the American Reform Society, a body of African-American men dedicated to the ''promotion of Education, Temperance, Economy, and Universal Liberty.'' Forten was the organizer of a number of local mass meetings advocating abolition and equality between the races. Again, in 1832, when the Pennsylvania legislature considered ending southern black migration to the state, Forten, along with his friends and colleagues, William Whipper and Robert Purvis, organized a petition drive against the proposals. In 1836 Forten prepared a memorandum to the state legislation that urged not only the abolition of slavery, but also the ending of all discrimination based on color. He pleaded, ''Let our motto be, the Law Knows No Distinction.''

There was no more unpopular cause than abolitionism and black equality in early nineteenth-century America, but Forten, despite his advancing age, continued his crusade until the fall of 1841, when he wrote to Garrison that he could exert himself in the cause of abolitionism no longer. He died a year later. His funeral, held on February 22, 1842, was one of the largest in Philadelphia's history. Several hundred whites and several thousand blacks marched in the procession. His son, Robert Bridges Forten, continued the sailmaking business, but the advent of steam soon caused it to be closed. The real mission of his children and grandchildren, however, was to continue James Forten's battle for abolition and civil rights. His son-in-law, Robert Purvis, became a prominent abolitionist, assuming James Forten's role in many organizations. Forten's son James, Jr., and daughter, Margaretta, were also involved in abolition and reform activities. Forten's granddaughter, Charlotte Forten, became a well-known abolitionist, and her diary is an important source for our understanding of the lives of the newly freed blacks during the Civil War.

When James Forten died, Charles Lyell, the eminent British scientist, happened to be traveling through the United States. In Philadelphia on the day of Forten's funeral, Lyell in his *Travels* describes the scene: ''A rare event, the death of a wealthy man of color took place during my stay here, and his funeral was attended not only by a crowd of persons of his own race, but by many highly respected white merchants, by whom he was held in high esteem.''

Sources

Although there are no family papers available for the Fortens, information can be secured from a number of collections. See the William Lloyd Garrison Papers in the Department of Rare Books and Manuscripts at the Boston Public Library and at the Houghton Library, Harvard University. The City Archives at City Hall, Philadelphia, has James Forten's will, and the records of the Anti-Slavery Society are on microfilm at the Historical Society of Pennsylvania in Philadephia. There are also some items in the Moorland-Spingarn Collection at Howard University and in the Frederick Douglass Papers in the Library of Congress. There is a full-length biography of James Forten by Esther M. Doughty entitled *Forten the Sailmaker, Pioneer, Champion of Negro Rights* (1968). There is a briefer biography of him by Ray Allen Billington in *Negro History Bulletin* XIII, 2 (November 1949), 31–36, 45; an abridged version of this is printed in Billington, *The Journal of Charlotte Forten* (1953), 6–14. Rayford Logan has a good short biography in *Dictionary of American Negro Biography* (1982), and there is a brief sketch by Benjamin Brawley in the *Dictionary of American Biography* VI: 536–39. W.H. Quick, *Negro Stars in All Ages of the World* (1898), Edgar A. Toppin, *Biographies of Notable Black Amer-*

icans (1971), 297–99, and Ingham, BDABL have brief treatments. Janice Sumler Lewis has done a study of the Forten family in her "Fortens of Philadelphia: An Afro-American Family and Nineteenth Century Reform," Ph.D. diss., Georgetown University, 1978. See also Charlotte Forten's "Life on the Sea Islands," *Atlantic Monthly* 13 (May and June 1864), 587–96, 666–76.

There are some early discussions of James Forten and his family in William Douglas, *Annals of the First African Church in the U.S. of A. Now Styled the African Episcopal Church of St. Thomas* (Philadelphia, 1862), 107, 110; Lydia Maria Child, *The Freedman's Book* (Boston, 1865), 102–3; William C. Neil, *Colored Patriots of the American Revolution* (Boston, 1855), 172–74; Samuel J. May, *Some Recollections of the Antislavery Conflict* (Boston, 1869), 287; Robert Purvis, *Remarks on the Life and Character of James Forten, Delivered at Bethel Church, March 30, 1842* (Philadelphia, 1842); and Henry M. Minton, "Early History of Negroes in Business in Philadelphia," in *The Philadelphia Colored Business Directory* (Philadelphia, 1913). The Forten family generally is discussed in *Negro History Bulletin* X, 4 (January 1947), 75–79; and in Gerri Major, *Black Society* (1976), 78–82ff. See also Joseph A. Barome, "Robert Purvis and his Early Challenge to American Racism," *Negro History Bulletin* 30 (May 1967), 8–10; and "Robert Purvis, Wendell Phillips and the Freedmen's Bureau," *Journal of Negro History* 42 (October 1957), 292–95.

The Forten daughters and Charlotte Forten, James's granddaughter, are discussed in Sylvia Dannett, *Profiles of Negro Womanhood*, 2 vols. (New York, 1964–66). There is a full-length biography of Charlotte Forten by Esther M. Douty, *Charlotte Forten, Free Black Teacher* (1971). See also *Black Enterprise*, June 1976, *U.S. News and World Report,* February 23, 1976; *Crisis* 83 (August 1976), 258 for recognition of Forten during the bicentennial year.

Fraunces, Samuel (c. 1722–October 10, 1795). Tavern owner: Fraunces Tavern, New York City. That we know anything today of Samuel Fraunces is a historical accident and says much about the nature of past historians and keepers of records. The Fraunces Tavern, which Fraunces bought in 1765, is revered today as the oldest building in New York City. It received its original fame, and was spared the wrecker's ball in the later nineteenth century, not because Samuel Fraunces, an African-American, owned it, but because George Washington dined there and the Sons of Liberty met there. Until very recently the fact that Fraunces himself was black was often ignored. Even in a relatively enlightened 1981, the guide published by the museum that had been established in the Fraunces Tavern failed to mention the fact that Fraunces was an African-American. Little wonder American blacks have often complained about being written out of America's past.

Samuel Fraunces (perhaps spelled Frances in his early years) was born and raised in the West Indies. Little is known of his early years, other than the fact that he was one of seven children. Even this fact, however, is in some dispute, since in the 1790 census he was listed as a native of New York. Of course, he and his wife were also called "free whites." In any event, he does not appear in New York City until about 1855, when he was about thirty-three years of age. He had obviously learned a great deal about food preparation while in his native land, and also probably had accumulated a good sum of money, since he was able to engage in the catering profession almost immediately upon his arrival. There is some speculation that he served as an officer's cook on an English ship, and that this is what brought him to New York.

There were about 2,500 African-American slaves in the city at that time, and there were also a certain number of free blacks. Even forty years later, however, there were still just 10,000 blacks in the city. This represented just over 10 percent of the entire population. It would be many years before blacks again would form that large a percentage, as their growth in the nineteenth century did not keep pace with that of other immigrant groups. Most of these blacks in the late eighteenth century worked as servants, laborers, sailors, and mechanics. A report of the American Colonization Society in 1797, however, indicated that a number of these early free blacks had done fairly well, since "[m]any in the town and country were freeholders, several worth from $300 to $1,300." Samuel Fraunces was obviously among this favored group.

The catering business in New York was one of the few in which blacks were able to achieve a measure of success. The tradition at that time was for wealthy families, such as the Rhinelanders, Goelets, Robinsons, and Gerrys, to hire catering firms to provide them with some or all of their meals on a regular basis. By the time Fraunces arrived in New York, at least a few African-Americans had moved into this field, including some black women. Fraunces had been a partner in a catering operation for about five years, when he decided to strike out on his own. During this same time he had married Elizabeth Dalles.

In 1859 Samuel and Elizabeth Fraunces went into business for themselves, opening a tavern called Mason's Arms on the corner of Broadway and Warren Streets. In addition to the regular meals and wines they served the customers there, the tavern featured "potable soup and sweetmeats, ketchup, bottled gooseberries, pickled walnuts, pickled or fried oysters fit to go to the West Indies, pickled mushrooms" and other colonial confections. In 1762 Samuel and Elizabeth acquired a building at the southeast corner of Broad and Pearl Streets, not far from the wharves at the tip of the island, so that their establishment could also become a depot for supplying ships docking in the vicinity. This building, the former residence of Stephen Delancey, a New York merchant, had been erected in 1719. Samuel bought the property from Delancey, Robinson & Co., for the sum of £2,000.

By the spring of 1763, Samuel and Elizabeth had converted the Delancey house into an inn, which they called the Queen's Head Tavern. This was, according to one account, "a typical eating place offering complete meals at a fixed, single price. The bountiful repasts to be had at Landlord Fraunces's table attracted diners from all over town." Four years later, Fraunces branched out in a new venture, developing a garden in upstate New York called Vauxhall. There, patrons could visit a wax museum for four shillings. This latter venture, however, was not a success, and in 1770 he sold it and devoted himself entirely to his inn.

In the early 1770s, as the tensions between Britain and America escalated, Fraunces's tavern became a popular meeting place for some major figures in the struggle. In 1774 the Sons of Liberty met in his establishment before dumping East Indian tea in the river. Samuel Fraunces himself also reputedly spied on the conversation of British officers drinking in his inn, relaying their words to revolutionary partisans. There is some evidence, however, that things may have been getting a bit too hot for Fraunces with all this chicanery and conspiracy going on in his establishment. He put his inn on the market in 1775, but it did not sell. When the revolution broke out in 1776, he decided it was prudent to change the name from Queen Anne, which reeked of colonial ties, simply to Fraunces Tavern, or, later, City Tavern.

Sometime during this period, Samuel Fraunces began to develop a close association with George Washington. For one thing, his daughter, Phoebe, evidently worked as Washington's housekeeper at Mortimer House on Richmond Hill, and it was she who supposedly uncovered a plot to assassinate the general. Washington also dined fairly often at Fraunces Tavern, and it was there that he met with British officials to draw up peace terms, and, when the British finally evacuated New York, it was at the inn that Washington gave his emotional farewell speech to his officers.

In 1785 Fraunces sold his tavern for £1.950 to George Powers and retired to country life in New Jersey. Three years later, however, he was back in New York, where he set up another tavern at 16 Nassau Street. Shortly afterward, when Washington left for the seat of the new government in Philadelphia, he called for Fraunces to join him there as his personal steward, and he served for several years at the executive mansion on Market Street. Washington wrote to an associate: "Fraunces, besides being an excellent cook, knowing how to provide genteel dinners and giving aid in dressing them, prepared the dessert. . . . " All the provisions and supplies for that early "White House" were purchased by Fraunces with monies advanced by the president's secretary. After a little over five years in this capacity, Fraunces wanted to return to running a tavern. In the spring of 1794 he was succeeded by Fred Kitts, and, upon leaving government service, "Black Sam" Fraunces, as he was called, received honors for his service both from the Continental Congress and the state of New York.

At that point Fraunces set up a tavern at 166 South Second Street in Philadelphia, followed a year later by one at 59 South Water Street in the same city. The latter was a large establishment, and Fraunces in addition owned two brick houses and lots on the north side of Filbert Street in that city. One of these homes was conveyed to his son, Andrew Gautier Fraunces, and both men were designated "gentlemen" in the city directory. A year later, Samuel Fraunces passed away. He was buried in St. Peter's Churchyard in Philadelphia, leaving his wife, a son, and five daughters. His widow later married Cornelius Smock, with whom she opened a "house of entertainment" in 1798. Fraunces's inn and homes in Philadelphia fell victim to progress in the nineteenth century and were destroyed. Not so his Queen Anne's Tavern in New York.

In 1905 the Sons of the Revolution purchased the Fraunces Tavern in New York and restored the building as a historical memorial. Even in the 1990s, food and drink are served on the lower level of the building; the upstairs houses "The Many Faces of George Washington," a private collection of eighteenth- and nineteenth-century engravings. In 1965 the building was officially designated a historical landmark by the New York City Landmarks Preservation Committee. By that time it was New York City's oldest building, and sat nestled among the skyscrapers in lower Manhattan. In all of this restoration, however, Samuel Fraunces, at least as he really was, became lost. The Sons of the American Revolution made no mention in a 1901 description of the building's history that he was African-American, insisting he was called "Black Sam" because he had a "swarthy complexion." In 1932, when there was a celebration of the 200th anniversary of George Washington's birthday at Fraunces Tavern, the black *New York Amsterdam News* complained that "Washington Turns Up, Samuel Fraunces Missing," since there was no mention of Fraunces having been black, and "no Negro was on hand to depict owner" during this event. Only recently have African-Americans moved to claim Samuel Fraunces as their own and is he being restored to rightful recognition. Perhaps not a great man, Fraunces, nonetheless, was a highly successful caterer and tavern owner in New York, one who attracted the "power elite" of the city to his establishment and parlayed that into a position of importance and visibility with President Washington. For this he deserves recognition.

Sources

The most useful collection of materials on Samuel Fraunces and his tavern is located at the New York Historical Society. In its collection are deeds, a will, and a few other personal materials relating to Fraunces's life. These are held in a variety of collections there. Certainly the most curious series of items on Fraunces are in the McCurdy Family Records, housed at the New York Historical Society. In these are records from Trinity Church of New York, where Fraunces was married, along with items from the 1790 U.S. Census, and Christ Church in Philadelphia, where Samuel Fraunces's daughter was baptized, along with other materials. The point of all of that is that Mrs. John Fraunces McCurdy, a descendant of Samuel, attempts to prove that he (and his family) were "Caucasian" and not "Negro."

In addition, there is a useful vertical file on Fraunces, with newspaper and magazine articles, most of which detail the fate of the building in which the Fraunces Tavern was located, and of the efforts to preserve it for future generations. Some useful material on Samuel Fraunces and his tavern can be found in *Black Enterprise*, June 1976; *New York Times*, December 18, 1926; Barbara Peyser, "Manhattan's Oldest Sits among City Skyscrapers," *Antique Monthly*, April 1934; Robert Hendrickson, "Washington Dined Here," *Americana*, May 1974; *New York Amsterdam News*, May 1932; *New York Herald Tribune*, February 23, 1942; *New York Sunday News*, February 20, 1955; *Philadelphia Evening Bulletin*, February 22, 1934; and *Our Town*, July 4, 1975. Fraunces Tavern Museum, *Guide to the Museum* (New York City, 1981) gives a history of the tavern, stressing its relationship to George Washington and the American Revolution. It never mentions the fact that Fraunces was an African-American.

Other materials of some value include Henry Russell Drowne, *The Story of Fraunces*

Tavern (New York, 1966); Richard Griffen, *A Tale of Fraunces Tavern, A.D. 1765 and Other Poems* (New York, 1914); Melusia Pierce, *The Landmark of Fraunces' Tavern: A Retrospect, Read December 4, 1900* (New York, 1901); and Freemasons, New York State, Grand Lodge, *The Washington Masonic Shrine at Tappan* (New York, 1934).

Fuller, S. B. (1905–October 24, 1988). Beauty supply firm founder, entrepreneur, and race leader: Fuller Products, *Pittsburgh Courier*, Regal Theater, and Fuller Department Store. "If there had been no you, there would have been no us," one former employee effused. John H. Johnson,* the publishing magnate, at a testimonial eloquently asserted, "We are here to say to a prophet in his own time, and in his own community that we have been touched and transformed by your life—and we are profoundly grateful. The great flame who honors us in this way represents, in his person and his achievements, that spirit of manliness and self-determination of the pioneer black businessman, who knew that nothing is given to men and women in this world . . . and that the God of history helps black businessmen who help themselves." And George Johnson,* the man responsible for the success of Johnson Products, graciously offered, "Everybody talks about Booker T. Washington* as a leader in the field of black economic development, and about a lot of other people. But very few people knew a thing about Fuller. We figured it this way: let's honor the man, let us show him how we feel while he is still alive and with us." The Fuller he so admiringly refers to is S. B. Fuller, whose early achievements provided inspiration for these other noted entrepreneurs. Such accolades were delivered in Chicago during a 1975 testimonial dinner honoring this pioneer businessman. However, the dinner differed from similar such occasions in that the proceeds of $70,000 (each guest paid $50), as well as the additional gift of stock certificates valued at $50,000 granted by George Johnson, were raised not only as a tribute to Fuller's achievements but also as a charitable donation to the honoree to deal with his trying times. It is true that S. B. Fuller had showed the way for many African-Americans with entrepreneurial aspirations and had even attained the status of being the engineer behind the largest black-owned company in the 1950s. Why, then, was Fuller the recipient of $120,000 in cash and stock certificates in 1975? As is often the case in business, especially in the African-American community, the tides can turn and the fruits of labor can be lost. Such was the case with S. B. Fuller.

Fuller was born in Monroe, Louisiana, in 1905 to a poor sharecropping family. Although he received nothing more than a grade six education, he had learned the value of door-to-door sales at the age of nine years. When he was fifteen, the family moved to Memphis, Tennessee, and when his mother died two years later, her seven children refused out of shame to accept government assistance. As Fuller recalls, "We were embarassed just because the relief woman came to talk to us. We did not want the neighbors to know we couldn't make it for ourselves. So we youngsters made it for ourselves."

In 1928, Fuller, penniless, arrived in Chicago, a city heavily populated with African-Americans who had migrated from the South during the first two decades of the twentieth century. Although Chicago had been a city with volatile racial problems, the climate had settled somewhat by that time for Fuller to find employment with little trouble. Initially, he accepted work in a coal yard, and then moved ahead as an insurance representative for Commonwealth Burial Association. Within in a short time, he was promoted to a managerial position. Another individual might have found comfort and security in such a white-collar job, but Fuller's quest for advancement could not be satisfied within the confines of a salaried position. Early on he had realized that self-employment provided opportunities far greater than any employer would be willing to bestow on an employee. In 1935, acting on this knowledge, with a mere $25 and the support of his wife, Fuller bought soap to sell door to door. Shortly thereafter, the $25 was multiplied into $1,000, and he was on his way. Fuller hired salespeople to market his thirty products door to door throughout the black community, primarily in the South Side of Chicago where the vast majority of African-Americans resided. The small space above a store that he had originally chosen as an office was soon abandoned for a small factory in 1939 also located on the South Side. Sales were escalating among black customers, his sales force had grown, and Fuller was finally enjoying a prominence he had not previously experienced.

The turning point in his career came in 1947 with the purchase of Boyer International Laboratories, a white cosmetics firm. The business transaction between the white firm and Fuller, an African-American, was done clandestinely to avoid criticism and boycotts from the white customers who were loyal to the products Boyer distributed—Jean Nadal Cosmetics and H. A. Hair Arranger—but were unforgivingly racist. Primarily, these customers resided in the southern states, in such segregated cities as Atlanta, Montgomery, Birmingham, and Dallas, and almost all of North Carolina. Fuller's business soared with this acquisition. By the early 1960s, with a line of 300 products, the company had an annual gross of $10 million and employed 5,000 salespeople with approximately 600 employees on the direct payroll. Since Fuller hired on merit rather than on skin color, both black and whites were on his payroll, and he established eighty-five branches in thirty-eight states. With this financial windfall came the economic freedom that allowed Fuller to diversify. He held interests in J. C. McBrady and Company and Patricia Stevens Cosmetics, which further complemented his already well-endowed line of beauty products.

As Fuller continued to diversify his operations, he purchased a major share of the Pittsburgh Courier Publishing Company, whose publications included the *New York Age*, the oldest black newspaper, and the *Pittsburgh Courier*, which had the largest circulation of any African-American newspaper. Fuller ventured into real estate; he owned a real estate trust in New York and many of the buildings in which his offices were located. He also bought the Regal Theater, which rivaled the Apollo Theater in Harlem as a showcase for black entertainment. His empire even included farming and beef cattle production. In addition, he owned several smaller black firms, such as the Fuller Guaranty Corporation and Fuller-Philco Home Appliance Center. Nothing was beyond this entrepreneur's grasp.

The 1960s surely held a promising future for S. B. Fuller. He had achieved the status of a black powerhouse tycoon who could afford what others could only dream of, including a $250,000 home in Chicago, and a designation in a national magazine as one of the wealthiest blacks in the United States. But an unexpected turn of events caused the premature demise of a man that had seemingly had it all. The effort to conceal the sale of Boyer International to a black man was ill founded. In a few years time, the White Citizens' Council uncovered the truth of the company's ownership and proceeded to ravage the organization with boycotts when they deemed it totally inappropriate for a black businessman to be selling products to white customers. In retrospect, a number of years later, Fuller expressed his sentiments regarding this issue: ''I have always believed that black producers should sell to white customers, the same way whites sell to blacks.'' No doubt he had similar feelings at the time of the boycott but was hardly equipped to counter the overt hostility that pervaded the South.

The fury of the South's wrath caused the downfall of Fuller. The far-reaching boycott led to the removal of the aforementioned products from the shelves of retail stores, primarily from white drugstore chains. This ploy had a devastating impact on Fuller Products because 60 percent of the company's sales had been achieved through the Boyer line in the South to white customers. The sales of the Jean Nadal products decreased to zero! This was one of the many ways the racially intolerant attitudes of whites manifested themselves during these explosive times. Fuller had virtually no choice but to reassess his situation and shift his focus to the white northern market and the African-American consumer, both in the North and the South. He was forced to sell the Jean Nadal line to raise capital and to rid himself of a white elephant. A New York liquor concern with headquarters on Park Avenue had expressed interest in buying the line for $1 million and $600,000 in royalties over a fourteen year period. Fuller banked on this company's letter of intent to purchase his company and proceeded to borrow $500,000 to open Fuller Department Store, which was formerly the South Center Department Store on the South Side of Chicago. Unfortunately, the liquor company reneged on their promise, and Fuller was left overextended (to say the least). Pushed to the limit financially as a result of this debacle, he was forced to sell the mortgages he held on $3 million worth of real estate. The worst outcome of such an unfortunate state of affairs became reality—he had no other choice but to declare bankruptcy in 1969 for the Fuller Products Company. After riding on the sails of success, Fuller's dreams seemed to shatter one by one.

In 1964 Fuller was confronted with accusations from the Securities and Exchange Commission for illicit practices of misstating material acts to purchasers of promissory notes and selling the notes in interstate commerce without registering them (for selling unregistered 10 percent notes on his business). Buyers ranged from individuals who bought as little as $100 or $200 of the notes to the

Antioch Missionary Baptist Church, which had invested $100,000. Fuller was placed on five years' probation and ordered to repay $1.6 million to creditors. In addition to that trouble, a Chicago social worker charged Fuller with giving credit to welfare clients. Such allegations stemmed from the policy whereby a welfare client could charge up to $100 in goods for only $30. Welfare customers were urged by the Social Service administrator not to honor their debts with the department store. Obviously the clients heeded these words of advice since it was in their best interest, and Fuller was left with over $1 million in unpaid charges. Ultimately, an arrangement was settled upon whereby Fuller was ordered to pay creditors 10 cents on the dollar. Mill Factors Corporation, a major secured creditor, found Fuller to be remiss in his payments. As a result, Fuller lost ownership of the department store.

As well, the publishing interest and the retail store were draining his cash flow. He divested himself of the publishing concern late in 1968, when he sold it to Sengstacke Enterprises, which owns the *Chicago Defender*. Suits were filed against him for unpaid bills and, although he had declared bankruptcy, he was permitted to continue operating the business pending a reorganization of the company. Close to 2,000 creditors came to the fore, many of whom were salespeople, note holders, and members of the Fullerite Club. Such club members had paid a $40 fee to permit them to purchase Fuller cosmetics at the wholesale price. It was then expected that they, in turn, would sell the products to friends and family members at the retail price. When a club member opted out of the club, he or she received the original investment of $40 in Fuller merchandise. However, the New York City members had understood that the $40 would be returned to them in cash rather than merchandise, and thus they were listed among the creditors. When summarizing the turn of events that brought on his troubles, Fuller stated that things were going well when he was allowed to operate Fuller Products as a business and that the troubles began when he "was forced to operate as a Negro business."

Not only had problems emerged from external sources, but Fuller's opinionated manner had ruffled some feathers as well. Although Fuller had suffered the direct consequences of overt discrimination, he rarely seemed bitter toward the white society. On the other hand, he tended to focus his criticism on the African-American community. He felt compelled to speak out without reservation in 1963 when addressing the issue of black poverty and lack of motivation: "Negroes," he said, "lack initiative, courage, integrity, loyalty and wisdom." And he had accused the National Association for the Advancement of Colored People (of which he was a former president of the South Side Chicago chapter) for only working to change the attitudes of whites rather than focusing on where the real problem lay—with the blacks. Fuller's frustration apparently originated in his upbringing, when he suffered the ravages of poverty and was forced to work at an early age to help the family make ends meet. The ambitious spirit was nurtured and from it emerged a driven man who failed to see any credible reason for the absence of motivation and entrepreneurial spirit among those of his own race.

Although he did concede that blacks did have some legitimate complaints, they were fewer than they claimed. He agreed that whites had not taught blacks sufficiently, particularly in matters of business. Fuller asserted that the key to success was owning a business, for, by doing so, the money would stay within the black community and give blacks a sense of pride and power. During the 1960s, when the civil rights movement was in full force, Fuller felt the energies of African-Americans were misdirected; that is, blacks were focusing on their status as second-class citizens rather than on defining themselves as first-class citizens and moving forward from that belief.

Needless to say, the black community reacted vehemently. Such harsh criticisms needed to be answered, especially when they were asserted by one of their own. The strategy implemented to respond to Fuller was one that proved so successful for the White Citizens' Council—boycotts. It was actually staged in response to a speech delivered by Fuller at the National Association of Manufacturers (of which he was the first black member), in which he said that "a lack of understanding of the capitalist system and not racial barriers was keeping blacks from making progress." This was certainly the same song he had sung before that had so enraged members of the black community. Although Fuller admitted that his business suffered from the boycott, he never retracted the words; rather, he felt that he had been misunderstood.

After reorganization under the federal bankruptcy laws, Fuller's firm reported profits of $300,000 in 1972. This number hardly compares to the $10 million achieved in the company's glory days, but it does attest to the tenacity of Fuller. The company continues to distribute beauty products with centers in Atlanta, Los Angeles, New York, Richmond, Washington, D.C., Greensboro, Cleveland, and Newark, relying on a broad regional network. These distributors have approximately thirty salespeople who market their wares door to door, the same strategy that Fuller utilized so successfully in the beginning. For $1,000 an individual can purchase a Fuller distributorship franchise, which also includes Fuller Product merchandise worth $26,000. In 1975 the cosmetic line was made up of sixty products, including lipsticks, perfumes, lotions, and other beauty paraphernalia. The sales volume was under $1 million, and Fuller was no longer a millionaire, but the company was on the road to recovery.

The black business community took note of the once-dominant, but now struggling African-American businessman who had provided a role model for many prominent entrepreneurs. At one time, these individuals had been employed by Fuller and they felt indebted to him for having shown them the way. They recognized that he was an individual responsible for paving the way for them, since no white financial institutions were willing to finance their business ventures and the Small Business Administration had not yet been established. Fuller had to rely on loans from some black benefactors who provided him with assistance, and in turn he has offered financial or other assistance to those who have followed in his footsteps. George Johnson, a former employee of ten years, was helped by Fuller. When Johnson's small cosmetics firm, a direct competitor to Fuller

Products, was burned out of its building in the 1950s, Fuller provided temporary space in his own offices for Johnson. Fuller preached the gospel of success in motivation classes that were started in his first few years of business and have persisted throughout the years. He continued to take pride in his achievements and never expressed remorse or bitterness at having lost everything only to start over again. Illinois Governor Walker declared June 15, 1975, S. B. Fuller Day. His death on October 24, 1988, was certainly mourned by many, and he will be remembered as a trailblazer with an indomitable spirit. As he remarked during his thank you speech at the testimonial dinner, "I saw in the paper this morning where I had retired. Now, I'm not going to no senior citizens' home, nor am I going to quit work. . . . We are going to do the job that I set out to do." And so he did.

Sources

No personal or business papers of S. B. Fuller are currently available. Nor has there been any strictly biographical material published on him. Information for this biography was composed from a variety of magazine and newspaper articles, including his obituaries in the *Chicago Defender*, October 25, 1988; *Chicago Tribune*, October 26, 1988; *Chicago Sun-Times*, October 29, 1988; and the *Afro-American*, November 26, 1988. See also Rutai G. Ladipo, "Salute to the 'Godfather' of Black Business: S. B. Fuller," *Chicago Defender*, June 15, 1985; "A Negro Businessman Speaks His Mind," *U.S. News & World Report*, August 19, 1963; "A Man and His Products," *Black Enterprise*, August 1975; Pamela Sherrod, "The Dean of Black Entrepreneurs," *Chicago Tribune*, June 9, 1987; "NAACP Raps Negro's Attack on Own Race," *New York Post*, December 8, 1971; Leonard Wiener, "S. B. Fuller's Downfall Tied to Race Tension," *Chicago Daily News*, August 15, 1988; *Chicago Defender*, November 14, 1988; *Jet*, June 26, 1975; *Ebony*, September 1975; *Chicago Tribune*, October 1, 1971; *Chicago Sun-Times*, May 20, 1972, and September 8, 1975; *Chicago Daily News*, May 14, 1975; and *Fortune*, September 1957.

G

Gardner, Edward G. (February 15, 1925–). Founder of hair products company: Soft Sheen Products, Incorporated. Edward Gardner is almost the prototypical contemporary black American business leader. He was born and raised in a time of severe racial discrimination and came into his adulthood at the end of World War II, at a time when black Americans were beginning to demand a "bigger piece of the pie" as a result of their "Double V" campaign. Taking advantage of the relative openness of education during these years, Gardner went to college, obtained an advanced degree, and worked his way up within the educational establishment. Then, in the 1960s, when pressures for greater economic opportunities for blacks intensified, Gardner began operating his own business. Unlike most of the blacks who started small businesses during those years, however, Gardner's grew into an enormous national concern and became the sixth-largest black-owned business in the United States in terms of sales.

Edward Gardner was born in Chicago, was educated in the city's public school system, and graduated from Fenger High School in 1943. He later admitted, however, that his "business training came from the streets" rather than from his formal education. Nothing else is known of Gardner's home life or experiences during this time, but he grew up in the city during the years when it was being made famous as the "Black Metropolis" of America. In the words of St. Clair Drake and Horace Cayton, authors of *Black Metropolis*: "Black Metropolis is the second largest Negro city in the world, only New York's Harlem exceeding it in size. It is a city within a city—a narrow tongue of land, seven miles in length and one and one-half in width, where more than 300,000 Negroes are packed solidly." It was a city with a tradition of violence against blacks, one in which the patterns of segregation and discrimination were firmly established and clearly delineated. Further, the Great Depression of the 1930s worsened the economic condition of African-Americans in Chicago; they were often the first to be fired or laid off from increasingly scarce positions. One can presume that Gardner's situation did not deviate much from the norm for Chicago blacks.

Upon graduation, Gardner was drafted into the U.S. Army, where he experienced his first sense of "combat" when he went through basic training in Pennsylvania. Going into nearby Indiantown Gap to see a movie, Gardner sat himself down in the middle of the theater. Soon a military policeman appeared with his club drawn and told Gardner that "Negroes don't sit in the middle of the theater." Gardner completed his training without further incident. He was sent overseas and served in the Pacific theater in New Guinea, the Philippines, and Japan before being discharged as a staff sergeant.

After the war, Gardner was able to go to college on the G.I. Bill, and he received his B.A. from Chicago Teachers College. He then got a job as an elementary schoolteacher in the Chicago school system. Sometime during the next decade he also received his master's degree at the University of Chicago. Later he was made assistant principal, serving first at Carver Elementary School in Altgeld Gardens and four years at Beethoven Elementary in the Robert Taylor Homes, one of the roughest housing projects in the city. Sylvester Monroe, a reporter for *Newsweek* who was growing up in the Taylor Homes at the time Gardner was a principal there, commented, "Generally speaking, poor people in the projects like the Robert Taylor Homes don't place much stock in dreams. They see little point in it." Edward Gardner differed greatly from the students he came in contact with each day in that he was highly ambitious and had dreams that greatly transcended his position as a civil servant in the Chicago school system.

Not content with his stable, secure life, or with the $10,000 a year he was earning, Gardner began dabbling in sales in his spare time. He had a friend who had a business selling hair-care products manufactured by others. The friend took Gardner on as a part-time salesman in 1957. Gardner worked evenings and weekends, making the rounds of various black beauty parlors with a cardboard box full of products under his arm. After a few years, however, he decided that even this was not enough—he wanted to start his own business. Furthermore, he was not going to just distribute products made by someone else; he was going to manufacture his own. In 1962 Gardner and his wife Bettiann set up the E. G. Gardner Beauty Products Company, which he ran from his basement. His friends did not see much wrong with that end of Gardner's plan; it was when he said he was going to quit his job as a principal and devote his full time to his dream that they reacted negatively. A typical reaction was, "You must be losing your mind giving up that good $10,000 a year job to go sell grease products up and down 4th Street." In a reflective mood many years later, Gardner said, "They were probably right. I didn't know anything more about what I was doing than the man in the moon."

Entrance into business activities during these years was difficult for African-Americans in Chicago and elsewhere. As Drake and Cayton point out, although success for blacks was inevitably measured in terms of their ability to attain positions of power in the city's business world, these same positions were almost universally closed to them. Those few that were open tended to be small-scale, retail operations. That is, it was much more likely for a black to be a barber or a beautician than a manufacturer of beauty products. Yet blacks had particular needs as far as hair care was concerned, needs that were little understood by whites, and almost totally ignored by them. As a consequence, the hair-care and hair-straightening fields had long been lucrative for blacks in America. Madame C. J. Walker (see Walker, Sarah Breedlove) was one example of a black entrepreneur who made a sizable fortune catering to these needs of the black market. She was also a great hero and a role model for a generation of blacks growing up in the 1920s and 1930s.

As a result, there were a number of small-scale hair-care manufacturers like Edward Gardner, who mixed products in their basements and distributed them from the trunk of their cars. By 1945 Drake and Cayton report there were about fifteen such companies in the black ghetto of Chicago, constituting one-third of all black manufacturing enterprises in the city. Gardner joined this group in 1962. Calling his new company Soft Sheen, he began mixing a number of hair-care products for blacks in his basement. With the help of his wife and four children, Gardner hawked his products out of his car, going from block to block and from store to store in his South Side Chicago neighborhood.

At that time, however, Gardner's company was merely the copycat of an emerging giant in the black hair-care field in Chicago. George Johnson,[*] a sharecropper's grandson, had founded Johnson Products in 1954 to market a hair product called Afro Sheen. When the Afro hairstyle became a great fad among blacks in the 1960s, Johnson Products was able to garner 80 percent of the black hair-care market in the United States. Publishing magnate John H. Johnson[*] also had successfully entered the field. Earlier, S. B. Fuller[*] pioneered the manufacture and sale of these products in the city. Gardner and a number of other manufacturers divided up the remainder.

Gardner's products were hardly an immediate hit in the market. He had taken various chemicals into his basement and mixed up several potions that he then carted around to hair stylists, giving out introductory samples. When he returned to some of them, however, they said, "Mr. Gardner, wherever you got this product from, don't ever bring it around here again." Either the product did not work, or it smelled so bad that it drove the customers out of the shop. Gardner admitted the hit-and-miss nature of his research, saying, "I usually ended up filling the house with acrid smoke." Finally, though, Gardner came up with a good conditioner, which he called Soft Sheen Hair and Scalp Conditioner. It was a quintessential family business: Edward Gardner handled the direct sales, Bettiann served as the bookkeeper, and their four children early on were expected to keep busy filling bottles and packing boxes.

As Soft Sheen became more popular, Gardner felt it was time to move the production facilities out of his basement. He set up his first plant, which was about the size of a studio apartment, in Chicago Heights. There the Gardner family labored away, turning out about four or five dozen bottles a week. "That was a big deal," Gardner later recalled. During the next fifteen years or so, the company experienced gradual expansion, setting up new production facilities in the black ghetto of South Side Chicago. In the 1970s, when the Afro hairstyle lost its allure, Johnson Products began to lose market share, and Soft Sheen captured an ever-larger portion of the so-called "ethnic" market. As Gary Gardner, Edward's son, said, Soft Sheen had "consistent growth patterns of 5 to 10 percent per year, which was pretty good, considering the fact that we were continually undercapitalized and had little money for new material and equipment." By 1979 the company had about 100 employees and sold about $500,000 worth of product a year.

Gardner and Soft Sheen were a success, but their great breakthrough came with the introduction of Care Free Curl in 1979. A year earlier, the Jheri curl, a loose-perm look popularized by black stars, such as Michael Jackson, that required a large number of hair maintenance products, burst on the scene. The new hairstyle involved a two-step process—first African-American hair had to be straightened, and then it was curled into a looser, freer look. At first, the leading maker of these new hair products was Revlon, the giant white-owned cosmetic firm. Their product, however, was a liquid, and black beauticians have always preferred cream products for straightening hair. Gary Gardner, who was then pursuing a dual MBA–JD program at Northwestern, recognized that there was an enormous market potential for Soft Sheen if they could create the right product. Also, since the Revlon process was very costly and time consuming, a product that could be used more quickly would be attractive to beauty parlors. In concert with his father, he came up with a product he called Care Free Curl. It was an instantaneous success.

From 1978 to 1982, the new hairstyle spurred the growth of the black hair-care industry at a 32 percent annual rate. Soft Sheen, as the first of the black-owned hair products firms to enter this new market niche, quickly reaped huge revenue increases. Before long, it surpassed Johnson Products as the largest, most profitable black hair products manufacturer. Melvin Jefferson, owner of Superior Beauty Supply in Detroit, said, "In our case, five or six years ago I wasn't doing $10,000 a year with [Soft Sheen], today I do that much in three days." Jefferson said that Gardner was simply "in the right place at the right time with the right product." As early as 1983, Soft Sheen controlled some 55 percent of the hair curl market, which had not even existed prior to 1978. By the early 1980s, sales of Care Free Curl and allied products for Soft Sheen amounted to some $34 million annually. By 1987 Soft Sheen had sales of over $81 million, while Johnson Products had only $38 million.

In the mid–1980s, however, Soft Sheen was faced with a challenge from white hair products manufacturers. Prior to that time, the cosmetics giants had not paid much attention to the ethnic market. They had never bothered to do much research on it, and most of the products they tried to market to blacks were greasy, petroleum jelly–based products that were not compatible with black hair. Revlon, one of the industry giants, in the mid–1980s, began packaging a number of ethnic hair-care products that were similar to Soft Sheen's Care Free Curl. Gardner was determined that massive white-owned conglomerates would not displace him from his hard-won market. "I heard that the people at Revlon say, 'We don't want just part of the market, we want *all* of it.'' Gardner said. "Well, they're not going to get it."

But the black hair-care market, which by 1988 was worth $1 billion, was very attractive to large white-owned cosmetics companies that found their growth stymied in other areas. It was particularly so because blacks spend significantly more on hair and skin products per capita than whites, and the larger and more prosperous black middle class that emerged in the 1980s represented an increasingly attractive market. By 1988 white-owned businesses owned 50 percent of the ethnic hair-care market and had made plans to take all of it from the far smaller, struggling, black-owned businesses. Gardner and other black hair-care manufacturers regarded this as unfair competition.

There were two aspects of this new competition that bothered them most. First of all, the white-owned firms had enormous capital resources to draw from, allowing them to overwhelm the far smaller African-American firms with their advertising, merchandising, and distribution power. Second, black firms are restricted from entering the larger white market. To the white cosmetics giants, it was purely a question of economics. James Alexander, vice president at Revlon, said, "Our approach is color blind. We see green. We will sell to blacks, whites, Hispanics." But Nate Bronner, Jr., vice president of the black-owned Bronner Brothers hair-care firm in Atlanta, said, "It is very similar to what white companies are experiencing from Japanese companies. The Japanese industries to a large degree are government-subsidized, and the white companies that come into the ethnic hair care market are subsidized by their large parent companies. They also have access to both markets and black companies do not have equal access to the white market, just like American companies don't have equal access to the Japanese market." Edward Gardner commented, "If we had equal access to the white market, it [white competition] wouldn't bother me at all." An executive at a large national distribution company essentially agreed with Gardner: "A product made by an ethnic company would always be looked at as a black product, and it would be hard to sell to white beauticians and white customers."

But the black-owned hair-care businesses were not about to roll over and play dead to the white conglomerates. When Irving Bottner, head of Revlon's professional products division, told a reporter that companies like his would take over all black-owned firms because the black firms produced poor-quality products, the black business community united as seldom before. Gardner, along with his cohorts, mounted an intensive campaign against this penetration. Reverend Jesse Jackson's Operation PUSH launched a boycott of Revlon products, and Edward T. Lewis[*] of *Essence* refused to accept any of the company's advertising, as did John Johnson of *Jet* and *Ebony*. In addition, picketers marched in front of a Chicago store selling Revlon's products. Most important, the boycott galvanized the membership of the American Health and Beauty Aids Institute (AHBAI), a twenty-two-member minority trade association of which Edward Gardner was a prominent member. They kicked off a $3 million campaign to induce black consumers to buy black products, all of which were marked with the AHBIA "proud lady" logo. It was a remarkable response, but it was not Gardner's only strategy to ensure his firm's survival in turbulent times.

Gardner's other response was to diversify his operations. During a period of eighteen months, from mid–1986 to early 1988, Soft Sheen made a number of important moves. It first sold a company it had picked up earlier—Perfect Pinch, a condiment manufacturer—on the grounds that it did not fit in with the new approach the company was taking. Edward Gardner as chief executive officer, along with his son Gary, who was president and chief operating officer, devised a strategy for Soft Sheen whereby they would create and manage a portfolio of companies that did business in related areas. Therefore, they set up Brainstorm Communications, an advertising agency that promoted Soft Sheen's products, among others, but which also did business in the general advertising market. They established Bottlewerks, which packaged Soft Sheen products, and *Shop-talk*, a trade magazine distributed to black beauticians.

Soft Sheen also launched a massive advertising campaign for their products. One of the ways in which Revlon and other companies were able to penetrate the black hair-care market was by using testimonials from such African-American media superstars as Billy Dee Williams and Jayne Kennedy. They were able to offer far more money than the black companies could afford. But the "black pride" campaign of AHBIA and other black organizations brought a certain disdain of blacks who promoted Revlon and Alberto Culver products. Soft Sheen signed black singing star Anita Baker as the spokesperson for their products and also sponsored a nationwide musical tour of Baker and Luther Vandross in a series entitled "The Heat." The series was a huge success, selling out everywhere, and Anita Baker helped the firm develop a new line of products called Optimum Care, for which she served as celebrity spokesperson.

In addition, Soft Sheen purchased Dyke and Dryden, the largest black-owned importer, manufacturer, and distributor of black personal-care products in Great Britain. With the growth of the black population in Britain, the Gardners felt that Dyke and Dryden had great potential and viewed it as "a gateway to the African market." Dyke and Dryden had a great deal of experience selling products to Africa, which gave Gardner access to a market of about 600 million blacks. Soft Sheen also established Soft Sheen West Indies, Ltd., in Kingston, Jamaica, to manufacture and market its products throughout the West Indies. Soft Sheen purchased Alaion Products, a manufacturer of lower-priced, black men's hair-care products, in Newark, New Jersey. This gave them an entrée to a portion of the hair-care field where they had previously had no penetration.

Gary Gardner has been the principal architect of Soft Sheen's global strategy. In a fairly short space of time, he set up a worldwide distribution network for the more than 150 products the firm makes. This was his master plan for the 1990s. "We see growth through globalization. We want to strategically market products to people who look like us around the globe," he said. "This becomes more significant as we see competition from majority-owned firms like Helene Curtis and Alberto Culver. We want black men and women to feel great about themselves and they will use Soft Sheen products or products provided by Soft Sheen.'' This dramatic, aggressive approach caused *Black Enterprise* magazine in 1989 to name Soft Sheen its ''company of the year.'' There is some caution on the part of many analysts, however, to see the same potential for success in globalization that Gary Gardner predicts. They point out that both M&M Products of Atlanta and Johnson Products realized heavy losses when they tried to expand onto the African continent.

Also, the idea that black hair-care products will somehow create self-confidence is not accepted by all black activists. The whole phenomenon of blacks straightening their hair, wearing wigs, coloring their hair, and so forth has always engendered a great deal of controversy in the black community. Ralph Wiley has summarized that whole aspect well:

The hair trip is an endless ongoing curling circling mass of people who have been straightening, frying, processing, conking, waving, texturizing, cutting, shaving, parting, hot-ironing, cold-waving, stocking-capping, Jheri-curling, activating, reactivating, oiling, braiding, Afrotiquing, natty dreading, Quo Vadising and otherwise fiddling with their hair for years. . . . Black hair care has become a one-billion-dollar-a-year business, thanks to the ideas of Madame C. J. Walker.

One of the keys to Soft Sheen's success in the domestic market remains its close ties to black beauticians and hairstylists. Fully 40 percent of its sales were to salons, rather than over the counter, and after 1978 it followed a dual strategy of pitching the same products to consumers as they did to salon owners. But Soft Sheen also maintained a staff of eighty-five hair-care experts to educate salon owners on how to apply Soft Sheen products. ''One thing Mr. [Edward] Gardner has always stressed,'' says his daughter-in-law, Denise, who is vice president of marketing, ''was not to forsake salon owners. We marry ourselves to them and we literally take professional vows.'' This alliance between Soft Sheen and black salon owners helps retard the penetration of white-owned firms into that vital segment of the market.

In recent years, Edward Gardner has moved out of the day-to-day management of Soft Sheen, leaving that to his son Gary and other family members. Daughter Terri heads the advertising agency and son Guy manages the bottling operation. Edward Gardner and his wife, meanwhile, have become intimately involved in community development in Chicago. Their roles were especially important in the $5 million renovation of the Regal Theater, owned at one time by the black beauty products mogul S. B. Fuller, on Chicago's South Side. During the 1950s and 1960s, the Regal rivaled Harlem's Apollo Theater as a showcase for black talent, and it represented in the 1980s a major investment in community concerns on the part of the Gardners and Soft Sheen.

Perhaps Edward Gardner's most dramatic contribution to the black community came with his support, to the tune of some $200,000, of a massive voter registration campaign among blacks in Chicago. In 1982 and 1983, an umbrella organization called VOTE Community, set out to sign up an additional 200,000 African-American voters to influence the mayoral campaign in 1983. The candidate that year was Harold Washington, a black, but he was given little chance of winning unless there was a large-scale black turnout. Gardner became the driving force in a tremendous campaign that energized the black community in a manner unlike anything that had been seen before. Gardner provided the bulk of the money for print and electronic ads, posters, buttons, and flyers. The registration drive was an overwhelming success, and Washington became Chicago's first and, so far, only African-American mayor.

After one of his female employees was brutally assaulted by a black male, Gardner founded the Black on Black Love campaign to combat black-on-black violence. As part of an effort to promote greater love and respect among all members of the black community, and to enhance individual and community self-image, the Black on Black Love Program initiated No Crime Day, which was also promoted in cities outside Chicago. For these works, and innumerable others, Ed Gardner has received numerous awards from the city's African-American community. This prompted a black Chicago journalist to announce, "What the black community needs is a few more Ed Gardners." Dempsey J. Travis,* another prominent black business leader and activist in Chicago, said of the Gardners, "They have made more unselfish contributions to the community than anyone else I know."

What Ed Gardner regards as his most important contribution to the city's black community, though, is simply the fact that he is a black manufacturer with his plant deep in the heart of the city's black ghetto, hiring some 625 workers from the community. "My ultimate goal," Gardner said, "is to provide jobs for the black community. In that respect our goals should be unlimited. We'd rather have blacks work here than make them go to Melrose Park." But Edward Gardner was worried about the next generation of black business leaders. When he was growing up, black businesses served a black market and tended to have important roots in the black community itself. Bright and talented young blacks in the 1980s, however, "get the MBA and go right to work for the major corporation and forget about building their own businesses," said Gardner. As a result, he argues that blacks will never break the cycle of poverty, that the black underclass will have an increasingly bleak future. Many black leaders concur. Alice Bussey, an Atlanta florist, and once head of the mostly black Atlanta Business League, saw it in much the same way. "After integration, a lot of blacks got into the system and made it," she said. "But now they have become so individualized that they forget they are supposed to be active in the community. That's why we're not as cohesive as we need to be." Tony Brown, host of a popular television show about blacks, is even more blunt: "You can talk about the other problems of our community, but the real cause is that we have failed to get into business. We have to do something to shore up our economic institutions, to generate jobs within the community. When we take care of that, the other stuff—the family problems, crime, our political needs—will start taking care of itself." The head of the black cosmetics industry trade group echoed the same line: "It's the younger blacks, who didn't live through the civil-rights movement, who don't understand why they should care." To most blacks and whites in America, Edward Gardner's Soft Sheen products are just yellow and red bottles that cater to particular black cosmetic needs. To many black leaders, however, they represent the future.

Sources

No personal or business papers are currently available on Edward Gardner or Soft Sheen. In fact, any kind of information on either is somewhat difficult to uncover. Gardner tends to be quite private about his background and personal life, and Soft Sheen, as a privately held company, chooses not to disseminate much information. There is no full-scale biography of Gardner, and information must be unearthed from a number of sources. The most useful bits of information come from various magazines and newspapers: *Jet*, August 16, 1982, and August 20, 1990; *Newsweek*, October 13, 1986; *Inc.*, September 1986; *Black Enterprise*, June 1987, June 1988, June 1989; June 1990, and June 1992; *Minorities and Women in Business*, January/February 1987; *Chicago Tribune*, June 8, 1983, and June 9, 1985; *Atlanta Journal & Constitution*, March 2, 1987; *Crain's Chicago Business*, June 6, 1983, and October 16, 1989; *Chicago Defender*, December 4, 1985, and February 21 and September 9, 1989; *Chicago Sun-Times*, November 16, 1983, August 14 and November 3, 1987, and January 10, 1989; *Counterparts*, Summer 1987 and Summer 1988; *Chicago Journal*, February 15, 1984; *Metro*, November 19, 1983, and June 7, 1986; *Metro News*, April 4, 1987; *Dollars & Sense Magazine's Blackbook International Reference Guide* (1985); *Class*, September 1990; Frank J. Johnson, *Who's Who among Black Millionaires* (1984), 120–21; *Who's Who among Black Americans* (1988). Also used in preparing the present biography were a number of press releases provided by Soft Sheen Products.

Gaston, Arthur George (July 4, 1892–) Banker, insurance company founder, real estate investor, entrepreneur, and community leader: Citizens Federal Savings Bank, Booker T. Washington Insurance, A. G. Gaston Motel, Booker T. Washington Business College, Vulcan Realty and Investment, Finley Park Garden Apartments, New Grace Hill Cemetery, and A. G. Gaston Home for Senior Citizens. On the eve of his 100th birthday, *Black Enterprise*, in its twentieth anniversary edition celebrating black business in 1992, bestowed upon A. G. Gaston the title "Entrepreneur of the Century." Despite stiff competition, this Birmingham, Alabama, entrepreneur has withstood the test of time, and he has excelled in a city where racial unrest and discrimination have prevailed throughout the century. Against these odds Gaston has created and sustained a business empire that not only provided him and his family with wealth and comfort, but also provided unprecedented opportunities for members of the black community. Throughout the decades of the twentieth century, numerous Birmingham black entrepreneurs have achieved some measure of success, but they have been unable to weather either the hostile racial environment or the unfavorable economic climate. Yet, Gaston could and did. How has this unique African-American achieved and sustained his success over the course of eighty years? The following biography provides glimpses into the tenacity and optimism of Gaston, a man whose patriotism to America and whose commitment to his race might seem contradictory but are, in reality, consistent with the philosophy of Booker T. Washington,[*] his hero.

Self-help, words key to the understanding of A. G. Gaston, touched him as a young child growing up in poverty in Demopolis, Alabama. Raised for a time by his grandmother, a former slave, Gaston was exposed to the dark menace of Ku Klux Klan parades throughout the streets of his town. Rather than harboring deep-seated resentment or hatred of whites after witnessing these exhibitions of white supremacy and suffering other abuses, Gaston declared that he learned to respect whites. After the turn of the century, Gaston joined his mother in the "Magic City" of Birmingham. Having been incorporated as a city in 1871, Birmingham held great promise for workers and speculators alike because of the vast coal, iron ore, and limestone deposits that lay in the hills and valleys of northern Alabama. Railroad developers and land speculators swarmed to the area with the hope of sharing the wealth of what was to become the "Pittsburgh of the South." With the creation of jobs in this budding metropolis, workers converged on the city in large numbers. Blacks, in particular, saw opportunities in an urban environment that had long been denied them in the rural regions of Alabama, where the sharecropping system still exploited their labor. Despite a lull in economic activity in response to the depression of 1873, Birmingham proved resilient, a pattern that was to be repeated several times. The dominance of Tennessee Coal and Iron, Alabama's largest and most powerful coal and iron company, and other companies such as DeBardeleben Coal and Iron, relied heavily on a large supply of black unskilled laborers who could be employed at low wages.

Without considering the social repercussions of recruiting mass numbers of blacks into the region, these industrialists provided the impetus that changed the racial composition of Birmingham. By 1890 blacks made up 43 percent of Birmingham's population, and in both 1910 and 1920 they accounted for 39 percent. Clearly, their presence in the city unsettled whites, who used Jim Crow laws to their fullest extent to segregate the races. As a young child, Gaston seemed immune to the limitations placed on him because of his skin color. Living apart from his mother, who was employed as a cook by the wealthy white owners of Loveman's department store, Gaston attended Tuggle Institute, which was located in the finest black residential neighborhood, Enon Ridge. For a time Gaston resided with Carrie Tuggle, founder of the institute, who greatly influenced Gaston. Tuggle Institute had a similar mandate to Booker T. Washington's Tuskegee Institute—industrial training and self-help. Undoubtedly this training, as well as a guest appearance by Washington himself in Birmingham, shaped young Gaston's own philosophy which empowered him as an astute entrepreneur for years to come.

As a young man Gaston worked at a number of jobs, including selling subscriptions for Oscar Adams' black newspaper, the *Birmingham Reporter*. After Gaston earned a diploma from the institute in 1910, he joined an all-black unit in the U.S. Army, where he claims to have "learned the value of obedience." Upon his return to the United States, Gaston looked ahead to his economic future and did not dwell on the poor treatment he and his fellow soldiers received upon their return to American soil. He secured employment at the Tennessee Coal and Iron Company, where he built railroad cars. His frugality early began to pay off handsomely. To earn extra income, Gaston loaned money to fellow workers, who spent frivolously, and charged them 25 cents on the dollar every two weeks. He also sold box lunches prepared by his mother.

Despite the hostile environment toward blacks throughout Birmingham's history, and most especially during the early part of the twentieth century, black entrepreneurs were taking advantage of the comprehensive segregation. African-Americans were denied access to public facilities, and in response they created parallel institutions to satisfy their own community's needs. Gaston, therefore, was reared in a city where black business people provided role models for an enterprising young man. Reverend T. W. Walker, Reverend William R. Pettiford,[*] Charles M. Harris, and T. C. Windham are just a few of the many black entrepreneurs who created a vital community for Birmingham's African-Americans.

Gaston's unique gift for recognizing and responding to the absence of services and facilities for blacks first revealed itself on a large scale during his efforts to establish a burial society. As early as 1899, Charles M. Harris had founded the Davenport and Harris Funeral Home, and then, in the 1920s, he started the Protective Burial Association. During the 1920s and 1930s, numerous black-owned burial and insurance companies were founded that offered services to the black community and guaranteed a respectable funeral upon the death of the policyholder. The largest black-owned insurance companies operating in Birmingham at this time were Atlanta Life, based in Atlanta, Georgia, and North Carolina Mutual Life Insurance Company, based in Durham. Many of these companies had their origins in the benevolent societies that provided the foundation and training upon which the insurance companies were based. Gaston was a member of several benevolent societies when he was a youngster in the late 1890s and early 1900s. Clearly realizing the benefits accruing to Harris, Gaston, with his father-in-law Abraham Lincoln "Dad" Smith, established the Booker T. Washington Burial Society. (Gaston credits Carrie Tuggle with suggesting the idea.) Quickly, Gaston earned the respect and support of the black community in Westfield and the surrounding towns. Resigning his position at Tennessee Coal and Iron to devote all of his time and effort to this promising venture, Gaston was on the road to success. Soon thereafter, the burial society purchased a funeral home, which catered solely to blacks. The Booker T. Washington Burial Insurance Company was incorporated in 1932, and it offered life and health insurance. All subsequent ventures were financed through this corporation.

The Great Depression that swept across the country in 1929 was completely indiscriminating—it destroyed small and large businesses alike, and white-owned and black-owned enterprises, too. Only the most fortunate businesses survived the ravages of this mighty economic panic. Severe unemployment affected classes of people that were generally immune from economic panics. During the 1930s, almost 8 million families (comprising 28 million individuals) received federal relief nationally. In Birmingham, the casualties among black-owned businesses were high—the number of black-operated retail stores fell from 200 in 1929 to 132 in 1935. And all the black newspapers, including the *Birmingham Eagle*, the *Birmingham Wide Awake*, the *Birmingham Weekly Voice*, and the *Birmingham Reporter* collapsed during the Depression. Yet, Gaston's businesses survived, and his ambitions flourished.

In 1939, when Gaston was unable to find sufficient numbers of black clerical workers to fill vacancies within his companies, he and his wife Minnie established the Booker T. Washington Business College. Ultimately, Gaston hired most of the students who received training there to work in his own enterprises. Under Minnie's guidance, the business college expanded more quickly than the couple's other businesses. The graduating students were the first in Birmingham to be able to take advantage of federal antidiscrimination laws when they came into effect during the 1960s. When blacks were denied access to overnight accommodations while traveling through Alabama, Gaston erected a motel and restaurant that catered to both whites and blacks. Located in downtown Birmingham, it was praised as "one of the finest in the Southeast," by white hotel operators, and hailed as a "wonderful step we hope will encourage the opening of other all-Negro motels and hotels over the Southeast," by race leaders. Gaston claims that he built the motel to fill a need: "I don't look on it just as a business step— but a real adventure in providing something fine that I believe will be appreciated by our people." In 1957 Gaston founded Citizens Federal Savings and Loan Association, later Citizens Federal Savings Bank, in response to the difficulty blacks were encountering when attempting to borrow money to finance their homes and churches. Clearly, Booker T. Washington's philosophy of self-help and diligence was influencing Gaston's every step. Further, in true Washingtonian tradition, Gaston's enterprises were benefiting not only himself, but the black community as well. William R. Pettiford had initiated a similar enterprise, the Alabama Penny Savings Bank, to assist blacks at the turn of the century, and whether or not Gaston appreciated his predecessor's efforts, he was clearly repeating a proven strategy.

Gaining confidence from his growing empire, Gaston continued to enhance and diversify his holdings. Real estate has long been considered a tried and true investment through which substantial earnings can be realized. Some of the richest individuals in America have achieved their wealth through wise and prudent real estate purchases. Gaston ventured into this arena in 1952, when he incorporated the Vulcan Realty and Investment Corporation to buy, sell, and manage real estate in the growing Birmingham market. Although Birmingham failed to experience the dramatic growth of Atlanta, Gaston was nonetheless able to make large profits by astutely exploiting the changes that did occur.

During the 1960s, when urban renewal had peaked and downtown business districts were being overhauled and enhanced at the expense of black housing, Gaston built the A. G. Gaston Building, which was the first new office building built in downtown Birmingham in over thirty years. He moved Citizens Federal Savings and Loan Association into new headquarters in the building and also completed the A. G. Gaston Home for Senior Citizens. Despite social and economic obstacles, Gaston moved forward to create facilities and employment for the black community. In addition to these ventures, Gaston purchased a gospel radio station and an FM rhythm and blues station, which has, on occasion, reached number one while casting wavelengths beyond Alabama's boundaries. Gaston has moved into numerous other business ventures, as diverse as opening a drugstore, purchasing a 2 percent interest in a horse-racing track and buying a bottling company. One might be inclined to conclude that this aggressive entrepreneur had spread himself too thin. Could financial failure just be waiting to happen? The answer is an uncontested, "No." Gaston's businesses have survived economic hardships but, with the exception of one miserable failure, the varied arms of the umbrella company have fared well.

When Gaston, early in his career, ventured into the soft drink business, his "get rich quick" scheme faltered. The young entrepreneur established the Brown Belle Bottling Company when he acquired the Joe Louis Punch franchise in 1938 or 1939. The products were marketed specifically for the black community through advertising of "pretty black women" painted on the panels of the company's trucks. But the revenues were minimal. After the company records and money were stolen, Gaston terminated his involvement as a bottler. Years later, J. Bruce Llewellyn* would illustrate the degree of success possible in the soft drink industry when he purchased the Philadelphia Coca-Cola Bottling Company in 1985. Gaston attributes his failure to his inexperience in the industry and to his desire to make a lot of money quickly. A. G. Gaston would never again repeat these mistakes.

The Booker T. Washington (BTW) Insurance Company's steady growth during the decades of the twentieth century has provided Gaston with security and financial flexibility with which to expand and diversify his holdings. Starting as a mutual aid society that offered life and health insurance, the insurance company consistently addressed the needs of the African-American community and ensured blacks a suitable burial. In 1942 the United States Department of Commerce's *Second Annual Report of Insurance Companies* listed Booker T. Washington Burial Insurance Company's total admitted assets at $112,098, with a total income of $189,407. Almost twenty years later, in 1961, Gaston's insurance company was ranked fifteenth on a list of "Negro-Managed Insurance Companies by Asset Strength." It showed assets of $3,969,476.02 in comparison to the top-ranked North Carolina Mutual Life Insurance Company's assets of $71,133,572.72. Gaston was riding a winning horse.

Black Enterprise's tracking of BTW Insurance over several decades illustrated that this growth continued thoughout the 1970s, 1980s, and into the 1990s. The dollar amount of insurance in force nearly tripled from 1970 to 1983 and passed the half-billion dollar mark for the first time in 1982. The company's total income from premiums and investments climbed from $3.8 million in 1970 to $7.5 million in 1982. Its assets of $24.8 million by the end of 1983 won it a ranking of eighth largest black-owned insurance company. In the 1980s, when merger fever was rampant throughout corporate America, Gaston jumped on the bandwagon in 1983 and acquired the controlling interest of both Unity Life Insurance Company in Mobile and Bradford Industrial Insurance. The friendly takeover added $3.5 million in assets to BTW's coffers. Patricia Walker Shaw,* of Universal Insurance in Memphis, had only praise for Gaston during this time: "I think that BTW is one of the most well-thought-of-insurance companies in the National Insurance Association," of which she was president. "It is very growth-oriented and progressive."

Gaston's original goals for entering the insurance business—to make money and to help his people—have unquestionably been realized. Although he does employ senior executives to direct and coordinate the company's activities, Dr. Gaston (as he came to be called because of the numerous awards and degrees bestowed upon him) is definitely a hands-on manager, director, owner, and operator. In 1984, when *Black Enterprise* named BTW the magazine's "Insurance Company of the Year," Donald L. Solomon, senior vice president for marketing, asserted, "He manages every detail every day. Nothing is done without his permission. Gaston's ability to manage money once he gets it has kept us out of the real problem of survival." Although black-owned insurance companies' earnings and assets cannot and should not be compared to those of white insurance companies, Gaston clearly set his goals high when, in 1984, he declared, "I'd like to take the company up there with the big boys like Aetna and Prudential. I want a piece of the rock." Despite the unlikelihood of Gaston's ever achieving these goals in his lifetime, the statement illustrates his ability to think on a grand scale and to ignore any limitations placed on him because of his skin color. The company has remained in touch with the black community it was originally intended to serve; most of BTW's policyholders are blue-collar workers, many of them female heads of households. As Donald Solomon stated in *Black Enterprise* in June 1984, "Our company is immersed in the philosophy of sharing. Our philosophy has been to stay close to those in our market. They are loyal to us because of our commitment to them. We sell our product to our market, but we invest our premiums back into the community, where they can see, feel and touch it."

Although critics of Gaston's limited market approach predicted that his company would be unable to survive in the future, he has thus far proved them wrong. Without significantly expanding his market, the insurance firm has continued to succeed. Plans articulated for the future, however, did include targeting the burgeoning black middle class. White insurance companies have moved into the black middle-class market, which has seen growth since the 1960s, but lower-class and working-class blacks remain unattractive liabilities for these main-stream, white-owned, insurance giants. On the other hand, black insurance companies have yet to capture a white clientele. Certain vestiges from a time gone by exist at BTW Insurance. Despite its use of computers, the company in 1984 still relied on home service, with its high operational costs. Plans for implementing new marketing strategies were in the developmental stages.

By 1989 BTW Insurance ranked seventh on *Black Enterprise*'s list for black-owned insurance companies, with assets totaling $36,795,000 and $10,213,000 in premium income. These are remarkably healthy returns given the sanguine state of affairs among black insurance companies on the national scene. Mergers and bankruptcies have consumed weaker companies that were unable to reorganize efficiently. Black insurers have difficulty riding out a downward turn in the market because they offer policies primarily covering funeral expenses or provide limited group coverage and reinsurance. Although overall black insurers were failing to share a piece of the pie, Gaston's BTW Insurance was able to withstand the pressure, particularly as middle-income blacks turned to majority-owned insurers which offered a broad array of investment-protection insurance products and better returns for the dollar. Clearly, the executives at BTW Insurance made some wise decisions. By 1991 the climate was bleak. Over the course of twenty years, fifteen companies had dissolved, and the future showed little promise for improvement. The recession was taking its toll among the smaller players, and the bigger firms were either divesting some of their assets or reaping the rewards of mergers, as was the case with the indomitable North Carolina Mutual. Nonetheless, BTW Insurance weathered the storm and emerged sixth among black-owned insurance companies, with assets of $39,398,000 and a premium income of $10,915,000.

Gaston's self-help philosophy incorporates certain rules which he has closely followed and urges others to follow: Pay yourself first; never borrow what you could not repay upon demand; and start a business only when there is a demand for a service. His response to the black community's need for assistance in financing gave sufficient cause for him to found a financial institution. When blacks were suffering from an acute shortage of housing, Gaston established the Citizens Federal Savings and Loan Association, which provided mortgages to blacks who were denied loans from white-owned banks. As Gaston perceived the situation, "There had always been a dual lending policy for home loans in Birmingham." This resulted in African-Americans living in substandard housing and paying exhorbitant rates of interest, if any money at all was available to them at the white lending institutions. White-owned banks counter that charge, claiming they have long loaned money to blacks. The literature suggests otherwise. Gaston's initial attempt at organizing Citizens Federal was opposed by white-owned savings and loan companies which claimed that it was not necessary. Gaston and lawyer and civil rights activist Arthur Shores persuaded the

Federal Home Loan Bank Board of the need for an institution that would lend money to blacks. The board approved the application provided Gaston could raise $350,000 from potential depositors in six months. In just three months, he raised more than $500,000 and subsequently was granted the charter in 1957. This opened opportunities to blacks to share in the American dream of home ownership.

In the same year, when blacks in Tuskegee staged an economic boycott to gain their voting rights, white banks pressured everyone having outstanding mortgages or business loans. But Gaston, a neophyte in the banking industry, loaned mortgage money to those being pressured. Many blacks withdrew their savings from white institutions and deposited them with Gaston's savings and loan. In June 1962 Citizens showed assets of $6,079,680 with $4,736,034 invested in first mortgages on homes and churches in the black community. In 1975 Gaston claimed that he had no intention of making a profit from this venture: "I don't need the money. I already pay over $30,000 a year in income taxes, after legitimate expenses and contributions to charity. I am already in the 80 percent tax bracket—every dollar I make, the government gets 80 cents. Why should I be greedy and take money I don't need from an institution that was founded to fill a social need?" The bank, which was chartered in 1957, had, at the end of its second year, assets of $2,482,946, and by December 31, 1961, the company recorded ledger assets of $5,120,633.85. Among black-managed S&L associations, Citizens Federal ranked eleventh in 1961.

Steady growth continued, and by 1968 $9.6 million in assets had been achieved and more than $6 million had been invested in mortgages on homes and churches owned by Birmingham's blacks. A decade later, Citizens Federal showed total assets of $26,113,458. Mortgage loans had increased, as did the general reserves and surplus, despite the uncertain economic conditions that prevailed at the time. In 1980 the S&L continued to grow, albeit slowly, posting assets of $28,900. These figures clearly reflect the support of the community as well as the astute management and business skills of Gaston and his senior executives. According to Louis J. Willey, vice president, secretary, treasurer, and one of the original seven directors of the S&L, "We've tried to stick with the purpose for which we were organized. . . . We've chosen in the great majority to stay with financing of new and existing homes. . . . Housing is changing to take care of the needs of the entry-level buyer. Many of them don't have all the accessories. Lot sizes are decreasing and the homes as well—just not much point in building homes that do not come within the range of people's ability to buy them."

In 1987 Citizens had assets of $62 million, and among its depositors were the city of Birmingham, Jefferson County, Greene County, and the state of Alabama. By maintaining its conservative philosophy in making loans, the bank has remained financially sound. What has set Citizens apart from its competition is the personal touch, the hometown service it offers the customers, according to Willey, who resigned his presidency of the S&L in 1988. In 1989 Citizens

Federal Savings Bank was rated the safest savings and loan company in Birmingham by Bauer Communications, Inc., of Miami—a respectable feat, given the steady decline of thrifts since 1980.

In 1989 the threat of a takeover emerged when an investor group applied to the Federal Home Bank Board of Atlanta to acquire up to 25 percent of Citizens' stock. Several hundred savings and loan institutions nationwide were being threatened with liquidation or mergers at this time, and Citizens took protective action to prevent a takeover. It established an employee stock ownership plan, which allowed workers to purchase up to $500,000 worth of the bank's common stock. This strategy made a takeover more difficult, although officials of the bank denied that this maneuver was instituted primarily to stymie this threat. Since 1980 more than 1,000 thrifts have failed according to the June 1992 issue of *Black Enterprise*, and between 1987 and 1990 S&Ls lost $43 billion. The steady erosion of black S&Ls over twenty years is evident in the loss of twenty-six of the forty-four black thrifts. Just eighteen remain. During the same period, deposits of the remaining black-owned thrifts grew, as did Citizens'. As of December 31, 1991, assets stood at $72,084,000 and deposits totaled $65,563,000.

During the 1960s, Gaston bought a considerable amount of downtown property, upon which he erected office buildings and a parking lot. The modern buildings symbolized the success of Gaston's numerous enterprises and offered space to house offices and a large auditorium. Vulcan Realty, the real estate development arm of Booker T. Washington Insurance, also addressed the needs of the black community. The firm built several black subdivisions and continued to purchase properties for future development. At his peak, Gaston owned the A. G. Gaston Motel, the New Grace Hill Cemetery, the Finley Park Garden Apartments housing development, considerable real estate, a business school, an insurance company and an S&L, rental housing, radio stations, retirement homes, and so forth. Gaston, as early as 1955, said he could offer "protection from the cradle to the grave." From that point forward, his empire grew and diversified, and during the 1990s Gaston continued to keep abreast of community affairs.

Gaston, well into his nineties, kept his finger on the pulse of his vast empire and showed little interest in retiring. Despite occasional setbacks from poor health, Gaston always bounced back. In 1987 he engineered a transaction that industry observers declared was a first for a black-owned firm: Gaston, who held a 97 percent controlling interest in Booker T. Washington (the remaining 3 percent was held by his wife, Minnie, and his employees), sold his company to his 400 employees for $3.5 million, a fraction of its worth. The firm had $34 million in assets, with $726 million worth of insurance in force. All the subsidiaries were included in the transfer of property, including Booker T. Washington Broadcasting, which owns radio stations WENN and WAGG, and the A. G. Gaston Construction Company. Blazing another trail, Gaston, unlike most business owners who pass their enterprises on to family members, chose an alternative that would benefit most people. Thus, his employees reaped the rewards of his ingenuity, diligence, and generosity and their own hard work. Reflecting on his decision, Gaston commented,'' I could have sold it for a whole lot more, but I'd have had to sell it to some company that would not be able to retain the employees' jobs. They helped me build this thing, and [I] couldn't see throwing them out of jobs.'' His employees in turn expressed their gratitude, and they intended to retain Gaston's strategies: a lean company with clear goals. According to one employee, ''We won't try to fix anything that's not broken.'' Why change a tried and true game plan? Gaston became chairman emeritus of the insurance company, but his position as chairman of the board of Citizens Federal Savings Bank remained unchanged, since the S&L was not included in the transaction. As a public corporation with 400 stockholders (as reported in 1988), the bank's major stockholder was Gaston, who holds 10 percent of the stock.

Gaston contributes generously to the African Methodist Episcopal Church, where he has served as general officer and as secretary treasurer of the Board of Church Extension of the AME Church. He admits that his reasons for involvement in the church are twofold—he believes in the church and he recognizes that his business has a captive audience among those who attend the church services and social functions. ''That's where the money is. Most of the shareholders in our savings and loan association are 'little fellows.' If you stick with the little fellows, if you give them your devotion, they'll make you big. . . . The important thing is what you do with the money you have.'' Gaston has proved that his commitment to the black community stands firm.

Gaston has nonetheless been the target of considerable criticism, particularly during the civil rights movement of the turbulent 1960s. Birmingham has a sad history of violence and bigotry in its race relations. During the 1950s, homes owned by blacks were dynamited repeatedly when they threatened to alter the homogeneity of a neighborhood; subsequently, the city earned the monicker ''Bombingham.'' The city never pressed charges, and blacks were systematically denied their rights despite the passing of federal legislation. Several local African-Americans led a crusade to challenge segregation, but it was not until Martin Luther King, Jr., attracted media attention to Birmingham that the city's politics were exposed nationwide. King pressed for demonstrations to draw attention in his concerted effort to dismantle the deep-seated and institutionalized racism that plagued the city. Local leaders, somewhat overshadowed by King's presence, nonetheless participated in the marches. Although Gaston had long been in touch with the black community and had been identified as race leader of the city by the white power structure, he was unwilling to participate directly in overt challenges to the status quo. He seemed more prepared and better equipped to negotiate with the city's power structure, but he failed to gain the confidence of many local blacks. His position of accommodation was far too conservative for the civil rights movement of the 1960s; a more aggressive approach had been adopted on a national scale. Charges of ''Uncle Tomism'' were repeatedly directed at Gaston, who determined that his options were limited.

Undoubtedly, Gaston's decisons were influenced by selfish concerns. He had taken many decades to build his business empire, and he had carefully nurtured relationships that had earned him the respect of blacks and whites alike. There was far too much at stake to risk. Gaston believed a more gradual, calculated approach was a more appropriate solution to racial discrimination and segregation. When King included young children in the demonstrations, Gaston publicly criticized the strategy. Yet, behind the scenes, Gaston was operating to assist the movement in his own way. He provided free accommodations at his motel for King and Southern Christian Leadership Conference officials, and he supplied them with necessary office equipment. Gaston also donated significant amounts of money to Project C, King's master plan, despite his opposition to their aggressive methods. Gaston put up bail for King when King's "Letter from a Birmingham Jail" was penned. He provided the bail primarily because he knew King was needed to curtail the masses and forestall the splinter groups of more militant protestors. In spite of his nonconfrontational tactics, Gaston too was vulnerable. His motel and his home were bombed during this time.

Gaston's role as liaison between the two races allowed for more open lines of communication during intense hostilities. Overall, his relations with the white community have been reasonably favorable. His appeal for harmony and open communication has been a common theme in his philosophy. He founded Operation New Birmingham's Community Affairs Committee, which was credited with helping to change the racial climate in the city from one of confrontation to one of cooperation and reconciliation. The label of Uncle Tom never seemed to bother Gaston: "[I]f wanting to spare children, save lives, bring peace was Uncle Tomism, then I wanted to be a super Uncle Tom," he said. In the 1992 issue of *Black Enterprise* he proudly declared, "If [he] hadn't been an Uncle Tom, there wouldn't be what we have today."

Birmingham was forced to take a good look at itself after watching the media's ugly portrayal of a city rampant with rage and intolerance. Its politicians recognized a make-over was long overdue, and they responded with aggressive strategies. By the 1990s, Birmingham had become a highly reputable cultural and medical center in the Southeast, whose medical centers have gained national recognition. The tight grip of the white racist power structure was loosening, particularly when the city's first black mayor, Richard Arrington, was elected to office in 1979. The victory achieved by dismantling segregation, however, came at great cost as black businesses suffered considerably. Their once captive audience had been lost to white merchants who offered goods and services at lower prices. Even Gaston was not immune to this development; his motel was forced to close when it lost its lock on the market.

Despite progress in terms of race relations and opportunities, Birmingham lags far behind in affording the opportunities to blacks that they receive in other major urban centers across the nation. Yet, Gaston emerges proud and victorious. During the 1980s and early 1990s, Gaston's attention and interest shifted more to social concerns. In 1966 the A. G. Gaston Boys' Club of America was founded with a $50,000 donation from its namesake. Through this organization and others, Gaston has touched the lives of many young people. He recognizes that the future lies with the young, who need positive role models and opportunities. Gaston has assumed responsibility to make these ingredients available to those less fortunate than himself. Both he and his wife Minnie are devoted to their race and community, and over the years they have exhibited their dedication. Their accomplishments have been recognized worldwide, and, over the decades, A. G. Gaston has been given numerous awards and honorary doctorates, including one from Tuskegee Institute, the school that was founded by his role model Booker T. Washington. The United States Commission on Civil Rights, the Birmingham Area Chamber of Commerce, and the U.S. Small Business Administration have all honored his remarkable accomplishments. Yet, he is most proud of the diploma he received from the Tuggle Institute which he earned himself. Gaston has served on the boards of numerous organizations and has held the position of president in the National Negro Business League, founded by Washington.

A. G. Gaston has had remarkable achievements, as this biography attests. This small, balding man who celebrated his 100th birthday on the 4th of July, 1992, has watched a century pass where social, cultural, economic, and technological advancements have changed the social fabric of American society. He bears no resentment toward whites, nor completely understands nor tolerates blacks who cannot help themselves. He overcame huge obstacles, and he fails to see why others cannot do the same. The acquisition of money, according to Dr. Gaston, is the key to his success, which explains the title of his autobiography, *Green Power*. "The power in this country is money. We got it just like other folks got it. It's a matter of using it in the right way. You can make it whether you are black or white or what side of the tracks you were born on, if you follow the rules, touch all the bases." Gaston is living proof that one individual can take responsibility for his own actions and make a difference for himself and his race.

Sources

Although there are no personal or company papers available at the time of this writing of A. G. Gaston, there is a wealth of information in a few primary sources and secondary source material. Gaston's own personal account of his life and business philosophy appears in *Green Power: The Successful Way of A. G. Gaston* (1968). He also contributed a chapter entitled "Investment in Life," in Stanton L. Wormley and Lewis H. Fenderson, *Many Shades of Black* (1969). An oral history conducted by Ann Elizabeth Adams on November 17, 1975, and June 1, 1977, is held at the Sterne Library of the University of Alabama, Birmingham. The focus of the interviews are Gaston's early years as a businessman, and the influential role Carrie Tuggle played in his life, along with his role in the civil rights struggles in the city. At the office of Booker T. Washington Insurance Company are numerous clippings of Gaston's business career and social contributions. In addition, a quasi-museum within the building displays trophies, certificates, photographs, awards, and memorabilia. The Birmingham Public Library has an excellent collection of well-organized clipping files where numerous articles can be found on A.

G. Gaston under such headings as Banks and Banking, Negroes—Birmingham, and Negroes—Birmingham—Biography—Gaston.

For more general information on Gaston and his business activities, see Geraldine Moore, *Behind the Ebony Mask* (Birmingham, Alabama, 1961); *Ebony Success Library* (1973), vol. II and the following more complete journal articles: *Ebony*, June 1955 and November 1975; *Down Home*, Summer 1982; and *Black Enterprise*, July 1976, and the particularly good article that appears in the twentieth anniversary issue, June 1992, in which Gaston is named "Entrepreneur of the Century." Local Birmingham papers that offer good general accounts of Gaston's business and social activities include the *Birmingham Post-Herald*, April 7 and 8, 1980, June 28, 1981, and July 14, 1987; and *Birmingham News*, October 2, 1978, and July 4, 1982. Another account of his life appears in Frank J. Johnson, *Who's Who of Black Millionaires* (1984).

For information on Citizens Federal Savings and Loan, see *Shades Valley Sun*, July 2, 1980, and the *Birmingham News*, August 21, 1989. An account of the bank's attempt to foil a takeover is recounted in the *Birmingham News*, September 30, 1989. To place Gaston's S&L in a broader framework, see the following articles on black-owned savings and loans: Timothy Bates and William D. Bradford, "Lending Activities of Black-Owned Controlled Savings and Loan Associations," *Review of Black Political Economy*, Winter 1978; William D. Bradford, "The Performance and Problems of Minority Controlled Savings and Loan Associations," *Federal Home Loan Bank Board Journal*, August 1976; William D. Bradford, "The Viability and Performance of Minority Controlled Savings and Loan Associations," working paper no. 62, Office of Economic Research, Federal Home Loan Bank Board, December 1975; Thomas A. King, "The Performance of Minority Controlled Savings and Loan Associations," *Federal Home Loan Bank Board Journal*, November 1980; Lewis Spellman, et al., "The Operating Efficiency of Black Savings and Loan Associations," *Journal of Finance*, May 1977. Also see *The State of Black America 1985*, published by the National Urban League, January 16, 1985, for a comparision of black-owned banks and savings and loans, and for a brief analysis of the contemporary issues facing these institutions.

Data concerning the Booker T. Washington Insurance Company is abundant. A particularly good article can be found in *Black Enterprise*, June 1984. An account of Gaston's move in handing BTW Insurance over to its employees appears in the *Birmingham News*, December 20, 1987; and *Black Enterprise*, June 1988. For an overview of black-owned insurance companies, see *Black Enterprise*, June 1990. C. A. Spencer's "Black Benevolent Societies: The Development of Black Insurance Companies in Nineteenth Century Alabama," *Phylon* XLVI, 3, 1985, offers an analysis of the transformation of benevolent societies to insurance companies. Spencer expresses gratitude to Gaston for providing information and insights into the process. One of the few accounts of Gaston's short-lived Brown Belle Bottling company appears in Vishnu V. Oak's *The Negro Entrepreneur* (1948), which offers a personal account of the business by Gaston. An editorial comment on the controversy that emerged around Gaston's purchase of his radio stations appears in *The Ferrous Journal* VIII, 6, March 1976 (?).

Numerous books have been written about the civil rights movement and the dynamics in Birmingham during the 1950s and 1960s. Gaston's role in the movement is examined in *Ebony*, June 1987, and his opposition to the use of children appeared in the *Birmingham News*, January 14, 1966, and the *Birmingham Post-Herald*, September 9, 1963. The most outstanding works that analyze Gaston's role in the movement and the machinations of Martin Luther King in Birmingham are Howell Raines, *My Soul Is Rested: The Story of the Civil Rights Movement in the Deep South* (1977); Taylor Branch, *Parting the Water: America in the King Years: 1954–63* (1988); and David J. Garrow, *Bearing the Cross: Martin Luther King, Jr., and the Southern Christian Leadership Conference* (1986). For challenges to de facto segregation in Birmingham during the 1950s, when bombings were the norm, see Leavy Oliver, ''Zoning Ordinances in Relation to Segregated Negro Housing in Birmingham, Alabama,'' Master's thesis, Indiana State University, 1951.

Gates, Clifton W. (August 13, 1923–   ) and **James Hurt, Jr.** (1923–?). Bankers, entrepreneurs, civic activists, realtors and developers, supermarket operator, beer distributor, auto dealer, newspaper publisher: Gateway National Bank, C. W. Gates Realty, St. Louis Police Board, Central City Foods, Lismark Distributing, Vanguard Redevelopment Corporation, Employees Loan and Investment, Vanguard Bond and Mortgage, Mid-Central Mortgage and Investment, *St. Louis Sentinel*, Community Redevelopment Corporation, Vanguard Volkswagon, St. Louis School Board, and St. Louis Housing Authority. Clifton Gates and James Hurt in many ways stand as allegories for African-American businessmen after the 1960s. Both men, one from a relatively privileged background, the other a poverty-striken orphan, burst on the scene in St. Louis in the 1960s in dramatic fashion. Coming at a time when the civil rights crusade was dismantling de jure segregation and the future seemed to promise full access to the American mainstream for blacks with talent, drive, and creativity, they both strove mightily to move black business in the city out of the mom-and-pop enterprises of the previous half-century and into the ranks of prominent business enterprise. Their accomplishments were staggering and excited nearly everyone, black or white, during a heady decade and a half. In the end, though, their careers were at least partially tarnished and their empires began to crumble. Both were tainted by scandal, and James Hurt was forced to flee the city in disgrace.

Both Gates and Hurt were born in 1923, but their births were separated by an enormous gulf, geographically and psychically. Clifford Gates was born in tiny Moscow, Arkansas. By the time he moved to St. Louis three years later, he was motherless, and when he was twelve his father died. Orphaned before he was a teenager, Gates, as well as his brother, was taken in by an uncle. The Depression years were difficult, as Gates later recalled: ''Both my wife and I grew up poor. My uncle raised me and my brother through the Depression. My wife was one of six children of a chauffeur.'' Despite these disadvantages, though, Gates was able to graduate from Sumner High and attended Stowe College in St. Louis for two years. Later, he joined the U.S. Army and was sent to Europe, where he landed at Normandy Beach at D-Day-plus-six and became part of the force that advanced into Germany. Upon his discharge, Gates returned to St. Louis, where he got a job with the post office. Working as a timekeeper, he labored for the next twelve years as a civil servant. But he was not satisfied with his economic prospects, and he began to sell real estate in his spare time. As a result, Gates did not get much sleep. He later recalled: ''Since

I was twelve I've always done two things. During my last years with the Post Office, I got by on about four hours of sleep a night."

James Hurt's early years were quite different. Born in St. Louis, his father was a physician and respected businessman in the city's black community. James Hurt, Sr., was from a poor family, whose mother worked as a washerwoman, but he was determined to become a physician. He attended Meharry Medical College in Nashville, but was forced to alternate his work years and his years of study in order to get through. During his alternate working years, the elder Hurt operated a number of business ventures, including an automobile-repair shop and a newspaper in New Jersey. After finally securing his medical degree, he went to St. Louis in 1913. There he practiced medicine for fifty-one years, until his death at the age of seventy-nine in 1965. During all the years he was a doctor, he also continued to run a number of successful business ventures.

St. Louis had long been attractive to blacks from elsewhere and, as a result, had developed a significant business community in the late nineteenth century. Foremost among its early business leaders were James Thomas,* Cyprian Claymorgan, and others, who made fortunes in barbering and real estate. In the early twentieth century both Annie Turnbo-Malone* and Madame C. J. Walker (see Walker, Sarah Breedlove) started their fabulously successful hair preparation concerns in the city. As St. Louis, like other American cities, became increasingly segregated in the early twentieth century, a number of successful black businesses arose to take advantage of the situation. Among them were the Russell and Gordon Funeral Home, which was started in 1894 by W. C. Gordon. Gordon also later set up the Acme Steam Laundry, at one time one of the largest of its kind owned and operated by African-Americans. A few years later, L. S. Williams started Williams Undertaking, another successful establishment. New Age Federal Savings and Loan Association was started in 1915 by Frank L. Williams, a school principal, who ran it until his death in 1952. Carper Casket Company, which had its origins in 1932, also continued as a successful business, and its founder, George Carper, Sr., became an officer in New Age Federal Savings.

Despite these successes, the Great Depression of the 1930s was very hard on black business in St. Louis. According to a study conducted by Atlanta University and the Union League in 1944, "Negro business enterprise hit a new low." Conceding there were 244 business enterprises run by blacks in St. Louis that year, it pointed out they were mainly service establishments and retail stores. Mostly one-man operations, they were largely marginal operations. Such did not seem to be the case with James Hurt, Sr.'s, enterprises. He started his major business endeavor in the teeth of the worst years of the Depression. It emerged out of a benevolent concern. In the early 1930s he had established the Negro Welfare League to help blacks find jobs. In 1938 the elder Hurt founded the Employees Loan and Investment Company with an investment of $2,000. Designed to provide small loans to blacks who were considered bad risks by white lending institutions, Employees Loan survived and prospered because, as James, Jr., later commented: "We had a unique ability to trace bad accounts because we used every method known.'' Like all these finance companies, Employees Loan had to borrow a good deal of money in order to have something to lend its clients. Since the elder Hurt and his other directors got loans on their own personal credit, the correspondingly high interest they charged their own customers was repaid in monthly installments. The elder Hurt suffered a crisis during these early years when he was accused in 1939 in the death of a female patient due to the result of an ''illegal procedure,'' probably an abortion. Nonetheless, his business continued to grow and prosper.

James Hurt, Jr., grew up and went to public school in St. Louis, and at age twelve he began working before and after school at Employees Loan, doing janitorial duties. After graduating from high school, Hurt wanted to go to college in his hometown but found that both St. Louis University and Washington University had a whites-only policy. He therefore went to Ohio State University, where he majored in business administration. After just a short time there, however, his education was interrupted by military service in World War II. He served three years in the China-Burma-India theater of operations and, after the war, returned to St. Louis where he was finally able to enter St. Louis University. There he received his B.A. in commerce and finance in 1948. After graduating, James, Jr., went to work for his father's Employees Loan and Investment, where he watched his father build the business and developed many of his own business practices and philosophies.

One thing he learned was the importance of blacks developing and supporting their own business institutions. Many years later he commented,

My dad used to tell a little story. When my sister and I were children he was going to take out some insurance and he was talking to agents from Metropolitan Life [a white firm] and Atlanta Life [a black firm] and he said he was going to take the insurance that was cheapest for him.

Then he told the man from Metropolitan Life he was going to take out his insurance with Atlanta Life. ''But how can you do that? We've shown you our premiums are cheaper,'' the Metropolitan Life agent told Dad.

My Dad said, ''Yes, your premiums are less but my son might be president of Atlanta Life someday or my daughter might marry the president some day. So, in the long run, the Atlanta Life premiums are cheaper for me and better for my children. (*St. Louis Globe-Democrat*, March 23, 1972)

After seven years with his father's business, James decided to go to work for the St. Louis Housing Authority and spent two years as a manager in the infamous Pruitt-Igoe project. In 1956 Hurt's stepmother died, and his father decided to take the less-active role of chairman of the board of Employees Loan. James, Jr., in 1957, returned to his father's company, replacing him as president and chief executive officer. He quickly began to expand its assets by selling investment certificates and stock.

By 1960, James, Jr., had made a name for himself and had begun attracting the attention of prominent blacks and whites. In that year he was approached by the Citizen's Association for the Public Schools about running for a position on the St. Louis Board of Education. His wife, a graduate of Stowe Teachers College in St. Louis, had been teaching in the St. Louis school system for some twelve years at that point. In December 1960, Hurt won a six-year term on the board, and in 1967 he was elected president of that body. After two years in that position, he continued to serve on the board as a member for a number of years. It was his participation in school board politics that gave Hurt tremendous visibility in the city. Although he protested some elements of segregation within the school system, he was generally viewed by white business elements as a voice of conservatism and moderation. This was of great benefit to him in gaining access to white capital and support for this later endeavors, but it also put him at odds with many black political leaders, some of whom referred to him as an Uncle Tom, as someone too closely allied to white business interests. It was at the end of his two-year term as school board president that Hurt began his great foray as an aggressive entrepreneur.

In the meantime, Clifton Gates was gaining great prominence also, and the two men would unite to create one of the most important economic institutions in black St. Louis. He diligently worked for years in the post office while his wife, like James Hurt's, taught school in the public school system. In 1958 Gates quit the security of the post office "because," he later remembered, "I decided there was something bigger and better." The bigger and better was to become president of his own real estate firm, C. W. Gates Realty. His real estate business, either because of, or in spite of, policies of housing segregation in the city, flourished. He also helped form and became vice president of Mid-Central Mortgage and Investment Company. By 1964 Clifton Gates had become one of the most prominent young black businessmen in the city. As a result, when discussions began about forming, for the first time in the history of St. Louis, an all-black bank, both Gates and James Hurt, Jr., played prominent roles.

In April 1964, Hurt and Gates, along with M. Leo Bohanon, regional director of the National Urban League, and Howard B. Woods, executive editor of the *St. Louis Argus*, and a number of other prominent blacks, made application for a national bank charter. This was to be the first completely black-owned bank in the state of Missouri and the first bank of any kind chartered in St. Louis since the dark days of the Depression. They received a charter on May 19, 1964, with capital of $500,000. Benjamin Davis, a local black dentist, was named chairman of the board, and Clifton Gates became president and chief executive officer of the new bank. Hurt played a less active role, serving on the board of directors.

Gateway National found the going difficult, especially during its first years. Gates and the other officers had hoped to have $5 million on deposit by the end of their first year of operation but, instead, found they had just $2.35 million. Gates announced, "We are not satisfied with the growth," and he cut back capital from $500,000 to $385,000. Gateway's deposits and general business began to pick up after 1966, however, when Gates was appointed the first African-American member of the St. Louis Board of Police Commissioners by Governor

Warren E. Hearne. By 1968 Gateway was showing a profit. A key decision on the part of Gates and the board was to bring in I. Owen Funderburg. A graduate of Morehouse College and the Graduate School of Business at the University of Michigan, Funderburg had worked for many years at the well-established Mechanics and Farmers Bank in Durham, North Carolina. Gates brought him to Gateway in 1966 as executive vice president. The principal decision made at that time was to partially shift the focus of the bank. When it was organized in 1964 Gateway's goal had been to provide loan funds to the city's black community. After Funderburg arrived they decided also to begin pursuing commercial accounts from nearby, largely white, businesses. They also expanded the bank's services in other credit areas, including the establishment of longer banking hours. Funderburg also set up a training program for bank workers, which had been a problem in the early years.

According to Funderburg and Gates, Gateway's mission continued to be as a source of venture capital for fledgling black businesses, and in 1970 they pointed with pride to a number of enterprises in the black community they had supported, such as an excavating company, two trash-hauling firms, several large midtown service stations, and a McDonald's fast food franchise. Another firm that used Gateway's services was the Willie Dennis Moving Company, which expanded to eight trucks, three tractors and trailers, and a large storage warehouse. Irma Dennis, who operated the business with her husband, explained how they had been refused financing by white institutions: "The only time we were able to get a loan on a truck was when a white man co-signed for us. The money in this business is in storage and long-distance hauling, and you know you can't expand into those things without financing." By that time, Gateway ranked thirteenth among the seventeen black banks in the United States.

Yet, Gateway encountered its share of criticism from the black community, particularly for not providing financing for new African-American economic ventures. In March 1969, Gateway turned down a group of blacks who applied for a loan to establish a restaurant on Olive Street which needed an additional $7,700 in capital. "We tried to get a loan from the Gateway National Bank, but our application was turned down because we didn't have enough business experience. And for a couple of other reasons," Allan Clay recalled. "We did finally get a loan from the St. John's Community Bank." Gateway, like its sister black financial institution, New Age Federal Savings, suffered from periodic robberies that strained its resources and credibility. There were times when the new institution's own employees were accused and convicted of acting as accomplices of the bank robbers.

By 1972 Gateway had a staff of thirty-nine people and was exercising an increasing influence on the black community, though the resignation of Funderburg as president in 1974 to join Citizen's Trust Bank in Atlanta was a blow. Nonetheless, Gateway continued to grow and expand throughout the decade. In 1980 Gateway suffered when it was caught holding over $173,000 in bad checks from the Yeatman Community Development Corporation. That was a complex situation that tested the capacity of the bank, but it emerged in good shape. A year later, Gates was elected chairman of the board while still serving as vice chairman of the St. Louis Board of Police Commissioners and retaining his other extensive business interests.

After a time, however, Gates began a power struggle with the board of directors. In August 1987, he was ousted by the board and replaced by Dr. Jerome Williams, Sr., another of the founding members. The bank had lost over $500,000 in the previous year and had the highest percentage of nonperforming loans of any bank in the St. Louis area. Its assets stood at $19.9 million. The bank had also sued Gates over a $52,000 loan in January of that year, a loan for which Gates denied he had any responsibility to repay. Two years later, however, in November 1989, Gates and Williams were elected cochairman to oversee all loans made by Gateway Bank. By 1990 Gateway continued to slip, as it ranked just twenty-fourth among black banks in America and had assets of $21.5 million. By 1992 it was no longer among the largest black banks as ranked by *Black Enterprise* magazine.

During these same years, Clifton Gate's economic and political interests continued to expand. He served as president of the Urban League and was a prominent member of the NAACP. In 1968 he and several other blacks received a license to operate a radio station, KWK. It experienced some financial difficulties but was able to return to the air in 1969 with a $500,000 loan from the Ford Foundation. Gates explained, "We were compelled to terminate the employment of some persons because they were associated with [another broadcasting firm] . . . a group seeking to wrest control of the station away from [Gates]. . . . We were in a situation whereby our own paid employees were trying to sabotage our control of the station." A few years later, however, the station again left the air, this time for good. Gates also had problems with radical black groups in the city, and in 1968 Black Liberation, a militant group, claimed credit for tossing a fire bomb at Gates's home on Union Boulevard. In 1974 he ran for the Democratic nomination for U.S. Congress, but was unsuccessful.

Gates's failure in electoral politics, however, worked to his advantage in business. The Miller Brewing Company had decided to set up a black distributor in St. Louis to go along with the two they had in Los Angeles and Chicago, and Gates, partially because of his visibility on the police commission and as a candidate for political office, was able to acquire it. He set up Lismark Distributing Company, which became very successful. Gates commented at the time about the distributorship: "Things were getting kind of dead in the real estate business. I like action and there's plenty of it out here." There certainly was. In 1987 Lismark also picked up the inner-city distributorship for 7-Up. Gates celebrated by buying himself a large mansion in a swank section of the city. By 1990 Lismark was the ninety-seventh largest firm on the *Black Enterprise* 100 list, with 1989 sales of $7.4 million. In 1984 Gates also became a member of the St. Louis Housing Authority. A Roman Catholic, he continued to live in St. Louis.

Meanwhile, James Hurt, Jr., was experiencing his own version of the American Dream. His first step outside his father's finance operation came when he moved into the furniture business. He explained how this came about: "We had been financing furniture sold by other companies and saw no reason we shouldn't sell the furniture we were financing. That took us into the furniture business." To do this, he set up Vanguard, Inc., which over the years became a mini-conglomerate. Some years later, Hurt's contacts with the public housing authority brought him an opportunity to organize a company to take over some of the management functions. He set up Vanguard Bond and Mortgage Company, which took over the management of a public housing project in the Kinloch section of St. Louis, and was supervising the construction of two others. Another project involved the sale, on a subsidized basis, of attached one-family houses to low-income people. Vanguard also had the contract to provide training and orientation to home ownership for these new owners.

James Hurt's most sensational breakthrough, however, came in 1967, when he announced, in conjunction with eleven ministers, his intention to build and operate a supermarket in the heart of black St. Louis. In April 1969, the new market, called Central City Foods, opened for business at the corner of Grand and Delmar. Clean, orderly, tastefully designed, well-lighted and well-maintained, it made an extremely favorable impression on all who saw it. The store's owners and managers were all black, most of its employees were black, and black subcontractors did most of the construction. A dazzling accomplishment, it fulfilled many of Hurt's long-term goals and dreams.

"We are the biggest single ethnic group in St. Louis," he declared. "There are more Negroes in St. Louis than there are people, black or white, in Little Rock or Louisville, or Kansas City, Kansas. We can achieve something by coming together." The *St. Louis Post-Dispatch* declared this was "James E. Hurt, Jr. Practicing His Own Version of Black Power." Years later, Hurt expanded on this theme: "Black people get paid on Friday and by Monday 90 percent of the money has left the black community. We've got to stop it." Central City Foods was a valiant attempt to do just that.

The genesis of the enterprise came at the Wednesday Morning Breakfast Club, where Hurt and various black ministers had met for years. Its purpose was to develop both ownership possibilities and jobs for black residents. "Basically," Hurt said, "we wanted to prove to black people that if anybody else in this country can do it, we can do it too." The First National Bank of St. Louis had advanced the construction money for the project, and they purchased the land with a loan from General American Life Insurance. It was financed by selling 20,000 shares of stock at $10 each in the black community. "I would say," Hurt claimed, "that 80 percent of the investors in Central City Foods never had any concept of what the word 'stock' meant. Maybe 70 percent of them still don't." Hurt contacted General Grocer Company for advice on site selection and layout and design. In its initial months, the new supermarket was a huge success. With a break-even point of about $2 million a year, it was doing $73,000 a month—or $3.8 million annually—in its early going.

National and local magazine and newspapers, reeling from riots in black ghettoes during the 1960s, and from rhetorical assaults from radical black leaders, crowed Hurt's praises and that of his new supermarket. Hurt himself tried to keep it in some perspective, telling the *Post-Dispatch*:

We are doing nothing with the [supermarket] Project that hasn't been done 100 times before in the white business community. However, I don't think we have reached the point yet where we could do it outside a predominantly black area. The potential is there— but until blacks and whites accept stores as stores and regard the color of the owners as completely incidental to the business, the climate will not be favorable for black enterprises scattered throughout the area.

Doing much of the organization and financing of Central City Foods was Hurt's Vanguard Redevelopment Corporation. Vanguard bought the land, constructed the building, and rented it to Capital City Foods. The U.S. Small Business Administration guaranteed that the rent would be paid. To help finance the operation, Hurt also leased part of the land to Ralston Purina, which built a Jack-in-the-Box restaurant there. Even before the supermarket was completed, Hurt was moving Vanguard and its twelve-man operating staff into new areas. They commenced a $1.6 million, 116-apartment, low-income housing project and also applied for other developments totaling 1,204 apartments costing $15.8 million. Employees Loan, the mother company, by this time had expanded its assets to $1.1 million.

By the early 1970s, the *St. Louis Globe-Democrat* was calling Hurt an "empire builder." The empire by then included the *St. Louis Sentinel*, a weekly newspaper he had started in 1968 with Howard B. Woods, formerly of *The Argus*, as editor. At about the same time, Hurt also announced he wished to expand Central City Foods into a nationwide supermarket chain. Speaking at the Grocery Manufacturers of America's meeting in New York City, he asked for the assistance of that group in acquiring twenty black supermarkets in inner cities across the nation. A year later, his Vanguard Bond and Mortgage Company, with Dr. Jerome Williams as president and Hurt as vice president, purchased a section of the Grandel Urban Project, the first parcel of urban renewal property the U.S. government ever sold to blacks.

In 1970 Hurt became the first black Volkswagon dealer in the United States, setting up Vanguard Volkswagon on Page Boulevard. At the same time, he got together with a group of black architects and subcontractors to form a loose association designed to attract more building projects for black companies. "We are just out to get as much of the action as we can," Hurt said. "The only way black people can succeed is by uniting ourselves together." Not all blacks, especially the more militant ones, were impressed with Hurt's activities. Like Gates's company, in 1969, his loan company was firebombed.

By the early 1970s Hurt had four large, dynamic business operations. His Central City Foods, which employed forty people, was finally beginning to show a profit; his Vanguard Bond and Mortgage, which was developing and managing housing projects costing some $3.7 million, provided housing units for 252 lower income families. Vanguard Volkswagon was making money, and Vanguard Bond was also expanding into new areas, having won approval to build 550 homes in the DeSoto-Carr area for $11 million. From this latter project, Hurt developed a grandiose plan to "save the city." Reflecting on the warning from the National Urban League that St. Louis and other American cities might become "urban ghost towns," Hurt proposed to use his project in the DeSoto-Carr area as a candidate for what he called "intensive care."

The DeSoto-Carr area in 1960 had a total of 310 businesses and 3,600 families, not including those living in nearby housing projects. Ten years later, there were just 160 businesses and 253 families there. Under Hurt's plan, the neighborhood would be given the highest level of every kind of service possible. Through special grants from the federal government and private foundations, it would get extra policemen to patrol its streets, the best teachers assigned to its schools, a new park department, and improved street cleaning and repair; all other city services were to be upgraded. Hurt also sought approval to locate the city's new convention center in the eastern portion of the project. A short time later, Hurt also bid successfully to build a hotel as part of the city's redevelopment of a sixteen-block area around the convention center. This was accomplished with the creation of a new company, a racially integrated firm called Community Redevelopment Corporation. Doing all of this, of course, greatly enhanced the project that Hurt's Vanguard Bond was developing in the area. Hurt couched his plans for the hotel and convention center in the area in politically cogent terms. "A vast majority of Americans," he said, "have only been exposed to blacks in positions of servitude. They are convinced that we can never be successful because they have never seen blacks in positions of responsibility."

About this same time, however, Hurt's empire began to unravel. As early as 1972 he was being pestered for the payment of $12,000 in delinquent property taxes on his late father's estate. Two years later, he had paid off only a portion of that. Then, in 1974, he ran into all sorts of problems. In one court decision he was ordered to repay $250,000 to Vanguard Bond and Mortgage. In another, the court threatened to take over the property from his father's estate for back taxes, and a third suit filed by stockholders of Employees Loan and Investment asked that the firm be dissolved and Hurt and several others be fired from their positions in the company. As a result of these suits, the financial records of the six firms controlled by Hurt were examined by court authorities for possible fraud.

By December 1974, Hurt's Vanguard Construction and Development had defaulted for the second time on low-income apartments that it was building for the St. Louis Housing Authority. Hurt at the same time was being sought by authorities in connection with a bad check charge and was facing grand jury indictments. In January 1975, Hurt was arrested and held for a few hours. Hurt himself blamed Department of Housing and Urban Development policies for the predicament he was in, and he announced various plans for turning his business around. In August 1976, however, he was arrested on a bad check charge. When he was released, he disappeared from St. Louis, his empire in shambles and his reputation ruined.

Black business in St. Louis had fallen a long way in the twentieth century, and its situation seemed not unlike what happened to James Hurt. Full of optimism in the early years of the century, many new businesses were created. The Depression destroyed many of those, but others were born, including James Hurt, Sr.'s, Employees Loan. The 1960s and 1970s brought heady times for both Gates and Hurt and seemed to foretell a glamorous and prosperous future for black business in the city and nation. But it did not quite work out that way. George S. Price, Jr., the black president of Kemi-Kol Building Maintenance Company, in 1971 predicted this would happen. Sardonically, he claimed, "In St. Louis, black capitalism is a bust." It seemed that way. St. Louis, with one of the largest black populations in America, had just one firm among *Black Enterprise*'s largest companies in 1992—Leader Motors, Inc.—started in 1983 by Jesse Morrow, the eighteenth largest black auto dealer in America. But the others, Gateway National Bank, Central City Foods, Vanguard Company, and even Lismark Distributing, had all slid from national prominence. Black capitalism in St. Louis had turned out to be a tragic affair.

Sources

The only primary source material available that deals with Gates and Hurt are the annual reports of Gateway National Bank from 1965 to 1979, held in the Black History Collection in the Thomas Jefferson Library at the University of Missouri at St. Louis. The most extensive information on Clifford Gates can be obtained from the clipping files at the St. Louis Mercantile Library, which has a large number of newspaper articles from the *St. Louis Post-Dispatch* and the *Globe*. Articles from the city's black newspaper, *The Argus*, generally are not held. There is a brief biography of Gates in *Who's Who in Black America, 1990–91*. There is a useful chapter on James Hurt in John Seder and Berkeley G. Burrell's, *Getting it Together*, (1971) 147–59. Most information on Hurt came from the clipping files at the St. Louis Mercantile Library. In addition, see an article in *Business Week*, May 10, 1969.

Geddes Family (see DeJoie, Geddes, and Misshore Families).

Gibson, Truman Kella (see Dickerson, Earl Burrus, Truman Kella Gibson, Sr., Truman Kella Gibson, Jr., and Frank L. Gillespie).

Gibson, Truman Kella, Jr. (see Dickerson, Earl Burrus, Truman Kella Gibson, Sr., Truman Kella Gibson, Jr., and Frank L. Gillespie).

Gidron, Richard D. (October 10, 1938–   ). Car dealer: Dick Gidron Cadillac & Ford Inc. African-Americans historically have faced enormous barriers gaining access to the mainstream economy. Traditionally, blacks have operated in what could be considered a dual-market economy, whereby they served solely the segregated black population. Exceptions to this rule have provided a few black entrepreneurs with the means by which to cross over into the mainstream economy. One of these notable exceptions is the opportunity to own car dealerships. Blacks had long been denied positions in the automobile industry other than as car jockeys or service personnel. However, that scenario changed when the Chrysler Corporation granted the first black-owned dealership to Ed Davis of Detroit. This now defunct agency helped to open the doors for people like Dick Gidron, whose success helped pave the path for other entrepreneurially minded African-Americans.

Richard D. Gidron was born on the notorious South Side of Chicago on October 10, 1938. At fourteen years of age he lost his father to an accident in the kitchen of a railroad car where he worked as a chef. His schoolteacher mother was responsible for rearing their three children on her own. The young Gidron survived those years without incident due to the staunch disciplinarian ways of his mother and grandmother. While attending school he worked part-time for General Motors as a car jockey in 1958 and moved into servicing cars within two years. He attended Bryant Stratton College as a business major with financial assistance from General Motors and graduated in 1959. Having little interest in settling for a career in the automobile industry, Gidron did not take an aggressive approach in shaping his future. However, his abilities were being recognized and he became the first black salesman of Cadillacs in the history of the company at the tender age of twenty. He worked as a service salesman for five years, learning the nuts and bolts of cars and customer service, an invaluable lesson in years to come. In 1966 he was promoted to the position of new car salesman, another first. A year later he became the top salesman in the country, netting $100,000 in income. Clearly, his abilities were earning him the attention of senior executives. The color barrier was about to be broken.

By 1967 Gidron was the top Cadillac salesperson in the country, an honor he held for four consecutive years. From that success, he was granted the position of assistant branch manager of the Chicago dealership for which he worked. The clientele of this agency was from 70 to 80 percent white. This fact taught him one of the realities of the marketplace: He could not survive by selling to a restricted market, since the bulk of his earnings was coming from white customers. His recognition of this fact shaped his approach as an entrepreneur in the future. As *Black Enterprise* stated, in its April 1975 issue, there were approximately 5,000 Cadillac salesmen in the United States, and Gidron's success in these early years was derived from converting many of his customer service accounts into new car buyers. He was again rewarded for increasing sales at the Cadillac dealership by a promotion to general manager. It was a relatively slow climb, but one that provided him with insight into all the operations of a dealership. As he succinctly articulated in 1975, "I went from the back end to the front end."

Taking all he learned during his years as a car jockey, serviceman, salesman, branch manager, and general manager, Gidron was ready to take a giant step. His accumulated knowledge was about to be put to the test. Although he was a native Chicagoan, and felt most comfortable working in a familiar market, an opportunity arose that he felt compelled to take. In 1972 a GM dealership became available in the Bronx, one of the five boroughs making up New York City. Having previously worked in the district of Chicago known as the Loop, Gidron had grown accustomed to serving an ethnically mixed clientele. The Bronx, too, was racially and ethnically diverse, which would provide Gidron with a familiar customer base. More important, the location was central and could draw from all of the five boroughs. "It was close to Manhattan and Harlem and the dealership was in a totally integrated community," he recalled. The dealership was located directly across from the renowned Jesuit institution Fordham University and near the world-famous Bronx Zoo.

Gidron could not have landed the Bronx dealership without the assistance of General Motors, who he claims has been "a good ally." Two black executives at GM worked very closely with Gidron to plan for the dealership. Gidron recalled, "We worked very closely together before we made this kind of investment in New York, because I really wanted to be a dealer in Chicago." GM was clearly committed to the concept of having more black dealers and they wanted them to succeed. Their diligence paid off in the persona of Dick Gidron. He was GM's second black auto dealer; the first was Albert W. Johnson* in 1967, a comrade and competitor. Despite GM's Minority Dealer Development Academy, designed to give minority business persons a better chance in winning and sustaining a car dealership, Gidron had sufficient background to succeed without the aid of the program. Johnson recalls that "Gidron had the tenacity to accomplish his goals and that he was a strong competitor. And he also has a knack for dealing with people." Gidron bought the business for $650,000— including a down payment of $150,000, with the remainder financed by GM. Gidron recalled in 1989 that he was not surprised that GM had considered him for the dealership because "[I] had the training, the money, the discipline and the knowledge to get along with everyone and to become a success."

However, New York has long been a tough nut to crack. A unique market, it has challenged the best of business people. Not only did he have to deal with being a black Cadillac dealer but he had to contend with the fact that no one knew him in New York City. Connections are very important in any market, but particularly in New York. However, Gidron used wile to insinuate himself into the ranks of the city's movers and shakers. Within six months, through extensive advertising and public relations, his visibility had increased dramatically. He received skilled advice from Percy Sutton* and James Bruce Llewellyn,* who, Gidron claimed, "knew the ropes and the players." Llewellyn introduced Gidron to several of the city's power brokers and engineered his entrée into the influential 100 Black Men organization. Both Sutton and Llewellyn speak very highly of Gidron. As Llewellyn recalled in 1989, "This guy knew the auto business and he had a real warmth about him. There are no false pretenses about Dick Gidron."

The odds were not in his favor. At this time the short history of black car dealerships had been marked by a large number of failures due to lack of experience and training. Gidron overcame the odds and emerged victorious through hard work and hiring well-trained employees. In 1973 the dealership sold 1,100 new cars and had earned a reputation as one of the largest and best-run dealerships in the nation. Upon assuming control, Gidron retained the personnel already in place since they had a proven track record. Because he runs a tight ship and has an engaging style, he quickly earned the respect of the managers and employees alike. He learned to tailor his more extravagant style, which took some adjustments. "I had to find out that I wasn't a millionaire because my name was up in lights and I had a lot of people running around the office calling me boss." Yet, curbing his style did not interfere with Gidron's attempt to create a certain environment by redecorating the Cadillac showroom. He clearly understood the symbolic significance of a Cadillac at that time. It was the car of prestige and status. As he stated in the late 1970s, "Really, the average American dreams of owning a Cadillac." And at that time he was right. The smaller, more fuel-efficient cars did not give the major three car manufacturers a run for their money until the 1980s. Gidron also took aggressive steps toward consolidating the dealership's operations by relocating the downtown accounting office to the Bronx. His new electronic accounting system allowed him to keep on top of the company's financial position, which in turn enabled him to engage in more spontaneous decision making.

The key to his success as one of the black pioneers of owning a car dealership was the emphasis Gidron placed on service. He provides "total" service to his customers, of which 50 or 60 percent are white. To his staff in just two years, he added three black salesmen, a reflection of the increasing black trade his dealership is attracting. When Gidron assumed control, the company had a customer ratio of white to black of 75:25; by 1975, the ratio had altered to 62:38. His agency was in the black from the beginning, which enabled him to pay off the loan of more than $500,000 from GM in just eighteen months. And much of his customers patronize his dealership on a referral basis—"word of mouth advertising."

Yet, not all was rosy for Dick Gidron and his entrée into dealer ownership. Within fifteen days of assuming title to the company, Gidron was faced with a labor dispute that centered around an agreement negotiated between New York City Cadillac salesmen and the dealers. A citywide strike ensued. He pushed ahead in spite of this rocky initiation rite, and his agency actually made money during the strike. His indomitable spirit has kept him above water even during the most trying times. A nationwide energy crisis challenged the domestic car industry during the late 1970s, when a gasoline shortage resulted in enormous lineups at the pumps. Americans became enraged with the escalating prices and long waits. The time was ripe for foreign car makers to take advantage of disgruntled Americans. Yet rather than focusing on the negative, Gidron concluded that motorists would use their gasoline more wisely if they were required to pay more. His optimism was commendable, if not wholly accurate.

By the late 1970s and early 1980s, car sales were down, and car dealers across the nation were suffering, including Gidron Cadillac. Sales fell as consumers were faced with high interest rates, the uncertainty of the administration, and high gasoline prices. Inevitably, black-owned car dealerships were hit the hardest. As Gidron asserted, "Blacks haven't been in this business long enough to accumulate the kind of capital that white dealers have." He survived the "crash of '79" and the subsequent inflationary years that financially toppled more than fifteen black dealerships across the United States. In 1980 he ranked in the top ten of the 1,600 Cadillac dealers in the United States and has one of the largest minority-owned corporations in the country. The second-largest Cadillac dealer in New York City, he has had an impressive client roster including former heavyweight champions Muhammed Ali and Larry Holmes and social activist Dick Gregory. Rather than dwelling on the possible repercussions of this downward trend, Gidron looked on the brighter side: "I think it has bottomed out. I have to be an optimist. I've got so much invested." His positive thinking worked to his benefit: He grew and profited during the 1980s, showing sales of $17 million in 1982. His strategy of cutting overhead and cutting some personnel reaped rewards. By the early 1980s, his agency was doing the same amount of business with thirty-five fewer employees.

After much cajoling, Gidron finally succumbed to offers from Ford Motor Company to buy a dealership. His devotion to GM ultimately gave way to an attractive deal. His reason for investing $650,000 in cash in a Ford agency was "that the Ford Motor Company has one of the finest lines of cars for 1984 of any carmaker in the country, and I thought it would be another profit center and another challenge for Dick Gidron." Ford had the number-one-selling car in the world in 1983—the Escort—and Gidron saw dollar signs. In 1982, the year before Gidron purchased the Ford agency, it had sold 395 cars and 166 trucks in the Bronx. By 1988 Ford had sold 1,120 cars and 52 trucks in the borough. As an executive with Ford asserts, "We would not be doing this well in the Bronx without him." Gidron's skills were transferable, and Ford was reaping the rewards of his extensive training with GM. He was in it for the long haul.

Gidron's aggressive salesmanship and enthusiasm ensured his success, even during troubling times. By 1989 his empire included 300 employees and four profitable franchises—the flagship Cadillac dealership and three Ford stores, two in the Bronx (which had combined gross sales of $19 million in 1988) and one in Mount Kisco, New York (which netted $11 million). This success earned him the title of *Black Enterprise*'s "Auto Dealer of the Year" in 1989. Like all astute business people, Gidron diversified. He entered into insurance and real estate in the Bronx and in Scarsdale and has a $1 million stake in NYT Cable TV. The cable TV station was purchased for $420 million by a joint venture group that included J. Bruce Llewellyn and Queen City Broadcasting, a Buffalo, New York, television production company that Llewellyn runs. Gidron was playing in the major leagues.

As the auto industry became increasingly competitive with the onslaught of foreign imports, Gidron in 1989 was less sanguine than he had been a decade earlier. He does not count himself among those who are destined to fail during a time when the quality of American cars are being questioned. He provides his sales staff with training seminars to keep them informed about their competition and to hone their sales skills. As he declared in the 1989 issue of *Black Enterprise*: "You have to be much sharper today to run a business than you had to be 20 years ago because the consumers have changed the business a lot." The same issue offered his insight on what it will take to survive in a changing market: "The dealers who will do successful business in the 1990s will have to be megadealers. We're talking about dealers with six, seven, eight franchises. That's the way to do business in the '90s." Gidron is definitely following his own advice. In the late 1980s, he was eyeing a foreign dealership—Mercedes. At that time there was only one black-owned foreign dealer—Robert P. Ross of Bob Ross Buick Mercedes, GMC in Ohio. Gidron recognizes the stiff competition to land a foreign dealership, particularly because "[foreign dealers] have a way of ignoring the black and Hispanic community." He was also entertaining the idea of buying a franchise in southeast Florida, where the market is growing by leaps and bounds. These were dreams that could not yet be realized because his franchises were feeling the effects of the foreign competition. By 1991 Dick Gidron Cadillac and Ford had slid to fourteenth place from eighth a year earlier, and from its third place standing in 1989 on *Black Enterprise*'s list of the 100 top black auto dealers. Its sales stood at $39,500,000, well behind those of the top black auto dealer—Shack-Woods and Associates of Long Beach, California, with sales of $287,000,000. Gidron no longer led the pack though he did blaze the trail.

The early 1990s proved to be a trying time for automobile dealers across the nation, particularly black car dealers. Americans seemed to have lost faith in the Big Three car manufacturers, as their cars failed to keep pace with the quality offered by such foreign firms as Toyota, Saab, Mazda, and Honda. And, at the higher end of the market, GM's Cadillac had to compete with Mercedes Benz, BMW, and Audi. It appeared that the key to success in the 1990s was to own a foreign car dealership. Mel Farr, who owns Mel Farr Automotive Group in Oak Park, Michigan, did just that. In 1989 he added a Toyota dealership to his other franchises, only the fifth black-owned Toyota agency in the country. This strategy enabled him to weather the storm of the first two years of the decade and granted him the title of *Black Enterprise*'s "Auto Dealer of the Year." Gidron's aspirations to own a Mercedes dealership still remained unrealized in late 1992. These were brutal times for others too. New strategies were required to survive the recession—do more with less. *Black Enterprise* reported in 1992 that its Auto 100 list employed 4.6 percent fewer people in 1991 than in 1990. Also, several companies either shut down or sold a dealership if they had more than one franchise. Even Baranco Automotive Group of Decatur, Georgia, one of the shining lights among black dealerships, was forced to sell one of its franchises as it watched its sales fall 13.9 percent from the previous year. Forty of the dealerships represented on *Black Enterprise*'s 1992 list showed lower sales, and seventeen dealerships reported gross revenues that dropped by more than 10 percent. The economic climate was bleak and they were feeling it firsthand. Thus, survival alone was a challenge, and Gidron rose to the occasion. As he has proved in the past, diligence and optimism pay off.

Dick Gidron's interests extend beyond himself. He is committed to participating in the rejuvenation of the Bronx, a borough that strives to overcome the negative image of the poverty-ridden, drug- and crime-infested South Bronx. The epithet "Mr. Bronx" is fitting, for he is personally dedicated to orchestrating the renaissance of the borough. He serves on numerous boards and has served as president of the Bronx Chamber of Commerce and has helped raise $65 million for Fordham Plaza, a luxury office tower that has pumped money and life into the borough. His community work was cited by President Reagan, who awarded him a citation for his outstanding contribution to the Bronx. As Gidron assesses his responsibility,

A dealer has to be community-minded, not only to take money out of the community, but to be also concerned about putting something back. You have to remember that an auto dealer doesn't have any competition within eight to ten miles of his or her franchise of the same make. Therefore, since I'm a Cadillac dealer in the Bronx, when people talk about Cadillacs, they refer to Dick Gidron. So it's my responsibility to be a part of this city in a positive way. (*Black Enterprise*, June 1989)

Gidron has considered entering the political arena where he could wield greater influence. J. Bruce Llewellyn had suggested that Gidron "wanted to be a big political power in the Bronx," but Gidron's aspirations supersede the Bronx. He turned down the opportunity to run for Bronx borough president because it did not have "the kind of power I wanted." His commanding presence and resourcefulness are definite assets in politics, where the bureaucratic hierarchy can hamper and impede progress. Gidron's tenacity has ensured his longevity in a cutthroat business that has seen more than its fair share of failures. And, he intends to remain a commanding figure in the years to come. His two children are waiting in the wings to take Gidron Cadillac and Ford a step farther. As Richard, Jr., aspired: "We'd like it to be on the same sales level as a *Fortune* 500 company." They have a long road ahead of them, but with dreams like that there is no telling what lies ahead.

Sources

Dick Gidron's personal or business papers are not available. Gidron appears in *Who's Who among Black Americans, 1980–1981*. The following articles track Gidron's career from its inception to the 1990s: *New Yorker*, December 23, 1972; *Black Enterprise*, April 1975; *News World*, 1977(?), and June 17, 1979; *New York Times*, June 2, 1980; *New Yorker*, October 31, 1983; *Black Enterprise*, November 1983; "The Making of Black Car Dealers," *Black Enterprise*, May 1974; and *Black Enterprise*, June 1989. The literature is scarce on African-American participation in the automobile industry. By far the best analysis appears in the annual listings of *Black Enterprise*'s largest black businesses, which also includes the rankings of black-owned car dealerships. *Black Enterprise*,

May 1974, analyzes General Motor's special training program for minorities to become car dealership owners.

Gillespie, Frank L. (see Dickerson, Earl Burrus, Truman Kella Gibson, Sr., Truman Kella Gibson, Jr., and Frank L. Gillespie).

Gordy, Berry (see de Passe, Suzanne Celeste, and Berry Gordy, Jr.).

Graves, Earl (1935–   ). Publisher and entrepreneur: *Black Enterprise* Magazine, Pepsi-Cola of Washington, D.C., and Earl G. Graves, Ltd. Earl Graves is in many respects a late twentieth-century reincarnation of Booker Taliaferro Washington,* perhaps with a little W.E.B. Du Bois and Marcus Garvey thrown into the balance. In the pages of his *Black Enterprise* magazine, he has promoted the prospects of African-American business and black economic development for over two decades, while at the same time demonstrating an acute entrepreneurial bent in his own right. In the black community of the 1980s and 1990s, which was increasingly rudderless and leaderless, Earl Graves's was one voice that was heard above the crowd.

Earl Graves was born and raised in the Bedford-Stuyvesant area of Brooklyn. His father also grew up in Brooklyn, graduating from Erasmus Hall High School. By the time he graduated, however, his father had died, and the elder Graves was forced to go to work as a $17-a-week shipping clerk to help his siblings finish high school and go on to college. As a result, Earl Graves's father never made a great deal of money, but he always urged Earl and his brother and sisters to succeed. Earl Graves's parents stressed the values of cleanliness, thrift, and academic excellence. His father always insisted that a good education was a "must" and "*not* an option." Later Graves said, "My father, who died at 47 when I was 19, used to say that he wanted me to *own* something." This early instilled in Graves the twin notions of owning a business and of developing a strong economic base for the black community. "I have always believed," he said, "that we must develop our own economic base if we are to make an impact on this society and protect our interests." Earl Graves also graduated from Erasmus High School, the second oldest school in America, and one with few blacks: "My father graduated from the same high school that I did. He was the only black in his high school class, and in my class I think there were only two of us."

Graves early showed an entrepreneurial interest, selling $150 worth of Christmas cards at five years of age. After graduating from high school, he went on to Morgan State University in Baltimore, Maryland, on a scholarship, where he ran on the track team and majored in economics. Graves made the dean's list in college, and was an officer or member of eight campus organizations. Since his father had died by this time, Graves had to earn money to put himself through school. He worked summers as a lifeguard in New York City and also operated several business enterprises on campus during the year, including a food and snack service and a flower, gardening. and landscaping operation.

After graduating from Morgan State in 1958 with a B.A. in economics, Graves joined the U.S. Army. While at college he had been in the Reserve Officer Training Corps, so he was commissioned a second lieutenant. While in the service Graves attended the elite Airborne and Rangers School and finished his army career with the rank of captain as a member of the 19th Special Forces Group—the famous Green Berets. Upon being mustered out of active service, Graves went to work as a narcotics agent with the U.S. Treasury Department. He did not remain at this long, however, and was soon back in Bedford-Stuyvesant, working for a real estate firm. Within a year he became the manager of that company, and he continued to sell and develop real estate until 1965, when he volunteered to assist in Senator Robert Kennedy's office.

A year later Graves was asked to join the Kennedy staff as a full-time, salaried administrative assistant, and he worked with the Kennedy team until the senator's assassination in the spring of 1968. The experience had a profound impact on Graves: "The main thing Kennedy did was to continue to foster my attitude that anything could get done once you made up your mind to get on with the work. There was no such thing in Kennedy's mindset as we *can't* do, it was just a matter of how long it would take us to get it done." After Kennedy's death, Graves formed his own management consulting firm—Earl G. Graves Associates—to advise corporations on urban affairs and economic development. He was able to attract a number of multinational corporations as clients. But this was not enough for Graves—he had been inspired throughout his life not just to become successful, but also in some way to make his success contribute to broader African-American economic development.

Graves believed that the black community needed "some kind of vehicle that could hook us all together to see what our mutual concerns, problems and opportunities were as black people in this country." Graves at that time was in Fayette, Mississippi, working on the campaign of Charles Evers to become the first black mayor of that city. The campaign was a success, and that set Graves thinking. Evers had made a good deal of money as a businessman in Mississippi, but he was now using that prestige and success to further the interests of the African-American community. Perhaps this could be done on a national level also. The Nixon administration had taken power in early 1969, and it had little sympathy for civil rights or black protest. What they did want, it seemed, was for blacks to enter the mainstream of American economic development. "Somehow the Nixon Administration," said Graves, "struck on the idea that black economic development was something they could run with. To a certain extent it felt it could do cosmetic-type things that made it appear a great effort was being made toward the growth of black business."

"Because of this," recalled Graves, "the time was absolutely right for *Black Enterprise*. There was a need for a magazine such as ours, and it got off the ground because of our commitment to it." Back in 1969," Graves said, "we started formulation of the germ of an idea that became *Black Enterprise* magazine, and the first issue came out in August 1970." Graves began making plans for the magazine with the help of Thomas A. Johnson, a veteran reporter with the *New York Times*. "Earl and I agreed first of all that this had to be a good, substantial magazine," Johnson later recalled. "This was not going to be a cut and paste type of magazine, something just put out there." This, of course, would be expensive; so Graves had to get the support of major African-American organizations and the financial backing of some important white financial institutions.

Graves's first task, then, was to sell the concept of *Black Enterprise* to the black community. This was not as easy as it might seem. The whole thrust of African-American thought and ideology from the end of World War II to the 1960s had been on integration into the mainstream of white society, and the use of the weapons of moral suasion and protest to achieve that. To many black militants and mainstream black organizations, black business was considered a charade as far as benefiting the mass of African-Americans. This view had been articulated as early as the 1930s by Abram Harris in his *Negro as Capitalist*, was picked up by the Carnegie-Myrdal study in the 1940s, and received its fullest expression in E. Franklin Frazier's *Black Bourgeoisie* in 1957 and Earl Ofari's *Myth of Black Capitalism* in 1970. They had generally been critical of black business because no really large-scale black businesses, like General Motors or IBM had emerged; they were not major employers of black labor; most were doomed to failure; and even individual black success did not bring group success.

Graves had to try a somewhat different approach to get the support of most of America's leading black organizations. Most important, Graves had to emphasize that *Black Enterprise* would not simply be a monthly listing of "Horatio Alger stories" of blacks who made it. Rather, its emphasis would be upon the economic conditions that would encourage black economic development as a basic element of the economy, and of the aspirations of most blacks to succeed in some form of business enterprise. Thus, it would also have to create usable role models for blacks, and this would entail portrayals each month of some black success stories. "The concept also had to show blacks that their careers were not restricted to either civil service or school teaching," said Johnson. "It would have to help people's minds soar beyond the traditional thought processes." Thus, what Graves had to achieve was a tough balancing act that would please all groups.

He was largely able to convince a prestigious group of African-American individuals and organizations of the worth of his proposal. Whitney Young, Jr., then head of the National Urban League, gave his endorsement. That was followed by similar support from the National Business League, the NAACP, the Interracial Council for Business Opportunity, the Congress of Racial Equality, the Organization of Industrial Centers, Capital Formation, the National Association of Marketing Developers, the Office of Minority Business Enterprise, and the Black Advisory Council of the Small Business Administration. The end result was a list of 100,000 "present and future leaders of the black community" who had endorsed the concept (for which they received free subscriptions). Graves was then ready to pursue financing.

With a rough draft of the magazine in hand, Graves approached Lewis Allen, who was president of Chase Manhattan Bank's Manhattan Capital Corporation. The bank agreed to give *Black Enterprise* a loan of $150,000 with $25,000 in equity. With that taken care of, Graves, who was not a trained journalist, had to find someone who would be responsible for the total look of the magazine and who would hire writers and set editorial policy. He settled upon Pat Patterson, an award-winning journalist from Long Island's *Newsday* newspaper. The first issue of *Black Enterprise* in August 1970 featured a cover and lead story on Charles Evers, who they said had "started small and made it big" in both politics and business in Mississippi. Evers was also a member of the magazine's board of advisors.

Earl Graves in that maiden issue set forth his ideas about black business and economic development:

The economic problems of our cities, where a majority of black people live, will not yield simply because we decry conditions there. Nor will stubborn rural poverty disappear because we bemoan that fact. What has become increasingly clear is that black people need economic power if conditions are to be changed. . . .

We shall cover the careers of those who are "Making It" in the corporate world and the problems of the shopkeeper who wants to improve his business. We shall include the thoughts of the theorists and practitioners alike. In short, *Black Enterprise* is your magazine, providing information and a wealth of experience for those who venture into the precarious world of business.

As readership grew, reaching 125,000 by 1973, new departments were added. There was also an innovative use of colorful graphics, illustrations, and photographs which were the work of art director Edward L. Towles, who joined the magazine in 1971. *Black Enterprise* began making money with its tenth issue, and by the end of its first year had $900,000 in advertising revenue. It continued to grow over the years, with yearly revenues at some $15 million by the early 1990s. By that time it had a guaranteed circulation of 230,000 and a readership of more than 1.9 million. It was carried on most major airlines, and it could be found at better newsstands nationwide.

The one area where Graves had some difficulty in the early years was in getting major Fortune 500 corporations to advertise in the pages of *Black Enterprise*. Wayne Sobers, who managed the advertising department in the 1970s and 1980s, asserted, "It's a fact that there are many [advertisers] who don't give any thought to the black consumer." Although he believed that only 10 percent of the executives were actually bigots, the majority were nonetheless swayed by arguments that "[all] blacks are on welfare and don't want to work." By the 1990s, however, Graves and his staff had done a commendable job of convincing major multinational corporations to advertise in *Black Enterprise*. By 1992 the magazine had a staff of sixty-three and revenues of some $17.5 million. It ranked number 73 on the *Black Enterprise* annual list of the 100 largest black-owned industrial-service companies.

As *Black Enterprise* became successful, Earl Graves began to develop a number of other business interests. In addition to the parent company—Earl G. Graves, Ltd.—and the Earl G. Graves Publishing Company, there was also Earl G. Graves Marketing and Research and EGG Dallas Broadcasting. The marketing and research company led to the development of the Minority Business Information Institute, which set up a library filled with census tract data on microfilm and microfiche, along with "two full-time professionals answering questions all day long on a non-cost basis to people who come in and want to use the material." EGG Dallas Broadcasting operated an AM and an FM station in the Dallas–Fort Worth area—the eighth largest market in the United States. In the mid–1980s Graves also instituted a series of "networking seminars" to "take the printed word—*Black Enterprise*—out to our audience." In the first year of its operation, seven of the seminars were conducted and fourteen were offered the next year. Graves appears at all of them and helps set the tone through comments at the beginning of the seminar.

Another big breakthrough for Graves came in 1990 when he gained the franchise for Pepsi-Cola in the Washington, D.C., area. Teaming with Earvin "Magic" Johnson, the star basketball player for the Los Angeles Lakers, Graves was elected chairman and chief executive officer of the firm, the largest minority-controlled Pepsi-Cola franchise in the United States. The $60 million franchise was acquired by Graves and Johnson in July 1990. With headquarters in Forestville, Maryland, the company covered a territory of 400 square miles including Washington, D.C., and Prince Georges County, Maryland. Key accounts handled by Pepsi-Cola of Washington, D.C., include the White House, the U.S. Capitol, the vice president's residence, and Air Force One. Graves commented on his being awarded the franchise, "Today's announcement is especially meaningful for me. In a very real sense, this is a preview to the diversity of business involvement to which I look with great anticipation in the next decade of my business career."

Earl Graves and his wife had three sons. The eldest, Earl G. "Butch" Graves, Jr., graduated in economics from Yale, and then went to Harvard Business School for his MBA. He had been drafted as a professional basketball player by the Philadelphia 76ers but decided to devote himself to business instead. Upon completing his degree at Harvard, he joined *Black Enterprise* as vice president of advertising and marketing. When his father and Magic Johnson were trying to obtain the Pepsi-Cola franchise, it was Butch Graves who was responsible for the bulk of the negotiations. In recognition of his achievement, he was made vice president of Earl G. Graves, Ltd., in 1992. "Johnny" Graves, the second son, majored in history at Brown University and received his law degree from Yale. After graduating, he became a Wall Street lawyer. The youngest son, Michael, attended the University of Pennsylvania, where he played football and majored in communications and sociology. He then became the business development manager at the Pepsi facility in Washington.

Earl Graves, Sr., has been involved in a number of civic organizations. One of the most important to him was the Boy Scouts, with which he was affiliated all his life, receiving the organization's highest awards for volunteer service: the Silver Buffalo Award in 1988, the Silver Antelope Award in 1986, and the Silver Beaver Award in 1969. He has also served on the executive committee of the Council for Competitiveness, the Stroh's Advisory Council, the National Minority Business Council, the Visiting Committee of Harvard University's Graduate School of Business Administration, and the President's Council for Business Administration at the University of Vermont. In addition, he was a trustee of the Council for Economic Development, the American Museum of Natural History and Planetarium Authority, and the New York Economic Club, and a board member of the New York City Partnership. In 1979 he was appointed a member of the Presidential Committee on Small and Minority Business, and he has served as a civilian aide to the secretary of the U.S. Army from 1978 to 1980.

On the occasion of the twentieth anniversary of *Black Enterprise* (June 1990), Earl Graves was cautiously optimistic about the future of black business and economic development. He recognized that the severe recession of the time, coupled with the neglect of African-Americans by the Reagan and Bush administrations, had created a terrible sense of malaise in the black community.

I strongly believe that we will emerge from this economic slowdown more powerful than ever. I believe that we will innovate and find new ways to market our goods as industrial sectors wax and wane. I strongly believe that we will continue to cultivate our businesses despite the assaults on affirmative action and business development programs. Endurance and growth have always been the business tradition of the *Black Enterprise* 100s. It is a path that we will continue to take.

Critics like Manning Marable, who wrote *How Capitalism Underdeveloped Black America* (1983), thinks that Graves's confidence has been misplaced. Only time will tell if Graves was a prophet, or if he was just "whistling in the dark."
Sources

No personal or business papers of Earl Graves are currently available. Information on his background and activities is rather scanty, but the best sources are as follows: Michael L. LaBlanc, *Contemporary Black Biography*, vol. I (New York, 1992), 95–96; Carolyne S. Blount, "Advocate for Economic Development: Earl G. Graves, Publisher, *Black Enterprise* Magazine," *About . . . Time*, April 1987, 14–16; *Ebony Success Library* (1973), vol. 1, 130; *Encyclopedia of Black America*, 408; *Black Enterprise*, May 1972, August 1980, 106–8 +, October 1984, 106–8 +; August 1988, 9, August 1990, 63 +, October 1990, 110–11, and June 1992, 308; *Los Angeles Times*, April 9, 1974; *San Francisco Examiner*, April 28, 1974; "Economic Integration and the Progress of the Negro Community," *Ebony*, August 1970; *Jet*, February 21, 1974, January 12, 1978, April 28 and August 18, 1986, and February 9, 1987; *Biographical News*, May 1975, 542–43; *Time*, July 15, 1974; Russell Miller, "Earl Graves: Change Comes from the Top," *Management Review*, April 1985, 57–58; Mark M. Colodny, "Publisher Takes the Pepsi Challenge,'' *Fortune*, August 27, 1990, 104; *Franchising World*, January-February 1992, 37–39; D. Moreau, ''Earl Graves Is the Publisher of *Black Enterprise*, and He Practices What He Preaches,'' *Changing Times*, November 1990, 112; Walter C. Daniel, *Black Journals of the United States* (Westport, Conn., 1982), 59–63. Earl Graves's business philosophy and ideology can be traced in the monthly issues of *Black Enterprise*, where he has an editorial. Information on Graves was also obtained from ''Earl G. Graves,'' Press Release, Earl G. Graves, Ltd.; Pepsi-Cola of Washington, D.C., News Release, July 25, 1990; and ''Fact Sheet.''

Greenlee, William Augustus (''Gus,'' ''Big Red'') (1897–July 1952) and **Cumberland Willis (''Cum'') Posey, Jr.** (June 20, 1890–March 28, 1946). Negro Baseball League owners, Baseball League official, saloon and nightclub owner, numbers operator, and politician: Pittsburgh Crawfords, Homestead Grays, Crawford Grill, National Negro League, Pittsburgh Board of Education. Gus Greenlee and Cum Posey could not have been more different. Posey was a refined, college-educated man from a middle-class African-American family. Greenlee was a street-smart hustler, numbers operator, and member of the city's criminal underworld. Ted Page, former outfielder for the Pittsburgh Crawfords, Greenlee's great Negro League team, summed it up well: ''Greenlee and Cum Posey didn't get along so good together. Posey was a Penn State man and Greenlee a street fellow. Cum was on the school board; he was an educated fellow, liked refined things. Gus was just a run-of-the-mill fellow; liked the numbers business, gambling.'' The two men had one thing in common, though, they owned two of the greatest Negro League ball clubs of all time—the Pittsburgh Crawfords and the Homestead Grays.

Cumberland Posey was born in Homestead (then Harding Station), Pennsylvania. His grandfather had been a slave who came to Washington, D.C., when he was freed after the Civil War. There he became a preacher. Posey's father, Cumberland Willis Posey, Sr., went to western Pennsylvania, where he began working on the rivers as a deck sweeper. Later, he began studying ship engines and became a riverboat pilot and engineer on the Ohio River, the first black to receive a license to follow that trade. ''Cap'' Posey soon left that occupation and began to seek his fortune in Homestead. He began constructing river barges in a shipyard there and became the owner of a large fleet; he also began investing in various coal companies and was reputed to be one of the first investors in Robert Lee Vann's[*] *Pittsburgh Courier*. The elder Posey was general manager of the Delta Coal Company and later owned the Diamond Coal and Coke Company, which became the largest black-owned business in Pittsburgh. He was a member of the Warren Methodist Episcopal Church and the prestigious Leondi Club, and he belonged to the best secret societies in the black community. At his death in 1925, he was buried with full Masonic honors and eulogized as one of the city's most prominent and wealthy African-Americans. The *Courier* mourned the passage of a ''pioneer in industry.''

Cum Posey's mother was Angelina Stevens. Daughter of a Civil War veteran, she was the first black to graduate from Ohio State University, as well as the first African-American to teach there. She was dignified and refined, an artist who covered the walls of the Posey home with her paintings. All members of the family were so light skinned they could easily have passed for white. Thus, Cum Posey was reared in the comfort of a well-to-do family, one that was an integral part of the city's older black elite.

But Posey's own interests were hardly genteel or academic. A marvelous athlete, he early became attracted to the far more raucous sports scene of Homestead and Pittsburgh's Hill District. He played for sandlot football and baseball teams; he also began playing and then coaching in the basketball program at Homestead. He was educated in local schools and went to Pennsylvania State University to study chemistry. Posey's real love, however, was sports. A small (5'9" 140 pound) man, his principal sport was basketball. He made the freshman team his first year and the varsity in his second. Academics, however, was another matter. Lack of attention to his studies caused his grades to fall, and after he was dropped from the basketball team for low marks, Posey quit school. This was generally his pattern as a young man. Wendall Smith, the great sportswriter for the *Pittsburgh Courier*, called Posey "an adventurous and turbulent spirit [who] brooked no faculty interference with his desires and he never stayed anywhere long enough to win the recognition which might have been his." Smith did, however, call Posey the "outstanding athlete of the Negro race" and "perhaps the most colorful figure who has ever raced down the sundown sports trail."

Posey returned to Homestead, where, with his older brother Seward ("See") Posey, he organized the Monticello-Delaney semipro basketball team. It was a tough existence. Basketball was still in its infancy in the years before World War I, and black basketball was played in crowded, sweaty gymnasiums and dance halls. There was little or no space to practice; Westinghouse Field House was open to blacks just twice weekly for two hours. In 1911 Posey's Monticello team took on Howard University's varsity champions in what Posey remembered as "the first colored game ever played in Pittsburgh." The Monticellos upset the heavily favored college team, and Posey and his teammates were thrust into the national spotlight. Posey was soon being hailed as the finest African-American basketball player in the country. His team eventually became known as the Leondi Club, because it was sponsored by that organization, and was a fully professional organization. Cum Posey was not only the team's star player, he also managed its finances and promoted and booked its games during a four-year period. Posey is credited with doing more than anyone else in this early period with putting professional basketball on a secure footing. But, before it reached its heyday in the later 1920s, Posey had already turned to another sport—baseball.

The Homestead Grays had emerged out of the sandlots in the early 1900s, at about the same time Posey was launching his basketball career. They began as the Murdock Grays, playing in Homestead Park on weekends. The players were black workers at local plants like Harbison-Walker brickyard and Carnegie-Illinois Steel. In 1910 they were renamed the Homestead Grays, and Posey, who was nineteen at the time, signed up to play in their outfield, playing basketball in the winter and baseball in the summer. Having learned the craft with his basketball team, Posey in 1912 approached its manager, Terry Veney, about booking the Grays' games. During this same period (1912–1913), he married Ethel Truman, with whom he would have five daughters, and enrolled at the University of Pittsburgh to resume his academic career. He did not play sports at Pitt and did not remain there long; he transferred to Holy Ghost College (now Duquesne University) under an assumed name in order to retain his sports eligibility. There he played basketball and was the team's leading scorer, in addition he was captain of the golf team. In 1917 Posey became the manager of the Homestead Grays.

At a time when Posey's Leondi Club achieved national prominence in basketball, the Homestead Grays were still small time, but already had a number of top-notch players. Two of these were Mo Harris and "Lefty" Williams, both of whom remained with the team when it became a national powerhouse in the 1920s. Posey during this period was no longer in college, and he worked full-time for the Railway Mail Service until 1920. He worked for the mail service and managed both the basketball and baseball teams for a number of years. In 1917 Posey also became manager of the Grays, and it was at this time that he began creating a black baseball dynasty in Pittsburgh. Finally, Posey decided to quit his job with Railway Mail, and to devote himself full-time to sports promotion and management.

To build his dynasty, Posey first attracted the very best of the local sandlot players, forcing most of the original part-time Homestead players to the bench. One of his first acquisitions was Oscar Owens, a top-flight pitcher. Next, he attracted some of the best black national talent such as Bobby Williams, a shortstop from the Chicago American Giants, and Sam ("Lefty") Streeter. The Grays, who played all over the tristate area of Pennsylvania, Ohio, and West Virginia, nearly totally dominated the competition. Posey's first crisis came in 1922 when black pitching great William ("Dizzy") Dismukes brought a group of powerful coal miners from Birmingham, Alabama, to Pittsburgh and used them as the nucleus of a team he called the Pittsburgh Keystones. Dismukes put his players on salary, as opposed to the variable, game-by-game pay style used by Posey. Posey knew he would have to pay his players accordingly, or he would lose them to the Keystones. So, he went to Charlie Walker, who had started with the club as a batboy and was elected the club's president in 1916, and asked him to bankroll a dramatic new salary strategy. Some of the Grays' players from those early years recalled the two men: "Charlie Walker was a great guy," said Clint Thomas, "but I didn't like Cum Posey. He was kind of a greedy guy." Jake Stephens commented, "Walker had the money. Posey had the brains. Every fall Walker would buy me a suit of clothes and an overcoat.

Posey knew where to go and get the players. They were two good men. Charlie Walker liked the booze—he'd wine and dine, pal. Cum Posey liked the women. Every town he was in he had a woman.''

Posey went to the Pittsburgh Pirates and made an agreement with them to use Forbes Field (but not the locker room) for games when the Pirates were on the road. The combination of salaries, superb ball players, and the ability to play before large crowds at Forbes Field gave the Grays an advantage the Keystones could not match, and Posey soon drove the Keystones out of the city. In 1923 the Eastern Colored League was formed and operated for six years with such teams as the Lincoln Giants, the Baltimore Black Sox, and the Brooklyn Royal Giants, but the Grays could not afford to give up their lucrative barnstorming to join the league. Posey continued to raid these teams for their best players. His shrewdest acquisition came in 1925 when he signed ''Smokey Joe'' Williams, who many consider the best black pitcher ever. Williams was forty-nine years old that year, and a veteran of twenty-five seasons, but he pitched for the team until 1932. In 1952 a poll conducted by the *Pittsburgh Courier* had Williams leading the voting for all-time best pitcher in the Negro leagues, even beating out Satchel Paige, who by that time was in the major leagues.

The next year, Posey added two more immortals to the Grays: Oscar Charleston, a Hall of Fame center fielder, and John Beckwith, a power hitter who could play any infield position. Over the next few years, Posey signed a number of other players for the Grays who would later be considered among the greatest players, black or white, ever to play the game: Martin Dihigo, ''Cool Papa'' Bell, Judy Johnson, and Willie Foster. All of these players, save Williams, Foster, and Beckwith, are currently in baseball's Hall of Fame at Cooperstown, New York. *Pittsburgh Courier* writer William G. Nunn, Sr., cautioned other black teams: ''For the information of all players and fans in general, the Homestead Grays have played to more paid admissions than ever before in their history. Posey has the happy facility of satisfying his men. They are all perfectly contented to play with him. Watch yourselves you Easterners.'' Historian Rob Ruck put it succinctly, ''[Posey] brooked no opposition in his drive to make the Grays the best team possible.''

By the late 1920s, Posey's Grays spent much of their time playing against white semipro and sandlot clubs, and the fans came out in droves to see the contests. The Grays also began to play exhibition games against teams of white major league all-star players, of which they won more than their share, and played many games throughout the season with Negro National League and Eastern Colored League teams, winning most of those. In 1925 they supposedly played 158 games against various opponents, won 130 of those games, lost just 23, and tied 5. The following year, they won 102 of the 114 games they played. By the end of the 1920s, Posey, who had continued to play in the field as well as manage the team both on and off the field, benched himself at age thirty-seven. In 1930 he pulled off what is widely considered his shrewdest move as a baseball owner and manager—he signed the young catcher, Josh Gibson, to a Grays' contract. Gibson may have been the greatest player to ever play in the Negro leagues and perhaps was the best catcher and power hitter of all time, black or white, major or Negro league. Cum Posey was on top of the sports world in Pittsburgh. He had the best black baseball team in the world and perhaps the best team regardless of color. He and the Grays were making money, and he had also been named head of the Greater Pittsburgh Colored Baseball League in 1930.

In 1931, Posey and the Grays reached their zenith. The team won a staggering 136 of the 153 games they played, Josh Gibson smashed an astounding seventy-two home runs, and in the fall of that year they played Connie Mack's All Stars, which contained some of the best players in the major leagues, including several future Hall of Famers: Harry Heilmann, Lefty Grove, Rube Wahlberg, Jimmy Dykes, Heinie Manush, and others. They played at least two games, drawing 20,000 for the first and 12,000 for the second. The Grays won both games, the second by a devastating score of 18 to 0. Cum Posey and his Homestead Grays were on top of the world and the future looked bright. Then, disaster struck— a new team, the Pittsburgh Crawfords, owned and operated by Gus Greenlee— burst on the scene to challenge Posey's predominance.

Greenlee, who was born in Marion, North Carolina, a small textile and furniture manufacturing town, was the son of a masonry contractor. Greenlee's father was perhaps the most prominent black in the town, having built the courthouse, the town hotel, and many other significant buildings. Gus's mother instilled in all her children a fierce racial pride; two of Greenlee's brothers became doctors and a third became a lawyer. Gus, however, had little interest in school. "Gus wasn't easily disciplined and dropped out his second year of college," his brother recalled. "After that, he was on the dogs with father." As a result, in 1916, at age nineteen, Greenlee joined the migration north to Pittsburgh. The *Pittsburgh Post-Gazette*, sixteen years later, described Greenlee's arrival in Pittsburgh: "It wouldn't be a surprise to hear that the daddies up there [the Hill District] gather their brown-skinned little ones to their knee at night and tell how Gus came to town on a freight train as a poor boy. . . . He got off the freight in the middle of winter, wearing patched pants and white canvas shoes." The city's black population was swelling with migrants during these decades. With an African-American population of just over 10,000 in 1890, it surged to nearly 26,000 in 1910 and over 37,000 in 1920. In the decade that Greenlee arrived, 87 percent of the city's increase in black population came from southern migrants like him. Pittsburgh's place as a center of heavy manufacturing with many jobs for unskilled and semiskilled men was a great attraction, as were worsening economic conditions in southern agriculture and a deteriorating racial climate in the South.

Before the arrival of southern migrants like Greenlee, blacks had lived in every ward of Pittsburgh. Increasingly, however, the new entrants were being clustered into an area known as the Hill District. "The Hill" had been home to hordes of previous migrants, including large numbers of Jewish immigrants. By

1910, over 40 percent of Pittsburgh's blacks lived there, although blacks continued to be dispersed throughout the city. It was the Hill, however, that became the cultural and symbolic center of black life in Pittsburgh. Gus Greenlee's background on the surface was much like Posey's: He was from a prominent and well-educated black family; he was very light skinned; and he had several years of college but preferred to play baseball and other sports. But the similarities ended there. When Greenlee left North Carolina, he hopped a freight train and "rode the rods," arriving in the city nearly penniless. He began his career there shining shoes, then worked at the Jones and Laughlin steel mill and drove a cab for a local undertaker, later buying his own taxi. When the United States entered World War I, Greenlee was shipped overseas where he was wounded in battle.

When Greenlee returned to Pittsburgh after the war, he found the Hill District a fertile ground for racketeering since the passage of the Prohibition amendment. He went back to driving his taxi, but he also carried bootleg liquor around with him and came to be known as "Gasoline Gus." It was a natural transition for him, as he became more successful, to open his own speakeasy, the Paramount Club, on Wylie Avenue in the Lower Hill. To go with the liquor, Greenlee began booking entertainment, particularly jazz artists, into the club, and it became known as a notorious "black and tan cabaret." The police raided and closed the club in 1922, but Greenlee reopened it with a partner in 1924. They again ran afoul of the law, however, when the *Pittsburgh Courier* alleged that young white girls were "running wild" in this "plague spot of a city infested with vice." The club's dance license was revoked, but Greenlee had it in operation again within a year.

At about the same time, Greenlee moved into the promotional end of the entertainment industry, organizing the Musical Booking Agency, with offices on the Paramount's third floor. This group handled the booking of talent for many of the city's clubs. Greenlee also owned the Workingmen's Pool Hall on Fullerton and ran the Sunset Cafe. By the late 1920s he was one of Pittsburgh's more prominent black businessmen, but his pride and joy was the world-renowned Crawford Grill, the classiest club on the Hill and a mecca for jazz fans. The Crawford Grill attracted most of the greatest musicians in America at one time or another and held countless late-night jam sessions. It was not unusual for patrons to hear Count Basie, Duke Ellington, Cab Calloway, Louis Armstrong, the Mills Brothers, and other noted black musicians there on a regular basis. Lena Horne, the singer, got her start there, where her father, Teddy Horne, was Greenlee's right-hand man, supervising the numbers of business as well as the liquor enterprise. The club catered to both blacks and whites and included many of the city's notables among its regulars. Art Rooney, owner of the Pittsburgh Steelers, and a close friend of Greenlee's, was a regular. The food and drink at the Crawford was reputed to be the best in Pittsburgh, and the club was noted especially for its daiquiries. The Crawford Grill became the hub for Greenlee's increasingly widespread, and often illegal, operations.

Gus Greenlee's main enterprise, and an economic staple of black Pittsburgh for at least two decades, was the so-called numbers racket. This is essentially a lottery, not unlike that run by many states in the United States in the 1980s and 1990s, in which the bettors wager that a three-digit number they select will be the number that "hits" on that particular day. The amount wagered was usually quite small, in the early years as little as a penny or a nickle, so the numbers were often referred to as the "poor man's lottery." Innocuous as it may seem, the numbers game was illegal in Pittsburgh and nearly everywhere else in the early twentieth century. By the late 1920s, the numbers industry was attracting more than just black bettors and had become a lucrative operation. In 1928 the *Pittsburgh Press* estimated that "nearly two millions of dollars flowed into the coffers of the city's 'numbers kings.' " Greenlee was one of these kings, and some estimated he brought in $20,000 to $25,000 a day or more on his operation.

Greenlee had learned the mechanics of the numbers business on a visit to New York City. There Gus went to Harlem, where he met Alessandro Pompez, owner of the Cuban Stars and later the New York Cubans baseball teams, and head of Harlem's highly lucrative numbers business. Pompez agreed to help finance Greenlee's numbers operation and provided him with the needed expertise to get it going. As Greenlee became more successful and was able to adopt a flamboyant life-style similar to that of Pompez, he was often referred to as the "Caliph of 'Little Harlem' " by the newspapers in Pittsburgh. By the early 1930s, Greenlee availed himself of the best food, the liveliest entertainment, and the most expensive clothes; he bought a new Lincoln convertible every year, owned a beautiful home on Frankstown Road, and engaged in continuous gambling. He had become a legend on the Hill.

Although the numbers trade was illegal and Greenlee was regularly "busted" and fined minimal amounts for his participation, it was not part of any organized crime operation until the early 1930s. When Prohibition ended many former bootleggers moved into the numbers business, trying to force the blacks out or to take a secondary role. As a result, gangland slayings became a regular occurrence in Pittsburgh in the early 1930s, but Greenlee and other blacks retained their positions, and the organized crime element in the numbers racket disappeared. Greenlee and other numbers barons simply paid off the police and politicians to be allowed to operate in their neighborhoods with relative impunity.

There was no stigma to being involved in numbers in Pittsburgh's black community. It provided jobs for poor blacks during the Depression. As Greenlee told the *Post-Gazette* in 1932, "If it hadn't been for the numbers, my people would have been a lot worse off than they were." His payroll was estimated at $1,500 a week, with about seventy people sharing in it. Like the older machine politicians, Greenlee was also expected to use his largesse to help those blacks suffering most. When a black family on the Hill needed money for rent, a doctor, groceries, or a load of coal, they knew they could turn to Gus Greenlee. As one of his outfielders, Ted Page, said, "He was never slow when a fellow needed a favor. His hands were just as fast as you could hope they would be when he'd come across people who needed help." At Thanksgiving and Christmas he handed out hundreds of turkeys, and he ran a soup kitchen across from the Crawford Grill throughout the Depression. One of his bitter enemies at this time could still grant him status as a man who helped his community, remembering his "standing there in the restaurant cooking food and just giving it away to the people all up and down the street." Walt Hughes, a former sandlot athlete, recalled, "Gus Greenlee was a beautiful man . . . a wonderful person who'd help anybody." Another said, "Gus? One of the best." A third commented that Greenlee was the "best man I ever knew. He never looked down on nobody. . . . If someone needed help after they got into whatever they went into, Gus would be right there to help out."

But it was also expected that he would provide other kinds of support for the black community, most particularly by bankrolling various sporting activities. His role in this area soon brought him another sobriquet: "Jesus of Negro Sport." Few blacks in the 1930s had the money to bankroll sports teams; as a result, most Negro League teams and other sports figures turned to the numbers men in the community for financial backing. Greenlee's foray into black baseball came in 1930, when he was approached by one of the city's best semipro clubs, the Crawford Colored Giants. The Crawfords were sponsored by the Crawford Recreation Center located close to Greenlee's Crawford Grill. When first approached, Greenlee declined, saying he knew nothing about sports. But he did offer to help the team pay some of its transportation and other expenses. A week later, he changed his mind and agreed to buy the team. Greenlee called them together and told them he was putting them all on salary. Bill Harris, a team member, recalled the players' reaction: "Man, gee whiz! A salary. We just blew up. A salary! So he says, 'I'm going to give you all the same price—$125 a month. And if you say you're better than this or whatever it might be, I'll raise your salary.' That was a dream to us. We never thought about no salary. We just wanted to play ball."

Before long, Greenlee dreamed of creating a great black baseball dynasty. He brought in shortstop Bobby Williams to manage the club, and Williams began recruiting some of the best black ball players in the nation, picking up Sam ("Lefty") Streeter, Jimmie Crutchfield, Chester Williams, Pistol Russell, and, most important of all, the great Satchel Paige. Paige later recalled his first meeting with Greenlee: "When I got to Pittsburgh, the first place I headed was Gus Greenlee's restaurant, the Crawford Grill. Gus had a real good thing in Pittsburgh in 1931. . . . As soon as Gus heard I was in, he came bustling over. 'We're gonna open against the Homestead Grays,' he said. 'They're the best there is, Satch. You beat them and you're number one right from the start.' " As these new men were added, they displaced many of the locals who had played for the Crawfords for years. Greenlee told those who remained that they would have to quit the team or quit their regular jobs so that they could concentrate on being better ball players.

Greenlee's next move was a truly breathtaking step for a black team—he decided to build a state-of-the-art stadium for the Crawfords at 2500 Bedford

Avenue on the Hill. Called Greenlee Field, it cost him $100,000, had a seating capacity for 7,500, and, most important, included superb locker room facilities for both the home and visiting teams. As James Bankes commented, "No longer did black players have to dress and shower in the dingy atmosphere of the Pittsburgh YMCA because the white managers of Ammon Field or Forbes Field refused to let them use their sacred establishments." Next, Greenlee went to Cum Posey to see about bringing his Crawfords into Posey's East-West League. Posey, however, set too high a price for entrance, so Greenlee began raiding the Grays of the cream of their talent. He was highly successful in both endeavors.

Posey's Grays were in dire financial straits in 1931–1932 because of the effects of the Depression. Greenlee, whose numbers business knew no depression, began opening up his bank account to the best of the Grays' players. Greenlee picked up the aging but brilliant Oscar Charleston to manage and play first base. He also enticed third baseman Judy Johnson and the magnificent catcher Josh Gibson to join the Crawfords in 1932 along with outfielder Ted Page. Greenlee also brought in some top-notch players from other clubs, picking up the incomparable Cool Papa Bell to play center field, Ted ("Double Duty") Radcliffe to pitch, and John Henry Russell. In 1932 Greenlee had the Crawfords barnstorming around the United States, and from that year until 1937 his team and Cum Posey's Grays battled for supremacy of black baseball in Pittsburgh and in the nation.

Playing the Grays nineteen times during the 1932 season, Posey's team managed to win ten of the encounters, but most ball fans by then considered the Crawfords the most exciting black ball team in the nation. That fall, the Crawfords barnstormed against Casey Stengel's white all-stars, which included the likes of Hack Wilson, and beat them five games out of seven with relative ease. Greenlee, however, was frustrated; he wanted a league for his Crawfords to play in. In 1933 he resurrected the Negro National League. Despite a wobbly beginning, it soon became the most successful of the various black baseball leagues. The "new NNL broke ground for black professional sport, achieving a measure of financial stability and a public presence unprecedented for a black sporting venture, thanks mainly to its architect, prime innovator, and president during the first five seasons—Gus Greenlee." One of his most important innovations came in 1933, when he organized the league's first East-West, or All-Star, game, to be played in Chicago's Comiskey Park about a month after the first major league All-Star game was played there. In later years the game would grow into the biggest spectacle of the NNL, drawing crowds of from 30,000 to 50,000.

Like Greenlee, many of the owners of the other clubs in the NNL were from the ranks of black organized crime—numbers bosses and others—because they had the most money. Owning the New York Cubans was Alex Pompez; the New York Black Yankees were owned by Ed "Soldier Boy" Semler; the Philadelphia Stars were owned by Ed Bolden; Tom Wilson owned the Baltimore Elite Giants; and Effa and Abe Manley owned the Newark Eagles. Cum Posey refused to join the NNL until 1935, by which time he was also forced to turn to gangster money in order to survive. He allied himself with Rufus "Sonnyman" Jackson, king of the numbers racket in Homestead and owner of many of the jukeboxes in the entire district.

By that point Posey had no choice. At the end of the 1933 season, he did not have enough money left to pay his players. Buck Leonard, later a Hall of Fame first baseman, a raw recruit picked up by Posey, later recalled, "I was wondering why he picked me up, I guess it was because he didn't have any money to pay us. I got $125 a month, plus 60 cents a day on which to eat—sixty cents!" In 1934 Leonard remembered that "we just scraped around and scraped around" trying to put together a team of nine men. Some saw this turn of events as a kind of justice for Posey. He was fighting for his baseball life; his league had collapsed; his players were raided by the Crawfords; and, as a Pittsburgh sportswriter commented, he was being raided "by the same ruthless methods he had used against other owners in past years." Rollo Wilson, another sportswriter, said, "The Crawfords have taken the play away from the Grays and no longer do Smoky City fans consider Cum Posey's bunch the penultimate in baseball."

Roy Welmaker, who was signed by Posey in 1936, talked about the rigors of travel in those days: "The bus we had was like a school bus. It didn't have the comfort of a Greyhound or Trailways bus. We had these school buses that these kids take across town—something like that. You couldn't sleep on that kind of bus." Quincy Trouppe, who played briefly with the Grays, recalled how hard it was to get his money: "They always promised me money, but I never got it. That's why I left. I was with the Grays maybe a couple of months or maybe a month and a half—something like that. . . . I got sick of that because I wanted to send some money home and have a little money when the season was over. But I didn't get it."

Sonnyman Jackson was Posey's salvation. Posey convinced him to put his money into the Grays as a way of laundering it and keeping clear of the Internal Revenue Service. Leonard said, "Baseball was just a cover-up," but it made a real difference. Leonard later said, "I played with the Homestead Grays 17 years and never missed a payday." Greenlee and Jackson, fierce competitors in the numbers business, now also became antagonists in the world of baseball, but it was Posey who made all the baseball decisions for the Grays. The Grays, however, were hardly a match for the brilliant Crawfords, who totally dominated the world of black baseball over the next several years.

In both 1933 and 1936, the Crawfords played before more than 200,000 paying fans, a tremendous feat for a black club playing in a relatively small stadium. Greenlee, who had a tremendous gift for promotion, began billing Satchel Paige as the "World's Greatest Pitcher" and Josh Gibson as the "World's Greatest Hitter." In neither case was much hyperbole involved. His advertising promised Paige would strike out the first nine men and that Gibson would hit a home run. It was often correct. Paige, who was a master of self-promotion himself, later recalled these years with the Crawfords: "The Crawfords played everywhere, in every ball park you could find. And we won, won like we invented the game.

Every time Gus announced I was going to pitch, they had to get cops to watch the gates because there were so many trying to crowd their way inside. If the cops hadn't kept them out, the fences would have split right in two.''

By 1936, however, Greenlee's magic with the Crawfords began to fade. By that time the Crawfords were not the same organization they had been the preceding five seasons. However artistically successful the team had been during those years—and they were, from the marvelous collection of baseball talent, to the flashy uniforms and sleek green bus with their name on the side—they had never turned a profit. Greenlee perhaps had never expected them to, but by 1937 his numbers racket was feeling the pinch. Frequent raids by the police were hampering operations, and he began to cut corners in many areas. In that year Greenlee got into a contract dispute with his prize slugger, Josh Gibson, who demanded a "stunning" salary increase and was traded, along with the aging Judy Johnson, to the crosstown Grays. It was a great coup for Cum Posey and a setback of untold proportions to the prestige of the Crawfords as it gave the Grays two of the greatest sluggers in black baseball—Gibson and Leonard. That same year Paige and Bell jumped to the Dominican League, and Greenlee's team was devastated. A season later Greenlee disbanded the Crawfords, and Greenlee Field was razed in 1938 to make way for Bedford Dwellings, a public housing project. A bitter John Clark wrote in the *Pittsburgh Courier*: "Regardless of what mistakes were made, or who made them, a purer racial interest should have been manifested to keep Greenlee Field out of the list of failures. . . . Greenlee Field joins the list of banks, industries, and other enterprises which should not be attempted in this city for the next 100 years." Greenlee then left the baseball business until 1945.

Greenlee's main sporting interest after 1938 was boxing. Since the early 1930s, he had kept a stable of boxers, the best of whom was John Henry Lewis, the first black American light-heavyweight champion in 1935. In 1939 Greenlee pitted Lewis against Joe Louis, the magnificent black heavyweight champion, at Madison Square Garden. It was a debacle; Lewis was defeated by a TKO in the first round. After that, Lewis retired, and Greenlee soon tired of the fight game also. The ring he had set up in the backyard of his home was dismantled, and his fighters left for other cities and other occupations. Greenlee's dream of becoming a big-time, prominent black boxing promoter was picked up several years later by Truman K. Gibson, Jr.,[*] of Chicago.

Cum Posey and his Homestead Grays had risen, phoenixlike, from the ashes to again reassert their dominance of black baseball. In 1937 Posey had been voted secretary of the NNL, and in 1940 the team began to rent Griffith Stadium in the "U" Street district of Washington, D.C. The home of the major league Senators, Griffith Stadium was also in the middle of that city's major black community. Thereafter the Grays played their home games in both cities, using Forbes Field when they were in Pittsburgh. Gate receipts with this arrangement were tremendous, and in 1942 they drew 170,000 fans to Griffith Stadium alone. Black baseball overall had a boom period in the 1940s, and Posey claimed in

1942, when the teams overall drew over 3 million fans, it was the largest black enterprise in the world except for the insurance companies. Posey and the Negro leagues, however, were living on borrowed time. As did the white major leagues, they lost several players to the draft; others left to work in defense plants. Then the Mexican League was formed, which enticed Josh Gibson and several other players south of the border for a season or two. But the big challenge was just around the corner—an adversary that for both political and economic reasons the Negro leagues could not, dared not, hope to defeat—the integration of major league baseball.

Cum Posey did not live to see this. In January 1946, Josh Gibson died of a drug overdose, and Posey passed away two months later, at fifty-four years of age, just three weeks before Jackie Robinson made his historic debut in organized baseball with the Montreal Royals. Posey's one-time pitcher, Ted Radcliffe, said of him:

Cum Posey owned the Grays, and he was as good a baseball man as ever lived. He had gone to college and he could have passed for white. He treated a man like a human being, and he'd look out for his ball players, just like Wilkinson [of the Kansas City Monarchs]. The best hotels, the best everything. They operated like big-league teams. They were the only ones who treated the ball players half-decent about riding all night. If they didn't go to bed, they gave them their room rent just the same. And Posey paid good salaries. You know he must have been a good man when he was paying Josh Gibson $1,200 a month and Buck Leonard and Sam Bankhead $1,000. Cum Posey was a genius.

Ric Roberts, a sportswriter, commented, "Posey and Wilkinson and the other owners, those were the guys who had persevered and risked their own personal equity to see that black baseball had some cash creditability. Cum Posey did a hell of a job. And nobody knows it." Thousands of mourners of both races filed past Posey's casket, paying final tribute to, in the words of sportswriter Chester Washington, "the sagacious sportsman who made the Homestead Grays as magic a name in the baseball world as Joe Louis in the fistic firmament."

For several years after he disbanded his team, Greenlee tried to get another NNL franchise for the Crawfords. After repeated rebuffs, he began to investigate other avenues. He assembled a new semipro Crawfords team and began raiding some of the established NNL teams for players. In 1945 and 1946, in conjunction with the Brooklyn Dodgers' Branch Rickey, Greenlee organized and ran the United States League. It had its headquarters on the second floor of the Crawford Grill. The new league was considered by many to be a stalking horse for Rickey's plans to integrate major league baseball with black players. There appears to be much truth to this. Six months after assisting in the formation of the league, Rickey announced the signing of Jackie Robinson to a contract. The color line in white-organized ball had been broken, and the following year Robinson made his debut with the Brooklyn Dodgers. Rickey's involvement with the USL gave his Dodgers first crack at much of the top black talent at the time. Nor did he pay the organized black teams for the talent he raided from them. Major league owners justified their actions on the very legitimate score that they were giving black players an opportunity they had long been denied and justly deserved. Conversely, Negro League owners who obstructed the signing of their players were castigated as unprogressive, backward, selfish individuals who put their own profit ahead of the welfare of their players and the race as a whole. See Posey, Cum's brother who continued to run the Grays, saw it differently. Ric Roberts recalled his last meeting with him:

The last time I talked to See Posey, he was in his office, almost in tears, on his way to the hospital. He gave me hell: 'How can you write about my ballplayers being snatched up by a pirate, didn't need a gun, hiding behind freedom for blacks?' He said it was like coming into a man's store and taking the commodities right off his shelf without paying a dime. 'You don't know how much it cost me to build this team. I guess I won't live to fight anymore.' (Holway, *Blackball Stars*, p. 326)

See Posey dissolved the Grays in 1950, after having lost $30,000 over the past two years. He died the following year.

After 1946 Gus Greenlee retreated to his Crawford Grill, which remained one of the top-grossing entertainment spots in town. In 1948, at the prestigious black Leondi Club, Greenlee was chosen the outstanding local businessman of the year by the Business and Professional Association of Pittsburgh, citing his role in promoting better race relations and advancing the civic and economic status of blacks in the city. But Greenlee's numbers business was dwindling rapidly as whites moved in to take over lucrative parts of it, and the federal government took him to court for nonpayment of back income taxes. He ultimately was forced out of the numbers racket and was in increasing financial trouble after the Crawford Grill burned down in 1951. A year later, "Big Red," the king of black sports in Pittsburgh, was dead. He was, in many respects, a man larger than life in the black community of the 1930s and 1940s. His former second baseman, Dick Seay, recalled him: "Greenlee was big, above six-three, about 225 pounds. He looked like the racketeer that he was. Dressed neat, big expensive hats, always a big crowd around him. I imagine he was something like Diamond Jim Brady, you know, always had a crowd." Ted Page, one of his pitchers, said, "A big man and a fine guy. Not the joking type of fellow, not the humorous type. He was all business. Not an educated man, but he was of the smart illiterate types—although he wasn't really illiterate by any means, he could read and write. He was the type of man who could see far into the possibilities, something that could turn you into some good money. And his heart was as big as his automobile. He'd give you money in the middle of winter. . . . Maybe he was too liberal. He was a gambler, made wild investments in sports. Boxers—he had a stable of fighters. Built a home for them. These things cost money." Another pitcher, Jesse "Mountain" Hubbard, put it succinctly: "Greenlee was the swellest fellow you ever met in your life . . . ball players—he'd give them his heart."

The once bustling, thriving Hill District declined rapidly in the years after

Greenlee's death. Once a magnet for drawing the top entertainers in America, the last blow was delivered by the riots after Martin Luther King, Jr.'s, assassination in 1968. Joe Robinson had opened a new Crawford Grill in the area, and although it was not burned down in the riots, it could just as well have been. Robinson commented, ''When they killed Martin Luther King, they killed me.'' Pictures of the jazz greats who had played the club in its heyday still decorate the walls, but by 1975 the place stood mostly empty. ''We're stuck here,'' Robinson told the *Post-Gazette*. ''We'd move if we could, but who wants this type of place? We're too big to be a neighborhood bar, and we aren't going to do enough business to continue the way we did in the past.'' Another long-time resident commented, ''The Hill could be made into a beautiful place. It's prime land. There's a whole lot of hope for the Hill District if the right people get behind it.'' But they did not, and by the early 1990s Wylie Avenue and the Hill were bleak reminders of another era.

In 1988 the Pittsburgh Pirates and members of the city government finally gave the Crawfords and the Grays the recognition they so richly deserved. They unveiled a plaque which said in part: ''[T]he Grays and the Crawfords made Pittsburgh the center for Black Baseball in America during the years when the color line barred blacks from the major leagues.'' One of the old Negro League players at the ceremony regarded it all rather wistfully: ''It was hard to see the Negro Leagues die,'' he said. ''The end of the color line opened the door for a lot of players, but it also closed it on a lot of players. Many Negro players found themselves out of a job. Some had played baseball all their lives. It was hard on them.''

Sources

There are no family papers for either Greenlee or Posey. Some of the best primary information on the black leagues and teams comes from interviews conducted by a number of scholars. For the Crawfords and the Grays, see especially the interviews conducted by Rob Ruck deposited with the Archives for Industrial Society, Hillman Library, University of Pittsburgh. Other useful interviews were conducted by Allen Richardson and are at San Jose State University.

The best secondary literature on Greenlee and Posey is in Rob Ruck, *Sandlot Seasons: Sport in Black Pittsburgh* (Urban, 1987), but see also ''Cum Posey and Gus Greenlee: The Long Gray Line,'' in John B. Holway, *Blackball Stars: Negro League Pioneers* (Westport, Conn., 1988), and Holway's short biography of Posey in *Dictionary of American Negro Biography* (1982). There is a short biography of Greenlee by Rob Ruck in *Biographical Dictionary of American Sports*, ed. David L. Porter (Westport, Conn., 1987). Some useful insight into some of Greenlee's nonbaseball activities can be gotten from the *Pittsburgh Post-Gazette*, October 10, 1932, and March 25, 1975. The Crawfords are also outlined in two articles by Rob Ruck: ''Black Sandlot Baseball: The Pittsburgh Crawfords,'' *Western Pennsylvania Historical Magazine* 66, 1 (January 1983), 63–67; and ''Kings of the Hill,'' *Pittsburgh* (December 1985), 23–24; and in a popular history: James Bankes, *The Pittsburgh Crawfords: The Lives and Times of Black Baseball's Most Exciting Team!* (Dubuque, Iowa, 1991). See also Debra Rowland, ''Black Baseball Pioneers Honored,'' *Pittsburgh Courier*, November 30, 1988. Other information on the two men, their teams, and the National Negro Baseball League can be obtained from books by or about older Negro League stars: William Brashler, *Josh Gibson: A Life in the Negro Leagues* (New York, 1978); Leroy [Satchel] Paige, *Maybe I'll Pitch Forever* (1962); John B. Holway, *Josh and Satch: The Life and Times of Josh Gibson and Satchel Paige* (Westport, Conn., 1991); and Quincy Trouppe, *Twenty Years Too Soon* (Los Angeles, 1977); along with a number of interviews in John B. Holway, *Voices from the Great Black Baseball Leagues* (New York, 1975); and Allen Richardson, "A Retrospective Look at the Negro Leagues and Professional Negro Baseball Players," Master's thesis, San Jose State University, 1980.

Griffey, Dick (November 6, 1943–   ). Concert promoter and recording company founder: Dick Griffey Concerts, Dick Griffey Productions, and SOLAR Records. Most whites would just dismiss Dick Griffey as a good A&R (artists and repertory) man and record producer. Successful at what he does, and wealthy, the attitude of the business press is generally that his activities are better handled in *Variety* or, better yet, *Ebony* or *Jet*. There is a tendency to trivialize music and popular culture as the stepchild of real business and real culture. Dick Griffey disagrees. He views himself as a man with an important mission: "I want to see the world give credit to black people for the heritage and art that they have given to the world musically. . . . When it comes to our art form, nobody has really stood up and said black people have given something beautiful to the world. Black music is the most widely accepted music there is, it's not only being done by black people. The largest selling album in history, "Saturday Night Fever," was the Bee Gees doing black music." Griffey is not the first black man to bring his music to the broader public in a major way; Berry Gordy, Jr.,* preceded him with Motown Records in the 1960s, and Kenny Gamble with his "Philadelphia Sound" was important in the 1970s, but Griffey has built his firm into one of the most important and fastest growing black entertainment enterprises in the 1980s. By the end of that decade it was the eleventh largest black-owned firm in the United States, with sales in 1987 of nearly $44 million.

Dick Griffey was born in Nashville, Tennessee, the home of country and western music in the United States, and one of the centers of the recording industry in the country. There is no information available on his father, but his mother, Juanita Hines, was one of the most popular gospel music singers in America and later became one of Griffey's recording artists. Griffey was raised and educated in his birthplace and attended Tennessee State University, where he was a defensive lineman on the football team. Also a promising drummer, he played in bands with Hank Crawford and others. Unlike many blacks who view athletics as a means to instant fame and fortune, Griffey was what he calls "entrepreneur-minded" from the very beginning. His mother says that even when he was a small boy he never wanted to work for white people, and when he was at Tennessee State this idea became further crystallized. "When I was in school, I never wanted to play on the football team as much as I wanted to own it. Look at Gale Sayers. He was a great player for the Chicago Bears, but when he hurt his knees after six years, he was out of football. But George Halas is almost 90 years old and he still owns the team.''

After Tennessee State, Griffey went into the Air Force, but it was not a happy time. "I didn't like the Air Force much," Griffey said later, "I never liked to punch a clock." When he got out in 1966 he began to think about a career in the entertainment field. Griffey and a classmate of his from Tennessee State, Dick Barnett, who was then a player-coach for the New York Knicks basketball team, decided to become coowners of a black nightclub in Los Angeles called Guys and Dolls. Griffey was responsible for booking acts into the club. Bringing in renowned black groups like the Temptations, the Impressions, and the Four Tops, Griffey helped build the nightclub into a popular institution for blacks in the city. After a time, he decided to become a music promoter on a broader level. "By the time I decided I wanted to be a show promoter," he said, "I already was one. Instead of trying to get 500 people into the club seven nights a week, I found myself thinking I'd rather rent a big place and fill it with people for just one night." Beyond that, some of the old ideas he had when he played football at Tennessee State returned: "As I got older, I kept thinking how entertainers come and go, but the promoters are always here. And the promoters were usually white. I felt it was time for black promoters to make their mark."

Griffey's first attempt at a concert promotion was not a success. He scheduled Count Basie and the Four Tops at a San Bernadino auditorium. The concert was for a Wednesday night, and he did not begin to advertise it until the Friday before. The result was that only 85 people showed up in a place designed to hold 10,000. The concert was cancelled. Griffey did not lose money on this because, as he says, "I didn't have any money to lose, but I sure lost a lot of somebody else's money." He was undeterred, however, and he set up Dick Griffey Concerts to continue booking concerts. By the early 1970s, Griffey had established himself as one of the major promoters in the Los Angeles area, and he was also beginning to have an impact on the national scene. He was one of the founding members of the Black Concert Promoters Association, and he forged strong alliances with black superstars, such as Stevie Wonder, for whom he arranged a highly successful world tour in 1974.

A year earlier Griffey was approached by Don Cornelius, producer and host of television's *Soul Train*, who asked him to handle booking responsibilities for the series. Two years later, they cooperated in the founding of Soul Train Records. They secured a limited distributing deal with RCA Records, which at the time was very weak in its black music division. Griffey and Cornelius, however, did not have great success with their record ventures. Their first attempt, "Soul Train '75" by the Soul Train Gang, never went higher than seventy-fifth spot on the pop record charts, and an album by the same group fared worse.

Griffey, however, was not disillusioned. He bought the recording rights to a group he managed called the Whispers from Chess/Janus records and started recording tracks for their next album. RCA liked what they heard, and despite the failure of Soul Train Records' first attempt, they distributed the Whispers' album with moderate success. The big breakthrough for Griffey and Soul Train Records, however, came with two very popular disco singles: "I Gotta Keep Dancin'," by Carrie Lucas (who became Griffey's wife), and "Uptown Festival," a medley of disco-ized Motown tunes by Shalamar. Disco was a curious phenomenon of the mid- to late–1970s. It was, in the words of *Rolling Stone*'s writers, "the most self-contained genre in the history of pop, the most clearly defined, and the most despised." A great generator of disco music in the 1970s was Gamble's Philadelphia International Records, but the sound was picked up by all the major recording companies and became a world sensation. Griffey's company was a minor player in this massive, highly profitable, largely studio-created dance music. The profits he made from these records, however, allowed him to consider bigger things.

In 1978 Griffey and Cornelius amicably parted company, and Griffey took sole control of the record company. He first changed the name to SOLAR (Sounds of Los Angeles Records) and signed another distribution contract with RCA. Recognizing that disco was dying out, Griffey had to find a new sound, one that would appeal to both black and white audiences, but mainly to the former. Synthesizing pop, soul, funk, and disco, he arrived at a formula that other black producers such as Quincy Jones and Maurice White also found highly successful. Griffey continued making successful records with Shalamar, but he also signed a group called Lakeside, with which he had several moderate hits. Lakeside was what was called a "funk band." Funk was a less accessible music than disco. With the rougher edges that disco usually smoothed over, funk had closer ties with the older traditions of rhythm and blues and pre-Motown soul music in its gritty instrumentation and studio production. Lakeside, whose best funk record was "Fantastic Voyage" in 1980, changed their wardrobe for every album— appearing as cowboys for one, and as pirates for the next. To a certain extent, critics viewed Griffey as attempting to create a "Los Angeles sound," similar to early manifestations of a "Motown" or "Philadelphia" sound, but he denied it. In large measure he was correct, since the music has tended to resist any geographic identification.

Griffey's company was successful, and at least a fair portion of his records were popular. If he did not have any of the enormous, worldwide hits of the 1980s, he did have a fair number of respectable-selling records. This prompted *Rolling Stone* to comment that "Solar is becoming to the Eighties what Philadelphia International was to the Seventies and Motown was to the Sixties—a veritable pop factory." Griffey also expanded into the gospel area, not only recording his mother, but also signing some other gospel artists. Griffey announced plans to bring out jazz records, although he would not say much about the venture other than the fact that it would not be called jazz, since jazz records seldom make a profit.

In 1981 Griffey switched his distribution contract from RCA to Elektra-Asylum records. He was able to get a highly lucrative contract with Elektra because, as *Black Enterprise* said," it is a well-known axiom in the business that blacks buy records regardless of what the economic climate may be.'' As the vice president of marketing at Solar commented, ''RCA never lost money on any Solar record they distributed. Black music accounts for one-third of all money generated by the entire record business, so a good black company is necessary to ensure corporate success.'' The Solar sound is very much a middle-of-the-road sound within the spectrum of black music. Not overly smoothed-over as in much of the white disco music, neither does it have the truly rough edges of real funk and rhythm and blues. It is commercial music, but commercial music that attempts to retain some sense to its roots in the black community. Griffey also demands that all his groups maintain a ''squeeky-clean'' image. ''I won't deal with self-destructive artists,'' he has said. ''There's enough negativity going around and I don't want to perpetuate it.''

Griffey also has had a major impact as a promoter, serving as president of the United Black Concert Promoters and as head of Dick Griffey Concerts. The key to its success is Griffey's knowledge of his product. ''I know what's good,'' he has said. ''When it comes to black music I think I'm probably the best A&R man in the country. I know how to recognize a good act and how to pick out a good song.'' Griffey also believes that his concert promotions and record company were closely intertwined. ''My philosophy is that you don't build a great company with hit records, you build it with hit acts.'' Thus his recording stars had to be able to go on tour and electrify live audiences, not just be successful in the studio. By the late 1980s Griffey's company provided employment for nearly 100 individuals, and did its share in providing a fund of money coming into the black community.

As Griffey's concert and record businesses became successful, he expanded into a number of allied areas. He founded Griff-co Management, which manages Griffey's artists; Spectrum Seven and Hip Trip publishing companies, which handle the music rights to all Solar songs; and Dick Griffey Productions, a video production company which sold a series called ''Sultans of Soul'' to cable television and has a number of other credits. Griffey also has Solar Stables, his pride and passion, which consists of seventeen thoroughbreds that race under Griffey's royal blue and white colors and are worth more than $1 million. ''We are building a successful entertainment conglomerate,'' said Griffey. ''That's the key to going forward in the Eighties, not diluting our ability to perform up to the full measure of our potential. We don't sign any acts that aren't superstar potential, and we don't have a crap shoot approach. We wait until we have minimized risks toward zero and we spend time making sure an act will succeed.''

Dick Griffey has also become an important civic leader in the African-American community, both in Los Angeles and in the nation. But his approach in this area differs from that of older, traditional civil rights leaders. ''All the marchin' and hummin' was cool at first.'' says Griffey. ''Of course, I wouldn't have done it. I just don't have the patience for that type of thing . . . if one of them honkies put a cigarette butt on my neck, my switch blade would open automatically. I got a .38 that shoots 15 times and after that it throws bricks.

So you know I can't stand none of that." What he did do over the years was to work with a number of youth gangs in Los Angeles, and he also provided support to Boys Clubs and the Sugar Ray Youth Foundation.

Griffey has taken a particularly strong stand on keeping the money made by popular black entertainers in the black community. "My main thing," Griffey said, "is to see that the $100,000 [a performer earns] circulates back into the community and not have some white promoter like Dick Clark take it to Beverly Hills." It particularly irritated him when young black music groups used black promoters to get started and then switched to a white firm when they became established. "You know," he said, "the main problem a black promoter has is that once a black act gets large, it goes up town and signs with the white cats. Which means the brother who promoted them when they were small and lost money gets nothing."

But Griffey's concern goes beyond simply protecting jobs and creating fortunes in the African-American community. "Music is the greatest natural resource in the African community," he says, "and the industry generates more dollars by and for African-Americans than any other single industry. Therefore it is important that African-Americans who are successful in the music business return something to the community which helped them succeed." To put these ideas into practice, Griffey provides a good deal of support to the Black Music Association, PUSH Trade Association, Black Entertainment Lawyers Association, the United Negro College Appeal, and a number of other organizations. On a national level, Griffey has been closely associated for a number of years with Reverend Jesse Jackson, and he was one of Jackson's key advisors in his bids for the presidency in 1984 and 1988.

In 1987, when Berry Gordy put Motown Records on the block, Dick Griffey was one of the major contenders to purchase the pioneer black record film. His bid was the one favored by most people in the black community, since if he was successful, the company would have remained black-owned. Gordy was asking over $60 million for Motown, and many questioned whether the floundering record firm was worth that, feeling that all that was left was its name. Griffey, however, said its name "is the most important name in American music. There is no Warner Brothers sound, no CBS sound, no MCA sound. But the Motown sound was so successful that they now call Detroit 'Motown'—they named the city after the company! That's worth something!" Finally, after protracted negotiations, Gordy sold Motown Records to MCA and Boston Ventures for $61 million.

One of the problems in the black ghettos in the 1980s has been the fact that black-owned businesses have been dying out, and bright, well-educated blacks have been moving into mainstream, white-owned corporations. As a result, the black community has been losing its institutional business base. Dick Griffey, like Edward G. Gardner* and other black business leaders, is keenly aware of this problem. As he commented in the early 1980s: "The reason the ghetto is a ghetto is because black folks spend the dollar once and that's it. The money doesn't circulate, it evaporates. I'm concerned with more money from black concerts being donated to the United Negro College Fund. I want to see more black ushers, ticket-takers, and caterers, so that more of us can profit from the money our music generates.'' Motown, once the largest black-owned music firm, was owned by whites by the 1990s. Other black firms in the media field, like Inner City Communications, which owned radio stations, and the Apollo Theater in Harlem, were experiencing difficult times. Dick Griffey Productions, however, continued to grow and show a profit. By 1992 Griffey's African Development Public Investment Corporation, which handled various African commodities and ran an air travel service, had sales of $23 million. Dick Griffey Productions had sales of $22 million. As a result, Griffey was viewed as some-what of a ''miracle man'' in the music business, finding success where others were experiencing difficulty. Called ''one of the most powerful new figures to emerge in black music in years,'' Griffey doesn't belittle the importance of his role. ''I hold firm in my belief that black music is the only national resource black people in America have,'' he said. ''Black music generates more dollars for black people than any other industry in America, and I think we should use our music in the same way that the Arabs use their oil.''

Sources

There are no personal papers for Griffey or his companies, nor have any full-length biographical studies been done. The most comprehensive biography is Ingham and Feld-man, CABL. Information comes from a number of articles on Griffey and his companies: *Rolling Stone*, June 12, 1980; *Black Enterprise*, July 1976, July 1982, June 1987, and June 1988; *Los Angeles Times*, August 9, 1973, December 6, 1981, and July 18, 1988; *Los Angeles Sentinel*, May 6, 1982, April 14, 1983, and May 15, 1986; *Sepia*, April 1974, and July 1980; *Ebony*, December 1985, 152; and *Who's Who among Black Americans* (1988).

H

Henderson, Henry F., Jr. (March 10, 1928–   ). Manufacturer and entrepreneur: H. F. Henderson Industries. In 1988 there were approximately 340,000 black-owned companies in the United States. Of those, just 1 percent were manufacturers, according to a staff member of the Small Business Administration's New York regional office. Despite this bleak figure, H. F. Henderson Industries of West Caldwell, New Jersey, has ranked in the top twenty of *Black Enterprise*'s top black-owned companies over the past several years. This is not just *any* manufacturing company. Henderson Industries is a high-tech firm whose customer roster reads like a *Who's Who of Finance and Industry*: Dow Chemical, Hershey Chocolate, Union Carbide, Goodyear, and General Electric. The U.S. government, however, is its largest customer. Henderson Industries, furthermore, is so critical to American industry that Henry Henderson, Jr., can state very matter of factly: "If all the systems we've contributed to stopped right now, everybody in the United States would be affected." Who is Henry Henderson, Jr., an African-American who has engaged in business with the giants of industry?

Henry F. Henderson, Jr., who prefers to be called Hank, was born in Paterson, New Jersey. His father was the only general contractor of African-American descent in northern New Jersey at the time, and he prospered. The younger Henderson attended Passaic Valley Regional High School in Little Falls, where he was the only black male (his cousin was the only black female). In high school, a very able and competitive athlete, he became a three-letter man in baseball, basketball, and track. Henderson won a fourth letter as manager of the football team. Upon graduation from high school, he attended New York University where he enrolled in several pre-law courses. After a year and a half he moved on, after deciding that law was not for him. He transferred to the State University of New York at Alfred and graduated in 1950 with an associate degree in electrical machinery and power distribution. He also completed graduate courses at William Paterson College, Seton Hall University, and New York University. During his studies at Alfred, Henderson had begun a painting business, hiring other students to work for him. His father supplied him with the necessary equipment and he was off and running.

Henderson was eager to begin his career, and he landed his first job grinding the insides of propeller blades at Curtiss-Wright, an aircraft manufacturer in Caldwell, New Jersey. This work hardly required the skills and knowledge of an engineer, but it was the best job he could find at the time. Henderson's sights were set on transferring to the electronics department, but this was not to be. Impatiently awaiting an opportunity to move into this division, Henderson was informed after several months that a position had opened up. Excitedly awakening the next morning to apply for the job, Henderson's dreams were soon dashed when he learned that no opening existed. Realizing that his skin color was the reason for the negative response, Henderson decided that Curtiss-Wright was not a company he cared to work for, and he resigned his position. He then answered an advertisement for a job at Richardson Scale Company in Clifton. When he appeared in person at the company, the personnel manager informed him that no job was available. Again, discrimination had reared its ugly head. Upon exiting the building, Henderson fortuitously encountered a high school colleague who introduced him to Enrico Klein, the firm's chief electrical engineer. Klein interviewed Henderson and offered him the job. Initially, Henderson was part of an engineering team that pioneered complex control systems for material control by weight. Research and Development included digital weight systems, electromechanical servo units, motion-detection equipment, load sensors, high-speed printers, and recording equipment. From there, Henderson went on to estimating. For fourteen years, from 1953 to 1967, he estimated virtually every electrical system job for Richardson Scale.

In 1954, with retired postal worker John Dotson, Henderson began a small electrical contracting company. They operated the company from the basement of Henderson's home (which he had built in 1952 in an all-white neighborhood). During the days Henderson worked at Richardson, Dotson took responsibility for their fledgling enterprise, and then Henderson worked evenings out of his house. They managed to keep the business alive primarily by doing commercial or industrial buildings that required them to work in the evenings or on weekends. Henderson later acknowledged that working two jobs provided him with an outlet on which to focus his energy constructively. His big break came when Richardson was caught in a backlog of work orders that they were unable to fill on time. Henderson took this opportunity to offer his services as a subcontractor, offering to complete the projects from his basement. Richardson complied, and H. F. Henderson Industries (HI) was born. (Henderson admits he would be reluctant to provide the same opportunity to one of his employees.)

Henderson's first job involved building a manual, push-button console to mix ingredients for animal feed. Henderson subcontracted out the steel work and cabinet work, and hired a man to wire it, while he built the console. Henderson recalled, "It wasn't much of a contract, it was for approximately $1,000 job and we put in about 30 man-hours on it, showing a profit of around $100. But it was a profit, and it gave us the incentive to continue.'' Although the revenues were minimal, the work was good and it was delivered on time, which set the stage for landing future projects from Richardson. Henderson was careful not to compete with his employer, and so, while manufacturing scales for Richardson, Henderson branched out on his own into the production and marketing of instrumentation and control panels. The move to panels was an easy one for a scale manufacturer, as Henderson noted. He took the panels that were used in scales and manufactured them separately, often fashioning them for special situations. The universality of panel use in most manufacturing processes helped ease the transition. His second job was a system for M&M Candies, which he built in his garage because it was too big for his basement. To this day, Henderson still cannot understand why the console fit into the garage; when the job was completed, he was unable to get it out. He had no other choice but to cut out three beams in the garage to remove the console.

Early on, Henderson marketed his panels through sales representatives—a strategy used by most small manufacturers. These representatives, independent salesmen who sell a line of products for a commission, helped keep fixed costs down while providing the distribution base the company needed. Eventually the sales force was reorganized and the representatives were replaced by an in-house sales staff that could provide improved service. As the company grew, its operations expanded beyond the capacity of the garage. The firm moved into rented quarters in a Little Falls, New Jersey, factory located in a more suitable commercial setting. While Henderson continued to work at Richardson during the day, Dotson managed the daily affairs of the business. The company moved again in 1965. Although the original 500 feet had expanded to 2,300 feet, the company still required more space. This time, they relocated to Paterson in a 5,000-square-foot building.

Then, in 1967, Dotson sold his interest in the company to Henderson, who until this day owns 99 percent of the stock. Henderson's wife is a minority shareholder. In that same year, Henderson took the plunge—he resigned from Richardson and devoted all of his attention and time to nurturing H. F. Henderson Industries, which Henderson saw as a lateral move that provided him with more independence and increased control. By this time the rapidly growing company needed a more hands-on management style that could keep abreast of every aspect of its growth. ''I saw that I could increase my income by not trying to work two jobs at once. I now had a business that needed full-time direction.'' And the self-motivated entrepreneur recognized his need for autonomy when he stated, ''I didn't make the decision because I thought owning a business was glamorous. I knew it was the thing for me to do, because I'm the type of person who doesn't like to work for somebody else.''

Henderson bought three acres of land in the West Caldwell Industrial Park in 1969 and built his own 17,000-square-foot plant and moved his operations into it in 1971. When he was questioned by friends how he would manage the financing of the plant, he responded in his typically optimistic manner, ''I'll manage, there isn't anything that I'm not capable of doing.'' He mortgaged his house and applied to a bank for further financing. The loans officer turned down the request for $5,000. A loan was finally approved when Henderson's father cosigned the loan application. With each additional request, the same bank required both father and son to sign the necessary documents. After four or five of these requests, the younger Henderson strongly asserted that he would not have his father act as cosigner again. His refusal was heeded, undoubtedly because all the previous loans had been paid on time. By 1986 Henderson had a $2 million line of credit, and by 1990 the plant had grown to encompass approximately 44,500 square feet.

H. F. Industries over the years became a high-tech electronics company that specializes in the design and manufacturing of control panels and automatic weighing systems, including mixing and conveying scales. From the early days of manufacturing less complex systems in the garage, the panels became bigger, more complicated, and computerized. The company also became involved in integrating several pieces of machinery to create manufacturing systems. It has made a significant contribution to the quality of high-precision systems and controls which automatically weigh and mix the ingredients going into the manufacture of hundreds of consumer products ranging from milk chocolate to rubber tires. Its products touch our lives in every way imaginable. Its instruments are used to can meats, package crackers, guide fleets of subway cars, and move oil through the Alaskan pipeline. Many would literally be in the dark without Henderson Industries, since it distributes electricity to millions of people.

Its diversity of specially designed products includes systems such as multiple reactor control systems for the preparation of plastic resins, a nuclear reactor simulator control room, and thousands of other special designs, including some of the most complex automatic weighing material handling systems ever installed. It utilizes automated and semiautomated equipment for the design, fabrication, and testing of printed circuit boards, electromechanical assemblies, wire harnesses, and cables. As a complete turnkey operation, Henderson Industries performs MIL and commercially approved printed wiring and electronic module assembly. It has always offered and specialized in providing in-house services custom tailored to meet client specifications. Henderson's modern electronic manufacturing facility is designed and equipped with the latest automated production and test equipment. It takes pride on the extent to which it can test all its equipment, thus ensuring the reliability of its products. The company has testing facilities right on its premises, including a separate electrodynamic shaker, three mechanical shakers, a humidity chamber, and a high/low temperature chamber. It also has complete capabilities for environmental testing to monitor pollutants to meet with government regulatory requirements. Henderson Industries employs highly skilled engineers who are considered experts in computer programming, data acquisition, structural design, stress analysis, and high-frequency amplifiers, as well as in navigational systems, radioactive waste systems, and cable sets.

The company's growth is largely due to the expertise gained through Henderson Industries' involvement with the government's 8(a) program administered by the Small Business Administration. The program, established by the Nixon administration, was designed to promote minority entrepreneurs and ensure their acceptance as viable competitors for government and private-sector contracts. The company benefited directly from this program; it gained expertise in advanced technology and state-of-the-art design of electronic systems. But it must be kept in mind that these contracts are not awarded indiscriminately. The competition is stiff, and the auditing procedures of the Small Business Administration are rigorous. According to Henderson, "It is certainly no give-away program. However, to those who say that it's too difficult, or that the red tape is too much, I say 'Learn how to work with the government.' " He has certainly mastered the skill behind winning a government contract, although he is quick to point out that "the majority of defense contracts are given without any competitive bidding." It was an 8(a) contract from the Federal Aviation Administration in 1977 which went awry that ultimately moved Henderson Industries into manufacturing a new product line—a specific type of navigation device. The company was to build Doppler VOR navigational-aid equipment (which eliminates signal interference when planes fly over mountainous terrain) that was being designed by Edo-Aire Avionics, a Fairfield, New Jersey, firm that specialized in VOR technology. Before the design was completed, the firm relocated to Texas. Henderson was left in the lurch. But, with typical Henderson resourcefulness, he took charge and completed the project. As he recalled, "I felt uncomfortable. Not just because we would have to deal with them long-distance, but I was really concerned that the original group of designers would not stay with the [company] through the move." True to his philosophy, "At HI our number one priority is to deliver." He bought the product line and the design team, thus ensuring design continuity, and named the subsidiary Systems Control Corporation. This strategy protected his reputation but cost the company $1.8 million.

Some of these 8(a) government contracts have given Henderson Industries national recognition, most notably from the design and manufacture of a material handling system that maintains the temperature of the insulation around the space shuttle. The company's experience with weighing systems and automated controls provided it with the leverage to compete successfully for the project, as did its scales, feeders, and bins that helped mix the chemicals that were sprayed by robot onto the shuttle's fuel cell. Henderson Industries was one of two bidders for the job, and it won the project hands down. One of the company's most difficult contracts was when it was required to develop a reliable method for molding resilient, waterproof, and shockproof casing around the cable assemblage for the fire control ballistic computer in the U.S. Army's M-60 tank. Henderson takes pride in meeting the military's stringent requirements. In 1987 the company was awarded a government contract for spare parts for an artillery battery computer system. The total contract, with options, totaled about $125 million and will carry into 1995–1996. In 1985 it was estimated that government contracts accounted for 50 percent of the company's domestic market, which, in turn, accounted for 75 percent of its sales. The other 25 percent was from the growing international market.

It took Henderson great nurturing and patience to land his first contract with the People's Republic of China, an accomplishment in which he takes great personal pride. In 1979 Henderson participated in a trade mission organized by the International Trade Department of the Port Authority for New York and New Jersey. The venture took him to China, where a door was opened that provided a complete array of possibilities for the growth of his business into international markets. After four years and three trips to China, and with the help of the Port Authority personnel stationed in the Far East, Henderson's tenacity bore fruit. Ta Chung Hua Rubber Tire Plant and Henderson Industries signed a contract for the design and manufacture of tire control consoles and material handling equipment. This marked the first time a black-owned corporation embarked on a business venture with a company in China. Despite the meager $300,000 contract, it did open doors whereby Henderson established a name in China and was able to negotiate other contracts with Chinese companies.

The Port Authority also entered into an agreement with Henderson in 1983 to provide overseas services designed to increase international sales. Henderson sees significant advantages to exporting that are not immediately evident, particularly the increase of jobs for Americans with every $30,000 of new exports. It increases tax revenues for the state and federal governments while lessening the balance of payments. Henderson's good fortune in the arena of exportation has made him an avid supporter and promoter of New Jersey Trade Missions. Since the 1960s Henderson Industries has sold systems to other countries, including Japan, Canada, Spain, and England, as a result of doing business with multinational companies based in the United States. However, he is cautious when considering other international contracts just to satisfy his ego, "If it's going to cost us more to supply and maintain equipment overseas, then just doing it for an ego trip doesn't make much sense."

During the 1970s and 1980s, Henderson Industries built up a stable of clients that secured the company a place in the future. This was achieved through a carefully orchestrated plan that was carried out by dedicated employees who understood the company's culture. Teamwork provides the backbone of the company under the stewardship of Henry Henderson. Although he is approachable and the perennial optimist, he likes to have things done *his* way. He stresses the necessity for perfection, and his employees echo his sentiments. Over the years he has displayed his willingness to be flexible because he recognizes that small businesses have to adapt in order to survive. His modest manner and soft-spoken approach fits with his self-effacing moniker—"a sophisticated scale-maker," yet his indomitable spirit has propelled him to achieve in an arena where many others have failed. He has never let his African-American heritage impede his progress, even when others have attempted to undermine his aspirations. He holds no bitterness and honestly feels that his race has not been a disadvantage. ''I never thought about being black when I went after something I wanted to achieve. I went after it and got it. I never felt held back because I was black.'' When he was first trying to recruit customers who would visit his place of business, he had Ben Martyn, his manager of engineering, stand in as the boss because he was white, and Henderson thought it best not to ''advertise'' that the company was owned by a black. One might consider this action to be somewhat compromising, but it was called survival in the business world of the 1960s, a time when no government programs were in place to assist minority-owned enterprises. In 1977 he declared, ''The majority of my customers don't even know that we're a black-owned company. We don't hide the fact, and we don't advertise it. In this business, the customer is looking for a good job at a good price, with service. They do ask how long you've been in business. When I give them our list of clients, we have no trouble. They say, 'Hey these people must be good.' And I think we are.'' This confidence has taken Henderson Industries a long way. Although the bulk of their customers are not among the giants, but are in the middle range of industrial America, they have shown their ability to compete against the larger companies, particularly because they implement the state-of-the-art creativity to reduce downtime. Henderson Industries has the same capabilities, equipment, and procedures as the giants, but with only a third of the overhead. This enables them to be price competitive.

Henderson Industries underwent a major reorganization in 1988. After considerable brainstorming over new ideas to improve the company's position in a market that had become increasingly competitive, Henderson decided to divide the company into two separate entities—commercial and government. The commercial unit sells only to private markets; the government unit pursues government contracts. The two departments are totally autonomous, self-contained operations that do not overlap in any way. Henderson's early reservations about this strategy were ill-founded: in 1987, HI had reported gross sales of $42 million, up from $20 in 1986, and a work force that doubled to 152. The commercial division alone, in 1988, generated about $4.2 million annually or 10 percent of the company's total sales. Henderson expressed confidence when he projected, ''[I see] the commercial group getting up to the $5 or $6 million per year figure in sales in the next two years.'' Henderson also asserted that the government division and high-quality manufacturing facility have given it a distinct selling advantage. He knows his facilities are top notch and that the government's prime contractors, such as Honeywell, United Technologies, and Martin Marietta, are ''awed'' by the type of equipment, the quality of people, and the cleanliness of the environment. To further impress the government contractors, the facilities meet the federal government's most stringent and all-encompassing quality-assurance standards. Major contracts have been won by this division: the Dummy Load and the Battery Computer System, both militarily oriented and both secured through the 8(a) program. In 1988, 100 percent of Henderson Industries' government contracts were secured this way. Service continues to be the company's number one concern, which has taken it from sales of $20,000 in its first year, to $42 million in 1986, with 152 employees. By 1990 Henderson Industries could proudly boast sales of $50 million, with a staff of 200. A year later, however, *Black Enterprise* magazine reported its sales as just $19.2 million, a drastic decline from the previous year. This drop was largely attributed to the effects of the recession that was ravaging America at that time, made even more serious by the cutbacks in defense spending by the government. Henry Henderson has begun to look forward to a time when he will ease himself out and grant his two sons, David and Ken, more responsibility.

Unusual as it may seem for a man who has, at various times in his life, experienced rejection because of racist attitudes, Henderson Industries employs very few African-Americans. One might feel compelled to jump to conclusions and criticize Hank Henderson for not employing members of his own race. For many years, the company had only a handful of blacks on its staff, including Henderson himself, his family members, and one other longtime employee. By 1984 just one-quarter of the seventy-five employees were minorities. Unfortunately, the harsh reality was that very few blacks had the skills to work in this high-tech firm. Henderson recognizes the injustice of the educational system and has implemented an aggressive affirmative action program with the assistance of the Port Authority, one of the company's largest clients at the time. Henderson's strong commitment to his race was exemplified when he stated,

I'm not altruistic. My first responsibility is to make Henderson Industries show a profit. But after making a sufficient profit, a successful minority businessman has a responsibility to his race and to his community: to help it grow, to increase the economic vitality of the community by creating jobs. Increased employment for minority race members is one of the best ways for solving some of the ills of society. (*Minority Business Entrepreneur*, Sept./Oct. 1986)

The relationship that the Port Authority and HI developed resulted from Henderson's being appointed as a commissioner of the Port Authority of New York and New Jersey in 1983 by Governor Kean of New Jersey. Henderson was the first African-American to occupy this unsalaried position, and he used this opportunity to introduce new concerns, such as the development of venture capital investments for local business and efforts to further a policy of affirmative action for minority participation in business. Peter Goldmark of the Authority, who was impressed with Henderson's ability, praised him in the following manner: "He is a very pragmatic, very tough-minded man. He participates in all the difficult issues." Henderson was also appointed to head the Essex County Economic Development Commission, responsible for making capital more accessible to local businesses and attracting businesses into the area and establishing a successful resource network. It was an astute appointment because Henderson is deeply committed to the state of New Jersey. He is unable to separate his business from the community; he feels that they are deeply enmeshed: "[T]echnology has meaning only when it is used, directly or indirectly, to improve the quality of life of the people who inhabit this planet." When he is awarded a large contract, he interprets the benefits as reaching beyond the confines of his company's walls to the people of the state in all types of industries, from truck drivers to assemblers, "people you wouldn't think would be involved in high-tech industry."

On a personal level, Henry Henderson has received numerous distinguished awards: In 1985 he was named Small Business Person of the Year, and in the same year he was cited by the New Jersey Business and Industry Association as the Distinguished Business Citizen of the Year. In 1986 he received the National Black MBA Association's award for outstanding contributions to the business community. He has achieved his overall goal of maintaining a solid reputation as a person who has been effective in helping minority entrepreneurs and all working people in the metropolitan New Jersey area to better themselves through his involvement in the Port Authority and other organizations that are helping businesses. His zest for life continues as he approaches his later years, flying his private plane, and enthusiastically taking pride in his accomplishments. This is shown when he responded to a question about how he feels when he sees the huge Henderson Industries sign above the headquarters' entrance each morning: "It feels fantastic. I have to pinch myself. It's really awesome."

Sources

No personal or business papers are currently available for Henry Henderson or Henderson Industries. Nor is there much detailed biographical information on Henderson himself. Most information on him and the company must be assembled from a variety of newspaper and magazine articles, along with some printed informational materials and videos supplied by Henderson Industries. Some of the most useful information is contained in William Hoffer, "Black Entrepreneurship in America," *Nation's Business*, June 1987; "Quiet Success of a Talented Engineer," *Ebony*, February 1977; "Company of the Year: H. F. Henderson Industries," *Black Enterprise*, June 1984; Mark Fortune, "Divide and Conquer," *Black Enterprise*, June 1988; *Minorities and Women in Business*, March/April 1989; "Black Enterprise," *New Jersey Business*, September 1987; *Business Direct to Business*, June 1985; Charles Q. Finley, "Executive Finds Hard Work Repaid by Success," *Newark Star-Ledger*, May 23, 1983; and *Minority Business Entrepreneur*, September/October 1986.

See also the following: *Nation's Business*, October 1974; *New Jersey Monthly*, March 1981; *New Jersey Business*, October 1976; *Trade World New Jersey*, April 1985; *Daily Record*, March 29, 1987; *Via*, January 1984 and September 1985; *Caldwell Progress*, August 21, 1986; *Newark Star-Ledger*, October 1, 1983, November 9, 1984, March 5 and December 8, 1985, and June 5, 1988; *Carib News*, January 29, 1985; *Star Scanner* (Lockheed Electronic Company Bulletin) XXVII, 11 (July 10, 1987); *Philadelphia Inquirer*, May 31, 1984; *The Connection*, May 18–31, June 1–14, 1985; *School Engineering Technologies*, April 24, 1985; *New York Times*, October 14, 1984; and "United Minority Business Brain Trust of New Jersey," March 18, 1988.

From Henderson Industries, we secured the following: three videotapes: (1) Henderson Industries, "Growing a Business," (2) Henderson Industries Capabilities, Commercial

Systems Division 1990 and, (3) Henderson Industries, Government Systems Division Capabilities II 1990; a curriculum vitae for Henry Henderson; general information about the firm put out by the company, and a Henderson Industry Company brochure.

Herndon, Alonzo Franklin (June 26, 1858–July 21, 1927), **Norris Bumstead Herndon** (July 15, 1897–June, 1977), and **Jesse Hill, Jr.** (1927–   ). Insurance company executives: Atlanta Life Insurance Company. Atlanta Life Insurance Company, founded by Alonzo Herndon in 1905, has nearly always been number two among African-American insurance firms, trailing the venerable North Carolina Mutual. Yet, it has been a profitable, stable institution, and it remains, unlike North Carolina Mutual, virtually entirely black owned. As such, Atlanta Life has been a pillar of the African-American upper class establishment in Atlanta, as well as a source of support for movements for black civil rights over the years. It remains a monument to the vision and ideals of its founder, an ex-slave and wealthy barber.

Alonzo Herndon was born on the Herndon plantation in Walton County, Georgia. His mother, Sophonie, was a slave woman, and his father was a white man, perhaps his master. Alonzo Herndon was so light skinned that W.E.B. Du Bois claimed that "anywhere but in the United States he would have been regarded as a white man. His father was white and probably seven of his eight great-grandparents were white; but he was classed as 'colored.' " Nothing is known of Herndon's life in slavery, but at seven and one-half years of age he and his family were emancipated. The newly freed family, consisting of his mother, brother, and grandparents, were in a state of extreme destitution. In the early years, only Alonzo's mother was able to work, and she hired herself out by the day. All the family had was a corded bed and a few quilts, which she put in a one-room log cabin also occupied by four other families. The space allotted to the family was so small that there was just room for the bedstead, under which she stored the family's meager possessions.

Sophonie Herndon did not earn money from her labors, but rather she was paid in kind with potatoes, molasses, peas, and other foodstuffs. It was usually enough to keep the family minimally fed, but it afforded no money to buy clothes or other necessities, so young Alonzo went to work with his grandfather, Carter Herndon, pulling a cross-cut saw. Alonzo continued this until he was thirteen, when he went to work as a farmhand for his old master, signing on for a period of three years. He was to receive $25 for his first year's labor, $30 for the second, and $40 for the third. In the limited spare time he had, Herndon peddled peanuts, homemade molasses candy, and axle grease made from burnt pine knots. All of his earnings, save a small portion that was put into savings, was turned over to his family to help them through their difficult times. During this time, Herndon managed to get just twelve months of formal education.

At age twenty, in 1878, Herndon left Walton County with just $11 in his pocket and a small hand truck, determined to make his way in the world. Herndon walked until he got to Senoia in Coweta County, where he again found work as a farmhand. To supplement his income Herndon began cutting hair on Saturday afternoons in a small space he rented in the black section of town. After a few months in Senoia, Herndon again moved on to Jonesboro, in Clayton County, just outside of Atlanta. There he opened his own barber shop and turned his full attention to that trade. Soon Herndon's shop became very popular and profitable, but he did not remain there long either. Just where Herndon went when he left Jonesboro is not clear, but some accounts have him going as far north as Chattanooga. What is clear is that Herndon had settled in Atlanta by early 1883 and that he was working as a journeyman barber in a shop on Marietta Street owned by a black man, Dougherty Hutchins. Herndon was reportedly making $6 a month at this job.

Herndon rapidly acquired a reputation for both his skill as a barber, and for the respectful demeaner he demonstrated toward the white clientele in Hutchins' shop. Herndon soon became the most requested barber in the shop. Within six months he had purchased a half-interest in the business, and the shop was renamed Hutchins and Herndon. It was quite an extraordinary achievement for Alonzo Herndon, even if he had gone no farther than that. Here he was, with just one year of formal education, and only five years removed from a life of the most grinding poverty imaginable, and he was already a part proprietor of a thriving business. Further, he had been in the city only six months when he achieved it. One cannot help but be impressed with the drive and determination of the young man. But he had only just begun.

In 1886 Herndon opened his own barbershop, on busy Whitehall Street in downtown Atlanta. Called the A. F. Herndon Barbershop, he operated it for one year until Mr. Silvey, the owner of the Markham House, then the city's finest hotel, offered to rent him space if he would relocate his shop there. This was a potential gold mine for Herndon, since, although it was somewhat of a novelty at the time, servicing the hotel trade generally became a lucrative end of the business for a barber. So Herndon accepted, setting up what would become a twelve-chair shop in the hotel, which he operated with great success. Over the years Herndon enlarged it several times and hired a number of assistants. One of those was C. H. Faison, a lifelong friend who later became one of the directors of Atlanta Life. This new venture, however, hardly quenched Herndon's ambition. In fact, he discovered that he thirsted for more. The one thing that rankled him about the hotel shop was that he was still essentially in the employ of someone else. Herndon desperately wanted to open a shop of his own, one that would be the envy of every other barber in the city. He had saved up enough money during the ten years he ran the hotel shop to fulfill his ambition. But Herndon could hardly walk out on the deal Silvey had given him. To do so might alienate segments of the white clientele Herndon had worked so hard to cultivate. Deliverance of a sort for Herndon came when the Markham House was destroyed by fire on May 17, 1896.

Herndon then opened two shops of his own, but these were just stopgap measures; he had plans to open the largest, most elegant barbershop Atlanta had ever seen. He opened that shop at 66 Peachtree in 1902, and it was quite an extraordinary place, which became increasingly grand over the years. After Herndon remodeled and enlarged it in 1913, it was an awesome sight for native Atlantans and visitors alike. The shop measured 24 by 102 feet, had twenty-five chairs and eighteen baths with tubs and showers. And Herndon, in his extensive European travels, had outfitted it with crystal chandeliers, gilt-framed mirrors and fittings, massive sixteen-foot front doors of solid mahogany, and beveled plate glass which he had copied from those he had seen in Paris. Herndon's shop, as always, catered only to the white trade, while all of the barbers were black. The whites who frequented Herndon's shop were the elite of Atlanta: judges, lawyers, politicians, ministers, and businessmen. It was, according to the *New York World*, "known from Richmond all the way to Mobile as the best barbershop in the South," and Herndon himself was recognized as "the king of boss barbers." The shop continued for at least ten years after Herndon's death in 1927, existing as a gracious monument to the southern tradition of blacks servicing whites in the old master-servant relationship that was a relic from the days of slavery. But Herndon, like so many other African-Americans during the seventy-five years from 1865 to 1940, made a fortune on this trade.

During the years after 1885, Herndon also invested heavily in real estate, continuing to do so throughout his life. By the time of his death he was the owner of an extensive portfolio of realty holdings. His first opportunity to purchase real estate came in 1885 from a white customer in his shop. Herndon seized the opportunity, and over the years he continued to add to his holdings. Eventually he owned more than 100 houses in the black section of Atlanta, a large block of commercial property on Auburn Avenue—the "main street" of the African-American business district—and a large estate in Florida, which he sold just before the land bubble burst in the 1920s. By the time of his death the value of his real estate holdings alone was assessed at $324,107. His total estate by that time was well over a half million dollars.

As Herndon's wealth and prestige accumulated during these years, his social prestige grew also. He became a recognized leader in the city's African-American community. This leadership emanated not only from his economic position, but also from his providential marriage. In 1893 he married Adrienne Elizabeth McNeil, of Savannah, a cultured and refined graduate of Atlanta University. A member of the older black elite, she introduced the largely self-educated ex-slave to culture, refinement, and education. Prior to her marriage, Adrienne NcNeil had been hired as one of the first black faculty members at Atlanta University, and she continued to teach dramatics there after her marriage. It was through his wife that Alonzo Herndon developed a strong attachment to Atlanta University, and they built a magnificent mansion near the campus that serves today as the elegant Herndon Museum. And it was through his wife that the Herndons were able to gain access to the more refined African-American elite in the city, assuming a position of leadership among this group.

It was Herndon's unquestioned position of economic and social leadership in the black community that brought two African-American ministers, Reverend Peter James Bryant and Reverend James Arthur Hopkins, to see him in 1905. Bryant, pastor of Wheat Street Baptist Church, had organized the Atlanta Benevolent and Protective Association a year earlier, and then had brought Hopkins in as manager. The business was run first out of Hopkins's home, and then from the Rucker Building on Auburn Avenue. Associations like the one these ministers organized were ubiquitous in the black communities of the South and North. African-Americans since emancipation had found it difficult to get insurance of any sort. Their poverty and low social standing made it nearly impossible for the masses of blacks to join the fraternal and other organizations that provided death benefits and other insurance services to many working-class whites, and white industrial insurance companies often refused to write policies for blacks since they were considered to be poor risks. So black churches throughout the nation stepped in to fill the void. For a nominal fee of from five to twenty-five cents weekly, the association provided minimal sickness benefits and a decent burial at death. As such, then, they filled a vital need in the struggling black community at the turn of the century.

Many of these associations, as might be imagined, were undercapitalized and poorly managed, and some were even outright frauds. As a result, a number of poor blacks found they were not able to receive their benefits when they were due. For this reason, and because some white insurance companies resented the growing competition from these burial associations, a new law was passed in Georgia in 1905. This law required that all industrial insurance companies (that is, insurance firms that collected weekly premiums) had to deposit $5,000 with the state treasurer as a guarantee that claims would be paid in case the company failed. Reverends Bryant and Hopkins realized that there was no way their association could come up with that kind of money, so they began looking for an "angel" in the black community who had enough wealth to put $5,000 in the state coffers and who would buy the association for a minimal sum and run it.

Hopkins realized that whites might try to take over the firm, but he and Bryant were determined it remain in African-American hands. As he later recalled, "When there were bids by white institutions, [we were] fully decided to let this institution remain as it began, a race institution." This was important because it truly defined Atlanta Life as it was then, and as it has remained. It is an economic entity, and a successful one at that, but it has also remained an important community or race institution. The man they turned to to save the struggling enterprise was Alonzo Herndon. He put up the $5,000 to deposit with the state and also paid the ministers $140 to purchase the association's assets. Herndon then set in motion a plan of reorganization for what was to be called the Atlanta Mutual Insurance Association, and later would become Atlanta Life Insurance Company.

For many in Atlanta's black community, Herndon's purchase of Atlanta Mutual was final confirmation of his role as a race leader. Truman K. Gibson,[*] a contemporary of Herndon's and a prominent insurance executive in his own right, expressed these sentiments, in assessing that Herndon came forward at a "critical hour" and "to the help of his race and to the succor of the enterprise of his people. With the dollars he had accumulated by toil and sacrifice . . . he deposited $5,000 with the state and restored the confidence of the people. By that act he averted a crisis which might have swept all our race enterprises out of existence."

In addition to Hopkins's and Bryant's association, Herndon brought two other small assessment associations, the Royal Mutual Insurance Association and the National Laborer's Protective Union, under his management. Herndon had to pay out an additional $8,500 in agency and promotional fees before he could get Atlanta Life going, but it soon began operating out of new quarters at 202 Auburn Avenue in a building Herndon owned. The fledgling enterprise, however, was hardly out of the woods. Herndon, who was elected president, could not devote much time to its operation in the early months. Nor did he know much about insurance. Therefore, Herndon looked for men in the black community who could provide the time and expertise the enterprise demanded. To this end he hired John H. Crew who, for ten years, had run a branch of the Birmingham-based Union Central Relief Association of Georgia in Atlanta. Crew was named secretary of Atlanta Life and given primary responsibility for running the organization. Crew and Herndon in the last three months of 1905 hired agents and opened offices throughout the state; by the end of the year, the company had 6,324 policies worth a total of $180,962.

Early on, Alonzo Herndon established a pattern for growth that came to characterize Atlanta Life throughout its history—he extended it through acquisition and merger. In early December of his first year of operation, Herndon took over the Empire Industrial Insurance Association, headed by the eminent Bishop Joseph S. Flipper and Reverend H. N. Newsome. By the end of 1907 Herndon had also acquired the Metropolitan Mutual Benefit Association and the Great Southern Home Industrial Association. During the twenty-two years Herndon ran Atlanta Life, it took over, in addition to those firms mentioned above: Alabama Protection, Atlanta Benevolent, Benevolent Union, Liberty Mutual of Savannah, Metropolitan Mutual, Royal Association, and Union Mutual of Georgia. These reinsurance deals, as Alexa Henderson has noted, also "made for great advertising for Atlanta Mutual, and the firm quickly gained the public's confidence."

Perhaps the most significant of these early mergers was with Union Mutual in 1915. Organized in Birmingham, Alabama, in 1894 by Reverend Thomas W. Walker, for years it had been a major competitor of Atlanta Mutual and had done a substantial business in Georgia for nearly twenty years. It fell on hard times after 1912, however, and when Atlanta Mutual took over its assets and reinsured its policyholders. Union Mutual did a great deal to increase the prestige of both the insurance firm and Alonzo Herndon. As Ben Davis, caustic editor of the *Atlanta Independent* commented a few years later, "When people buy a policy in Atlanta Life they are buying Alonzo Herndon.'' This faith was largely promoted by Herndon's reinsurance deals: Blacks who thought they would lose all they had invested in their policies to failed black insurance firms were grateful to Herndon for saving their nest eggs. And he never let them down.

By 1910 Atlanta Life was a substantial, stable business entity, and Alonzo Herndon had unquestionably emerged as the city's preeminent African-American business leader. In that year Herndon took Atlanta Life in a new direction in terms of expansion: He took the firm into Alabama and, by the end of the year, had sold over $70,000 worth of insurance in that state. The following year he extended operations into Kentucky. This move was made in conjunction with Heman Edward Perry's* Standard Life Insurance Company. A complex arrangement, typical of the deals put together by Perry, it fell apart after a few months, reportedly because of personal differences between the two men. At the end of 1915 Herndon and Atlanta Life had reached a momentous benchmark—it now had over a million dollars of insurance in force. Although, as with most industrial insurance firms, it suffered a high lapse rate over the years, the firm was nonetheless able to grow and prosper throughout Herndon's management.

In 1916 capital stock amounting to $25,000 was subscribed and sold—nearly all of it to Herndon himself. In that same year, Atlanta Life set up a department of industrial straight life, allowing it to sell small policies without the sickness provisions. In 1922 Herndon again increased the capital stock of the firm, this time to $100,000, of which Herndon again was the principal purchaser. By this time Atlanta Life's insurance in force had reached a stunning $9.75 million, a nearly tenfold increase over what it had been a scant seven years before, and some fifty-eight times greater than at the end of its first year of operation. With this growth it was also necessary for Atlanta Life to move into its own new quarters. To this end, in 1918 Herndon purchased an old, two-story brick building at 132 Auburn, which had formerly housed the local black YMCA, and began renovating it. The company moved into the building in 1920. By this time, Auburn Avenue was the vibrant commercial hub of a growing black community. Known affectionately as ''Sweet Auburn,'' it was the ideal location for the dynamic and aggressive Atlanta Life.

The 1920s were dubbed the ''golden years'' by the company, a decade that witnessed the laying of a secure foundation for future growth and development. Atlanta Life began to write ordinary life insurance policies, thereby extending its insurance coverage to segments of the black middle class. It also began expanding into a number of states that bordered Georgia—Florida, Tennessee, and, again, Kentucky. Atlanta Life also moved into Missouri, Kansas, and Texas during the early 1920s. This expansion drive was curtailed after 1924, however, as Herndon was concerned about the dangers of spreading the organization too thin through overexpansion. Particularly difficult for the insurance firm was finding enough educated blacks to hire as agents. It used Atlanta University as the recruiting base, but the overall lack of experience of many of these young agents was a constant source of trouble for the company.

It was during the early years of the decade that Herndon expressed himself most eloquently as to what he wished Atlanta Life to become:

I hope to live to see the Atlanta Life Insurance Company the largest Negro insurance company in the world. I intend to do all that is within my power to help make it so. I am willing to exert every ounce of influence I possess to help it move upward and I will go with it, but if it goes down, I will not go down with it.

Atlanta Mutual had not quite achieved Herndon's goals by the time he died, but in 1927 it was a solid, strong second among African-American insurance companies, trailing only perennial front-runner North Carolina Mutual. In that year, Atlanta Life had a total income of over $1.8 million, with profits of nearly $190,000. It was a very good year, indeed, although difficult years lay ahead during the Great Depression.

As a prominent black business leader in one of the South's most dynamic cities, and one which was gaining renown as a center of African-American business enterprise, Alonzo Herndon quite obviously became a prize to be captured in the ideological debate that raged during the first decade and a half of the twentieth century between Booker T. Washington* and W.E.B. Du Bois. Washington in 1990 had organized the National Negro Business League, and Herndon attended the first conference as one of the Atlanta delegates. He played little other part in the organization, however, and efforts on the part of Washington to get a stronger commitment from Herndon, especially after the founding of Atlanta Life, were fruitless. Yet, Herndon appears to have agreed with Washington's philosophy of self-help and business enterprises since he gave many speeches on that topic.

Efforts of Du Bois to enlist Herndon in support of the Niagara Movement and the NAACP were similarly short-circuited. As with the National Negro Business League, Herndon was among the twenty-nine men who founded the Niagara Movement in 1905, but he quickly appeared to lose interest. Whether it was because of pressure from Washington and his forces, or just because Herndon preferred to shy away from essentially political controversies of this type, is difficult to say. But he continued to maintain cordial, though relatively cool, relations with both sides for years.

Other critical race issues arose during the years to test Herndon's mettle, but his stance was usually to avoid making a direct confrontation against them. The most devastating for him was the terrible Atlanta Riot of 1906. In this riot, mobs of whites went wild, attacking black homes and persons throughout the ghetto, killing a number of persons. Herndon was personally affected by the rampage when the front window of his stately Peachtree Street shop was smashed. Worse, four of his barbers were shot, and a bootblack in the shop was kicked to death by enraged whites. Herndon had made his fortune catering to the needs of the white community, and now it had turned on him in unaccustomed virulence.

Herndon's response was not rage but a muted sense of tragedy. His initial reaction was simply to move away; to go north to start a new life for himself and his family. He wrote to Booker T. Washington: "The riot and the unsettled conditions here make us feel that I can never hope to have [a home] in this ungodly section." But that feeling soon passed, and Herndon stayed on to build his insurance company and his fortune. A few years later, his first wife died, and in 1912 he married Jessie Gillespie from Chicago. From a politically active family, she brought a heightened sense of the black mission to her new husband. As a result, the Herndons became increasingly involved in the social life of black Atlanta. They gave their support to a number of black orphanages and generally came to be considered leaders in both the business and social uplift activities in the community.

By the time of his death, in addition to Atlanta Life, Herndon had taken an active role in the Southview Cemetery Association, Atlanta Loan and Trust, and Atlanta State Savings Bank. He was also one of the founders of Gate City Drug Company, which opened the first black-owned drugstore in the Auburn Street area. In addition, he erected the Herndon Building at 251 Auburn, which housed a number of black businesses, professional offices, and organizations. It also housed one of the earliest black-owned hotels. At his death, he was eulogized by a large number of persons who attended his funeral. George W. Lee,* head of the Memphis office, said, "The Captain of our army has made his last stand." C. C. Spaulding* of North Carolina Mutual commented, "His life, character and integrity speak so loud among Negro business men of the country that what we might say would not be necessary. The Negro business men of America regarded Mr. Herndon as one of the sanest and most successful men of the Race."

But perhaps the most eloquent words were spoken later by someone who was not there. W.E.B. Du Bois said of Alonzo Herndon:

Alonzo Herndon was an extraordinary man and illustrates at once the possibilities of American democracy and the deviltry of color prejudice. . . . He did this in the face of every discouragement. He had no right to vote; he was continually in danger of mob violence; laws were passed to put him out of business; white men who were his moral, mental, physical and business inferiors called him "Alonzo," and he could be insulted with impunity by any white Atlanta hoodlum.

Yet, Herndon rose above that. Born a slave, experiencing the most grinding poverty imaginable, living his manhood and making his fortune during one of the most virulently racist times in the American South, he still persevered and conquered.

When Alonzo Herndon died, he was succeeded by his son, Norris. Norris Herndon was very nearly a recluse, so much so that *Ebony* magazine in 1955 tagged him as "The Millionaire Nobody Knows" and talked about how he remained largely secluded in the stately mansion his father had built. Norris Herndon, at least by the 1950s, was not listed in *Who's Who in America* or in *Who's Who in Colored America*; he was not even listed in the phone book. When a reporter asked an executive in a social service agency how someone got in to see Herndon, he shot back: "Impossible! He is the most inaccessible Negro in the world." What do we know about Norris B. Herndon, and what role did he play in the growth and development of Atlanta Life? Neither question is easy to answer.

Norris Herndon was born in Atlanta and, unlike his father, was raised in the lap of luxury. Although the elder Herndon was a stern taskmaster in many ways, he had a tendency to dote upon his only child, especially after his first wife died in 1910. Alonzo Herndon admitted to friends that he spoiled "everyone that I have anything to do with." Norris Herndon was a good and conscientious student who graduated from Atlanta University in 1919. He thereupon went to Harvard University Graduate School of Business and received his master's in business administration in 1921. Young Herndon, who had worked for Atlanta Life during summers for a number of years under his father's tutelege, then joined the firm as cashier and first vice president. Norris's first big assignment came in 1925, when his father asked him to head up a motorcade to the firm's twentieth-anniversary planning conference in Tavares, Florida. At the conference young Herndon gave the opening speech, highlighting the difficulties and accomplishments over the past twenty years. He worked in close conjunction with his father from that point until the latter's death.

Norris Herndon was elected the second president of Atlanta Life in January 1928. His administration, which lasted for some forty-five years, represented a period of unprecedented growth and prosperity. There can certainly be little question about that. First of all, the firm continued to grow steadily throughout the 1930s, despite the severity of the Depression. Total insurance in force had nearly doubled during that decade, total income went up over 50 percent, and the firm's total assets escalated by a similar amount. Then, with World War II and postwar prosperity, the expansion became even more impressive. During the entire period of Norris Herndon's stewardship of the company, insurance in force went from about $25 million in 1930 to $346 million in 1973. Total income advanced from $1.8 million in 1930 to nearly $21 million in 1973. Over the same period, total assets went from just under $1.7 million to over $84 million. Furthermore, Atlanta Life remained the second-largest black insurance company, and, unlike North Carolina Life, remained black owned (in fact, Herndon owned, since he held about 95 percent of the stock) during this time.

Beyond that, however, it becomes difficult to assess Norris Herndon's role in the firm. His reclusiveness was not just limited to reporters and the "outside" world. Few of his own employees, or even his other executives, knew him well, and some hardly ever saw him. Norris Herndon had an extreme distaste for what he called "conspicurarity," and he seldom came into direct contact with most people in the firm, especially in the field and the branch offices. A famous story is told of Norris Herndon showing up at a branch office on Auburn Avenue, just a block from the home office. The cashier there, who liked to lighten her day with good humor, approached the tall man whom she had never seen and announced, "Good morning, I'm Mrs. Norris Herndon. What may I do for you?"

Herndon paused and stammered, "W-e-l-l, since I am Norris Herndon, I'm having a little trouble understanding why I haven't met my wife before." This was particularly perplexing for him since he never married.

Nor did Norris Herndon really take an active part in most of the day-to-day activities usually associated with the chief executive of a company. He left the details of the operation to a team of executives who also conducted most of the public affairs of the firm. Yet, many associated with the company defended his position there, insisting he was really running things. Even in later years, when he spent much of his time in Florida, and would only visit the home office in short spurts, a prominent educator said, "He goes to his office seldom now, but when he does he can do more work in two weeks than an ordinary man can do in two months." Another called him "brilliant, a genius," while a fellow business executive commented that Herndon could "raise more money tomorrow morning than any Negro in the world."

Whatever the truth of the matter, it is clear that Norris Herndon, years before Howard Hughes discovered the routine, had become a recluse out of touch with much of the outside world. An unostentatious man, he drove himself around in an old Ford, and, although he retained on his staff a chauffeur, a yardman, a cook, and a housekeeper, he seldom gave any of them anything to do. The reclusive, shy, and sometimes inarticulate Norris Herndon perhaps met his match one day at his lavish home in Atlanta. Joe Louis, the great heavyweight boxing champion, was invited there once after an exhibition. Louis walked in, looked around, and said, "Nice place you got here." Then he said nothing else the entire evening, and, knowing Norris Herndon, he probably didn't either. Those close to the firm insist that most of the real work of the chief executive during the years of Norris Herndon's tenure was handled by Eugene Martin.

Yet Norris Herndon, despite his reticence in public, continued much of his father's concern for humanitarian and philanthropic issues, although this was never done directly. He gave generously to the NAACP, National Urban League, United Negro College Fund, his First Congregational Church, the local black YMCA, Atlanta University, Morris Brown College, and many others. His most important creation, however, and one that is virtually unique in the African-American community was the Alonzo F. and Norris B. Herndon Foundation in 1950. This nonprofit corporation was set up to hold the vast majority of Atlanta Life's stock after Norris's death. He also agreed to contribute shares of stock to the foundation every year until that time. All of the earnings of the foundation were to be returned to the black community for various religious, scientific, educational, or literary purposes. The magnificent family home reverted to the foundation upon Norris's death to become a museum open to the public. By the time of Norris Herndon's death in 1977, the Herndon Foundation was one of just two black-endowed foundations with capital assets in excess of $1 million. Most of its philanthropy was directed to black colleges, dispensing over $47,000 in 1975.

Jesse Hill, Jr., Norris Herndon's successor as president in 1973, is referred to by most people as a "human dynamo." Hill brought a vastly different management style to Atlanta Life, both in terms of its internal operation and communication and in terms of its relationship to the problems of race and class in Atlanta in the 1970s and 1980s. Hill, like Alonzo Herndon, was born into grinding poverty. He was the son of Nancy Dennis Martin and Jesse Hill, Sr. His father and mother were divorced when Jesse, Jr., and his sister were young, and his mother raised them in a family with her own father. Hill's mother had had a hard life also. The oldest of fifteen children, she had ended her formal education early in order to help her parents raise her younger brothers and sisters. After her own early marriage ended in divorce, she worked in a Pullman steam laundry to provide the educational opportunities she never had to her son and daughter.

Jesse Hill recognized the important role his mother played in his life: "I was fortunate," he said, "to grow up under the guidance of a mother who, although she never attended high school, worked hard to fulfill a dream to make it possible for me and my sister to secure an education. She always impressed upon me the importance of two things: (1) giving praise to God from whom all blessings flow and (2) always pursuing excellence and giving my very best at all times no matter what the task." Hill received his business acumen from his grandfather, who drove a horse-drawn wagon, selling watermelons in the summer and ice and coal in the winter. Hill remarked about his grandfather, "As a young child I learned the fundamental principles of business sitting beside him."

Hill grew up in the tough southeast section of St. Louis alongside the Mississippi River. After graduating from local high school there, he enrolled in Lincoln University in Jefferson City, Missouri, founded after the Civil War by black Union veterans. Hill quickly became a top student at the school, majoring in mathematics and physics and graduating with honors in 1947. He then went on to the University of Michigan where he enrolled in graduate school studying actuarial science and business. At that time there were still very few blacks with degrees in actuarial science, but, as would be characteristic of Hill in later life, that simply acted as a spur to him. Hill got his degree and headed for Atlanta, a city that he had heard a lot about from his mother and from the chairman of the mathematics department at Lincoln. The story they kept repeating to him was about an ex-slave named Alonzo Herndon and how he had started this big insurance company. "The attraction to me without question," said Hill, "was two things, Alonzo Herndon and the city of Atlanta. I had heard so much about Atlanta and I wanted to be part of it."

Hill arrived in the city in 1949, got a room at the Butler Street YMCA, and began working as an actuarial assistant at Atlanta Life. During his first three years there, Hill served in a number of capacities and got started on his impressive program of community involvement. Hill's first step in that direction was to do volunteer work for the YMCA where he was living, but soon he was also teaching Sunday School at the Big Bethel AME Church, was serving as secretary of the Atlanta Negro Business League, was a scoutmaster, and was a member of the

Community Chest, the NAACP, and the Urban League. He was also an active campaign worker for the Atlanta Negro Voters League. Clarence Coleman, who was a staff member of the Atlanta Urban League chapter, recalls Hill just walking in off the street and taking out a membership: "He said that he wanted to work with us in any way that he could, and that was very unusual for a person who was new to town." Hill's early community work was so remarkable that, at the tender age of twenty-five, he became one of the youngest citizens to be honored for his work in the community.

Hill's first stint with Atlanta Life, and with the community, was interrupted in 1952, when he served for two years with the U.S. Army in Korea. He returned a decorated veteran in 1954 to resume his duties at Atlanta Life as acting actuary, and a year later he married Juanita Azira Gonzales, a native of Cuba who had graduated from Grady School of Nursing. It was also during this time that Hill and Atlanta Life became linchpins in the black community's burgeoning civil rights movement. He had become, by the late 1950s, what Atlanta school board president Benjamin E. Mays called a "total community character." Hill's great crusade in the 1950s was for black voting rights. He served as chairman of the All-Citizens Registration Committee, whose goal it was to add 50,000 black voters to the poll lists. He also became a member of the Atlanta Committee for Cooperative Action (ACCA), which began to tackle the issues of school segregation.

Hill and the other young black professionals who were members of the ACCA decided in the late 1950s to concentrate their attack on the state's colleges and universities. They tried first to secure desegregation of the University of Georgia's law school, and, failing that, turned their attention to a general drive to rout Jim Crowism from the university system's undergraduate admissions. They waged a long battle to secure the admission of two black students to the University of Georgia, which was finally accomplished in 1961. The next campaign rose naturally out of the first, when, in 1960, a group of black students at the Atlanta University Center colleges decided to stage sit-ins at the lunch counters of public buildings, bus and train stations, major department stores, and at the five and dime stores. Hill was one of the few black business leaders in the city to support this movement, and from the beginning he acted as an advisor to the Student Nonviolent Coordinating Committee. The switchboard and offices of Atlanta Mutual became the command center for the movement.

Since none of the city's newspapers, white or black, were supportive of these disruptive sit-in movements, Hill took the leadership in founding *The Atlanta Inquirer*, which became the mouthpiece of the more radical black movement in the city. Elected president of the corporation formed to publish the paper, he served in that position for a number of years. While the students were out demonstrating and boycotting, Hill worked behind the scenes as a master negotiator and coordinator, working out deals with the white power establishment. In this manner, the student movement was able to gain most of their demands, and Hill, who had proved himself a tough, but fair and rational negotiator, found he was gaining access to the highest reaches of the white establishment. It began a bittersweet transformation for Hill and the black movement. He increasingly became its leader, sometimes it seemed like its only leader, and was able to exert great influence at the highest possible levels to wrest concessions. At the same time, however, he became farther removed from the rank and file of the movement, and by the late 1980s much of his support from the black community, which had been unquestioned previously, began to erode.

During the 1960s, however, Hill was still close to the people and was jousting with the white power elite. One of his most dramatic victories came over massive demonstrations that had been organized to protest portable classrooms set up for black high school students in the Buttermilk Bottoms slum. Hill called the portables the "disgrace of the Atlanta school system." In the end, Hill was able to get the school board to capitulate and build a new school for the displaced students. It was during this time, also, that some of the conservative middle-class blacks who had policies with Atlanta Life decided that Hill's involvement with civil rights was endangering the firm and the security of their policies. They threatened to picket the company and withdraw their policies unless Norris Herndon put Hill on a tighter leash. Herndon, ever uncommunicative, simply ignored their demands, and in that manner gave full support to Hill and his dramatic civil rights activities.

By the early 1970s Hill's "radical" civil rights stances had taken on an air of respectability, and so had Hill himself. He was appointed to the Metropolitan Atlanta Rapid Transit Authority and also became the only black to be put on the board of directors of the Atlanta Chamber of Commerce. Hill also became increasingly involved in electoral politics, supporting Sam Massell's successful bid to become mayor of Atlanta in 1969, and the candidacy of Andrew Young for Congress in 1970. He also was a frequent guest at the White House during the administrations of both Lyndon Johnson and Richard Nixon. By this time, also, he had become vice president and chief actuary of Atlanta Life. When Norris Herndon stepped upstairs to the board chairmanship in 1973, Hill was named to replace him as president. This advance was just one of three that came to Hill within the space of a few weeks. He was also named by Governor Jimmy Carter to the State Board of Regents and was elected to the board of directors of Rich's, a local department store he had led pickets and boycotts against just a few scant years earlier. Atlanta's blacks by that point could truly paraphrase Pogo and say, "We have met the establishment and it is us." Jesse Hill, Jr., after 1973 was part of the power structure of Atlanta and Georgia.

It was then that some of the resentments emerged over Hill's role as a black leader. Reverend William Holmes Borders, a prominent Baptist minister, called out to Hill on the street in 1973, saying, "Come here, Jesse . . . what you are doing is fine, but what I want you to know and I want the white folks to know, that Jesse Hill is not the only black man with brains." But Hill just pushed deeper and deeper into the white establishment. He joined the Action Forum in 1971, organized by Mills B. Lane, Jr., to bring white and black leaders together to discuss problems of race. A year later Hill was named chairman of the Atlanta Crime Commission and in 1975 was elected a director of Atlanta-based Delta Airlines. Hill was also chairman of the National Alliance of Businessmen for Metro Atlanta and North Georgia. Then, when Jimmy Carter was elected U.S. president in 1976, Hill, who had been a longtime backer of Carter, began to acquire clout on the national level also. He became chairman of the Minority Business Resource Center, which had been created by Congress to ensure that minority businesses got their share of the $6.4 billion to be spent on renovating and restructuring America's railways. Hill rightly cautioned blacks and other minorities not to assume all of this would just fall in their laps. Earlier he had commented on the pitfalls of black capitalism: "Many people have found out the hard way that while 'Black Capitalism' has a nice ring to it, slogans aren't a whole lot of help when you come up against keen competition in the marketplace."

Hill in many respects capped his astonishing rise to power and influence in political and business circles in 1977 when he was elected the first-ever chairman of the Atlanta Chamber of Commerce. This gave Hill and Atlanta's black community an important new forum. Hill soon let it be known that, although there was necessity for reform and social change, his "primary concern [was] to promote the economic growth and development of Atlanta and the region": pretty much what white chamber presidents had been saying all along. He did assure blacks, however, "that it would be quite a serious omission if as a result of my serving in this position we came back ten years from now and found that some of the barriers that existed for blacks and other minorities were still here." One of his harshest critics, however, was Hosea Williams, who announced, "Blacks will be looking for Mr. Hill to deliver the bacon home, meaning they expect under his administration to penetrate, participate in the economic mainstream of the city." Hill cautioned that "nothing will change overnight."

As Jesse Hill grew more and more powerful in Atlanta, Georgia, and the nation, he did not neglect Atlanta Life. In fact, he continued to insist that Atlanta Life was what was really important. As he stated in 1978, "I love this company. I love its history, growing pains, and what it means to the future of black business and poor people. I want it to continue to succeed." And indeed it did. While involved in all his other activities, Hill also launched Atlanta Life on an incredibly ambitious acquisition campaign. Over a short period of time, it bought the People and Keystone Life Insurance Companies of New Orleans, Louisiana, and the Southern Aid Insurance Company of Richmond, Virginia, which was the oldest black insurance company in existence at that time. Atlanta Life paid in excess of $3 million for these firms and increased its overall value of assessment by $10 million, giving Atlanta Life total assets of over $90 million. In 1976 it was one of only two black insurance companies to receive "excellent" ratings by *Best's Insurance Reports*, the "bible" of the insurance industry.

One of Hill's goals in taking over these firms, he told the press, was to ensure that they continued to be black controlled. Several black insurance firms had been taken over by white firms in Louisiana, thus prompting Hill's move into that state. In 1979 Jesse Hill began making plans for the completion of a new office building for Atlanta Life. The new building, a magnificent six-storied structure of rose-hued marble and glass, was dedicated in September 1980, in time for the firm's seventy-fifth anniversary. The structure cost $10 million, and was paid for in full on opening day. Located next door to the old office, the new Herndon Plaza was viewed by many as the westernmost anchor to a hoped-for rebirth of Auburn Avenue. Atlanta Life itself was aware of its mission in that regard. Helen Collins, vice chairman of the board, said, "We built it here because we hoped to enhance the area, we certainly didn't want to leave our roots." By that point Atlanta Life had more than 800,000 policyholders, 1,500 employees, sixty offices in twelve states, and the highest net earnings of any black business in the nation.

Hill continued Atlanta Life's expansion in the 1980s. His biggest coup came in 1985 when he battled North Carolina Mutual's William J. Kennedy III[*] for control of Mammoth Life and Accident Insurance Company of Louisville, the eighth-largest black insurance firm in the nation. Hill was successful, and this pushed Atlanta Life's assets up over the $155 million mark and its insurance in force to almost $2 billion. And he had ambitious plans for the future, saying, "We project over three to five years an average of at least one acquisition per year." North Carolina's Kennedy dismissed Hill's acquisition strategy, saying, "They can merger all the [black] companies out there and they won't catch us. . . . In fact, I've told Jesse Hill we'd consider taking him over."

Hill also announced that Atlanta Life would be altering its strategy in selling insurance somewhat. Always an industrial policy provider for the black poor, Hill wanted to target more business from the black middle class, much of which was going to white insurance firms. One area Hill had no interest in entering was the lucrative group insurance market—a strategy used successfully by both North Carolina Mutual and Golden State Mutual. In 1989 Hill was forced to announce that attempts to lure more middle-class policyholders had not been as successful as he had hoped. "Our goal has eluded us," he said. "We have not been as nearly successful as we'd like." The share of the life insurance sales to African-Americans by black-owned companies has declined or not kept pace. Yet, he continued to envision Atlanta Life as a "race institution" as Alonzo Herndon had visualized it eighty-five years earlier. "I think my determination to make a quest for human dignity has to be tied to the quest for economic dignity, and vice versa," said Hill. "I think that is the spirit of our founder . . . who was a former slave, he launched this quest and frankly, I think I want to carry that tradition."

But some in the black community felt Jesse Hill was no longer either speaking to or for the African-American community of Atlanta. Cynthia Tucker, associate editor of the *Atlanta Constitution* and a black woman, said that Hill "may well be the victim of his own success." She went on, adding that Hill and "others of the old guard belabor a stereotypical and one-dimensional view of blacks," when, in fact, there was now a "cacophony of black voices." She predicted that a "mature black community will hardly be led around by Jesse Hill—or any other single person or group." But Jesse Hill showed little indication that he was loosening the reins of power he held either at Atlanta Life or in Atlanta's black community. Hill was, in fact, part of Alonzo Herndon's magnificent legacy to black Atlanta.

Edward L. Simon, chairman of the board of Atlanta Life in the early 1980s, talked of Alonzo Herndon's influence, and what it meant for the company's later years. Saying that good management has always been the key to Atlanta Life's success, he elaborated:

My father used to play checkers with Mr. Herndon. We went to the same church, First Congregational. He was more renowned for his barber shop then than for an insurance company. But I remember one thing, you always heard people saying Mr. Herndon had some of the smartest people in town working for him. . . . Mr. Herndon knew the value of high-caliber personnel. (*Ebony*, June 1981)

Helen Collins, vice chairman of the board took up another theme:

I would think our history refutes the notion that when a Black businessman dies, his business must die also. We have a strong record of service to our policyholders. Our investment portfolio is strong; we are respected in the community. I think the miracle of the ages is that Mr. Herndon, by setting up a foundation, left his company to Black America. (Ebony, June 1981)

Jesse Hill felt a deep indebtedness to this same tradition, remarking in 1981:

The baton of this quest [for economic dignity] was passed from the founder in 1927 to N. B. Herndon and a dedicated team of management associates . . . who guided Atlanta Life to its position of financial strength. In 1973 the baton and challenge was passed to my generation.

Jesse Hill embodies in quantities perhaps unimagined by Alonzo Herndon a dedication to the quest for economic security, along with a fierce and powerful race pride. He stands fully in the tradition of the Herndon family and Atlanta Life.

Sources

The Herndon Family Papers are located at the Herndon Museum in Atlanta, Georgia. Although they are open to researchers, they have little of interest on the business side. For that kind of information, there are the Atlanta Life Insurance Company Files, but these are currently restricted. Alexa Benson Henderson, however, was able to use these files for her biography of the company: *Atlanta Life Insurance Company: Guardian of Black Economic Dignity* (Tuscaloosa, Al., 1990). There are a few letters from Alonzo Herndon in the Booker T. Washington Papers in the Library of Congress, and some material relating to Atlanta Life in the Robert Russa Moton Papers at Hollis Burke Frissell Library, Tuskegee University, Tuskegee, Alabama. There is also some useful information in the National Negro Business League Papers at the same location.

Biographical information on Alonzo Herndon, most of which also has much to say about Atlanta Life, is found in Alexa Benson Henderson, "Alonzo F. Herndon and Black

Insurance in Atlanta," *Atlanta Historical Society Bulletin* (Spring 1977); M. S. Stuart, *Economic Detour* (1940), 117–25; *Atlanta Daily World*, May 30, 1959, September 21, 1980, August 21, 1983, and August 20, 1987; *Atlanta Constitution*, July 31, 1989; an unpublished paper on "Alonzo Franklin Herndon" by Samuel W. William in the Fulton County-Atlanta Public Library; *The Vision* (Atlanta Life company organ), June 1932, September 1966, and June and July 1969; Clement Richardson (ed.) *National Cyclopedia of the Colored Race* (1919) (although Herndon is called "Henderson" here); *Crisis*, May 1914, March 1921, and September 1927; *New York World*, July 31, 1927; *Atlanta University Bulletin* (September 1974), 18–21; *Ebony*, April 1949; Ingham, BDABL; and Dan Durrett and Dana F. White, *An-other Atlanta: The Black Heritage, a Bicentennial Tour*, sponsored by Atlanta Bicentennial Commission, 20–21, held in the Martin Luther King, Jr., Center for Social Change, Atlanta. See also *Who's Who of the Colored Race* (1915).

There are some useful brief histories and analyses of Atlanta Life in *Ebony*, June 1981; *Atlanta Daily World*, August 8, 1937, May 30, 1959, and September 21, 1980; *Atlanta Constitution*, August 14, 1985; *Black Enterprise*, June 1977, June 1982, and June 1989; "The Atlanta Life Insurance Company," *Underwriters' Forum*, January 1947, 7; Truman Kella Gibson, "The History of Industrial Insurance and the Story of Atlanta Mutual," in W.E.B. Du Bois, ed., *Economic Cooperation among Negro Americans* (Atlanta University Publication 12, 1907), 37–38; *Atlanta Life*, 1977 (publication commissioned by Atlanta Life for its 75th anniversary). Information on the Herndon Foundation is found in Robert S. Browne, "Developing Black Foundations: An Economic Response to Black Community Needs," *The Black Scholar*, December 1977, 25–28.

Information on Norris Herndon is limited. See *Who's Who in Colored America*; *Ebony*, October 1955; and *Atlanta Constitution*, July 16, 1984. He wrote "The Progress of Atlanta Life Insurance Company," published in *The Vision*, January 25, 1932.

Information is abundant on Jesse Hill, Jr. See *Minorities and Women in Business*, March/April 1989; *Atlanta Inquirer*, September 5, 1960; *The Vision*, July 1971; *Atlanta Constitution*, September 8, 1971, May 4 and 24, and November 27, 1973, June 29, 1974, May 21, May 11, and June 11, 1978, January 20 and August 13, 1984, August 15, 1985, and October 24, 1987; *Atlanta Journal and Constitution*, May 13, 1973, July 23, and August 20, 1978, September 21, 1980, August 18, 1985, and December 3, 1989; William Schemmel, "Profile of Jesse Hill," *Atlanta Magazine*, January 1971, 26–32; *Jet*, August 14 and 27, 1974, August 14, 1975, May 11, 1978, and July 11, 1988; Robert J. Sye, "Jesse Hill, Jr.: Atlanta's Human Dynamo," *Sepia*, June 1978; *Birmingham News*, December 15, 1977; Ann Wead Kimbrough, "The Long Road to Success," *Atlanta Weekly*, January 26, 1986; *Black Enterprise*, June 1977 and June 1988; *Trailblazers among Black St. Louisans* by the National Sorority of Phi Delta Kappa (St. Louis, 1978); *Ebony*, August 1971; Frank J. Johnson, *Who's Who of Black Millionaires* (1984), 127; *Jet*, May 6, 1991.

Hill, Jesse, Jr. (see Herndon, Alonzo Franklin, Norris Bumstead Franklin, and Jesse Hill, Jr.).

Houston, Ivan James (see Beavers, George Allen, Jr., Ivan James Houston, Norman Oliver Houston, and William Nickerson, Jr.).

Houston, Norman Oliver (see Beavers, George Allen, Jr., Ivan James Houston, Norman Oliver Houston, and William Nickerson, Jr.).

Hurt, James, Jr. (see Clifton W. Gates and James Hurt, Jr.).

J

James Family: Charles Howell James (1862–February 2, 1929), Edward Lawrence James, Sr. (1893–June 18, 1967), Charles Howell James II (November
22, 1930–), and Charles Howell James III (1959–). Food processors and
wholesale and retail distributors: James Produce Company and C. H. James &
Co. C. H. James & Co., at 109 years of age was called, in 1992, America's
oldest black business by *Black Enterprise* magazine. That is a bit surprising,
since it is in a state, West Virginia, with a small black population, and as part
of Appalachia is an area that has had a marginal economic climate for decades.
There are many communities with far older and larger black populations, but
the African-American businesses in those areas, or for that matter, the vast
majority of the white businesses, have not managed to last as long. What has
been the secret of success of this four-generation firm?

The founder of the enterprise was Charles Howell James, who was born in
Gallia County, Ohio, while his father was fighting for the Union Army during
the Civil War. His father, Francis James, was discharged from the army in West
Virginia and decided to settle there. Before entering military service, he had
decided to become a minister, and after the war he was ordained the first black
Baptist minister in West Virginia. He and his sister, Lucy, also became teachers
in the new public schools set up for blacks. It is not clear from available evidence
what happened to Charles James's mother, Elizabeth Courtney James, but
Charles was sent to live with his grandfather in Ohio, where he grew up and
was educated. At age eighteen, in 1880, he and his three brothers, along with
the rest of the family, joined their father in West Virginia.

Upon his arrival in West Virginia, Charles James decided to follow his father's
career as a teacher. This proved to be a mistake. Charles had little interest in
the classroom or teaching, and he yearned to engage in some form of business.
By 1883, and perhaps as early as 1881, he and his three brothers (Edward R.,
H. Alex, and Garland D. James) were working as peddlers, selling a variety of
wares. They had pooled what little money they had to buy an assortment of
items. According to a company history written by C. H. James III, they "sold

ginseng roots and herbs and barks for medicinal purposes'' but also carried a number of novelty items, the most popular of which were pictures of the recently assassinated president, James A. Garfield. ''The cash flow generated from the sale of these pictures and other small articles carried by the brothers,'' said James, ''laid the foundation for a business that ultimately survived the Great Depression of the 1930s and the Great Recession of the 1970s.''

As the four brothers traveled about the hardscrabble countryside, they discovered a number of things: first, cash was a rare commodity among their rural customers, and, second, there was a demand for fresh produce in urban areas. So the James brothers began bartering their items for local produce, which they then took into Charleston, West Virginia, to sell. Before long, the farm produce they were carrying back to the city became too heavy to carry in their packs. They took part of their proceeds and purchased a mule and wagon to transport the produce back to Charleston. By the mid–1880s their business pattern was established: They went to wholesale dry goods and notion houses in Charleston, where they acquired on credit the merchandise they intended to sell to their rural customers. They, in turn, would sell these goods to farmers for cash or in trade for produce. The James brothers would then return to Charleston, where they sold the produce to hotels, restaurants, and grocers. With the proceeds they paid their bills to the wholesalers and pocketed whatever profits remained.

It was actually a propitious time to be in West Virginia and in Charleston. The fate of southern West Virginia, where Charleston and the James family's enterprises are located, from the early years was tied to the rise of bituminous coal mining. An area of preindustrial, subsistence agriculture was transformed over a short space of time into a critical adjunct of the nation's massive industrial system. This provided a great stimulus to both general economic activity and to the growth of the area's black population. Southern West Virginia, which had just 4,794 African-Americans constituting 6 percent of the population in 1880, thirty years later had over 40,000 blacks who made up 13.5 percent of the population. Charleston, which had just 3,000 people in 1870 when it became the state capital, had ballooned to 23,000 in 1910. Most of the blacks who came to West Virginia after 1890 went into coal mining, although a number were also involved in building the massive rail network in the state. Both occupations, compared to southern agriculture, offered blacks greater potential for money-making. During these early years, both Booker T. Washington[*] and Carter G. Woodson, the great African-American historian, worked in Kanawha County mining and railroad jobs.

Although blacks suffered less mob violence and overt racism in West Virginia than in the Deep South, segregation and discrimination nonetheless grew tremendously during the period around the turn of the century. As a result, almost every aspect of life in West Virginia, as in the rest of the South, became segregated. This was a horribly bitter pill for blacks, but it also worked to their benefit in some respects. Since whites would not service black needs, and blacks were restricted from participating in the white mainstream on so many levels, it opened the opportunity for a parallel black middle class of professionals and business people to develop. The number of blacks in professional, business, and clerical occupations in West Virginia increased from fewer than 1,000 in 1990 to over 1,600 in 1910, an increase of more than 60 percent in just ten years. Comparatively large numbers of black physicians emerged to take care of the health needs of black miners and their families, and a smaller number of African-American lawyers also set up practice. The lawyers often expanded into real estate. A few blacks went into coal mining, setting up firms like Eagle Coal Company. Black-owned restaurants, hotels, theaters, and funeral parlors were also created to cater to the black community. What was different about Charles H. James's business was that it catered to whites, rather than to blacks. This has been true of the firm throughout its history. As Charles H. James II, grandson of the founder commented in 1976, ''I can count my black customers on two hands and still have some fingers left over.''

The James family, in a state with one of the smallest black populations in the country, from the very beginning pegged its chances for success on a white clientele. First, as noted above, it was selling trinkets and notions mostly to white farmers. Later, the family's success depended almost solely upon white businesses in Charleston and upon the coal companies in the mountains which maintained full-line company stores for their employees living in their mining communities. Perhaps 10 percent of these miners were black, but that was incidental; Charles James and his heirs did their business with whites and operated in the economic mainstream. This has been a source of their staying power and growth over time, but it has also put them at a serious disadvantage, and even in some danger, at various points.

Although race relations were generally less violent in West Virginia than farther south, there were lynchings and outbreaks of other kinds of overt hostility, particularly in the 1890s. This had a direct impact on the James family. Often they were threatened with violence. ''It became,'' C. H. James II said, ''a question as to whether they would be permitted to trade in these areas or be frightened and driven out.'' The brothers persevered, but not without great personal tragedy. Charles James II told *Black Enterprise*, ''I probably shouldn't mention this, but one of my grandfather's brothers was shot out in Boone County.'' The gunshot was fatal, but Charles James, a pragmatic man, did not let it deter him or the development of his business. He simply detoured around that particular spot and continued to go about taking his goods to the coal mine company stores in the hills and fruits and vegetables to Charleston to sell to white-owned restaurants and hotels. He was just following a maxim he preached often to his children: ''Business is business, and race has no business in business.''

During the late 1880s and early 1890s, the James business continued to grow. Before long, they had four horses or mules hitched to each of four huge wagons which were ''veritable department stores on wheels.'' They carried bolts of cotton, calico and muslin, thread, pots, pans, sugar, coffee, and other goods that were scarce in outlying areas. When they found that there was a great demand for fresh eggs in Charleston, they began bringing eggs and fresh poultry to the city. As a result, they decided to expand into retail activities also and set up an outlet on Quarrier Street, one of Charleston's principal business arteries. Charles H. James at that point retired from the road to take charge of that end of the business, while his brothers continued as before.

In the late 1890s the business was reorganized. As noted above, one brother, Garland D. James, had been shot and killed in 1894, and another brother, Alex, died during this same period. Edward R. James, the oldest brother, decided to give up the business and leave the United States. He went first to New Zealand and then to São Paulo, Brazil, where he launched a construction business. C. H. James was left on his own, but "with more than a touch of fierce determination," he continued as before. He maintained the commercial outlet himself but hired other men to haul the merchandise into the hills and do the buying and selling. As his business continued to expand, James moved to larger quarters on Summers Street, by then the main business thoroughfare.

In 1885 Charles H. James had married Roxy Ann Clark, and they had six children. The only male child to reach adulthood was Edward Lawrence James. He graduated from Garnet High School in Charleston and then went to Howard University. In 1916, however, his father asked him to leave school and come back home to help with the business because he had decided to transform his business that year from a primarily retail operation to wholesale food distribution. He made Edward a partner in the enterprise and then embarked upon construction of a large, modern, three-storied warehouse on the corner of Virginia Street and Park Avenue, with access to the Kanawha and Michigan Railroad. The warehouse was constructed for just over $3,000, and the new firm was inaugurated with a sign reading, "C. H. James & Son, Wholesale Produce."

The father and son team began to import fresh fruits and vegetables into the region, procuring them from as far away as Cincinnati and Richmond. These sources, in turn, gave the firm access to produce coming from every part of the United States and abroad. Within two years, the newly focused C. H. James & Son was doing enough business for the elder James to be asked to join the Charleston Chamber of Commerce. The firm was "grossing well over $350,000 a year, or roughly one and a half million by 1976 standards," according to C. H. James III, "and had become the largest wholesale food operation in the state of West Virginia." The company had ten trucks with thirty employees. All seven of the company's salesmen were black and were furnished with company cars.

In 1926 C. H. James, the company founder, retired from active participation in the business, and Edward L. James took over as chief executive officer. By this time, the business assets of C. H. James & Son amounted to $140,000, of which the elder James held an equity position of $70,000. He lived an elegant life-style in a twelve-room home with a lawn tennis court on Virginia Street in the fashionable end of Charleston. He employed domestic servants in addition to a uniformed chauffeur to drive the company's luxurious Pierce Arrow limousine.

By this time, C. H. James was an integral part of a small but dynamic black middle class that had emerged in Charleston and in the state. In the state as a whole, black males made up 3.8 percent of those engaged in business, and black females accounted for 10.8 percent of the women running businesses in 1920. In sum, just over 950 African-Americans of both sexes ran businesses. Ten years later, 4.1 percent of the businesses run by males were owned by blacks, and 10.5 percent of the businesses run by females were owned by black females. A total of 1,350 individuals were so engaged. The vast majority of the black male businessmen were barbers (343) or tailors (243) or ran retail establishments (134). Of the females, most ran beauty parlors (109) or boarding houses (224). By that time, there were about 2,000 black males and females who were professionals or clerical workers.

In addition to the James family's thriving enterprise, a hotel was opened by G. E. Ferguson for blacks in the city (Hotel Ferguson), which the local black paper said "ranks as one of the foremost most modern and elaborately furnished and equipped hotels catering to Negro patronage around the country." There was also a black-owned life and casualty company (Union Insurance Company), which was capitalized at $150,000 with cash resources of $50,000. The firm invested in first mortgages on black-owned property in the state. There were, in addition, a large number of restaurants, poolrooms, taverns, undertakers, and other business enterprises of varying scope to serve the black community. C. H. James, who was an integral social part of this growing black bourgeoisie, however, continued to service primarily a white market.

C. H. James continued to worship and serve as an elder in the Baptist church that had been founded by his father in 1867. John W. Davis, who became president of West Virginia Collegiate Institute (now West Virginia State College) in 1919, had this to say about the elder James: "Charles James helped to make West Virginia a state. He helped improve race relations and there was a lot that had to be done . . . and there was the matter of getting jobs for Blacks. James was involved in all of that. He helped to establish West Virginia State College, which has become a pillar of the black community."

C. H. James had also become an early supporter of the National Negro Business League, founded by Booker T. Washington. There was occasional correspondence between James and the officers of the NNBL, and in July 1922 Albon Holsey of that organization implored James to give a speech at the upcoming convention. James demurred but said he would attend and might say a few words about his business. He also gave assistance in trying to establish NNBL locals around the nation. In addition, James was a director of the Mutual Savings and Loan and the Mountain State Building and Loan Association in Charleston. In politics, James was essentially an independent. He was first a Republican, later supported Theodore Roosevelt's Bull Moose or Progressive party, and later affiliated with the Democratic party. In the latter he served as treasurer of the Negro Democratic Club of West Virginia.

Charles James was also one of the founders of the National Association for the Advancement of Colored People in Charleston. He and Reverend Mordecai W. Johnson, pastor of James's First Baptist Church and later president of Howard University, led a protest against the showing of the film *Birth of a Nation* in Charleston. As a result, they expected to take charge of the new chapter of the NAACP in the city, but a rival faction, headed by a local painting contractor, I. M. Carper, met first and applied for a charter. James claimed that Carper's group lacked "full public confidence by reason of their conduct of public affairs" and asked to be given the charter instead. Ultimately the two factions agreed to merge, but there was always a split between the two in terms of goals and tactics. James remained an important presence in the organization throughout his life.

In 1928 C. H. James became increasingly frail, and in February 1929, he passed away. He was eulogized in local papers. The *Charleston Gazette* proclaimed

It is with great regret that *The Gazette* records the passing of C. H. James. He was one of the leading merchants of the city, and was a Negro of nationwide prominence. He built up a business that carries his name through industry, ability of a high order and scrupulous integrity. Irrespective of color, C. H. James was held in high esteem by citizens of all walks of life. He was a man who would have loomed large in any community. In his death we feel that we have lost a good citizen and a useful one. When that can be said of any man, he has made a success of his life.

James's death was perhaps a way of sparing him a wrenching agony. Shortly after his demise, Edward L. James was forced to petition for bankruptcy. Although this occurred several months before the outbreak of the Great Depression, the James family recalls that the reason for the bankruptcy was the inability of E. L. James to collect his own accounts receivable. The firm's 1927 balance sheet indicated that it had over $51,000 in that category. When E. L. James filed the bankruptcy papers, they showed assets of $20,000 and liabilities of $160,000. It was a bitter pill for James to swallow. He had been raised in affluence and privilege. He had grown up in a home filled with servants, and pictures of him in the early 1920s show a dandy dressed in tuxedos with high, starched collars, white gloves, spats, and a walking stick. In 1918 he had married the daughter of a prominent Methodist minister who herself had graduated from prestigious Oberlin College. While the Jameses' business expanded during the 1920s, Edward James moved his growing family into a fifteen-room apartment over the company's headquarters, where they had their own servants and a chauffeur-driven Pierce Arrow. It was a wrenching blow to lose all of that—business, home, servants, automobile—in a tragic moment in 1929.

A crushed Edward James quietly moved out of Charleston with his wife and seven children, settling in nearby Institute to begin a new life. By then, of course, the Great Depression was in full swing, and thousands were out of work. E. L.

James joined the masses in working on a WPA project, as a timekeeper for various road-building ventures. His son, Charles H. James II, remembers, "The Crash had a profound effect on my father. He had to sell everything to pay off the business debts. He lost his house, he lost everything. He had nothing when he moved us to Institute." He was offered a job as postmaster in Institute in the following year, but he turned it over to his wife, who filled the position for the next seventeen years. Instead, Edward James was able, since the family now had a steady source of income, to get back into the produce business in a small way.

Setting up a small produce stand in the farmer's market on Charleston's Patrick Street, Edward James began his long climb back to economic viability. He was able to do it by displaying the same sort of entrepreneurial flare his father had used. Traveling to rural areas in a truck he bought on credit to pick up produce to sell in Charleston, E. L. James started selling eggs he picked up on neighboring farms. James purchased eggs from farms as far away as Ohio, traveling there three times a week. Then he rushed back to Charleston in his battered old truck, using the "Blue Ribbon" brand to identify his product. Charles James II commented, "My father was the first man to introduce fresh eggs to the Charleston market. Before that people either had to go to the farms to get them, or buy eggs that had been held in cold storage, sometimes for weeks at a time." The James Corporation continues to use the Blue Ribbon brand for its produce to the present day. The James family became so expert at judging eggs that, when the state decided to enact laws to grade eggs, they turned to the family as chief experts on the subject.

At some time during the 1930s James also added fresh-killed poultry to his business, and by the end of the decade he was renting a 4,000-square-foot warehouse with refrigeration space for eggs and dressed poultry, live poultry pens, and an eviserating plant. By then the company had four trucks. Despite increased competition from national food giants, James Produce, as it was by then called, continued to thrive because it sold fresh eggs and poultry as opposed to cold-stored eggs or frozen poultry. By the end of the decade the company was finally showing a profit again, enough so that Edward James could send his children off to expensive medical schools and prep academies. By 1942 sales totaled $78,800, and the firm's net profit was $4,800, 6.1 percent of sales. This may seem a paltry amount, but just 5 percent of American families in 1941 earned more than that. The James family had managed to climb back to economic respectability and into the upper middle class. But it had not been easy.

Charles H. James II recalled the trials of those years: "I have to admire my father, swallowing all that had to be swallowed. He could have taken the job of postmaster and just made a living. My mother persuaded him to go ahead doing what he knew best, being a businessman. My father often said that the only thing he had going for him at that time was his personal image of the business and the recognition of the James name. He literally clawed his way back up."

The next crisis for the James company and family came in 1952, when two suspicious fires destroyed their poultry processing operation. At the same time, the city had passed an ordinance forbidding any new processing plants from being built, and new federal laws tightened regulations on sanitation in the industry. As a result, James Produce began buying its fresh-dressed poultry from other suppliers, and became the largest distributor of fresh-dressed poultry in the state. In most respects this turned out to be a blessing in disguise. The new regulations were such that only the giant processors could really afford to stay in the business, and Charles James II reflected, "The handwriting was on the wall. So we got out of the business of dressing poultry ourselves. It was a dirty, nasty business anyway. The blood, the feathers, the cold wetness."

In 1961 James Produce passed the one million dollar mark in sales for the first time. Part of the reason for this great expansion during the 1950s was Edward James's decision in 1952 to begin brokering frozen food for the firm's rural customers. James Produce did not inventory the product, but instead took orders from customers who needed frozen food, then purchased the product from suppliers. The frozen food business increased the company's sales volume by more than 50 percent in just the first year it began its brokerage service, and it was a powerful engine of growth thereafter. In 1957 Edward James took out a mortgage and built a 7,000-square-foot warehouse, to which he later added a 5,000-cubic-foot freezer. The freezer allowed James Produce to stop brokering frozen foods and to go into the business on a full-time basis. He also added institutional-sized canned goods for use in hotels, restaurants, and so forth to further diversify the company's operations. As C. H. James II later said, "We would not be in business today if we had stayed exclusively in poultry and eggs. And companies that handled nothing but frozen foods are out of business. In this business, you must diversify to survive."

In 1961 James Produce was incorporated, and Edward James retired at about the same time. His son, Charles, reflected on his father's contribution to the business:

My father worked so hard. His business wasn't glorious like my grandfather's, and I have to ashamedly admit that I could not appreciate what my father did until he died. I used to hear so much about my grandfather, that all I knew was that I wanted to be just like him when I grew up. Actually, my father should get more credit than my grandfather. It was a shattering experience for him to have fallen from the pinnacle to the depth of despair. My grandfather had nothing to lose. He started with nothing. My father had this weight all his life to pull himself up in his own eyes as well as in the eyes of others.

At the time of Edward James's death in 1967, the firm was grossing over $1 million a year, and there were fourteen workers, five trucks, three automobiles, and a newly constructed brick building.

Edward James, when his business became profitable, built a fine ten-room home for his family in Institute. He sent all of his children to college; the youngest, Daniel, earned a Ph.D. and went to work for DuPont before starting his own hair-care manufacturing concern in Wilmington, Delaware. E. L. James, Sr., served as vice president of the National Poultry, Butter and Egg Association, was a member of Charleston's Chamber of Commerce, and was an active supporter of Future Farmers of America. He also served on the board of a number of civic organizations. In politics he was a Democrat, and on several occasions he was a delegate to that party's national conventions.

Two of his sons entered the business early on. The eldest son, Edward L. James, Jr., joined the family business on a full-time basis in 1945 after graduating from West Virginia College and serving in the U.S. Navy during World War II. After a time he became president and general manager of the company, while his father was chairman. Business did not seem to suit his interests, however, and in 1963 he left the family concern. After that time, Edward, Jr., worked at a number of jobs for the state and never returned to the family enterprise on a full-time basis. Suffering from chronic heart disease, he died in 1972. The successor to E. L. James, Sr., was his younger son, Charles H. James II.

Charles James II was educated at local schools and then attended West Virginia State College for several years. Charles James transferred to the Wharton School of Finance at the University of Pennsylvania, where he graduated with honors in 1953. According to James, he had never even heard of Wharton when his father told him he should transfer there. After a tour of duty in the U.S. Air Force, where he achieved the rank of captain, in 1956 young Charles James joined the company on a full-time basis as sales manager. Serving first as secretary treasurer of the company, then as general manager, he became president and the third chief executive officer of the James concern upon his father's death. Upon taking control, Charles James continued the process of diversification begun by his father. In 1969 the firm's sales had increased to $1.5 million. The profit generators were still poultry and eggs, but frozen foods and canned and dry goods also contributed greatly to the operation.

Charles H. James II continued to build James Produce during the 1970s. In 1973 he built a large new warehouse on Dunbar Avenue on the outskirts of Charleston. The new facility had a 12,000-square-foot warehouse and an 88,000-cubic-foot freezer, which management believed to be the largest in the state. James used an innovative plan to finance the new warehouse, which he called "a coup in itself." He arranged to finance the $350,000 facility with Industrial Revenue Bonds that bear interest at a 6 percent fixed rate for twenty-five years with no prepayment penalties. This was a 35 percent discount from the 9.25 percent conventional mortgage financing rate then available. He also took out a $41,000 loan from the Small Business Administration to install a computer to handle billing, bookkeeping, inventory, and sales reports.

Like his father, the younger James was always concerned about maintaining a low debt-to-equity ratio. Memories of the Depression years, and of the long, hard struggle Edward James had to restore the family to economic respectability bore heavily on his son. By the mid–1970s James Produce was grossing about $4 million a year. After that time, however, the firm became stagnant and there was virtually no growth during the next decade; sales in 1987 totaled just $4 million. Worse, profits, which had continued even after growth stagnated, ceased in 1983. Two years later the fourth generation of the James family, Charles H. James III, joined the firm. That year, James Produce dropped off the *Black Enterprise* 100, and the youngest James was determined to get it back on. "We dropped off the BE 100 when I first came back," said James. "I wanted to get back on the list, and I wanted to get federal contracts for national distribution accounts." This caused friction between young "Chuck" and his risk-averse father.

Chuck James had graduated from Morehouse College in Atlanta and then had joined Chicago-based Continental Illinois Bank as a banking associate for two years. At the end of that time he went to his father's alma mater, Wharton School, where he received his MBA. While there, Chuck James had written his thesis paper on the family business, chronicling the previous three generations of entrepreneurial success. When he returned to Charleston in 1985, James was itching to take control of the enterprise and return it to its former glories. Charles H. James II, who had been schooled by his own father to be cautious and deliberate, was most comfortable laboring at his desk and avoiding any risky ventures. His wife, Lucia, daughter of the renowned black historian C. A. Bacote, recognized the difference between father and son: "My husband sees the glass as half empty all the time, my son always sees it as half full."

Despite these temperamental and philosophical differences, the two men never had a confrontation. Chuck James explained how he managed this: "I would say to my father: 'Daddy did you run this business the way your daddy did in the 1940's and '50's?' And he'd say, 'No.' Then I'd say, 'Well then, how do you expect me to run it today based on a formula that was successful more than twenty years ago?' " Although Chuck James largely ran the concern after 1985, the business officially changed hands in 1988 when the elder James lightened his work load after suffering several heart attacks. He then liquidated the business and sold it to his son. The deal was financed by the Charleston-based Commerce Bank, which normally extends a $5 million line of credit to the company. Chuck James repaid the loan in just eighteen months. Another change was formally implemented in 1989 in the name and structure of the firm. James Produce Company, Inc. became the James Corporation, which in turn was merely a holding company for the family's principal assets. The operations of the company were then conducted through a wholly owned subsidiary, C. H. James & Co., Inc. This was done to protect the family's principal assets should the operating company ever again be forced into bankruptcy.

C. H. James II in 1984 was named the Small Business Administration's minority business person of the year for his region, and he was invited to the White House to receive his commendation from President Reagan. In 1970 he was the first black asked to join Charleston's Rotary Club, and he has been very active in family, political, civic, and social activities. He served as chairman of the Charleston Chamber of Commerce and was vice president of the Mountain

State Businessman's Association of West Virginia, along with other concerns. He is a life member of the NAACP and a trustee of the First Baptist Church. He and his wife had four children whom they reared in a comfortable, fourteen-room home in Charleston's exclusive Louden Heights section. Politically, he affiliated himself closely with Senator and then Governor Jay Rockefeller. For a time, he served at the governor's request on the Private Industry Council, which locally administered a federal program to provide job training to new entrants to the labor market and displaced workers who need new skills.

Chuck James's first mission upon assuming control of the family firm was to install a more professional management structure which encouraged the firm's twenty-five employees to participate fully in implementing a "mission statement" he distributed to them. There were some problems with changing the corporate ethic and structure at first, but he ultimately won them over. One of the firm's managers commented, "Chuck allows people to become more involved in the company and the decisions that are made. That makes you feel more responsible for your job and the outcome." She also remarked that James "cut back expenses, revamped a lot of jobs and streamlined operations to become more productive."

But James's most important change was to make the company a competitor for national contracts. "I've never viewed this company as a local business selling food in Charleston," he commented. "I always saw it as a base from which to build an international food distribution empire." Most industry analysts agreed that James had little choice in the matter. "Food distribution has gone the same way a lot of other industries have," said Darryl Breed of the U.S. Department of Agriculture. "The big companies get bigger and the small companies go out of business." So Chuck James saw his mission as one of "do or die." Either he made James Products a player on the national and international scene, or he would have to close it up and peddle his MBA to some big company. He chose the former.

The critical element was to gain large-scale contracts, and Chuck James was having a good deal of success along this line. In 1991 half of the firm's business came from large, competitively bid contracts. Matthew D. Smith, an assistant vice president at Commerce Bank, where James is on the board, said, "Chuck is always aggressive. He prefers to spend more time working on larger scale projects that are going to make more money in the long run." Chuck James himself commented, "We started looking at some of the government direct-bid contracts and bids servicing veterans on a regional and national basis. Those contracts are literally designed for firms like ours that are out there slugging it out in the trenches." His slugging seemed to be paying off. Maintaining his staff of twenty-five persons, James increased sales from $4 million in 1987 to $10 million in 1989, and to $18 million in 1991. Fully 77 percent of their contracts have come from national contracts. When Chuck became president in 1987, the firm did not have a single national contract.

Another device Chuck James took advantage of that his father would not, was to pursue what are called "set aside" contracts for minority businesses from the federal government. Of those, James commented that, although they were good revenue generators, "We have always viewed the 8(a) program as gravy on the meal—something nice to have, but nothing to predicate our entire business strategy on." Through this program, the company has an ongoing relationship with the Department of Veteran Affairs to supply VA hospitals with juices and canned goods amounting to sales of over $1 million a year. This sort of thing can cause problems also. One of its largest contracts, a $4.7 million deal to provide canned goods for Operation Desert Storm for the invasion of Iraq in 1991, was terminated when the war ended so quickly. The firm was left holding $2.5 million in goods, and it was negotiating a settlement with the government on that.

Looking for other ways to expand and diversify, in 1990 James approached John A. Wendling, who had sold his wholesale meat and cheese business to his son. Wendling purchased 49 percent of C. H. James & Co.'s local distribution business and a new firm—James Food Service—was established. Wendling, who served as president, distributed goods from his son's Dixie Provisioners to the local Charleston market.

Chuck James served as treasurer of the West Virginia Economic Development Authority and on the board of trustees of Charleston University and the board of directors of the Charleston Area Medical Center. His business captured the U.S. Department of Agriculture's Minority Contractor of the Year awards in 1988, 1989, and 1990. James himself was chosen as the Small Business Administration Mid-Atlantic Region Minority Small Businessman of the Year.

Chuck James is young, aggressive, and highly entrepreneurial, much like the original C. H. James who had started the firm over 100 years earlier. Chuck James often feels the weight of that legacy: "Every day when I walk into my office, I have to face my great-grandfather, and my grandfather, and my father is just a phone call away. Over the years I've come to realize that I'm not just managing a family business. What I'm really overseeing is a family trust. . . . The goal is not just to maximize wealth. The goal is to turn over the business in a healthy condition—so that the next generation will be able to enjoy the same things that you did."

Sources

No personal or corporate papers on the James family or business are currently available, although members of the James family are willing to give interviews to researchers. There are also a few letters between C. H. James and various officials of the National Negro Business League in the Booker T. Washington Papers at the Library of Congress, and in the National Negro Business League Papers at Tuskegee University. The best source for family and company history is "A History of the James Corp. of Charleston, West Virginia, the Oldest Black Business in the United States, 1883–1984," by Charles H. James III, his honors thesis in the MBA program at the Wharton School, University of Pennsylvania. It has also been excerpted extensively in James D. Randall and Anna E. Gilmer, *Black Past* (1989). Other useful information on the company and family is found in *Ebony*, September 1961, 51–58; and *Black Enterprise*, June 1976, 66–74, 223 and

June 1992, 142–50. In addition, there is some biographical information on the family founder, C. H. James, in *Who's Who of the Colored Race*, vol. I, (Chicago, 1915), 152; and *National Cyclopedia of the Colored Race*, 428. There is a brief biography of Charles H. James II in *Who's Who among Black Americans* (1990).

Johnson, Albert W. (b 1923?–   ). Owner of car dealerships and cable television: Al Johnson Cadillac-Saab and Continental Cablevision/Stellar Group. *Black Enterprise*, the business publication owned by Earl Graves[*] has taken the responsibility of documenting black business activity in the United States. From its inception in 1970 the magazine has attempted to focus on specific industries and the progress African-Americans have made within such arenas. An industry into which blacks have entered with a vengeance is automobile dealerships, which has proven to be a highly lucrative, if somewhat volatile, business. In 1987 *Black Enterprise* reported that more than half of its BE 100 members (the top 100 black businesses, with at least 51 percent black ownership) were car dealers. Fifty-three auto dealers had $1.35 billion in total revenues and were responsible for 41 percent of the BE 100's gross sales. Apparently car dealerships, both new and used, provide African-Americans with the opportunity to prove their mettle in business. However, this entrée by blacks into car dealer ownership is a relatively recent phenomenon. The Big Three white-owned American automobile manufacturers—General Motors, Ford, and Chrysler—were hardly cooperative in the earlier decades when blacks were desperately trying to win a place among whites in the working world. It was not until 1967 that a tenacious young man took the first ground-breaking steps when he was finally awarded the first GM dealership. That trailblazer's name was Al Johnson.

Albert W. Johnson was born in East St. Louis, Illinois. His father was a prominent physican who afforded his only child an affluent upbringing. The younger Johnson attended the University of Illinois, graduating in 1943 with a B.S. degree in business. He then moved on to Northwestern University where he earned a graduate degree in hospital administration. Johnson's first job was as a regional director for the United Public Workers, and from there he assumed the position of assistant to the administrator at the Homer Phillips Hospital in St. Louis, Missouri, at a salary of $12,000. Johnson's father was one of the founders of the hospital, which caused his son some grief, since it was expected that he would follow in his father's footsteps and become a doctor. After twenty years of service at the hospital, Johnson was ready to make a change. He had developed a passion for selling cars in 1953 when he had purchased a Buick and had been offered a deal by the person who had sold it to him: For every paying customer Johnson brought in, he was to receive $25. His appetite whetted, Johnson soon realized that he could make more money if he sold the cars himself. He identified a dealer in Kirkwood, Illinois, for whom he began moonlighting. As he recalled, ''I was actually selling cars out of a bag. Many people bought cars from the Olds Fact book. Being black didn't hurt me, especially since many dealers acted as if they didn't want black business.'' That untapped market gave

Johnson $1,100 in commissions in his first month. Although he was working two jobs, having not yet resigned his position at the hospital, he was selling twice as many cars in an eighteen-hour week as were some of his full-time white colleagues.

I did well not so much because I was a super salesman as that I was a super follow up man. Whatever the problem, my customers would call me. And I'd do anything I could for them. I'm not a mechanic, but I even learned to write out repair orders that a service guy could understand. Then I'd take the car into the repair shop myself.

When he had earned enough money to leave the hospital, Johnson was still denied the right to work on the showroom floor because of his color. Unwilling to accept such limitations, Johnson began actively to pursue purchasing a dealership. A precedent was about to be set. No black dealerships yet existed, although forty such businesses were owned by persons classified as minorities. That situation did not deter Johnson. The civil rights movement was in full swing, and blacks were asserting themselves as they had never done before. Local civic leaders even sent recommendations to General Motors, urging the company to grant dealerships to blacks. The timing was right for Johnson to chase his dream. After considerable pestering of General Motors, Johnson was finally granted an Oldsmobile franchise in Chicago in 1967. Although he was reluctant to leave his home, this was the opportunity he was looking for. GM had finally capitulated when it decided that a visible indication of its commitment to minority economic development would be supported by the initiation to establish several black-owned dealerships.

Johnson readily became acutely aware that he had been oversold on a failing dealership that had not made money in years. He had proven his outstanding sales ability prior to this acquisition but knew virtually nothing about how to run a dealership. Sales is just one component of this business, a fact which became immediately apparent to Johnson when he found himself deeply immersed in a new business with no training or experience in running a company. To finance the business, he had borrowed money from General Motors Corporation's dealer development program. When a bank first refused Johnson's loan application, GM offered assistance and granted him a loan of $355,000. For the real estate on which the dealership stood, the First National Bank loaned him $250,000. Johnson became the first black among the then 18,000 holders of GM new-car franchises. Once the financing was settled, Johnson faced another, perhaps less expected, problem. He remembers, ''Negroes had never spent this kind of money with their own people before, and they were scared. I just told them, 'Well, if you're going to be overcharged any way, then wouldn't you rather I do it?'' On October 1, 1967, the dealership officially opened. Sales were hardly brisk: Within just two months the business was losing money—fast— and complete failure was imminent after only six months. Fortunately, his desperate situation did not go unheeded; his cry for help was heard. Johnson approached John Watson, a competitor who owned an Oldsmobile dealership in

Harvey, just a short distance away. Although he was Johnson's closest competitor, Watson willingly assisted Johnson. As Johnson nostalgically recalls:

Boy, did he ever help. He got together four dealers who are really sharp on various aspects of the business. They would meet with me weekly, going over my daily and weekly expense sheets to point out what I was doing wrong here and why I was losing money there. For four months those guys gave me constant help. The company showed a marginal profit in the third month. Getting the benefit of their many years of experience in the auto business was like having the world's best in-service training. Since the company made that first small profit, we've never looked back.

The combination of this generous help and Johnson's strong interpersonal and sales skills helped make Al Johnson, Inc., one of the most profitable Oldsmobile dealerships in Chicago. In his first three years Johnson drove his net profits before taxes up from $20,550 to $66,400 and then to $142,405. In 1971, when he sold this franchise to Rufus Dukes, another black entrepreneur, it had an annual net of $250,000. Johnson proceeded to purchase a Cadillac dealership, which was partially financed through the General Motors finance division. In the first full year of this business, profits before taxes totaled $650,757, and he became the first black dealer to pay off the loan in only nine months. Thus Johnson had again achieved a first—the first black man to *own* a General Motors Corporation dealership. He became known as the Cadillac King of Tinley Park (the suburb of Chicago where his dealership is located). In 1972 his net profits before taxes increased from the previous year to $727,606. However, due to the energy crisis in 1973, which caused an across-the-board slump, the company's net profits fell to $645,316 that year. Once the crisis no longer posed a threat, Johnson could optimistically boast a net worth in 1974 of about $2.8 million.

This hard-earned success, according to Johnson, would not have been possible without the attention of the white dealers, or the aid of a strong regional director who gave more support to him than to any other dealer. Johnson's dealership has a relatively large number of white clients; almost 40 percent of his business is elicited from white customers. He maintains an interracial and interfaith staff of sales people, managers, and service personnel, which may be one reason why customers of different races patronize his business. Johnson also stresses the importance of good service, which is reflected in his assertion, "Black is beautiful only when you treat the customers properly—otherwise you're ugly as sin."

In 1974 Johnson was recognized by *Time* magazine as one of the top ten automobile dealers in the country. Such national media attention inspired other enterprising blacks to try their hand at owning an automobile franchise. After Johnson's near failure with his first dealership was saved with the assistance of well-seasoned dealers, General Motors, in conjunction with Johnson and others, developed an official program to provide training for those entering the business without any prior experience or training. The program was officially started in 1972 by GM personnel, interested dealers, and the Jam Handy Organization, a sales training and management development firm. GM had responded without delay to Johnson's success, particularly in light of the fact that so many other black dealerships were failing at a staggering rate. When questioned by GM officials as to why he had emerged victorious where others had failed miserably, Johnson responded, "We had fallen heir to historically unprofitable dealerships, without knowing beforehand, that just because you are a black man in a black community, it doesn't mean that you will be instantly successful and that a major factor was that we didn't understand the business—how it should be run."

A partial solution to this problem, according to Johnson, was training programs. Johnson's assessment proved correct. After months of extensive research, conducted by GM, the manager of the car manufacturer's program stated that, "it was determined that we made several mistakes in such areas as the selection of dealer candidates, the location of dealerships, and the degree of management assistance required for these new entrepreneurs." What emerged as a result of this study was the need for intensive training sessions that would condense from twelve to fifteen years of practical experience in car retailing into eighteen months of high-intensity training. After an individual completed the training, he or she was then eligible to buy a franchise. Johnson urged GM and other car manufacturers to provide training programs also for middle-management positions, in addition to the programs for ownership, to ensure progress at all stages. The dedication Johnson offers to the business sector can be seen to a similar degree in the commitment he feels to the black community.

With the training programs being adopted by the three major automobile manufacturers, Johnson was no longer one of the few blacks to succeed in this line of business. Shortly thereafter, numerous companies surpassed his success and boasted larger earnings. Richard D. Gidron[*] in 1972 opened the first Cadillac dealership in the Bronx owned by an African-American. In later years, Gidron's business would grow at a remarkable rate that would leave Albert Johnson's trailing behind.

Many dealerships weathered a downturn from the energy crisis during 1973–1974, which had caused unending lineups at the gas pumps and astronomical fuel increases. They were again challenged in the late 1970s with the advent of a four-year decline in their profits, an unfortunate reflection of the severe effects of another energy crisis. And the 1982 recession caused further fatalities among auto dealers. Undeterred, Johnson chose to capitalize on the foreign car market that was beginning to take America by storm, although as a rule blacks are politely refused franchises by Japanese and other foreign auto manufacturers. The National Association of Minority Automobile Dealers (NAMAD) has challenged Japanese importers to adopt the domestic car manufacturers' policies of offering blacks dealerships. Into the 1990s the issue had not been resolved, but the Japanese may be forced to adopt the policies of the domestic companies with which they have partnerships, which could include the granting of minority dealerships.

Johnson was granted a foreign car dealership, but not from the Japanese. The

Swedish car company, Saab, awarded Johnson a franchise in 1981, and Johnson was the first black to receive a Saab dealership. By the 1980s, with the overwhelming response of Americans to foreign imports, the Big Three were struck a blow. Big cars had lost their élan, and were replaced by the smaller, more fuel-efficient European models. Johnson's business represented both the American and the European car manufacturers. His Cadillac business was suffering in 1987, due to the lack of interest in the down-sized Eldorados and Sevilles; conversely, his Saab sales were exploding and he was unable to get a sufficient supply to satisfy the demand. No doubt the "yuppie" phenomenon of the 1980s contributed to the overwhelming demand for Saabs, one of the designated symbols of success of the status-seeking young, urban professionals. The combined sales of Johnson's Cadillac-Saab dealership was $21.4 million, ranking seventy-first of the top 100 black businesses according to *Black Enterprise*. This left him well behind Dick Gidron's Cadillac and Ford, Inc., which ranked fourteenth, with gross sales of $46.5 million in 1986. By 1989 Gidron's ranking among car dealers was fourth, with sales of $57.5 million, while Johnson's ranked twelfth on the list with sales of $37.2 million. His plans for the future were to purchase additional franchises—"anything that's a good deal." He recognized the need for expansion; his competitors have proven that an effective strategy to ensure growth and competitiveness is the acquisition of additional dealerships.

Johnson has demonstrated his abilities as a competent businessman whose tenacity has benefited a substantial number of enterprising African-Americans. Blacks were more readily accepted by the Big Three carmakers as viable risks once Johnson had laid the groundwork. And Johnson has enjoyed the fruits of his labor by indulging in extravagances that others might find excessive: He sports a pinky diamond ring and chartered a jet to see Muhammad Ali fight Larry Holmes in 1980. His multimillionaire status has afforded him the luxury of pursuing other interests, such as harness racing and condominium development in South America. He is also a major partner in a cable television group, Continental Cablevision/Stellar Group. But Johnson is not only generous with himself. He was one of the moving forces behind the election campaign of the former mayor of Chicago, Harold Washington. In return, Washington appointed Johnson as a $1-a-year special adviser to liaison between the mayor's administration and the Chicago business community.

Johnson is a civic booster who is the champion of minority business interests. As early as the time he was awarded his first Oldsmobile dealership, he immediately became involved in the community in which his business was located. He has been known to give money away. In 1980 he contributed $125,000 to a variety of local civic and church groups. Some of the recipients were park districts in Orland Park and Tinley Park, where his Cadillac-Saab dealership is located; Ingalls Hospital; the Christian Action Missionary; and Operation PUSH, of which he is ex-treasurer. Johnson is not an entrepreneur who has taken from the community and not given something in return. "You make it from the community and that's why we give it back,'' he states matter of factly. He is a member of Chicago United, a director of Seaway Bank, and vice president of the Variety Club of Illinois.

Success can only be measured personally and Albert Johnson clearly is unsure whether he is successful. "It's very difficult to say whether I'm successful. Success is where you set your goals. Some people say they're successful because they've made a few million dollars. I measure success by the accomplishments I've made. I think a lot of minority business men feel this way. They've made it in spite of the obstacles.'' And no doubt the obstacles were there. But Johnson managed to reach beyond the limits and succeed in his pursuit. However, despite his pride in having achieved that first black dealership, he did find room to criticize the American system.

Sure, I was happy, but the *sad* part is that, as long as they've been making automobiles, the first black dealer had to come seventy-five years later. I hope no one is so naive that he thinks a black man just says "I want to go into business" and it happens. I *begged* for an agency for years. Hell, my money wasn't green enough. Black people have been consumers. Until recently, we didn't own anything, we didn't manufacture anything, we didn't sell anything—we were simply consumers. That was part of slavery.

Strides in the right direction have been taken, and although blacks still have a long way to go to achieve any semblance of equality, Johnson is one man who can take pride in the fact that he contributed to changing how the white power structure perceived African-Americans. No mean feat.

Sources

No personal or business papers are available at this time. Little published information exists on Albert Johnson, his car dealership, and other enterprises. Several articles appear in mainstream publications: *Saturday Review*, August 23, 1969; Vernon Jarrett, "A Success Story of a Black Man," *Chicago Tribune*, October 4, 1972; "Al Johnson— Making It in Spite of the Obstacles," *Chicago Daily News*, June 17, 1971. See also several articles: *Chicago Tribune*, October 18, 1972, July 4, 1972, November 6, 1974, and April 19, 1981; *Chicago Daily News*, February 26–27, 1977; *Chicago Metro News*, April 23, 1977; *Chicago Defender*, March 27, 1973, and November 29, 1983; *Chicago Lawyer*, October 1983; and *Chicago Sun-Times*, August 25, 1983. Johnson's appointment as special adviser to Mayor Washington appears in *Southtown Economist*, August 28, 1983; GM's special training program is documented in "The Making of Black Car Dealers," *Black Enterprise*, May 1974, in which Johnson's role in the program is covered. More recent articles include *Black Enterprise*, June 1987, June 1988, and June 1990. The company's standing among other black-owned automobile dealerships is tracked annually in *Black Enterprise*'s Special Anniversary Issue.

Johnson, Edward Austin (see Coleman, Warren Clay, Richard Burton Fitzgerald, and Edward Austin Johnson).

Johnson, George (June 16, 1927–   ). Hair products manufacturer and entrepreneur: Johnson Products. George Johnson was the founder, former chief executive officer, and chairman of Johnson Products Company from 1954 until
1989, when he lost control of the company to his wife, Joan Johnson, in a divorce
settlement. Johnson resigned and turned over his shares, 49.5 percent of the
company, to his wife, who then assumed the position of chairperson with 61
percent of the shares. Until 1993 George Johnson acted in the capacity of a
consultant for the company at a salary of $190,000 a year. To lose control of
his company must have caused great pain for the man who had nurtured Johnson
Products, like an infant from birth, only to watch it slip through his fingers into
the hands of his estranged wife. One can only imagine the bitterness and frustration he felt. Yet, Johnson proved himself a gentleman when he acknowledged
that the settlement was the best way to keep the company in the family and in
the black community. With resignation, he uttered, "I can live with it."

George Johnson was born in Richton, Mississippi, the grandson of poor sharecroppers and the son of a lumber mill worker. His mother, Priscilla, had married
when she was very young, as was often the practice among rural Americans.
She had given birth to three sons early in the marriage and soon realized that
she and her husband were incompatible. When she learned from her siblings in
Chicago that conditions were far better there than in the South, Priscilla packed
up her children and moved north to that city in 1929–1930. This pattern was
repeated by thousands of blacks migrating to Chicago and other northern cities
in search of a better life. Upon arrival, she immediately secured a job with
Michael Reese Hospital to support herself and her sons. When George Johnson
was old enough to work, he shined shoes, peddled junk, and shared a paper
route with his brothers. He attended public grammar schools and Wendell Phillips
High School up to the eleventh grade. Choosing to work rather than continue
his education, in 1944 Johnson followed in the footsteps of his older brother
who was employed by Fuller Products, the large cosmetics company owned by
the ambitious African-American entrepreneur S. B. Fuller.* For three months
Johnson worked as a door-to-door salesman, then became a production chemist.
Although Johnson had only studied basic chemistry in high school, he found
greater pleasure in this capacity than in sales. In the early 1950s he was promoted
to production manager, a job from which he resigned in 1954. Times were
difficult for Johnson and his wife Joan during the first years of their marriage,
and Johnson was faced with working also as a busboy at a hotel, earning a total
of $150 from these two jobs. Although the fifteen-hour days proved exhausting,
Johnson also worked weekends in door-to-door sales and at a car wash.

After ten years of employment at Fuller Products, Johnson wanted more
rewards in return for his hard work. Having met Orville Nelson, a barber, Johnson
became interested in the hair-straightening techniques Nelson used on such notable male entertainers as Duke Ellington and Nat King Cole. Noting that these
products were somewhat crude and damaging to the scalp and hair, Johnson
modified the formula with the assistance of Herbert A. Martini, a chemist with

Fuller Products. Together, Martini and Johnson created a new formula that would provide similar results with less harmful side effects. Upon presenting this new product to Nelson, Johnson and he became partners, whereby Nelson took charge of promotions and sales, given his built-in client base, and Johnson oversaw the manufacturing responsibilities. In 1954 Johnson resigned his position at Fuller, eager to launch his Ultra Wave Hair Culture. The two partners determined that $500 would suffice to start up the company. Nelson came up with $250, but Johnson faced obstacles in his attempt to do likewise. His appeal to a white loan officer was rejected on the grounds that blacks are not capable business people. Undeterred, Johnson approached another branch of the same company and requested a loan of $250 for an (ostensible) vacation to California with his wife. In no time the loan officer complied with the request. Such overt discrimination has embittered Johnson over the years.

After just one day, only one dollar remained of the starting capital of $500, after all the equipment and supplies were purchased. Without delay, Johnson began manufacturing this new product, while Nelson was supposed to be recruiting customers to purchase it. Johnson worked nights and weekends in rented space, manufacturing the product he dreamed would revolutionize the hair-straightening industry and bring him financial security. Within a short time, Johnson realized that Nelson was reneging on the agreement. The product was so good that Nelson was kept busy using it on his clients, giving him no time to market it. Johnson, upon realizing that Nelson was not pulling his weight, sued him and ended the partnership. Although Nelson knew the formula and became Johnson's chief competitor, Johnson owned the name Ultra Wave Hair Culture, a name that had become stamped on the minds of African-Americans.

Again faced with insufficient capital to start his own business, Johnson, now twenty-six years old, appealed to S. B. Fuller to invest in his fledgling cosmetics firm, which certainly took some gumption considering that Johnson might at some time be a potential competitor. Fuller refused, "Barbers are the worst businessmen in the world," when he realized that Johnson's customers would be barbershops. Despite this disappointment and the fact that Johnson's mother was overtly critical of his dreams of starting a business when he had a secure job, Johnson's wife Joan and the chemist Martini provided him with the encouragement and support he needed to forge ahead.

In 1955 Johnson recruited his wife to work in the office as a bookkeeper and order taker and perform other duties, and he hired his brother John to manufacture a new hair straightener for men. Johnson, despite his distaste for sales, went on the road to build a national market for distribution. In the first year the company did $18,000 in sales, and a year later sales had increased to $75,000. Johnson leased space in the back of a beauty supply company and then moved elsewhere when the company expanded beyond the capacity of this location. In 1958 the company moved to a three-storied building to accommodate the rapid expansion. Until this time the company sold only to barbershops and, despite this somewhat limited market, had achieved $250,000 worth of business in that year.

It was during this time that Johnson identified the relatively untapped market of hair-care products designed specifically for black women's needs. Ultra Sheen was introduced as a unique product in that it was the first no-base hair relaxer, a claim that suggested that it was a product safer than other hair relaxers because it contained a protective cream that shielded the scalp against powerful acids. Women's hair was exposed to the same potential hazards as men's hair.

Although hair-straightening procedures had been introduced in the nineteenth century when blacks were attempting to emulate whites, it was the introduction of the hot comb method by Madame C. J. Walker* that really gave the industry a boost. Fortunes have been made in this industry by such notable black women as Madame Walker and Annie Turnbo-Malone.* Johnson's product line consisted of a cream press permanent, cream shampoo, and Ultra Sheen conditioner which could be applied at home between visits to the hair salon. Initially, he sold only to beauty salons, whose personnel were educated by Johnson employees on the correct use of the product. It took three years to establish a market, but when it finally achieved acceptance, the word spread quickly. On the heels of this success came a potentially major setback. In 1964 an all-consuming fire destroyed the Johnson Products' plant and inventory. To the rescue came S. B. Fuller, who provided Johnson's company with temporary facilities until they could locate a permanent home. The prospects of what might have been were tempered by the generous nature of the man who later welcomed an equally generous gesture of financial assistance from Johnson (see S. B. Fuller biography). In 1966 Ultra Sheen was finally made available to the general public. A massive advertising campaign was launched, reaching the female market primarily through advertisements in *Ebony* magazine. Drugstore chains, discount outlets, and supermarkets were the primary distributors of the lower priced Ultra Sheen line. To accommodate the overwhelming demand for Ultra Sheen, a new factory was built, equipped with fully automated production lines.

An unexpected turn of events caught Johnson off guard. When the civil rights movement was appealing to the black community to recognize their roots and embrace their heritage, a new hairstyle was adopted as a way to take pride in the African-American experience. And thus was born the Afro, a hairstyle that abandoned the notion that straight hair was more desirable. The new look displayed a more natural hairstyle which severely cut the demand for straighteners and other traditional products for blacks' hair. Johnson was slow to respond, as he admitted, "I didn't know if it was a fad or not, so I took a wait-and-see attitude until I was sure it was a trend." When Johnson finally took action, he introduced Afro Sheen for the natural look, a product line that included hair spray and a "comb easy" shampoo. Despite his reluctance to jump on the bandwagon, Afro Sheen was a hit and earned the number one spot in the marketplace.

Late in 1969 Johnson Products Company was the first African-American-owned firm to be listed on the American stock exchange. It was one of two companies of size owned by blacks to be publicly traded; the other was H. G.

Parks, Incorporated, owned by Henry G. Parks of Baltimore. The decision to go public was borne out of the desire to raise enough capital to expand and acquire new concerns. The public stock offering provided Johnson with the necessary capital: 300,000 shares of common stock were sold at $28 a share for a cash total of $8,400,000. The firm had a market value of $56 million with slightly more than 2,000,000 shares outstanding of common stock. The company in 1971 had 2,500 shareholders (mostly white) who invested in Johnson Products, but the Johnson family retained ownership of 83 percent of the total outstanding stock worth $44 million, which parlayed into $80 million when the stock was selling near $30 in the fall of 1973. In 1969 the company had annual sales from hair preparations of $12.6 million, and before-tax profits of $4.5 million, with a long-term indebtedness of only $221,000, a small amount for a business with that sales volume. This relatively low figure for indebtedness reflects the true nature of the cosmetics business—product costs are only about 30 percent of the sales price at the distributor level. However, vast amounts of money are spent on advertising and on promotional and administrative costs, substantially more than on the actual cost of the goods produced.

In 1970 Johnson began test marketing cosmetics, a completely separate line from any of the hair products. Again he focused on a low-priced line of products, with such items as liquid makeup, face powder, and skin cleansers. Shades that complemented the black skin tones were offered as a marketing ploy that would appeal to African-American women. The same stores that proved themselves reliable customers of the hair-care products were the primary distributors of this line, too. White cosmetic companies, which still had not taken note of the highly lucrative black market that Johnson had so effectively reached, were content to market extensions of their ''white'' lines to blacks. Johnson's products were an instant success. It is important to note that African-Americans buy almost one-third of the approximately $1 billion spent on hair preparations each year. The $2.5 million advertising campaign, 17 percent of total sales, that raised public awareness of the Johnson product lines focused on selling through the use of billboards in black-dominated communities, black radio stations, and black magazines (although the company had boycotted *Ebony* and *Jet* when John H. Johnson,* the owner of both publications, ventured into cosmetics with the Fashion Fair line and gave his products preferential space in these magazines), and by sponsoring the television program ''Soul Train.''

Continued success was enjoyed by Johnson during the first half of the 1970s. In 1972 the company grossed $17,567,507 in sales, considerably more than any other black manufacturing company. Through the years from 1968 to 1973, Johnson Products' sales quadrupled and its net worth more than tripled. In 1971 sales were $14 million, in 1973 they had increased to $24 million, and in 1976 they reached $39.4 million. These were truly halcyon years for the hard-driving entrepreneur, who was proving that blacks were astute business people, even in manufacturing, an area where African-Americans seldom had a chance to prove their mettle. Although the recession of 1971 caused the company's net income to drop 10 percent, the firm remained aggressive and increased its advertising budget to keep sales steady.

The second part of this decade proved to be the undoing of Johnson Products. Troubles began in 1975, when the company introduced Black Tie, a men's fragrance line that was intended for *all* men, black or white. Although Johnson had not yet attempted to reach the white market, he felt that he had the right to do so since white companies continually market their products to the black community. However, several factors were operating against him. Johnson himself made a grave error in his decision to distribute Black Tie through the same channels he used to sell his other merchandise. Black Tie was intended for a more upscale male public that did not purchase colognes in drugstores or supermarkets, but rather in department stores. The other problem stemmed from the fact that the distributors placed the fragrances in the ethnic section of the stores, which sabotaged Johnson's efforts to reach the white male market. The campaign was termed a "real disaster" by one industry analyst. Johnson's assessment of the situation clearly reveals his anger:

Most of the retailers across the country had displayed the fragrance in the black hair care sections of stores, not with the other fragrances. Black Tie never had a chance. It was clear that the hangup was the fact that this particular fragrance, specifically developed for the general consumer market, was produced by Johnson Products, a black manufacturer. When all the dust settled, this debacle cost our company around $8 million.

Perhaps this could be considered a minor setback, however, when compared to the next episode in Johnson's troubles.

In 1976 the Federal Trade Commission ordered Johnson Products Company to issue warnings on its hair products and on its advertising, informing the public that the items contained lye that could be caustic if used improperly. Johnson Products was singled out by the FTC, which ignored the much larger white companies that manufactured the same products. When challenged by Johnson, the FTC claimed that it went after Johnson's company because it was the market leader. Revlon quickly took advantage of Johnson's disadvantage and went on a full-scale marketing campaign. One year later, when the FTC finally required Revlon to issue a warning, the wording was far less strict than the one Johnson was forced to comply with. After one more year Johnson was permitted to adopt the less rigid Revlon standard. Such practices certainly appeared to many African-Americans to be a textbook case of overt racism.

After eighteen months of suffering, Johnson's sales were lagging considerably. As Johnson angrily complained, "The FTC gave Revlon 22 months to rip off my market and put me in a straight jacket." Although Johnson blames the FTC's decision for his declining sales, an industry analyst felt that the problem was ineffective marketing. It could not compete with Revlon's Polished Amber line, its Realistic Hair Straightener, or its Dermanesse cosmetics line, nor could it match the appeal of John Johnson's Fashion Flair, which had a classier panache. To add fuel to the fire, Johnson was unable to find a suitable individual to run the research lab and thus came up short in the area of new product development. Johnson encountered embittered retailers when he accused them of not providing his products with shelf space in proportion to their sales. A black competitor, on the other hand, thought that Johnson's squabbling over shelf space was really indicative of his inability to accept the fact that the smaller companies were encroaching on his territory. Finally, in 1978, some of Johnson's largest distributors became antagonistic in response to Jesse Jackson's campaign urging them to buy ethnic products from black distributors. The retailers were critical of the effort because Jackson's Operation PUSH received nearly $190,000 from Johnson's personal foundation. The problem of lagging sales was probably a combination of these factors, nevertheless the bottom line was still the same—the company was seriously faltering.

Johnson Products' market share had dropped from 60 percent to approximately 40 percent in 1980, and the books showed an unhealthy color—red. The company was feeling the effects of its failure to keep up with fashion trends. It was also suffering from heavy-handed management. It desperately needed new products to maintain the market share it had enjoyed in the early 1970s. In 1980 the company introduced Precise, a combination hair relaxer and conditioner that was sold through professional hairdressers, and Moisture Formula, a line of lipsticks and other related products for the retail market. However, this decade held problems of its own for Johnson. Losses were suffered in three of the four years from 1981 to 1985. The company's image had lost its élan and it was tarnished even further in 1985 during a vetoed business venture featuring two controversial individuals—Muslim leader Louis Farrakhan and Libyan President Muammar Khadafy. Farrakhan had received a $5 million interest-free loan from Khadafy to develop black economic enterprises in the United States. The New Jersey–based company POWER (an acronym for People Organized and Working for Economic Rebirth) was organized to woo African-American consumers away from white marketers to keep black consumer dollars, estimated at $204 billion a year (1985), in the black community. Johnson Products and four other black-owned companies supported the basic idea of keeping black consumers' money in the black community and offered to manufacture products for the group. When challenged on the decision to support Farrakhan, who has openly expressed anti-Semitic and antiwhite sentiments, a Johnson Products' spokesperson assured the critics that the company did not support his philosophy, but it did support the concept of POWER. After considerable pressure from the media and distributors, Johnson Products pulled out of the program. Johnson addressed the decision: ''Our discussions (with POWER) reflected a business decision that would have enabled the company to use excess manufacturing capacity. The recent publicity about the program, however, has falsely given many the impression that we are anti-Semitic.'' Ultimately, four of the five original companies withdrew support.

The company's downward slide is clearly reflected in the reduced revenues in 1985 of $37.8 million. The figure represents a decrease in revenues of 9 percent from those of 1984, and an even more dramatic decrease of 17.5 percent from 1983. What had begun as a temporary decline became a struggle for survival. Plans for a turnaround involved the introduction of a private label offering such products as nonethnic shampoos, conditioners, and other items. Johnson, however, was still reluctant to take more aggressive measures. He refused to offer deep wholesale discounts and overlooked an opportunity to capitalize on the then current popularity of the curly styles. In addition to these oversights was the stark reality of the company's spotty distribution system offering inefficient shipping and order filling. Johnson did take steps to reorganize the unmotivated sales force, and he cut consumer advertising spending 40 percent in 1985 to $6 million, well below the level of $7.2 million in 1983.

Perhaps the internal confusion that was pervasive at the time was the source of all these problems. Johnson addressed this issue by cutting 18 percent of the work force between September 1985 and April 1986, and by reducing the salaries of the highest paid employees. In August 1986 the research and development division finally provided the company with four new products to introduce, all of which sold well. The advertising budget was increased 21 percent, retrenching continued, and an all-out effort was made to get back to basics. It appeared that Johnson was on the right track. But 1986 sales were sagging at $30 million and the family holdings were a relatively meager $6 million when compared to the value of its holdings in earlier years. Johnson expressed his bitterness at the turn of events over the years: "This company built the ethnic market and now the others are reaping the rewards." His revenues were far surpassed by another African-American cosmetics company based in Chicago—Soft Sheen Products, Incorporated founded by Edward G. Gardner.* But Soft Sheen too was feeling the encroachment of the white cosmetics giants, such as Alberto Culver and Revlon. To counter this trend, Johnson Products Company, Soft Sheen, and M&M Products of Atlanta began a campaign to encourage black consumers to buy black. A special logo from AHBAI (American Health and Beauty Aids Institute, a Chicago-based consortium of black-owned hair-care companies) was printed on their products to identify them as products of African-American-owned companies.

In 1987 Johnson acquired a much-needed $10 million loan; he sold eleven acres near the company's headquarters for a profit of $1 million; and he sold Debbie's Beauty Schools, an investment that was profitable until 1985, when it started to lose money. Previously, it had been a bright spot in the company, so much so that Bristol-Myers Company, owner of Clairol, had expressed interest in taking over the schools. Without hesitation, Johnson responded firmly, "Not for sale." By 1985, though, the "for sale sign" was put up. Additionally, Johnson sold the assets of Ultra Precise Beauty Boutique, a beauty salon.

Along with these divestments came a major change in the company's management. Eric, Johnson's eldest son, in 1988 succeeded his father as president of Johnson Products and continued in the capacity of chief operating officer. The elder Johnson, who held the positions of chief executive officer and chairman, was highly confident that his son possessed the qualities to turn the company around. Eric Johnson had joined the business permanently in 1977 after selling toothpaste for Procter & Gamble Company, the biggest consumer-products company. This was an interesting training ground given that Johnson Products was once referred to as the "black Procter & Gamble." Eric Johnson's primary challenge was to keep the company competitive. By the fall of 1989 he had trimmed employment and introduced two product lines, and the firm responded with three profitable quarters. With sales of $33.5 million by the end of December 1989, Johnson Products ranked only twenty-fourth on the *Black Enterprise* list of Industrial/Service companies. It lagged far behind Soft Sheen Products, which ranked sixth, with sales of $87.2 million. The younger Johnson certainly had his work cut out for him. Eric Johnson has identified the European market, specifically France, Great Britain, and Belgium, as his intended target for expansion. He is a hands-on type whose goal is "to be operating a profitable business and to build up employment as business merits it." Eric Johnson's cost-cutting management style is in contrast to his father's more expansive methods, and he probably will not achieve the popularity his father did in the black community. "We're not a social organization that has memberships."

George Johnson was truly committed to the black community. In 1985 it was reported that he had contributed an estimated $5 million to black causes, including voter registration drives, 200 charities, civil rights crusades, and college scholarships. He personally contributed $1.5 million to assist 1,600 students graduate from college. The Johnson Foundation was created to provide scholarship aid to black students in business administration. For a time Johnson operated a factory in Lagos, Nigeria, which provided employment for numerous Nigerians. The project proved too costly to maintain due to high energy costs, the exorbitant cost of imported raw materials, and an epidemic of smuggling, which undercut profits. In 1989 Johnson Products sold its interest in the plant for $375,000—a third of what it cost to open it ten years earlier. In spite of these notable contributions, he has been harshly criticized for having a "profound white orientation": He had hired whites as senior executives; he elected to reside in a "palatial estate in Glencoe, Illinois, an area noted for its 'exclusivity';" and he refused to seriously support or initiate black programs. To be fair to Johnson, he did jump at the chance to organize a black bank as early as 1964 after having experienced racism and discrimination when applying for loans. The Independence Bank was founded to give African-Americans an easier time in acquiring financial assistance than he had had when he was attempting to start his business.

Such biting attacks were difficult for Johnson to swallow but not as difficult as the final chapter in his reign over Johnson Products Company. In 1989, when Johnson relinquished control of the company to his ex-wife Joan, the vacant CEO position was filled by then president Eric. The transition was achieved with little fanfare, although the media attempted to highlight the breakdown of a marriage and a family. George Johnson appeared to be a man without a company—that is—his company. However, he continued to act as chairman and remained the largest shareholder in Indecorp, Inc., the holding company that owns the Independence Bank and the Drexel National Bank. Johnson was also one of the largest landowners in his native Mississippi; he owned two farms in Kentucky, with 6,700 in total acreage; and the family owned a vacation spot in Jamaica. These investments were also divided during divorce negotiations, but since Joan Johnson won control of the company, George Johnson probably received a larger share of the other assets. No doubt they are worth a princely sum. Only time will reveal what George Johnson intends to do next. Entrepreneurs are rarely idle for long.

Asked to comment by the financial magazine, *INC.*, on his son's running of the firm in 1991, George Johnson replied; "I'm not here to be anything but supportive," referring to his role as a paid consultant. A moment's reflection, however, brought another comment: "But if you look at the numbers, we're not going great guns. I hope Eric's moves are right, but we have to see. His mother sure has a lot riding on it."

Sources

No family or company papers were available to researchers during the writing of this biography. Johnson Products is a public company and thus is required to publish annual financial information concerning revenues, sales, and profits. The bulk of information about the company and George Johnson appears in magazine articles. However, John Seder and Berkeley G. Burrell's *Getting It Together* (New York, 1971) also profiles Johnson, as does Gerri Major's *Black Society* (1976), 382–83. In addition, Johnson is briefly profiled in Frank J. Johnson, *Who's Who of Black Millionaires* (1984). By far the best accounts of the early years of Johnson Products appear in a broad array of mainstream publications: "Hair: The Fastest Way to Make a Million in the Black Business World," *Sepia*, April 1971; "He's Good to Hair, Hair's Good to Him," *New York Times*, June 30, 1976; "Making Black Beautiful," *Time*, December 7, 1970; "From an Idea for a New Product Has Grown a Giant Cosmetics Empire," *Ebony Success Library* (1973), vol. II; "The New Black Cosmetics Magnate," *Black Enterprise*, June 1973. Other articles following the company's early growth are found in *Business Week*, September 8, 1973; *Chicago Defender*, June 21, 1971; *Chicago Daily News*, November 25, 1972; *Jet*, November 27, 1969, January 6, 1972, and December 14, 1972, among many other issues. Gwendolyn Robinson, "George Johnson: Mississippi Experiences," *Sunbelt*, February 1, 1980, offers general information on Johnson as well as his property investments in Mississippi. The *Chicago-Sun Times* and the *Chicago Tribune* have featured numerous stories on Johnson products, and the researcher is advised to check their respective indices for citations. Johnson Products' decline and Johnson's efforts to revitalize the company are documented in "A Healthy Paranoia," *Forbes*, March 9, 1987; "Limping Johnson Products Struggles to Survive," *Crain's Chicago Business*, April 14, 1986, and "Restructuring New Products Help Johnson," *Crain's Chicago Business*, December 15, 1986. The introduction of Black Tie is covered in the *Chicago Tribune*, February 17, 1980. Criticism of Johnson's white orientation as exemplified in living in Glencoe, Illinois, appears in an editorial by Charles Harris in *Chicago Metro News*, May 21, 1977. His problems with the FTC rulings and rivals such as Revlon are covered in the following articles: *Wall Street Journal*, January 23, 1981; *Chicago Defender*, December 18, 1978 (specifically Revlon's challenge); and *Jet*, September 9, 1976. The controversy over Johnson's involvement with POWER and Khadafy was covered in the following articles: *Chicago Sun-Times*, September 15, 1985, October 24, 1985, and October 28, 1985; *Crain's Chicago Business*, September 9, 1985; *Chicago Metro News*, October 26, 1985, and December 24, 1988; and *Advertising Age*, September 16, 1985. The divorce settlement between Joan and George Johnson was covered extensively by the press. See *Chicago Tribune*, October 3, 1989; *Wall Street Journal*, October 3, 1989; *Black Enterprise*, December 1989; and *Jet*, October 16, 1989. Eric Johnson's assumption of power and his management style are examined in *Crain's Chicago Business*, December 4, 1989; *Chicago Defender*, October 3, 1989; *Chicago Metro News*, December 24, 1988; *Jet*, October 16, 1989; and *Inc.*, March 1991.

Stephen Birmingham's *Certain People* (Boston, 1977), 36–51 provides an analysis of the controversial relationship between George Johnson and publisher John Johnson, as does the *Chicago Sun-Times*, February 18, 1979. George Johnson's Johnson Foundation and other black foundations are discussed in "Developing Black Foundations: An Economic Response to Black Community Needs," *Black Scholar*, December 1977. An interview appears in "In Pursuit of Excellence," *Black Collegian*, September/October 1973, in which Johnson offers his opinions on building a successful career and the outlook for blacks in America.

Johnson, John Harold (January 19, 1918–). Publisher of magazines and books, founder of cosmetics and hair-care products firm, insurance company executive, entrepreneur, and race leader: Johnson Publishing Company, Supreme Beauty Products, Fashion Fair Cosmetics, Supreme Liberty Life Insurance, and Radio Station WGRT. African-Americans have perhaps never had a "crossover" hero in American business to equal John Johnson. Certainly, Booker T. Washington,[*] in his time, was known to virtually every white American, but it was as a social philosopher. Later popular culture icons like Louis Armstrong or Joe Louis also acquired that kind of fame, as did protest leaders like Martin Luther King, Jr., but Johnson is probably the only black business leader whose name almost automatically comes to a white person's lips when the term "black business" is mentioned. And with good reason. Over a period of some fifty years, Johnson has built a giant publishing empire and has added a cosmetics company, a large insurance firm, radio stations, and other interests. He is the most important African-American business leader of the last half century. He might well have been named *Black Enterprise*'s "Entrepreneur of the Century" were it not for the incredible record of longevity of A.G. Gaston.[*] Make no mistake, though, in both black and white America, John Johnson is considered the preeminent African-American business leader.

Johnson was born in the rural mill town of Arkansas City, Arkansas, the son of Leroy Johnson, a mill worker, and Gertrude Jenkins. Gertrude Jenkins, who was born in Lake Village, Arkansas, was the daughter of two ex-slaves. Reared in desperate poverty, Gertrude managed to finish just the third grade before she was forced to work in the fields and kitchens of the Mississippi Valley. She later moved to Arkansas City, where she worked as a domestic until she met her first husband, Richard Lewis. They had a daughter, but this marriage did not last, and she later married Leroy Johnson. Fourteen years after her first child,

Beulah, was born, John Johnson came into the world. Johnson's father was killed in a mill accident when the boy was six years old, and his mother soon married James Williams, another mill worker. Williams was a hard-working man, but, in the words of his wife, "the trouble was, Williams just couldn't hold on to any money. He spent the whole of it on drink and gambling." There is no question that Johnson's mother was the dominant force in his life. As he later reflected, "She was a short, forceful woman then, not quite five feet, with the family bowlegs and a big smile and a will of steel. She walked straight up, her head held high, a woman of stature and quality."

The family was forced to live in a situation of dire poverty. Since James Williams was not able to support his family adequately, both Gertrude and young John Johnson went to work also. Gertrude Johnson often ran field kitchens for a dredging company crew and followed the levee camps, washing and ironing clothes for the laborers and cooking in the levee kitchens. John Johnson tagged along, learning at an early age how to wash and iron clothes. Despite the family's poverty, however, Johnson made the point in his autobiography that they were not "poor." This was a crucial distinction to him, as he explained: "Our poverty, in other words, couldn't be compared with the soul crushing poverty in the slums of modern America." But this poverty was made worse by the almost complete lack of opportunities for blacks in the town. It was a time of intense racism and segregation in the Mississippi Delta, and the Johnson family encountered it at nearly every turn.

The schools in Arkansas City were segregated, and, as throughout most of the South, black schools received far less funding than white ones. The black teachers had to teach several grades at once; however, according to Johnson, the school "stressed excellence and brought better results than most contemporary schools." The real problem came after Johnson graduated from elementary school—there was no public high school for blacks. The only option if he wanted to go on—and both Johnson and his mother were determined that he would—was to go away to a private boarding school in Pine Bluff or Little Rock. His mother made him repeat the eighth grade, which he resented deeply, while she worked even more, trying to save enough money to send him away. By 1933 John Johnson was fifteen, and Gertrude Johnson was fed up with Arkansas City and the lack of opportunities there. A friend had told her about Chicago: "I had a friend in Chicago," said his mother, "and she wrote me and said that things were much better for colored folks up there. So I said to [James Williams], 'I'm going. You can come too if you like, but if you don't like I'm going anyway. You can't stop me and nobody can stop me.' " Williams decided to remain in Arkansas City, and his wife and stepson set off for Chicago on the bus and arrived in the city during the height of the Great Depression in 1933.

Things were certainly tough in Chicago at that time, especially for blacks. Unemployment was high and times were hard and blacks were crowded into dilapidated housing. The situation was so bad that the great migration of blacks from the South decreased dramatically during the decade of the 1930s. Even at its best, Chicago must have seemed foreboding to the recently arrived migrants from the South. Richard Wright, in *American Hunger* (1944), described his first view of Chicago:

My first glimpse of the flat black stretches of Chicago depressed and dismayed me, mocked all my fantasies. Chicago seemed an unreal city whose mythical houses were built of slabs of black coal wreathed in palls of gray smoke, houses whose foundations were sinking slowly into the dank prairie. Flashes of steam showed intermittently on the wide horizon, gleaming translucently in the winter sun. The din of the city entered my consciousness, entered to remain for years to come.

Despite how Chicago first appeared to Richard Wright, and probably to most newly arrived black migrants, the city nonetheless remained an irresistible magnet for southern blacks. Throughout the 1920s and 1930s, and for some twenty years after World War II, Chicago was a mecca for upwardly mobile blacks. The hub of the nation's railways, the railroads themselves provided innumerable jobs for African-Americans as conductors, porters, brakemen, and so on. A number of jobs were also available in construction and in the stockyards and other industries in the city, as well as higher status positions in the post office and the local government. Practically every southern black knew at least one black family in Chicago who owned their own home and car and were sending their children to college. "The hopes," as Stephen Birmingham has said, "of Chicago's blacks were high." Gertrude and John Johnson joined that procession of southern blacks hitching their wagon to Chicago's rising star.

John Johnson years later remembered his own first impression of Chicago in 1933: "I stood transfixed on the street. I had never seen so many Black people before. I had never seen so many tall buildings and so much traffic." But as soon as he saw the better kind of housing available to blacks in Chicago, as compared to Arkansas City, Johnson was impressed. "Chicago," Johnson said, "was my kind of town. . . . Tough, brutal, unforgiving, it lived on the edge and close to the edge. The city challenged you, provoked you, and dared you. . . . If you could make your dream come true anywhere, you could make it come true in Chicago." His mother found a job as a domestic, and they moved into an apartment building at 5610 Calumet in the massive black ghetto on the city's South Side.

John Johnson went to high school that fall, attending Wendall Phillips High, a nearly all-black institution at 39th and South Parkway. "Nothing in my experience," Johnson recalled, "prepared me for Wendall Phillips, which had a student population larger than the total population of Arkansas City." Before long, however, Wendall Phillips burned down, and the student body was transferred to a new black school—Du Sable High. This was to become the gathering place for the "best and the brightest" of the city's South Side blacks. During Johnson's student years there were such future notables as mayor Harold Washington, jazz great Nat "King" Cole, John Elrod Sanford, better known as the comedian Redd Foxx, jazz pianist Dorothy Donegon, entrepreneur Dempsey J. Travis,* and Charles Murray, Jr., the son of the founder of Murray Hair Pomade.

At first, Johnson's reception by his classmates was not warm. Although most of the blacks at school were poor, they were not "rural poor." That is, they tended to dress fairly well and to know the proper styles and customs. Johnson did not. He wore homemade shoes and suits, just as he had in Arkansas, and the other students poked fun at his "mammy-made" clothes and also made fun of his deep southern accent. As soon as he complained to his mother, though, she made sure he was wearing good clothes, and he was soon the best-dressed student in his class. Nothing, if Gertrude Johnson had anything to say about it, would keep her talented son from success.

During John Johnson's first year in Chicago, his stepfather decided to join them. This caused a family crisis, since he was not able to find a job anywhere in the city. They were forced to apply for welfare, and from late 1934 to 1936 the family was on relief. Finally, his stepfather secured a WPA job, and John himself began working part-time with a division of the National Youth Administration. He had also during this time emerged as a student leader at Du Sable. He was an honor student, a member of the debating team, president of the student council, and president of the senior class in 1936. As such, Johnson was chosen as the only student speaker at the school's commencement on June 11, 1936. He gave a talk entitled "Builders of a New World." In recognition of his achievements, Johnson received a $200 scholarship to attend the University of Chicago. His problem was to find a way to finance a year's study there in just two months.

Providence looked down on John Johnson. He was invited to attend an Urban League dinner honoring the top black high school students in the city. The principal speaker that day was Harry H. Pace,* the president of Supreme Liberty Life Insurance, the largest black business in Chicago, and one of the most versatile and charismatic black business leaders of all time. He gave what Johnson called a "brilliant" speech, and afterward young John told Pace how much he appreciated his remarks. Pace asked him what he planned to do, and Johnson replied that he wanted to go to college but did not have enough money. Pace offered him a job working part-time at Supreme Life, allowing Johnson to finance his education in that way. It also opened up the world of black business to John Johnson in ways that he would be able to exploit to the fullest.

Johnson began working at Supreme Life in September 1936 while attending the University of Chicago. As time went on, Johnson found his duties as assistant to Pace more and more exciting, and he began losing interest in his studies. Finally, after two years, he dropped out of college to work full-time at Supreme Life. As he later remembered, "[M]y real school from 1936 to 1941 was the university of Supreme Life." Johnson viewed Supreme Life as being on the "cutting edge" of the dream of African-American economic success. "The company," he said, "had succeeded in building a strong presence in a field where the high Black mortality rate had frightened off white investors. It was so successful in this effort that it survived the Depression and continued to make loans to Black property owners when White banks and realtors were routinely turning down Black applicants. Supreme survived, in other words, not because it was inferior to White corporations, but because it was superior in dealing with the challenges of an unfavorable business environment.''

The big thrill for Johnson at Supreme Life, however, was watching Pace, Truman K. Gibson,* Earl B. Dickerson,* and the other executives wheel and deal. "It was the dare, it was the gamble, it was the deal that captivated me. I was on the bottom rung at Supreme, but coming to work and watching Pace and his associates play with millions gave me a physical, almost a sexual, thrill.'' Johnson was also drawn into journalism at this time. Pace had started one of the first black general-interest magazines in America, *The Moon*, with W.E.B. Du Bois in Memphis. At Supreme Life, Pace established a monthly company newspaper called *The Guardian*. Pace served as editor of the journal, and Johnson was named assistant editor in 1939. This assignment was not quite as mundane as it sounds, since it involved more than simply reporting company news. Supreme Life, in the 1930s and 1940s, was at the virtual epicenter of black Chicago. "It can be said with only slight exaggeration," said Johnson, "that practically every major event in Black Chicago between 1936 and 1942 was planned, organized, or financed by people who orbited around the Supreme sun.''

The man who became Johnson's closest mentor during these years, Earl Dickerson, also introduced him to the arcane world of black politics in the city. "Working with and around Dickerson and his team stretched my mind and vision," said Johnson. "For three or four months [in Dickerson's 1939 aldermanic campaign] I lived and breathed politics, rising at dawn and working until the early hours of the morning, doing research for speeches, writing articles for local papers and our ward newspaper.'' When Dickerson rather surprisingly won the aldermanic race, he named Johnson to the key post of political secretary. Johnson thought this was the beginning of a long political career, but Dickerson was ousted in the next election. By then, Johnson was on to bigger things.

In 1941 Johnson made another important step in his emergence as a young man of promise on the Chicago scene. He made a highly beneficial marriage to Eunice Walker. Also from Arkansas, she was from very different roots than Johnson. A graduate of Talladega College, her grandfather, William H. McAlpine, had founded the school. He was also a close friend of Booker T. Washington. Eunice's father was a physician and her mother was principal of the local high school. Eunice and John Johnson met while she was studying for her master's degree in social work at Loyola University in Chicago. As Stephen Birmingham has said, the marriage "was a distinct move upward in the social scale [for Johnson], and for Eunice her marriage to John Johnson was considered a 'catch' since by 1941 he was already a young man whose star was visibly on the rise.'' The couple later adopted two children, John Harold, Jr., and Linda Johnson.

Johnson's next big step was to start his own magazine. Pace, in the last year of his life, gave Johnson a new assignment, to make up a digest of what was happening in the black world. Johnson began clipping items on African-Americans from the black press and from an occasional white news source. Pace then selected which ones would be reprinted in *The Guardian*. When Johnson told his friends about some of the articles and news items he had seen, he was struck by their inmmediate interest. Almost invariably they wanted to know where they could find the article. Soon, Johnson realized he was "looking at a black gold mine." He decided he wanted to begin publishing a black version of *Reader's Digest*, publishing a digest of articles about blacks from the African-American press. The problem was to find someone who would give financial backing to the project.

Everyone Johnson turned to, including Roy Wilkins of the NAACP, discouraged him from trying. He went to a number of black business leaders in Chicago, but none of them would give him financing. He decided to send out a mailing to the Supreme Life policyholders, some 20,000 in all, offering them charter subscriptions at $2 each. Pace gave him permission to use the company's addressing machine to send out the letters, but in order to do it, Johnson had to raise $500 to pay for the stamps. He tried the First National Bank of Chicago, but a clerk there laughed in his face and said, "Boy, we don't make any loans to colored people." The clerk did, however, send him to Citizens Loan Corporation, which agreed to give him the loan if he had some collateral. The only thing Johnson could think of that he could use for this purpose was his mother's furniture. At first she was understandably hesitant but ultimately gave her consent. With the $500 in hand, Johnson was able to send out the letters. Three thousand people responded with $2 each, and with the $6,000 Johnson was able to do a first-issue press run of 5,000 of the *Negro Digest* in November 1942.

Johnson's dream magazine was launched, but it was not smooth sailing during the first few months. At several points more money was needed, but, again, he found wealthy individuals unwilling to give him support. An important innovation by Johnson was to set up a system of agents around the country to get *Negro Digest* into black-owned drugstores, newsstands, and other outlets. *Negro Digest* grew slowly, and nothing spectacular happened until Johnson hit upon a winning idea: to have various prominent whites contribute to a column entitled, "If I Were a Negro." Marshall Field, Pearl Buck, and others had attracted some attention, but not until Johnson persuaded Eleanor Roosevelt, wife of the president, to write an entry did interest abound. Almost overnight circulation of the *Negro Digest* jumped to 150,000. John Johnson was on his way. He added other highly popular features such as "My Most Humiliating Jim Crow Experience," which often featured the contributions of prominent blacks.

With the success of the *Negro Digest*, Johnson was able to quit his job at Supreme Life in September 1943. A few months later he bought the first building for Johnson Publishing, paying $4,000 for a property at 5619 South State Street. A typical Chicago storefront, Johnson filled it with used furniture and started assembling a permanent staff. By 1945, with World War II at an end, America seemed to be looking forward to a future of unparalleled prosperity. With the status of blacks in that society almost certain to change dramatically due to the growing impatience of a new generation of African-Americans who had served in the war, Johnson readied to make another dramatic move. For some time he had studied the success of *Life* magazine, a supremely successful glossy picture magazine put out by Henry Luce. Johnson decided to bring out his own black verson of that magazine, calling it *Ebony*.

With *Ebony*, Johnson was determined to show a more positive side of black life than had usually been displayed in black magazines. The tendency, even with *Negro Digest*, was to focus on discrimination, segregation, and the shameful way in which blacks were treated. In *Ebony*, Johnson wanted to "show not only white people but also Negroes got married, had beauty contests, gave parties, ran successful businesses, and did all the other normal things of life." In his first editorial in *Ebony*, Johnson said, "Sure, you can get all hot and bothered about the race question (and don't think we don't) but not enough is said about all the swell things we Negroes can do and will accomplish. *Ebony* will try to mirror the happier side of life—the positive, everyday achievements from Harlem to Hollywood." The first press run of 25,000 was sold out in hours, and Johnson went back to press and printed another 25,000. Almost overnight, *Ebony* became the largest circulation black journal in America, surpassing its sister publication, *Negro Digest*. Before long, *Ebony* had a readership of over 400,000 an issue and was still growing. At that point Johnson began to look for advertisers. But he did not want the tiny "hair straightener" ads and the other staples of the black press. He wanted big, four-color ads paid for by the major white American corporations.

The problem Johnson faced was that the more copies of *Ebony* he sold, the more money he lost. Since he had no large advertisers in the magazine, and since he wanted to keep the price low to build readership, he lost money on each and every issue. The steady, inexpensive *Negro Digest* was paying the bills during this period and subsidizing *Ebony*. Johnson recalls in his autobiography that "I intended to deal with the problem by persuading corporations and advertising executives to give *Ebony* the *same* consideration they gave to *Life* and *Look*." In May 1946, Johnson got the first large ads from white companies— Chesterfield and Kotex—along with two other ads for Murray's Hair Pomade and Supreme Life. The great turning point for Johnson and *Ebony* came when he persuaded Zenith to advertise in its pages.

Johnson had discovered that almost all blacks owned radios, and for some reason most of these were Zeniths. He got an appointment to see Eugene F. McDonald, the hard-driving head of Zenith, and was able to persuade him to place Zenith ads in *Ebony* on a regular schedule. McDonald also helped Johnson get ads from Swift Packing, Elgin Watch, Armour Foods, and Quaker Oats. That was the turning point; from then on, *Ebony* was off and running. Before long, Pepsi-Cola, Colgate, Beech-Nut, Old Gold, Seagrams, Remington Rand, Roma Wines, and Schenley were advertising in its pages.

Johnson and *Ebony* went through a period where they were glamorizing nearly all aspects of black life in a manner that bordered on the sensational—running pictures of black beauty models on its cover, running sexy articles, and featuring picture reports on conspicuous consumption by the black elite. After a time, however, *Ebony* settled into a family publication pattern similar to that of *Life* and *Look*. Slick and eye-catching, it was seldom titilating or suggestive. There were articles on various aspects of black life, including politics and business; there were black success stories; and there were comprehensive articles on black history and racial problems. It took a stance on civil rights in the 1950s and early 1960s that was geared to the pace of the black community as a whole but seldom, if ever, played any kind of a leadership role in that area. As a result, the magazine came under withering attack from black militants in the 1960s. Kenneth B. Clark, the noted black psychologist, however, defended *Ebony* by noting, ''It is almost impossible to measure the morale-building value of such a magazine. The mere fact of its existence and success has been an inspiration to the Negro masses.''

With the success of the slick *Ebony*, Johnson in 1951 brought out *Jet*, a pocket-sized newsweekly. Far more sensational and colorful than *Negro Digest*, the *Digest* was retired that year, only to be brought back ten years later. Johnson also brought out a true-confessions type magazine called *Tan* in 1950, which later became a general women's service magazine. He began publishing *Hue* in 1951, but it was abandoned soon after its inception. Johnson also began publishing books in the 1950s and soon had a very successful book publishing arm. By 1972 Johnson Publishing was so successful that it was able to build and open a large new headquarters downtown in Chicago's Loop area. An eleven-storied, steel, concrete and marble structure, it cost $8 million and was the first one built by blacks in downtown Chicago. By that time Johnson Publishing was conservatively estimated to be worth between $50 million and $60 million, and it was wholly owned by Johnson, his mother, and his wife. During these same years, Johnson was also developing a number of other business interests.

Johnson became involved in other businesses primarily as a way of creating advertisers for his magazines. His first business outside of publishing was Beauty Star Cosmetics, which also marketed several hair-care products, including Santene. He started Linda Fashions, a mail-order business that sold dresses and clothes. He also sold vitamins, Star Glow wigs, and, through the *Negro Digest* Book Club, books. These ventures became quite successful, and ultimately they evolved into Supreme Beauty Products, which marketed Duke and Raveen hair-care products, and Fashion Fair Cosmetics, along with Ebony Jet Tours, a travel service, and Ebony Fashion Fair, which evolved from Linda Fashions. Eunice Johnson is the head of Fashion Fair. Johnson's hair-care products and most other lines have generally been rather minor, though profitable, players on the scene. The one nonpublishing venture that has had a major impact on the industry is Fashion Fair Cosmetics.

Although one small black cosmetics company, Flori Roberts, Inc., had been founded in 1965, nobody, especially such large white cosmetics firms as Revlon and Estée Lauder, paid much attention to the special needs of African-American women. Johnson was motivated to start his own cosmetics company when he started his Ebony Fashion Fair Shows and observed the trouble black models had trying to mix different shades to suit their skin color. Johnson approached several white manufacturers to bring out a cosmetic line for blacks, including Charles Revson of Revlon, but none were remotely interested. He and his wife, Eunice, went to a private lab and had a number of formulas put together, which they then tried out on their models. Finally, in 1973, they put out a cosmetics kit that was advertised in *Ebony* and in *Women's Wear Daily*. There was an encouraging response, forcing Johnson to make a critical decision. "There is a high road and a low road in the cosmetics field," he said, "and the two roads seldom if ever meet. You either marketed your products in high-line department stores or in mass merchandising outlets, such as drugstores and discount houses. I decided from the beginning to go the high-line route."

The key for Johnson, if he was to take the "high-line" route, was to get Fashion Fair Cosmetics into the prestigious Marshall Field & Company store in Chicago. If Marshall Field bought it, others would follow. If it did not, then no one else would either. Marshall Field agreed to carry it, and Johnson was then able to convince Bloomingdales and Nieman-Marcus to do likewise. With these three leading stores in line, others followed rapidly. The most fruitful account for Fashion Fair, however, was Dillards Department Stores, which was based in Arkansas. When Johnson approached William Dillard, the owner, Dillard greeted him warmly and said how proud he was that an Arkansas native had done so well. He then put Fashion Fair in all his stores, which numbered 35 then, and had grown to 130 by the end of the 1980s. It was by then Fashion Fair's largest account. William Dillard and Johnson developed a close relationship, and Johnson was elected to the board of directors of the department store chain. By the end of the 1980s, Fashion Fair was the largest black-owned cosmetics firm in America, selling its products in over 1,500 stores nationwide.

Johnson has also had a variety of other business interests. In the summer of 1972, when he purchased radio station WGRT, renaming it WJPC, he became the first black to own a radio station in the city. Johnson had wanted to buy an FM station, which was where the real money was in radio, but was not successful. Therefore, he paid $2 million for a station that had sold for less than half that much several years before. Next Johnson bought WLOU, the second-largest station in the Louisville market. Both of these AM stations were, according to Johnson, "transitional investments leading to the FM bonanza." He finally purchaed FM station WLNR which operated in a suburb but could be heard in Chicago. Johnson also entered the expanding television market, sponsoring two major shows—the "Ebony Music Awards" show and the "American Black Achievement Awards" show. Johnson has never been much interested in real estate, but he did make a major investment in Lawson Gardens, a government-sponsored, middle-income complex which houses 750 families in Chicago. He also paid $250,000 for a deteriorating hotel next door to Johnson Publishing to erect a parking lot and $1.5 million for an indoor parking lot across from the Hilton Towers.

Johnson also maintained his interest in Supreme Life over the years, and he continued to buy stock in the company when it was available. After a time he was the largest stockholder in the firm, and he was elected chairman of the board. Johnson had planned to remain a somewhat passive voice, but when he found that administrative costs were far too high, he fired the president and assumed that office himself. He has been the chief executive officer and the principal force in running the insurance firm in recent years. Supreme Life's performance between 1989 and 1992 was curious. In the former year, it had $2.3 billion of insurance in force, premium income of $21 million, and assets of over $55 million. In 1991, however, Supreme Life appeared to hold a virtual fire sale of its assets. During that year, Johnson sold off $39 million worth of assets to the United Insurance Company of America, cutting its total from $53 million to just $12 million. Johnson also claimed he wrote off nearly $4 million in real estate loans between 1985 and 1990. In 1987 he stated, "The real reason Supreme Life hasn't run into serious financial problems is because I put more money into it. It's that simple. We've written off just about all our bad properties; now we have a strong, viable real estate portfolio." He said that he wanted to sell the assets to black insurance companies, but they declined after reviewing the asset portfolios.

In 1992 Johnson claimed he had Supreme Life in "fighting trim." "All claims have been paid," he said, "the staff has been trimmed; and Supreme Life still handles group and real estate insurance." Yet, Supreme Life was hardly the giant, dynamic firm it had been for decades. It had settled into an apparently profitable niche in the market but was hardly the "largest Negro business in the North" any longer, nor was it even close to being the third-largest black insurance company, and it continued slowly sliding down *Black Enterprise*'s listings of top firms, resting at tenth place in 1992.

The crown jewel of Johnson's empire is still Johnson Publishing. By 1992 it was the second-largest black-owned firm in America, with sales in 1991 of over $260 million and a staff of 2,700. It continued to be wholly owned by Johnson and members of his family. John Johnson also intends a dynastic transference of power in the firm, grooming his daughter, Linda Johnson Rice, to succeed him. She earned a degree in journalism from the University of Southern California, and in 1987 she received her master's degree in business administration from Northwestern University. At the same time, she also enrolled in a special training program that her father had created for her to learn business leadership. He then brought her into the firm right after graduation as president and chief operating officer of Johnson Publishing. It was not a move that impressed all analysts. Louis W. Stern, one of Rice's marketing professors at Northwestern, said, "There aren't many 20-year-olds capable of running a $175 million company." However, Earl Graves,* publisher of *Black Enterprise*, replied, "Clearly she is ready. She certainly has the sophistication and training for the job." She married André Rice, a stockbroker with Goldman-Sachs, in a ceremony that one Chicago writer called "the most elaborate wedding in Chicago history." Others estimated it cost at least $500,000. Johnson responded, "I'm the only person who knows for sure [what he paid]—and I'm not saying." He did make one thing clear: When he and Eunice Johnson got married in 1941, they could not afford a honeymoon. "What the hell, I've got the money, she's my only daughter; and Eunice and I paid our dues driving from Alabama to Illinois on the 1941 honeymoon we never had."

John Johnson is not just business. He is a race and civic leader of the first order. He served on the board of directors of the Urban League from 1958, and in 1954 he was elected to the board of trustees of Tuskegee Institute. In 1951 he was named one of the ten outstanding men of the year by the United States Junior Chamber of Commerce. He won the Freedom Fund Award of the NAACP in 1958, its Spingarn Medal in 1966, and the Horatio Alger Award in 1966. In 1982 he received the Drum Major Award from the Southern Christian Leadership Conference. He has served on the board of directors of Twentieth Century Fox, Marina City Bank of Chicago, Service Federal Savings and Loan Association of Chicago, Opportunities Industrialization Centers, and the National Conference of Christians and Jews. He is a fellow of Sigma Delta Chi, the professional journalism society, and he received the Newspaper Publishers Association's John Russwurm Award in 1966, along with the Magazine Publishers Association's Henry Johnson Fisher Award. He has been a major philanthropist for such black causes as the United Negro College Fund.

Johnson, a complex man, has attracted praise and criticism in nearly equal doses. On one hand, there is a dispute over what kind of person he is to work for. All agree he has an autocratic management style, but the question is whether he is a benevolent despot. Although he has always run a nonunion shop, Johnson claims his first concern is with the welfare of his employees. "I genuinely care about the welfare of the employees," he said. "I get to know them well. I have a policy here that no one is ever employed unless I personally meet them. I learn the names of the people I come in daily contact with. I know most of their birthdays and I inquire about their families. Above all, I pay them a good salary and I give them good benefits. People should not make a sacrifice to work for a black company."

On the other hand, black employees at Johnson Publications often refer to the company as the "plantation." For many years Johnson posted himself at the entrance to catch tardy employees, and he has strict rules concerning dress and behavior. One former employee said, "When you travel for Johnson, you travel first class and you live first class. . . . The disagreeable aspect is the constant insecurity. I don't think any of us would go back to work for him . . . but I don't think any of us regrets for a moment the time we spent there. We came out of Johnson Publishing with a professional education that, as Negroes, we couldn't have gotten anywhere else in the country.'' *Fortune* magazine in 1985 named Johnson one of the toughest bosses in America, saying that employees complained of his ''wild temper tantrums and firing threats.'' Johnson responded, ''It's a fact. I'm tough, but I'm fair. Tough does not mean going around bullying people. Tough does not mean insulting people. Tough means you hold people accountable. . . . I would much rather be known as tough and fair than to be thought of as soft.''

There has also been much criticism of the style of journalism that Johnson has fostered, even though it has been incredibly successful. Johnson points out that he is trying to inspire the black middle class and to emphasize the more positive aspects of black life. Yet, Johnson argues, ''[W]e're not a happiness magazine. We still live in a country where there's lots of racism. We must challenge that. But we must do everything we can do to improve the situation.'' Many blacks think he does not do enough. Grayson Mitchell, once an employee at Johnson Publications and later with Johnson Products, founded by George Johnson,* said, ''I don't buy that rah-rah approach. *Ebony* is very much a reflection of Johnson's own estimation of the black intellect—and it's a perception not much different from whites. He thinks black people must be entertained. He thinks you must make them sing and dance. He doesn't view them as serious people who want to be informed about the world around them. The black educated household is tremendously more enlightened than that. This is 1980, not 1945. And *Ebony* essentially looks like it did in 1945.''

Johnson replies to charges like this in the following manner: ''When Stokely [Carmichael] first screamed black power on the road to Memphis, we dispatched a reporter immediately. When Angela Davis was in prison, we sent a reporter. Anytime anybody does anything important, we're up there photographing.'' He explained in another context, ''Many people assume that *Ebony* is saying everything is great, but we're not saying that. We're saying we have to deal with the world as we find it.'' When the criticism of his stance on these issues becomes too intense, Johnson often replies, ''Remember, I'm a businessman, not a social worker.'' And, after all, somebody is still buying his magazines.

''I don't say everyone can be a John Johnson,'' he once said. ''You have to be in the right place at the right time. You have to have a bit of luck. But I'm saying whatever you're in, if you apply yourself you'll do better.'' That, according to Johnson, is all he really wanted to do anyway. ''When I started *Negro Digest* I was making fifty dollars a week. I thought that if the magazine succeeded, I could make two hundred.'' He also knew something else: ''[N]o matter how much money you acquire or what sort of positions you hold, you're still black. And you're never free of that. There's no way to free yourself of that. . . . Now, when I step out of this building, I'm a black man. I'm not John Johnson, the publisher . . . and if they don't respect black people, in general, they won't respect me. And our country, in general, does not respect black people.'' John Johnson was perhaps the greatest black entrepreneur of the twentieth century, and he was always one to trumpet the positive side of things in the pages of his magazines. But even he realized in the end that however rich and powerful he was he was still black, and America was a racist society. Some things do not change.

Sources

John Johnson's papers and those of the Johnson Publishing Company have not been made available to researchers, but much of these materials are held at the Johnson Publishing Company Library. The most complete biographical information on Johnson is his autobiography, written with Lerone Bennett, Jr., *Succeeding against the Odds* (New York, 1989). There are briefer (though sometimes more objective) accounts of his life in the following sources: *Current Biography* (1968); *Ebony Success Library* (1973), vol. II, 132–37; John Seder and Berkeley G. Burrell, *Getting It Together* (New York, 1971), 205–10; Stephen Birmingham, *A Certain People* (Boston, 1977), 19–35; Ingham, BDABL; *Chicago Tribune*, June 4, 1955, November 25, 1973, and November 10, 1975; *Fortune*, January 1968, 152ff.; Nick Thimmesch, "John H. Johnson: The Man behind *Ebony*," *Saturday Evening Post*, October 1975, 36ff.; Ponchitta Pierce, "The Man Who Turned Ebony into Gold," *Reader's Digest*, December 1975, 161–66; *Washington Post*, September 14, 1980; Jonathon Greenberg, " 'It's a Miracle,' " *Forbes*, December 20, 1982, 104ff.; Dan Rottenberg, "Atop the Ebony Empire," *United Airlines Magazine*, January 1985, 39ff.; Edgar A. Topping, *A Biographical History of Blacks in America* (New York, 1971), 338–39; Lerone Bennett, *Before the Mayflower* (Chicago, 1984), 374 +; Philip Drotning and Wesley South, *Up from the Ghetto* (New York, 1970); Jane Hurley and Doris McGee Haynes, *Afro-American Then and Now* (Sacramento, 1969), 120–23; Frank J. Johnson, *Who's Who of Black Millionaires* (1984), 102; Meyer Stein, *Blacks in Communications, Journalism, Public Relations and Advertising* (New York, 1972), 33–36 +; "Ebony Publisher John H. Johnson," *San Francisco Chronicle*, November 23, 1980; "Ebony Publisher Johnson," *Black Enterprise*, June 1980, 212–13; "John H. Johnson," *Black Enterprise*, May 1983, 88; "Publisher John Johnson," *Chicago Sun-Times*, October 19, 1980, 1–23; Martin Fletcher, *Our Great Americans* (1953), 56; Louie Robinson, Jr., *The Black Millionaire* (New York, 1972), 7–21; Edwin Darby, *The Fortune Builders* (New York, 1986), 197; Robert Sobel and David Sicilia, *The Entrepreneurs* (New York, 1986), 32–37; Nelson George, *The Death of Rhythm and Blues* (1988), 22–23; *Who's Who in America* (1992–1993); and *Who's Who among Black Americans* (1992–1993).

There are also a number of useful interviews of Johnson over the years. See "John H. Johnson of *Ebony*: Setting a Goal and Reaching It," *Nation's Business*, April 1974, 45–50; "John H. Johnson," *Ebony*, November 1985, 45–58; Paul Lindsey Johnson, "Interview: John H. Johnson," *The Crisis* 94, 10 (January 1987), 32–48; Derek T. Dingle, "Doing Business John Johnson's Way," *Black Enterprise*, June 1987, 150–64; and "Failure Is a Word I Don't Accept: An Interview with John H. Johnson," *Harvard Business Review*, March-April 1988, 79–88. Johnson's own writings can also be revealing at times. See "Black Capitalism: Little Improvement in Past Decades," *New York Times*, April 21, 1974; "Blacks Must Abandon Politics of Poverty, Philosophy of Despair," *Jet*, March 1, 1973, 16–17; "Downtown Retailers Rely Heavily on Negro," *Advertising Age*, April 13, 1959, 96; "Five Major Myths of Black Business," *Ebony*, December 1971, 4–6; "Greening of the Black Consumer Market," *The Crisis*, March 1976, 92–95; "Individual Responsibility and the Negro Image," *Negro Digest*, January 1965, 4–6; "Negro Market Will Be Controlling Factor in Profit Margins of Big U.S. Companies in Fifteen Years," *Advertising Age*, September 21, 1964, 119–20. See also his "Publisher's Statement" which runs in each issue of *Ebony*. Excellent, complete bibliographies on works by or about Johnson and his economic empire can be found in George H. Hill and Michael Nelson, eds., "John Harold Johnson, Publishing Magnate," *Bulletin of Bibliographies* 42, 2 (1988), 89–94.

There is a veritable mountain of information on Johnson and his publishing and other interests. Articles featuring briefer information on Johnson include *Printer's Ink*, October 27, 1950, 100; *Reader's Digest*, April 1987, 56–57; *Time*, October 23, 1950, September 22, 1952, and December 9, 1985, 68; *Newsweek*, November 7, 1949, October 19, 1953, and November 10, 1975; *Chicago Sun Times*, October 25, 1951, May 19, 1963, May 20, 1964, May 14, 1972, November 18, 1973, October 19, 1980, May 20, 1984, November 3, 1985, May 25, 1986, May 6, 1987, March 27, May 11, and June 8, 1989; *Chicago Tribune*, June 4, 1955, November 10, 1975, May 6 and 7 and October 27, 1987, May 14, 25, and 30, 1989; *Ebony*, December 1971, 156; *Washington Post*, December 3, 1975; *The Afro-American*, May 25, 1985; *Fortune*, August 6, 1984, 23, and July 31, 1989, 186; *New York Times*, December 4, 1982; *Black Enterprise*, June 1992; *Business Week*, July 13, 1987, 40; *USA Today*, April 16, 1986; *USA Weekend*, November 1–3, 1985; *Crain's Chicago Business*, April 4, 1953, and August 14, 1989; *Chicago Defender*, December 22, 1981; *Product Marketing*, March 1979; *Toronto Globe & Mail*, August 8, 1989, B8; *Editor & Publisher*, June 3, 1989, 13; *Black Enterprise*, June 1989, 41; and *The Crisis*, October 1989, 14ff. (reviews). Articles on his economic concerns include *Los Angeles Sentinel*, May 19, 1983; *Time*, August 21, 1968, 32; *Chicago Tribune*, November 25, 1973; *Business Week*, March 23, 1968, 70–76; *Advertising Age*, September 23, 1963; *The Reporter*, November 12, 1959, and December 24, 1959; *Ebony*, November 1955; *Black Enterprise*, March 1989; *Madison Avenue*, December 1984, 84–85; Walter C. Daniel, *Black Journals of the United States* (Westport, Conn., 1982), 93–96, 159–65, 213–14, 262–64; Donald Freeman Joyce, *Gatekeepers of Black Culture: Black-Owned Book Publishing in the United States, 1817–1981* (Westport, Conn., 1983), 94–96, 195–97 + .

For Supreme Liberty Life, see Robert C. Puth, "Supreme Life: The History of a Negro Life Insurance Company," Ph.D. diss., Northwestern University, 1967. Portions of his research have also been published as "Supreme Life: The History of a Negro Life Insurance Company," *Business History Review* XLIII, 1 (Spring 1969), 1–21; and "From Enforced Segregation to Integration: Market Factors in the Development of a Negro Life Insurance Company," in *Business Enterprise and Economic Change: Essays in Honor of Harold F. Williamson*, edited by Louis F. Cain and Paul J. Uselding (Kent, Ohio, 1973), 280–301. There is some other useful information on the company in *Ebony*, August 1946, November 1956, and October 1973; and *Chicago Defender*, November 18, 1969, and January 18, 1975.

Johnson, William (1809–June 17, 1851). Businessman, barber, and diarist, Natchez, Mississippi. William Johnson was a highly successful businessman and barber in antebellum Natchez, Mississippi. Owner of the largest barbershop in the city, he was also a successful moneylender, real estate speculator, and planter. This in itself was an extraordinary accomplishment in Mississippi, which had little patience for free blacks. As Charles Sydnor has pointed out, this group in Mississippi was always comparatively small, and the white response to their very existence was "hostile and fearful," resulting in much restrictive legislation. So, the fact that William Johnson could survive and prosper in such an environment is remarkable. What he is best remembered for today, however, is the extraordinary diary he left. The discovery of this thirteen-volume, 2,000-page journal caused historian Allan Nevins to call Johnson "one of the most . . . interesting of American diarists." Hodding Carter III, in the *Delta Democrat Times*, concluded that Johnson's diary was "the most unusual personal record ever kept in the United States," saying that "not only does the diary depict the more provincial happenings, it also pictures his thoughts and opinions on state and even national and international affairs."

William Johnson was born a slave in 1809, to Amy, a slave on the plantation of one William Johnson, who was probably his father. In 1814 the white planter emancipated Amy, by going to Louisiana and undertaking the manumission procedure there. Four years later, young William's older sister, a "mulatto girl named Delia aged about thirteen years," was also freed. She was then sent to Philadelphia to live. In 1820, the planter William Johnson petitioned the Mississippi legislature to free Amy's eleven-year-old child, William. This was a very difficult procedure in the state, but ultimately on February 10 of that year, a bill was signed by Governor Poindexter which said in part: "That the mulatto boy named William, son of Amy, a free woman of color, and the slave of William Johnson of Adams County, be, and he is hereby emancipated and set free from slavery."

Amy, meantime, had become a peddler in Natchez. She was also a woman of tempestuous nature who was involved in a number of court suits while William was a young boy. At least one of these suits involved charges of assault against a local barber in which Amy was granted damages. In others, however, she was not so fortunate, and young William was often troubled by her quarrelsome nature in later years. In the same year that William was emancipated, another of Amy's daughters, Amelia, married the Philadelphia-born free-black James Miller. Miller established himself as a barber in Natchez, and ran a successful business until 1830. When William Johnson was freed, he was apprenticed to his brother-in-law's shop to learn the trade of barbering, which had become the vocation of choice for free African-Americans in the river towns of the South.

James Miller was William Johnson's new "master," but more than that, he was a surrogate father, who taught him the legalities and intricacies of surviving and prospering as a free black in the tightly controlled racial situation in Mississippi. By 1827 Miller had attained such status in Natchez that forty-four prominent white men in the community petitioned the state legislature asking for the removal of all civil disabilities as a free man of color, save those of voting and jury duty. In 1828 the nineteen-year-old William Johnson struck out on his own and opened a barbershop in Port Gibson, Mississippi. He did quite well in this location, according to his own records, "The amount taken in during my stay in Port Gibson which was twenty two months was one thousand and ninety four dollars and fifty cents. This was by Hair Cutting and Shaving alone."

In 1829 James Miller began contemplating a move to New Orleans, and a year later, he sold the unexpired portion of his lease to William Johnson for $300. Miller by this point was a highly successful businessman in Natchez, owning four slaves and having $3,750 "loaned at interest." Why he left is not clear, but perhaps the somewhat more comfortable racial climate for free blacks in Louisiana was the reason. In any event, Johnson took over the shop and made a ringing success of it. By 1833 he was able to move from his rented quarters to a brick building he purchased on Main Street. Within the next several years, according to his biographer, he had become "the most enterprising young businessman in Natchez." Johnson was also a rather carefree, man-about-town during these years, who dated many young women, gambled, occasionally drank, and attended musical performances and stage shows and other events. During much of this period, one of the women he dated was Ann Battles, a young, free, mulatto girl. In 1835 the twenty-year-old Battles married Johnson, the most eligible bachelor in the free black community. At the time of the nuptials, Johnson was running the town's most popular barbershop, owned four slaves, and had real property worth at least $2,700. Their marriage, which lasted until Johnson's untimely death in 1851, produced ten children.

Johnson's ownership of slaves brings up an important issue—why would recently freed slaves like Johnson, Andrew Durnford,* and William Ellison*— own slaves themselves if they had so recently experienced the degradations and hardships of that position? Did they feel a sense of racial solidarity with their brothers in chains, so that perhaps, as Carter Woodson stated many years ago, this was an act of benevolence on their part—an attempt to protect family members and others from the worst effects of slavery? There are a number of things to understand in answering these questions.

First of all, slave ownership was the key to enhanced prosperity in the South, for both blacks and whites. If Johnson wished to become something more than a simple tradesman he needed to use the labor of slaves, since the acquisition of each slave allowed him to expand his business activities beyond his barbershop. There were essentially only two kinds of labor available to Johnson. He could hire other free blacks to work in his shops, which he did, but they were rather scarce in antebellum Mississippi. Johnson used a number of free black apprentices and journeymen, but they often left to start their own shops, and they were not available for other kinds of labor. Johnson did sometimes hire illiterate whites, the only ones who would work for a black, but he had relatively little control over their labor, and they regularly cheated him. Thus, he was left with the second alternative, and the ownership of slaves was the most secure way in which he could expand his enterprises.

Also, owning slaves protected Johnson and his family, as free African-Americans, from insinuations that they might be antislavery advocates. How could they be, if they shared a stake in the South's "peculiar institution?" Nor was skin color and cultural heritage necessarily a link between Johnson and his slaves. He and his family were light-skinned mulattoes, while most slaves were classified in the federal census as "black." The evidence for this insistence on a racial difference by light-skinned African-Americans to differentiate them from their darker-hued brethren is legion, both in contemporary accounts and historical analyses. Nor is there any evidence that Johnson owned slaves out of benevolent or philanthropic motives. None of his slaves were family members, none were emancipated out of kindness, and his slaves were treated no better and no worse than slaves owned by whites in Natchez.

In the middle 1830s Johnson usually owned four or five slaves; his mother owned five, and his mother-in-law owned one. By the 1840s Johnson's slave-holdings rose to eight or nine, and by the time of his death he owned fifteen. Of the thirty-one slaves he had owned in total over his lifetime, Johnson sold three of them at a profit, six died, and one escaped or had been stolen. Johnson often used whipping to discipline his slaves, but it should be recalled that this form of discipline was not unusual in the early nineteenth century. Not only were black slaves regularly beaten; white apprentices, criminals, schoolboys, soldiers, and sailors were disciplined in a similar manner.

Johnson's barber business was conducted entirely by blacks catering exclusively to whites. His barbers were all free blacks, along with a few slaves he was able to train. Out of the number of slaves he tried to train, however, only two of them proved satisfactory. Rather, he brought in young free blacks as apprentices, as James Miller had done with him, and taught them the trade. The boys were usually placed in his shop when they were between ten and fifteen years of age, and they served until they were eighteen. During that time, they were subject to Johnson's discipline and control, and in return for their labor, he gave them a rudimentary education, fed, and, in some instances, clothed them. When they graduated into the journeyman class, he regularly paid them from $100 to $150 per year.

As time went on, and Johnson became wealthier and more successful, he was able to expand his enterprises. First of all, he made a number of significant improvements in his shop on Main Street. In 1837 he installed nearly fifty "shaving boxes," which he rented to customers for 25 cents a month. By 1839 he was dressing his barbers in linen coats, and by the time of his death his shop had two couches, six barber chairs, four mirrors, thirty-one framed pictures, two washstands, a coatrack, a small writing desk, a table, a "small stand," "razors Scissors &c," and a "showcase and perfumery." In 1838 and 1839, Johnson participated in the general renovation of Main Street, tearing down his old building and constructing a new three-storied brick building on the property at a total cost of nearly $3,400. The shop always opened early and closed late. It was also open Sunday mornings with Johnson and at least one of the barbers at work cutting hair.

At about the same time, Johnson built a three-storied brick home on State Street, which was to serve as the family home for more than a century, and which in recent years was renovated and put on the National Register of Historic Places. The William Johnson House was described by the Mississippi Department of Archives and History as "a three-bay, two-and-one-half-story townhouse that survives as a typical example of a nineteenth century middle-class dwelling in the Greek Revival style. It is constructed of brick laid in common bond with the facade stuccoed and scored in imitation of ashlar masonry."

After a time, Johnson expanded his business to include a bathhouse and two smaller barbershops. The bathhouse, erected in the summer of 1834 at a cost of $170, included four "tubbs." This was part of a new concern on the part of Americans for cleanliness, and also was due to the lack of running water in many homes. It was a luxury that was popular in the summer months and in prosperous times, but it was slow in winter and in times of recession. He ran the bathhouse for about a decade. He opened two small, one-man barbershops, one in the Tremont Hotel, just around the corner from his Main Street shop, and the other in the Natchez-under-the-Hill district, the rough waterfront area. Each shop was run by free blacks employed by Johnson, or by Charles, one of the few slaves who had been successfully trained. Charles, unlike most of Johnson's other slaves, was exceedingly well treated, and in most respects he was as free as any of his journeymen.

Johnson also developed a number of business interests outside his barbering and bathhouse trade. Like James Miller, he became a leading private moneylender in the town by loaning money to many of his white barbershop customers. By 1836–1837 his moneylending operation was in full swing and brought Johnson fair profits in most years, although he probably never earned more than $300 in any year. His interest rates varied from 5 percent per month to 6 percent per year. His largest single loan was $1,000 to the firm of Gemmell & Taylor. He also augmented his income by buying and selling and by a number of other small enterprises. He conducted a toyshop, sold wallpaper, and used two of his slaves to haul coal and sand and water barrels. For a brief period, he operated with Henry Melin, a drayman. Johnson also speculated in farmland, and he developed a small but steady income from rental properties he owned in town. In addition, he received a small income by hiring out his slaves for periods ranging from one day to six months. In all, he hired out nine slaves in the twenty years he was a slaveholder.

Like many other urban businessmen in the South, Johnson developed a strong urge to own farmland and to become a planter of sorts. He bought his first tract of rural land in 1835 but disposed of it quickly when he had a chance to double his investment. Soon, however, he made a more permanent investment, buying 120 acres of "Hard Scrabble" land on the Mississippi River for $600. Thirteen months later he spent $3,000 to acquire 242 acres of adjoining land. He began farming some of this acreage but also harvested timber from portions of it. From the summer of 1845 until his death six years later, Johnson devoted increasing amounts of his time and energy to his farming and timber ventures. Since he could not be at the farm full-time, however, he hired illiterate whites to act as overseers and laborers on the land. He hired a succession of whites for this purpose, but none worked out very well. It is not clear whether the farm was profitable or not, but the land purchase was profitable, since his widow was later able to sell the property he had purchased for $4,300 to planter James Surget for $7,812.50.

By the time of his death in 1851, William Johnson was a comparatively wealthy man. His fifteen slaves were valued at more than $6,000, his farmland at nearly $8,000, his farm tools and stock at $1,600, and his two Main Street properties at about $7,500. His estate was thus worth at least $25,000 at his death, a tidy sum in antebellum America. He was by this time the most successful and prominent free black in Natchez, and he had a solidly entrenched position in both the black and white communities. In the free black community he was viewed as a successful businessman and philanthropist, and he was close friends with many of the other leading blacks in the town. He was, in the context of the town's black community, probably their leading aristocrat, and he lived a life that befitted that station.

His relationship with whites was more complex. As his biographers have stated, "William Johnson's position as a free person of color was that of a man who had reached the top of his class but who possessed elements of two conflicting cultures in his heritage—that of the slave and that of the planter." In his own mind, however, Johnson viewed himself as part of the gentry, and he always wholeheartedly believed that one day character and success, not color, would determine a man's worth in society. Thus, as a young man, Johnson adopted a Ben Franklin–like approach to developing high standards of conduct, hoping that the white citizens of Natchez would one day accept him socially. That day never came, and in death it became clear that, in the eyes of most whites, Johnson was still little more than a slave.

Nonetheless, it is apparent that Johnson was allowed a considerable degree of latitude in his relations with whites. He rented rooms to them, he lent them money, he sued them in court, he employed skilled whites to erect buildings for him and illiterate whites to work on his farm. At times, he had long man-to-man conversations with whites that lasted until deep into the night. But always that color line was there—sometimes obscure and tenuous, other times daunting and unbridgeable. The white with whom he had the closest relationship, and the one who was most faithful to him after his murder, was Col. Adam L. Bingaman. Bingaman, the scion of a wealthy and aristocratic Adams County family, graduated from Harvard in 1812 as its top-ranking scholar. He was also a nationally known turfman; it was this love of horses and horse racing that initially bonded the two men, black and white. Over the years, however, it is clear that they developed a relationship of mutual respect and admiration that, to some extent anyway, transcended the racial divisions of the time.

Johnson's murder in 1851 came as the result of a boundary dispute with Baylor Winn, another free black, who had bought swampland adjoining Johnson's property. The two men had known each other for a long time, although they had never been friends. After Winn purchased the land next to Johnson's, he began engaging in timbering operations on his neighbor's land. Johnson complained many times, and once, when Johnson sent in surveyors to determine the boundary line, Winn drove them off with a shotgun. Johnson finally decided to bring Winn to court on the matter, and while it was in litigation, Winn shot Johnson from ambush on June 16, 1851, as he was returning to his farm. Critically wounded, Johnson died the following morning. The headline in the local *Courier* screamed: "SHOCKING MURDER." "[A] horrible and deliberate murder has been committed upon an excellent and most inoffensive man. . . . This murder has created a great deal of excitement, as well from its atrocity, as from the peaceable character of Johnson and his excellent standing."

While on his deathbed Johnson identified his assailant as Baylor Winn, but since the only other witnesses were two free blacks and a slave, a problem emerged. Blacks could not testify against whites in court, and, although Winn was "presumed" to be a free black, the prosecution failed to establish the fact that he was not white to the satisfaction of the jury. He was put on trial three times for the offense, but he was ultimately freed and served no more than a token amount of time. As Johnson's biographers commented, "[Johnson's] death by murder was avenged by the law no more than if he had been a common slave."

After his death, Johnson's widow headed the family for fifteen years until her own death. She constructed a new brick building on Main Street in which her sons and employees continued to conduct the successful barbershop through the Civil War and afterward. Just before her death, her eldest son, William Johnson, Jr., became mentally ill and had to be confined to a mental institution in New Orleans. Col. Bingaman demonstrated his friendship then and at other critical times, taking the responsibility for securing care for the sick boy and comforting the family in its double affliction of their mother's death and the boy's confinement. Young Byron Johnson, who became head of the family after 1866, worked as a successful barber and plasterer until his own death in 1872. In 1868 Col. Bingaman wrote at least two letters to Byron from New Orleans, in which he informed him that "Teeny and your sister are both well," and ended with "My love to your sisters and accept the same for yourself." By this time, Bingaman was living in New Orleans with his free black mistress and their children.

After Byron's death, his sister, Anna L. Johnston (by this time the family name was spelled this way) was head of the family. A schoolteacher in Adams County, she lived in the family home until her death in 1922. In her later years she was ably assisted by Clarence M. Johnston, William Johnson's youngest son, a blacksmith, and a grandson, Dr. W. R. Johnston. Dr. Johnston, who graduated from Wilberforce College and the medical school at Howard University, became the leading black physician in Natchez until his death in 1838. Edwin Adams Davis discovered William Johnson's diaries in the attic of the family home, one of the greatest historical findings of that period. The diaries not only tell us much about the life of an antebellum free black family, and of the way in which Johnson conducted his business and personal life, but also a great deal about the social life of whites at the time. Johnson's barbershop was the largest in town, and it was a major clearing house for the news and gossip of that community. Johnson, never one to gossip himself, or to betray confidences, nevertheless recorded these items faithfully in his journals.

Sources

William Johnson's sixteen-year diary (1835–1851) is in the William Johnson Papers at Louisiana State University, Baton Rouge. There is a detailed description of these papers in William R. Hogan, ed., *Guide to the Manuscript Collections in the Department of Archives, Louisiana State University* (University, La., 1940), 33–35. The diary is in book form in *William Johnson's Natchez: The Antebellum Diary of a Free Negro*, edited by W. R. Hogan and Edward A. Davis (Baton Rouge, 1951). See also their *The Barber of Natchez* (1954 reprint edition, Port Washington, N.Y., 1969), and E. A. Davis, "William Johnson: Free Negro Citizen of Antebellum Mississippi," *Journal of Mississippi History* XV (1953). The Mississippi Department of Archives and History has a subject file on William Johnson, containing a wide variety of items dealing with his life and with the Natchez district, both during his lifetime and later. Some of the newspaper accounts of value in that file include *Concordia Intelligencer*, June 21, 1851, which contains an account of Johnson's murder; and *Natchez Democrat*, July 13, 1976, September 25, 1978, and December 13, 1979; *Washington Post*, March 5, 1989; *Clarion Ledger*, July 18, 1976, and June 19, 1977, all of which deal with the restoration of Johnson's family home listing on the National Register of Historic Places. Edwin A. Davis wrote a short biography of Johnson for the *Dictionary of American Negro Biography* (1982), and there is another brief treatment of him by George A. Sewell and Margaret L. Dwight, *Mississippi Black History Makers* (Jackson, 1984), 149–54.

K

Kennedy, William Jesse, Jr. (June 15, 1889–July 8, 1985), **William Jesse Kennedy III** (October 24, 1922–   ), **Charles Clinton Spaulding** (August 1, 1874–August 1, 1952), and **Asa T. Spaulding** (July 22, 1902–September 5, 1990). Insurance company executives: North Carolina Mutual Insurance Company. The historian Walter Weare has said, "If Charles Clinton Spaulding— the leading black businessman of the first half of the twentieth century—had not existed, America would have invented him." There is much truth to this observation. If John Merrick* was the man who got North Carolina Mutual and Durham's black business community off the ground, it was C. C. Spaulding who institutionalized it and made it part of the American mythology. C. C. Spaulding ran North Carolina Mutual from 1900 until his death in 1952, a time of entrenched racism and segregation throughout the South. Spaulding represented, for both blacks and whites, what could be done within that system. Whereas civil rights leaders and others always focused upon the various restrictions placed upon blacks, C. C. Spaulding was always a highly visible example of how ambitious, intelligent, but deferential, blacks could succeed in America. Yet, as Weare astutely notes, Spaulding was more than this—he was a "race man." That is, he was a leader who combined the doctrine of self-help with racial solidarity. Over his career, Spaulding became as important a political leader as he was a businessman, although he himself never admitted it. He always simply replied, "I am a businessman, not a politician." But, as a race man, Spaulding increasingly was both.

C. C. Spaulding was born near Whiteville and Clarkton, in Columbus County, North Carolina, not far from Wilmington. This area was the home of an extraordinary African-American population, with a maze of kinship ties that formed generations of intermarriage within the community. Dr. A. M. Moore, one of the organizers of North Carolina Mutual, was Spaulding's uncle, and three of the first five presidents of the company hailed from this area. Although the white media later called Spaulding the son of an ex-slave, it is quite clear that both Spaulding's father and grandfather were born free, but that the family had originally been slaves on plantations near Wilmington. Charles Spaulding's father, Benjamin McIver Spaulding, was by all accounts a special man. He was not only a successful farmer, but also a blacksmith, cabinetmaker, and community leader who served as county sheriff during Reconstruction. Much later, when C. C. Spaulding was being lionized as "the most successful Negro," he responded, "[My father's] success story is vastly more impressive than mine could ever be, because—starting with the Emancipation—he had to work out a completely new pattern of existence. All I have had to do was to try and follow the excellent pattern he developed."

Education, however, was not a major element of Benjamin Spaulding's pattern for his ten children. C. C. Spaulding received only a smattering of formal education while in Columbus County. Most of his time was spent working for his father in the fields on the family farm, mending harness, or scrubbing the floors of their cabin. As a result, the younger Spaulding was able to complete only the early elementary grades before he moved to Durham. Spaulding in later years, though, viewed those years on the farm as his most important formative experience: "I was well on my way to success before I ever left the farm. My father had already taught me the most important lessons I have ever learned."

When Spaulding, at age twenty came to Durham in 1894, he was barely literate, and his uncle, Dr. Aaron McDuffie Moore, took him under his wing. Spaulding enrolled in Whitted School and worked at a succession of menial jobs to support himself while attending school. He worked as a dishwasher, a bellhop, and a waiter, but when he found it difficult to keep up with his schoolwork, Spaulding spent two years as a cook with a wealthy white family. He finished his formal education in 1898, with what amounted to a high school diploma for the time. Upon graduation Spaulding became manager of a local cooperative grocery store. Twenty-five of Durham's leading blacks had each invested ten dollars to start the venture, but when the company suffered financial trouble, most of the members withdrew their investment. Spaulding was left with bare shelves and around $300 of debt. At that point, however, opportunity knocked loudly for Spaulding.

His uncle and John Merrick had established the North Carolina Mutual Insurance Company in 1898, but by 1900 the firm was on the brink of collapse. Moore and Merrick bought out their other partners and prepared to reorganize the company on a sound basis, but they recognized that they needed someone to devote himself full-time to the management of the fledgling enterprise. Spaulding's grocery enterprise may have folded, but he had shown entrepreneurial ability during the two years he ran it, and, besides, he was family. Moore and Merrick offered the twenty-six-year-old Spaulding the position of general manager of the company. It was an exalted title for a young man, but as Spaulding pointed out several times in later years, their first office was rented for the princely sum of two dollars a month. "When I came into the office in the morning," he once said, "I rolled up my sleeves and swept the place as the janitor. Then I rolled down my sleeves and was an agent, and later I put on my coat and became the general manager.''

That was no doubt true, but Spaulding's major task in the early years was to sell policies and recruit agents. Spaulding has been described by those who knew him as a ''go-getter'' and a ''natural-born salesman.'' He certainly displayed those characteristics during his first years with North Carolina Mutual. He sold insurance policies on street corners, went door to door, and was the classic life insurance salesman who would not take no for an answer. He was even able to turn potential disaster into advantage. In the very early days of his sales push, the owners of one of the first policies he sold unexpectedly died. North Carolina Mutual would have to come up with the $40 to pay his benefactors. To do so, the three partners had to put up money out of their own pockets. Spaulding used the receipt from that claim, and others in later years, as proof of the financial stability of the company: He paid off on its claims, and asserted that ''only a foolish Negro could not afford a policy.''

As Spaulding signed up policyholders, the company's premium income was double what it had been the year before. North Carolina Mutual was now more solvent, and Spaulding began recruiting a sales force. At first he signed up mostly black teachers and ministers to do the work, and within six months he had agents in twenty-eight towns in North Carolina. Although this greatly increased premium income, it also doubled expenses. Spaulding, Moore, and Merrick could hardly extract more than a hand-to-mouth existence out of North Carolina Mutual alone. Moore and Merrick had other business interests to provide them with income, but for Spaulding it was a difficult time. Nonetheless, in 1900, the same year he joined the insurance firm, he married Fannie Jones, of Washington, D.C., John Merrick's half sister.

Perhaps the most critical years in North Carolina Mutual's early history, however, were 1901 and 1902. Sick claims and death claims ran very high in 1901, and Spaulding's office and travel expenses from expansion were lofty. Thus, in the fall of 1901, Moore and Merrick had to loan the company $300 to save it. Losses continued to outrun profits in 1902, and claims for February of that year exceeded premium income by a whopping $300. Again, Merrick and Moore had to advance money to the company. But Spaulding continued with his unflagging optimism, and by March the worst crisis was past. By 1903, despite a deficit, premiums exceeded claims for the first time, and the firm had turned an important corner. Early in 1903 the triumvirate made another momentous decision—Spaulding became the first of the three to receive a set salary—$15 a week. With things now relatively stabilized, it was decided that the only way North Carolina Mutual would continue to prosper was if it aggressively pursued greater expansion. And the way to do that, Spaulding reasoned, was by advertising. In 1903 the firm began a multipronged advertising approach that would prove very successful.

What Spaulding decided to do was brash and rather extraordinary—he decided to publish a company newspaper that would also serve as a community newspaper for the black community of Durham and as a powerful advertising tool. Therefore, he founded the *North Carolina Mutual*, and got the prominent Duke family to donate a printing press. That monthly magazine was a successful venture in every respect, but the company also distributed advertising novelties—pencils, matches, fans, thermometers, cuspidors, blotters, and art calenders with black subjects.

At that point Spaulding began to expand the insurance firm outside of North Carolina, most particularly into the adjacent state of South Carolina. At the same time he began expanding the firm's range of insurance offerings. Previously, the firm had sold combination life, sickness, and accident policies on an "industrial" basis. Industrial insurance was a device whereby the poor, by paying small weekly premiums, were able to afford insurance policies. It was more expensive for the policyholder, and more costly for the company to administrate, since the agent had to "make the rounds" each week to collect the premiums. Now, however, Spaulding began to offer the option of industrial "straight life" policies, without the sickness and accident benefits, and in 1904 introduced its first ordinary whole life plans and twenty-year endowment plans. North Carolina Mutual was becoming a full-line life insurance company.

In that same year the three men made another important decision for the future growth of the company—they decided to erect a new office building. They at first considered building it in Hayti, the center of the black community, where most of the rest of their real estate investments were located, but ultimately decided to build a handsome brick edifice on Parrish Street on the edge of the white-dominated downtown. Within two years, the company had purchased additional lots and added to the building, forming a large black business complex there. It contained, besides the offices of the insurance company, the domicile of the Royal Knights of King David, the Oddfellows, two black lawyers, Dr. Moore's medical offices, two clothing stores, a barber shop, a large drugstore, a tailoring shop, offices of the black newspaper, and the Mechanics and Farmer's Bank. In 1920, when Spaulding decided to improve this complex, he built a magnificent marble-trimmed, ultramodern, six-storied office building which the company moved into in 1921. It was a vitally important symbol of the importance of North Carolina Mutual to Durham's black community. As Walter Weare has commented:

As long as it stood six stories tall as a black institution in a southern town of squat warehouses and dimestores, and in the white rather than in the black business district, it commanded attention. . . . It came to represent in the white mind a self delusory promise of what the black community might be.

Spaulding had shepherded North Carolina Mutual through a decade of impressive growth by 1911. By that time the firm had premium income of about $250,000, assets of nearly $120,000, insurance in force of over $2 million, and nearly 500 employees. It was hardly big business, but it was an impressive institution in the newly emergent black business community of the New South. By this time, too, North Carolina Mutual had helped the black community of Durham found Lincoln Hospital and set up a library, North Carolina Central College, and three newspapers. It also lent invaluable support to the area's African-American churches, especially the Baptists, with which Spaulding was affiliated. Also, as Spaulding hired increasing numbers of bright college graduates, a thriving black intellectual community began to flourish in Durham. As early as 1903 the town supported an African-American literary society, which was soon joined by a myriad of others. Durham had more than its share of the "talented tenth" of black society.

The next two decades witnessed continual growth by the dynamic company. It survived John Merrick's death with barely a ripple, in 1920, and continued to expand and grow more profitable during the first half of the next decade, but problems in southern agriculture forced cutbacks after 1926. Insurance in force in 1929 stood at $39 million, down from $46 million in 1926. To address this problem, Spaulding instituted an austerity program to meet the rising demand for policy loans and surrender values, which became particularly severe during the depression years of the 1930s. The Great Depression severely tested North Carolina Mutual's and Spaulding's mettle, and they passed the test with flying colors. By 1939 insurance in force had recovered to surpass the previous peak year of 1925, while premium income was restored very nearly to that prior level. Surviving the Depression added greatly to the already healthy mystique of North Carolina Mutual in the black community.

During World War II and the postwar years, North Carolina Mutual grew rapidly under Spaulding's guidance. By the time of his death, the firm had assets of nearly $38 million, and insurance in force of over $179 million. It was at that time, and remained for a number of years, the largest black business in the United States. A longtime member of the National Negro Business League, Spaulding rescued that failing organization in 1938 and served as its president for a number of years. He was also a founder of the somewhat less successful Negro Insurance Association in 1921, vice president of Bankers Fire Insurance of Durham, and a member of the National Negro Bankers Association. Because of the great success of North Carolina Mutual, and the way in which Spaulding dominated the firm after the mid–1920s, most people thought he was a multimillionaire. The *New York Times* at his death called him "One of the Richest U.S. Negroes." But, in fact, he was a salaried employee all of his life, owned no stock in the firm, and amassed far less wealth than most people assumed. At his death his estate was estimated at a comfortable, but not staggering, $200,000.

As long as he lived, though, there was never any question that C. C. Spaulding dominated North Carolina Mutual, despite the fact that he had assembled an exceptionally able cadre of executives to aid him. Viola Turner, longtime secretary at the firm, who later became treasurer and director, told Walter Weare:

There was never nobody behind C. C. Spaulding. C. C. Spaulding was his own man in every way. The only somebody that governed him just a teensey weensey little bit was his wife, Mrs. Charlotte Spaulding [his second wife, whom he married in 1920]. And when I say teensey weensey, I mean teensey weensey.

One of the great sources of Spaulding's power both within and outside the company was his contacts with influential whites. William Clement, longtime executive vice president of the firm, said:

C. C. Spaulding built North Carolina Mutual by being Mr. Cooperation. He knew how to deal with white people. And he knew how to select men and put them in positions to carry out a task, and he stayed out in front, in the public image, and developed North Carolina Mutual.

If Spaulding was not extremely wealthy, he was extremely powerful and important—and not just within the confines of North Carolina Mutual. He was, as Weare noted, a race leader, and this was manifested in a number of important ways. One of the most significant of these was in the area of education. Here Spaulding formed a close alliance with James E. Shepard, one of the early founders of North Carolina Mutual and president of North Carolina Central College. Shepard had been an important leader in Fusion politics in North Carolina, but after founding North Carolina Central became the almost quintessential accommodationist black leader. Serving until 1947, Shepard along with Spaulding patronized, flattered, and cajoled influential white legislators to get sufficient appropriations for the school over the decades. Spaulding also served on the boards of trustees of Howard University and Shaw University, and over the years he campaigned to save many financially strapped black colleges from extinction.

The Depression of the 1930s energized Spaulding's political instincts and sympathies in new ways. He became a fervent supporter of Franklin Roosevelt's New Deal, and he was a key figure in leading blacks from the Republican to the Democratic party in North Carolina. He early became an advocate of black political participation in Durham and in North Carolina, and soon he began to acquire political influence on both the state and national levels. The governor of North Carolina appointed Spaulding to the state Council on Unemployment and Relief, and he became national chairman of the Urban League's Emergency Advisory Council. Spaulding also cultivated access to President Roosevelt's "black cabinet," by which he was able to help southern blacks get federal jobs and to assist black property owners in acquiring federal farm loans. Spaulding soon came to be recognized as the leading black Democrat in North Carolina.

Spaulding's most important political and community contribution, however, came with his leadership of the Durham Committee on Negro Affairs (DCNA). Organized in 1935, the group frankly stated that its goal was to put the vote in the hands of blacks. According to political scientist Everett C. Ladd, Jr., the DCNA became the South's most effective "peak organization," designed to push for black political, economic, and civil rights victories. It was strikingly effective in bringing about political and social reforms for blacks, and Spaulding termed his own role as a "shock absorber between the races." Part of his success always lay in the fact that, for the white community, he posed as more conservative than he actually was; and, for the black community, he appeared more radical than he wished to be. For whites he was always expressing aphorisms that reeked of patriotism and sycophancy. In 1948, for example, Spaulding wrote an article entitled "What America Means to Me." In it, he said, "I shall always feel grateful that my ancestors were transplanted to North America. It is the best place in the world that I have found to live and work." Five years earlier, he had assured white America that blacks did not desire social equality, but just wanted a chance to succeed on their own turf—the old Booker T. Washington* philosophy. This did much to soothe white fears and allowed Spaulding, like his mentor Washington, to extract money from their pockets, along with compromises on a variety of social and political issues. Whites often referred to C. C. Spaulding as "Mr. Cooperation," but he did remind them that cooperation "does not mean Negroes do the co-ing whites did the operating." On other occasions Spaulding commented, "It takes both the black and white keys to play the Star Spangled Banner." Behind the scenes, Spaulding often encouraged more radical black organizations to make threats to frighten whites, while in the background he "stroked the big whites."

When C. C. Spaulding died in 1952, it was front-page news in Durham and the surrounding area. E. J. Evans, the mayor of Durham, in an unprecedented move, issued a proclamation in which he declared the day of Spaulding's funeral to be "a day of respect to the memory and works of Dr. Spaulding." His funeral, said to be the largest ever held in the city, was attended by some 3,000 persons who overflowed the White Rock Church auditorium, lawn, and sidewalks. It was perhaps fitting that Dr. Mordecai Johnson, president of Howard University, in his memorial address at the rites said he did not come to grieve Spaulding, but to build upon his heritage. Johnson used the occasion to deliver a blistering attack on the institutions of white racism in the South and cautioned Americans to improve the situation for its 15 million blacks, "lest the brown races of the world turn to some nation other than ours."

In 1980 C. C. Spaulding became the first black to be inducted into the national Business Hall of Fame by *Fortune* magazine and Junior Achievement. William Clement, an executive at North Carolina Mutual, idolized Spaulding: "So, C. C. Spaulding was a great man. Yeah, he was my man. They've never developed another man like C. C. Spaulding. . . . Oh, he built it, he built it. We've never had an entrepreneur like C. C. Spaulding." Even more succinctly, William J. Kennedy III, the sixth president North Carolina Mutual, said of Spaulding: "He had charisma."

With Spaulding's death, as with John Merrick's a generation earlier, the transition to new leadership caused barely a ripple. During that latter generation another triumvirate had ruled North Carolina Mutual. During the first twenty-five years, it was John Merrick, Dr. A. M. Moore, and C. C. Spaulding; after 1925, it was C. C. Spaulding, William J. Kennedy, Jr., and Asa T. Spaulding.

The connecting link in those two triumvirates that ruled North Carolina Mutual for nearly seventy years was C. C. Spaulding.

William Jesse Kennedy, Jr., was another of the extraordinary men who were attracted to North Carolina Mutual. He was born in Andersonville, Georgia, in 1898, to a unique family. His grandfather was a huge, six-foot, eight-inch, slave-craftsman who continued to build bridges after emancipation. Over time, the grandfather was able to develop a substantial family farm of some 400 acres. Young William took up his family's carpentry trade, but he also received a good education, graduating from the Americus Institute, a Baptist academy in Americus, Georgia. Kennedy then worked several years as a carpenter and traveling salesman. He then went to Savannah, where he sold insurance for another black firm. In 1916 the directors of North Carolina Mutual convinced Kennedy to become manager of their Savannah office. During the three years he ran the office, revenues in Savannah increased 500 percent. Following Merrick's death in 1919, the head office asked Kennedy to come to Durham to manage the Ordinary Department. William Clement, whose father, Arthur J. Clement was head of the Charleston office of North Carolina Mutual at this time, claims that "there was a struggle between the Merrick family and the Spaulding family, which really got the Kennedys involved." In any event, in 1917, Kennedy married Margaret Lillian Spaulding, sister of C. C. Spaulding, and the business remained in the complex family web being woven at North Carolina Mutual during these years.

In 1920 Kennedy advanced to the board of directors, and in 1923, after the death of Dr. Moore, Kennedy emerged as the new third man of the triumvirate. He served as assistant secretary and office manager under John Moses Avery during the 1920s, until he became a master of the entire operation. And this was always Kennedy's forte: He was an organization man, a detail man. C. C. Spaulding had a great flair for salesmanship and public relations, but as Kennedy's son has said, "While C. C. was president, he was Mr. Mutual to the public, but my father was the inside man. He was a stickler for proper corporate form—minutes, ledgers, journals. He's largely responsible for the systems and records we've developed." One of the results of Kennedy's passion for details and written records was the company history he published in 1970.

In any event, during the thirty years before he ascended to the presidency, Kennedy was the firm's principal problem solver. He handled much of the correspondence, dealt with personnel problems, set up communication systems between departments, and generally managed the firm during these difficult years. Even in the early 1920s Dr. Moore praised Kennedy as a "Moses sent to North Carolina Mutual." A decade later, Asa Spaulding wrote to Kennedy: "I often wonder what would have been the history of the company for the last decade without your stabilizing influence." During the 1930s Kennedy was corporate secretary of the firm, and in 1932 he was also named vice president and helped C. C. Spaulding steer the company through that turbulent decade.

In 1952 Kennedy succeeded C. C. Spaulding as president. His ascension had little impact, since he had, in effect, been running the day-to-day operations of the firm for decades anyway. There was a new, quieter style to the head office of North Carolina Mutual, but otherwise things did not change much. During Kennedy's seven-year term as president, North Carolina Mutual grew significantly, as assets increased from nearly $38 million to over $67 million. Insurance in force went from $179 million to $337 million. As Walter Weare has noted, "The mood of the Mutual during the 1950's was quiet, steady, and optimistic— much like the man who ran the company." Yet, by the 1960s, the life of blacks in America was on the verge of a massive transformation, and this upheaval would have an impact upon North Carolina Mutual and Kennedy's successor as president. Kennedy, who advanced to the chairmanship of the board of directors in 1959, was succeeded as president by Asa T. Spaulding. Although he served as chairman for only two years, becoming honorary chairman, Kennedy was hardly a figurehead in his new position; he took a remarkably active role in virtually every aspect of the firm. He was also chairman of the board of Mechanics and Farmers Bank and of the Mutual Savings and Loan Association. Like C. C. Spaulding, Kennedy was involved in community issues outside the firm, but he performed them in his generally less visible way. He was a member of the North Carolina State Board of Higher Education, trustee and treasurer of the White Rock Baptist Church, and one of the founders of the NAACP in Durham. In 1977 he was honored at its Freedom Fund Dinner. He died in 1985.

Kennedy's successor, Asa T. Spaulding, was the second cousin of C. C. Spaulding, and Dr. A. M. Moore was his great-uncle. Asa Spaulding, like those two men, was born in Columbus County, North Carolina, son of Armstead and Annie Bell (Lowery) Spaulding. His mother's first husband was A. McL. Moore, a relative of Dr. Moore. Spaulding's father operated a farm, but he was also a businessman who ran a general store, cut timber, and operated a still that produced turpentine and rosin. Asa Spaulding was educated in a one-room school in his home community, but the level of education he received was not of the highest quality. Very early he displayed an uncanny ability to "figure in his head," and his great-uncle, Dr. Moore, soon heard of him. As Spaulding tells it, Moore on one of his return visits to his hometown confronted Spaulding's father: "What are you going to do with that boy? Where's he going to school now?" "Well, he's thinking about going to Biddle," Spaulding's father replied. "Why don't he come to Durham? I'll take charge of him," commanded Moore. And so he did. Spaulding came to Durham in 1919, where he enrolled in the National Training School, a private institution. This was the same year that Kennedy came to Durham.

Asa Spaulding got a tuition scholarship to attend school, and he stayed with Dr. Moore and his family doing odd jobs to earn room and board. During the summers Spaulding worked for the insurance company. In 1923, when he graduated, he received every honor the school could bestow. Spaulding then returned to Columbus County to teach at his old one-room school. Within a year, however, he was back working at North Carolina Mutual, and in 1924 he went to Howard

University for a semester. Again, Spaulding returned to North Carolina Mutual to work and save money for his education, and in 1927 he enrolled at New York University to study accounting. At that time there was only one black CPA in the entire country, and Dr. Saul B. Ackerman, one of Spaulding's professors, suggested that he consider becoming an actuary—a specialist in the calculations related to mortality and life expectancy. There was not a single black actuary in the United States at that time, and North Carolina Mutual itself, which was not equipped to do its own actuarial tables, farmed that work out to a white consulting firm. It had seemed an insurmountable hurdle for years to black-owned insurance companies. As M. S. Stuart commented, "The belief was prevalent that the standard of actuarial qualification was so rigid it could only be reached by persons of extreme mathematical genius. Actuaries were regarded as rare and infallible supermen."

When Spaulding presented his plans to North Carolina Mutual, they were delighted with the idea, and after getting his B.S. in accounting at New York University, he went to graduate school at the University of Michigan to study actuarial science. Spaulding got his master's degree in actuarial science in 1932, at which time he served an apprenticeship first at the renowned actuarial firm of Haight, Davis, and Haight, and then with F. B. Dilts, actuary of the white Home Security Life Insurance Company in Durham. In January 1933, Spaulding joined North Carolina Mutual, establishing and staffing the actuarial department and becoming its supervisor. As Walter Weare said, Spaulding came to North Carolina Mutual in 1933 carrying a message: "Like Jackie Robinson a decade later, he was one of the celebrated 'Negro Firsts' . . . he was the heroic black tactician on his way to battle. Perfecting the operations of the North Carolina Mutual, ostensibly a mundane task, was a symbolic act of improving the race and another exemplary lesson for white folks."

Undoubtedly Asa Spaulding's contributions to the Mutual during the depression decade were not as heroic as some saw them, but they were crucial in many respects. As he once commented, "One of the first things I had to deal with was that the mortality among our policyholders had always exceeded our life expectancy figures . . . the premium was not adequate to take care of expenses and set up a reserve . . . we set up an underwriting committee, consisting of the medical director, the claims supervisor and the actuary. . . . No policy was issued if I rejected an application." Without his insights and expertise, the firm probably would have continued its marginal existence of the last half of the 1920s. He had worked such a remarkable transformation in his first two years as actuary that, in 1935, Asa Spaulding was elected assistant secretary, just one notch behind W. J. Kennedy in the organization chart. Three years later he became the youngest member of the board of directors. In 1945 Spaulding became controller of the firm, and in 1952 he advanced to the post of vice president. Finally, in 1959, Asa Spaulding assumed the presidency of North Carolina Mutual and served until his own retirement in 1967.

One of Spaulding's great accomplishments during his presidency was the completion of a new twelve-storied office building in 1966. Built on the highest point in Durham, it is situated on a site formerly occupied by the mansion of James B. Duke. It was, to that point, the largest private building ever constructed in Durham. The dedication was attended by dignitaries from across the nation. And, when some commented that the North Carolina building was the biggest in Durham, Asa Spaulding feigned surprise and remarked, "Way over there's Duke University, Chapel Hill and American Tobacco. Our building the biggest in Durham? You have to judge for yourself, 'cause we don't brag." But if the new building and glamorous dedication ceremonies impressed whites, they alienated some blacks. They were upset that the formal banquet was held at the Gothic "Great Hall" at Duke University, and that white dignitaries like Vice President Hubert H. Humphrey and North Carolina Governor Dan K. Moore dominated the scene. To many blacks, who were becoming increasingly militant in the late 1960s, it seemed as if they had been shut out—North Carolina Mutual was becoming more a firm devoted to success in the white marketplace than a black institution devoted to improvement of the race.

North Carolina Mutual, despite the fact that integration and civil rights crusades had caused white insurance companies to hire more blacks and also to write more insurance for blacks, continued to grow impressively. With assets of just over $60 million in 1958, and $255 million of insurance in force, by 1968 there were over $94 million in assets and $467 million in insurance in force. By 1968 the company served some 800,000 policyholders through thirty-six branch offices.

Asa Spaulding, like his cousin, C. C. Spaulding, became a dynamic force in race relations and politics in Durham and the nation during his lifetime. Unlike C. C., however, Asa Spaulding was living in a more complex and volatile time, and perhaps he was not as astute in his ability to walk a fine line between powerful whites and militant blacks. As a result, he came under a great deal more criticism, especially from blacks. Upon C. C.'s death, Asa, who inherited his mantle, sat on the Durham Human Relations Committee, serving as vice chairman from 1957 to 1964, was chairman of the North Carolina Advisory Committee to the Commission on Civil Rights, and was on the subcommittee of the voluntary home mortgage credit program of the Federal Housing and Home Finance Agency. He tried during most of this period to work behind the scenes as his predecessor had successfully done. In October 1957, he wrote to Rencher N. Harris, a North Carolina executive and the first black city councilman in Durham, telling him that he wished "to meet with a small interracial group and quietly and dispassionately discuss matters that might tend to disturb the peace and harmony of our community." Those days of backroom negotiations in Durham, however, were very nearly at an end.

In 1954 Asa Spaulding made his first try for elected office, running for county commissioner, but he was not successful. After he retired Spaulding again made a run at the county commission seat, and this time he was successful, becoming the first black in history to be elected to the position, despite the fact that the

county was 70 percent white and only 30 percent black. But he found himself
under increasing pressure from black groups during these years for not being
militant enough. In 1971 he ran for mayor of Durham but was not successful.
In 1967 Spaulding had joined with other wealthy black business leaders in
forming the National Negro and Professional Committee, an attempt to raise $1
million to finance lawsuits for the NAACP to gain enforcement of civil rights
legislation. Later, his wife, Elna Spaulding, was elected county commissioner
and served from 1974 to 1984. Their son, Kenneth Spaulding, became a powerful
figure in the Durham Committee on the Affairs of Black People, and he served
in the North Carolina legislature. Both of them, like Asa Spaulding, ran into
charges of being too accommodationist. Asa Spaulding's advice to his wife when
she ran for office was, ''The best role you can play is that of a mediator, arbitrator.
You have the protagonists on both sides. If you line up with either side, you'll
destroy your effectiveness and credibility with the other.'' That, of course, was
the old C. C. Spaulding technique, but it did not work nearly as well in the
world of the highly charged racial politics of the 1970s.

Asa Spaulding won an impressive number of awards during his lifetime.
Perhaps dearest to him was when Howard University, which he served as head
of the board of trustees, renamed their insurance society the Asa T. Spaulding
Insurance Society. He was also a trustee at Shaw University. Spaulding represented the United States at the inauguration of President William Tubman of
Liberia, and he made a trade tour of Central America for the secretary of commerce. His speech, ''Discrimination and the Negro in the United States,'' originally delivered in India, was reprinted in the *Congressional Record* and was
much quoted by people over the years. Despite his honors, and the magnificent
work he did for North Carolina Mutual during his lifetime, not everyone in the
firm was impressed with his contributions. Just as in politics, some people felt
he was looking out for his own interests. This was expressed by William Clement,
who commented, ''Asa was a 'different breed.' Asa was selfish, and he built
himself.''

One of the problems that Asa Spaulding and the other leaders of North Carolina
Mutual had by the late 1960s was the extent to which it was still actually a black
institution. Beginning in 1969, just about a year after Asa Spaulding turned the
presidency of the company over to John Goodloe, the Mutual signed a number
of large group insurance contracts with such corporate giants as IBM, General
Motors, Chrysler, Procter & Gamble, Sun Oil, and Atlantic Richfield. This
brought about a massive increase in insurance in force for the firm, the largest
increase it had ever experienced. By 1971 insurance in force, which stood at
$483 million two years earlier, had soared to over $1 billion. About $400,000
of the increase came from those group contracts. Walter Weare caught the
dilemma the Mutual and its officers faced: ''The Mutual now possessed a large
number of white policyholders, and conversely these now owned a part of the
Mutual. No longer could the company identify itself as black-owned.''

Although this factor made it difficult for Asa Spaulding or his successors to adopt radical black stances, and they therefore came under a good deal of criticism from those farther to the left, it is instructive just how well they have maintained power. The key to black political power in Durham, and equally the key to the continuing influence of the Mutual, is the Durham Committee on Negro Affairs. Begun in 1935 by C. C. Spaulding, it has always been dominated by the "Parrish Street Gang," as the officials of North Carolina Mutual were called. Nonetheless, the local black newspaper, the *Carolina Times*, which is usually well to the left of Spaulding and the other officers of the Mutual, has enjoyed a cordial relationship with the Mutual elite, which has done much to ensure that the committee remained focused on the problems of the poor blacks of the city. A key player on the Durham Committee during the 1970s and 1980s was Kenneth Bridgeforth Spaulding, son of Asa. He also served in the North Carolina legislature, quite openly representing the "business wing" of the Durham Committee. As such, he forged close ties with white developers in the area, which enraged his white liberal allies. He apparently has retained the support of most African-Americans.

William J. Kennedy III, son of W. J., Jr., became the seventh Mutual president in 1972. Born in Durham, he went to area schools and graduated from Virginia State College in 1942. After limited action in World War II, he earned an MBA from Wharton School at the University of Pennsylvania in 1946, and a second MBA from New York University in 1948. William Kennedy then joined his father at North Carolina Mutual, where he worked his way through various departments. He was named controller in 1959, vice president in 1970, and president and chief executive officer two years later. Kennedy was still at the helm twenty years later. Since the company had so many white clients, Kennedy hired increased numbers of white insurance salespeople to service this market, which incurred the rancor of many African-American groups.

By 1989 North Carolina Mutual had $215 million in assets, and insurance in force of $7.9 billion, making it far and away the largest black-managed insurance company in the world. Since it was a mutual firm, though, which meant policyholders were also shareholders in the company, the actual ownership of the firm by then rested in the hands of white corporate giants. North Carolina's growth during the 1980s had been slow, and Kennedy decided that the problem was the firm's old staple—industrial insurance. His remedy was to begin phasing it out, and he also moved toward an important diversification of the company.

In 1986 Kennedy set up NCM Capital, an investment advisory firm that planned to pursue aggressively the massive pension and corporate fund management business. "We see a need to develop another vehicle to help us diversify into mutual funds and pension management," Kennedy has explained. By 1990 NCM Capital was managing $500 million worth of assets for thirty clients, including Chrysler, IBM, and the Chicago Transit Authority. Other attempts at diversification have been less successful. In 1988 North Carolina Mutual had to write off a $3 million investment in Rolling Hills, a 170-unit Durham residential subdivision. On the other hand, it met with success with the $500,000 twenty-six-unit Ivy Arms project in Winston-Salem, and it has become involved in a venture to develop cellular radio systems. But the company has retained an aura of social responsibility, as well, supporting United Durham Incorporated, a local community development group, in its plans to develop an industrial park near the Research Triangle. "My goal before I retire," Kennedy said in 1986, "is to get North Carolina Mutual in the top 100 companies in the country. We are already in the top 200, but I am working on getting us into the top 100."

Those ambitious men in 1898 who founded North Carolina Mutual had grand visions and plans for how the company would become a powerful economic institution; would form the basis of a strong local, regional, and national black economy; would uplift the black race; and would prove to whites once and for all that blacks could achieve success in every way. As they looked down on the company in 1992 they must have been elated and saddened at the same time. The growth and economic prosperity of North Carolina Mutual surely have exceeded their wildest fantasies. And certainly the creation of a solid, black, middle class in the city and elsewhere is satisfying, as is the fact that the firm handles so much white business. North Carolina Mutual has been more substantially integrated into white society than they could have dared hope in the dark days of 1898. Yet, the insurance firm has not "uplifted" the race or solved all its problems. Poverty remains a severe problem, violence and social disorganization are a tragic legacy. "Race men," like Merrick, Moore and Spaulding could not rejoice in that.

Sources

The Charles Clinton Spaulding Papers are in the possession of the North Carolina Mutual Insurance Company. Access is restricted to researchers. The Manuscript Department at William R. Perkins Library at Duke University has the papers of Asa T. Spaulding, but these are also restricted. There are a very few letters between Booker T. Washington or Emmett J. Scott and C. C. Spaulding in the Booker T. Washington Papers at the Library of Congress. There are also some items of interest on C. C. and Asa Spaulding and North Carolina Mutual in the W. A. Clement Papers and in the Southern Oral History Collection in the Southern Historical Collection at the University of North Carolina in Chapel Hill. The Rancher Nicholas Harris Papers and the James Richard Young Papers at Duke University also have a number of letters to or from the two Spauldings. Also of value is the collection of materials by William J. Kennedy, also held at North Carolina Mutual. Asa T. Spaulding was interviewed by Walter Weare. The interview is in the Southern Oral History Collection at the University of North Carolina.

Biographical material on both the Spauldings in voluminous, since each seemed to cultivate publicity and the press with a fine hand. C. C. Spaulding biographies include: Sylvia M. Jacobs, *Dictionary of American Negro Biography* (1982); Arvarh E. Strickland, *Dictionary of American Biography* (1977), supplement 5; Walter Weare, "C. C. Spaulding: Middle Class Leadership in the Age of Segregation," in *Black Leaders of Twentieth Century America*, edited by John Hope Franklin and August Meier (Urbana, *National Cyclopedia of American Biography* (1958); XLII, 449; *Who's Who in Colored America*: Ingham, BDABL; Edgar A. Toppin, *Biographies of Black Americans* (1971), 413–14; J. A. Rogers, *World's Great Men of Color*, vol. II (New York, 1947), 679–81; M. W. Williams and George W. Watkins, *Who's Who among North Carolina Baptists* (1940) 366–67; William S. Powell, *North Carolina Lives* (1962), 1142–43. Obituaries appear in the *New York Times*, August 2, 1952; *Norfolk Journal and Guide*, August 9, 1952; *Carolina Times*, August 9, 1952; *Negro History Bulletin* XVI (December 1952); *Time*, August 11, 1952; *Durham Morning Herald*, August 2, 1952; *Durham Sun*, August 1, 1952, and August 4, 1952; *Journal of Negro History* XXXVII, 4 (October 1952); *The Carolinian*, August 9, 1952; *Raleigh News and Observer*, August 2, 1952; *New York Daily News*, August 2, 1952; and the *Greensboro Daily*, August 13, 1952. See also *Who's Who of the Colored Race*, (1915).

For speeches and writings of C. C. Spaulding see "Life Insurance and Its Benefits," National Negro Business League, *Annual Report* (1915), 114–19; "Dangerous Tendencies in Negro Business," *The Messenger*, July 1927; "Is the Negro Meeting the Test in Business?" *Journal of Negro History* XVIII, 1 (January 1933), 66–70; "What This Country Means to Me," *American Magazine* (December 1948); "Fifty Years of Progress in Business," *Pittsburgh Courier*, 1950 Commemorative Issue; "The Administration of Big Business," *Pittsburgh Courier*, August 13 and 20, 1927; "Business in Negro Durham," *Southern Workman* LXVI, 12 (December 1937); "Business Is My Business," *Negro Digest* I (February 1943), 32–33.

There is an extensive clipping file on C. C. Spaulding in the North Carolina Collection Clipping File, University of North Carolina, Chapel Hill, Library, and in the clipping file in the Durham Public Library. Some other miscellaneous articles about C. C. Spaulding include Archibald Rutledge, "They Call Him 'Co-operation,' " *Saturday Evening Post*, March 27, 1943; *Fortune*, April 21, 1980; *Black Enterprise*, June 1976; and *Opportunity* V, 4 (April 1927).

Biographies on A. T. Spaulding appear in NACB, L, 581–83; John Seder and Berkeley G. Burrell, *Getting It Together* (1971) 192–204; *100 Years, 10 Men, 1871–1971* (n.p., n.d.), 335–37; William S. Powell, *North Carolina Lives* (1962), 1142; Auren Uris, *The Strategy of Success* (London, 1969), 79–94; *Durham Morning Herald*, March 27, 1960; and *Who's Who among Black Americans* (1990). There is a very brief obituary in *Jet* (September 24, 1990). There are large numbers of clippings on various aspects of A. T. Spaulding's life in the North Carolina Collection Clipping File at the University of North Carolina, Chapel Hill, Library, and at the Durham Public Library. Some of the more important of these include *Durham Morning Herald*, May 27, 1951, March 27, 1960, April 12, 1962, May 17, 1965, March 21, 1967, June 27, 1971, September 6 and 8, 1979, June 27, 1980, September 7, 1982, and July 29, 1984; *Durham Sun*, January 13 and 15, 1976, January 4 and 22, 1980, and August 8, 1983; *New York Times*, March 20, 1967; *New York Times Magazine*, July 23, 1967; *The Masonic Journal* XII 1 (Spring and Summer 1972); *Howard Underwriter* II, 2 (December 1979); *Ebony*, December 1984; *Black Enterprise*, June 1974, 141–47; *The Crisis*, May 1966; *Time*, February 7, 1964; *Sepia* 8, 1 (January 1960), 45; *Norfolk Journal and Guide*, December 12, 1952; *Christian Science Monitor*, September 16, 1960; *The Independent*, December 19, 1986, and January 15, 1987. A. T. Spaulding also did some writing on North Carolina Mutual and black business. See "Dedication Festival, March 28–April 2, 1966," and "Rising Insurance Firm a Symbol of Enterprise" (North Carolina Mutual brochure available at Perkins Library, Duke University).

William J. Kennedy, Jr.'s, papers are also held at North Carolina Mutual. For biographical material on the Kennedys, see *The Carolina Times*, August 8, 1953; *Durham Sun*, April 1, 1959; *Atlanta Daily World*, June 18, 1976; *Minorities and Women in Business*, July-August 1986; *The Ebony Success Library* I (Chicago, 1973) 190; *Ebony*, September 1955 and June 1966; *Black Enterprise* December 1979, 57–59, and June 1990,

214–18; *Business Week*, November 11, 1972; *Who's Who in Black America*, (1990); and *Who's Who among North Carolina Negro Baptists* (1940). An obituary of William J. Kennedy, Jr., appeared in the *New York Times*, July 13, 1985. William J. Kennedy, Jr., did much writing about North Carolina Mutual. See "Historical Sketch, 1899–1949, North Carolina Mutual Life Insurance Company, Durham N.C." and "The Negro's Adventures in the Field of Life Insurance" (North Carolina Mutual Life Insurance Company, 1984), both in the Peabody Collection of Hampton University, available on microfilm. William J. Kennedy III is treated briefly in Frank J. Johnson, *Who's Who of Black Millionaires* (1984), 128; and *Who's Who among Black Americans* (1990).

General articles on North Carolina Mutual and its allied firms are equally voluminous. There is a good deal of valuable information in William J. Kennedy, *The North Carolina Mutual Story* (1970), but by far the most incisive account is Walter B. Weare, *Black Business in the New South: A Social History of the North Carolina Mutual Life Insurance Company* (1973). See also Jesse Edward Gloster, "North Carolina Mutual Life Insurance Company: Its Historical Development and Current Operations," Ph.D. diss., University of Pittsburgh, 1955. Shorter, often laudatory treatments of the firm and its executives can be found in both the black and white press. See, for example, *National Cyclopedia of the Colored Race* (Montgomery, Alabama, 1919), 344–46; *Norfolk Journal and Guide*, November 11, 1910, February 3, 1917, January 16, 1918, and February 14, 1920; *New York Age*, February 21, 1920, and October 8, 1920; *Atlanta Independent*, February 10, 1917; *Brown American*, July 1940; *The Crisis*, April 1941; *Ebony*, September 1955 and June 1966; *Durham Sun*, April 1, 1959; *Business Week*, November 11, 1972; *Atlanta Daily World*, June 18, 1976; *Black Enterprise*, December 1979, June 1981, June 1989, and June 1990

For information on the Wheeler family and the Mechanics and Farmers Bank, see *Atlanta Independent*, December 12, 1921; *Business Week*, May 16, 1964; *Durham Herald*, February 2, 1988; *Durham Sun*, June 21, 1989; *Black Enterprise*, June 1987, June 1989, and January 1990; *Minorities and Women in Business*, March-April 1989; *Who's Who among Black Americans* (1990). Financial statements for the bank are located at the Perkins Library, Duke University.

King, Horace (September 8, 1807–May 28, 1885). Covered bridge builder and contractor, Georgia and Alabama. On April 22, 1979, the city of Phenix, Alabama, through the joint efforts of the Russell County Historical Society and the Historic Chattahoochie Commission, erected a historical marker to Horace King. It was the first marker erected to an individual in Russell County, and Charles Tigner, the county historian, said, "Despite the fact that much has been written about Horace King, he was not generally known to the area. Having a marker to his name is a dream come true. . . . Our first attempts to get funds through the state failed." Who was Horace King, and why was there such a fuss about honoring his memory?

King, who was born a slave in the Chesterfield District of South Carolina, was the son of a mulatto slave named Edmund King and Susan or "Lucky," of Catawba Indian and African-American heritage. In 1829 Horace King's old master died, and, since his estate was insolvent, the family's slaves were sold. Horace King was purchased by Jennings Dunlop of Cheraw, South Carolina.

Within a short time, however, King was purchased again, this time by John Godwin, an experienced house builder and bridge contractor in the area. Perhaps Godwin already knew something of the twenty-two-year-old King's skills, which would explain why he made this fortuitous purchase; it is certain that he put them to use very quickly.

King began working alongside Godwin almost immediately. Godwin had been involved with the Connecticut architect, Ithiel Town, who had developed what was called the Town lattice truss, an innovative new procedure to build covered bridges using inexpensive common sawmill lumber and the labor of less experienced carpenter's gangs. Godwin had worked with Town when Town came to supervise the construction of a bridge over the Pee Dee River in 1822, using his new design. There is some evidence that King worked on this bridge, which may have originally brought Godwin and King together. In any event, it is fairly evident that, by the time King came to Alabama with Godwin in 1832, he was well acquainted with bridge building using the Town truss technique.

John Godwin, who was the son of a prominent South Carolina businessman, decided that he wished to seek his fortune on the frontier, reasoning that the crude road systems being built in Georgia, Alabama, and elsewhere, would need bridges to span the numerous rivers. In the early 1830s, when Godwin learned that the city of Columbus, Georgia, was planning to build a bridge to span the Chattahoochee River to connect it with the vast new area that would be ceded by the Creeks to the state of Alabama in the Treaty of Cuesseta in 1832, he decided to go after the contract. When the city of Columbus advertised for bids for a bridge in the local paper, Godwin submitted a bid which was quickly accepted by city officials. He and Horace King moved to Columbus in 1832 to commence construction of the bridge.

This was no simple task. As William H. Green has pointed out, "The Chattahoochee was not an easy river to span, particularly with the technology of 1832. Bridgebuilding was an art, not a science. The material was wood; construction machines were men and mules, axes, hammers, ropes, and wooden beams, and success depended upon the skill of one man, a master bridgebuilder who supervised the crews of carpenters, masons, and laborers." That man was Horace King. It is clear that from the very beginning that King was, in the words of Thomas L. French, Jr., and Edward L. French, "more of a junior partner in Godwin's company than a slave. Godwin developed proposals; King supervised construction."

Their first bridge, called the City Bridge, and later the Dillingham Street Bridge, was to use the Town patent, have stone piers, and be "built high, strong and of good materials." It was to cost $14,000. The completion of this bridge was quite an achievement on King's part, and it impressed everyone who used it. As William H. Green said, "[King] was a man who understood how to throw a two-hundred-yard bridge of wooden beams across swirling water, a man who was to construct most of the bridges across the Chattahoochee for a period of fifty years." With that success behind them, King and Godwin next built a 540-

foot-long bridge south of Columbus at Irwinton (Eufala), Alabama, at a cost of $22,000. This was followed by bridges at West Point, Georgia, in 1838–1839, Tallassee, Alabama, and perhaps another at Florence, Alabama, in 1839.

What distinguished the bridges of King and Godwin was the superior workmanship that was due largely to King's skill and ingenuity. His bridges were so well constructed that Godwin was able to guarantee them for five years, even against flood damage. Occasionally, of course, flood damage did occur, but Godwin then took full responsibility and repaired or replaced the damaged bridge. During his lifetime, including the period after he had his own independent business, King oversaw the construction of more than 25 bridges spanning 500 feet or more, along with about 100 shorter bridges. All of these were made with the Town lattice truss design, and all had exceptional strength and endurance.

During this same period when King and Godwin were building bridges, King also constructed a number of houses in conjunction with the Godwin firm in Girard (Phenix City), Alabama, and Columbus. King's ability to supervise such a diversity of massive construction projects, and to produce end products of such superior workmanship, attracted the interest of a number of southern businessmen. It is said that Godwin refused offers of $6,000 for King. This was an enormous sum in the 1840s, at a time when a fine home cost around $1,000. And, since Godwin later encountered severe financial difficulties, the offers for King must have been enormously attractive to him. In this case, at least, the old southern myth about paternalism and the love of master for slave and vice versa seems to have had some validity. Godwin would not sell King, and King always was more of a partner than a slave in their enterprises.

In the 1840s, however, King began working with Robert Jemison, Jr., a wealthy lawyer and state senator from Tuscaloosa, Alabama. Jemison had large plantations and a number of large and well-organized businesses, including a stagecoach company, a turnpike and bridge firm, and large sawmill operations. In the early 1840s Jemison began contracting with Godwin for bridges to be built in west Alabama. Jemison's mills furnished the lumber, Godwin supplied the work crews, and King supervised all the construction. In Lowndes County, Mississippi, where Jemison built seven bridges in the area to improve his transportation needs, Jemison often delayed the work until he could be certain that King would be available to design the bridge and supervise the construction. Jemison and King did much work together in the 1850s, after King became an independent businessman.

In 1839 King married Frances Thomas, a free-born black, who was part African-American, part Creek Indian, and part white. They had four sons and a daughter, all of whom ultimately joined Horace King in his bridge-building business. John Godwin was not so fortunate, however, as he suffered a series of business reversals in the 1840s. Godwin had badly overextended himself, and he was concerned that as his estate became entangled with lawsuits and creditors, someone might attach Horace King as part of his property. Godwin therefore arranged for his freedom. Godwin had Robert Jemison petition the Alabama

General Assembly for King's emancipation from slavery, and on February 3, 1846, by an act of the legislature, King was declared a free man. A short time later, the Georgia legislature took a related action, guaranteeing King's freedom in both states. Horace King was now free to bid on and build bridges without Godwin's participation, and he was encumbered with none of the other drawbacks connected to a condition of servitude.

Horace King bid on and completed many projects on his own during the 1850s, including a large bridge across the Flint River at Albany, Georgia. In this venture, Nelson Tift, a Georgia entrepreneur, secured the contract, and he hired King to oversee the construction. Some of King's most frequent and lucrative projects during that decade, however, were in conjunction with Jemison. Jemison was a member of the state Ways and Means Committee in Alabama, and this helped to steer a lot of work their way. In 1850–1851 the two men bid on construction for Madison Hall, a dormitory at the University of Alabama, but they were not successful. They also maintained a constant correspondence and consultation with one another, even when they were not doing a project together.

For example, King and Jemison began corresponding about submitting a bid for construction of the Alabama Insane Hospital in 1852. On December 9, 1852, Jemison wrote to King, ''I have no further information as to our Insane Hospital, at any rate nothing it would be prudent to trust to a very uncertain and often treacherous medium as a letter.'' Five days later Jemison wrote again, asking King, ''What would the additional cost of the machinery for making sash, doors, blinds—be[?] If you can give me any information as to cost, utility proffit [sic]— of such machinery I would be pleased to get it as early as convenient.'' They got the contract, one of the most massive undertaken in Alabama to that time, and completed it in 1860.

In 1853 the two men discussed whether to bid on building an additional dormitory at the University of Alabama. Jemison wrote in August 1853: ''If you would like to undertake this carpenters work either by yourself or jointly with me I would be pleased to have you do so. The job is small and may therefore suit you best to be unconnected with any other, if so have no delicacy or hesitancy in saying so.'' There was obviously a certain sense of respect, equality, and shared dignity between King and Jemison, just as there had been between Godwin and King. One might speculate that King was fortunate to encounter such fair-minded and generous men in the South of the 1850s, and indeed he was. But we must also be cognizant of the enormous ability and intelligence that Horace King demonstrated. These qualities seemed to allow him to transcend, even in the minds of die-hard southerners, the boundaries of involuntary servitude and white racism.

This was demonstrated when R. M. Patton of Florence, Alabama, who was interested in constructing bridges, inquired of Jemison as to competent bridge builders. Jemison responded on June 25, 1854: ''I would recommend to you Horace King a free mulatto (formerly the property of Mr. Jno. Godwin of Girard).

... I regard Horace as the best practicing bridge builder in the South. He has worked for me while bond and free. I have had extensive [dealings?] with him and have never dealt with or settled with a more correct and honest man of any color, and will seek him for the job you propose doing if not before any man I know." Jemison's letters to Horace King in 1852 were closed with "truly." By 1853 and thereafter, he closed with "your friend, R. Jemison, Jr." Horace King, on the other hand, was always much more cautiously deferential. Whereas Jemison's salutation was always "Dear Horace," King's was "Mr. Jemison, Dear Sir," and the closing was "Your humble servant," and this did not change as the years progressed. Even in the 1870s, when one might have thought some sort of social equality had been achieved between the two men, King did not alter his manner of address to Jemison.

Meanwhile, John Godwin's fortunes deteriorated during the 1850s. When he died in 1859, his estate was insolvent, largely because of the failure of the Girard-Mobile Railroad. The Godwin children, evidently as devoted to Horace King as was their father, were worried that King might be held accountable for their father's debts. Therefore they took one additional step to ensure his freedom; they recorded in the Russell County courthouse that "the said Horace King is duly emancipated and freed from all claims by us." Out of regard for his former master, King spent $600 erecting an imposing obelisk at his grave which reads: "This stone was placed here by Horace King in lasting remembrance of the love and gratitude he felt for his lost friend and former master." Ironically, this inscription was the brilliant Horace King's major claim to fame for nearly a century.

The fact of King's affection and devotion to his master was the stuff of folktales and legend in the post–Civil War South. Southerners continually used the fact of King's tombstone for Godwin to demonstrate that slavery was never the odious sort of institution that northerners claimed it was. Finally, Henry Moses took a picture of the gravestone and sent in to Robert Ripley's "Believe It or Not." Ripley wrote: "John Godwin has been dead for 82 years, and Horace King his faithful and devoted slave has long since crumbled to the same common dust, but as a reminder of both lives and their friendship and affection, the sturdy monument still stands steadfastly pointing toward heaven." Horace King became a perhaps unwitting endorsement of the South's "peculiar institution."

King was in Ohio being inducted into the Masons, since the branch in his home state would not allow him to join, when the Civil War broke out. He could have remained in the North, but his home, business, and family were in the Confederacy. Thus, he returned and managed the Godwin Sawmill and contracting business, while also operating his own firm in conjunction with his sons. These were difficult years for King. His wife died in 1864, and it was very taxing on him to run his own business and keep the Godwin enterprises running profitably. King did have a wealth of construction jobs during the war, but, like most southern businessmen, he was paid in Confederate currency, which lost value rapidly, and became worthless at war's end. King's descendants supposedly kept the Confederate money until the 1920s, when they decided to throw it out as "trash."

The two decades after the end of the Civil War brought good times for King and his family. All his sons, and his daughter, became partners in his business, forming King Brothers Bridge Company. As a team they rebuilt a number of bridges, factories, and other structures that had been destroyed during the war. Jemison again was a useful contact for much of this work. On February 22, 1867, he wrote to King: "I wish you to build the Bridge, also any mills. We have sold our R.R. to a company who will undertake to complete it to this point in three years. This will include the bridges across both the Tombiebie and Warrior Rivers besides sundry and minor bridges and a large amount of trestling. If you should want any of the contracts and I can serve you in any way I need not tell you it will afford me great pleasure to do so."

It was during this time that King was remarried, in 1869, to Sarah Jane McManus, and also became involved in politics, evidently against his own wishes in the latter instance. There is some discrepancy in the accounts, but King was evidently urged to run for the Alabama House of Representatives by white friends, who wished to counter the influence of more radical blacks and whites in the "black and tan" legislatures. King won election twice, without actively campaigning, and served from 1868 to 1872. He introduced several bills, including one for "the relief of laborers and mechanics" and one that required Russell County commissioners to use convict labor on public works and road projects. King was also a magistrate for Russell County for a time, served as registrar in Girard in 1870, and was compiler of the federal census in one portion of the county.

In the mid–1870s the King family moved from Alabama to LaGrange, Georgia. There King became involved in the work of the Freedman's Bureau, being particularly concerned with their education program. Citing his motto, "Ignorance breeds poverty," King wanted to establish a colony in Georgia where former slave men and women could study. It was to be essentially a trade school, not unlike what Booker T. Washington[*] would establish a few years later in Tuskegee, Alabama. It is not clear whether King's project ever got off the ground. Horace King and his children also acquired a great deal of property on the eastern side of LaGrange. There they built their gracious homes and maintained their shops and mills for their construction business. Many of the houses built in LaGrange after 1872 were built by King Brothers', and King Street in the city is named after Horace King.

King's company, of course, continued to build a large number of structures during this period. King Brothers' construction built a new chapel for the Southern Female College in 1875–1876 and also built the LaGrange Academy at about the same time. The academy was the city's first black school. By the early 1880s, King had largely retired from active business interests, but his sons and daughter continued running the business profitably. The key factors in the family firm after Horace King's death were his sons, John Thomas and George, and his daughter, Annie Elizabeth. John Thomas King was the guiding light of King Brothers' in his father's declining years and after. As a prominent contractor in LaGrange, he built many houses, bridges, and other buildings. Washington W. King, the oldest son, had been a member of the firm for many years, but when his father died, he moved to Atlanta, where he set up his own construction business. He built a number of important bridges in that area.

By the time Horace King died, however, the days of the covered bridge, of wood construction, and the Town truss were virtually over. Steel was rapidly replacing wood as the preferred material for bridges, and the Town lattice bridge, which had been so innovative when King learned it in 1832, was largely obsolete by the time of his death. His sons continued to build these bridges for years after his demise, but it was a declining craft, much admired for its beauty, but increasingly less practical as new materials and new methods took its place. The most famous of these bridges was the Glass Bridge that spanned the Chattahoochee River at West Point and was erected by John T. King and his brothers in the 1890s. Built on the old Town lattice truss design, it had seven spans resting on six piers of stone. The bridge was closed in 1954, but was still so sturdy that the only way it could be taken down was to burn it. Two of the covered bridges built by Washington King were still standing in the 1980s. The longest and most spectacular is the Watson Mill Covered Bridge, which became the focal point of Watson Mill State Park in Georgia. Another is the Stone Mountain Covered Bridge.

At the memorial for Horace King in 1979, Dr. Green summed up King's life and accomplishments with rare eloquence:

Horace King was a Southern Everyman, born a slave but winning his freedom, sprung from the three noble races of the early South. Laborer and legislator, his life was an astonishing symbolic bridge—a bridge not only between the states, but between men. Like one of his own stately Town lattice bridges, Horace King's life rises above the murky waters of historical limitation, of human bondage and racial prejudice. He did not change the currents of social history, but he did transcend them and stand as a reminder of our common humanity, the potential of the human spirit, the power of mutual respect.

Sources

There are a number of letters to and from Horace King in the Robert Jemison Papers at the University of Alabama Library, Special Collections. The official account of the legislative act securing King's emancipation is in the *Journal of the House of Representatives*, State of Alabama, Act Number 292, February 3, 1846, pp. 207–8. There is also a vertical file on Horace King at Chattahoochee Valley Community College, Phenix City, Alabama. The LaGrange Memorial Library in LaGrange, Georgia, has a scrapbook on Horace King composed by James G. Bogle for his article on Horace King, and the Reference Department, Bradley Memorial Library, Columbus, Georgia, has a Horace King Folder with various materials. Thomas L. French, Jr., of Columbus, Georgia, has also collected extensive materials, including a number of interviews and oral histories on King, for his research.

There are a number of good short biographies of Horace King: Thomas L. French,

Jr., and Edward L. French, "Horace King, Bridge Builder," *Alabama Heritage* 11 (Winter 1989), which is based on letters in the Jemison Papers, as well as on other materials; W. Warner Floyd, "Horace King Built Bridges to Freedom and Fame," *Down Home* (n.d), 48–49; Charles Tigner, "Russell Remembers a Master Bridge Builder," *Phenix Citizen*, May 4, 1979; James G. Bogle, "Horace King 1807–1887: Master Covered Bridge Builder," *Georgia Life* IV, 4 (Spring 1980), 33–35; Harold S. Coulter, *A People Courageous: A History of Phenix City, Alabama* (Columbus, Ga., 1976), 115ff.; and a biography by Thomas L. French, Jr., in *American National Biography* (forthcoming). There were obituaries in the *Atlanta Constitution*, May 30, 1885, and the *LaGrange Reporter*, June 4, 1885. See also Susie Fowler, "Hoarce King Gravesite, Found, Marked by Society," *LaGrange Daily News*, July 12, 1978. There are also several extensive, older, accounts of Horace King's life and career; for example, Rev. F. L. Cherry, "The History of Opelika and Her Agricultural Tributary Territory," *Opelika Times*, October 19, 1883. This has been reproduced several times, first by the Works Progress Administration, "Sketches of Alabama Towns and Counties: A Collection," vol. 3, supplement (Public Library, Birmingham, Ala., 1937); and in *Alabama Historical Quarterly* XV, 2 (1953), 193–97. See also *Birmingham News*, April 17, 1944; Jim Green, "Slave Famed for Bridges," *Columbus Ledger-Enquirer*, October 14, 1951; *Columbus Ledger*, June 9, 1982; State of Alabama, Department of History and Archives, "Negro Members of the Alabama House of Representatives and Senate, 1869–70, 1870–71, 1871–72, Horace King, Russell County"; and the *Montgomery Examiner*, February 19, 1948.

Other information on King, John Godwin, and covered bridges of the area is found in Etta Blanchard Worsley, *Columbus on the Chattahoochee* (Columbus, Ga., 1951), 405; Peter A. Brannon, "Bridges Then and Now," *Alabama Highways* II, 11 (February 1929), 6; Richard Saunders Allen, *Covered Bridges of the South* (1970); Thomas L. French, Jr., and Edward L. French, *Covered Bridges of Georgia* (1984); Tom Sangster and Dess L. Sangster, *Alabama's Covered Bridges* (1980); George Landry, "Covered Bridges Played a Colorful Role in Georgia, Alabama History," *Columbus Ledger-Enquirer*, October 1953. Accounts of historical plaques or other awards for Horace King are in *Phenix Citizen*, April 17 and 19, 1979; *Alabama Heritage*, 15 (Winter 1990), 47; *Montgomery Advertiser*, May 1, 1979.

L

Lafon, Thomy (December 28, 1810–December 22, 1893). Businessman and philanthropist. In most nineteenth-century cities, Thomy Lafon would have been part of the old "colored aristocracy." In New Orleans, with its long-entrenched Creole aristocracy, he was a bit of a parvenue, a man of "new money." The city's "Creoles of Color" were the wealthiest group of African-Americans in the United States prior to the Civil War. In 1836, 855 free persons of color in New Orleans paid taxes on property worth $2,462,470. This was an average of nearly $3,000 per property owner, and not far below that of the wealthiest whites in the same area. The great majority of New Orleans' free colored population had come to the city from Santo Domingo, and were mostly French-speaking, slaveholding mulattoes who had fled during the Haitian revolution. By 1850 fully 81 percent of the free black population in the city was mulatto, while very few slaves were of mixed blood. Skin color was an important badge of status in New Orleans.

The Creoles of New Orleans often called on a distinctive upper class culture that set them apart from the city's slaves. They lived in one section of the city, in magnificent, luxuriously furnished homes, were devout Catholics who attended St. Louis Cathedral, spoke flawless French, and sent their children to private academies. They were a highly educated and cultured people who viewed themselves as French before all else. They also identified so strongly with the dominant white society that they repeatedly participated in catching runaway slaves, uncovering slave plots, and suppressing revolts. Of course, since so many of them (nearly one-third) owned slaves, that behavior is perhaps not surprising.

Thomy Lafon shared most of these characteristics with his Creole cohorts, but his money was newer and his status was far less certain. Lafon, who left an estate when he died in 1893 of over $600,000, was born in poverty. To his benefit, however, he was born a member of Louisiana's *gens de couleur libres* (free people of color), which gave him an important status advantage over slave-born blacks. Little is known about his parents or his early life. His mother was Modest Foucher, probably of Haitian extraction, and his father was probably

Pierre Laralde, who may have been a Caucasian from France, or was at least of French extraction. It is not known where the surname Lafon came from. Both parents were free people of color, and although his father may have deserted the family when Thomy was still a child, Thomy was still somehow able to secure a fine education for the time. Lafon's fluency with languages, especially French and English, led to his assertion that he was partially educated in Europe. This claim was backed up in 1935 by Lafon's lawyer, Rene Metoyer, who said Lafon attended the School of Louis XIV in Paris. There is no other evidence to support the claim, but it is possible, since a large number of the city's Creoles did, in fact, go to France for part of their education.

Little else is known of Lafon's rise to wealth and success in the years prior to the Civil War. Popular accounts, or perhaps myths, have it that Lafon began his career selling cakes to the workmen along the wharves. It is more certain that he taught school for a time. In 1842, when he was thirty-two years old, he was listed as "T. Lafon, Merchant" in the New Orleans city directory, with a business at 387 Rampart Street. He does not appear in the directory again until 1861, when his business had moved to 97 Exchange Street. Melvin J. White, in the *Dictionary of American Biography*, states that Lafon was "operat[ing] a small store in Orleans Street" and that "just before the Civil War he began to lend his savings at advantageous rates" and to invest in real estate. Whether or not that was the case cannot be determined with complete assurance, but evidence indicates that he remained in business at the same location throughout the war, and then, in the 1867 directory, he was listed at a new business address at 16 Exchange Place, with his residence now listed separately at 242 Ursuline. A year later, for the first time, he is identified as a "broker" in the directory.

Whatever Lafon was doing during these years and whenever he began acting as a broker, it is clear that by 1870 he was a very rich man. In 1860 he held $10,000 worth of real estate, and over the following decade, despite the trauma of the war, he purchased $60,000 in property and sold $26,000, dealing mostly in swamplands. By 1870 he was worth $55,000. During the decade from 1871 to 1880, Lafon purchased $41,000 worth of property and sold $22,000, thereby further increasing his fortune. Later, he moved his office to 46 Royal Street, and after 1887 he either retired or else began operating his business out of his home, since only his home address at 242 Ursuline is listed in the directory.

One of the reasons Lafon was able to accumulate so much wealth during his lifetime is that he lived exceptionally frugally. Although his property included several very fine houses, he elected to live with his sister in a shabby-looking house on Ursuline Street. He never married, and he dressed as niggardly as he lived. Although always impeccably attired in a frock coat, a top hat of beaver, and a cane, his clothes were serviceable and inexpensive, rather than fashionable and expensive. Tall and gaunt, he was very light-skinned, with steel-grey, straight hair. Lafon also comported himself with utmost dignity, and was evidently revered by members of the Creole, white, and black races. The *Picayune* noted in his obituary that Lafon was "courteous to everyone, and maintained a gentlemanly bearing and dignity in all his transactions.'' He evidently held directorships in several banks, and supposedly the bank had a special chair reserved for him when he arrived to conduct his business affairs. Lafon, a devout Roman Catholic, was a highly cultured man, with an interest in music and art.

Although, as will be shown below, the extent of Thomy Lafon's philanthropies was exceptional, his business success was not. Numerous other Creoles had similar careers in New Orleans. The best-known free black businessperson in the 1830s and 1840s was a woman, Cécé McCarty, who had inherited $12,000 and built up a fortune of $155,000 in the importing business by the time she died in 1845. Merchant tailors in the city, such as Julian Colvis and Joseph Dumas, accumulated fortunes of $150,000 through that business and astute investments in real estate. Even wealthier was François LaCroix, another merchant tailor, who built a fortune of $242,000 during this time. Drosin McCarty, Cécé's son, who also operated as a real estate broker, was worth over $60,000. Bernard Soulie, a merchant broker and capitalist, had a fortune estimated at a half million dollars. Peter Casanave, an undertaker and commission merchant, inherited $10,000 from his white benefactor and built a fortune in excess of $100,000. Honore Pottier, a commission broker in cotton, had a fortune estimated at $200,000.

During the decade prior to the Civil War, the free colored population of the city was subject to a concerted attack on their status and privileges by the dominant white society. During this decade, the free black was considered a challenge to southern institutions and a potential threat to stability, so the city and state governments took steps to control many areas of their lives and freedoms. This was abetted by a savage attack in New Orleans by white newspapers on the free black, in which the dignified and highly cultured members of the Creole aristocracy were held up to ridicule and scorn. As a result, some free blacks began to emigrate from New Orleans, going to Haiti and Liberia. According to Robert C. Reinders, this involved the loss of a number of the most able potential leaders of the free black society, while the ones who remained went into ''hibernation.'' Sufficient numbers remained, however, to provide a potential cadre of leadership in the city when the Union troops invaded in 1862. These individuals, including Thomy Lafon, organized a campaign for increased rights and privileges for all blacks.

Lafon, along with Dr. Louis Roudanez, J. B. Roudanez, Aristede Mary, Victor Macarty, Paul Trivigne, and other Creoles, formed the leadership of the Radical Club in New Orleans. This group supported the Union troops upon their arrival in the city, and demanded the vote and access to white public schools for all blacks. They were also involved in supporting and running *The Tribune*, the first black-owned newspaper in the South after the war, and an unstinting advocate for black rights during this critical period. This movement, as in all southern states, was a failure, and as the rights of blacks began slipping away, the position of the old mulatto aristocracy also eroded.

Although a few members of the older black aristocracy did well financially during these years (John Racquet Clay increased his fortune from $5,000 to $21,500, and Drosin McCarty raised his from $45,000 to $77,300, and, of course, Lafon's increased enormously), the rest were either static or suffered a decline. Worst of all, for most of the members of this aristocratic group, was the loss of status. Whether their wealth remained the same, or even if it increased, they now found that white authorities lumped them into the same category as masses of ex-slaves.

The effect of this decline in status on members of the old aristocracy was traumatic. Three men—Jean Baptiste Jourdain, Aristede Mary, and John Racquet Clay—committed suicide out of despair for their declining financial situation or diminished social status. François LaCroix, once one of the wealthiest and most esteemed of the group, watched with a "vacant smile" as his estate was auctioned off to pay his debts. Facing an increasingly hostile world in New Orleans in the late nineteenth century, the old aristocracy retreated to nostalgia, geneology, and traditions: "The old community, forged before the war, whatever its infirmities, was all that many of the free coloreds had left, and they eagerly sought refuge within its narrow confines, where neither blacks nor whites were admitted."

Thomy Lafon evidently retreated more deeply into his private world, and into a world of philanthropy. He began giving more and more generously to various charities during his lifetime. Besides contributing to established charities, he also frequently assisted individuals whom he knew were in need. During his lifetime he established the Lafon Orphan Boys' Asylum and the Home for Aged Colored Men and Women, while also giving liberally to other charitable institutions. After his death, Lafon's will left an ample amount of money to care for his sister during the balance of her life, and some other monies and property were given to relatives, totaling $49,000 in cash, plus some property. The balance of $92,000 in cash and more than $500,000 in property was donated to a variety of institutions. Ample real estate was given to the Catholic Institute for the Care of Orphans and the Louisiana Asylum. He also left money for a hospital and for Straight [later Dillard] University and New Orleans University, in addition to the old folks home and to religious orders. It was the greatest benevolence left by a black to the city.

Thomy Lafon's generosity has not gone completely unrecognized. Although it is claimed that the Louisiana legislature authorized a bust to be cast of him, none was completed, and there is no record that it was ever authorized. His name, however, does grace a number of New Orleans institutions. In 1898 the Thomy Lafon Public School was completed and dedicated to him. It was the first school in the city to be named for a black man, and the second to be named for a black person.

Upon Thomy Lafon's death in December 1893, the *Daily Picayune* was moved to make the following tribute to him:

There passed away yesterday shortly after noon, one of the most remarkable and distinguished colored men in Louisiana. His name was Thomy Lafon, and owing to the immense real estate interests which he owned and controlled, in almost every section of the city, he was well-known to many. Not alone on account of his vast possessions, however, was he popular, for he was extremely charitable to all.

Thomy Lafon was, as Rudolphe Desdunes commented, "a true philanthropist."
Sources
    Very little information, published or otherwise, is available on Thomy Lafon. There is some rudimentary information on him in records at St. Louis Cathedral and at the City Hall in New Orleans. There is also a copy of his will in the office of the Clerk of the Civil District Court for the Parish of New Orleans. There are good, short biographies of him in *Dictionary of American Biography* V (1932, 1933) and *Dictionary of American Negro Biography* (1982), 546–47. The most detailed account, which stresses Lafon's philanthropy, is Charles E. Wynes, "Thomy Lafon: Black Philanthropist," *Midwest Quarterly* 22, 2 (1988), 105–12. There is also some useful information about him in Stella Weber, "History of Certain Charitable Donations in New Orleans," Master's thesis, Tulane University, 1935, 127–31; *Riders' Digest*, January 17, 1977; *Negro History Bulletin*, May 1941 and October 1943; Rudolphe Lucien Desdunes, *Our People and Our History*, trans., Dorothea O. McCants (Baton Rouge, 1973); James E. Winston, "The Free Negro in New Orleans, 1803–1860," *Louisiana Historical Quarterly* 21, 4 (October 1938), 1080; *Times Picayune*, February 21, 1988; and *Journal of Negro History*, January 1917 and April 1922. He is also mentioned in important economic and political contexts in John Blassingame, *Black New Orleans, 1860–1880* (Chicago, 1973); and Donald Everett, "Demands of the New Orleans Free Colored Population for Political Equality, 1852–1865," *Louisiana Historical Quarterly*, April 1955, 60–61, and "Free Persons of Color in New Orleans, 1803–1865," Ph.D. diss., Tulane University, 1952.

Lee, George W[ashington] (January 4, 1894–August 1, 1976). Businessman, political leader, association executive, fraternal leader, and author: Mississippi Life Insurance, Atlanta Life Insurance, Lincoln Republican League, National Negro Insurance Association, and Benevolent and Protective Order of Elks. George W. Lee had a myriad of accomplishments in business and politics, but he is remembered most for his connection with Memphis' famous Beale Street. Often called the "Sage of Beale Street," Lee made that street famous throughout the land as a center of African-American music and culture. His books were full of colorful stories of Beale's people and businesses, and his stories created a powerful portrait of the community. Lee himself was a regular fixture there, often seen strolling along its sidewalks with his wide-brimmed hat and a "loglike cigar" jutting out of his mouth. Just as Lee in many respects created Beale Street for America, he also created himself. Born a sharecropper's son in Mississippi, he became a black Horatio Alger, and in the process fashioned a mythic portrait of himself. A spellbinding orator, captivating writer, and a man always alert to the media, Lee did all he could to produce a powerful public image. He hired a clipping service to collect newspaper articles about himself, and when David M. Tucker was writing his biography, Lee cooperated fully, until he found that he could not control the final manuscript. He then withdrew permission to quote from his unpublished writings and ceased to cooperate. As Tucker commented, "Lieutenant Lee would have preferred a eulogy." By all accounts, however, he was a powerful, dynamic man who had a profound impact on the development of African-American business and politics in Memphis.

Four miles west of Indianola, Mississippi, in the tiny hamlet of Heathman, George W. Lee was born. His father, the Reverend George Lee, preached at the crossroads Negro Baptist Church on Sundays, and during the week he worked the land he purchased with the nickles and dimes his parishioners donated each week. Shortly after George was born, however, his parents separated, and not long after that Reverend Lee died. George's mother, Hattie Stringfellow Lee, was left to raise him and his older brother. The family farm was soon seized by Reverend Lee's brother, forcing Hattie Lee to move her family to a sharecropper's cabin, where, in return for planting the land, she received the cabin and a bare subsistence to buy cornmeal at the single plantation store. Hattie, the daughter of house servants, was hardly content with a future of fieldwork, so she made sure her sons received an education at the nearest country school.

Before long, Hattie sent her older son Abner to find a job in Indianola, where he was hired in the cotton-seed mill. Not long after, the owner of the land where she was sharecropping, ran Hattie and her family off the land, so the entire family joined Abner in Indianola. That town, which has become famous in sociological literature because of the many academic studies conducted there, then had some 2,000 residents, more than half of whom were black. The town was rigidly segregated, and it was a time when Mississippi was experiencing a resurgence of virulent racism, championed by James K. Vardaman. Vardaman preached that "education ruined good field hands" and only led to rapes and murders, which in turn brought on lynchings and burnings. The only remedy, he counseled, was to bring an end to the education of blacks in the state.

These issues of black equality with whites came to a head in Indianola with the "Minnie Cox Affair." Minnie Cox and her husband, Wayne, were the leaders of the local black community. Wayne Cox was a graduate of Alcorn College in 1884 who had moved to Indianola to establish a school for blacks, invested in real estate, founded the Delta Penny Savings Bank and Mississippi Life Insurance Company, and had gotten his wife installed as postmaster of the town through his connections with the Republican party. In October 1902 Indianola's whites circulated a petition to ask Minnie Cox to resign. President Theodore Roosevelt, however, intervened, instructing the Postmaster General to refuse her resignation and ordering the post office closed until the town reinstated her. This only fortified the resolve of white Mississippians, and two years later Roosevelt finally capitulated and appointed a white to the office. The reverberations of this great national controversy had an impact on young George himself.

George Lee had gotten a job in Mr. Holme's grocery store. Holmes had evidently fired a young white boy for stealing, and he hired Lee in his place to run various errands. Soon, however, whites demanded that Lee be replaced with a white, and ultimately Holmes acquiesced, saying that he had only hired him in the first place because "a nigger wouldn't have the nerve to steal as much as a white boy." George Lee had a propensity for landing on his feet, though, and soon he got a job as houseboy for Charles Klingman, a powerful cotton planter and buyer in the town. When Lee grew too old for that job, Klingman got him a position as a dray driver for Greshman's mercantile store. This delivery job enabled George Lee to earn more money than ever before, and he began to buy Buffalo Bill and Horatio Alger novels. The poor but ambitious young boys in Alger's books became an inspiration to Lee, so when his mother insisted he leave his job to go to Alcorn Agricultural and Mechanical College in order to improve his chances in life, he was willing and eager to comply.

Alcorn at this time was hardly a true college, but it did provide a fairly solid high school education for the blacks who went there, and in Mississippi at that time there was no real alternative. George Lee soon proved an exceptional student at the school, and he remained there for three years until he decided to go north to Memphis in 1912 to find a summer job. His brother had earlier moved to the bustling city of 100,000, and Lee himself had spent some weekends in the metropolis. As in Indianola, more than half of Memphis was made of up black inhabitants, but the range of jobs and other opportunities there far exceeded those available in the small Mississippi town. There also, blacks had their own grocery stores, restaurants, drugstores, laundries, harness shops, newspapers, funeral parlors, beauty parlors, and other establishments. The most important black family in the city was the Churches, whose head, Robert R. Church, Sr.,* died the year Lee arrived in Memphis. Other important black business leaders were Thomas H. Hayes and J. W. Sanford, who had joined with Church to organize the Solvent Savings Bank and Trust. Memphis was a vibrant, exciting city, filled with what seemed like a myriad of opportunities for the young Lee.

The commercial and cultural center of Memphis was boisterous, rollicking Beale Street. Despite the relatively great opportunities Beale Street offered a young man like Lee, it was not an easy challenge. Beale Street and Memphis then had the highest homicide rate in the nation, was rife with political and police corruption, and was filled with underworld gangsters, gambling, drinking, prostitution, and other assorted urban ills. It was, as Lee later commented, a street "owned by Jews, policed by whites and enjoyed by Negroes." Throughout most of its history until the 1960s, Beale Street was known variously as "the murder capital of the world," "Saturday night heaven," and "the street where the blues began," because it was here also that southern country blues musicians like W. C. Handy, Ma Rainey, Bessie Smith, Alberta Hunter, and others played. George Lee later recalled:

Beale Street was a main street of Negro America where its pulse beat highest, where richly dark brown women, hang-jawed country rubes mixed with spruce urban Negroes in an atmosphere pungent with barbequed pig, alive with the music of those who sit around in cafes trying to ease their souls with ready-made song. The night cries of carefree people, the midnight serenaders twanging on their guitars blended with the traffic noise to create a sound triumphant. Back of the sound of this red-hot syncopation lies the plantation Negro who, if he was sometimes lost in the vast apathy of a decaying system, was also often impelled to seek Beale Street where it was always Saturday night. (*West Tennessee Historical Papers*)

Whereas Memphis had defeated some rural migrants, such as the parents of novelist Richard Wright, George Lee was undaunted. Lee got a job as a bellhop at the prestigious Gayoso Hotel, found he could make a good deal of money, and continued working there during five summers. By 1917, however, America was caught up in the excitement of World War I. As war fever grew, many African-Americans were determined that they be given the opportunity to participate. The NAACP petitioned for an end to racial discrimination in the U.S. Army and called for the commissioning of black officers. The army finally yielded to these demands and set up a black officer training camp in Des Moines, Iowa. George W. Lee was determined to be chosen one of the African-Americans to participate in the program. Despite the fact that he was only twenty-three, much younger than the minimum set for officers, he was able to secure an appointment. He became one of just twenty-seven Tennesseans selected. In October 1917 he became one of 133 southern and 506 northern blacks commissioned second lieutenants. Lee was sent to France, where his battalion of black soldiers, and Lee himself, were cited for bravery by the French. Lee was promoted to first lieutenant and honorably discharged on March 27, 1919. He would thereafter always be known as "Lieutenant Lee of Beale Street," a brilliant strategem on his part. At that time, white newspapers refused to use honorific titles, such as Mr. and Mrs. for blacks. Only doctor or reverend were allowed, but Lee was able to convince whites and blacks alike to refer to him by his military title.

In 1919 Lee returned to Memphis a hero and found his employment opportunities had been greatly enhanced by his exploits abroad. He called upon Robert Church, Jr., who had become the most important political power in the black community and a force to be reckoned with in the state and national Republican party. Church wanted Lee to work as his aide in political affairs, and he offered him a job as a plainclothes detective on the city police force. Lee, however, was not sure he wanted a bureaucratic position. He had watched the Cox family in Indianola make a small fortune in business with a bank and an insurance company, so instead he got a job as a ten-dollar-a-week salesman with Mississippi Life Insurance. After a few weeks he was promoted to district manager of the Memphis office, with responsibility for recruiting and training new agents.

Mississippi Life had been conceived and organized by Wayne Cox and several other men in Indianola. It was part of a trend among blacks during that time, which saw the organization of firms such as North Carolina Mutual, Atlanta Life, National Benefit Life of Washington, D.C., and Supreme Liberty Life of Chicago. Coming up from Indianola to organize the Memphis branch was Joseph E. Walker (see Walker Family), who had succeeded Cox as president of the firm. Walker decided to move Mississippi Life's home office to Memphis because of deteriorating race relations in Indianola. Along with Walker came several other men from Indianola, including Merah Steven Stuart, who was the firm's general manager.

Mississippi Life, like most other black insurance companies, specialized in industrial insurance, whereby small amounts were sold and agents had to collect tiny premiums, usually a nickle or a dime a week, from the policyholders. Lee's technique was to stress that purchasing insurance would not just buy a death benefit, but would also "increase happiness, stabilize the future home, and make poorhouses a relic of the past." Lee and his agents in Memphis were extraordinarily successful, and by 1920 his district sold more insurance than any other company office. As a consequence, Lee was promoted to vice president of Mississippi Life. In that capacity, he attended the annual meeting of the National Negro Business League. There he discovered that the insurance segment of the organization was almost totally dominated by representatives of the African-American benevolent orders and that the larger black insurance companies were relegated to the background. Although Lee was a staunch member of the Elks, he felt this situation was wrong. Thus, when he returned to Memphis, he and Merah Stuart, C. C. Spaulding,* and others set about organizing the National Negro Insurance Association, a trade association, in Durham, North Carolina. Lee was a member of the executive committee of that organization for many years.

During the first four years George Lee was with Mississippi Life, his salary soared, reaching $6,500, a princely sum for the time. Then, suddenly, one of the greatest crises in the history of black insurance in America erupted, and it was at this time that Lee may have had his finest, most noble, hour. In 1923 Minnie Cox and her son-in-law sold the controlling shares in Mississippi Life to Heman Perry* of Atlanta. Perry, who was one of the most dashing and daring entrepreneurs in African-American history, had organized Standard Life in 1913, using this as a base to create a truly massive and wide-ranging business empire, with a bank, construction firms, laundries, and drugstores. But it was an empire that was heavily leveraged, and he had borrowed heavily from the white-owned Southeastern Trust Company. This was evidently unknown to Walker, Stuart, and the Coxes, who thought they were plugging Mississippi Life into the vast resources of Perry's empire. They soon learned differently.

Within weeks after taking over Mississippi Life, Perry had skimmed well over $100,000 from its cash reserves, and then sold it to a white firm, Southern Life, for $240,000. This meant that Mississippi Life, the oldest black-owned legal reserve firm in America, had suddenly passed into white hands, and this created a furor in Memphis and throughout black America. George Lee decided he would not tolerate it and staged a revolt. Lee announced to the new owners: "We refuse to work for you, we will rather go back to the anvil and the forge, to the work bench and to the cotton patches of Mississippi." Lee and sales managers from three states picketed the offices of Southern Life and resigned their positions. By this action, they rendered Mississippi Life worthless, since there was no one to collect the premiums, the only source of income. Officials of Southern Life tried to buy Lee off with an offer of a $7,000 salary if he would return to work, but he refused. Instead, he and his agents continued their fight.

At the rally held in front of Southern Life, Lee, who was a spellbinding orator, dramatically presented the situation to his managers and to the world:

[Mississippi Life] was builded upon the blood and sweat money of the women from the wash tubs, the men from the farms, the anvils and the forge. It has established a brand of efficiency that represents the highest expression of a struggling people, who stand trembling on the borders of the economic universe and are looking to this and similar institutions to establish the trademark of Negro competence.

He also issued a warning:

The white South is going to have a hard time explaining to the world just why they are making efforts to take from the heart of the Negro one of the biggest insurance companies they have. . . . We have gathered here not to temporize or to mince our words; nor to make you believe that if you win this case in the courts we are going to continue in your employ. This thing either belongs to you or it belongs to us. If you get it we want no part of it.

Lee had a harder time dealing with the machinations of a black man like Perry than he did with the underhanded play of the whites. He could not bring himself to believe that an African-American had betrayed his race. So, he blamed it on the Ku Klux Klan. Although Lee's biographer believes this was a figment of Lee's imagination, it allowed him to view Perry as an unwitting dupe of the Klan. The rest of Mississippi Life's agents and staff were less kind to Perry. When he arrived in Memphis, the displaced employees drove him out of town with spit, bottles, and threat of even greater bodily harm. At this point, Lee might have taken his agents, and the thousands of Mississippi Life policyholders whom he held in the palm of his hand, and organized his own insurance company. But, despite his success as a businessman and a leader, he had little entrepreneurial spirit. He wanted the security of working for someone.

George Lee approached Alonzo Herndon[*] of Atlanta Life, who opened a branch of his firm in Memphis, making Lee manager. Atlanta Life by this time was the second-largest black insurance company in America, and Lee continued to service most of his old Mississippi Life customers with a crew of thirty-five agents, also largely from his old firm. Atlanta Life was to be his "home" for the rest of his long life. Lee rose to senior vice president and was a member of the board of directors. In 1946 he was notified by Atlanta Life that he was being considered for a post at the head office in Atlanta. They changed their minds, however, when they received a letter signed by 500 Memphians pleading that Lee be allowed to remain in their city. In later years Lee helped establish the Herndon Foundation, which ensured that Atlanta Life would remain in African-American hands after Norris Herndon's[*] death. Lee was also a founder of *The Vision*, the corporate magazine. In 1927, Lee became a director of Universal Life Insurance, which Joseph Walker had created out of the rubble of Mississippi Life.

Lee, along with Joseph Walker, Robert Church, Jr., and a few others, was a major spokesman for the benefits of black capitalism in the 1920s. This was sometimes difficult to maintain. In 1922 Bert Roddy's Citizen's Cooperative Stores, a major black venture, went bankrupt, shortly after receiving a $100,000 loan from Solvent Savings, Church's bank. Hobbled by this loss, Solvent struggled for another five years, and in 1927 merged with rival Fraternal Savings Bank. This was of no benefit. On December 29, 1927, after depositors had withdrawn money to pay for Christmas shopping, the bank faltered and a run ensued by its 28,000 depositors. It was a terrible scandal; six bank officers were jailed, including its president, Alfred F. Ward, and vice president, Thomas H. Hayes; and much of Beale Street's black business establishment was embarrassed by the tragedy. Wayman Wilkerson, chairman of the board of the bank, head of Tri-State Casket, and husband of the head of the local NAACP chapter, committed suicide.

The reaction of most black Memphians to the bank failure was that of shock and horror. When Ward, the bank's president, appeared at a depositors' meeting at St. Andrews AME Church, indignities were heaped on him. George Lee, however, chose to remain optimistic and to transmit that optimism to the black populace of the city. In an article in the *Memphis Triangle* in January 1928, he said that "disaster is as much a part of life as success. . . . It's God's plan for teaching us that we are but mortals living in an atmosphere of imperfection." He further stressed that "crookedness is not a racial trait, but an individual trait," and he urged, "We must step forward and build upon the ashes of the ruins. To turn back means disintegration and economic slavery." Economics was the key for Lee. As he once said; "America is a commercial country, its aristocracy is built upon the dollar. He that has the most dollars is prince." Blacks must thus build a new bank, and get about the business of creating a viable African-American business community. It would be another twenty years, however, before black Memphians created a bank. Joseph E. Walker was the organizer of the Tri-State Bank, and Lee served on its board of directors.

George Lee also became a civil rights and political leader of the black community during the 1920s. As David Tucker has demonstrated, Lee was a staunch advocate of "black pride" during this decade. Over the course of hundreds of speeches and articles, Lee insisted, "The development of race consciousness by stressing and lauding of things Negro creates a line of defense against white newspapers and white propaganda that plays the Aframerican up as an underling. It saves his pride and self-respect from the effects of Jim Crowism." Lee's main competitors in the area of race relations were the ministers of Memphis, especially Reverend T. O. Fuller of the First Baptist Church and Reverend Sutton E. Griggs of the Tabernacle Baptist Church. Like Lee, both were relative newcomers to Memphis, and both advocated a form of accommodationism to whites that Lee could not abide. Together with a number of white businessmen, they had formed the Inter-Racial League to secure civic improvements and better treatment of African-Americans. Griggs, a one-time charismatic militant in Nashville, particularly distressed Lee. By the time he got to Memphis, Griggs had accepted the social Darwinist thought that blacks were less advanced than other races. Nor was this an alterable condition; according to Griggs, blacks were racially inferior, lacking a series of critical "Anglo-Saxon" traits. David Tucker reports that "the better classes of Negro Memphians called Griggs an 'Uncle Tom,' the working class termed him a "white folks" nigger.' "

Lee decided to directly confront Griggs in the press, where Lee protested that the minister overemphasized black criminality and social problems and neglected what he called a "healthy race consciousness" which would lead "the Negro to realize equal rights within the next century." Blacks would find, Lee claimed, that "all find the path leads to the world of economics. Industry equality will bring all else." In this way, Lee theorized, segregation would lose its economic foundation. Racial pride and business success were the keys to ending black economic and social inferiority, and this in turn would bring an end to segregation. Lee also joined the local NAACP during this time, which, although it laid less stress on economic development, did countenance a more militant approach to race relations. What Lee and the NAACP had in common was a willingness to protest injustice. As Lee commented; "We have too many apostles of peace at any price, too many preaching about the glories of the other world and too few pointing out the hell of the world in which we now live." So long as injustice existed, said Lee, "I for one, shall love confusion and despise peace." Lee had become an eloquent spokesman for the black community. When he was offered a position in Atlanta in 1930, the *Memphis Triangle* declared; "Memphis Can't Lose Lieut. George W. Lee."

It was also during this time that Lee became Bob Church's right-hand man. Lee, of course, had rejected Church's offer of a job in the police department when he returned from France, but he willingly became involved in the wealthy African-American's political machine. Church had little interest in running the family's vast business empire, but rapidly became a leader in Republican politics in Memphis, western Tennessee, and the nation. The source of his influence was the Lincoln League, which he organized with T. H. Hayes, Wayman Wilkerson, J. T. Settle, Jr., Levoy McCoy, J. B. Martin, and Bert Roddy in 1916. The league organized clubs in each black ward in Memphis and held political revival meetings in Church's Auditorium in Church Park. The technique was a resounding success, and Church was appointed to the National Republican Advisory Board. He then expanded the league's activities to the national level in 1919. Roscoe Conkling Simmons, Booker T. Washington's* nephew, was named president, Walter Cohen* of New Orleans was made treasurer, and Church gained the powerful backroom position of executive committee chairman.

Church, who shunned publicity and preferred being a backroom manipulator, needed an associate who had charisma and enjoyed basking in the limelight. The ideal man was George W. Lee. It took little coaxing for Church to convince Lee to climb on board the bandwagon. Lee established his office of Atlanta Life above Bob Church's office at 392 Beale Street, and the two men met daily to discuss strategy. Lee became Church's leading speaker, and after 1927 was second only to Church himself in political influence among blacks in Memphis. David Tucker claims that Lee was attracted to politics not for any personal gain, but because it was one of the "few opportunities of integration in the South." It also offered Lee a national forum for race leadership, which he greatly desired. It gave him a broader platform upon which he could preach his philosophy of black pride, economic progress, and protest over injustice and segregation.

In later years, however, Lee and Church drifted apart and became antagonists. On the local level, Church, Lee, and black Republicans had exerted their influence in an uneasy partnership with the Democratic political machine of Edward H. Crump. Crump, a native of Holly Springs, Mississippi, came to Memphis in the 1890s where he became a successful buggy manufacturer. He also became involved in political reform, pushing for establishment of the commission form of government. Subsequently, in 1909, he ran for mayor of the city on a reform platform. He had W. C. Handy compose a campaign song for him, a song that became world famous as the "Memphis Blues." During his terms in office from 1910 to 1916, Crump did much to court the black vote through a series of paternalistic policies. In 1911 Harry H. Pace,* organizer of the Colored Citizens Association, and Church helped secure black support for Crump.

For the next two decades, Crump and Church, leaders of two powerful "ethnic" political organizations in the city, developed an informal arrangement with one another based upon mutual respect of the power each of them wielded. Crump, for his part, rarely used the race-baiting tactics commonly employed in southern politics at that time. Church, on the other hand, despite his Republican loyalties, seldom interfered with Crump. This arrangement began to fragment in the late 1920s. In 1927 Church, Lee, and other blacks organized the West Tennessee Civil and Political League, with George Lee as president. Its goal was to register more blacks in order to force white city leaders to provide more services and greater sensitivity to black needs. The result was a bitter election in which there was a great deal of race baiting by Mayor J. Rowlette Paine. Crump opposed Paine's candidacy, and Lee and his organization turned out blacks in large numbers to bring about Paine's defeat. Lee interpreted this as a triumph for the "new Negro" leadership in Memphis and called it "one of the greatest victories ever achieved by Negroes in the South." In hindsight, it is difficult to agree with that, as the city under Crump again became crime and violence ridden, and corruption seeped into every pore.

During the 1930s Lee became increasingly conservative as he turned his back on his older ideas of protest leadership. He and Church both withdrew from active support of the NAACP, with control passing to J. E. Walker. Lee and Church put all their emphasis on the Republican party, but since it no longer held power in Washington, it was of less significance at home, particularly as more and more blacks began voting for the Democrats. But Lee would not switch. Nor would he recant his relations with the Crump machine, which had become increasingly unpopular with blacks. Crump turned against Church, and the city sued Church for $89,000 owed in back taxes on his property. When it was not paid, the city confiscated Church's property and sold it at an auction. Church moved to Chicago, but Lee stayed in Memphis and remained committed to the Crump machine. Church was furious and accused Lee of acquiescing to "Mr. Crump." It ended their once-cordial relationship.

As black leadership in Memphis became more radical in the 1940s and 1950s, Lee recoiled in horror. Crump fought every attempt at racial equality on the part of blacks, and Lee could not oppose him. In this manner the once fiery radical came to be perceived increasingly as a tame house pet of Crump. In 1948 Estes Kefauver challenged Crump's leadership, and Joseph Walker, Taylor C. D. Hayes, along with others, supported Kefauver's candidacy. George Lee played no role in this rebellion, but he remained tied to Crump in Memphis and to conservative Republicans at the state and national levels. In 1952 Lee made one of the speeches nominating the conservative Robert A. Taft at the Republican National Convention. Lee in later years became a fixture of Beale Street, tolerated, and even loved, because of his nostalgic connection with a rapidly disappearing era. Lee was a bachelor who had always lived with his mother. After she died, however, he married a former Miss Bronze America in 1947, but the marriage did not last long. It did, however, produce one daughter, Gilda Lee Robinson.

When the civil rights revolution came to Memphis in the 1950s Lee was totally unprepared. As David Tucker noted, Lee thought of integration as a "fantastic dream" that was unattainable in his lifetime. He did not think it would help to push for desegregation legislation, since whites would not obey the law anyhow. By the 1960s Lee had become an anachronism, and in 1964 the conservative Goldwater faction of the party purged him from office. Lee became an increasingly reactionary voice in the rapidly radicalizing America of the 1960s. He used his position as grand commissioner of the Elks to travel around the country giving speeches criticizing black power advocates and other black radicals. Lee had always believed the best way for blacks to gain concessions from whites was to play upon white guilt. Riots and violence, along with impassioned racial rhetoric, he believed, would eliminate the white guilt complex and increase racial hostility.

By then the elderly Lee was little more than a curiosity in black Memphis as he took his daily stroll up and down Beale Street. Beale Street, of course, was just a shell of its former self also. Lee's books and novels of Beale Street were revered, and he was called the "Bard of Beale Street." In 1976, at age 82, Lee was killed in a car wreck in Memphis. Many in the city mourned his passing, which signaled the end of an era as well as the passing of a dynamic and charismatic leader. As State Representative Alvin King, a Democrat, said, Mr. Lee "was a great man, a great historian and humanitarian. I feel that Memphis and the black community have lost a great leader." The mantle of leadership, of course, had long before fallen to younger and more militant blacks, and during his final thirty-five years George W. Lee spoke only for a small group of conservative, middle-class African-Americans. But there is still that magnificent image of the thirty-year-old Lee protesting against Southern Life and proclaiming:

These managers who stand before you white men cannot assist you in carrying out your plans to take over the Mississippi Life without sinking into the basest ingratitude and handing their names down to posterity to be linked with Benedict Arnold and Judas as the arch traitors of their time. We cannot under any consideration continue in your employ. (Tucker, *Lieutenant Lee of Beale Street*)

It was, indeed, a glorious moment.

Sources

The George W. Lee Papers are held in the Shelby County Library in Memphis with scrapbooks and folders of letters and other material. The library also has an extensive newspaper clipping file on him, mostly with articles in the two local Memphis white newspapers. There is an interview with Lee, conducted in April and May, 1966, filed in the Oral History Research Office of Memphis State University. Lee's three main books were *Beale Street: Where the Blues Began* (1934); *River George* (1937); and *Beale Street Sundown* (1943). He also wrote a number of short stories and other articles. Those of some interest to historians of business include "These Colored United States: Tennessee—The Last Stand of Justice in the Solid South," *The Messenger*, July 1925, 252–53; "Poetic Memories of Beale Street," *West Tennessee Historical Society Papers*; "Insurance—Its Necessity and Value," *The Messenger*, March 1927; "Group Tactics and Ideals," *The Messenger* IX (April 1925); "The Negro's Next Step," *Memphis Triangle*, January 28, 1928; and "The Political Upheaval in Memphis," *The Messenger*, February 1928.

There is a solid biography of Lee entitled *Lieutenant Lee of Beale Street* by David M. Tucker (Nashville, 1971). See also Tucker, "Black Pride and Negro Business in the 1920's," *Business History Review* XLIII (Winter 1969). Lee's memoir, *Beale Street: Where the Blues Began*, is valuable and fascinating, but Lee was a master of self-promotion, and it must be used with some care. A shorter biography is found in George A. Sewell and Margaret L. Dwight (n.p., n.d.) *Historic Black Memphians*. Obituaries appeared August 2, 1976, in the *Commercial Appeal* and *Press Scimitar* and on August 3, 1976, in the *New York Times*.

There is also useful information on Lee and his activities in Lester C. Lamon, *Black Tennesseans, 1900–1930* (Knoxville, 1977); Linton Weeks, *Memphis: A Folk History* (Parkhurst/Little Rock, 1982) 163–64; M. S. Stuart, *Economic Detour: A History of Insurance in the Lives of American Negroes* (New York, 1940), 275–77; *Ebony*, September 1950; *Pittsburgh Courier*, March 8, 1924; *Encore American and Worldwide News*, October 4, 1976; *Congressional Record*, April 10, 1973; *Press Scimitar*, July 2, 1964; *Commercial Appeal*, August 29, 1967; *Pilot*, Fall 1976; Hugh R. Gloster, *Negro Voices in American Fiction* (Chapel Hill, 1948), 238–41; G. P. Hamilton, *The Bright Side of Memphis* (Memphis, 1908); and *Beacon Lights of the Race* (Memphis, 1911), 510–13.

Leidesdorff, William Alexander (1810–May 18, 1848). Merchant, financier, land speculator, and government official. William Leidesdorff was born on the island of St. Croix, in the West Indies, which then belonged to Denmark. His father, William Leidesdorff, was a white Danish merchant, and his mother was Anna Maria Spark (some sources list her as Maria Ann Sparks), a mulatto or

Creole woman with an indeterminate amount of Negro blood. The two were never legally married, and William was born out of wedlock, but the laws of Denmark allowed the father to legalize his son as his heir, which he did in the courts of St. Croix in 1837. This allowed young Leidesdorff to inherit his father's property, which evidently came about a year or two later when the father passed away. Young William was educated on St. Croix, but the extent of his education is difficult to ascertain. It is generally assumed that, following the custom of the day for the sons of merchants and planters, he was sent to Europe for advanced training. One source claims he was trained in banking and finance there. What is clear is that Leidesdorff had complete command of a number of languages, which he used to great advantage in his business relations.

In the meantime, young William had come to the United States in 1834, settling in New Orleans. There he became a ship's captain, sailing between that city and New York. There is a story, which seems to have no particular substantiation, but which nonetheless has acquired the status of folklore in some quarters, that Leidesdorff was the victim of a tragic love affair in New Orleans. According to legend, young William, who was "copper-skinned and handsome" and had "wavy hair and a full mustache," was not known to be of African extraction while in New Orleans, and the racial line there at that time was rather mutable anyhow. In any event, he was attracted to a "young, beautiful socialite of English extraction. Her name was Hortense." Another "source" described her thusly, "Hortense, the girl with the golden hair and blue eyes. Her family traced its ancestry to the aristocracy of Louis XIV's France." Terribly smitten with the young white woman, Leidesdorff proposed to her, and she accepted. He had not, however, informed her of his racial background. One evening just before the wedding, the story goes, he revealed his background, probably assuming her love for him would be too great for Hortense to reject him. He was mistaken: "Weeping bitterly, Hortense replied that her father would never consent to the match, but [that] she would love him until she died." Then, according to one report, a few days later, the crestfallen Leidesdorff noticed a funeral procession and asked whose it was. "A young society girl's"—Hortense of course. Utterly disconsolate, the story then says that he purchased the 160-ton schooner *Julia Ann* and sailed for South America.

More careful historical authorities have less to say about Leidesdorff's years in New Orleans. It is clear that he never married and never had any children. But according to extant records, he left New Orleans to live in New York for a time, and then became captain on the *Julia Ann*, which was owned by one J. C. Jones. He did sail around South America, reaching the California coast in Monterrey in 1841. Sometime after arriving in California, Jones was forced to put his ship up for sale, and Leidesdorff was out of a job. He therefore decided to go into the mercantile trade, choosing a tiny village called Yerba Buena to start his business. Destined to become the city of San Francisco, Yerba Buena at that time was a community of just thirty families. Leidesdorff rapidly became its most prominent and respected citizen.

Leidesdorff prospered in trade, being involved primarily in the export of tallow and hides and, by 1843, had accumulated enough money to purchase a lot in the town at the corner of Clay and Kearney Streets. A year later he built a warehouse at the beach on the corner of California and, what would later be, Leidesdorff streets. Also, in the same year he decided to become a naturalized Mexican citizen, since California was still under the coutrol of that country and there were certain advantages to Mexican citizenship. One of those was that Leidesdorff received a grant of 35,000 acres, located in the Sacramento Valley, on the left bank of the American River. The property was adjacent to that of John Sutter, and Leidesdorff named his undeveloped estate Rio Rancho Americano. He acquired other large city lots on one of which he built a store and on another of which he constructed what was said to be the finest residence in the city. It was the site of many lavish parties for visitors to the Bay Area during this time. Leidesdorff also built the City Hotel on his lot at the corner of Clay and Kearney, which was reputed to be the "most pretentious" in the town until it burned down in 1851.

San Francisco was growing rapidly during the years Leidesdorff lived there and positively exploded after the discovery of gold in 1848. During the 1850s, San Francisco became an entrepôt for the goldfields then, in later years, dominated both the mining country and the agricultural hinterland. By 1870 it was the ninth-largest American city, and as a port it rivaled New York, Boston, and New Orleans. In 1850 its exports amounted to nearly $5 million and its imports, $7 million. Twenty year later, exports were $35 million and imports, $48 million. Manufacturing grew more slowly, but by the end of the century its product exceeded imports and exports combined. The African-American population of San Francisco, however, was small. In 1852 there were just 464 blacks in the city, and this increased to just 1,654 a half century later. Total population meantime had grown from nearly 35,000 to over 340,000. Most of the African-Americans attracted to the city in the nineteenth century were sailors and maritime workers, along with a number who worked on the railroads.

During the time of his residence in California, Leidesdorff became greatly involved in civic and political affairs. It is not clear the extent to which he ever admitted or claimed his mixed-African ancestry during this time. A number of people who were in California claimed they were aware of his ancestry. Mrs. Annie Peters, one of the first black women there, was from St. Croix and said that she knew his mother was a "Negress." Jacob Wright Harlan, who traded with Leidesdorff, said, "I believe [Leidesdorff] had a dash of Negro blood in his veins." Several accounts also mentioned the same fact, so it seems apparent that Leidesdorff was able to achieve his prominence to economic and civic affairs in spite of the fact that his ancestry was known. That is quite a testament to his character and personality, since these were not generous times for African-Americans.

Leidesdorff served as a member of the City Council of Yerba Buena, was appointed treasurer of that body, and because of his prominence, was appointed to many committees of that group. One of these committees was given the responsibility for establishing a public school for the community. This was accomplished in April 1848, shortly before Leidesdorff's death. He also became very active in the affairs leading to the uprising Americans in California against Mexican rule. Thomas A. Larkin, the American counsel to California, stationed at Monterrey, had been a close friend of Leidesdorff's since the latter's arrival. In 1845 Larkin appointed Leidesdorff vice counsel for the Port of San Francisco. This was done despite the latter's Mexican citizenship. The letters between Leidesdorff and Larkin are powerful evidence of the degree to which the two men and other Americans were plotting to overthrow the Mexican government during this period. When the explorer John C. Fremont came to California, he met with Leidesdorff and others, apparently to plot the seizure of California by the United States. During this time, Leidesdorff nonetheless continued to receive land grants from the Mexican government. When Captain John Montgomery landed in Yerba Buena with seventy marines in July 1846, he asked Leidesdorff to translate the proclamation of the commander in chief into Spanish, so that all would clearly understand what was happening. This, according to W. S. Savage, "was the real contribution of Leidesdorff in securing California for the United States."

With the takeover of California complete, Yerba Buena was renamed San Francisco, and Leidesdorff asked to be released as vice consul so that he could concentrate on his mercantile pursuits. To this end, he also planned to establish a twenty-four-hour express service between Sacramento and San Francisco. He purchased a steamship called the *Sitka*, which had been constructed by an American company in Russia. Its maiden voyage on the Sacramento River was a disaster. The trip took six days—longer than it would have taken a man to walk the distance—since the ship was far too small and too slow. He was, nonetheless, the first person to operate a steamboat "that ever sailed into San Francisco Bay."

Shortly thereafter, on March 15, 1848, gold was discovered on Sutter's Creek near Leidesdorff's property on the American River. There is some evidence that had he lived, Leidesdorff planned to try to develop gold on his own properties. James Forbes wrote to him on May 15, 1848, offering his services in mining the land. Leidesdorff was not able to take advantage of this because, three days later, he died of typhus. His death took him by surprise; he had not prepared a will. This fact opened his estate to litigation, and that developed into one of the most sensational struggles over an estate in the city's history.

When he died, Leidesdorff's property was $60,000 in debt, but it was clear that the value of his properties would escalate rapidly with the discovery of gold and expected rapid growth of San Francisco. Thomas Larkin first applied to be executor of the estate, but then found that he could not act in that capacity, since Leidesdorff was still a Mexican citizen. At that point, since Leidesdorff had no children, the state of California began litigation to take over the property because it was not legal for persons who were not American citizens to inherit California land. In the meantime, another player entered the scene—Captain James L.

Folsom. Folsom, a graduate of West Point, was in charge of the Quartermaster Depot at San Francisco. When he learned of the potential value of Leidesdorff's estate, he decided to travel to Saint Croix, where he offered Leidesdorff's mother, Anna Maria Spark, $50,000 for the property. She agreed but later decided she was not getting enough for it, and Folsom was forced to give her another $25,000. Ultimately, he got the property from her for a total of $75,000.

Folsom was not home free, however. He next had to convince the state of California that Anna Maria Spark was indeed able to inherit the land; otherwise, her transfer of the land to him would not be valid. The California High Court ultimately decided in Folsom's favor, and Leidesdorff's property at Folsom's own death in 1855 was judged to be worth some $1.5 million. Because of this, many call Leidesdorff America's first black millionaire. This is not quite true. Had he lived and held on to the property, it would have been worth that amount, but he was never worth that much during his own lifetime.

Nonetheless, William Leidesdorff was a figure of gigantic proportions in the early history of California and San Francisco. As W. S. Savage has written, "William Alexander Leidesdorff was without doubt one of the great men of early San Francisco and the State of California. He played a major role in establishing the United States on the Pacific Coast and should be better known. ... The city had a street named in his honor; it is a very small street and may be overlooked by many who visit San Francisco. William Alexander Leidesdorff is one of California's illustrious citizens."

Sources

There are several collections of William Leidesdorff's papers. The California Historical Society Library in San Francisco has a collection of his correspondence, account books, orders, and receipts from 1834 to 1848. See also the Leidesdorff Collection at Bancroft Library, University of California, Berkeley, and the William Alexander Leidesdorff Collection at the Huntington Library, San Marino, California. There are also some of his letters in the William Heath Davis Papers, the Joseph Libby Folsom Papers, the Thomas C. Larkin Papers, and the Dingerfield Fauntleroy Papers; there is also some information in the Minutes of Proceedings of the San Francisco City Council, all at the California State Library. There is also information dealing with the settlement of the Leidesdorff and Folsom estates in the Halleck, Pinckney, and Billings Papers at the University of California, Los Angeles Library. Many of Leidesdorff's letters have been published in John A. Hawgood, ed., *First and Last Consul, Thomas Oliver Larkin and the Americanization of California* (San Marino, 1962).

There is no full-length biography of Leidesdorff, but biographical information is available in a number of published sources: *Dictionary of American Negro Biography* (1982); W. S. Savage, "The Influence of William Alexander Leidesdorff on the History of California," *Journal of Negro History* XXXVIII, 3 (July 1953), 322–32; W.S. Savage, "Intrigue in California (1846)," *Midwest Journal* (Winter 1949), 63–68; W.S. Savage, *Blacks in the West* (Westport, Conn. 1976), 129ff.; Sue Bailey Thurman, *Pioneers of Negro Origin in California* (San Francisco, 1949), 1–5; Delilah Beasley, *The Negro Trail Blazers of California* (Los Angeles, 1919); Hubert Howe Bancroft, *The History of California* (San Francisco, 1884–90), vol. 4, 279, 711, and vol. 5, 566; Robert Ernest Cowan, "The Leidesdorff-Folsom Estate: A Forgotten Chapter in the Romantic History of Early San Francisco," *Quarterly of the California Historical Society* VII, 2 (June 1928), 106–11; Edgar A. Toppin, *A Biographical History of Blacks in America* (1969), 349–51; "The First Negro Millionaire," *Ebony*, November 1958; Robert O'Brien, "San Francisco's Street of Tragedy," *Coronet*, April 1951, 36–37; Rockwell D. Hunt, *California Firsts* (n.p. 1957), 206–8; *Encore American and World Wide News*, June 6, 1977; William L. Katz, *Black People Who Made the Old West* (1977), 72–75; *Tuesday*, November 1969, 28–30; Mirriam Allan De Ford, "Who Was Leidesdorff?" *Westways* 45 (March 1953), 18–19; John E. Morgan, "Comparison Study of the Lives of W. A. Leidesdorff and Joseph L. Folsom," typescript at Bancroft Library; James F. Manning, "William A. Leidesdorff's Career in California," Master's thesis, University of California, Berkeley, 1941; and Ingham, BDABL. See also *California Star*, September 18, 1847, for news of Leidesdorff's appointment as city treasurer; and *Blacks and Their Contributions to the American West: A Bibliography and Union List of Library Holdings through 1970* (1974), compiled by James de T. Abajian.

Lewis, Edward T. (May 15, 1940–   ). Publisher; Essence Communications, Inc. For generations, blacks were relegated to the fringes of the American economy. Black business, as understood from the time of Booker T. Washington* until the 1960s, was small, local, and often marginal. Characteristic black business activities included funeral parlors, ethnic hair-care products, barber and beauty shops, and the like. After World War II a small number of blacks began achieving more substantial success in new areas. One area in which blacks had enjoyed some measure of attainment was the media, where a number of highly successful newspapers were created to serve the local and national black communities. Most of these, too, remained fairly small. The one exception emerged after World War II when John H. Johnson* developed the phenomenally successful Johnson Publishing Company, a vast media and manufacturing empire, which published *Ebony* and *Jet*, and had nearly 2,000 employees and sales of over $200 million in 1987. For a long time, people assumed there was no room for other black publications. Johnson had cornered the market. Then, in 1969, Edward Lewis and three other young blacks had an idea for a new black-oriented magazine, and from that they built from scratch a massive and rapidly growing black media empire.

Edward Lewis was born in the Bronx, educated in the public schools there, and graduated from DeWitt Clinton High School, where he excelled in football as the team captain. Lewis was named to the all-city team and was the recipient of the Lou Gehrig Award for Courage and Sportsmanship. Not much is known about his parents, although his mother and father were divorced and his mother later remarried. When asked about his childhood, Lewis's most vivid memories were of being sent to his grandparents' farm in Virginia each summer. It was there, he felt, "that my family instilled, along with my mother, all the values that I hold today in terms of perseverance, in terms of hard work, family, working together, black history, supportive of blacks in terms of working together." Another great influence on Lewis's life during these years was an uncle: "He had his own business," Lewis remembers, "and he used to talk to me, as I was growing up, about having control over one's destiny. And I wanted to be like him. He was a generous man, a hard-working man, but he said: 'I like having some control over my own life and the only way I know one can do that is to have something of your own.'" The other thing that influenced Lewis's development was the darkness of his skin. There was a certain prejudice against darker skinned blacks in the African-American community, and this affected him adversely. It made him feel inferior and he had to work hard to overcome that.

Upon graduation from high school, Edward Lewis went to college at the University of New Mexico on a football scholarship. He later recalled, "I must tell you the only thing I knew about New Mexico then was that the atomic bomb was built at Los Alamos and exploded at Alamagordo." At New Mexico, Lewis studied political science and international relations and graduated in 1964. His time there was not without controversy. Lewis lost his football scholarship when he became a vocal supporter of Malcolm X. He was a member of the student council and had used that as a "bully pulpit" to advance Malcolm's views. Otherwise, however, he did not involve himself in the civil rights issues of the time. Despite some problems, Lewis recalls that New Mexico turned out to be "a wonderful experience." In 1963 he served as a lecturer in the Peace Corps program at the university and worked for two years in the city manager's office as an administrative analyst. He then went back to the University of New Mexico, where he got his master's degree in 1966. Lewis's next step was to enroll in Georgetown Law School, from which he promptly flunked out. This was a devastating experience for him. Lewis recalls, "It was very difficult because, not having failed before, I began to realize that in life you have your ups and downs and you've got to pick yourself [up]. I must say I felt so bad about it, I never did tell my family about it. I couldn't tell my friends about it. I couldn't deal with the fact that I had really flunked out of law school."

Lewis's spirits improved, however, when a friend got him a job at First National City Bank (Citibank) in New York City as a financial analyst. He also was a part-time student in the Ph.D. program in public administration at New York University. By 1969 Lewis was regarded as one of the "bright young blacks" on his way up in the New York financial world. As a result, he was one of fifty young blacks invited to a local black capitalism conference sponsored by the prestigious Shearson-Hammill and Company brokerage firm. Shearson, Hammill called the conference to encourage the development of initiatives in black capitalism. That incentive, in turn, had been prompted by the Nixon administration and Maurice Stans of the Commerce Department, who viewed it as an antidote to the violence and radicalism then coursing through the black ghettos of America.

The idea of a slick, new magazine to appeal especially to black women was advanced by Jonathon Blount, a twenty-four-year-old ad salesman for New Jersey Bell Telephone Company. The Shearson, Hammill advisor got Blount together with Cecil Hollingsworth, a black who had experience in the print industry; Clarence Smith, a salesman for Prudential Insurance; and Ed Lewis, who was well trained in financial planning. The four young black men met in the evenings after their regular jobs, making plans for their new magazine. The mood of white America in 1969 and 1970 was one of absolute panic over the possibility of a black revolution, so the men found a great deal of help and support for their project among denizens of Madison and Sixth avenues during this period. Providing assistance by way of advice and training were *Time-Life*, *Newsweek*, *Psychology Today*, *New York* magazine, CBS, Young & Rubicam, J. K. Lasser Tax Institute, Cowles Communications, McCann-Erickson, and Lorillard Corporation, among others.

The young men came back to Shearson, Hammill with their first budget proposal—for a whopping $5 million. The brokerage company told them it would be impossible to raise that much and advised cutbacks. Finally, they came forward with a more modest $1.5 million proposal. As it turned out, even this was optimistic. Just as they hit the money markets, the steep recession of 1970 brought things to a halt. Ultimately, they were able to collect just $130,000 in cash, and 52 percent of that represented their own funds. They did, however, get commitments to cover the balance up to $1.5 million (and ultimately $2 million) from a consortium of investors that included First National City Bank, Chase National Bank, and Morgan Guaranty Bank. They also approached Playboy Enterprises for support in this initial period but were turned down.

In any event, the four young men allocated enough money to finance publication of the first and several subsequent issues of a magazine named *Essence*. The first issue came out in May 1970 amidst great fanfare. It was a slick, glossy, stylish magazine, what *Time* called "*Vogue*-cum-*Ramparts*" in style. That referred to the rather uneasy combination of two disparate elements in the magazine. The first was twenty pages of high-fashion color photography, similar to that found in *Vogue*. The second, evidenced in an article entitled "Five Shades of Militancy," ran throughout the magazine's text. In response to the heightened black activisim of the time, the new magazine tried to strike a note of revolution and militancy. Most of all, however, what *Essence* presented was something new in black magazines. The dazzling full-page color photos of gorgeous black models clad in bikinis and miniskirts had seldom been seen previously. White magazines, of course, almost never used black models, and *Ebony* and *Jet* were generally more sedate and dignified in their presentation of blacks. Then, too, there were pointed articles that one did not find elsewhere: "Sensual, sexy black man . . . What are you doing with that white woman?"

"*Essence* tapped a need in the market," said Lewis. "When we started, black women did not have a publication that spoke to them as the intelligent, beautiful and talented people that they are or recognized their contributions to their race and country." *Essence* was new, exciting, and different. And it was black. But it almost folded early on. Lewis and his three partners had an optimistic initial press run of 200,000 copies which were distributed to 145 cities. Of this, they sold just 50,000 copies. Worse still, *Essence* had managed to sell just thirteen pages of advertising. The infant enterprise was teetering and was further being torn apart by editorial and managerial dissension. A major bone of contention was the strident political tone of the magazine. Because of that, the editor of the first issue, Ruth Ross, left when she believed her editorial independence was being undercut. During the first year, Ross was followed by two more editors, each of whom quickly came and went. By the second year, a number of important changes had been made. First of all, Marcia Gillespie was installed as editor in chief, and she stabilized the magazine and provided a clear and successful focus. Most important, however, Edward Lewis and Clarence Smith ousted their two partners from control of the operation, and Lewis became publisher and chairman of Essence Communications. Smith was named president of the corporation. The two men, along with Marcia Gillespie, battled hard to bring *Essence* to respectability and profitability.

By 1975 *Essence* was a success. When interviewed by *Advertising Age* that year, however, Ed Lewis seemed more relieved than ecstatic. "We've survived," he told them. He also recalled that their investors "took a helluva risk with us." By 1975, though, *Essence* was still the only black women's service magazine, and it had experienced a 40 percent circulation gain from 1973 to 1974, a larger increase than any other woman's magazine. Its ad volume also grew by a respectable 13 percent. The first profitable issue came out in 1974, and for fiscal 1975 *Essence* earned a tiny but significant profit of $90,000 on $3.4 million in revenues. By this point, circulation had climbed to 450,000, and was expected to rise another 50,000 in the following year. *Essence* also moved to new and more spacious offices at 1500 Broadway. A critical intervention had been made on *Essence*'s behalf during its first year, when it almost went under. Playboy Enterprises, which had earlier refused to help, came up with much-needed backing, as did a number of other mainline companies. All told, Lewis collected about $2 million from investors before the magazine began showing a small profit.

Edward Lewis and *Essence* hit a snag in 1977 when his former partners, Blount and Hollingsworth, in coalition with filmmaker Gordon Parks, who had provided early editorial supervision for the magazine, sued for control of the magazine. By this point, *Essence* was a profitable operation, having shown a second full year of profit, and its circulation was projected at 600,000. Parks, speaking for his group, said he thought Lewis, Smith, and Gillespie did a marvelous job, but that he and his group could do better. The battle went on for two years before Lewis finally took the company private and settled with his ex-partners. During those two years, *Essence* operated in the red, but as soon as the dispute was over it returned to profitability. In 1980 Essence Communications earned profits of $300,000, about the same as it had in 1979. As Lewis remarked at the time: "I'm not hearing any complaints these days." He credited the profitability to an "extraordinarily better job of controlling expenses," especially ending the magazine's dependence on Publisher's Clearing House, which saved 90 percent on new subscriptions.

By this point, *Essence*, which was ten years old, had a circulation of 600,000 and ran an all-time high of 109 ad pages in its tenth anniversary issue. At a time when ad pages in women's magazines were decreasing at an alarming rate, *Essence*'s were increasing. This was due in large measure to two interrelated factors: the increasing affluence of an important segment of the black population, and the ability of *Essence* to reach a huge proportion of this group. Lewis claimed it reached 46 percent of all black women between the ages of eighteen and forty-nine, and that most of these women were in the black upper income group. A market research study conducted in 1990 showed that 81 percent of *Essence*'s readers had attended college and their average household income was $37,300.'' *Essence* was a unique and dependable way for advertisers to reach an increasingly important market. To build on this profitability, Lewis took an important step in 1980—he set up a direct marketing operation in conjunction with the magazine. Called Essence Direct Mail, it began with an eighteen page catalog mailed at random to a sample of 20,000 *Essence* subscribers. As Lewis noted, ''Direct Mail is a booming market, and, to my knowledge, there are no other specifically black mail order houses operating now.'' Lewis had found another potentially important niche in the black market.

By 1988 Lewis had built a rather robust little communications empire. Circulation of *Essence* had climbed to 850,000, and profits remained very high. The mail order business was a success, and Lewis, in association with Bruce Llewellyn,* Percy Sutton,* and others, purchased television station WKBW, the ABC affiliate in Buffalo, New York, for $65 million. It was the largest of about a dozen television stations owned by blacks in the United States. Years before, Lewis had expressed a dream of creating a black-owned media giant, and by 1988 he was well on his way to achieving that goal. Essence Communications had revenues of $31 million in 1987, and Lewis expected them to reach between $45 and $50 million in 1988. It was the twentieth largest black business in America in 1987.

By 1990 the situation was not quite so rosy at *Essence*. Advertising pages fell 7 percent in 1989, and dropped another 15 percent in the first quarter of 1990. This, however, was part of an overall softening of advertising in the early 1990s and was not out of step with the experience of mainstream magazines. But Lewis was particularly upset over the fact that some white companies, especially white cosmetics firms, refused to advertise in *Essence*, despite the fact that black women buy more cosmetics than the average consumer. By 1992 Essence was the twenty-third largest black-owned firm in the United States, with sales of over $43 million, and a staff of sixty-nine. Edward Lewis had come a long way from the young management trainee in New York City twenty years before. No wonder he could say; ''I'm a capitalist. I believe in the system.''

Sources

Personal and business papers for Edward Lewis and for Essence Communications are currently inaccessible. There is no full-scale biographical treatment of Lewis, but the best short biography is Ingham and Feldman, CABL. See also *Who's Who among Black Americans* (1988); and Doris F. Innis, *Profiles in Black* (New York, 1976) 44–45. The best sources of information appear in magazine and newspaper articles: *Newsweek*, May 11, 1970; *Time*, May 4, 1970; *National Review*, November 8, 1974; *Advertising Age*, July 28, 1975, April 9, 1977, and August 11, 1980; *Essence*, June 1975 and May 1980; *Black Enterprise*, June 1980, June 1988, and June 1992; *Toronto Globe & Mail*, May 24, 1988; *New York Times*, April 5, 1985, and May 7, 1990; *Wall Street Journal*, March 24, 1992; *Television/Radio Age*, January 6, 1986; *Product Marketing*, February 1980; Walter C. Daniel, *Black Journals of the United States* (Westport, Conn., 1982), 170–74. See also the transcript of an interview of Edward Lewis by Beverly Schuch on "Pinnacle," CNN Business News, June 16, 1990, and a press release containing biographical information on Lewis from Essence Communications.

Lewis, James (see Walter Cohen, James Lewis, and James Lewis, Jr.).

Lewis, James, Jr. (see Walter Cohen, James Lewis, and James Lewis, Jr.).

Lewis, Reginald F. (December 7, 1942–January 19, 1993). Arbitrager and conglomerate executive: TLC Group, Incorporated. Move over Donald Trump, look out Carl Icahn, here comes Reginald Lewis. Wall Street and black America were stunned in 1987 when Lewis, an African-American attorney and hitherto bit player in the high-stakes game of arbitrage and deal making, netted the largest offshore leveraged buyout in business history. His TLC Group first sold its holdings in McCall Pattern Company for a staggering 90-to-1 return on its original investment and then invested the proceeds and more to finance the $985 million purchase of Beatrice International Foods. In the twinkling of an eye, TLC Group became by far the largest firm owned by a black American, with revenues of $2.5 billion. In the previous year, the largest black-owned firm, the venerable Johnson Publishing Company, owners of *Ebony*, *Jet*, and a number of other interests, had sales of $173.5 million. TLC Group, the sixth-largest black company that year, had revenues of just $63 million. As Lewis later commented, "It was something like the gnat swallowing the elephant, which frankly appealed to me."

Lewis was born in Baltimore, Maryland, and was raised along with five half brothers and sisters in what Lewis called a "tough but stimulating neighborhood" in the city. He preferred not to talk much about his early years, saying, "I usually like to think ahead rather than go back." His upbringing, however, was essentially middle class. His mother, Carolyn, and father were divorced when he was young (some reports say when he was six, others when he was nine). The divorce must have brought some pain to young Lewis, but he said, "They were divorced but they were always good friends and certainly always supportive of each other when it came to their dealings with me, so the divorce didn't really adversely affect the love and affection I received from them." Because of the divorce, however, he and mother lived for several years with Lewis's grandparents, who also played an influential role in his upbringing. Lewis's mother, who was a postal worker, later married Jean Fugett an elementary schoolteacher.

in conjunction with his grandparents, evidently provided Lewis with an extremely supportive environment.

While attending Catholic elementary school, Lewis demonstrated the first glimmers of an entrepreneurial bent. Growing up in a black, working-class section of Baltimore, he got a paper route delivering the *Baltimore Afro-American* when he was nine. Lewis recalled that it "ultimately became a $15 to $20-a-week business—a lot of money in those days." Responding to the advice of his grandfather, Lewis put away a good deal of the money he was earning. "My grandfather used to tell me: 'save some, don't spend it all'—and I did. I would pay my own way to camp and buy my own clothes." When he did go off to camp for the summer, he did not give up his paper route—he turned it over to his mother. She said later, "He paid me a salary, but he made sure he made a profit, believe me." Lewis remembered well the values he learned from his grandparents, saying they were "[v]ery important, exceptional, very American, just very American in values and just honest, hard working, every day diligent type of people. I think of them often. They are very important to me." Later, after Lewis had "made it" on Wall Street, he paid his grandfather back by taking him to lunch at the Harvard Club in New York. Lewis recalled the incident fondly, "My grandfather was in his 80's and we knew he didn't have much time to live and he was brought up to New York by my stepfather actually and the two of us walked into the Harvard Club and we had a wonderful time together that I will always remember."

After elementary school, Lewis went on to Dunbar High School, where he captained the baseball, football, and basketball teams. Until he was fifteen, Lewis assumed that he would make a career in professional sports, retire when he was thirty, and then become a lawyer or businessman. That summer, however, he got a high-paying job as a waiter in a Baltimore country club, and he was able to play less and less baseball. He said too that the decision was based partly on the fact that he "[c]ouldn't hit the low outside curve ball." Throughout this time, however, he had never been completely focused upon sports, as is the case with many athletically gifted African-American children. "He put a lot of time into his studies," said his mother, "He didn't goof off." Judge Robert Bell, of the Court of Special Appeals in Baltimore, who was a classmate of Lewis's, says that Lewis "always knew where he wanted to go and he moved in that direction. . . . Reggie was a good guy, very ambitious. He always knew he'd make it."

Upon realizing that money was more important to him than athletics, he gave up his earlier dreams. Even as a teenager he had an eye for value. His mother later recalled that when Lewis was sixteen he wanted to buy an expensive pair of loafers. His mother demurred, but Lewis insisted, "Mother, they are worth every penny I'm going to pay for them." The shoes, it turned out, lasted Lewis through the rest of high school, four years of college, and three years of law school. He also early on seemed to shrug off the effects of racism and discrimination. When asked about his encounters with racism during these years, he replied, "After all, I was born in 1942. You can't be an American of African descent and not have experienced racism. Our high school teams didn't play white high school teams until my sophomore or junior year in high school." Despite this, he cautioned that "it would be unfair to suggest that I was denied opportunities. But that wasn't because of the absence of racism, but because of the support of my family and the belief they instilled in me that I could do whatever I wanted to do." He added, "I don't like to dwell on racism because I think it's unhealthy."

Lewis went on to Virginia State University, where he played quarterback on the football team for a year, until he injured his shoulder. What really captivated him was, of all things, basic economics. According to Lewis, it was "love at first sight." He thereupon focused all his energies on studying, and he compiled an enviable record at Virginia State. "He was so serious in school that we used to call him Lawyer Lewis," a classmate remembers. That was fitting, for from there Lewis went on to Harvard Law School, where he specialized in securities law. "I took a third-year seminar under Lewis Loss, the big man in securities regulation, and found it completely fascinating," Lewis says. "I wrote my third-year paper on take-overs. That, plus my general interest in economics, moved me in that direction." He also enjoyed the ambiance at Harvard and in Cambridge. "I enjoyed Harvard very much," says Lewis. "Cambridge was a very exciting place then. Everyone seemed to be very excited about what the future did hold. Of course, the Vietnam War was very much on everyone's mind at that time." Lewis, did not, however, engage in protests against the war.

After graduating in 1968, Lewis worked for the New York firm of Paul Weiss Rifkind Wharton & Garrison. Also, about the same time, he met his wife, Lolda Nicholas, who was also a lawyer. Lewis did well at Weiss, Rifkind, but the work did little to fuel his entrepreneurial ambitions. A colleague of his there recalls that Lewis "worked hard and was well-regarded by everybody . . . [but] like the other young lawyers at the firm at that time; they wanted to do something on their own." Lewis left in 1970, before finding out if he would become a partner, and before his pay got so high he could not afford to leave. In that year he became a partner in Murphy, Thorp & Lewis, the first black law firm on Wall Street.

After three years with that firm, Lewis decided to start his own company— Lewis & Clarkson—to specialize in venture capital work, with offices at 99 Wall Street. In that role Lewis was very successful, helping corporations such as Aetna, Equitable, and General Foods lend money to minority-owned firms. Lewis felt in later years that this work sharpened his appreciation for the "quantitative aspects of business and how businesses are analyzed." He had no formal business training, and he felt his interaction with a number of bright MBAs, both in the minority businesses and in the large corporations, gave him an invaluable education. After a decade of this, however, Lewis became bored. "There was not a lot I could do with the law firm besides making a good living unless I did the deals myself," he recalled. His partner, Charles Clarkson, recalled, "For years we did basic corporate law. [Lewis] always had this drive and an attitude that nothing could stop him from getting what he wanted. And more and more, Reg wanted to establish a vehicle for doing business ventures." In the meantime, Lewis was appointed in May 1979 to the Off Track Betting Corporation by Mayor Edward Koch, where he served for four years. This was a fruitful experience, since at OTB Lewis was an outspoken force in getting more black and Hispanic companies in the bidding for contracts. "I think I brought a different perspective to the board," Lewis said.

In 1983 Lewis started TLC Group as his vehicle to engage in business ventures. A year later he took $1 million in cash and a $24 million loan and bought the McCall Pattern Company, a 113-year-old sewing-pattern firm, that was suffering from a shrinking market and rapidly declining profitablity. Most analysts at the time thought it was a poor move on Lewis's part, but he proved them wrong. As he later said, "A lot of people had written off [McCall Pattern Company] as not having much of a future. The more I researched the facts, the more I thought it had a great future." The biggest advantage Lewis saw for McCall was that the shrinking market left it free of serious competition, an aspect he intended to capitalize upon. He developed a line of knitting patterns and began plans to export them to China, and he also branched into greeting cards, using McCall's distribution network. After Lewis ran the company for three and a half years, it showed a profit of $14 million. In all its previous years of operation, profits had never exceeded $6.5 million. Then, in a recapitalization plan in December 1986, McCall paid stockholders $19 million. All of this activity made the formerly weak concern a target for takeover. In the summer of 1987, Lewis sold McCall Pattern to Britain's John Crowther Group for $63 million in cash, at which time it also absorbed $32 million in debt. Lewis, who had invested $1 million in McCall, had sold it for ninety times what he paid for it. This astonishing achievement caught the notice of Wall Street, in particular Michael Milken, at that time Drexel Burnham Lambert's mastermind of leveraged buyout financing.

Without batting an eye, Lewis set out after bigger game. He found that Beatrice Food International was available, and he determined to make a bid for it. Lewis put the deal together, arranged much of the financing, and submitted a bid to Beatrice. At that point, Milken invited Lewis out to his office in Beverly Hills, where upon his arrival Milken suggested they work on something together. Lewis replied; "Mike, I just bid $950 million for Beatrice. How about that?" Milken's precise reaction is not recorded, but he and Drexel Burnham quickly took 35 percent of the action on Beatrice. Although Lewis welcomed Milken's assistance, all connected with the deal agree that Lewis himself masterminded it. Before submitting the bid, Lewis already had signed agreements to dispose of three of Beatrice International's units for nearly $430 million. He financed the rest of the deal with a $450 million line of credit from Manufacturers Hanover Trust and the profits from the McCall sale.

When the deal went through in August 1987, Lewis acquired a massive operation. With sixty-four separate companies in thirty-one countries, it had over

20,000 employees. To put that latter figure in some perspective, Johnson Publishing, previously the largest black-owned firm, had just over 1,800 employees. Lewis had acquired one of the giants of world food production, and Lewis found himself running an empire that ranged from the manufacture of ice cream in Italy to the making of potato chips in Ireland. And it was another venerable, mainline American firm that Lewis had acquired. Beatrice Foods, the parent firm of Beatrice International, was the thirty-sixth-largest industrial corporation in America, manufacturing over 8,000 product lines under more than 200 different brand names. In the early 1980s Beatrice acquired other food giants, picking up the Northwest Industries in 1981 and the giant Esmark (formerly Swift & Co.) in 1984. Esmark had in 1983 acquired another food giant, Norton Simon. Beatrice had used the leveraged buyout technique in acquiring these various firms, in the process accumulating an enormous debt load. In a complex series of manuevers, Donald P. Kelly, formerly head of Esmark, joined with the Wall Street firm of Kohlberg, Kravis and Roberts to engineer a leveraged buyout of Esmark. As a result, Beatrice needed to sell off some portions of these recent acquisitions to finance the purchases. This opened the door for Lewis's acquisition.

News of Lewis's coup staggered both Wall Street and the nation's black community. James Norton, a managing partner at UNC Ventures, a Boston-based black venture capital and investment banking operation, said that Lewis's acquisition "does a lot for me. When I go in to do a 10- or 20- or 30-million dollar deal, it strengthens my hand. It says to the people on the other side of the table that black folks can get things done." Jim Haddon, a black vice president at Paine Webber, the New York investment firm, said; "People think they've done something when they buy a house for $150,000 and sell it a few years later for $300,000. This says you can think a lot bigger, and think it realistically." The African-American economist, Andrew Brimmer, said; "The importance of Reginald Lewis is that he has demonstrated that he can attract Wall Street financiers and run a business not anchored in the black community."

Lewis was obviously very proud of his successful buyout of Beatrice, but the subsequent media focus on his skin color made him very uncomfortable. There was a tendency for both the black and white media to refer to him as the "Jackie Robinson of Wall Street," the man who broke the color barrier in large-scale mergers and acquisitions and leveraged buyouts. In an interview with *Black Enterprise*, Lewis said in response to the above description: "I really don't spend a lot of time thinking about that." At another time he said, "I'm trying not to take that too seriously, it's tough enough to operate without the added pressure that if I make a mistake, I let down 30 million people." He preferred simply to be considered a businessman who made a shrewd and intelligent business deal. "I'm very proud of the accomplishments of African-Americans," he said, "and I'm delighted that people feel this accomplishment adds to that list. But to dwell on race—to see that as something that becomes part of my persona—is a mistake, and I do everything I can to discourage it."

Some observers questioned whether Lewis had the background or ability to run an operation like Beatrice International, but others were confident he did. A managing director at Drexel Burnham said, "Reg is a tough, aggressive guy. He's going to be a highly successful fellow." Most agree he was strong willed and pursued what he wanted with utter confidence. Lewis approached the job as a corporate strategist, leaving the day-to-day operations to the managers already in place. As *Fortune* commented, "Lewis is expert at getting people to devote their best energies to a problem they may not have recognized." A partner in one of TLC Group's law firms concurred: "He has a way of making people set their goals a little higher, and helps them see what is possible if they spend a little more energy." The *New York Times*, in June 1991, reported that Lewis was doing an excellent job of running the Beatrice empire. "If one looks at the numbers that have come out of TLC Beatrice in recent quarters, the company has been financially successful by any measure under Reg Lewis," said Leonard G. Teitelbaum, a food analyst with Merrill Lynch Research. What he did soon after taking over, in order to finance his buyout, was to sell off 80 percent of the firm's Canadian operations, as well as businesses in New Zealand and Thailand. Lewis concentrated on Beatrice's European operations, and moved rapidly into Eastern Europe when the Iron Curtain fell. "Under the current management," says Kurt Kalm, of Dillon, Read & Company, "they are working the assets hard and doing better than ever before." In 1992 TLC-Beatrice remained by far the largest black-owned firm, with $1.542 billion in sales and 5,000 employees.

Lewis, despite his discomfort at being called a black pioneer or trailblazer, was very concerned with the fate of blacks in America, and he was one of Reverend Jesse Jackson's largest contributors in his run for the presidency in 1988. Lewis had first encountered Jackson in 1984, when Lewis was engineering the McCall deal and Jackson was making his first try at the presidency. They became close friends, and Jackson even claimed that Lewis got his courage to tackle Wall Street from watching Jackson try for the presidency. "It came to Reg that if I could function in that environment against those odds," Jackson said, "then he could function in the Wall Street environment against *those* odds." Whether or not that was true, Lewis did develop a deep admiration for Jackson, telling *Black Enterprise*: "I believe in the man. I also believe that the country really needs leadership [Jackson] has a vision of what the country should be. That's not to say I agree with everything Jackson says—I don't. But he has a clear vision of the direction in which he wants to take the country, and it's one that I share."

Whether Lewis's vision was exactly like Jackson's "rainbow coalition" is not clear. What is clear is that Lewis's vision of the future for blacks in American business was quite different from that of such other prominent black business leaders as Edward G. Gardner* and Dick Griffey.* Both Gardner and Griffey believe that black-owned businesses are the lifeblood of the black community, and they fear that the tendency of the most talented of young blacks to enter mainstream corporations will doom the residents of the black ghetto to remain an underclass in America. In response, Lewis pointed out that, in the 1940s and later, "you had great men like John Johnson* and later Berry Gordy*, and many, many others who started their businesses from scratch. That was fine. In fact, that was the way most companies were built in those days, black or white." Lewis thought that there were new and greater opportunities for blacks. Discussing his ability to obtain financing for massive takeovers of large corporations, Lewis said, "It's reassuring to know that the market will reward performance notwithstanding the problems that our society continues to have with Americans of African descent moving into the mainstream." Yet, he did not feel these "problems" were of great consequence. As far as whether it was possible for blacks to achieve success in the white corporate world, he said, "I think the sky is the limit. When it comes to African-Americans, I think our experience in this country puts us in a position to know that you achieve through very, very hard work, and that's very much in vogue these days." Horatio Alger wrote popular stories in the nineteenth century, extolling the ability of bright and plucky young men to achieve fame and fortune in the capitalist system. With Reginald Lewis, it seems that Alger had been reborn a black man.

Sources

No personal or business papers of Reginald Lewis or his companies are currently available. The best biography is in Ingham and Feldman, CABL. See also *Who's Who among Black Americans* (1988). The principal sources of information are articles in magazines and newspapers. See also the vertical files at the Schomburg Center and the New York City Research Center of the New York Public Library. A detailed obituary appears in *USA Today*, January 20, 1993. Some of the most useful articles include *Business Week*, June 3, 1985, and August 24, 1987; *Fortune*, September 14, 1987, and January 4, 1988; *Black Enterprise*, May 1974, January 1979, June, October, and November 1987, June 1988, February 1990, and June 1992; *U.S. News and World Report*, August 31, 1987; *Fortune*, September 14, 1987, and January 4, 1988; *Time*, August 24, 1987; *The Crisis*, October 1989; *Afro-American*, August 22, 1987; *New York Times*, March 20, 1988, and June 9, 1991; *New York Daily News*, May 9, 1990; *Newsday*, August 11, 1987, and November 19, 1989; *Atlanta Constitution*, September 11, 1987; *Wall Street Journal*, August 11, 1987; *News & Observer*, August 11, 1987; *Washington Post*, December 21, 1989. See also the transcript of an interview of Reginald Lewis by Beverley Schuch on "Pinnacle," CNN, August 20, 1988. For historical background on Beatrice, see Harry C. McDean, "Beatrice: The Historical Profile of an American-Styled Conglomerate," in *American Business History Case Studies*, edited by H. C. Dethloff and C. J. Pusateri (1987). There are some interesting articles written by Lewis in *Black Enterprise* dealing with business practices before he hit the "big time": "The Public Offering," June 1973, 127, 132; "Preparing for the Venture Capitalist," February 1973, 45; and "Acquiring a Business," March 1973.

Llewellyn, James Bruce (July 16, 1927–   ). Entrepreneur and public official: Fedco Stores; Coca-Cola Bottling Company of Philadelphia; Queen City Broadcasting; Garden State Cable; and Overseas Private Investment Corporation. In the 1980s, rock star Bruce Springsteen was often known simply by his sobriquet—"The Boss." For many blacks in the 1970s and 1980s, there was another

Bruce who was known to them as "the Boss"—J. Bruce Llewellyn. And with good reason. Perhaps no black businessmen has ever had a career to rival Llewellyn's. True, there were magnificently powerful older black businessmen who, like John H. Johnson* and even Berry Gordy, Jr.,* made a fortune merchandising aspects of black culture to white America and to blacks themselves. There was also a younger generation of black business leaders—men like Edward T. Lewis,* Reginald F. Lewis,* and Thomas J. Burrell*—who were making a fortune as blacks moved into the mainstream of white America. But Llewellyn— well there had never been anybody quite like him. He was a successful businessman, one who made fortunes with businesses that served the black community along with ones that served the broader public. But he was also a public official, serving in important, sometimes high-profile positions. In addition, he served as head of at least one prominent black social service organization and of the black community's highest profile bank. He was the closest thing the black business community has had to a Business Roundtable–type businessman. And Llewellyn even had a bit of show business in him. In several of his economic endeavors he collaborated with Julius Erving, the charismatic "Dr. J" of professional basketball, Bill Cosby, the most popular television star and performer in America, and football star and sportscaster O. J. Simpson and baseball star Dave Winfield. This "boss" did it all.

Bruce Llewellyn was born in Harlem, New York, son of recent immigrants to America from Jamaica. His parents, who came to the United States in 1921, were ambitious, highly motivated people, who wanted the best for themselves and their two children. At first his father, Charles Wesley Llewellyn, worked as a linotype operator for the old *New York Herald Tribune*. After two years, the family moved from Harlem to suburban Westchester County, settling in White Plains, a predominantly white, middle-class environ. Llewellyn recalled, "Basically I grew up like everybody else in a segregated section of an integrated neighborhood." That is, although White Plains had few blacks, and those who lived there were not segregated in a black area, they, nonetheless, tended to congregate near one another. But Llewellyn went to integrated schools, and he felt this was an important reason for his later success. "It's important that you have no sense of inferiority about what you're learning or about your abilities," he said. "In the real world you're up against everybody, so you ought to know if you can play or not."

Llewellyn's parents were great believers in the work ethic, and they instilled this in Bruce and his sister, who became a New York District Supreme Court judge. Even in his early years, Bruce Llewellyn worked in his father's bar and restaurant in White Plains and sold magazines and Fuller Brush products. "My father used to tell me that this is a great country with great opportunity but that you're going to have to work twice as hard to get half as much." In 1943, when he was sixteen, Llewellyn joined the U.S. Army and pursued advancement there with the same determination and zeal he demonstrated in later life. Since the army could not put him into combat until he was eighteen, Llewellyn studied engineering at Rutgers for more than a year as part of the army's specialized training program for aviation cadets. He graduated as a second lieutenant from Engineer's Officer Candidate School and was commissioned as the youngest officer in his battalion. The war came to an end in that year, however, and Llewellyn soon found himself in charge of a dump truck company.

Llewellyn was not satisfied with this turn of events, and he applied to West Point in a roundabout attempt to get out of the service. "I was trying to get out of the Army and I couldn't get out any other way because they were making me pay back the time I'd gone to college. So I took the exam, won the appointment, resigned my commission, refused to go to West Point, and got discharged." The discharge was also tied up with the fact that his father was seriously ill at this point and would die of a heart attack in 1949, one year after Llewellyn was discharged.

When Llewellyn came home in 1948, at just twenty-one years of age, he took his severance pay from the army and opened and operated a liquor store in Harlem. He was to prove in this endeavor, as he did with his army discharge, an astute student of laws and rules that he could use to his advantage. "The state government had a special kind of program for veterans," he said, "to get liquor licenses. It wasn't a bad business for a veteran to get into." He used the income from the store, along with his GI benefits, to meet living expenses while attending City College of New York in the mid–1950s. At first Llewellyn wanted to become a hospital administrator, but he soon changed his mind and decided to pursue a career in business or law. After getting his B.A., he entered the School of Business at Columbia University, where he concentrated on economics, but he did not write his thesis. He continued at New York Law School, where he received his J.D. in 1960 in an honors program.

When he got his law degree and passed the state bar in 1960, Llewellyn decided to go into politics and government service, feeling he would have his best career advancement in that area. As he later noted, "You got involved in politics, which in turn got you a job in city, state, or federal government. You weren't going to get a job with some major Wall Street firm, that's for sure." This was before the civil rights movement began to put pressure on the white establishment in the North to open up career opportunities to blacks, and Llewellyn believed that the most he could hope for was to be appointed a judge. He entered New York government in 1961 in the District Attorney's office, where he had worked as a student assistant while attending law school. He also was a partner in his own small law firm, which he had formed with a classmate, Sam Berger, during this time. Llewellyn then moved on to the city's Housing and Redevelopment Board in the mid–1960s. From there, Llewellyn went on to become regional director for the Small Business Administration and later executive director of the Upper Manhattan Small Business Development Corporation. In this post, he supervised the agency's five multiservice centers for minority businessmen. Then, in 1968, he became deputy commissioner of the city's Housing Commission. Llewellyn had come a long way, and it was clear that a judgeship was within his grasp by that point. It was also clear to him, however, from his work in the Small Business Administration, that the business world had opened up for blacks in ways that had not been true a decade earlier. Llewellyn determined to take advantage of this new, more favorable business climate.

Further, he had become frustrated with the public sector and its leviathan bureaucracy. "Most of the time," he said, "I found the places loaded with bureaucratic red tape and with a bunch of dumb people who retired from the moment they got the job. And they sure didn't want to hear a new idea about doing something. That really threw them into a tizzy. I decided the first chance I got, I was getting out of this." His chance came in 1969, when Sam Berger told him Fedco Foods Corporation, a chain of ten food stores in the economically devastated South Bronx, was for sale. Although the store chain was quite profitable, and had experienced significant growth, buyers shied away because of the stores' location. Llewellyn was undeterred. The main problem he had was raising the $3 million asking price for the chain. Llewellyn went to a longtime friend, Robert Towbin, who was a managing partner with the investment banking firm of L. F. Rothchild, Unterberg, Towbin. What Llewellyn proposed was, in effect, a leveraged buyout before leveraged buyouts became the rage. A leveraged buyout is a method of taking over a company by issuing securities backed by the target corporation's assets to finance the purchase. Towbin remarked that "Fedco was really one of the first leveraged buyouts that was ever done, before they became popular." He arranged for Llewellyn to meet with Prudential Insurance Company to arrange financing. "It was a co-operative effort between the buyer, seller, and lender," Towbin recalled.

It was still not easy. Llewellyn had to mortgage his house and cash in everything he owned, but Prudential did give him a $2.5 million loan to make the purchase. They also gave him a piece of advice. "They told me," said Llewellyn, "if it doesn't work we can guarantee that it will hurt you a hell of a lot more than it will hurt us." He reflected, "You had to learn or go out of business." Llewellyn was determined he would not fail. He kept the existing management at Fedco, including the former owners Ralph and Herbert Poses, as consultants until he was able to learn the business. The grocery business was all new to Llewellyn. Although he had retail experience with his Harlem liquor store in the 1950s, this was something else again. "It's much more complicated than a liquor store," he commented. But Llewellyn put an enormous effort into revamping the store's operations, and the results were soon apparent.

He was faced with a number of difficult problems. Like everyone else in the retail end of the food industry in the early 1970s, Llewellyn encountered escalating wholesale prices of farm products. Unlike many other grocery chain owners, however, most of his customers had incomes well below the median. Also, as an operator of inner-city stores, he had to contend with other special problems. There was high turnover among personnel, and minor theft by employees and shoplifters was a continual problem. There was also a different pattern of business in the inner city. "Stores in the central city do most of their business on Fridays and Saturdays," he said. "Whereas on weekends we can hardly keep pace, during the week the workers can coast. It's an unreasonable way of doing business." Nor did he get any special consideration from area residents because his stores were black owned. They wanted lower prices; and if Llewellyn could not provide them, they would go elsewhere. "It all boils down to where I can get the most for my money," said a local resident. "It's [Fedco] a major market in the area, but I have a car, so I go" to wherever she can get the best deals. Llewellyn realized that, saying, "Whenever we can, we try to undersell the major chains, but it's getting harder and harder to do that."

As Fedco became increasingly profitable—by 1983 it had sales of $85 million and had expanded to twenty-seven stores—Llewellyn's success greatly affected both the black and white business communities. Very few blacks, prior to this, had gotten multimillion dollar financing, and Llewellyn had shown that blacks could be successful. Towbin said, "Bruce established for a lot of people the fact that you back a black businessman and it could be successful." Llewellyn's success helped open up opportunities for the next generation of black business leaders.

As Llewellyn became a success with Fedco, he was called upon to assume greater visibility in the black business community. One of these roles involved the troubled Freedom National Bank in Harlem. The bank had been founded by Hall of Fame baseball star Jackie Robinson, but by 1971 it was in desperate need of help. It was $1.9 million in the red and facing bankruptcy. Robinson asked Llewellyn to join the board of Freedom National, and when Robinson died two years later, Llewellyn succeeded him as chairman. Llewellyn, while still running Fedco, beefed up the bank's management staff and loan portfolio, and got the backing of such heavyweights in the white business community as Goldman, Sachs, Morgan Stanley, and the Ford Foundation to help recapitalize the bank. He left as board chairman in 1975 with Freedom in relatively sound condition. Llewellyn's salvation of Freedom National, however, could not forestall its eventual demise, and its doors were finally shuttered in November 1990.

By the early 1980s, Llewellyn looked to move in a new business direction. He had long been impressed with the business possibilities of becoming a bottler for one of the major soft drink manufacturers. "I knew back in 1974 that I wanted to own a bottling company," Llewellyn said. The problem was getting one. Highly profitable enterprises, they were very scarce. Llewellyn initially pursued his interest with officials at Coca-Cola, but when that did not seem to be going anywhere, he made a bid for a Pepsi-Cola franchise that covered practically the whole state of Connecticut. Just three days before closing, however, the seller backed down. So, Llewellyn was forced to continue playing the waiting game. During this time he had a number of other interesting and attractive offers. In 1978 President Jimmy Carter asked him to become secretary of the army, but Llewellyn declined, suggesting that Carter appoint Clifford Alexander, his former law partner. A short time later, Carter called back and offered Llewellyn a job with the Overseas Private Investment Corporation (OPIC), a fifteen-year-old institution which had been started under the Nixon administration to provide insurance underwriting for American corporations conducting industrial operations in foreign countries. Llewellyn accepted the attractive offer. It was, first of all, in the business field, which would enhance Llewellyn's own profile in that area, and, second, it was a challenge that few blacks had ever been offered. The job involved negotiating with the heads of state and foreign ministers on some twenty foreign projects. Llewellyn made the organization far more efficient than it had been in the past, distributing $65 million in financing for projects and issuing $1.12 billion in risk insurance to corporations. The agency took in record profits during the years Llewellyn headed it.

When the Reagan administration came to power in 1981, Llewellyn had to leave the OPIC post, but he was even more determined to make his dream a reality. When he returned to the South Bronx, Llewellyn teamed with Julius Erving and Bill Cosby, and the three of them began to push for a Coca-Cola bottling franchise. They were immeasurably helped in their quest by a month-long boycott staged in 1981 by Reverend Jesse Jackson and his Operation PUSH. In its settlement with PUSH, Coca-Cola agreed to increase the participation of blacks in the company's business. Still, things did not happen overnight. It took two more years, but finally Llewellyn got his bottling company—or at least a piece of one. In the summer of 1983, Llewellyn, Erving, and Cosby purchased 36 percent of the Coca-Cola Bottling Company of New York. This made the group the largest single stockholder in the company, and it secured Llewellyn a seat on the board and the chairmanship of its subsidiary, the Philadelphia Coca-Cola Bottling Company.

In 1984 Llewellyn sold the Fedco stores, getting $20 million for the chain. With that money, Llewellyn made his first move toward media ownership, heading an investment group of black businessmen who joined with other minority investors to build a UHF station in San Diego, California. The investors, however, did not see eye to eye, and after a time the group of blacks from the East Coast, including Llewellyn, pulled out. "I don't like having a lot of partners," he said. "The fewer the better." The following year, however, was to be a red-letter one for Llewellyn.

In 1985 Bruce Llewellyn fulfilled two goals—he got his own bottling plant, and he controlled a major-market, network-affiliated television station. Ever since Llewellyn had bought into New York Coke, he had been negotiating with officials of the parent company to take over the Philadelphia bottling subsidiary. Finally, by the end of 1985, the terms for the purchase of the Philadelphia Coca-Cola Bottling Company were set. The three partners converted their New York Coke shares, got a loan of $75 million from various financial institutions, and bought out the Philadelphia operation. It was, at the time, the fifteenth-largest Coke bottling plant in the country, and the fourth-largest black business in America. Over the next several years, Llewellyn increased business at the plant some 300 percent as a result of adding thirty-six new routes and because of the enormous popularity of Julius Erving in Philadelphia, where he played basketball. In 1987, with sales of $166 million, Philadelphia Coca-Cola Bottling had moved up to the eighth-largest bottler in the Coke system, and was now the third-largest black-owned business.

In 1985 there were already eight other black-owned television stations in America, but most were small, independent UHF operations. The station Llewellyn pursued was different. When Capital Cities Communications had purchased the ABC Television network, the FCC had required that it divest itself of WKBW-TV (channel 7), the ABC affiliate station in Buffalo, New York. Putting together a coalition of investors to buy the station, Llewellyn enlisted Edward T. Lewis* of Essence Communications, Julius Erving, former U.S. Ambassador McDonald Henry, auto dealer Richard D. Gidron,* Richard Clarke, an executive recruiter, and several others in a new company called Queen City Communication. They put in a highly leveraged bid of $65 million for the station, but another bidder had already offered over $90 million. The one advantage Llewellyn and his group had going for them was that, if Capital Cities-ABC sold to a group of minority businessmen, it would get a tax certificate worth $30 million. Llewellyn and his group got the station. Two years later, WBKW-TV ranked first among the seven noncable stations in its market, and it was reputed to be a highly profitable entity.

When the sale was consummated, there was some criticism, most of it focusing on the highly leveraged nature of the buyout. Some businessmen said they felt Llewellyn and his group were getting in over their heads with the purchase, but Llewellyn dismissed the idea. ''That whole notion is ridiculous,'' he said. ''In the first place, we bought the station for $30 million less than it was worth at the time. The leverage is not really important.'' In 1987 Llewellyn arranged with Goldman, Sachs & Co. to help him raise $55 million by selling debentures to private investors for Queen City Communication Broadcasting. He said the cash would be used to acquire new stations and to pay off debt. All of this was a signal, however, that the situation with Queen City was not as rosy as Llewellyn had claimed. It had become clear by the late 1980s that the station was not generating enough cash from its operation to pay the cash part of its interest bill. The station for several years paid its bills by borrowing and by tapping the $10 million in cash that Llewellyn and his group had used to buy their stock. Worse still, the prices for television stations were starting to drop.

Llewellyn, yet again, proved himself to be a financial genius in getting rid of Queen City and by doing it at a profit to himself and his partners. In August 1990, he persuaded Prudential Insurance, his old backer at Fedco, to pay $13 million for 45 percent of the station, of which $12 million went to Llewellyn's investors, who continued to own 55 percent of the station. Allen Sloan, a financial columnist for *Newsday* wrote that Llewellyn ''has made the greatest escape seen in Buffalo since the Amazing Randi was stuck in a straitjacket, suspended by a crane over Niagara Falls and emerged to tell the tale.'' Prudential would not comment on the sale, other than to say, "We did it to make money." In the meantime, it freed Llewellyn to pursue his other business interests.

Llewellyn's newest love affair in business was with cable television. To this end, in January 1989, among with several others, he purchased New York Times Cable Company, headquartered in Cherry Hill, New Jersey. Llewellyn had a 20 percent stake in this venture, along with Julius Erving, Bill Cosby's wife, and members of Michael Jackson's family. His group was to contribute at least $25 million of the equity and will assume 20 percent of the debt. Joining them in ownership was Comcast Corporation and Lenfest Communications, each of which owned 40 percent. Llewellyn, all conceded, would be the active, managing partner of the business. The other partners credited Llewellyn with being the key player in the negotiations for the cable company. Gerry Lenfest, one of the other partners, said that when lawyers for the *New York Times* questioned whether enough equity could be raised: "At that point, Bruce just looked them in the eye and said 'I guarantee you that I will raise it. I have done it before, and I will do it again.' Without that pledge, I don't think we could have satisfied them." Llewellyn was no longer considered a "black" businessman—he was a real business heavyweight. "He insists on paying his own way," said Ralph Roberts of Comcast. "It was clear to us that he isn't looking for any special edges because he is a member of a minority group. To him, we are all the same. I have not met too many people like this."

Other African-Americans viewed this deal as a significant event for the black community. Marolyn L. Bailey of Comcast said; "This deal is highly significant for minority companies because, to date, it [the cable industry] was always thought to have been too capital-intensive. But this deal was structured with a minority partner being at risk with a good portion of the equity." Edward Lewis of *Essence* said, "This is just another wonderful step in the right direction for blacks in business. It's a major deal which shows that we will continue to grow and to expand to have something of our own." NYT Cable had 165,000 subscribers in fifty-nine municipalities in southern New Jersey, in an area with about 263,000 households. With 309 employees, its revenues in 1988 were over $57 million. With the cable company in his pocket, Llewellyn indicated that he was also in the market for a professional sports team, but as of 1992 nothing had come of that desire.

By 1992 Bruce Llewellyn had a tidy little business empire. He was the only person who during the twenty years of the existence of *Black Enterprise*, had had four different firms on its list of the 100 largest black businesses. Fedco stores was for years the fourth-largest firm on the list until he sold it to non-minority investors in 1984. Llewellyn was soon back on the list in 1986 with two ventures, Philadelphia Coca-Cola Bottling and Queen City Broadcasting. In 1991 his third firm on the list was Garden State Cable, the old New York Times cable firm. In 1992 Philadelphia Coca-Cola was the third-largest black business, with sales of $256 million and over 1,000 employees. Garden State Cable was the sixth-largest firm, with $88 million in sales and 300 employees.

Queen City Broadcasting had fallen to forty-eighth on the list, with revenues of just over $25 million and 130 employees.

Bruce Llewellyn's most important area of leadership in the black community outside of business was his presidency of 100 Black Men. This was an extraordinarily influential group of black business and professional leaders, which had started in New York City in 1965, but later expanded to become a national organization. As president, Llewellyn commented; "Together we encompass the most accomplished group of blacks in this country, and we are—without a doubt—the most powerful black organization in the city. And 100 Black Men is using its influence to elect meaningful change for the total black community." Some agree with that assessment, and some do not. Walter Page, president of Morgan Guaranty Trust Company, commented; "These men are honestly seeking to secure a place for themselves within the system. They are not asking for handouts." Charles Luce, chairman of the board of Con Ed, remarked; "We have had frequent contact with 100 Black Men, both as individuals and as a group. We appreciate their efforts on behalf of the community." Some black community leaders, however, are less positive. "I can't truthfully tell anyone that 100 Black Men has managed to improve the quality of life in Harlem," said Marshall England, head of Haryou, a community development corporation. William Hatcher, president of a self-help group in Harlem, comments; "I've been active in community affairs for almost twenty years, and I had never heard of 100 Black Men until a year ago. Frankly, most people in Harlem are too busy trying to get their heads out of the sand to be concerned about 100 Black Men."

Bruce Llewellyn, a six-foot, 5-and-a-half-inch, 250-pound, almost larger-than-life, man effects a casual and modest appearance, but he is a tremendously driven and ambitious man. Richard Clarke, a longtime friend, said of Llewellyn; "When you eat with Bruce, as soon as you are done, he'll grab the plates, wash them, and come back with the brandy and cigars. He's always anxious to get on to the next step." Llewellyn's outlook is tough and determined, but decidedly upbeat. "My father always told me," he told *Business Week*, "that brains and education can defeat prejudice within society." Edward Lewis, another business associate and friend, said of Llewellyn, "He's a very, very smart guy who can get to the heart of whatever the problem or situation is." Bruce Llewellyn, in the 1980s, was leading black businessmen into an area that was relatively new to them—the general market. Llewellyn himself was keenly aware of what he was doing: "In the old days black business people had to be based in the black community," he said. "You had generations of the John Johnsons and the Berry Gordys who expanded the black community from local neighborhoods to the national community. Now we're dealing with the entire community. I've never really been a general marketer." But by 1992 he was, and a highly successful one to boot.

Sources

No personal or business papers of Bruce Llewellyn are currently available. There is no full-length biography; the best short treatment is in Ingham and Feldman, CABL. See also *Who's Who among Black Americans* (1986); and Frank L. Johnson, *Who's Who among Black Millionaires* (1984). The best information on Bruce Llewellyn comes from various magazine and newspaper articles, including *Black Enterprise*, June 1972, 32+, June 1973, 36, October 1983, 19, March and September 1986, June 1987, June 1988, March and June 1989, and June 1992; *Forbes*, May 5, 1986; *Business Week*, November 16, 1987; *Nation's Business*, September 1990, 41–44; *Fortune*, March 1990, 52–54; *Jet*, February 21, 1974, 15, June 28, 1979, 54, December 2, 1985, 16, and August 14, 1989, 37; *Ebony*, October 1975, 72–80, and June 1987; *Sepia*, September 1971, 28–35; *Datamation*, September 1977, 266–67; *The Crisis*, October 1989; *Los Angeles Times*, May 29 and August 6, 1990; *Minorities and Women in Business*, November/December 1986; *Atlanta Journal/Constitution*, July 9, 1983; *New York Post*, March 19, 1975; *Wall Street Journal*, January 19, 1989, B1; *New York*, January 24, 1977. A press release from the Philadelphia Coca-Cola Bottling Company was also used in the preparation of this biography.

M

Merrick, John (September 7, 1859–August 6, 1919). Insurance company and bank founder, real estate investor, entrepreneur, barber: North Carolina Mutual Insurance, Mechanics and Farmers Bank, Merrick-Moore-Spaulding Land Company, Bull City Drug Store, Durham Textile Mill. In October 1898, John Merrick, a wealthy African-American barber and entrepreneur, brought together six black men in the skilled trades and professions in Durham and nearby Raleigh, North Carolina. Each man put $50 into the infant enterprise. They created what was to become the North Carolina Mutual Insurance Company. Although this was not the first black-owned and black-managed life insurance firm, it soon grew to become the largest of its type. It was Merrick's organizational ability, his contacts with the white community, and his status in the broader African-American community that did much to make the venture the success it became.

John Merrick was born a slave in Sampson County, North Carolina. He never knew his father, but his mother was apparently very loving and supportive of John and his brother. Virtually nothing, however, is known of John Merrick's early life. How much education he received, or how good it was, is not recorded. We do know that in 1871, at the age of twelve, Merrick began working in a brickyard in Chapel Hill to help support his family. Six years later he and his mother and brother moved to Raleigh, where John began working as a hod carrier. Working on the first buildings on the Shaw University campus, Merrick advanced from hod carrier to brick mason. The ambitious Merrick, however, knew that manual labor would not provide the sort of upward mobility he craved. Therefore, he left to take the more menial job of a shoe shiner in a barber shop. This might seem a strange step down, from skilled brick mason to bootblack, but Merrick knew that barbering was one of best professions for a young black man who wanted to open his own business. Therefore, while shining shoes, he learned the barbering trade.

Merrick's regular customers in the Raleigh shop included members of the Duke family and Julian S. Carr, all of whom were wealthy tobacco manufacturers of nearby Durham. They soon persuaded Merrick and his senior associate, John

Wright, to come to Durham to set up a decent barber shop there. Merrick agreed, but it was, in the context of the time, an unusual choice. Raleigh at that time was one of the beacons of black business in North Carolina, while Durham was then little more than a bump in the road. John Merrick and Durham, however, proved to be well matched. Merrick was one of those rare entrepreneurs who radically transform their environment, and Durham was a relatively blank slate on which he could make his mark.

Durham was a "new city" in the late nineteenth century. For a young man on the make, someone rising rapidly from the very depths of servitude and poverty to comfortability and respectability, Durham held out alluring prospects. Created to take advantage of the industrialization of the "New South," Durham boasted that it had "no aristocracy but the aristocracy of labor." Within obvious limits, Durham's white businessmen, like Washington Duke and Julian S. Carr, encouraged black enterprise. The town's first African-American newspaper caught the spirit: "Everything here is push, everything is on the move, every citizen is looking out for everything that will make Durham great. The Negro in the midst of such life has caught the disease and . . . awakened to action." As Walter Weare has commented; "As a raw city of the New South, Durham possessed neither a white aristocracy nor a 'cream of colored society,' which one would find in older cities like New Orleans or Charleston." Durham was hardly a utopia in race relations, no city in America could make that boast, nor was it a society completely open to talent. But, compared to most venues in the South during this time, there was more latitude for African-Americans of ability, drive, and a willingness to show a certain deference to their white "superiors" to achieve success.

Still a tiny frontier town in the 1870s, Durham began attracting a small cadre of black migrants during that decade. Several, including George Pearson and Robert G. Fitzgerald, managed to accumulate substantial amounts of property. Merrick and Wright came to Durham in 1880, and Merrick worked as the senior man's assistant for six months. He then bought a share of the shop. The two men ran the shop together until 1892, when Wright sold out to Merrick. Wright later commented about his relationship with John Merrick: "Merrick and I were in business many years and during that time we never disagreed. I always found him congenial and ready to serve the customers and likewise courteous . . . Merrick continued to succeed [after Wright left] in all lines of business and everything he turned his hands to turned to money."

Indeed it did. Few blacks in late nineteenth-century America showed such a knack for business success. With little capital, Merrick had to start in a small way. First, in 1881, he purchased a lot in the black section of town known as Hayti and built a small home there next to one Wright had constructed for his family. This was the beginning of Merrick's real estate purchases. Into this home he moved his wife, Martha Hunter, and their first two children were born there. After buying out Wright's share of the business, Merrick's entrepreneurial bent showed itself, as he rapidly began expanding the enterprise, soon owning five barbershops in the city, and for a time as many as nine. During these same years, he also continued to buy lots, build houses on them, and rent them out. He soon had a rather comfortable little real estate empire in the Hayti section.

It was during these years also that Merrick developed a dandruff cure, which he had been working on since 1890. He wrote a series of ads for his treatment, which demonstrate his creativity and business sense, but also his lack of formal education: ''No Dandruff cure has ever been put upon the market that has found such favor with the Tonsorial Profession as Merricks Dandruff Cure. No greec [sic], no fussy oder [sic] its quick erfeck [sic] its cooling and clensing [sic] Power make it wonderful.'' Merrick also became involved with a fraternal organization in 1883, in conjunction with John Wright and some other black businessmen, purchasing the Royal Knights of King David from Reverend Morrison of Georgia. The Royal Knights, like most African-American fraternal orders of that time, had insurance features and was run on the assessment plan. They began expanding the order throughout the southern states, and by 1918 it had 21,000 members, was bringing in $8,000 per month, and owned $22,000 in bonds and securities and $40,000 in property.

Merrick's fifteen years at the helm of the Royal Knights, however, must have given him some doubts about the capacity of fraternal orders to provide adequate insurance service for African-Americans. They, in effect, just provided burial insurance, whereas Merrick and others were already thinking in terms of offering a wider variety of life insurance options. But something else sparked Merrick's decision to found North Carolina Mutual in October 1898—the ghastly Wilmington, North Carolina, race riot earlier that year. The Wilmington riot came about when conservative white Democrats, angry over black political influence in the city, staged a night of terror, in which between eight and thirty blacks were killed, large numbers were wounded, and masses, including many of the black political and business leaders, were run out of town. It also killed Wilmington as a center of black economic and social life in North Carolina.

The riot also had a profound effect on John Merrick, and he became a staunch proponent of Booker T. Washington's[*] ideals of self-help, free enterprise, and accommodation on issues of political and social equality. Merrick was so upset by what had happened that he made one of his very rare public speeches in announcing the formation of North Carolina Mutual: ''The Negroes have had lots of offices in this state and they have benefited themselves very little. . . . Had the Negroes of Wilmington owned half the city . . . there wouldn't anything happened to them [to] to compare with what did. Let us think more of our employment and what it takes to keep peace and to build us a little house.''

Merrick joined with Edward Austin Johnson[*] and James E. Shepard, both of Raleigh, Dr. Aaron McDuffie Moore, William Gaston Pearson, Dock T. Watson, a roofing contractor, and Pinkney William Dawkins, a schoolteacher, to found the new insurance firm. Later, Robert G. Fitzgerald would become an investor and director of the company. Fitzgerald by that time owned a brickyard, the largest black business in Durham, and was reputed to be the wealthiest African-

American in the area. Aaron McDuffie Moore had come to Durham in 1888 from Columbus County, North Carolina, near Wilmington. This area was the home of several future executives of North Carolina Mutual, including C. C. Spaulding* and Asa T. Spaulding.* Moore, a graduate of Shaw University, was Durham's first black physician, and later, with Merrick, and Robert's brother Richard B. Fitzgerald,* founded the Bull City Drug Company. Moore and Merrick, with the aid of the Duke family, also established Lincoln Hospital, one of the better private hospitals for blacks in the South.

William Gaston Pearson was secretary and manager of the Royal Knights of King David, running it until his death in 1928. He was also intimately involved with Merrick in practically every one of his business ventures. Pearson was the son of George Pearson, the principal developer of the Hayti region, and one of the earliest black settlers of Durham. Edward A. Johnson and James E. Shepard had each been deeply involved in Republican politics in Raleigh, and both men became eminent educators. Johnson and Shepard had gotten burned by the volatile fusion issue in North Carolina politics, and they left Raleigh in despair at their political fortunes there. Shepard, who had been born in Raleigh, graduated from Shaw University in 1894. In Durham, Shepard became the founder and leader of what is today North Carolina Central University. Johnson was born a slave in 1860 and graduated from Atlanta University in 1883. In Raleigh he became the principal of Washington High School, and he wrote *A School History of the Negro Race* to teach black children about the contributions of members of their race to history. He was also involved with Warren C. Coleman* in establishing the first cotton mill owned by blacks in the state. Johnson was a sizable realty holder in Raleigh, and in 1902 he was one of only two black residents of the city whose income was sufficient to warrant payment of state income tax. These men Merrick chose to join with in founding North Carolina Mutual, then, were the cream of Durham and Raleigh's black elite—the wealthiest and most well regarded African-Americans in the area. Nonetheless, the company nearly foundered during its first year of existence.

North Carolina Mutual actually began operations in April 1899, and within six months was on the brink of collapse. Merrick called a meeting, and he and Moore bought out the interests of the other five investors. It was at this time that Robert Fitzgerald joined the firm. The most important decision Moore and Merrick made this time, however, was to recognize that neither of them had the time to engage in full-time management of the concern. So Moore hired a relative from Columbus County, Charles Clinton Spaulding, to be full-time manager of the operation. This bit of nepotism turned out to be a stroke of genius, since Spaulding became the firm's driving dynamo during its first half-century. Spaulding talked about the roles of the three men during these early years: "I was manager, agent, clerk and janitor and had to do local collecting as well as organize new fields in the adjacent counties. Dr. Moore and Mr. Merrick served without salaries, each continuing to follow his chosen business while I took the field on a commission basis.''

If Merrick was not the day-to-day manager of North Carolina Mutual, he was the firm's public relations man and figurehead at a critically important time. At first North Carolina just wrote industrial insurance, but in 1904 it began to write industrial straight life, followed a year later by ordinary life insurance. It also began to offer a number of endowment policies. It took a number of years before the company really became solvent, and after they decided to advertise in the *Blade*, a black newspaper in Raleigh, growth truly began to spurt. Income, which in 1899 was just $840, stood at $1,662,527.28 in 1919. Insurance in force was at over $16 million by that time.

For Merrick, however, North Carolina Mutual was in many respects merely the cornerstone of a large financial empire he created in Durham. Although Durham was just a small city of 6,000 in 1900, about one-third of its population was black, and black people formed the basis of the economic enterprises Merrick created at this time. One of the most important of these was the Mechanics and Farmers Bank. This institution was actually begun by R. B. Fitzgerald and W. G. Pearson. They each put up $1,000 to start the bank and persuaded Merrick to subscribe $1,000. Mechanics and Farmers was not actually organized until 1907, however, when another $7,000 was pledged. Dr. Moore and James E. Shepard were other subscribers to this venture, and Shepard became one of the critical factors in its early success. The bank had its offices in the North Carolina Mutual building, with Fitzgerald as president, Merrick as vice president, and Pearson as first cashier. The bank became an important element in the development of black capitalism in Durham and, by the early 1920s, had deposits amounting to over $600,000 and resources of $800,000. In 1920, the bank saved more than 500 homes and farms belonging to blacks in Durham by lending the purchasers over $200,000.

Merrick and Moore were also responsible for the founding of a number of other significant black business ventures in Durham. Merrick had long been accumulating real estate in the city, as had North Carolina Mutual. After the state insurance commissioner advised that the insurance firm unload much of its real estate, replacing it with more secure bonds and mortgage loans, the company complied. In doing so, it set up the Merrick-Moore-Spaulding Land Company to own and manage these properties. In 1906 North Carolina Mutual set up its own newspaper, the *Durham Negro Observer*. This was not a success, but the *North Carolina Mutual*, also published by the company, continued for decades as the only black newspaper in the city. In 1908, the same year the bank was opened, Merrick, Moore, Pearson, Fitzgerald, and Shepard also started Bull City Drug Company, to operate drugstores in the black section of town. One of the most important ventures started by Merrick, Moore, and Spaulding was the Durham Textile Mill in 1914. The three men raised $10,000 to start the mill but found it difficult to operate because of a shortage of skilled black labor and problems of establishing a market for its products. Also, none of the three owners was able to commit enough time to manage the facility, and C. C. Amey, who was chosen as manager, was inexperienced.

In 1907 Edward R. Merrick, John Merrick's son, entered North Carolina Mutual. Born in 1888, he graduated from A. and T. College in Greensboro. Edward Merrick soon became a director of the firm, and in 1923, upon the death of Dr. A. M. Moore, he was elected treasurer of the company. Edward Merrick served in that position until he retired in 1957. In 1952 he also became president of Mutual Savings and Loan, another venture developed under the aegis of North Carolina Mutual and advanced to chairman of Mutual Savings in 1962. He died in 1967. His 1916 marriage to Lydia Vivian Moore, daughter of Dr. Moore, cemented an alliance between perhaps the two most powerful black families in the state. In 1952 Lydia Moore Merrick founded the *Negro Braille Magazine*, the only national publication directed toward sightless black people.

In 1906 North Carolina Mutual moved to a new and larger office building on the margins of the white business community. It formed the center of a new black business complex there. In the building were two clothing stores, a barber shop, a large drugstore, a tailoring shop, the newspaper, and the Mechanics and Farmers Bank. By 1910, when Booker T. Washington visited Durham, the small city of 18,000 had a vibrant black business community. Washington was so impressed that he praised Durham as the most progressive city in the South and cited Merrick as the unquestioned leader of its business community. Few if any questioned Washington's judgment on that score. Merrick was considered by virtually everyone in Durham, black or white, as the unquestioned leader of the black community.

E. Franklin Frazier, evaluating North Carolina Mutual as an emblem of the "New Negro" of the 1920s, contrasted Merrick's more subservient "slave" mentality with Spaulding's more modern, independent personality. There can be little doubt that Merrick's early success owed much to his access to white capitalists. As his biographer has noted, "Mr. Merrick's contact with the leading businessmen of Durham had as much to do with his success as his own personal gifts." He was observed on some occasions "toadying up" to influential whites. But to view Merrick solely as a "white man's nigger" is to badly miss the point. Like so many slaves and ex-slaves, he learned, as Langston Hughes said, to "wear the mask." Walter Weare points out that contemporary blacks knew well that Merrick could with "great poise, tip his hat to a white man and at the same time call him a son-of-a-bitch under his breath." In the urban South at the turn of the century, race relations were balanced on a knife edge. It took a man with abilities as unique as Merrick's to walk that line with perfect balance—he persuaded wealthy whites to subsidize a number of black ventures with both money and moral support, but never once did he compromise the independence or success of these ventures in doing so. That is the mark of an exceptional man.

Sources

John Merrick's papers may not exist. There is just one letter from Merrick to John Carlise Ilgo in the Duke University Archives, and a scattering of letters between Merrick and Booker T. Washington and Emmett J. Scott in the Booker T. Washington Papers at the Library of Congress. Material on North Carolina Mutual, in the Charles C. Spaulding

Papers held at the insurance company, is not currently open to researchers. There is some material on the early founding and operation of the firm in the Southern Historical Collection, Southern Oral History Program at the University of North Carolina at Chapel Hill. These largely consist of interviews conducted by Walter Weare with various members of North Carolina Mutual. Most of the interviews, conducted in the 1980s, of necessity focus on the period after Merrick's death. There is also an interview with E. R. Merrick, John Merrick's son, about James B. Duke in the Duke Endowment Archives, Oral History Division, Duke University.

The only full-scale biography of Merrick is Robert McCants Stewart, *John Merrick: A Biographical Sketch* (1920), which was written just after his death. There is a good deal of valuable information in William J. Kennedy, *The North Carolina Mutual Story* (1970), but by far the most incisive account is Walter B. Weare's *Black Business in the New South: A Social History of the North Carolina Mutual Life Insurance Company* (1973). See also Jesse Edward Gloster, "North Carolina Mutual Life Insurance Company: Its Historical Development and Current Operations," Ph.D. diss., University of Pittsburgh, 1955. There are shorter biographies of Merrick in Benjamin Brawley, *Negro Builders and Heroes* (Chapel Hill, 1946); George W. Reid and Freddie L. Parker in *Dictionary of American Negro Biography* (1942); Ingham, BDABL; *Black Enterprise* VI (June 1976), 121; A.B. Caldwell, *History of the American Negro*, vol. VI (1921); C. H. Hamlin, *Ninety Bits of North Carolina Biography* (1946), 124–26; *Durham Herald-Sun*, July 11, 1943; *Durham Herald*, February 2, 1988; Roi Ottley, *Black Odyssey* (1949), 234–40; *Paths toward Freedom* (1976), 174. An early listing of Merrick, his profession and residence, can be found in *Directory of the Business and Citizens of Durham City for 1887*, compiled by Levi Branson (Raleigh, 1887), 93.

For information on some of those who joined with Merrick in founding North Carolina Mutual: On Robert G. Fitzgerald, see Pauli Murray, *Proud Shoes: The Story of an American Family* (New York, 1956); *Durham Recorder* (April 16, 1900); *Crisis* (June 1920), 93; *Dictionary of North Carolina Biography*, vol. I (1979); Fitzgerald Family Papers, Southern Historical Collection, University of North Carolina at Chapel Hill. There are also several Fitzgerald letters in the Duke Papers at Duke University. On William G. Pearson, see Albon L. Holsey, "Pearson: Brown Duke of Durham," *Opportunity* VI (April 1923), 116–17. On Dr. Aaron McDuffie Moore, see "Aaron McDuffie Moore, M.D.," *Journal of the National Medical Association* XVI (January-March 1924), 72–74; *Durham Herald*, February 2, 1988; Louis D. Mitchell, "Aaron McDuffie Moore: He Led His Sheep," *The Crisis*, August-September 1980; M.W. Williams and George W. Watkins, *Who's Who among North Carolina Negro Baptists* (1940), 189. There are also some letters from Moore to Booker T. Washington in the latter's papers in the Library of Congress. On Edward R. Merrick, see *Durham Morning Herald*, June 9, 1966, and February 9, 1967. On his wife, Lydia Merrick, see North Carolina Clipping File at the University of North Carolina, Chapel Hill Library; *Raleigh News and Observer*, June 1, 1977; *Public Libraries* 20: 3 (Fall 1981); *Durham Morning Herald*, February 15, 1987; *Hope and Dignity: Older Black Women of the South* (Philadelphia, 1983), 69–71; and the Oral History Collection in the Duke Endowment Archives. On Edward A. Johnson, see *Raleigh News and Observer*, January 14, 1951; and June 10, 1976; *Crisis*, April 1933; *Dictionary of North Carolina Biography*, vol. I (1979), 288–89; G.F. Richings *Evidences of Progress among Colored People* (1897); *Who's Who in Colored America* (1928–1929); *School and Society*, July 29, 1944; *Journal of Negro History*, October 1944; *New York Times*, July 25, 1944. On James E. Shepard, see George W. Reid,

"James E. Shepard and the Public Record of the Founding of North Carolina College at Durham, 1909–1948"; *Negro History Bulletin* 41, 6 (November–December 1978), 900–901.

Milton, Lorimer D. (see Jesse B. Blayton, Lorimer D. Milton, and Clayton R. Yates).

Misshore Family (see Dejoie, Geddes, and Misshore Families).

Mitchell, John, Jr. (July 11, 1863–December 3, 1929). Banker, publisher, politician, entrepreneur, and editor: Richmond *Planet*, Mechanics Bank, Repton Land Company, and Unique Amusement Corporation. America, and certainly Virginia, was hardly prepared for the likes of John Mitchell, Jr., at the turn of the last century. Proud, brilliant, charismatic, and fearless, Mitchell was accomplished in many fields. He was a powerful, if somewhat bombastic, writer of crusading editorials for black rights, and he was an astute businessman and pioneering banker, an accomplished politician and political leader, and a bluntly outspoken opponent of segregation and white racism. Mitchell was a social leader of Richmond's African-American community and head of one of the city's leading fraternal groups. He was also, in the bargain, tall, handsome, and dashing, and always dressed impeccably in the latest of fashion. A source of constant attention from the city's black females, Mitchell never married. He was, in all respects, a renaissance man.

John Mitchell, Jr., was born in Laburnum, just outside of Richmond, Virginia, of slave parents. His father and mother, John and Rebecca Mitchell, who have been described as "exceptional slave parents," were house servants on the plantation of James Lyons, a wealthy and aristocratic lawyer, and a member of the Confederate Congress. At the end of the Civil War, John and Rebecca, along with their young son, deserted the Lyons plantation in the first flush of their newly acquired freedom. Where they went is not certain, but what is clear is that they were soon persuaded to return to work for Lyons. It is difficult to estimate what emotional traumas these tumultuous years visited upon the elder Mitchells, but in many respects their return to the Lyons plantation no doubt worked to young John Mitchell's advantage.

Whatever indignities and drudgery John and his parents experienced on the Lyons estate during the postwar years, there is little question that he had advantages unavailable to most African-Americans in Richmond at the time. Young John was not only able to learn all the "rules of polite society," which would be of great benefit to him in later years, but was also able to make contacts with important white families which were to prove invaluable, if also rather constraining. As Ann Field Alexander has stated, "Like his former master (James Lyons), John Mitchell would long be remembered for his distinguished appearance, his courtly manners, and his aristocratic bearing."

The greatest influence on Mitchell's life, however, was his mother. An intelligent and ambitious woman, she had somehow learned to read and write as a slave and was determined that her son would have all the advantages that education and learning could bring. She also gave Mitchell his fierce racial pride and unwillingness to brook any racial insults. When James Lyons refused to allow John Mitchell to attend school, Rebecca taught him at home while he worked as a carriage boy on the plantation. In 1870, when Mitchell was seven years old, Reverend Anthony Binga, Jr., a black abolitionist who had recently come to Richmond from Canada, opened a private school for blacks. Young John was one of his first pupils, and he remained with Binga for two years until he entered the public schools of the city. Since only one of five black children in Richmond in the 1870s was able to attend school, Mitchell was indeed fortunate during these years. Becoming a fine student, in 1876 he entered Richmond Normal and High School, the best black high school in the state, which had been founded nine years earlier under the auspices of the Freedman's Bureau by R. M. Manly, a northern, white carpetbagger.

Mitchell flowered at "Colored Normal," as it was called, and, when he graduated in 1881, he was chosen to give the valedictory address. He now stood ready to conquer black Richmond, and perhaps even Richmond itself, since at that time most African-Americans viewed the future in rosy terms. It seemed to be a world open to men of talent, and, all agreed, no young African-American in the city had more charm and talent than John Mitchell. But Mitchell was hardly the only talented black striving for success during this time. In the years since the Civil War, a vigorous black middle class had emerged in the city, and young men of Mitchell's age added to that during the next quarter century. Whereas the earlier black businessmen had catered to the white community, those of Mitchell's generation turned to servicing the needs of African-Americans, so much so that the streets of "Africa" in Richmond by the turn of the century were lined with black banks, funeral parlors, law firms, newspaper offices, groceries, and churches. Among that younger generation of blacks, John Mitchell emerged preeminent.

Upon graduation from Colored Normal, Mitchell applied to teach in the Richmond public school system. Despite his evident credentials, however, he did not secure a position, and he was forced to accept a job teaching in the public schools of Fredericksburg, Virginia. Two years later, however, with the victory of the "Readjuster" faction in state politics, a new school board was put in place in Richmond. Far more sympathetic to blacks, they fired about thirty white teachers in the city's black schools and hired a number of African-Americans to replace them. Mitchell was among those hired in 1883, and he began teaching at the Valley School that year. At the same time, he became the Richmond correspondent to the *New York Globe*, a leading black newspaper edited by T. Thomas Fortune. This was Mitchell's first introduction to the world of journalism.

Mitchell's most important career move came in December 1884, when he was chosen editor of the year-old Richmond *Planet*. The paper had been founded by a number of politically conscious young blacks, including three men who were principals in Richmond's schools. The paper's first year was a rocky one, as it had to compete for the African-American reader's attention with two other black journals in the city. Important for its early survival, however, was its subsidization by the Independent League, which had been founded by D. Webster Davis, another Richmond teacher. John Mitchell was one of the founding members of the league and thus was drawn into the affairs of the *Planet* from the very beginning.

In November 1883, however, the Readjusters suffered an ignominious defeat at the polls, and African-American leaders in Richmond were despondent. The fortunes of the *Planet* suffered a corresponding decline during the following year, since one of the purposes of the infant paper had been to act as a spokesman for the Readjuster politicians. Further, the conservatives, when they got control of the city's board of education, fired a host of black teachers, including ten of the seventeen involved in the founding of the *Planet*. Mitchell was one of those given the axe. When the twenty-one-year-old Mitchell, in December 1884, offered to assume the debts of the *Planet*, the rest agreed to elect him as editor.

One of the first things Mitchell did was to make plans for the *Planet* to acquire its own printing company, thereby freeing it from dependence on a white printing firm. To this end, Mitchell organized the Planet Publishing Company to subsidize the *Planet* and to acquire a printing press. By the end of the year, the publishing company had bought a secondhand press, and Mitchell had become publisher as well as editor of the Richmond *Planet*. Important to the success of the newspaper during these early years was Mitchell's entrepreneurial skills, and a calculated gambler's attitude that prompted him to take risks in expanding the *Planet*'s facilities during lean times. Although these expenditures plunged both him and the newspaper into debt, they also provided the means whereby it could outgrow its infancy and become an organ of no little importance in the South and nationally.

Another source of strength for Mitchell and the *Planet* was Richmond's fraternal organizations. During its early years, Mitchell was closely tied to William Washington Browne[*] and his Order of True Reformers, the largest African-American organization in the state. In 1894 Mitchell broke with Browne, and after 1900 he became an important factor in the Knights of Pythias, serving as its grand chancellor. Both organizations provided extensive subsidies to the *Planet* in return for coverage in the paper. In addition, as with nearly all black newspapers, the *Planet* was closely tied to African-American businesses in the city, providing them and their owners with a good deal of flattering exposure, in return for paid advertisements.

What propelled Mitchell to the front ranks of African-American newspaper editors and publishers during these early years, however, was his militant approach to race relations, most especially his emotional crusade against lynching. Although militant stands against white racism were not unusual for black newspapers, Mitchell's approach was uniquely dramatic. On the masthead of his paper, for example, he placed a drawing of a powerful black arm with flexed biceps and a clenched fist, symbolizing the strength and power of the black community. Mitchell's approach was to suffuse the *Planet's* pages with continual assertions of black pride: "We have no desire to be identified with any other race but the Negro, the blacker the better," and "Every man should be glad that he is a Negro. . . . Great is the Negro. . . . We don't believe in being ashamed of one's race and constantly trying to be engrafted onto some other." Perhaps Mitchell's most remembered editorial, however, concerned a lynching in 1890. In that he urged his fellow African-Americans to arm themselves for self-defense: "The best remedy for a lyncher or a cursed night-rider is a 16-shot Winchester rifle in the hands of a Negro with enough nerve to pull the trigger."

Nor was this simply empty rhetoric on Mitchell's part. On several occasions he involved himself personally in trying to achieve retribution for lynchings, and when personally threatened for his actions, he armed himself and walked directly into the stronghold of the lynchers. These actions not only revealed Mitchell's courage, but also his flair for the dramatic, which greatly helped to increase his newspaper's circulation. He did, however, also involve himself quietly in a number of court cases concerning blacks in Richmond, using his influence in whatever way he could.

Until 1902 Mitchell also took a prominent role in fighting the forces of segregation and discrimination that were attempting to impose a series of Jim Crow laws segregating the races in all aspects of life, and also to take the vote away from them. These twin campaigns really got under way in the 1890s, just at the time Mitchell was coming into his own as an editor and publisher, and he took the lead in Richmond in opposing them. It was his stance on these issues that did much to distance him from the more accommodating W. W. Browne, who believed in race pride and advancement, but, like Booker T. Washington,* did not feel it was productive to push for social and political equality in the South's current climate. Although Browne and Mitchell could at times agree to protest Jim Crow laws like those concerning streetcars, they generally parted company on whether to fight for political equality.

Browne felt the black's vote was an overrated, too contentious issue, and he counseled acquiescence to white demands on the issue. Mitchell, who was deeply involved in politics himself, was far more militant on the topic. An affair that symbolized rather clearly the passions and issues involved came when Mitchell in 1895 had dinner at the Virginia governor's mansion. Richmond's whites flew into a rage over the incident, and Browne, who was sharply critical of Mitchell's temerity, wrote an obsequious letter to the *Richmond Dispatch* in which he apologized for his colleague's indiscretion. Mitchell responded with a stinging letter to the *Richmond Times* defending his actions.

Mitchell himself served on Richmond's city council as a representative of Jackson Ward from 1888 to 1896, when he was defeated in a fraudulent election. He ran again in 1900 but was defeated again in a rigged election. Meanwhile, his militant stands on the race issue were causing him to lose the support of white Republicans, and when blacks were disfranchised in Virginia, just after the turn of the century, his political career was over. This, combined with his move into increasingly more important business activities, marked Mitchell's transition to a more conservative, accommodating stance on political and social issues, similar to that of Browne and Washington. By 1905 the *Planet* was considered by most observers to be a conservative journal which only very occasionally, and then quite cautiously, challenged Washington's leadership.

The critical turning point in Mitchell's business career came in 1902, when he founded the Mechanics Savings Bank of Richmond. This action was a direct result of Mitchell's increasing involvement in the Knights of Pythias. As with W. W. Browne and the True Reformers, Mitchell felt he needed his own institution to handle the savings of the fraternal society. The bank became so interwoven with the order that it was known as the Knights of Pythias Bank. Also, like Browne, Mitchell envisioned the bank as the cornerstone for the creation of a large, multifaceted black business empire. At the same time, the *Planet* began urging Richmond's blacks to start their own businesses and to patronize those black enterprises that had already been started. This was a litany similar to that preached by Booker T. Washington on the national level, and it brought the philosophies of the two men into closer harmony.

Mitchell's bank, in conjunction with the business enterprises of the True Reformers and Maggie Lena Walker's* Order of St. Luke, propelled Richmond into the front ranks of black business enterprise in the South. By 1920 many considered the city's African-American banks and businesses the most important in the country. In recognition of his success, and his increasing conservatism on the race issue, Mitchell was elected the first black member of the American Bankers Association. At its convention in 1904, he spoke out publicly: "I love the white man. There is no quarrel between me and him. . . . I am proud of the South. You men of politics told us to eschew politics and take to business. . . . Here we expect no discrimination: A man is judged by his worth." The remarks were so stunning that they received extensive coverage in the *New York Times*, and John Mitchell became a national figure symbolizing accommodation with the white community.

Yet, it would be a mistake to think that Mitchell, or any of the other black leaders in Richmond and elsewhere, had moved too far along the path of accommodation during these trying years. The black vote had been eliminated from politics, business was the new stairway to eventual equality, and this all implied a new, less confrontational stance. It is well to remember, though, that at the very time that Mitchell was so unctuous in his comments to the bankers, he was also leading the crusade against Jim Crow laws for Richmond's streetcars. Organizing a successful boycott of the streetcars by the city's blacks, he used the slogan "Walking Is Good Now! Let Us Walk!" It was a stunningly successful boycott, so much so that a local transit official commented "[t]hat the trolley car lines give the impression that Negroes had left the city." After seven months of the boycott, a judge placed the trolley company in receivership, and for a short time, at least, Richmond was the only southern city that tolerated an integrated seating arrangement on its public transportation facilities.

Nor did Mitchell ever really forsake politics. A lifelong Republican, in 1921 he was nominated, along with a number of other disenchanted blacks, as a candidate for governor under the Black Independent, or so-called lily black ticket. Of course, by this time, about 90 percent of the African-American voters in the state had been disfranchised, and Mitchell was certainly not serious about winning the election. It did, however, serve to make clear to the Republicans that some blacks, at least, were not content with the situation. Although Mitchell received only about 5,000 votes in the election, he felt vindicated by the results, since it was enough to provide a margin of victory for the Democratic candidate and show the Republicans an important lesson. It also secured from the new Democratic governor a promise (not fulfilled) of fairer treatment for African-Americans in the state.

Mitchell's primary concern in the years after 1902, however, was the bank and his budding business empire. The Mechanics Bank used the funds deposited with it by the Knights of Pythias and the *Planet* to create an interlocked series of business enterprises controlled by Mitchell. Among the most important of these were the Repton Land Corporation, which was formed to operate the Woodlawn Cemetary for blacks, the Unique Amusement Corporation, which was created to finance the Strand Theater, and the Pythian-Calanthe Industrial Association.

The Strand Theater turned out to be a socially significant but economically troubled investment. The theater, located in the white business section, formerly had been patronized by whites. When Mitchell purchased it and announced his intention to turn it into a theater for a black clientele, white hostility was intense. As a result, the venture turned out to be a constant money loser. Whites reportedly offered Mitchell a handsome sum for the building, but his intense race pride would not allow him to sell it. The bank therefore continued this unprofitable operation on its books for a number of years.

All of this came to a head in May 1923, when the Mechanics Bank was closed, and Mitchell was later charged and convicted of making false entries into the bank's books. He was sentenced to three years in the state penitentiary, which he immediately appealed. The specific charge was that Mitchell had falsified bank records so that he was able to conceal some $83,000. In November, the Virginia Court of Appeals exonerated Mitchell of wrongdoing, but he was by this time a visibly shaken man. Mitchell thanked the blacks of Richmond who had stood by him during this ordeal. Mechanics Bank survived, but neither it nor Mitchell was ever quite the same again. In 1926 Mitchell pleaded with Reverend Beverly D. Tucker, of St. Paul's Episcopal Church, to intercede with Col. Thomas B. McAdams, a prominent Richmond financier, to secure additional funds for the troubled bank. Nothing of significance was accomplished, however.

During the last years of his life, Mitchell continued to edit and publish the Richmond *Planet*, which by 1927 had grown from four pages to fourteen. Although it, like most African-American newspapers of the time, began using an increased number of syndicated columns from other papers, and covered a good deal of "light" news, such as sports, music, theater, and the operations of black society, the front page was still reserved for Mitchell's crusades. Although they were fewer and farther between in the later 1920s, Mitchell never wholly forsook his militancy. After he died in December 1929, the paper was continued by his stepson, Roscoe C. Mitchell, who in turn was succeeded by N. A. Norrell. In 1938 the *Planet* was merged with the *Baltimore Afro-American* and continued to be published as the *Afro-American Planet*.

Mitchell's death left an enormous vacuum in the African-American leadership of Richmond. Although the city was blessed with a number of powerful and effective business and political leaders, such as W. W. Browne, Maggie Lena Walker, and Giles Jackson, it was Mitchell who garnered the greatest attention. A handsome, dashing man, who was a highly successful businessman, crusading editor, fighting politician, and fraternal leader, he was a powerful symbol for blacks of all classes in the city, state, and nation. The regard Richmond blacks had for Mitchell was formally recognized nationally nearly fifty years after his death when he became the first black newspaperman to be chosen to the Hall of Fame of Sigma Delta Chi, the national professional journalist society. At the unveiling of his plaque, Mitchell was praised as a man "whose lifelong dedication to human dignity and social justice exemplifies the finest spirit of courageous journalism."

Sources

Few letters or personal records of John Mitchell remain. The Virginia Historical Society in Richmond has several letters he wrote to a local minister when his bank was floundering in 1926. There are also some letters in the Reed Family Papers either by or about John Mitchell, and some letters written in 1897 by Mitchell in the Republican Party of Virginia Papers, all of which are deposited at the Virginia Historical Society. In addition, there is some very limited correspondence between Mitchell and Booker T. Washington in 1905 in the latter's papers at the Library of Congress. Several letters to Robert H. Terrell are found in the latter's papers, also at the Library of Congress. The Valentine Museum in Richmond has some valuable clippings on black business in Richmond. The best single source for Mitchell's life and work, however, are the issues of the Richmond *Planet*, a nearly complete run for which exists from 1890 to 1929. Another useful, though eclectic, source for some aspects of Mitchell's life is in the Peabody Collection clipping file of Hampton University, which is available on microfilm. There are various clippings in it from the *Nashville Banner*, *New York Sun*, *New York Times*, *New York Age*, *Commonwealth*, and *Cleveland Gazette*, among others. There are also clippings from the *Richmond Planet* and additional sources on black banks in Richmond taken from local newspapers. The *Norfolk Journal and Guide* also had occasional articles on Mitchell and black business in Richmond.

The most authoritative source for Mitchell is Ann Field Alexander, "Black Protest in the New South: John Mitchell Jr. (1863–1929) and the Richmond 'Planet,' " Ph.D. diss.,

Duke University, 1973. A master's thesis at Virginia State University by George Henry Johnson, Jr., entitled "Richmond Negro Business during the 1920's" (1969) has some useful material on Mitchell and his business activities. Abram L. Harris, *The Negro as Capitalist* (1936) provides the best analysis of the Mechanics Bank, its collapse, and Mitchell's role in all of that.

Besides the above named, the best sources for Mitchell's early life are Ann Field Alexander, "Between Two Worlds: John Mitchell's Richmond Childhood," *Virginia Cavalcade* 40 (Winter 1991), 120–131; and William J. Simmons, *Men of Mark* (1887). There is a good biography of Mitchell by Field in the *Dictionary of Negro Biography* (1982) and a shorter one in Ingham, BDABL. There is also an obituary in the *Richmond Times-Dispatch*, December 4, 1929, 2; and December 5, 1929, 11. The *Richmond Afro-American* (a direct descendant of the *Planet*) published rather extensive stories commemorating Mitchell on January 20–24, 1976, and March 26, 1983. There are also brief accounts of his life in *Who's Who in Colored America* (1928–1929), *Who's Who of the Colored Race* (1915), *The Negro in Virginia* (1940), and W. H. Quick, *Negro Stars in All Ages of the World* (1898).

James Wesley Smith, *The Strange Way of Truth* (1968), which deals with Mitchell's fight against segregation, is based almost solely on the *Planet*. A number of other sources deal with Mitchell's work as an editor and crusader for racial justice: Willard B. Gatewood, Jr., "A Negro Editor on Imperialism: John Mitchell, 1889–1901," *Journalism Quarterly* 49, 1 (1972), 43–50; Clay Perry, "John P. Mitchell, Virginia's Journalist of Reform," *Journalism History* 4, 4 (1977–1978), 142–47, 156; Fitzhugh Brundage, "To Howl Loudly: John Mitchell, Jr. and the African-American Campaign against Segregation in Virginia," *Canadian Review of American Studies* (Winter 1991), 325–42; I. Garland Penn, *The Afro-American Press* (reprint, 1988), 183–97; James H. Brewer, "Editorials from the Damned," *Journal of Southern History* 28 (1962) 225–3; James H. Brewer, "The War against Jim Crow in the Land of Goshen," *Negro History Bulletin* VVIV, 3 (December 1960), 53–57; August Meier and Elliot Rudwick, "Negro Boycotts of Segregated Streetcars in Virginia, 1904–1907," *Virginia Magazine of History and Biography* 81 (1973), 470–83; Henry Lewis Suggs, *The Black Press*, 392–97. An excellent general analysis of African-American newspapers during this time is Emma Lou Thornborough, "American Negro Newspapers, 1880–1914," *Business History Review* XL (Winter 1966), 467–90.

James H. Brewer focuses on black politics and Mitchell's role in that in "The Ghosts of Jackson Ward," *Negro History Bulletin* XXII, 2 (November 1958), 27–30. A good general source on Richmond during this period, and the role of Mitchell and the black community within it, is Virginius Dabney, *Richmond: The Story of a City* (1976), see especially 254–61, 270–71, 294–95.

Montgomery, Benjamin Thornton (see Charles Banks, Benjamin Thornton Montgomery and Isaiah T. Montgomery).

Montgomery, Isaiah T. (see Charles Banks, Benjamin Thornton Montgomery, and Isaiah T. Montgomery).

Moore, Frederick Randolph (1857–March 1, 1943). Journalist, black business advocate, and race leader: *New York Age*, *Colored American Magazine*, National Negro Business League, Afro-American Building and Loan Association, Afro-American Realty Company.

Fred Moore had a varied career. He was the publisher of one of the most important black newspapers in America, the national organizer for the Negro Business League during its first critical years, one of the founders of the National Urban League, a dynamic business entity in the development of the African-American community in Harlem, and an important spokesman for the black community on a number of issues. A close confidant of Booker T. Washington,* Moore has been almost totally overshadowed by the Tuskegean. Moore, in fact, is often viewed simply as Washington's mouthpiece or puppet. This is understandable, but unfortunate. Fred Moore deserves more credit than that. He was an important figure in the development of a coherent business philosophy for blacks in America, and he was a key player in black business development in New York City, especially in Harlem.

Fred Moore was born in Virginia, the son of a slave mother and a white father. While Moore was still an infant, his family moved to Washington, D.C. There Moore attended public schools and helped support the family by selling newspapers. After high school, Moore got a job as personal messenger for the secretary of the Treasury Department, a position he held through seven secretaries, also serving as a confidential aide in later years. In addition, Moore was with President James Garfield when he was assassinated in 1881, and six years later he accompanied Secretary Daniel Manning for three months in Europe while on departmental business. Upon their return to the United States, Manning took a position in the Western National Bank and brought Moore with him into that institution. There Moore became a vault and delivery clerk and then went to the New York Clearing House, where he took charge of all shipments during the eighteen years he served there. During this long period, Moore was also involved in the intricate battlefield of politics.

The period was an extraordinarily difficult one for African-Americans, one Rayford W. Logan in *The Betrayal of the Negro* (1954) has referred to as the "nadir." The commitment of the Republican party to blacks in both the North and South was dwindling rapidly. As Logan perceptively commented:

> The last decade of the nineteenth century and the opening of the twentieth century marked the nadir of the Negro's status in American society.... The nadir was reached, however, not because of lack of attention. On the contrary, the plight of the Negro worsened precisely because of the efforts made to improve it.

Fred Moore was among those engaged in trying to enhance the position of blacks economically, socially, and politically, and also among those who suffered for his efforts.

While still in his position at the bank, Moore was involved in an abortive effort to organize a chapter of the Negro Protective League, designed to safeguard the interests of blacks. The national Protective League had been organized by T. Thomas Fortune, with whom Moore became very close friends. Fortune had developed this idea in 1887, but it was not until two years later that local leagues began being formed. Fortune conceived of the league as a militant group. At its first convention, he proclaimed, "It is a narrow and perverted philosophy which condemns as a nuisance agitators." He counseled blacks to "fight fire with fire . . . it is time to face the enemy and fight inch by inch for every right he denies us." This organization ultimately evolved into the Afro American League.

The Afro American League as a national organization persisted for two decades with varying degrees of success. The group, which emphasized race solidarity, increasingly came to advocate various self-help schemes. Fortune proposed an Afro-American bank, a bureau of industrial education, and a bureau of cooperative industry in order to stimulate business enterprises among blacks. He also proposed a "bureau of emigration" to scatter blacks throughout the country. The league protested against disfranchisement, inequitable distribution of school funds, exclusion from juries, lynchings, and other barbarous acts committed against African-Americans. Among those at the founding convention were John Mitchell, Jr.,* of the Richmond *Planet*, W. Calvin Chase, Sr.,* of the *Washington Bee*, and P.B.S. Pinchback,* a prominent black politician and businessman. Despite great optimism, the league as a national venture soon foundered. By 1893 most of its local leagues, including the New York City branch, were defunct. In 1898 it was revived as the Afro-American Council under the leadership of Fortune and AME Zion bishop Alexander Walters. This group passed under the control of Booker T. Washington after the turn of the century.

The most lasting aspect of the Protective League in New York City, and the one Moore was most involved in, was its offshoot, the Afro-American Building and Loan Association, which was successfully launched in 1892. It was designed to provide loans to blacks who wanted to build homes and start businesses. Although no detailed accounts are available, the organization returned only minimal dividends during its existence. Moore served as president of the organization, and was still in that capacity in 1901, when Fortune bought a home in Red Bank using funds provided by it. This was a visible symbol of a friendship and alliance between the two men that intensified over the years.

Sometime in the 1890s, Fortune and Booker T. Washington also became close personal friends and political allies, and Fortune, in turn, probably introduced Moore to the Tuskegean. This led to Moore's involvement in the founding of the National Negro Business League with Washington, Fortune, and others. Fortune, in fact, had been among those encouraging Washington to develop a national forum for black business leaders, and when the league was organized in Boston 1900, he was among the founders and was named chairman of the executive committee. Moore at this time took no prominent part in the activities of the Negro Business League since he was deeply involved in partisan political activities in New York City.

An avid Republican, Moore served as a district captain of the party in New

York, and in 1902 he made an unsuccessful bid for a Brooklyn seat in the state assembly. Two years later, Washington interceded to secure Moore a position as deputy collector of internal revenue. Moore held this position for only a few months, though, when he resigned at Washington's behest to take a position as national organizer for the Negro Business League.

Moore's first duty as national organizer was to survey the status of local league chapters throughout the country. His report to the 1904 national convention was not encouraging. He stated that the local leagues were "in a chaotic condition with no general line of policy and no general interest manifested in them," strongly condemned local league officials whose cooperation with the national organization was insufficient, and bemoaned the fact that there was no central clearinghouse of information for the national organizer to draw upon. He urged more funding for the organizer's office and lamented the attitude of many blacks who saw the local leagues simply as "a money making business."

The year between the convention in 1904 and the next one in 1905 saw Moore deeply involved in the enhancement of the organizer's position and putting the league itself on a sounder financial basis. For this latter job, Washington had encouraged Moore and his economic ally in New York City, Philip A. Payton, Jr.,* to put the house in order. One of their major recommendations was the incorporation of the league under the laws of the state of New York. At the same time, the executive committee met at Stevens House in New York and added field service duties to the job of the national organizer. For this new job, Moore was allotted an annual salary of $1,400. In accepting this as a full-time position for the first time, Moore agreed to give up all his other activities except the publication of the *Colored American Magazine* and his involvement in the building and loan company.

At the same time Moore was upgrading the economic and organizational foundation of the league, he was urging Emmett J. Scott, Washington's right-hand man and corresponding secretary of the organization, to expand the league's political base in New York. He particularly urged that the *New York Age*, then being run by Fortune, be tied more directly to the local New York Business League's organization. Moore then offered his own services, saying, "There's money in it, and I can be had." Washington, as Moore well knew, had been expanding his efforts to control aspects of the black press and had a particularly strong position with Moore's *Colored American Magazine*.

For some time, Moore had worked part-time for the *New York Age*, most probably placed in that position by Washington, but in 1905, with funds secretly supplied by the Tuskegean, he became editor and publisher of the Boston-based *Colored American Magazine*. It had been founded in 1900 by William H. Dupree, a postal superintendent, civic leader, and businessman in Boston. Washington evidently bought a few shares of stock in the magazine in 1901, but later disposed of them. By 1904, however, the paper was suffering severe financial difficulties, and Washington agreed to purchase the magazine, but only if he could install Fred Moore as editor. Moore was to be assisted by the nephew of Washington's wife, Roscoe Conkling Simmons. They both agreed that Washington would never be publicly identified with the journal.

There is abundant correspondence between Washington and Moore in 1904 and 1905 concerning finances. Moore repeatedly requested money from Washington, but there is no clear evidence whether Washington acceded to these demands. Despite Moore's efforts, the *Colored American Magazine* remained a losing proposition. By 1909 Washington concluded that he could no longer afford to support the magazine and ended his connection. By this time, though, Moore was long gone. What made Washington's support of Moore, who was not an experienced journalist, palpable, was that he, unlike Fortune and several others, was perfectly willing to allow Washington to remain actively, but secretly, involved in the editorial affairs of the journal.

Moore succinctly stated his editorial policies for readers when he took over the *Colored American Magazine*: "It seeks to publish articles showing the advancement of our people along material lines, believing that the people generally are more interested in having information of the doings of the members of the race, rather [than] the writings of dreamers or theorists."

Moore frankly admitted his admiration for Booker T. Washington and his philosophy, but he maintained that he, Moore, alone was responsible for the editorial content. There is no evidence that Moore's own ideas, however, deviated much from Washington's. Moore published articles detailing the achievements of black businessmen and often bitterly attacked the higher education. Moore also emphatically agreed with Benjamin J. Davis, editor of the *Atlanta Independent*, when he declared that the "civilization of a race must rest upon economic fundamentals and not politics." Moore advocated racial pride, self-help, racial solidarity, and economic chauvinism, most particularly in the idea that blacks should support African-American business.

"The Negro should awake to the necessity of relying more on his own resources," Moore proclaimed, "as an impetus to race progress. The race cannot expect the whites to do for it what it can do for itself. We must learn to walk alone. If race prejudice shuts the door of hope in our face, we must turn our face in other directions. If opportunity does not come, let us make other opportunities. How can this be better done than by promoting race enterprises?" Moore, however, was much less willing to adopt Washington's accommodating attitude toward the white South. On the contrary, he continually attacked the South in terms that must have grated on Washington:

The American people have stood by and allowed the Negro to be 'jim-crowed' in politics, in religion, in education, in business, on the railroads, and in the theaters and hotels, without a ripple of dissent. [The South] has repressed the Negro in almost every . . . conceivable way in the states and now its aim is at the national bulwark of Negro citizenship. . . . The 'Jim-Crow' system is a constant proclamation to the Negro people that they are an inferior race. . . . To have this sting constantly flaunted in our faces all the time is likely to breed in us a self-contempt that will dwarf our aspirations and make us hate those whom we inevitably must consider our oppressors. (*Journal of Negro History*, 1953)

Although Moore considered himself a militant in many respects, he also always distinguished between his brand of militance and that of the members of W.E.B. Du Bois's Niagara Movement. At one point, in responding to criticisms from the intellectuals in that movement, Moore said that the black race needed something more than "vigorous talk and loudmouthed railings in newspapers." He urged them to "spend [their] energies in urging Negroes to buy homes and educate children." To Moore, race salvation lay primarily in economic development, not in civil and political rights. The Niagara group saw things in nearly completely opposite terms. As August Meier has commented, "Both were militant, but in different ways."

At the same time, of course, Moore continued as national organizer of the National Negro Business League. In order to encourage wider black interest in the league, Moore and Fortune proposed to Washington that he create "a National Cooperative Association," to be modeled on the Afro-American Investment and Building Company, of which Moore was president and Fortune a director. This was to expand on a national basis Moore's concept of a lending agency for blacks to help them buy homes and start businesses. Moore sought to convince Washington that it would enhance the league's image if they could be seen as aiding blacks who were "burdened by the exorbitant rates of interest charged by people who seek their enslavement rather than their freedom." The proposal, however, did not get off the ground.

After 1906 Moore's field activities as national organizer began to be curtailed. He was, first of all, increasingly involved in his own affairs, and he complained when field trips took him away from these activities. Also, some critics felt that his frequent and expensive travel was unnecessary. Thus, in 1907, the executive committee temporarily abolished the position of national organizer and replaced it with a number of state worker positions coordinated by Scott. This never worked well, and finally, in 1913, a new national organizer, Ralph W. Tyler, was appointed. At the same time, Washington asked Moore to resign his seat on the executive committee in order to remedy a situation that "places us in an awkward situation before the country." It is not clear just what Washington was referring to by this statement.

The National Business League had held its 1905 meeting in New York City, and Washington had asked Moore and Philip Payton to organize the affair. The two men expected great benefits to accrue both to the general black business climate in New York, and to their own business activities. Moore was involved in a number of interests in the city, and Payton by this time was the most successful black realtor. The keystone of Payton's real estate empire was the Afro-American Realty Company, which he had organized in 1904 in conjunction with some of the most eminent black businessmen in the city. Although Washington made no personal investment in the firm, Emmett Scott and his wife purchased $600 worth of stock. The company, according to Maceo C. Dailey, was thus "sucked into the vortex of Tuskegee politics." By the summer of 1905, several of Washington's strongest supporters—Charles W. Anderson, Wilford Smith, and Emmett Scott—in addition to Moore, were either officers or directors in the firm.

The goals of Afro-American Realty were to earn a profit for its founders and to provide adequate housing for blacks in New York City. This had long been a problem. First settling in lower Manhattan, blacks had been forced out of this area. They then settled in the Five-Point District (near the site of the present city hall), but were also forced out by the arrival of Irish immigrants. African-Americans then settled in the "Little Africa" area in Greenwich Village, only to be pushed out again, this time by arriving Italians. By the early twentieth century they were located in the Tenderloin and San Juan Hill districts, from 37th to 58th streets, but they were once more feeling pressure because of commercialization and redevelopment. Payton secured apartments in Harlem in 1903, then in a newly built suburb, enabling blacks to move into this area, thereby providing the best housing the race had yet seen in the city. For this, Payton was called the "Father of Colored Harlem."

By the fall of 1905, however, Payton and Moore were at loggerheads with one another. Payton, a charismatic idea man, was impatient with details and rules. Other members of the firm were continually bailing him out of potential legal jams. Moore wrote to Washington that Afro-American Realty would have to follow a more "conservative policy" if it was to survive. By this, Moore meant that the company had to improve its financial image and sell more stock. Although Payton generally agreed, he was concerned about losing control of the firm and preferred reducing the shares of stock held by the original company members to reach this goal. Payton was able to convince Scott of this plan, and Moore took his complaints to Booker T. Washington. Moore also urged Scott to tender his resignation. Scott refused, and this was the beginning of a long and bitter relationship between Moore and Scott. In April 1906, Payton gained full control of Afro-American Realty with the backing of Emmett J. Scott, forcing the resignation of Wilford Smith. Moore, however, remained a director of the firm until its demise in 1908. Its failure, ironically, was caused by Payton's speculations, precisely the sort of thing Moore had earlier warned against.

Moore, meanwhile, was set to move on to the next stage in his career, the one that would prove to become his life's endeavor. The internecine politics in the black community of New York at this time were complex and constantly changing. Various individuals and factions were trying to gain the ear and good favor of Booker T. Washington, and they seemed to be almost constantly at each other's throats. In 1906, Charles W. Anderson, collector of internal revenue for New York, a close Washington operative and Moore's boss several years before, warned Washington about Moore. At one point, Anderson described Moore as a "summer coon, neither fit for fur or [sic] meat." At the same time, however, T. Thomas Fortune was causing Washington even greater concern.

Although Fortune continually defended Washington in the pages of the *New York Age*, he often attacked his policies, causing the Tuskegean consternation. A critical turning point, however, came in late 1906, when Fortune publicly stated that Washington owned half of the *Age*, a disclosure that Washington immediately and vehemently denied. This was not an isolated instance. Fortune, who was an alcoholic, was becoming increasingly unstable, and Washington was concerned about the necessity of replacing him.

For his part, Fortune was desperately in need of money and was willing to sell the *Age*. Moore appeared to be the ideal purchaser. Long a close friend of Fortune's, in 1905 Moore had written to Washington chiding him for ignoring Fortune in his time of troubles: "It is time for you to stand by him—since he has supported you in the past. You should tell him frankly where he stands with the administration." In 1907 Washington encouraged Moore to begin negotiations with Fortune and indicated that he thought William H. Baldwin, Jr., one of Tuskegee's white benefactors, would advance him the money needed to buy the paper. Moore offered to buy the paper for $7,000 from Fortune and his partner and promised to provide employment to both men.

Just as the arrangements were about to be completed, however, Moore found that Baldwin had refused to loan him the money. It came, he said "as a stunner—I certainly thought we had the matter O.K." What happened thereafter is not clear, but on September 4, 1907, Fortune agreed to transfer his interest to Fred Moore in exchange for a $300 deposit. Fortune, however, who was alternately ill or drunk during this period, soon reconsidered the bargain and attempted to cancel it, and his partner Peterson claimed that the terms of the original partnership gave him an option to purchase Fortune's stock. In any event, Moore moved in to run the *Age*, and Fortune and Peterson attempted to return the $300 and regain control of the operation. Moore refused to budge, and ultimately it was agreed that he would pay Fortune $7,000 for the stock over a three-year period. Washington, in turn, agreed to advance Moore the money to cover the payments. The offer of employment for Fortune was no longer part of the package.

Moore no sooner took control of the *Age* than he found himself burdened with the same sort of financial problems that had bedeviled Fortune and virtually all other black publishers. Washington and Scott were also dismayed by what they perceived to be a distinct fall in the editorial and composition quality of the paper under Moore. Once, Scott complained that the front page looked like a "huge handbill," and Scott and R. W. Thompson, an experienced newspaperman, agreed that Moore's ideas of journalism were "pitched too low" and that some of the material that he featured was "cheap." They felt that he would fail to attract the "superior class of readers" they desired. During this same period, Charles Anderson and others continued to attack Moore unmercifully to Washington.

Communications between Moore and Washington were equally complex and difficult to analyze during this period. Washington certainly wanted to influence the content of the *Age*, but he did not want people to suspect that he was backing the operation financially. Thus, Washington time and again counseled Moore to stop discussing "political matters" in the pages of the *Age* and to deal with the economic advancement of the race instead. In 1908 Washington even urged Moore not to give so much attention to lynchings: "Each of four headlines on the front page this week deals with lynching. That is unfortunate."

In other respects, the Tuskegean had little more success in controlling Moore's writings or actions than he did Fortune's. Moore was even close with some of Washington's more vocal opponents, such as AME bishop Alexander Walters. At the same time, Washington wrote to Moore that he hoped "you will be careful to keep as many attacks on individuals and organizations out of your paper as you can. I fear that your paper is getting the reputation for attacking people." An increasingly acrimonious element in the relations between Washington and Moore was Moore's running conflict with Emmett J. Scott. The two men had not gotten along for some time, but in 1914 Scott loaned Moore $200 to buy back some of Scott's stock in the *Age*. Moore, then, for the next several months, refused to pay back this money, claiming that it had been paid for by free advertising in the *Age*. The conflict, however, remained rather muted until after Washington's death in 1915. Then, in the struggle for control of the National Business League and the "Tuskegee Machine," Moore openly sided with Albon Holsey and Robert R. Moton against Scott. The Moore, Moton, Holsey faction was successful, and Scott ultimately was sent packing to Howard University.

Moore continued as a significant presence in the National Negro Business League throughout most of the rest of his life, most of which he served on the executive committee. Perhaps his most significant work for the league in his later years was his involvement in the Colored Merchants Association (CMA). Long an advocate of racial solidarity and cooperation, Moore, in conjunction with John E. Nail,* advocated in the late 1920s that the league sponsor a co-operative venture to improve the status of black business. Albon Holsey decided that the league should sponsor a national cooperative grocery store venture. The goal was to organize black grocers into cooperative buying units, create a standardized store service, promote cooperative advertising, and use the local league chapters as the coordinating agencies.

By the summer of 1929, the CMA was being developed in at least twenty-five cities with a secret advance from the Tuskegee Institute General Fund. The general headquarters of the group was located in New York City, and it was the Colored Merchants Association of Harlem that became the demonstration project for the entire nation. Incorporated in New York, the CMA, Harlem had capital of $100,000 and issued 10,000 shares of stock. In April 1930, a former bankrupt black grocery store became the first model CMA store in Harlem. By this time, however, the Great Depression was ravaging the black community in Harlem and elsewhere. With the Depression as a backdrop, the CMA elected its first permanent officers and directors in 1931. Holsey was elected president, John E. Nail vice president, and Fred Moore treasurer. They faced an uphill, if not impossible battle, which was made no easier when the officers and board itself were beset with internecine warfare.

Most of the complaints about the CMA came from the black consumers, who continually complained that they could get better bargains at white-owned stores. Holsey, Moore, and Nail chastised blacks for being more concerned with price than with the betterment of the race, and they explained that their local black grocer had higher overhead costs. But most blacks, who had never shown much propensity to patronize African-American enterprises anyway, simply could not afford to do so during those desperate times. The situation had become so critical by February 1933, that the league held an emergency meeting to deal with the CMA. At the meeting, Moore openly attacked the CMA for its association with the National Negro Business League. Holsey, on the other hand, appealed to the executive board to stand by the CMA in its time of trial. C. C. Spaulding[*] supported Holsey, and the league voted to continue its support. Within a year, however, the CMA was in receivership.

Moore also continued to run the *Age* until his death in 1943. Although he was not recognized then, or later, as one of the great African-American journalists, the *Age* was a successful, influential, and well-read paper during the nearly four decades he ran it. Although Moore continued to advocate economic advancement and race building, the paper was also militant in attacking many aspects of white racism. It fought the policy of "lily-white" Republicanism in the Taft administration and later; it was steadfast in attacking the Ku Klux Klan when it was reborn during World War I; and Moore never stopped his condemnation of lynching and mob rule in the South. In 1932 Moore and the *Age*, although staunchly Republican, vigorously attacked Herbert Hoover in his reelection bid. Perhaps paradoxically, though, Moore opposed the reelection of Franklin D. Roosevelt in 1936, even though he had supported him four years earlier.

Moore and the *Age* also became part of the growing black business community in Harlem after World War I. In 1919 the *Age* joined the great exodus to Harlem. New offices were on 135th street, and a modern printing plant and warehouse were set up in the area. This helped bring Moore into the center of the power structure of that important community, a position he held for many years. Much of Moore's leadership role was expressed through politics. He not only attended every Republican National Convention from 1908 to 1920, but he also served on every National Negro Republican Committee during presidential campaigns. Even more important, he tirelessly promoted black capitalism in Harlem throughout the 1920s and 1930s and, partially in conjunction with the CMA, was an early sponsor of Harlem's "Don't Buy Where You Can't Work" campaign. Moore won election as a New York City alderman in 1927 and 1929. In 1924 he helped nominate a black congressional candidate, and five years later he was instrumental in electing an African-American to the state assembly.

Moore was also actively involved in the organization and development of the National Urban League, and he served on the board of that organization for more than three decades. His involvement began as early as 1905, when he arranged for a meeting of various black social organizations at the Mount Olivet Baptist Church. Working with Moore on this was Booker T. Washington, Mary White Ovington, Elizabeth M. Rhodes, and Mrs. Elizabeth W. Tyler. By 1910 this loose coalition had come together as a more cohesive force, and Moore was named chairman of the New York chapter of the organization. At the meeting in that year, Moore spoke out strongly against Jim Crow practices in the South. Elected a board member at the first national meeting, Moore served as a powerful, often behind-the-scenes, force in the National Urban League throughout his life. In 1919 it fell to Moore to lead a delegation of blacks to try to woo the officers of the American Federation of Labor to the cause of African-American workers. Although he and his colleagues had some success in their quest, the response of the AFL was too general to be of real value to black workers.

While a young man in Washington, D.C., in 1879, Moore had married Ida Lawrence. They had eighteen children, only six of whom lived to adulthood. Three of them later worked on Moore's staff at the *Age*, prompting Roi Ottley in the 1940s to comment that ''[the *Age*'s] present staff has been recruited largely from his family, leaving the *Amsterdam News* as the only paper to which the section's remaining Negro newspapermen may turn for employment.'' One of his daughters married Lester Walton, a journalist who became a U.S. minister to Liberia. Moore, an untiring advocate of black capitalism, by the time of his death must have felt little optimism. The Great Depression had destroyed much of the nation's once-thriving black business enterprises, and World War II spending had yet to provide an uplift. His crusades against racism and discrimination were beginning to bear some fruit, as a new generation of ''angry young men'' was emerging during World War II. It was this generation who would provide the leadership for the great ''Second Reconstruction'' of the 1950s and 1960s. They, of course, did not recognize Moore as an inspiration. He was viewed as an accommodationist, an Uncle Tom. Walter White, volatile executive secretary of the NAACP caught the change taking place in the war years:

A wind *is* rising—a wind of determination by the have-nots of the world to share the benefits of freedom and prosperity which the haves of the world have tried to keep exclusively for themselves. That wind blows all over the world. Whether that wind develops into a hurricane is a decision which we must make now and in the days we form the peace.

For all of Moore's militance, the postwar world would be one he could not understand. With his passing went one of the last of a generation of black leaders who had come to adulthood in the waning days of Reconstruction, had cut their political eyeteeth on the philosophy of Booker T. Washington, and had vacillated between militance and accommodation thereafter. The new world would demand more of its black leaders, but in his own time Fred Moore was a force to be reckoned with.

Sources

There are numerous letters to and from Fred Moore in the Booker T. Washington Papers at the Library of Congress. There are also a number of letters in the Emmett J. Scott Papers in Roper Library at Morgan State University in Baltimore, Maryland, and in the Robert R. Moton Papers, the Albon Holsey Papers, the Booker T. Washington Papers, and the National Negro Business League Papers, all located in the Tuskegee Institute Archives at Tuskegee University. See also the National Negro Business Leagues, Proceedings of Annual Conventions, 1900–1924, available at Hampton University. There is no full-length biography of Moore, but a good short treatment is by John B. Wiseman in the *Dictionary of American Negro Biography* (1982). An obituary appeared in the *New York Times*, March 3, 1943. There is a good deal of information on Moore and his association with Booker T. Washington in Emma Lou Thornbrough, *T. Thomas Fortune: Militant Journalist* (Chicago, 1972). Moore's role as national organizer for the Negro Business League is found in John Howard Burrows, "The Necessity of Myth: A History of the National Negro Business League, 1900–1945," Ph.D. diss., Auburn University, 1977; and August Meier, *Negro Thought in America, 1880–1915* (Ann Arbor, Mich., 1963). Moore's relationship with Booker T. Washington and the *Colored American Magazine* is found in August Meier, "Booker T. Washington and the Negro Press: With Special Reference to the *Colored American Magazine*," *Journal of Negro History* XXXVIII, 1 (January 1953), 67–90. Moore's association with Philip Payton and Washington in the Afro-American Realty Company is superbly covered in Maceo C. Dailey, "Booker T. Washington and the Afro-American Realty Company," *Review of Black Political Economy* VIII (Winter 1978), 184–201. His involvement in the Urban League is covered in Guichard Paris and Lester Brooks, *Blacks in the City: A History of the National Urban League* (Boston, 1971). There is a fairly good overview of the history of the paper during most of Moore's regime in Ludlow W. Werner, "The New York Age: Lusty Veteran," *The Crisis* 45, 3 (March 1934), 74–75, 91–92. Back issues of the *New York Age* are available at the Schomburg Research Collection of the New York Public Library and on microfilm. Copies of the *Colored American Magazine* are available at the Cleveland Public Library and at the Mooreland Research Center at Howard University. A copy of *Afro-American Realty Co., Prospectus* (New York, 1904) is also there; the original is located at the New York City Hall of Records.

N

Nail, John Bennett (May 29? 1853–February 14, 1942) and **John (Jack) E. Nail** (August 22, 1883–March 6, 1947). Businessmen, realtor, and hotel, cafe, and billiard hall proprietor: Nail & Parker and Nail Brothers Restaurant. Harlem today is hardly considered a real estate investor's dream. Shells of deteriorated buildings line several blocks, and high crime rates plague neighborhoods. Yet, not all of Harlem has suffered this fate. Within its boundaries are not only ravaged and dilapidated multifamily dwellings, but also small apartment buildings and brownstones that are well maintained and highly desirable. Affluent middle- and upper-middle class blacks own and occupy these dwellings. Furthermore, the buildings that are deteriorating or abandoned were once properties that earned well-respected white and black real estate brokers handsome incomes. Prior to and during the Harlem Renaissance, property in New York City escalated at previously unheard of rates. The massive migration of blacks from the South during the first two decades of the twentieth century had created an enormous demand for housing that far outweighed the supply. And, too, the choices available to blacks in search of accommodations were limited to areas deemed appropriate for them. Harlem, located in the northern reaches of Manhattan, was rapidly changing from an affluent white neighborhood to an overcrowded black ghetto. Philip A. Payton, Jr.,[*] a young, black entrepreneur had seen and taken advantage of the opportunities unfolding in Harlem real estate. His company not only rewarded Payton; his coterie of real estate agents also fared well—if not financially at least in terms of experience. When Payton's business began to falter, two salesmen employed by his Afro-American Realty Company, John E. Nail and Henry C. Parker, promptly created their own real estate firm.

John E. Nail was the son of John Bennett Nail, an entrepreneur in his own right. John B. Nail was born in Baltimore and, as a young man, migrated to New York City with only 59 cents in hand. Nail first did odd jobs until he was hired to work in the aristocratic Washington Square Club. Ten years later, after saving a sufficient amount of money, the elder Nail and his brother Edward opened a tavern, which then became a restaurant, hotel, and billiard parlor on lower 6th Avenue. They proceeded to purchase the building in which their businesses were located, which was the first midtown Manhattan property purchased by blacks. The Nail brothers' various business enterprises initially thrived, but when earnings began to decrease in 1909, they systematically began to sell off all of their business interests, including the building.

As Harlem became an increasingly attractive community for blacks, the Nail brothers continued their real estate activities. Although at this time there were only about 8,000 African-Americans residing in what was to become a ghetto completely dominated by blacks, the Nails saw the advantage of investing in real estate there. White speculators had long seen the gold mine that lay in Harlem property, and overwhelmingly blacks were denied the opportunity to participate in this prosperous activity. The Nail brothers, along with such visionaries as Lillian Harris, better known as Pig Foot Mary, Philip Payton, and St. Philip's Episcopal Church, began purchasing property in Harlem. The Nails bought a row of five apartment houses, and like Payton and St. Philip's, dispossessed the white tenants then occupying them and rented the apartments to blacks. Undoubtedly they sensed a surge in demand for housing, but the boom that ensued likely exceeded their wildest dreams. They all fared remarkably well as neophyte property owners, and John B. Nail provided a sturdy foundation on which his son could build his own real estate empire.

At the age of fifty, John B. Nail became the first black to receive a credit rating by the Wall Street credit rating organization of Dun and Bradstreet. By the early years of the twentieth century, he was one of the largest African-American realty holders in the city, and when Booker T. Washington[*] was organizing the National Negro Business League, Nail, along with Fred R. Moore,[*] Payton, and prominent black politician Charles W. Anderson, was among the New Yorkers he chose to aid him. These men were selected because of their prominence in business and political affairs. Nail not only engaged in real estate activities, he also was a philanthropist and the first lifetime member of the National Association for the Advancement of Colored People. In addition, he established a fine collection of prints, lithographs, and paintings on the subject of sports, which he eventually disposed of for a sizable sum. Nail was one of the earliest patrons of black art and literature, and he owned a large collection of paintings and sculptures by African-American artists, and in his library were all of the works of black authors. He also developed lasting relationships with such notable individuals as Robert G. Ingersoll and Dr. Felix Adler, with whom he shared his pursuit for absolute truth. He was one of the original founders of the Ethical Culture Society. John B. Nail, although he retired from active business in 1903, remained a silent partner in his son's business until the elder's death in 1942.

John (Jack) E. Nail was born in New London, Connecticut, and was educated in New York City. At an early age, Jack Nail was an observer and then a participant in his father's real estate business, which gave him an entrée into the profession. The younger Nail opened his first real estate office in the Bronx, a rapidly growing area at that time. He then accepted employment with Philip Payton, whose Afro-American Realty Company, along with John B. and Edward Nail, were actively blazing trails in the Harlem real estate market. After some heady times, Payton's company in 1907 suffered a downturn. Two of its star salesmen, Jack Nail and Henry C. Parker, a North Carolinian by birth, resigned their positions and established their own Harlem realty firm of Nail & Parker, Inc. Following in Payton's footsteps, they were motivated by their desire to serve the black community while, at the same time, earning large profits.

Because racial discrimination was rampant at this time, blacks were frequently denied housing anywhere in most areas of New York City. But, as the city's black population moved farther north, Harlem was quickly transformed into a black belt that was squeezing out white residents. Crowding became a severe problem that could be rectified only by providing additional affordable dwellings to the rapidly escalating numbers of blacks who were competing for space. Nail and Parker correctly assessed the situation. They purchased property which they then rented to blacks, and they urged other members of their race to follow suit. Harlem real estate was a windfall, and they reasoned that it was far better to have blacks own the property and collect rents than whites, who would abuse their black tenants either by charging exorbitant rents or by failing to maintain the property.

Nail and Parker deserve credit for breaking the "covenant," the unspoken agreement that certain blocks in Harlem must remain white. On these designated blocks, properties could not be rented or sold to blacks. Lending institutions cooperated with this discriminatory practice by refusing mortgages to blacks. Nail and Parker fought this custom (which came to be called "redlining") and gradually earned the respect of a lending institution, but this did not come until after World War I. Although segregation persisted, blacks could rent or purchase property that was previously denied to them. As these restrictions were gradually lifted, Harlem became increasingly black and Nail & Parker served the community by offering first mortgages and by buying, selling, and managing property. Nail was the moving force of the company, which quickly earned a respectable reputation. He took a dominant role in engineering real estate transactions, and became an authority on Harlem property. The firm not only engaged in the buying and selling of real estate, but also offered appraisal services, consulting, and rent collecting, which in 1925 amounted to more than $1 million. Nail emerged as an expert in condemnation proceedings, and even the city of New York sought his expertise.

Nail & Parker was involved in numerous large-scale real estate transactions which were noteworthy even in New York City, where property values had escalated higher than in most other cities in the United States. Their first large transaction involved the sale of downtown property worth $1,070,000 to St. Philip's Episcopal Church. In 1911 Nail and his pastor, the Reverend Hutchens C. Bishop, who had passed for white on several occasions, purchased land for the church's new building and for several apartment buildings which the church would then rent. The annual collection from these properties was $25,000. This transaction was a coup for the church, for Nail and Parker, and for the black community: Only a few days earlier these lavishly decorated apartments had been reserved for whites only. The firm's most noteworthy client, by far, was Madame C. J. Walker,* a wealthy entrepreneur in beauty products. She purchased a property in Irvington-on-the-Hudson that cost $200,000. Other notable transactions included the sale to the Copeland Realty Company, a black corporation, of a large elevator apartment for $250,000, and the sale to a holding company of the Wage Earners' Savings Bank on a corner in Harlem for $250,000. In 1929 Nail & Parker contracted for the management of Harlem's largest and finest apartment building, which was owned by the Metropolitan Insurance Company. Then, in 1931, the firm acted as brokers in the sale of the twenty-one-acre McGlynn estate in Verplanck, a Hudson River town south of Peekskill, Westchester County, to the New York Urban League for development as a convalescent home and recreation center for blacks. Although Nail & Parker earned respectable profits from these various transactions, the firm served the black community well by providing housing and financial services to African-Americans at a time when few others did.

Despite Nail's success in providing housing for blacks and promoting black businesses to open in Harlem, he encountered accusations that his Harlem rents were exorbitant. He acknowledged the fact that Harlem rents were high, but he asserted that white people living under similar conditions elsewhere in New York City paid equally high rent. Nail was particularly troubled by the practice of black tenants suing black owners, who then charged higher rents to cover their increased carrying costs. Nail believed that these legal challenges were fostered by white real estate agents bent on returning the property to white hands. Nail, like Booker T. Washington, strongly held that property ownership was the only means by which blacks could retain Harlem as a black residential community. Decreased rents would result in defaults and foreclosures on the property. Nail was always a champion for Harlem, and when concern was expressed that blacks were leaving Harlem in pursuit of cheaper rents elsewhere, he calmed the fears that a massive exodus was ensuing. He was correct.

Several black entrepreneurs took advantage of the Harlem real estate market. Watt Terry, who hailed from Brockton, Massachusetts, founded the Terry Holding Company in New York City, and replicated the success he had achieved in New England. Having created something of a real estate empire in Brockton during the early twentieth century, Terry was reputed to be one of the wealthiest blacks in the United States at the time, rivaling other black speculators during the 1920s. It was also during the third decade of the twentieth century that black institutions moved into Harlem. Nail had earlier encouraged William Washington Browne's* United Order of True Reformers and several fraternal organizations, such as the Masons and Elks, to establish branches there; and social service agencies, including the Urban League and the NAACP, opened offices in Harlem. Nail & Parker became the agent for the African-American branch of the YMCA when it, too, relocated in Harlem. The firm also handled the sales and rental of the apartments designed by Stanford White. (These apartments had been turned over by the Equitable Life Insurance Company.) By 1930 Nail estimated that blacks owned and controlled Harlem property worth between $50 and $60 million, compared to 20 years earlier when very few blacks could claim ownership of any property in Manhattan. Times had changed considerably during the 1910s and 1920s, although blacks by no means held property in value comparable to whites. Nonetheless, African-Americans had made great strides, and there was no reason to believe that further advancements could not be achieved. The 1929 stock market crash, however, dashed any hopes that enterprising blacks had entertained.

The storm of the Great Depression ravaged numerous businesses, irrespective of color. Throughout the country enterprises fell by the wayside, unable to bear the economic burden. Harlem was on a downspin from which it never fully recovered. Despite efforts of Harlem's black leaders to assist the unemployed and destitute, the damage seemed to be irreversible. The median family income in Harlem declined 43.6 percent in less than three years, but rentals ranged from $12 to $30 a month higher than the rest of Manhattan. The Harlem ghetto was visibly deteriorating, transforming into a slum almost overnight. Harlem businesses fell like dominoes, including the well-respected, successful firm of Nail & Parker.

In 1933 the company went bankrupt and was dissolved. Of the 100 shares of stock outstanding at the time of the bankruptcy, Nail and Parker each held 45 shares; the remaining 10 shares were held by Isador D. Brokow, a white man who was a silent partner. The partners went their separate ways: Henry Parker entered a branch of the financing business, and Jack Nail's ambitious spirit motivated him to initiate another real estate business just down the street from the original enterprise. He assumed the presidency of his business, and a white realtor was secretary and treasurer. Nail maintained his drive, engineering several real estate transactions on his own. When St. Philip's Church fell victim to the Depression and almost lost its property, Nail, in his role as its agent, saved it from foreclosure. He identified the Jackruth Realty Corporation, a downtown white firm, which agreed to lease the property for ten years, during which time the church was forced to forego any revenue. When the federal government allocated funds during the New Deal for rehabilitation of urban communities, Nail attempted to secure, with the help of the noted novelist James Weldon Johnson (who was married to Nail's sister, Grace), funds to improve Harlem. The quest went unfulfilled, and Harlem was left to decay. Nonetheless, some black real estate companies fared well enough. Augustine A. Austin organized the Antillean Holding Company in 1919, and, despite the Depression, by 1936 it claimed assets of approximately $1 million.

Nail achieved recognition beyond the boundaries of Harlem, although he took great interest in representing Harlem in all business and housing issues. He became one of the most influential and highly respected black realtors in New

York City. He was the first black member of the Real Estate Board of New York, the only black member of the Housing Committee of New York, and a member of the Harlem Board of Commerce. He was brought in as a consultant for President Herbert Hoover's Commission on Housing during the Depression. Nail's awareness of his race's problems went far beyond housing concerns. He served for a time as one of the directors of Harry Pace's* Black Swan Phonograph Company and, through Pace, also became involved in the Marcus Garvey controversy in New York.

The early 1920s was the period of Marcus Garvey's greatest influence in New York and the nation as a whole, and he incited a great deal of controversy among prominent black leaders. Pace had become one of the most important members of the anti-Garvey movement, and on January 15, 1923, he joined with Robert S. Abbott,* publisher of the *Chicago Defender*, John E. Nail, and five other "respected leaders" to write a letter to Attorney General Harry M. Daugherty, protesting the delay of nearly a year in the trial of Garvey. This self-styled Committee of Eight condemned Garveyism as a philosophy that was "seeking to arouse ill-feeling between the races" and attacked Garvey himself as "an unscrupulous demogogue, who has ceaselessly and assiduously sought to spread among Negroes distrust and hatred of all white people." Garvey attacked the group venomously: "Like the good old darkey, they believe they have some news to tell and they are telling it for all it is worth—the liars and prevaricators that they are." Garvey also referred to them as "Uncle Tom Negroes," "wicked malingers," and other ad hominem epithets, claiming they were performing "the greatest bit of treachery and wickedness that any group of Negroes could be capable of." Garvey also claimed they were "nearly all Octoroons and Quadroons" or were "married to Octoroons."

Another important venture Jack Nail was involved in was the Colored Merchant Association (CMA) in Harlem. Long an advocate of racial solidarity and cooperation, Nail, in conjunction with Fred R. Moore, advocated in the late 1920s that the National Negro Business League sponsor a cooperative venture to improve the status of black business. Albon Holsey, head of the league, decided that it should sponsor a national cooperative grocery store venture. The goal was to organize black grocers into cooperative buying units, create a standardized store service, promote cooperative advertising, and use the local league chapters as the coordinating agencies. By the summer of 1929, the CMA was being developed in at least twenty-five cities with a secret advance from the Tuskegee Institute General Fund. The general headquarters of the group was to be located in New York City, and it was the Colored Merchants Association of Harlem that became the demonstration project for the entire nation.

Incorporated in New York, the CMA, Harlem had capital of $100,000 and issued 10,000 shares of stock. In April 1930, a formerly bankrupt black grocery store became the first model CMA store in Harlem. By this time, however, the Depression was ravaging the black community in Harlem and elsewhere. With the Depression as a backdrop, the CMA elected its first permanent officers and directors in 1931. Holsey was elected president, John E. Nail vice president, and Fred Moore treasurer. They faced an uphill, if not impossible, battle, which was made no easier when the officers and board itself were beset with internecine warfare.

Most of the complaints about the CMA came from the black consumers. They continually complained that they could get better bargains at white-owned stores. Holsey, Moore, and Nail chastised blacks for being more concerned with price than with the betterment of the race and explained that their local black grocer had higher overhead costs. But most blacks, who had never shown much propensity to patronize African-American enterprises anyway, simply could not afford to do so during those desperate times. The situation had become so critical by February 1933, that the league held an emergency meeting to deal with the CMA. At the meeting, Moore openly attacked the CMA for its association with the National Negro Business League. Holsey, on the other hand, appealed to the executive board to stand by the CMA in its time of trial. Charles Clinton Spaulding* supported Holsey, and the league voted to continue its support. Within a year, however, it was in receivership.

Jack Nail was for a time vice president of the New York Urban League, and he worked for the YMCA and the NAACP. He had grand dreams for his race, dreams that were never realized, for America was not yet ready to embrace equality for African-Americans. Upon his death in 1947, Harlem lost one of its great cheerleaders.

Sources

There are no personal papers of either John B. or John E. Nail. Included in the James Weldon Johnson Papers, however, is the John E. Nail Scrapbook, which contains some helpful information on both father and son and on Nail & Parker Realty. Newspaper clippings were collected by Johnson on various subjects, including several articles on Harlem real estate, letters of condolence, and assorted current events. This collection is held at the Beinecke Rare Book and Manuscript Library at Yale University. A biography of John E. Nail appears in *The Dictionary of Negro Biography* (1982). Gilbert Osofsky, *Harlem: The Making of a Ghetto* (1966) provides information on John B., John E., and Nail & Parker. The papers of the Works Progress Administration in the Schomburg Center for Research in Black Culture, New York City Public Library, contains valuable information, including a project entitled "Negroes of New York, An Account of the Nail and Parker Business Enterprises," July 26, 1939, by Arthur Gary. Also Wilfrid R. Bain's "Negro Real Estate Brokers" offers additional material on Harlem brokers, including Watt Terry, Philip Payton, and others. A good, though somewhat disorganized, account of Harlem is offered in Myrtle Evangeline Pollard, "Harlem as Is: The Negro Business and Economic Community," Master's thesis, City College, 1937; included in her second volume is an interview with John B. Nail, conducted on November 12, 1936. Odetta Harper, a WPA researcher, conducted an interview with John E. Nail, in which Negro Harlem in the first decade is described.

John E. Nail authored an article entitled "$20,000,000 in Negro Holdings," which appeared in the *New York Evening Mail*, January 26, 1918. A valuable profile of John E. Nail appears in *The Crisis*, March 1925. Several letters between John B. Nail and Booker T. Washington appear in container 243, reel 247 of the Booker T. Washington

Papers. These letters briefly address the issue of the Washington–Du Bois controversy during 1905. There are also some letters between John E. Nail and Albon Holsey in the Albon Holsey Papers, Tuskegee Institute Archives, Tuskegee University.

Accounts of the activities of Nail & Parker appear in the *New York Age*, March 30, 1911, and August 31, 1920; *New York Sun*, September 2, 1912, May 19, 1931, and May 20, 1931; and *Interstate Tattler*, January 2, 1931. Later business activities of John E. Nail's real estate firm appear in the *New World Telegram*, December 8, 1932; *New York Amsterdam News*, March 1933, and December 20, 1933; *New York Herald Tribune*, December 17, 1933; *New York American*, December 17, 1933; and *New York Age*, December 23, 1933.

Obituaries of John B. Nail appeared in the *New York Age*, February 21, 1942; the *New York Star News*, February 21, 1942; and the *New York Herald Tribune*, February 16, 1942. Obituaries of John E. Nail appeared in the *New York Times*, March 6, 1947; the *New York Herald-Tribune*, March 6, 1947; and the *New York Age*, March 15, 1947. For some information on the relationship between the Nails and the National Negro Business League and the Colored Merchants Association of Harlem, see John Edward Burrows, "The Necessity of Myth: A History of the National Negro Business League, 1940–1945," Ph.D. diss., Auburn University, 1977.

Napier, James Carroll (June 9, 1845–April 21, 1940). Lawyer, banker, politician, association official, and racial activist: One-Cent Savings Bank, Citizens Savings Bank, and National Negro Business League. In 1990 Willard Gatewood has written about the "Aristocrats of Color," whom he has defined as a group of individuals "who came from the ranks of free people of color and privileged slaves and who constituted a mulatto elite [which] moved in disproportionate numbers into positions of leadership." James Napier was an almost perfect example of that phenomenon in the South prior to World War II. Although he was prominently involved in a number of business activities, his influence greatly transcended that genre—he was a "race leader"—not just in Nashville and in Tennessee, but on the national level also. There were few African-Americans in the period from 1900 to 1925 who had greater visibility and respect in the nation's black community.

Most accounts assert that James Napier was a freeborn son of recently emancipated parents. A more recent account by Herbert L. Clark, however, claims that young Napier was born a slave and that the family was freed by their master's will upon his death in 1848. Clark's account appears to be more accurate. James Napier's parents were William Carroll Napier and Jane E. Napier. They were slaves on the plantation of Dr. Elias W. Napier, located about six miles west of Nashville. They were, however, "privileged slaves," and James's grandmother, Judy, had worked as Dr. Napier's seamstress and bore him four sons and one daughter. In recognition of this status, Judy's family was emancipated upon the master's death and was also bequeathed "a certain sum of money," on condition that they leave Davidson County by March 1, 1849. In response, Judy and her children purchased a farm near Cincinnati and then one in New Richmond, Ohio.

At that point William Carroll Napier decided to take his family back to Nashville, where he went into the livery business. William Napier, with a few other free blacks, also founded an illegal school for Nashville's African-American children, but it was later closed by whites. In response, William sent young James, along with his mother and brother, back to Ohio to be educated. The two brothers were enrolled at Wilberforce University near Xenia. When the main building of that school was destroyed by fire, James transferred to Oberlin College, which he attended until his junior year. In 1867, with blacks rising to positions of power in politics in Tennessee, James, just twenty-two years old, returned to Nashville, where he began his fruitful political career as a page in the Tennessee State Senate. A year later, he was appointed a county claims commissioner for Davidson County by Governor William G. Brownlow.

Shortly thereafter, John Mercer Langston, an Ohio free black who had become a powerful Republican politician and congressman, visited Nashville. Langston had become friends with the elder Napier in Ohio, and, upon meeting James in 1870, prevailed upon him to attend the law school at Howard University, where Langston served as dean. Because James Napier did not have the funds to attend school on his own, Langston secured him a clerkship in the office of the Bureau of Refugees, Freedmen and Abandoned Lands. A few months later, Napier passed his civil service exam and was appointed clerk first class in the office of the sixth auditor of the U.S. Treasury.

In 1872 Napier graduated from Howard Law School and was admitted to the bar in the District of Columbia. Nonetheless, he immediately returned to Nashville, where he passed the Tennessee bar exam and set up practice. The law, on its own, was hardly a lucrative practice for blacks in the nineteenth century. It was, instead, an entrée into business and politics. On the business side, Napier began selling real estate and also began to accumulate a small amount of property in his own right. Over a twenty-year period, Napier's real estate holdings grew from just two lots valued at $250 each to fifteen parcels of property with a value of $23,300. He continued to hold property until his death in 1940, at which time he had seventeen pieces with an assessed valuation of $43,016. It was hardly enough to make him wealthy, but it did provide him with a steady source of income throughout his life.

Napier also used his legal position to help him get started in politics. His political career in the Republican party was enormously enhanced in 1878 when he married Nettie, the daughter of John Mercer Langston. Their wedding was the biggest social event in black Nashville in the nineteenth century. A contemporary account gushed: "The marriage of J. C. Napier to Miss Nettie Langston, in Washington City, two months ago, threw Nashville colored society into a general flutter of excitement. . . . The church was completely packed, both upstairs and downstairs, and the doors were blocked to such an extent that many who desired to get in were compelled to content themselves with a few inches of standing room on a bench in the hall.''

Napier's political connections in 1875 got him an appointment as internal revenue gauger for the fifth collection district of the state of Tennessee. He later advanced to deputy collector, which he held until he resigned in 1878 to take a Nashville city councilman position he had won in the election of September of that year. Napier had run on a platform that demanded that African-American teachers be employed in the city's black schools. He was reelected for two more terms, serving until 1884, and acquitted himself very well during his tenure in office. As he promised, Napier was instrumental in the hiring of the first black teachers for the public schools, and he was also partially responsible for the erection of the first modern school buildings—Meigs and Pearl schools—for blacks in the city. In addition, Napier secured the appointment of the first African-American firefighters to the city's fire department. After Napier's official tour of government with the city ended, he continued to serve as an unofficial financial advisor for the city.

While still in municipal government, Napier began to acquire greater influence in the affairs of the state's Republican party. In 1882 he was elected to serve on the most powerful organ of the state party—the executive committee. As such, Napier became an integral part of the decision-making process of the party, and he also served for a quite some time as chairman and for six years as its secretary. From this position of influence, Napier was nominated three times to run for state elective offices. In 1882 he was a candidate for the state legislature and later for the circuit court clerk of Davidson County. In 1898 Napier was a candidate for Congress for the Sixth District, but he lost the general election. That was Napier's last try for an elective office, but he would continue to have a great deal of influence in the Republican party on the local, state, and national levels, serving as a delegate to the Republican National Convention four times in the period from 1880 to 1912.

In the meantime, Napier developed an extremely close friendship and professional association with Booker T. Washington* of Tuskegee. Napier first met Washington in 1891, and the two men, despite the fact that Napier was fourteen years older, had an instant affinity for one another. Washington once said, "I have been associated with him for twenty years. . . . During all the years I have known him I have never heard Mr. Napier express a narrow or bitter thought toward the white race." Napier reciprocated in kind about Washington, saying, "Contrary to the judgement of his friends, in opposition to what almost all the leaders of his race advised, he commenced his work of reconciliation of the relations of the two races of the South."

The two men, Napier and Washington, became what was known at that time and thereafter as "accommodationists," men who espoused conciliation by blacks in race relations and gradualism in the procurement of civil rights. Yet, as shall be shown, they were hardly Uncle Toms, as many critics later claimed. Indeed, they both possessed a strong strain of black nationalism and race pride, and both also worked fervently behind the scenes to secure the political and civil rights they discounted in public.

Washington, in his Atlanta Exposition speech in 1895, had advocated that

African-Americans achieve equality through economic progress. This was to be accomplished through industrial education of the masses of unskilled and ill-educated blacks, but also through a new program of black business activity. Whereas older black business ventures, like barbershops, restaurants, caterers, and so forth, had serviced the white community, Washington encouraged the development of a whole range of business institutions, owned by blacks, to service the various needs of the developing black communities in urban areas. To this end, Washington also established the National Negro Business League (NNBL) to encourage and coordinate these efforts. This new theory and organization was to capture the interest, enthusiasm, and talent of James Napier.

Napier was a delegate from Nashville to the first convention of the NNBL held in New York City. Upon his return, Napier pushed for the creation of new business ventures by blacks in the city, organized the first Tennessee chapter of the NNBL in 1902, and persuaded Washington to hold the national convention of the organization in Nashville the following year. Chapters soon sprang up throughout the state, and by 1909 African-American business leaders in sixteen communities in Tennessee had organized branches. Napier continued as a national official of the league throughout these years, and, upon Washington's death in 1915, he succeeded him as president. Napier shepherded the organization through the difficult years of World War I and, particularly, took a stance against the massive migration of blacks from the South to the North that went on during this time. He laid the fault for this exodus from the South squarely at the feet of whites and their racist Jim Crow legislation and violence. Napier was evidently a strong and progressive president who established a nationwide advertising campaign in an effort to increase black business activities. He turned the reins over to Robert R. Moton in 1919.

Napier also took a number of important steps himself or in conjunction with others to bring Washington's dreams for black business to fruition. Quietly, but with great significance for the later development of the city's black business community, Napier made his office building—Napier Court, at 411 Fourth Avenue, near the corner of Cedar and Fourth—the center of black business activity. A number of black lawyers and other professionals had offices in his building, and the area rapidly became the apex of a developing business and amusement district, with restaurants, theaters, and a whole range of black service enterprises. This was capped in 1912 when Albert N. Johnson, a successful African-American undertaker and fellow member of the NNBL, opened the Majestic Theater, which was described by the *Nashville Globe* as a "magnificent playhouse erected at enormous expense."

The first and most lasting step in this direction came in 1903 when, in conjunction with Richard H. Boyd,* local undertaker Preston Taylor, and six other prominent blacks, Napier helped found the One-Cent Savings Bank, one of the first banks in the United States owned by blacks to actually go into operation. Each invested $100 in the venture, and when the bank opened on January 6, 1904, 145 patrons deposited $6,392.86. Capitalization at the founding was

$25,000. Napier served without pay as chief cashier and advisor of the institution for many years, and he gave the bank temporary quarters in Napier Court. He also pledged his personal fortune as security for the bank's operation during the first year. Under his guidance and that of the Boyds, the One-Cent Savings Bank (later Citizens Savings Bank) followed a remarkably conservative fiscal policy. It announced its purpose was to "encourage frugality and systematic saving among our people, to secure the safe keeping and proper investment of such savings and set in motion business enterprises." Because of the earlier collapse of the Freedman's Bank, and a general lack of confidence in black-owned banks by the African-American populace, One-Cent, as one officer later recalled, put emphasis on "first confidence, and second, financeering." This resulted in excruciatingly slow growth, as its capital grew to just $60,000 in the first thirty-three years, and deposits thirty-five years later were only $209,942.85. To the Boyds and James Napier, growth was never as important as stability, and most scholars have traced this caution primarily to Napier's influence. (Greater detail on the bank's operation over the years is given in the biographies of Richard and Henry Allen Boyd.)

With the bank in operation, and black business beginning to flourish in Nashville, Napier and the local NNBL played a leading role in the city's famous streetcar boycott, an event which, more than any other, demonstrates the complex relationship between public pronouncements of accommodation, on one hand, and the reaction to real crises in race relations on the part of Washington, Napier, and other black business leaders, on the other. Although Napier was not one of the key leaders in this confrontation, the NNBL chapter he had founded spearheaded the boycott, and Richard H. Boyd and Preston Taylor, both closely associated with Napier, emerged as the principal actors in the drama.

The controversy began to build in 1903, when the West Nashville trolley line added an extra car for black workers traveling to the fertilizer plants in that area. This fed into growing demands by whites to segregate the trolley lines completely, and by January 1905, the state legislature enacted a Jim Crow streetcar law for all Tennessee cities, to go into effect on July 5. In the spring, well before the law was in operation, black leaders in Nashville began preparing the African-American populace for a boycott. Reverend Edward W. D. Isaac, editor of the *Nashville Clarion*, advised its readers "to trim their corns, darn their socks, wear solid shoes . . . and get ready to walk." When the law went into effect, it was clear that few blacks were riding on the cars. After three weeks of the boycott, the leaders of the local chapter of the NNBL, then headed by Richard H. Boyd, but including Napier, Preston Taylor, and several others, met on July 31 and declared that blacks should use the trolleys only in "absolute necessity" and that owners of express wagons in the city should use them to transport people to their destinations. Shortly afterward, they quietly went about organizing their own traction company.

Taylor, Richard Boyd, and Napier emerged as the leaders of this new race-conscious enterprise, called the Union Transportation Company. Taylor, an ex-slave and native of Shreveport, Louisiana, who became pastor of the Lea Avenue Christian Church and owner of a prosperous funeral parlor, was named president of the concern. The firm purchased five steam-driven "auto buses," which were in operation in black neighborhoods by October 1905, but they soon proved to be underpowered to handle Nashville's hilly terrain. In response, Taylor, Boyd, and Napier brought in fourteen electric buses, each capable of carrying twenty passengers, to replace the steamers. Rather than purchase power from the white-owned Nashville Railway and Light Company, the main culprit in the Jim Crow dispute, the company installed its own dynamo in the basement of Boyd's National Baptist Publishing Company.

The whole enterprise, however, was undercapitalized, and the city fought back by levying special taxes on the buses. The operation was also strained by the great dispersion of Nashville's blacks, who lived and worked in all parts of the city. The company was able to continue operations until July 1906, but a short time thereafter it went out of business. By this point the boycott had been abandoned by most of the city's blacks. Yet, it was one of the longest boycotts in the history of American cities, and it provided a beacon for blacks in the 1950s when they prepared their successful protests against segregated transit systems in Montgomery, Alabama, and elsewhere. James Napier's role in all of this was more muted than either Taylor's or Boyd's, but it was important. Whereas those two men were perceived as "rabble-rousers" to some extent by the leaders of the white community, Napier was viewed as an "accommodator," as a reasonable man, or perhaps, a "good nigger." Thus, he proved to be a quiet and effective negotiator with whites during the boycott, since most believed that Napier only wanted fairness and equality for both races.

From this point onward, Napier's attention was more on political than business affairs, and the focus of his activity increasingly shifted from the local to the national level. A key event in this transition was Booker T. Washington's success in getting Napier appointed to the board of trustees of the Anna T. Jeanes Foundation in February 1908. The foundation had a one-million dollar trust fund for the purpose of establishing schools for southern blacks, and also on the board were prominent whites like William Howard Taft, then secretary of war, George Peabody, a Massachusetts financier, and Andrew Carnegie, the steel magnate. Napier impressed these eminent gentlemen with his ability, and before long he was appointed an executive committee member and vice chairman. Napier's leadership role in this organization soon brought him offers from presidents to enter governmental service on the national level.

Washington and Napier decided that they should focus on getting Napier placed in the Treasury Department. They particularly wanted him to be appointed registrar of the U.S. Treasury, the highest appointive office available to blacks. President Theodore Roosevelt instead offered Napier the post of consul to Bahia, Brazil, in 1908. Napier refused the appointment, stating his preference for the treasury post. They continued to lobby Taft for the position when Taft became president, but he also tried to buy them off in 1910 by offering Napier the position of minister resident and consul general of Liberia. Again, Napier refused. Finally, in March 1911, Taft appointed Napier to succeed W. T. Vernon as registrar of the Treasury. The job was, in effect, that of the official bookkeeper of the United States, and Napier countersigned all U.S. currency and submitted an annual report to the secretary of the treasury on the business transacted by his office during the year. Napier headed a staff of seventy-three in the office.

In this office, Napier continued his crusade to expand opportunities for African-Americans in the government and to promote self-improvement efforts. A particularly important act on his part was to ensure that historically black land-grant colleges got their full share of the federal funds due them under the Morrill Acts of 1862 and 1890. He obtained funds to conduct an investigation into the use and distribution of these funds, and in April 1913 he testified before the House Committee on Agriculture to promote passage of the Page Bill, which was designed to eliminate discrimination in the allocation of these funds. He also proposed an amendment to this bill which provided that none of the federal money to land-grant colleges be appropriated or paid out in states that practiced discrimination.

By this time, however, Woodrow Wilson had ascended to the presidency, and Napier's days were numbered with the Treasury Department. He most likely would have been replaced anyway, since he was a Republican appointment, but Wilson's determination to pursue a rigid Jim Crow policy in federal departments set the two men on a collision course. When Wilson sanctioned a segregation order that required white and black employees to use separate toilets in the Treasury Building, Napier protested. Wilson asked for Napier's resignation which he supplied, and Napier left federal service at the age of sixty-eight. Napier returned to Nashville, where he resumed his law practice and continued his earlier political, banking, and civic activities.

One of Napier's most important achievements was the creation of the Tennessee Agricultural and Industrial School in 1913 (later Tennessee State University) in Nashville, to be funded by the Morrill Act of 1890. Napier, in conjunction with a number of other black leaders in Nashville, had begun campaigning for the creation of the school in 1909, and in 1910 and 1911 he had appeared before Davidson County's fiscal body to encourage it to issue bonds for establishing a normal school. Each time, he was able to get passed bond appropriations of $80,000.

The following year, Napier was elected president of the Board of Trade of Nashville, an organization involved in school improvement, sanitary housing, business development, public order, and increased opportunities for employment for the city's blacks. A few years later, he was also appointed chairman of Nashville's Community Chest's Negro Division, a position he retained for virtually his entire life. He also lectured at Meharry Medical College each year, served as a lifelong trustee of Fisk University, and was generally recognized as the dean of the city's black community. When the Nashville Housing Authority was organized during the 1930s, the aged Napier was appointed by Mayor

Thomas L. Cummings to represent blacks. In 1940 the city proposed to name a new housing project, built by the Federal Housing Administration for blacks, J. C. Napier Court. When the local newspaper interviewed Napier, ninety-four years of age, for his reaction to this announcement, he replied, "Why I'm just a plain, old colored man who has lived a long time and seen many things."

The last years of James Napier's life were filled with many such honors. In 1934 students of the Negro history class of Tennessee State College publicly honored James and Nettie Napier with a pageant called "From Africa to America." The following year, Fisk University awarded Napier an honorary doctor of laws degree to commemorate his ninetieth birthday. Upon his death in 1940, funeral services were held at the Fisk Memorial Chapel with Reverend Henry Allen Boyd officiating. Napier was, in most respects, the last of an extraordinary generation of blacks in America—the freeborn or privileged slave mulattoes of the post–Civil War generation. They had formed an ambitious corps of prosperous builders, hotel men, caterers, waiters, and small farmers before the war, and they became the political, social, and economic leaders of the emerging black community in the late nineteenth century. Increasingly, however, they were superceded by darker skinned ex-slaves who came to dominate the community. Napier spanned all these worlds with relative ease. He was respected by whites, doted upon by the light-skinned elite, and revered by most of the black masses. This was reflected by the fact that Citizen's Bank and Trust was always called "Napier's Bank" by the masses, even though Richard Boyd and others were far more influential in its management. This "small, quiet, dignified, and light-skinned patriarch was a source of pride and continuity" in Nashville's black community. He represented individual success and accomplishment, but he was also, as was commented at his funeral, a "drum major for racial justice."

Sources

James Napier's papers are found in the Special Collections at Fisk University in Nashville. There are also a large number of letters between Napier and Booker T. Washington and Emmet J. Scott in the Booker T. Washington Papers at the Library of Congress. There are some letters and handwritten corporate materials by Napier regarding the organization of his bank in the Tennessee State University Archives in Nashville. See also the papers of the National Negro Business League at Tuskegee University in Tuskegee, Alabama. Napier's own writings include "Negro Members of the Tennessee Legislature," *Journal of Negro History* 5 (July 1920), 117–18. Several of Napier's speeches on business issues in the *Proceedings* of the Annual Meeting of the National Negro Business League, 1901 and 1906, are contained in the Special Collections at Hampton University.

There is no full-scale, published biography of Napier, but see Cordell Hull Williams, "The Life of James Carroll Napier from 1845 to 1940," Master's thesis, Tennessee State University, 1954, for the fullest account of his life; and Herbert L. Clark, "The Public Career of James Carroll Napier: Businessman, Politician and Crusader for Racial Justice, 1845–1940," D.A. diss., Middle Tennessee State University, 1980; and his "James Carroll Napier: National Negro Leader," *Tennessee Historical Quarterly* 49 (Winter 1990), 243–52, for his role as a businessman and national race leader. See also a good short biography by Lester C. Lamon in *Dictionary of Negro Biography* (1982) and obituaries in the *Journal of Negro History*, July 1940; *Negro History Bulletin*, February 1942, 114; *The Tennessean*, April 22, 1940; and the *Nashville Banner*, April 22 and 23, 1940. Short biographical treatments appear in T. O. Fuller, ed., *Pictorial History of the American Negro* (Memphis, 1933), 288; Clement Richardson, ed., *National Encyclopedia of the Colored Race*, vol. I (1919); *Leaders of Afro-American Nashville*, project of 1983 Nashville Conference on Afro-American Culture and History; and *Who's Who of the Colored Race* (1915). The basic outline of Napier's life and accomplishments can be found in typewritten biographical material contained in the Fisk University Library, Special Collections; and there is another typewritten account of his life in the Archives at Tennessee State University.

There are some other materials on Napier in Helen Dahnke, "An Old Colored Man," *Tennessean Magazine*, May 4, 1937, 2; *Commonweal*, August 9, 1940, 324; *Crisis*, April and May 1911 and January 1939; *The Tennessean, Focus*, January 1, 1986, and March 2, 1988; *Nashville Banner*, September 13, 14, 16, and 17, 1886, and June 10, 1938; *Nashville Globe*, November 11, 1910, and February 24, 1911; *Nashville American*, September 13, 15, and 16, 1886; *Negro History Bulletin*, June/July 1974, 267–68; and Linda T. Wynn, "Building Confidence: The Survival of a Financial Institution," *The Courier* (Nashville: Tennessee Historical Commission, 1981). For Napier's role in the Nashville streetcar boycott, see Lena R. Marbury, "Nashville's 1905 Streetcar Boycott," Master's thesis, Tennessee State University, 1985; and August Meier and Elliott Rudwick, "Negro Boycotts of Jim Crow Streetcars in Tennessee," *American Quarterly* XXI, 4 (Winter 1969). Lester C. Lamon, "The Tennessee Agricultural and Industrial Normal School: Public Education for Black Tennesseans," *Tennessee Historical Quarterly* 32 (1973), 42–58 has some information on Napier's role in the founding of that institution, as does Raymond Lloyd Grann, "Tennessee Agricultural and Industrial State University, 1912–1962: Fifty Years of Leadership through Excellence, 1912–1962," *Nashville*, 1962.

Nickerson, William, Jr. (see Beavers, George Allen, Jr., Ivan James Houston, Norman Oliver Houston, and William Nickerson, Jr.).

O

Overton, Anthony (March 21, 1865–July 3, 1946). Entrepreneur, cosmetics manufacturer, insurance and bank founder, realtor, and newspaper publisher: Overton Hygienic Manufacturing, Victory Life Insurance, Douglass National Bank, Great Northern Realty, *Half-Century*, and *Chicago Bee*. In the first quarter of the twentieth century, Anthony Overton was one of the few African-American businessmen in Chicago who had created a highly diverse conglomerate. One could consider him a role model for having achieved such success against all odds. However, time has taken its toll on Anthony Overton, for he is hardly remembered today. How could someone who had so dominated a generation of black business in Chicago be nearly totally forgotten? The OGBVD Syndicate of Chicago was a business empire including the Overton Hygienic Manufacturing Company, the Great Northern Realty Company, the *Chicago Bee*, the Victory Life Insurance Company, and the Douglass National Bank. The fact that such a diversified conglomerate was owned by an African-American in the early part of the twentieth century in the racially forbidding climate of Chicago is truly remarkable.

Although blacks were not an integral or integrated part of the larger white society during the late nineteenth and first decade of the twentieth centuries, they were treated with a mixture of consternation and tolerance. Even this situation soon began to deteriorate. Between 1900 and 1914, Chicago's Black Belt (a narrow stretch of land where an enclave of black housing had developed) reached its saturation point in terms of population. Between the years from 1914 to 1918, a mass migration of African-Americans from the South overwhelmed the city of Chicago. The population of 34,335 blacks in 1910 swelled to 92,501 in 1920, a nearly 60 percent increase in one decade. With the cessation of construction during the war, housing became a problem of insurmountable proportions. When the more established black middle class elected to move to areas occupied primarily by whites, overt hostility erupted with an unprecedented vengeance. How Anthony Overton and his OGBVD Syndicate thrived during this racially explosive climate requires a closer look.

Anthony Overton was born into slavery on March 21, 1865, in Monroe, Louisiana, to Anthony and Martha (Deberry) Overton. With the end of the Civil War, Overton attended public schools and received a college education at Washburn College in Topeka, Kansas, and at the University of Kansas, where he earned a bachelor of laws degree in 1888. He was admitted to the Kansas state bar upon graduation and began practicing law in Topeka. Shortly thereafter he served for one year as a judge of the municipal court in Shawnee County. Moving on to Oklahoma, in 1892 Overton was elected treasurer of Kingfisher County. Despite his success in the field of law, Overton had grander dreams. He ventured out into business, first purchasing a general store in Oklahoma City, and then moving on to create the company that would ultimately afford Overton greater opportunities.

In 1898 he established the Overton Hygienic Manufacturing Company in Kansas City, Missouri, with a starting capital of $1,960. Initially, the company manufactured and marketed one product—Hygienic Pet Baking Powder. From there, he moved on to manufacture toiletries and flavor extracts. Within a short time, Overton realized the potential profitability in cosmetics, specifically for African-American women. During the company's formative years, Overton assumed the role of a traveling salesman, trying to establish a solid market for his new product line. The company expanded rapidly despite a setback during the first nine months of business when the company realized a loss of $40 per month. A relatively quick recovery took place but was then frustrated by the flood of 1903 which engulfed the manufacturing districts of Kansas City, and the company's total investment was lost. The resulting bankruptcy was known to no one outside the company, and business proceeded as usual.

Overton's integrity was manifested in his conviction to manufacture products of the highest quality and his refusal to manufacture any products deemed degrading, such as skin bleaches. He also employed a sales force that acted as home sales agents, who reached a market that was ripe for tapping. The products had an international appeal in markets as remote as Egypt, Liberia, and Japan, among numerous other countries, and it imported from such international locations as India, Japan, and the Philippines. The receptive response of the African-American public in the southern and some midwestern states allowed for further expansion. The next stage of growth focused on the Atlantic Coast states from New York to the Carolinas.

In 1911 Overton moved his company to Chicago, which was becoming a center of African-American business activity in the North, with a network of railroads that facilitated the distribution of the company's products. A full line of cosmetics and perfumes was marketed under the patented trade name of High Brown. Also Overton Hygienic was now marketing shoe polish, hair preparations, baking powder, toilet water, and flavoring extracts, and it was one of the few cosmetic manufacturing firms in the United States that made the odor bases for its perfumes. By 1912 the product line consisted of fifty-two items which were marketed by a salaried sales force of five, all black, in addition to 400 house-to-house agents. The products were sold at wholesale only to merchants, large schools, and public institutions. At the end of June 1912, the firm had done a business of $117,000. By 1915 the company was capitalized at $268,000, with thirty-two full-time employees and a line of sixty-two products.

In 1927 Bradstreet, the credit rating service, assessed Overton Hygienic Manufacturing Company at a value in excess of $1 million. The *Chicago Bee* (a newspaper owned and operated by Overton) in that same year reported that more than 150 black women and men were employed in the home and branch offices; that the company manufactured 250 products; and that it distributed its items worldwide. Although these figures may or may not be true representations of the company's achievements, it is difficult to ascertain the full array of products because the company manufactured products for other companies that marketed items under their own brand names. Nevertheless, Overton's company did enjoy an impressive level of success. He stood his ground despite fierce competition from Annie Turnbo-Malone* in St. Louis and Chicago and Madame C. J. Walker* in Indianapolis, among other African-American beauty supply manufacturers.

The wealth that Overton amassed as a direct result of the company's success provided him with the springboard from which to engage in diverse business activities. The *Half-Century*, which Overton began in 1916, was his first attempt at diversification. This monthly publication (although it was occasionally published bimonthly) was a variety magazine that appealed to black middle-class conservatives, primarily educated and prosperous southerners. The magazine provided its readers, mostly women, with general information, news reports, and articles with a cultural focus. It has been suggested that this magazine was the precursor to *Ebony*, an African-American women's magazine started in 1945 by publishing magnate John Harold Johnson.* Overton excessively advertised the High Brown cosmetic line in *Half-Century*, and he used the publication as a vehicle to put forth his own interests and ideologies. The dominant theme of *Half-Century* was the creation of a separate black economy and society, with a particular emphasis on race pride, racial independence, and self-help. Overton, an advocate of Booker T. Washington's* philosophy, strongly urged African-Americans to embrace the concept of race pride and ambition and to aspire to what he considered the correct standards of living.

Overton opposed the symbols of the old elite, and as early as the first issue of *Half-Century*, Overton set the tone for his intolerance of W.E.B. Du Bois's intellectual elitism.

It will not be our sole ambition to make this magazine a "literary gem" either for our own gratification or to suit the fancy of the "high-brows," but to present facts in plain, commonsense language, so that the masses may read and understand; or, in the words of Brother Taylor, we propose to call a "spade a *spade*" and not an "excavating instrument for manual manipulation."

With the massive influx of southern blacks migrating north and specifically to Chicago during World War I, the *Half-Century* reflected the fears and concerns of older Chicago residents. It never encouraged the migration, which was a policy in sharp contrast to that of the Robert Abbott's* *Chicago Defender*. Rather, the *Half-Century*, like the Urban League, discouraged the northbound exodus. Despite the magazine's policy of accommodation, its conservative tone changed when Chicago's racial tensions exploded during the summer of 1919. The riots that ensued destroyed whatever dreams there had been of racial integration. When the final casualty figures were calculated, 23 blacks and 15 whites had died, and 342 blacks and 178 whites had been injured. An African-American instrument like the *Half-Century* could not hold its tongue in view of the injustice that its people had suffered. This heightened racial antagonism led the *Half-Century* to focus on politics and interracial conflict; it temporarily took a militant stance as did almost all black publications. Stories of racial oppression replaced columns on music and art. In the face of racial strife, the *Half-Century* became an ardent supporter of the NAACP and urged its readers to support the organization. However, by 1992, the magazine had resumed its former policy of renouncing protest as futile.

On April 18, 1925, Overton phased out the *Half-Century*, replacing it with the weekly *Chicago Bee*. (For a time, Overton also backed at least two other publications: the *Chicago Whip* and *Champion* magazine.) This newspaper was a direct challenge to the *Chicago Defender*, although the *Defender* appealed more to the black masses, and the *Bee* continued in the tradition of the *Half-Century* in its appeal to the middle class. It was harsher in its criticism of the lower class, urging its members to adopt the middle-class values of their well-established northern counterparts. Although the *Bee* suffered the same financial difficulties during the Great Depression of the 1930s as many other publications, it had a significant national following, which allowed it to survive into the 1940s.

As the *Half-Century* was establishing a place in the publishing marketplace, Overton pursued a completely different avenue for his next business investment. In 1922 he opened the Douglass National Bank, the first black-owned bank to receive a national charter. This was an important evolution in the way in which black banks were protected; previously, African-American banks were privately owned, small organizations or were building and loan associations free from the protective safeguards of state or national charters. As early as 1919, an article had appeared in the *Half-Century* addressing the need for African-American banks, and Overton had probably considered entering the business of banking at this time. Although the shrewd black businessman Jesse Binga* had beat Overton at opening a black bank in 1921, Binga's bank operated under a state charter. Throughout its lifetime, the financing of Douglass National Bank took many twists and turns.

In its first year of operation, the bank's total deposits were $56,030, and total deposits had peaked at $1,507,336 in 1929; then, in 1931, in response to the

Depression, its total deposits suffered a dramatic decrease to $542,455. Despite the fact that the bank required and received Overton's conscientious attention over and above his other business interests, it was unable to weather the Depression or the three major runs it suffered in 1932 due to public hysteria over numerous bank closings. It officially closed in 1932, never to reopen its doors to the public.

Overton's final entrée into a new line of business occurred in 1923 when he launched the Victory Life Insurance Company, which was incorporated under Illinois law. It was granted the authority to write business on March 3, 1924, with a paid-in capital of $100,000 and a surplus of $50,000. Overton's goal in establishing the insurance company was to encourage thrift, create estates, protect widows and orphans, and provide lucrative jobs for middle-class African-Americans. Without delay, the original capital was invested in real estate—first mortgages on blacks' homes, probably engineered through Overton's Great Northern Real Estate Company. The public response to the Victory Insurance Company was very favorable. By the end of 1924, the company's assets had reached $167,000, with a surplus of $157,000, and an income of $14,719. Insurance in force was $680,000. The year 1925 proved to be a time of remarkable expansion. The company successfully opened offices in Texas, Missouri, Ohio, West Virginia, Kentucky, the District of Columbia, Maryland, and New Jersey. Its assets equaled $170,000, its net reserve was $30,000, its capital and surplus had reached $132,000, and insurance in force had more than tripled to $2,250,000.

In 1927 Victory Life Insurance accomplished an unprecedented feat—it was the only company chartered by the state of Illinois to accomplish entry into New York State—one of the few to gain admittance in some twenty-five years. Its entrance into this lucrative market was facilitated primarily by such prominent African-American New Yorkers as Dr. P.M.H. Savory, Dr. C. B. Powell, and John W. Duncan. Savory had visited the facilities of the Douglass Bank and the Victory Life Insurance in 1924, and he was sufficiently impressed to invest $3,750 in exchange for fifty shares. He also engineered Victory Life's admittance into New York State. Savory's intervention proved successful and catapulted Victory Life's name and reliable reputation into the public eye. The New York expansion brought tremendous returns to Victory Life Insurance: Nearly $7,000,000 of paid-for business was placed on the company's books from 1927 to February 1932, derived solely from New York City and the metropolitan area. It is important to note that the actual amount in cash, $282,000 paid on stock subscriptions, was greater than in all of the other states combined.

From New York, Victory Life gained access to the Indiana market—the first African-American old-line company to be admitted into that state. Shortly thereafter, Virginia was added to its stable of territories. By 1927, with the addition of Michigan, the company's income reached $283,000, its capital and surplus was $262,000, and it had $8.5 million of paid-for business on the books. During the first five years of operations, a total of $246,000 had been loaned on properties owned by blacks, and $114,000 had been paid to beneficiaries of deceased policyholders. The company enjoyed continued growth and progress from 1929 through 1931, when its insurance in force escalated to $16,350,633, with assets of $1,216,730, and capital and surplus reaching $222,287. This surge in business proved to be short lived.

Despite the seemingly smooth transition to a larger insurance company, unethical practices, occurring behind the scenes, caused Overton to lose control of his insurance firm. Savory took issue with several policies Overton had instituted, including Overton's investment practices. As was mentioned earlier, Overton provided Douglass Bank with the most nurturing of any of his companies. What appears to have happened was his inability to separate the bank and the insurance company, which resulted in an entanglement of affairs.

Between 1919 and 1929, Chicago experienced a boom in the real estate market. The value of property escalated to a level of inflation that gave real estate holders a false sense of security. In 1929, with the onset of the Great Depression, values plummeted. What transpired for Overton was devastating, since it was noted earlier that the entire original capital of the Victory Life Insurance Company was invested in mortgages on blacks' homes. With the nation's economy in a tailspin, the market value of the entire mortgage holdings was far less than the amount shown on the books, and less than the State Insurance Department would appraise it. Overton erred in investing the total amount of the original capital in one vehicle.

Some examples of Overton's indiscretions are helpful in understanding the dismantling of his empire. In January 1927, Overton invested $70,000 in Douglass National Bank stock three weeks before a directors' meeting. A short time later, before another meeting and in the face of a protest from the New York Insurance Department's opposition to the first investment, another $60,000 cash was taken out of the treasury of the company to purchase some additional bank stock. In 1931, Michigan, Missouri, and New York wrote to criticize the collateral loans, demanding an examination as of June 30, 1931. They were suspicious of the presence of bank stock and two collateral loans, one for $40,000 to Overton's daughters, and a personal loan of $15,000 in the name of George A. Gaughn, who was subsequently found to be Overton himself. The New York State Insurance Department suspended the company twice in 1932, and New Jersey followed in response to the unethical practices.

The New York directors' sensitivity to these public transgressions, as well as the dangerous policies practiced by the Victory Life Insurance Company, caused them to take direct action against Overton. They voted their stock collectively, thereby achieving a voting strength to avert what they feared to be impending disaster. Overton's attempt at diverting this action proved fruitless. The result of a directors' meeting was to oust Overton; this action was followed by putting the company into receivership, at which time it had in excess of $15 million of paid-for insurance on the books.

Savory and Powell took the reins and reorganized the company as the Victory Mutual Life Insurance Company on April 5, 1933. After several months of business operation under this new name, death claims of $100,000 were settled, and $78,000 was paid to the Reconstruction Finance Corporation, and $300,000 had been acquired in new business. In 1938 Victory Mutual's total admitted assets of $36,633 paled in comparison to Supreme Liberty Life's admitted assets of $2,261,564, but the fact that it had survived a total restructuring is noteworthy nonetheless. By 1961 the company had achieved a ranking of twelfth among all black-managed insurance companies in the United States, with assets of $7,408,192. Victory Life Insurance Company was listed as a separate firm through 1970. From 1971 through 1989, it was listed as a division of the American Benefit Life Insurance Company. Neither company was listed after 1989.

To house his multitude of business enterprises, Overton erected the Overton Hygienic/Douglass National Bank Building. The building was constructed in 1922/1923 at a cost of $250,000. A monument to black thrift and industry, more important, it was a symbol of the success of one man—Anthony Overton. The structure also supplied rental office space for African-American professionals such as Walter T. Bailey, Chicago's first black architect, and the Theater Owners Booking Association, which managed and booked black entertainment. Again, the financial troubles he faced during the 1930s resulted in a keen disappointment: the abandonment of the Overton Hygienic/Douglass Bank building for more consolidated quarters in the *Chicago Bee* building, which was erected in 1929 as a newspaper office and an apartment building. With the failure of the bank and the loss of control of the insurance company, the *Bee* and Overton Hygienic Manufacturing continued to share the same building until the early 1940s when the newspaper ceased publication.

Why, after such a notable achievement in business as Anthony Overton's, did such a rapid decline occur? As mentioned previously, the Depression played a pivotal role in the decline of not just Overton's conglomerate, but also numerous smaller companies that were denied the federal government's assistance and were faced with frozen assets and ultimately bankruptcy. However, it would be remiss to blame the economic panic as the sole reason for Overton's failure. Despite Chicago's tense race relations, many black entrepreneurs were able to take advantage of the large African-American market who had no other choice but to patronize African-American-owned businesses. Jesse Binga, the banker who had opened the first state bank owned by a black man, had diversified his business interests and grew to enjoy wealth and recognition. But Overton and Binga had an ongoing rivalry that may have contributed to the demise of both their empires, since neither was able to weather the storm of the 1930s.

Although Overton had taken a cautious approach when he first started out in business, his ambition and competitiveness appear to have led him astray. Fortunately for Overton, he managed to retain some assets and live a relatively comfortable life in his later years. On July 3, 1946, Overton's death was cited in a short obituary in the *New York Times*. He was awarded the Spingarn Medal of the National Association for the Advancement of Colored People in 1927, the first businessman to receive such an honor for his achievements in business, and the Harmon Award from the Harmon Foundation in 1928 for similar accomplishments. It is important to remember Anthony Overton for his dreams and achievements, not for his defeats.

Sources

Anthony Overton's personal and business papers are not extant, although his unpublished memoirs at least at one time were in the possession of Olive Diggs, former business manager of the *Chicago Bee*. No full-length biography has been written about Overton, but several pieces have been written about the man and his various business ventures: John McKinley, "Anthony Overton: A Man Who Planned for Success," *Reflexus* I (April 1925, Chicago), 14, 15, 56; *National Cyclopedia of American Biography* 47: 256–57, 1965; James J. Flynn, *Negroes of Achievement in Modern America* (1970), 109–20, offers a lengthy although somewhat flawed biography of Overton; Ingham, BDABL; *Who's Who in Colored America*, vol. I, 1927, and 1928–1929; *Crisis* 10 (September 1915), 242; "Some Chicagoans of Note," *Crisis* 10 (Sept. 1915), 242; Dewey R. Jones, "Chicago Claims Supremacy: *Opportunity* 7 (March 1929), 92–94; and "The House That Overton Built," *Pittsburgh Courier*, July 27, 1929, 10. Overton is briefly mentioned in "The Negro as a Local Business Man," by J. Harmon Jr., *Journal of Negro History*, April 1929; and in the Marcus Christian Collection held at the University of New Orleans, which cites Overton in "The Negro as a Business Man," 23, 79, 105; and "Noted Men and Women of Illinois," *Crisis*, May 1942. Several letters of correspondence between Overton and Booker T. Washington and Emmett J. Scott appear in the Booker T. Washington Papers, container 15, reel 13, held at the Library of Congress. A lengthy obituary of Overton appears in the *Journal of Negro History* XXXII, 2 (July 1947), 394–96; additional obituaries appear in the *New York Times*, July 4, 1946; and *Chicago Tribune*, July 4, 1946. Some general articles about Overton and his varied business ventures and his rise to success appear in the *Pittsburgh Courier*, the *Chicago Bee*, the *New York Age*, the *Chicago Whip*, and other African-American publications.

The Victory Life Insurance Company and the Victory Mutual Life Insurance Company are covered in Myrtle Pollard, "Harlem As Is: The Negro Business and Economic Community," Master's thesis, City College, 1937, vol. II, app. B2. "History of the Rise and Fall of Victory Life and the Birth of Victory Mutual Life Insurance Co." is held at the Schomburg Center for Research in Black Culture at the New York Public Library. The *New York News*, October 14, 1935, included an editorial entitled "The Victory Mutual Life Insurance Company"; the *Chicago Bee*, May 21, 1927, cites the licensing of Victory Life in Virginia; M.S. Stuart's *Economic Detour* (1940) follows the company's growth and its subsequent demise; Claude McKay's *Harlem: Negro Metropolis* (1940) describes the reorganization of the Victory Life Insurance Company into a mutual company; the IWP Business Survey provides a comparison of the 1938 financial standing of black-owned insurance companies in Chicago, including Victory Life, Supreme Liberty, Protective Mutual, and Unity Mutual. The *Birmingham World*, March 3, 1962, describes the battle for control of Victory Mutual Life. Information about Dr. P.M.H. Savory and Dr. C. B. Powell, who engineered the reorganization of the company, can be found in M.S. Stuart, *Economic Detour*; *Crisis*, 45, 4 (1938); and Claude McKay, *Harlem: Negro Metropolis* (1940). The Moorland-Spingarn Research Center at Howard University has a very extensive run of *The Victor*, which was Victory Mutual Life Insurance Company's monthly publication. The OGBVD Syndicate is treated in the *Chicago Bee*, December 17, 1927. A report on the Douglass National Bank of Chicago appeared in *Opportunity*, September 1928.

The *Half-Century* and *Chicago Bee* are analyzed in Albert Lee Kreiling, "The Making of Racial Identities in the Black Press, 1878–1929," Ph.D. diss., University of Illinois, Urbana, 1973; and in Ralph Nelson Davis, "Negro Newspapers in Chicago," Master's thesis, University of Chicago 1939. See also, Illinois Writers Project, "Newspapers," p. 20, and "Bronzeville Finds Its Voice," p. 7, in *Negro in Illinois*. (n.d.). held at the Carter G. Woodson branch of the Chicago Public Library.

A valuable resource at Hampton University is the 1901 Proceedings of the National Negro Business League, in which appears Overton's address entitled "Negro as Manufacturer and Jobber," and the *Report of the Thirteenth Annual Convention of the National Negro Business League*, August 21–23, 1912, includes a report by Overton entitled "The Largest Negro Manufacturing Enterprise in the United States—"The Overton-Hygienic Mfg Co., Chicago, Ill." This presentation details the early years of the manufacturing concern, offers encouragement to aspiring business-minded people, and addresses the issues of prejudice and the importance of race pride. Chicago Historical Society, "Overton Hygienic/Douglass National Bank Building," in *Black Metropolis: Historic District* (March 7, 1984), 15–18,31 offers a chronological approach to Overton's rise to prominence and focuses on the architecture and structure of the building itself. Page 31 focuses on the Chicago Bee Building.

Articles about Overton's winning the Spingarn Medal and his business appear in such publications as the *Pittsburgh Courier*, June 18, 1927; the *Chicago Whip*, June 18, 1927; and the *Chicago Bee*, June 11, 1927. Additional articles citing the winning of the medal include the *World*, June 12, 1927; *New York Age*, July 2, 1927; *New York News*, June 18, 1927. *Opportunity* 6 (February 1928), 47 cites Overton as being awarded the Harmon Award for Distinguished Achievements among Negroes. Overton wrote *Successful Salesmanship* (1915) and an undated, untitled newspaper article that outlines the role of banks and the role that protective legislation play in protecting banks and their depositors.

P

Pace, Harry Herbert (January 6, 1884–1943). Entrepreneur, newspaper and sheet music publisher, banker, insurance executive, record company founder, author, and race leader: *Moon Illustrated Weekly*, Solvent Bank and Trust Company, Standard Life Insurance; Northeastern Life Insurance, Supreme Liberty Life Insurance, Pace and Handy Music, Black Swan Phonograph, Grand Exalted Ruler of the Elks, Grand Treasurer of the Odd Fellows, and Secretary of the Georgia State Republican Committee. Harry Pace was an extraordinary man. Handsome, dashing, and well educated, he was the founder or cofounder of a impressive number of important African-American companies, at times introducing blacks into industries where before they had no standing. He was tightly networked with most of the prominent African-Americans of the time, to the extent that he operated at the very apex of the status and power pyramids in the black communities of Memphis, Atlanta, New York City, and Chicago at various points in his life. He also found time to write song lyrics, novels, and expository articles and to act as a national or local leader of black social, cultural, and political organizations. Harry Pace was bigger than life: the sort of individual who, if presented in fiction, would never be believed. Yet he has been virtually forgotten today. This short biography is an act of historical reconstruction and rehabilitation much needed for a giant of a man who has slipped through the cracks of historical memory.

Harry Pace was born in Covington, Georgia, the son of Charles Pace, a blacksmith, and his wife, Nancy Francis. While Harry was still an infant, his father died, but he nonetheless was able to secure the advantages of a good education. A precocious child, Harry Pace finished elementary school in Covington by the time he was twelve, and seven years later he graduated as valedictorian of his class at Atlanta University. Pace's educational achievements, despite the loss of a parent, as well his later rapid climb in the business world may have been aided by family connections. Although there is no concrete evidence, there is a strong possibility that he was related to Solomon Pace, a prosperous barber in Atlanta who was also an early director of Atlanta Mutual

Life Insurance. If so, it would help explain Harry Pace's ability to attend college and to rise in the business world.

Pace as a youth learned the trade of printer's devil, determined to pay his way through Atlanta University in this way, working in the college's print shop. He soon found, however, that they were paying white union workers more for doing the same work as blacks, and he refused to work under such conditions. As a result, he was forced to work as a common laborer on campus, performing the most menial tasks, to pay his tuition and expenses. After graduation, Pace put his print shop training to use by taking a job in a new firm established by a group of prominent blacks in the city. The owners were Alonzo Franklin Herndon,* a wealthy barber and later the founder of Atlanta Mutual Life; Bishop Holsey of the AME church; Benjamin J. Davis, the head of the Odd Fellows Grand Lodge of Georgia; and William Driskell, the grand treasurer of the same organization. Pace served as foreman and shop manager, but the venture was not a success and soon closed. It was nonetheless beneficial for Pace inasmuch as it gave him some valuable experience in the printing trade and connected him with several prominent members of Atlanta's emerging African-American middle class.

Pace's next position was as an instructor at the Haines Institute in Augusta, Georgia, where he planned to save enough money to enter law school at Columbia University in New York, since becoming a lawyer had been his childhood ambition. Pace was to remain at the Haines Institute for only one year when W.E.B. Du Bois, who had been one of his teachers at Atlanta University, persuaded Pace to join him and another former student, Edward Simon, in launching the *Moon Illustrated Weekly*, a weekly magazine for blacks published in Memphis, Tennessee. Du Bois served as editor of the journal, while Pace was manager and Simon printer. Although the venture was relatively short lived, it had significance for a number of reasons. First, it was a precursor to Du Bois's *The Crisis*, one of the most important African-American journals. Second, it was one of the earliest efforts at a weekly magazine for blacks. Finally, it provided Pace with a favorable introduction to the rising black business community of Memphis.

The genesis of the *Moon* came in March 1904, when Du Bois formed a partnership with Simon in his print shop at 358 Beale Street. Simon, who graduated from Atlanta University, was a printing instructor at LeMoyne Institute in Memphis. Du Bois invested his entire savings, $1,600, in the venture. Since he made only $1,200 a year teaching at Atlanta University, it was a great gamble and sacrifice on Du Bois's part. In 1905 he wrote of his decision to start the magazine:

[Memphis] is a city of 49,910 Negroes with one rival Negro shop and numberless white shops. Mr. Simon has managed the plant entirely, receiving a salary of $60 a month. We are at present housed in a rented building, which we have leased for 5 years @ $40 a month. We use the first floor and cellar and sub-rent the second for $22 a month.

During their first year, Du Bois and Simon earned $1,343 for printing jobs, but spent $2,734 for the plant and equipment.

Du Bois's goal, however, was not to run a print shop, but to publish a national magazine for African-Americans. From 1888 to 1904, he had written articles for a number of national publications, and he often expressed his desire to found a black-owned and black-managed journal. To this end, he had several times approached a number of northern white philanthropists, without success, to fund the venture. Failing that, Du Bois decided to start publishing a magazine, intending to impress potential donors with the quality of the product he was able to produce. Thus, late in 1905, he persuaded Harry Pace to join the partnership with him and Simon, with the intention of putting out a national magazine.

The three men pooled their resources of $3,000, and the *Moon* commenced publication in December 1905. Du Bois, although editor in chief of the publication, continued to live and teach in Atlanta; Pace managed the day-to-day affairs of the journal in Memphis, and Simon did the printing. As Miriam DeCosta-Willis has said, "The *Moon* was DuBois' brainchild, but in many respects it was Pace's baby." George W. Lee,* a young Memphis business and political leader at the time, described the effort Pace put into the venture:

With no money to pay the salaries of the editorial staff most of the work of getting out the paper fell upon the shoulders of Harry Pace, who not only solicited and edited material, but set its type, made up the paper, put it on the press and ran it off. . . . At four o'clock Saturday morning the milkman would see him dragging a United States mail sack down the streets to the post office.

Despite the effort Pace put into the publication, Du Bois was disappointed with the quality of the product. In January 1906, just a month after the *Moon* got started, Du Bois wrote to Jacob Schiff, a wealthy banker, appealing for a $10,000 subsidy, saying, "The samples [of the *Moon*] are far below my ideal— the best possible on the present small capital." Later he wrote to Isaac Seligman, another wealthy capitalist, in the same vein, saying that the *Moon* was "only a faint approximation of my ideal; the mechanical make-up is poor and the general appearance a little slovenly." Whether this was just a tactic to persuade them to donate funds, or whether Du Bois was truly disappointed, is impossible to determine. In any event, Du Bois soon lost interest in the project and withdrew his support, and the magazine survived for just eight issues. It was Pace who battled most valiantly to save it. M. S. Stuart has commented that Pace "spent everything he had to meet the expenses of getting out the magazine. Soon he found himself penniless, his last suit of clothes threadbare, and hunger, almost his daily lot."

But Pace's courageous struggles to save the publication did not go unnoticed in Memphis. First of all, he had been responsible for soliciting advertising and, in that way, had met most of the top black business leaders of the city, as well as some prominent whites. Among the whites from whom Pace was able to secure advertising revenue were the Guardian Real Estate Company, which offered "Lots for Good Colored People Only," the Union Painless Dentist, which featured "Special Reductions for Colored People Only," and Duke Cayce Bowers, an influential white, whose small chain of grocery stores advertised for black clientele.

Far more important to Pace's future, however, were the African-American business leaders he met and impressed with his energy and determination. Among those were Thomas H. Hayes, Sr., owner of the largest and most prosperous black funeral parlor in the city, a close associate of Booker T. Washington,* and one of the leaders of the African-American financial community; the Gillis brothers, who ran grocery stores; Dr. A. N. Kittrell; Reverend J. Jay Scott; and H. Wayman Wilkinson who also advertised in the *Moon*. Pace also secured advertisements from several prominent black Atlantans, including Alonzo Herndon, who advertised his Atlanta Mutual Insurance Association, Dr. F. B. Badger, the city's first black dentist, and People's Shoe Store, which claimed to be "the only first class shoe store in the city owned by colored people." In addition, Pace made some contacts among younger African-Americans which were to benefit him greatly in later years. The *Moon*, which had a circulation of just 250 to 500 copies per month, used agents to sell it in various parts of the country. Two of those were Truman K. Gibson,* Pace's future partner in Supreme Liberty Life, and Bishop Richard R. Wright, Jr.,* later the head of Citizens and Southern Bank in Philadelphia.

In any event, one bleak Saturday night in November 1906, Pace was sitting in the back of his dirty little printing office. Just twenty-two years old, he considered himself an utter failure. He had left a good teaching job and given up his dream of going to law school to join Du Bois in putting out the *Moon*—and now dark failure stared him squarely in the face. According to his own account, he was considering suicide as the only way out, when two persons entered his shop. One was a postal telegraph messenger, with a telegram on which 80 cents was due. The other was Ruben Ware, cashier of Solvent Savings Bank, Memphis' first and only black-owned bank. When the messenger presented the telegram, Pace responded, "Take it back, I haven't a dime in the world; and the only news that telegram could bring me would be bad news, and I don't want any more of that." Ware, however, upon overhearing the conversation, said, "Wait a minute, leave it. I'll lend him 80 cents."

Ware paid the fee and handed the telegram to Pace. In it Pace was offered a position as a professor of Latin and Greek by President B. F. Allen at Lincoln University in Jefferson City, Missouri. Pace's spirits, however, were hardly buoyed by the news. "Why, how can I take it," he said to Ware. "I have no clothes, no means of transportation and no way to get any money." Ware appealed to Thomas H. Hayes to help the young man. Hayes gave a Memphis merchant orders to let Pace have all he needed in men's apparel, and Ware gave Pace some money to tide him over. Pace left for Lincoln University to assume the professorial position and remained there for a year. In 1907 trouble at Solvent Savings Bank caused the officers to reorganize the firm. Milton L. Clay, a successful grain merchant and barber, and owner of the Panama Club on Beale Street, who had been impressed with Pace's work with the *Moon*, asked the young man to join the bank. Pace also received a similar letter from Robert R. Church,* the bank's president, asking him to join.

Pace, however, was reluctant to return to Memphis. He was happy and secure in his teaching job, and he had already given up one such job to take on a business venture with Du Bois that had almost destroyed him. Further, he knew nothing about banking and told the directors of the bank that. "Why," he asked, "do you want me to take this job when you know that I know nothing about it?" Clay and the other directors, however, implored him to come. Pace finally agreed, even though his salary would be just $83 a month, compared to the $110 he was earning at Lincoln. Pace became cashier of the bank, succeeding Ware in that position. The assets of the bank when he came were about $50,000, and it had a deficit of $7,000. Pace, although untrained in banking, proved himself an excellent businessman. Within four years he had increased the bank's assets to $600,000, had made it an exceedingly profitable venture, and saw his own salary increase to $200 a month.

In 1912, however, Pace decided to make another major change in his career path. In that year, Robert Church, Sr., the bank's president died, and his son, Robert, Jr., also resigned. With those changes in the bank's upper management, Pace felt it was wise to look elsewhere. In the meantime, Pace had met Heman Edward Perry,* the charismatic entrepreneur and owner of Standard Life Insurance Company of Atlanta, who had persuaded Pace to sell fifty shares of stock in his company at $200 a share. Perry then offered Pace the position of secretary of Standard Life, which he accepted, and he moved to Atlanta. Again, however, Pace had to accept a decrease in salary—from $2,400 to $2,000 a year—as he moved into this new field.

Pace decided to go to Atlanta, in spite of a counteroffer from W.E.B. Du Bois, who wrote to Pace on April 3, 1912:

I should propose that on September 1st, you join our staff [at *The Crisis*] as either "Business Manager," or "Traveling Representative." That your salary be $100 a month and traveling expenses. That your job for the first one or two years be to raise the circulation of the *Crisis* from 20,000 to 100,000 by traveling over the country.

Du Bois described the financial growth of his magazine, which was the official organ of the NAACP, and he predicted that the journal would be "an enterprise of gigantic proportions." Pace, however, perhaps fearing a repeat of his Memphis experience, turned down Du Bois's offer and decided to join Standard Life in Atlanta.

One of Harry Pace's first jobs as secretary of Standard Life, however, must have filled him with dread and foreboding. Under the laws of Georgia, Standard had to have fully $100,000 on deposit to function as an insurance firm. By the end of 1910, Perry had raised just $60,000 of the $100,000 needed. By 1912 Perry had $70,000 of that, so he instructed Pace to return all money to subscribers as required by law, along with 4 percent interest. In the letter, however, Pace asked if the interest would be voluntarily returned, since Perry had taken no salary, nor even any expenses during the two-year ordeal, and could sorely use the money. Only about $60 was returned to them.

Undaunted, Perry just started all over again with Pace as his right-hand man. This time, however, Perry decided to apply for the state charter after he had raised the $100,000. Again, he spent two years traveling throughout the South soliciting funds, and once more he fell short. But this time Perry had developed stronger relations with important individuals in Atlanta. One of those influential Atlantans who provided Perry with monetary support in his second attempt was Alonzo Herndon. He persuaded the board at Atlanta Life to agree to invest $5,000 in Standard Life stock. With Herndon's endorsement, and that of several of his associates, along with the money from Atlanta Life and the stock Perry had been able to sell, he was able to get a $50,000 loan from a white bank in Atlanta and deposit the full $100,000 with the Georgia insurance officials. Perry received a charter on March 22, 1913, and began operating the company that June. Pace was finally part of a going concern again.

Standard Life became the first black insurance company organized solely for the purpose of selling ordinary life insurance, and it was just the third firm, after Mississippi Life and North Carolina Mutual, to achieve legal reserve status. With the company in operation, Perry and Pace assembled an impressive cast of supporters and aides. On the board of directors were Emmett J. Scott, Booker T. Washington's secretary; F. C. Brown, of the Brown and Stevens Bank in Philadelphia; Robert R. Church, Jr., and Thomas H. Hayes of Memphis; Truman K. Gibson, later of Supreme Life; Henry A. Boyd,* of the National Baptist Publishing House in Nashville; Sol. C. Johnson, publisher of the *Savannah Tribune*; Walter S. Scott, president of Savannah Banking and Savings; John Hope, president of Morehouse College in Atlanta; and a number of others.

As a result of Perry's enormous drive and charismatic personality, coupled with Pace's great organizational ability and financial acumen, Standard Life grew rapidly over its first ten years. By 1923 it had increased its capital stock to $250,000, held assets of $2.25 million, had $6 million of ordinary life insurance in force, and had a cash income of $1 million that year, enabling it to pay a 12 percent dividend on its stock. By this time, however, Harry Pace had been gone from the scene for a number of years. Pace installed business systems at Standard, but the exacting regulations of these systems did not exactly suit the entrepreneurial personality of Perry. Perry was very impatient of details and regulations of accounting, and the two men clashed often over Perry's cavalier methods. Nonetheless, Pace managed to work with Perry until the summer of 1917, when petty friction finally exploded into a confrontation. The story of that parting smacks of melodrama.

In June 1917, Pace had married Ethlynde Bibb, and the two went to Jacksonville, Florida, for their honeymoon. While there, Pace learned that his enemies in Standard Life were plotting with Perry to oust him. Pace hurried back to

Atlanta, where he found Perry strangely cool. Standard was then subjected to a rigid state examination, and the examiners found the firm lacked some $60,000 in required reserves under the law. Pace, to handle this crisis, devised an ingenious scheme. "Why not," he said, "offer the policyholders a nonparticipating type of policy requiring less reserves." Under the direction of Pace, the policyholders, with few exceptions, were persuaded to accept the new policies, and the firm was saved. This intervention on Pace's part, however, merely served to widen the breech between him and Perry. Finally, by 1920, Pace knew that his usefulness as secretary was over, and he tendered his resignation.

The *Atlanta Independent* took Pace's side:

> Mr. Pace leaves us and quits the Standard Life after giving this institution six of the best years of his eventful life. We will all miss him but the Standard Life will miss him more; for around his constructive ability, more than around any other one man has the Standard Life been built. . . . The board of directors has made a blunder that will not only bear the stock of the corporation in the market, but we fear, prophesy the downfall of Standard Life. Their mistake smacks of the betrayal of a sacred trust. . . . Whither is the Standard drifting?

Upon his resignation, Pace headed for New York City, for yet another adventure in the world of African-American business and culture.

In New York, Harry Pace joined with William C. Handy, the great composer and compiler of blues, in establishing a sheet music publishing company. The two men had long been associated with one another. Handy, a native of Florence, Alabama, was the son of an AME minister who preferred the vernacular music of country blacks to religious compositions. He began traveling about the countryside around the turn of the century, collecting the tunes of guitar-picking country blues singers, the "primitive" beauty of whose music haunted Handy. In the early twentieth century, Handy moved to Memphis, where he formed a band that became regarded as the city's best. There they played for Beale Street saloons, picnics, funerals, and political campaigns. In 1908 Handy composed a song for Mayor Ed Crump's political campaign called "Mr. Crump." Later retitled the "Memphis Blues," the song in 1912 became the country's first published blues composition and a big hit for Handy.

In the meantime, Handy and Pace had begun working together in Memphis. Handy described their meeting in his autobiography:

> [In 1907] I first became a tenant of the Solvent Savings Bank. The cashier of the bank was Harry H. Pace, a handsome man of striking personality and definite musical leanings. Pace had written some first rate song lyrics and was in demand as a vocal soloist at church programs and Sunday night concerts. In 1907 we wrote "In the Cotton Fields of Dixie" which was published by a Cincinnati firm. It was natural, if not inevitable, that he and I should gravitate together. We spoke the same language. We collaborated on songs. Finally we became partners in the "Pace & Handy Music Company—Publishers."

The origins of Pace and Handy Music actually went back to 1917, when both Handy and Pace were at turning points in their careers. Pace was under fire from Perry and the board of directors, and Standard Life was close to losing its charter. Pace sensed that his days there were numbered. Handy's troubles were more prosaic. Handy had taken his band to play an engagement in Atlanta, and from there they were to go to play a booking at the University of North Carolina in Chapel Hill. The band made so much money from the Atlanta engagement, however, that the members just wanted to return to Memphis, where they could go back and "strut their stuff on Beale Street." Handy came to Pace, who advised him to let the band members return to Memphis and told Handy to go to New York City to market the songs of Handy and Pace. So Handy moved there that year and established the Pace and Handy Music Company in the Gaiety Theater Building. Handy had very little money, but he brought with him to New York a song, "A Good Man Is Hard to Find," which he had purchased for $125. The song created an overnight sensation on Broadway, and its popularity helped make a success of Pace and Handy Music. This success encouraged Pace to quit his position with Standard Life and join Handy in New York.

Pace and Handy conducted a dynamic and successful music business in New York for a number of years. Pace was president of the firm, Charles Handy (William's brother) was vice president, and W. C. Handy was secretary treasurer. Pace bought a fine home on what was called "Striver's Row" in Harlem, a group of townhomes designed by Stanford White, and he settled in to manage the firm. As Handy later recalled:

With Pace installed in the president's office, a new day dawned for the Pace & Handy Company. A valuable and capable man, Pace installed a new system, enlarged our financial contacts, opened up lines of credit with five leading colored banks in the South and otherwise demonstrated his worth.

The company began to grow rapidly and, outgrowing its quarters, moved to 232 West 46th Street, where it took over the entire building.

When Pace came to New York, his greatest success was in selling "St. Louis Blues," written earlier by Handy, to the nation, making it into a huge hit. He hired a female singer to record the song for Victor Records; it was an almost instantaneous hit, and soon thereafter nearly every other record company wanted to record it. It rapidly became one of the most popular songs in the history of songwriting. Despite this success, however, Pace was frustrated. White-owned record companies bought their songs, but then recorded them using white artists. Or, if they did employ blacks, they refused to let them sing and play in their own, "authentic" style, insisting on molding them into what they considered "acceptable" styles. Pace determined to start his own record firm, the first to be owned by blacks in the United States. Although most scholars have assumed that Handy was involved in this firm, that was not the case. As Handy himself stated,

To add to my woes, my partner withdrew from the business. He had disagreed with some of my business methods, but no harsh words were involved. He simply chose this time to sever connections with our firm in order that he might organize Pace Phonograph Company, issuing Black Swan Records, and making a serious bid for the Negro market in this field. With Pace went a large number of our employees, persons especially trained for the requirements of our business and therefore hard to replace. . . . Still more confusion and anguish grew out of the fact that people did not generally know that I had no stake in the Black Swan record company.

Pace in later years described the founding of Black Swan Records to Roi Ottley:

[P]honograph companies were not recording the voices of Negro singers and musicians . . . and I therefore determined to form my own company and make such recordings as I believed would sell. . . . I organized Pace Phonograph Corporation Incorporated under the laws of New York sometime in March, 1921 with a capital stock of $30,000. Associated with me as directors were Dr. W.E.B. Du Bois, Mr. John E. Nail,[*] Dr. Matthew V. Boutte, and Mrs. Viola Bibb. I opened offices at 257 West 138th Street, New York.

In his advertising promotion in African-American newspapers, Pace stressed the race issue, saying, "The Only Genuine Colored Record—Others Are Only Passing for Colored."

Pace did not have an easy time getting the firm established. White record companies threw up innumerable obstacles to him. When he attempted to purchase a record-pressing plant, a large white company bought it just to keep him out. Ultimately, however, he was able to set up recording studios and a pressing laboratory, and obtain other supplies necessary to produce records. The first record put out by Black Swan was "Dear Little Boy of Mine," by Carole Clark, followed closely by "Thank God for a Garden," by Revella Hughes, and "Blind Man Blues," by Katie Crippen. At the end of the first month, Black Swan had cash receipts of just $674.64.

The big breakthrough for Black Swan came with the discovery of a fantastic young singer, the legendary Ethel Waters. Pace recalled their first meeting:

I went to a cabaret [in Atlantic City] . . . and heard this girl and invited her over to my table to talk about coming to New York to make a recording. She very brusquely refused but at the same time I saw that she was interested and I told her that I would send her a ticket and she came to New York and made two records. "Down Home Blues" and "Oh Daddy." . . . the records were enormously successful. I sold 500,000 of these records within six months.

Waters remembered her first meeting at the Black Swan offices:

The Black Swan office was, I think, in the home of one of the owners. The day I went there I found Fletcher Henderson sitting behind a desk and looking very prissy and important. . . . Mr. Pace paid me the one hundred dollars and that first Black Swan record I made had "Down Home Blues" on one side, "Oh Daddy" on the other. It proved a great success and a best seller among both white and colored, and it got Black Swan out of the red.

It was not clear, though, just what kind of music Waters would sing, and she recalled, "There was much discussion of whether I should sing popular or 'cultural' numbers." Although Pace wanted the firm to promote black artists and African-American music, he did not want it to appear "too colored." On that basis, Pace rejected Bessie Smith when she auditioned, because of her "unmistakable nitty-grittyness."

Pace not only hired great singers, he also brought in talented people to co-ordinate the technical and artistic side of recording. William Grant Still, the superbly talented composer, was named musical director, and Fletcher Henderson, the great bandleader and arranger, was recording manager. After the success of her records, Pace decided to send Waters out on tour with Fletcher Henderson's band, which was called the Black Swan Jazz Masters for the occasion. It was during this tour that Henderson's band began playing jazz, but jazz that was not in the prevailing New Orleans style. This set the standard for a host of later big band jazz ensembles.

With the success of this tour, Pace hired more staff for the office, including Fredi Washington and her sister Isabelle. Isabelle Washington later became the wife of Reverend Adam Clayton Powell, Sr. They also made other changes, as Pace recalled,

Business became so great that we bought a plant in Long Island City that we were using as a recording laboratory and a pressing laboratory, and shortly afterward transferred all shipping over to the plant. We were selling 7,000 records a day . . . [but] could make only 6,000 records daily, so that we were running behind. We ordered three additional presses in 1923.

The future for Black Swan Records seemed very bright in 1922 and 1923. Pace wrote to many of his friends and business associates, encouraging them to invest in the concern. One of those was Robert L. Vann,* publisher of the *Pittsburgh Courier* and a close friend. Vann wrote back on July 7, 1922: "I want some stock—in fact, I mean to have some." Vann proposed to pay for the stock partially by running free advertising for the record company in the *Courier*. Their enthusiasm, however, proved overly optimistic. The advent of radio as a popular, and much cheaper, way of transmitting music destroyed the prospects of Black Swan Records and threatened to send even white record companies into bankruptcy.

As a result, Pace decided to sell his company to Paramount Records. A company press release at the time stated: "It is to be hoped that the retirement of the Black Swan from the operating field will not mean the dropping of the large number of singers previously employed." Although many of Pace's artists—Ethel Waters, Carol Clark, Revella Hughes, Fletcher Henderson, and others—continued to be recorded, much of the authenticity of earlier black music was lost. Most important, blacks were largely shut out of the management side of the record business. Although another black company, Black Patti operated by J. Mayor Williams, functioned for a brief period in 1927, it was not until Berry Gordy, Jr., *established his Motown Records that a black-owned company would achieve major success.

During this same period, Pace found time to become involved in the internecine politics of the African-American community. The early 1920s, of course, was the period of Marcus Garvey's greatest influence in New York and the nation as a whole. Garvey incited a great deal of controversy among prominent black leaders. Pace became one of the most important members of the anti-Garvey movement. On January 15, 1923, Pace, along with Robert S. Abbott,* publisher of the *Chicago Defender*, John E. Nail, the wealthy black Harlem realtor, and five other "respected leaders," wrote a letter to Attorney General Harry M. Daugherty, protesting the delay of nearly a year in the trial of Garvey. This self-styled "Committee of Eight" condemned Garveyism as a philosophy that was "seeking to arouse ill-feeling between the races" and attacked Garvey himself as "an unscrupulous demagogue, who has ceaselessly and assiduously sought to spread among Negroes distrust and hatred of all white people." Garvey assaulted the group venomously: "Like the good old darkey, they believe they have some news to tell and they are telling it for all it is worth—the liars and prevaricators that they are." Garvey also referred to them as "Uncle Tom Negroes," "wicked malingers," and other ad hominem epithets, arguing that they were performing "the greatest bit of treachery and wickedness that any group of Negroes could be capable of" and claimed they were "nearly all Octoroons and Quadroons" or were "married to Octoroons."

In 1925 Pace participated with a number of other wealthy blacks in the organization of Northeastern Life Insurance Company in Newark, New Jersey. Although the firm struggled in its first several years, Pace operated it fairly successfully until 1929, when he began talking with his old Atlanta University classmate and friend, Truman K. Gibson, about the possibility of merging Northeastern with Supreme Life and Casualty of Columbus, Ohio. According to William J. Trent, it was Pace who conceived the idea of uniting together the major African-American insurance companies of the Northeast. Supreme Life had large holdings of industrial insurance, with salesmen trained to sell it, while Pace's Northeastern had an excellent investment portfolio and first-rate management. Neither firm, however, had been profitable in 1928, so they began seeking another company that had larger cash reserves. This turned out to be Liberty Life Insurance of Chicago, one of the largest and most successful black companies in America.

As the merger was coming to fruition, Pace in 1929 appealed to his old friend and fellow Boule brother, Robert L. Vann, for editorial support:

I have been counting on your support in this matter and the support of all of the Pittsburgh group because as I realize that both as the man of vision and as a Boule brother you would throw your weight and strength into a proposition which affects as it happens three Boule men who happen to head each of these three organizations which are now being consolidated into one.

The new firm, called Supreme Liberty Life Insurance, had combined capital of $400,000, insurance in force of $25 million, total assets of over $1.4 million, and 1,090 employees. Harry Pace was named president and chief executive officer of the new company.

The history of Supreme Liberty Life is covered most fully in the combined biographies of Frank L. Gillespie,* Truman K. Gibson, and Earl B. Dickerson,* but Pace's achievements with the firm will be summarized here. The early years of Supreme Liberty Life were ones of survival. Just after the merger in 1929, the devastating Great Depression struck. The young firm had not even fully coordinated its procedures at that point, but the great problem was simply to survive in an economic crisis of unprecedented proportions. The Depression hit urban blacks in the North harder than any other group, and African-American unemployment reached astounding levels. Even as late as 1940, fully 36 percent of the black males in Chicago were still unemployed or had only relief work. As they lost their jobs, and as income levels fell, blacks could not afford to keep up their insurance premiums. The effect on black insurance companies nationwide was traumatic, and two of the larger black-owned firms went out of business during the decade.

The situation for Supreme Liberty Life was more desperate than for many other insurance concerns for two reasons. First, they relied more heavily on the ordinary life market, which was more expensive, and blacks were more likely to allow these policies to lapse. Second, the company had invested very heavily in the real estate market, and with the rapid devaluation of that commodity, especially in black areas, the value of these assets held by the firm shrank accordingly. Then, too, as hard-pressed blacks, unemployed and underemployed, could not meet their mortgage payments, Supreme Liberty Life was put into a difficult situation. Foreclosures would only saddle the firm with property that either could not be sold, or could only be liquidated at a fraction of its former value.

To deal with these crushing problems, Pace, and his coleader Truman Gibson, reduced operating expenses and cut the par value of the stock from $10 to $2.50 a share. They also focused the firm more on the industrial insurance market, which, with its low weekly premiums, was the only area of even moderate growth among the black population. The key element was to maintain the policyholders' confidence. To do so, the executives made sure they paid off all death claims, and they were even ready and willing to continue loaning money at up to 50 percent of the cash surrender value of the policy. It was a difficult time, as Supreme Liberty Life's assets fell from $1,830,000 in 1930 to $1,575,000 in 1934 and investment income virtually disappeared.

Then Pace was faced with an even more critical situation. In 1933 the Illinois Department of Insurance began an examination of all insurance firms. In the course of their examination, they drastically reduced the book value of most of the real estate items in Supreme Liberty's investment portfolio. As a result, its real estate holdings were revalued from $743,000 to just over $380,000. Since the company had only a small surplus of just over $76,000, and was not making profits on current operations, bankruptcy seemed inevitable. At that point, Earl Dickerson, the corporate counsel, came up with a brilliant and unorthodox scheme. He persuaded the company's policyholders to sign a lien by which they acknowledged an indebtedness to the firm of either 50 percent or the entire amount of their policies' reserves. It was a maneuver of somewhat questionable legality, which was, in fact, later make illegal by statute, but after a court battle the Illinois Supreme Court allowed the use of the liens as admitted assets. Dickerson, who was also assistant attorney general of Illinois at this time, was a key factor in the firm's legal victory. However dubious they were as assets, the action saved Supreme Liberty Life, allowing it to add some $300,000 in policyholders' liens to the asset list.

That was the turning point. Supreme Liberty Life became increasingly profitable in the late 1930s. The liens were retired in 1937, surplus funds grew from $100,000 in 1935 to $280,000 in 1941, and in 1941 a dividend of 30 cents a share was declared. This recovery, as suggested above, was based largely on the sales of industrial life insurance. The key figure in this drive was James G. Ish, the agency director, who developed a concept he called "mass production." Under this system, largely untrained agents were sent out to write as many policies as they could without requiring any financial settlement at the time of signing. After the policy had been processed and issued, the agent would try to get the client to sign it, stressing the very small weekly premiums to be paid. This technique allowed a rapid expansion of Supreme Liberty's industrial insurance holdings, as $460,000 of these policies were sold from 1935 to 1942. This brought the company's total industrial insurance in force by the latter year to over $53 million.

This expansion, however, was very expensive. Supreme Liberty's lapse rate was the highest among black insurance firms, with thirteen policies issued for every one remaining in force. Then, too, the expense of collecting the premiums on those policies in force was also high, and there was a very high turnover among the inexperienced and untrained agents. Nor did it do much for the reputation of Supreme Liberty Life. As Robert Puth (1969) has commented; "Agents learned almost nothing about the sales approaches necessary to sell life insurance as a long-term contract, or in selling large policies—both sources of reduced operating expenses. Supreme Liberty Life agents were not well paid, and the company lost many of its better sales personnel to other firms."

After American entrance into World War II, black employment and wages began rising rapidly. Black mortality rates also began falling sharply, becoming closer to the national average. On one hand, this increased the opportunity for Supreme Liberty to sell more profitable ordinary life insurance; on the other hand, it made the black market more attractive to large white firms. These new challenges, however, had to be met by Truman Gibson, as Harry Pace passed away in 1943.

Pace, as has been noted above, was a man of many parts and a multitude of interests. He had wanted to be a lawyer since the time he was a young boy, but he had given up his chance at law school when he got involved in the *Moon* with Du Bois. In 1930 he at last decided to pursue a law degree, despite the heavy responsibilities he carried as head of Supreme Liberty Life. He began attending law school and studying three hours a day for a period of three years until he got his degree. He graduated fourth in a class of forty, most of whom were white. He then became a member of the law firm of Bibb, Tyree, and Pace until the end of his life.

Pace was also a prominent member of the National Negro Insurance Association, serving as its president from 1928 to 1929, statistician from 1929 to 1930, and general counsel from 1934 to 1938. The National Negro Insurance Association was an outgrowth of the National Negro Business League in 1921. Its purposes were to advance "the best interest of insurance among Negroes in America," to "publish a journal," to recommend "courses of study in insurance in various Negro colleges and universities," and to "drive from the business all unworthy agents and employees." It was, in a word, a trade association designed to increase the degree of cooperation among black insurance firms, and it was relatively successful in its aims over the years.

Partially because of this position, Pace became an influential writer on insurance issues among blacks. In 1926 he wrote a seminal article in *The Crisis* in which he outlined the emergence of African-American insurance firms. This was followed a year later by an article in *The Messenger* which analyzed the contributions that black insurance companies had made toward racial development. In 1928 he wrote a very important and influential article for *The Southern Workman* in which he outlined the poor treatment of blacks by white insurance firms, thereby providing rationale for the growth and development of black insurance companies. Throughout the 1920s and 1930s, Harry Pace was probably the single most important spokesman for the African-American insurance industry.

Pace was also very involved in social organizations and issues. A dedicated member of the Elks, Pace had assumed a number of leadership roles in the organization. In 1907 he had written an article in the *Voice of the Negro* entitled "The Case of the Negro Elks," in which he detailed the rise of the Elks among blacks and investigated the nature of white opposition to black Elks. Pace founded the first Elk's Lodge in Memphis, and at the age of twenty-four he was grand secretary of the order, becoming grand exalted ruler three years later. He was ousted from this position in 1913, however, and spent several years trying to regain the post. Finally, in 1926, he asked George W. Lee* to speak in his behalf at the national convention. The *Pittsburgh Courier* reported on Lee's speech:

The audience was on tip-toe while the fighting lieutenant [Lee] painted in colorful hues the merits of his candidate. He was in a happy frame of mind and his words were silver lined, while his climaxes fell with burning conviction as he soared from description to narrative. When he had closed, he was beseiged by men on all sides and given a warm and hearty platform appreciation by the fifty and more prominent Race leaders from all parts of the country. It was a gem.

Lee was not able to transfer that enthusiasm to his candidate, however, and Pace was again defeated.

In 1933 Pace was chosen by Secretary of Commerce Roper as a member of the advisory committee regarding the activities of blacks, and two years later he was appointed assistant counsel of the Illinois Commerce Commission. He was elected a member of the Diocesan Council of the Protestant Episcopal Church in the Chicago Diocese in 1935, the first black man to serve in such a position, and he served for many years on the national board of directors of the NAACP. He was a member of the local board of the Urban League, and president of the Citizens Civic and Economic Welfare Council of Chicago. In addition, he wrote a book of inspirational essays in 1934 called *Beginning Again*, and a serial novel which was published in the *Chicago Defender*.

According to John H. Johnson,* in *Succeeding Against the Odds*, Pace, in the last year or so of his life, decided to "pass over" into the white race. "Pace was so light that you'd never believe he was Black unless he told you. His whole family, in fact, was light-skinned, and there were rumors, never substantiated, that his children were passing for White. Pace himself had recently opened a law office in downtown Chicago, and he'd recently moved to a White suburb of River Forest." Black employees at Supreme Life were evidently incensed at this, and several planned to demonstrate at Pace's home to embarrass him in front of his white neighbors. According to Johnson, when Pace heard about the plan, he went through a personality change: "From that day until his death a year later, he was a changed man, more cautious, more withdrawn, more secretive." After his death, his heirs sold their Supreme Life stock and, according to Johnson, "disappeared from the Black limelight."

Whatever happened in his last year, throughout most of his life Harry Pace was what was called a "race man." He believed that African-Americans should own their own companies and develop their own economic power. Only in that way, he reasoned, could they achieve true equality in America. He viewed black insurance firms in just that way:

Some day—and the day is not so far away—Negroes will come to the realization of the economic power to be derived from the free use of life insurance facilities and they will build up their own companies into the giants that they can become. There is no longer any excuse for any Negro to take a policy in any company that does not want his business or is lukewarm about it. . . . And in taking insurance in his own companies he creates opportunities for employment that must be created by Negroes for Negroes. And he develops a financial reservoir that will eventually make him economically free.

Harry Pace dreamed big dreams—America has yet to fulfill them.

Sources

There are no family or business papers of Harry Pace, but portions of his correspondence can be found in several collections. A number of references to Pace, along with the words to one of his early songs, appear in the W. C. Handy Collection at the Memphis-Shelby Public Library. There are at least two letters from Pace to Booker T. Washington in the

Booker T. Washington Papers at the Library of Congress. The most interesting and useful, however, are a number of letters between Pace and Robert L. Vann concerning Black Swan Records in the Percival L. Prattis Collection at the Moorland-Spingarn Research Center at Howard University. Pace himself was a rather prolific author who wrote articles on insurance and other matters for a number of newspapers and magazines. Several of his early articles appeared in the *Voice of the Negro*: "The Question of Education," May 1906; and "The Case of the Negro Elks," June 1907. There were also numerous short items either by or about Pace in the *Atlanta Independent* from 1913 to 1920, the years Pace lived in that city. In later years, he wrote articles on the insurance industry, including "The Possibilities of Negro Insurance," *Opportunity*, September 1930; "Premium Income and Jobs," *Amsterdam News*, October 1, 1930; "The Attitude of Life Insurance Companies toward Negroes," *Southern Workman*, January 1928; *Chicago Defender*, May 4, 1935; "The Business of Insurance among Negroes," *The Crisis*, September 1926 and May 1928; and "The Business of Insurance," *The Messenger*, March 1927. In addition, he penned insurance-related articles that appeared in the *Chicago Defender*, May 4, 1935, and in the *Savings Bank Journal*, September 1927. He wrote a book of inspirational essays entitled *Beginning Again*, published in 1934, and he wrote a novel with W.E.B. Du Bois around the turn of the century entitled *Voice of the Negro*. Only two issues of the *Moon Illustrated Weekly* survive, and are held at the Memphis-Shelby County Public Library.

There is no book-length study of Pace, and relatively little scholarly analysis of any kind. The fullest source (although somewhat biased since he was an associate of Pace) is M. S. Stuart, *An Economic Detour: A History of Insurance in the Lives of American Negroes* (New York, 1940), 75–81. There are brief contemporary biographies in the *Amsterdam News*, December 25, 1929; George P. Hamilton, *The Bright Side of Memphis* (1908), 102; and *Who's Who in Colored America* (1915, 1928–1929, 1938–1940). Pace's association with W.E.B. Du Bois in the *Moon Illustrated Weekly* is covered most fully in Paul G. Partington, "The *Moon Illustrated Weekly*—The Precursor of *The Crisis*," *Journal of Negro History* XLIVIII (July 1963), 206–16; and Miriam DeCosta-Willis, "DuBois Memphis Connection," *West Tennessee History Society Papers* XLII (December 1988), 30–38. Pace's connection with this enterprise, as well as with the Solvent Bank, is covered in George W. Lee, *Beale Street: Where the Blues Began* (New York, 1934); and David M. Tucker, *Lieutenant Lee of Beale Street* (Nashville, 1971). There is information on Pace's role in Standard Life and Citizens Trust in Atlanta in a number of sources, including Eric D. Walrond, "The Largest Negro Commercial Enterprise in the World," *Forbes Magazine* 13 (February 1924), 503–5, which gives a wildly exaggerated account of the development of Standard Life. See also *Pittsburgh Courier*, July 15, 1961. Pace gave his own account of things there in "A New Business Venture," *Crisis* 8 (January 1914), 143; and in an address before the Annual Meeting of the National Negro Business League, 1913, in Philadelphia, in which he gave extensive information concerning the goals and ambitions of Heman Perry and Standard Life. Bobby J. Lamar, "Citizens Trust Company and Its Role in the Development of the Atlanta Black Community with Emphasis on the Loan Function," Master's thesis, Atlanta University, 1969, is a study of those aspects of the bank. For more information, see the biography of Perry in this volume, and see *Atlanta Independent*, January 31, 1920, for an impassioned, and probably biased, account of the controversy between Perry and Pace that forced Pace's departure.

Information on Pace's association with W. C. Handy in the music business can be obtained from Handy's autobiography, *Father of the Blues* (New York, 1941), and from

Ethel Waters's autobiography, *His Eye Is on the Sparrow* (New York, 1950), 141–42, 145–47. See also Roi Ottley and William J. Weatherby, eds., *The Negro in New York* (reprint, Dobbs Ferry, N.Y., 1967), 232–36, which reprints an important letter on Black Swan from Pace to Ottley; *New York Age*, December 31, 1949; and *Memphis Commercial Appeal*, September 9, 1973; along with the works by and about George W. Lee mentioned above. See Eileen Southern, *The Music of Black Americans: A History* (New York, 1971) for information on Fletcher Henderson, William Grant Still, and black music generally. William Barlow, *Looking Up at Down* (1989) is a good history of the blues. For information on Pace's conflict with Garvey, see Amy Jacques-Garvey, ed., *Philosophy and Opinions of Marcus Garvey* (New York, 1923); and E. David Cronon, *Black Moses: The Story of Marcus Garvey and the Universal Negro Improvement Association* (Madison, Wis., 1955).

There is abundant information on Pace's role in Northeastern Life and Supreme Liberty Life. See Robert C. Puth, "Supreme Life: The History of a Negro Life Insurance Company," Ph.D. diss., Northwestern University, 1967. Portions of Puth's research have been published as "Supreme Life: The History of a Negro Life Insurance Company," *Business History Review* XLIII, 1 (Spring 1969), 1–21; and "From Enforced Segregation to Integration: Market Factors in the Development of a Negro Life Insurance Company," in *Business Enterprise and Economic Change: Essays in Honor of Harold F. Williamson*, edited by Louis F. Cain and Paul J. Uselding (Kent, Ohio, 1973), 280–301. There is other useful information on the company in *Ebony*, August 1946, November 1956, October 1973, February 1974, and March 1990; and *Chicago Defender*, November 18, 1969, and January 18, 1975. For additional information see the biography of Dickerson, Gibson, Gibson, and Gillespie in this volume.

Payton, Philip A., Jr. (February 27, 1876–September 4, 1917). Realtor: Brown and Payton Realty and Afro-American Realty Company. Harlem was not always the largest, most infamous of black ghettos in the world, nor, for that matter, was it always a ghetto. Prior to the twentieth century, Harlem was a highly desirable community in which to live, with residences owned and sought after by some of the most affluent and influential members of New York's high society. During the 1870s and afterward, upper- and upper-middle-class residential dwellings emerged that appealed to people of taste and money. Sprinkled among these society types were a substantial number of blacks, although they were fewer in number and more dispersed than the blacks who lived within the traditional boundaries of Manhattan.

In 1900 there were 60,666 African-Americans scattered throughout the five boroughs of New York City. About 5,000 of these were foreign born, mostly from the islands in the Caribbean. With the onset of the first wave of mass migration of African-Americans to the North, many chose New York City as their destination; between 1890 and 1914, the population of blacks increased dramatically. The black population of Manhattan increased by 24,288 between 1900 and 1910, at which time it reached 91,709—the majority of whom had migrated from the South. Manhattan housed 78 percent of the city's industry in the early twentieth century, and blacks gravitated to the numerous unskilled jobs offered by these factories. Among this poverty-stricken majority of unskilled black laborers was a small black middle class who defined themselves as the elite of the race. Caterers, doctors, lawyers, small businessmen, and other professionals made up the core of this elite group of individuals. Although they preferred to live apart from their lower class counterparts, to their dismay, whites lumped them together as one group.

In the area that lies just west of Harlem, a large-scale real estate development took place at the turn of the century, which was ultimately to become the first section of the neighborhood known as "Negro Harlem." Although public transportation had not yet extended thus far, speculators banked on the idea that it would. Luxury buildings that offered the finest of amenities were erected to appeal to white families who wanted high-class flats, and who could afford such gracious living. But they proved to be too expensive, and the developers' optimism about the extension of the transit system proved to be ill-founded. To the chagrin of many hungry real estate developers, the market collapsed, and they were faced with foreclosing on their properties. An alternative solution, one they were reluctant to try, was available to them: to rent their properties to blacks. Philip Payton took advantage of this opportunity to convince the African-American community to move to the highly desirable neighborhood of West Harlem, which laid the foundation for what became the most luxurious black community the world had seen to that time.

Philip A. Payton, Jr., was born in Westfield, Massachusetts. His father, Philip Payton, Sr., was a native of the South who was educated at Wayland Seminary in Washington, D.C. In 1872, when he migrated to Massachusetts, he became a merchant and a barber, and his barbershop served as a gathering place for the small black community in Westfield. The younger Payton, one of four children, attended public schools and then attended Livingston College in Salisbury, North Carolina. After he graduated in 1899, Payton chose to settle in New York City, the metropolis of dreams for many blacks migrating from the South. His first job was in a large department store as an attendant at the penny-weighing and picture machines at a salary of $6 a week. Upon returning from a brief absence, he learned that he had lost his job. With no other employment possibilities in sight, Payton relied on the barbering skills he had learned from his father and mastered as a young man. He kept the job, which paid from $5 to $6 each week, until a seemingly better opportunity came along in 1900, the job of a janitor at $8 a week in a real estate firm. Payton had unwittingly landed in the right place at the right time. His first exposure to the real estate business came in a flurry of activity, for the industry was in the midst of a boom at the turn of the century. Having observed from the sidelines for only a brief time, Payton's appetite was whetted. His aggressive nature and hard-driving spirit were finally, at the tender age of twenty-four, going to be challenged.

In October 1900 Payton and a partner opened the Brown and Payton Realty Company. The partnership was short lived because Brown found himself unsatisfied with the inactivity and resigned after six months. Payton's relentless spirit forged him ahead, despite his inability to pay the rent, since his gross receipts after seven months totaled no more than $120. He was evicted and moved into another apartment from which he was also evicted for nonpayment of rent. Although Payton had been marketing himself as a real estate agent specializing in the management of colored tenement property, it took more than a year for him to get a colored tenement to manage. His first opportunity came in 1901, when two white landlords were embroiled in a dispute about a property on West 134th Street, in the heart of Harlem. One of the landlords got even with his adversary by handing the property over to Payton with instructions to fill the units with "colored tenants." Payton successfully rented all the apartments and proceeded to manage the property. With that success, he was able to recruit other white landlords to use his services. His acute awareness of business strategy is illustrated in his decision to advertise for colored tenements in white real estate publications: "Colored man makes a specialty of managing colored tenements; references; bond. Philip A. Payton, Jr., agent and broker, 67 West 134th." He also advertised in subways, trains, and outdoor billboards, and it was reported by the *New York Age* on July 12, 1917, that he was the first black businessman to see the value of the media. Such aggressive advertising brought in additional business, which caused Payton to seek out other black businessmen to help him expand his business.

Payton's sights were set on establishing a full-scale real estate operation, but without the financial backing of cooperative investors his dreams could not be realized. In 1903 he participated in the National Negro Business League's conference in Nashville, Tennessee, as one of nine business delegates from New York. There he addressed the audience on the "Possibilities of the Negro in the Real Estate Field" and took the opportunity to encourage investment in real estate operations. In his attempt to recruit investors with the assistance of Wilford H. Smith, a black attorney from New York who ultimately became the corporation's counsel, Payton focused primarily on Emmet J. Scott, the personal secretary and right-hand man of Booker T. Washington.* Payton's goal was to organize the Afro-American Realty Company as a partnership, and no doubt he sought Scott's support as a means of gaining access to Washington.

In 1904 Payton, and the highly successful black mortician and astute real estate investor (and likely Payton's key backer) James C. Thomas, pooled their resources and blocked an attempt by a white syndicate, Hudson Realty, to evict blacks from three homes sold to them by the Afro-American Realty Company. Hostilities emerged over the rapid expansion across Lenox Avenue into the fashionable St. Nicholas Park area. White residents, alarmed at the black invasion into what they perceived as their territory, joined forces to impede any further encroachment. When Hudson had gained the momentum (with financial backing from members of the Harlem Property Owners' Improvement Association) to proceed with the eviction of all the black tenants, Payton and Thomas aggressively interceded and secured the residences for the blacks. This courageous and remarkably successful strategy garnered the attention of Booker T. Washington, who praised the men for their race loyalty and business acumen.

Payton valued Washington's opinion and influence, and he eagerly sought his financial support. Although Washington praised his actions, he would not invest in his real estate ventures. Nonetheless, several other noted black businessmen and professionals invested in the young real estate firm. James C. Thomas became the company's first president, a largely ceremonial position; Payton, as vice president and general manager, was the real moving force. James E. Garner, owner of Garner's Manhattan House Cleaning and Renovating Bureau and treasurer of the New York branch of the National Negro Business League, was an early investor and corporation secretary and treasurer. Wilford H. Smith, one of Washington's closest allies and one of the most highly respected black Manhattan lawyers, was also an early investor. In time, other well-connected men invested in the company: Fred R. Moore,* who was on the Tuskegee payroll and was the editor of the *New York Age*; Emmet J. Scott, who finally conceded to "get in on the ground floor"; and Charles W. Anderson, another well-heeled confidant of Washington's, who had been appointed a collector of the internal revenue in New York with the aid of Washington.

Payton, "the only maverick among Washington's lackeys," remained outside New York's elite clique. He had chosen to remain aloof from the political ties that were part of the package when one accepted the economic benefits of the "Tuskegee Machine." Washington's decision to keep Payton outside the fold was probably due to the fact that Payton was unwilling to be a Washington pawn. Payton's goal was to acquire property to ensure that residential restrictions were abolished and that individuals of means could enjoy the luxury of residing where they so desired. Noble as his aspirations were, his refusal to be manipulated denied him the "right" to penetrate Washington's well-protected fortress. What becomes clear is that, although Washington declined an invitation to invest in the Afro-American Realty Company, he was well-represented and could keep abreast of the company's activities as long as he had his people in place. These individuals, unlike Washington, seemed to feel a particular fondness and fraternity for Payton. As Maceo Dailey so effectively put it, "The company was thus sucked into the vortex of Tuskegee politics. Washington and his omnipresent Tuskegee Machine obsessively sought to be informed and control the activity of black businesses in order to put forward what he considered the correct and acceptable image to the white power structure."

New York had long eluded the grip of the Tuskegee Machine, and Washington was keenly aware of the importance of penetrating perhaps the most influential of all the cities in the union. Northeastern black urban communities, like Boston and New York, had been emboldened by W.E.B. Du Bois, and they were highly critical of Washington's accommodationist philosophy. In 1905 they sought to disassociate themselves from him by creating an organization—the Niagara Movement—that espoused a more aggressive appeal for civil and political rights. Washington's enemies had clearly laid down the gauntlet, and Washington was deeply upset by the affront.

The 1905 meeting of the National Negro Business League was slated to be held in New York City. Washington no doubt chose this location as a means of establishing a network of businessmen who were sympathetic to his tactics for advancing the concerns of the African-American race. Payton also saw the business league as a vehicle with which he could further impress the black business community, most specifically Booker T. Washington. Payton had by then conquered Harlem's black real estate market by exhibiting keen judgment and by cultivating relationships with influential people. After the officers of the company were appointed and their investment dollars were in place, Payton appealed to the black working class via advertisements in various black-owned newspapers, including the *New York Age*. His advertisements asserted the importance of supporting an enterprise that promised to terminate "relentless race prejudice." In the company's "Prospectus," Payton offered his business as a symbol of business acumen and as a means of securing housing wherever individuals aspired to live, within their means.

No doubt Payton was interested in the betterment of his race, which he so precisely articulated in his speech entitled "Meeting the Realty Needs of the New York Negro" at the 1904 National Negro Business League convention in Indianapolis. However, public reports falsely reported that stocks were rapidly selling, while in reality salesmen were hired to promote the company's stocks at a 20 percent commission. Only rarely were more than a few shares sold to an individual with the exception of the initial investors. The realty company was misrepresenting its assets and was unable to deliver on its promises, as illustrated in its inability to pay out dividends to its shareholders.

Payton was a driven salesman who had complete confidence in his own business judgment despite the reservations expressed by others. He was compelled to move on to bigger transactions which only led to further internal strife and financial difficulties. The company originally specialized in acquiring five-year leases on Harlem properties owned by whites, and then renting them back to blacks at a rate higher than the market dictated. When he was challenged on this issue, Payton justified the higher rents on the grounds that he had to borrow money at higher interest rates than his white counterparts and thus had to pay substantially more for his properties. As long as he could find blacks who were willing to pay the rents, he continued to charge them higher rents.

The company was capitalized at $500,000 and was authorized to issue 50,000 shares at $10 each. Ten of the eleven original members of the all-black board of directors subscribed to 500 shares each. The company began with an estimated capital of $100,000. In 1904 it controlled ten flathouses, and it held ownership in four five-storied flats valued at $125,000. By 1905 it had control of twenty New York apartment dwellings valued at $690,000, six of which were owned by the company and fourteen of which were on long-term lease. It appeared that Payton's ambition was being realized, demonstrating "that there is executive and business ability in the Negro race, and that the Negroes' business capacity equals that of any other race when given the necessary capital to work with."

The company was suffering, however, from an internal power struggle that undermined its future. Charles Anderson, the one person other than Emmett J. Scott, who was the closest and most useful individual to Washington, had resigned after serving only two months as vice president when he realized that he was unable to devote enough time to the company. Moore and Smith, on the other hand, fought for control, in October 1905, when they strongly opposed Payton's business decisions. Moore was concerned with the company's financial image and urged that it sell additional stock. Payton agreed with Moore's concerns but chose to achieve the same results by reducing the shares held by the directors of the company and, by doing so, reduce their power. A reorganization resulted, and Payton maintained his dominant position in the company.

Having lost several of his allies, Payton sought out the support of Emmett J. Scott, who was urged by Moore and Smith to resign. To appease all parties concerned when Scott refused to resign, Washington wielded his influence and kept Scott occupied at Tuskegee in order to prevent him from aligning himself with Payton. Thus the storm had been weathered, but only temporarily. The jockeying for position among the remaining directors reemerged. Control for the company between Moore and Smith against Payton ensued again, and ultimately Smith resigned his position. These developments illustrate the diminishing control of the Tuskegee Machine over the Afro-American Realty Company, and more important, its declining presence in New York City.

Payton secured a position of authority for himself in the company by purchasing additional shares from J. C. Thomas. Now he could act independently, implementing policies that had been opposed earlier. To provide housing for blacks, Payton purchased an apartment at 525 West 151 Street and issued an eviction notice to the white tenants. The white press, which jumped at the opportunity to sensationalize the event, accused Payton of undermining the white community's cohesiveness by saturating it with black tenants. This maneuver totally contradicted and challenged the cardinal strategies of Washington: "secret offensive maneuvers and counterdefensive moves." Washington's accommodationist philosophy did not allow for any behavior that challenged the dominance of the white race. Thus, New York City remained outside of Washington's grasp.

The Afro-American Realty Company, which continued to be riddled with internal dissension, endured three major organizational overhalls in just four years. The strife finally came to a head in October 1906, when forty-three stockholders, represented by Smith, sued Payton and the company for having issued a fraudulent prospectus, which misled and cheated the general public, particularly African-Americans. The stockholders charged that the company's financial statements were "highly exaggerated"; that the contracts for the ten apartment buildings the company claimed to control on five-year leases contained sixty- and ninety-day cancellation clauses; that "nearly all of them had been cancelled" when the prospectus was issued; and that most of the houses the company claimed to own free and clear were, in reality, mortgaged to their full value. In 1907 Payton was arrested on charges of fraud, but he was immediately released when the judge ruled the suit a civil, and not a criminal, action. Over and above that decision, Payton could not be held liable for damages because he was just one of the officers in the company.

Although Payton was spared the embarrassment and trauma of serving time in prison, his company suffered from a tainted image. Payton continued to do business through 1907 and into the early part of 1908. He conceded to issue the first and last dividend the company paid to its shareholders as a way of enhancing its image, but it was to little avail. In 1908 the Afro-American Realty Company closed its doors and ceased doing business.

If one were to ask why the company failed, the answer could possibly be found in the relentless character of Philip Payton. It appears that his speculations were ill conceived and thus doomed to failure. Even after the suit had been filed, Payton indiscriminately continued to purchase property at a whirlwind pace, and true to his character, he refused the counsel of those who advised him on the value of moderation. His timing proved to be his undoing also, for in 1907–1908, when he went on a buying spree, the economy was suffering from a recession. The black community, on which he depended to occupy his buildings, was as always, hardest hit by the downturn. They were unable to afford his high rents and thus were forced to accept inferior housing. Payton was left with many new tenements, but with few new tenants. The property that remained vacant was subsidized by the rent paid on the occupied dwellings. The company was unable to meet its mortgage payments of from $10,000 to $20,000 to keep solvent. Desperation set in once Payton realized that the company was on the verge of collapse, and he was unable to solicit loans from anyone.

Payton's final appeal to Booker T. Washington, which in retrospect seems an incredibly brazen move, went unheeded. He requested that Washington arrange a meeting with Andrew Carnegie. Washington refused. When Payton directly appealed to both Carnegie and Oswald Garrison Villard for assistance, his requests were denied. Payton's final request that Washington underwrite the company's notes was also denied, either because Washington lacked the funds to do so, or more likely because the company was on the verge of collapse anyway, and it was never one of Washington's pet projects. However, it would be remiss to put the blame solely on the shoulders of Philip Payton, since the company had other officers who could be held liable. But, by the time of the collapse of the Afro-American Realty Company, all the officers had resigned, with the exception of Payton and Moore, neither of whom ever bothered to write a letter of explanation to the stockholders, despite Scott's request for ''an explicit statement giving the reasons which led to the failure of the Company. As honorable men I do not see how the company could do less than this.'' No public statement was ever issued.

Payton's indomitable spirit lifted him up from this tragedy. Although he no longer enjoyed the spotlight, nor could boast being the richest black landlord, he managed to continue operating privately in the real estate business. Documentation of his activities is scarce after the downfall of his firm, but what is available indicates that he continued to have modest success, interspersed between periods of struggle as evidenced in a letter to Emmett J. Scott on September 23, 1914, in which he complained that "business is rotten." Payton also commented that people were hanging on to their money, except for blacks, who were still "spending money like drunken sailors." And, he fretted in the same letter, "I am afraid I am Colored." Yet, despite his dejected spirit, correspondence with Scott reveals that Payton was actively pursuing business deals, including one with Heman Perry,* from whom Payton purchased shares in Standard Life.

Just one month before his death in 1917, Payton closed the most lucrative deal of his career, when he acquired six apartment buildings on West 141 Street valued at $1.5 million. Upon his death, the Payton Apartments Corporation was formed in March 1918, with a capital of $250,000. Watt Terry took over the transaction, with the support of bankers Edward C. and W.H.C. Brown from Philadelphia and Washington, Emmett J. Scott, and Heman Perry. The corporation assumed control of the modern elevator apartments; however, it fared no better than Payton. The buildings were not equipped with heat, which became readily apparent during a bitterly cold winter. The suffering tenants moved out of the building, and the partners in the venture were unable to earn any income from this property.

Payton's real estate business set the stage for John E. Nail* and Henry C. Parker, formerly his salesmen, who picked up where Payton left off and became known as the "Little Fathers" of Negro Harlem, in contrast to Payton's well-respected moniker as the "Father of Colored Harlem." It was Payton who encouraged blacks to invest in property in what was to become the artistic and intellectual capital of black America, and it was he who laid the foundation for the largest black ghetto in the world.

Sources

There are no personal or company papers available, nor is there a full-scale biography of Philip Payton. The original Afro-American Realty Company "Prospectus" (New York, 1904) is held in the New York City Hall of Records, as is the "Certificate of Incorporation of the Afro-American Realty Company, June 15, 1904," and "Crowder vs. Philip A. Payton, Jr. and the Afro-American Realty Company" (1907), the stockholders' suit against Payton. A short history of the Afro-American Realty Company appears in the Booker T. Washington Papers at the Library of Congress; as does important correspondence between Payton and Washington and especially with Emmett J. Scott. However, there are some useful materials, including the following: Gilbert Osofsky, *Harlem: The Making of a Ghetto*, chapter 7, "Race Enterprise: The Afro-American Realty Company," 92–104 (New York, 1966), which offers both biographical information about Payton and details the company's history; and Booker T. Washington, *The Negro in Business*, chapter XIX, "Philip A. Payton, Jr., and the Afro-American Realty Company," 197–205 (1907). James Weldon Johnson, *Black Manhattan* (1930, 1968) provides some limited information on Payton; Clement Richardson, *National Cyclopedia of the Colored Race* (1919) offers numerous biographies of successful African-Americans in business, including Payton. Brief biographies of Payton appear in *National Cyclopedia of the Colored Race* (Montgomery, Alabama, 1919), Ingham, BDABL, and *Black Enterprise*, June 1976. An obituary appears in the *New York Age*, September 5, 1917.

L. B. Byron's "Negro Real Estate in New York," a WPA Project, is held in the Schomburg Collection of the New York Public Library. Myrtle Evangeline Pollard's "Harlem As Is: The Negro Business and Economic Community, Master's thesis, City College, 1937, Vol. II, offers a brief account of Payton and other real estate brokers Allon Schoener, ed., *Harlem on My Mind* (New York, 1968) includes a collection of newspaper clippings dealing with blacks, some of which cover real estate issues in Harlem. A superb article about the Tuskegee Machine and Washington's efforts to gain control in New York City through Payton's realty firm is Maceo Dailey, "Booker T. Washington and the Afro-American Realty Company," *Review of Black Political Economy* VIII (Winter 1978), 184–201. The National Negro Business League's Fifth Annual Convention, August 31 and September 1 and 2, 1904, and the National Negro Business League's Ninth Annual Convention 1908, available at Hampton University, include an address given by Payton on his business ventures.

Several articles on Payton appear in various publications: The Peabody Collection at Hampton University consists of numerous newspaper clippings on Payton and the realty firm from a variety of publications, including the *New York Sun*, July 26, 1904; *New York World*, July 27, 1904; and *New York Age*, July 28 and August 11, 1904. *The New York Age*, August 4, 1904, is a lengthy article that is a response to a *New York Times* editorial, July 26?, 1904, on the creation of the Afro-American Realty Company and its goals. See also *Houston Daily Post*, August 4, 1904; *St. Louis Globe Democrat*, May 3, 1914; and *Philadelphia Tribune*, May 11, 1918. Articles appearing elsewhere include the *New York Age*, December 5, 1912, an important interview, and July 31, 1920; *New York Sun*, March 14, 1918; the *New York Tribune*, July 26, 1904; the *New York Evening Mail*, January 26, 1918; and the *Interstate Tattler*, January 2, 1931.

Perry, Christopher James (September 15, 1854–May ? 1921) and **Eugene Washington Rhodes** (October 29, 1895–June 24, 1970). Newspaper publishers and political leaders: *Philadelphia Tribune*. Perry and Rhodes, father- and son-in-law, created an important newspaper dynasty in Philadelphia, when their paper, the *Philadelphia Tribune*, became a bastion of economic and political conservatism, and a repository of the mores and values of the city's eminent African-American middle class. Perry, who had been born in Baltimore, Maryland, the son of Christopher and Rebecca (Bowser) Perry, freeborn blacks, was educated in public schools. He came to Philadelphia as a young man to seek his fortune. Black Philadelphia when Perry arrived in 1873 was bustling with activity and optimism. By 1880 there were over 30,000 African-Americans in the city, constituting 3.7 percent of the total population. The number of blacks continued to grow rapidly during Perry's lifetime, reaching 134,000 by 1920.

Perry had wanted to start his own newspaper but soon realized that he was not prepared to cope with the complexities of the city he found. Therefore, he began to work for a white family while he attended night school at the Lombard Street Presbyterian Church. Over the next several months, Perry developed his reputation as a thinker and speaker, and he was offered the opportunity to write a regular column for the *Philadelphia Sunday Mercury*, entitled "Flashes and Sparks." He immediately accepted the offer and began writing the column for the paper, reporting on social events and other aspects of the black community.

He was given a series of promotions at that paper and then became editor of the "Colored Department." In 1884, however, the paper folded, and Perry now without a job, decided it was time to start his own venture. In May of that same year he married Cora Harris of Philadelphia and on November 28, 1884, he brought out the first issue of the *Philadelphia Tribune*.

The *Tribune* came into existence at a time when the African-American press of the United States was beginning to take on the vitality and dynamism that characterized it during the first half of the twentieth century. Under these more favorable new circumstances, along with Perry's vigorous editorial style, the *Tribune* soon became the largest black weekly in the city. Setting up his office at 725 Sansom Street, Perry focused on the problems that were affecting the lives of the massive numbers of black men, women, and children who were pouring into Philadelphia from the South and filling up the "Negro Wards" of South Philadelphia. Perry himself was a familiar figure on the streets of South Philadelphia, as he "pounded the beat" looking for news items. His smart and sassy young paper caught the fancy of these southern newcomers, who saw a kindred soul in Perry, since he too was from "down South." Circulation increased, advertising revenues grew, and soon Perry had to move out of his rented quarters to more spacious accommodations at 717 Sansom, where he rented two floors and installed a press for outside work. He also added two more people to the *Tribune* staff.

Perry's *Tribune*, however, was not without competition in the black community. The great spurt in the city's African-American population provided an attractive market to would-be entrepreneurs of all kinds. The *Philadelphia Sentinel*, started by George W. Gardner in 1884, was published until 1896. In the mid–1890s, however, other black papers emerged. One of the most important was the *Philadelphia Standard-Echo*, published by William Simpson. Nonetheless, W.E.B. Du Bois, in his *Philadelphia Negro*, published in 1899, reported that the *Tribune* was "the chief news sheet [in the city's black community] and is filled with generally social notes of all kinds, and news of movements among Negroes over the country. Its editorials are usually of little value chiefly because it does not employ a responsible editor." He did allow, however, that it was "an interesting newspaper and represents pluck and perseverance on the part of its publishers." The editor of the *Tribune* for some fourteen years was John W. Harris, Perry's brother-in-law.

In the early twentieth century, several other competing newspapers, such as the *Philadelphia Defender* and the *Courant*, also were published. There are no extant copies of the *Tribune* prior to 1912, but between that date and 1920, the basic format of the paper was developed. The editorials were written by the new managing editor, G. Grant Williams. These editorials covered a wide variety of subjects of local, national, and sometimes even international importance. Regular columns were written by William C. Bolivar, whose contribution, called "Pencil Pusher Points," dealt with a wide variety of subjects. Reverend Robert H. Pierce of Creditt Point Baptist Church edited a column on "Churches and Their Pastors,'' and Perry continued his column on social news called "Flashes and Sparks.'' What was most unique about Perry and the *Tribune* during this time is the fact that the paper did not just write about the issues facing the black community, it involved itself in them in a very direct and personal manner.

Perry participated in a number of crusades during the thirty-five years he ran the *Tribune*. He constantly campaigned for better jobs and better working conditions for blacks, for greater African-American representation in city government, and against discrimination and corruption in politics. He also used his influence as an editor and an increasingly powerful political figure to push for "cleanups" of the black ghetto. Although the cleanup was accomplished, it came at a time when black influence in Philadelphia politics was at a nadir. After winning the election of three common councilors to the city council in 1890–1891, black political prospects declined drastically. Perry, however, was able to increase his own political power, along with the influence of his paper, during this time. He had earlier been appointed, with the support of the Republican organization, the first black clerk in the Sheriff's Department, where he served for fifteen years, and also was made an inspector in the Department of Highways for three years. His crowning political achievement, however, came in 1895, when Perry was elected to the common council.

Perry had a difficult road to travel on the council. On the one hand, he had to tread carefully along the boundaries established by the Republican machine. On the other, Perry viewed himself and his newspaper as representatives of his race. With the increasing racism and disregard for blacks exhibited by his colleagues, it made Perry's job difficult. One local ward politician at that time succinctly summarized white politicians' attitudes toward blacks: "There are some Negroes in my division, and they've been coming to me and telling me what they want, but I tell them to go to hell.'' The turn of the century, however, began to change the situation somewhat. During the decade from 1900 to 1910, the city's black population grew by 35 percent to nearly 90,000. Race riots, such as those in Wilmington, North Carolina, and Atlanta, Georgia, along with the general growth of virulent white racism and discrimination in the South, fueled this massive increase. The larger black population increased marginally the political power of blacks, and Perry used the size of this black population to serve on the common council until 1905.

One of the greatest problems faced by black newcomers to Philadelphia at this time was the shortage of available housing, as they found themselves crowded into already overcrowded "colored sections'' of the city. The *Philadelphia Tribune* became active on a number of levels in assisting the new arrivals to the city. It publicized and supported the activities of the Philadelphia Association for the Protection of Colored Women. The Armstrong Commission, an affiliate of the city's Urban League, also received extensive support from the *Tribune* during its fund-raising drives and its campaigns for greater employment opportunities for blacks. Perry also supported the work of Reverend William D. Creditt, the principal of Downington Industrial School and the pastor of the First African

Baptist Church, in his quest to improve the employment, housing, and sanitation conditions of black workers. In 1917 a Negro Migration Committee was formed to keep in touch with the changing conditions produced by migration, and the *Tribune* openly supported and publicized its work.

As white violence against African-Americans increased during these decades, the *Tribune* (January 18, 1916) not only reported these attacks, but also issued strong editorials condemning them, urging blacks to defend themselves:

When violence has been shown such persons in the damaging of their property and the threatening of their lives, the police and the courts have not afforded sufficient protection and redress to the outraged citizens. The lawless public opinion has been allowed to have its way. . . . Treading upon our rights in Philadelphia is becoming common. Unless we organize and fight it, we shall soon be in as bad a mess as we are in Maryland and other Southern states.

But the *Tribune* went farther than that. On June 30, 1916, G. Grant Williams presided over a protest meeting concerning these attacks on blacks. At that meeting, a coalition of leading black fraternal, social, and religious organizations agreed to support a boycott of white-owned businesses on South Street. The boycott was successful in forcing some changes.

As more and more of these African-American newcomers from Virginia and North Carolina poured into the city, Perry continued to use the *Tribune* to appeal to their interests. He understood that many of them wanted news from their former homes, so Perry used his extensive contacts in other southern communities to get from them the requisite news items. In turn, these new Philadelphians bought copies of the *Tribune* to send back home to friends and relatives, hoping to convince them to come north to this land of relative peace and prosperity. Circulation and advertising revenues of the *Tribune* continued to rise sharply, and Perry became a wealthy man. By 1913 the paper boasted a circulation of 20,000 and it was "knee-deep in prosperity."

As a result, Perry found that the rented quarters at 717 Sansom were inadequate, and he leased a large building at 526 S. 16th Street. Four years later, he added two large linotype machines and then a flatbed press. With the money he made from his newspaper, Perry began to engage in other business activities. He developed some real estate interests in conjunction with John W. Harris, and he served as treasurer of The Conservative Co., which bought and sold real estate and managed properties. A member of the Lombard Street Presbyterian Church, Perry died unexpectedly in 1921.

At the time of Perry's death, there was no successor to take his place at the *Tribune*. He had a wife and four daughters, along with a son, Christopher Perry, Jr. Beatrice Perry, one of the daughters, became president of the firm, and Bertha, another daughter, became managing editor and women's editor. Chris, Jr., was composing room foreman. To replace the elder Perry as editor, they chose Grant Williams, who met his own death a year later. This paved the way for the next stage of the *Tribune*'s history, under the dynamic leadership of Eugene Washington Rhodes.

Rhodes was born in Camden, South Carolina, the son of Charles Rhodes, a carpenter, and Laura Boykin. Although the Rhodes family was not affluent, Laura Rhodes was determined that her thin, sickly, sometimes moody and inarticulate son would have a good education. She therefore dipped into the family's meager savings to send him to a good Presbyterian private school in Camden, and then to Benedict College in Columbia, South Carolina, a prep school for blacks. In 1918 Rhodes entered Lincoln University in Pennsylvania and earned his bachelor's degree there four years later. Since there was little family money, Rhodes worked at a series of odd jobs during the school year to help finance his education, and he worked during the summers in Philadelphia, selling advertising space for the *Tribune*. While still in school, he also began writing editorials for the paper, preparing to join the company full-time when he graduated in 1922.

While at Lincoln University, Rhodes made a number of friendships that would serve him well in later years. The most important of these friends was his roommate, the aggressive and dynamic Robert N. C. Nix, but there were also other men who later became prominent in the economic and political life of Philadelphia. When Rhodes came to Philadelphia and joined the *Tribune* in 1922, things were highly unsettled, and he continued to sell advertising space full-time while attending law school part-time at the University of Pennsylvania. Late in that year Grant Williams died, and Rhodes, with precious little experience, was named his successor.

On one hand, this was a risky move, given Rhodes's youth and inexperience; on the other hand, the *Tribune* had virtually no competition at that time, was making a good deal of money, and was growing rapidly. In addition, Rhodes seemed to have good business and political sense. A year after assuming the editorship, on June 22, 1923, Rhodes married Bertha Perry. The marriage cemented Rhodes's right to succession in control of the paper, and he immediately embarked upon ambitious plans for expansion. He requested that the board of directors approve the purchase of new equipment, and in 1925 the paper's first linotype machine, which had been installed in 1912, was replaced by a new model. In 1930 the *Tribune* purchased a Monotype and Rule Caster to make type for headlines, and in 1931 it finally purchased their own building at 526 S. 16th Street. At the same time, they purchased a forty-page Hoe Press as a replacement for the old flatbed press Perry had installed. In 1926, when Christopher Perry's widow died, Rhodes was appointed the paper's general manager.

These technical improvements were but a small part of Eugene Rhodes's contribution to the growth of the *Tribune* during the 1920s. Rhodes and the *Tribune* propounded a dual philosophy during this period that enhanced the paper's popularity until the 1930s. He and his paper were, first of all, very self-conscious representatives and voices of the emerging black middle class in the city. They propounded middle-class values of thrift, hard work, education, self-help, and free enterprise. These values gave the paper a conservative cast during this time that fit well with Rhodes's own strong Republican orientation. He had gotten his law degree in 1926, after attending Temple University part-time. When Rhodes was admitted to the state bar in that year, he was appointed by the reigning Republican administration to the post of assistant U.S. attorney for the Eastern District of Pennsylvania. He served in that post until 1933. Rhodes was also a law partner in the firm of Nix, Rhodes and Nix, run by his friend and political ally, Robert N. C. Nix.

What tempered or moderated the conservatism of Rhodes and the *Tribune* was his profound racial consciousness. As an ally and advocate of the new black business group that had emerged in the city, he championed racial separation in many elements of life, and he strongly supported the need for blacks to patronize these businesses. The *Tribune* under Perry, Williams, and Rhodes regularly published articles extolling the virtues of black business and businessmen. They also filled their pages, week after week, with articles alternately praising and cajoling, scolding and praising, pleading for and bemoaning the lack of support of black businesses. This race consciousness, however, also at times gave the *Tribune* a tougher edge. Extremely proud of his race, highly sensitive to slights of any kind to himself or other blacks, Rhodes and the *Tribune* often engaged in militant crusades against aspects of white discrimination and racism.

This stance was demonstrated by Grant Williams and Christopher Perry in 1918, when white mobs and gangs of sailors attacked black homes and roamed the streets beating up blacks while the police seemed to stand by and do nothing. The *Tribune* joined with R. R. Wright, Jr.,[*] and others in protesting this action, and the paper ran a long series of articles on the riots and on police brutality; Williams wrote angry editorials castigating everyone involved. They were successful in their campaign. After Rhodes took control of the paper, it conducted a long and strident campaign against the evils of segregated schools. Although the *Tribune* supported segregation in some areas, segregated schools tended to be inferior schools, and Rhodes would not tolerate that. Thus throughout the 1920s and on into the 1930s, Rhodes and the *Tribune*, in conjunction with middle-class black organizations, fought for integrated or mixed schools. Rhodes began his assault on segregated schools with an editorial calling on blacks "to open fire on segregated schools." Although the *Tribune* was successful at times, it was severely hampered by the inability of middle-class black organizations to work together. That was particularly true of the NAACP. Because of this, Rhodes angrily attacked the organization, saying it needed "new blood, clearer vision, and a will to fight." This kind of internal friction in the black community did little to help end segregation policies.

Perry also campaigned editorially for the election of black members to the board of education, and the first African-American member of that board was elected in 1932. In addition, Rhodes challenged what he termed the Jim Crow policies of the Philadelphia police department, pointing out that there were fewer black police than there had been a decade before, and that police tended to treat black and white suspects differently. Regardless of its ineffectiveness at times, in a decade of continuing racial hostility, Eugene Rhodes and the *Tribune* were one of the few visible signs of defense and solidarity for the city's lower class blacks.

Nonetheless, the *Tribune* was hardly considered an exceptional or dynamic newspaper, even by other blacks. A survey conducted in the mid–1920s by Eugene Gordon for *Opportunity* ranked the *Tribune* seventh out of the twelve papers considered. The *Norfolk Journal and Guide*, no radical rag itself, in 1931 called the *Tribune* "one of our most conservative papers in editorial content and mechanical makeup." This relative conservatism and complacency, along with Rhodes's continued alliance with the Republican party during the Depression, opened the way for a vigorous new competitor—the *Philadelphia Independent*, published by the irascible J. Max Barber. Barber was a longtime thorn in the side of Booker T. Washington* as publisher of the *Voice of the Negro* in Atlanta, and one of the most consistently radical black voices during the first half of the twentieth century.

The *Independent*, more liberal than the *Tribune* and less stridently race conscious, tried to reach all the blacks in the city. Unlike the staunchly Republican *Tribune*, the *Independent* identified itself as a "paper whose present political leanings are definitely pro-Democratic." It asserted that the "basic principle of freedom of speech and the espousing of the weaker cause" would be its aim. The *Tribune* under Rhodes, although it fought racism and discrimination, did not really view itself as an instrument for social change. It was a business, and Rhodes intended to manage it in a business-like manner. As he once said, "Newspapers despite apparent belief to the contrary are materially-minded as well as idealistically minded organs. Without money, newspapers could no longer exist to serve the general purpose they are serving." But Rhodes's conservatism did not serve the *Tribune* as well as it might have.

The paper had grown steadily throughout the 1920s, largely because there was no real competition. But the *Independent* rapidly took readers away from it in the 1930s. With a circulation of just 10,000 in 1931, the *Independent* had 30,000 readers in 1935. It was clear that the younger paper had found a voice that the black masses in Philadelphia, struggling under the yoke of the Depression, found refreshing and reassuring. Rhodes, however, never deviated from his more elitist, middle-class format and Republican orientation. To attract more readers he used other devices. He added more features to the paper, with more columns featuring gossip about prominent blacks, and he introduced comics, more pictorial spreads, and other features. These more expensive options, which the less well-capitalized *Independent* would have a hard time adopting, appealed to another dominant 1930s mood—escapism.

One area of vital concern to the city's blacks, and one that also fit into the prevailing middle-class values of the *Tribune*, was the need for jobs during the Depression. Early on, Rhodes announced in an editorial: "The *Philadelphia Tribune*, working with the Armstrong Association, . . . intends to initiate a campaign to secure jobs for Negroes in Philadelphia on the cold basis of money spent with merchants by colored people.'' Although this sort of approach had some attraction to lower class blacks without jobs, it is also clear it had the interests of the black middle class more at heart. It was a classic case of "trickle down.'' The *Independent*, as a Democratic paper, supported the various job programs and other acts passed by the Roosevelt administration. Rhodes, on the other hand, tended to attack the National Recovery Administration, the Works Progress Administration, and other New Deal measures as being discriminatory. He castigated the NRA editorially as the "Negro Removal Act,'' since employers now had to meet federal standards for equal wages, which he felt would cause low-paid black workers to be replaced with white workers. But most blacks, even most of the African-American middle class, came increasingly to view the New Deal measures as benefiting the black community. Rhodes and the *Tribune* thus became increasingly out of step with the population it serviced. In response, Rhodes resorted to some of Christopher Perry's old issues. In 1937 the *Tribune* teamed up with the North Philadelphia Civic Betterment Leagues and veteran's organizations to sponsor the country's first Clean Black Campaign, which led to the cleaning and beautification of several of the city's black neighborhoods.

Nonetheless, the *Tribune* under Rhodes's leadership continued to grow and expand. By 1941 it changed from a weekly publication with a circulation of 7,000 to a twice-weekly paper whose circulation had grown to 50,000 by the time of Rhodes's death. In 1967 the Tribune Company grossed about $900,000 from subscribers and advertisers. Although most of its readers were black, one of the secrets of Rhodes's success was his ability to convince whites to advertise in the publication. Between 60 and 70 percent of the advertisers were white.

Honors also continued to come Eugene Rhodes's way. In 1933 he was elected president of the National Bar Association and served until 1935. He was appointed chairman of the State Commission to Study Conditions of the Urban Population from 1939 to 1944, and from 1954 to 1956 he served as the first black appointed to the Pennsylvania Parole Board. He was also a member of the County Board of Law Examiners (1947–1953), director of the NAACP (1948–1962), and had a number of other affiliations. In 1947 he established the Tribune Charities, of which he served as treasurer until his death. Tribune Charities established scholarships and sponsored award banquets, a cooking school, fashion shows, and other activities to instill race and community pride. In 1958 Rhodes was appointed a member of the Philadelphia Board of Education, becoming just the second black to serve on that body. From 1962 to 1965 he served as president of the National Newspaper Publishers Association, and in 1966 he won the Distinguished Editor Award from that organization.

Rhodes was a member of the Union Baptist Church, which he served as a deacon. Rhodes's first wife died in 1963, and two years later he married Jeanne (Simmons) Scott of Mon2 Mononghela, Pennsylvania. He had no children. Christopher Perry and Eugene Rhodes were not "Old Philadelphians,'' members of that light-skinned group of African-Americans in the city who traced their lineage back to the early nineteenth century, had assimilated the values of the white majority, and had taken on an aristocratic, upper class demeanor. Perry and Rhodes, both migrants from the South, tended to identify strongly with the generally darker skinned members of that group who formed the bulk of Philadelphia's black population. Yet they retained a strong affiliation with middle-class values, and had little regard for lower class members of their race. As Charles T. Haley commented, "Although middle class Black Philadelphians, such as E. Washington Rhodes . . . were dedicated to improving their race, their race pride was instilled with an acceptance of middle class values."

Sources

No personal or business papers of either Christopher Perry or E. Washington Rhodes are currently available. Back issues of the *Philadelphia Tribune*, however, are available on microfilm. Back issues of the *Tribune* after 1912 are available at the Free Library of Philadelphia, the Chicago Public Library, and the University of Illinois Library. Biographical information on Perry and Rhodes can be obtained from John A. Saunders, *100 Years after Emancipation* (Philadelphia, n.d.); *National Cyclopedia of American Biography* vol. 56 (1975), 48–49; *Who's Who of the Colored Race* (1915); *Who's Who in Colored America*, vol. I, 1927, 7th ed. 1950; R. R. Wright, Jr., *The Colored Directory of Philadelphia* (Philadelphia, 1908); Charles Frederick White, *Who's Who in Philadelphia* (Philadelphia, 1912); *Nixon's Classified Directory of Negro Business Interests and Professions in Pennsylvania* (Philadelphia, 1928); Roy L. Hill, *Who's Who in American Negro Press* (Dallas, 1960), 27–28; G. F. Richlings, *Evidences of Progress among Colored People* (1896); WPA Writer's Project, "The Negro in Philadelphia" (Philadelphia, 1938), microfilm copy available at Balch Institute for Ethnic Studies; *Philadelphia Bulletin*, December 7, 1958, and May 8, 1967. See also V. P. Franklin, "'Voice of the Black Community': The Philadelphia Tribune, 1912–41," *Pennsylvania History* vol. 51 no. 4 (October, 1984). E. Washington Rhodes wrote "The Negro Press Takes Up Its Burden," *The Brown American* (Philadelphia, Spring-Summer, 1942). Two dissertations do an excellent job of putting the *Tribune* and the work of Perry and Rhodes into a proper historical context: Charles Ashley Hardy III, "Race and Opportunity: Philadelphia during the Era of the Great Migration, 1916–1930," Ph.D. diss., Temple University, 1989; and Charles T. Haley, "To Do Good and Do Well: Middle Class Blacks and the Depression, Philadelphia, 1929–1941," Ph.D. dissertation, State University of New York at Binghampton, 1980.

Perry, Heman Edward (March 5, 1873–January 4, 1929). Insurance and bank founder and entrepreneur: Standard Life Insurance Company, Citizen Trust Bank, and Service Corporation. Heman Perry has been called by some the "Commercial Booker T. Washington,[*]" but in many respects a more accurate appellation would be the "black William C. Durant." Durant, the founder of General Motors, was, like Perry, a man of enormous vision and gigantic dreams. Durant was a marvelous salesman, promoter, and organizer, who, because of his inability or disinterest in the mundane, day-to-day details of running a massive enterprise, lost control of General Motors twice, and ultimately died a nearly forgotten man. Perry, like Durant, had dreams and visions that fired the imagination of the African-American community of the entire nation, but he, as Alexa Henderson has said, "received low marks as a skillful manager," and his empire fell apart. But, like the Brown and Stevens Bank in Philadelphia, Perry and his failed visions are often remembered more fondly than the more staid and stable enterprises that succeeded. Perry, like Durant, dared to dream the impossible dream, and although each lost control of his creation, at least parts of it continued on as important elements of American business life.

Heman Perry was born in Houston, Texas, the second child of John and Lucy Compton Perry. Heman Perry had three brothers and five sisters. His father had been born a slave in Georgia, reputedly on the plantation of Judge Heman Perry in Waynesboro. According to Heman Perry's sister, the elder Perry and his sister ran away to Texas. John Perry had no formal education, and followed no specific occupation, but rather dabbled in a number of activities and enterprises. He owned several drays which he rented out to haul commodities for various stores and individuals in the area. He also operated a farm at times, and he bought and sold cotton and a number of other commodities. In addition, he ran a grocery store for a few years and worked as an insurance agent on a part-time basis from time to time.

Despite his lack of schooling, John Perry believed strongly in the concept of education for his children. Family poverty and racial discrimination restricted Heman Perry's formal education to the seventh grade level. John Perry thus supplemented young Heman's book learning with business experiences. As Olive Perry, Heman's sister, commented, "Anything my father thought would be educational to Heman, he exposed him to it. Father would carry Heman with him when he bought and sold cotton, and would carry Heman to the courthouse whenever there were trials so he could learn something about the legal procedures."

After young Heman finished seventh grade, he got a job in a cotton factory as a cotton sampler and stenciler. During this time Perry also moonlighted for white insurance companies in Houston selling policies to blacks. He enjoyed the challenge of selling, and the independence of working for himself, along with the possibilities that entailed for making money. As he once commented later, the "salary business never appealed to me; it was too slow a game." He also tried running a 250-acre cotton farm during this period, but it was not a success. Perry went to Cincinnati, where he worked as an attendant im a Turkish bath, until his father died and he returned to Houston.

A short time later, sometime in the 1890s, Perry decided to go to New York City. He began working for a number of large white insurance companies upon his arrival in New York, spending about twelve years as a solicitor for the Equitable, Manhattan Life, Fidelity Mutual, and the Mutual Reserve. But this was not enough for Perry, since, as he later told a reporter for *Forbes* magazine, "I went to New York with the idea of getting rich." From his experience in Texas, Perry thought he knew cotton well, and he was determined to make his fortune as a trader in that commodity. As he told it, "I went to New York a bear on cotton and a bull on stocks. . . . I went into the stockmarket with $800 or $900, and within a few weeks I ran it up to $10,000. Then, like everything else, I got caught in one of those reactions dealing with a bucket shop and lost everything I had. . . . Knowing that New York is a cold place for a person who was broke,'' Perry continued, ''I decided to go to Georgia and start all over again in cotton.''

Perry pawned his cuff links to buy passage on a boat to Savannah, Georgia, in 1908, made 65 cents in tips while on the journey, and finally arrived in Atlanta stone broke, eating ten-cent meals at two-day intervals while he tried to get a job as a cotton broker. He finally found a job in that field, and later worked in a warehouse, but during this time he began to dream of creating an insurance empire. His work for white insurance companies in New York had convinced him that there was a market among blacks for whole or ordinary life insurance, rather than the industrial insurance sold by nearly all of the African-American firms. Industrial insurance was sold for small face amounts, with relatively high weekly premiums collected to cover the costs. Basically burial insurance, it did not build equity for the blacks who held the insurance and it was costly for the companies to administer. So, thought Perry, why not set up a company selling higher value insurance policies to blacks that would help his people better themselves, but also provide a profitable new business arena for black businessmen? Perry soon found that getting into the insurance game in this way was much harder than he imagined. So, less than a year after Perry arrived in Atlanta, he embarked on a pursuit of what, in retrospect and probably even at the time, seems like a fantastic dream.

Atlanta in the years after Perry's arrival in 1908 was a dynamic, yet deeply scarred, environment. The tragic Atlanta riot in 1906 had deeply shaken the faith of the city's African-Americans in their city, and in the South generally. On the other hand, the self-defense tactics they had used against the white mobs during the riots had gone a long way toward creating an autonomous, independent black community in the city. Auburn Avenue was emerging as the center of black business, cultural, and social life, and a whole range of dynamic new enterprises was springing up, giving renewed optimism to the people. It was an optimism based not on the older ideas of integration into the mainstream of white society, at least in the near future, but more on the concept of developing a powerful parallel black community that could eventually merge with the white community on a more nearly equal basis.

That optimism, that sense of ''can-do-ism'' that infected African-Americans in the Booker T. Washington era, perhaps explains why Perry, a man with virtually no capital, no tenure in the city, and no track record to speak of, could manage to attract a number of the city's most prominent individuals to a meeting at the black YMCA in January 1909 to discuss proposals for setting up an insurance company. Although there were several back insurance firms in the country in 1909, and Atlanta itself had the thriving Atlanta Life Insurance Company, these were all industrial insurance ventures which could be started and maintained with relatively little in the way of capital or reserves. An ordinary life company, however, had to meet strict requirements, even in Georgia. In that state there was for, example, the demand for a minimum $100,000 in capitalization.

When Perry announced to the assembled audience at the YMCA his need for $100,000 in capital, most reacted with incredulous disbelief. After all, even the city's largest black financial institutions at that time did not have capital anywhere near that amount. Atlanta Life, for example, had been started barely four years earlier with just over $5,000; Atlanta Savings Bank, the first black bank in the city, had capital of around $10,000 in 1909 and raised it to just $25,000 in 1913. What Perry proposed to these men was indeed astonishing. As Perry himself commented later; "It was something new among our people, and you couldn't get them to see it." Perry, as usual, was undaunted. A few days later, he organized a corporation with prestigious black contractor Henry A. Rucker as president, set up offices in the Rucker Building, and got a charter from the state of Georgia. The charter stipulated that he had two years from its granting to raise the $100,000 in order to embark in business.

Perry at this time reminds one of the classic definition of a salesman—"A smile, a hearty handshake, and a shoeshine"—for, indeed, he did not have much else. He set out upon a two-year odyssey, criss-crossing the country on Jim Crow railroads, meeting with wealthy and influential blacks in an attempt to raise what seemed to most to be a mammoth sum. One old Atlanta resident, who was a neighbor of Perry's, described him as a soft-talking Texas "pretty boy," and others attested to his eloquence and sales ability. The neighbor also said that Perry could "paint pictures and make people buy Standard stock." W.E.B. Du Bois more prosaically commented, "Perry got hold of colored men who had some savings or a business, and especially the professional Negroes, and laid before them his scheme for an old-line insurance company. Perry had facts and figures; he showed people that it was possible to establish a Negro insurance company and carry it on by business and scientific methods and make money." Perry also resorted to racial pride to convince blacks to buy stock. He reminded them of the slights they had all suffered at the hands of white insurance agents, and of the fact that blacks were never sold insurance at the same rates as whites. All of this helped Perry move closer to his goal, but it was not easy.

For two years, Perry traveled the country, securing the endorsement of such eminent blacks as Booker T. Washington, through the intercession of his childhood friend, Emmett J. Scott, the Tuskegean's personal secretary. By the end of 1910, Perry had raised just $60,000 of the $100,000 needed. A herculean task, to be sure, but still far short of the mark. By the end of January 1911, Perry had still not reached his goal, having only added another $10,000 to his total. Thus, he instructed the secretary of the company, Harry Herbert Pace,* to return all money to subscribers as required by law, along with 4 percent interest. In his letter, however, Pace asked if the interest might be voluntarily returned, since Perry had taken no salary, nor even any expenses, during the two-year ordeal, and could sorely use the money. Only about $60, however, was returned to them.

Any other man would probably have read the handwriting on the wall and abandoned what seemed to be a fruitless, unappreciated project. But not Heman Perry; he just started all over again. This time, however, he decided to apply for the state charter after he had raised the $100,000. Again, Perry spent two years traveling throughout the South soliciting funds, and once again he fell short. But this time he had developed stronger relations with important individuals in Atlanta. One of those influential Atlantans who provided Perry with monetary support in his second attempt was Alonzo Herndon.* Herndon persuaded the board at Atlanta Life to agree to invest $5,000 in Standard Life stock. With Herndon's endorsement, along with that of several of his associates, and with the money from Atlanta Life and the stock Perry had been able to sell, he was able to get a $50,000 loan from a white bank in Atlanta and deposit the full $100,000 with the Georgia insurance officials. Perry received a charter on March 22, 1913, and began operating the company that June.

Standard Life became the first black insurance firm organized solely for the purpose of selling ordinary life insurance, and it was just the third firm, after Mississippi Life and North Carolina Mutual, to achieve legal reserve status. With his company in operation, Perry assembled an impressive cast of supporters and aides. On his board of directors he featured men such as Emmett Scott; F. C. Brown, of the Brown and Stevens Bank in Philadelphia; Robert R. Church,* the wealthy black Memphis entrepreneur; Thomas H. Hayes, a prominent undertaker and head of the Solvent State Savings Bank in Memphis; Truman K. Gibson,* later of Supreme Life in Chicago; Henry A. Boyd,* of the National Baptist Publishing House in Nashville; Sol. C. Johnson, publisher of the *Savannah Tribune*; Walter S. Scott, president of Savannah Banking and Savings; John Hope, president of Morehouse College in Atlanta; and a number of others.

Perry also had an uncanny ability to find and encourage a number of highly qualified and well-educated individuals to join his staff. Harry H. Pace, his right-hand man in early years, later organized Supreme Life in Chicago along with a number of other ventures. When Pace left, he was replaced by J. A. Robinson, an English-trained Guyanan who was dean of the Commerce Department at Morris Brown College. Perry also recruited Jesse B. Blayton,* a professor of accounting at Atlanta University and the first black certified public accountant in Georgia, and Lorimer D. Milton,* a graduate of Brown University and professor of economics at Morehouse College. Blayton commented that Perry's "official staff . . . read like a blue book or social register of Negroes at the time."

As a result of Perry's enormous drive and charismatic personality, coupled with the highly competent staff he had assembled, Standard Life grew rapidly; Perry and his salesmen sold $400,000 worth of insurance in the first two weeks. He was even able to impress whites of his goals and purpose and attain their support. The *Atlanta Constitution*, which seldom even noticed doings in the black community at that time, was agog over Standard Life's prospects:

Nothing less than an epoch in the material history of the Southern Negro is comprised in the organization and chartering of Standard Life with H. E. Perry as president.... The launching of the company under these particular auspices is nothing less than a milestone in the upward history of the race. It illustrates what the Negro can do for himself.

Over the first ten years, Standard Life grew impressively, and by 1923 had increased its capital stock to $250,000, held assets of $2.25 million, had $6 million of ordinary life insurance in force, and had a cash income of $1 million that year, enabling it to pay 12 percent dividends on its stock.

Perry was hardly content with the success of Standard Life; he wanted to create a large, rationally integrated black business empire. Perry's first step was to organize The Service Company in 1917, with capital stock of $100,000 borrowed from the insurance company. Perry started in a small way with a laundry in Augusta, Georgia. Although there were some problems in the beginning, by 1919 it was thriving, and Perry set up a branch of the laundry in Atlanta. The Service Company devoted its energies almost exclusively to the laundry business until 1920, when Perry decided that it should focus on housing problems for blacks. Middle- and working-class blacks were forced to depend upon the "filtering process" for their housing. Restricted by discrimination and segregation to undesirable parts of the city, they got additional housing stock only when whites were through with it. As a result, it was usually substandard and dilapidated. As Homer Nash, a neighbor of Perry's, commented,

Up to Heman's time, if a Negro wanted a decent home to live in, he waited until some white person wanted to sell his. Then, Perry came along and showed that you didn't have to wait for a white man to die or get ready to sell his house. You can have a new one of your own. So he started building these houses.

Heman Perry focused his attention on an area west of downtown and of the Auburn Avenue district, near the Atlanta University complex. Buying 300 acres in this area, Perry set off what came to be known as the "West Side Boom" of 1923, as he began building some 500 new homes for blacks in the vicinity. Organizing a subsidiary known as Service Realty Company, to handle real estate purchases and sales, and Service Engineering and Construction Company, to handle the building of houses and other structures, Perry began a mammoth enterprise. Perry ultimately spent more than $600,000 to acquire land on the west side, and he sold lots to blacks for $350 if they were unimproved and $750 if they were improved. He also built homes that he sold to African-Americans for between $3,000 and $8,000. These bungalow-style homes were similar to those being built for whites in other parts of town.

C. C. Hart, a plumber who did a good deal of work on Perry's homes, recalled what it was like: "They'd go out and buy a piece of land, develop it and build homes and sell it to our people. I had a lot of that work, putting plumbing into new homes that they built. And our people started expanding, getting into these new homes." In 1922 Perry sold a portion of this land to the city as a site for

Booker T. Washington High School, the first public high school for blacks, and he won a $212,000 contract to build the Howard Junior High School for African-Americans.

Perry also played a part in getting the city to set up Washington Park, the first public park for blacks, on the west side. To the west of his housing development there was Mosley Park, which had a swimming pool for whites. Perry would pass by that area and comment, "I sure wish I could get that so my boys could swim there." He got Washington Park instead, and it became an important neighborhood and community resource on the west side. Estelle Clemmons, who lived in the area, recalled,

Everybody from across town and everywhere else came over to Washington Park. It was a place of recreation and the only park for blacks at that time, you see . . . we thought we had something when we could come to Washington Park, because there was a swimming pool there, and there was a pavillion where people used to dance during the week.

This enhancement of the lives of black Atlantans instigated by Heman Perry was not accepted without protest in the white community. Throughout the 1920s, the Ku Klux Klan and other white supremacists held rallies, burned crosses, used firebombings and other acts of violence in an attempt to intimidate the black families moving into this area. One former resident remembered, "The white people bombed a house right there at 333 Ashby Street one night. Colored people were living in it. Just a few of them sneaked back another time to bomb that house, and those colored people were waiting with guns and pistols, and they just went to shooting."

Perry had started a revolution in housing for blacks in Atlanta, and by 1940 fully 40 percent of the city's African-Americans were living on the west side. Even though both de jure and de facto segregation continued in Atlanta for decades, and much remains to the present day, Heman Perry was the first to provide large numbers of the city's blacks with a large stock of decent housing in areas formerly considered reserved for whites. The Empire Real Estate Board in Atlanta paid fitting tribute to Perry in 1958 when it proclaimed,

The most significant move toward better housing for Negroes started back in the early Twenties during the time of Heman Perry of the Standard Life and Service Company. Whatever errors of judgement or administration overtook this great combine . . . [t]he spirit and intent have never been liquidated, nor did it bankrupt the minds of Atlanta Negroes to reconstruct from their ashes a sounder foundation on which to build.

Another source said, "The opening of the West Side was the greatest single contribution to the improvement of living conditions in Atlanta for Negroes made in 25 years."

In addition to this massive real estate project, Perry developed a number of other enterprises as part of the Service Corporation. He set up the Service Printing Company, primarily to do in-house printing for Standard Life, but also to produce publications for churches and colleges throughout the southeast. He took over the failing Gate City Drug Company, which had two stores, one on the west side at Hunter and Ashby, and one at the corner of Butler and Auburn. The Service Farm Bureau was set up to deal with the problems black farmers were having with the boll weevil and with the agricultural depression of the early 1920s. It counseled them on growing more and better crops, and helped to facilitate the marketing of these crops. He also established the Service Foundation, which was to be an African-American version of the Carnegie and Rockefeller foundations. It gave substantial gifts to educational institutions, such as Meharry Medical College and Fisk University, and also made bequests to the community chest, YMCA, and other organizations.

One of the key elements of Perry's business empire was the creation of a bank. Unlike just about every other group of blacks who started an insurance company, Perry was relatively slow to establish a bank. It usually seemed like a natural move to the executives of insurance firms since there was a large cash flow coming into the company on a regular basis. Perry, however, retained the Standard Life deposits in Atlanta State Savings Bank. Atlanta's first black-owned bank, it had been started in 1909 by John Oliver Ross, a merchant and real estate broker. For some time, since Perry depended upon the goodwill of the city's black elite, it seemed important to keep Standard's deposits in Atlanta State Savings. In 1918, however, as Perry's vision for a new business empire began to take shape, he realized a bank was needed as a centerpiece.

In June 1918 Perry initiated stock sales for a new bank. After a three-year campaign, he had raised enough money to open the bank with capital of $250,000. He opened Citizens Trust as a full service bank for blacks, offering nearly every type of service to its customers. It engaged in commercial banking, savings, farm and business loans, discounts and collections, safety deposit vaults, liberty bonds, a woman's department, and administration of estates, and it acted as an agent for individuals and corporations. The massive deposits of Standard Life, of course, were placed in Citizens Trust, which severely weakened Atlanta Savings. The older bank was further weakened as others followed Perry's lead. Wheat Street Baptist Church withdrew $5,000, followed by Ebenezer Baptist Church's withdrawal of $10,000 in its building fund, forcing Atlanta State Savings to close.

Citizens Trust played a key role in Perry's business empire, as it allowed the use of Standard premiums to finance the buying of homes on the west side. The bank would ''act as a medium in lending funds for the building of homes from the reserves which the insurance company had piled up.'' By March 1923 Citizens Trust had deposits totaling over $469,000; there were 1,882 demand accounts, and 3,558 savings accounts. The bank held $1,132,845 in outstanding loans, a large number of them mortgages on real estate on the west side. It was by that time the largest black-owned banking institution in the country, and the provision of those banking services was vitally important to the blacks of Atlanta. The financing for the purchase of homes and capital for black businesses that Citizens Trust was providing was difficult, if not impossible, to get at white institutions.

Atlanta University professor Samuel Nabritt stated, "It didn't matter what the law said, you couldn't get it because nobody would give you the loan. They could restrict your living by simply economic control of money, where you borrowed." Perry's bank changed that, at least for a time.

In total, Perry's empire contained eleven firms at various times between 1917 and 1925, with an estimated value of around $11 million. At its peak in 1923, Perry's companies employed in excess of 2,500 people, which was about 2 percent of the black population of Atlanta. Perry also had visions of expanding this empire beyond Atlanta; he hoped to use his Atlanta model in other cities to create similar entrepreneurial endeavors. Perry envisioned creating nothing less than a self-sufficient national black economy. He was quoted in 1923 by the *Atlanta Independent*: "I am more convinced every day that the ultimate solution of our problem must rest upon the foundation of nationwide economic development." It was a grand vision, a noble dream, but overexpansion, mismanagement, and a number of other difficulties caused it to unravel quickly and tragically in 1924 and 1925.

Perry's magnificent plans, no matter how beneficial to the black community overall, placed an enormous financial drain on the resources of Standard Life. Perry's expansionist activities, and his "creative" financing schemes, had earlier caused dissension within the company, and Harry H. Pace, the secretary, had resigned in late 1919. Without Pace's restraining influence, Perry plunged headlong into ever more dangerous plans. A remarkably robust entity in 1922, with assets of $2 million, of which fully $900,000 was in cash, Standard Life was bled virtually dry by the real estate development demands of Service Realty. As J. B. Blayton wrote to W.E.B. Du Bois: "[T]he company resorted to the practice of making loans on real property in amounts beyond that permitted by law. This unsound investment policy (which proceeded under the guidance of white lawyers, actuaries, and accountants) led to another impairment considerably larger than the former." It therefore became necessary to increase the capital stock of Standard Life, and 1,250 new shares were issued at $300 per share, doubling the capital stock of the firm. Perry then had Service Company buy the entire issue, giving it a one-half ownership of Standard Life. Service Company, of course, did not have that kind of money, so Perry arranged for Citizens Trust to loan Service Company the cash to make the purchase.

This maneuver put a severe strain on the cash resources of Citizens Trust, and it did not have the necessary funds to meet its daily clearings. At that point, Perry approached the Southeastern Trust Company to furnish the funds needed by Citizens Trust. To secure the agreement, a large portion of the real property assets of Service Company were deeded in trust to the loan company. The president and attorney of that firm were then given the roles of executive managers of the Service Enterprises. This arrangement, however, did not solve the larger money problems. Southeastern provided Citizens Trust with small sums of from $2,000 to $5,000 at a time to meet emergencies, but it did not rectify the more serious problems. This became evident in 1924 when the Georgia Insurance

Department ruled that Standard Life was impaired. This ruling was based largely on the amount of real estate appearing among the insurance firm's assets, which was due to the high number of mortgages foreclosed by the company.

But Perry did not cut back, in fact, he proceeded to get involved in ever more expensive, and possibly corrupt, dealings. The most dramatic and controversial concerned Mississippi Life Insurance, the first black, old-line, legal reserve company. Mississippi Life had been organized in 1908 in Indianola, Mississippi, but it had struggled until 1917 when it moved its operations to Memphis, Tennessee. There the company had apparently flourished for a number of years under the guidance of Joseph E. Walker (see Walker Family). It had come under attack from a number of sources in 1922 and 1923, and despite having assets of reportedly more than $500,000, was in precarious condition. Heman Perry entered the scene with a check for $80,000, with which he bought out the company. At that point, Perry's empire was still intact and, to the outside observer, powerful and prosperous. So, Mississippi Life officials were willing to sell their company for the rather small amount offered by Perry in order to combine the supposedly enormous resources of Standard Life with those of Mississippi Life to create a large, impregnable, black ordinary life insurance company. In February 1924, however, Perry turned around and sold Mississippi Life to Southern Insurance Company of Nashville, a white-owned firm.

The oldest black-owned legal reserve firm in America had suddenly passed into white hands. The news of this development created a furor in Memphis and in black communities around the country, and Mississippi Life's black insurance agents, led by George W. Lee,[*] staged a revolt. Lee announced to the new owners: "We refuse to work for you, we will rather go back to the anvil and the forge, to the work bench, and to the cotton patches of Mississippi." Lee, who became an important leader of the black community in Memphis, was also bitter in his condemnation of Perry, saying that Nashville whites "had made Perry an unwitting dupe in their scheme to sap the black man's economic strength." When Perry went to Mississppi Life's home office in Memphis after committing what they viewed as an act of racial and financial treason, the company's displaced employees drove him out of town with spit, bottles, and threat of even greater bodily harm. This was merely a portent of what was to come for Perry.

Perry's Faustian deal with Southern Life did little to stave off collapse of his tottering empire. Unable to secure a loan from traditional lending sources, and with the failure of a coalition of prominent blacks headed by Atlanta Life's Alonzo Herndon to raise enough money to purchase Southeastern's share of Standard Life, Perry was forced on July 24, 1924, to make a second deal with Southeastern Trust, an arrangement one source has likened to "pawnbrokering." What Perry did was to sign a loan agreement assigning 51 percent of Standard Life stock (that portion owned by Service Company) absolutely to Southeastern Trust as security for a loan of $135,000. The loan had a term of six months, in which Southeastern agreed not to foreclose on Standard Life. This gave Perry an extension until December 15, 1924, on the life of his insurance company and crumbling business empire.

The pending demise of Standard Life energized the national forces of black America as had few previous incidents. John Hope issued a clarion call to blacks around the country to step forward to help the beleaguered enterprise, and a number of blacks responded. The most important plan was put in motion by Robert Russa Moton, head of the National Negro Business League and Booker T. Washington's successor at Tuskegee. Moton appealed to white philanthropist Julius Rosenwald for funds to save Standard Life, and in August 1924 he received provisional approval of funds totaling in excess of $400,000 coming from Rosenwald, John D. Rockefeller, and Trevor Arnett. There was just one catch—Heman Perry would have to step down as head of the enterprises—since they saw the need for "securing a qualified individual for management." They, in turn, asked Moton to take Perry's place. Perry would have none of this. Whether he was too proud to admit defeat, excessively optimistic about the future of his firm, or too egotistical concerning his own abilities to bring about a transformation, Perry turned his back on Standard Life's last chance at survival.

When Perry could not pay back the loan to Southeastern Trust in December, Southeastern foreclosed on Standard Life in January 1925, acquiring fee simple title to 51 percent of Standard Life stock. At the same time, as majority stockholder, it voted to merge Standard Life with Southern Life, the white Nashville firm Perry had sold Mississippi Life to a few months earlier. The agreement required that all of the assets of Standard Life, including a large amount of real estate, become part of the assets of the new Southern-Standard Life Insurance Company. Despite opposition from minority stockholders, the merger could not be stopped, and it was finalized on January 15, 1925. Southern Life, and white America, had gotten control of two of the oldest and largest African-American-owned legal reserve insurance companies within the space of a few months, all due to the actions of Heman Perry. Southern Life controlled Standard Life until the end of 1927, bled it virtually dry, and then transferred what was left of Standard Life's business to the National Benefit Life Insurance Company, which would itself be forced out of business in later years.

The effect of the death of Standard Life and the Perry empire on the nation's black community was devastating. As noted by the *Philadelphia Tribune*,

An organization is wrecked. An ideal is smashed. The Standard Life Insurance Company of Atlanta, Georgia, has floundered, wavered and crashed. The institution that was the pride, the joy of thousands of Negroes is no more. . . . The passing of the "Standard" is more than the failure of a big business institution. It means the shattering of hope and confidence.

The Chicago *Whip*, never a newspaper to exercise restraint, proclaimed: "White folk of the South took the Standard Life Insurance Company away from us: It was a thing of beauty, but now it is gone forever. . . . The future of black boys who had hoped to rise in this company was blighted, the hearts of those who put their money in it as a monument to their race hung heavy."

The outcry against Perry in Atlanta for allowing these precious companies to fall into white hands was intense, and he was soon shamed out of the city. A few years later, he resurfaced in Kansas City, where he attempted to start another insurance venture. He died, alone, a bachelor as he had been all his life, of heart failure. He was just fifty-five years old.

What had happened? Why had Perry's grand dreams and plans turned to dust so quickly? There were many theories afloat in the black community in the months and years after Standard Life's failure. For instance, a conspiracy theory held a great deal of credence among African-American business leaders. They believed that Perry's downfall was all part of a well-orchestrated plan on the part of whites to destroy all successful black businesses. This theory was especially occasioned by the involvement of John A. Copeland, a white who was with both state insurance agencies and Southeastern Trust. He also worked as an actuary for Standard Life and Southern Life, and was in a good position, at least so the theory went, to steer Perry's firm into compromising situations. Copeland himself blamed everything on Perry: "Standard Life was never impaired. It was sound as a rock. Perry was an excellent organizer but he was not a supervisor. He could not handle money. He ruled with iron hands. He was a dictator. Perry was an adventurer; he would make a debt to pay a debt."

Others saw the conspiracy as part of an economic war waged by the Ku Klux Klan to destroy the achievements of urban blacks. This accusation especially surfaced over the sellout of Mississippi Life to Southern Life. Several claimed that the "Klan's program was not only to intimidate the Negro with the rope and the torch, but also to strike at the foundations of his economic strength." And Eugene Martin, a rather sober, rational official of Atlanta Life, said, "I am absolutely sure that the failure of the Standard Life was down-right deliberately planned . . . to break down the confidence in Negro enterprises."

But most of Perry's own employees with Standard Life and his other enterprises thought it was Perry's own fault. L. D. Milton said, "Possibly the company would have been standing today if Mr. Perry had not disobeyed three laws: (1) the laws of expansion, (2) the business cycle, and (3) the law of capital structure." He criticized Perry for expanding too rapidly, for not paying more attention to trends in the broader economy, and for using up too much of the capital reserves in his program. Cyrus Campfield, an executive with Atlanta Life, agreed in part, saying, "One reason for Mr. Perry's failure was, he expanded too rapidly. The money his institutions handled was not large enough to cover the expenses. The Service Company was one of the main sources of his failure. Too much money was wasted." But Campfield also saw other factors: "Another reason why he failed is that he was influenced by certain white men to invest his assets in certain enterprises. He was encouraged to make the investments because they were supposed to have been 'get rich over-night' schemes." We may never know the whole truth about this.

Whatever the tragedy of Perry's fall and the loss and destruction of Standard Life, parts of his business empire continued to prosper under black control in

Atlanta. Citizens Trust, which later became Citizens Trust Bank, ended its affiliation with Perry in 1924, was reorganized and ultimately came under the control of Jesse Blayton, L. D. Milton, and Clayton R. Yates,* who ran it successfully for over fifty years. It still continues under African-American control in the 1990s. Service Printing was purchased by William Alexander Scott II,* who used it to finance the creation of the *Atlanta World* in 1928, and later built a chain of Southern black newspapers around it. Yates and Lorimer also bought the drugstore chain from Service Company, renaming it Yates and Milton Drugs, Inc., which was run successfully for decades. In fact, the Blayton-Lorimer-Yates combine used the remnants of Perry's business empire to build the dominant black business operation from the 1930s to the 1960s. Also, although Perry's vast real estate entity was not continued in any formal manner, he did give example to Walter A. "Chief" Aiken, who later became the most successful builder of multiple housing for blacks in America. Aiken himself claimed he was inspired by the work of Perry, as "the first man in Atlanta to buy subdivisions."

As passions cooled over the years, people were able to look back and reflect upon Heman Perry with a degree of detachment. His appraisal has gained stature with time. Cyrus Campfield, who was well aware of Perry's faults, nonetheless said,

It is no doubt about it, Mr. Perry was one of the greatest organizers I have ever known. I say now, and have said in the past, that if Mr. Perry had devoted all of his attention to insurance, Standard Life would have been one of the greatest organizations in existence today.

Dr. George A. Howell, who had been a member of the board of directors of Standard Life, remarked,

Mr. Perry was an earnest man. It never was his idea to hurt anyone. He was a gentleman in every respect, and was void of any veneer and glamor. Mr. Perry was one of the greatest optimists in the world. He was a great dreamer and was not afraid to venture into anything.

Olive Perry, somewhat embittered over the treatment of her brother in Atlanta, reflected some twenty years after his death: "The people of Atlanta do not give my brother credit for what he did. He encouraged Negroes of Atlanta to build better and more attractive homes."

This generally favorable assessment of Perry is shared by present-day analysts. Judy Simmons, in *Black Enterprise* magazine in 1978, summarized Perry as "the financial 'artist' of the Harlem Renaissance Era, a striver who didn't know his limits because he had already smashed all the orthodox boundaries of caste and class." Perry was, she concludes, "an intransigent black visionary." Alexa Henderson concurs, saying that "it is in large measure because of Heman Perry's efforts that Atlanta became a major center of business activity among African-Americans . . . he boldly initiated a grand design for economic development and attempted to realize it without access to adequate capital or sufficient credit to conduct activities on an expanding scale.'' Perry's passing at the end of the decade was the end of an era, and, according to Lerone Bennett, ''[T]he old spirit of daring, the old idea that black businessmen could create and manage billion-dollar enterprises, faded and was replaced by a new spirit of caution and even timidity.'' Heman Perry, a tragically flawed giant of African-American enterprise, appeared like a brilliant meteor across the skies of early twentieth-century America, nearly simultaneously stimulating hopes and smashing dreams for blacks all over the country.

Sources

There is no collection of Perry family papers, but there are some letters and other materials available in a number of sources. The records of Perry's various enterprises are not generally available. The richest source is perhaps the Thomas W. Jarrett Papers, which are privately held in Atlanta, Georgia. These, however, are not completely open to all researchers. There is a description of some of these materials in Thomas D. Jarrett, ''A Study toward a Biography of Heman E. Perry, Pioneer in Negro Business,'' in *Summaries of Research Projects, 1947–52*, edited by Nathaniel Tillman (Atlanta, 1953). There are also some interesting letters to and from Perry in the Booker T. Washington Papers at the Library of Congress and in the Robert Russa Moton Papers at Hollis Frissell Library, Tuskegee University. In addition, numerous helpful printed materials on Perry and Standard Life were collected by Comradge Leroy Henton for ''Heman E. Perry: Documentary Materials for the Life History of a Business Man,'' Master's thesis, Atlanta University, 1948. The Robert W. Woodruff Library, Atlanta University Center, Division of Archives, Special Collections has the *Standard Life Insurance Company Rate Book*, dated June 1921, a small handbook issued for agents of the company which has instructions regarding policies, rates, and so forth.

In addition, there are some published biographical materials on Perry that are helpful. The best is Alexa Benson Henderson, ''Heman E. Perry and Black Enterprise in Atlanta, 1908–1925,'' *Business History Review* 61 (Summer 1987), 216–42, which is based, in addition to the above-named sources, on a series of interviews conducted with people who knew and worked with Perry. See also a good business biography of Perry by Judy D. Simmons, ''Heman Perry: The Commercial Booker Washington,'' in *Black Enterprise* (April 1978), 41–48, which was reprinted later in *Atlanta World*, February 18 and 24, 1983. There was also an early biography of Perry in Clement Richardson's *National Cyclopedia of the Colored Race* (1919). There is a wealth of useful information on Standard Life and Citizens Trust, including Eric D. Walrond, ''The Largest Negro Commercial Enterprise in the World,'' *Forbes Magazine* 13 (February 1924), 503–5, which gives a wildly exaggerated account of Perry's career and the development of Standard Life; *Pittsburgh Courier*, July 15, 1961; Merah Steven Stewart, *An Economic Detour: A History of Life Insurance in the Lives of Negroes* (New York, 1940); and Harry H. Pace, ''A New Business Venture,'' *Crisis* 8 (January 1914), 143. Pace also gave an address before the Annual Meeting of the National Negro Business League, 1913, in Philadelphia, in which he gave extensive information concerning the goals and ambitions of Perry and Standard Life. Bobby J. Lamar, ''Citizens Trust Company and Its Role in the Development of the Atlanta Black Community with Emphasis on the Loan Function,'' Master's thesis, Atlanta University, 1969, is a study of those aspects of the bank. There is also some helpful material in George Washington Lee, *Beale Street: Where the Blues*

Began (New York, 1934); David M. Tucker, *Lieutenant Lee of Beale Street* (Nashville, 1971); and T. J. Johnson, *From the Driftwood of Bayou Pierre* (1949), which covers Perry and Standard Life's role in the takeover of Mississippi Life by Southern Insurance Company from the perspective of Joseph E. Walker, the young head of Mississippi Life and later the dynamic founder of Memphis' Universal Life Insurance.

Some additional materials on Perry and his enterprises can be found in the Peabody Collection of Hampton University, which is available on microfilm. See the category, Negro Insurance and Real Estate. Some of the relevant articles include *American Baptist*, May 30, 1913; *Norfolk Journal and Guide*, July 31, 1915; *New York World*, February 10, 1920; *Nashville Globe*, July 23, 1920; and *Atlanta University Bulletin*, November 1916. See also the *Atlanta Independent*, January 18, 1919; and *Atlanta World*, August 18, 1937, and June 18, 1976; *Crisis* 10 (June 1915), 65–66, and 25 (January 1923); and *Afro-American*, May 7, 1932.

Pettiford, William Reuben (January 20, 1847–September 21, 1914). Educator, pastor, businessman, banker, realtor, race leader: Sixteenth Street Baptist Church and Alabama Penny Savings and Loan Company. The once vibrant black business district of Birmingham, Alabama, is no longer the thriving community it was. The now rundown buildings sit vacant, and the absence of pedestrian street life is glaringly evident. No longer does Birmingham have a vital black business district where the city's blacks once congregated and patronized their own race's theaters, cafes, hotels, and other business establishments. When Birmingham, "the Magic City," emerged from the cornfields in 1871 at the proposed intersection of the Alabama & Chattanooga Railroad and the South & North Railroad, it rapidly rose to the status of a bold new boomtown. Coal, iron ore, and limestone lay in the hills and villages of northern Alabama, and it was on the foundations of these natural resources that Birmingham's economy flourished.

Blacks gravitated to this emerging urban center from the rural regions in search of employment. The large white-owned coal, iron, and steel companies (and one small, black, coal mining company owned by Reverend T. W. Walker) were keen to employ cheap, unskilled labor, and blacks provided the ideal source of labor for the grueling jobs within this industry. With the rapid industrialization of this region, the population increased dramatically. By 1890 blacks constituted 43 percent of Birmingham's population, and in 1910 and 1920 they made up 39 percent—the highest black percentage of any American city with a population exceeding 100,000. Their presence was evident most noticeably in factories, where they made up 90 percent of the unskilled labor. Although their pay could never be considered generous, it was the first time that many of these workers had ever earned even meager wages. Thrift was a virtue that rarely needed consideration, since survival was their overriding concern. For these people to enhance their lot in life, they needed to be educated in matters of finance and planning for the future. The person who accepted this mission was William R. Pettiford.

William Reuben Pettiford was born in Granville County, North Carolina. His parents, William, a farmer, and Matilda Pettiford, were free blacks, a status which was inherited by their children. When William was ten years old, his father sold the farm, and the family moved to Person County, North Carolina, where he purchased another. William, the eldest of the four offspring, was denied the opportunity to attend school since he had responsibilities on the farm. Although young Pettiford worked diligently for long hours during the day, in the evenings he recruited his siblings to provide him with a rudimentary education which was supplemented with instruction he received from a district school-teacher who boarded with the family. William early on showed entrepreneurial tendencies while working on his father's horse farm. At seventeen, he bought his first pig from his brother, and with a parcel of land that his father had granted him, he raised hogs which he then sold at a profit. The accumulated savings from this business venture, in addition to a tanning enterprise, were without value at the close of the Civil War.

At twenty years of age Pettiford was hired to work in a tobacco factory in Roxbury, North Carolina. After a few years, he left the factory out of sheer boredom and began to engage in a variety of low-paying jobs. As a young man, Pettiford had been interested in the church, but in the summer of 1868 he went through an intense conversion experience and was baptized by Ezekiel Horton of Salisbury, North Carolina. When employed as a clerk at the Pleasant Grove Baptist Church in Roxbury, Pettiford "heard the calling" and decided to pursue a vocation of pastoral work. The wages he received were insufficient to sustain him and his wife, Mary Jane Farley, whom he had married in 1869. In response to a letter he sent out in search of employment, Pettiford was offered a job helping to build a railway in Marion, Alabama, but he refused the position. By this time, however, he had already relocated in Marion, so Pettiford took a one-year contract to work on a farm near Uniontown, Alabama. At the end of the year, his wife Mary died. Pettiford enrolled at the Marion Normal School, and he continued studying there for seven years. He pursued knowledge during the winters and continued working summers to support his studies. During this time Pettiford also became a school principal for four years in Uniontown.

Following the death of his second wife, Jennie Powell, in September 1874, Pettiford continued teaching while pursuing his education. When he was hired in the winter of 1877–1878 as an assistant teacher by the board at Selma University, Pettiford studied theology at the Baptist Normal Theological School for three years. He had a deep-seated commitment to building a school and providing an education for aspiring young ministers in Alabama. Pettiford engaged in missionary work for Selma University, vigorously recruiting students and collecting monies. He proved himself a committed teacher and financial agent. When he was called to ordination by the Berean Baptist Church in Marion, Pettiford resigned after only one year, to accept the pastorate of a church at Union Springs, Alabama. He moved there with his third wife, Della Boyd, whom he had married in September 1880, to assume his new position at the pastorate and to take on the duties of principal of the public school. In 1883 he accepted a lower salaried position (than he had held in Union Springs) with the

Sixteenth Street Baptist Church in Birmingham, Alabama. Pettiford was urged by the leaders of the state (perhaps Booker T. Washington* had been instrumental in this recruitment, since documentation reveals a close relationship between him and Pettiford) to accept this post because they felt he could provide the necessary guidance to Birmingham's rapidly growing black population. Pettiford accepted when he was convinced that Birmingham was a place where people could more substantially benefit from his leadership.

Birmingham was a young, raw, frontier city in the early 1880s, and its black population was composed exclusively of migrants from elsewhere, mostly young men and women barely two decades removed from slavery. Already, however, a significant black business community was coalescing there. The key figure in the early development of black Birmingham was Reverend Thomas Walker. Walker was a former slave and a preacher who, by 1881, had already founded several black churches in the community. As a pastor, Walker was often called upon to assist his congregants in financial matters that affected their general welfare. Deciding that the black community was in dire need of its own business institutions, Walker organized a coal company, a brick manufacturing concern, a shoe store, a drugstore, a livery stable, a funeral home, and a cemetery. Deciding something else was needed to make black families more self-sustaining economically, Walker also organized a bank and a mutual aid association. Called the Afro-American Benevolent Association, it was a small, church-related organization.

In December 1894, however, the Afro-American Benevolent Association was expanded into a full-fledged business enterprise, the Union Central Relief Association of Birmingham. Designed to provide burial insurance for the black community in Birmingham, and later in all of Alabama, it grew rapidly. In February 1901, Union Central became the first black insurance association to be chartered officially in Alabama. Also, in 1897, Walker expanded the firm's business into Georgia, organizing the Union Mutual Relief Association of Atlanta, the first to be so-chartered in that state. These were both thriving organizations for a number of years. The Georgia branch finally ran into financial difficulties in 1915 and was sold to Alonzo Franklin Herndon's* Atlanta Life Insurance Company. Then, in the early 1930s, reeling from the Depression, Union Central Relief in Birmingham was also taken over by Atlanta Life.

In 1883, when Pettiford arrived in Birmingham, he assumed responsibility of 150 congregants who convened in a downtown storeroom. The informal organization was burdened by a debt of $500, which Pettiford had eliminated by 1884. His congregation grew rapidly, as he was a pastor committed to the betterment of his parishioners. At that time Pettiford also invested the accumulated monies of $14,000 from the building fund in a new building. Pettiford proved to be a progressive clergyman from 1883 to 1893, and in 1892 he held the presidency of the Baptist State Convention of Alabama. However, his most significant contributions, according to the available literature, were as an astute businessman. In 1890, when Reverend W. W. Browne,* president of the Savings

Bank of the Grand Fountain United Order of True Reformers of Richmond, Virginia, announced that he intended to open a branch of his bank in Birmingham, the local black business leaders responded quickly. Pettiford, with the assistance of the Negro Progressive Association, a business club of Birmingham, convened to address the issue. In response to Browne's designs, the Birmingham cooperative asserted that they were better equipped to serve the blacks of their own city.

A nucleus of Birmingham's black leaders—J. O. Diffay, N. B. Smith, A. H. Parker, T. W. Walker, Peter F. Clarke and B. H. Hudson—united to organize a bank. Without having investigated the laws fully, these leaders issued capital stock of $25,000 in shares of $25 each, elected a board of directors, and leased a building for three years at $30 per month. After a brief financial setback, the Alabama Penny Savings and Loan Company finally opened on October 15, 1890. During the postponement of the opening, it was decided that rather than abandon the project, and thus risk the loss of the confidence of the people they were hoping to serve, they would organize under the common law and operate as a private bank. When the bank opened, with Pettiford in place as president, there were just three other black banks in the United States.

Although Browne's inquiries had provided an impetus for Birmingham's black leaders to commence a banking institution, Pettiford's primary stimulus derived from Birmingham's blacks themselves. From the time he had accepted the pastorate at the the Sixteenth Street Baptist Church, Pettiford had been sensitive to the plight of the people of his race. Waves of blacks had migrated to Birmingham during its emergence as a boomtown in 1871 in search of employment, and although they received only meager wages for their labor, they often squandered those monies that briefly lined their pockets. Pettiford had noticed that his people were being denied their due rights in matters of property transfers, loans, and so forth, and so he took corrective action. The bank emerged as a bank for the people, where they could deposit their savings confidently. Pettiford recognized the need for an institution that could assist the unfortunate and provide instruction on the value of thrift and investment. Thus, Alabama Penny Savings, as was true of many other black business ventures, was a mixture of profit seeking and race betterment.

The panic of 1893 challenged not only the stability of the Alabama Penny Savings Bank, but all of the banks in the United States. One hundred ten banks closed their doors during this time. Birmingham felt the effects of this depression when one of the national banks failed to cash a check of $82,000 drawn by the Tennessee Railroad and Mining Company, which forced the bank to close permanently. Consequently, many depositors, black and white, panicked out of fear of losing their savings. The Penny Savings Bank was able to withstand the pressure and emerged unscathed. This success enamored the bank to the community, particularly when it opted to pay out cash rather than certificates, which other banks had done to weather the storm. Pettiford recalled, ''Being able to survive the panic was a good investment for us. It gave us the confidence of the people that, perhaps, we should not have gained in any other way.''

In 1895 the bank was incorporated by a special act of the Alabama state legislature with a capital stock of $25,000 and the privilege of increasing it to $100,000. During the bank's first decade, Pettiford engineered numerous real estate transactions that proved to be highly insightful and lucrative. In 1896 the bank bought a building for $6,500 and sold it one year later for $20,000. Pettiford also bought a house for $18,000 and sold it for $35,000 a few years later. The bank built its own home in 1913, which became a symbol of black pride and sophistication for Birmingham's African-American community. The impressive building was designed by Wallace A. Rayfield, a prominent architect in Birmingham, and was erected by the firm of Windham Construction Company, owned by T. C. Windham, both of whom had also participated in the erection of the Sixteenth Street Baptist Church. Both of these individuals were African-Americans, which is a testament to the fact that Pettiford practiced what he preached, namely the importance of building a self-sufficient black community whereby the members of the community patronize their own institutions. By contracting the work to Rayfield and Windham, Pettiford offered a tangible example of his philosophy.

Despite the tense racial climate of the South during the 1890s, the bank and Pettiford maintained positive relations with the white banks of Birmingham. Pettiford determined that the good relations between the races was based on the fact that the white banking community did not feel threatened by the Alabama Penny Savings Bank. He even went so far as to suggest that the black banks benefited the white financial institutions in several ways. The Penny Savings Bank took an aggressive advertising approach that emphasized the merits of thrift, which apparently reached lower class whites also. He also believed that the creation of his bank allowed white financial institutions to focus on servicing the white community, a component of the city's population which they were more in tune. Over the course of the Alabama Penny Savings' life, it's white counterparts on several occasions offered assistance—they provided training for the bank's first employees and even offered financial aid.

In 1900 Booker T. Washington established the National Negro Business League to unite African-Americans engaged in business for the purpose of sharing their experiences and to stimulate entrepreneurial pursuits. This forum provided Washington with the opportunity to further promote his basic philosophy of self-help: it was essential for blacks to lay down an economic foundation on which to uplift the entire race. Early on, Pettiford had expressed similar sentiments when he and others established the Alabama Penny Savings Bank. Pettiford's primary focus was on laborers, the working class, and the common men and women. He believed that, with the proper education, these African-Americans would adopt the virtues of saving and investment propounded by Washington.

In the proceedings of the several business-oriented meetings in which Pettiford participated—the Hampton conferences and the National Negro Business League sessions—his commitment to the philosophy of self-help is clearly evident. In 1903, at the seventh Hampton Negro Conference, Pettiford's address entitled, "The Importance of Business to the Negro," stressed this concept: "[N]o substantial progress can come to any race unless the race is developed in a very large degree along business lines." He also emphasized the essential concept of race pride, whereby blacks must patronize businesses of their own race in order to perpetuate the financial growth and longevity of these enterprises. It is apparent from the proceedings of several NNBL meetings that Pettiford played a prominent, though little-recognized, role among the African-American business communities across the United States. His accounts of Birmingham's black response to his "teachings" illustrate the success of what he identified as his "missionary work." Pettiford was a strong advocate for homeownership and, at the sixth annual NNBL convention in 1905, Pettiford boasted that of 8,000 depositors, 1,000 owned homes, and the overwhelming majority were black. During the same year, the aggregate amount of deposits with the bank equalled $709,277. He also estimated that 90 percent of the depositors had never taken advantage of the services any previous bank offered, and that some of the depositors had mobilized themselves with the assistance of bank loans to open small businesses. Pettiford's personal ambitions were being realized.

In 1906 Pettiford helped create the National Negro Bankers' Association "to foster and encourage the establishment of banks among our people and to look after the interests and welfare of those already organized." As he articulated during one of the organization's meetings, "The man who controls your money will dictate where you must stand." His persistent belief in the necessity and importance of black banks was illustrated during the NNBL's thirteenth convention when he referred to banking institutions as "the practical means of financial self-defense." By that, he meant that such institutions ensure that blacks are supported in their endeavors to erect schools and churches and businesses which, he believed, were seen by all individuals as signs of racial progress. Pettiford clearly envisioned the role of the bank as multifaceted: to provide financial assistance, to educate the masses in areas of thrift and investment, to furnish the race with training in jobs relating to banking, and to encourage a sense of unity and cooperation in the black community.

William Pettiford had been forced to resign his pastorate during the early years of the bank when he was urged to accept the presidency permanently. In response to his decision, he protested, "I'm still a preacher." Evidently he always considered his missionary work for the bank as an extension of his duties as a clergyman. His scheme to establish a trust to reach out beyond Birmingham manifested itself in the creation of branches of the Alabama Penny Savings Bank. Although Pettiford never achieved the expansive network of branch banks across the country when the Alabama state legislature passed a law prohibiting the further extension of them, he, nevertheless, opened branches in Selma, Montgomery, and Anniston. Despite the restrictions imposed on realizing his dream,

Pettiford's influence was far-reaching. He published pamphlets, wrote newspaper articles, and went on tour to different cities lecturing his philosophy. By October 1911, the Alabama Penny Savings Bank had resources of $421,596.51. It was thriving, and was capable of paying 4 percent interest on savings accounts and offering shares in the company for $5 each.

At the time of William Pettiford's death on September 21, 1914, Alabama Penny Savings Bank was the largest, strongest, African-American-owned bank in the United States, with a capitalization of $100,000 and an annual business exceeding $500,000. The bank's last flush of prosperity came when it absorbed the Prudential, a rival black bank. That acquisition, coupled with a surge of unemployment in the steel and mining industries of the city, spelled its doom. Perhaps if Pettiford were still alive, and able to exert his influence and tap into his established networks in the white banking community, Alabama Penny Savings might have survived. But that was not to be. Long-term loans to churches and individuals necessitated the freezing of assets, and heavy withdrawals at Christmas time and the inability to make customary loans from a large bank in Birmingham resulted in the permanent closing of the Alabama Penny Savings Bank on December 23, 1915, after providing service to the black community for twenty-five years. The Grand Lodge Knights of Pythias bought the bank's building which was ultimately sold to A. G. Gaston,* the high-profile African-American entrepreneur.

Pettiford served as the bank's president for twenty-three years, and prior to his death he was president of the National Negro Bankers' Association and a director in the National Economic League. He was also instrumental, in 1901, in establishing Industrial High School (later renamed Parker High School), the first high school for blacks in Birmingham. This institution continues as a source of race pride into the 1990s. Pettiford was president of the Ministerial Association in Birmingham and of the Negro American Publishing Company which published the *Negro American Journal*, and he had many other affiliations. He garnered respect from blacks and whites alike, which was evident in the overwhelming numbers who paid their respects at his funeral service. It is estimated that, at the time of his death, Pettiford was one of the wealthiest African-Americans in Alabama.

Although Pettiford succeeded in reaching numerous individuals and could boast of assisting black-owned grocery stores, drugstores, undertaking establishments, and mutual aid associations to thrive in Birmingham, many of these enterprises were short lived. By 1935, when the Department of Commerce issued a census report, Birmingham ranked fourteenth, among the fifteen U.S. cities with 50,000 or more blacks, in the number of retail stores operated by blacks. Sixty-eight fewer stores were operated by blacks in Birmingham in 1935 than in 1929.

The decline came to a halt in the 1940s and 1950s. The black business district enjoyed a renewed activity whereby new businesses were operating and thriving to such a degree that Danny Holloway, a Birmingham barber reminisced, ''We had more business than we knew what to do with. This was the only place we had to come. All the movies, all the clubs, all the restaurants, everything was here'' (*Birmingham Post-Herald*, July 14, 1987). However, when integration came, black customers ceased to patronize black businesses. The migration of middle-class blacks to the suburbs also contributed to the ultimate disintegration of the once-bustling black business community between 16th and 18th streets on Third, Fourth, and Fifth avenues.

In 1981 Birmingham's African-American community was attempting to revitalize the downtown community and was pressuring the city's government to redevelop the black business community as well as the white, uptown business district. Their success is questionable, given the results of a 1987 national survey that counted the number of black-owned firms in metropolitan areas of 100,000 or more black residents. Birmingham was at the bottom of the list in terms of the percentage of these firms. Birmingham's black business community, by the late 1980s, was bemoaning the absence of leadership, particularly the inability to provide the community with a sense of unity and organization.

William R. Pettiford had the qualities Birmingham urgently needs in the 1990s. A historical marker honoring him stands in the vestibule of the Sixteenth Street Baptist Church—a reminder of the valuable contributions this leader provided for the African-American community. Where is the desperately needed leader who can stimulate black entrepreneurship in Birmingham today?

Sources

There are no personal or business papers remaining of Pettiford. Some of the Alabama Penny Savings Bank are in private hands. A few biographical resources are available to researchers, including the following: C. O. Boothe, *The Cyclopedia of the Colored Baptists of Alabama* (Birmingham, 1895); *Who's Who of the Colored Race* (1915); William J. Simmons, *Men of Mark* (1887), 460–65; G. F. Richings, *Evidences of Progress among Colored People* (1896); and Booker T. Washington, *The Negro in Business* (1907), 126–37, which was compiled with the assistance of those included in the volume. A brief account of Pettiford and his role in the bank and its success can be found in the Edweena Reed and Dr. Charles A. Brown, ''Ceremony of Dedication of a Historical Marker in Honor of Dr. W. R. Pettiford,'' February 1, 1979, held at the Birmingham Public Library; August Meier, *Negro Thought in America, 1880–1915* (Ann Arbor, Mich. 1966), 143. *The Journal of Negro History* XIV (1929) offers a retrospective on Pettiford and the bank. See also ''The Negro as a Business Man,'' *World's Work* XVI, 2 (June 1908). Obituaries appear in the *Nashville Globe*, October 25, 1914; the *Birmingham News*, September 20 and 21, 1914; and a laudatory tribute to Pettiford's rise to prominence appears in Clement Richardson, ''The 'Nestor of Negro Bankers,' '' *The Southern Workman* XLIII, 11 (November 1914), 607–11. There is also a small amount of information in Harry H. Pace, ''The Business of Banking among Negroes,'' *The Crisis,* February 1916, 186.

A few examples of Pettiford's writings include ''How to Help the Negro to Help Himself,'' *Southern Workman,* XXX (November 1901), 387–89; and his *God's Revenue System* (n.d.). Both the *Hampton Conference Proceedings* and the *National Negro Business League Proceedings* are available at Hampton University, and the following cited articles provide insight into Pettiford's philosophy and business practices: ''The Importance of Business to the Negro," *Hampton Negro Conference*, no. VII (Hampton, July 1903), 38–40; "Growth of Banking Business," *Proceedings of the Sixth National Negro Business League* (New York City, 1905); "History of the Alabama Penny Savings Bank," *Proceedings of the Seventh National Negro Business League* (Atlanta, 1906); *Proceedings of the Eighth National Negro Business League* (Topeka, 1907); "The Work of a Bank as an Agent in Developing the Many Interests of the Race," *Proceedings of the Thirteenth National Negro Business League* (1912), in which other bankers also offer personal accounts; and "The Negro Banker," *Proceedings of the Fourteenth National Negro Business League* (Philadelphia, 1913). Numerous letters of correspondence between Washington and Pettiford appear in the Booker T. Washington Papers, including reels 67, 115, 166, and 295, held at the Library of Congress.

A pamphlet of the Alabama Penny Savings and Loan Company (no imprint, n.d.) can be found in the Booker T. Washington Papers. The Peabody Collection at Hampton University contains numerous newspaper clippings (some of which are lacking complete citation information) on blacks in business, including the *Informer* (Urbana), April 1908; the *Freeman* (Indianapolis), February 22, 1908; and the *Reformer*, March 7, 1908.

Pinchback, Pinckney Benton Stewart (May 10, 1837–December 21, 1921). Politician, businessman, and editor: *New Orleans Louisianian*, Mississippi River Packet Company. P.B.S. Pinchback could have been Andrew Carnegie's double. Very light skinned, short, with straight white hair and a full, trimmed beard, Pinchback not only could easily have passed for white, he probably could have convinced most of the people in America at the turn of the century that he was the dynamic Scotsman. Pinchback also shared Carnegie's penchant for verbosity and oratorical flourish, and both had a dash of the flamboyant. Carnegie, of course, has gone down in history as one of the greatest of America's entrepreneurs, while Pinchback is largely forgotten. But there was a time in the 1870s when the two men, Carnegie in Pennsylvania and Pinchback in Louisiana, were working veritable revolutions on their respective societies. Most southerners, at least, probably would have bet that Pinchback was the more important—not better—just more important. Although Pinchback had significance as a businessman, it was as a politician that he made his greatest mark, and political involvement brought him most of his economic success.

Pinchback was born near Macon, Georgia, the son of Major William Pinchback, a white plantation owner, and Eliza Stewart, of mixed African, Indian, and Caucasian ancestry. From the time Eliza had been a young slave on the elder Pinchback's plantation in Virginia, she had been his favorite, and by 1836 she had borne him eight children. Major Pinchback decided that he wanted to move to the rich delta lands in Mississippi. He purchased extensive acreage in Holmes, Mississippi, but before he moved there, he decided to emancipate Eliza. That meant that any other children born to her would also be free. While en route to Mississippi P.B.S. Pinchback was born, and he inherited his mother's newly granted free status.

Young Pinchback received rudimentary training on the plantation, but at an early age he displayed a good deal of intelligence and ability. As a result, in

1846, when he was nine, Pinchback and his older brother, Napoleon, were sent to Gilmore's High School in Cincinnati, Ohio, to further their education. Pinchback remained there a year and one-half before returning to the Mississippi plantation when his father took ill. Major Pinchback died soon after, and the administrator of the estate, realizing that the major's relatives, who had already "purloined their inheritance," would try to re-enslave Eliza and her children, instructed them to flee to Cincinnati. Shortly after arriving there, Napoleon became mentally unstable and was placed in an asylum. Thus, at age twelve, P.B.S. Pinchback became the sole provider for his family.

Displaying the kind of energy and ingenuity that would characterize his later career, Pinchback found employment as a cabin boy on canal boats operating on the Miami, Toledo, and Fort Wayne canals. From there, he began working on steamboats plying the Mississippi River, where he toiled from 1854 to 1862. During this time he learned to gamble and become a con man, but also rose to the position of steward, the highest an African-American could obtain on a riverboat in those days. It was his experience with the "rough trade" who frequented these boats, however, that would haunt his later career.

Pinchback's introduction to the world of gamblers and card sharks came from George Devol, one of the most infamous of the breed. The two men met in a riverboat barbershop, and the elder man, immediately attracted to young "Pinch," made him his protégé. As Devol later recalled in his memoirs: "He was my boy. I raised him, and trained him. I took him out of a steamboat barbershop. I instructed him in the mysteries of card-playing, and he was an apt pupil." Devol taught Pinchback seven-up and poker, taught him how to throw monte, and also showed him how to be a confidence man, taking financial advantage of the black roustabouts on the boats. Devol remembered, "We sent Pinch to open a game of chuck-a-luck with the niggers on deck, while we opened up monte in the cabin." Pinch also acted as the personal manservant to Devol and another gambler, "Canada Bill" Jones. In the nineteenth century, the term "riverboat gambler" was often used to characterized any shifty, dishonest person. P.B.S. Pinchback was a riverboat gambler, and his later critics never let him forget it.

Because of this background, many rumors later circulated about Pinchback's romantic life during these years. How much is fact and how much fiction is impossible to know. Certainly by all accounts it was a bawdy and boisterous life on the river, and Pinchback fully participated in that life-style. According to legend, he was married once before 1860, at the point of a shotgun, but that union was later dissolved. He also supposedly had relationships with other women, one of whom he impregnated, and whose brother attacked him with a knife. In 1860, however, he met Nina Emily Hawthorne, a young girl of sixteen. They were married in that year; the union produced six children, and despite rumors of affairs that Pinchback had with a number of other women over the years, their marriage lasted until their deaths. A grandson of Pinchback was Jean Toomer, the famous poet and writer.

By 1862 Pinchback had advanced to the position of steward on the boats, but the Civil War was raging, and New Orleans had just fallen to Union troops. In May of that year Pinchback decided to jump ship at Yazoo City, and he headed for New Orleans, where he was determined to volunteer to fight for the Union cause. Shortly after his arrival, he was attacked by his knife-wielding brother-in-law on the street for reasons that have never been revealed. Pinchback pulled his own knife, stabbed his assailant, was arrested, and spent two months in the workhouse.

Pinchback finally secured his release and then volunteered to serve in the First Louisiana Volunteer Infantry, a white regiment. Shortly thereafter, an executive order from President Abraham Lincoln authorized the employment of "persons of African descent" in the armed services, and Pinchback was assigned the task of recruiting black volunteers. Within a week, Pinchback had organized the "Corps d'Afrique," and he was made a captain in charge of Company A. Trouble soon developed. Pinchback had intended that the units be composed of black enlisted men commanded by African-American officers, but the blacks he recruited for the latter positions could not pass the qualifying exams and were replaced by white officers. Only Pinchback among the blacks was found qualified. He raged against this injustice, but military officials turned a deaf ear. Finally, in September 1863, Pinchback tendered his resignation, saying, "I find nearly all the officers inimical to me and I can foresee nothing but dissatisfaction and discontent, which will make my position very disagreeable indeed."

That action coincided with Pinchback's decision to become actively involved in the campaign for political rights for blacks in the city. On November 5, 1863, Pinchback addressed a meeting of "Free Colored Citizens" at the New Orleans Economy Hall. He demanded that blacks, as a matter of right, be given the vote, but he did not ask for social equality. If they had political rights, Pinchback reasoned, they could be men, and they could also fight in the war with renewed zeal. A short time later, Pinchback approached General Nathaniel P. Banks for permission to raise a company of black troops, and that request was granted. Pinchback spent $1,000 of his own money to recruit the company, and by the middle of November he had a full complement of free black men. When it came time to get the commission, however, it was not approved. Disheartened and discouraged, Pinchback gave up all attempts to serve the Union Army in Louisiana.

In 1865 Pinchback headed north to Washington, D.C., intending to visit President Lincoln to promote the cause of black political rights. While he was there, however, Lincoln was assassinated, and Pinchback left the capital, going to Alabama, where he gave speeches to recently freed black audiences in a number of cities and towns and advocated adherence to Radical Republican principals. In all, Pinchback remained in Alabama for two years, trying to decide his future course of action. Following the enactment of the Reconstruction Acts in Louisiana in 1867, however, Pinchback decided to return to that state to establish his permanent home in New Orleans, since that city had become a mecca for ambitious blacks. There, Pinchback entered the political arena, where he soon received recognition as an astute and shrewd politician.

Pinchback made his most important move on April 9, 1867, when he organized the Fourth Ward Republican Club to serve as a political base, reportedly the first black political organization in Louisiana. As leader of this organization, Pinchback was elected a delegate to the state constitutional convention in September 1867 where he played a prominent role in drafting the new state constitution. Pinchback's most significant contribution was the drafting of a civil rights article, which granted to African-Americans equal rights and privileges on common carriers and in public and private places of business. Pinchback emerged as the champion of this bill, and soon he acquired a reputation as the foremost champion of black rights in the state. He also worked for passage of articles establishing free, tax-supported schools, universal suffrage, and other such measures. By the time the convention ended in March 1868, Pinchback had emerged as one of the most important figures in Louisiana's fledgling Republican party. He particularly impressed Henry Clay Warmoth, a young native of Illinois who had come to New Orleans in 1865, and who became the Republican candidate for governor in 1868.

In the election of 1868, Warmoth won the governor's office, with Oscar J. Dunn, a black ex-slave, as his lieutenant governor. Pinchback, with Warmoth's backing, ran as Radical Republican candidate for the state senate in the Second District. Pinchback, however, found he had been defeated by his opponent, 899 to 819. Charging fraud, Pinchback immediately called for a recount. When the new Republican (and largely black) legislature sat, they decided in Pinchback's favor, and he was seated. This was the beginning of a pattern for Pinchback in all succeeding elections: He would be defeated by a close vote, would call for a recount, and the decision would be made, either in his favor or against him, largely on the basis of political considerations rather than on an actual investigation of the charges. In the end, he lost more races than he won.

Upon taking his seat in the legislature, Pinchback was involved in two situations that helped to shape his future political career. First of all, he was shot at on the street by S. C. Morgan, a mulatto opponent of the Warmoth administration. Pinchback returned the fire, and both antagonists were arrested by police. Pinchback, however, was immediately released, and the white Democratic newspapers in the city had a field day with his predicament. Pinchback was enraged, and he gave a speech in the legislature the next day that was reputed to be the most incendiary in its history. Blacks, he said, had reached the end of their patience. He refuted the slanders in the press, and at the climax of the speech, he exclaimed, "The next outrage of the kind which they [white Democrats] commit will be the signal for the dawn of retribution, of which they had not yet dreamed—a signal that will cause ten thousand torches to be applied to this city; for patience will then have ceased to be a virtue and this city will be reduced to ashes.''

His speech shocked the press and white Louisianians, who took this as proof of "the utter unfitness of this class of which Pinchback is a type to be Senators and rulers in the land." It was also contended that his speech, delivered in early September, sparked an escalation of violence against blacks, and was ultimately one of the root causes of the disastrous riot in October of that year. On the other hand, unlike the riot of 1866, when armed whites attacked defenseless blacks at will, in this altercation blacks armed themselves with guns and axes and took to the streets attacking every white person in sight. Pinchback by then was a major leader of the Republican party and one of the two most prominent blacks in the state, but he was also a lightning rod for massive white resentment against Reconstruction and black political involvement that was building in Louisiana. Warmoth, his patron, recognized these two sides to Pinchback, calling him "a restless, ambitious man . . . [who] had more than once arrayed himself against me. He was a free lance and dangerous and had to be reckoned with at all times."

In 1869 Pinchback began to expand his interests from politics to include business. On April 19, he and C. C. Antoine,* a colleague in the senate, opened a factorage concern in New Orleans called Pinchback and Antoine. Located at 114 Carondelet Street, the partnership was a success and lasted for several years, until the two men had a falling out over other matters. On December 25 of that same year, Pinchback and Antoine founded the *New Orleans Louisianian*, a semiweekly paper. After about two and a half years, Antoine left the paper, and Pinchback continued to run it until 1881.

The *Louisianian* not only served as Pinchback's own personal political mouthpiece, but also became an important organ of the black race in the state. The paper's masthead proclaimed its political orientation: "Republican At All Times, and Under All Circumstances." Pinchback and his editor, William G. Brown, stated the goals and ideals of the paper in the first editorial: "We shall advocate the security and enjoyment of broad civil liberty, the absolute equality of all men before the law, and an impartial distribution of honor and patronage to all who merit them." The *Louisianian* also advocated a policy of fair and just taxation and supported the establishment of a public school system open to all citizens, regardless of race. Although the *Louisianian* was a less forceful advocate of black rights, as opposed to Republican political interests, than its predecessors, like the *Tribune* and the *Black Republican*, it was more successful in terms of longevity—being continuously published for a dozen years. As William Brown once explained, "With resolution that our vocabulary contained no such word as 'cannot,' we were determined to 'get it out,' and we did it."

In 1870 Pinchback secured passage of an act establishing the Mississippi River Packet Company, of which he was one of the incorporators. A year later, the act was amended so that the state included an appropriation of $250,000 to aid the corporation. There were no apparent benefits accruing to the state, although one of the purposes of the bill was ostensibly to provide better traveling facilities on the Mississippi River for blacks. Nothing, however, was accomplished by the company, but Pinchback and other black Radical Republicans, such as C. C. Antoine, P. G. Deslonde, and others who were incorporators, presumably made a handsome profit.

It was also during this same period that Pinchback, who had been appointed one of the park commissioners for New Orleans, used his political position to economic advantage. The commissioners were appointed to select and purchase land for a public park. They acquired title to a piece of land, paid $65,000 down on a $650,000 property, with the rest mortgaged, divided it in half, and sold the other portion to the city at a much higher sum. The commissioners collected their share of the proceeds in cash and bonds and transferred their original debt to the city. This transaction produced a permanent split between Antoine and Pinchback, as the former accused the latter of somehow cheating him out of $40,000 that he felt was due him on the deal.

Politics in Louisiana were becoming increasingly bitter and complex, and Pinchback was in the center of it all. In 1871 the lieutenant governor, Oscar Dunn, passed away, and the senate met to choose a new president pro tem. Warmoth backed Pinchback's candidacy, and in another extremely close election marked by charges of corruption, Pinchback was elected in December of that year. Then, in 1872, there was a confused, heated battle among Republicans for control of the party. Opponents of Governor Warmoth, led by C. C. Antoine, had coalesced into what was called the Custom House Ring. Pinchback and Warmoth also warred with one another, but Pinchback remained allied with the governor, and at the Republican convention two slates appeared. The Custom House Republicans nominated William Pitt Kellogg for governor and Antoine for lieutenant governor. The Pinchback Republicans, on the other hand, put forward Warmoth for governor and Pinchback for lieutenant governor. The two groups ultimately reached a compromise, however, when Pinchback agreed to support Kellogg and Antoine, while Pinchback, himself, ran as a congressman at large.

The result was another election riddled with fraud and corruption in which the Kellogg ticket was ultimately placed in office by President Ulysses Grant himself. One result of the election was the instigation of impeachment proceedings against Governor Warmoth. To avoid prosecution, Warmoth fled Louisiana, and he was replaced as governor during the period from December 9, 1872, to November 30, 1873, by Pinchback, who served as acting governor. In the meantime, Pinchback was also declared the winner of his congressional race, and while serving as acting governor, the state legislature elected him to a six-year term in the United States Senate. Both elections, however, were hotly contested, and he was never seated in either case. There were charges and countercharges of fraud and corruption, and finally, the Senate voted him a sum of money equal to his senatorial pay during the time that the contest was being decided.

Pinchback, in the meantime, had remained involved in political, economic, and social affairs in New Orleans. Throughout the Republican regime in Louisiana, he had served as a member of both the state and city boards of education. In 1875 he had engineered the appointment of E. J. Edmunds, a brilliant black graduate of the University of Paris, as professor of mathematics at Central High School for boys. Upon his arrival, Edmonds was accosted by several of the white students and told he was nothing but a "nigger." Whites then held a mass meeting to protest the appointment, and newspapers publicly castigated Pinchback for his decision. Pinchback, however, stuck to his position, and Edmonds was ultimately able to resume his teaching duties with little difficulty.

Pinchback also challenged the city's segregation ordinances in several instances. He had long refused to ride in the Jim Crow streetcars reserved for blacks, and when he boarded a "white" car, the conductors moved all the whites out, and Pinchback rode alone in utmost dignity. In 1871, when Pinchback purchased a ticket for his wife on the Jackson Railroad, and the company refused to honor the ticket, he filed a $25,000 lawsuit against the company and tried to get its charter revoked. Company officials were most apologetic, and the suit was dropped. Then, at Redwitz's beer saloon, in May 1874, where Pinchback had been served along with whites for several years, Redwitz refused to serve him. The *Louisianian* took up the cause in this case and advised New Orleans blacks to challenge various segregation statutes at every opportunity. Despite this strategy, however, by 1875 Pinchback was advising patience on the issue of civil rights. In a speech in March of that year, he counseled blacks that they "should so prudently and courteously exercise the rights it [the civil rights act of 1875] gave us so as not to make the measure an irritant and aggravation of the evils and prejudices it was intended to correct." Historian John Blassingame believes that this advice was detrimental to blacks getting enhanced civil rights during this time.

In 1879 Pinchback served as a delegate to the state constitutional convention, where he sponsored a bill which resulted in the creation of Southern University. For this, he was bitterly attacked by New Orleans' Creole community, led by aristocratic Aristede Mary. Mary and 1,300 Creoles petitioned the convention, protesting that the "foundation of a *colored* university" would retard "the death of prejudice." Pinchback, through the *Louisianian*, countered that the Creole's views were sentimental, "impractical and visionary" and that they should recognize the immutability of white racism and accept "the best available means for educating the black masses."

This issue resulted in a deep rift between Pinchback and the city's elite Creole community. According to David Rankin, they perceived Pinchback as the "leader of the 'American' Negroes who had 'never done anything for the Creoles.' " At a political meeting held by Pinchback's Republican faction in 1882, a young Creole lawyer, Louis Martinet attended and castigated "Pinchback and the like" by saying, "What have they ever done that has not been of more profit to them than to their race? *They have grown rich fighting the race's battles*; that's the kind of patriots they are."

Because of increasing white racism, and the growing split with the city's

Creoles, Pinchback became all the more disillusioned over the prospects for African-Americans in post-Reconstruction Louisiana. From 1882 to 1885, he served in the post of surveyor of customs at the port of New Orleans, which was his last political appointment of any consequence. In 1885, at the age of forty-eight, Pinchback decided to become a lawyer. He resigned his position as surveyor and entered Straight University law school. A year later he graduated and was admitted to the Louisiana bar, although he apparently never actually practiced. Sometime between 1892 and 1895, Pinchback moved with his family to New York City, where he served as a U.S. marshall. After that, he relocated to Washington, D.C., where he was active in political affairs behind the scenes.

Sometime during the 1890s, Pinchback also became closely allied with Booker T. Washington,* and the two corresponded on a number of subjects over the years. After a time, Pinchback and Robert Terrell became Washington's principal allies in the nation's capital. In January 1904, when Edward H. Morris, a supporter of W.E.B. Du Bois and Monroe Trotter, viciously attacked Washington at a meeting of the Bethel Literary and Historical Association, Pinchback rose to the Tuskegean's defense. Pinchback was also responsible for arrangements for Washington's trip to the capital shortly thereafter to reply to the criticism. When the trip went off well, Pinchback wrote to Washington, full of self-congratulations. Emmett J. Scott, Washington's assistant, wrote in the margin of the letter to his boss: "You can see how the *Governor* feels!" Pinchback was never one for understatement.

In the same year, Pinchback and Washington led the crusade to get William D. Crum appointed collector of the customs for the port of Charleston, South Carolina. Pinchback and Whitefield McKinlay were primarily responsible for waging the battle on the District of Columbia front, while Booker T. Washington corresponded with President Theodore Roosevelt. Pinchback also helped Walter Cohen,* a fellow New Orleans black business leader and politician, to secure a federal post. After Washington's death in 1915, Pinchback's political influence declined, and he spent his remaining years in rather splendid decay. He and his wife were attended to by their grandson, Jean Toomer, a painful vigil which he later referred to as watching "Pinchback's breakup." Pinchback died at the age of eighty four in 1921. His body was taken back to New Orleans, where the funeral was held, and he was interred in the family vault at Metairie Ridge Cemetery. It was a lonely funeral, a far cry from the crowds Pinchback had attracted in earlier years. Just Toomer and Walter Pinchback, a son, had accompanied the body to New Orleans, and only a handful of local blacks came to the funeral. P.B.S. Pinchback died a largely forgotten man.

Pinchback had been criticized by many people for a number of things throughout his life. He was an extraordinary individual. Reared on a plantation, he became a riverboat gambler, a founder of the Republican party, and a leader of his race in a city in which he was a relative stranger. He was elected to the state legislature, became lieutenant governor, and then acting governor. He was elected to both the U.S. Congress and the U.S. Senate, but he never served.

Pinchback owned a number of successful businesses, ran an important black newspaper for over a decade, and became an important ally of Booker T. Washington in the late nineteenth and early twentieth centuries. And he, like so many other blacks in that tempestuous time, was fiercely proud of his race and heritage. As W.E.B. Du Bois said of him in his *Black Reconstruction*; "To all intents and purposes he was an educated, well-to-do congenial white man, with but a few drops of Negro blood, which he did not stoop to deny, as so many of his fellow blacks did." As the poet, Bruce Grit, commented on Pinchback's eightieth birthday; "He is one among the last of the old guard and he has fought the good fight."

Sources

Pinchback's letters and other materials are held in Special Collections at the Moorland-Spingarn Research Center, Howard University, as is some correspondence in the Blanche Kelso Bruce Papers. In the Pinchback papers is a biographical sketch, with no author or date, but which supposedly was written by his secretary. There is also extensive correspondence between Pinchback and Booker T. Washington and Emmett J. Scott, in the Booker T. Washington Papers at the Library of Congress. There is a full-length biography of Pinchback by James Haskins, *Pinckney Benton Stewart Pinchback* (New York, 1973). Agnes Smith Grosz's 1943 master's thesis at Louisiana State University, "The Political Career of Pinckney Benton Stewart Pinchback," *Louisiana Historical Quarterly* XXVII (April 1944), 527–612, is useful for that topic. There are shorter treatments by Emma Lou Thornbrough in *Dictionary of American Negro Biography*, (1982) and Ella Lonn in the *Dictionary of American Biography* (1934), in addition to William J. Simmons, *Men of Mark* (1887). Obituaries appeared in the *Washington Post*, December 22, 1921; the *New Orleans Times-Picayune*, December 22, 1921; and the *Baltimore Afro-American*, December 30, 1921. Jay Matthew, "Black Because He Wanted to Be," *The Washington Post*, October 24, 1982, is also useful. There is some additional biographical information in A. E. Perkins, "Some Negro Officers and Legislators in Louisiana," *Journal of Negro History* XIV (1929), 526; *New Orleans Times*, March 11, 1872; *Ouachita (Louisiana) Telegraph*, May 18, 1877; and *New Orleans Republican*, September 2, 1871. Pinchback's career as a riverboat gambler is recounted in George H. Devol, *Forty Years a Gambler on the Mississippi* (New York, 1887), esp. 216–17. The evolution of the *Louisianian* is briefly described in Thomas J. Davis, "Louisiana," in Henry Lewis Suggs, ed., *The Black Press in the South, 1865–1979* (Westport, Conn., 1983), 160–62.

Pinchback's role in Louisiana Reconstruction is covered in a number of sources, including Ella Lonn, *Reconstuction in Louisiana after 1868* (New York, 1918); Henry Clay Warmoth, *War, Politics and Reconstruction* (New York, 1963); Sidney James Romero, Jr., "The Political Career of Murphy James Foster, Governor of Louisiana, 1892–1900," *Louisiana Historical Quarterly* 28 (1945), 1134–35, 1138; John Edmond Gonzalez, "William Pitt Kellogg, Reconstruction Governor of Louisiana, 1873–1877," *Louisiana Historical Quarterly* 29 (1946), 403–6; Hilda Mulvey McDaniel, "Francis Tillou Nicholls and the End of Reconstruction," *Louisiana Historical Quarterly* 32 (1949), 399–400; Ted Tunnell, *Crucible of Reconstruction: War, Race and Radicalism in Louisiana, 1862–1877* (Baton Rouge, 1984); Joe Gray Taylor, *Louisiana Reconstructed, 1863–1877* (Baton Rouge, 1974); Charles L. Dufour, "The Age of Warmoth," *Louisiana History* VI (Fall 1965), 335–64; Francis Byers Harris, "Henry Clay Warmoth, Reconstruction Governor of Louisiana," *Louisiana Historical Quarterly* XXX (April

1947), 523–653; Althea D. Pitre, "The Collapse of the Warmoth Regime, 1870–72," *Louisiana History* VI (Spring 1965), 161–87; A. E. Perkins, "James Henry Burch and Oscar James Dunn of Louisiana," *Journal of Negro History* XXII (1937), 324–34. Worth noting also is a fictional treatment of the period, Ben Ames Williams, *The Unconquered*, (Boston, 1953) which gives a feeling for the passions of the time. Pinchback's role in the William D. Crum affair is briefly summarized by Willard B. Gatewood, "William D. Crum: A Negro in Politics," *Journal of Negro History* LIII (October 1968), 301–20.

Posey, Cumberland Willis (see Greenlee, William Augustus, and Cumberland Willis Posey).

Proctor, Barbara Gardner (1932–   ). Advertising executive: Proctor and Gardner Advertising, Incorporated. The setting is Black Mountain, a rural community outside of Asheville, North Carolina, where African-Americans were insulated from the pressures of urban life. Many blacks lived in rundown shacks without the necessities of running water and electricity. Self-reliance and strong bonds developed among the blacks of this tarheel community where a severe housing shortage required tolerance of overcrowding. Racism prevailed in this community where many blacks were forced into menial jobs just to survive. Such was the environment into which Barbara Gardner Proctor, the first black woman to own and operate an advertising agency, was raised.

Born in 1932 to William Gardner and Bernice Baxter, an unmarried couple, Proctor was essentially raised by her grandmother, Coralee Baxter, when her mother went off to attend secretarial school. Her grandmother provided Barbara with a healthy upbringing and proved to be the driving force in her life. She taught her grandchild "to accept whatever your circumstances are, but first admit that you can deal with it." When white matrons would coo over Proctor as a young child, her grandmother would quickly correct their effusions of her granddaughter's cuteness, by stating, "Not cute. But right smart." Proctor has proved her right.

Barbara Gardner Proctor received a scholarship when she completed high school, and then went to Talladega College in Alabama. When the scholarship failed to cover all her expenses, Proctor worked part-time, and her mother provided additional financial assistance to pay for her education. In 1954 she graduated with two degrees, one in English literature and education and one in sociology and psychology; she intended to return to North Carolina to become a teacher. However, after working at the Circle Pine Center summer camp in Kalamazoo, Michigan, Proctor stopped in Chicago on her way home. Having spent her transportation fare on clothes, Proctor had no choice but to remain in the sprawling metropolis.

Proctor's first job was as a social worker with the Chicago Union League, but she resigned when she found the job too depressing and she was unable to maintain her objectivity. She was then hired as office manager by the Oscar C. Brown Real Estate Company, where she remained for six years. The undemanding job provided Proctor with sufficient free time to write profiles of jazz stars such as Ray Charles, Cannonball Adderly, and Nancy Wilson for several magazines and recording companies. Ultimately she free-lanced for *Downbeat*, a high-profile jazz publication, continuing to write articles for twelve years. She also authored several television specials, produced a column for a South Side newspaper in Chicago, and contributed to seven books on jazz. These accomplishments gained Proctor entry into the Veejay Record Company, where she wrote the blurbs on the backs of album covers. This work was a stepping stone to more responsible positions, which culminated in Proctor's promotion as director of the International Division. In this capacity, she traveled to seventeen countries in Europe four times each year, looking for new acts to sign. Her biggest coup came when she arranged to bring The Beatles to the United States in 1962, in exchange for sending The Four Seasons to Europe.

During her employment in the music industry, Proctor met Carl Proctor, then Sarah Vaughn's road manager, and shortly thereafter they married and she became pregnant. Proctor admits that it was only out of boredom that she got married, and she only stayed in the marriage for two years because she felt that was a respectable amount of time to stay married. "I require freedom. I'm not a marriageable person. You can be whole without being married," she has commented. Not coincidentally, on the very same day that she left her marriage (their second wedding anniversary), Proctor also resigned her position with Veejay Records. The time had arrived for her to reassess her life. For eighteen months she was unemployed, and, by her own admission, suffered a crisis. It was her "battle with destiny."

Proctor opted to pursue a new direction in advertising, whereby she could continue writing, but on a different level. After the Leo Burnett Agency denied Proctor a job because she was "overqualified," she was hired by the Post-Keyes-Gardner advertising agency in 1964 at $8,500 a year, and she "learned everything from scratch, writing Pine-Sol labels." Although Proctor had used her maiden name, Gardner, throughout her professional career, she was forced to adopt her married name to avoid sharing a name with one of the principal partners of the firm. She absorbed the pain and complied, assuming the name Barbara Gardner Proctor. During her employment there, she wrote many notable advertisements that won her recognition by the people in the industry; she won twenty-one awards in three years. After five years Proctor did a brief stint as a copy supervisor with Gene Taylor Associates, and then moved on to North (which became Grey-North) Advertising, where she was hired as a copy supervisor for a salary of $26,000 in 1969. Her employment with this agency was short lived. When she realized that she had been pidgeonholed into servicing the traditional women's accounts, Proctor was embittered, particularly because she found it objectionable to be stereotyped as a black, as a woman, or as anything. Also there was an obvious conflict of philosophies between Proctor and the company, and she felt compromised by their methods. Proctor perceived that the company's focus was misplaced: on the client rather than on selling a product. Their "establishment ways'' of conducting business were antithetical to her ideals and techniques, and so it was time to move on.

Proctor started her own agency when she realized that her philosophy conflicted with the vast majority of advertising firms in the United States. This was a courageous decision for a black woman in Chicago in 1970. At that time there were no other black advertising agencies in Chicago, and obviously no black agencies owned by a woman. Although the feminist movement was gaining momentum, it had not yet gained enough ground to encourage Proctor's valiant move. But Barbara Proctor was unflappable. As she stated, rather defiantly, "They loved my work when I worked for someone else. Let's see how much they love me now."

Proctor and Gardner Advertising, Incorporated, began business on June 1970. The decision to use both her names was based on the idea that people doing business with her would assume that Gardner was the man standing behind her and that would provide comfort for the clients who had not yet adopted a progressive attitude toward women in positions of power. Initially, financing proved to be an insurmountable problem, since the only collateral she had to offer was her talent. To convince the Small Business Administration that she was worth the risk of a $100,000 loan, she ingeniously suggested that the administration check with three advertising agencies for the market value of Barbara Proctor. As she proudly recalled, "I was a hot property." At this time, when Mary Wells had emerged as a force to be reckoned with in the business, and was receiving a lot of media attention upon the opening of her Manhattan agency, a magazine article had referred to Proctor as a "black Mary Wells." This comparison enhanced her credibility and profile. The query of her net worth brought three different responses: $65,000, $80,000, and $110,000. She was granted a loan for $80,000.

Proctor and Gardner's first home was above a restaurant, in less than ideal conditions. The staff consisted of Proctor, an account person, an art director, and a media director, hardly a full complement of professionals, but sufficient to get the ball rolling. The pain of waiting seven long months to land an account taught the firm's employees the virtue of thrift, since they had only $26,000 to run the business from its inception until February 1971. By 1972 they had moved to a swank, new office on East Wacker Street in downtown Chicago. Since clients frequently visit their advertising agency's facilities, it was essential to the company's livelihood to have an impressive address and office. An integrated staff of eleven, who were assessed by Proctor as a group of malcontents whose talents were stifled at other agencies, occupied the firm's offices. She takes credit for having engineered a clan of superstars who were granted the autonomy to be creative and responsible. She resisted controlling her staff, declaring, "I can't do that heavy role, bossing grown people around."

Proctor's ability to delegate responsibility was an asset she learned in time. When the company was establishing its footing, Proctor felt compelled to do everything herself. She wrote all the copy, sold all the copy, and chaired all the client meetings. Was she displaying a keen sense of prudence or was this an ego running rampant? Perhaps a bit of both, since there is no uniform opinion on this issue. To be fair to Proctor, whatever the case, she built the company from the bottom up in a less than welcoming climate. By working seven days a week, she pursued the golden ring that had thus far eluded her. She handled difficult assignments, particularly ones that required her to market generic products to African-Americans. Initially, the black response to generic goods was that it was cheap junk. Her successful campaign, using television, radio, and newspapers, reached the people. The advertisements typified her style of clear, direct messages that endorsed the idea of "value for your money."

In 1973 the company's billings were approximately $4.5 million, the following year they increased slightly to $4.8 million, and in 1976 they were $5.4 million. By 1978 billings had reached $6.8 million. Growth continued at a gradual pace over the next decade, and Proctor succeeded in spite of her race or her sex, which she considers challenges not obstacles. "I happen to be born female and Black but I am much more than that. To view every circumstance in small biological characteristics is very self-limiting." In 1981 she could proudly boast of billings estimated at $12.2 million, which decreased just slightly the following year. Fifteen million dollars were projected for 1982, and $13 million in 1983, but in 1984 the agency suffered the loss of its largest client, Alberto-Culver, who took with it 20 percent of the agency's billings. This was a loss the agency could not afford, and in response Proctor took drastic measures when she reshaped the agency's management team by replacing longstanding employees with new, young blood.

Proctor and Gardner's client list was an impressive one, particularly considering her refusal to compromise her values—the primary reason she started her own agency in the first place. The agency's first account was with Ghana-American, and six months later it landed Jewel Food Stores, a Chicago-based food chain. Sears-Roebuck, Alberto Culver, and E. J. Gallo Winery followed shortly thereafter. These companies wanted to reach the African-American consumers who had thus far been ignored. It was reasoned that a black agency could best address this market, since it could identify habits and trends unique to blacks. The irony lies in the fact, that prior to opening the agency, Proctor had never worked on products specifically for the black consumer market. Initially, she had intended to pick up white clients that she had cultivated when she was employed elsewhere: however, most of the agency's revenues are in small amounts from promotions and public relations budgets geared to the black consumer. Nevertheless, she refused to be stigmatized as an ethnic agency and had a broad range of nonethnic billings. Proctor is frustrated by the kind of thinking that "lumps all blacks into one homogeneous market," as many companies have a tendency to do. She correctly assesses the black community as a segmented market, and as such, for an agency to develop an effective advertising campaign, it must acknowledge these inherent differences. She has targeted what she calls the bulk of blacks, that is, if they were white, they would be the Silent Majority.

The philosophy that Proctor adheres to and requires her clients to support is a commitment to the development of business, to secure a future for blacks, economically. She has been known to turn away business that contradicts her philosophy, which has cost her billings, but not her conscience. She tends to select clients whose products and services are constructive influences in the consumer communities. Proctor rejects products or accounts that reinforce negative black or female stereotypes, or are not in the best interest of African-Americans or the family, whose stability is being threatened. She assumes a sense of responsibility as evidenced in the following: ''I have the opportunity to show the strength, beauty, humor and family respect that is a very proud tradition in the Black experience. And I have a magnificent client base which agrees with that projection and supports me in sharing it.'' The sincerity of these commitments was illustrated when both Kraft and Jewel Foods elected to withdraw sponsorship from violent television programs. Proctor and Gardner had never developed a relationship with a company that either manufactured cigarettes or liquor, the only black-owned advertising agency able to make such a claim. However, in 1984, when Alberto Culver ended its association with the agency, Proctor and Gardner landed the account of G. Heileman Brewing Company—to formulate a separate advertising strategy for black consumers, who were a critical segment of the beer-drinking market. Was this out of sheer desperation given the volume of the business lost, or did Proctor assess beer as less harmful than hard liquor, or had she compromised her principles?

With her commitment to the African-American race and to women, Proctor has used her high visibility to reach members of the power structure. Her outspoken, and often aggressive, nature (by her own admission) have frequently worked to her detriment, but she has not relinquished her pursuit for fair treatment and equality. However, at times, she has taken what one might consider an unpopular stance. In 1980 she openly criticized the white establishment's hold on the marketing field, a grip that she feels is dominated by the Green Giants, who are male, white, and very rich. In contrast, she perceives women as little sprouts who must exercise their options to challenge the old boy network. Her patience had worn thin fighting the conservative standards of the chauvinistic business community. In 1979, as a member of the White House Task Force for the Small Business Council, Proctor attempted to direct the government into providing additional support for those already in business rather than helping more people get into business. She felt that there were far too many failures, and such failures could be minimized with the imposition of stricter guidelines for those requesting loans from the Small Business Administration. Her criticism transcends the U.S. government and dares to identify a problem that she finds inherent in numerous black businesses. The absence of good service and quality merchandise contributes to the failures, according to her assessment of the sorry situation. When once asked why she felt black businesses were not supported by blacks, she responded vitriolically:

It is not that blacks do not support black businesses, they don't support shabby businesses. Blacks are some of the most sophisticated shoppers in the world. They have less money to spend so that means they have to be good shoppers. They are not going to buy a black product just because it is black. If the service is not up to standards they are not going to buy. They expect their customers to accept dirty windows, accept that they added too much to their bill last month or that they don't offer credit. This is the problem with too many black companies. This is exactly what I mean when I say those people should not have been in the business in the first place.

Proctor's suggestion to blacks who are eager to start a mainstream business is to practice teamwork. She speaks from experience, and she is keenly aware that her criticisms of the black community have likely lost her some business. She is impatient with the black upper class who have adopted the negative aspects of elitism—the ostentatious displays of material things—the jewels, the big cars, the big apartments and houses—all symbols of a nouveau riche who feel compelled to exhibit the excesses of their achievements. She finds it absolutely intolerable that there are black nursing homes where the elite "shove" the elderly when they become a burden. The symbol of black nursing homes speaks to her loud and clear: "Economically we move up, but morally we move down." She is puzzled that there are enough African-Americans who dispose of the elderly to support the abundance of nursing homes, when the family ties that she grew up with were so strong despite the conditions in which she was reared. Needless to say, she has been harshly criticized for publicly denouncing her own race.

In addition to the backlash she receives for these "inappropriate" pronouncements, there are some African-Americans who have concluded that Proctor's success, like that of other African-American women, make them, if not an outright competitor, then at least an impediment to the advancement of the black man. Advocates of this judgment argue that a black woman on the middle or upper management level preempts a position that could be held by a black man. These critics propose that a woman should take a back seat so that her male counterpart can assume a prominent and primary position and dispel the image of a matriarchal black society. Such antifeminist thinking was a reaction to the women's movement, which allowed African-American women to enhance their economic standing more than black men. Proctor's success has obviously ruffled some feathers, but it has failed to keep her down.

Proctor's presence in Chicago is recognized by both the white and black business communities. In 1976 she was elected president of the Cosmopolitan Chamber of Commerce, the first African-American woman to achieve this position. This organization was preceded by the Negro Chamber of Commerce, which was organized in 1933 by a small group of black entrepreneurs. Their goal was to transform the anemic black community into an economically viable capitalistic one. In 1955 the Chamber of Commerce adopted a new name to represent its new membership affiliation. When the white business community refused to admit black business people into its industrial world, blacks took the initiative to invite their white counterparts to join their organization. From that time onward, the Cosmopolitan Chamber of Commerce has operated as an integrated body, and it has achieved the status of being the nation's largest interracial trade association. Upon accepting the post of president, Proctor proceeded to criticize the association for being self-serving by primarily favoring a few highly paid staff members, consultants, and others with funds received by federal grants, corporate contributions, and small monetary gifts from those in the community the chamber supposedly served. Her primary goal was to overhaul completely the organization's image and policies to eliminate any individual or organization that might be serving its own selfish desires.

In addition to her affiliation with the Cosmopolitan Chamber of Commerce, Proctor has served on numerous boards, including Illinois Bell Telephone, the DuSable Museum, the Council of Chicago Better Business Bureaus, and Operation PUSH (for whom the agency has designed advertising campaigns); she is also a lifelong member of the NAACP. Proctor also served as president of the National League of Black Women from 1978 to 1982. In 1983–1984, she received a special appointment from the governor of Illinois, as cochair of the Gannon-Proctor Commission, which was designed to study the role of women in Illinois. Proctor expressed the role of the commission as one that addressed the need for society to develop solutions to issues responsible for the "tragic reality of women's roles in the home, in industry and in society." Her success in business has provided her with the opportunity to speak out on issues that are important to her, and she has proved herself to be a formidable opponent and spokesperson.

In 1984 Proctor was cited by President Ronald Reagan in his State of the Union Address. He honored her as a woman who "rose from a ghetto shack to build a multi-million dollar advertising agency," and that she, among others, have sparked a "spirit of enterprise" in the United States. Her response to this honor was to acknowledge that her drive to excel was a large factor in her success, but she pointed out that the agency could not have been started without government support and aid from the private sector. "The only point I would want to emphasize is that the conditions when I started my company were very fertile for entrepreneurs. I think that (those) opportunities are at risk at the moment." In 1986 Proctor was again honored by President Reagan for her contribution to the nation's economy as a leading woman entrepreneur. She was chosen as one of eighty-five leading women entrepreneurs by a special report, "Risk to Riches: Women and Entrepreneurship in America." Proctor has also received numerous awards for her outstanding achievements in the field of advertising and for her contributions in the community. Such citations include the 1974 Chicago Advertising Woman of the Year and the 1975 Advertising Person of the Year by the sixth district of the American Advertising Federation.

Barbara Proctor's achievements as an astute business person have rewarded her sufficiently so that she can afford the finer things in life. No one knows better than she what life is like without the luxuries or even the basic necessities.

Although her upbringing in the back hills of North Carolina could hardly be expected to play a significant role in the success she enjoys today, she says, "My absolute super inspiration everything in the whole world in terms of what you can be and do was Lena Horne. Way, way back in Black Mountain, when I was running around barefooted, ignorant, and Black, in the South, Lena was all we had. I like to think that some young person will look out at my example, the way I've looked at those who inspired me, and develop a drive to win." She is featured in the Smithsonian Institution's "Black Women Achievements against the Odds" Hall of Fame. This acknowledgment will surely place her permanently in history as an African-American woman who achieved entrepreneurial excellence.

Sources

Barbara Proctor's personal papers and the company records are inaccessible to researchers, and there is no full-scale biography. There are several shorter biographies of Proctor, including Lois Rich-McCoy, *Millionairess: Self-Made Women of America* (New York, 1978), reprinted in the *Chicago Sun Times*, February 18, 1979; Caroline Bird, *Enterprising Women* (1976); Stephen J. Birmingham, *Certain People* (1977), 72–78; Mariann Davis, *Contributions of Black Women to America* vol. I (1982); Laura French and Diana Stewart, *Women in Business* (Milwaukee, c. 1979); and briefer treatments such as, the *National Who's Who in Finance & Industry* (1988); and Frank J. Johnson, *Who's Who of Black Millionaires* (1984).

There have been numerous newspaper accounts and magazine articles following the career of Proctor, and some of the more detailed accounts can be found in the following: *Essence*, July 1972; *Working Woman*, August 1979; *Ebony*, August 1977 and August 1982; *Money*, September 1981; *Black Enterprise* August 1974; *Chicago Tribune Magazine*, April 19, 1981; *Chicago Metro* October 30, 1976; *Raleigh News and Observer*, November 27, 1978; and *United Airline Magazine*, May 1982. Numerous other articles cover Proctor and her business and personal affairs and can be located in the clipping files of the Chicago Municipal Library and the Chicago Historical Society as well as the Raleigh Public Library. The innovative advertising techniques of Proctor Advertising have been included in such university texts as Courtland Boveé and William F. Arens, *Contemporary Advertising* 3rd edition (Homewood, Ill, 1989), John Wright, et, al., *Advertising* (Toronto, 1984); Gerhard Gschwandtner *Supersellers* (New York, 1986); and "Highest Form of Persuasion: Barbara Proctor," published by the American Management Association, 1986.

Proctor's criticism of the white male power structure appears in the *Atlanta Daily World*, March 21, 1980; and her role in and criticism of the Cosmopolitan Chamber of Commerce is in the *Chicago Metro*, December 6, 1975, and February 14, 1976. President Reagan's acknowledgment of Proctor's accomplishments were noted in the *Chicago Sun Times*, January 26 and 27, 1984; *Chicago Defender*, January 28, 1984; and *Chicago Tribune*, January 26, 1984. Articles dealing with race and business are in the *Chicago Tribune*, February 24, 1972, and June 13, 1972; and *Chicago Defender*, June 3, 1979. Articles on gender, race, and business are in the *Chicago Sun Times*, July 6, 1982; *Black Enterprise*, August 1974; *Women's Wear Daily*, reprinted in the *Chicago Tribune*, September 5, 1971. The Gannon-Proctor Commission Final Report is available at the Chicago Historical Society. The WTTW public service television station produced a half-hour special on Proctor and Gardner Advertising Agency in 1976, and the highly rated news program "60 Minutes" profiled her in a segment.

R

Rhodes, Eugene Washington (see Perry, Christopher James, and Eugene Washington Rhodes).

Russell, Herman Jerome (December 23, 1930–   ). Entrepreneur, contractor, property manager, real estate investor, communication company founder, food and beverage concessions owner, and publisher: H. J. Russell and Company, H. J. Russell Construction, Interstate Construction, H. J. Russell Plastering, Wet and Dry Walls, Inc., Paradise Management, Diversified Project Management, Gibraltar Land, Georgia Southeastern Land, Concessions International, Russell-Rowe Communications, and the *Atlanta Inquirer.* "The people here have not yet placed the blame on white folks for their problems. They don't realize that when they look at those pretty buildings downtown there's nothing that belongs to them." What they also may not realize is that Herman Russell, an African-American, built some of those glistening towers. In the 1960s civil rights activists were challenging Atlanta's racial status quo. Although the city's segregation policies were deeply embedded in the psyche of the white power structure, Atlanta was forced to relax its discriminatory practices to solidify its newly won status as the regional center of finance, transportation, trade, and of the entire service sector of the economy. Reluctantly, the barriers began to crumble, and self-motivated, hard-driving, African-American entrepreneurs were gradually beginning to take advantage of the changing climate.

As Atlanta emerged as "the promising city," "the black mecca," and "the New York of the South," Herman Russell, the contractor, also came forth as a force to be recognized. He is not a member of the black elite that has persisted since the time when Auburn Avenue, better known as "Sweet Auburn," provided the stimulus for many ambitious African-American entrepreneurs. To this day, a few of the enterprises from those early years continue to thrive—Atlanta Life Insurance Company and Citizens Trust Bank. However, Auburn Street in the 1960s fell on hard times, and although the old black aristocracy clings to tradition, they no longer dominate either the social or the economic scene for African-

Americans. Herman Russell is one of those outsiders who has made a name for himself, and his reputation extends well beyond the traditional boundaries of black business in Atlanta.

Herman Russell was born in Summerhill, a rundown black neighborhood in Atlanta, adjacent to the present Atlanta Braves ballpark. Russell, the youngest of eight children, was raised by parents who instilled in him the self-help philosophy of Booker T. Washington.* Russell's industrious father, who worked as a plasterer, stressed the importance of hard work and thrift, words that made a lasting impression on his son when he preached, "If you make a dollar you ought to save a portion of it, even if it's only 1 percent." He was employed by his father as a hod carrier, laborer, and plasterer, among other jobs. Herman Russell had learned the plastering trade by the age of twelve, and by the time he reached sixteen, while still attending David T. Howard High School, he bought his first piece of property for $250. When Russell continued his schooling at the Tuskegee Institute in Alabama, he worked summers building a duplex on this piece of land with the help of friends. Russell also worked during the school term as a plasterer to pay for his college education.

In 1953, upon graduating from Tuskegee with a diploma in building construction, Russell returned to Atlanta to start a business. With little start-up capital, Russell bought an old pickup truck for $150, hired one worker, and offered services in plastering and repairing under the company name of H. J. Russell Plastering Company. Soon thereafter he took on larger projects—building new homes, bidding on hot contracts, and buying land (initially purchasing the property next to his first real estate investment). His relative success afforded him the opportunity to purchase three pickup trucks and hire twenty-five employees and then, in 1957, he inherited from his father the Rogers Russell, Sr. Plastering Company, with an estimated value of $15,000.

Herman Russell was not the first African-American in Atlanta to build houses for his race on a large scale. The original developer of the west side of the city for blacks was Heman Perry,* with his Service Company, which went bankrupt in the early 1920s. A number of years later, Perry's mantle was assumed by "Chief" Aiken, who built a large number of homes in many sections of the city for blacks up to the 1950s. Thus, Russell was building upon an important tradition in Atlanta when he built his first houses in the late 1950s.

In 1959 Herman Russell established the H. J. Russell Construction Company, which offered general contracting services. By this time, he had received a good credit rating and was eligible for financing through commercial banks, providing him with sufficient capital to expand the size of his jobs from duplex construction, to 4- and 8-unit apartments, and then to 400- and 500-unit complexes. Russell focused on building housing for low- and middle-income families, but rather than selling the properties he retained ownership. Various Department of Housing and Urban Development (HUD) programs financed the construction of these endeavors. By 1978 Russell had completed twenty-nine projects (4,000 units) or more, and he had $12 million worth of HUD work and another $28 million on the drawing board. Clearly he had significantly benefited from such government financing programs introduced by the Nixon administration, which gave $315 million in loans, grants, and contracts primarily to African-American firms located in the South.

In the 1960s H. J. Russell Plastering Company experienced rapid growth, which Russell partially attributes to the sensitivity of then Mayor Ivan Allen, Jr. Under Allen's leadership, Atlanta and the federal government expanded programs to assist residential construction, which, in turn, provided financing to Russell's company. The real turning point for H. J. Russell Company came in the late 1960s, when it landed work on large commercial projects and on Atlanta Stadium. Russell's successful bid on the thirty-four-storied Equitable Life Insurance Building in downtown Atlanta was his entreé into the "big time." By the early 1970s, he had won many contracts, including the Martin Luther King Community Center, his first major public project, which was partially financed with funds Russell had raised from the white power structure. When Maynard Jackson, Atlanta's first African-American mayor, introduced mandatory affirmative action programs in the 1970s, which required white companies involved in city construction contracts to hire minority companies as subcontractors or to develop joint partnerships with minority business, Russell's companies benefited substantially. These arrangements finally gave him and other African-Americans the opportunity to prove their mettle. It is important to keep in mind that although H. J. Russell benefited from such Minority Business Enterprise (MBE) programs, he was successful before the implementation of such mandatory programs. In 1987 Egbert Perry, a key executive in Russell's empire, felt compelled to defend Russell's climb to the top. He asserted that from 75 to 80 percent of the company's joint venture projects had been for private companies, firms with neither a public mandate nor any minority participation requirements. "He has made it in the private sector," Perry asserted, "bidding head-to-head with older and more established firms." Although Russell acknowledges the positive aspects of such programs, he is quick to assert that they fall short of their potential:

They just make good, common economic sense. When you give a man a meal ticket, a good way to earn a living that he can use to support his family and educate his kids properly and get some of the necessary things that every human being is entitled to, then the Government is not going to have to give him those things. Consequently, you make a better situation for the country and for the world. He becomes a foundation, not a burden.

H. J. Russell Company's most lucrative jobs are those taken on as joint partnerships with such prominent white construction companies as J. A. Jones Construction of Charlotte, North Carolina, and Holder Construction of Atlanta. As Ron Holder, chairman of the Holder Construction, noted, "We have helped create a formidable competitor and that was what the Minority Enterprise [Program] was suppose to do." Russell's total commitment on such joint contracts as the Metro Atlanta Rapid Transit Authority (MARTA) train station, the $18 million construction of parking decks at the Hartsfield International Airport, and the $115 million Georgia Pacific fifty-two-storied office tower for its corporate headquarters (then the largest office building in the Southeast and Atlanta's second-tallest building) has brought him a significant increase in business and has earned him considerable respect from both the private sector and the public domain.

Russell is selective on the number of collaborations he accepts because, as he readily admits, "[T]hat kind of growth scares me." He also suspects some white firms of improperly using minority firms as a front:

We [blacks] will only control our destiny when we learn to master whatever we are doing. I always insist not only that we pick up our equal part in the proceedings, but that we have black people in key positions where they can learn. If all we are going to get out of it is a buck and we don't develop the human resources, then we are missing the boat. (*Black Enterprise*, June 1987)

While keeping in mind the philosophy of controlled growth, Russell has created H. J. Russell and Company, an umbrella organization for several vertically integrated firms of which Russell is chairman and chief executive officer. The real estate division, Gibraltar Land Inc., was established in 1985 to control all aspects of the development process. It oversees activities in the areas of housing, office, and industrial park development. Paradise Management, Inc., which emerged in 1959, supervises all types of property management from federally assisted programs to turnarounds of struggling properties. In 1984 the project management division—Diversified Project Management (DPM)—was organized. It originally operated, from 1976 to 1984, under the name DDR International, Inc. DPM functions as a consulting firm of professional architects, engineers, and contractors who coordinate and manage information services to organizations involved in capital improvement programs. Finally, four operations—H. J. Russell Construction Company, Interstate Construction, H. J. Russell Plastering, and Wet and Dry Walls—constitute the construction division, which offers a range of services from general building construction to fireproofing, plastering, drywalling, and so forth. Typically, these subdivisions are regionally active, providing both union and nonunion labor to the hiring companies.

Despite Russell's tendency to invest conservatively, he has diversified outside the construction industry. He owns Russell-Rowe Communications, which operates WGXA-TV, an ABC affiliate in Macon, and he also owns City Beverage Company, with $20 million in sales in 1986, which distributes such brands of beer as Coors, Strohs, and Becks throughout southern Atlanta. To complete the corporate file, Russell owns Concessions International Corporation, which is valued at $10 million, a company that manages food concessions in major airports across the United States, including Chicago, Louisville, and Seattle. He also owns a liquor store which one of his brothers runs, and two grocery stores, and he is a partner in two nursing homes.

All told, in 1987 the estimated value of "The Company" was $118 million, with Russell's personal wealth estimated at $10 million. In 1989 the company could boast a staff of 1,500 across the United States. To ensure continued growth and consistency of service, Russell employs highly qualified professional people, who are "10 times sharper" than he, by his own admission. This strategy has proven itself successful, by the very fact that the company has not suffered a losing year since its inception. In the 1980s his many contracts included such notable projects as the Robert W. Woodruff Library at the Atlanta University Center, the Carter Presidential Center, the Atlanta City Hall Complex, the McGill Place Condominiums (in a revitalized area of downtown), and the joint partnership arrangement in the $24 million addition to the Atlanta Merchandise Mart. Such projects contributed to the more than $103.8 million sales the company achieved in the 1980s.

Russell has expanded well beyond the borders of Georgia, into South Carolina, North Carolina, Massachusettes, and Colorado. In the 1990s his company has provided general contracting services to the Peachtree Tower in Atlanta, project management consulting to the Birmingham Airport Terminal, and property management services to the Durham County Jail, among numerous other business commitments. His company is one of the most sought after construction interests for joint partnerships, evidently due to its proven track record.

Russell's astute sense of timing has provided him with opportunities unique to African-American entrepreneurs. In 1972 he was invited to join the Omni Group, a group of investors that purchased the National Hockey League (NHL) franchise that ultimately became the Atlanta Flames (later sold and moved to Calgary, Alberta, Canada); bought the management rights to the new Omni, a 17,000-seat sports-convention center complex; and ownership of the Atlanta Hawks, a National Basketball Association (NBA) team. Russell's investment in this $12 million package was $1.8 million, the equivalent of 10 percent. This was a profound accomplishment in view of the fact that never before had an African-American been involved in ownership of either an NHL or an NBA franchise. His keen business sense paid off handsomely when the Citizens Trust Bank, Atlanta's only black bank, needed additional monies to finance the construction of its new building in downtown Atlanta. Russell bailed out the institution with $250,000, in return for $250,000 worth of the bank's stocks. One less successful venture was the dream town of Shenendoah, located thirty-two miles south of Atlanta. In 1973, according to *Ebony*, this was intended to be a model city designed to show the world that a society integrated by race and economics could succeed. In 1981 HUD, which had guaranteed $25 million for the project, wanted to take it over from Russell and his partner in the venture. It is unclear whatever became of the debacle.

Although Herman Russell has achieved remarkable success and is highly revered in Atlanta, he still admits receiving the most satisfaction in building housing for low-income families. This really is the key to what drives the entrepreneur. As Jesse Hill, Jr.,* chief executive officer of Atlanta Life recalls: "Herman has created a tremendous number of jobs for blacks and whites, too.

He's brought dignity to the hard hat and blue collar workers. Under federal housing programs, he's got the best track record I know of for upgrading housing for lower and middle income families.'' Having never forgotten his roots, Russell is constantly ''giving back'' to the place from where he came. As he asserts, ''We represent ourselves not as a minority business but as a business with a minority commitment.'' Russell sees his business as a vehicle for creating institutions that are lacking in the black community. He donates land to black churches, participates in fund-raising geared to youth programs, and supports Little League ball in the the projects. Although he could well afford a sleek office building in a classy part of Atlanta, he has chosen to house his headquarters in a modest building in a dilapidated part of the city. He is committed to inner-city development; early on he dreamed of renewing this area, to make downtown a living experience, but thus far it remains an undesirable district.

Russell's commitment to Atlanta's black community was demonstrated when he helped start the *Atlanta Inquirer*, a weekly instrument through which the 1960s civil rights movement's crusaders could express their philosophies, frustrations, and criticisms. His home was a retreat for Martin Luther King, Jr., during the movement, and it is a meeting place for Atlanta's black power elite and political strategy sessions. His commitment is also evident in the construction of the Maggie Russell Tower, a senior citizens' residence named in memory of his mother; the General Daniel ''Chappie'' James Center for Aerospace Science and Health Education at Tuskegee University, his alma mater; and the renovation and expansion of Grady Memorial Hospital, Russell's birthplace.

A high-profile political position is often the pursuit of individuals who have realized their business goals. Nothing could be farther from reality for Herman Russell. He has never expressed, either publicly or privately, political ambitions of any kind. Although he has achieved a prominence that could easily transcend business, his preference is to remain behind the scenes, influencing those who choose to bask in the limelight. Russell's political connections are far reaching, all the way to the White House; he has had the honor of visiting with Presidents Lyndon Johnson, Richard Nixon, and Jimmy Carter. At the local level, he has been instrumental (albeit behind the scenes) in the campaigns of Andrew Young, Maynard Jackson, and others in their pursuits of various political offices. Although he seldom publicly endorses any candidate, many political hopefuls seek his support, because, as Andrew Young has reflected,'' [H]ardly anyone would run without going to see him. A word from him. A word from him can make you or break you in a lot of circles.''

Russell is a founding member of the Atlanta Forum, an influential group of Atlanta's business elite, and he was also the first black member of Atlanta's Chamber of Commerce. When the organization inadvertently sent him an invitation to become a member—they had not realized that he was black—he accepted nonetheless. He was acting president of the Chamber of Commerce in 1981, the second African-American to hold that position; the first was Jesse Hill of Atlanta Life Insurance Company. In 1986 Russell was voted CEO of the Year by the Atlanta Business League, and in 1987 *Black Enterprise* cited H. J. Russell and Company as their "Company of the Year," and in the same year Russell was honored during Black History Month by the nineteen-member city council. He sits on the board of directors of numerous organizations, both purely business-oriented companies and those that have the public welfare as a priority, and he is a lifetime member of the NAACP. Russell has been the recipient of various honors, among them the Salute to Greatness Award by the Martin Luther King Center for Nonviolent Social Change and the Distinguished Humanitarian Award by the National Jewish Center for Immunology and Respiratory Medicine.

As his company continues to broaden its empire, it will no doubt aggressively bid for contracts in light of the massive construction required to accommodate the 1996 Olympics. Atlanta and the Atlanta Olympic Organizing Committee (on whose advisory board Russell served) invested in excess of $7 million to land the bid, and Mayor Maynard Jackson expects the Olympics to be the "single biggest continuous infusion of economic development to Atlanta in the history of the city, under any circumstances. Nothing will compare to it." Jackson's confidence and enthusiasm is shared by Atlanta's black business community; they are prepared to compete actively for licensing, for the opportunity to provide business and consumer services, and for participation in joint ventures. No doubt Herman Russell will reap significant rewards from this coup.

To this day Herman Russell remains a very humble man who lives a moderate life-style and is a devoted family man. He has groomed his three children to carry on the traditions of the family business when he reluctantly retires. His shrewd business persona contradicts his gentler nature, which surfaces when he speaks of those less fortunate than he:

I work very hard. My mind is still on when I was such a poor child. To never own a bicycle, never have central heat or air conditioning as a boy . . . all the other things your kids and my kids have today. It wasn't there. That makes me aware there's a lot of human need out there. There's a lot to do.

These memories are what drives this "Quiet Giant" to succeed so that he may share the fruits of his labor.

Sources

No personal or company papers are accessible to the researcher; however, the company provides the researcher with a package of materials, mostly promotional. No full-scale biographies have been written about Herman Russell, although his company is one of the largest minority-owned businesses in the United States. Brief biographies appear in Frank J. Johnson, *Who's Who of Black Millionaires* (1984); *Who's Who in Black Corporate America* (1982); and *Who's Who among Black Americans* (1990).

Numerous articles about Russell and his business appear in mainstream publications and business journals. The following articles provide good material on these subjects: *Atlanta Magazine*, May 1974; *Ebony*, May 1973; *Engineering News-Record*, February 23, 1978; *New York Times*, March 5, 1981; *Atlanta Journal and Constitution*, August 8, 1983, and March 22, 1985; *Cascade Chronicle*, August 1984; *Atlanta Business Chronicle*, June 28, 1987; *Nation's Business*, January 1987; *Business Atlanta*, May 1989; and

Black Enterprise, June 1987. *Black Enterprise*, January 1991, deals specifically with black business and the Olympics, and controversies over the MBE program were documented in the *Atlanta Constitution*, September 6, 1987. Numerous additional articles are available in the *Atlanta Journal*, *Jet*, *Black Enterprise*, *Minorities and Women in Business*, and so forth. The clipping service at the WMC of the Atlanta Public Library has a separate file for Russell.

S

Scott, Cornelius Adolphus (February 8, 1908–) and **William Alexander Scott II** (September 29, 1902–February 7, 1934). Newspaper publishers: *Atlanta Daily World, Birmingham World, Memphis World,* and Scott Newspaper Syndicate. By the 1990s once-proud Auburn Avenue was crumbling. It was anchored by national historic sites at both ends and in the middle. On the east end was the home where Martin Luther King, Jr., was born; in the middle, the Martin Luther King, Jr., Center for Social Change and the Ebenezer Baptist Church; and to the west, the somewhat dilapidated offices of the *Atlanta World.* But it was not always thus. Seventy years earlier it had been what John Wesley Dobbs called "Sweet Auburn," the leading street in America for black business, cultural, and religious activities. In the 1920s, according to black banker Lorimer D. Milton,[*] "Every type of business that an individual Negro had sense enough to run, he first headed to Auburn Avenue because that was the center of Negro activity. It was the hotbed." In 1920 there were 72 black businesses and twenty professionals located on Auburn; by 1930, 121 businesses and thirty-nine professionals were there. It was, as a former resident noted, "the pride and joy of black people." It was to Auburn Avenue—to that mecca of black commerce— that the young William A. Scott was drawn in 1928 to start his newspaper enterprise.

William Scott and his brother Cornelius were born in Edwards, Mississippi, the sons of William A. Scott, Sr., a preacher, and Emeline Southall. The large family, there were nine children, moved to Jackson, Mississippi, where the elder Scott owned the Progress Printing House, and Emeline Scott worked as a printer. Both the young boys worked in their father's shop, doing every sort of odd job they were given. Young William then went to Jackson College, a junior college for blacks, from which he graduated in 1922. A year later, in June 1923, he married his childhood sweetheart, Lucille McAllister. That this may not have been an entirely voluntary union on young William's part is attested to by several facts. First, the couple's son, William A. III, was born before the nuptials.

Second, they were separated and divorced fairly early. Lucille was the first of William A. Scott's four wives.

In 1923 William Scott went to Morehouse College in Atlanta, where his older brother, Aurelius Scott, had preceded him. Aurelius was a bit of a wunderkind, and there was an intense but friendly rivalry between the brothers. Aurelius had made a distinguished record at Morehouse. He had been a star football player, had made the debating team, and then went on to occupy a professor's chair at West Virginia State College. William Scott was convinced that, if Aurelius could do it, he could too. He went to Morehouse—wife, child, and all—and became a top football player, a member of the debating team, a highly ranked student, and a recognized talent in music. Whether those accomplishments satisfied his urge to excel, or whether it was the pressures of raising a growing family (a second son was born in 1925), William Scott left Morehouse before graduating in 1925 and went to Jacksonville, Florida. There he worked as a railway clerk on the run from Jacksonville to Miami, but also began to get involved in the publishing trade. While still in Jacksonville, he published the *Jacksonville Negro Business Directory* in 1927.

It was during this time in Jacksonville, probably in 1926, that William Scott's first marriage broke up, and Lucille Scott took the children and went to live with her parents in Shreveport, Louisiana. Some fifty years later, Lucille talked about her long-deceased ex-husband. He was, she said, "the grandest guy in the world" and such a salesman that he could have "sold ice to an Eskimo," but as much as she loved him, she just could not live with him. From all accounts, William A. Scott was an extraordinary individual, in ways both good and bad. Ric Roberts, a columnist and cartoonist for the *Atlanta World* from the very beginning, and a close friend (or at least as close as anyone got) of William A. Scott, had this to say about him: "He was one of the most unrelenting persons I ever knew. . . . He was brilliant, cynical and hard. He was definitely amusing. He was so typical of the newspaper racket that, to write about it, you just wrote about W. A. Scott. . . . He had all the wiseness and cruel smartness and the flashy veneer." He went on to say, "W. A. Scott's honesty was a strange thing. It was the honesty of complete independence."

Frank Marshall Davis, editor of the *Atlanta World* in the 1930s, and later executive editor of the Associated Negro Press, wrote years later in the *Negro Digest* (November 1946) that Scott was "trigger-brained, daring, capable and determined, and enjoyed himself most when matching wits with an opponent. . . . He made enemies freely, drove his car with the same recklessness with which he ran for touchdowns as a halfback at Morehouse College, led an active love life and ruled his family with an iron thumb." William Scott was a dynamic man with enormous appetites, who crammed more into thirty-one years than most people do into seventy-five.

W. A. Scott arrived back in Atlanta in 1928, determined to start a newspaper. This was a characteristically audacious move on Scott's part. The leading black newspaper in the city at that time was the *Atlanta Independent*, published by Benjamin J. Davis, Sr., one of the most powerful blacks in the city—in fact, in the state and in the entire South. He had, furthermore, through his involvement with the Odd Fellows, become the virtual king of Auburn Avenue. Davis had started the *Independent* in Dawson, Georgia, in 1903, and moved it to Atlanta in 1909. It was, at that time, the most militant black paper in the Deep South. Unable to secure advertisements from either white or black businesses, Davis developed a strong alliance with the Odd Fellows, which supplied the paper with a healthy subsidy. Davis had given invaluable assistance to the Odd Fellows when they built their massive six-storied complex on Auburn Street in 1912. With a 2,000-seat auditorium, and space for black businesses and offices, it immediately became the commercial and cultural center of Atlanta's black community. Davis, meantime, was becoming a power in the state Republican party, serving for many years as secretary of the Georgia State Republican organization. Then, in 1925, he became the Georgia member of the Republican National Committee, making him one of the three most politically powerful blacks in the South. As such, Davis controlled all federal patronage positions in the state. In 1929, however, he was dismissed from his post by President Herbert Hoover, who wished to rid the party of what he called "rotten boroughs." Then, with the onset of the Depression, the Odd Fellows experienced severe financial difficulties, cut their subsidy to the *Independent*, and sold their Auburn Avenue complex. Davis was therefore forced to close down the *Independent* and leave the field to Scott's *Atlanta World*.

The imminent demise of Davis' and the *Independent*, however, was not apparent to Scott or anyone else in Atlanta in 1928. Davis was the giant, virtually unchallenged for decades in the city, and Scott was David come to give battle. Things, though, had a way of going Scott's way. While at Morehouse, Scott had taken an economics course from L. D. Milton. Milton, at this time, fortuitously for Scott, was employed at Citizens Trust, which had received the Service Printing Company for debt when Heman Perry's[*] empire crashed in the mid–1920s. Scott knew Citizens Trust was sitting with the printing equipment, not knowing what to do with it, so the brash young man approached Milton. Milton later recalled the encounter:

I started that paper. W. A. went to Morehouse College while I was teaching at Morehouse, and that's how he got to know me. I had a printing company which I took from Perry and his crowd when they failed in running the printing company successfully. And when Scott knew that I owned that printing shop, that is, my bank owned that printing shop, then he came to me to let him use it. And so I let him use the damn equipment. I didn't charge him a damn thing for it.

The Scott family recalls that it was a "reasonable rental," not free, but it is clear from both accounts that Scott, a "born salesman" had persuaded someone else to give him a deal.

Ric Roberts recalled the origins of the *Atlanta World* from his perspective.

He was sitting one day at the soda fountain at Yates and Milton Drugstore when Scott walked and said to him, "Say Ric—I'm going to print a newspaper. Ben Davis' *Independent* seems on the downgrade—the time is ripe for a paper in this town." Roberts was enthusiastic about the idea, but wondered where Scott, who had little capital, would get the money. Scott replied, "I don't need a lot of money. It will be a healthier way to start. I won't waste money—I'll use just enough to get going and then I'll work and work and work—see?"

According to Roberts, nearly everybody in Atlanta's black community thought Scott was a fool for starting the paper—good deal on the printing equipment or not. But Scott soon proved them wrong, as he hit the city's newspaper world like a whirlwind. In the first issue of the *Atlanta World*, on August 5, 1928, Scott wrote a column entitled, "A Dedication to the Public." In it, he outlined his ambition for the infant enterprise. "The publishers of the *Atlanta World*," he wrote, "have felt the need of a Southern Negro newspaper, published by Southern Negroes, to be read by Southern Negroes." Of course, blacks in Atlanta already had the *Independent*, but Scott ignored that. The problem, he wrote, is "that the Negro is viewing his race news, such as it is—chiefly crimes of thieves and murderers—primarily through the optics of a host of prejudiced white papers which take pride in flaunting the black man as a vicious enemy to society."

Scott's verve and style caught the imagination of the African-American reading public in Atlanta and his paper began selling. But Scott was not one to leave anything to chance; besides, he was a salesman, and he knew how to sell newspaper just like any other commodity. Starting the *World* primarily as a business, rather than a political venture, Scott hired scores of agents, who worked like door-to-door insurance salesmen, soliciting subsriptions in the black community. This was something new, and it assured the infant paper of a healthy circulation, almost overnight. With this circulation, Scott could turn to both black and white businesses to solicit advertisements. He was highly successful in securing weekly ads from the largest, most prosperous firms in the black community, and he began getting support from white firms too. By 1931 Sears, Roebuck and Company was advertising in its pages, and shortly thereafter Rich's, the city's premier department store, also began running ads. Benjamin Davis, who had viewed his paper primarily as a political venture, was completely outdone by Scott's aggressive, businesslike approach. As Frank M. Davis commented about Scott, "What the *World* contained was of no great interest to him but how many copies were sold was of primary importance. . . . His concentration was on home delivery." By 1930 the *Atlanta World*, a weekly paper, was doing extremely well.

Scott divided Atlanta into sections or districts, with managers responsible for the routes. The delivery boys were expected to sell the paper, aggressively, to the majority of the families along their route, and collect from them on a weekly basis. Any newsboys who began to slip in this soon found themselves replaced by someone else. The system worked, and it made money for both the *World* and the newsboys. As Frank M. Davis said, "a good many graduates of Atlanta colleges can thank the *World* for providing them with a means of getting their education.''

From that point on, Scott gave Atlantans ''something new each year.'' In 1930 he began publishing the paper twice a week, and in 1931 he took a bigger plunge. He not only began printing the *Atlanta World* three times a week, but he began the *Chattanooga Tribune*, the *Birmingham World*, and the *Memphis World*. The Tennessee paper soon folded, but the other two continued on for over forty years—W. A. Scott had created the first chain of black newspapers. On March 3, 1932, the *Atlanta World* became a daily. All this change, growth, and dynamism had black Atlanta agog. Ric Roberts reported that those people who had chided Scott in 1928 for his foolishness in starting a newspaper now thought: ''He was a miracle man. He was a genius. Their hats were off— W. A. Scott was insuperable.''

Scott also began creating what came to be known as the Scott Newspaper Syndicate at this time. One reason he had moved toward publishing a daily was that he had a great deal of excess, expensive, printing capacity in his shop. Daily print runs took up some of that slack, but not all of it. So, Scott began contacting the editors and publishers of small black weeklies throughout the South, and later the North. He offered to print their papers for them, providing them with bits of news from the general news agencies that went into all the papers, and then printing up the local news that they sent in also. It was a good deal for all concerned, and soon the Atlanta plant was doing the printing for dozens of newspapers. When he switched to a daily, Scott could begin bringing out a Sunday paper, and for that he developed a rotogravure section. According to the *World*, ''[N]o Negro paper anywhere, unless it is published by the Southern Newspaper Syndicate [what the Scott Syndicate was then called], gives its readers a rotogravure section.'' Also called the ''brown sheet,'' it was ''filled with pictures of Negroes and their activities gathered from here and every part of the world.'' He also put in a series of regular comic strip features.

As the *Atlanta World* grew, and became more profitable, W. A. Scott continued to expand his business interests. But even here there was a sense of malice, of beating an old enemy and beating him soundly. When the Depression hit, and real estate values fell and old financial empires tottered, Scott knew it was time to get rich. In a daring move, he decided to buy the massive Odd Fellows complex, the biggest black edifice in the South at that time. There were three reasons for this. First, it would provide adequate space to house the *Atlanta World* and Scott's increasing business interests. Second, it would be a sweet final victory over Benjamin J. Davis and his Odd Fellow supporters. Third, it gave him the enjoyment of ousting his third wife from the premises, since she operated a beauty parlor on the third floor of the building.

By 1934 William A. Scott was rich and famous. He had one of the few daily black newspapers in America, he had the only chain of black newspapers, he had a large printing and syndication service for small African-American weeklies, and he had a fortune in Atlanta real estate and other enterprises. Then, suddenly, on a cold January night it all came to an end. Scott had parked his car in his garage, and as he was heading for his house, he was shot in the back and killed. He died in the hospital eight days later. A suspect, the brother of Scott's fourth wife, was charged with the murder, but he was never convicted, and the case remains officially unsolved.

Ric Roberts wrote the day after William Scott's funeral, "I looked down on his bier yesterday . . . on the effigy or caricature of William Alexander Scott that the mortician has created with a little paint and powder. . . . There he lay looking so cold and aged admist [*sic*] the piles of living blossoms. Little more than a week before, W. A. had met a few of us at the door of his office." In a July 1976 article, *Jet* magazine called W. A. Scott II one of the 200 most important black people in the United States during its first 200 years. Sherman Briscoe, executive director of the National Newspaper Publishers Association, an organization of black publishers, called him one of the top twenty-four black journalists in the past 150 years. William Scott's son, W. A. Scott III, who was eleven years old when his father was killed, summed it up best in 1971: "It has been over thirty-seven years since his death and I have never met another man like W. A."

With William A. Scott II's death, there ensued a ferocious battle for control of the newspaper and Scott's financial empire. His estate was inherited by eleven legatees, including his two sons, his sisters, his brothers, and his mother. Although they all shared to some extent in the enterprise, it was his brother, C. A. Scott, who emerged in control of the *Atlanta World*, proclaiming, "We shall carry on!" C. A. Scott was virtually the total antithesis of his brother. A quiet, conservative, family man, he resembled W. A. only in his dedication to putting out the paper in a crisp, businesslike fashion. In that respect, then, there was little change in the editorial or business policies of the paper after C. A. Scott took over.

C. A. Scott grew up in Jackson, Mississippi, and Johnson City, Tennessee. He moved to Atlanta in 1928, where he attended Morris Brown College for a year, and then went to Morehouse College from 1929 to 1931. During these years, he worked with his brother on the founding and growth of the *Atlanta World*. C. A. then went off to journalism school at the University of Kansas in Topeka from 1931 to 1932. In 1932 C. A. returned to Atlanta and became assistant manager of the publishing concern.

During a one-month period in 1945, the content of the *Atlanta Daily World* was analyzed. Certain patterns were evident that reflected the general editorial thrust of C. A. Scott and the Scott Newspaper Syndicate. The study found that the *World* was "a special pleader for human rights, [but] does not protest too much on local issues and news." Rather, it found, the emphasis was on "general issues, politics and news from distant points." In its analysis of headlines, the study found that not one local issue was deemed worthy of inclusion during that period. Issues that were given strong coverage by the *World* during these years often dealt with race relations, particularly lynchings, but virtually all of these took place outside Atlanta. Similarly, during the 1930s, the *World* took up the cause of the Scottsboro boys, convicted of rape in Alabama. It also opposed discrimination in the nation's capital during the 1930s, mistreatment of black soldiers during World War II, and segregation in the schools.

One local issue that was stressed in the paper was what is today called "black-on-black" crime. Since this issue was almost totally ignored in the city's white press, the *World* took upon itself the mission of dealing with these matters. In its coverage of the issue in 1945, the paper advocated that crime should be met with strict justice and less leniency by the local courts, and that more black policemen should be hired to enhance the respect for police and the law in the black neighborhoods. As early as 1931, however, the *World* came under some criticism for its heavy reporting on black crime. The paper responded editorially, defending the practice by saying that the issue was of the greatest interest to the largest number of readers.

Numerous other matters of local importance were stressed by the *World*, especially during the first thirty years of C. A. Scott's tenure. There was, for instance, a constant call for support of black businesses. Without this support, it warned, "business cannot be built up or places made for capable and well-trained members of the race." It particularly urged support be given to black insurance companies, which were the largest and most significant financial institutions in the black community. A major reason for the *World*'s advocating support for black business was because it would provide jobs for the black community. And this fed into the conservative, Republican, anti–New Deal philosophy of C. A. Scott. During the Depression, Scott argued that blacks wanted jobs rather than relief, and, like Eugene Washington Rhodes[*] of the *Philadelphia Tribune*, opposed both the National Recovery Act and the passage of the minimum wage on the grounds that they would discriminate against blacks.

A staple of the *World*, as with virtually all other black newspapers, are the various social columns, dealing with the comings and goings of the city's black elite, and with the various clubs and organizations. This practice has come under withering attack from both outside and within the community of the black press. Charles Tisdale, publisher of the *Jackson* (Mississippi) *Advocate* in the 1980s, for example, said, "Many major black publications are more concerned about who got married or bought a new dress than the concerns of working-class black people." Although there is much truth to this accusation, it does overlook a critical fact of the period from the 1920s to the 1960s. As one scholar has commented, during that time "the 'white press' carrie[d] personal items on Negroes only when they [were] dead and these in paid advertisements of undertakers." It may have seemed trivial to many activists, both black and white, but the "social news" of the *World* and other black papers was important for creating a sense of community during a time when practically nothing else functioned to provide this essential communication function.

Three other areas covered in great detail by the *World* were news on the churches, the schools, and sports. For church news, there were not only regular columns by ministers, but also much "social" news of the various churches and their activities. The *World* also gave full reports on church conferences and other major events in the religious life of black Atlanta. School news revolved around not only the six major black universities in the city, which had been combined to form the Atlanta University Center, but also the black public schools, especially Booker T. Washington High School. BTW High was the first, and for many years the only, high school for blacks in the city, and its graduates including Dr. Martin Luther King, Jr., were illustrious. Finally, the sports activities of the local black schools and colleges were covered in much detail, and there were also reports on local, semiprofessional teams in a variety of sports. "Major league" sports did not receive much coverage until the 1960s, when Atlanta got the Braves, the Falcons, the Hawks, and, for a time, the Flames.

The most contentious issue, and the one most difficult to analyze, for C. A. Scott and the *World* was civil rights. On one hand, Scott and his paper have always trumpeted their longstanding devotion to the cause of black equality and rights. On the other hand, the paper has endured relentless and harsh criticism from black militants, particularly after 1960, for what was seen as its ultraconservative stance on this issue. There is little question that Scott and the *World* have been fighting for political rights for blacks for a long time. In 1945 Scott formed the Citizens Democrat Club of Fulton County to challenge the legality of the white primary, and in 1959 he cochaired a committee that raised funds to successfully defend a black man who had been convicted and sentenced to die for the alleged rape of a white woman.

Yet a natural conservatism in politics and social activities colored Scott's thinking and set the tone for the *World's* editorial positions. As he once noted, "My mother sorta made me . . . a natural born conservative," and he and the paper became increasingly Republican in political affairs after 1952. Scott and the *World* endorsed every Republican presidential candidate from 1952 through 1988, except Barry Goldwater in 1964. This same conservatism became particularly obvious after the civil rights crusade became more militant and direct action–oriented in the 1960s. The key shattering point was the student sit-ins of the early 1960s. Scott could not bring himself to support this action, and this caused a deep fissure between the paper and the increasingly mobilized black community.

The first critical issue emerged over the decision on the part of college students to stage sit-ins at the major public restaurant facilities in downtown Atlanta that were closed to blacks. This included Rich's Department Store, and several other major advertisers in the *World*. The paper faced a major dilemma. If it supported the sit-in, it would alienate some of the *World's* major advertisers. On the other hand, if it opposed the sit-in, or remained silent, it would be betraying its long history of support for civil rights. Stanley Scott, a family member and officer at the paper, explained that "they were really walking on a tightrope. Because on one hand they had to depend on the department stores for their life blood— advertising. And they had to stand up and be counted in respect to the civil rights movement." C. A. Scott had to choose, and he chose to oppose the sit-in. He editorialized that blacks should place more emphasis "on removing segregation in education, more voting and political influence, equal consideration in the administration of justice at the state level and improved economic opportunities than on places to eat." The temper of the times demanded support—and Scott failed to provide it.

Of course, there was another aspect to this, too. Scott and the *World* had long promoted the success of black business—"shop where you can work" campaigns were common. Integration of white business institutions would sound the death knell for the thriving black business community on Auburn Avenue of which Scott and the *World* were so much a part. Scott never said that this was one of the reasons why he did not support the sit-in, but it is clear that most of the old black elite in the city, those whose roots and fortunes were deeply embedded in the black business establishment, did not support the sit-ins. It was, perhaps, a case of self-interest all around.

When the *World* and the older black establishment refused to support the sit-ins in the 1960s, the world of black newspapers and black leadership in the city began to change. On July 31, 1960, the *Atlanta Inquirer* was founded by Jesse Hill, Jr.,[*] a young executive with Atlanta Life, with the financial support and backing of Herman Russell.[*] Hill and Russell were strong supporters of the newly energized civil rights crusade. In the *Inquirer*'s first editorial, it said that the paper was "the brain child of a group of young men who felt a void existed in the reporting of news in the Atlanta Negro community." Hill further promised that the *Inquirer* would take a "firm, unequivocal stand on controversial issues involving the interest" of blacks. They were going to take on the "twin evils of segregation and discrimination," and the time of gradualism and restraint (i.e., Scott) were passed. Members of the old order, the *Inquirer* said, should retire and pass on the mantle of leadership to younger and "more able" personalities. "You must either join hands and lead us together down the path of freedom or step aside."

C. A. Scott later defended his stance on the sit-ins:

When the sit-ins began in 1959, I thought it was a great idea for the young people to get involved. We played it right up and I defended Dr. King's right to come to Atlanta. We sent him money to help the Montgomery bus boycott. When the sit-ins came to Atlanta, and one of the large stores said it would desegregate when the schools did, I thought this was fair. . . . I told the white business people they shouldn't be stampeded into hiring Negroes and I told the civil rights leaders to give whites time to adjust to the change, for the best interests of both sides.

But the black community would not accept this explanation; readers switched to the *Inquirer*, and later on to the *Atlanta Voice*. The *World*'s circulation, which had been about 30,000 in 1960, had dropped to 20,000 ten years later. At that time, *Atlanta* magazine called it "the weakest, professionally, of the three black newspapers . . . the two weeklies are more aggressive, fatter, more interesting, more attractive."

But C. A. Scott did not mellow or surrender his contrary attitudes. In 1983, when there was a campaign to establish Martin Luther King, Jr.'s birthday as a national holiday, Scott wrote an editorial in the *World* opposing it. He argued that it would be too expensive for the economy to give everyone a day off on that day, and, besides, only one president had been so honored. Again, this stance hardly endeared Scott to the black community, especially since the Martin Luther King, Jr., Center for Social Change, with King's tomb in its courtyard, was being built just up Auburn Avenue from the *World*'s offices. Despite his rather cantankerous statements, Scott continued to be honored as a "hero" of the civil rights crusade. In 1981 the Atlanta Urban League gave its annual Jesse O. Thomas Service Award to Scott for his service to Atlanta and the *World*. Two years later, he was made a Life Fellow in the Southern Regional Council in recognition of his fight for "racial equality." Rather ironically, by 1990, Martin Luther King Day had become a major holiday and celebration, especially in Atlanta, and Scott and the *Atlanta World* milked it for all it was worth. Each year they printed a special three-color "King Holiday Edition" and lauded the fact that "Dr. M. L. King's Nonviolent Change Helps Masses Fight for Freedom."

One long-term struggle of C. A. Scott received more respect by the 1990s than his earlier stands on civil rights demonstrations. This had to do with his fight to save Auburn Avenue as a significant area for black business and culture. In 1950 the Metropolitan Planning Committee had designated Auburn Avenue and the surrounding area a "slum" to be sold to the Atlanta Housing Authority using the right of eminent domain, and then sold to private, white, business to be developed as a "respectable" and profitable adjunct to the downtown business area. Scott argued before the commission that "Auburn Avenue must remain and become a part of the 'Golden Heart' which is the apparent pride of the Commission." His intervention was critical in saving the area, and Scott has devoted himself to bringing about its transformation in the forty years since that time. In 1987 he urged the Atlanta chapter of the Frontiers International Club, a service organization, "to take the initiative and boldly help rehabilitate and preserve Auburn Avenue." To this point, however, his crusade, despite some historic preservation money, and "Sweet Auburn" tours, has been largely unsuccessful.

In 1983 the Atlanta Business League, long affiliated with Booker T. Washington's* National Negro Business League, celebrated its fiftieth anniversary. C. A. Scott, at seventy-five years of age, reminisced about earlier, "golden" days. He pointed out that his father had helped Washington found the National Business League in 1900, and that he and his brother became active supporters of the Atlanta branch when they arrived in the 1920s. "I firmly believe in economic activity, and that is why the organization was founded—to promote economic development, to help in any way it could to get black people involved in business." Fifty years before, that had been the message, and that had been the answer. By the 1980s, however, things had changed. Charles Tisdale in

1987 spoke eloquently against Scott and his ilk: "The black press has evolved to the point where it generally responds only to middle-class injustices. . . . In the past, great black editors, such as Robert S. Abbott[*] of the *Courier* [*sic*] and Percy Green of the *Advocate* were interested in grassroots justice against the evils of lynching, segregation and second class citizenship." Once, the *World* and the Scott family were too, but C. A. Scott's stodgy business orientation, allied with his political conservatism, diluted that stance to the point where the *World* attracted little praise. Its complacent mediocrity stood in stark contrast to the dynamism with which the paper had been founded in 1928.

Sources

No personal papers of the Scott family are currently available. Company records are located at the *Atlanta World* office on Auburn Avenue in Atlanta, but they are not open to researchers at the present time. A full run of back issues of the *Atlanta World* is available on microfilm, as are substantial runs of the *Birmingham World* and *Memphis World*.

Biographical information on W. A. Scott II is found in *Atlanta Daily World*, June 18, 1976, and February 12, 1984; *Negro Digest*, November 1946; *Who's Who in Colored America* (1928–1929); and Ric Roberts, "W. A. Scott, Jr.—The Man," in the Schomburg Collection in the New York Public Library. Information on C. A. Scott comes from press releases from the *World* offices, from *Atlanta Daily World*, May 31, 1981, February 12, 1984, October 25, 1987; and January 14, 1990; *Who's Who in Colored America* (1950); *Who's Who among Black Americans* (1988); *Black Enterprise*, June 1980; *Atlanta Constitution, Intown Extra*, February 17, 1983; *Atlanta Journal and Constitution*, November 13, 1983; and *Birmingham Post-Herald*, March 9, 1960.

For information on the *Atlanta World* itself, see Henry L. Suggs, *The Black Press*, (1983) 127–39; Sadie Mae Oliver, "The History and Development of the *Atlanta Daily World* (The Nation's Only Negro Daily Newspaper)," Master's thesis, Hampton University, 1942; *Atlanta Constitution*, July 30, 1978; *Atlanta Daily World*, June 18, 1976, August 5, 1982, and March 2, 1986; *Pittsburgh Courier*, July 15, 1961; "Press: Black Voices Filling a Void," *Atlanta Magazine*, May 1970, 48–54; and Robert J. Alexander, "Negro Business in Atlanta," *Southern Economic Journal* 17, 4 (April 1951), 455–56.

Sengstacke, John Herman Henry (see Abbott, Robert Sengstacke, and John Herman Henry Sengstacke).

Shaw, Patricia Walker (see Walker Family).

Sims, Naomi (March 30, 1949–). Fashion model, entrepreneur, wig and cosmetics manufacturer, and author: Naomi Sims Collection; and Naomi Sims Beauty Products, Ltd. Naomi Sims has been lucky; and she has been good. She was lucky to have been born tall and beautiful. She was lucky to have come of age at a time, the 1960s, when the world of fashion and modeling opened up to African-Americans for the first time—when "Black Is Beautiful" became a common catchphrase. But there were other beautiful black women of Sims's generation—only she was bright enough, ambitious enough, and good enough to translate that ephemeral advantage into stunning business success as an entrepreneur and manufacturer.

Sims was born in Oxford, Mississippi, and later moved to Pittsburgh, where she graduated from Westinghouse High School. Other than that information, reports of her early life, supposedly based upon interviews with Sims herself, are contradictory. In one, she is reported to have been born into a poor family, and to have moved to Pittsburgh to live with foster parents, Mr. and Mrs. Albert Talbot, when she was nine. In another account, it says she moved to Pittsburgh with her parents when she was three. In an interview, she said; "My parents weren't dirt-poor. They were a lower-middle class couple who took great pride in rearing three girls. My father was a working man and my mother, who is no longer living, didn't work. They owned land in Mississippi." In an earlier interview, however, she had said; "My parents were divorced when I was a baby and I knew nothing of my father except that my mother told me he was a absolute bum." In yet another account, there was another twist on the story. Explaining that she had only vague memories of her father, and that her mother was the dominant influence on the family, it states that when Naomi was eight years old her mother had a nervous breakdown, which caused her daughter to be sent to live with foster parents. Naomi Sims stated, "I moved around a lot," which gave her a "complex," but that her family situation also "forced [her] to be self-reliant." In another interview, she stated; "At the age of nine I was taken away from my mother to live in a home for girls and a series of foster homes. It took me a long time to get over it. I used to cry at night and say 'I want my Mommy.' "

In any event, after graduation, all accounts agree that Sims left for New York City to live with her sister, Betty, who was an airline stewardess and who later also became a model. Naomi Sims obtained a small scholarship and attended the Fashion Institute of Technology, where she studied merchandising and textile design. At the same time, she also got another small scholarship to study psychology at New York University, where she went in the evenings. Before long, however, Sims found herself short of funds, and a counselor at the Fashion Institute suggested she try modeling. Not really knowing how to approach this, Sims called various fashion photographers, until she contacted Gosta Peterson, one of the "stars" of the profession. Incredibly, Peterson agreed to meet with Sims. Peterson was overwhelmed with the beauty and grace of the 5-foot, 10-inch, dark-skinned, black beauty. He immediately contacted his wife, Patricia Peterson, who was a fashion editor at the *New York Times Magazine*. Patricia Peterson put Sims in a high-profile fashion layout in the magazine in her first modeling session, and Sims's fairytale career as a fashion model was launched.

Although Naomi Sims's entrance into the world of modeling seems so easy as to have been almost automatic, she was actually just in the right place at the right time. For decades, black women had been virtually banned from the mainstream modeling profession. As *Life* magazine stated when it put Sims on its cover in 1969: "Until 1945 virtually no black faces appeared in ads, except for

Aunt Jemima. Then they began to appear regularly in the black publication *Ebony* but only to tout such products as skin bleaches and hair straighteners." The first really successful black model was Helen Williams. But she got layouts only for black magazines because she was considered too dark skinned for mainstream magazines. "The light-skinned girls get the jobs," she explained to *Newsweek* in 1962. "It's very difficult for a dark-skinned girl." Yet, she was credited by every African-American model who came later for opening the door for them. "She was," an article claimed, "every Black girl's dream come true in their aspirations to model. She [was] the first dark model to gain acceptance in the industry and has opened doors for all women of darker than olive complexion. Her exquisite Budweiser Beer and Modess ads became a trademark."

The big breakthrough for blacks, prior to Naomi Sims, however, was Donyale Luna, who in 1964 was featured on the cover of *Harper's Bazaar*—the first black model to be so featured and also the first black model to earn top fees. Sims, however, in 1967 became the first "Black model superstar, flanked by the twin attendants of fame and fortune. Within two years from the time she began modeling, Sims was on the cover of *Life*, described simply as 'top model,'" *Black Enterprise* reported in 1976. "She has appeared in virtually every fashion magazine in the world." What was the secret of Naomi Sims's meteoric rise in the fashion world? As in most cases like this, it was a combination of luck, talent, hard work, and burning ambition.

After she appeared in the *New York Times* layout, Sims contacted the top white agencies, assuming they would be eager to sign her up. She soon learned otherwise. According to Sims, when she showed them her layout in the *Times*, they all said, "Well, that is very nice, but I really don't think I can get you work." As a result, Sims approached Wilhelmina Cooper, who was starting her own modeling agency. In one account, Cooper said, "[W]hen that lady [Sims] walked through the door, nobody else existed," and she signed her on the spot. In Sims's own telling the situation was much different. Cooper, like the other modeling agency heads, told her, "I just don't think you will make it." But Sims was undaunted. She told Cooper that she wanted to send out 100 copies of her fashion layout to people listed in the *Madison Avenue Handbook*, and she asked if she could just list Cooper's number at the bottom. It was a no-risk deal for Cooper and she agreed. If people called, she had a model and modeling commissions, if not, she had not spent any time or money on the project. To Cooper's surprise, the response was overwhelming. A few days later, she sent a telegram to Sims, saying. "We have so many calls for you (stop). Please contact us right away (stop). We want to represent you (stop)."

In the first week after she signed with Cooper, Sims did a national television commercial with a white and an oriental model for AT&T which launched what was to prove to be a short, but brilliant, career in modeling. During the next six years, Sims graced the covers of just about every major fashion magazine in the world, and she won an armful of awards in the industry. She was the first black woman to be featured on the cover of a major woman's magazine, *Ladies*

Home Journal, and the first black to be featured in a multi-colored magazine spread in *Vogue*. Twice, in 1969 and 1970, she was voted the top model of the year by International Mannekins. "When she put on a garment, something just m-a-arvelous happened," gushed the designer Halston. "She could make any garment—even a sackcloth—look like sensational haute couture," proclaimed Cooper. But Sims was lucky too. The late 1960s was a time when "Black Is Beautiful," as *Essence* has stated, "sounded a vigorous call to confront and love our authentic African selves." Sims became "the first Black woman accepted as a beauty in her own right." "Never," said *Essence*, "had a model so dark-skinned received so much exposure, praise and professional prestige."

Naomi Sims also did much to revolutionize the fashion industry itself. The *Kansas City Star* reported, "Her walk became her hallmark. It wasn't like the glide or bounce of many models. Her serpentine movements of the arms, torso and legs were beautiful to watch and as subtly controlled as a dancer's." This was the beginning of a larger transformation that has rocked the fashion world. Frederick Murphy, in *Encore*, said,

Black female models are credited with dramatically changing the manner in which clothes are introduced at "trade-only" fashion shows. Until the mid-sixties, when designers began using Black models, the high fashion mannekin was stiff, lifeless—almost other worldly. But . . . Black models danced and strutted. They brought to the runway an attitude that delighted fashion editors and buyers alike. And they made designers and manufacturers happy because they helped boost sales.

Other top black fashion models commented on the change; "Just ain't none of them white girls got as much rhythm in their whole body as we got in our little fingers." "We grew up with the rhythm and the beat," another said. "My first Clovis Ruffin show, I jiggled, I hammed, I boogied, I cut it up, man, and those poor tired buyers loved it." By the mid–1970s, black models were in great demand for just those reasons, and Naomi Sims was among the most requested. But at the peak of her success in modeling, she retired to pursue other goals and dreams.

By 1972 Sims had become rather disillusioned with modeling, and most especially with her agency. As a result, she wrote to Eileen Ford, head of Ford Modeling Agency, telling her, "During this past year I have become more than disillusioned with the performance of my present agency. I am not concerned about my bookings . . . I am involved in various non-specifically modelling [*sic*] enterprises that my agency is incapable of handling or even giving intelligent advice, let alone assistance, upon. . . . When I began modelling, four years ago, age eighteen, fresh from the sticks, I obviously had no idea of the potential complexities involved. Having achieved a certain degree of notoriety in the field I want to take advantage of it professionally with no-nonsense, expert management." It is not known if Ford wrote back, or what she might have said, but Sims soon found new outlets for her intelligence and ambition.

When she gave up modeling in 1973, Sims was just twenty-four years old, and she had a potentially long career ahead of her. When asked a few years later why she retired, she replied, "Modeling was never my ultimate goal. I started to model to supplement my income to go to college. And even while I was modeling I was always fighting the reputation models have for being vapid and unintelligent. But the idea of starting my own business had always appealed to me, and I was fortunate that my first career led to my second." Early on, Sims had shown an entrepreneurial bent. Writing to an unknown manufacturer in 1969, she announced, "It is my intention to sell your products in the United States of America, starting in New York and Pittsburgh and extending the sales to other states afterward." She then outlined in a precise and cogent manner exactly how she planned to do it, what she thought her expenses would be, and how successful she would be at it.

For her second career, Naomi Sims began manufacturing wigs for African-American women. Again, the time was right. The Afro hairstyle, which stressed the "natural look" for black women, had just about run its course by 1973, and many black women who were going into the business world wanted a look that was presentable, yet easy and quick to achieve. Sims's wigs were designed to provide that. Sims had come upon the idea of wigs from her own experience: "I never wore a wig before I went into the business because they didn't match the texture of my hair. They were made of Caucasian hair. Our hair is totally different. It is porous in structure and has a strong wave pattern." But she also had problems managing her own hair while modeling: "I was sort of driven to distraction in terms of how to vary my hairstyle," she said, "because to increase your life as a model, depends on how different you can look in each picture, and that meant being able to change your hairstyle."

Since there was nothing on the market in the way of wigs that suited what Sims wanted, she began experimenting with synthetic fibers. "I got hold of a current best-selling fiber for white women, wet the fiber down, put it in my oven at a very low temperature, and baked it for maybe five or ten minutes." The results were encouraging in terms of texture, but she had many other problems to solve. There were numerous variations of colors, shades, and textures of women's hair in the black community, so when Sims traveled as a model and a speaker she would take scissors along with her. "Wherever I went—streets, theater—I'd ask for hair samples."

Convinced that she had a winning idea, Sims approached several wig man-ufacturers, but she was rejected. Finally, Metropa Company, an import-export firm that had been in the wig business for ten years and sold a line of wigs for black women, agreed to put up some money and to make its research and chemist facilities available to Sims. She also put up some money and founded her own company in 1973, called Naomi Sims Collection. "Those were scary days in the beginning," she later recalled, but finally a breakthrough came. A fiber was produced that looked exactly like straightened black hair, was light in weight and construction, and did not have to be set. The fiber was patented and trade-marked under the name Kanekalon Presselle. With that advance, the Naomi Sims line of wigs went into production. During the first three years, Sims did practically everything with the firm herself, designed the wigs and the ads, and traveled around the country promoting her product to department store buyers.

A few stores took the wigs immediately, but then Sims began encountering resistance. The white buyers essentially refused to believe that there was any difference between white and black hair, and they assumed that black women would buy and wear wigs made for whites. Sims was thus forced to conduct what she called "a crash course to completely re-educate everybody about the anatomical structure of black hair, and what straightening black hair meant." Ultimately she was highly successful; first year sales reached $5 million. The sales were fueled by the fact that 40 percent of black women wear wigs, but had been dissatisfied with the products for years. Thus, when Naomi Sims's wigs came on the market they fulfilled a great need, and customers hurriedly searched them out. This forced other department stores to begin carrying her line.

Sims was not entirely happy with the performance of Metropa during this early period. She wrote to Robert Lasky in 1973, complaining that her "product is selling well, it has put them on the map. Now, they simply don't give a damn. They seem to fatally combine the drawbacks of being both greedy and small-minded. Bad wigs are being sent to stores . . . I could bore you to tears with stories of their sheer stupidity, arrogance, racism and general incompetence. . . . Bob, an awful lot depends on this. My future is going to lie in these kinds of products. One day soon I will have the largest company in this country marketing every damn thing from perfume to corn-remover. . . . For this reason, Metropa has got to perform."

Sims finally resolved her problems with Metropa, and her company was spun off into a separate division. Employing sixteen people in 1979, Sims's division accounted for the lion's share of the total sales of the Metropa firm. Meantime, every other wig company also came out with wigs for black women, which provided more competition for Sims, but also proved how right she had been about the need for the product. By the early 1980s her wigs were sold in 2,000 department stores throughout the United States, Canada, Great Britain, the West Indies, and Africa. The products were manufactured in Hong Kong and Korea. Some have called Naomi Sims's wig collection the greatest beauty aid to black women since Madame C. J. Walker (see Walker, Sarah Breedlove) marketed the straightening comb in the early twentieth century.

In order to help promote her wigs, and to enhance her own visibility and prospects, Naomi Sims also became an author during this time. In 1976 she wrote *All about Health and Beauty for the Black Woman*, a comprehensive guide to every aspect of black beauty care, along with tips on diet and health. "For years," she said, "my publishers approached me to write a book describing my own beauty tips. I didn't feel comfortable with just that, though, so I took the idea further and interviewed 100 Black women, from all walks of life, across the country. . . . And I spent countless hours on my own, researching and compiling information.'' The book sold very well, and it was in its tenth printing three years later.

By the late 1980s Naomi Sims was ready to take her next step in creating the business empire she had envisioned in her letter to Robert Lasky in 1973. She brought out her own line of cosmetics. As with the wigs, it was first picked up by a few high-status stores, including Carson-Pirie-Scott, Abraham & Straus, Saks Fifth Avenue, Nordstroms, and R. H. Macy's. She toured the country to promote her products and to convince buyers to put them in their stores. Although many other firms produced cosmetics for black women, Sims claimed that her line was the first allergy-free skin-care line with conditioners, cleaners, and moisturizers to alleviate black skin problems. In 1988, three years after founding her cosmetics line, Naomi Sims Beauty Products was grossing about $5 million. By 1989, however, Sims's firm, along with other black-owned cosmetics companies, were being seriously challenged by the large white firms, which had decided to come out with special lines of cosmetics to appeal to the black woman. A division president of Revlon was quoted as saying, ''In the next couple of years, the black-owned businesses will disappear. They'll all be sold to white companies.'' Reverend Jesse Jackson's Operation PUSH organized demonstrations to protest this remark. As for Naomi Sims, her comments were not recorded, but one can imagine her saying under her breath, ''Over my dead body!''

Sims, who married Michael Alistair Findlay, an art gallery owner who had immigrated to America from England, has one son. She is very involved in the affairs of the black community of New York, where she serves on a number of boards. One of the most important to her is the Harlem Northside Center for Child Development, which was designed to provide help for troubled young people. In other respects, however, she has maintained a low profile socially, preferring to spend time with her husband and child at home.

Naomi Sims, by the early 1990s, stood as probably the preeminent black woman entrepreneur in America. Yet she was not without her critics, particularly because many viewed her beauty business as an attempt to exploit the black woman's desire to adapt to the white concept of beauty propagated in the media. Feminists of all colors also often disparage the emphasis on the superficial aspects of women. Sims confessed, ''I am sure I have my share of Black female critics and enemies. It doesn't matter. I adore women and I know I am a woman's woman. . . . I would be nowhere if it weren't for Black women.'' She was not apologetic. Her vision of herself and her work was probably best expressed to her young son, who questioned why she worked. She replied, ''Mommy loves Black women very very much, and I make products that make all of us black women look just a little bit more beautiful, and give us more confidence to go out into the world.'' She recalls her own teenage years, and states, ''Black wasn't beautiful then. The darker your skin the less good-looking you were considered; and I was too tall, and too skinny. But somewhere within me I just always had that confidence in my looks and my intelligence.'' And that is what she sees herself and her products imparting to other African-American women.

Sources

Naomi Sims's papers have been deposited at the Schomburg Center for Research at the New York Public Library. There are audiovisual tapes of Sims giving fashion advice, as well as copies of her books and articles on fashion. The collection also contains a limited number of personal and business letters, along with clippings on Sims's activities from various magazines and newspapers. There is nothing in the collection after 1976. There is no book-length biography of Sims, but there are shorter biographical treatments in Marianna Davis, *Contributions of Black Women to America* (1982), vol. I; *Ebony Success Library* (1973), vol. II; and short listings in *Who's Who among Black Americans* (1990); Anne Stegemeyer, *Who's Who in Fashion* (New York, 1988); and *Afro-American Encyclopedia* (North Miami, Florida, 1974).

Some useful magazine articles include *Newsweek*, September 3, 1962, 69, and May 5, 1975, 68; *Ladies Home Journal*, November 1968, 114, 14; *Life*, October 17, 1969; *Ebony*, May 1970, 152*ff.*; *Mademoiselle*, September 1974; *Kansas City Star*, June 22, 1975; *Millinery & Wig Research*, March 26, 1975; *Encore*, April 19, 1976; *Black Enterprise*, September 1976, 41, July 1979, 41–46, and March 1989, 45–49; *Redbook Magazine*, May 1977, 60, 62; *People*, August 22, 1977, 14, 16; *Pittsburgh Courier*, June 16, 1979, 14; *The Afro-American*, October 16, 1982, 11, and April 23, 12; *Essence*, January 1987, 38*ff.*; *Chicago Sun-Times*, November 25, 1987; and *New York Daily News*, June 26, 1983. She was, in addition, interviewed several times on television, and some of these tapes are available. See especially an interview by Barbara Walters on the "Today Show", February 1976. A useful account of Sims's entry into the cosmetics field is found in Patricia O'Toole, "Battle of the Beauty Counter," *New York Times Magazine*, December 3, 1989.

Naomi Sims has written at least three books dealing with fashion and hair care for African-Americans: *All about Health and Beauty for the Black Woman* (New York, 1976); *How to Be a Top Model* (New York, 1979); and *All about Hair Care for the Black Woman* (New York, 1982). She also has written several articles, including, "It Takes More Than Beauty to Make a Model," *Essence*, August 1970, 14; and "A Gift Truly Liberating," *Encore*, June 23, 1975.

Smith, Stephen (1797?–November 4, 1873). Businessman, reformer, abolitionist, and philanthropist. Stephen Smith was born in Paxtang, Dauphin County, Pennsylvania, the son of Nancy Smith, a slave. On July 10, 1801, he was indentured to General Thomas Boude, a Revolutionary war hero who had large-scale lumber interests. Before Smith reached maturity, he assumed the management of Boude's lumber business in Columbia, Pennsylvania. With a loan of $50, Smith was able to purchase his freedom on January 3, 1816; in November of that year, he married Harriet Lee, sister of Isaac Harford Lee. Smith soon established his own lumber business in Columbia and began to engage in large-scale real estate operations, while his wife ran an oyster and refreshment house.

In 1842, while continuing to run his operations in Columbia, Smith moved to Philadelphia, where he purchased the home of his friend, Robert Purvis, son-in-law of James Forten,* at 921 Lombard Street. In that city Smith opened a large coal and lumber yard at Broad and Willow streets, while his long-time associate, William Whipper, ran the Columbia operations. Smith's partner in the Philadelphia operations was Ulysses B. Vidal. During his first decade in Philadelphia, Smith acquired thirty-six properties and had substantial investments in securities. In 1849 Smith and Whipper had an inventory of several thousand bushels of coal, 2.25 million feet of lumber, and twenty-two cars running on the rail line from Columbia to Philadelphia and Baltimore. Their firm owned $9,000 worth of stock in the Columbia Bridge Company and $18,000 worth of stock in the Columbia Bank. Smith was the largest stockholder in the bank. Smith himself was said to own fifty-two solid brick houses in Philadelphia, plus a number of homes and other real property in Columbia.

By the 1850s, according to the R. G. Dun credit reports, Smith was grossing $100,000 annually in sales; and by 1864, his net worth was estimated at $50,000. An 1857 credit rating in the Dun report described Smith as "King of the Darkies w. 100m." His partner, Whipper, was worth about $20,000 in 1853 and Vidal, the other partner, in 1865 "w. 30–50m." By 1849, when Martin R. Delany was compiling his report on the condition of blacks, Smith's coal and lumber business was reputed to be one of the largest in the city. Delany described Smith as "decidedly the most wealthy colored man in the United States." His principal business activity, though, as Delany noted, was "that of buying good negotiables and other paper, and speculating in real estate."

Like James Forten and other wealthy blacks in Philadelphia, however, Smith's life was not easy. He suffered much from racism and discrimination, and these factors, together with his own race pride, caused him to become active in movements to end slavery and bring about the equality of the races. Smith had become one of the initial subscribers to the *Freedman's Journal*, and later he became a contributor to that publication and to the *Emancipator*. In 1831 he conducted a meeting of free blacks in Columbia to protest against the policies of the American Colonization Society, which sought to deport freed slaves to Africa. In 1832 Smith purchased a church building for the use of the Mount Zion African Methodist Episcopal Church. Two years after that, Smith's office in Columbia was attacked by a mob during the antiblack riots on 1834. A year later he was publicly warned to leave the community by whites who were resentful of his business success. Other prominent white citizens, however, rallied to his support, and he was able to remain in Columbia for a few more years.

In 1836 Smith became a member of the General Conference of the African Methodist Church, and two years later he was ordained to preach. He also became actively involved in the operations of the Underground Railroad in both Columbia and Philadelphia with Whipper and William Still.* During this same time, Smith attended the national conventions of free blacks in New York and Philadelphia, and he participated in the organization of the American Moral Reform Society, a group of African-American black men dedicated to temperance reform. He attended the first meeting of the Pennsylvania Anti-Slavery Society in 1837 and was active in a number of conventions and associations for free blacks prior to the Civil War. He became an ardent supporter of the Republican party after its organization in the 1850s. On March 15, 1858, John Brown met at Smith's house with a group of prominent black leaders with his plan for freeing the slaves.

Smith, a major philanthropist for Philadelphia's black community, gave to the Institute for Colored Youth, the Home for Destitute Colored Children, the House of Refuge, and the Olive Cemetery. He was also one of the incorporators of the House for Aged and Infirm Colored Persons, which was later renamed the Stephen Smith Home for the Aged. He also built the Zion Mission at Seventh and Lombard, a church in Chester, Pennsylvania, and another in Cape May, New Jersey. Smith was a member of the Bethel African Methodist Church, and he preached in all the churches of his denomination in Philadelphia. He left $15,000 in his will for the Stephen Smith Home in West Philadelphia.

Smith's partner, William Whipper, also achieved prominence in many areas. He was born in Little Britain township, Pennsylvania, in about 1804. By 1828 he was living in Philadelphia, engaged in steam scouring, a process for cleaning clothes. In 1834 he operated a "free labor and temperance grocery" there. A year later Whipper moved to Columbia, where he became associated in the lumber business with Smith. Like his older mentor, Whipper became involved in a variety of abolition and reform groups, playing a leading role in the founding of the American Moral Reform Society. He was editor of the society's journal the *National Reformer*, the first magazine edited by a black. In 1853 Whipper went to Canada, where he purchased land near Dresden, Ontario. Several of his relatives emigrated there, and Whipper himself was planning to go also when the Civil War broke out. He financially aided the Union cause during the war, and after 1865 he ended his business association with Smith to enter a partnership with his nephew, James W. Purnell. In 1868 Whipper moved to New Brunswick, New Jersey, where the 1870 census recorded his fortune at $108,000. He was the cashier of the Philadelphia branch of the Freedman's Savings Bank from 1870 until it was closed in 1874. In 1873 he returned to Philadelphia, where he died in 1876.

Sources

There is little information of substance available on Stephen Smith. Richard P. McCormick has written a good short biography of him in *Dictionary of American Negro Biography* (1982), and there is another account of Smith in William Frederic Worner, "The Columbia Race Riots," *Lancaster County Historical Society Papers* 26 (October 1922), 175–87. There is also some information in Juliet E. K. Walker, "Racism, Slavery, and Free Enterprise: Black Entrepreneurship in the United States before the Civil War," *Business History Review* 60 (Autumn 1986), 353–54. See also Lawrence Spraggins, "The History of Negro Business prior to 1860," Master's thesis, Howard University, 1935, deposited in the Moorland Spingarn Research Center, Howard University. There is some biographical data on William Whipper in the Leigh Whipper Papers, at the Moorland Spingarn Research Center and an autobiographical memoir in William Still, *The Underground Railroad* (rev. ed., 1879). Richard McCormick has a good biography of him in *Dictionary of American Negro Biography* (1982).

Spaulding, Asa T. (see Kennedy, William Jesse, Jr., William Jesse Kennedy III, Charles Clinton Spaulding, and Asa T. Spaulding).

Spaulding, Charles Clinton (see Kennedy, William Jesse, Jr., William Jesse Kennedy III, Charles Clinton Spaulding, and Asa T. Spaulding).

Still, William (October 7, 1821–July 14, 1902). Businessman, abolitionist, and writer. William Still's father, Levin Steel, was born a slave in Maryland. He had been permitted to purchase his freedom in around 1807, whereupon he left wife and family behind to move to New Jersey. The attraction of this area for Steel was that a number of his relatives lived there. In fact, the first member of the Steel (or Still as they were later called) family in this area arrived in the 1630s. That part of Gloucester County came to be known as Guineatown and endured for three centuries; the last resident, a Mrs. Still, lived there until the 1930s. Levin Steel soon arranged for the escape of his wife, Sidney, who took her two daughters, but left behind her two oldest sons. She changed her name to Charity and joined him in New Jersey, where they also changed their last name to Still to avoid being captured and taken back into slavery.

In was on his father's farm in the New Jersey Pine Barrens that William Still was born, the youngest of eighteen children. It was a hardscrabble life for the Still family and for William. He began working on the family farm at an early age, and he was never able to get more than a few hours a year of formal schooling. To further aid the family, William hired out to chop wood and work in the nearby cranberry bogs. An avid reader, he spent every spare hour pouring over every book he could get his hands on. In 1841, at the age of twenty, young William left home to seek his fortune. He first signed on with Joshua Borton of Eversham Mount at $10 a month doing general farm work. During this time, in December 1842, Still's father died, and William began to think in terms of leaving the area to find better job opportunities.

In 1844 he arrived in Philadelphia with just three dollars in his pocket and a tattered, meager wardrobe. He soon found, like so many other rural migrants to the city, that Philadelphia's streets were hardly paved with gold, especially for a young black man with scant formal education, no money, little urban polish, and few marketable skills. He picked up day labor jobs, and other kinds of casual work, until he decided to go into business for himself. He opened a store that sold oysters, but soon found that he was not at all prepared for the business world, and closed it up. Undeterred, he decided to go into the second hand clothing business, which at that time was dominated by blacks, but he went bankrupt in short order. Facing a desperate situation, Still answered an ad by a widow in the city who needed a handyman. Still got the job and worked over a year for the woman, enabling him to acquire a small nest egg, learn some urban polish and skills, and read voraciously. When that job ended, Still waited on tables for a time and got a job in a brickyard. In 1847, however, Still's life changed profoundly.

In that year he married Letitia George, and at the same time answered an ad for a clerk's position at the Pennsylvania Anti-Slavery Society on 107 North Fifth Street, in center city Philadelphia. Although his duties at the organization in the beginning were strictly clerical and janitorial, Still soon began to involve himself in aiding the fugitives from slavery. Becoming one of the most active agents for the Underground Railroad, Still is said to have aided as many as sixty runaways a month, keeping meticulous, secret records of his activities. Still used his own home to provide room and board for these runaways, since they often stopped in Philadelphia for several days before resuming their journey to Canada. He also met often with fellow Underground Railroad operatives, such as Harriet Tubman. One of Still's most dramatic episodes came in 1850 when he interviewed a grey-haired, bedraggled man who had spent more than forty years in slavery, and had just completed a long desperate journey from Alabama to Philadelphia to be reunited with his mother. William found out that the man was his long-lost brother, Peter Still. His story was one of those that most effectively awakened the nation to the evils of slavery.

Still was also involved in other aspects of the antislavery movement. In 1850 Frederick Douglass informed Still of John Brown's pending raid on the Harper's Ferry arsenal, and Still gave aid to several of Brown's accomplices who were seeking arms to foment a nationwide slave revolt. Brown's wife stayed at William Still's home for a time after her husband's arrest. Brown's daughter sent Still a lock of her father's hair in a gold locket. These are held as part of the William Still Collection at the Pennsylvania Historical Society. Still's last major act in conjunction with the Underground Railroad came in 1860, when he traveled to Canada to report on the conditions of runaway slaves there. The *Philadelphia Public Ledger* had reported that ex-slaves in Chatham, Ontario, had taken control of the public schools, locking out the whites, and that a near-riot situation existed. Still reported that the blacks in Chatham were living peaceably and respectably, indicating that once freed in America, they could develop a stable, peaceful existence, if allowed to do so.

With the outbreak of the Civil War, the Pennsylvania Anti-Slavery Society closed, and Still was out of a job. By this time, however, he had purchased property worth about $2,000, had $300 in the bank, and was well versed in the ways of the business world. He decided to start a secondhand stove business, renting his old offices at the Anti-Slavery Society. He bought old stoves in the summer, when they were cheap, fixed them up, and resold them in the winter for a substantial profit. While engaged in this business, Still also began dealing in coal on commission. In the second year of operation, as the sales of coal increased, he also added the manufacture of gas stoves, boilers, large appliances, and heaters. During the next four years, Still's business increased annually, until by 1864 he had a very successful enterprise.

At that time, Edward M. Davis, son-in-law of Lucretia Mott, offered Still the position of post sutler at Camp William Penn, located eight miles outside of Philadelphia, where black troops were stationed. Although acceptance of the offer would mean a severe financial hardship for Still, since it would disrupt his business activities, it was nonetheless a great honor to be offered the position, and he accepted it and served until the end of the war. At that point Still decided to expand his coal business well beyond the modest operation he had run during the war. He bought a deserted site, built a shed there, laid the necessary railroad tracks, and erected improvements that greatly enhanced the value of the entire area. He then stocked his yard with coal and supplies, and bought coal wagons and good teams to deliver the coal. He established an excellent reputation for dealing honestly and promptly with all his customers. He ran this business successfully until his death in 1902, becoming one of most influential African-American business leaders in the city, and being elected to the predominantly white Philadelphia Board of Trade. His business was sold when he retired it to the Baldi Brothers.

Still also served as the first president of Philadelphia's oldest black-owned banking institution, the Berean Savings Association, which had been founded by his son-in-law, Reverend Matthew Anderson, in February 1888. Anderson was a native of Pennsylvania who had graduated from Oberlin in 1867. He entered Princeton Seminary, where in 1877 he was one of the first three blacks to graduate. Anderson spent the next two years doing graduate work in theology at Yale. At that point he went to Philadelphia, where he first was connected with the Gloucester Mission in North Philadelphia. In 1880 he helped organize, and became pastor of, Berean Presbyterian Church. Anderson brought together a group of citizens to help solve the problems of housing newly arrived black migrants. The venture was successful, and Berean Building and Loan continues in the 1990s as one of the oldest and strongest associations in the United States.

During the last half of William Still's life, he continued to fight his race's many battles, although he could not always count on the support of his own people in many of his crusades. In 1859 he had first started a campaign to end segregation on Philadelphia's streetcars, by sending a letter to the press. The war intervened, but in 1862, after Frederick Douglass complained about his treatment on the city's public transit, Still secured the signatures of 360 prominent whites to a petition protesting this situation. Finally, in 1867, the state legislature enacted a law to end segregation, but the issue was debated at length in the newspapers, and some of his fellow blacks accused Still of opposing this legislation. In reply, Still wrote *A Brief Narrative of the Struggle for the Rights of the Colored People of Philadelphia in the City Railway Cars*, which was read before a large public meeting in Liberty Hall on April 2, 1867, as an explanation and justification for his actions.

A few years later, Still again incurred the wrath of some members of the African-American community. In 1874 he bolted from his people's traditional support of the Republican machine to back Col. A. K. McClure, a "reform" Democratic candidate. In response, Still again took pen in hand, arguing in *An Address on Voting and Laboring* that blacks should support candidates, not parties. In 1872 he published his records on his antislavery activity in the book, *The Underground Railroad*. At the Philadelphia Exposition in 1876, Still proudly exhibited the book in a heavy glass case, and it became for a time one of the most widely circulated works on the antislavery network. In addition to these activities, Still in 1861 helped finance and organize an association to collect data about blacks in the city, and later he helped found a Mission Sabbath School in North Philadelphia. In 1880 he was a founder of one of the earliest YMCAs for blacks, and he also helped manage homes for aged blacks and destitute African-American children, as well as a home for the children of black soldiers and sailors. He remained president of the Pennsylvania Anti-Slavery Society until a year before his death in 1902. An important black business leader in nineteenth-century Philadelphia, William Still is primarily remembered as the "Father of the Underground Railroad."

Sources

Parts of William Still's journal of the Philadelphia Vigilence Society, along with some of his personal letters, are in the William Still Papers at the Historical Society of Pennsylvania. His book, *The Underground Railroad*, which was first published in 1872, has a biographical sketch written by James P. Boyd. That publication is available on microfilm as part of the History of Women Collection of Research Publications, New Haven, Connecticut. Still's *Brief Narrative of the Struggle for the Rights* (Philadelphia, 1867) has been reprinted as part of vol. 10 of the Afro-American History Series by Scholarly Resources (Wilmington, Del., 1970). Still's *An Address on Voting and Laboring* is available at the Pennsylvania Historical Society. Larry Gara has a biography of Still in *Dictionary of American Negro Biography* (1982), and there is also a brief biography in *Dictionary of American Biography* (1935, 1936) by Harold G. Villard. Alberta S. Norwood, "Negro Welfare Work in Philadelphia Especially As Illustrated by the Career of William Still, 1775–1930," Master's thesis, University of Pennsylvania, 1931, has some useful information; as does his obituary in *Philadelphia Public Ledger*, July 15, 1902; and a short biography in W. J. Simmons, *Men of Mark* (1887). See also Lawrence Spraggins, "The History of Negro Business prior to 1860," Master's thesis, Howard University, 1935; Linn Washington, Jr., "The Chronicle of an American First Family," *Philadelphia Inquirer*, October 11, 1987; and Lureyt Khan, *One Day, Levin . . . He Be Free, William Still and the Underground Railroad* (1972), available at the Charles A. Blockson Collection at Temple University.

Information on Matthew Anderson and the Berean Savings and Loan can be found in *Berean Savings and Loan Association, Anniversary, 1888–1988* (brochure at the Balch Institute); *Berean Manual Training and Industrial School, 1936 Yearbook* (Balch Institute); *"Founder's Day" Berean Presbyterian Church, Broad & Diamond Streets, Philadelphia, Pa., Sunday December 13, 1987* (pamphlet, Balch Institute); William P. White and William H. Scott, comps., *The Presbyterian Church of Philadelphia* (Philadelphia, 1895); Matthew Anderson, *Presbyterianism: Its Relation to the Negro* (Philadelphia, n.d.).

Sutton, Percy Ellis (November 24, 1920–   ). Lawyer, politician, civil rights activist, and communications entrepreneur: Inner City Broadcasting Corporation, Queens Inner Unity Cable Systems, Apollo Theatre Investor Group, *Amsterdam News*, *New York Courier*, and Percy Sutton Incorporated. Picture this scenario: a young man with a penchant for taking chances and a longing to escape from Texas ventures into the highly risky business of stunt flying. "Red" Dawson taught Sutton the ropes of flying in exchange for the young boy's help in washing his planes. After pulling some strings of his own by cutting classes, Sutton accompanied a friend on a barnstorming circuit. He performed such acrobatic stunts as loop-the-loop, roll-overs, and delayed parachute jumps for small county carnival crowds in East Texas, Alabama, Oklahoma, and Louisiana. Sutton's flying career came to an abrupt end when Red Dawson miscalculated a maneuver and was decapitated in an accident. As Sutton recalled, ''I remember feeling relieved by his death. I also remember feeling guilty for feeling that relief. Until then I had had no idea how much I hated that flying.'' Although Sutton never barnstormed again, this account illustrates just one phase in the life of a man who was continually challenging himself and the status quo. Who is Percy Sutton and how have his accomplishments made a difference in the lives of African-Americans?

Percy Ellis Sutton was born on a farm near Prairie View, in eastern Texas, the youngest of fifteen children (although three had died prior to Sutton's birth) born to S(amuel) J. a former slave, and Lillian Sutton. His father was a capable businessman, activist, and educator, whose wife was also a teacher. S. J. Sutton was the principal of the San Antonio high school that all of his children attended, and he was a moderately wealthy man with a variety of business interests in that city, including undertaking, funeral supplies, mattress making, burial insurance, and real estate. His eye for wise property investment is best illustrated in one of his first purchases—a parcel of land he bought before the turn of the century that was adjacent to the center of what was then just an outpost cattle town known as San Antonio. That property became a valuable piece of real estate in downtown San Antonio.

S. J. Sutton was keenly aware of the importance of preparing his children for the harsh realities of the world. His youngest son recalled, ''All of us worked in the various businesses and in farming. So I had some idea of what business was about as a youngster.'' Percy Sutton's reverence for his father was revealed when he stated, ''He was a short man, but I always thought my father was 10 feet tall.'' Young Percy attended public schools, all the while dreaming of enriching his life by seeing more of the world. Like most African-Americans, Percy Sutton experienced discrimination and segregation as a youngster. As a child of twelve years, while handing out NAACP flyers in a white neighborhood in San Antonio, a policeman slapped him for engaging in inappropriate activity in a district reserved for whites. Sutton involuntarily kicked the officer in the shins, which resulted in a severe beating. A year later, young Sutton was arrested for having settled in the wrong place on a public bus. His memory of these incidents linger, for the Sutton children were never taught ''where [they] couldn't go. [They] had access to the better things and [he] never realized until about that time that anybody would beat you up for being in the wrong neighborhood.'' S. J. Sutton had raised his children in a highly charged household that taught discipline, ambition, and the importance of involvement in community affairs. They were prepared for success, but not the kind of success that meant making money.

It meant involvement, it meant caring, it meant doing something in the community. We were given a lot of opportunities because our father and mother always reminded that you're going to succeed and it was a punishment if you didn't succeed, so if you're structured like this, it's not too difficult, when you go in, you try something, you fall on your face, and you say, well, yes, I fell on my face, but I'm going to get up again, because we were required to do that as children.

With this philosophy deeply ingrained in his mind and soul, Percy Sutton was well equipped to reach for the stars.

From San Antonio, young Sutton went to Prairie View College, an all-black institution, when he was denied entrance to a veterinary school elsewhere in Texas because of his color. He had been accepted at a school in Iowa, but once his application had been processed through the courts, the term had already begun. After Prairie View, Sutton went on to study agriculture at Hampton Institute in Virginia, and then on to Booker T. Washington's* Tuskegee Institute, both black schools.

When World War II broke out, Sutton attempted to enlist in the Army Air Force. Thinking that the North would be less racist than the South, he relocated in New York. After considerable persistence, Sutton was recruited in 1942. His unit went overseas—in a segregated boat—where he was employed as an intelligence officer (after having attended Air Intelligence School in Pennsylvania) assigned to British Intelligence. Although racism prevailed there, too, Sutton became the first black intelligence officer involved in combat intelligence in the Air Force.

Sutton's experiences with injustice in the service, in addition to the unpleasant obstacles he had encountered over the course of his life thus far, inspired him to become a lawyer—someone who could assist others in fighting for their rights. In that capacity he could carry on the family tradition of community involvement and social responsibility. In 1945, upon his release from the Air Force, Sutton applied to Columbia University in New York City. He staged a sit-in to gain admittance into class, and he worked at two full-time jobs to pay for his education. From 4 P.M. to midnight, he worked at the post office, and from 12:30 to 8:30 A.M., he was employed as a conductor with the transit authority. From Columbia he went on to study at Brooklyn Law School, where he earned an LL.B. degree. His classes went from 9:00 A.M. until 2:00 P.M., at which time Sutton went to work. In total, he worked sixteen hours a day, attended law school, and on the weekend, when he was not taking review courses for the bar exam, he worked as a waiter at Lundy's at Sheepshead Bay in New York.

When Sutton took the bar exam in 1950 he was so certain of failure that he applied for readmission to the military. By this time the Air Force had been desegregated, and he offered his services as the first black judge advocate (a skill he had learned while enrolled at U.S. Judge Advocate School at Air University, Maxwell Field, Alabama). After serving for two and a half years in Korea, Sutton returned to the United States and resumed his position with the transit authority as a token booth operator from midnight until 8 A.M. For the remainder of the workday, he volunteered his services to Assemblyman Joseph Pinckney's Central Democratic Club, whose office was located in Harlem. Sutton worked on the projects that most interested him because he was not receiving remuneration, and he used this opportunity to learn all that he could. He practiced law free of charge for the club's regulars, organizing tenant groups and pushing voter registration.

Sutton chose a Harlem office to work in because, as a black, he knew that if he wished to enter politics in the 1950s, Harlem was the place to begin. Bitten by the politics bug, he ran for assemblyman in 1954 but lost his bid. Sutton continued to lose elections for the next ten years. He ran every year—or worked for someone else—for assemblyman, or district leader, or state committeeman. "People rejected me and everybody I supported, year after year after year," said Sutton. He claims that each year he went farther into debt, at least $10,000 deeper into debt, either financing his own losing campaigns or someone else's. Finally, his labor bore fruit: In 1964 he was elected assemblyman. The lessons of persistence he had learned from his parents were paying off.

During these years, Sutton learned the Byzantine politics played in New York: unkept promises, payments of graft to win favors, voluntary jamming of voting machines, and other practices. This was a difficult but valuable lesson for a neophyte in politics to learn. From this lesson, Sutton mastered the technique of evasion—a skill that earned him the alliance of individuals from opposing factions in the political forum. Undoubtedly, his fastidious style of dress and his self-controlled, smooth manner drew colleagues to him. Those who criticized Sutton's "riverboat-gambler style" were intolerant of his perfectly pressed suits and his carefully articulated speech, qualities that were markedly atypical of most other city politicians.

In his first year in office, Sutton was selected "Assemblyman of the Year" by the Students Association of New York. In 1966 he introduced the first modern-day divorce reform and abortion reform bills. In the same year, Sutton was elected Manhattan borough president, a position that he held for almost twelve years. In 1977 he took the big plunge into a high-profile bid for the mayoralty of New York City, a city that basks in excessive media coverage. The bid carried with it an array of possibilities for Sutton. It propelled him into the media spotlight, perhaps because of his skin color. Never before had an African-American been elected mayor in New York City. Sutton was directly challenging the city's long-proclaimed liberalism in racial matters. Although other metropolises, such as Los Angeles and Atlanta, had matured enough to elect black mayors, New York City lagged behind.

Sutton, during his years of public service, developed excellent relations with all the ethnic groups in the city. As early as 1974, he appeared on the front page of the fleet owner's newspaper, *City Life & Taxi News*, as the man "considered by many political leaders as 'most likely to be our next mayor.' " His qualifications were outstanding, as exhibited in his remarkable leadership abilities and his performance as a lawyer and public official. He campaigned not as a black candidate, but rather as a candidate who represented all of the people. On paper, it appeared that the odds were in his favor, but the overwhelming number of issues and the competition of numerous candidates worked against him. Sutton lost his bid for mayor to Ed Koch, who served as mayor for twelve consecutive years. It was not until 1989, when David Dinkins was elected, that New York City had its first black mayor. Ironically, it was Percy Sutton and two other Dinkins mentors, Congressman Charles Rangel and lawyer Basil Paterson, collectively known as the Harlem Mafia, who had controlled black politics and who had pushed Dinkins into the campaign. Their financial backing, political connections, and experience helped Dinkins win the campaign over the incumbent. On the night of his victory, Dinkins stood before a cheering crowd and declared, "Tonight I know full well that I stand on the shoulders of Percy Ellis Sutton." As *M Inc.* noted, "A rare public acknowledgment for the man who has helped determine the political fortunes of an entire generation of black leaders including Representative Charles Rangel, Basil Paterson and Jesse Jackson." Obviously, Sutton was able to see beyond his own self-aggrandizement to engineer another African-American's campaign for the coveted office of mayor.

Sutton's own unsuccessful bid for mayor in 1977 proved to be his swansong in electoral politics. Once he left the political arena, he devoted full attention to his business interests. When he was asked in 1980 whether he missed being directly involved in politics, and particularly missed the opportunity to become the city's first black mayor, he candidly responded, "Of course, I do. I think about it all the time, I think of how it could have been me as mayor. But I keep very busy and try not to look back. There is a time and place for everybody. It wasn't my time. But I'm not doing too badly, not at all." As a politician he was unable to be actively involved in the day-to-day affairs of his company, due to his busy schedule. Now he was free to return to the fast pace and big money of the business world. Sutton had his sights set on the communications industry, and he felt that he was well qualified to become a media mogul: "Communications has always been a strong force in my family. We were always involved in it—attempting to influence, attempting to persuade."

In 1971, Sutton and a coterie of political allies founded a company called AM-NEWS, Inc. This group of black investors was intent on making a political statement. They criticized how blacks were treated by the mainstream white-owned media, and they organized to challenge and change the white power structure. These primarily Harlem-based investors bought the *Amsterdam News*, Harlem's long-established weekly, which then had a circulation of 80,000. They paid $2 million for the paper, $1.5 of which was borrowed from the Chemical Bank (the remaining $500,000 was raised from unrevealed sources). James H. Anderson founded the venerable newspaper in 1909, and for most of the time he was the acting editor, reporter, advertising manager, sports writer, circulation manager, and financier. In 1936 the paper was purchased by the Powell-Savory Corporation and achieved an increased circulation. Over the decades, the *Amsterdam News* survived trying times and in the late 1960s, it had a circulation of approximately 250,000. The paper was riding a roller coaster when Sutton and his cohorts rescued it. Their goal was to transform the paper into an "instrument of black liberation."

The purchase of the *Amsterdam News* was the group's first foray into communications, but they had greater plans for the future. On the back burner rested their real dream—to turn their fledgling company into an all-encompassing entertainment empire. Sutton was joined in this venture by Wilbert A. Tatum, a former aide to Sutton and treasurer of the *Amsterdam News*; H. Carl McCall, a former state senator and former chairman for the city's Council against Poverty; Clarence Jones, then editor and publisher of the *Amsterdam News*; and John Edmonds, secretary of the *Amsterdam News*, vice chairman of the Harlem Urban Development Corporation (HUDC), and former director of the Harlem–East Harlem Model Cities Committee. Sutton's 37 percent ownership in the company made him the second-largest stockholder in the newspaper. However, in 1975, he sold his stock because the paper became a political liability for him while he was in office. (Clarence B. Jones, the publisher and major stockholder had withdrawn a year earlier.) By 1987 the circulation of the *News* had declined to 50,000. Its reduced budget allowed for only a skeleton staff that struggled to produce a paper of quality. Sutton explained that "he was suffering both personally and politically," having come increasingly under fire from both within and outside of the press as a result of the "mistaken belief" that he was controlling the editorial content of the paper. It is likely that he was uncomfortable being linked with the paper's militant philosophy. "I was blamed for everything that people thought was wrong with the paper."

Only one month later, Sutton founded the Inner City Broadcasting Corporation with his regular cast of partners: Tatum, Jones, Edmonds, and McCall. State Supreme Court Judge Oliver Sutton (Sutton's brother), Pierre Sutton (Percy's son), and M. S. Woolfolk also joined the group of investors. The company laid the foundation from which other business interests would emerge, and Sutton personally fine-tuned the organization with a substantial amount of research and planning:

I had this body of knowledge, but I had no experience. I drafted the certificate of incorporation putting together Inner City Broadcasting, and the way I did that was, though I was a lawyer, I went down to the County Clerk's office, the same way I do much of my research, and I pulled out all of the companies that I thought were powerful, whose certificates of incorporation I thought were prescient. I made photocopies of them, I went through all of these ten or twenty odd certificates of incorporation and I took the best elements out of all of them to structure what is now Inner City Broadcasting Corporation.

Inner City proceeded to buy radio station WLIB-AM for $2 million, with yet another loan from the Chemical Bank of $1.7 million. The opportunity to buy the station was presented to Sutton by Harry Novik, then owner of WLIB. Novik remembered that Sutton had expressed interest in buying the station during the 1960s, when he was on the air advocating civil rights issues. Several years later,

Novik offered the station to Sutton, who jumped at the opportunity to purchase a radio station—a dream he had carried from his years in Texas: "It's just that since childhood I had wanted to be a radio announcer, and I thought the way to do this is to own a station, so you can be sure of being the announcer." When the deal was completed, Sutton began building his media empire. As the moving force behind the company, he was given the first option of buying any shares put on the market. Later in the year, the stock was divided into Class A and Class B shares. Under the retrenchment, the 10,000 Class A shares controlled 60 percent of the voting power, and the 1,470 Class B shares had 40 percent of the power. The Class A shares were divided between two people, and Sutton was one of the lucky two. Several notable media personalities—the Reverend Jesse Jackson, pianist Billy Taylor, and singer Roberta Flack, among others—were original investors who bought between $500 and $5,000 worth of company stock at a $100 a share.

Early on, WLIB-AM's chances of survival were questionable: Its Harlem headquarters was poorly equipped, it lacked experienced management, and there was a shortage of capital. In addition to these formidable obstacles, WLIB's license restricted its broadcasting hours to daylight only, which limited its potential profits. To counteract this unchangeable and depressing situation, the company purchased WBLS, an FM station, for $1.35 million. This proved to be a coup, for WBLS became the company's profit center in New York. The station altered its format to appeal to white listeners as well as black, a strategy that catapulted the station to the top of the New York ratings charts for FM stations in 1980, 1981, and 1983. It was the first time a black radio station had moved into the number one slot in the number one market where blacks constituted only approximately 11 percent of the population. Every week in 1981, over 2 million people listened to WBLS, which meant that every 15 minutes a quarter of a million people were tuned in. That audience was larger than the total populations of Boston, San Francisco, Washington, D.C., and St. Louis at that time. By 1989 a rating service placed WBLS eighth in listeners among the more than thirty FM stations heard in New York, and analysts ranked the station tenth in revenues in the city's FM market. For first-time investors in a radio station, who were considered ill equipped to own and manage one, they quickly learned how to turn it into a money-making machine.

Revenues from WBLS were used to fuel Inner City's expansion and subsidize WLIB, which was eventually converted to a news-talk format. The station's mandate was to take radio to the streets; leaders in the black community used the station to reach the people. Program guests have ranged from the Reverend Jesse Jackson, to former Mayor Ed Koch, to the controversial Reverend Al Sharpton, who called the station "the heartbeat of the black community." As the publisher of the *City Sun*, a black publication, asserted; "It is the only station black people can turn to and listen to serious news and get information and talk back to. It takes black people seriously, when white radio across the board does not take black people seriously at all." The station appears to have achieved its goals—"to communicate with one another, without going through the filter of someone else"—and has served as an "electronic marketplace of African and African-American ideas."

The power of the media can never be overestimated: In 1988, Police Commissioner Benjamin Ward revealed that the Police Department had been monitoring WLIB programs to get information on the activities of a local black extremist group. And, in 1990, when callers used the station to make denigrating remarks about Mayor David Dinkins during a week of racial tension, Sutton threatened to close down the station rather than have WLIB used as a "bashing ground." Although the station continued to operate within the truncated hours the license mandated, it, nonetheless, realized a profit from 1984 to 1988.

During the early 1980s, Inner City expanded and purchased five additional radio stations in San Francisco/Berkeley, Detroit, Los Angeles, and San Antonio. In 1988 Inner City sold its Detroit station for a reported $6 million (to finance its cable franchise in Queens), and *Black Enterprise* reported that the company sold its Los Angeles station for $15 million. Beyond these radio stations in the United States, Sutton runs the only full-time Caribbean radio station, WLIB, and services eighteen stations in Italy and elsewhere in the world. He also has the music market virtually cornered in Africa where he has engaged in goodwill work. His strong sentiments concerning the value of the media are reflected in the following assertion: "Black people must control elements in the news media in order to liberate themselves. We must begin to define ourselves, not always be defined by someone else."

In 1982 *Black Enterprise* cited Inner City Broadcasting Corporation, with sales of $24.5 million, as its "Company of the Year," and *Ebony* presented Sutton with its award for "Businessman of the Year." Sutton's original dream to create a vast communications network was taking shape when he branched into cable television. In 1983 Inner City Broadcasting Corporation and Unity Broadcasting Network (another black-owned company) joined forces under the collective name Queens Inner Unity Cable Systems. The newly formed company won the right to negotiate on a franchise to provide cable television for one-third of New York's borough of Queens, which would give them access to a market the equivalent in size of a Milwaukee- or Boston-based cable market. Sutton entered the major leagues when he was forced to compete with such formidable opponents as Westinghouse Electric's Teleprompter unit and Cablevision Systems Development Corporation. He also had won a bid for a lease on one of the coveted transmitters on RCA's Cable Net 2 communications satellite, from which he broadcasted music and other entertainment.

Sutton's entrée into the much sought after cable business was facilitated by his political connections. "When you are on the board of estimate"—a powerful New York City board whose fiscal policies can make or break business and real estate ventures, and which granted rights to negotiate the new cable franchises— "you don't destroy your power base." Sutton clearly used his connections to his benefit. However, he was unable to follow through with his obligations: By

1987 he had not yet started building his cable franchise because, he claimed, he was unable to raise the money.

We found great difficulty in being able to raise money, not equity money, but debt money. We'd experienced that before when we began radio. We found it was difficult for black people to borrow money. It had nothing to do with your ability. It had to do with the color of your skin. (*New York Times*, October 23, 1989)

Finally, homes in Queens began receiving cable when Queens Inner Unity formed a partnership with the media giant, Warner Communications. Each partner put up $3 million in equity, and Warner assumed management responsibilities and agreed to provide or find bank financing for an additional $60 million.

Sutton's empire was growing by leaps and bounds. In 1980, as the general partner in the Apollo Theatre Investor Group, he purchased the then bankrupt Apollo Theatre for $220,000. The Apollo had long been a shining light and a historic landmark in Harlem. For years, beginning in 1935, it was the most important black performance hall in the world. Such notable talents as James Brown, Sarah Vaughn, Ella Fitzgerald, and Billie Holiday performed there over the years. Although Sutton's purchase was not considered a wise investment, he was attempting to make a symbolic gesture that could provide blacks with a sense of pride and heritage. He had first patronized the Apollo in 1943 when he was in the Air Force, and he continued to attend the performances every week, except when he was involved in the Korean conflict and World War II. Sutton gave back to an institution—more than $25 million—that gave to him pleasure over the years. His ambition to make it a citadel of entertainment took shape with state-of-the-art production facilities and a music publishing arm and a record label. As recently as 1990, Sutton was still pouring money into the struggling Apollo. In that same year, a deficit of $1.9 million was projected and one of $2.9 million was projected for 1991.

Sutton's sensitivity toward people and their attitudes led him and psychologist Kenneth Clark to found Data Black public opinion polls—the nation's first black opinion polling organization. Other business ventures have extended his business network far beyond the East or West coasts of the United States. His communication empire reaches far and wide—to Africa, the Caribbean, and Europe—and he directs twenty-three corporations that invested in oil and coal, built plants, and constructed a record manufacturing company in Africa. Sutton had ventured into "spot oil" as early as 1977, when he found himself debt-ridden from his costly mayoral campaign. In 1989 Sutton boasted of his easy access to capital and a personal net worth of $170 million: "Now I can go to a bank and borrow, 10, 20, 30, 40, 50 million dollars. I have access to $100 million or more through people I have come to know in the last few years and who would invest with me."

In 1979 Sutton and a group of black businessmen, from the United States and Nigeria, convened to organize a multimillion-dollar corporation called NATRAL (Nigerian-American Tapes and Recordings Associates, Ltd.) to manufacture and sell records and tapes in the United States and Africa. Sutton also established Percy Sutton Intercontinental, a holding company for several partnerships which he is developing in Africa. The late oilman Charles Wallace, president of Wallace and Wallace Fuel Oil Company in New York, the nation's tenth largest black-owned firm, had been doing business with OPEC many years earlier, long before the more recent trend toward international trade. The entrée of blacks into international trade was facilitated by the high visibility and efforts of former African-American ambassador to the United Nations, Andrew Young.

Sutton's son Pierre (called Pepe) has also carved out a niche for himself in international trade. He is president of Percy Sutton International, Inc., an investment trade company doing business in Nigeria and in several other African and Southeast Asian nations. His father is chairman of the board. Among other projects, the company built a flour mill and macaroni manufacturing plant in Nigeria, and also purchased commodities such as meat and sugar from Brazil, processed and canned them, and then sold the finished product overseas. The Sutton family has taken advantage of the trend toward increased international trade, where the Third World countries are more eager to conduct business with minority-owned firms who treat them with more respect than do the large companies. Cheryl Sutton, Percy Sutton's daughter, was vice president and general manager of the Apollo organization, and vice president of a subsidiary called Inner City Management and Consultants. Pepe, who studied political science at Pennsylvania and New York universities, is also president of the Inner City Broadcasting Company, and took over the chairmanship of Inner City Broadcasting from his father in 1990. In the same year, the company had sales of $26 million, a decline from its 1989 sales of almost $33 million. Pepe Sutton was formerly the managing editor of the *New York Courier*, a black newspaper that the elder Sutton bought in 1968 and successfully increased its circulation in two years from 2,400 to 25,000. Pepe plans to expand the firm's entertainment division and its cable TV business. Both Pepe and his father expect Inner City to grow 15 percent each year throughout the 1990s.

Percy Sutton's accomplishments in business are noteworthy indeed. He has proven his aptitude for politics and business, and he has the comfort of knowing that there are those who deem him one of the wealthiest and most powerful black men in America today. But, above all, his commitment to social issues is what propels him forward. As a young child he was raised in a household that stressed the importance of social activism. He has carried these lessons with him throughout his entire life. His striving for achieving his goals to be the first black man in a variety of capacities in the private and public sectors have provided African-Americans with a role model. As a lawyer in the 1960s, during the civil rights movement, Sutton was a Freedom Rider who was jailed more times than he can remember. He is a Pan-Africanist and activist in demonstrations, negotiations, and fund-raising efforts on behalf of the African Freedom Movement, in general, and South Africa, Mozambique, Namibia, Zimbabwe, and Angola, in particular. He is the founder and a board member and supporter of TransAfrica, a lobbying group in support of African causes. In 1976 Sutton developed the concept and founded the now internationally famous Five Borough, New York City Marathon. His affiliations and honors are far reaching and diverse: He was for a time counsel in the law firm of Phillips, Nizer, Benjamin, Krim & Ballon of New York; and he took on the responsibility with his late brother, former New York State Supreme Court Justice Oliver C. Sutton, of defending, among others, the militant Black Panthers and Malcolm X, for whom he continues to have great respect. "Malcolm X would hold them all in the palms of his hand." Sutton was an early supporter of Jesse Jackson and his Chicago-based organization PUSH—the People United to Save Humanity, of which Sutton is a board member. And, during the 1984 Jesse Jackson presidential campaign, Sutton served as national finance chairman and confidant to Jackson. Sutton's commitment to his race and his optimism is far reaching. In 1987 Sutton received the NAACP's Spingarn Medal.

I have great hope for the cause of civil rights and black economic advancement. I know that which can be accomplished, but I don't think it's going to come with blacks being mild and meek and accepting the status quo. I think the time has come again for black organizations to protest, to be militant without being violent. You have to agitate, demonstrate, sit in and vote aggressively in order to attract the attention that is necessary.

Percy Sutton takes pride in his achievements, his connections, his wealth, and the other accoutrements of his position, but nothing seems to give him more satisfaction than his involvement with his people:

I wouldn't trade anything for being black and having had all the experiences, all the jail terms I've had, all the rest that have occurred to me, all the things that have occurred to me, all of these are part of living for me. I wouldn't trade anything for it and I wouldn't want to go back and relive any of it, but if I had to relive my life over, I would want to do it the same way.

Sources

Currently there are no personal or company papers of Percy Sutton and his varied business interests. No full-length biography has been written of Sutton, but there are various materials available that proved useful. Very brief biographies appear in Frank J. Johnson, *Who's Who of Black Millionaires* (1984); *Ebony Success Library* (1973), vol. II, 252–55; *Who's Who among Black Americans* (1988); and *Minorities and Women in Business*, March/April 1987. The Sutton vertical file at the Schomburg Centre holds numerous newspaper clippings from a variety of local sources, including the *Village Voice*, *New York Post*, *New York News*, *New York Times*, and *New York News World*. For articles about Sutton's political involvements see Nicholas Pileggi, "Guess Who's Coming to Gracie Mansion," *New York*, May 27, 1974, which deals with Sutton's bid for the mayoralty and New York politics in general; *New York News*, September 12, 1983; *New York Times*, January 8, 27, and 28, 1977; and numerous other articles that appear in local papers. Sutton's business interests have been followed closely and covered extensively: *New York Times*, January 22, 1983; *News World*, April 20, 1986; *Soho Weekly*, August 5, 1976; *New York News*, March 16, 1980, and October 16, 1988; *Wall Street Journal*, December 22, 1981; *New York Daily News*, May 23 and 29, 1990; *M.*

Inc, September 1990; and *New York Sunday Post*, March 12, 1987. Sutton's cable interests were reported in *Village Voice*, February 3 and April 7, 1987. Articles dealing with international trade and Sutton's entrée into Africa are the following: *New York News*, November 23, 1979; *New York Post*, November 17, 1977, and February 6, 1979. The *Amsterdam News* is covered in *The Crisis* XLV (April 1938), 105–6; David Hatchett, "The Black Press," *Crisis* XCIV (January 1987), 14–19; and *New York Times*, November 13, 1975, and August 17, 1987. Also an interview with Sutton was conducted on "Pinnacle" and the transcript is available to researchers from the Cable News Network, New York.

T

Thomas, James (1827–December 17, 1913). Barber, real estate developer, and businessman; Nashville and St. Louis. James Thomas's life reads like some sort of gruesome fairy tale. Born into slavery, abandoned by his white father, who repeatedly tried to sell him, and emancipated when his mother bought his freedom, Thomas rose to prominence as an African-American entrepreneur in not one, but two, cities. At one point in his life worth at least a quarter of a million dollars, when he died in 1913 Thomas left meager savings of just $1.45.

Thomas was born in Nashville, Tennessee, the son of Judge John Catron and an African-American slave, Sally. Catron had no interest in Sally or his young son, and they ended up in Virginia, belonging to Charles Thomas, an Albermarle County plantation owner. When Charles Thomas died, the executors of his estate in about 1833 put his slaves up for sale. Sally and James became the property of young John Martin, who took them back to their former home in Nashville. In his autobiography, James remembered, "My recollections of early life are many, but none are so vivid as the one instance where I was [load]ed in a vehicle of some sort bound for Charlottesville, [Virginia]." Upon returning to that city, Martin immediately put James Thomas up for sale to the highest bidder. Sally had faced the same crisis with her two older sons, and in each instance she had prevented the sale. This time, she went to Ephraim Foster, a prominent Tennessee planter, lawyer, and politician who had a reputation for fairness to blacks. Sally told him, "I want you to talk with him [Martin] and learn what he will take for the boy." Foster got an asking price of $400 for the eight-year-old boy, an amount she considered exorbitant.

Nonetheless, Sally, who owned a small clothes-cleaning business, had managed to save $350, and she asked Foster to loan her the balance. On January 20, 1834, the deal was made, and a short time later she paid off the debt and received young James's freedom papers. The problem, however, was not yet solved. Tennessee law required freed blacks to leave the state, or they could be legally returned to bondage. This legal technicality did not seem to deter either James or his mother. He ran errands for Sally, worked as an assistant to a young

Nashville physician, and during the winter attended school in a drafty one-room schoolhouse. Even though school was often canceled because there was no teacher, James was an apt pupil and soon mastered the rudiments of reading and arithmetic.

By age twelve, James Thomas felt he was ready to take on the world. As he noted, ''At the age of twelve, I thought I had played the part of washerwoman long enough,'' and he decided to ''see something of the great world.'' Thomas booked passage on a river steamer that took him to New Orleans, where he discovered a world far different from that of the city of his birth. He saw magnificent hotels, raucous saloons, and gambling establishments, and he visited the bustling French market. All of this seemed to fire his imagination, and when Thomas returned to Nashville a short time later, he determined to learn a trade that would allow him to live like the whites and blacks he had seen in New Orleans. In about 1841, Thomas hired out as an apprentice barber, working for free-slave, Frank Parrish. Thomas's brother, who had taken the name of John Rapier, had established a barbershop in Florence, Alabama, so James had a powerful example to follow. John Rapier said of his younger brother, ''James are still with Frank Parrish and has the character of a good barber, So a Gentleman told me and is well though[t] of by the Gentlemens.'' After his five-year apprenticeship, James Thomas opened his own shop at 10 Deaderick Street, his family home where his mother also still ran her cleaning business.

Thomas's barbershop was well located, being within walking distance of banks, law offices, the courthouse, market square, and the state capitol. As a result, like nearly all successful black barbers at this time, he was able to develop a successful white clientele, and Thomas used this environment to cultivate his relationships with influential whites. ''The old time barber shop,'' he later recalled, ''was the best of all places to learn the ways and peculiarities of the old time gentlemen.'' He further reflected, ''In a city the size of Nashville in those days it did not take long to learn people's names, where they lived and where they did business. Many gentlemen wore pleasant faces after saying good morning, others looked not altogether pleasant.'' In Nashville, as in most other southern cities, barbering offered an attractive avenue for economic independence. Of the eight barbers advertising in the city directory in 1853, six were African-Americans.

Thomas soon built a lucrative business, and his fame spread so far that in 1848 he was contacted by Andrew Jackson Polk, cousin of President James K. Polk and owner of more than 300 slaves, to accompany him north as his personal servant. When Thomas demurred, saying that he had just bought this business, Polk replied, ''Don't tell me about your business. I'll buy it and shut it up.'' So Thomas went with Polk, traveling to Cincinnati, Buffalo, Albany, and New York City. There the two men stayed at the Astor Hotel, but Thomas was denied a seat on a bus, was rudely ejected from a theater, and encountered jeers and catcalls on the street. He was disgusted by the hypocrisy of the North in these matters, and he became convinced that he would rather remain in the South.

Upon his return to Nashville, Thomas was well paid for his trip with Polk, and he decided to take a second trip to the North to visit Saratoga, Boston, Newport, and New York City. Despite the fact that Thomas was still technically a slave, he considered himself better off than most northern blacks: He could come and go as he pleased, he could attend the religious, cultural, and political functions of his choice, and blacks and whites in Nashville intermingled in a number of ways, in sharp contrast to the situation in the North. It is well to remember, however, that James Thomas was an exceptionally privileged black in Nashville. Since the 1830s, various laws had been passed to segregate blacks and whites, and to restrict the activity of blacks in a number of areas. These restrictions did not affect Thomas much, but he was the definite exception.

By 1851 James Thomas had become so economically successful, and so well respected, that he decided to ask Ephraim Foster, his nominal owner, to present a petition to the Davidson County Court seeking his emancipation. The petition was successful, and the court proclaimed that "the said Slave James, otherwise called James Thomas, be emancipated, and forever set free." Next, as a free man, Thomas himself begged the court that the law requiring free blacks to emigrate from the state not be enforced. An immunity was granted, and on March 6, 1851, Thomas became the first black in Davidson County to gain both freedom and residency. Thomas continued happily and successfully to run his shop in Nashville for the next several years, earning as much as $100 per month. He soon had earned enough to buy himself a $3,000 house on Ewing Street, and by the mid–1850s, his large advertisements in city directories indicate he was running one of the largest "tonsorial establishments" in the city. It is well to note that there were other free blacks in Nashville at this time who owned their own businesses also, such as Peter Lowrey and Jerry Southard.

In 1855 Thomas decided to go back to New Orleans, sixteen years after his first visit. This time, in addition to revisiting his earlier pleasures, he went to the opera and to a thoroughbred horse race. By this time, Thomas was no longer content with the small-town atmosphere of Nashville, and he craved new adventures and perhaps a new home. His first foray came when he learned that William Walker, a boyhood friend in Nashville, who had invaded Nicaragua with a handful of compatriots, was organizing a new confederation of states in Central America. Thomas was offered free land there, so he and his nephew, John Rapier, Jr., embarked for Central America in February 1856. Soon after their arrival, however, Thomas found that Walker planned to declare himself dictator and to reinstate black slavery. Thomas and Rapier departed immediately, and, years later, when asked by an American why he had ventured so far from home, Thomas said, "I told him I didn't know." That hardly ended Thomas's wanderlust, and upon his return home he began to dream of resettling in the Old Northwest. As he commented, the "old town of Nashville" no longer held much charm for him.

Thomas began to collect outstanding debts that were owed him, put his house on the market, and made preparations to close his business. Shortly thereafter,

Thomas left Nashville, went north to Wisconsin, and then cruised down the Mississippi River looking for an appealing place to resettle. This took some time, and he returned to Nashville several times for short periods before finally deciding to resettle in St. Louis, Missouri, in July 1857. St. Louis probably appealed to Thomas because of its similarities, in certain respects, to New Orleans. With a French, Spanish, and Creole heritage, it had a more ambivalent set of racial attitudes than most other southern cities. Cyprian Claymorgan many years later noted that affluent free blacks were "separated from the white race by a line of division so faint that it can be traced only by the keen eye of prejudice—a line so dim indeed that, in many instances that might be named the stream of African blood has been so diluted by mixture with Caucasian, that the most critical observer cannot detect it."

There, Thomas secured employment as a waiter and barber on the luxury steamboat, the *William Morrison*. During layovers in St. Louis, Thomas worked as a barber in the shop of Henry Claymorgan, who managed one of the busiest shops in the city. Through him, Thomas made contact with many of the wealthiest and most influential blacks in the city, including Cyprian Claymorgan (Henry's brother) and William Johnson, both of whom had made a good deal of money in real estate. Thomas also met twenty-year-old Antoinette Rutgers, whose mother, Pelagie, was the richest free black in Missouri, owning more than $50,000 in property, and who had been married to a Claymorgan. Thomas soon began a long courtship with the younger Rutgers woman. They married in 1868, and the white *St. Louis Dispatch* crowed in its headline: "Rich Nigs Wed," and said of their wedding, "It was a most imposing affair. The elite of the city were present." The paper further commented, "The bride has property and money to the value of $400,000. The husband is worth nearly the same amount." They were married at St. Vincent de Paul Roman Catholic Church, where Thomas would belong for the rest of his life.

Although the *Dispatch* grossly overestimated the wealth of both Thomas and his bride, he had done very well during his years in St. Louis. Cyprian Claymorgan in 1858 listed Thomas as a "man of mark," and said he would "do honor to the proudest white man in the land." Claymorgan went on to comment that Thomas was "a Tennessean by birth, and is worth some $15,000. . . . He is very genteel in his manners, attentive to business, and is a remarkably fine looking man." For several years, Thomas ran a barbershop in partnership with Claymorgan, but in the 1870s opened a magnificent establishment in the new Lincoln Hotel in downtown St. Louis. A ten-chair operation, it was one of the most successful in the central business district, but, more important, he began to invest in real estate like so many other enterprising blacks in the city. He began buying and selling real estate in several parts of the city, and also began building and improving rental apartments, mostly on Rutger Street and Jefferson Avenue. In addition, Thomas began buying railroad and insurance stocks in the stock market.

Thomas was a shrewd and innovative real estate operator. For instance, in one transaction he made a down payment on a few lots, traded one of them for a share in a building company, used those shares to finance the construction of a small apartment building, and then, with the rental units, paid off the mortgage. By such techniques, Thomas soon built a large empire. He often grossed as much as $2,000 a month. By the early 1870s there was no question that he was the richest African-American in St. Louis, with a fortune of at least $250,000. He was at least twice as rich as his nearest competitor. Thomas continued to increase his wealth, despite the depression of that decade. By the late 1870s he owned nearly two entire blocks of downtown property, rented forty-eight apartment units, and controlled real estate as far away as Memphis and Nashville. By 1879 his fortune was worth a solid $400,000.

With this prosperity in business, Thomas soon began to display an opulent personal life-style. He owned two mansions, one in town and one in the country in Alton, Illinois, and furnished them with imported Persian carpets, mahogany furniture, and a magnificent $2,000 rosewood piano. In 1873 Thomas embarked on a long tour of Europe. There he was impressed by the relations between persons of color. He wrote, "In Paris, I saw people who could pass for colored in America without trying, but [judging] from their general demeanor and bearing, [they] have never worn the yoke." Upon his return to America, Thomas said, "Every colored man ought to know, although he has been treated as a companion [in Europe], on American soil all that comes to an end. [Negroes] are supposed to take [their] regular place. Custom, which has a heap to say, has so ordered it."

With his economic success, Thomas became involved in activities for the betterment of the masses of freed blacks. He had accepted a position as financial advisor to the St. Louis Freedmen's Savings and Trust Bank, and when that bank failed in 1874, he lashed out bitterly at the trustees, who he felt had robbed more blacks of their hard-won savings. Thomas lamented quite rightly that many blacks would never again trust a bank, particularly one run by or for blacks. In 1879 he helped organize, along with J. Milton Turner, another black businessman in the city, the Colored Immigration Association to provide food, shelter, and clothing for thousands of displaced blacks who were fleeing racial oppression in the South.

During the 1880s, Thomas and his family began spending more of their time at their country home in Alton. There, the local newspapers had made them feel welcome by calling them "among Alton's most respected families." James Thomas, now in his fifties, began to phase out his business activities in St. Louis, and in 1890, when just sixty-three, he retired. Thomas had looked forward to a life of leisure and comfort in his declining years, but was badly jolted three years later by the outbreak of a severe depression. Unlike the downturn of the 1870s, this depression severely affected Thomas's holdings. He suffered a sharp decline in income, defaulted on several $1,000 notes, and lost some of his property in a St. Louis subdivision. To survive this situation, Thomas mortgaged his property, ultimately taking out more than $50,000 in mortgages. Then, in

1896, a tornado hit St. Louis, zeroing in on the neighborhood where Thomas held most of his property. Without adequate insurance coverage, he was forced to take out a number of new mortgages, and he never recovered from the catastrophe. A year later, his wife died of a kidney disease.

Shortly after the funeral, Thomas went to live with his daughter Pelagie and son-in-law, Jefferson Blair, in Chicago. During this time, he had so little money that he could not forestall the auctioning off of their home in Alton, including the piano and several family portraits. He did manage to save one of his apartment buildings in St. Louis, and in 1898 he returned to the city to live in one of the units. Thomas received just a modest income from these apartments, since the area had begun to decline badly, and he spent most of his time reading, writing, and walking to a nearby park. In 1903 Thomas began to write his autobiography. He completed it in about a year, and then revised it in later years.

Thomas's autobiography was a collage of memories of slaves and free blacks, of "poor whites" and wealthy planters, and of the excitement of the decade preceding the Civil War. His writing tended to celebrate the achievements of blacks, especially those who managed, despite a lack of education or advantage, to start and run successful business enterprises. He also recounted the harsh savagery of race relations in the South, particularly a lynching he had witnessed. These brutal incidents, however, he tended to blame on lower class whites, while retaining a fondness and admiration for many wealthy white slaveholders. Yet, as his experiences in Europe taught him, blacks in America were always circumscribed by custom, and this rankled him greatly throughout his life.

During the last few years of his life, Thomas suffered from a number of illnesses, including arthritis and frequent pulmonary infections. He lived in a dingy, two-room apartment, possessing just a few sticks of furniture, warming himself in winter next to a leaky coal stove. In 1913 he caught influenza, which quickly developed into pneumonia. He died soon after, virtually penniless. He had not, however, been forgotten. At his funeral at St. Vincent de Paul, several hundred mourners, including some of the wealthiest and most respected people in the city, attended a two-hour high mass. The *St. Louis Globe-Democrat* ran his obituary on the front page, proclaiming, "James P. Thomas, 87, Dies." It went on to stress what Thomas had contributed to various civic organizations, and how he had provided for the city's poor. The article also contained a long list of prominent Americans that Thomas had known or met.

St. Louis, by the first decade of the twentieth century, had changed greatly from the city it had been when Thomas arrived there in 1857. The small (about 1,700 free blacks and a slightly smaller number of slaves, in total less than 2 percent of the population), but relatively prosperous and dynamic, prewar black population had been inundated by masses of poor, newly freed slaves in the decades after the war and Reconstruction. By 1900 there were slightly more than 35,000 blacks living in the city, and St. Louis ranked second only to Baltimore in the percentage of blacks in the total population. Although it was a large and dynamic community, with black men involved in the building trades, in hauling dray wagons, entertaining in music halls, waiting on tables in restaurants, working in the post office, and unloading merchandise in warehouses and stores and African-American women caring for children, washing clothes, and cleaning houses, it was a far more segregated environment than it had been over fifty years earlier. Denied access to the mainstream of American society, blacks in St. Louis and elsewhere constructed their own infrastructure of schools, clubs, professions, and organizations. They also developed their own cadre of professionals, teachers, doctors, and lawyers to service that community. And, they operated a variety of small businesses. These new businesses differed from Thomas's barbershop in that their intended clientele were fellow African-Americans, not whites. They had, by this time, their own newspaper, the *St. Louis Argus*, which would service the black community for over half a century. Many years later, in the early 1980s, when a group of blacks attempted to reconstruct the history of the participation of African-Americans in St. Louis in business, James Thomas was not even mentioned. Understandable, perhaps, since his barbershop thrived on a white clientele, and he had lost his entire fortune. But James Thomas for over fifty years, in both Nashville and St. Louis, gave a shining example of what an African-American could do with diligence, perseverance, some luck, and good connections in the white community.

Sources

The single most important source for James Thomas's life and career is his autobiography, the manuscript copy of which is located in the Moorland-Spingarn Research Center, Howard University. Loren Schweninger edited this, and provided an excellent introduction in his *From Tennessee Slave to St. Louis Entrepreneur: The Autobiography of James Thomas* (Columbia, Mo., 1984). The book also has an excellent bibliography of primary and secondary sources on Thomas, particularly the state, county, and church records of the details of Thomas's life. There is also some information available in the "John Rapier, Jr. Diary, 1856–1860," at the Moorland-Spingarn Research Center, and the Rapier-Thomas Papers at the same locations.

The best short biography of Thomas is by Loren Schweninger in the *Dictionary of American Negro Biography* (1982). He has also written several excellent articles dealing with aspects of Thomas's life: "The Free-Slave Phenomenon: James P. Thomas and the Black Community in Antebellum Nashville," *Civil War History* 22 (December 1976), 293–307; "A Negro Sojourner in Antebellum New Orleans," *Louisiana History* 20 (Summer 1979), 305–14; "A Slave Family in the Antebellum South," *Journal of Negro History* 60 (January 1975), 29–44; and "Thriving within the Lowest Caste: The Financial Activities of James Thomas in the Nineteenth Century South," *Journal of Negro History* 63 (1978), 353–64. Schweninger deals briefly with Thomas in the larger context of black property owners in *Black Property Owners in the South, 1790–1915* (Urbana, Ill., 1990). A contemporary biographical account is in Cyprian Claymorgan, *The Colored Aristocracy of St. Louis* (n.p., 1858). Thomas and his barbershop are listed in Nashville's first city directory *Nashville General Commercial Directory*, 1853, and in *Edwards Annual Directory of St. Louis*, 1871. Thomas's obituary is in the *St. Louis Post-Dispatch*, December 16, 1913.

Travis, Dempsey J. (February 25, 1920–   ). Realtor, insurance executive, banker, trade association founder, publisher, author, and race leader: Travis Realty, Travis Insurance, Sivart Mortgage Corporation, Travis Security and Investment, United Mortgage Bankers of America, Urban Research Press, and Seaway National Bank. In 1945 Dempsey Travis thought the world was his oyster. He had graduated from Du Sable High School, the training ground for Chicago's South Side black elite. His classmates included John Johnson,[*] who was about to establish his vast publishing empire, Harold Washington, just beginning a political career that would see him become the first black mayor of Chicago, Nat "King" Cole, the great jazz pianist and pop singer, and Dorothy Donegon, another jazz pianist. Travis was twenty-five years old, a veteran of World War II, where he had held responsible clerical positions, and an accomplished jazz musician who had headed his own band. But, when he applied to go to college, he was rejected by every school in the Chicago area. Travis took entrance exams, and failed each one of them. For some of the schools he could have rationalized the failure as an example of white racism, since they had quotas for blacks. But he was also rejected by Roosevelt University, which had no such quotas. Travis later wrote, "[T]hey told me I was illiterate! They said I could barely read and write, that it was hopeless for me to try to go to college. They said I should be a plumber or a laborer of some sort."

Stunned by the news, with his good-sized ego enormously shaken, Travis took a job as a "mule," hauling hams at the Armour Packing Company. But Travis soon realized he wanted more than that, and he still believed that he had the ability to achieve more. The problem was his inadequate training at Du Sable. There, he later said, "the teachers spent most of their time in the hall gabbing with each other while the class sat and did nothing. In twelve years of public school I can remember only three teachers that *tried* to teach us something. Du Sable was a jungle. There's only one good thing I can say about it—and it's a terrible thing to say—it wasn't as bad then as it is now." Travis, then, was one of the casualties of the black urban ghetto, but he was able to overcome these obstacles to become one of the wealthiest, most successful and powerful blacks in Chicago.

Dempsey Travis was born in Chicago. His father, Louis Travis, was one of a legion of young blacks who came north from Alabama in the early twentieth century. Although his father was musically inclined and played the piano, the elder Travis spent his life as a laborer in the stockyards. Louis Travis later married another native of Alabama, Mittie Sims, a daughter of slaves who was born in Birmingham and came to Chicago in 1916. She and Louis Travis were married two years after her arrival in Chicago, and Dempsey was born two years after that. The Travis family was quite poor while Dempsey was growing up, particularly during the dark days of the Great Depression. As Dempsey Travis later recalled, though, "We always had something to eat, but sometimes it was beans three times a day. My clothes were clean, but they weren't always new.

I graduated from high school in a suit that had been handed down from my uncle to my father to me.'' Although Louis Travis could not provide a great deal in material possessions, he instilled in Dempsey a great respect for the honor of work. His method of punishing his son was to refuse to let him work, so that it soon came to seem like a privilege to do so. The elder Travis died in 1943, however, and it was Dempsey's mother who provided her son with the greatest support and guidance throughout his life.

"My mother really deserves credit for a great deal of what I have accomplished,'' Travis said. "She is the warmest, most outgoing kind of person— she just loves people. She will go over and get on a bus to go downtown, and by the time she gets there she has made at least one friend. They take down each other's names and phone numbers and after that they visit back and forth. She has a whole book full of names of people she met on the bus or the elevated train.'' Mittie Travis, who called Harold Washington her "second son'' because he was in the house so much when he was growing up, played a supportive role in her son's business affairs, and lived across the hall from him and his wife until she died in 1989 at the age of ninety-one.

Dempsey Travis grew up in the black ghetto of Chicago's South Side, an area referred to by Gwendolyn Brooks as "Bronzeville.'' St. Clair Drake and Horace R. Cayton described that community in their classic *Black Metropolis* (1945):

Stand in the center of the black belt—at Chicago's 47th St. and South Parkway. Around you swirls a continuous eddy of faces—black, brown, olive, yellow, and white. Soon you will realize that this is not "just another neighborhood'' of Midwest Metropolis. . . . In the nearby drugstore colored clerks are bustling about. (They are seldom seen in other neighborhoods.) In most of the other stores, too, there are colored salespeople, although a white manager or proprietor usually looms in the offing. In the offices around you, colored doctors, dentists, and lawyers go about their duties. And a brown-skinned policeman saunters along swinging his club and glaring sternly at the urchins who dodge in and out among the shoppers.

Bronzeville was a "world within a world''—a ghetto where nearly everyone was black. This gave Dempsey Travis and other Chicago African-Americans a certain sense of empowerment—nearly everyone they met, including the faces and voices of authority and influence in Bronzeville, were black. But there was another side to the area too: its horrific poverty and the violence and criminality that came in its wake. Richard Wright, in *12 Million Black Voices* (1941), recalled his own impressions of Chicago and its impact on poor southern blacks who migrated there:

Perhaps never in history has a more utterly unprepared folk wanted to go to the city; we were barely born as folk when we headed for the tall and sprawling centers of steel and stone. We, who were landless upon the land; we, who had barely managed to live in family groups; we, who needed the ritual and guidance of institutions to hold our atomized lives together in lines of purpose; we, who had known only relationships to people and not relationships to things; we, who had had our personalities blasted with two hundred years of slavery and had been turned loose to shift for ourselves—we were such a folk as this when we moved into a world that was destined to test all we were, that threw us into the scales of competition to weigh our mettle.

It was in this environment, this self-contained world, one of shared struggle but also of severe economic and cultural deprivation, that Dempsey Travis came of age in the 1920s and 1930s.

Like his father, Dempsey Travis began playing the piano at an early age, and at age six made his debut as a pianist at the West Point Baptist Church, which the family attended. Seven years later, Travis took important steps toward a career as a professional musician. The first came when his maternal grandmother, Winnie S. Sims, arrived from Birmingham, Alabama. A Seventh Day Adventist, she pushed him to pursue his piano playing with great discipline. With his cousin, Joe Strickland, Travis attended his grandmother's Shiloh Seventh Day Adventist Church for 106 straight weeks, thereby hearing good music and also learning to play religious songs. In this way, Travis learned to read music well. At the same time, he organized his own trio which began playing at the Savoy Ballroom and other nightspots over the next several years.

At the same time, Travis entered Du Sable High School, and there he came under the tutelege of music director Captain Walter Dyett, who also launched the careers of Nat Cole, Dorothy Donegan, and John Young. Dyett and Travis, however, did not get along very well, since Dyett considered the young man a "know-it-all" and always called him "the little big shot." Travis later admitted that Dyett had a point: "I was a cocky kid," he said. "I had an attitude that I knew it all. And, man, I was *out there*." Travis later wrote about his participation in the jazz scene of Chicago during the late 1930s in a book called *An Autobiography of Black Jazz*. He said, "Benny Goodman took jazz out of the whorehouse and put it into a virgin's white gown, made it respectable. White folks in '36 or '37 just went wild about black music. They didn't even know it was black music—they called it swing." During this time, Travis also acted as the local booking agent for his band, putting his organizational and promotional abilities to good use.

Travis graduated from Du Sable in 1939 and went out to find a steady job, but found there was little that appealed to him. Walking the streets looking for a job, he was met with signs that said "White Help Only." He finally paid $10 to get a job as a "porter" and cleaned toilets for $11.20 a week at the Apex Box Company on West Cermak. He also began to despair of following a career in music at this time. "I wasn't really the gutsy kind of jazz pianist," he later recalled. "My style was more classic in its structure. It was on the order of Oscar Peterson rather than Count Basie, Duke Ellington or Albert Ammons or Fats Waller." Travis plodded along until early 1942, when he was inducted into the U.S. Army. There he had some of the most traumatic experiences of his life.

In the army, Travis became a band conductor at a USO center, which was a posh placement. But it was not long before he got into trouble with a sergeant, who resented the fact that Travis got special privileges, and demanded he be paid a half pint of whiskey a week. Travis refused, and the two men had a confrontation in front of the entire platoon. As a result, Travis was transferred to Shenango, in western Pennsylvania, where he experienced prejudice such as he had never before seen. The army post was completely segregated, with markedly inferior facilities for blacks. There were a series of minor altercations between white and black soldiers, but those escalated to full-scale violence. Travis remembered the incident with great bitterness:

[A]ll of a sudden, without any warning, without anybody giving us an order to disperse or anything else, all the lights went out and *they* [the white soldiers] *started shooting at us*. The United States Army just deliberately opened fire on a peaceful assemblage of black men.

Travis himself was shot twice and the man next to him was killed instantly. An "investigation" was undertaken, but the incident never received any media publicity. Travis was then transferred several more times, and he finally ended up at the Aberdeen Proving Grounds in Maryland. He was made manager of the post exchange and became the first black man there to have a staff of whites working for him. He was honored with the Best Manager's Award there and stayed in the army until 1946.

With these successes, as noted above, Travis thought he could rise rapidly in postwar America, with a college education under the GI Bill as his first step. When he was rejected by all the area colleges, he had to reassess his career plans. Working in the stockyards, and preparing tax returns for members of a black congregation, Travis began to attend Englewood Junior College, which did not require entrance exams, on a part-time basis. He did well in his accounting and sociology courses, and that, he said "made me feel a little better." Travis then entered Wilson Junior College, where he was told he would have to take remedial reading and remedial English. By this time he was twenty-seven years old, and it was a crushing blow for his ego. But Travis's ambition knew no bounds and he pushed forward.

Travis plowed through the remedial courses. It was not easy. "I'd wrestle my way through Hawthorne or Thoreau or Sinclair Lewis and write a report on it," said Travis, "and the teacher would just look at me sadly. . . . I'd say 'What did I do wrong?' and he'd say, 'Well, you just didn't understand what you read . . . but why don't you try again?' And so I'd try it again." Finally, it came clear to Travis as if in a revelation: "Then one day it all paid off—all that hard work, all that struggle. I was wrestling through a book on political science in my usual way, one word and one phrase at a time—when suddenly it clicked! It became clear, it all fell into place." Upon successful completion of his remedial courses, Travis applied for entrance at Roosevelt University, and this time he was accepted. He got his bachelor of arts degree there in 1949.

For some time, Travis had wanted to be a lawyer, so he enrolled at Chicago Kent School of Law. While there, he took a course in the principles of real estate, and that aroused his interest in the subject. Then, too, he was discouraged by the lack of prospects for black lawyers. Most were in small-time criminal practice, with clients who either could not pay at all for the service, or could afford very little. Travis wanted more than that, so he decided to pursue a career in real estate. After finishing his real estate course, Travis applied for a license as a real estate broker in Chicago. His application was approved, but the fee was $50, and he had only $25. Travis borrowed the other $25 from his mother, who then became a lifelong partner in the business, handling the internal office affairs. Travis's wife, Moselynne, whom he had married earlier in 1949, did the typing for the firm after hours from her own job. Travis's first office was in space he borrowed from a lawyer. His desk was an orange crate and his chair was an upturned wastebasket. Travis warmed a bologna sandwich on the steam radiator for his lunch each day. It was a lean and difficult time, but he was determined to succeed.

Travis soon found that being a black real estate broker was probably worse than being a black lawyer. It was not until May 1950 that he made his first sale, but then he found he had to share his commission with lawyers for the buyer and seller, even though technically he was not required to do so. At that point, Travis decided that he would use his intelligence, imagination, drive, good humor, and charm to attract prospects to his company. An excellent salesman, he got a number of listings and made many sales, but, again, not without problems. Thousands of South Side blacks wanted to buy homes, and they had good, steady jobs and sufficient savings for a down payment, but they had difficulty securing conventional mortgages from any financial institutions. Instead, they were usually forced to take what were called "land contracts," which stipulated that if the purchaser missed even one mortgage payment, he or she defaulted on the loan to the mortgager, and they lost their property and all the equity that had supposedly accumulated in it. These evictions were carried out without any notice. Overnight, dependable, hardworking, responsible black families, who happened to miss just one payment because of a layoff or illness, found their furniture out on the sidewalk. They never got back even one penny of their investment.

Travis decided that he had to find a way to provide regular mortgages to blacks, to help his people, and also to allow his realty company sell more homes. In 1953 he organized Sivart (Travis spelled backward) Mortgage Company with capital of $25,000. It was one of the characteristics of Travis that he was always able (at least in his own mind) to combine a drive for financial success on his part with a wish to uplift his people. He has always rejected the label of "capitalist," and instead has defined himself as a "humanist," saying that black people cannot afford the luxury of having sheer capitalists in their midst. Travis was then able to get the backing of several Polish-American savings and loan associations, which agreed to back mortgages cleared by Sivart. This allowed Travis's mortgage business to expand and grow throughout the 1950s.

Travis's main preoccupation in real estate in the 1950s was finding decent housing for the hundreds of thousands of blacks crammed into the South Side ghetto. He did this largely by finding white clients who were willing to sell to blacks, especially in areas of west Chicago. Travis was good at placing blacks in the Douglas Park area of the West Side. This was largely a Jewish area, and Travis found that the residents there did not react violently when blacks began moving in, as they did in Cicero and some other parts of West Chicago. Moselynne Travis typed out letters to property owners in the Douglas Park area, asking if they were interested in selling. At the same time, she also sent letters to some 3,000 owners and tenants being displaced by urban renewal in the 100-acre Lake Meadows development site. These families had from $3,000 to $5,000 in equity from their homes in the former area, so they were able to afford homes in Douglas Park. "I got to be very good at matching South Side people with West Side housing," Travis recalled. "Many Blacks chose Douglas Park because the West Side Jewish residents being displaced by black South Side immigrants never reacted violently, as did the Irish and Poles on the Southeast and Southwest sides."

All of this, however, was very controversial. On the one hand, Travis viewed the Lake Meadows slum clearance program as an opportunity for blacks to advance themselves, whereas most African-Americans bitterly opposed the program. Lake Meadows was the first major urban redevelopment project in Chicago. It was supported by Marshall Field & Company and the Chicago Title and Trust Company, along with nearby Michael Reese Hospital and the Illinois Institute of Technology, which wanted to see their neighborhoods "cleaned up." Thousands of slum-dwelling blacks were to be displaced and relocated. Some were to be placed in new public housing projects, and others were to be relocated into private housing units; this was the market that Travis was intent on servicing. Emotions in the affected area, however, ran high. Handbills warned blacks not to be "Duped again by Lyers [sic] and Land-Grabbers who seek to herd you like INDIANS and JEWS to Reservations or Consentration [sic] Camps in the Bad Land." Many blacks feared that "slum clearance" was, in the words of local alderman Archibald Carey, really "Negro clearance." Although Travis did assist his people by helping them find housing and get mortgages, he was also part of, and profiting from, a deeply hated and resented program designed to destroy a portion of the black community.

Second, there was also reaction to the so-called block-busting tactics of Travis and other realtors. The seemingly innocuous letters that Moselynne Travis sent out to white owners often caused panic to set in—blacks were moving into their neighborhoods and therefore the value of their houses would plummet rapidly if they did not sell immediately, or, at least, so they feared. Travis offered whites an easy way out: He would handle the sale of their homes to blacks, securing for them a much better price than if they waited until the neighborhood had "turned"—that is, become more than 50 percent black. None of this was illegal or immoral, but it did engender much fear and hatred among whites, and Travis and others were often labeled "block busters" or "panic peddlers," though certainly blacks did not view that end of Travis's operations with the same disdain as they did his support of slum clearance.

Despite Travis's success during the 1950s, he was still frustrated by the fact that the large white banks and lending institutions refused to provide mortgage money to blacks. One survey of 141 commercial banks and 229 life insurance companies revealed that they refused to make "even a token number of conventional mortgages . . . for the typical Negro home buyer." Travis challenged this primarily because white-owned insurance firms held literally millions of dollars from blacks in policy premiums, but refused to even consider providing mortgage money to the same people. Travis also fought against the "redlining" practice of casualty and fire insurance companies which refused to provide black areas with fire insurance. This gave white financial institutions a convenient excuse to deny mortgages to blacks.

Travis was one of the leaders in the battle against these discriminatory practices, and he was elected to the presidency of the Dearborn Real Estate Board and the local NAACP. His presidency of the Dearborn Real Estate Board was analyzed by James Q. Wilson in *Negro Politics: The Search for Leadership* (1960):

Dempsey J. Travis, a real estate broker, is a young and energetic businessman who has sought to organize Negro real estate and insurance men into a campaign to alter a policy of fire insurance companies that results in an inability to insure properties in Negro areas against fire losses. His energy has carried him to the presidency of the Dearborn Real Estate Board, a professional association of Negro real estate brokers . . . [and] has brought Travis to the forefront as an organizer and a spokesman.

As head of the Chicago chapter of the NAACP, Travis led a march on the Republican National Convention when it was held in Chicago in 1960, and later helped organize Dr. Martin Luther King, Jr.'s first protest march in the city.

Travis's protests finally bore fruit during the administration of John F. Kennedy. Robert C. Weaver, an African-American, was named secretary of Housing and Urban Development, and, soon after, Kennedy issued an executive order directing federal housing agencies to cease their policies of racial discrimination in the issuance and insuring of home mortgages. This opened up the flood of money from white financial institutions to black borrowers, and also to black mortgage brokers like Travis, for the first time. To take advantage of this, Travis organized an association of black mortgage bankers called the United Mortgage Bankers of America in 1961. At that time there were few black mortgage bankers, and they were not allowed membership in the white Mortgage Bankers Association (MBA). Travis found that, as an individual mortgage banker, he still had difficulty getting access to the capital of the largest white lending institutions.

The United Mortgage Bankers was designed to increase the individual and collective clout of black mortgage bankers. Finally, in the later 1960s, the MBA allowed Travis and several other African-American mortgage bankers to join their ranks.

Travis, meanwhile, had to open up channels of white capital to black home owners through his firm. His first breakthrough came in 1960, when he began to handle the paperwork on FHA mortgages for Chicago Metropolitan Assurance, a black-owned insurance company. Then, after 1962, the International Ladies Garment Workers Union agreed to invest $10 million with Travis and other black mortgage bankers. Travis's next breakthrough came when he got a line of credit with the Central National Bank, which by 1971 had risen to $2.2 million. Ultimately, he got the backing of Equitable Life Assurance, the New York Bank for Savings, and many other mainstream white financial institutions.

As white money and other opportunities began opening up for Travis in the 1960s and 1970s, he pursued several somewhat contradictory courses. In the early 1960s, he became very involved in slum clearance and replacing those torn-down or "cleared" buildings with new ones. His first big project was a dreary slum in the 4700 block of Calumet on Chicago's South Side. It was the first move by a black firm in Chicago to engage in a huge urban renewal program. "You seem mighty pleased to see that old slum being knocked down," one resident told Travis. "Frankly," replied Travis, "I wasn't thinking so much about that old building as I was about the new ones which are going to rise on this site. We plan to erect some of the finest middle-income housing here that this city has ever seen." Travis continued to avail himself of public monies to clear slum areas and build housing with the support of HUD throughout the 1960s and early 1970s. In 1972, however, things changed dramatically.

In that year, HUD rejected Travis's three proposals to provide over 1,000 low-income housing units. He charged that HUD's new site selection policies made it virtually impossible for home buyers or owners in black areas to get access to the 235 and 236 programs that had been used previously to subsidize their payments. "Where are black people supposed to go?" Travis asked at one of the rallies he staged to protest the actions. "They cannot build or rent where they live. They are not welcome in white suburbs. It looks to me like this is an attempt to move the niggers into the swamps." Travis complained that the new HUD regulation would funnel federal housing money into the suburbs rather than the inner city. And it was in the inner city where Travis had made his money. Since he could no longer get the federal government to fund low-income housing and public housing in the black ghetto, Travis changed his tactic—he began advocating a return of the black middle class to the area.

Travis started his campaign slowly. In the mid–1970s, Travis gave a series of speeches in which he pointed out that the potential economic power of the black community was being dangerously dispersed, and with that, their political, social, and economic power was being undermined. He pointed out that "the only thing we are willing to buy in any quantity from each other is gasoline," since there were some 6,300 black-owned filling stations in the country. He further said that small food stores, and eating and drinking establishments, were the other areas where blacks bought from blacks. It therefore seemed to him "that the only things some blacks buy from each other with any consistency are those things that would be difficult or inconvenient to buy someplace else." Appealing to racial pride, Travis called for the development of a "black magnificent mile" on South Cottage Grove from 71st to 95th as a "major step in the business rejuvenation of the South Side." This challenge was accepted without much controversy among other black leaders, although most probably thought it was a pipe dream.

By the late 1970s, however, Travis had extended his argument, and it was causing great concern—he became blunt in his demand for the return of the black middle class to the ghetto from the suburbs. Taking a page from Booker T. Washington's* famous Atlanta Exposition address in 1895, Travis advised Chicago's blacks to "cast down their bucket where you are." By this he meant middle-class blacks should not forsake the ghetto, and, in fact, should rush to reclaim the inner city before whites came in to reap all the profits. To this end, Travis was pushing for the redevelopment of an area called the Gap, an area wedged between the Lake Meadows apartment complex and the Illinois Institute of Technology—an area of gracious old homes that had been spared the redevelopment of a quarter century earlier. "Unless the black community realizes the asset that it has geographically," Travis argued, "and invests its money, time, and talent into [its near-Loop] neighborhoods and builds new housing that our people need, close to the jobs and economic power of the Loop, our odyssey will have come full circle by the year 2000, and once again, poor blacks will ride trains to the Loop through white and middle-class neighborhoods sold to [those whites] by blacks whose myopia saw only the nearest suburb."

Although many urbanologists and housing experts agreed with Travis's analysis and solution, a number of other leaders, both black and white, were very upset. Those who had led the crusade for integrated housing in Chicago for decades felt betrayed and threatened by Travis's stance. Deborah Haines, a housing researcher for the Urban League, put it bluntly, "Ever since the housing market opened up for blacks, blacks have been spreading out. . . . The poorer areas have a lot of public housing, and middle-class blacks don't want to live around public housing—it's not safe and there's no status." Nedra Sims, project coodinator for another housing program, concurred, "Success means to get out, to get away. . . . To return is to overcome a psychological barrier. If they're making 15 grand, they aren't going to go back." The most vehement and vocal opposition to Travis, however, came from Thomas M. Gray, executive director of Home Investments Fund: "To ask blacks to hold onto predominently black areas," Gray said, "is to appeal to racial prejudice. Dempsey couches his argument in overtly racial terms, and in that sense much of what he says is against the spirit of open housing. That spirit, which began in the early 1960's, envisioned a biracial community as the outcome of civil rights activities. . . . I'm uncomfortable with any kind of statement that seems to define territory as black or white'' (*Chicago Leader*, February 9, 1979).

Others, however, supported Travis's stance. Clyde H. Brooks, president of the Southern Christian Leadership Conference's local chapter, said that ''Dempsey is saying that to live in the inner city is an alternative.'' Sharon Morgan, director of community services at Provident Hospital agreed: ''I don't dislike white people. I'm not a racist, but I like being around black people. I feel very comfortable around them. They are the people I know. I'm not particularly interested in being in an integrated society, and the city isn't really integrated anyway.'' Perhaps Travis's most eloquent support, however, came from Joseph Jefferson, president of the Douglas Corporation, which was involved in developing the Gap area with $106,000 in grants from the city. Jefferson was alive when Jesse Binga* was ''king'' of the South Side. He pointed out, ''Jesse Binga went throughout the south side telling churches and large groups to invest in the Gap. Dempsey's telling us to keep what we've got and do something with it—nothing wrong with that'' (*Chicago Leader*, February 9, 1979).

No one, however, could dispute Travis's success. By the early 1980s his realty firm was generating $15 million a year in real estate transactions and insurance sales. It ranked as the city's largest black-owned realty firm, and the firm managed and sold—through Sivart—real estate projects, including Lake Grove Village at 35th and Cottage Grove, and Vistra Gardens at 62nd and Michigan. The bulk of his real estate business, however, was in smaller parcels scattered throughout the South Side. He also got a boost politically and economically when his boyhood friend, Harold Washington, was elected mayor of Chicago in the early 1980s. Travis was appointed head of the Mayor's Real Estate Review Committee, which had a great deal to say about how the city's real estate was developed. Travis and his wife live in an apartment building they own, and his mother until her death lived across the hall. Travis neither smokes nor drinks, and has had only two cups of coffee in his life. ''What wakes me up in the morning,'' he claimed, ''is the excitement of another day. I jump out of bed because I want to get started. I don't understand why people need drugs and stimulants. Life itself—doing things—that's plenty of stimulation for me.'' Rising at daybreak, Travis bicycles twenty miles along the lakefront each morning, comes home and writes his books and articles for two hours, and arrives at his office, refreshed, by 9 A.M.

Travis was among the founders of Seaway National Bank, which, by the early 1990s, had become the largest black-owned bank in the United States. The moving forces behind the organization of the bank were Jasper Williams, a local doctor, and Ernie ''Stu'' Collins, owner of a small string of South Side grocery stores. Seaway National was founded in response to a need felt in the South Side black community for decades. As the *Chicago Defender* said, ''A call was repeated by business leaders for decade after decade: 'We should have a bank of our own.' '' This had been thwarted, however, by the reluctance of the State Treasury Department to charter such a bank, and also by the fact that black leaders were long concerned with a different set of issues. The founding of Seaway was in response to claims by black business leaders in the area that white lending institutions were ignoring their needs. The officers of Seaway Bank explained the need for their bank in the 1960s:

The heavily Black-populated South Side area needed a financial institution—a "friendly bank"—knowledgeable in the community's history, and concerned with needs and growth. What was required was a responsive bank that would be eager to make an investment in the community and grow with it.

Collins and Wilson were able to raise the required $1 million in capital through the support of Travis and a number of other South Side black business leaders. The bank first opened for business in a storefront at 8555 Cottage Grove Avenue, a middle-class black neighborhood. An instant hit in the community, it ended its first year with assets of over $5 million. It soon moved into a permanent headquarters nearby, and its growth over the next few years was steady. By the early 1990s it had four branches, along with automatic tellers in a number of other locations. It proudly proclaimed itself a "full service" bank.

A major turning point for Seaway, as for much of the city's black community, came in 1983 when it made a $149,000 loan to Harold Washington's mayoral campaign. After Washington's election, Seaway's business expanded rapidly, as it opened 115 new accounts a week. Even more important, Seaway became a depository for some city funds, a move by Harold Washington that engendered a good deal of controversy from political opponents. In any event, this led to increased corporate financing by Seaway, as it was able to open large lines of credit for such mainstream firms as Batus and Sears, Roebuck. Later, they also did business with Levi, Strauss & Co., and Borg-Warner Corporation. This, in turn, enabled Seaway to make large loans to fledgling black enterprises in the ghetto, such as the $1.5 million it loaned Christ Tech Corporation, a holding company made up of black people. By 1992 Seaway was the third-largest financial institution listed in the *Black Enterprise* survey, with assets of over $170 million and capital of nearly $13 million. It employed one hundred sixty people, and held deposits totaling over $150 million and loans of $49 million. By that time, however, Travis was no longer involved with the bank.

Travis, like many other successful blacks, sees himself as a role model for young African-American males. "Look, America has more to offer these kids than cotton fields and slums, and they should know that. I know it. . . . Every youngster should know there's a certain high to be had from a sparkling glass of champagne." Travis also believes that black businessmen must retain a strong social conscience: "I think every black entrepreneur has to have a whole lot of socialworker in him. And yet I've found that you can deal fairly with people and make a lot of money at the same time. Seems to me there are quite a few businessmen who don't understand that, including some in the biggest companies in this country."

Yet Travis is not just a Pollyanna about the American Dream for blacks. "I know that I am an exception,'' he once said. ''The opportunities are just not there for blacks, I don't give a damn how you cut it. And I think one of the things that successful black businessmen have failed to do is to speak out for fear of rocking the boat and endangering the thing they've got going. You have to face the fact that there's just a different set of rules for black people, if there are any rules at all. . . . The way I look at it, a black person is in a trap. But you can't let that rule your life. You can't let the jaws of that trap close down on you. You just have to know how to avoid that.''

Sources

Dempsey Travis's papers have been deposited with the Chicago Historical Society and are open to researchers. The collection consists of four boxes of materials from the United Mortgage Bankers Association, four boxes of Sivart Mortgage Corporation records, another four boxes of miscellaneous materials, and a large number of unsorted newspaper clippings and photographs. Travis is the author of a number of books, some of which are autobiographical in nature. See especially *An Autobiography of Black Chicago* (Chicago, 1981) and *An Autobiography of Black Jazz* (Chicago, 1983). Portions of the former book were excerpted in the *Chicago Tribune*, February 7, 1982. Another book, *Don't Stop Me Now* (Chicago, 1970), is also autobiographical, but intended for a juvenile audience. There are a number of shorter biographical treatments of Travis including ''The Jazziest Renaissance Man in Town,'' *Chicago Sun Times*, November 21, 1983; Lori Granger, ''A South Side Horatio Alger,'' *Chicago Tribune Magazine*, October 11, 1981; ''Dempsey J. Travis: Mortgage Banker,'' John Seder & Berkeley Burrell in *Getting It Together* (1971), 44–63; Frank J. Johnson's *Who's Who of Black Millionaires* (1984), 108–9; *Ebony*, May 1983; and *Chicago Sun Times*, September 24, 1970.

Besides the books mentioned above, Travis was the author of an impressive number of books and articles: *Racism: American Style* (Chicago, 1990); *Harold: The People's Mayor* (Chicago, 1989); *Real Estate Is the Gold in Your Future* (Chicago, 1988); *An Autobiography of Black Politics* (Chicago, 1987); ''Barriers to Black Power in the American Economy,'' *Black Scholar*, October 1971; ''The Black Businessman: Obstacles to His Success,'' *Black Scholar*, January 1973; ''Can Black Builders Survive?'' *Black Scholar*, February, 1974; and ''The 1980 Homestead Act,'' *Black Scholar*, November/December 1979.

A staggering number of newspaper and magazine articles deal with various aspects of Travis's career, or review his books and other writings. Some of the most useful of those include *Chicago Tribune*, June 14, 1970, September 21, 1983, February 7, 1982, September 21, 1983, December 28, 1986, and August 14, 1988; *Parade*, October 11, 1981; *Chicago Defender*, June 12, 1975, June 30, 1977, March 20, 1980, March 27, 1982, November 14, 1983, December 3, 1983, January 3, 1984, May 21, 1984, April 4, 1987, March 22, 1988, and February 11, 1989; *Ebony*, June 1967, July 1969, September 1972, and February 1976; *Black Enterprise*, August 1972; *Ebony Secrets of Success* (1973), vol. II, 256–59; *Sepia*, July 1962; *Chicago Sun Times*, September 9, 1983, and June 4, 1989; *Chicago Lawyer*, April 1984; and *Chicago Reader*, February 9, 1979.

Information on Seaway National Bank appears in the *Chicago Defender*, September 26, 1969, September 22, 1973, August 1 and 25 and September 14, 1985, June 25, November 23, and December 12, 1988, and May 16, 1989; *Black Enterprise*, June 1988, and June 1992; *Chicago Sun Times*, December 21, 1987; and a twenty-fifth anniversary brochure put out by Seaway in 1990.

Turnbo-Malone, Annie Minerva (August 9, 1869–May 10, 1957). Hair and toiletry preparations manufacturer, entrepreneur, and philanthropist: Poro Manufacturing, Poro College, and St. Louis Colored Orphans' Home. The 1976 *Guinness Book of World Records* acknowledges Annie Turnbo-Malone, the hair- and skin-care pioneer, as the earliest recorded self-made female millionaire. Although perhaps one takes for granted the vast array of hair- and skin-care products available today, when Turnbo-Malone began her career she targeted what was then an untapped market. African-American women had long been treating their hair with numerous homemade products, but Turnbo-Malone, with keen foresight, trailblazed a field that would become big business operations for such enterprising black businessmen as George Johnson,* S. B. Fuller,* and Edward G. Gardner.* The field is now dominated by men telling women how to care for their bodies and hair, despite the fact that the industry was essentially conceived of by Annie Turnbo-Malone and her ''sisters''—such notable figures as Madame C. J. Walker (see Walker, Sarah Breedlove) and Sarah Spencer Washington.

Annie Minerva Turnbo-Malone was born in Metropolis, Illinois, to Robert and Isabella (Cook) Turnbo. There is speculation, although there is no substantiated evidence, that her parents were former slaves. This is based upon the historic framework in which they matured to adulthood. Robert had become a farmer who, according to family tradition, had served with the Union troops during the Civil War. His wife and children fled from Kentucky to find refuge in Illinois, and they were reunited later with their father in Metropolis. Turnbo-Malone was the second youngest of eleven children, and she was raised by her older siblings when her parents died. She attended public schools in Metropolis, and then went to high school in Peoria, where she had moved to live with a married sister. Turnbo-Malone never completed high school; she withdrew from her studies due to a debilitating illness. During these formative years she had had a fascination with dressing her sisters' hair, which obviously developed into more than merely a passing fancy. Turnbo-Malone later claimed that once she was well enough to continue with her schooling, she studied chemistry to enhance her understanding of how to improve on the sheen and texture of hair.

In 1900, when Turnbo-Malone was living in the all-black town of Lovejoy (named after the abolitionist Elijah Lovejoy and now is Brooklyn), Illinois, she began to manufacture and sell her ''Wonderful Hair Grower,'' a hair growth preparation that she had developed single-handedly. For $5 per month, she rented space in the rear room of a small building, which the business soon outgrew. When the demand for her hair and scalp products transcended the local boundaries of Lovejoy, Turnbo-Malone recognized the importance of assuming a higher profile. She relocated to a larger city where she could expand her manufacturing facilities and meet the public's demand. In 1902 she decided to move to 2223 Market Steet in St. Louis, a strategic location from which to spread the word of her highly successful hair-care products. Turnbo-Malone began to reach out to the public by traveling door to door with her three assistants. Once she had sufficiently interested a prospective customer, she would personally treat her hair and scalp at no charge, giving her the opportunity to demonstrate the effectiveness of her products at no initial cost to the customer.

To further enhance her products' salability, Turnbo-Malone engaged in a massive advertising campaign in 1904. The impetus for this was impressive response for her products following the St. Louis World's Fair, which convinced her that she had not yet begun to reach the vast market that was just waiting to be taught professional hair care. She embarked on a massive tour throughout the South, demonstrating her preparations and techniques, and recruiting women whom she then trained to administer and sell her line of products. Claude Barnett, the founder of the Associated Negro Press and the company's public relations officer for years, claimed that one of Turnbo-Malone's agents in St. Louis in 1905 was Sarah Breedlove (Madame C. J.) Walker,* who founded a highly successful beauty product empire which also had its origins in St. Louis. In addition, Turnbo-Malone advertised in many of the black newspapers and magazines. The response was so overwhelming that fraudulent claims made by imitators were sprouting up across the country. To stymie charlatans' efforts, Turnbo-Malone in 1906 adopted and copyrighted the trade name "Poro." From that time forward, the hair-care products were sold under that name, which succeeded in confounding the fraudulent imitations.

By 1910, having built a well-established national enterprise that required larger accommodations to house the expanding operations, Turnbo-Malone relocated to new quarters at 3100 Pine Street. Although competition was fierce in the specialized area of hair staighteners and pomades, Poro's sales far surpassed the others, most likely due to an efficient franchising system. When facilities again proved to be inadequate, Turnbo-Malone constructed a magnificent new building on expansive grounds, which came to be known as Poro College. Ground was broken for the original structure in October 1917, at Ferdinand and Pendleton Streets, and was completed in 1918. This impressive five-storied factory and beauty-training school in the heart of St. Louis' upper-middle-class black neighborhood incorporated much more than simply the company's operations. In addition to modern classrooms, auditorium, cafeteria, bakeshop, dormitory, guest rooms for travelers, roof garden, and business offices, the building had facilities to accommodate the needs of religious, fraternal, civic, and social functions. The choice of the word "college" implies Turnbo-Malone's vision: a campuslike environment that offered a broad array of facilities for those within and outside of the company.

Such prominent figures as Mary McLeod Bethune, the Mills Brothers, Lena Horne, and Joe Louis were guests at the complex. The National Negro Business League (of which Turnbo-Malone was an active member) had made its headquarters there in 1927, and black St. Louisans, who were denied admittance to venues in the city's popular restaurants and hotels, were welcome to take advantage of the modern facilities that also offered a club room and a well-appointed dining room. So magnificent was this structure and the opportunities it provided the black community that it came to be known as the "Showplace of St. Louis."

The fact that no other black enterprise in the world at that time encompassed under one roof such high-quality accommodations and services to guests earned Poro College an unmatched reputation throughout the United States. To address the increased volume of business, in 1920 an annex and garage were added to house the Poro plant, and represented an investment of over $1 million.

In 1922 Turnbo-Malone introduced a line of soap, cold cream, and and bleaching cream, which soon enjoyed the popularity of the earlier products. In that same year, Poro employed 175 people in St. Louis alone. African-American women from throughout the world represented the Poro product line in such locales as Canada, the Philippines, Africa, and South America, where, in total, almost 75,000 jobs were created. Branches were set up in major American urban centers such as Washington, Baltimore, Cleveland, Detroit, and Chicago, where education on beauty techniques was offered through franchise schools. At its peak, the company was identified as the largest mail-order house in the city of St. Louis. Turnbo-Malone was riding on the wave of success: Her products had gained international acclaim and were selling at an unprecedented rate; she had acquired the esteem of not only her fellow St. Louisans, but also her business colleagues and peers. In 1924 her income tax of $38,498 and the reported profits of Poro suggest that Turnbo-Malone had achieved the status of a millionaire.

Turnbo-Malone was determined to act as a unifying force for the women of the world. In her advertising brochures she called for "ambitious women to enter a profitable profession" and promised them economic independence as Poro agents. Turnbo-Malone had long enjoyed the fruits of financial independence and encouraged women to seek a similar goal with Turnbo-Malone as a role model. She had what has been called a "benevolent, if autocratic," concern for Poro's "beauty culturists." Turnbo-Malone had devised for her employees a system of incentives to reward their outstanding achievements and to encourage promising trainees to work harder. One of the several awards given annually was a gold gift presented to those who invested in real estate or helped their parents to do so. To each longtime (five-year) employee, Turnbo-Malone awarded a diamond ring; there were also prizes for punctuality and attendance, and raincoats and umbrellas for all, admonishing the "Poro family" to "guard their health."

Turnbo-Malone's activities and energies transcended her business interests. Her dedication to her race was documented throughout her life, from the money she gave to a variety of black organizations, including hospitals, churches, and schools, to the way in which she depicted her race in advertisements in such activist publications as W.E.B. Du Bois's *The Crisis* magazine. She truly saw it her mission to promote and help her race in any way she could, and she succeeded both in providing thousands of jobs for African-Americans in a variety of capacities, ranging from representatives to teachers to factory workers, and in donating sizable sums of money to the black institutions that provided the community with important services.

Turnbo-Malone's generosity extended beyond her employees. She was a philanthropist who provided generously to numerous worthy causes. Following the disastrous St. Louis tornado in 1927, Poro College provided thousands of destitute St. Louisans with shelter, food, and clothing. Upon awarding Howard University's Medical Endowment Fund an additional $5,000, which increased the total of her donation to $10,000 in 1927, Turnbo-Malone stated,

With the wish that this amount may be of some assistance in aiding in the uplift of our race, I gladly make this contribution for the worthy cause, believing that in turn the results will come from the earnest endeavors of the youth in their contribution to humanity and that they feel it their obligation. For value received, I promise to pay.

Twenty five thousand dollars was donated to St. Louis' 1925 black YMCA campaign "to show that the Negro . . . is willing to bear his share of responsibility." In 1919 Turnbo-Malone donated a $10,000 site for the St. Louis Colored Orphans' Home (which was founded by Sara W. Newton in 1888 and incorporated in 1889), and she raised an additional $120,000 for its construction. After serving on its board as president from 1919 to 1943, the trustees in 1946, despite her objections, renamed it the Annie Malone Children's Home. Her gifts are still appreciated and remembered by the various recipients of her donations: a maternity ward at Barnes Hospital, the Ferrier-Harris Home for the Aged, and the Phillis Wheatly branch of the YWCA. All remain vital forces in St. Louis' black community.

Although Turnbo-Malone had been married in 1903 to a Mr. Pope, the union was short lived when she filed for divorce, citing his interference in her business affairs as the cause of the breakup. After remaining on her own for several years while she developed her business and concentrated on expanding the operations and increasing the company's revenues, Turnbo-Malone again married in 1914. Her second husband, the dapper Aaron Eugene Malone, was a former teacher and traveling Bible salesman. After thirteen years of marriage, Aaron Malone filed for divorce, in a suit that was closely scrutinized by the press and public alike. On July 1927, *The Messenger*, in an article entitled "The Malone Case," addressed the issue of the wider implications of the Turnbo-Malone divorce suit. The journal asserted that the suit's outcome would have racial consequences that would transcend the two individuals directly involved. It went on to say, "Therefore, the lesson is that we who climb the heights are obligated beyond our personal desires to hold hard to what we have or where we are, because the impact of a crash strikes the whole group." Mr. Malone, in his suit, demanded half of her business, which forced Poro College into a court-ordered receivership. The public reaction was split in black St. Louis: For political reasons, half the community sided with Aaron Malone, who had become prominent in local and state Republican politics (which was partially financed by his wife's business). In the other camp, black church leaders, the black press, Poro employees, and such national figures as Mary McLeod Bethune, supported Annie Turnbo-Malone. After considerable deliberation, an out-of-court settlement was arrived at on May 9, 1927, that affirmed Turnbo-Malone's position as sole owner of

Poro. Although Aaron Malone had alleged that he helped build the company, and thus was entitled to half of its assets, he ultimately accepted cash (reportedly $200,000) and real estate as his final settlement. One editorial covering the suit noted that Poro College had prospered "without the guiding hand of man," which apparently was substantiated by the court's ruling. A divorce was granted on May 23, 1927, which allowed Turnbo-Malone to run the company independently again.

Having suffered the pain and indignity of a publicized divorce and the subsequent loss, Turnbo-Malone elected to absent herself from the unpleasant memories of St. Louis. She moved her business to Chicago's South Parkway in August 1930. There she purchased an entire city block, which came to be known as the Poro Block, to house her ever-expanding operations. Information on Poro's operations is scarce after her move to Chicago. One can only speculate from the data that are available that Turnbo-Malone never enjoyed the fruits of her labor to the same degree as she had in St. Louis. She had moved to Chicago during the worst days of the Depression in the early 1930s, and the city's blacks suffered greatly during this time. Also, competition had become fierce in the hair-care and beauty treatment field, and undoubtedly she felt the impact of companies infringing on the territory she had dominated. Although the best-known and most successful competitor was Madame C. J. Walker, there were many other enterprising black women who jumped on the bandwagon and developed their own lines of hair and beauty products to rival the deeply entrenched Poro products. In 1913, Sara Spencer Washington, originally from Virginia, founded a small hairdressing establishment in Atlantic City, New Jersey, where she instructed students on her techniques. Seven years later, she organized Apex News and Hair company, which, at its peak, manufactured a line of over seventy-five kinds of beauty preparations, and had 35,000 agents across the United States. As recently as 1976, the *Atlanta Daily World* stated that there were still thousands of agents handling the Apex line. Turnbo-Malone certainly had her hands full devising a strategic plan to counteract the effects of such formidable competition.

As if the changing climate of the cosmetic industry and the Great Depression were not enough to challenge Turnbo-Malone's abilities as an entrepreneur, 1937 appears to be the year of her undoing. In that year, she lost a suit that had been filed against her many years earlier by a former employee, who claimed that he had been discharged within six weeks after being appointed general manager of the college. He claimed he had been hired with the understanding that he was to receive a third of the net profits of the company for two years, and thus was demanding what he believed was his share of the profits. The settlement forced the sale of the much cherished St. Louis property.

Turnbo-Malone had long suffered at the hands of dishonest and incompetent managers, who had failed to provide assistance and advice on how to manage her vast empire. On January 28, 1937, Poro College was foreclosed upon by Missouri Valley Trust Company, which held a defaulted $65,000 mortgage on the building. Turnbo-Malone had an aversion to paying excise taxes levied against her by the federal government. Paying taxes never became part of her operational system, so between 1933 and 1951, she was sued time and time again. In 1951 the government finally took control of her business for delinquent taxes, which left Turnbo-Malone with considerably fewer assets, and undoubtedly more regrets for not having managed her money with more care. The combination of these setbacks contributed to the decline of Turnbo-Malone as the ''Queen of Manufactured Beauty.'' She lost all her property in Chicago, which was sold through tax foreclosures. At the time of her death on May 10, 1957, Poro Colleges still operated in over thirty cities, although her active participation had declined over the years.

What a sad state of affairs for a woman who had showed the world that women were capable and responsible business people who had the initiative and good sense to run a large enterprise. Unfortunately, the absence of professional advisors led to her demise. More important, it must be remembered that Annie Turnbo-Malone achieved far greater accomplishments than most women and men of the early twentieth century, and not only those of African-American descent. Fortunately, Turnbo-Malone's hard work was not in vain, as her contributions are not forgotten: To this day, the Children's Home in St. Louis still honors her memory with an annual May Day parade. Perhaps the most eloquent testimony to Annie Turnbo-Malone's influence comes from the African-American women whose lives were changed as a result of the opportunities she opened up to them. One of those was Dr. Ruth J. Jackson, who opened a Poro College of Beauty Culture in Birmingham, Alabama, in 1936. Interviewed in 1981, she said,

There is more money made in cosmotology [sic] than in any other, if they treat their patronage right. They make more money than the teachers if they stick to it. When I started in cosmotology [sic] people were getting one dollar, and a dollar and a quarter per patron. Now, no operator gets less than fifteeen dollars for any patron. . . . I tell anyone, cosmotology [sic] or beauty culture is my lifelong living. That's all I've ever done all my life.

And she owed it all to Annie Turnbo-Malone.

Sources

Although a comprehensive collection of Annie Turnbo-Malone Papers is not available, a variety of material is accessible at several sources. The Claude A. Barnett Papers at the Chicago Historical Society contain correspondence, clippings, photographs, press releases, publications, and a typescript biography of Annie Turnbo-Malone. The Western Historical Collection at the University of Missouri at St. Louis has a biographical checklist as well as research materials on Poro College and the Children's Home. Included in that collection are the Herman Dreer Papers, which contain an interview with Turnbo-Malone for Dreer's dissertation entitled ''Leadership in St. Louis: A Study in Race Relations,'' Ph.D. diss., University of Chicago, 1975. The Schomburg Center in the New York Public Library system has a collection of paraphernalia including letters and papers, such as a two-page instruction manual for ''The Proper Treatments to Improve Scalp Ailments.''

A small number of letters were found among the Booker T. Washington Papers housed at the Library of Congress.

Several books acknowledge Turnbo-Malone's national stature: J. L. Nichols and W. H. Crogman, *Progress of a Race* (1920); Carter Woodson, *The Negro in Our History* (1927); Edwin R. Embree, *Brown American: The Story of a Tenth of the Nation* (1943); and E. Franklin Frazier, *The Negro in the United States* (1969). *Who's Who in Colored America* (1928–1929 and 1930–1931–1932) also provides a synopsis of her career and achievements. Gladys Porter, *Three Negro Pioneers in Beauty Culture*, (1966), and Eva DelVakea Bowles, "Opportunities for the Educated Colored Woman," *Opportunity*, March 1923, provide several biographies of women in the beauty field that allow a comparison of careers. A comprehensive profile of Turnbo-Malone appears in *Notable American Women* (1980) by Jeanne Conway Mongold; shorter yet helpful biographies appear in *Show Me Missouri Women: Selected Biographies*, edited by Mary K. Dains (1989); and *Profiles in Silhouette: The Contributions of Black Women of Missouri* by the St. Louis Alumnae Chapter (1980).

Much briefer sketches of Turnbo-Malone appear in the *Official Manual—State of Missouri* (1971–1972); *Missouri Historical Review*, July 1973; *Journal of Negro History* 9 (1924); *Negro History Bulletin*, May 1952; *The Ville: The Ethnic Heritage of an Urban Neighborhood* (1975); *St. Louis: Its Neighborhoods and Neighbors, Landmarks and Milestones*, edited by Robert E. Hannon; *Trailblazers among Black St. Louisans*, by the National Sorority of Phi Delta Kappa (1978), *Missouri's Black Heritages*, by Lorenzo J. Greene et al. (1980). Numerous articles chronicling Turnbo-Malone's career and business activities appear in the St. Louis *Globe Democrat* and the St. Louis *Post Dispatch*, which are available in clipping files at the Mercantile Library in St. Louis. Articles also appear in the *Interstate Tattler*, *Chicago Daily Defender*, *Guardian*, *New York Age*, *New York World*, and *Atlanta Daily World*. Turnbo-Malone's obituary appeared in the following newspapers: *St. Louis Argus*, May 17, 1957; *St. Louis Post-Dispatch* and *St. Louis Globe-Democrat*, May 12, 1957; and *Chicago Daily Defender*, May 13, 15, and 16, 1957. The interview with Dr. Ruth J. Jackson was conducted by Otis Dismuke on January 9, 1981, and is held in Birmingham Find, an oral history collection in the Archives at the Birmingham, Alabama, Public Library. See also Albert Anderson, "The Amazing Inside Story of the Malone Case," *The Light and "Heebie Jeebies"* 3, 13 (19 February 1927), 14–22; Louis W. George, "Beauty Culture and Colored People," *Messenger* 2 (July 1918), 26; Evelyn Northington, "About Cosmetics and Other Things," *Half-Century* (October 1919), 11; and "Beauty Is a Business," *Brown American* (August 1944), 12–14.

V

Vann, Robert Lee (August 27, 1879–October 24, 1940). Newspaper publisher, politician, entrepreneur, race leader, and government official: *Pittsburgh Courier, The Competitor: The National Magazine*, Assistant City Solicitor (Pittsburgh), and Assistant to the U.S. Attorney General. Andrew Buni, Robert Vann's biographer, said that "Vann's real monument was the *Pittsburgh Courier*." That the statement is true is beyond question. There were a number of important African-American newspaper editors and publishers (John Mitchell, Jr.,* Eugene Rhodes,* C.A. and W.A. Scott II,* Fred Moore,* W. Calvin Chase,* William Monroe Trotter, and P. B. Young, among others), but only Vann and Robert Abbott* built black newspapers with truly national circulation. As such, the *Courier* and Abbott's *Chicago Defender* were able to influence millions of blacks beyond the boundaries of their particular cities. Those two newspapers strove to create patterns of migration from the South to the North, to define issues and tactics for fighting discrimination nationwide, and to build at least some sense of community among blacks in the American diaspora. On top of that, they were able to make money doing so, to create viable economic institutions that nonetheless managed to be politically sensitive and aware, and which acted as a voice for African-Americans during a particularly crucial time in the nation's history.

Robert Vann was born in the tiny hamlet of Ahoskie, in Hertford County, North Carolina. Like much of the rest of northeastern North Carolina at that time, the area was mostly agrarian and more than 50 percent black. African-Americans in the area, most of whom had been slaves prior to the Civil War on surrounding plantations, by the end of Reconstruction were growing tobacco or peanuts on small plots, either as farm owners or sharecroppers. A small number of other blacks worked in timbering or fishing. Vann's mother, Lucy Peoples, was the daughter of Fletcher Peoples and Martilla Holloman, ex-slaves who operated a small general store in the hamlet of Ahoskie. Lucy worked as a cook and a domestic for nearby white families, and in her teens, when Robert Vann was born, worked for the Albert Vann family. As was the custom, she bestowed the surname of her employers on her young son. She herself remained Lucy

Peoples until she married a few years later. She chose the names Robert Lee in honor of his great-grandfather. There is no record of Robert Vann's father. When asked about his father in later years, he simply replied, "I came of a family named Peoples, and my mother gave me the name of her grandfather, who died before the war of 1860. I don't even know his name or where he was born, but my family, the Peoples, still live in North Carolina."

A few years after Vann's birth, his mother married Joseph Hall, a black field hand on the same farm where Lucy was working as a cook. Subsequently, Hall deserted the family, and Robert's mother had to raise her young son by herself. According to Andrew Buni, Lucy was able to retain the favored position of cook to support herself and her son because of the "hierarchy of skin color"—Lucy was very light skinned and attractive, and her son inherited those characteristics. When Robert was six, Lucy got a cook's job with a very affluent family, and, although they lived in a cabin nearby, Robert Vann was nonetheless able to experience the gracious and serene way of life of the Askew farm. Throughout his life, this example was an important factor in the motivation that drove him out of rural North Carolina, toward the North and Pittsburgh, to make a success of himself in the newspaper business, politics, and the law.

Lucy Peoples was a strict disciplinarian, and she made sure Robert was introduced to religion at an early age, baptizing him at the New Ahoskie Baptist Church. Vann was educated at the Springfield Colored School located in the area. That one-room, unpainted school, like so many schools for blacks in the South at that time, provided only a rudimentary education, but Vann was an apt pupil and graduated in 1892. That same year, Lucy Peoples married John Simon, a local dirt farmer, and instead of going on to secondary school, Vann found himself spending the next few years either toiling on his stepfather's farm, or being hired out as a cook, seine fisher, or tobacco picker. Vann later commented, "My stepfather thought that I was big enough to work but he never knew how the first ten years of my life constantly rebelled against the six years of torment I encountered under his jurisdiction." Vann not only had to do hard, physical labor, which he never before had experienced, but also suffered a diminution in status, as he was no longer the child of a favored servant, but now the stepson of a poor dirt farmer—perhaps as low a ranking as one could have in that limited society. As a result, Vann learned to detest his stepfather and, throughout his life, remembered John Simon as "the world's most worthless man."

Vann's escape from this life came in 1895, when he had a chance to work as a janitor and part-time clerk at the Harrellsville Post Office. By the end of that summer, he had saved $16, and he was determined to secure an education. He chose the private, Baptist-run Waters Training School in Winton, the Hertford County seat. Vann still had to work to put himself through school, either taking a term off to labor in the nearby tobacco fields, or working during the summer as a waiter in Boston, and in odd hours also shining shoes. These latter occupations also taught him about the world outside of rural North Carolina, and of the importance of good grooming—for the rest of his life, Vann would be meticulous about his clothing and appearance. Vann graduated as valedictorian from Waters in 1901, but he felt the need for further training before he attempted college. Therefore, he enrolled at Wayland Academy, the university preparatory school of Virginia Union University in Richmond. By 1902 he had received a degree there, and he enrolled in Virginia Union as a college student. It was during this time, also, that Vann became acquainted with the militant leadership, in the city's black community, of John Mitchell, Jr., editor and publisher of the *Richmond Planet*.

Increasingly, at Virginia Union, Robert Vann's interests shifted toward debate, oratory, and politics. Two of his closest friends at the school remained friends throughout his life: J. Max Barber, who later became editor of *The Voice of the Negro* and a "radical" on the race issue; and Eugene Kinckle Jones, later executive secretary of the National Urban League and a moderate on these same issues. Vann, interestingly, would fluctuate between radicalism and moderation on matters of race throughout his life, taking contrary stands not only from issue to issue, but sometimes on the same issue during a short space of time. By the time Vann graduated from Virginia Union in 1903, things looked bleak for blacks in North Carolina. The incredibly vicious race war waged by whites on the black community in Wilmington in 1898 had been followed by the difranchisement and wholesale segregation of blacks and whites in nearly every aspect of life in the state. Robert Vann, degree in hand, stood little chance of occupational or political success in his home state. He resolved instead to go north to continue his studies and applied at Western University of Pennsylvania (now the University of Pittsburgh), where he won a $100 Avery scholarship.

Although Vann was one of very few blacks at the University of Pittsburgh, he continued to grow in eminence as an orator and debator, and he also served for two years as a regular contributor to the school's newspaper. In his senior year, Vann was chosen editor-in-chief, and when he graduated in 1906, he was chosen class poet. As in North Carolina, Vann's extremely limited finances forced him to work after school and during summers in a resort at Bar Harbor, Maine. It was also during this time that Vann made his first excursion into politics, developing what would become a lifelong passion. A loyal Republican at that time, Vann worked for Pittsburgh's Magee-Flinn machine in the 1906 election when they were challenged by a group of reformers. The one dark spot during this period came in 1904 when his mother passed away in North Carolina, leaving him utterly alone in the world—no father, no siblings, no close relatives.

In 1906 Robert Vann finally, at age twenty-seven, had his bachelor's degree. It was, as Andrew Buni pointed out, an exceptional feat. Between 1823 and 1909 just 693 blacks in the entire country had graduated from white colleges. Vann decided to enroll in law school at the University of Pittsburgh, and he received his law degree there in June 1909. Thirty years old, Vann began to practice law in the city and met a woman who became his wife and lifelong companion—Jessie E. Matthews. They were married on February 17, 1910, shortly before Vann got involved in another lifetime venture, the *Pittsburgh*

Courier. In the year between June 1909 and May 1910, though, Vann tried his hand at making a living as a criminal lawyer. He found the work challenging but hardly remunerative. He had a few major cases, performing well in those, but most of the blacks accused of truly serious crimes chose white lawyers. So, Vann spent his time working on mundane cases with small monetary rewards. By the spring of 1910 he was ready for a new challenge, and for a chance to make more money than he could as a criminal lawyer.

Pittsburgh, at the turn of the century, was a city bursting with economic vitality, but cursed with pollution, dilapidated housing, corrupt city government, and heavy industry. It represented, perhaps, the best and worst of American industrialism. Although African-Americans had been in Pittsburgh for many years, the group was still tiny in the latter decades of the nineteenth century. Despite the fact that the black population doubled between 1870 and 1880, and doubled again in the next decade, the number reached just 10,000 in 1890. In the early decades of the twentieth century, the city's black population was swelled with migrants from the South like Vann. The number of blacks surged to 26,000 in 1910, and to over 37,000 in 1920. In the decade of World War I, 87 percent of the city's increase in black population came from southern migrants. Pittsburgh's place as a center of heavy manufacturing with many jobs for unskilled and semiskilled men was a great attraction, as were worsening economic conditions in southern agriculture and the deteriorating racial climate in the South. At the time Vann arrived, though, most blacks in the city were still limited to domestic or personal service, with 58 percent of the men and over 90 percent of the women so employed. Very few had yet been able to crack the racial barriers in the steel or coal industries of the city and surrounding area.

Before the arrival of southern migrants, blacks had lived in every ward of Pittsburgh, and Vann himself first lived in a small pocket of middle-class African-Americans in Allegheny, just across the river from Pittsburgh. Increasingly, however, the new entrants were being clustered into an area known as the Hill District. "The Hill" had previously been home to hordes of earlier migrants, including large numbers of Jewish immigrants. By 1910, over 40 percent of Pittsburgh's blacks lived on the Hill, although they continued to be dispersed throughout the city. It was the Hill, however, that became the cultural and symbolic center of black life in Pittsburgh. It was a bustling, vibrant area, but the conditions were deplorable. Helen Tucker, who came from Hampton Institute to investigate the Hill in 1908 said, "I think I never saw such wretched conditions. In some alleys there were stables next to the houses and while the odor was bad at any time, after a rain the stench from these and from the dirt in the streets was almost unendurable."

Many of these middle-class blacks, as in the South, were ministers and teachers, but as the city became more ghettoized, and there was a greater need of services for blacks, a number of African-Americans established their own businesses. In the decade from 1900 to 1910, there were eighty-five black-run businesses, ranging from poolrooms to contractors, to caterers, to print shops that employed over 300. Only 1 percent of the black population worked as professionals during this decade, and most of them were clergymen.

A small group of Pittsburgh blacks came to visit Robert Vann's office in March 1910. They wanted him to draw up incorporation papers for a new newspaper, to be called the *Pittsburgh Courier*. The men had been trying to run the scraggly affair, which Vann referred to as a "two-page sheet initiated by a Negro in a pickle factory," since 1907. It was begun by Edwin Nathaniel Harleston, who worked in the H. J. Heinz plant and had developed the paper as a vehicle to publish his poems. In 1909 Harleston decided to put his paper on a more businesslike footing, and he began searching for financial backers. He was not really successful in this pursuit, but he did get a number of other blacks to join with him in putting out the new, larger paper in 1910, which was when they came to see Vann. Vann agreed to draw up the papers, and since they had no money to pay him, he was given stock in the firm instead. He then helped the group get some financial backing in the African-American community. Among those investing money was Cumberland Posey, Sr., who owned a fleet of river boats and was the father of Cumberland Posey,* future owner of the Homestead Grays Negro League baseball team.

The *Courier* struggled valiantly during its first few months, but when Harleston was forced to leave in the fall of 1910, Vann was asked to take over as editor, publisher, and practically everything else on the paper. For all of this he received $100 a year, to be paid in *Courier* stock. Vann gave his own account of these events in a letter to Elizabeth Amelia Pinckney in 1936: "On March 10, 1910 I secured the certificate of incorporation for the Pittsburgh Courier Publishing Company and remained as its attorney until the fall of 1910 when, due to some disagreements, Mr. Harleston withdrew entirely from the company and left the City of Pittsburgh and I became the editor as well as the lawyer for the company. These joint positions, whatever they represent, I have held ever since." The advantage for Vann at the time was that he used the *Courier*'s pages to trumpet his successful court cases; in this manner, he was able to increase his legal revenues. But he was hooked. He loved the challenge and notoriety of being a newspaper publisher; he loved to express his opinions in print, to influence the broader black community in Pittsburgh and elsewhere. He also provided a sorely needed service to the black community of the city. With over 25,000 black inhabitants in 1910, there was no African-American newspaper before the *Courier* to provide news to that group. The only white Pittsburgh paper that had been doing so was the *Press*, and it discontinued its "Afro-American News" after 1914. So, Vann and the *Courier* were, in many respects, a lifeline for the nascent black community in the city, and the *Courier* billed itself as "Pittsburgh's Only Colored Newspaper."

Without any significant advertising from the white community, and hampered by the fact that white newsstands refused to carry the *Courier*, the paper had to survive on subscription sales, which were erratic at best. By 1914, however, Vann had finally gotten the paper on a solid footing, and in that year he made a critical decision; he hired Ira F. Lewis as his full-time aide in running the paper. A native of North Carolina, like Vann, Lewis's mother had died shortly after his birth, and he never knew his father. Lewis had gone to Biddle University (later Johnson C. Smith University) in Charlotte for a time, then had come north, first to Washington, D.C., and then to Pittsburgh. After a time, Lewis became the business manager of the paper, and the combination of the two men, as unlikely a pair as they were, was most successful. Where Vann was conservative and withdrawn, Lewis was flamboyant and outgoing. Where Vann was somber, Lewis was cheerful and boisterous. Vann in 1914 seemed to have new resolve and new plans for his paper. In an editorial in the Christmas edition of that year, he forecast a new, dynamic role for himself and the paper "having weathered the storm without the loss of a single issue," he wrote. He rededicated the newspaper "to the cause of the Negro and all that pertains to his interests. We propose to continue our fight for the general advancement of the Negro . . . to abolish every vestige of Jim Crowism in Pittsburgh. . . . Let us leave no stone unturned which will lead [us] toward advancement."

Robert Vann built up the *Courier* in the years before and during World War I by conducting, in its pages, a number of crusades that enhanced the paper's popularity. He tackled the problems of housing that African-Americans in the city were experiencing. In the two years between 1916 and 1918, 18,500 blacks had poured into Pittsburgh from the South. The overcrowding in the Hill district, as well as the quality of the housing available there, was deplorable. The *Courier* pushed to eliminate the laws and customs that created a segregated environment in the city. It also urged blacks to establish their own building and loan associations and real estate development operations to address the problem. Vann also campaigned in the pages of the *Courier* to establish decent medical facilities for blacks and to upgrade the very poor educational opportunities afforded members of his race in the city.

Another area where Vann pushed for change was in the kinds of jobs available to African-Americans. They were relegated to the worst, poorest paying jobs in the community; union rules and other devices were employed to keep them out of heavy industry and from working in better jobs with other white companies. Vann achieved a great symbolic victory for blacks and for the *Courier* when Kaufmann's, the city's oldest department store, in the midst of union problems with its white drivers, dismissed them all and replaced them with blacks. Seventy-six black drivers were hired, and Vann was jubilant, proclaiming, "The entire service, including mechanics, helpers, greasers, oilers, shifters, gasoline men, vulcanizers, chauffeurs, and delivery men was turned over to our men with the hope that we can take hold of this opportunity and make good or die in the effort." Of course, this hampered relations between white unions and the black community, but, given the unions' attitudes toward blacks, Vann's reaction was appropriate.

As more and more poor, ill-educated, and poorly prepared blacks flooded into Pittsburgh during the years around World War I, the white press became increasingly racist in its handling of the situation. Blacks were almost universally treated in a degrading and humiliating manner; questions were continually raised about their willingness to work, their intelligence, their high crime rate, and their living habits. Vann believed it was important to counter these negative stereotypes in the *Courier*. Creating more positive images of blacks, in turn, would help create the racial pride necessary to build the bonds of community among his people. Along the same line, it was important simply to provide news of the black community. White newspapers seldom reported anything positive that happened among African-Americans, so the *Courier* was an important source of news and uplift for the people. Much of the coverage seems minor on the surface: accounts of meetings of social clubs, such as the Frogs or the Leondi, recording of events at various black churches, news of the comings and goings of the black elite of the city—but all of this was designed to give blacks a more positive sense of the nature of African-American life.

Vann also crusaded about various laws and customs that permitted discrimination in public places, such as streetcars, theaters, and restaurants. To that end, he campaigned for passage of a state law in 1915 to outlaw such practices. He personally went to Harrisburg to lobby for its passage, and it was cleared through both the upper and lower houses. The governor, however, vetoed the bill, calling the law "unnecessary." Various civil rights bills were introduced over the next several years in the state legislature, and Vann campaigned strenuously for each of them, until he finally despaired after another defeat in 1923. Vann and the *Courier* did not win all the battles they waged during these years, but they gave blacks in the city a sense of empowerment and belonging, and these battles increased the popularity of his paper.

During this period of time, Vann also became more involved in politics on a local level, and he received his first important political appointment. He had continued to support the Republican machine, by then headed by William A. Magee, but in 1917 Vann made a critical decision to defect to a reform coalition headed by Edward Vose Babcock. Babcock had promised Vann a political appointment if elected. Vann campaigned strenuously for the reform coalition. Babcock was victorious in the general election, and the black vote had been crucial for his victory. In return, Babcock rewarded Vann with the post of assistant city solicitor at a salary of $2,650 annually. This was a real plum, the highest political office a black had ever received in Pittsburgh's municipal government. Ira Lewis was also given a clerkship with the sheriff's office. These political jobs did much to relieve the financial pressures on the two young directors of the *Courier*, and allowed the paper more freedom to pursue its various campaigns.

During World War I, unlike a number of other black leaders and newspapers at that time, Vann and the *Courier* gave full endorsement to the nation's war effort. This support transcended the paper's editorials, as Emmett J. Scott obtained an appointment for Vann to a "Committee of One Hundred," a group of blacks formed to report on conditions encountered by African-Americans in the armed forces and in the nation generally. Vann helped create a black National Publicity Bureau to publicize African-American wartime achievements, and neither he nor the *Courier* criticized a series of devastating race riots that rocked the nation during and immediately after the war. In 1917 Vann actually supported the hanging of black soldiers accused of rioting in Houston, and two years later he was cautious in his response to riots occurring in Chicago and elsewhere: "We had just as well view the situation sanely." He also criticized what he viewed as the Communist sponsorship of much of the antigovernment activity of the postwar Red Scare, and he was particularly critical of union leadership during the great steel strike of 1919 for, in his view, being under Communist influence. As a result of these actions, the government never investigated Vann or the *Courier* during these years.

In the 1920s Robert Vann engaged in a number of grandiose entrepreneurial efforts, none of which was successful. He was very much a follower of the self-help, free enterprise philosophy of Booker T. Washington,* and the pages of the *Courier* were often filled with praise for the entrepreneurial exploits of wealthy blacks like Robert R. Church* of Memphis. Vann was also intimately involved in the activities of the National Negro Business League, and he addressed its annual convention several times. This connection brought him into contact with black businessmen in many areas. Vann seemed to have an almost maniacal desire to get rich with some kind of enterprise. A series of letters between Vann and Harry Pace* of Chicago demonstrated that insatiable appetite. Pace had founded Black Swan Records, a black-owned recording company designed to record black artists, most particularly the music of W. C. Handy. Vann wrote to Pace in 1922: "I want some stock—in fact, I mean to have some. My ideas about the method of purchase and the amount must be governed by what amount you can set aside under my proposition."

As a result of these activities and attitudes, Vann began to pursue his own entrepreneurial dreams during the "go-go" period of the 1920s. The first of these was publication of *The Competitor: The National Magazine*. An expensive and ambitious venture, *The Competitor* was designed as an illustrated magazine for a national black audience. It published some of the top black writers of the day, was printed on glossy stock, and had a large number of photographs. But the magazine was too expensive and appealed to only a small number of highly educated and literate blacks. As a result, it failed almost before it began. It must be recognized, though, that in many respects Vann was simply ahead of his time. In 1936, a similar magazine, *Life*, began being published by Henry Luce for whites with phenomenal success, and after World War II, John H. Johnson* brought out *Ebony* magazine for blacks, around which he built a vast publishing empire.

In 1925 Vann became involved in the rashest venture of his career. Prompted by the intense interest in Africa generated by Marcus Garvey, Vann and some friends tried a series of schemes for investing in the Gold Coast of Africa. The undertakings included exporting manganese and animal skins and growing cocoa and rubber. None of the ventures succeeded. In the same year, Vann also tried to start a black-owned bank in Pittsburgh. He tried to capitalize the venture with an unrealistic figure of $500,000, but had no luck, and the dream died before it became a reality.

Vann also continued his interest in politics during these years. During the 1920s he served as director of Negro publicity for the National Republican campaigns of 1920, 1924, and 1928. He also ran unsuccessfully for local office several times during the decade. By the end of the 1920s, Vann had become disillusioned with the Republican party's unwillingness to do anything constructive for blacks. Thus, when Franklin D. Roosevelt ran for the presidency in 1932, Vann switched his allegience to the Democratic party. The Great Depression of the early 1930s had hit the blacks in Pittsburgh with extreme severity, and Republicans on the national, state, and local level seemed unable to do anything constructive. Vann's conversion to the Democrats was also aided by his increasing alliance with Michael L. Benedeum, a wealthy oilman who helped fund expansion of the *Courier*, and Senator Joseph E. Guffey. These men gave Vann some personal incentive, in the form of the possibility of high political appointive office in the party. In September 1932, Vann made tremendously effective speech at a political rally in Cleveland:

It is a mistaken idea that the Negro must wait until the party selects him. The only true political philosophy dictates that the Negro must select his party and not wait to be selected. . . . I see millions of Negroes turning the picture of Lincoln to the wall. This year I see Negroes voting a Democratic ticket.

That image, "turning Lincoln's picture to the wall," was an effective use of public relations, and it did much to create a Democratic majority for Roosevelt among blacks in Pittsburgh and elsewhere. In return, as will be covered below, Vann was rewarded with a political appointment in Washington, D.C.

During the later 1920s the *Courier* had its heyday as circulation soared, and revenues and profits were high. A key factor was that Vann gave the paper his full attention, and he also made a number of administrative and organization changes that improved the quality and profitability of the paper. To improve advertising revenues, he hired the William B. Ziff Company to secure national advertising contracts. Ziff was a white businessman who had succeeded in securing national accounts for virtually all the black weeklies. He charged extremely high rates for this service, but he guaranteed payment to the newspaper and eliminated collection problems for them. The fact that ads for prominent national firms, such as Pillsbury or Proctor and Gamble, now ran in the *Courier*, also gave the paper an enhanced respectability among its black readers. It was a badge of acceptance for them by the white community.

Vann also made important changes in the staff of the paper, hiring a number of talented reporters and writers. The most important of these was George S. Schuyler, who had a grand reputation from years with *The Messenger*. Vann also hired Wilbert Holloway, a cartoonist, and Floyd Calvin, a special features writer who was based in New York. Entertainment and society writers were hired, as were a number of people to handle black sports news. Chester Washington became the most important of these, but "Cum" Posey, owner of the local Homestead Grays, was a popular columnist for a number of years also. By the end of 1928, the *Courier* had been declared America's best black weekly, and first in editorial standing by Eugene Gordon, a *Boston Post* reporter.

Vann's largest project for the *Courier* during the 1920s was building the paper's own printing plant. By 1926 circulation stood at 55,000, the staff was highly competent, and the paper was of increasing national importance. In fact, both a city and a national edition of the paper were being published. Erection of a printing plant seemed necessary, as the cost of having the *Courier* printed by an outside company was becoming exorbitant: $25,000 a year by 1925. Vann thus raised the capitalization of the *Courier* from $50,000 to $75,000 and got a substantial loan from Benedeum, one he did not have to repay, to build the plant. The building and first-rate, though second-hand, equipment cost far more than Vann had anticipated and saddled the *Courier* with an enormous debt just as the Great Depression commenced. For years, the paper hovered on the edge of bankruptcy because of the cost of the new plant, but, in the long run, its lower printing costs were largely responsible for the fact that the *Courier* was able to weather the crisis.

In payment for his political activity in the 1932 election, the Roosevelt administration rewarded Vann with the post of special assistant to the U.S. attorney general in Washington, D.C. Vann left Pittsburgh with great fanfare and much anticipation but soon found he was given only insignificant duties to perform in that office. Nonetheless, Vann did become part of what was known as the "black cabinet" in Washington at this time, which advised Roosevelt on matters affecting the black community. Vann resigned that post in 1935, but supported Roosevelt in the election of 1936. The *Washington Tribune*, a black newspaper in that city, ran a headline when he left his justice post saying he had quit "because of the lack of dignity of his office," remarking that an official claimed that "Vann handled no case of importance during his tenure of office." Increasingly, Vann became disillusioned about the depth of commitment of the president and New Dealers to the cause of African-Americans, and soon he began to devote most of his energies to supporting Democrats in Pennsylvania. By 1940 he had become nearly completely alienated from the national party and supported Wendell Wilkie for president. This resulted in his nearly total banishment from the councils of the local, state, and national Democratic party.

Vann and the *Courier* had continued to mount a number of highly visible crusades throughout the late 1920s and 1930s. Some of these were successful, others were of questionable utility. Vann protested against the "Amos 'n' Andy" show, then the most popular radio program in America, for its use of offensive racial stereotypes. Editorials filled the pages of the *Courier*, and a petition drive was commenced, stressing the whole issue of self-respect and racial dignity. But Vann's goal of getting a million signatures in protest failed by nearly 400,000, and ultimately the issue died down. Vann also provided a good deal of support for Marcus Garvey at a time when Robert Abbott's *Chicago Defender* and several other organs of black opinion were severely critical of him. Garvey's arrest, trial, imprisonment, and ultimate deportation blunted that crusade also.

The two campaigns during the 1930s that were most successful for the *Courier* concerned Italy's invasion of Ethiopia and Joe Louis, the "Brown Bomber" and heavyweight champion of the world. Both issues represented the black man's struggle for survival and self-respect against seemingly insuperable odds, and both were sources of pride for African-Americans in a gloomy, depressed time. These two subjects ballooned the *Courier*'s circulation to 250,000 by 1938, allowing the paper to pay shareholders its first dividend in seven years in 1939.

The *Courier*'s support of Joe Louis had a particularly dramatic impact on black life. Louis himself recounted in his autobiography *Joe Louis: My Life* (1981),

I started noticing some things I thought were strange. A lot of black people would come to me and want to kiss me, pump my hand. I thought they were congratulating me for my fighting skills. Now they started saying things like, "Joe, you're our savior," and "Show them whites!" and sometimes they'd just shout, "Bomber, Bomber, Brown Bomber!" I didn't understand then.

Maya Angelou later in *I Know Why the Caged Bird Sings* (1969) told of how Louis's exploits had brought joy and an enhanced sense of dignity to blacks even in isolated, small towns in the Deep South, a factor in which the *Courier* played a major role:

Champion of the world. A Black boy. Some Black Mother's son. He was the strongest man in the world. People drank Coca-Cola like ambrosia and ate candy bars like Christmas. Some of the men went behind the store and poured white lightening in their soft drink bottles.

The historian Lawrence W. Levine reported in *Black Culture and Black Consciousness* (1977) that "For the young Malcolm X and his peers the career of Joe Louis was a testament to the fact that defeat at the hand of the white man was no longer to be taken for granted."

With the increasing success of the *Courier* in later years, and with his own political prominence, Robert Vann was able to enjoy many of the trappings of luxury and honor that came his way. After trying for decades to join the Pittsburgh Chamber of Commerce, he was finally invited to join that organization in 1939. Two years earlier, he was elected vice president of the Associated Weekly Publishers of Allegheny County, and at about the same time he bought a magnificent, eleven-room Tudor home on wide lawns in the Pittsburgh suburb of Oakmont. Costing $50,000, it was Vann's pride and joy in his later years, when he added a greenhouse and spent countless hours putting around in the rock garden.

At about this same time, Vann also began his last crusade for racial equality for blacks in the armed services during the months and years prior to his death when the country began gearing up to enter World War II. He protested against the demeaning duties assigned to blacks in the services, and about the small number of black officers available to command black troops. He assigned Percival L. Prattis, then city editor of the *Courier*, to publicize these protests. Vann and others advocated the formation of a separate Negro division in the army, and Vann and Prattis supported the Committee on Participation of Negroes in the National Defense Program, with Rayford W. Logan of Howard University as chairman, but over which Vann had enormous influence. This crusade, which continued after Vann's death, was a key factor in the rising popularity of the *Courier* during the war.

By 1940 Vann was becoming increasingly weak. In January of that year he was operated on for abdominal cancer, but he died in October in Shadyside Hospital. A bronze plaque was placed in his honor at the *Courier* offices, which said, "In Loving Memory of Robert L. Vann: Publisher, Lawyer, Statesman, Brilliant Editor, Loyal Friend, Fearless Champion of Rights. Erected by His Admiring Employees Who Profited Greatly by His Precepts and Examples." Elmer H. Carter, writing in *Opportunity*, said, "The passing of Robert L. Vann . . . came as a shock to Negro America which had come to look upon him as a leader without fear of power whether it was the power of entrenched wealth or of political party or organized labor. . . . He never chose his enemies with an eye to his personal future." Public schools were named for him in his birthplace and in the Hill district of Pittsburgh. Scholarships were established in his name at Virginia Union University and at the University of Pittsburgh. In 1942 a liberty ship bearing his name was launched at the Portland, Maine, shipyard, joining the *Booker T. Washington* and the *George Washington Carver*. At Virginia Union, the Robert L. Vann Memorial Tower was erected. But his real monument, as Andrew Buni, said, was the *Courier*. Alas, Vann's paper experienced extreme vicissitudes over the next half-century.

World War II and the immediate postwar period was the time of the greatest influence and prosperity of the *Pittsburgh Courier*. During the war, the paper, under the guidance of P. L. Prattis, conducted a highly popular and successful "Double V" campaign, standing for "Victory abroad and Victory [against discrimination] at Home." In May 1947, circulation of the *Courier* reached an all-time high of 357,212. It was indisputably the most influential black newspaper in America, and it had the largest circulation, reaching into every corner of black America. The *Courier*'s circulation began to fall rapidly over the next few years; by 1950, it stood at 280,000. In 1953 it undertook a "Double E" crusade for education and equality, in which it raised funds to support the NAACP's legal fight in *Brown vs. Board of Education*, which resulted in a major victory for civil rights forces in 1954. But, that was the *Courier*'s last glorious moment. Circulation continued declining throughout the 1950s, to just over 100,000 in 1960. Jessie Vann, who had been titular head of the paper after her husband's death, retired in 1963 and died four years later.

In 1960 the *Courier* was taken over by a board of directors headed by S. B. Fuller,* a cosmetics manufacturer in Chicago. The paper continued to limp along until 1965, when it was sold to John H. Sengstacke,* publisher and owner of the *Chicago Defender*, the *Courier*'s longtime rival on a national level. The sale was made with great fanfare, and Sengstacke announced that only the "intangible assets" of the *Courier* had been purchased (good will, circulation, advertising, accounts receivable), but not the other physical assets, including the *Courier* building on Centre Avenue in the Hill district. "It would be tragic," said Sengstacke, "if the *Pittsburgh Courier* was no longer published." The paper continued as the *New Pittsburgh Courier*, and Sengstacke promised to pump in the funds needed to keep it going. Three years later, the old *Courier* building in the Hill district was sold to the Union Baptist Association, which planned to develop the property as senior citizen's apartments.

By the late 1970s the *New Pittsburgh Courier* was in deep trouble. Its circulation was way down. Where once it had been close to 400,000, by then the Pittsburgh circulation was 15,000, and the seven-city-edition circulation was 50,000. Bill Nunn, who was a *Courier* staffer in the 1950s, believed the problem lay in the fact that large white advertisers no longer used the *Courier* after its circulation fell. "That was just a product of the time," he said. "There were not enough black businesses to pick up the slack." "The only advertising we could get," remarked longtime staffer Hazel Garland, "was skin bleachers and hair straighteners. Cheap ads, Fortune tellers." Where once 300 people had worked for the *Courier*, by the late 1970s they were down to just a few. Many felt the *New Pittsburgh Courier* was no replacement for the old paper. Frank Bolden called it "a creature of John Sengstacke of Chicago. It's not like the old *Courier* at all. The old *Courier* died." Bill Nunn concurred; "I really don't think the product they put out meets the standard [of what it was]." Sengstacke conceded that black newspapers like the *Courier* and the *Defender* had lost much of their one-time readership but said, "[W]e'll be in business as long as there is segregation and discrimination in the United States. There will always be a need for black newspapers."

In 1985 the *Courier* celebrated its seventy-fifth anniversary, but there was little optimism about the future, just nostalgia for a glorious past. "We took on the issues," said Hazel Garland. "We were particularly strong in the South. We crusaded the rights of the Scottsboro Boys. During this period, Blacks relied on the *Courier*. Many grew up on the paper and it was the only way they found out what was happening in the country." Several years later Mark Southers, who used to work for the paper, was cynical of its future: "Before the *Courier* was the only means of news when other papers weren't reporting fairly. Now blacks tend to pick up the *Press* or *Post-Gazette* first. It's not the *Courier*'s fault. Their only way to compete is to go daily. It's now an outlet for local stories on local people, very featurish. News doesn't support it; advertising does." A longtime reader of the paper, who no longer subscribed to it, said; "There's nothing in it for me." The *Courier*, she added, is filled with "junk."

A sad denouement for a once great newspaper founded by a dynamic, crusading journalist.

Sources

Robert Vann's papers are deposited with the Carnegie Library in Pittsburgh. Also very important are the papers of Percival L. Prattis, which are located in Special Collections at Howard University, and have much of Vann's correspondence to a number of people. Other collections of papers that have items of interest for Vann are the NAACP Papers in the Library of Congress, and a few items in the Booker T. Washington Papers held there for an earlier period. For information on Vann's political involvements, see material in the National Archives on the role of blacks in the government and the Franklin D. Roosevelt Papers at Hyde Park, New York. The best source is the *Pittsburgh Courier* itself, which is available on microfilm for its entire run from 1910 to the present.

An excellent published biography of Vann is Andrew Buni, *Robert L. Vann of the Pittsburgh Courier: Politics and Black Journalism* (Pittsburgh, 1974). There are shorter, but useful biographies of him by Rayford Logan, *Dictionary of American Negro Biography (1982)*, and Ingham, BDABL. There are other, less satisfactory, short accounts in Edgar A. Toppin, *A Biographical History of Blacks in America* (1969, 1971), 433–35; *Paths toward Freedom* (1976); Charles L. Blockson, *Pennsylvania's Black History* (Philadelphia, 1975), 89; and *Encyclopedia of Black America*, 825. Obituaries of Vann are found in *Opportunity*, December 1940; *Brown American*, November 1940; *New York Times*, October 25, 1940; and *Pittsburgh Post-Gazette*, October 25, 1940. See also James H. Brewer, "Robert Lee Vann and the *Pittsburgh Courier*," Master's thesis, University of Pittsburgh, 1941; and Henry G. LaBrie III, "Robert Lee Vann and the Editorial Page of the *Pittsburgh Courier*," Master's thesis, University of West Virginia, 1970. An interesting unpublished source is a typescript at the Carnegie Library, Pittsburgh: Harry B. Webber, "Vann of Pittsburgh" (n.p., n.d.). This should be used with some care. Much of it is a "dialogue" in quotation marks but with no footnotes or attribution as to where the quotes come from. A clipping file on Vann at the Schomburg Collection in the New York Public Library contains a number of newspaper accounts of his activities.

For some studies of Vann's political activities, see James H. Brewer, "Robert L. Vann: Exponent of Loose Leaf Politics," *Negro History Bulletin* 21 (February 1958), 100–103; *Time*, October 31, 1938, 13–14; Lee Finkle, "Quotas or Integration: The NAACP versus the Pittsburgh *Courier* and the Committee on Participation of Negroes," *Journalism Quarterly* 52 (1975), 76–84; and an editorial by Vann, "What Should We Expect of the National Administration?" *Opportunity* XV (January 1937), 14–16. For some later accounts of the *Courier* and its fate see *Our World*, March 1948, 21; *Pittsburgh Post-Gazette*, January 6, 1968, January 5, 1980, and January 16, 1981; *Pittsburgh Courier*, December 14, 1985, and February 2, 1989; *Pittsburgher* November 1978, 43–44; and *In Pittsburgh*, June 29–July 5, 1988.

W

Walker Family: Antonio Maceo Walker (June 7, 1909–); **Joseph Edison Walker** (March 31, 1880–1958), and **Patricia Walker Shaw** (June 26, 1939–June 30, 1985). Insurance company executives, bankers, and race leaders: Mississippi Life, Universal Life Insurance, Delta Penny Savings Bank, and Tri-State Bank. The Walker family, who were newcomers in Memphis in 1923, seventy years later had ascended to the top of the city's African-American aristocracy. They controlled Universal Life Insurance, the city's largest black business, and the fourth-largest African-American insurance company in the nation. They also dominated the city's largest black-owned bank, and were the most visible and dynamic black family in the city, successors to the Church family, which had dominated the city's black community from Reconstruction until World War II. But there were massive differences between the Memphis of the Church family in the early twentieth century, and the Memphis of the Walkers in the 1990s. The only other black businesses of any consequence in Memphis by the 1990s were two automobile dealerships, Shelby Dodge, owned by H. Steve Harrell, and Southland Chrysler-Plymouth, owned by John Willie Roy. Memphis had fallen a long way from when it was a major center of black business enterprise in America.

Joseph Edison Walker was born in Tillman, Mississippi, to George and Patsy Walker, who were sharecroppers. Young Walker was educated in local schools and graduated from Alcorn Agricultural and Mechanical College with a bachelor's of science degree in 1903. From there Walker went to Nashville, Tennessee, where he attended Meharry Medical College, graduating in 1906. He financed his education by doing carpentry, farm work, and summer teaching, and he earned a First Grade teaching certificate to replace his provisional certificate. Upon completing his education, Walker left Nashville and moved to Indianola, Mississippi, where he set up a practice of general medicine.

Indianola had some 2,000 residents, more than half of whom were black. But the town was rigidly segregated, and this was at a time when Mississippi was experiencing a resurgence of virulent racism, championed by James K. Vardaman. Vardaman preached that "education ruined good field hands" and led to rapes and murders, which in turn brought on lynchings and burnings. The only remedy, he preached, was to bring an end of the education of blacks in the state. This was not an environment conducive to accept educated, well-trained African-Americans. The arrival of a black doctor, then, incurred the wrath of racist whites, and Walker felt the consequences of this racism on a daily basis. He, nevertheless, practiced medicine from the time of his arrival in 1906 until 1923.

These issues of black equality with whites came to a head in Indianola with the "Minnie Cox affair." Minnie Cox and her husband, Wayne, were the leaders of the local black community. Wayne Cox, a graduate of Alcorn College in 1884, who had moved to Indianola to establish a school for blacks, invested in real estate, founded the Delta Penny Savings Bank and Mississippi Life Insurance Company. By the time Walker arrived in Indianola, Wayne Cox was reportedly the richest black in the Mississippi Delta. Cox had "struck gold" in real estate when he purchased thousands of acres of Delta land at a reduced rate ($.25 to $1 an acre), which he later sold off portions for $50 to $75 an acre. Cox was networked with the most prominent black leaders of the Delta—Isaiah T. Montgomery* and Charles Banks,* the founder and financier of Mound Bayou; Reverend W. A. Scott, the father of W. A. Scott II* of the *Atlanta World* Syndicate; and Dr. W. A. Attaway, who founded the Mississippi Beneficial Life Insurance Company.

Cox had also managed to get his wife installed as postmistress of the town through his connections with the Republican party. In October 1902, Indianola's whites circulated a petition asking Minnie Cox to resign. President Theodore Roosevelt, however, intervened and instructed the Postmaster General to refuse her resignation, ordering the post office closed until the town reinstated her. This only strengthened the resolve of white Mississippians, and two years later Roosevelt finally capitulated and appointed a white to the office.

Sometime during Walker's years in Indianola, he succeeded Wayne Cox as president of the Delta Penny Savings Bank. While Walker served as president, the bank operated as the center of influence among the blacks of Mississippi, particularly of the Delta. It helped blacks purchase homes and financed many black business enterprises. After the Board of Examiners' rigorous examination to determine the worthiness of the bank, the Delta Penny Savings Bank received its designation as a bank with guaranteed deposits—the only black bank in the world at the time that could boast such an accomplishment.

When affluent blacks of the Delta convened to organize Mississippi Beneficial Life, Wayne Cox provided the bulk of the initial investment and thus garnered significant bargaining power. Although Cox had favored Walker to serve as president of the insurance company, this did not materialize until after the death of Cox. Initially, Walker refused the position due to lack of capital, but Cox's widow offered Walker a financial arrangement that provided him with the necessary funds. In 1917 Walker was installed as the third president of the Mississippi Life Insurance Company. Walker proved to be a highly capable president when he assumed the leadership role. The company's premium income in 1917, $201,168, in five years increased to $943,671. Assets of $85,832 also increased to $467,671; and insurance in force, which was $1,970,280, rose to $14,896,848. To manage this growth, additional employees were recruited to Indianola. White residents could no longer tolerate the perceived threat of their town being overrun by affluent, middle-class blacks, and their distorted perception enormously increased racial tensions. Walker, at the urging of his comrade and fellow executive, M(erah) S. Stuart, left the hostile environment and moved north to Memphis in 1923.

Memphis, situated in the western region of Tennessee, has long posed a conundrum for historians. In the 1840s and 1850s, the city exhibited remarkable growth, which led many to believe that a promising future was in store. With a population of only 2,000 in 1840, by 1870 more than 40,000 people inhabited the Bluff City. The black population quadrupled between 1860 and 1870, and increased from 17 percent of the population to 39 percent. However, the boom years suddenly came to a halt. Historians have speculated that the three yellow fever epidemics that swept through the city during the 1870s ravaged the economy and depleted the population, either through death or through emigration. Other variables in conjunction with this theory provide a more comprehensive explanation for the demise of Memphis as a major urban center. Prior to the onslaught of the epidemics, Memphis had been suffering from serious fiscal problems. By 1880 Memphis had the largest per capita debt of any city in the United States. Also contributing to Memphis' stagnation was the obvious absence of effective leadership. The business elite and the elected officials frequently pursued divergent goals which inhibited growth. In view of the divisive nature of the city's politics in addition to the above noted factors, Memphis remained at a standstill until the 1880s.

Whites were not alone in the pursuit of economic gain. The African-American community began to come into its own, with Beale Street as its center of business activity. An overwhelming number of black business leaders entered the city and opened enterprises such as undertaking establishments, grocery stores, drugstores, and laundries. As in Indianola, real estate proved to be the ticket to success, and many enjoyed the fruits of their investments. The real transformation of the black business community occurred after 1900. Robert Church, Sr.,[*] proved to be the guiding light of black business with his astute investments in real estate and in other business ventures. Despite the persistence of racism throughout the South and in Memphis, blacks were able to establish a solid economic foundation.

Memphis in the early 1920s seemed to be a prime location in which to expand Mississippi Life. With a black population of more than 100,000, Walker undoubtedly believed that a market was waiting to be tapped. But the transition to Memphis was not as smooth as Walker had expected. First, the company's directors encountered difficulty with the state's Insurance Commissioner, who was unwilling to allow the securities of $100,000 on deposit with the treasurer of Mississippi to be transferred to Tennessee. Arrangements were finally settled when the company agreed to remain legally and theoretically domiciled in Mississippi. A greater difficulty surfaced when the company physically relocated its offices to Memphis. The presence of Walker, who did not realize that the deeply entrenched black elites of the city might (and did) resent the arrival of a newcomer who would infringe on their territory, aroused hostility and criticism. Walker overlooked the protocol of introducing himself and outlining his professional intentions to the black business community—an oversight that proved to be highly injurious to him personally and to Mississippi Life. What Walker quickly learned was that he was no longer a big fish in a small pond but a small fish in a very large pond.

Refusing to be so easily shunned and rejected, Walker and his fellow executives proceeded to carry on with their plans. What appeared to irritate the older black business elite was that its own interests in insurance companies were being threatened by someone who appeared to them to be just a country doctor, an "outsider." There were agencies in the city representing Standard Life of Atlanta, the National Benefit Life Insurance Company of Washington, D.C., in which it was rumored that Robert R. Church, Jr.,[*] had a financial interest, Atlanta Life, North Carolina Mutual Life Insurance, and Supreme Liberty Life. These well-established business enterprises were owned and operated by some of the most elite members of black America. When Mississippi Life began to show signs of increased momentum, the established black business community accused it of infringing on established territory. While it has been suggested that a concerted effort to stop Walker and his officers was engineered by the corps of elites determined to run them out of Memphis, it was clearly Heman Perry[*] of Atlanta Life who was at the helm, either acting independently or urged on clandestinely by the powerful Memphis elite.

Perry's intentions of creating a vast business empire, based in Atlanta, had begun when he established Standard Life Insurance Company, after considerable difficulty in raising the required capital of $100,000 in 1913. Sitting on his board of directors were such notable and influential figures as Emmett J. Scott, Robert R. Church, Jr., Truman K. Gibson,[*] Sol C. Johnson, and John Hope. One of his key officers was Harry H. Pace,[*] who acted as the secretary treasurer of the company until 1920. Standard Life rapidly expanded into twelve states, and sales increased at an impressive rate. From this successful venture, Perry pursued other avenues. In 1917 he organized the Service Company, which focused on real estate activities and later became a holding company for all his enterprises. He went on to found the Citizens Trust Bank as a depository for his enterprises and as a full service banking facility for the black community.

Perry used Standard Life's funds to finance other branches of his business empire. By 1922 Standard Life's financial statement showed assets of over $2 million, $900,000 of which was in cash. Borrowing heavily from these resources, Standard Life's cash assets were depleted quickly. Mississippi Life, meantime, was experiencing difficulties. An official Mississippi state examination revealed that the firm was impaired in the amount of $20,000, a loss that had been sustained in the Ordinary Department. Perry, realizing the highly tenuous future his own companies were facing, but concealing that from Mississippi Life officials, presented himself as a possible savior. Mississippi Life at the time was a hornet's nest of intrigue and dissension.

Joseph Walker and Minnie Cox had originally rescued the company from its shortfall, contributing $20,000 in securities to the surplus of the company, to which they had to relinquish all title in favor of the company. At a subsequent stockholders' meeting, Minnie Cox increased her holdings in the company and gained control of a majority of the shares. This acquisition entitled her to make demands that could not be overridden, mainly that her son-in-law, Dr. Wayne Cox Howard of Alabama, be installed as president of the company. Although Walker had been elected to a two-year term, he was forced to resign, effective February 22, 1923, upon receiving financial compensation. Dr. Howard then reluctantly assumed the presidency, an office which he treated with indifference from a distance.

A company without strong leadership is destined for disaster, and Perry, forever the opportunist, moved in surreptitiously. As Perry's biography details, his attempt to overtake Mississippi Life was a disaster, and the company fell into the hands of Southern Life of Nashville, Tennessee, a white-owned insurance company. Perry suffered indignities beyond reproach for this maneuver and was driven from Memphis by furious employees of Mississippi Life. No doubt Joseph Walker was relieved to be free from any involvement with the Mississippi Life Insurance Company when these events transpired. After resigning his position at Mississippi Life, Walker immediately pursued a new career. He organized the Universal Life Insurance Company as a Tennessee corporation and began business in Memphis on September 6, 1923. In April of that same year, Walker formed a stock sales agency to sell the stock, and by September the entire authorization of $100,000 had been sold, with the financial assistance of Dr. J. T. Wilson, who purchased $40,000 worth of the $100,000 capital stock. Wilson's reputation ensured further investments in the new company that allowed the outstanding $60,000 worth of stock to be sold in smaller denominations. A. W. Willis, an employee of North Carolina Mutual Life of Durham, invested in the stock also, as did Dr. Preston Taylor, a prominent Nashville undertaker. With the exception of M. W. Bonner, who had assisted Walker in organizational tasks, none of the officers of Mississippi Life supported Walker in this ambitious endeavor.

Universal Life was organized as an old-line, legal reserve, stock corporation, which specialized in home service or industrial insurance—a form of premium collection pioneered by the John Hancock Company in the 1800s for workers in the then-burgeoning industries who brought home weekly pay checks. This plan was well suited to black workers in the South, who were not paid sufficiently to engage in long-term budgeting. With its market identified and the capital in place, Universal Life was on its way.

Despite the relative ease with which Walker raised the necessary capital and organized his company, the first two years were very lean. The public's reluctance to deposit money in Walker's enterprise appears to be one of confusion, absence of faith, and bitterness over the demise and subsequent takeover of Mississippi Life. Undoubtedly, the remnants of animosity between the officers at Mississippi Life and Walker further detracted from Walker's integrity. When Universal Life began to make inroads into competitors' territories, they responded with unethical practices. Fortunately, Walker had the support of several influential people, including A. F. Ward, the cashier of the Fraternal Bank, in whose building Universal Life's offices were located. Over the years, Walker's relationship with Ward intensified, until Ward paid Walker the compliment of recommending him as one of the directors of Fraternal Bank.

In 1924 Universal Life opened in the state of Missouri to increase the firm's revenue and create a reserve, and a year later, it opened in Texas. In just three years it was operating in three states and appeared to be a healthy company, but insiders knew differently. The Insurance Examiners recognized Universal Life's problems, but they showed faith and patience, as the company struggled during its early years. Walker proved to be an effective leader, who paid himself a meager wage in order to help defray the company's overhead. Walker's prudence elicited the Nashville examiner's attention, who offered Walker the debits of Mississippi Life for $154,000, which Southern Insurance had assumed when it took over the company. Now that Southern Insurance was in the red, it was willing to unload the debits. Universal Life was granted three years to pay for the debits. The hitch in the proposal was that the Stuart and Anderson agency (founded by M. S. Stuart, formerly of Mississippi Life) held a ten-year contract with Southern to collect these debits on a profit-sharing basis. When approached, Stuart rebuffed Walker's offer, and claimed that he was selling the contract to C. C. Spaulding* of North Carolina Mutual. However, when Stuart and Walker met with the commissioner, an agreement was settled upon.

A more pressing problem than amending a longstanding battle with Stuart was the issue of where to get the money to finance the deal. Walker borrowed $5,000 from A. F. Ward and, after considerable difficulty, received a loan for an additional $5,000 from the Citizens Saving Bank in Nashville (owned by Richard Henry* and Henry Allen Boyd*). The signing of the sale contract for the Mississippi Life debits was the largest financial transaction transferred from whites to blacks at that time, but it created problems for Universal Life. After the first two years of the three-year contract, a black bank in Memphis where Universal deposited its securities went under. When Walker attempted to gain entry into the bank to withdraw his firm's funds, he was arrested. Released on bond, Walker again desperately sought financial assistance from individual property owners in Arkansas, whose names and property he used as collateral; it was placed on record as security for the remaining part of the $154,000 obligation for the Mississippi Life debits. Before the end of the three-year term, the mortgages against the Arkansas properties had been cancelled, and the Mississippi Life debits had been fully paid. Walker had met the terms of the agreement in spite of the obstacles.

The restored alliance of M. S. Stuart and J. E. Walker provided Universal Life with an unprecedented match of men with complementary abilities. Walker continued to serve as president, and Stuart assumed the positions of vice president and general manager. The reuniting of these two men also restored the confidence of the black community. Mississippi Life's debits annually amounted to $800,000 in income for Universal Life, which enabled Universal to move forward and concentrate on building a prosperous company. When Walker was derided in the press, the widow of Dr. J. T. Wilson (the original investor in the firm), fearing for the future of Universal Life, sold a large portion of her shares to Walker, who scrambled desperately to raise sufficient capital to acquire shares that would make him the largest stockholder in the company. Most important, this acquisition gave him a controlling interest over the future of Universal Life.

Under Walker's stewardship, the company had fared remarkably well. It survived the ravages of the Great Depression, when other, seemingly more stable, companies fell by the wayside. Walker built a solid company that benefited from his selflessness and single-mindedness. He expanded the company's activities into three separate geographic regions in the United States: the South, the Southwest, and the Midwest. The bulk of its insurance business at this time was on the weekly premium basis, a principle that had been established from the company's inception. It also offered a selection of ordinary insurance contracts, from which 20 percent of its business was derived. A comparison of statistics illustrates the growth of the company under Walker's direction, and a sense of the stability the company provided African-Americans. In 1925 the assets of Universal Life were $130,000, with capital of $100,000 and surplus of $12,327. The industrial insurance in force totaled $3,568,049. By 1930 the company had increased the weekly premium amount to $9,473,704, while it had ordinary insurance in force of $2,087,165. Assets had grown to $540,495, capital was $108,750, and surplus amounted to $48,423.

Universal Life survived the Great Depression but remained stagnant during the 1930s. In 1930 its assets amounted to $540,495, which increased to only $597,123 in 1935. However, the toil of these depression years was well worth the effort. In the next five years the company essentially doubled in size: Assets increased to $1,129,786; reserves also rose, from $340,867 to $756,583; and the capital-surplus funds amounted to $272,628. In 1947 Universal Life had more than $50 million of insurance in force, with assets exceeding $5 million. In addition it had surplus funds in excess of $1.6 million. Walker increasingly viewed himself and Universal Life as the financial bedrock of the black business community, often rescuing troubled firms. In 1932 he came to the rescue of the Woodmen Union Life Insurance Company of Hot Springs, Arkansas, which was struggling financially. An agreement was entered into with John L. Webb, president, and B. G. Olive, secretary, whereby Universal became the liquidating trustee for the purpose of collecting the premiums of the insurance company, liquidating its assets, and paying all claims against the latter company. Universal also reinsured the Great Southern Insurance Company of Arkansas in 1927, and it offered financial assistance to several other smaller mutuals and associations.

Walker also ventured into the highly uncertain business of banking. Although he had experienced first-hand the risky nature of banks in general, and black-owned banks specifically, Walker felt compelled to create a banking institution that would offer financial opportunities to the struggling black community in Memphis. In 1946 he opened the Tri-State Bank. The sale of bank stock, which was primarily instigated by Walker's son A. M. Walker, proceeded with greater ease than the elder Walker could have imagined. Within seven months, $243,000 had been collected, and the unpleasant memories of two failed black-owned banks were fading rapidly. As president of the bank, J. E. Walker actively recruited depositors and preached the benefits of thrift. The younger Walker assumed the vice presidency, and R. R. Wright III (the grandson of Richard R. Wright*) was appointed cashier. Other distinguished members of the board included George W. Lee* and M. W. Bonner. The bank began business with capital of $200,000 and a surplus of $40,000. In two years its deposits surpassed $1 million, and its assets reached beyond $1.5 million. In 1958 it had 5,000 depositors, $2,680,000 in deposits, and $3,136,000 in resources. Its rapid growth illustrates the fact that Memphis blacks were eager to reap the benefits of what Walker's bank had to offer.

Walker's involvement with the black business community was far reaching. His involvement in the National Negro Business League, founded by Booker T. Washington,* not only kept Walker abreast of the achievements of African-Americans in business, but also provided him with insight into the problems and concerns of black business across the United States. His dedication to the organization was finally rewarded when he was unanimously elected president of the league during the 1939 conference held in Oklahoma City. Walker was also involved with the National Negro Insurance Association, of which he was elected president at New Orleans in 1926, serving two full terms. His commitments were also evident at the local level as early as 1916, when he was a delegate from the Third Mississippi Congressional District to the Republican Convention in Chicago. He later served as chairman of the Democratic Club of Memphis.

Universal Life moved into its new $500,000 headquarters in a primarily white neighborhood to celebrate its twenty-fifth anniversary in 1949. The property on which the building was erected was purchased by a light-skinned black employed by Walker, in order to ensure that the transaction would be completed. With a new home for Universal Life, which was enjoying healthy returns, J. E. Walker relinquished his position as president in 1952 to his son, Antonio Maceo (better known as A. M.) Walker, who was promoted from the position of vice president and secretary. In December 1950, according to *Ebony* magazine, Universal Life "rank[ed] fourth largest among 52 Negro insurance firms in the United States though it is scarcely more than a quarter of a century old. It has blossomed into big business faster than any other Negro institution in the South.'' Joseph Walker had built a mighty insurance company.

The younger Walker was well equipped to assume his new role. Born in Indianola, Walker moved to Memphis with his parents in 1920. He attended the primary schools in Indianola, and completed his grammar and high school courses at LeMoyne Institute (now LeMoyne Owen College) in Memphis. Walker received his bachelor's degree from Fisk University in Nashville. From there he went on to do graduate work as the only black student at New York University, where he studied actuarial mathematics, and graduated with a master's degree in business administration. Walker also studied at the University of Michigan where he earned another master's degree in actuarial science. An ''educational pioneer,'' he was the first black MBA in Tennessee, and the second black actuary in the country, after Asa T. Spaulding.*

A. M. Walker served as a field auditor for Universal Life during school vacations prior to 1935, and upon finishing his course work at the University of Michigan in that year, he was appointed actuary of Universal Life. When he entered the company on a full-time basis, Walker recognized that Universal Life was not as healthy as it appeared to be. As he recalled, ''Mortality was a problem, in the sense that we were having too many deaths for the premiums we were charging.'' The problem stemmed from the fact that the company's actuaries were using standard, that is white, mortality tables to calculate premiums, although the life spans of blacks were seven or eight years shorter than those of whites. Walker rectified the discrepancy, and gradually the company's fortunes improved.

In 1944 Walker helped implement the company's data-processing operation, which only two other black insurance companies had at this time—North Carolina Mutual and Atlanta Life Insurance Company. By 1946 Universal Life's financial status had improved to the point where it could consider expansion into a completely new area: banking. As mentioned earlier, Tri-State Bank opened its doors in 1946, with a resounding reception after A. M. Walker's success in selling the bank's shares. Over the years the bank has performed well: In 1964, when its offices were moved from Beale Street to Main Street, its resources were slightly above $3 million, and its assets were $15 million. In the early 1980s it could proudly boast $28 million in resources and assets of $58 million. Tri-State's position on the *Black Enterprise* list of top black-owned banks in the United States has held its own with a ranking between eleventh and thirteenth in the late 1980s and early 1990s. By December 31, 1989, it had achieved assets of $59.301 million, with $52.374 million in deposits and loans of $22.836 million. By 1992, however, it was no longer on *Black Enterprise*'s list.

When A. M. Walker assumed the reins of Universal Life from his father in 1952, the company had $10 million in assets and $83 million worth of insurance in force. The new president's expansion program enhanced Universal Life's portfolio. The company aggressively sought a larger portion of the Memphis market and of the surrounding area; the sales force was increased; investments were made in bonds; and mortgage loans for homes and churches were made. The generous policy in making and securing mortgage loans not only made better housing available for blacks, but also encouraged home ownership. Since 1958, when J. E. Walker tragically died from a gunshot wound, the concern has acquired five life insurance companies—Excelsior Life of Dallas, 1958; Louisiana Life of New Orleans, 1961; Richmond Beneficial Life of Richmond, Virginia, 1963; Afro-American Texas Debits, 1975; and Union Protective of Memphis, 1980.

A. M. Walker stepped down as president of Universal Life in 1983, after running the company for a total of thirty-one years. He passed the torch to his daughter, Patricia Walker Shaw, who after serving only two years in the capacity of president, succumbed to cancer at the pinnacle of her career. A. M. Walker once again assumed the presidency when Universal Life was faced with a crisis of leadership previously unheard of at the firm. At seventy-five years of age, Walker resumed his aggressive strategy during a time when the United States' thirty-five black insurance companies were facing increased competition from the white financial institutions. In June 1987 *Black Enterprise* concluded that this was "an exceptionally tall order for a man most people considered well past his prime. But Walker has more than risen to the occasion."

During the fall of 1986, true to form, Walker engineered the $1.2 million purchase of Security Life Insurance of Jackson, Mississippi, which provided an additional $1.3 million to the company's annual income. To justify his continued expansion strategy, Walker explained, "Every time you buy a company, you buy more income, and this is where you make your money." Universal Life achieved the "Company of the Year" designation by *Black Enterprise* in 1987 because of its "consistent prosperity." The company ranked fourth among black insurance companies, and its insurance in force had nearly doubled from $333 million in 1976 to $611 million in 1986. In addition, its assets rose by $15 million during that same period, increasing from $50 million to $65 million. The company continues to be publicly owned, and it has been paying its stockholders dividends since 1936. A. M. Walker has proved his mettle as a remarkable business leader. As the largest shareholder in both the Tri-State Bank and Universal Life, Walker has become a financial success and a well-respected man. However, one disappointment continued to frustrate him: "Whites simply don't trade with blacks in business. Now, the money's in the white race; very little of it is in the black race. My two businesses just simply can't develop like they should, 'cause I've got no white trade."

As a man who has fought for racial equality and integration, he has not reaped the rewards, in a business sense, from this difficult task. Every one of Universal Life's policyholders is black, as are 98 percent of Tri-State's depositors. In addition, not one of the employees of either institution is white; however, the institutions are not segregated by choice. "There's nothing to stop a white man from buying shares in either Universal Life or Tri-State—he would be absolutely welcome. I would welcome white employees, white consumers, white anything.

I would welcome them.'' The reasons for this de facto segregation are varied and complex—lower salaries, higher premiums, vestiges of a racist heritage, and other variables.

A. M. Walker's accomplishments in business are exemplary and have provided him with financial security and recognition, but his commitments extend far beyond the business arena. As young man he suffered at the hands of racism; he knows what it means to be considered a "nigger"—he was treated as one for most of his life. Like so many other young, well-educated African-Americans, he was unable to get a job, even as a delivery boy. He readily acknowledges the situation was intolerable and that it took a thick skin to endure the pain. "[I]t did require a bit of self-discipline not to shout back, not to fight back. I kept working, I kept smiling, I kept plunging ahead. I never had room in my mind for both bitterness and progress. I had to blot out the bitterness if I expected the progress to take place.'' This discipline has enabled Walker to use his energies constructively, to address the real problems of the community and to fight to right the wrongs.

The Walker family has been the leading force in Memphis' black community for years in terms of business and civil rights. Since the advent of the modern civil rights movement, Universal Life, with the backing of A. M. Walker, has been the black political power center in Memphis. According to Jesse Turner, Jr., the bank's president, "Whenever the movement was in a financial pinch, the Walkers were there to bail it out. If people needed money or financial advice they could go to them.'' J. E. Walker had provided the groundwork for such commitment, and his son has carried on with the tradition. As early as the 1940s and 1950s, long before it was fashionable or safe to be involved, the Walkers championed the civil rights cause. As A. M. Walker reminisced, "We [blacks] just about set this city on fire. We made it hot. I mean *HOT*.'' He was instrumental in integrating Memphis State University in 1964, and he raised the money for the tuition for qualified black students who wished to enroll there. A. M. Walker was also the first black to break the segregated seating arrangement at the Malco Theater in Memphis. Over the years, the company has financed the construction of three low-income housing projects, including the 700-unit J. E. Walker Housing Projects. The J. E. Walker school is nearby.

The Walkers also became involved in electoral politics. J. E. Walker unsuccessfully attempted to enter politics when, in 1951, he ran for a position on the school board. After he was appointed to the Transit Authority ten years later (the first black man to sit on a major city board in modern history), A. M. Walker appeared to be well positioned for the legislature. Instead, he bowed out of active politics. As the younger Walker stated, "We realized that we would never get anywhere unless we got some black voting strength.'' The Walkers, along with Jesse Turner, their right-hand man at the Tri-State Bank, organized the Non-Partisan Voters' Registration Club to increase the black electorate. Bit by bit they built the voting strength. A. M. Walker's decision not to pursue politics on a grand scale is explained in *Memphis*, 1987:

The problem at that time was that it was hard to find good black executives. And a white executive would not work for us. A lot of blacks just didn't understand this, but I had to make a decision as to whether I was going to stay with these two businesses, or leave 'em and go into politics. So I just sat down one day and asked myself: Maceo Walker, what are you better trained for? I thought about my experience, so I said, "Well, it's obvious you're better trained for business."

His track record certainly verifies this claim. Although he chose to remain outside of politics officially, Walker continued to involve himself in the social and political issues that directly affected his race.

A. M. Walker has been the recipient of numerous awards and citations by such organizations as the National Association for the Advancement of Colored People, which named him "Man of the Year" in 1973. (The NAACP was granted rent-free office space by Universal Life when it first began operations in Memphis.) Universal Life, in 1979, also invested $200,000 in a pilot project to help six black colleges build their endowments over the next twenty years through low-cost loans. When the fund was established, Walker said the investment was made as "a matter of a social point of view."

In 1983, when A. M. Walker decided to pass the torch to his daughter Patricia, she had already proved herself a capable, hard-driving business person. Born in Little Rock, Arkansas, Patricia Walker attended Oakwood High School in Poughkeepsie, New York, from which she graduated in 1956. From there she went to her father's alma mater, Fisk University, where she earned a bachelor of arts degree cum laude in the field of business administration in 1961. She attended the University of Chicago's graduate school of business administration briefly in 1961, but then altered her career path and earned a teacher's certificate from Tennessee State University in Nashville in 1962. Continuing in this direction, she attended the Graduate School of Social Work in 1966 at the University of Tennessee in Memphis. For a time, Patricia Walker worked intermittently in the social service field as a caseworker and then as a welfare worker.

Ultimately, the lure of Universal Life enticed the young woman to enter full-time the business in which her father and grandfather had shown such outstanding ability. She was first hired as a clerk in the underwriting department, from which she moved on to the position of keypunch operator. In 1967 Walker Shaw was promoted to chief clerk of the lapse division of the data-processing department. After three years of serving in that capacity, her career moved forward rapidly. In 1970 she was promoted to supervisor of the same department, and in 1971 she assumed the responsibility of supervisor-cashier in the accounting department. Within that same year, Walker Shaw took a giant step; she became assistant vice president, assistant controller, and research analyst, which provided her with the chance to do audits of every department and to work with officers across the United States. By 1974 she was promoted to the position of vice president and associate controller. In 1981 she was named executive vice president in charge of developing a new marketing thrust for Universal Life, where she proved her abilities as a highly competent senior executive.

The long-awaited moment finally came to pass on February 24, 1983, when the board of directors of Universal Life Insurance Company elected Patricia Walker Shaw the company's new president. She became the third chief executive in the firm's sixty-year history and the first female to head a major American life insurance organization. A. M. Walker, who stayed on as chairman of the board of directors and finance and investment committee, proudly announced his daughter's promotion: "I am very pleased that my chosen successor is such a highly experienced and proven executive. A leader who knows our business from the bottom up . . . who has the kind of forward-looking ideas the company will need in the years ahead." Perhaps the announcement was not a surprise, since she had spent the previous two years under the direct tutelage of her father preparing for the day when she would be his successor.

During her truncated career as president of the company, Patricia Walker Shaw displayed her power and keen sense of judgment. Upon assuming her new position, Walker Shaw identified her goals: "I am convinced that by combining our traditional commitment to basic principles with our new and broader marketing profile, Universal Life will grow profitably in the years to come." She emphasized the fact, as her father did before her, that Universal Life is a black company that sells insurance only to black people. She acknowledged that it was a full-service firm that offered insurance coverage to millions, black and white, who otherwise might be unable to afford it. This assertion provided the foundation for her aggressive marketing approach: "[to] develop our basic products to meet the needs of an extended potential customer base," although she recognized that Universal Life could not challenge head on such big, white firms as Prudential or John Hancock. Her pursuit of a larger share of the ordinary or monthly payment insurance business preferred by the middle class did not imply that Universal Life would abandon any of its home service, or industrial, insurance. She was aware of the value of the small policyholders who needed Universal's protection, and that Universal Life needed their business also. "Our system of delivery is very important for many of our people. It's a social service as well as a business service."

This attitude represents the fact that Patricia Walker Shaw inherited her family's commitment to improve the plight of her race. However, her outspoken nature hit hardest when she spoke of the back-to-basics philosophy: "We're reclaiming our own. This brain drain and this dollar drain from our community needs to come to an end." She expressed frustration at the situation in which companies, such as Universal Life and others, have supported educational institutions and programs to increase blacks' social mobility, only to watch some of the best talent and much of the money sent off to work in the white world. Her attempt to reverse this trend is an extension of her father's effort to achieve a sense "of giving back" to the community which he helped to build. Walker

Shaw's involvement in the community mirrored the efforts of her grandfather and father.

We believe we are the mother ship of black economic development, and as the mother ship we have spawned all kinds of smaller ships in the black community. We will continue to finance projects through loans, that build black businesses and black churches, and we will continue to help black colleges survive. (*Essence*, June 1984)

Walker Shaw was the first woman president of the National Insurance Association, and she served as chairperson of the board of directors of the Federal Reserve Bank, Memphis branch. Her activity on a local level was far reaching: She sat on the board of directors of the Economic Club of Memphis, the Memphis Development Foundation, and the Memphis-Plough Community Foundation. Her civic affiliations were numerous, and she had the honor of being awarded the C. C. Spaulding Award for extraordinary achievement in the field of insurance.

Unfortunately, Walker Shaw's status as a leader in the black community was short lived. She died of cancer on June 30, 1985. One can only imagine the grief A. M. Walker felt when he resumed his role at the helm. Walker temporarily took control until he had the opportunity to reflect on the apparent leadership crisis the company was facing. In 1990 he finally selected the person to succeed him—G. T. Howell—the first vice president of the insurance firm and a longtime employee, who became chief operation officer and president. A. M. Walker stayed on as chairman of the board and chief executive officer.

The Universal Life Insurance Company has weathered various storms, from the early years when J. E. Walker was betrayed and slandered and financially challenged, to the highly changeable tide of the economic climate of the 1970s and 1980s under the leadership of A. M. Walker and Patricia Walker Shaw. The strength of character of the Walkers and their dedication to the African-American people have been consistent. When A. M. Walker was asked in the early 1980s about the future, he responded, "Let me tell you what my father used to tell my wife and me. He said, 'Don't get discouraged. You are going to see some things in your lives that you never thought would happen. Cause I've seen some in my life that I never thought would happen. Now here you are decrying the fact that you can't ride in this kind of cab or that kind of cab.' He said, 'You watch, in about fifteen or twenty years you'll be riding in any cab you want to, hear?' And he was so right." That kind of optimism and patience has won the Walkers a significant place in history, and a major role in the black community of Memphis.

Sources

No company papers are currently available to researchers, J. E. Walker's papers are also unavailable, but there is some useful information in the following: a somewhat sentimental and biased biography of Walker is T. J. Johnson, *From the Driftwood of Bayou Pierre* (1949); in addition, brief biographies of Walker appear in *National Cyclopedia of American Biography* 50: (1968), 730; the *Clarion Ledger*, July 27, 1975; George A. Sewell and Margaret L. Dwight, *Historic Black Memphians* (n.p., n.d.) 170–76; *Commercial Appeal*, January 15, 1982; and Robert Fulton Hotzelaw, *Black Magnolias*

(1984). Some correspondence between Lee and Walker can be found in the George W. Lee Papers held at the Memphis Shelby Public Library, which also has clipping files on J. E. Walker. Another vertical file on Walker can be found at the Schomburg Centre for Research, New York Public Library. Obituaries of Walker appeared in many newspapers including *Press Scimitar*, July 28, 1958, which also provides an account of the incident that resulted in his shooting death, and the *New York Times*, July 28, 1958. Tributes to Walker appear in the *Commercial Appeal*, August 3, 1958; *Press Scimitar*, July 29, 1958; and *Tri-State Defender*, February 14, 1976. A reprint of Walker's address delivered at Fisk University, December 5, 1927, appears in "History and Progress of Life Insurance," *Messenger*, April 1928, 80.

A. M. Walker's papers are also unavailable. He is mentioned in the Johnson biography of J. E. Walker mentioned above. A brief biography of him appears in Frank Johnson, *Who's Who of Black Millionaires* (1984); and a well-researched article appears in *Memphis Magazine*, 1987, which can be found in the vertical file of the Hollis J. Price Library at LeMoyne-Owen College. Numerous other clippings of value are held in this collection. He is also mentioned in the George W. Lee Papers held at the Memphis Shelby Public Library.

Patricia Walker Shaw's papers, available to researchers at Memphis State in the Mississippi Valley Collection, include biographical information, family background, general correspondence, Universal Life miscellanea and newspaper clippings. There is a vertical file on Walker Shaw at the Memphis Shelby Public Library. *Mid-South Business*, March 4, 1983; *Press-Scimitar*, February 12, 1983; *Commercial Appeal*, February 12, 1983; and *St. Louis American*, February 24, 1983, all address her promotion to the presidency at Universal Life. She also appears in *Essence*, June 1984, which features other successful black women entrepreneurs; and *Connection* XII, 2 (February 19, 1974). In the *Commercial Appeal*, December 29, 1983, appears an interview with Walker Shaw. *Memphis Business Journal*, February 28, 1983, offers insight into her back-to-basics economic philosophy. Obituaries are numerous and appear in such publications as the following: *Tri-State Defender*, July 6, 1985; *Commercial Appeal*, July 1, 1985; and *Afro-American*, July 27, 1985.

The following materials contain information on the Universal Life Insurance Company's early years and J. E. Walker's role both in Mississippi Life and Universal Life: Alexa B. Henderson, "Heman E. Perry and Black Enterprise in Atlanta, 1908–1925, *Business History Review* LXI, 2 (Summer 1987), 216–42; M. S. Stuart, *Economic Detour: A History of Insurance in the Lives of American Negroes* (New York, 1940); the George W. Lee Papers at the Memphis-Shelby Library; and *Ebony*, December 1950. A portion of G. A. Maclean, *Insurance up through the Ages*, reprinted in *From the Driftwood of Bayou Pierre* offers an account of the organization, development, growth, and financial rating of Universal Life in the early years. Additional articles about Universal Life are *ULICO* (Universal's quarterly newsletter) XX, 3 (Fall 1971), which includes a brief history of the company; and Fiftieth Anniversary Edition, *ULICO* XXII, I (Fall 1973), which provides a decade-by-decade analysis of Universal Life and a tribute to A. M. Walker. See also "Universal Life Fetes Economic Advance of Black Life Insurers," *The National Underwriter*, April 14, 1973; *Commercial Appeal*, March 24, 1973, June 4, 1978, July 30, 1980, and October 14, 1979; and *Black Enterprise*, June 1987, which acknowledges Universal as the Insurance Company of the Year, and June 1989. Information on the Tri-State Bank is scarce. The *National Cyclopedia of American Biography*

(1968) offers a brief mention in its biography of J. E. Walker, and *From the Driftwood of Bayou Pierre* includes an entire chapter entitled, "Birth of Tri-State Bank."

Walker, Madame C. J. (see Walker, Sarah Breedlove).

Walker, Maggie Lena (July 15, 1867–December 15, 1934). Banker, business leader, race leader and philanthropist, St. Luke Penny Savings Bank, Consolidated Bank and Trust Company, *St. Luke Herald* and St. Luke Emporium. Black businessmen were a rather rare breed in turn-of-the-century America, but black businesswomen were virtually unknown. Yet, Maggie Lena Walker was not just a business leader, she was also a dedicated champion of the rights of women, particularly black women, at a time when hardly anyone else gave them any thought. By example, rather than by theory, Maggie Lena Walker showed the way for African-American women and men, and for the black community in general. The first woman bank president in America, black or white, she was an astute businesswoman, an able organizer, and a charismatic leader in a city with some of the most important black male leaders in America.

Maggie Walker born in Richmond, the daughter of Elizabeth Draper, a former house slave and then cook in the home of Elizabeth Van Lew, a wealthy spinster. Elizabeth Van Lew, one of that rarest of breeds, a southern abolitionist, supposedly participated in running an "underground railway" for black slaves to the North and Canada. During the Civil War, as a noted Yankee sympathizer, she was often referred to as a "Union spy." Van Lew was protected, however, by her family's great wealth and prestige. At the time of Maggie Walker's birth, Elizabeth Van Lew was postmistress of Richmond. Family tradition claimed that Maggie's father was Eccles Cuthbert, a northern abolitionist author. Whatever the case, Elizabeth Draper soon married William Mitchell, a butler in the Van Lew household. Maggie Walker's earliest years were spent at the Van Lew estate, a palatial mansion perched upon the top of Church Hill.

William Mitchell soon became the headwaiter at the St. Charles Hotel, and he decided to move his family out of the Van Lew home, to a small cottage in what later became known as Maggie Mitchell Alley. This was a short path running from Broad to Marshall Street in what would later become Jackson Ward, the heart of Richmond's African-American community. A half-brother, John, was born at the cottage, and the family's life went smoothly for a time, with Maggie's mother taking in washing and ironing for white people to help them meet expenses. This tranquil life was soon shattered, however, when William Mitchell disappeared. A few days later he was found floating in the James River, and, although his killer was never found, the consensus was that he had been robbed and murdered, and his body had been thrown in the river.

In addition to the personal tragedy of losing their husband and father, the Mitchell family was faced with an economic crisis all too familiar to nineteenth-century working-class families—the loss of their principal breadwinner. With no savings and no insurance, Maggie's mother was forced to work full-time as a laundress, and Maggie assisted by taking care of her younger brother. It was a hard life for both of them, as Maggie Walker found that her days of carefree playtime were behind her, and her days were filled with housework and care for her younger brother. Despite this financial difficulty, Maggie Walker was able to get as good an education as was available to blacks in Richmond at that time. She went first to Lancaster School, the elementary school in her neighborhood. Located across the street from the jail, it was in many respects a daunting experience for a young child. But the southern white women who taught there seemed to provide a good education to Maggie Walker and the other black children. Walker's childhood friend, W. P. Dabney, who also attended the .school, later testified that "[t]here was little sign of the prejudice so frequently seen now" at Lancaster School.

Walker progressed well during these years and, at eleven years of age, had an important conversion experience and was baptized into the Baptist church. As she grew older, she became an assistant Sunday school teacher, and later a full-fledged instructor. Another important stepping-stone in her life came when she was fourteen and joined the Independent Order of St. Luke. In future years, Maggie Walker held many elective offices in the order. That organization would literally become Walker's life, and she, in turn, molded St. Luke into a reflection of her own vision for the African-American race. Meanwhile, she continued to do well in school, going on to Armstrong Normal School. It was at this school, also, that she demonstrated her rebellious side. The tradition was that commencement ceremonies for Armstrong, a black high school, were held in a black church, while graduates of white schools had their ceremonies in the city theater. She and Wendell P. Dabney, as members of the class of 1883, took the lead in opposing this practice, refusing to participate in the ceremony. A compromise was offered: The blacks could have their ceremony in the city theater if they agreed to segregated seating for the two races. Dabney, Walker, and the other students refused, and the diplomas were handed out in the auditorium of the school. This in itself was quite an achievement for Maggie Walker. Generally only members of the city's black elite, such as Dabney, whose father was a leading caterer, could afford to attend high school. The fact that Walker, from a poor, single-parent household, could accomplish this was testament to the dedication of both Maggie Walker and her mother.

After graduation, Maggie taught school at her old alma mater, Lancaster School, for three years. During this time, Maggie also took courses in accounting and worked part-time as an agent for the Women's Union, an insurance company. This experience would serve her well in the future. The Women's Union was a female insurance company, which took as its motto, "The Hand That Rocks the Cradle Rules the World." Although Walker's time there was relatively brief, the Women's Union introduced her to two important concepts that were to influence her life. The first was the importance of insurance for African-Americans, particularly for black women, since she had experienced first-hand the trauma faced by families when the primary breadwinner died without leaving insurance. Second, she learned the importance of establishing women's networks. These would, if done properly, greatly increase the power and prestige of African-American women. Deborah Gray White in *Ar'n't I a Woman* (1985) has recognized the importance of these networks during the days of slavery: "Strength had to be cultivated. It came no more naturally to them than to anyone.... If they seemed exceptionally strong it was partly because they had functioned in groups and derived strength from numbers.... [T]hey inevitably developed some appreciation of one another's skills and talents. This intimacy enabled them to establish the criteria with which to rank and order themselves." These same ideals remained with Maggie Lena Walker, and intensified as she grew older.

Maggie Mitchell married Armstead Walker in 1886, a man several years her senior, who was involved with his father in the construction business, which erected some of the "finest buildings in Richmond." The Walkers had two sons, Russell and Melvin, and another who died in infancy. Maggie Walker had married a member of the city's African-American elite, and as such she was expected to remain at home, taking care of her sons and doing housework. Her free time was to be filled with participation in Richmond's many social clubs and entertainments. She was, in sum, destined to become a woman of relative leisure. Nothing could have suited her less, as her boundless energy was hardly sated by the demands of her home and family. As Wendell Dabney noted, "Her renunciation [of a world of work outside the home] was a veritable martyrdom. Naturally a happy, laughing, rollicking girl, with strongly marked histrionic ability . . . her desires were crushed by conditions beyond her control. While others danced and sang, she made music with the wash tub and ironing board." And Maggie Walker did not like it one bit. It was soon clear that, if she was to maintain her sanity, she would have to find some fulfillment outside the home. She found it in the Order of St. Luke.

The Independent Order of St. Luke was organized in Baltimore, Maryland, in 1867 by Mary Prout, a former slave. The purpose of the order was to aid the sick and provide benefits for proper burial of the dead. From Baltimore, the order soon spread to other states, with the most noted chapter in Virginia. This group, like the Women's Union, had started as an organization for women only, but as the order grew, men were also admitted. Elsa Barkley Brown has commented that "societies like the Independent Order of St. Luke had a nonexclusionary membership policy; any man, woman, or child could join." This meant that it was a "mass-based organization that played a key role in the political, economic, and social development of its members and of the community as a whole."

Walker had maintained her interest and affiliation with the order since her teenaged years, but after her marriage she increased her involvement. She became a national deputy, organizing councils throughout Virginia and West Virginia. In 1889 she was elevated to the position of executive secretary of the order. At about the same time, Magdalena Council no. 125 was formed and named after her. She had, by this time, already become a major force in the organization.

In 1895 Maggie Walker organized the juvenile branch of the order to establish social programs and address itself to other social concerns of youth. Walker made a great success of this venture, and in 1899 she was elected executive secretary treasurer of the organization. This was, by far, the most important job in the entire organization, and from this position Maggie Walker led the work of St. Luke for some thirty-five years. The duties in the position were onerous. She had to collect dues, verify cases of illness and death, keep the books, and pay the claims. This was made all the more difficult by the poor financial condition of the order. At the time Walker assumed control, there was just $31.61 in the treasury, collected from 1,080 members, with bills amounting to over $400.

Maggie Walker's dynamic leadership transformed the Independent Order of St. Luke into one of the strongest, most important black financial organizations in America. Just two years after assuming leadership, she reported at the August 1901 meeting of the order that there were 1,400 new members, but she had hardly begun her massive restructuring of the institution. At that 1901 convention, she called for a number of dramatic and revolutionary changes. Following the lead of W. W. Browne* of Richmond's True Reformers, Walker organized an insurance department in the order. This soon provided the Order of St. Luke with a large cash flow. Most of this was due to Maggie Walker. "Success came almost immediately," remembered W. P. Dabney. "The earnestness, diplomacy and oratorical ability of [Maggie Walker] served as a magnet."

But Maggie Walker and the women in the Order of Saint Luke were not just concerned with business issues. They were also deeply involved in the social life of the community. A key element in this was the creation of a journal—the *St. Luke Herald*—to unite members and provide a uniform means of communication. Over the next several years, in concert with Walker's sometime enemy John Mitchell, Jr.,* the *Herald* came out strongly against segregation, lynching, Jim Crow railroad cars, unequal educational opportunities for blacks, and other discriminatory practices. Although started with a narrow organizational purpose, the *Herald* soon became an important community-building device among Richmond's African-Americans and helped stir the fires of jealousy between Mitchell and Walker. An important period of cooperation, however, came during Richmond's streetcar boycott in 1904, when the women of St. Luke, along with Walker and Mitchell, assumed leadership of that important effort.

To Mitchell, the passage of new Jim Crow legislation for Richmond's streetcar lines represented the passing of an old era of "traditional harmony" between the races. In his *Planet*, he expressed fear that the city's blacks would be subject to mistreatment at the hands of "poor white trash"—conductors and motormen. Maggie Walker and the *St. Luke Herald* concurred, predicting that "the very dangerous [police] power placed in the hands of hot headed and domineering young white men," who were already hated by blacks for their overbearing and insulting conduct, would "certainly provoke trouble." One of the reasons Walker and Mitchell advocated a boycott was to avoid occasions for friction and disorder.

Allying with Walker and Mitchell in organizing the boycott were J.R.L. Diggs, a professor at Virginia Union University, Benjamin Jackson, a grocer and former city councilman, and W. P. Burrell, Browne's successor as general secretary of the True Reformers. The boycott lasted for several months, but in the end it was unsuccessful in its main purpose. It did, however, have a galvanizing effect in promoting the cohesion of the city's African-American community.

Maggie Walker's greatest venture was to organize a black-owned bank in 1903. It was not the first black bank in America, not even the first in Richmond— that had been pioneered by Browne—but it became one of the most important economic and social cogs in the black community of the city, allowing Walker to become the first female bank president in America. It also became the most successful venture of the Order of St. Luke, but from the first it viewed itself as more than an economic institution. It also played an important social role in Richmond's black community. At its founding, Walker stated, "We need a savings bank, chartered and officered and run by the men and women of this order" in order to fulfill the destiny of the black community.

The bank, then called the St. Luke Penny Savings Bank, was to be a depository for the funds of the order, but each St. Luke member was requested to purchase one share of stock in the bank for $10, and each was urged to open a separate account for his or her savings. The fact that it was called a *penny* savings bank was indicative of the meager resources of blacks, particularly women, in Walker's time. Elsa Barkley Brown reports that many of the bank's early supporters were washerwomen, including Maggie Walker's mother. Throughout the years that Walker directed the bank, it continued to stress its special commitment to "the small depositor." Maggie Walker, in her charismatic way, persuaded depositors that the bank "will take nickles and turn them into dollars." The bank was an immediate, if modest, success, taking in over $9,000 in shares and deposits during the first day of operation. It continued to grow, and by 1904 it was able to move to 112 Broad Street, in a property that cost $13,500, of which $3,500 was paid down. The following year the bank moved to yet another new building.

By 1910 deposits at Penny Savings had risen to over $85,000. In that same year, the True Reformers Bank failed, which created a sense of crisis in Richmond's black community. The confidence of African-Americans in banks owned by members of their own race was tenuous at best, and this latest failure made them even more wary. One black termed the failure of the True Reformers Bank "the downfall of Africa." Maggie Walker simply said that "[i]t was a time to try men's souls," and she set about restoring confidence in her own institution. W. P. Dabney stated that "Mrs. Maggie L. Walker and her forces stood as steady as the rock of Gibraltar." St. Luke Penny Savings Bank survived the crisis and became the most powerful black financial institution in the city.

An important goal of Maggie Walker's in all of this was to provide economic opportunity for African-American women. In 1900 the U.S. Census reported that 83.8 percent of all employed black women worked as domestics or in personal service. The economic plight of black women had long concerned

Walker, whose comments on the problem sound surprisingly contemporary. "How many occupations have Negro women?" asked Walker. "Let us count them: Negro women are domestic menials, teachers and church builders." When two Richmond black men, Daniel Webster Davis and Giles Jackson, wrote a textbook for black children that counseled black women to remain in the home, "being supported by their husbands" and spending "time in the training of their children," Walker responded indignantly: "The old doctrine that a man marries a woman to support her is pretty nearly thread-bare today."

As early as 1901, in an address to the delegates at the St. Luke convention, Maggie Walker implored them to have concern for their sisters:

Who is so helpless as the negro woman? Who is so circumscribed and hemmed in, in the race of life, in the struggle for bread, meat and clothing as the negro woman? They are even being denied the work of teaching negro children. Can't this great Order, in which there are so many good women, willing women, noble women, whose money is here, whose interest is here, whose hearts and souls are here, do something towards giving to those who have made it what it is.

Walker was concerned throughout her life in developing enhanced employment opportunities for black women, and the offices of the Order of St. Luke and the bank provided clerical jobs not available elsewhere. Mary White Ovington, when she visited Richmond, commented on the St. Luke offices: "The clerks are nearly all women, all colored of course. They wear white uniforms which they don after they arrive in the morning. Order is everywhere evident and work moves with expedition." Black women were similarly employed in the bank, at the *St. Luke Herald*, and in a shop established to manufacture regalia for the order. In 1902 Walker described herself as "consumed with the desire to hear the whistle on our factory and see our women by the hundreds coming to work." These same motives and concerns led Walker and other St. Luke women to affiliate with the National Association of Wage Earners. This women's organization attempted to pool the energies of housewives, professionals, and managerial, domestic, and industrial workers to protect and enhance the economic position of black women.

Another important attempt to assist in the development of the black community, as well as promote economic opportunities for African-American women, was the establishment in 1905 of a department store by the order. Called Saint Luke Emporium, it was to be a large department store located right in the core of the white downtown business community. Maggie Walker, along with twenty-two women from the Independent Order of St. Luke decided to establish the department store with the aim of providing quality goods at more affordable prices to the entire community, while at the same time providing a place where black women could get jobs and a business education. Fifteen black women were employed in the store as salesclerks.

St. Luke Emporium closed after a number of years, and its failure is usually blamed on poor management by blacks. W. P. Dabney commented, "Our race has much to learn both as salesmen and purchasers." Elsa Barkley Brown, however, views the situation differently. She reports that Walker's plans for a department store encountered stiff opposition from the white business community from the very beginning. A coalition made several attempts to buy them out before it ever opened, and after it was open they made various other efforts to hinder its operations. A white Retail Dealers' Association was formed for the purpose of crushing "Negro merchants who are objectionable . . . because they compete with and get a few dollars which would otherwise go to the white merchant." Wholesale merchants were asked not to supply St. Luke Emporium with goods, and other tactics were also employed. The efforts were ultimately successful, although the Emporium managed to operate for seven years before closing.

Another of the problems faced by St. Luke Emporium, however, was endemic to black retail businesses—lack of support from the black consumer. This made Maggie Walker furious, and about a year after the store opened, she called for a mass gathering of black men in the community to talk about support for the business. She rose to her full magnificence as an orator on this occasion:

Hasn't it crept into your minds that we are becoming more and more oppressed each day that we live? Hasn't it yet come to you, that we are being oppressed by the passage of laws which not only have for their object the degradation of Negro manhood and Negro womanhood, but also the destruction of all kinds of Negro enterprises?

She went on to warn:

There is a lion terrorizing us, preying upon us, and upon every business effort we put forth. The name of this lion is PREJUDICE. . . . The white press, the white pulpit, the white business associations, the legislature—all . . . the lion with whom we contend daily . . . in Broad Street, Main Street and in every business street in Richmond. Even now . . . that lion is seeking some new plan of attack.

"[T]he only way to kill the Lion," she concluded, "is to stop feeding it."

One purpose of Penny Savings Bank was to encourage home buying among blacks and to finance mortgages at 6 percent. By 1920 there were 645 black homes "entirely paid for through our bank's help," according to Walker. Like almost every thing else Maggie Walker did, this home buying program was designed to assist black women. "When any one of our girls is advanced to making as much as fifty dollars a month," said Walker, "we begin to persuade her to buy a home. As soon as she saves enough for the first payment, the bank will help her out." Although housing conditions for blacks in Richmond were hardly better than elsewhere, the Knight survey in the 1930s showed that blacks in the city did own 39 percent of the dwellings they occupied. A large share of the credit for this must be given to Penny Savings Bank. The bank continued to grow rapidly during these years, so that deposits were at $376,288 by 1919. The 1920s witnessed a further expansion of the bank's services, and its name was changed to the Saint Luke Bank and Trust Company.

The next great crisis for Maggie Walker and the bank came in 1929, when, in order to weather the Great Depression, she merged it with two other black banks. This was a complicated procedure. Walker was engaged in negotiations with two banks, Second Street Savings Bank and the Commercial Bank and Trust Company. After several meetings, Commercial Bank and Trust withdrew but in 1930 reentered the alliance. At that time, the new merged institution was renamed the Consolidated Bank and Trust Company. Maggie Walker remained chairman of the board of Consolidated until her death in 1934. Consolidated Bank and Trust continued to grow over the years, and by 1970 had total resources of over $14 million. In 1992 it was the fifth-largest financial institution on *Black Enterprise*'s list, with assets of over $143 million and deposits of nearly $138 million. Of all the black-owned banks listed, it was the oldest.

Maggie Walker was not simply a business leader. Like so many other African-Americans of her generation, she carried out a multitude of roles in the black community. On both the formal and informal levels, Maggie Walker was at the center of an increasingly large network of black women in the city who expanded their role in a series of political issues. What alarmed her, and many of the other women in the St. Luke Order, was the systematic way in which blacks were being disfranchised in Richmond and elsewhere. In the city, between 1885 and 1915, all blacks were removed from the city council, and predominantly black Jackson Ward was gerrymandered out of existence. Further, a new state constitution disfranchised the vast majority of black Virginians. Walker came to the conclusion that the development of the black community could not be achieved by men alone, or by men on behalf of black women. They would have to work together. According to Elsa Barkley Brown, "Strong race consciousness and strong support of equality for black women were inseparable. Maggie Walker and the other Saint Luke women therefore came to argue that an expanded role for black women in the black community itself was essential in the community fight to overcome the limitations imposed upon the community by the larger society."

Because of this involvement, Walker spearheaded the local movement for women's suffrage and voter registration after passage of the nineteenth amendment. The campaign was so successful that fully 80 percent of the eligible black voters in the 1920 elections were women. As Elsa Barkley Brown has noted, "[U]ndergirding all of their work was a belief in the possibilities inherent in the collective struggle of black women in particular and of the black community in general." Maggie Walker was at the center of many of the most important black organizations in Richmond. In 1912 she founded and acted as president of the Richmond Council of Colored Women, which raised funds for black causes, including the development and maintenance of the Girl's Industrial School in Peaks, Virginia, and the Community House in Richmond. Its motto was "Lifting as We Climb," which symbolized well both its purposes and the dominant ideology of the African-American community of that time. Maggie Walker was also president of the state branch of the NAACP, and she served on the board of the National Association of Colored Women's Clubs. In addition, she was a founding member of the Negro Organization Society, an outgrowth of a Hampton Conference, which was designed to focus on the health concerns of the black community.

Maggie Walker had to deal with tragedy in the midst of her triumphs. In 1915 her older son, Russell, accidentally shot and killed his father when he mistook him for a burglar. He was charged with murder but cleared after two exhausting trials. The situation was made worse by her rival John Mitchell, whose *Planet* fanned rumors of foul play in the death of her husband. He was evidently jealous of Walker, since her bank was succeeding after his had failed. Alvin E. White reports that "Richmond's black newspaper, the *Planet*, had a Roman holiday [with the slaying]. It ran extras with glaring headlines and the wildest kind of 'background' stories, all unproven." This episode incited opposition to Maggie Walker within the order. Protests were staged against her leadership at the next annual convention, and for many years later. White reports, "[T]he wolves howled, snipers took potshots." Finally, at the 64th annual convention in the early 1930s, she stood before the group and poured out her sentiments:

Forty-five years in actual St. Luke harness, 31 as your right worthy grand secretary-treasurer . . . my whole life has been with you. While at school before graduation, I was your grand officer. Married and become a mother, still your grand officer. A widow with home reponsibilities, still with you. Deprived of the use of my limbs for nearly four years, I am still in your employ, your officer, your friend. (*Sepia*, December 1977)

The convention reportedly "went wild," as objectors were "hooted down." White reports that "Alphonse, her chauffeur, pushed her wheelchair down the aisle, [as] the crowd continued to cheer. It was the most moving day of any St. Luke convention."

Walker suffered a number of other setbacks during her life. In 1906 she fell and broke her kneecap, which never healed completely, and increasingly incapacitated her after 1907. She had an elevator installed in her home and needed a wheelchair to get around. It was that injury that ultimately took her life in 1934, when she died of diabetic gangrene. Walker's husband died in 1915, her mother died in 1922, and Russell died a year later—all of which taxed Maggie Walker's emotional strength.

As she lay dying, Maggie Walker appealed to the "Negroes of America and the World," urging them to "[h]ave hope, have faith, have courage and CARRY ON." Her funeral was one of the largest ever held in the history of Richmond, with some 200 cars in the procession, and many dignitaries in attendance. Seldom, if ever, had a black in Richmond received the accolades Maggie Walker garnered on her death. At her funeral, the mayor of the city called her "a magnificent character," and added that "her influence made this a better city in which to live." The white *Richmond News Leader* called her "A Remarkable Woman" and said her influence was "constant and wholesome." Perhaps the most ironic comment came from E. Lee Trinkle, governor of Virginia, at a mass meeting held at the City Auditorium: "If the State of Virginia had done no more, in fifty years, with the funds spent on the education of Negroes than educate Mrs. Walker the State would have been amply repaid for its outlay and efforts." In October of the year she died, she was honored by African-Americans all over America when it was declared that for all black organizations in the United States it would be known as "Maggie L. Walker Month."

In 1979 Maggie Lena Walker's home became a National Historic Site and museum. The house at 110½ Leigh Street was built originally in 1883 as a two-storied, red-brick structure. It was in a prime location in Jackson Ward, the center of black Richmond's social and economic life. She and her husband purchased the house in 1904, added electricity, a furnace, and radiators, enclosed porches, and eventually increased its size to twenty-two rooms. The restoration of Walker's home became part of an effort to bring about a rebirth of the old Jackson Ward area of Richmond. When the deed to her home was turned over to the National Park Service, many dignitaries again extolled the great virtues of Maggie Lena Walker.

Reverend E. D. McCreary, president of the Maggie Walker Foundation, talked about her charisma, saying that it helped her "work miracles, almost, and made people flock to her." Mrs. Ada Fisher, a "resident historian" of Jackson Ward, recalled Walker as "gracious, easily approachable . . . she had a soft voice." She added, however, that Walker was a "controversial figure . . . men resented her, were sort of jealous of her." McCreary agreed that Walker could be an "authoritarian," but he added that she was "gracious in every sense of the word. . . . She represented real FFV [First Family of Virginia] living in terms of blacks." Elsa Barkley Brown summed up Walker's importance best: "Maggie Lena Walker and the Saint Luke women demonstrated in their own day the power of black women discovering their own strengths and sharing them with the whole community. They provide for us today a model of womanist praxis."

Sources

The largest collection of source materials on Maggie Lena Walker is located at the Maggie Lena Walker National Historic Site in Richmond, run by the National Park Service of the U.S. Department of the Interior. These materials, unfortunately, are not currently completely available to researchers. The site does not have a completed catalog, and the museum curator has complete control over access to the collection. Nonetheless, it does contain some personal letters, diaries, newspaper clippings, and photos of Walker. There are also some materials from the Order of St. Luke, including a journal from 1901, and some canceled checks. The collection contains oral histories of Maggie Walker's grandchildren, which are restricted. In addition, there are some public records from the city of Richmond relating to Maggie Walker, as well as a number of secondary materials.

The Valentine Museum in Richmond has the records of the Independent Order of St. Luke, along with a good collection of newspaper clippings and secondary materials on Walker, the Penny Savings Bank, and the Order. The Virginia State Library in Richmond has some secondary materials on Walker, as does the Virginia Historical Society, in addition to a useful 1975 master's thesis "Maggie Lena Walker (1867–1934): An Abstract of Her Life and Activities" by Sallie Chandler held at the Virginia Union University

Library, and a number of good photographs. Virginia Commonwealth University Library in its Special Collections has an oral history by Leah Pollard Jones-Johnson, which has some interesting material on the home life of Maggie Walker. The Schomburg Collection of the city library of New York City has a number of clippings on Walker, as does the Peabody Collection at Hampton University, the latter of which are available on microfilm. Hampton University also has the proceedings of the Hampton Negro Conference, where Maggie Walker first made her national presence felt in 1903.

Although there is no full-length biography of Maggie Walker, there are a number of useful published short biographies. The most comprehensive and analytical is Elsa Barkley Brown, "Womanist Consciousness: Maggie Lena Walker and the Independent Order of St. Luke," *Signs: Journal of Women in Culture and Society* 14, 3 (1989). An article more closely focused on her banking activities is Charles Willis Simmons, "Maggie Lena Walker and the Consolidated Bank and Trust Company," *Negro History Bulletin* 38, 2 (1975). See also, Suse Field, "Maggie Walker: Lifting as We Climb," *Richmond* 1 (1976). Sadie Daniel St. Clair has a biography of Walker in *Notable American Women* (1971), as does Rayford Logan in the *Dictionary of Negro Biography* (1982). See also, Caroline Bird, *Enterprising Women* (1976); Daniel Porter Jordan, "Indomitable Maggie Walker," *Commonwealth* 48, 3 (March 1981); *Encyclopedia of Southern Culture* (1989); and Ingham, BDABL. Older accounts include Wendell Dabney, *Maggie L. Walker and the I. O. Order of Saint Luke* (1927); Sadie I. Daniel, *Women Builders* (1931); Beatrice J. Fleming, *Negro History Bulletin* V, 4 (January 1942); Mary White Ovington, *Portraits in Color* (1927); Sylvia G. Dannett, *Profiles of Negro Womanhood* 2 vols. (New York, 1964–66); and *Who's Who in Colored America* (1928–1929).

Obituaries of Walker appeared in a number of magazines and newspapers: *Journal of Negro History*, January 1935; *Richmond News Leader*, December 18 and 20, 1934; *Richmond Times-Dispatch*, December 16, 1934; and *Opportunity* 13, 6 (June 1935). African-American newspapers often carried stories about Walker. Schomburg has a number of these, including, *New York Age*, August 14, 1926, and September 30, 1933; *Pittsburgh Courier*, January 4, 1930; and *New York Amsterdam News*, August 24, 1927. *Sepia* had a tribute to Maggie Walker by Alvin E. White in December 1977. *Black Enterprise* also had a tribute in June 1976. There was another spate of articles on Walker and her home when it was turned over to the National Park Service. See *Richmond News Leader*, July 16, 1979, among others. That paper also carried a story on Jackson Ward, where the Walker house is located, on October 10, 1973.

Walker, Sarah Breedlove (Madame C. J.) (December 23, 1867–May 25, 1919). Pioneer African-American business woman, manufacturer, and philanthropist: Madame C. J. Walker Manufacturing Company. Sarah Breedlove was born in a desperately poor family of sharecroppers in Delta, Louisiana, just two years after the end of the Civil War and slavery. Her parents struggled mightily against the system of racism and oppression in the postwar years, but they were defeated by it and died, leaving Sarah an orphan when she just six years old. She left Louisiana to live with her married sister, Louvenia, in Vicksburg, Mississippi. Life was not much better for her there, and in 1881, at the age of fourteen, she married for the first time, to Moses (Jeff) McWilliams. Their daughter, Lelia (later to call herself A'Lelia) was born in 1885, and two years later McWilliams was killed, said to be a victim of a lynching during a race riot. Sarah Breedlove, twenty years old, barely literate, unskilled, and with a two-year-old child, faced a tragic situation. Reactionary racism was on the rise in Mississippi, there were few opportunities for blacks in the state, and virtually none for black women. She headed up the Mississippi River, hoping to find a haven, a place where at least she could survive. She finally arrived in St. Louis where she obtained employment as a washerwoman. Thus, Sarah Breedlove Walker's life resembled that of so many other poor black women at the turn of the century. Left without a mate to raise a child on her own, she faced racism and sexual discrimination in a society that offered little hope for the future. For many years thereafter she struggled as a common laborer and a domestic for whites. But she had an idea, a new concept of hair care for African-American women, and she put this idea into practice. Amazingly, the concept caught on, and Walker toured the country promoting her products. By the time she died a scant fifteen years later, she was the owner of one of the largest black-owned companies in the United States, and she was said to be the first self-made female black millionaire. How did she accomplish this?

Sarah Walker was just one of thousands of African-Americans who were fleeing an increasingly racist and violent South in the 1880s and 1890s. As they steamed up the Mississippi River, many of them recognized St. Louis as the first place of relative freedom outside the South. From just over 3,300 blacks in 1860, there were already over 22,000 there in 1880. And many more came during the decade that Walker arrived, so that the African-American population reached 35,000 by 1900, and over 44,000 ten years later. By this time, St. Louis ranked second only to Baltimore in the percentage of blacks in the total population.

Although it was a large and dynamic community, with black men involved in the building trades, in hauling dray wagons, entertaining in music halls, waiting on tables in restaurants, working in the post office, and unloading merchandise in warehouses and stores and African-American women caring for children, washing clothes, and cleaning houses, it was a far more segregated environment than it had been fifty years earlier. Denied access to the mainstream of American society, blacks in St. Louis constructed their own infrastructure of schools, clubs, professions, and organizations. They also developed their own cadre of professionals, teachers, doctors, and lawyers to service their community. They operated a variety of small businesses that catered to the black community, and they had their own newspaper, the *St. Louis Argus*, which published for over half a century.

Sarah Walker experienced both the favorable and unfavorable features of St. Louis' black community. On the one hand, she was forced to work terribly hard, often fourteen to sixteen hours a day, six or seven days a week, to support herself and to ensure that her young daughter would receive the kind of education that had been denied her mother. Every day, hour after hour, Sarah Walker stood over the steaming hot washtubs, her hands, face, and hair assaulted by the hot water and the steaming vapors of chemicals and fumes. As a result, like many other black women forced to work in this situation, she began to lose her hair. She could not help but contrast her own life with the pampered lives of the white women for whom she worked, with their smooth, creamy skin, their well-coiffed and pampered hair and nails, and the various vanities that they had the time and money to indulge themselves in. Walker began experimenting with the various chemicals she used everyday, trying to find some kind of preparation that would aid in the care and grooming of the hair and skin of black women. Like most black women of the time, Sarah Walker did not get much help from society, but there was one organization in St. Louis that did come to her aid—the National Association of Colored Women. Black women in this club ran an orphanage for young black children and had a daycare for the children of women who had to work every day. This allowed Walker to provide care for her daughter while she was making enough money to send her off to school at Knoxville College, a small, private, black institution in Tennessee. It also gave Walker some extra time to work on her hair-care product.

Sometime between 1900 and 1905, Walker came up with a new hair-care formula for black women. Just what it was has always been kept secret by her and the company, but the highly touted "secret ingredient" was probably sulphur. In any event, one of the great "myths" that drove the company in the early years and helped contribute to the hagiography of Walker herself was the story of how she came upon this formula. According to Walker, it came to her in a dream:

He answered my prayer, for one night I had a dream, and in that dream a big black man appeared to me and told me what to mix up for my hair. Some of the remedy was grown in Africa, but I sent for it, mixed it, put it on my scalp, and in a few weeks my hair was coming in faster than it had ever fallen out. I tried it on my friends; it helped them. I made up my mind to sell it.

Other, more cynical, individuals attributed the discovery to something more prosaic—industrial piracy. They claim that she probably obtained the product made by Annie Turnbo-Malone's* Poro Company, analyzed it, and copied it.

At about the same time, Walker also developed an improved version of the hot comb. There has been some dispute about this over the years. Later, some said she invented the device, but a longtime employee, Dr. Joyner, made the same claim for herself. Walker denied inventing it, but she did redesign the handles and teeth, and she had the comb made out of steel to make it more useful for the hair of African-Americans. With her ointment and her steel hot comb, Walker developed what came to be known as the "Walker system" for straightening hair. She and later company officials, however, disputed this, saying, "[We] are not 'hair straighteners,' but hair culturists and scalp specialists." They insisted Walker's major contribution was to the growing, not the straightening, of African-American hair. Nonetheless, a major emphasis of the Walker system was on the removal of "kinks" from the hair of black women—

to straighten their hair—to the point where it was often referred to as the "anti-kink Walker system."

Walker, according to her own story of her firm's origins, started out with just $1.50 in capital. She mixed up a batch of her product and began selling it door to door in the black community in St. Louis. Meeting with some success, she decided a few months later, in July 1905, to move to Denver, Colorado. There she joined her recently widowed sister-in-law and nieces, got a job in a laundry for $30 a month, had cards printed up advertising her company, and soon began peddling her product in her spare time. Soon thereafter she met Charles J. Walker, a newspaperman and publicist, who gave her tips for marketing and advertising her product. It was he who evidently convinced her to use the name Madame C. J. Walker, either to dignify the products, or to avoid having some condescending name like "Aunt Sarah" applied to them.

The Walker business proved highly successful in Denver, and Charles and Sarah were married a few months later. Charles Walker handled advertising and promotion and tended to affairs at the home "office" while Madame Walker continued to go door to door, marketing the product. As the popularity of her hair-care products grew, it was obvious that Madame Walker alone would not be able to service all of her customers. She began training "agents-operators." Calling them "hair culturists" or "scalp culturists," she instructed them in care methods and in how to manufacture the products themselves. Once the business in Denver became relatively self-sustaining, Madame Walker began traveling extensively in the South and East, giving lectures and demonstrations at black clubs, homes, schools, and churches; the popularity of her products grew enormously. In 1906, she put her daughter, who had moved to Pittsburgh in 1903, in charge of mail-order operations there.

The Walker system had become so popular in the eastern states that Madame Walker decided it was imperative to establish an office closer to those markets. Therefore, in 1908, she set up a temporary office in Pittsburgh, with A'Lelia in charge. There the two women also founded the Lelia College to give instruction in the Walker method in a $25 correspondence course. Meanwhile, Madame Walker continued to search for an ideal permanent location as headquarters for her company. She wanted someplace that was centrally located with access to good transportation. While on her travels in 1910, she stopped in Indianapolis, and was greatly impressed by what she found there. She moved the headquarters of the firm there in that year and established a large-scale manufacturing operation. She proclaimed proudly, "I have built my own factory on my own ground." Later would come a training center for her salespeople, along with research and production laboratories, and another beauty school.

Business expansion, constant traveling, and a change in location put a severe strain on Madame Walker's marriage, and in 1912 she and her husband divorced. As she later remembered, "When I started in business . . . with my husband, I had business disagreements with him . . . for when we began to make ten dollars a day, he thought that amount was enough and that I should be satisfied," she told the *New York Age*. "But I was convinced that my hair preparations would fill a long-felt want, and when we found it impossible to agree, due to his narrowness of vision, I embarked in business for myself."

Indianapolis had an old, well-established African-American community. As early as 1880 there were 6,500 blacks in the city, and it continued a slow, but steady, growth during the next quarter century. There were several well-established black businesses and newspapers there, with George L. Knox's *Indianapolis Freeman* having national distribution and recognition. Black elite families included the Bagleys, Alberts, Christys, Thorntons, McCoys, and Hills, among others. Most of these families were descended from antebellum free black families or were descendants of escaped slaves. By the time Madame Walker arrived, they were employed as teachers, journalists, physicians, and attorneys.

In Indianapolis Madame Walker set up a laboratory and a beauty school, and her enterprise continued to grow more rapidly than perhaps she had ever dared dream. In 1911 she decided to incorporate the company, with herself as the sole stockholder. By this time, her profits were running about $400 per month, and within a few years the company was grossing in excess of $100,000 monthly. She had fifteen employees in the factory in Indianapolis, along with several thousand agents scattered throughout the country. Madame Walker in no sense started to relax; in fact, she traveled and worked nearly incessantly. Her business system has been described in the following manner:

Although Madame Walker owned the business, her actual participation reflected that of an employee more than that of an employer . . . [she] labored in the field from cabin to cabin pushing her goods . . . orders were sent back to her daughter for processing. A'Lelia would fill the order and mail the products back to C. J. Walker.

Madame Walker developed a full line of products for growing and beautifying hair, including hair grower, temple grower, shampoo, glossine (a pressing oil), and tetter salve, which was a remedy for scalp diseases. But C. J. Walker's technique was not simply sales; it was education. Her agents not only sold Walker products but also educated their customers about hygiene and the value of a clean and healthy personal appearance. In an editorial after her death, *Crisis* magazine stressed that Madame Walker had "revolutionized the personal habits and appearance of millions of human beings" and counted that among her greatest accomplishments.

As her business expanded, Madame Walker endeavored to further systematize its operation. During her travels, she had met Freeman B. Ransom, who was then working as a train porter, but was also a student at Columbia Law School. He became enthusiastic about the business potential of her products, and when he graduated, C. J. Walker hired him to head the manufacturing and head office operations in Indianapolis. This solved a nagging problem at the company. A'Lelia Walker was not a well-organized business person, and this had caused confusion in production, order filling, and other matters. With Ransom in charge, Madame Walker was able to concentrate on increasing sales and developing a devoted cadre of agents. A'Lelia was then free to move to New York City, where her task was to expand the East Coast operation and to open a second Lelia College. She also set up a luxurious beauty salon in her expensively furnished Harlem town house.

Madame Walker at this time also began to organize her agents into a series of Walker Clubs which gave cash prizes to the clubs that did the largest amount of philanthropic work. These clubs became engines of both business growth and community and individual uplift. Then, in a technique that was later copied by such modern-day entrepreneurs as Mary Kay Ash, Walker began to bring her agents together in national conventions. The first of these was held in Philadelphia in 1917, when 200 Walker agents convened for the first meeting of the Madame C. J. Walker Hair Culturists Union of America. Hailing from the deep South, the North, and the West, they came together to learn new techniques, to share business experiences, and to tell their own personal success stories. Here, also, Madame Walker would personally hand out $50 prizes to the clubs that had been the most benevolent in supporting their churches and missionary societies.

The annual meetings became venues for the empowerment of African-American women. At the Philadelphia meeting, Madame Walker addressed the women on "Women's Duty to Women," reminding them of their obligation to show other women how to be independent. By this time, she was also urging her agents to get involved politically and socially. She promoted the education of black women, advocated extensive business participation, and took a particularly strong stand against lynching, which at that time was endemic in the South. The Walker agents in 1917 sent a telegram to President Woodrow Wilson urging him to support a law making lynching a federal crime, and to protest the murders of blacks in the recent race riot in East St. Louis, Illinois.

The Walker agents continued their annual meetings for many decades after Madame Walker's death. A gathering of the Walker agents in a city was front-page news in the city's black newspapers. For example, when they convened in Atlanta in 1925, the *Atlanta Independent* trumpeted the event in large headlines: "These people will leave thousands of dollars in our midst, and will immensely advance the economic welfare of our community. The *Independent* welcomes them, and calls upon Atlanta to give them such entertainment as Madame Walker's business so richly deserves." Hundreds of delegates, some from as far away as the West Indies, where Walker had expanded the market during her own lifetime, attended. A year earlier, when they had met in New York City, in addition to the formal proceedings, they had moonlight boat rides, sightseeing trips, shopping tours, and a pilgrimage to Madame Walker's gravesite in Wood-lawn Cemetery.

The Walker agents made quite an impression in their hometowns also. They made "house calls" dressed in their characteristic white shirtwaists tucked into long black skirts and carried black satchels which contained all the preparations and tools necessary for dressing hair. By this time the product was attractively packaged in tin containers whose covers bore Madame Walker's portrait, which, together with extensive advertising campaigns, made her perhaps the best-known black woman in America at that time. The Walker agents paid twenty-five cents a month to belong to Walker's Hair Culturists Union. In return, their estates at their deaths were entitled to a $50 payment. Mostly though, it was a way for black women to achieve economic, social, and psychological independence.

Marjorie Joyner, who became a Walker agent in 1916, recalled, "People would want to become agents and learn the trade so they could travel. They found out that they could make money plus have a new way of getting away from home." Lucille Wilson, another longtime company employee, commented, "All of the Madame C. J. Walker agents had a great love for Madame. They felt she had given them an opportunity to make a living for themselves, which was different from the living that most colored women were able to make at that time." By the end of the first decade of the twentieth century, the Walker Company had trained and employed 5,000 black female agents worldwide. Madame Walker's firm could best be called maternalistic, as she treated her agents in a motherly way, taking infinite pains to show them how to operate efficiently. The company provided two new ways in which black women could make a living: as beauty culturists and as sales agents. As Charles Latham, Jr. has commented, "In an age when black women had very few choices for jobs beyond domestic service and manual labor, this was a major accomplishment."

C. J. Walker may have learned the technique for holding annual motivational conventions from Booker T. Washington[*] and the National Negro Business League (NNBL). In 1911 the local Knights of Pythias brought Washington to Indianapolis for a visit. While Washington was there, Walker invited him to tour her factory and home. He was greatly impressed by her hospitality and also with the magnitude of her business and the wealth it had brought her, as letters from Washington to Walker on July 18 and July 25, 1911, attest. The following year, at the Thirteenth Annual Convention of the NNBL, held in Chicago, C. J. Walker was invited by Washington to address the gathering. When she arrived, however, she found herself either ignored or trivialized by the gathering of males. After waiting through the morning and afternoon sessions to be heard, and listening to speech after speech from black men who recounted their rise from rags to riches, she finally rose to her feet in frustration and demanded to be heard. Her remarks reflected her anger:

Surely you are not going to shut the door in my face. I feel that I am in a business that is a credit to the womanhood of our race. . . . I went into a business that is despised, that is criticised and talked about by everybody—the business of growing hair. They did not believe that such a thing could be done, but I have proven beyond the question of a doubt that I do grow hair!

The audience erupted in laughter and applause, and Madame Walker then launched into a traditional survey of the growth of her firm, explaining that "my object in life is not simply to make money for myself or to spend it on myself in dressing or running around in an automobile, but I love to use part of what I made trying to help others."

Over the next several years, Walker tried to get Washington to include hair-dressing in the curriculum at Tuskegee and to endorse her work publicly. To the first end, in 1914, she sent Washington a check for $300 to cover the expenses of five students for one year, plus another $50 which she gave to the general operating expenses of the school. Washington accepted the checks but curtly informed her that the amount was not really sufficient and that the size of her business ought to enable her to make a larger donation. Nor would he publicly endorse her business, probably because of the widespread skepticism about the effectiveness of hair and skin products, and also because men, black or white, did not take very seriously business operations run by women. Nonetheless, Walker addressed the NNBL convention again in 1914 at Muskogee, Oklahoma. Saying she was surprised to be asked to speak, she said, ''I simply want to ask a favor of you in order that I, in turn, may be able to do more favors for our race. . . . I have come before you this evening to ask you to endorse my work. . . . I ask it because it will help me in the struggle I am making to build up Negro womanhood. I have inspired, and made it possible for hundreds of women of our race to earn a decent, upright living.'' A resolution of endorsement of Madame Walker was read, and James C. Napier* of Nashville seconded it. Washington then considered the resolution passed. A year later, at the convention held in Boston, Washington praised Walker and the success she had found with her hair preparation products. It was a great victory for C. J. Walker.

Madame Walker also became increasingly involved in club and philanthropic work. In 1904 the National Association of Colored Women had met at her church in St Louis, and this began her association with that group. This facilitated her entry into a uniquely educated and progressive group of African-American women, including Mary McLeod Bethune. Bethune and Walker became fast friends, and both were introduced to the 1912 convention of that group. Madame Walker became a staunch benefactor of Bethune's college in Florida, leaving it $5,000 in her will. Walker increasingly became part of an influential group of black leaders during these years and, with them, did much to enhance race pride and to protest injustices. C. J. Walker began a suit against the Central Amusement Company in Indianapolis to protest her exclusion from the Isis Theater. During World War I, she was a member of a delegation, which also included Richmond's Maggie Lena Walker,* sent to Washington, D.C., to protest President Wilson's segregation policies. Shortly before her death, Madame Walker also considered going to the Versailles Conference as an alternate delegate of the National Equal Rights League to ask for a provision concerning the rights of Americans of African descent to be included in the treaty. She, like other members of the delegation, was denied a passport. Walker was also briefly involved in 1919 with Reverend Adam Clayton Powell, Sr. in the formation of the International League of Darker Peoples.

Her philanthropies were equally well known and well regarded. She gave sizable contributions to the National Association for the Advancement of Colored People, a $1,000 donation to the YMCA of Indianapolis, and money for homes for the aged and the needy in that city. In addition, she maintained scholarships for young women at Tuskegee, and gave money to the Palmer Memorial Institute in Sedalia, North Carolina. Through her membership in Indianapolis' Bethel AME Church, Walker gave a good deal of money to several important missionary groups working in Africa. Ultimately, she wanted to build a replica of the Tuskegee Institute for girls in West Africa, and in her will she left money to that end.

As she became wealthier from her hair preparation business (the firm by 1917 had business amounting to $500,000 annually, and was the largest black-owned business in the United States), Madame Walker began to invest her profits in other endeavors, particularly real estate. In Indianapolis, she purchased the entire 600 block on Indiana Avenue where the large Walker Building would later be built. She also bought vacant land and developed homes on it called Hilltop additions. Walker also bought property in Los Angeles, Chicago, Savannah, St Louis, and Gary, Indiana. From 1913 to 1915 she purchased two houses in Harlem at 108–10 West 136th Street. After being extensively remodeled, these were converted into a beauty parlor and school, with the upper floors as living quarters. Later, she bought an apartment house at 374 Central Park West and a house at 1447–49 Boston Road in the Bronx.

In 1916 Madame Walker left Indianapolis to live in New York City, where she enjoyed an increasingly more opulent life-style. She moved into a house in Harlem, and, at the same time, bought a four-and-a-half acre estate in Irvington on the banks of the Hudson. John E. Nail,[*] the prominent Harlem realtor, was her broker in this transaction. There she commissioned a black architect, Vertner W. Tandy, to build a gracious mansion with a formal Italian garden and a swimming pool. The final product cost her nearly $350,000 and severely drained her resources. She named the estate Villa Lewaro at the suggestion of the opera star Enrico Caruso. It was an acronym made up of the letters of the name of her daughter, Lelia Walker Robinson. Among the luxurious furnishings of the home was a Weber grand piano covered in gold leaf, a Victrola to match, and an Estey pipe organ. To complete it, however, Walker had to take out a large mortgage on the house, and the furnishings were not fully paid for many years.

To Madame Walker, it was probably all worth it. The estate was to be eloquent testimony, visible to all, of what someone of her race and gender could accomplish. It seemed to have worked. The *New York Times* gushed in a headline about the "Wealthiest Negro Woman's Suburban Mansion." It went on to say, "Twelve years ago she was a washerwoman, glad of a chance to do any one's family wash for $1.50 a day. Her friends now acclaim her the Hetty Green of her race. They say she has a cool million, or nearly that." It went on to describe the house: "It is fireproof, of structural tile with an outer covering of cream-colored stucco, and has thirty-four rooms. In the basement are a gymnasium, baths and showers, kitchen and pantry, servant's dining room, power room for the organ, and storage vaults for valuables. . . . The main entrance is on the north side. The visitor enters a marble room, whence a marble stairway leads to the floor above. . . . Plans for furnishing the house call for a degree of elegance and extravagance that a princess might envy.''

By this time, though, Madame Walker's health began to fail. She had lived an exceptionally strenuous life, working inhumanly long hours, traveling constantly, and dealing with the constant stress of running a large organization and answering a myriad of outside requests as a public speaker. Her doctors had warned her for years that she had hypertension and needed to slow down, but she ignored them. Suffering also from periodic bouts of kidney failure, she took rest cures at Hot Springs, Arkansas, in 1916 and at a Battle Creek, Michigan, sanitarium in 1917. But she would not slow down. In 1919, while on a trip to St. Louis, she became very ill. She was taken home to rest but did not recover and died there at just fifty-one years of age. Walker had been a washerwoman until she was thirty-eight, but when she died thirteen years later, she left a fortune between a half million and a million dollars.

Two years before her death, Madame Walker made out a new will, and modified that with a codicil in 1919. The documents, however, were unclear and sometimes contradictory, which complicated the settlement of the estate, with inevitable lawsuits from various injured parties. Essentially, the bulk of her estate, including ownership of the Walker Company, was left to her daughter, A'Lelia, although a group of trustees, including A'Lelia and F. B. Ransom, had oversight over much of the company stock. She also left over $100,000 to a number of charities, including $10,000 to establish the industrial school in Africa she had dreamed about.

After Madame Walker's death, A'Lelia Walker Robinson became president, but the actual operation of the concern fell to Ransom, as it had in the past. The firm continued to prosper throughout the 1920s, and in 1927 the Walker Building was built to house the company's operations. The building contained, in addition to the factory itself and offices, a theater, casino, drugstore, and coffee shop. It also rented out office space to other tenants. The cost of $350,000 was raised partly through mortgages. By that time F. B. Ransom claimed that the company's payroll amounted to $200,000. Just two years after the building opened, however, the Great Depression of the 1930s hit with full force, and sales dwindled rapidly. From a peak of $595,000 in 1920, the company plummeted to $130,000 in 1931 and just $48,000 in 1933. The company found itself saddled with enormous debt, not only for the Walker Building in Indianapolis, but also for the expense of Villa Lewaro, which ran to at least $13,000 annually. It also had to support the extravagant life-style of A'Lelia Walker Robinson and her estate, and pay heavy back taxes from World War I.

It became clear that cutbacks had to be made. A'Lelia's beauty parlors in New York and Philadelphia were closed, and the Harlem building was leased to the city of New York. They also tried to sell Villa Lewaro, but few could afford the home in the 1930s. Therefore, they decided to auction off the house's furnishings in 1930. The scene was chaotic. The *New York Sun* (November 28, 1930) reported, ''Buyers Storm Negro Palace,'' saying, ''More than seven

hundred residents of Westchester County—well-to-do white people—excitedly
engaged in spirited, even angry bidding this afternoon to possess at any cost,
some souvenir of the mansion . . . from the millions that a remarkable Negro
woman made out of a preparation to take the kink out of black people's hair.''
Despite the commotion, those "excited white people" were evidently not willing
to part with much hard cash, and the auction raised just $1,500. The mansion
itself was finally sold in 1932 for just $50,000.

A'Lelia Walker meanwhile was establishing another kind of reputation for
herself. She became the doyenne of the Harlem Renaissance. At the salon in
her lavish home in Harlem, know as the "Dark Tower," the most talented
African-American musicians, writers, and artists rubbed shoulders with wealthy
and influential white intellectuals, especially publishers, critics, and potential
patrons. A handsome, statuesque woman, A'Lelia Walker, who was often called
the "Mahogany Millionairess" was addicted to extravagant gowns and exotic
turbans. At her Dark Tower one met the cream of what Roi Ottley called "Cafe-
au-Lait Society": James Weldon Johnson, Zora Neale Hurston, Langston
Hughes, Countee Cullen, Jean Toomer, and many others. One social reporter
reported the reactions of a patron: " 'What a crowd!' she exulted. 'All classes
and colors met face to face, ultra-aristocrats, bourgeoisie, Communists, Park
Avenuers galore, bookers, publishers, Broadway celebs, and Harlemites giving
each other the once over. The social revolution was on.' " Wallace Thurman,
a black writer, called those gathered in the Dark Tower the "niggerati." In
1931, however, A'Lelia died suddenly at the age of forty-six, and a colorful era
of black life in Harlem came to an end. Five years later, her home at 108–10
West 136th, which had enjoyed such a fabled existence, became a city health
center.

After A'Lelia's death, half of her stock in the Walker Company went to F.
B. Ransom, and the other half to her adopted daughter, Mae Walker Perry. Perry
remained president of the firm until she died in 1945, and Ransom continued as
general manager until his own death. In later years other members of the Walker
and Ransom families continued to run the Walker concern, but it did not fare
well against the dynamic new competition of the postwar period. Although it
had introduced Satin Tress, which had been developed by Marjorie Joyner, with
great fanfare in 1948, it was not enough to defeat new challengers like George
Johnson's* Johnson Products and later Edward G. Gardner's* Soft Sheen, both
of which were based in Chicago. The Walker company was sold in 1985, and
the plant was relocated to another site in Indianapolis in 1987. Net sales remained
tiny, and what was once the largest black business in America was by then
nearly dormant. The Walker Building was taken over by the city of Indianapolis.
It set up the Walker Urban Life Center and renovated the building as part of a
downtown redevelopment program, housing offices and a cultural center.

Madame C. J. Walker left, perhaps, an ambiguous legacy. Her once proud
business was a shell of itself by the late 1980s. And hair-care products, partic-

ularly straighteners for blacks, hardly seemed like an esteemed heritage to many. In 1940 Claude McKay had commented, ''Harlem's head is full of vaseline. For in the process of unkinking and ironing and plastering Negro hair, the barbers consume a vast quantity of vaseline.'' Fifty years later, Ralph Wiley echoed those comments:

The hair trip is an endless ongoing curling circling mass of people who have been straightening, frying, processing, conking, waving, texturizing, cutting, shaving, parting, hot-ironing, cold-waving, stocking-capping, Jheri-curling, activating, reactivating, oiling, braiding, Afrotiquing, natty dreading, Quo Vadising and otherwise fiddling with their hair for years. . . . Black hair care has become a one-billion-dollar-a-year business, thanks to the ideas of Madame C. J. Walker.

Perhaps Madame Walker and her descendents should be given the last word. Walker herself said,

I am a woman who came from the cotton fields of the South. I was promoted from there to the washtub . . . and from there I promoted myself into the business of manufacturing hair goods and preparations. . . . I have made it possible for many colored women to abandon the washtub for a more pleasant and profitable occupation. . . . The girls and women of our race must not be afraid to take hold of business enterprises. . . . My business is largely supported by my own people, so why shouldn't I spend my dollars so that it will go back into colored homes.

A'Lelia Perry Bundles, C. J. Walker's great-great-granddaughter, who in the 1980s was a field producer for NBC News in Atlanta, reflected,

It's almost as if all the things Madame Walker thought she wasn't, I am. It's almost as if there's this breeding in five generations. And now, nearing the twenty-first century, we are confident, educated, articulate and able to move in the world in a way she couldn't. After all, what she always tried to do was show people what *could* be done. (*Essence*, June 1983)

Sources

Some of Madame Walker's personal papers, as well as those of her company, amounting to some eighty boxes of material and forty-seven ledgers of business interests are deposited at the Indiana Historical Society. As of the early 1990s this collection was closed to researchers because the late Alex Haley and C. J. Walker's granddaughter, A'Lelia P. Bundles, were doing a history of her life. A number of very significant letters between Walker and Booker T. Washington and Emmett J. Scott, along with some Walker Manufacturing promotional materials, are found in the Booker T. Washington Papers at the Library of Congress. Walker's significant speech to the National Negro Business League in 1912 can be found in *Report of the 13th Annual Convention*, Chicago, 1912, 154–55. An important response by Booker T. Washington is in the *Annual Report of the 16th Convention*, Boston, 1915, 234–37. These are both available at Hampton University or at Tuskegee University. In addition, Walker's last letter to her daughter, along with a brief account of her life was published in A'Lelia P. Bundles, ''Madame C. J. Walker to Her Daughter A'Lelia Walker—The Last Letter,'' in *SAGE: A Scholarly Journal on Black Women*, I, 2 (Fall 1984), 34–35.

There is, as yet, no full-scale biographical treatment of Madame Walker. There are, however, a number of solid shorter accounts. The best and most recent, based on access to her personal and business papers, is Charles Latham, Jr., "Madame C. J. Walker & Company," *Traces of Indiana and Midwestern History* I, 3 (Summer 1989), 29–34. Also of value is Leon Davis, Jr., "Madame C. J. Walker: A Woman of Her Times," Master's thesis, Howard University, 1978. Useful short treatments are Martha Gruening, *Dictionary of American Biography* (1936); Walter Fisher, *Notable American Women* (1971); Rayford Logan, *Dictionary of American Negro Biography* (1982), A'Lelia P. Bundles, "Madame C. J. Walker, Cosmetics Tycoon," *MS Magazine*, July 1983, 91–94, and her "America's First Self-Made Woman Millionaire," *Radcliffe Quarterly*, December 1987; Mariana W. Davis, *Contributions of Black Women to America*, 2 vols. (Columbia, S.C., 1982); and Ingham, BDABL. There are a number of contemporary accounts which may profitably be consulted, but these, as well as the above accounts, should be used with some care: *The National Cyclopedia of the Colored Race* (1919), 263–65; *Who's Who of the Colored Race* (1915); "Life Story of Madame C. J. Walker," *Pittsburgh Courier*, March 8, 15, and 22, 1952. There were long obituaries in the *New York Times*, *New York Sun*, *Indianapolis News*, and *St. Louis Post-Dispatch* on May 27, 1919. The Peabody Collection of Hampton University, which is available on microform, has extensive clippings from various black and white newspapers on Madame Walker and her daughter. The Schomburg Collection at the New York Public Library also has a useful clipping file on the Walkers, as does the Moorland-Spingarn Research Center at Howard University.

Other sources containing varying degrees of biographical or business information are J. L. Nichols and William H. Crogman, *Progress of a Race* (1920), 202, 442–44; George Schuyler, "Madame C. J. Walker: Pioneer Business Woman of America," *Messenger* 6 (August 1924), 251ff.; F. B. Ransom, "Manufacturing Toilet Articles: A Big Negro Business," *Messenger* 5 (December 1923), 937; *Who's Who in Colored Louisiana* (1930); Gladys Porter, *Three Negro Pioneers in Beauty Culture* (1966), 39; Caroline Bird, *Enterprising Women* (1976), 130–31; E. A. Vare and G. Ptacek, *Mothers of Invention* (1987), 69–70; Albon L. Holsey, "Negro Women and Business," *The Southern Workman* LVI, 8 (August 1927), 343–49; *Literary Digest*, October 13, 1917; Edgar A. Toppin, "Madame C. J. Walker, Cosmetics Manufacturer," *Afro-American*, June 24–30, 1937; Jill Nelson, "The Fortune That Madame Built," *Essence*, June 1983, 84ff.; and Kathleen Doyle, "Madame C. J. Walker: First Black Woman Millionaire," *American History Illustrated*, March 1989. A'Lelia Walker's role in the Harlem Renaissance is discussed in Roi Ottley, *New World A-Coming* (New York, 1943), 170–74; Claude McKay, *Harlem: Negro Metropolis* (New York, 1940), 97–99; James Weldon Johnson, *Black Manhattan* (New York, 1940), 282–83; and David Levering Lewis, *When Harlem Was in Vogue* (New York, 1981). Briefer mention occurs in *Black Enterprise* June 1976, 214; *Ebony*, January 1949; and Douglas C. Lyons, "History's Children: Descendents of Legendary Figures Continue the Tradition," *Ebony*, February 1988, 33–34. Editorials in *Crisis*, July 1919 and the *African-American Episcopal Church Review*, July 1919 give a good sense of the importance that contemporaries put on Madame Walker's accomplishments. Also of value is *The Madame C. J. Walker Beauty Manual* (1928) which contains information on her beauty techniques, along with an inaccurate sketch of her life. Walker's home, Villa Lewaro, is described in the *New York Times*, November 29 and 30, 1930. *New York Times*, June 2, 1985, contains information on plans to convert Walker's Villa Lewaro to a museum, and "Madame C. J. Walker Exhibit Initiates Black History Collection," *Indiana Historical Society Newsletter* 12 (August 1979) deals with that subject. See also "Madame C. J. Walker: Two Dollars and a Dream," Video Documentary, Stanley Nelson and Associates, 1988. The reader can get a good sense of the tremendous impact that Walker agents had upon the African-American community by looking at the commotion that ensued when there was a convention of these individuals. See the *Atlanta Independent*, August 6 and 13, 1925, to recapture some of that flavor. The decline of the beauty business in Harlem, including A'Lelia Walker's salon, is covered in LeRoy Jefferies, "The Decay of the Beauty Parlor Industry in Harlem," *Opportunity*, 1936, 49–52. Some additional information on the beauty business and C. J. Walker Company was provided in an interview conducted by the authors at the *Chicago Defender* offices of Dr. Marjorie A. Joyner, one of the firm's early employees, who joined the firm in 1916, became research director, and developed Satin Tress in the 1940s. See also, Toni Costonie, "Profiles of a Legend: The History of Dr. Marjorie Stewart Joyner," *Beauty Classic* 2, 3 (1985), 50–51, 63; and *Beauty Classic* 6, 1 (1987) for information on Dr. Joyner.

Washington, Booker Taliaferro (April 5, 1856–November 14, 1915). Promoter of African-American business, race leader, and educator: National Negro Business League and Tuskegee Institute. Booker T. Washington was a man of many parts, but this biography will focus on his role as a promoter of business enterprise among African-Americans, along with his general role as a race leader. Washington was one of those larger-than-life individuals whose early years, and even later career, are shrouded somewhat in mystery, not because of a paucity of information, but because he and his aides practiced an early form of news management. Then, too, he became the subject of so much controversy and attack from various quarters during the last twenty years of his life, that these critics have tended to define the scope of inquiry concerning the "Wizard of Tuskegee's" life and career.

What we know of Washington's early life comes primarily from his own autobiographies, which place perhaps excessive stress on the poverty of his early years. Nonetheless, he was born a slave on a small farm in Franklin County, Virginia. His mother, Jane, was the slave cook in the home of James Burroughs, a small planter in the area. Washington's father was an unidentified white man from the neighborhood. His mother gave him the name of Booker Taliaferro, but the second name was later dropped. The young boy himself adopted the surname "Washington" when he first enrolled in school, believing the name gave him greater dignity. A few years after his birth, his mother married Washington Ferguson, a slave on a nearby plantation. According to Washington's *Up from Slavery*, the slave family lived in a one-room cabin with a fireplace and a "potatoe hole," but without a wooden floor or glass windows. Washington claimed that he "never remembered sleeping in a bed until after our family was declared free by the Emancipation Proclamation." Despite these hard conditions, Washington maintained that there was much mutual affection on the plantation between the slave and master. As his biographer, Louis Harlan, points out, as house slaves, Washington's family had a higher status than the other slaves and were probably treated better as a result. This relationship also might have accounted for the "mutual affection" referred to by Washington.

When young Washington was nine years old, he and his family were freed, whereupon they moved to Malden, near Charleston, West Virginia, where Washington Ferguson had gone earlier to work in the area salt furnaces. Booker T. Washington soon found himself working in the coal mines and at the salt furnace, pushed to work by his exploitive stepfather. These were hard times for the young boy, and in his autobiography he recalled the hard physical labor he endured there and the distaste he had for the town itself. They lived in a small cabin clustered among many others. With no sanitary regulations, the surrounding filth and stench from garbage and outhouses was appalling. Young Washington was also disgusted by the behavior of the poor whites with whom they lived in close proximity. Remembering them as "the poorest and most ignorant and degraded white people," he considered that class of white southerner for the rest of his life the enemy of his people.

At this time young Washington could neither read nor write. In fact, the only character he could recognize was "18," which was his father's number as a salt packer. When Washington was forced to work with his father, he had to learn to mark all his bags with that number. An "intense longing to read" was one of Washington's earliest memories, and he finally persuaded his mother to secure a speller so that he might begin to learn. She got the Webster's "Blue-Back Spelling Book," and Washington soon mastered the alphabet with it. Young Washington's first formal education outside of the home was in a Sunday school, where he began regularly to attend the African Zion Baptist Church in nearby Tinkersville, along with the rest of his family. Sometime after that, the blacks in Malden hired young William Davis to open a school for local black children, but Wash Ferguson refused to allow his son to attend. The young boy was forced to attend night school with adults until his stepfather finally relented and allowed him to go to regular school. In return, Washington had to work at the salt furnace from four to nine in the morning, and for two hours after school.

Sometime between 1867 and 1871, young Washington took a momentous step—he moved out of the cramped, foul-smelling family cabin, and the salt furnace toil that went with it, and went to work as a houseboy for the wife of General Lewis Ruffner, the owner of the area mines and furnaces. Ruffner owned the largest and best-appointed house in the town, which Washington referred to in his autobiobraphy as the "big house." Pictures of the home in the nineteenth century, however, reveal a rather modest structure, certainly not a mansion. General Ruffner's second wife, Viola, was a brilliant former schoolteacher from Vermont who had been rejected by Ruffner's children from his first marriage. A stern mistress, she had gone through a succession of houseboys before Washington arrived. But he was so glad to escape the rigors of the salt furnace and the stench of his home, that he was eager to please her every wish. For Viola Ruffner's part, the young boy was a godsend. Bright, eager, articulate, and completely devoted to her, she had finally found someone to mold and nurture. Mrs. Ruffner later remembered that "as there was little for him to do, he had much spare time which I proposed he should use by learning to read, which he readily accepted. I would help and direct, and he was more than willing to follow direction. He was always willing to quit play for study. He never needed correction or the word 'Hurry!' or 'Come!' for he was always ready for his book.'' Besides her own tutoring, she also allowed him to continue attending William Davis's school.

As much formal education as Washington received from Mrs. Ruffner, his most important lessons were informal ones—lessons of cleanliness, discipline, order, truthfulness, and punctuality. He also began to demonstrate a passion for greater achievement than would have been thought possible for a young ex-slave in the early 1870s. As Mrs. Ruffner recalled, ''He seemed peculiarly determined to emerge from his obscurity. He was ever restless, uneasy, as if knowing that contentment would mean inaction. 'Am I getting on?'—that was his principal question.'' During this time, Washington heard two miners talk about Hampton Normal and Agricultural Institute in Virginia, and he made plans to attend that institution. In 1872, at age sixteen, he left for Hampton, some 500 miles away, with a few dollars in his pocket. Walking the entire distance, he arrived filthy, broke, and hungry. Samuel Chapman Armstrong, principal of Hampton, asked Washington to take a broom and sweep a room. Booker, well-trained by Mrs. Ruffner, swept the room three times and dusted it four times. Armstrong was impressed, and he arranged for a white philanthropist to pay Washington's tuition.

As Washington later remembered, ''Life at Hampton was a constant revelation . . . the matter of having meals at regular hours, of eating on a tablecloth, using a napkin, the use of a bathtub and of the toothbrush, as well as the use of sheets upon the bed'' were all new experiences for him. At Hampton, Washington studied academic subjects, and he worked in the fields and cleaned pig stys. In addition, he learned the trade of a brick mason. During summers he worked at a Saratoga hotel as a waiter. Washington's special interest, however, was debate and public speaking, and he was jubilant when he was chosen to speak at his class's commencement. After graduating from Hampton, Washington returned to Malden, where he taught in the black school for three years. He later remembered this period as ''one of the happiest periods'' of his life because he had the opportunity ''to help the people of my home town to a higher life.'' But his ambition, his drive to achieve more than he could in the small town of Malden, continued to display itself. In 1878 Washington went to Washington, D.C., where he spent eight months as a student at Wayland Seminary, taking an entirely academic program. Washington disliked this experience, since he felt his fellow students were educating themselves to rise above, and live off, the mass of blacks. The fact that Washington did not perform well at Wayland may also have played a role in his negative reaction. In any event, this brief sojourn convinced him that Hampton's technique of industrial education was the most beneficial for his race. He also developed a strong distaste for big city life at this time.

At the end of his studies at Wayland, Washington returned to Hampton, where he taught in a program for American Indians and served as secretary to General Armstrong. In 1881 events began to unfold that had a profound impact on the young teacher's life. General Armstrong was involved in discussions with George W. Campbell, a banker, merchant, and former slaveholder, and Lewis Adams, a mechanic and ex-slave, about starting a normal school for African-Americans in Tuskegee, Alabama, where both men lived. The year before, the state had passed an act authorizing the establishment of such a school, giving it an appropriation of $2,000. In asking Armstrong to recommend someone to start the new school, they had assumed a white man would be recommended, but instead Armstrong suggested Booker T. Washington, who was not only black, but also just twenty-five years old.

In June 1881 Washington set out for Alabama to establish his new school. When he arrived in Macon County, in the heart of Alabama's black belt, Washington found there was no land or buildings for the projected school, nor was there any money with which to purchase them. He searched until he found a black church and a few dilapidated shanties in which he could begin instruction. He hired one black teacher, attracted thirty pupils to the school, and by the fall of that year Tuskegee Normal and Industrial Institute was in operation. The next year, a 100-acre plantation was purchased to provide more room and facilities for the growing student body. The Agricultural Department was set up in 1882 and the Brickmaking Department, a year later. The curriculum came to include carpentry, printing, cabinetmaking, wagon building, harness making, and shoe making over the next few years. A night school, a training school, a model country school, a preparatory department, a mechanical department, an industrial department, and industries for women were also set up. By the 1890s, more than forty buildings had been erected by student labor on 1,400 acres of land. The property was valued at $225,000 and was unencumbered by a mortgage. Seventy persons were employed as instructors of one kind or another, and there were nearly 1,000 pupils. By 1915 Tuskegee had an endowment of nearly $2 million, with 2,000 students, and a staff of some 200.

In addition, in 1890, Tuskegee instituted well-publicized annual conferences, such as the Tuskegee Negro Farmer's Conferences. Washington commented about these that "the matters considered at the conference are those that the coloured people have it in their own power to control—such as the evils of the mortgage system, the one-room cabin, buying on credit, the importance of owning a home and of putting money in the bank, how to build schoolhouses and prolong the school term, and to improve the moral and religious condition." At the school itself, reflecting Washington's training with both Mrs. Ruffner and at Hampton, strong emphasis was placed on personal hygiene, manners, and character building. Students were also required to attend chapel daily and a series of religious services on Sunday. Although Tuskegee was in some respects a replica of Hampton, in at least one important respect it was different—all the teachers, administration, and staff were African-American. At other "black" schools, often until well into the twentieth century, the top administrators and even much of the faculty were white. Tuskegee thus provided a daily model for its black students for what African-Americans could accomplish without the aid of whites. In addition, Washington's powerful personality penetrated every nook and cranny of the school, making Tuskegee more the reflection of him and his ideals than of Hampton or elsewhere.

The reasons for the growth of Tuskegee and the rise to prominence of Booker T. Washington were manifold, but a few can be isolated. He was often called the Wizard of Tuskegee, and much of the reason for this appellation had to do with his ability to extract large amounts of money from northern philanthropists, along with his ability to cool the growing racist ardors of southern whites. Through his fund-raising efforts, Washington became relatively close with a number of leaders of industry at the turn of the century, including John Wanamaker, Henry H. Rogers of Standard Oil, Collis P. Huntington, Robert C. Ogden, William H. Baldwin, Jr., and Andrew Carnegie. Carnegie became the largest single donor to Tuskegee and a close ally and confidant of Washington. Carnegie once called Washington "the combined Moses and Joshua of his people. Not only has he led them to the promised land, but [he] still lives to teach them by example and precept how properly to enjoy it." Washington also raised funds for Tuskegee from the Peabody Education Fund, the John F. Slater Fund, and the Julius Rosenwald Fund, and he helped establish the Anna T. Jeanes Fund and the Phelps-Stokes Fund.

Because he became close to so many northern capitalists, and because Tuskegee's rise was so dependent upon their largesse, Washington was careful not to criticize the existing capitalist system. In many respects, however, Washington was simply a man of his time, and his extolling of the virtues of free enterprise and capitalism was typical. Victorian America enshrined the virtues of thrift, hard work, abstemious behavior, self-help, and industry. These came naturally to young Washington, and these beliefs he naturally shared with other self-made men of the time. Thus, his pronouncement on this score, which made him so attractive to northern philanthropists, probably reflected Washington's deeply held beliefs. He did not have to temper his remarks, or become, as Kelly Miller has said, a "diplomat of the first water" to appeal to these men. Unlike some black leaders like Henry McNeal Turner or J. Max Barber, who saw little hope for the black man within the existing system, Washington had faith that over time these virtues would allow African-Americans to create their own thriving economic and social communities, which, in turn, would convince whites that blacks were fully deserving of inclusion in the mainstream of American life.

More problematic are Washington's attitudes toward southern whites and the institutionalized racism and segregation that was developing during this time. He began what came to be called his "accommodationist" philosophy early on. In 1884, in a speech before the National Educational Association, the twenty-eight-year old Tuskegean proclaimed, "Any movement for the elevation of the Southern Negro, in order to be successful, must have to a certain extent the cooperation of Southern whites. They control the government and own the property." Washington did not, however, counsel blacks to be obsequious Uncle Toms. As he noted later in the same speech, "Now, in regard to what I said about the relations of the two races, there should be no unmanly cowering or stooping to satisfy unreasonable whims of the Southern white man.'' He did advise, though, that southern blacks remain respectful of the southern traditions and etiquette on race relations, counseling them to respect the law, however racist in intent, and to cooperate with white authorities in maintaining the peace.

Washington's philosophy achieved national prominence in 1895 when he was invited to address the Cotton States and International Exposition in Atlanta. The offer in itself was extraordinary, as he was to speak before a racially mixed audience. He directed his attention primarily to the whites. Washington assured them that southern blacks were not demanding social equality, and, saying that he had a desire "to say something that would cement the friendship of the races," he made one of his most famous statements: "In all things that are purely social we can be as separate as the fingers, yet one as the hand in all things essential to mutual progress." To the blacks in the audience he said, " 'Cast down your bucket where you are'—cast it down in making friends in every manly way of the people of all races by whom we are surrounded. Cast it down in agriculture, in mechanics, in commerce, in domestic service, and in the professions."

White southerners were generally elated with the tone of Washington's address. Clark Howell of the *Atlanta Constitution* wrote that Washington's speech heralded the beginning of a moral revolution in the South, and found him a "wise and safe leader." Howell stated further, "The address was a revelation. The whole speech is a platform upon which blacks and whites can stand with full justice to each other." The *Montgomery Advertiser* praised Washington because there was "nothing of the agitator about him." The *Memphis Advocate* called him "an advocate of high morality, sublime ethics and bath tubs" and characterized him as a "diamond cast in a basket of charcoal." White southerners in general were pleased with the fact that Washington expressed a relative disinterest in fighting for political and civil rights for African-Americans, and that he placed his confidence in the benevolence of southern whites for good treatment of southern blacks, rather than insisting upon the need for federal or northern intervention. On this score Washington had commented, "Reforms have to come from within, since Southerners don't like to obey orders that come from Washington, D.C., telling them that they must lay aside at once customs that they have followed for centuries."

The reaction of blacks in the audience and elsewhere was more mixed. James Creelman, a reporter for the *New York World*, observed that at the end of Washington's speech "most of the Negroes in the audience were crying, perhaps without knowing just why." That statement has bedeviled historians ever since. Some have taken it as evidence that blacks believed they had just been "sold out" by their white-annointed leader. Others assert that blacks reacted in this way because at a time when relations between blacks and whites in the South were at their darkest, and at a time when "hollowness and despair gripped the nation," Booker T. Washington lighted the way to a new plateau of hope and progress. There is little question that the rapid rise of a virulent racist attitude, accompanied by white terror on a scale unimagined in the South, had intensified a separatist feeling among many southern blacks. Washington's speech spoke to that feeling. Washington, in effect, told blacks it did not really matter what whites did, they must go about building their own independent and self-sufficient communities. Certainly most of the black middle class, especially schoolteachers, of that time seemed to agree with Washington. August Meier reports that one black Virginia teacher said, "The Negro will have to work out his own salvation. Religion, education and money will make any race great." Another teacher claimed that the race's problems would be solved "when the more intelligent classes of the race united their effort to educate the ignorant classes by example rather than by precept."

It was the black intellectuals, especially in the North, who were most offended by Washington's utterances. Openly criticizing his recent speech, the black *Detroit Tribune* declared in 1895, "That latest Tennessee lynching should be exhibited at the Atlanta Exposition as a fine speciman of one of the staple products of the South." John Hope, president of Atlanta University, declared, "Now hold your breath, for . . . I am going to demand social equality. In this republic we shall be less than freemen if we have a whit less than that which thrift, education, and honor afford other freemen. . . . Come, let us possess this land. . . . Let your discontent break mountains high against the wall of prejudice, and swamp it to the very foundation. Then we shall not have to plead for justice nor on bended knee crave mercy; for we shall be men." Those criticisms, though, were rather rare in 1895. It was only after about 1901 that the intellectuals' attack on Washington grew more intense. W.E.B. Du Bois, in fact, who was to become the Tuskegean's sharpest critic, wrote to the *New York Age* to say that he thought there might be the basis for a real settlement between the blacks and whites of the South in Washington's speech.

Washington sought to encourage his students, and African-Americans generally, to build "system, order, regularity," into their lives. He was particularly concerned with the issues of the dignity of work and of the retention of skills. As far as work was concerned, Washington fretted that "[t]he Negro learned in slavery to work but he did not learn to respect labor. On the contrary, the Negro was constantly taught, directly and indirectly during slavery times, that labor was a curse. . . . The consequence of that teaching was that, when emancipation came, the Negro thought freedom, in some way, must mean freedom from labor." Washington's program was to instill a respect for work and labor in southern blacks. Also, noting that the "elder men and women trained in the hard world of slavery were dying out," he was concerned that there were not enough blacks in the younger generation with the necessary occupational skills for survival and prosperity in the twentieth century. He insisted on the need to provide training, particularly in agriculture, but also in home economics, stock raising, and a number of important mechanical trades, along with blacksmithing, brick masonry, carpentry, printing, tailoring, and a number of other trades.

This was the industrial and vocational training that Washington believed was necessary for the southern black. Yet, this was not at the exclusion of other academic training or occupational pursuits. As Washington commented, "I would set no limit to the attainments of the Negro in arts, letters or statesmanship, but I believe the surest way to reach those ends is by laying the foundation in the little things of life that lie immediately about one's door. I plead for industrial education and development for the Negro not because I want to cramp him, but because I want to free him. I want to see him enter the all-powerful business and commercial world." Washington, who accepted rather uncritically the dominant philosophy of American business, and the southern credo of segregation, began to push for the creation of powerful, free-standing, and independent black business communities in all cities and towns of the South and North.

Washington's single most important development on this score was his creation of the National Negro Business League (NNBL) in 1900, which was designed to foster business and industry among blacks. As August Meier comments, "It was this group that was especially instrumental in the burgeoning of the philosophy of racial solidarity, self-help and the group economy, the rationalization of the economic advantages to be found in segregation and discrimination—to use a phrase commonly employed in those days. Washington's National Negro Business League was the platform on which this group expressed its point of view." The NNBL, according to its historian, John Howard Burrows, "bore the characteristics of racial solidarity and the fervency of a religious revival. Guided by the administrative talents of Washington's secretary, Emmett J. Scott, the League continued to proclaim the Washingtonian ideal after Washington's death."

Washington in 1902 discussed what elements had impelled him to organize the league:

For several years previous to the formation of the Business League, as my work in connection with Tuskegee Normal and Industrial Institute had taken me about the country, both North and South, I had been surprised and encouraged to find so large a number of Negro men and women as I did find engaged in some business occupation. It is true that these enterprises were usually small—sometimes very small—and in general with small amounts of capital invested. It seemed to me interesting that they existed at all. . . . As I spoke of this to other men of our race in various parts of the country, I found that they agreed with me that a national organization which should bring together Negroes from all parts of the country engaged in business for the purpose of advising with one another, would be a source of beneficial encouragement and inspiration.

As John R. Bruce later commented, "There does not appear to be any good reason why Negroes should not thus organize for mutual benefit and self protection. If organization is good for white men in politics and business, it ought to be just as good for Negroes."

Washington was able to convince Andrew Carnegie to bankroll the fledgling organization, and it held its first annual meeting in Boston in 1900. The meeting, incidentally, was organized and run by a number of local black businessmen, none of whom were part of that city's African-American intellectual elite. It is perhaps not coincidental that the organized opposition to Washington's policies began the next year in Boston, and was spearheaded by William Monroe Trotter and George Forbes, Ivy League college graduates and members of the African-American intelligentsia.

As Washington described it, "The machinery of the League is very simple. Any Negro man or woman who is engaged in any business is eligible for membership upon the payment of an annual fee of two dollars." Immediately, local leagues began forming, and the expansion was so successful that, by 1906, 1,200 individuals attended the annual convention held in Atlanta. Although Washington gave the league its charismatic leadership, it was, contrary to most interpretations, a fairly decentralized affair. George M. Newstelle, head of the local league in Montgomery, Alabama, described his organization in 1915:

We did not organize a debating or literary society, but we met for business. We met regularly in a store or office, discussing only such things as had a practical bearing on the objects of our organization. Of course at that time we were not so well acquainted with the methods and mission of the National Negro Business League. We took it upon ourselves to give a barbeque with the two-fold purpose of increasing our funds and at the same time making an effort to increase our membership.

The national and local leagues not only provided encouragement for the creation of black-owned businesses, they also used every sort of moral suasion to convince African-Americans not to trade with whites. The local Kansas City league established a vigilance committee which "ferreted out those who failed to patronize Negro enterprises," according to Meier (*Negro Thought in America*, 1963), "and the League had put on such a campaign that it was accounted 'almost a crime' for a Negro who amounted to anything at all to patronize a white establishment for an article or service that could be obtained in a Negro place of business."

Booker T. Washington was also directly involved in the promotion of a number of business enterprises. Most prominently, he took an active interest from about 1900 onward in the development of the all-black town of Mound Bayou, Mississippi, founded by Isaiah T. Montgomery* and Charles Banks,* both of whom became officers in the NNBL. Washington also developed some close ties with businesses and business leaders in other centers of black enterprise. In Durham, North Carolina, he took a particular interest in the creation and growth of the North Carolina Mutual Insurance of Charles Clinton Spaulding* and John Merrick* and the Coleman Manufacturing Company, a black-owned and black-operated textile mill, founded by Warren Clay Coleman* and others. Washington, for a variety of reasons, also became very closely involved in the operations of Philip A. Payton, Jr.'s* Afro-American Realty Company in Harlem and the *New York Age*, which was run first by Thomas T. Fortune and then by Fred R. Moore.* Washington's interest in these ventures, however, was apparently more political than economic, as was his involvement with the *Colored American* and

W. Calvin Chase, Sr.'s* *Washington Bee* in Washington, D.C. Washington's involvement in these newspapers, and in the Afro-American Realty Company, was part of his campaign to control the dissemination of information concerning his activities, and also to retain influence over the black leadership in the important centers of New York and Washington.

Far too much ink has already been spilled concerning the attack on Washington by Du Bois, Trotter, and other black intellectuals. Suffice to say that their crusade against him focused on his "toleration of political and civil discrimination and his emphasis on industrial education as opposed to higher education." As Du Bois stated in his *Souls of Black Folk*,

There is among educated and thoughtful colored men in all parts of the land a feeling of deep regret, sorrow and apprehension at the wide currency of ascendancy which some of Mr. Washington's theories have gained . . . [and] the hushing of the criticism of honest opponents is a dangerous thing. . . . Mr. Washington asks that black people give up, at least for the present, three things, first, political power; second, insistence on civil rights; third, higher education of Negro youth, and concentrate all their energies on industrial education, the accumulation of wealth, and the conciliation of the South.

This form of criticism was accepted rather uncritically by historians for decades. Recently, however, there has been some revision of this stance. August Meier, for instance, shows that although publicly Washington took the stance of an accommodationist, privately he often followed other agendas. He often was, as Louis Harlan has observed, "neither a black Christ nor an Uncle Tom but a cunning Brer Rabbit, 'born and bred in the brier patch' of tangled American race relations." Although he publicly declined to attack disfranchisement of blacks, privately he lobbied against this, and he did all he could to subvert the lily-white Republican party in the South. Similarly, although he publicly acquiesced in segregation statutes, surreptitiously he wrote unsigned letters to black newspapers denouncing many of these statutes. In addition, he provided support to the various boycott movements against the Jim Crow streetcar laws in southern cities during the first decade of the twentieth century. As a result, many historians now view Washington not as an Uncle Tom, but as a hard-nosed realist who secured limited but significant gains for his race during a time when more militant leaders achieved far less. In addition, his call for blacks to achieve economic independence, to separate from the white mainstream, and to cultivate the virtues of their own African-American identity and culture, obviously has more salience in the racial climate of the 1980s and 1990s, than it had during the 1950s and 1960s, when integration and assimilation were viewed as the keys to dismantling white racism and achieving black equality. There is also the sense that, despite the fact that Kelly Miller claimed that Washington was "not a leader of the people's own choosing," he did, in fact, appear to be closer to the African-American masses, especially those in the South, than his critics. As Donald J. Calista and others have pointed out, "DuBois was the aloof New England idealist from Harvard Square," who, according to Arnold Rose, held the black masses in some contempt. Washington, in a sense, was far more "Afro-Centric," even though he counseled blacks that they should not consider returning to Africa. He placed much emphasis on black people knowing their African past and origins, and he always tried to assert the positiveness of their "blackness." Thus, when Reverend Richard H. Boyd* of Nashville developed an African-American doll for children, Washington was most supportive, saying it would "teach the children to admire and respect their own type."

In his later years, Washington's influence on all levels declined markedly. This was caused by a number of factors, not the least of which was constant attacks from Du Bois, Trotter, and members of the NAACP, especially after 1910. Then too, Washington was involved in the so-called Ulrich affair in New York City, in which he was attacked by an irate white man for supposedly peeping through the keyhole of the apartment of a white woman. When Woodrow Wilson won the presidency in 1912, Washington's "pipeline" to the White House was cut off, and he could no longer supply the sort of patronage he had been able to achieve from Republican presidents. Overworked, and suffering from continual exhaustion, Washington took ill and died of arteriosclerosis in Tuskegee on November 14, 1915. His funeral was to be a rather simple affair, but the little town of Tuskegee was mobbed by some 8,000 persons, including large numbers of dignitaries from the North. He was buried in a large brick tomb, made by the students at his school, on a hill with a commanding view of the entire institute.

Tuskegee and Washington's institute continued to expand during much of the twentieth century. Robert R. Moton, Washington's successor as principal, perpetuated the ideal of Tuskegee Institute as the "practical way" to educate blacks, and he advanced the idea of Tuskegee itself being a model community with ideal race relations, a view that was endorsed by area whites. For all its energy and fanfare, however, Tuskegee Institute had only limited success in its educational effort. Black education in Macon County, where it was located, was poorly funded, despite the generosity of the Rosenwald Fund, and farming practices in the area were no better than most of the rest of the South. Charles S. Johnson, in a study in the 1930s, concluded that black farmers in Macon County were little better off than they were when slavery ended, with 90 percent still working as tenants. Malnutrition and disease were rampant, and few blacks could afford adequate medical care. Ned Cobb, a sharecropper in Macon County whose recollections were immortalized by Theodore Rosengarten in *All God's Dangers* (1974), spoke eloquently of the exploitation he experienced.

To Washington's credit, however, Tuskegee was also a cradle of the black middle class. By 1940 the town had more than 1,000 black professionals, and the institute maintained Washington's policy that all its staff must live in the town. The campus itself retained its beauty as a showplace of black achievement. Rolling hills and imposing brick buildings nestled alongside comfortable homes with well-kept lawns. Blacks and whites in Tuskegee early established a truce in race relations which at least gave the appearance of tranquility and peace.

The 1940s and World War II, however, brought a new, more militant civil rights movement to Tuskegee, in contrast with the accommodationist mode of Booker T. Washington. In many respects, though, this was simply a vindication of Washington's deeper philosophy. As the historian of that era, Robert J. Norrell, has said, "Washington's experiment, which promised that blacks would realize full equality once they had made themselves useful to society, ultimately succeeded in Tuskegee. Well-educated, economically secure Institute professors successfully challenged white conservative control of Tuskegee after Washington's hands-off policy toward politics was forsaken in the late 1930s. Middle class blacks in Tuskegee demonstrated after 1940 that political rights would indeed follow from economic power. The Washington policy was vindicated, as least in its place of birth."

Claude McKay, who was once a student for a few weeks at Tuskegee, was moved to write a poem upon hearing of Booker T. Washington's death:

> O how I loved, adored your furrowed face!
>   And fondly hoped, before your days were done,
> You would look into mine too with paternal grace.
>   But vain are hopes & dreams!—gone: you are gone;
> Death's hand has torn you from your trusting race,
>   And O! we feel so utterly alone.

Sources

There is an extraordinary amount of material, both published and unpublished, available on Washington. The richest source is the Booker T. Washington Papers, at the Library of Congress. See United States Library of Congress, Manuscript Division, *Booker T. Washington: Register of His Papers in the Library of Congress* (Washington, D.C., 1958). A relatively small portion of these have been published by Louis R. Harlan and Raymond W. Smock in a fourteen-volume series: *The Booker T. Washington Papers* (Urbana, Ill., 1972–   ). Unfortunately, few of the published letters deal with Washington's attitude toward business or the NNBL. Tuskegee University has another important collection of Booker T. Washington Papers, as well as the papers of the National Negro Business League, the records of the Institute itself, and a scrapbook on Washington. Later events of the business league and Tuskegee can be found in the Robert R. Moton Papers, also at Tuskegee. There are also a number of letters from Washington to several benefactors of Tuskegee in the Booker T. Washington Papers at the Schomburg Collection, New York Public Library. The Peabody Collection at Hampton University, which is available on microfilm, has nineteen volumes of newspaper clippings dealing with Washington, along with the published proceedings of the Annual Conventions of the National Negro Business League. There is also a scrapbook there entitled "Attack on Booker T. Washington."

Washington himself published three autobiographies: *The Story of My Life and Work* (1909); *Up from Slavery* (1910); and *My Larger Education* (1911). These volumes, especially *Up from Slavery*, are fascinating, but highly sanitized and should be read with care. In addition, his most important speeches are collected in *Selected Speeches of Booker T. Washington* (1932), edited by his son, E. Davidson Washington. The elder Washington also wrote (or at least had published under his name), a staggering number of books and articles, including, *The Future of the American Negro* (1899); *Sowing and Reaping* (1900); *Character Building* (1902); *Working with the Hands* (1904); *Putting the Most into Life* (1906); *Frederick Douglass* (1907); *The Negro in Business* (1907); *The Story of the Negro* (1909); and *The Man Furthest Down* with R. E. Park (1912); and he edited *Tuskegee and Its People* (1905). In addition, see, *Black Belt Diamonds: Gems from Speeches, Addresses, and Talks to Students of Booker T. Washington* (New York, 1898, reprinted, 1969); "The Negro in Business," *Gunton's Magazine*, March 1901; "Progress of the Negro Race in Mississippi," *World's Work* (London) 13 (March 1909), 409–13; "Is the Negro Having a Fair Chance?" *Century Illustrated Monthly Magazine* LXXXV (November 1912); and "Durham, North Carolina: A City of Negro Enterprise," *Independent* LXX (1911).

The best and most comprehensive biography of Washington is a two-volume work by Louis R. Harlan, *Booker T. Washington: The Making of a Black Leader, 1856–1901* (New York, 1972), and *Booker T. Washington: The Wizard of Tuskegee, 1901–1915* (New York, 1983). These works, especially the second volume, are marred by Harlan's insistence on viewing Washington as a "machine politician." This tends to distort many of Washington's actions during the period from 1901 to 1915, especially relations with the NNBL and his promotion of African-American business. See also reviews of the second volume by William H. Harbaugh in the *New Republic*, July 18 and 25, 1983, and by Sherman Jones, executive vice president of the Tuskegee Institute, in *Change*, September 1983. See August Meier, "Toward a Reinterpretation of Booker T. Washington," *Journal of Southern History* XXIII (May 1957), 220–27, and his *Negro Thought in America, 1880–1915* (Ann Arbor, Mich., 1963), for some penetrating insights. Harlan has also written a shorter biography of Washington entitled "Booker T. Washington and the Politics of Accommodation," in John Hope Franklin and August Meier, eds., *Black Leaders of Twentieth Century America* (Urbana, Ill., 1982), 1–18. Many of Harlan's published essays on Washington have been collected in Raymond W. Smock, ed., *Booker T. Washington in Perspective: Essays of Louis R. Harlan* (Jackson, Miss., 1988). Other biographies of Washington include Emmett J. Scott and Lyman Beecher Stowe's hagiographic *Booker T. Washington, Builder of Civilization* (1916); Basil Matthews, *Booker T. Washington, Educator and Interracial Interpretor* (1948); and Samuel R. Spencer, Jr., *Booker T. Washington and the Negro's Place in American Life* (1955). See also Emma Lou Thornbrough, ed., *Booker T. Washington* (1969) and a short biography by her in the *Dictionary of American Negro Biography* (1982) and one by Anson Phelps Stokes in the *Dictionary of American Biography* (1936). There was an obituary in the *New York Times*, November 15, 1915, and nearly all other major newspapers on that date.

An excellent bibliographic compilation of published work on Booker T. Washington, which especially highlights economic and business elements, is Don Quinn Kelley, "The Political Economy of Booker T. Washington: A Bibliographic Essay," *Journal of Negro Education* XLV, 4 (Fall 1977), 403–18. Some of the most useful scholarly articles on Washington, especially discussing his ideas on business, include Donald J. Calista, "Booker T. Washington: Another Look," *Journal of Negro History* XLIX, 4 (October 1964), 240–55; Emma L. Thornbrough, "More Light on Booker T. Washington and the New York *Age*," *Journal of Negro History* XLIII, 1 (January 1958), 34–49; Emma L. Thornbrough, "Booker T. Washington as Seen by His White Contemporaries," *Journal of Negro History* LIII, 2 (April 1968), 161–82; Emma L. Thornbrough, "The National Afro-American League, 1887–1908," *Journal of Southern History* XXVII (November

1961), 494–512; Lawrence J. Friedman, "Life 'In the Lion's Mouth': Another Look at Booker T. Washington," *Journal of Negro History* LIX, 4 (October 1974), 337–51; John P. Flynn, "Booker T. Washington: Uncle Tom or Wooden Horse," *Journal of Negro History* LIV, 3 (July 1969), 262–74; Francis H. Shaw, "Booker T. Washington and the Future of Black Americans," *Georgia Historical Quarterly* LVI, 2 (Summer 1972), 193–209; Daniel Walden, "The Contemporary Opposition to the Political and Educational Ideas of Booker T. Washington," *Journal of Negro History* XLV, 2 (April 1960), 103–15; Michael L. Goldstein, "Preface to the Rise of Booker T. Washington: A View from New York City of the Demise of Independent Black Politics, 1889–1902," *Journal of Negro History* LXII, 1 (January 1977), 81–99; Melbourne Cummings, "Historical Setting for Booker T. Washington and the Rhetoric of Compromise, 1895," *Journal of Black Studies* VIII, 1 (September 1977), 75–82; Elliott M. Rudwick, "Booker T. Washington's Relations with the National Association for the Advancement of Colored People," *Journal of Negro Education* XXIX, 2 (Spring 1960), 134–44; Booker T. Gardner, "The Educational Contributions of Booker T. Washington," *Journal of Negro Education* XLIV, 4 (Fall 1975), 502–18; Willard B. Gatewood, "Booker T. Washington and the Ulrich Affair," *Journal of Negro History* LV, 1 (January 1970), 29–44, which was also published in *Phylon* XXX, 3 (Fall 1969), 286–302; Manning Marable, "Booker T. Washington and African Nationalism," *Phylon* XXXV, 4 (December 1974), 398–406; Alfred Young, "The Educational Philosophy of Booker T. Washington: A Perspective for Black Liberation," *Phylon* XXXVII, 3 (September 1976), 224–35; August Meier, "Booker T. Washington and the Negro Press: With Special Reference to the *Colored American*," *Journal of Negro History* XXXVIII, 1 (January 1953), 67–90, and his "Booker T. Washington and the Town of Mound Bayou," *Phylon* XV, 4 (1954); Maceo C. Dailey, "Booker T. Washington and the Afro-American Realty Company," *Review of Black Political Economy* VIII (Winter 1978), 184–201; and Herbert Aptheker, "The Washington-DuBois Conference of 1904," *Science and Society* (Fall 1949).

A massive amount of material was written on Washington in the mainstream press during his life and after. A few of those that shed some light on his business and economic attitudes are Charles S. Johnson, "The Social Philosophy of Booker T. Washington," *Opportunity* VI, 4 (April 1928), 102–5, 115; Henry R. Jerkins, "Apostle of Industrial Education," *Opportunity* XVIII, 5 (May 1940), 141–43; W. L. Brown, "Booker T. Washington as a Philosopher," *Negro History Bulletin* XX (1956), 34–37; O. K. Armstrong, "Booker T. Washington—Apostle of Good Will," *Reader's Digest* (February 1947), 25–30; Wesley C. Pugh, "The Inflated Controversy: DuBois vs. Washington," *The Crisis* (April 1974), 132–33; Broadus N. Butler, "Booker T. Washington, W.E.B. DuBois, Black Americans and the NAACP—Another Perspective," *The Crisis* (August-September 1978), 222–30, and his "The Great Debate," *The Crisis* (December 1980), 474–82; Richard M. Ketchum, "Faces from the Past—VIII," *American Heritage* XIII, 6 (October 1962), 11; Eleanor Fishburn and Mildred Sandison Fenner, "Cast Down Your Bucket!" *Negro Digest* (July 1944), 25–29; "The Other Side of Booker T. Washington," *Atlanta Daily World*, February 23, 1979; Benjamin Brawley, "Booker T. Washington and Industrial Education," *Negro Builders and Heroes*, 147–57; W.H. Quick "Booker T. Washington and the Tuskegee Institute," *Negro Stars in All Ages of the World* (1898); Edgar A. Toppin, *Biographical History of Blacks in America* (1969), 437–41; G. F. Richings *Evidences of Progress among Colored People* (1897); Earl E. Thorpe, *Black Historians* (1958), 59–61; *Ebony*, August 1969 and August 1972; and William J. Simmons, *Men of Mark* (1887), 1027–30.

Information on the town and school at Tuskegee can be gotten from Horace Mann Bond, *Negro Education in Alabama: A Study in Cotton and Steel* (New York, 1939); Stephen B. Weeks, *The History of Public School Education in Alabama* (Westport, Conn., 1971); Erwing W. Wadsworth, "A Historical Perspective of Education in Macon County, Alabama, 1836–1967," Ph.D. diss., Auburn University, 1968; Anne Kendrick Walter, *Tuskegee and the Black Belt: A Portrait of a Race* (Richmond, 1944); Pete Daniel, "Black Power in the 1920's: The Case of the Tuskegee Veterans Hospital," *Journal of Southern History* XXXVI (August 1970); Allen W. Jones, "The Role of the Tuskegee Institute in the Education of Black Farmers," *Journal of Negro History* LX (April 1975); James H. Jones, *Bad Blood: The Tuskegee Syphilis Experiment* (New York, 1981); Manning Marable, "Tuskegee and the Politics of Illusion in the New South," *Black Scholar* IX (May 1977); Robert J. Norrell, *Reaping the Whirlwind: The Civil Rights Movement in Tuskegee* (New York, 1985).

The history of the National Negro Business League is covered in John Howard Burrows, "The Necessity of Myth: A History of the National Negro Business League, 1900–1945," Ph.D. diss., Auburn University, 1977; and Louis R. Harlan discusses Washington's role with that organization in "Booker T. Washington and the National Negro Business League," in William G. Shade and Roy C. Herrenkohl, eds., *Seven on Black: Reflections of the Negro Experience in America* (Philadelphia, 1969), 73–91. These works, however, by focusing upon the pronouncements of the national leadership, and upon the undeniably powerful presence of Booker T. Washington, probably have seriously distorted the way in which the NNBL functioned, viewing it almost exclusively as yet another vehicle for the "Tuskegee Machine." That sort of top-down history will be replaced in the near future by the work of historian Kenneth M. Hamilton, who is looking at the records of various local NNBL affiliates. It is expected that his work will demonstrate the greater autonomy enjoyed by the various local leagues. See also, Booker T. Washington, "The Negro in Business," *Gunton's Magazine*, March 1901, 209–19, and his "The National Negro Business League," *The World's Work* IV, 2 (October 1902), 2671–75; Max Bennett Thrasher, "Negro Business Men," *Colored American*, November 1902, 41–44; J.R.E. Lee, "The Negro National Business League," and John E. Bruce, "The Necessity for Business Leagues," *Voice of the Negro*, August 1905, 327–30, 338–39; George M. Newstelle, "A Negro Business League at Work," *Southern Workman* XLIV (January 1915), 43–47; Gustavus Adolphus Steward, "Something New under the Sun," *Opportunity*, January 1925, 20–22; J.R.E. Lee, "Highlights on Early History of the National Negro Business League," *Quarterly Journal* IX (October 1940), 9–13; "The NNBL: Forty Years in Review," *The Crisis*, April 1941, 104–5; and "The National Business League," *Black Enterprise*, June 1972, 37–41. See also William Hughes and Frederick D. Patterson, *Robert Russa Moton of Hampton and Tuskegee* (Chapel Hill, N.C., 1956); and Carl Stanley Matthews, "After Booker T. Washington: The Search for a New Negro Leadership, 1915–1925," Ph.D. diss., University of Virginia, 1971.

For accounts of some of the principal contemporary critics of Washington, see Elliott Rudwick, *W. E. B. DuBois: A Study in Minority Group Leadership* (Philadelphia, 1960); Stephen R. Fox, *The Guardian of Boston: William Monroe Trotter* (New York, 1970); Emma Lou Thornbrough, *T. Thomas Fortune: Militant Journalist* (Chicago, 1972); and Hugh Hawkins, ed., *Booker T. Washington and His Critics* (Lexington, Mass., 1974). It is also helpful to read Du Bois's *Souls of Black Folk* (Chicago, 1903) and *Dusk to Dawn, An Essay toward an Autobiography of a Race Concept* (New York, 1940). Du Bois did alter some of his views of Washington's ideas in "Does the Negro Need Separate

Schools?'' *Journal of Negro Education* IV (July 1935), 328–29. See also Kelly Miller, ''Washington's Policy,'' *Boston Evening Transcript*, September 18 and 19, 1903, collected in *The Making of Black America*, vol. II, edited by August Meier and Elliott Rudwick (New York, 1971), 119–30, for a brilliant discussion of Washington's ideas.

Wormley, James (January 16, 1819–October 18, 1884). Hotelkeeper: Wormley's Hotel, Washington, D.C. Washington, D.C. is reknowned for its elite African-American community. Considered the oldest, most prestigious, and most cultured, it has stood as a model of black success in white America. At the very apex of that black social pyramid is the Wormley family, and it was the business success and resulting wealth of James Wormley that largely made that eminence possible.

James Wormley was the son of Peter Leigh Wormley and Mary Wormley. They had been born in Virginia, where they lived for a number of years as free people on a plantation before coming to Washington in 1814. Peter had served for a number of years as a coachman on the plantation, and in the 1820s he became the proprietor of a livery establishment in the nation's capital. His stable was located on Pennsylvania Avenue between 14th and 15th streets near the famous Willard Hotel. It was a prosperous business, and Peter Wormley was able to raise a family of five children, all of whom found some measure of success in the city. It was James, however, who laid the basis for real family wealth.

Little is known of James Wormley's early years, but it is clear that at a young age he began working as a hack driver for his father, transporting visitors to and from Washington's major hotels. It was not long before James Wormley purchased his own carriage and went into business for himself. While in this service, James met a number of the most distinguished public figures, an experience that was to serve him well in later years. Wormley, however, soon became restless and gave up his hack business to become a steward aboard a U.S. ship commanded by Allen McLane. After several years of this, Wormley worked as a steward on a number of the elegant Mississippi River boats. This experience in the West made Wormley susceptible to the lure of the California gold rush, and in 1849 he joined with thousands of others in emigrating to the gold fields there. Failing to strike it rich, he returned to Washington, where he became a steward at the eminent Metropolitan Club.

Shortly before the outbreak of the Civil War, Wormley started his own catering business on I Street near 15th, next door to a candy store run by Anna Thompson, whom he had married in 1841. Although Wormley's was destined to be the most successful and famous, it was hardly the only catering or hotel establishment in Washington run by blacks. It was, indeed, a very popular form of business enterprise, one in which African-Americans were assumed by whites to have a ''natural aptitude,'' and one, further, that maintained the old service relationship between blacks and whites which had existed from plantation times. Allowing blacks to become wealthy and successful, these occupations were, during most of the nineteenth century, considered servile by whites. Wormley, however, brought a measure of dignity and pride to his operation which, in turn, brought him fame from both whites and blacks.

By the mid–1860s Wormley had extended his catering business to include a restaurant on the premises at 314 I Street, North, an establishment that quickly became popular with many of the city's political elite. It was an especially attractive watering hole for many of Washington's Radical Republicans, and it was there that Wormley formed close associations with men like Senator Charles Sumner (after whom he named one of his sons), and Vice President Henry Wilson. Wormley's success as a caterer and restaurateur attracted the attention of Reverdy Johnson, a bumbling, blustering man who had just been appointed ambassador to the Court of St. James. Johnson persuaded Wormley to accompany him to England as his steward, leaving behind his wife and four children. It was a rather unusual decision, but it did much to secure the future success of James Wormley.

Johnson had decided that the English were far too stiff and cold, and that what was needed to "warm them up" was some American food, especially his favorite dish of diamondback terrapin from the Chesapeake Bay and the Potomoc River. It was Wormley's job as embassy steward to prepare these terrapin. It was a difficult task for Wormley to transport the terrapin across the Atlantic and then maintain them in good health until they were eaten. He was able to do this successfully, however, and then supervised the preparation of the dishes to the delight of Johnson's English guests. This meal and those succeeding it cemented Wormley's reputation as a connoisseur of fine foods, and greatly increased the demand for his services in Washington. Before returning home, however, he stopped off in Paris to learn yet more about food preparation and gracious service. Thus armed, Wormley returned to Washington, where he acquired a building on the southwest corner of H and 15th streets. With his older building serving as an annex, in 1871 he opened what came to be known as Wormley's Hotel. When Wormley ran into some monetary problems during the early going, and was unable to meet the terms of the sale, an arrangement was worked out with Congressman Samuel Hooper of Massachusetts, who purchased the building and rented it out to Wormley.

The location of the hotel was ideal, since it was near Lafayette Square, the White House, the Treasury Department, and the Navy Department. Immediately popular because of Wormley's political and social connections, and because of his notable reputation as a result of the "culinary diplomacy" in England, Wormley cemented that popularity with an elaborate and refined menu, excellent service, and gracious rooms. Wormley's Hotel soon became a favorite of congressmen and others in need of temporary lodging in the nation's capital. It also served as the Washington home for Vice President Schuyler Colfax, Assistant Secretary of State John Hay, and Senator Roscoe Conkling of New York. Wormley's Hotel was also very popular with many foreign dignitaries, the German legation was housed there during the 1880s, and members of the diplomatic corps of both France and Chile also resided there. During 1889 and 1890, delegates to the Pan American Congress also lived at Wormley's.

The hotel building, a five-storied structure, had offices and dining rooms on the first floor, and parlors and sleeping apartments on the upper floors. The halls and corridors were reputed to be wide and spacious, and the rooms were large and handsomely furnished. It could accommodate 150 guests and had all of the newest improvements, such as elevators, telephones, and electric bells. There were also a number of special touches. When his friend, Charles Sumner, died, Wormley purchased the furnishings from Sumner's home and placed them in the hotel in a ''Sumner Parlor.'' The basement of the hotel had a bar which was widely known for the excellence of its wines and liquors, and there was also a first-class barber shop located there. In 1876 the room charge at the Wormley Hotel was $5 a day.

The most famous and significant event in the history of Wormley's Hotel occurred in February 1877 between representatives of Rutherford B. Hayes and a group of southerners led by Major E. A. Burke, which resulted in the ''Wormley Agreement,'' known in the history books as the Compromise of 1877. Briefly, the presidential election of 1876 resulted in a constitutional crisis, in which the Democratic candidate, Samuel J. Tilden, was one electoral vote shy of the 185 needed for election; Hayes had 165 electoral votes; and 20 votes, 19 of them from three southern states still under the control of Radical Reconstruction, were under dispute. A commission was established to iron out the issue, and a compromise was reached whereby Hayes was to receive all 20 disputed electoral votes, giving him the election, and, in return, he would agree to withdraw the last of the federal troops from southern states. Although the basics of the compromise had been worked out earlier, it was at Wormley's Hotel on February 26 that the agreement was reiterated, and southerners were given further assurances concerning troop withdrawal. It is ironic, indeed, that the decision that signaled the abandonment of blacks in the South was reached at a hotel owned by an African-American, and that the subsequent agreement would bear his name. Wormley, however, took no part in it, and probably had no knowledge of those proceedings.

James Wormley continued to run his hotel and catering business profitably and successfully until his death in Boston in 1884. At that time his son, James T. Wormley, assumed management of the enterprise and ran it until he was undone by the financial crisis of the 1890s. In 1893 he sold the hotel to Charles E. Gibbs, who had served as manager of the famous Ebbitt House in Washington. Gibbs continued to operate it under the name of Wormley's Hotel until 1897, when it became the Colonial Hotel. Nine years later, the structure was torn down to make way for the Union Trust Building. When he died, James Wormley left an estate estimated to be well in excess of $100,000. This fortune, even when diminished somewhat by his son's financial problems in the 1890s, allowed Wormley's progeny to live in comfort, perhaps even luxury, for generations.

By the time of his death, James Wormley was one of the most revered African-

Americans in a city noted for the prestige and brilliance of its black population. He was depicted in an oil painting at the bedside of the dying President Abraham Lincoln, and he was an honorary pallbearer at Lincoln's funeral. He was also an honorary pallbearer at Vice-President Henry Wilson's funeral in 1875, and he marched in the black honor guard with Frederick Douglass at the funeral of Charles Sumner. At the time of his own death, the *Washington Star* called Wormley "one of the most remarkable colored men in the country." This status was attested to at his own funeral. All flags at Washington's hotels were flown at half mast on that day, and among his pallbearers were the white owners of the Arlington Hotel, the Ebbitt House, and the Riggs House. Another white pallbearer was the ex-mayor of the city, James G. Barrett. Among the eminent blacks were John F. Cook, head of the finest school for African-Americans in the city, and ex-Congressman Blanche K. Bruce.

James Wormley was a businessman, and hardly a radical or an activist in any sense. Yet, like so many other African-American business leaders of the time, he combined a fierce racial pride and dignity with his business acumen. Francis Grimke, a prominent black minister, said that Wormley "demanded respect from others and respected himself." This was shown most graphically in his reaction to Frederick Douglass's appointment on the United States Commission to Haiti. Although Douglass was a close friend, Wormley was highly critical of him for accepting a position as a "token black" on the commission, in which the real authority was given to a white man. Wormley claimed that, had President Ulysses Grant offered him this position, he would have turned it down. James Wormley was honored soon after his death in 1884 with the erection of a public school in his name on Prospect Avenue between 33rd and 34th streets, which was used for that purpose until the 1950s. Although merely a dim memory of a distant past 100 years after his death, James Wormley was a giant in Washington's eminent black community in the years of the Civil War and Reconstruction.

Sources

No family or personal papers of James Wormley or his family are available, nor is there a full-length biography of him. Information on Wormley must be garnered from a number of secondary sources. There is a good short biography of him by Rayford Logan in the *Dictionary of American Negro Biography* (1982), which is based in large measure on an article by Charles E. Wynes, "James Wormley of the Wormley Hotel Agreement," *Centennial Review* (Winter 1975), 397–401. Another good short biography is in Afro-American Bicentennial Corporation, *A Study of Historic Sites in the District of Columbia of Special Significance to Afro-Americans* (Washington, D.C., 1974). There is also information in the *Dictionary of American Biography* (1936), vol. 10, series 2, 534–35; John Clagatt Proctor, "Figures of a Vanished Past Linked with 15th Street," *Washington Star*, December 27, 1936; and W. S. Robinson, *Historical Negro Biographies*, 146–47. Other aspects of Wormley's life, and especially his heirs, are considered in C. G. Woodson, "The Wormley Family," *Negro History Bulletin* XI, 4 (January 1948), 75–84; "Washington's Negro Elite," *Look*, April 6, 1965; Geneva C. Turner, "For Whom Is Your School Named?" *Negro History Bulletin* XXIII, 8 (May 1960), 185; and Gerri Major, *Black Society* (1976), 40, 72, 171–72, 232–34, 401.

Wright, Richard Robert, Sr. (May 16, 1853–July 2, 1947) and **Richard Robert Wright, Jr.** (April 16, 1878–December 12, 1967). Bankers, businessmen, publishers, religious and educational leaders and trade association officials: Citizens and Southern Bank and Trust Company; *Weekly Journal of Progress*; *Weekly Sentinel*; and National Association of Negro Bankers. There hardly could be more unlikely candidates for business success than Richard Wright and his son. Both were highly educated intellectuals and academics, both were college presidents, and one was the bishop of a church, the editor of a national religious magazine, and an author of an armful of academic tomes. Furthermore, their banking enterprise was started almost as a whim, when the elder Wright was sixty-eight years of age. Yet they became among the most successful and important African-American business leaders in twentieth-century America.

The elder Wright's life was the stuff of which legends are made. He was born a slave on a plantation near Dalton, Georgia. His father, Robert Waddell, was the family coachman, while his mother, Harriet, was a house servant. When Wright was two years old, his father ran away to free territory, and he and his mother were taken to Cuthbert, Georgia, where she married Alexander Wright. His stepfather also escaped during the Civil War and joined the Union Army. After the war, Harriet moved to Atlanta to run a boardinghouse, and young Richard was enrolled in the Storrs School of the American Missionary Association. It was there that Wright's charmed life began. General Oliver O. Howard, head of the Freedman's Bureau, spoke at the school in 1868. At the end of his talk, he asked the children, "What shall I tell the children up north about you?" Richard raised his hand, stood up, and replied, "Tell them, General, we're rising." This dramatic incident inspired the poem, "Howard at Atlanta," by John Greenleaf Whittier.

A year later, Wright was chosen to attend the preparatory school of the newly established Atlanta University. To help finance his education, he taught during the summers. While teaching in Hannahatchee, Georgia, in 1875, he received a threat from the Ku Klux Klan to "leave the county in 24 hours or we will give your d—n carcass to the buzzards because we understand you are in favor of the Civil Rights Bill." Wright stayed on, and he graduated as valedictorian of Atlanta University's first class in 1876. Later that year, he married Lydia E. Howard of Columbus, Georgia, and the young couple moved to Cuthbert, Georgia, where Wright became principal of an elementary school. But his boundless energy could not be contained in that job. Wright also found time to organize farmer's cooperatives and the state's first county fair for blacks. In 1878 he called for a convention of Georgia's black teachers, organized them into the Georgia State Teacher's Association, and served as the first president. During this same period, Wright began to publish the *Weekly Journal of Progress*, later renamed the *Weekly Sentinel*. The following year, Wright went to Augusta, Georgia, where he founded Ware High School, the first public high school for blacks in the state. There, he taught the younger brother and sister of John Hope, cementing an alliance with another powerful black leader.

In 1879 Wright was chosen to represent Georgia's African-Americans at the First National Conference of Colored Men in the United States, held in Nashville. There he made a favorable impression on John Roy Lynch and P.B.S. Pinchback,* two important black Reconstruction politicians. That association paved Wright's way for his participation in Republican politics. The Georgia Republican party during Reconstruction had a large black voting base, but it was controlled by whites. In 1880 Wright was one of a group of aggressive young blacks who led an insurgency against this white domination. The revolt was temporarily successful, and Wright was chosen as an alternate delegate to the Republican National Convention. Although the black insurrection was soon rolled back, Wright was able to continue as a member of the state Central Committee, and he was active in party affairs for the balance of the century. He was also chosen as a delegate to national conventions through 1896. In return, Wright received a number of patronage positions, many of which he declined. One patronage job he did accept was the presidency of the newly established Georgia State Industrial College in 1891. He was, however, also the logical choice for the position, having spent some fifteen years as a teacher and administrator.

The increasingly conservative Georgia state legislature had cut off state funds to Atlanta University in 1887, but after passage of the Second Morrill Act in 1890, they passed a bill establishing a land-grant college for black students in Athens, Georgia. The bill mandated that blacks be given a vocational, as opposed to a "classical" education, which most white legislators considered unwise for "inherently inferior" blacks. When white citizens protested placing the school in Athens, it was moved to Savannah, and Wright was appointed its first president.

Wright was to have a difficult time during his thirty-year tenure as president of the college. He was forced to do constant battle with Peter W. Meldrim, chairman of the white board of trustees of the institution. Meldrim and most Georgia whites wanted Georgia State Industrial College to teach only "practical" arts to their black students, and they opposed any attempt to provide them with traditional academic subjects. In one speech, Meldrim said, "I do not believe in educating you niggras for things you cannot get. We must educate the best possible Negro and not a bad imitation of the white man." Then, too, the black students who entered the college were poorly prepared, and Wright had to establish a preparatory school for them to make them ready for college-level courses. It was seven years before the school had its first graduate—Richard R. Wright, Jr.—son of the president.

Recognizing these difficulties, many of which he shared with the heads of other black colleges, Wright, Sr., in 1901 brought together heads of these colleges and formed the National Association of Teachers in Colored Schools. Yet Wright could not seem to shake Georgia State Industrial out of its academic torpor. In 1910 W.E.B. Du Bois conducted a survey of black colleges, and the school was given a "poor" rating. It also came under fire in a survey conducted by Phelps-Stokes in 1916, and in response the legislature made a gesture to improve facilities. When, however, a survey by the federal government in 1921 found that Georgia State Industrial was still inadequate in both plant and equipment, Wright resigned his post. It is not clear to what extent the fault for this situation lay with Wright, and to what extent the blame was to be laid on the board of trustees and the legislature.

Over the years, Wright became an apostle of Booker T. Washington's* ideas of self-help and industrial education, and these had been put into practice at Georgia State Industrial. As part of that program Wright counseled his students and the broader black community in Savannah to participate in business activities. Two years before he was appointed president of the college, Wright gave a talk at the Beach Institute in Savannah in which he advised blacks to remain in the South. "[O]ur people are rising and the day will come when this southland will be theirs." Less than two years after his arrival in the city, he helped organize the Negro Civic Improvement League. This group purchased land for the erection of a home for the aged, and Wright also set up a home for delinquent African-American girls and introduced the first probation office to the city. He used his political influence to persuade the city to improve living conditions for poor blacks.

By the late 1890s, though, it was clear that blacks, even prominent political figures like Wright, were going to have little influence on the political decisions of Georgia and the South, and Wright began increasingly to turn to Washington's economic approach. Wright, in conjunction with black businessmen's associations, fraternal societies, and social welfare agencies, propounded that doctrine. Black banks, insurance companies, and other businesses were the tangible results of that approach in Savannah and elsewhere. Wright also increasingly turned his attention to business activities.

While still president of the college, Wright became involved in several commercial enterprises, particularly extensive real estate dealings in the Savannah area. Wright's entrance into the world of banking, though, came in a unique way. His eldest daughter, Julia, had gone downtown to the Citizens and Southern Bank to transact some business. The bank officer with whom she dealt called her "Julia" instead of "Miss Wright." When she requested that he call her "Miss" as he did his white customers, the officer screamed, "I am a white man and I call no nigger Miss." The two had an altercation, even exchanging blows. When the senior Wright went to the bank president (a man who had long professed to be his friend) for an apology, it was denied. At that point, in 1920, Wright, according to his own recollection, said, "I'm going to organize a bank where anybody may come and be treated like a lady or a gentleman." He contacted his son in Philadelphia, and plans were made to organize a bank in that city.

Richard R. Wright, Jr., in his autobiography, gave his estimation of why his father was so determined to enter the world of banking at a time when most men are retiring:

My father had lived nearly thirty years at Savannah, thought he had the respect of all citizens, and had been lauded time and again as an example for Negro-Americans in education, thrift, loyalty and honor. He had the professed friendship of the 'best Southern whites' but now not one was willing to help him . . . [my father] had made hundreds of speeches to the colored population to support the nation in war, because he felt that this was indeed a war to make the world safe for democracy. Now his own daughter could be insulted and physically assaulted and there was no redress.

Father and son joined together to create one of the largest, most successful black banks in the North.

Richard Wright, Jr., had a life nearly as extraordinary as his father's. Born in Cuthbert, Georgia, he attended the Haines Institute in Augusta and was the first graduate of Georgia State Industrial College in 1898. Deciding to continue his education, he went to the University of Chicago in 1898 and earned a bachelor of divinity degree in 1901 and the A.M. degree in 1904. He then went to the University of Pennsylvania, where he received his Ph.D. in 1911. During this same period, he also studied at the University of Berlin, 1903 to 1904, and the University of Leipzig, in 1904.

From 1901 to 1903 young Wright was an instructor of Hebrew and New Testament Greek at Payne Theological Seminary, and after he returned from Europe, he served as a pastor of churches in Pennsylvania and Illinois until 1909. He served as editor of the *Christian Recorder*, the official organ of the American Episcopal Methodist Church, from 1909 to 1936, and manager of the AME Book Concern from 1909 to 1912 and from 1916 to 1920. He also served as pastor of several other AME churches in the Philadelphia area. It was during this same period that Wright began to gain some valuable business experience.

According to his own account, Wright, Jr., "learned something about business" as field secretary to the Armstrong Commission and the 8th Ward Settlement Building and Loan Association. But his first real business job was as the manager of the AME Book Concern, a position he held until 1912, when the recession of that year forced him to begin to manufacture beauty products as a part-time job. During this same time, Wright completed his doctoral dissertation at Penn, writing his thesis on "The Negro in Pennsylvania, a Study in Social and Economic History." In his research, he conducted a survey of the deposits in white banks by black depositors, and the results, showing some $4 million on deposit, came as "a revelation to bankers and blacks." As a result, a group of blacks organized the People's Savings Bank in October 1907, with Wright as secretary. The bank lasted more than a decade before closing, as a result of its inability to find competent personnel to run its operations.

Several years later, Wright became involved in the real estate business in association with E. C. Brown, head of the important Brown and Stevens Bank in Philadelphia. Because of its close proximity to the South and the heavy concentration of munitions and shipbuilding industries in the city, Philadelphia became an attractive magnet for the exceptionally large number of southern migrants who surged north during World War I. Wright and Brown began to purchase homes in "changing" neighborhoods, selling them to recently arrived black migrants from the South. As this proved successful, Wright moved out on his own, ultimately owning about fifty houses in the neighborhood between 48th and 49th streets, Brown and Fairmount avenues. Wright held these until the early 1930s, when he went to Wilberforce. Young Wright had also become a political force in the city, serving as a member of the black "kitchen cabinet" of Mayor J. Hampton Moore.

In 1920 the elder Wright came to Philadelphia, where he and his son decided to start a private bank, hoping later on to sell stock in an incorporated state bank. This venture served the needs of both men well. The elder Wright wanted revenge and a new career; the younger Wright was keenly aware of the need for capital for mortgages and businesses in Philadelphia's burgeoning black community. For capital, Richard Wright, Jr., put up $11,200; his father put up $5,600; and a daughter, Lillian, who was Wright, Jr.'s, secretary, put in $200. Richard, Sr., was named president; Richard, Jr., secretary treasurer; and Lillian Wright, teller of the new institution. They rented the first floor of a building at 1849 South Street and opened the bank on September 15, 1920, receiving about $1,000 in deposits that day. The elder Wright then returned to Savannah, promising to resign from the college at the end of the school year and come to Philadelphia to take over the bank if it was successful. It should be noted that his job at Georgia State Industrial was on tenterhooks anyway at this time. In any event, in June 1921, he resigned his position of thirty years and moved to Philadelphia at age sixty-eight to start a new career in banking.

It was now time to incorporate the bank as a joint stock venture, and Wright had to raise capital of $125,000 to do so. He used the vast contacts he had built up over the years to get this backing. He traveled widely and persuaded blacks, rich and poor, in Texas, Georgia, Louisiana, and other southern states to invest in his bank. It took two years to sell the stock at $100 a share, but they were finally successful and opened the Citizens and Southern Bank and Trust Company on January 15, 1924. Besides the two Wrights, members of the board of directors of the bank included several important black ministers, *Philadelphia Tribune* editor Eugene Washington Rhodes,[*] merchant tailor Frank H. Hopkins, and builder L. B. Thompson. The ministers were particularly important because their presence gave the bank some legitimacy and respect among the city's black population. Nonetheless, it was a decade-long upward struggle for the Wrights, battling against its reputation as a "storefront bank," run by a schoolteacher and a preacher. Most of its deposits during these years were small, representing the savings of recent migrants from the South, as few native Philadelphia blacks trusted the institution.

Whereas the city's other black bank, Brown and Stevens, was primarily a commercial bank dealing in large real estate ventures and with commercial establishments, the Wrights positioned Citizens and Southern as a community bank appealing to the small depositor. Still an educator at heart, the elder Wright believed he had to teach his small depositors the values of thrift and savings and protect them from unscrupulous businessmen of both races. The Wrights publicized the bank by taking out advertisements in the local black newspapers, distributing advertising cards, and speaking in churches and private homes. To attract working-class customers, the bank stayed open until 9 P.M., and emphasized a policy of "POLITENESS, EFFICIENCY, AND CURTESY [*sic*]," on its advertising cards. As Charles Hardy has stated, "The Wrights used Citizens and Southern to provide working class blacks the skills to make wise investments and build capital."

In order to enhance the credibility of his bank with both the black and white communities, the elder Wright selected three white corresponding banks with which he maintained excellent relations. He also kept two lawyers, one black and one white, to cover any situation that might emerge. To further improve relations, Wright joined the Pennsylvania Bankers Association in 1922 and the American Bankers Association in 1923. When he found that the needs of black bankers were not fully addressed by these organizations, he founded and became first president of the National Association of Negro Bankers (later the National Bankers Association) in 1926.

By this time, Citizens and Southern was the first black bank in the country chartered to do a title insurance business, and it had also become a full-service financial institution with a trust department and a title and real estate department. The latter helped the Wrights to assist black home buyers by protecting their deposit money and providing full information about closing costs, and by presiding at the closing of sales. To provide competent management for the bank, Wright sent his daughter to Wharton School of Finance, and then hired Charles Ealy from Jacksonville, Florida, as manager of daily operations. Ealy, a godsend to the young firm, remained with it throughout its existence. Citizens and Southern practiced extremely conservative lending policies, overly conservative in the minds of some, but it did provide stability during the 1920s, and this ultimately allowed the bank to survive the Depression of the 1930s when many other black banks failed.

Two of Philadelphia's early black banks failed during the 1920s, and Citizens and Southern benefited from their troubles. The most dramatic collapse was that of the Brown and Stevens Bank in 1925, a concern that enjoyed an almost mythic regard in the city's black community. Although this failure tended to undermine confidence in black businesses of all kinds, and Citizens and Southern had to weather its own scandal in 1924 when its trust officer, John W. Parks, was jailed for embezzling bank funds, the Wrights' bank continued to prosper. This was accomplished especially through a high-profile public relations campaign in conjunction with the *Philadelphia Tribune*. The paper's publisher, E. Washington Rhodes, was chosen trust officer to succeed Parks, and his paper did much to burnish the image of Citizens and Southern.

The other bank failure was that of Keystone Bank, which had opened in 1922. Troubled with mismanagement from the beginning, the Pennsylvania State Banking Department approached Wright about taking over the firm. Wright determined that Keystone was small enough and solvent enough to take over its deposit accounts and assets. The "consolidation" took place in January 1927, and the new bank became known as the Greater Citizens and Southern Bank and Trust Company. Citizens and Southern continued to grow, and by 1928 it was one of the few black banks to specialize in commercial loans, with $100,000 in working capital and $500,000 in assets. The bank weathered the stockmarket crash in 1929, and it was one of the 100 banks to reopen in 1933 when President Franklin Roosevelt ended the bank holiday. In 1936, Abram Harris said that "it is perhaps one of the strongest and best managed of Negro financial institutions in existence. . . . Perhaps it is the type of bank best suited to the needs of the Negro community."

With the coming of World War II, the decade-long depression came to an end and massive numbers of southern blacks again began pouring into Philadelphia to take advantage of job opportunities in the war industries. This further stimulated the growth of Citizens and Southern. At the time of his death in 1947, Wrights, Sr.'s, bank had over $3 million in deposits. Despite his advanced age, running the bank hardly absorbed all of the elder Wright's abundant energies. In 1935 he organized the Haitian Coffee and Products Trading Company, which imported and sold coffee until the outbreak of World War II. He was also instrumental in getting the U.S. Post Office to issue a commemorative stamp honoring Booker T. Washington. Issued in 1940, it was the first U.S. stamp to honor a black. Wright himself received a host of honors throughout his lifetime, and his funeral in Philadelphia attracted 1,200 mourners, including Charles C. Spaulding* and J. Finley Wilson.

After the elder Wright died in 1947, he was succeeded as president of Citizens and Southern by another son, Emanuel C. Wright. Five years later, E. C. Wright was, in turn, replaced by Reverend W. C. Williamson, pastor of White Rock Baptist Church and a longtime friend of the family. That sparked a long-term struggle for control of the bank. A number of white politicians tried to take over the bank, and to counter this threat, Richard Wright, Jr., moved back to Philadelphia in 1954 to assume the presidency, with his sister Harriet as vice president. After two years, however, Wright found that he could not perform his duties as bishop of the AME church diocese in the Northeast and be a banker at the same time, and he resigned from the presidency.

Richard Wright, Jr., had gone to Wilberforce University as president in 1932, accepting $268,000 in university debt as his own obligation. Wright remained at Wilberforce for four years, when he was made a bishop in the AME church. Upon his nomination, Wright then accepted assignment to South Africa for the next four years. After his return to the United States in 1948, Wright was assigned to the bishopric in Kentucky and Tennessee, and he served in a succession of dioceses until 1956. He was then appointed historian of the AME church. He founded the R. R. Wright, Jr., School of Religion and the Crogman Community Clinic in South Africa, and he built some fifty churches and schools. He was also a prolific author, having written *The Encyclopedia of African Methodism*, *Church Financing*, *Handbook of the AME Church*, *The Negro in Pennsylvania*, and a host of other books and articles. He married Charlotte Crogman, daughter of Dr. W. H. Crogman, president of Clark College, in 1909.

The younger Wright reported that "[w]e searched a year and a half for a

Negro-American to succeed me and found no one. . . . We sold a majority of our stock to a group of colored and whites. . . . Myron Freudberg was made president, my sister Harriet remained vice-president, and I was still a member of the board.'' Under this new management, the bank underwent significant expansion, opening two new branches, one in West Philadelphia, and one in the center city. What had started as a black bank in the heart of the African-American ghetto was rapidly becoming, in Wright, Jr.'s, words, ''the most thoroughly integrated bank in the United States.'' Neither Freudberg nor S. Harry Gelfand, another of the new officers in 1956 were black, and of the ten employees, four were white.

Under the new leadership, Citizens and Southern began to grow more rapidly. The new management also changed the nature of the bank's business. Prior to 1956, its portfolio was almost entirely in U.S. government securities, home mortgages, and church loans. As a result, safety and liquidity were high, but profits were either low or nonexistent. By the early 1960s, however, corporate bonds, consumer loans, and commercial loans, all of which paid a higher return, made up a much larger part of the portfolio. The bank also established its own charge plan—the Citizens Charge Plan—to be used at some 250 stores throughout the city and suburbs. As a result, the bank for the first time was serving the needs of small business, consumers, and small industry, regardless of race. The new policy appeared to be successful, as deposits rose to over $5.5 million by 1966.

Things began unraveling for the bank in the late 1960s. Gelfand succeeded Freudberg as president in 1961, and he, in turn, was succeeded by Sander L. Field, who became chairman and principal stockholder in 1968. Field led the bank to the brink of collapse within a year, as it was caught up in a web of corruption and financial chicanery. He was forced to resign his chairmanship and sell his stock. When he did that, the state district attorney dropped charges against him. By this point, however, it hardly mattered to the black community of Philadelphia. None of the new officers was black, and Citizens Bank, as it was by then called, was no longer an African-American bank in any respect. Citizens and Southern was an extraordinary success story, and the Wright family was an authentic black version of fulfillment of the promise of the American Dream, but in the end it made little difference to African-Americans in Philadelphia. The city's massive black population remained largely poor and lived in substandard housing, and there was no black bank in the city to perform the community services for them that Major Wright had developed in the 1920s.

One of Major Wright's most quoted sayings as bank president was, ''No matter how little you make, save something.'' Perhaps the most fitting testimonial to what he accomplished came from the poor African-Americans he encouraged in this way. One of the bank's most enthusiastic early depositors was a bespectacled cook. From her meager earnings she put aside a small amount each week, which she brought to Citizens and Southern with her bankbook. This was a time, it is important to remember, when few banks would accept the tiny transactions of poor blacks. Finally, she had saved $125, enough to make a down payment on a small home. Coming into the bank one day, she could not restrain her enthusiasm for the elder Wright: "What y'all chillun doing here? Sho' better treat the President of this City Southern Bank right. Cause he done stop me from paying rent. I eats and sleeps, and boards under my own vine an' fig tree." When she passed away, she had over $200 on deposit at Citizens and Southern Bank and Trust.

Sources

Any papers of Wright father and son which may exist are in family hands and not available to researchers. There are scattered letters between Wright and Booker T. Washington covering the period from 1899 to 1912 in the Booker T. Washington Papers, Library of Congress. There is a book-length, informal biography of Richard R. Wright, Sr., by Elizabeth Ross Haynes, *The Black Boy of Atlanta* (Boston: Edinboro Publications, 1952). There are solid short biographies of him by Andrew Buni in *Dictionary of American Biography* Supplement 4, and James G. Spady in *Dictionary of American Negro Biography* (1982). Obituaries appeared in the *New York Times*, July 3, 1947; and *Journal of Negro History* XXXII No. 4, October 1947, 529–30; *Newsweek*, July 14, 1947, 44; *Time*, July 14, 1947, 76; *School and Society*, July 12, 1947, 25; *Savannah Morning News*, July 3, 1947; *New Yorker*, July 5, 1947, 16–17; and *Atlanta Constitution*, July 6, 1947. Extensive articles on Wright were done in *Ebony*, November 1945, 43ff.; and *Atlanta Constitution and Journal*, February 10, 1974.

Information on Wright, Sr.'s, early career as an educator can be found in June O. Patten, "Major Richard Robert Wright, Sr. and Black Higher Education in Georgia, 1880–1920," Ph.D. diss., University of Chicago, 1980; Clarence A. Bacote, *The Story of Atlanta University: A Century of Service, 1865–1965* (1969); Ridgeley Torrence, *The Story of John Hope* (1948); August Meier, *Negro Thought in America, 1880–1915* (1963); James G. Spady, *Umoja: Afro American Journal* (1975), 11–17; *Savannah*, December 1972, 26–27; Paul Allen Stewart, "How Georgia State Remained a College," *Negro Digest*, June 1949, 7–8; and Willard Range, *The Rise and Progress of the Negro Colleges of Georgia, 1865–1949* (1951).

There is a host of newspaper clippings either about Wright, Sr., or written by him. Many of these can be found in the Peabody Collection at Hampton University, where they are available on microfilm. Mostly from black newspapers from 1900 to 1915, they concern his activities as a college president and community leader. There are also items in the *Savannah Morning News* and *Savannah Tribune*, the latter a black newspaper, during Wright's years in that city. The files of the *Philadelphia Evening Bulletin* from 1969 to 1971 have a number of important articles dealing with the crisis in Citizens and Southern during that time. There are also scattered articles over the years in that paper dealing with both Wrights and their bank. The morgue files of that paper are available at the Urban Archives at Temple University. Abram Harris has a short description of the bank in his *The Negro as Capitalist* (1936), 143; and *Opportunity* also had a small article on it in September 1924. Charles Ashley Hardy III, in his Ph.D. dissertation, "Race and Opportunity: Black Philadelphia during the Era of the Great Migration, 1916–1930," Temple University, 1989, 331–70, has an excellent description and analysis of Citizens and Southern Bank and the dissertation overall provides superb background information on the growth of the black community in Philadelphia.

Biographical information on Richard Wright, Jr., can be gotten from obituaries in *New York Times*, December 14, 1967; *Jet*, December 28, 1967; Earl E. Thorp, *Black Historians*

(1958), 164–165; Clement Richardson's *National Cyclopedia of the Colored Race* (1919), 522. He wrote an autobiography entitled *Eighty Seven Years behind the Black Curtain: An Autobiography* (Philadelphia: Rare Book Company, 1965).

Both Wrights were active authors during their lifetimes, but the son's writings were far more significant. The principal publication on business by the elder Wright is his "Negro Banking or Banking by Negroes," in *The Crisis*, April 1941, 112. Another source for the elder Wright's ideas is *Radio Speeches of Major R. R. Wright, Sr.*, compiled by his daughter, Harriet Beecher Stowe Lemon (Philadelphia: Farmer Press, 1949). Important writings by Wright, Jr., are his *The Negro in Pennsylvania: A Study in Economic History* (1912) and "The Economic Condition of Negroes in the North: Negroes in Business in the North," *Southern Workman* XXXVIII, 1 (January 1909). He also contributed "One Hundred Negro Steel Workers," to *Wage Earning Pittsburgh*, vol. 6 of the famous *The Pittsburgh Survey*, edited by Paul U. Kellogg (New York: Survey Associates, 1914). Most of the writings by both men are difficult to obtain, but the Charles A. Blockson Collection at Temple University has many of them.

Y

Yates, Clayton R. (see Blayton, Jesse B., Lorimer D. Milton, and Clayton R. Yates).

BUSINESS LEADERS BY PLACE OF BIRTH

Alabama
 Gaston, A. G.—Demopolis
Arkansas
 Gates, C. W.—Moscow
 Gillespie, F. L.—Osceola
 Johnson, J. H.—Arkansas City
 Shaw, P. W.—Little Rock
California
 Houston, N. O.—San Jose
Connecticut
 Nail, J. E.—New London
Delaware
 Fitzgerald, R. B.—New Castle
Florida
 Amos, W. Jr.,—Tallahassee
Georgia
 Abbott, R. S.—St. Simons
 Beavers, G. A., Jr.—Atlanta
 Browne, W. W.—Habershaw County
  (s)
 Gibson, T. K., Sr.—Macon
 Gibson, T. K., Jr.—Atlanta
 Herndon, A. F.—Walton County (s)
 Herndon, N. B.—Atlanta
 Kennedy, W. J., Jr.—Andersonville
 Pace, H. H.—Covington

Pinchback, P.B.S.—Macon
Russell, H. J.—Atlanta
Sengstacke, J.H.H.—Savannah
Wright, R. R., Sr.—Dalton (s)
Wright, R. R., Jr.—Cuthbert
Illinois
 Burrell, T. J.—Chicago
 Gardner, E. G.—Chicago
 Gidron, R. D.—Chicago
 Johnson, A. W.—East St. Louis
 Travis, D. J.—Chicago
 Turnbo-Malone, A. M.—Metropolis
Iowa
 Alexander, A. A.—Ottumwa
Louisiana
 Antoine, C. C.—New Orleans
 Bartholomew, J. M.—New Orleans
 Boutte, A. J.—Lake Charles
 Cohen, W.—New Orleans
 Davis, W. D.—Lisbon
 DeJoie, E. B.—St. John the Baptist
  Parish
 Durnford, A.—New Orleans
 Fuller, S. B.—Monroe
 Geddes, J. P.—New Orleans
 Lafon, T.—New Orleans

N.B. (s) indicates person was born into slavery.

Lewis, J., Jr.—New Orleans

Misshore, W. J.—New Orleans

Overton, A.—Monroe (s)

Walker, S. B.—Delta

Maryland

Lewis, R. F.—Baltimore

Nail, J. B.—Baltimore

Massachussetts

Payton, P. A.—Westfield

Michigan

Binga, J.—Detroit

Gordy, B., Jr.—Detroit

Mississippi

Banks, C.—Clarksdale

Boyd, R. B.—Nexubee County (s)

Church, R. R.—Holly Springs (s)

Dickerson, E. B.—Canton

Johnson, G.—Richton

Johnson, W.—Natchez

Lee, G. W.—Heathman

Lewis, J.—Woodvale

Montgomery, I. T.—Davis Bend (s)

Scott, C. A.—Edwards

Scott, W. A. II—Edwards

Sims, N.—Oxford

Walker, A. M.—Indianola

Walker, J. E.—Tillman

Missouri

Hill, J., Jr.—St. Louis

Hurt, J., Jr.—St. Louis

New Jersey

Henderson, H. F.—Paterson

New York

dePasse, S. C.—New York City

Graves, E.—New York City

Lewis, E. T.—New York City

Llewellyn, J. B.—New York City

North Carolina

Coleman, W. C.—Cabarrus County (s)

Greenlee, W. A.—Marion

Johnson, E. A.—Wake County (s)

Kennedy W. J. III—Durham

Merrick, J.—Sampson County (s)

Pettiford, W. R.—Granville County

Proctor, B. G.—Black Mountain

Spaulding, A. T.—Columbus County

Spaulding, C. C.—Columbus County

Vann, R. L.—Ahoskie

Ohio

James, C. H.—Gallia County

Oklahoma

Blayton, J. B.—Garden

Pennsylvania

Dutrieuille, A. E.—Philadelphia

Forten, J.—Philadelphia

Posey, C.—Homestead

Still, W.—Paxtang (s)

South Carolina

Ellison, W.—Winnsboro (s)

King, H.—Chesterfield District (s)

Rhodes, E. W.—Camden

Tennessee

Griffey, D.—Nashville

Napier, J. C.—near Nashville (s)

Thomas, J.—Nashville (s)

Texas

Boyd, H. A.—Grimes County

Nickerson, W., Jr.—Cold Springs

Perry, H. E.—Houston

Sutton, P. E.—Prairie View

Virginia

Milton, L. D.—Prince William County

Mitchell, J., Jr.—Laburum (s)

Montgomery, B. T.—Loudoun County (s)

Moore, F. R.—birthplace unknown (s)

Walker, M. L.—Richmond

Washington, B. T.—Franklin County (s)

Washington, D.C.

Chase, W. C., Sr.

Wormley, J.

West Virginia

James, C. H. II—Charleston

James, C. H. III—Charleston

James, E. R.—Charleston

Outside United States

St. Croix

Leidesdorff, W. A.

West Indies

Fraunces, S.

BUSINESS LEADERS BY PRINCIPAL PLACE OF BUSINESS

Alabama

Birmingham

   Gaston, A. G.

   Pettiford, W. R.

Tuscaloosa

   King, H.

Tuskegee

   Washington, B. T.

California

Los Angeles

   Amos, W., Jr.

   Beavers, G. A., Jr.

   Davis, W. D.

   dePasse, S. C.

   Gordy, B., Jr.

   Griffey, D.

   Houston, N. O.

   Nickerson, W., Jr.

San Francisco

   Leidesdorff, W. A.

Georgia

Atlanta

   Blayton, J. B.

   Gibson, T. K., Sr.

   Herndon, A. F.

   Herndon, N. B.

   Hill, J., Jr.

   Milton, L. D.

   Pace, H. H.

   Perry, H. E.

   Russell, H. J.

   Scott, C. A.

   Scott, W. A. II

   Yates, C. R.

Augusta

   Perry, H. E.

Columbus

   King, H.

Savannah

   Wright, R. R., Sr.

Illinois

Chicago

   Abbott, R. S.

   Binga, J.

   Boutte, A. J.

   Burrell, T. J.

   Dickerson, E. B.

   Fuller, S. B.

   Gardner, E. G.

   Gibson, T. K., Sr.

   Gibson, T. K., Jr.

   Gillespie, F. L.

Johnson, A. W.
Johnson, G.
Johnson, J. H.
Overton, A.
Pace, H. H.
Proctor, B. G.
Sengstacke, J.H.H.
Travis, D. J.
Turnbo-Malone, A. M.

Indiana

Indianapolis
Walker, S. B.

Iowa

Des Moines
Alexander, A. A.

Louisiana

New Orleans
Antoine, C. C.
Bartholomew, J. M.
Cohen, W.
DeJoie Family
Durnford, A.
Geddes Family
LaFon, T.
Leidesdorff, W. A.
Lewis, J.
Lewis, J., Jr.
Misshore Family
Pinchback, P.B.S.

Michigan

Detroit
Gordy, B., Jr.

Mississippi

Davis Bend
Montgomery, B. T.
Montgomery, I. T.

Indianola
Walker, J. E.

Mound Bayou
Banks, C.
Montgomery, I. T.

Natchez
Johnson, W.

Missouri

Kansas City
Overton, A.
Perry, H. E.

St. Louis
Gates, C. W.
Hurt, J., Jr.
Turnbo-Malone, A. M.
Walker, S. B.

New Jersey

Newark
Pace, H. H.

West Caldwell
Henderson, H. F.

New York

Buffalo
Gidron, R. D.
Lewis, E. T.
Llewellyn, J. B.

New York City
Fraunces, S.
Gidron, R. D.
Graves, E.
Lewis, E. T.
Lewis, R. F.
Llewellyn J. B.
Moore, F. R.
Nail, J. B.
Nail, J. E.
Pace, H. H.
Payton, P. A., Jr.
Perry, H. E.
Sims, N.

Sutton, P. E.

Walker, S. B.

North Carolina

Concord

Coleman, W. C.

Fitzgerald, R. B.

Johnson, E. A.

Durham

Fitzgerald, R. B.

Kennedy, W. J., Jr.

Kennedy, W. J. III

Merrick, J.

Spaulding, A. T.

Spaulding, C. C.

Raleigh

Johnson, E. A.

Merrick, J.

Ohio

Columbus

Gibson, T. K., Sr.

Pennsylvania

Columbia

Smith, S.

Philadelphia

Dutrieuille Family

Forten, J.

Llewellyn, J. B.

Perry, C. J.

Rhodes, E. W.

Smith, S.

Still, W.

Wright, R. R., Sr.

Wright, R. R., Jr.

Pittsburgh

Greenlee, W. A.

Posey, C. W., Jr.

Vann, R. L.

South Carolina

Stateboro

Ellison, W.

Tennessee

Memphis

Church, R. R.

Lee, G. W.

Pace, H. H.

Perry, H. E.

Shaw, P. W.

Walker, A. M.

Walker, J. E.

Nashville

Boyd, H. A.

Boyd, R. H.

Napier, J. C.

Thomas, J.

Texas

Houston

Nickerson, W., Jr.

Virginia

Richmond

Browne, W. W.

Mitchell, J., Jr.

Walker, M. L.

West Virginia

Charleston

James Family

Washington, D.C.

Chase, W. C., Sr.

Graves, E.

Wormley, J.

BUSINESS LEADERS BY TYPE OF BUSINESS

Financial Services and Insurance

Banking

  Banks, C.

  Binga, J.

  Blayton, J. B.

  Boutte, A. J.

  Boyd, H. A.

  Boyd, R. H.

  Browne, W. W.

  Church, R. R.

  Davis, W. D.

  Fitzgerald, R. B.

  Gaston, A. G.

  Gates, C. W.

  Hurt, J., Jr.

  Kennedy, W. J., Jr.

  Merrick, J.

  Milton, L. D.

  Mitchell, J., Jr.

  Napier, J. C.

  Overton, A.

  Pace, H. H.

  Perry, H. E.

  Pettiford, W. R.

  Still, W.

  Thomas, J.

  Travis, D. J.

  Vann, R. L.

  Walker, A. M.

  Walker, J. E.

  Walker, M. L.

  Wright, R. R., Sr.

  Wright, R. R., Jr.

  Yates, C. R.

Loan Association, Money Lender, Factorage

  Antoine, C. C.

  Hurt, J., Jr.

  Johnson, W.

  Lafon, T.

  Moore, F. R.

  Pinchback, P.B.S.

Insurance and Benefit Societies

  Antoine, C. C.

  Bartholomew, J. M.

  Beavers, G. A., Jr.

  Blayton, J. B.

  Browne, W. W.

  Cohen, W. I.

  DeJoie Family

  Dickerson, E. B.

  Gaston, A. G.

Geddes Family

Gibson, T. K., Sr.

Gillespie, F. L.

Herndon, A. F.

Herndon, N. B.

Hill, J., Jr.

Houston, N. O.

Johnson, E. A.

Johnson, J. H.

Kennedy, W. J., Jr.

Kennedy, W. J. III

Lee, G. W.

Merrick, J.

Milton, L. D.

Nickerson, W., Jr.

Overton, A.

Pace, H. H.

Perry, H. E.

Shaw, P. W.

Spaulding, A. T.

Spaulding, C. C.

Travis, D. J.

Walker, A. M.

Walker, J. E.

Walker, M. L.

Wright, R. R., Jr.

Yates, C. R.

Investor/Arbitrager

Lewis, R. F.

Llewellyn, J. B.

Travis, D. J.

Retailing and Service Industries

Undertaking

DeJoie Family

Gaston, A. G.

Geddes Family

Misshore Family

Catering

Dutrieuille Family

Wormley, J.

Tavern Owner

Fraunces, S.

Nail, J. B.

Hotel Proprietor

Gaston, A. G.

Nail, J. B.

Wormley, J.

General Merchant

Antoine, C. C.

Leidesdorff, W. A.

Pinchback, P.B.S.

Still, W.

Drug Stores

Boutte, A. J.

Cohen, W. I.

Fitzgerald, R. B.

Gaston, A. G.

Merrick, J.

Milton, L. D.

Perry, H. E.

Walker, M. L.

Yates, C. R.

Supermarket Owner

Hurt, J., Jr.

Llewellyn, J. B.

Mail Order

Lewis, E. T.

Walker, S. B.

Car Dealership

Gidron, R. D.

Hurt, J., Jr.

Johnson, A. W.

Wholesale/Retail Distributorship

James Family

Manufacturing

Baked Goods

    Amos, W., Jr.

Food and Beverage Concessions

    Russell, H. J.

Beauty Supplies and Cosmetics

    Fuller, S. B.

    Gardner, E.

    Johnson, G.

    Johnson, J. H.

    Overton, A.

    Sims, N.

    Turnbo-Malone, A. M.

    Walker, S. B.

Miscellaneous

    Banks, C.

    Boyd, H. A.

    Boyd, R. H.

    Coleman, W. C.

    Davis, W. D.

    Fitzgerald, R. B.

    Forten, J.

    Henderson, H. F.

    Johnson, E. A.

    Merrick, J.

    Montgomery, I. T.

    Spaulding, C. C.

Real Estate, Construction and Agriculture

Real Estate

    Bartholomew, J. M.

    Binga, J.

    Church, R. R., Sr.

    Fitzgerald, R. B.

Gaston, A. G.

Gates, C. W.

Johnson, E. A.

Johnson, W.

Lafon, T.

Leidesdorff, W. A.

Merrick, J.

Mitchell, J., Jr.

Moore, F. R.

Nail, J. B.

Nail, J. E.

Napier, J. C.

Overton, A.

Payton, P. A., Jr.

Perry, H. E.

Pettiford, W. R.

Russell, H. J.

Smith, S.

Still, W.

Thomas, J.

Travis, D. J.

Walker, S. B.

Wright, R. R., Jr.

Planter

    Durnford, A.

    Ellison, W.

    Johnson, W.

Contracting/Construction

    Alexander, A. A.

    Bartholomew, J. M.

    Hurt, J., Jr.

    King, H.

    Perry, H. E.

    Russell, H. J.

WOMEN BUSINESS LEADERS

DeJoie, E. B.

de Passe, S. C.

Geddes, G.

Proctor, B. G.

Turnbo-Malone, A. M.

Shaw, P. W.

Sims, N.

Walker, S. B.

Walker, M. L.

BIBLIOGRAPHIC ESSAY

BIBLIOGRAPHIES AND GENERAL TREATMENTS

The principal collections of primary source materials on African-Americans are located in the Booker T. Washington Papers at the Library of Congress, Fisk University, Hampton University, the Moorland-Spingarn Research Center at Howard University, the Slaughter Collection at Atlanta University, the James Weldon Johnson Collection at Yale University, the Schomburg Center for Research in Black Culture at the New York Public Library, and the Vivian Harsh Collection at the Chicago Public Library. There are also numerous materials in other collections, as noted in the individual bibliographies.

An older bibliography which is still of some value is Monroe R. Work, *A Bibliography of the Negro in Africa and America* (New York, 1928). See also James M. McPherson, et al., *Blacks in America: A Bibliographic Essay* (Garden City, N.Y., 1971); Dorothy B. Porter, *The Negro in the United States: A Selected Bibliography* (Washington, D.C., 1970); Erwin K. Welsch, *The Negro in the United States: A Research Guide* (Bloomington, Ind., 1974); Erwin A. Salk, *A Layman's Guide to Negro History* (Chicago, 1969); Dwight L. Smith, ed., *Afro-American History* (Santa Barbara, Calif., 1974); and Elizabeth W. Miller, *The Negro in America: A Bibliography* (Cambridge, Mass., 1970).

The best general histories of African-Americans are John Hope Franklin and Alfred A. Moss, Jr., *From Slavery to Freedom: A History of Negro Americans*, 6th ed. (New York, 1988); and August Meier and Elliott Rudwick, *From Plantation to Ghetto: An Interpretive History of American Negroes*, 3d ed. (New York, 1976). See also Mary Frances Berry and John Blassingame, *Long Memory: The Black Experience in America* (New York, 1982). Biographical sources for African-Americans include Rayford Logan and Michael R. Winston, eds., *Dictionary of American Negro Biography* (New York, 1982); and Edgar A. Toppin, *A Biographical History of Blacks in America since 1528* (New York, 1971); and others noted in the text. Some prominent black leaders are also covered in the *Dictionary of American Biography*, although few business leaders are included. A better source for African-American women business leaders is *Notable American Women* (1971). There has been little done on black businesses in general, with the only partial exception being Abram L. Harris, *The Negro as Capitalist: A Study of Banking and Business among American Negroes* (Philadelphia, 1936), which is quite hostile to the notion.

GENERAL ITEMS ON POLITICS AND SOCIETY

A vast number of works deal with the institution of slavery on the national, state, and local levels. Some of the most useful are Kenneth M. Stampp, *The Peculiar Institution* (New York, 1956); Eugene Genovese, *The Political Economy of Slavery* (New York, 1965), and his *Roll, Jordan, Roll, The World the Slaves Made* (New York, 1974); John Blassingame, *The Slave Community: Plantation Life in the Antebellum South* (New York, 1974); Leslie Howard Owens, *This Species of Property: Slave Life and Culture in the Old South* (New York, 1976); and Charles Joyner, *Down by the Riverside: A South Carolina Slave Community* (Urbana, Ill., 1984). Slavery in southern cities is treated by Richard C. Wade, *Slavery in the Cities: The South, 1820–1860* (New York, 1964); and Claudia D. Goldin, *Urban Slavery in the American South, 1820–1860: A Quantitative History* (Chicago, 1976).

There are a number of works on African-American owners of slaves: Calvin Dill Wilson, "Black Masters: A Side Light on Slavery," *North American Review* 181 (1905), 685–98; Carter G. Woodson, ed., *Free Negro Owners of Slaves in the United States in 1830* (Washington, D.C., 1924); R. Halliburton, Jr., "Free Black Owners of Slaves: A Reappraisal of the Woodson Thesis," *South Carolina Historical Magazine* LXXVI (1976), 129–42; Larry Koger, *Black Slaveowners: Free Black Slave Masters in South Carolina, 1790–1860* (Jefferson, N.C., 1985); Edwin Adams Davis and William Ransom Hogan, eds., *The Barber of Natchez . . .* (Baton Rouge, 1954), and their *William Johnson's Natchez* (Baton Rouge, 1951); Philip J. Schwarz, "Emancipators, Protectors and Anomolies: Free Black Slave Owners in Virginia," *Virginia Magazine of History and Biography*, 95 (July 1987), 317–38; Michael P. Johnson and James Roark, *No Chariot Let Down: Charleston's Free People of Color on the Eve of the Civil War* (Chapel Hill, N.C., 1984), and their *Black Masters: A Free Family of Color in the Old South* (New York, 1984).

Information on free black slaves in the South generally can be gotten from *Afro-American Ledger*, December 21, 1907; Ira Berlin, *Slaves without Masters: The Free Negro in the Slave Era* (New York, 1974); Leonard P. Curry, *The Free Black in Urban America, 1800–1850: The Shadow of a Dream* (Chicago, 1981); E. Horace Fitchett, "The Free Negro in Charleston, South Carolina," Ph.D. diss., University of Chicago, 1950; "The Status of the Free Negro in Charleston, South Carolina, and His Descendants in Modern Society," *Journal of Negro History* XXXII, 4 (October 1947), 430–451; and his "The Origin and Growth of the Free Negro Population of Charleston, South Carolina," *Journal of Negro History* XXVI, 4 (October 1941), 421–437; Willard B. Gatewood, Jr., *Free Man of Color . . .* (Knoxville, 1982); Robert L. Harris, Jr., "Charleston's Free Afro-American Elite: The Brown Fellowship Society and the Humane Brotherhood," *South Carolina Historical Magazine* 82, 1 (January 1981), 289–310; Michael P. Johnson and James L. Roark, "A Middle Ground: Free Mulattoes and the Friendly Moralist Society of Antebellum Charleston," *Southern Studies* 21 (Fall 1982), 246–65; Bernard Edward Powers, Jr., "Black Charleston: A Social History, 1822–1885," Ph.D. diss., Northwestern University, 1982; Edward Forrest Sweat, "Free Negro in Antebellum Georgia," Ph.D. diss., Indiana University, 1957; Marina Wikramanayake, *A World in Shadow: The*

Free Black in Antebellum South Carolina (Columbia, S.C., 1973); Loren Schweninger, "Prosperous Blacks in the South, 1790–1880," *American Historical Review* (February 1990), 31–56, and his *Black Property Owners in the South, 1790–1915* (Urbana, Ill. 1990); and Joel Williamson, *New People: Miscegenation and Mulattoes in the United States* (New York, 1980).

Free blacks in the North during the antebellum period are covered in Leon Litwack, *North of Slavery: The Negro in the Free States, 1790–1860* (Chicago, 1961); James Oliver Horton and Lois Horton, *Black Bostonians: Family Life and Community Struggle in the Ante-bellum North* (New York, 1979); Leonard P. Curry, *The Free Black in Urban America, 1800–1850* (Chicago, 1981); and Robert Cottrol, *The Afro-Yankees: Providence's Black Community in the Antebellum Period* (New York, 1982). Information about free black women in the South is in Suzanne Lebsock, *The Free Women of Petersburg: Status and Culture in a Southern Town* (New York, 1984); and Ellen N. Lawson and Marlene D. Merrill, *The Three Sarahs: Documents on Antebellum Black—College Women* (Lewiston, N.Y., 1984).

Treatments of Reconstruction and its impact on blacks in the South are voluminous. Solid general histories are John Hope Franklin, *Reconstruction after the Civil War* (Chicago, 1961); and Kenneth M. Stampp, *The Era of Reconstruction* (New York, 1965). Works that focus upon the role of blacks during this time include W.E.B. Du Bois, *Black Reconstruction* (New York, 1935); Lerone Bennett, *Black Power, U.S.A.: The Human Side of Reconstruction, 1867–1877* (Chicago, 1967); Peter Kolchin, *First Freedom: The Responses of Alabama's Blacks to Emancipation and Reconstruction* (Westport, Conn., 1972); Leon Litwack, *Been in the Storm So Long: The Aftermath of Slavery* (New York, 1979). A helpful study of black political leaders during this time is Howard Rabinowitz, ed., *Southern Black Leaders of the Reconstruction Era* (Urbana, Ill., 1982).

General analyses of many of the issues that concerned blacks in the period from 1880 to 1930 can be found in Arnold A. Taylor, *Travail and Triumph: Black Life and Culture in the South since the Civil War* (Westport, Conn., 1976); Rayford W. Logan, *The Negro in American Life and Thought: The Nadir, 1877–1901* (New York, 1954); August Meier, *Negro Thought in America, 1880–1915* (Ann Arbor, Mich., 1963); Ray Stannard Baker, *Following the Color Line* (New York, 1908); Alfred H. Stone, *Studies in American Race Relations* (New York, 1908); I. A. Newby, *Jim Crow's Defense: Anti-Negro Thought in America, 1900–1930* (Baton Rouge, 1965); Arthur F. Raper, *The Tragedy of Lynching* (Chapel Hill, N.C., 1933); Ida Wells Barnett, "Our Country's Lynching Record," *Survey* XXIV (January 1913); E. B. Reuter, *The American Race Problem* (New York, 1927); Robert L. Zangrando, *The NAACP's Crusade against Lynching, 1909–1950* (Philadelphia, 1980); Nancy Weiss, *The National Urban League, 1910–1940* (New York, 1974); Emmett J. Scott, *The American Negro in the World War* (Washington, D.C., 1919); Arthur E. Barbeau and Florette Henri, *Unknown Soldiers: Black American Troops in World War I* (Philadelphia, 1974); Louise V. Kennedy, *The Negro Peasant Turns Cityward* (New York, 1930); Emmett J. Scott, *Negro Migration during the War* (New York, 1920); Ray Stannard Baker, "The Negro Goes North," *World's Work* XXXIV (July 1917); Henderson Donald, "The Negro Migration," *Journal of Negro History* VI (October 1921); Paul Baker, *Negro-White Adjustment* (Boston, 1925); and James Weldon Johnson, *Along This Way* (New York, 1933). The growth of antiblack prejudice in the North is treated in David A. Gerber, *Black Ohio and the Color Line, 1860–1915* (Urbana, Ill., 1976). Treatment of a border city is George C. Wright, *Life behind a Veil: Blacks in Louisville, Kentucky, 1865–1930* (Baton Rouge, 1985).

For general coverage of many of the political issues of the New Deal and World War II see Harvard Sitkoff, *A New Deal for Blacks: The Emergence of Civil Rights as a National Issue* (New York, 1978), and his "Racial Militancy and Interracial Violence during World War II," *Journal of American History* LVIII (December 1971); Lawrence J. Psazek, "Negroes and the Air Force, 1939–49," *Military Affairs* 31 (1967), 1–9; Leslie Fishel, Jr., "The Negro and the New Deal Era," *Wisconsin Magazine of History* 48 (1965), 111–26; William H. Hastie, *On Clipped Wings: The Story of Jim Crow in the Army Air Force* (New York, 1943); Walter White, *A Rising Wind* (New York, 1945); Richard Dalfiume, "The Forgotten Years of the Negro Revolution," *Journal of American History* 55 (1968), 90–106; Lee Finkle, "The Conservative Aims of Militant Rhetoric: Black Protest during WWII," *Journal of American History* 60 (1973), 692–713; W. Edward Orser, "Racial Attitudes during Wartime: The Protestant Church during World War II," *Church History* 41 (1972), 337–53; David K. Wiggins, "Wendell Smith, the *Pittsburgh Courier-Journal* and the Campaign to Include Blacks in Organized Baseball, 1933–1940," *Journal of Sport History* 10 (Summer 1983), 3–29.

For the period of the "Second Reconstruction," from 1945 to the present, see Harvard Sitkoff, *The Struggle for Black Equality, 1954–1992* (New York, 1992); Steven Lawson, *Black Ballots: Voting Rights in the South, 1944–1969* (New York, 1976); Paul Burstein, *Discrimination, Jobs and Politics: The Struggle for Equal Employment Opportunity in the United States since the New Deal* (Chicago, 1985); Louis Lomax, *The Negro Revolt* (New York, 1962); Robert Brisbane, *Black Activism: Black Revolution in the U.S., 1954–1970* (Valley Forge, Pa., 1984); Richard Kluger, *Simple Justice: The History of Brown v. Board of Education and Black America's Struggle for Equality* (New York 1975); Manning Marable, *Race, Reform and Rebellion: The Second Reconstruction in Black America, 1945–1982* (London, 1984); Taylor Branch, *Parting the Waters: America in the King Years* (New York, 1988); James Button, *Black Violence: Political Impact on the 1960's Riots* (Princeton, N. J., 1978); David J. Garrow, *Bearing the Cross: Martin Luther King, Jr. and the Southern Christian Leadership Conference* (New York, 1986); Howell Raines, *My Soul Is Rested* (New York 1977); and Mary Aiken Rothschild, *A Case of Black and White* (Westport, Conn., 1982).

BIBLIOGRAPHICAL INFORMATION ON INDIVIDUAL CITIES AND STATES

Atlanta and Georgia

For general information on African-Americans in Atlanta and Georgia see Edward Randolph Carter, *The Black Side: A Partial History of the Business, Religious, and Educational Side of the Negro in Atlanta* (Atlanta, 1894); John Dittmer, *Black Georgia in the Progressive Era* (Urbana, Ill., 1977); Alexa B. Henderson and Eugene Walker, *Sweet Auburn: Thriving Hub of Black Atlanta, 1900–1960* (U.S. Department of the Interior/National Park Service, 1976); Clarence Bacote, "Some Aspects of Negro Life in Georgia," *Journal of Negro History* 43 (July 1958), 186–213; August Meier and David Lewis, "History of the Negro Upper Class in Atlanta, Georgia, 1890–1958," *Journal of Negro Education* 28 (Spring 1959), 128–39; Michael Leroy Porter, "Black Atlanta: An Interdisciplinary Study of Blacks on the East Side of Atlanta, 1890–1930," Ph.D. diss., Emory University, 1974; Ronald H. Bayor, "Roads to Racial Segregation: Atlanta in the Twentieth Century," *Journal of Urban History* 15, 1 (November 1988), 3–21;

Glenn Sisk, "The Economic Condition of the Negro in Atlanta," *Negro History Bulletin* XXVII, 4 (January 1964), 87–90, and Sisk, "The Negro in Atlanta Politics (1870–1962)," *Negro History Bulletin* XXVIII, 1 (October 1964), 17–18; Jesse Max Barber, "The Atlanta Tragedy," *Voice*, November 1906, 473–79; Booker T. Washington, "The Golden Rule in Atlanta," *The Outlook*, December 15, 1906, 913–16; Benjamin G. Brawley, "Atlanta Striving," *Crisis*, May 1914, 27–31; Robert C. Vowels, "Atlanta Negro Business and the New Black Bougeoisie," *Atlanta Historical Quarterly Bulletin* (Spring 1977), 48–63; Eugene J. Watts, "Black Political Progress in Atlanta, 1868–1895," *Journal of Negro History* LIX, 3 (July 1974), 268–86; Charles Crowe, "Racial Violence and Social Reform—Origins of the Atlanta Race Riot of 1906," *Journal of Negro History* LIII, 3 (July 1968), 234–56, and Crowe, "Racial Massacre in Atlanta, September 22, 1906," *Journal of Negro History* LIV, 2 (April 1969), 150–73; Robert J. Alexander, "Negro Business in Atlanta," *Southern Economic Journal* XVII, 4 (April 1951), 451–64; *Atlanta Daily World*, June 18, 1976, and February 28, 1988; *Black Enterprise*, February 1974, 41–46; *Atlanta Constitution*, December 8, 9, 10, 11, 12, and 13, 1979; and Adrienne S. Harris, "City Profile: The Southern Magnet," *Black Enterprise*, June 1992, 335–47. See also *Pittsburgh Courier*, July 15, 1961.

Some general works on Atlanta history include James Michael Russell, *Atlanta, 1847–1890: City Building in the Old South and the New* (Baton Rouge, 1988); Harold E. Davis, *Henry Grady's New South: Atlanta, A Brave and Beautiful City* (Tuscaloosa, Ala., 1990); Clifford M. Kuhn, Harlon E. Joye, and E. Bernard West, *Living Atlanta: An Oral History of the City, 1914–1948* (Atlanta, 1990); Harold H. Martin, *Atlanta and Environs: A Chronicle of Its People and Events: Years of Change and Challenge, 1940–1976* (Atlanta, 1987); Robert A. Thompson, et al., "Atlanta and Birmingham: A Comparative Study in Negro Housing," in *Studies in Housing and Minority Groups*, edited by Nathan Glazer and Davis McEntire (Berkeley, Calif., 1960), 40–46; Robert D. Bullard and E. Kiki Thomas, "Atlanta: Mecca of the Southeast," in *In Search of the New South: The Black Urban Experience in the 1970s and 1980s*, edited by Robert D. Bullard (Tuscaloosa, Ala., 1989), 75–91; James Michael Russell, *Atlanta, 1847–1890: City Building in the Old South and the New* (Baton Rouge, 1988).

Birmingham and Alabama

Although information is lacking on black-owned businesses in Birmingham, an excellent study is offered by Franklin D. Wilson, "The Ecology of a Black Business District: Sociological and Historical Analysis," Institute for Research of Poverty Discussion Papers, University of Wisconsin-Madison, 1975. An abridged version of this paper appears in *The Review of Black Political Economy* 5 (Summer 1975), 353–75. Several more recent articles appear in the *Birmingham Post-Herald*, July 1, 1978, April 7, 1980, July 13, 1982, January 28, 1981, and July 14, 1987; and the *Birmingham News*, July 6, 1987. Geraldine Moore's *Behind the Ebony Mask* (1961) offers profiles on local black business people in Birmingham. *The Other Side: The Story of Birmingham's Black Community* (n.d.) is a brief description of the social, business, and political environment in Birmingham. Ernest Porterfield's chapter "Birmingham: A Magic City" in *In Search of the New South: The Black Urban Experience in the 1970s and 1980s*, edited by Robert D. Bullard (Tuscaloosa, Ala., 1989), offers historical data on the city's growth and the social, political, and economic position and contributions of local blacks. Jimmie Lee

Franklin's *Back to Birmingham: Richard Arrington, Jr., and His Times* (Tuscaloosa, Ala., 1989), focuses on the political climate of Birmingham and the contributions of the city's first black mayor. The changing nature of black leadership in Birmingham is examined, as Franklin recreates Arrington's rise. A. G. Gaston's accommodationist philosophy is presented, as is his loss of influence as a result of the adoption of more aggressive tactics by a new leadership corps. The most comprehensive and scholarly study of Birmingham's politics is Carl V. Harris, *Political Power in Birmingham, 1871–1921*. Although blacks are not studied in detail, Harris does provide an analysis of their passive role in settling and building Birmingham in the early years.

Several general interest books have been written about Birmingham, particularly about the city during its infancy. See Leah Rawls Atkins, *The Valley and the Hills: An Illustrated History of Birmingham and Jefferson County* (Windsor Publications Inc., n.d.); Florence Hawkings Wood Moss, *Building Birmingham and Jefferson County* (Birmingham, 1947); George R. Leighton, *Five Cities: The Story of Their Youth and Old Age* (New York, 1939); John W. DuBose, *Jefferson County and Birmingham, Alabama, Historical and Biographical* (Birmingham, 1887).

Biographies of prominent Birmingham blacks during the early twentieth century appear in *Leaders of the Colored Race in Alabama* (Mobile, 1918). On Thomas W. Walker and his business interests, see Alexa Benson Henderson, *Atlanta Life Insurance Company* (Tuscaloosa, Ala., 1990), 9–10; Isabel Dangaix Allen, ''Negro Enterprise: An Institutional Church,'' *Outlook* 88 (September 17, 1904), 179–83; T. W. Walker, ''Negro Coal Mining Company,'' speech presented at the First National Negro Business League Proceedings (Boston, 1900). Information on architect Wallace Rayfield is available in Charles A. Brown, ''W. A. Rayfield: Pioneer Black Architect of Birmingham, Ala.'' (Birmingham, n.d.), held at the Birmingham Public Library; and a very limited amount of information on contractor T. C. Windham is available in Marjorie Longenecker White, ''Images of Smithfield,'' *Journal of the Birmingham Historical Society* IX (December 1985). See also Harold Jackson, ''A Measure of Profits,'' *Black Enterprise*, June 1992; ''Bham Revisited,'' *Ebony*, 1971, 114–120; Marjorie Longenecker White, *The Birmingham District: An Industrial History and Guide* (Birmingham, 1981), Birmingham Historical Society. Several novels by Octavious Cohen were written about the social and moral character of Birmingham's black business district during the early twentieth century, including, *Black and Blue* (1926); *Polished Ebony* (1926); *Detours* (1922); *Highly Colored* (1921); *Dark Days and Black Knights* (1923); *Bigger and Blacker* (1925); and *Assorted Chocolates* (1922).

Information on African-Americans in Alabama includes William Rogers, *The One-Gallused Rebellion: Agrarianism in Alabama, 1865–1896* (Baton Rouge, 1970); Kelly Miller, *An Appeal to Conscience* (New York, 1918); Paul Lewison, *Race, Class and Party* (New York, 1959); John B. Clark, *Populism in Alabama* (Auburn, Ala., 1927); William Garrott Brown, *A History of Alabama* (New York, 1900); Jonathon M. Wiener, *Social Origins of the New South: Alabama, 1860–1885* (Baton Rouge, 1978); Peter Kolchin, *First Freedom: The Response of Alabama's Blacks to Emancipation and Reconstruction* (Westport, Conn. 1972); Rayford W. Logan, *The Negro in American Life and Thought: The Nadir, 1877–1901* (New York, 1934); T. Thomas Fortune, *Black and White: Land, Labor and Politics in the South* (New York, 1884); Ray Stannard Baker, *Following the Color Line* (New York, 1908), and Robin D. G. Kelley, *Hammer and Hoe: Alabama Communists during the Great Depression* (Chapel Hill, N.C., 1990).

California

Works on African-Americans in California and the West include Rudolph M. Lapp, *Blacks in Gold Rush California* (New Haven, Conn., 1977); Kenneth G. Goode, *California's Black Pioneers: A Brief Historical Survey* (Santa Barbara, Calif., 1973); D. Forbes, *Afro-Americans in the Far West: A Handbook for Educators* (Berkeley, Calif., 1967); William L. Katz, *The Black West* (New York, 1971); Robert F. Herzer and Alan M. Almquist, *The Other Californians* (Berkeley, Calif., 1971); W. Sherman Savage, *Blacks in the West* (Westport, Conn., 1976); Charles Wollenbert, ed., *Ethnic Conflict in California History* (Los Angeles, 1970); A. Odell Thurman, "The Negro in California before 1890," Master's thesis, College of the Pacific, 1945; James A. Fisher, "A Social History of the Negro in California, 1860–1890," Master's thesis, Sacramento State College, 1966; Sheila M. Skjeie, "California and the Fifteenth Amendment: A Study of Racism," Ph.D. diss., Sacramento State University, 1973; Larry George Murphy, "Equality before the Law: The Struggle of Nineteenth-Century Black Californians for Social and Political Justice," Ph.D. diss., Graduate Theological Union, 1973. General histories of California include Walton E. Bean, *California: An Interpretative History* (New York, 1968); Warren G. Beck and David A. Williams, *California: A History of the Golden State* (New York, 1972); Robert G. Cleland, *From Wilderness to Empire: A History of California* (New York, 1960); Andrew F. Rolle, *California: A History* (New York, 1967).

Charleston and South Carolina

General background information on free black slaves in South Carolina can be gotten from *Afro-American Ledger*, December 21, 1907; E. Horace Fitchett, "The Free Negro in Charleston, South Carolina," Ph.D. diss., University of Chicago, 1950, Fitchett, "The Status of the Free Negro in Charleston, South Carolina, and His Descendants in Modern Society," *Journal of Negro History* XXXII, 4 (October 1947), 430–51, and Fitchett, "The Origin and Growth of the Free Negro Population of Charleston, South Carolina," *Journal of Negro History* XXVI, 4 (October 1941), 421–37; Willard B. Gatewood, Jr., *Free Man of Color . . .* (Knoxville, 1982); Robert L. Harris, Jr., "Charleston's Free Afro-American Elite: The Brown Fellowship Society and the Humane Brotherhood," *South Carolina Historical Magazine* 82, 1 (January 1981), 289–310; Michael P. Johnson and James L. Roark, "A Middle Ground: Free Mulattoes and the Friendly Moralist Society of Antebellum Charleston," *Southern Studies* 21 (Fall 1982), 246–65; Larry Koger, *Black Slaveowners: Free Black Slave Masters in South Carolina, 1790–1860* (Jefferson, N.C., 1985); Gary B. Mills, *The Forgotten People: Cane River's Creoles of Color* (Baton Rouge, 1977); Bernard Edward Powers, Jr., "Black Charleston: A Social History, 1822–1885," Ph.D. diss., Northwestern University, 1982; Dale Rosengarten, et al., "Between the Tracks: Charleston's East Side during the Nineteenth Century," published by the Charleston Museum and Avery Research Center (Charleston, 1987); Marina Wikramanayake, *A World in Shadow: The Free Black in Antebellum South Carolina* (Columbia, S.C., 1973).

General information on antebellum Charleston and South Carolina is in Rosser H. Taylor, *Ante-Bellum South Carolina: A Social and Cultural History* (New York, 1970); George C. Rogers, Jr., *Charleston in the Age of the Pinckneys* (Norman, Okla., 1969). Willard B. Gatewood, in his *Aristocrats of Color* (Bloomington, Ind., 1990) discusses the Charleston antebellum black elite in the context of other upper class African-American families. For South Carolina during Reconstruction, see Thomas Holt, *Black over White: Negro Political Leadership in South Carolina during Reconstruction* (Urbana, Ill., 1977).

Chicago

There is quite a bit of information on a variety of African-American businesses in Chicago in the records of the National Negro Business League in the Booker T. Washington Papers at the Library of Congress. Other material on general black business in Chicago includes "Business in Bronzeville: The Center of U.S. Negro Business," *Time*, April 18, 1938, 70–71; "Chicago: Money Capital of Negro America," *Our World* 6 (September 1951), 15–19; "How Chicago Strikes It Rich," *Color* 11 (March 1956), 22–33; Barbara Reynolds, "Business without the Crystal Stair," *Chicago Tribune Magazine*, January 22, 1978; *Chicago Tribune*, June 12, and 13, 1972, May 4, 9, and 24 and July 31, 1976, and March 20, 1988; *Ebony*, September 1978; *Chicago Daily News*, June 23–24, 1973, and August 4, 1975; *Chicago Sun-Times*, June 16, 1976, and February 18, 1979; *Chicago Defender*, August 2, 1978, July 3, 1979, and February 15, 1986; *Crain's Chicago Business*, August 14, 1989; *Daily Press* (Newport News, Va.), July 29, 1979; *Richmond Times-Dispatch*, July 29, 1979; Robert Everett Weems, Jr., "The History of the Chicago Metropolitan Assurance Company: An Examination of Business as a Black Community Institution," Ph.D. diss., University of Wisconsin-Madison, 1987. Another useful source on black business in Chicago is Madrue Chavers-Wright, *The Guarantee— P. W. Chavers, Banker, Entrepreneur, Philanthropist in Chicago's Black Belt in the 1920's* (New York, 1985).

Information concerning African-Americans in Chicago is abundant. The classic overviews are St. Clair Drake and Horace R. Cayton, *Black Metropolis: A Study of Negro Life in a Northern City*, 2 vols. (New York, 1945); Allan H. Spear, *Black Chicago: The Making of a Negro Ghetto, 1890–1920* (Chicago, 1967); Thomas Philpott, *The Slum and the Ghetto: Neighborhood Deterioration and Middle Class Reform, Chicago, 1880–1930* (New York, 1978); Arnold R. Hirsch, *Making the Second Ghetto: Race and Housing in Chicago, 1940–1960* (New York, 1983); and several superb newer treatments of important aspects of the development of black Chicago: James R. Grossman, *Land of Hope: Chicago, Black Southerners, and the Great Migration* (Chicago, 1989); and Nicholas Lemann, *The Promised Land: The Great Black Migration and How It Changed America* (New York, 1991). A good general history of Chicago is Harold M. Mayer and Richard C. Wade, *Chicago: Growth of a Metropolis* (Chicago, 1969).

A superb source for finding information on African-Americans in the city is *The Chicago Afro-American Union Analytic Catalog: An Index to Materials of the Afro-American in the Principal Libraries of Chicago*, 5 vols. (Chicago, 1972), containing some 75,000 entries, held at the Carter G. Woodson Branch of the Chicago Public Library. Another valuable source is the Illinois Writers Project, part of the broader WPA undertaking, which is on microfilm at the Carter G. Woodson Library. There is also an excellent contemporary clipping file on many of the city's important blacks at the City Hall Library, and *Black Metropolis Historic District: Preliminary Summary of Information* (Chicago, 1984) is valuable. Other useful studies include D. A. Bethea, comp., *The Colored People's Blue Book of Chicago* (Chicago, 1906); Horace R. Cayton and George S. Mitchell, *Black Workers and the New Unions* (Chapel Hill, N.C., 1939); Chicago Commission on Race Relations, *The Negro in Chicago* (Chicago, 1922); Otis D. Duncan and Beverley Duncan,

The Negro Population of Chicago: A Study of Residential Succession (Chicago, 1957); Neil Filgstein, *Going North: Migration of Blacks and Whites from the South, 1900–1950* (New York, 1981); E. Franklin Frazier, *The Negro Family in Chicago* (Chicago, 1932), and Frazier, *Black Bourgeoisie* (Glencoe, Ill., 1957); Florette Henri, *Black Migration: Movement North, 1900–1920* (Garden City, N.Y., 1975); E. Marvin Goodwin, *Black Migration in America from 1915 to 1960* (Lewiston, Me., 1990); Isaac E. Harris, comp., *The Colored Men's Professional and Business Directory of Chicago and Valuable Information of the Race in General* (Chicago, 1885–86); Alma Herbst, *The Negro in the Slaughtering and Meat-Packing Industry of Chicago* (Boston, 1932); Michael Homel, *Down from Equality: Black Chicagoans and the Public Schools, 1920–41* (Urbana, Ill., 1984); Louise V. Kennedy, *The Negro Peasant Turns Cityward: Effects of Recent Migration to Northern Centers* (New York, 1930); Emmett J. Scott, *Negro Migration during the War* (New York, 1920); *Simms' Blue Book and National Negro Business and Professional Directory* (Chicago, 1923); Allan Spear, "From the South to the Southside," in *Blacks in White America*, edited by Robert C. Twombly (New York, 1971); Arvarh Strickland, *History of the Chicago Urban League* (Urbana, Ill., 1966); William M. Tuttle, Jr., *Race Riot: Chicago in the Red Summer of 1919* (New York, 1970); Junius B. Wood, *The Negro in Chicago* (Chicago, 1916); Chicago Urban League, *Urban Renewal and the Negro in Chicago* (n.p., 1968); Devereaux Bowly, Jr., *The Poorhouse: Subsidized Housing in Chicago, 1895–1976* (Carbondale, Ill., 1978); Frederick H. Robb, ed., *The Negro in Chicago, 1779–1929* (Chicago, 1929).

Articles of importance include Carroll Binder, "Notes by Carroll Binder on Chicago and the New Negro," *Journal of Negro History* (April 1928), 214–22; Lizabeth Cohen, "Encountering Mass Culture at the Grassroots: The Experience of Chicago Workers in the 1920's," *American Quarterly* 41, 1 (March 1989), 6–33; Stephen J. Diner, "Chicago Social Workers and Blacks in the Progressive Era," *Social Service Review* 44, 4 (December 1970), 393–410; Henderson H. Donald, "The Negro Migration of 1916–18," *The Crisis* 14, 2 (June 1917), 63–66; William L. Evans, "The Negro in Chicago Industries," *Opportunity* 1, 2 (February 1923), 15–17; E. Franklin Frazier, "Chicago: A Cross Section of Negro Life," *Opportunity* 7, 3 (March 1929), 63–72; Rita Werner Gordon, "The Change in the Political Alignment of Chicago's Negroes during the New Deal," *Journal of American History* LVI, 3 (December 1969), 584–603; Rollin Lynde Hartt, "When the Negro Comes North," *World's Work* XLVIII, 2 (June 1924); Joseph J. Parot, "Ethnic versus Black Metropolis: The Origins of Polish-Black Housing Tensions in Chicago," *Polish-American Studies* 29, 1–2 (Spring–Autumn 1972), 5–33; Karl Taeuber and Alma Taeuber, "The Negro as an Immigrant Group: Trends in Racial and Economic Segregation in Chicago," *Journal of American Sociology* 69 (January 1964); William M. Tuttle, Jr., "Contested Neighborhoods and Racial Violence: Prelude to the Chicago Riot of 1919," *Journal of Negro History* LV, 4 (October 1970); Edward E. Wilson, "Negro Society in Chicago," *Voice of the Negro* VI (July 1907); and St. Clair Drake and Horace R. Cayton, "Chicago Today," *Negro Digest* XXII (April 1963), 20–25. See also "The Negro in Chicago, 1790–1860," by L. D. Reddick, an unpublished manuscript in the Schomburg Collection of the New York Public Library.

Some dissertations and masters theses of value are Lizabeth Cohen, "Learning to Live in the Welfare State: Industrial Workers in Chicago between the Wars, 1919–1939," Ph.D. diss., University of California, Berkeley, 1986; Myra Hill Colson, "Home Work among Negro Women in Chicago," Master's thesis, University of Chicago, 1928; Vattel E. Daniel, "Ritual in Chicago's South Side Churches for Negroes," Ph.D. diss., University of Chicago, 1940; Michael Homel, "Negroes in the Chicago Public Schools, 1910–1941," Ph.D. diss., University of Chicago, 1972; Joseph E. Logsdon, "Reverend Archibald J. Carey and the Negro in Chicago Politics," Master's thesis, University of Chicago, 1961; Alice Q. Rood, "Social Conditions among Negroes on Federal Street between Forty-fifth Street and Fifty-third Street," Master's thesis, University of Chicago, 1924; Robert Lee Sutherland, "An Analysis of Negro Churches in Chicago," Ph.D. diss., University of Chicago, 1930; David A. Wallace, "Residential Concentration of Negroes in Chicago," Ph.D. diss., Harvard University, 1953; Frederick Burgess Lindstrom, "The Negro Invasion of the Washington Park Subdivision," Master's thesis, University of Chicago, 1941; Stanley Carlson Stevens, "Urban Racial Border: Chicago, 1960," Ph.D. diss., University of Illinois, 1972; Alvin Winder, "White Attitudes toward Negro-White Interaction in an Area of Changing Racial Composition," Ph.D. diss., University of Chicago, 1952; Ralph Davis, "Negro Newspapers in Chicago," Master's thesis, University of Chicago, 1939; Norman W. Spaulding, "History of Black-Oriented Radio in Chicago, 1929–1963," Ph.D. diss., University of Illinois, 1981; Monroe N. Work, "Negro Real Estate Holders in Chicago," Master's thesis, University of Chicago, 1903; John Chika Agboso Ndulue, "Urban Black Adaptation and Successful Entrepreneurship in Chicago: An Extended Case Study of a Black-Owned and Operated Construction Industry," Ph.D. diss., University of Illinois, 1984; Albert Lee Krieling, "The Making of Racial Identities in the Black Press: A Cultural Analysis of Race Journalism in Chicago, 1878–1929," Ph.D. diss., University of Illinois, 1973; and Steven R. Tallackson, "The *Chicago Defender* and Its Reaction to the Communist Movement in the Depression Era," Master's thesis, University of Chicago, 1967.

Detroit

African-Americans in Detroit are covered in David M. Katzman, *Before the Ghetto: Black Detroit in the Nineteenth Century* (Urbana, Ill., 1973); Francis H. Warren, ed., *The Michigan Manual of Freedmen's Progress* (Detroit, 1915); A. L. Turner and Earl Moses, *Colored Detroit, 1924* (Detroit, 1924); *The Negro in Detroit* (Detroit, 1926); John C. Dancy, "The Negro People in Michigan," *Michigan History Magazine* XXIV (Spring 1940), 221–40; Ulysses W. Boykin, *A Handbook of the Detroit Negro* (Detroit, 1943); John Marshall Ragland, "The Negro in Detroit," *Southern Workman* LII (November 1923), 533–40. There are several useful works on Detroit's 1943 race riot: Alfred McClung Lee and Norman D. Humphrey, *Race Riot* (New York, 1943); Robert Shogan and Tom Craig, *The Detroit Race Riot: A Study in Violence* (Philadelphia, 1964); and Dominic J. Capeci, *Layered Vision: The Detroit Riots of 1943* (Oxford, Miss., 1991), and his *Race Relations in Wartime Detroit: The Sojourner Truth Housing Controversy of 1942* (Philadelphia, 1984). Neil A. Wynn, *The Afro-American and the Second World War* (London, 1976), deals with that topic generally; Alan Clive, *State of Wartime Michigan in World War II* (Ann Arbor, Mich., 1979), gives good background on that topic. Harriet Arnow, *The Dollmaker* (New York, 1954) is a novel that gives a good feel for the lives of white southerners in wartime Detroit. The 1967 riot in Detroit is covered in *The Kerner Report: The 1968 Report of the National Advisory Commission on Civil Disorders* (New York, 1968); Leonard Gordon, *A City in Racial Crisis: The Case of Detroit Pre- and Post- the 1967 Riot* (Detroit, 1971); James H. Lincoln, *The Anatomy of a Riot* (New York, 1968); Hubert G. Locke, *The Detroit Riot of 1967* (Detroit, 1969); Van Gordon Sauter, *Nightmare: Detroit—a Rebellion and Its Victims* (New York, 1968);

Benjamin D. Singer, *Black Rioters: A Study of Social Forces and Communication in the Detroit Riot* (Lexington, Mass., 1970); Joe Feagin and Harlan Hahn, *Ghetto Revolts: The Politics of Violence in American Cities* (New York, 1973); and John Hersey, *The Algiers Motel Incident* (New York, 1968). Some contemporary works on Detroit include Dan Georgakas and Marvin Surkin, *Detroit: I Do Mind Dying: A Study in Urban Revolution* (New York, 1975); B. J. Widick, *Detroit: A City of Race & Class Violence* (Detroit, 1972); Melvin G. Holli, ed., *Detroit* (New York, 1976); Olivier Zunz, *The Changing Face of Inequality: Urbanism, Industrial Development, and Immigrants in Detroit, 1880–1920* (Chicago, 1982); John Bussey, "Detroit's Racial Woes Persist Two Decades after Devastating Riot," *Wall Street Journal*, June 17, 1987; Bill Peterson, "Twenty Years after the Riots: Inequalities Still Burden Detroit's Blacks," *Washington Post*, July 28, 1987.

Durham and North Carolina

A wealth of materials has been published on black business enterprise in Durham. Among those of the greatest interest are Walter B. Weare, *Black Business in the New South* (Urbana, Ill., 1973); Booker T. Washington, "Durham North Carolina: A City of Negro Enterprise," *Independent*, March 30, 1911, 642–50; W.E.B. Du Bois, "The Upbuilding of Black Durham," *World's Work* XXIII (January 1912), 334–38; Clement Richardson, "What Negroes Are Doing in Durham," *Southern Workman*, July 1913, 614–19; E. Franklin Frazier, "Durham, Capital of the Black Middle Class," in *The New Negro. An Interpretation*, edited by Alain Locke, (New York, 1925), 333–40; C. C. Spaulding, "Business in Durham," *Southern Workman*, December 1937, 364–65; and Pat Patterson, "Durham: Decades of Effort Pay Off in Black Economic and Political Strength," *Black Enterprise*, June 1974, 137–47. See also William Kenneth Boyd, *The Story of Durham: The City of the New South* (1927); David Lewis Cohn, "Durham: The New South," *Atlantic Monthly* CLXV (May 1940), 614–19; Margaret Elaine Burgess, *Negro Leadership in a Southern City* (Chapel Hill, N.C., 1960); Helen Grey Edmonds, *The Negro and Fusion Politics in North Carolina, 1894–1901* (Chapel Hill, N.C., 1951); Everett Carll Ladd, Jr., *Negro Political Leadership in the South* (Ithaca, N.Y., 1966); William R. Keech, *The Impact of Negro Voting* (Chicago, 1968); and Arthur M. Miller, "Desegregation and Negro Leadership in Durham, North Carolina, 1954–1963," Ph.D. diss., University of North Carolina, Chapel Hill, 1976.

Indianapolis and Indiana

Information on the African-American community in Indianapolis and Indiana can be obtained from Emma Lou Thornbrough, *Since Emancipation: A Short History of Indiana Negroes, 1863–1963* (Indianapolis, n.d.), her *The Negro in Indiana: A Study of a Minority* (Indianapolis, 1957), and her "Segregation in Indiana during the Klan Era," *Mississippi Valley Historical Review* 48 (Winter 1961), 594–618. Good insight into the black community of Indianapolis, especially its elite business community, can be found in Willard B. Gatewood, ed., *Slave and Freeman: The Autobiography of George L. Knox* (Lexington, Ky., 1979); Cyrus F. Adams, "George L. Knox: His Life and Work," *Colored American Magazine* 5 (October 1902), 465–68; and Darlene Clark Hine, *When the Truth Is Told: A History of Black Women's Culture and Community in Indiana, 1875–1950* (National Council of Negro Women, 1981). More detailed information can be found in extant copies of the city's three black newspapers: the *Freeman*, the *World*, and the *Recorder*. For general information on the city, see Jacob P. Dunn, *Greater Indianapolis: The History, the Industries, the Institutions, and the People of a City of Homes*, 2 vols. (Chicago, 1910).

Los Angeles

For general items concerning African-American business in Los Angeles, see "Black Leadership in Los Angeles," Celes King III interviewed by Robin D. G. Kelley, 2 vols., 1988, in the Oral History Collection at UCLA, which covers a wealth of interesting material. See also, "Whose Black Capitalism," oral history interviews of prominent black businessmen and Small Business Administration officials in Los Angeles, held at San Diego State University Library. See also, "The Soul Elite," *Los Angeles Times*, May 1984; Brenda Lane Worthington, "Blacks Who've Climbed to the Top of the Hill," *Los Angeles Times*, October 8, 1977; Harry Anderson, "Black Entrepreneurs: Lost in the Crowd?" *Los Angeles Times*, June 26, 1990; Karen Grigsby Bates, "Elite Fraternity Widens Agenda for Black Men," *Los Angeles Times*, July 18, 1990; Louis Sahagun, "Black Entrepreneurs Fight an Uphill Battle," *Los Angeles Times*, April 8, 1984; *Los Angeles Times*, May 7, 1987; and *Los Angeles Sentinel*, May 1, 1975, April 20, 1978, March 22, 1979, and October 17, 1985. More general sources of information on blacks in Los Angeles is in Lawrence Brooks de Graaf, "Negro Migration to Los Angeles, 1930 to 1950," Ph.D. diss., University of California, Los Angeles, 1962; J. Max Bond, "The Negro in Los Angeles," Ph.D. diss., University of Southern California, 1936; *Westways Magazine*, January 1976, 44–47; "The Los Angeles Negro," *Frontier*, June 1955, 6–15; Robert Lewis Williams, Jr., "The Negro's Migration to Los Angeles, 1946," *Negro History Bulletin* XIX, 5 (February 1956). The Watts riot of 1965 brought forth a flood of studies analyzing the causes of the riot and the nature of the African-American community in Los Angeles: Governor's Commission on the Los Angeles Riots, *Violence in the City—An End or a Beginning?* (Los Angeles, 1965); Jerry Cohen and William S. Murphy, *Burn, Baby, Burn! The Los Angeles Race Riot of August 1965* (New York, 1966); Bayard Rustin, "The Watts 'Manifesto' and the McCone Report," *Commentary*, March 1966; Robert M. Fogelson, "White on Black: A Critique of the McCone Commission Report on the Los Angeles Riots," *Political Science Quarterly*, September 1967; Robert Blauner, "Whitewash over Watts," *Trans-action*, March/April 1966; Robert M. Fogelson, ed., *The Los Angeles Riots* (New York, 1969); Spencer Curry, *Black Riot: Los Angeles: The Story of the Watts Tragedy* (Los Angeles, 1966); Nathan Cohen, ed., *The Los Angeles Riots: A Socio-Psychological Study* (New York, 1970); and Robert Conot, *Rivers of Blood, Years of Darkness* (New York, 1967). A retrospective look at the riot was Karl Fleming, "Burn, Baby, Burn: 25 Years Ago: A Los Angeles Community Erupts in Violence," *Memories*, August/September 1990, 60–69. See also Frank Clifford, "Watts, Wary of Huge Proposed Redevelopment," *Los Angeles Times*, July 18, 1990. A look at another black community in the city is Richard Elman, *Ill-at-Ease in Compton* (New York, 1967). The explosion of violence in South Central Los Angeles in May 1992, following the Rodney King verdict refocused attention on the city's black community. See *Newsweek*, May 11 and 18, 1992; *Business Week*, May 18, 1992; and *New York Times*, May 10, 1992. There is also a disturbing account of the possible long-term implications of the riot in Jack Miles, "Blacks vs. Browns: The Struggle for the Bottom Rung," *Atlantic Monthly*, October 1992, 41–68.

An excellent history of the development of Los Angeles in the early years is Robert

M. Fogelson, *The Fragmented Metropolis: Los Angeles, 1850–1930* (Cambridge, Mass., 1967). For analyses of the city in later years, see Rayner Banham, *Los Angeles: The Architecture of Four Ecologies* (New York, 1971); Mel Scott, *Metropolitan Los Angeles* (Los Angeles, 1949); Christopher Rand, *Los Angeles: The Ultimate City* (New York, 1967) and Mike Davis, *City of Quartz: Excavating the Future in Los Angeles* (New York, 1990). See also Carey McWilliams, *Southern California Country* (New York, 1946). A good study of the boom atmosphere of Los Angeles and its main promoters is Robert Gottlieb and Irene Wolt, *Thinking Big: The Story of the Los Angeles Times, Its Publishers and Their Influence on Southern California* (New York, 1977). See also David Rieff, *Los Angeles: Capital of the Third World*. An interesting novel of Los Angeles at the turn of the century is *A Place in the Sun* (Los Angeles, 1949) by Frank Fenton, an old-time resident of the city.

Memphis

Information on the black community of Memphis can be found in Shields McIlwaine, *Memphis down in Dixie* (1948); Lester C. Lamon, *Black Tennesseans, 1900–1930* (Knoxville, 1977); Marius Carriere, Jr., "Blacks in Pre-Civil War Memphis," *Tennessee Historical Quarterly* (1991), 3–14; Randolph Meade Walker, "The Role of the Black Clergy in Memphis during the Crump Era," *West Tennessee Historical Society Papers*, XXXIII (October 1979), 29–47; "The Impact of Yellow Fever on Memphis: A Reappraisal," *West Tennessee History Society Papers* XLI (1987), 3–18; Roger Biles, *Memphis in the Great Depression* (Knoxville, 1986); Francis H. McLean, "Memphis Today," *Survey* XXX (1913); "Business Enterprises Owned and Operated by Negroes in Memphis, Tennessee, 1944," Special Report of the Project to Study Business and Business Education among Negroes, Atlanta University and National Urban League; David M. Tucker, *Black Pastors and Leaders: Memphis, 1819–1972* (Memphis, 1975); Ron Walter, "Memphis' Upper-Class Blacks Fall into Distinct Social Groups," *Commercial Appeal*, March 31, 1981; Larry Moore, "Across the Great Divide: The Memphis Black Elite," *Memphis* VII, 8 (November 1982), 37, 47–49; Lynn Norment, "Memphis," *Ebony*, June 1981, 120–30; "One-Hundred Years of Memphis Black Newspapers, 1880–1980," compiled by Vandella Brown, Memphis Public Library, 1981; James Gilbert Ryan, "The Memphis Riots of 1866: Terror in a Black Community during Reconstruction," *Journal of Negro History* LXII No. 3 (July, 1977); Joseph H. Cartwright, *The Triumph of Jim Crow: Tennessee Race Relations in the 1880's* (Knoxville, 1976); J. Merton England, "The Free Negro in Ante-Bellum Tennessee," *Journal of Southern History* IX (February 1943), 37–58; David M. Tucker, "Black Politics in Memphis, 1865–1875," *West Tennessee Historical Society Papers* XXVI (1972), 13–19; Kate Born, "Memphis Negro Workingmen and the NAACP," *West Tennessee Historical Society Papers* XXVIII (1974); Fred L. Hutchins, "Beale Street as It Was," *West Tennessee Historical Society Papers* XXVI(1972); Roberta Church and Ronald Walter, *Nineteenth Century Memphis Families of Color, 1850–1900*, edited by Charles W. Crawford (1987); August Meier and Elliot Rudwick, "Negro Boycotts of Jim Crow Streetcars in Tennessee," *American Quarterly* XXI, 4 (Winter 1969), 755–63; John H. Ellis, "Disease and the Destiny of a City: The 1878 Yellow Fever Epidemic in Memphis," *West Tennessee Historical Society Papers* XXVIII (1974); William D. Miller, *Mr. Crump of Memphis* (Baton Rouge, 1964), and his *Memphis during the Progressive Era, 1900–1917* (Memphis, 1957); Benjamin Muse, *Memphis* (Atlanta, 1964); David M. Tucker, *Memphis since Crump: Bossism, Blacks, and Civic Reformers, 1948–68* (Knoxville, 1980); W.E.B. Du Bois, "Black Banks and White in Memphis," *Crisis*, May 1928, reprinted in *W.E.B. DuBois: A Reader*, edited by Meyer Weinberg (New York, 1970), 49–54; Miriam DeCosta-Willis, "Between a Rock and a Hard Place: Black Culture during the Fifties," *Memphis*, 1948–1958, Memphis Brooks Museum of Art, sponsored by First Tennessee National Association, n.d. and her "Ida B. Wells *Diary*: A Narrative of the Black Community of Memphis in the 1880s," *West Tennessee Historical Society Papers* XLV (1991) 35–47; Caleb Perry Patterson, *The Negro in Tennessee, 1790–1865* (Austin, Tex., 1992); Mingo Scott, Jr., *The Negro in Tennessee Politics and Governmental Affairs, 1865–1965* (Nashville, 1964); A. A. Taylor, *The Negro in Tennessee, 1865–1880* (Washington, D. C., 1941); David Bowman, "Beale Street Blues," *Southern Exposure* V, 1 (1977), 75–79; Susan Adler, " 'Black Capitalism' Fails First Test in Memphis," *Press Scimitar*, January 1, 1973; William C. Handy, *Father of the Blues: An Autobiography*, edited by Arna Bontemps (New York, 1934); Mrs. Jesse W. Fox, "Beale Street and the Blues," *West Tennessee Historical Society Papers* 13 (1959), 128–47; Hugh Davis Graham, *Crisis in Print: Desegregation and the Press in Tennessee* (Nashville, 1967); Lester C. Lamon, "The Tennessee Agricultural and Industrial Normal School," *Tennessee Historical Quarterly* 32,1 (Spring 1973), 42–58; A. A. Taylor, "Fisk University and the Nashville Community, 1866–1900," *Journal of Negro History* 39,2 (April 1954), 111–26; Joe Richardson, *A History of Fisk University, 1865–1965* (Tuscaloosa, Ala., 1980); Gloria Brown Melton, "Blacks in Memphis, Tennessee, 1920–1955: A Historical Study," Ph.D. diss. Washington State University, 1982; Lester Lamon, "Negroes in Tennessee Politics, 1900–1930," Ph.D. diss. University of North Carolina at Chapel Hill, 1971; James Hathaway Robinson, "A Social History of the Negro in Memphis and Shelby County," Ph.D. diss., Yale University, 1934; Joel M. Roitman, "Race Relations in Memphis, Tennessee, 1886–1905," Master's thesis, Memphis State University, 1964; Michael Honey, "Labor and Civil Rights in the South: The Industrial Labor Movement and Black Workers in Memphis, 1929–45," Ph.D. diss., Northern Illinois University, 1987; and Charles J. Williams, "Two Black Communities in Memphis, Tennessee: A Study in Urban Socio-Political Structure," Ph.D. diss., University of Illinois, 1982.

Mississippi

For information on African-Americans in antebellum Mississippi see Charles S. Sydnor, "The Free Negro in Mississippi before the Civil War," *American Historical Review* XXXII, 4 (July 1927), and his *Slavery in Mississippi* (New York, 1933). Natchez is treated most fully in D. Clayton James, *Antebellum Natchez* (Baton Rouge, 1968). See also Edith Wyatt Moore, *Natchez Under-the-Hill* (Nachez, 1958); Catherine Van Court, *In Old Natchez* (Garden City, N.Y., 1937); Noel Polk, ed., *Natchez before 1830* (Jackson, Miss., 1989); Pierce Butler, *The Unhurried Years: Memoirs of the Old Natchez Region* (Baton Rouge, 1948); Robert G. Pishel, *Natchez: Museum City of the Old South* (Tulsa, Okla., 1959); Michael Wayne, *Reshaping of Plantation Society* (Baton Rouge, 1983); Virginia R. Matthias, "Natchez Under-the-Hill as It Developed under the Influence of the Mississippi River and the Natchez Trace," *Journal of Mississippi History* VII (October 1945), 201–21. Some useful general material on Mississippi can be found in John K. Buttersworth, *Confederate Mississippi* (Baton Rouge, 1943); James W. Garner, *Reconstruction in Mississippi* (New York, 1901).

For the period after Reconstruction, see Charles Granville Hamilton, "Mississippi

Politics in the Progressive Period, 1904–1920,'' Ph.D. diss. Vanderbilt University, 1958); Anne Moody, *Coming of Age in Mississippi* (New York, 1968); William Henry Holtzclaw, "Present Status of the Negro in Mississippi," *Southern Workman* 59 (August 1930); James W. Loewen and Charles Sallis, *Mississippi: Conflict and Change* (New York, 1974); Richard Aubrey McLemore, ed., *A History of Mississippi*, 2 vols. (Hattiesburg, Miss., 1973); Albert Dennis Kirwan, *Revolt of the Rednecks: Mississippi Politics, 1876–1925* (New York, 1951). See also Willard B. Gatewood, "Theodore Roosevelt and the Indianola Affair," *Journal of Negro History* LVIII (January 1968), 48–70.

On Delta agriculture see Herbert Weaver, *Mississippi Farmers, 1850–60* (Nashville, 1945); and Hebron Moore, *Agriculture in Antebellum Mississippi* (New York, 1958). Hortense Powdermaker in *After Freedom: A Cultural Study in the Deep South* (New York, 1939) deals with the Delta town of Indianola, as do John Dollard, *Caste and Class in a Southern Town* (Garden City, N.Y., 1949); and Allison Davis et al., *Deep South: A Social Study of Caste and Class* (Chicago, 1941). See also Linton Weeks, *Clarksdale and Coahoma County: A History* (Clarksdale, Miss., 1982). For some general treatments of Mississippi, see John K. Bettersworth, *Mississippi: A History* (Austin, Tex. 1959); Richard A. McLemore, *History of Mississippi*, 2 vols. (Hattiesburg, Miss., 1973); Dunbar Rowland, *History of Mississippi, Heart of the South*, 2 vols. (Chicago, 1925); John Ray Skates, *Mississippi: A Bicentennial History* (New York, 1979); and Joseph G. Baldwin, *Flush Times of Alabama and Mississippi* (Americus, Ga., 1853).

Nashville

Works with information on blacks in antebellum Nashville or Tennessee include J. Merton England, "The Free Negro in Antebellum Tennessee," *Journal of Southern History* 9 (February 1943), 37–58, England, "The Free Negro in Davidson County, Tennessee, 1780–1860," Master's thesis, Vanderbilt University, 1937, and England "Free Negro in Antebellum Tennessee," Ph.D. diss., Vanderbilt University, 1941; Anita Goodstein, "Black History on the Nashville Frontier, 1780–1810," *Tennessee Historical Quarterly* 38 (Winter 1979), 401–20; Chase C. Mooney, "Slavery in Davidson County, Tennessee," Master's thesis, Vanderbilt University, 1936, Mooney, "Slavery in Tennessee," Ph.D. diss., Vanderbilt University, 1939, Mooney, *Slavery in Tennessee* (Westport, Conn., 1957), and Mooney, "The Question of Slavery and the Free Negro in the Tennessee Constitutional Convention of 1834," *Journal of Southern History* 12 (November 1946), 487–509; James Patton, "The Progress of Emancipation in Tennessee," *Journal of Negro History* 17 (January 1932), 67–102; William L. Imes, "Negroes in Tennessee before the Civil War: A Sociological Study," Master's thesis, Fisk University, 1912; and Caleb P. Patterson, *The Negro in Tennessee, 1790–1865* (Austin, Tex., 1922).

On African-Americans in Nashville after the Civil War, see John Egerton, *The Faces of Two Centuries, 1780–1980* (Nashville, 1979); Bobbie L. Lovett, ed., *Winter to Winter: The Afro-American History of Nashville, Tenn., 1870–1930* (Nashville, Tennessee State University, Department of History and Geography, 1981); Gloria H. McKissack, "Black Nashville during the 1890's," Master's thesis, Tennessee State University, 1985; Faye Welborne Robbins, " 'A World-within-a-world': Black Nashville, 1880–1915," Ph.D. diss., University of Arkansas, 1980; Mary Alice Harris Ridley, "The Black Community of Nashville & Davidson County, 1860–70," Ph.D. diss., University of Pittsburgh, 1982; "Structure of Nashville Society among the Negro Group" (E. Franklin Frazier Papers, Moorland-Spingarn Research Center, Howard University, Washington, D.C.); Charles

Foster Smith, "The Negro in Nashville," *Century Magazine* XLII (May 1891); Lester
C. Lamon, "The Black Community in Nashville and the Fisk University Student Strike
of 1924–1925," *Journal of Southern History* XL, 2 (May 1974), 25–44; James Sum-
merville, "The City and the Slums: Black Bottom in the Development of South Nash-
ville," *Tennessee Historical Quarterly* 40, 2 (1981), 182–92; "Business Enterprises
Owned and Operated by Negroes in Nashville, Tennessee, 1944," a special report of
the Project to Study Business and Business Education among Negroes, sponsored by
Atlanta University and the National Urban League, 1944; Leon H. Schuster, et al.,
"Business Enterprises of Negroes in Tennessee," a report by Tennessee Agricultural and
Industrial State University (July 1961); Helen Elizabeth Work, "A Historical Study of
the Colored Public Schools of Nashville," Master's thesis, Fisk University, 1933; and
D. N. Crosswait, "Nashville's First Black High School," *Negro History Journal* 37
(June-July 1974), 266–68.

General works on Nashville include Anita S. Goodstein, *Nashville, 1780–1860: From
Frontier to City* (Gainesville, 1989); Don H. Doyle, *Nashville in the New South, 1880–
1930* (Knoxville, 1985), Doyle, *Nashville since the 1920's* (Knoxville, 1985), and Doyle,
Nashville as a Historical Laboratory (Nashville, 1979); Williams Waller, *Nashville,
1900–1910* (Nashville, 1972); Lizzie Ellicott, *Early History of Nashville* [to 1797] (Nashville, 1911); Philip M. Hamer, *Tennessee: A History*, 4 vols. (New York, 1933); Stanley
J. Folmsbee, Robert E. Corlew, and Enoch L. Mitchell, *Tennessee: A Short History*
(Knoxville, 1969); Mary French Caldwell, *Tennessee: The Dangerous Example; Wataga
to 1849* (Nashville, 1974); W. W. Clayton, *History of Davidson County, Tennessee*
(Philadelphia, 1880); H. W. Crew, *History of Nashville, Tennessee* (Nashville, 1890);
and F. Garvin Davenport, *Cultural Life in Nashville on the Eve of the Civil War* (Chapel
Hill, N.C., 1941).

New Orleans and Louisiana

Important sources of information on free African-Americans in antebellum Louisiana
include Donald Everett, "Free Persons of Color in New Orleans: 1803–1865," Ph.D.
diss., Tulane University, 1952; Everett, "Free Persons of Color in Colonial Louisiana,"
Louisiana History VII (1966); and Everett, "Emigres and Militiamen: Free Persons of
Color in New Orleans, 1803–1815," *Journal of Negro History* XXXVII (1953), 377–
80; Robert Reinders, "The Decline of the New Orleans Free Negro in the Decade before
the Civil War," *Journal of Mississippi History* XXIV (1962), 88–98, and his "The Free
Negro in the New Orleans Economy, 1850–60," *Louisiana History* VI (1965), 273–85;
and Laura Foner, "The Free People of Color in Louisiana and St. Domingue: A Comparative Portrait of Two Three-Caste Slave Societies," *Journal of Social History* III
(1970), 408–11. See also David Rankin, "The Impact of the Civil War on the Free
Colored Population of New Orleans," *Perspectives in American History* XI (1977–78),
379–416; Richard Tansey, "Out-of-State Free Blacks in Late Antebellum New Orleans,"
Louisiana History XXII (1981); and Gary Mills, *The Forgotten People: Cane River's
Creoles of Color* (Baton Rouge, 1977). Another large, free, African-American planter
in Louisiana is discussed in Charles Vincent, "Aspects of the Family and Public Life of
Antoine Dubuclet: Louisiana's Black State Treasurer, 1868–78," *Journal of Negro History* 66 (Spring 1961), 26–36. On slavery in Louisiana, see Joe Gray Taylor, *Negro
Slavery in Louisiana* (Baton Rouge, 1963); and Joseph K. Mena, *The Large Slaveholders
of Louisiana, 1860* (New Orleans, 1964).

Useful information on New Orleans and Louisiana can be obtained from John Blassingame, *Black New Orleans, 1860–1880* (Chicago, 1973); Donald Everett, "Demands of the New Orleans Free Colored Population for Political Equality, 1852–1865," *Louisiana Historical Quarterly* (April 1955), 60–61, and Everett, "Free Persons of Color in New Orleans, 1803–1865," Ph.D. diss., Tulane University, 1952; Roger A. Fischer, *The Segregation Struggle in Louisiana* (Urbana, Ill., 1974); Grace King, *New Orleans: The Place and the People* (New York, 1912); Charles B. Rousseve, *The Negro in Louisiana: Aspects of His History and His Literature* (New Orleans, 1937); W. E. Sterkx, *The Free Negro in Ante-Bellum Louisiana* (Rutherford, N.J., 1971); Loren Schweninger, "Antebellum Free Persons of Color in Postbellum Louisiana," *Louisiana History* 30, 4 (Fall 1989), 356; Emma McGowen, "Free People of Color of New Orleans, 1803–1860," Master's thesis, Tulane University, 1939; and Dorothy Rose Eagleson, "Some Aspects of the Social Life of the New Orleans Negroes in the 1880's," Master's thesis, Tulane University, 1961.

Other sources helpful for understanding the African-American population in New Orleans and Louisiana include Arthe Agnes Anthony, "The Negro Creole Community, 1880–1920," Ph.D. diss., University of California, Irvine, 1978; *The New Orleans Architecture*, vols. IV and VI (Gretna, La., 1980); Dalt Wonk, "The Creoles of Color," *New Orleans Magazine* (1976); James Haskins, *The Creoles of Color of New Orleans* (New York, 1975); Roland Wingfield, "The Creoles of Color: A Study of a New Orleans Subculture," Master's thesis, Louisiana State University, 1961; Annie Lee West Stahl, "The Free Negro in Ante-Bellum Louisiana," *Louisiana Historical Quarterly* 25, 1 (1942), 301–96; Dale E. Somers, "Black & White in New Orleans: A Study in Urban Race Relations, 1865–1900," *Journal of Southern History* XL, 1 (February 1974), 19–42; David Rankin, "The Impact of the Civil War on the Free Colored Community of New Orleans," *Perspectives in American History* II (1977–78), 379–416, Rankin, "The Origins of Black Leadership in New Orleans during Reconstruction," *Journal of Southern History* XL, 3 (August 1974), 417–40, Rankin, "The Politics of Caste: Free Colored Leadership in New Orleans during the Civil War," *Louisiana's Black Heritage* 107–46, and Rankin, "The Forgotten People: Free People of Color in New Orleans, 1850–1870," Ph.D. diss., Johns Hopkins University, 1976; Robert C. Reinders, "The Free Negro in the New Orleans Economy, 1850–1860," *Louisiana History* VI, 1 (Winter 1965), 273–85, and his "The Decline of the New Orleans Free Negro in the Decade before the Civil War," *Journal of Mississippi History* XXIV, 2 (April 1962), 88–98; Roger A. Fisher, "Racial Segregation in Ante Bellum New Orleans," *American Historical Review* LXXIV (February 1969), 926–37, Fisher, "A Pioneer Protest: The New Orleans Street-Car Controversy of 1867," *Journal of Negro History* LIII (July 1968), 219–33, and Fisher, "The Segregation Struggle in Louisiana, 1850–1890," Ph.D. diss., Tulane University, 1967; Giles Vandal, *The New Orleans Riot of 1866: Anatomy of a Tragedy* (Lafayette, La., 1983), and his "The Origins of the New Orleans Riot of 1866, Revisited," *Louisiana History* 22, 2 (1981), 135–65; Donald E. Reynolds, "The New Orleans, Riot of 1866, Reconsidered," *Louisiana History* V (Winter 1964), 5–27; Melinda Meek Hennessey, "Race and Violence in New Orleans: The 1868 Riot," *Louisiana History* 20, 1 (1979), 77–91; Louis R. Harlan, "Desegregation in New Orleans Public Schools during Reconstruction," *American Historical Review* LXVII (April 1962), 663–75; Henry C. Dethloff and Robert R. Jones, "Race Relations in Louisiana, 1877–1898," *Louisiana History* IX (Fall 1968), 306–310, and V. P. Thomas' "Colored New Orleans," *The Crisis* (February 1916). A useful general work on New Orleans during this period is Joy B. Jackson, *New*

Orleans in the Gilded Age: Politics and Urban Progress, 1880–1896 (Baton Rouge, 1969). See also George M. Reynolds, *Machine Politics in New Orleans, 1897–1926* (New York, 1936); William Ivy Hair, *Bourbonism and Agrarian Protest* (Baton Rouge, 1969); Matthew James Schott, "John M. Parker of Louisiana and the Varieties of American Progressivism," Ph.D. diss., Vanderbilt University, 1969; and John H. Rohrer and Munro S. Edmonson, *The Eighth Generation Grows Up* (New York, 1960).

New York City and State

Information on African-Americans in New York in the early years can be obtained from Seth M. Scheiner, *Negro Mecca: A History of the Negro in New York City, 1865–1920* (New York, 1966); Arnett G. Lindsay, "The Economic Condition of the Negroes of New York prior to 1861," *Journal of Negro History* VI (April 1921), 190–99; Roi Ottley and William J. Weathersby, *The Negro in New York: An Informal Social History* (New York, 1967); Leo H. Hirsch, Jr., "The Negro in New York, 1783–1865," *Journal of Negro History* XVI (October 1931), 382ff.; Rhoda G. Friedman, "The Free Negro in New York City in the Years before the Civil War," Ph.D. diss., Columbia University, 1968; Herman D. Block, *The Circle of Discrimination: An Economic and Social Study of the Black Man in New York* (New York, 1969). There is also a wealth of valuable materials on the period housed in the Schomburg Collection of the New York Public Library.

Information on New York City during the early twentieth century can be found in Gilbert Osofsky, *Harlem: The Making of a Ghetto* (New York, 1966); David Levering Lewis, *When Harlem Was in Vogue* (New York, 1981); Nathan Irving Huggins, *Harlem Renaissance* (New York, 1971); James Weldon Johnson, *Black Manhattan* (New York, 1930); Claude McKay, *Harlem: Negro Metropolis* (New York, 1940); Seth Scheiner, *Negro Mecca: A History of the Negro in New York City, 1865–1920* (New York, 1966); George Edward Haynes, *The Negro at Work in New York City: A Study of Economic Progress* (New York, 1912); Roi Ottley and William J. Weathersby, *The Negro in New York: An Informal Social History* (New York, 1967); Roi Ottley, *New World A'Coming* (Boston, 1943); Myrtle Evangeline Pollard, "Harlem as Is: The Negro Business and Economic Community," Master's thesis, City College of New York, 1937; and Allon Schoener, ed., *Harlem on My Mind: Cultural Capital of Black America, 1900–1968* (New York, 1968). The "John E. Nail Scrapbook at Beineicke Library at Yale University has material on Harlem during the Depression. An interesting insight in issues of race and color in Harlem in the early twentieth century there is by Wallace Thurman, *The Blacker the Berry* (1929) as is James Weldon Johnson, *Along This Way* (1933). Other novels of relevance are Jessie Redmond Fauset, *Plum Bun* (1929) and Claude McKay, *Home to Harlem* (1928).

For information from the 1930s, see Roi Ottley, *New World A-Coming* (Boston, 1943); and Claude McKay, *Harlem: Negro Metropolis* (New York, 1940). A recent scholarly appraisal of Harlem during the Depression years is Cheryl Lynn Greenberg, *"Or Does It Explode?": Black Harlem in the Great Depression* (Oxford, 1991). Information on Harlem—housing and real estate markets—can be found in National League on Urban Conditions among Negroes, *Housing Conditions among Negroes in Harlem, New York City* (New York, 1915); Benjamin H. Locke, "The Community Life of a Harlem Group of Negroes," Master's thesis, Columbia University, 1913; New York Urban League, "Twenty-Four Hundred Negro Families in Harlem: An Interpretation of the Living Conditions of Small Wage Earners,'' typscript, Schomburg Collection, 1927; ''Harlem: Mecca of the New Negro,'' *The Survey* LIII (March 1, 1925), 629–724; E. F. Dycoff, ''A Negro City in New York,'' *The Outlook* CVIII (December 23, 1914), 949–54; Harlem Board of Commerce, *Harlem Survey* (New York, 1917?); Rollin Lynde Hart, ''I'd Like to Show You Harlem!'' *The Independent* CV (April 2, 1921), 334–35; Eric D. Walrond, ''The Black City,'' *The Messenger* VI (January 1924), 13–14; Chester T. Crowell, ''The World's Largest Negro City,'' *Saturday Evening Post* CXCVIII (August 8, 1925), 8–9, 93–94, 97; ''The Negro City,'' *American Review of Reviews* LXXIII (March 1926), 323–324; Owen R. Lovejoy, ''Justice for the Negro Child,'' *Opportunity* VII (June 1929), 174–76; E. Franklin Frazier, ''Negro Harlem: An Ecological Study,'' *American Journal of Sociology* XLIII (July 1937), 72–88; The Mayor's Commission of Conditions in Harlem, ''The Negro in Harlem: A Report on Social and Economic Conditions Responsible for the Outbreak of March 19, 1935'' (LaGuardia Papers).

Philadelphia

Information on blacks in Philadelphia includes W.E.B. Du Bois, *The Philadelphia Negro* (1899); Henry M. Minton, ''Early History of Negroes in Business in Philadelphia,'' in *The Philadelphia Colored Business Directory* edited by R. R. Wright, Jr. (1913); and Rev. George F. Bragg, Jr., *Men of Maryland* (Baltimore, 1925), on Thomas J. Dorsey. See also Charles Haley, ''To Do Good and Do Well: Middle Class Blacks and the Depression, Philadelphia, 1929–1941,'' Ph.D. diss., State University of New York at Binghampton, 1980; Eugene P. Foley, ''The Negro Businessman in Search of a Tradition,'' in *The Negro American*, edited by Talcott Parsons and Kenneth B. Clark (1966); Theodore Hershberg, *Philadelphia: Work, Space, Family and Group Experience in the Nineteenth Century* (New York, 1981); William W. Cutler III and Howard Gillette, Jr., eds., *The Divided Metropolis: Social and Spatial Dimensions of Philadelphia, 1800–1975* (Westport, Conn., 1980); Gail Stern, ed., *Philadelphia African Americans: Color, Class, and Style, 1840–1940* (Philadelphia, 1988); Edward Turner, *The Negro in Pennsylvania, Slavery—Servitude—Freedom, 1639–1861* (Washington, D.C., 1911); Theodore Hershberg, ''The Free Negro in Antebellum Philadelphia: A Study of Ex-Slaves, Freeborn, and Socioeconomic Decline,'' *Journal of Social History* 5 (1972), 183–209; Martin R. Delany, *The Condition, Elevation, Emigration and Destiny of the Colored People of the United States* (Philadelphia, 1852); Eugene Foley, ''The Negro Businessman: In Search of a Tradition,'' in *The Negro American*, edited by Talcott Parsons and Kenneth B. Clark (Boston, 1967), 555–92; and Emma Jones Lapsansky, ''Friends, Wives, and Strivings: Networks and Community Values among Nineteenth-Century Philadelphia Afroamerican Elites,'' *Pennsylvania Magazine of History and Biography* (January 1984), 3–24.

For other works on blacks in Philadelphia, see H. Viscount Nelson, Jr., ''Race and Class Consciousness of Philadelphia Negroes with Special Emphasis on the Years between 1927 and 1940,'' Ph.D. diss., University of Pennsylvania, 1969; Emma Jones Lapsansky, *Before the Model City: An Historical Exploration of North Philadelphia* (Philadelphia, 1969); Vincent Franklin, ''The Philadelphia Race Riot of 1918,'' *Pennsylvania Magazine of History and Biography* 99, 3 (July 1975), 336–50; George E. Simpson, ''Race Relations and the Philadelphia Press,'' *Journal of Negro Education* 6, 4 (October 1937), 628–30; John F. Bauman, *Public Housing, Race and Renewal: Urban Planning in Philadelphia* (Philadelphia, 1987); Emily Dinwiddie, *Housing Conditions in Philadelphia* (Philadelphia, 1904); John T. Emlen, "Negro Immigration in Philadelphia," *Southern Workman* 46 (November 1917), 555–57; Vincent Franklin, *The Education of Black Philadelphia: The Social and Educational History of a Minority Community, 1900–1950* (Philadelphia, 1979); William Fuller, "The Negro Migrant in Philadelphia," Negro Migrant Study Collection, Urban Archives, Temple University; Stephanie Greenberg, "Neighborhood Change, Racial Transition and Work Location: A Case Study of an Industrial City, Philadelphia, 1880–1930," *Journal of Urban History* 7,3 (January 1989), 67–68; James Gross, "Negro Labor and the Industrial Department of the Armstrong Association," Master's thesis, Temple University, 1957; Clara A. Hardin, "The Negroes of Philadelphia: The Cultural Adjustment of a Minority Group," Ph.D. diss., Bryn Mawr College, 1945; Eugene Hatfield, "The Impact of the New Deal on Black Politics in Pennsylvania, 1928–1936," Ph.D. diss., University of North Carolina at Chapel Hill, 1979; Arthur M. Johnson, "An Appraisal of the Industrial Program of the Armstrong Association," Master's thesis, University of Pennsylvania, 1946; Roger Lane, *Roots of Violence in Black Philadelphia, 1860–1900* (Cambridge, Mass., 1986); A. L. Manly, "Where Negroes Live in Philadelphia," *Opportunity* 1 (May 1923), 10–15; David McBride, "Black Health Care: Labor and the Philadelphia Medical Establishment: 1910–65," Ph.D. diss., Columbia University, 1981; Annetta G. McCall, *Supplementary Housing of the City Negro* (Philadelphia, 1916); Frederic M. Miller, "The Black Migration to Philadelphia: A 1924 Profile," *Pennsylvania Magazine of History and Biography* 107,3 (July 1984), 315–50; James E. Miller, "The Negro in Pennsylvania Politics, with Special Emphasis on Philadelphia since 1932," Ph.D. diss., University of Pennsylvania, 1945; Sadie T. Mosell, "Standard of Living among 100 Negro Migrant Families in Philadelphia," *Annals of the American Academy of Political and Social Sciences* 98 (November 1921), 173–218; Scott Nearing, "Negro Migrants in Philadelphia in 1923," *Monthly Labor Review* 19 (November 1924), 998–99; Howard Odum, "Negro Children in the Public Schools of Philadelphia," *Annals of the American Academy of Political and Social Sciences* 49 (September 1913), 186–203; Ruth Francis Paul, "Negro Women in Industry: A Study of the Negro Woman in the Clothing, Cigar, and Laundry Industries in Philadelphia," Master's thesis, Temple University, 1940; Harry Silcox, "The Search by Blacks for Employment and Opportunity: Industrial Education in Philadelphia," *Pennsylvania Heritage* 4,1 (December 1977), 38–43; John F. Sutherland, "A City of Homes: Philadelphia Slums and Reformers, 1880–1920," Ph.D. diss., Temple University, 1973; Thomas J. Woofter, Negro Housing in Philadelphia (Philadelphia, 1927). See also Edward R. Turner, *The Negro in Pennsylvania: Slavery—Servitude—Freedom, 1639–1861* (Washington, D.C., 1911).

Pittsburgh

For information on African-Americans in Pittsburgh, see Lawrence Glasco, "Double Burden: The Black Experience in Pittsburgh," in *City at the Point: Essays on the Social History of Pittsburgh*, edited by Samuel P. Hays (Pittsburgh, 1989), 69–109; John Bodnar, Roger Simon, and Michael P. Weber, *Lives of Their Own: Blacks, Italians, and Poles in Pittsburgh, 1900–1960* (Urbana, Ill., 1982); M. R. Goldman, "The Hill District as I Knew It," *Western Pennsylvania Historical Magazine* 51 (July 1968); Andrew Buni, *Robert Lee Vann of the Pittsburgh Courier: Politics and Black Journalism* (Pittsburgh, 1974); Helen Tucker, "The Negroes of Pittsburgh," in *Wage-Earning Pittsburgh, The Pittsburgh Survey*, edited by Paul U. Kellogg (New York, 1914), 424–36; Ira De A.

Reid, *Social Conditions of the Negro in the Hill District of Pittsburgh* (Pittsburgh, 1930); Richard R. Wright, Jr., *The Negro in Pennsylvania: A Study in Economic History* (Philadelphia, 1912), and his "One Hundred Negro Steelworkers," in *Wage-Earning Pittsburgh* (1914); Arthur J. Edmunds, *Daybreakers: The Story of the Urban League of Pittsburgh* (Pittsburgh, 1983, 1978); Dennis Dickerson, "Black Steelworkers in Western Pennsylvania, 1915–1950," Ph.D. diss., Washington University, 1978; J. Ernest Wright, "The Negro in Pittsburgh," unpublished WPA paper, 1940. An excellent study of the migration of blacks to Pittsburgh during this period is Peter Gottlieb, *Making Their Own Way: Southern Blacks Migration to Pittsburgh, 1916–30* (Urbana, Ill., 1987). See also Abraham Epstein, *The Negro Migrant in Pittsburgh* (Pittsburgh, 1918); and John T. Clark, "The Migrant in Pittsburgh," *Opportunity* 1 (October 1923), 303–7, and his "Negro in Steel," *Opportunity* 2 and 4 (October 1924 and March 1926), 299–301, 87–88.

A number of masters theses at the University of Pittsburgh are helpful for understanding the role of blacks in the city: Abram L. Harris, "The New Negro Worker in Pittsburgh," 1924; Ira De A. Reid, "The Negro in the Major Industries and Building Trades of Pittsburgh," 1925; Wiley Hall, "Negro Housing and Rents in the Hill District of Pittsburgh," 1929; Alonzo G. Morton, "Distribution of the Negro Population in Pittsburgh, 1910–30," 1933; John N. Rathmell, "Status of Pittsburgh Negroes in Regard to Their Origin, Length of Residence, and Economic Aspects of Their Life," 1935; Ruth Stevenson, "The Pittsburgh Urban League," 1936; and Jacqueline Wolfe, "The Changing Patterns of Residence of the Negro in Pittsburgh, Pennsylvania with Emphasis on the Period 1930–60," 1964.

INDEX

Note: Bold face entries are biographical subjects of this compilation.

About the Authors

JOHN N. INGHAM is professor of history at the University of Toronto. His earlier books include *Contemporary American Business Leaders* (Greenwood, 1990), *Biographical Dictionary of American Business Leaders* (4 vols., Greenwood, 1983) and *Making Iron and Steel: Independent Mills in Pittsburgh, 1820–1920* (1991). He is currently working on a study of African-American business in southern cities from 1880 to 1945.

LYNNE B. FELDMAN is an independent researcher and writer. She is currently working on a study of the African-American community in Birmingham, Alabama, and is the coauthor of *Contemporary American Business Leaders*.